Lecture Notes in Computer Science   8751

Commenced Publication in 1973
Founding and Former Series Editors:
Gerhard Goos, Juris Hartmanis, and Jan van Leeuwen

T0213678

Jarosław Wąs   Georgios Ch. Sirakoulis
Stefania Bandini (Eds.)

Cellular Automata

11th International Conference on Cellular Automata
for Research and Industry, ACRI 2014
Krakow, Poland, September 22-25, 2014
Proceedings

 Springer

Volume Editors

Jarosław Wąs
AGH University of Science and Technology
Dept. of Applied Computer Science
30-059 Krakow, Poland
E-mail: jarek@agh.edu.pl

Georgios Ch. Sirakoulis
Democritus University of Thrace
Dept. of Electrical and Computer Engineering
67100 Xanthi, Greece
E-mail: gsirak@ee.duth.gr

Stefania Bandini
University of Milano-Bicocca
CSAI - Complex Systems and Artificial Intelligence Research Center
20126 Milan, Italy
E-mail: stefania.bandini@disco.unimib.it

ISSN 0302-9743   e-ISSN 1611-3349
ISBN 978-3-319-11519-1   e-ISBN 978-3-319-11520-7
DOI 10.1007/978-3-319-11520-7
Springer Cham Heidelberg New York Dordrecht London

Library of Congress Control Number: 2014948675

LNCS Sublibrary: SL 1 – Theoretical Computer Science and General Issues

Typesetting: Camera-ready by author, data conversion by Scientific Publishing Services, Chennai, India

Printed on acid-free paper

Springer is part of Springer Science+Business Media (www.springer.com)

Foreword

This volume collects the papers selected for presentation at the 11th International Conference on Cellular Automata for Research and Industry (ACRI 2014), held in Kraków, Poland, September 22–25, 2014. ACRI 2014 was organized by the AGH University of Science and Technology as a forum for the presentation and discussion of specialized results as well as general contributions to the growth of the cellular automata approach and its application. Cellular automata represent a very powerful approach to the study of spatio-temporal systems where complex phenomena are built up out of many simple local interactions. The ACRI conference series was first organized in Italy, namely ACRI 1994 in Rende, ACRI 1996 in Milan, ACRI 1998 in Trieste and followed by ACRI 2000 in Karlsruhe (Germany), ACRI 2002 in Geneva (Switzerland), ACRI 2004 in Amsterdam (The Netherlands), ACRI 2006 in Perpignan (France), ACRI 2008 in Yokohama (Japan), ACRI 2010 in Ascoli Piceno (Italy), and ACRI 2012 in Santorini Island (Greece).

ACRI conferences have been offering since 1994 a biennial scientific meeting to both scientists and innovation managers in academia and industry to express and discuss their viewpoints on current and future trends, challenges, and state-of-the art solutions to various problems in the fields of arts, biology, chemistry, communication, cultural heritage, ecology, economy, geology, engineering, medicine, physics, sociology, traffic control, etc. The ACRI conferences have traditionally focused on challenging problems and new research not only in theoretical but application aspects of cellular automata, including cellular automata tools and computational issues. They are also concerned with applications and solutions of problems from the fields of physics, engineering, environment science, social science, and life sciences. The primary goal is to discuss problems from a variety of scientific fields, to identify new issues, and to enlarge the research fields of cellular automata. Since its inception, the ACRI conference has attracted an ever-growing community and has raised knowledge and interest in the study of cellular automata for both new entrants into the field as well as researchers already working on particular aspects of cellular automata.

This volume contains the invited contributions and the accepted papers presented at ACRI 2014. The submission and refereeing process was supported by the EasyChair conference management system. Each submission was reviewed by at least three referees and a total of 72 full and short papers, was selected for oral and poster presentation at the conference. There were two invited talks presented by Andrew Adamatzky and Gabriel Wainer. We warmly thank the invited speakers and all authors of the submitted papers and the members of the Program Committee as well as the Workshops Chairs and their Program Committees for their excellent work in making this selection. We also thank the additional external reviewers for their careful evaluation. All these efforts were the basis for the success of the conference.

In order to give a perspective in which both theoretical and applicational aspects of cellular automata contribute to the growth of the area, this book mirrors the structure of the conference, grouping the 72 papers into two main parts. The first part collects papers presented as part of the main conference and organized according to six main topics: (1) theoretical results on cellular automata, (2) cellular automata dynamics and synchronization, (3) modeling and simulation with cellular automata, (4) cellular automata-based hardware and computing (5) cryptography, networks, and pattern recognition with cellular automata. The second part of the volume is dedicated to contributions presented during the ACRI 2014 workshops on theoretical advances and challenging application contexts for cellular automata (CA): specifically Crowds and CA (5th edition, chairs: Sara Manzoni and Jarosław Wąs), Asynchronous CA and Asynchronous Discrete Models (3rd edition, chairs: Alberto Dennunzio, Enrico Formenti, and Thomas Worsch), Traffic and CA (3rd edition, chairs: Katsuhiro Nishinari and Andreas Schadschneider), and Workshop on Agent-Based Simulation and CA (chairs: Stefania Bandini, Kurt Dopfer and Giuseppe Vizzari).

Many people contributed to the success of ACRI 2014 and to the creation of this volume, from the initial idea to its implementation. Our first acknowledgement is to all the scientists that submitted their works, and to all Program Committee members and reviewers for their precious collaboration. A special thanks for their hospitality to the Municipality of Kraków, Małopolska Kraków Region, Fundacja Dla AGH, Department of Applied Computer Science and, of course to AGH University of Science and Technology, as well as for its generous contribution to the realization of this volume to the Centrum ISI. The collaboration with Springer for preparing this volume was very efficient and pleasant. We like to thank in particular Alfred Hofmann, Anna Krammer and Christine Reiss from Springer for their help. Finally, a special acknowledgement also to all the people involved in the organization of ACRI 2014 (in particular, alphabetically ordered, to: Edyta Kucharska, Robert Lubaś, Marcin Mycek, Jakub Porzycki, and especially to Anna Inglot) whose work was really fundamental for the actual success of the event.

Finally, we would like to thank the AGH University of Science and Technology and the Department of Electrical and Computer Engineering of Democritus University of Thrace, and all those institutes and organizations that financially supported the congress.

September 2014

Jarosław Wąs
Georgios Ch. Sirakoulis
Stefania Bandini

Organization

ACRI 2014 was organized by the AGH University of Science and Technology in Kraków.

Conference Chairs

Jarosław Wąs   AGH University of Science and Technology,
         Poland

Georgios Ch. Sirakoulis   Democritus University of Thrace, Greece

Workshop Chairs

Asynchronous CA and Asynchronous Discrete Models

Alberto Dennunzio   University of Milano-Bicocca, Italy
Enrico Formenti   Nice Sophia Antipolis University, France
Thomas Worsch   University of Karlsruhe, Germany

Crowds and CA

Sara Manzoni   University of Milano-Bicocca, Italy
Jarosław Wąs   AGH University of Science and Technology,
         Poland

Traffic and CA

Katsuhiro Nishinari   University of Tokyo, Japan
Andreas Schadschneider   University of Cologne, Germany

Agent-Based Simulation & Cellular Automata

Stefania Bandini   University of Milano-Bicocca, Italy
Kurt Dopfer   University of St. Gallen, Switzerland
Giuzeppe Vizzari   University of Milano-Bicocca, Italy

Organizing Committee

Edyta Kucharska   Jakub Porzycki
Robert Lubaś   Anna Inglot
Marcin Mycek   Jarosław Wąs

International Steering Committee

Stefania Bandini   University of Milano-Bicocca, Italy
Bastien Chopard   University of Geneva, Switzerland
Giancarlo Mauri   University of Milano-Bicocca, Italy
Hiroshi Umeo   University of Osaka, Japan
Thomas Worsch   University of Karlsruhe, Germany

Program Committee

Andrew Adamatzky   University of the West of England, UK
Ioannis Andreadis   Democritus University of Thrace, Greece
Jan Baetens   Ghent University, Belgium
Franco Bagnoli   University of Florence, Italy
Stefania Bandini   University of Milano-Bicocca, Italy
Olga Bandman   Siberian Branch of Russian Academy of
                            Science, Russia
Terry Bossomaier   Charles Sturt University, Australia
Bastien Chopard   University of Geneva, Switzerland
Alberto Dennunzio   University of Milano-Bicocca, Italy
Andreas Deutsch   Dresden University of Technology, Germany
Salvatore Di Gregorio   University of Calabria, Italy
Bernard De Baets   Ghent University, Belgium
Pedro de Oliveira   Universidade Presbiteriana Mackenzie, Brazil
Michel Droz   University of Geneva, Switzerland
Witold Dzwinel   AGH University of Science and Technology,
                            Poland
Samira El Yacoubi   University of Perpignan, France
Nazim Fatès   Inria Nancy, France
Ioakeim Georgoudas   Democritus University of Thrace, Greece
Tomasz Gwizdałła   University of Łódź, Poland
Teijiro Isokawa   University of Hyogo, Japan
Francisco Jiménez Morales   University of Santa Clara, Spain
Ioannis Karafyllidis   Democritus University of Thrace, Greece
Toshihiko Komatsuzaki   Kanazawa University, Japan
Krzysztof Kułakowski   AGH University of Science and Technology,
                            Poland
Martin Kutrib   Universität Gießen, Germany
Jia Lee   Chongqing University, China
Joseph Lizier   CSIRO Computational Informatics, Australia
Pradipta Maji   Indian Statistical Institute, India
Danuta Makowiec   Gdansk University, Poland
Sara Manzoni   University of Milano-Bicocca, Italy
Maurice Margenstern   Université Paul Verlaine, METZ, France

Genaro J. Martínez	National Polytechnic Institute, Mexico
Nobuyuki Matsui	University of Hyogo, Japan
Giancarlo Mauri	University of Milano-Bicocca, Italy
Michael Meyer-Hermann	Helmholtz Centre for Infection Research, Germany
Angelo Mingarelli	Carleton University, Canada
Shin Morishita	Yokohama National University, Japan
Katsuhiro Nishinari	University of Tokyo, Japan
Hidenosuke Nishio	University of Kyoto, Japan
Dipanwita Roy Chowdhury	Indian Institute of Technology, India
Franciszek Seredyński	Institute of Computer Science Polish Academy of Sciences, Poland
Roberto Serra	University of Modena and Reggio Emilia, Italy
Biplab K. Sikdar	Bengal Engineering and Science University, India
Georgios Ch. Sirakoulis	Democritus University of Thrace, Greece
Domenico Talia	University of Calabria, Italy
Paweł Topa	AGH University of Science and Technology, Poland
Leen Torenvliet	University of Amsterdam, The Netherlands
Hiroshi Umeo	University of Osaka Electro-Communication, Japan
Giuseppe Vizzari	University of Milano-Bicocca, Italy
Burton Voorhees	University of Athabasca, Canada
Jarosław Wąs	AGH University of Science and Technology, Poland
Thomas Worsch	University of Karlsruhe, Germany
Daichi Yanagisawa	The University of Tokyo, Japan

Workshop Program Committees

Asynchronous CA and Asynchronous Discrete Models

Alberto Dennunzio	University of Milano-Bicocca, Italy
Nazim Fatès	Inria Nancy, France
Enrico Formenti	Nice Sophia Antipolis University, France
Eric Goles	Universidad Adolfo Ibáñez, Chile
Jia Lee	Chongqing University, China
Ferdinand Peper	National Institute of Information and Communications Technology, Japan
Adrien Richard	CNRS and Nice Sophia Antipolis University, France
Hiroshi Umeo	University of Osaka Electro-Communication, Japan
Thomas Worsch	University of Karlsruhe, Germany

Crowds and CA

Andrew Adamatzky	University of the West of England, UK
Stefania Bandini	University of Milano Bicocca, Italy
Michael Batty	University College London, UK
Winnie Daamen	Delft University of Technology, The Netherlands
Mizar Luca Federici	CROWDYXITY, Italy
Ioakeim Georgoudas	Democritus University of Thrace, Greece
Hubert Klüpfel	TraffGo GmbH, Germany
Gerta Köster	Munich University of Applied Sciences, Germany
Tobias Kretz	PTV AG, Germany
Franziska Klügl	Örebro University, Sweden
Sara Manzoni	University of Milano Bicocca, Italy
Shin Morishita	Yokohama National University, Japan
Katsuhiro Nishinari	Tokyo University, Japan
Andreas Schadschneider	Institute of Theoretical Physics, Germany
Stefan Seer	Arsenal Research Vienna, Austria
Armin Seyfried	Jülich Supercomputing Centre, Germany
Georgios Ch. Sirakoulis	Democritus University of Thrace, Greece
G. Keith Still	Crowd Risk Analysis Ltd., UK
Harry Timmermans	Technical University Eindhoven, The Netherlands
Giuseppe Vizzari	University of Milano Bicocca, Italy
Jarosław Wąs	AGH University of Science and Technology, Poland

Traffic and CA

Stefania Bandini	University of Milano-Bicocca, Italy
Martin Evans	University of Edinburgh, UK
Henryk Fuks	Brock University, Canada
Rui Jiang	University of Science and Technology of China, China
Florian Knorr	University of Duisburg-Essen, Germany
Sven Maerivoet	Transport and Mobility Leuven, Belgium
Shin-ichi Tadaki	Saga University, Japan
Tetsuji Tokihiro	The University of Tokyo, Japan
Akiyasu Tomoeda	Musashino University, Japan
Antoine Tordeux	Juelich, Germany
Martin Treiber	University of Dresden, Germany
Peter Wagner	DLR Berlin, Germany
Daichi Yanagisawa	The University of Tokyo, Japan

Agent-Based Simulation and CA

Vincent Chevrier	Université de Lorraine, France
Jan Dijkstra	Eindhoven University of Technology, The Netherlands
Alexis Drogoul	IRD, France
Guy Engelen	Flemish Institute for Technological Research (VITO), Belgium
Nazim Fatès	LORIA - Inria Nancy, France
Andreas Pyka	Universität Hohenheim, Germany
Andrea Roli	Alma Mater Studiorum, Università di Bologna, Italy
Paul Torrens	University of Maryland, USA
Mirko Viroli	Alma Mater Studiorum, Università di Bologna, Italy
Jarosław Wąs	AGH University of Science and Technology, Poland
Roger White	Memorial University of Newfoundland, Canada

Table of Contents

Modeling and Simulation with Cellular Automata

Cellular Automata-Based Hardware and Computing

Cryptography, Networks and Pattern Classification with Cellular Automata

C&CA - Int. Workshop on Crowds and Cellular Automata

ACA - Int. Workshop on Asynchronous Cellular Automata and Asynchronous Discrete Models

TCA - Int. Workshop on Traffic and Cellular Automata

ABSim and CA - Int. Workshop on Agent-Based Simulation and Cellular Automata

Conductivity, Memristivity and Creativity in Cellular Automata

Andrew Adamatzky

Unconventional Computing Centre, University of the West of England, United Kingdom
andrew.adamatzky@uwe.ac.uk

Abstract. Cellular automata is a universal tool in literally any field of sciences and engineering yet more applications and weird discoveries are to come. We show how three barely related natural phenomena — conductivity of an excitable medium, networks of resistors with memory and structure of schizotypy versus cognitive control mental space — are represented in two-dimensional cellular automata with two or three states, and what discoveries we made using these models. This is an abstract of the talk at the conference on cellular automata, thus we do not provide any basics on cellular automata.

1 Conductivity

We introduce a two-dimensional excitable cellular automaton where resting cells excite depending on whether numbers of their excited neighbours belong to excitation intervals and boundaries of the excitation intervals are updated depending on ratio of excited and refractory cells in each cell's neighbourhood [1]. We define conductivity of a cell via size of its excitation interval and selected the excitation interval update functions that lead to formation of connected configurations of conductive cells (Fig. 1).

We demonstrate that by positioning elementary seeds of excitation we grow conductive wires (chains of cells in conductive states) and implement routing of the wires via collisions between the wires. Results presented might shade a light onto development of information pathways in excitable spatially extended media and contribute towards manufacturing of self-growing and self-organising circuits in ensembles of organic memristive polymers.

We show that it is possible to fine tune conductivity of an excitable medium by controlling local dynamics of excitation. Functions which stabilise excitation dynamics (where size of excitation interval increase with decrease of excitation and decreases when excitation dominates) generate fully conductive when a small number of initially resting cells are stimulated. A point-wise initial excitation can play a seed of a growing wire, a chain of cells in conductive states; directions of the wire grows in pre-programmed in the configuration of initial excitation. The growing wires can be routed in almost arbitrary manner, dependent on positions of their seeds. Several wires can interact with each other by changing directions of their growth, merging in a single wire and co-aligning.

We illustrate how to design and grow potential information pathways. Often extended patterns are formed at the sites of collision between growing wires. Chances are high

J. Wąs, G.C. Sirakoulis, and S. Bandini (Eds.): ACRI 2014, LNCS 8751, pp. 1–5, 2014.
© Springer International Publishing Switzerland 2014

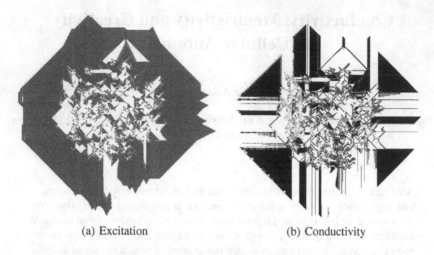

(a) Excitation   (b) Conductivity

Fig. 1. Snapshots of an excitation dynamics (a) and conducivity (b) in a two-dimensional excitable cellular automaton with dynamically adjustable excitation intervals [2]

that these patterns can implement a range of sensible transformations of input excitation to output excitation, which could be interpreted in terms of computation.

Memristive Automata

A memristive automaton is a structurally-dynamic excitable cellular automaton where a link connecting two cells is removed or added if one of the cells is in excited state and another cell is in refractory state.

We define a minimalistic model of a two-dimensional discrete memristive medium [3]. Every site of such medium takes triple states, and a binary conductivity of links is updated depending on states of sites the links connect. The model is a hybrid between classical, e.g. Greenberg-Hasting model, excitable cellular automata and classical structurally-dynamic cellular automata, e.g. Ilachinski-Halper model. A memristive automaton with binary cell-states would give us even more elegant model however by using binary cell-states we could not easily detect source and sink of simulated 'currents'. Excitable cellular automata provide us with all necessary tools to imitate current polarity and to control local conductivity. From topology of excitation of wave-fronts and wave-fragments we can even reconstruct relative location of a source of initiated current.

We discuss two type of memristive cellular automata and characterise their space-time dynamics in response to point-wise and spatially extended perturbations. We classify several regimes of automata excitation activity, and provide detailed accounts of most common types of oscillating localizations. We show types of oscillations typically found after perturbations caused by random spatially-extended stimulation are over. We illustrate how formation of conductive pathways could occur (Fig. 2) and demonstrate that opportunities to grow 'wires' in memristive automata are virtually unlimited.

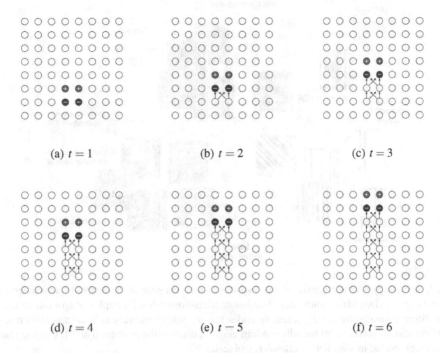

(a) $t = 1$ (b) $t = 2$ (c) $t = 3$

(d) $t = 4$ (e) $t - 5$ (f) $t = 6$

Fig. 2. Snapshots of excitation and links dynamics the memristive cellular automaton. In initial configuration two cells are excited, two cells are in refractory state, others are resting. Arrows symbolise conductive links.

Creative Cellular Automata

Creativity is ubiquitous yet elusive concept. Everyone knows what it means to be creative, e.g. to be successful in problem-solving and generation of novel thoughts, but few can define creativity rigorously. From a psychological and neurophysiological perspective there is a great similarity between creativity and psychoticism. Kuszewski (2009) provides plausible and psychologically feasible indicators of creativity: divergent thinking and lack of lateral inhibition; the ability to make remote associations between ideas and concepts; the ability to switch back and forth between conventional and unconventional ideations (flexibility in thinking); generation of novel ideas appropriate for actualities; willingness to take risks; and, functional non-conformity. Cognitive control of divergent thinking is a guarantee of creativity. A person with extremely divergent thinking yet unable to control it will be a'nutter'. Those who can fit their high schizotypy traits into a rigid cognitive frame incline to genious. Thus creativity could be positioned together with autism and schizophrenia in the same 'phase' space.

We uncover cellular automata analogies of Kuszewski's scheme by assuming that a cell neighbourhood configuration represents a 'thought', or some other elementary quantity of a mental process, and a degree of schizotypy is proportional to the diversity of global configurations generated by the cellular automata [4]. We speculate that

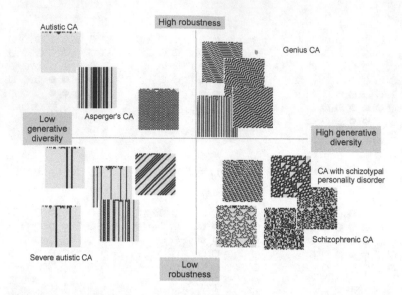

Fig. 3. Schizotipy versus cognitive control spaces as seen via generative morphological diversity and robustness (Derrida coefficients) of cell-state transitions rules. Examples of space-time configurations generated by autistic, creative and schizophrenic elementary cellular automata rules. Configurations evolved from initially random uniform distribution of states 0 and 1. Cells in state 1 are black pixels, in state 0 are yellow/grey pixels.

cognitive control is equivalent to robustness of automata evolution. An automaton is robust if trajectory of a disturbed automaton, with some cells' states changed externally, does not deviate, in terms of Hamming distance, too far away from a trajectory of an undisturbed automaton. The degree of deviation caused by a disturbance is measured by the Derrida coefficient.

Using measures of generative morphological diversity and the Derrida coefficient we classify elementary cellular automata rules onto a spectrum of autistic, schizophrenic and creative personality (Fig. 3). Autistic rules correspond to rule classes with fixed point behaviour, schizophrenic rules are chaotic and creative rules belong to a class of two-cycle behaviour.

There are two types of creativity: creative product and creative process. The creative automaton rules discovered correspond to a creative process; space-time configurations produced by a creative rule may not be creative. Rule 54 and 110 are computationally universal but why are they not creative? Because they lack autonomous cognitive control defined as a robustness. These rules perform computation only with strict initial conditions. The computational circuits in these rules do not emerge in their space-time configurations by themselves.

References

1. Adamatzky, A.: Reaction-Diffusion Automata. Elsevier (2013)
2. Adamatzky, A.: Patterns of conductivity in excitable automata with updatable intervals of excitations. Phys. Rev. E 86, 056105 [16 pages] (2013)
3. Adamatzky, A., Chua, L.: Phenomenology of retained refractoriness: On semi-memristive discrete media. Int. J. Bifurcation Chaos 22, 1230036 [19 pages] (2012)
4. Adamatzky, A., Wuensche, A.: On creativity of elementary cellular automata. Complex Systems 22, 4 (2013)

Cellular Modeling with Cell-DEVS:
A Discrete-Event Cellular Automata Formalism

Gabriel A. Wainer

Department of Systems and Computer Engineering
Carleton University, Ottawa, ON, Canada
gwainer@sce.carleton.ca

Abstract. In recent years, grid-shaped cellular models have gained popularity to understand physical systems. Complex cell spaces can require large amounts of compute time, mainly due to its synchronous nature; the use of a discrete time base also constrains the precision of the model. The Cell-DEVS formalism was defined in order to deal with these issues. We give a brief introduction to the main characteristics of Cell-DEVS, and show how to use the method to model complex cell spaces. We present different examples of application, and show how to integrate cellular models with external data collection and visualization.

1 Introduction

In recent years, there has been a trend in studying natural and humanmade systems using advanced modeling and simulation techniques. These problems were traditionally modeled with differential equations, and standard numerical methods. New methods based on Cellular Automata (CA) have provided new ways to solve these problems [1]. CA are represented as a cell space (a regular n-dimensional lattice whose cells can take discrete values). The states in the space are updated according to a local rule in simultaneous and synchronously, in discrete time steps, as dictated by a local transition function using the cell state and a finite set of neighbors. When CA are used to study complex systems, the use of a discrete time base poses restrictions in performance and in the precision of the model. In [2, 3, 4] we showed how the Cell-DEVS formalism solves these problems by using the Discrete Events Systems Specification formalism (DEVS) [5]. The goal is to build discrete event cell spaces, improving their definition by making the timing specification more expressive.

The DEVS and Cell-DEVS formalisms were implemented in the CD++ environment [3, 6, 7] which has been was used successfully to develop different types of systems: biological (ecological models, heart tissue, ant foraging systems, fire spread, etc.), physical (diffusion, binary, solidification, excitable media, surface tension, etc.), artificial (robot trajectories, networking, traffic, etc.), and others [3, 7-11]. We have developed different kinds of simulation engines (centralized, parallel distributed and real-time), which were used to execute the same models [12, 13].

In the following sections we give an introduction to Cell-DEVS, and show how to model cell spaces in an asynchronous environment.

J. Wąs, G.C. Sirakoulis, and S. Bandini (Eds.): ACRI 2014, LNCS 8751, pp. 6–15, 2014.

2   Background

DEVS is a formalism for discrete-event dynamic systems. It defines a way of specifying models whose states change upon the reception of an input event or the expiration of a time delay. It also allows for hierarchical decomposition of the model by defining a way to couple existing models. A coupled model can be regarded, due to the closure property, as another DEVS model. This allows for hierarchical model construction. A model that is not constructed as a coupled model is known as an atomic model.

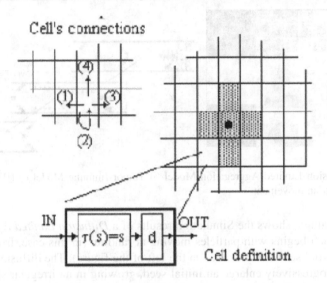

Fig. 1. Informal definition of a Cell-DEVS model [3]

Cell-DEVS is a formalism based on DEVS for cellular models. As in CA, a Cell-DEVS model is defined as a lattice of cells, each of which has a value and a local rule that defines how to obtain a new value based on the current state of the cell and the values its neighbors. Cell-DEVS defines a cell as a DEVS model and a cell space as a coupled model. It introduces a new flexible way of defining the timing for each cell (each cell defines its own update delay asynchronously from the others). A cell uses a set of input values to compute its future state, which is obtained by applying the local computation function τ. A delay function $\mathbf{d}$ is associated with each cell, deferring the output of the new state value. After the basic behavior for a cell is defined, the complete cell space will be constructed by building a coupled Cell-DEVS model.

The CD++ tool has been used to model numerous applications in different fields [3]. In http://cell-devs.sce.carleton.ca the reader will find a list of hundreds of models available for use, in different fields that range from basic chemistry and physics problems, up to advanced environmental and networking applications. Fig. 2 shows a number of different results obtained with the related tools.

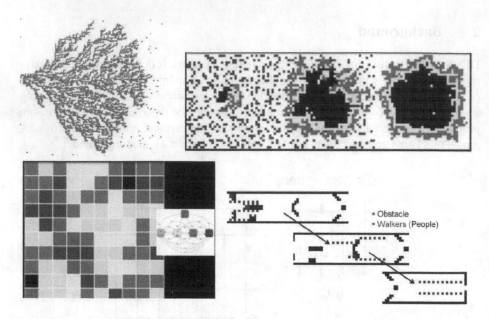

Fig. 2. a) Diffusion Limited Aggregation Model b) Tumor-Immune Model c) HIV Influence Model d) Pedestrian movement

The first example shows the Simulation results of a *Diffusion Limited Aggregation Model* [3], which begins with particles moving at random (in this case, from right to left), and an initial seed (in this case, on the left of the figure). The diffusing particles stick to and progressively enlarge an initial seed, growing in an irregular shape. This figure presents a case with concentration of 40%, showing fractal growth properties. The second example shows three different scenarios used for modeling tumor-immune systems [14]. The model shows how to model a core of necrotic cells, surrounded by a ring of dormant cells, surrounded in turn by a ring of proliferative cells. The immune cells attack the tumor in an attempt to stop it from growing. The next example focuses on the attitudes and influences of neighbors for intravenous drug user. Some people (green cells) affect their neighbors in a positive way (i.e., clinics and aid workers). The light green cells represent individuals that can be influenced by negative neighbors, or to remain drug free. The red cells represent HIV+ people who can be convinced to stop using. Finally the brown cells are users with HIV who will influence their neighbors negatively and will soon turn into a black square (someone who died of HIV). The last example shows a simulation scenario for a two dimensional pedestrian movement model in a corridor with obstacles.

The following sections are devoted to show how to define this kind of models and how to generate varied Simulation results based on the execution of the cellular models in CD++.

3   Basic Model: Human Circulatory System

The human circulation system transports oxygen and minerals through a network of arteries, veins and capillaries. The blood never comes into contact with any of the body's cells: the substances are diffused through the capillaries. In this section we present an example model of how oxygen is transported to the muscle cells using Cell-DEVS.

The first set of rules focus on the movement of blood cells. Since blood flow is a driven activity, a directional movement rule with fixed priority was defined. A blood cell will first attempt to move to the cell in front; if it is occupied it will then attempt to move into NE; if this cell is occupied it will try to move to the SE and if this space is full it will stop.

```
rule:{ if((0,-1)=1, if(((-1,-1)=6 or (1,-1)=6),
1, 2), 2)} 1 {((0,0)=0 and ((-1,-1)=7 or (-1,-
1)=6)) and ((0,-1)=1 or ((-1,-1)=1 and (-1,0)!=0
) or ((1,-1)=1 and (1,0)!=0 and (2,0)!=0) or ((-
1,1)=2 and (0,1)=2) or ((1,1)>=8 and (0,1)>=8))
```

A blood cell will have two states, oxygenated or deoxygenated. An oxygenated cell will become deoxygenated when it passes by a deoxygenated muscle cell. They will "re-oxygenate" in the lung cells when they pass an oxygenated cell. Muscle cells become oxygenated when an oxygenated blood cell comes into contact with them. An oxygenated muscle cell will become deoxygenated after some time. The code snippet above shows the de-oxygenation of cells. Like the muscle cells, lung cells become oxygenated after spending a period of time deoxygenated, and deoxygenated when a deoxygenated blood cell comes into contact with it, as follows:

```
rule : { if((1,0) = 1, 6, 7) } 1 { (0,0) = 7 }
%Muscle Cell Becoming Oxygenated
rule : { if((-1,0) = 0.1, 7, 6) } 1 { (0,0)=6 }
%Muscle Cell Becoming De-Oxygenated
rule : { if((-1,0) = 0.1 , 4, 5) } 1 { (0,0)=5 }
%Lung Cell Becoming Oxygen Enriched
rule : { if((1,0) = 2, 5, 4) } 1 { (0,0)=4 }
%Lung Cell Becoming Carbon Dioxide Enriched
rule : {(0,0)} 1 {(0,0) != 0 }
```

The counter is responsible for "resetting" the corresponding lung or muscle cell to either oxygenated or deoxygenate.

```
% Rate of Consumption = (0,1)/(0.004) = 25 s
{ if((1,0)=6, ((0,0)+0.005),0)}1{(1,0)} = 6 }
% Lung Cells Replenishing Oxygen Supply
% Rate of Regeneration = (0.1)/0.004 = 25 s
{ if((1,0)=5, ((0,0)+.025 ), 0)} 1 {(1,0)=5 }
```

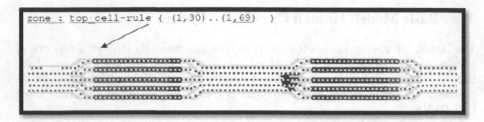

Fig. 3. Lung Model Simulation Results

4   Advanced Models: An Evacuation Cellular Model

The simulation of evacuation processes has been widely used to buildings, ships and the aviation industry. In [3, 5, 17] we presented various models in this area. The model introduced in this section represents people moving through a room trying to leave the building through an exit door.

The model is a 3D Cell-DEVS with two planes: one for the floor plan of the structure and the people, and the other for a Voronoi Diagram representing the orientation to the closest exit. The model characterizes a person's behavior: a normal person goes to the closest exit; a person in panic goes in opposite direction People move at different speeds; if the way is blocked, people can decide to move away and look for another way. The rules in Fig. 5 have two parts: the coupled model definition (size, neighborhood shape, initial conditions, etc.) and the local computing function. The first set of rules serves to define what path a person should follow using the orientation plane. The basic idea is to take the direction that decreases the potential of a cell. We have 8 rules to control the people's movement, one for each direction. A second set of rules governs the panic behavior.

In [15] this model was extended to conduct an integration between 3D visualization software and CD++, using as example the Society for Arts and Technology (SAT) building in downtown Montreal. Fig. 5 shows the results for this model. We can see the initial grid split into two layers. The left represents the walls, exits and initial positions of the people. Red cells represent people who want to escape. The black cells represent walls. On the right we can see the second layer which holds the distances to the exits. Fig. 5 considers a basic model with eight people without panic. In this simple scenario we could observe that they follow the second layer to exit the building without any complications. The building is almost empty (which is a normal condition for SAT). This evacuation is designed to give us a general idea of the exit directions people will follow, which will help us in developing the successive simulations.

```
type : cell dim : (49,27,2) delay : INERTIAL
defaultDelayTime : 1 border : wrapped
neighbors : (-1,-1,0) (-1,0,0) (-1,1,0)
neighbors : (0,-1,0) (0,0,0) (0,1,0)
...
[EvaRule]
% Rules to control the movement of individuals
rule : {#pos1+1} {1000/#pos0} {((0,0,0)>0 AND
#pos0 =0 ...
rule : {#pos1+3} {1000/#pos0} {((0,0,0)>0 AND
#pos0 =0 ...
rule : {#pos1+5} {1000/#pos0} {((0,0,0)>0 AND
#pos0 =0 ...
rule : {#pos1+7} {1000/#pos0} {((0,0,0)>0 AND
#pos0 =0 ...
rule : {#pos1+2} {1000/#pos0} {((0,0,0)>0 AND
  #pos0 =0 ...
```

Fig. 4. Evacuation rules as set in the CD++ Model file

5   Interfacing Cell-DEVS, External Input and Visualization

Several zoonotic diseases have emerged on the Asian landscape; Macaques have been affected by landscape changes caused by humans and these have increased the incidence of human interaction, potentially leading to bi-directional pathogen transmission to macaques.

The model in this section focuses on evaluating how landscape changes might influence pathogen transmission patterns [18]. Macaques can move to surrounding environment randomly, they may or may not carry pathogen, and can be infected by nearby neighbors. This model uses the landscape (the map contains only forest, water, and coastlines), temple (macaques live in their birth temple; females cannot cross the temple borders, while male macaques can), movement (at random into one of the 8 adjacent cells; collision avoidance is implemented), gender, and pathogen (each monkey may carry the pathogen; there are four phases of the transmission cycle: susceptible, latent, symptomatic, and acquired immunity).

The GRASS GIS was used to generate inputs for the model, combining information about the forests in Bali, and the water and coast map. The final map, shown in Fig. 6, is used to get the landscape values to be represented as cells and be used in the model simulation.

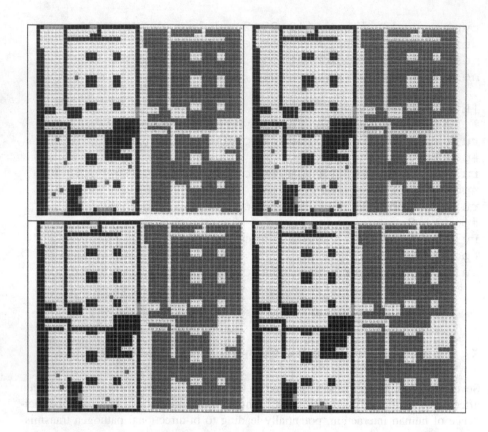

Fig. 5. a) SAT at time: 00:000–Initial placement of people; b) 00:834–First movement of people; c) 02:673–People proceed to the nearest exits; d) 13:015–Last person to leave the building

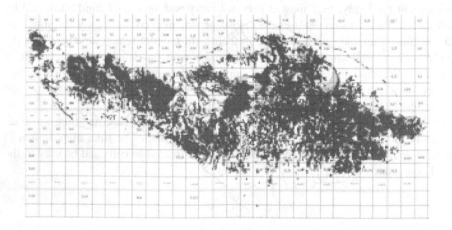

Fig. 6. The map divided into a cell space

Fig. 7 shows the model execution under 3 scenarios. The first one uses an initial monkey occupation of 10%, a river cross probability of 20%, a male ratio of 50%, and an initial pathogen infection ratio of 30%. The second test uses an occupation of 20%, a river cross probability of 20%, a male ratio of 40%, and an infection ratio of 50%. The third test uses a 30% occupation, a river cross probability of 50%, a male ratio of 70%, and an initial pathogen infection ratio of 80%.

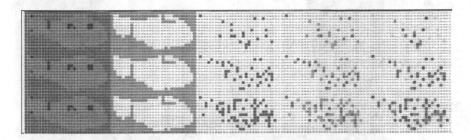

Fig. 7. Three test cases comparison

A closer look at what is happening in the pathogen layer can be seen in Fig. 8. The cell marked by a circle is currently in latent infection. On the next step of the simulation, the cell changes stage 3 (symptomatic). The cells in the square show two monkeys with immunity. Since the rules state that when a cell in stage 4 has surrounding cells which are also in stage 4, it will not change phases. The two cells adjacent to the circled cell represent two monkeys that attempted to move to the same cell.

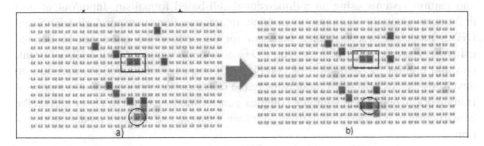

Fig. 8. Phase changes example

Fig. 9 shows the visualization of the simulation results in Google Earth. To do so, a KML file was generated from the CD++ simulation log file and the geographical information for the map generated above. The small white square on the map is the region that was used to test the pathogen transmission. The panel on the left shows visualization with the 5 layers in our model. Here, only the gender layer is shown (pink cells: females; blue cells: males).

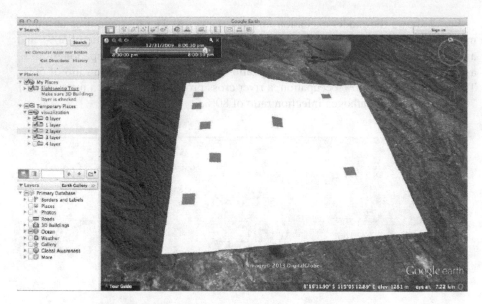

Fig. 9. Gender Layer in Google Earth

6 Conclusions and Future Work

We have presented the Cell-DEVS formalism, and introduced several features CD++, a toolkit for DEVS modeling and simulation. Cell–DEVS allows describing physical and natural systems using an n-dimensional cell-based formalism. Input/output port definitions allow the definition of multiple interconnections between Cell-DEVS and DEVS models. Complex timing behavior for the cells in the space can be defined using very simple constructions. The CD++ tool implements the Cell-DEVS formalism and entitles the definition of complex cell-shaped models. We showed how to develop several Cell-DEVS models using the CD++ toolkit, which provides a general framework to define and simulate complex generic models. Cell-DEVS simplifies the construction of complex simulations, allowing a simple and intuitive model specification.

We showed that different kinds of applications can be easily developed, allowing the study of complex problems through simulation, which, otherwise, could not be attacked. Finally, the use of a formal base improves the development, checking and maintaining phases, facilitating the testing and reuse of their components.

The tools are public domain and can be obtained at http://cell-devs.sce.carleton.ca.

Acknowledgement. This work was partially funded by NSERC. Numerous students participated in the construction of the models presented here, including Eman Al Disi, Rhys Goldstein, Joanna Lostracco, Emil Poliakov, Faezeh Rafsanjani Sadeghi, Michael Van Schyndel, Sixuan Wang and Myriam Younan.

References

1. Burks, A.W.: Von Neumann's self-reproducing automata. In: Burks, A.W. (ed.) Essays on Cellular Automata, pp. 3–64. University of Illinois Press, Champaign (1970)
2. Wainer, G., Giambiasi, N.: Application of the Cell-DEVS paradigm for cell spaces modeling and simulation. SIMULATION 71(1), 22–39 (2001)
3. Wainer, G.: Discrete-Event Modeling and Simulation: a Practitioner's approach. CRC Press, Taylor and Francis (2009)
4. Wainer, G., Giambiasi, N.: N-dimensional Cell-DEVS. Discrete Events Systems: Theory and Applications 12(1), 135–157 (2002)
5. Zeigler, B., Kim, T., Praehofer, H.: Theory of Modeling and Simulation: Integrating Discrete Event and Continuous Complex Dynamic Systems. Academic Press (2000)
6. Bonaventura, M., Wainer, G., Castro, R.: A Graphical Modeling and Simulation Environment for DEVS. SIMULATION: Transactions of the SCS 89(1), 4–27 (2013)
7. Wainer, G., Liu, Q., Dalle, O., Zeigler, B.: Introduction to Cellular Automata in Gaming. Simulation and Gaming 41(6), 796–823 (2010)
8. Wainer, G., Castro, R.: A survey on the application of the Cell-DEVS formalism in cellular models. Journal of Cellular Automata 5(6), 509–524 (2010)
9. Saadawi, H., Wainer, G.: Modeling Physical Systems Using Finite Element Cell-DEVS. Simulation Modelling Practice and Theory 15(10), 1268–1291 (2007)
10. Wainer, G., Davidson, A.: Defining a Traffic Modeling language Using Cellular Discrete-Event abstractions. Journal of Cellular Automata 2(4), 291–343 (2007)
11. Wainer, G.: Applying Cell-DEVS Methodology for Modeling the Environment. SIMULATION: Transactions of the SCS 82(10), 635–660 (2006)
12. Liu, Q., Wainer, G.: Parallel Environment for DEVS and Cell-DEVS Models. SIMULATION: Transactions of the SCS 83(6), 449–471 (2007)
13. Al-Zoubi, K., Wainer, G.: RISE: A General Simulation Interoperability Middleware Container. Journal of Parallel and Distributed Computing 73(5), 580–594 (2013)
14. Wainer, G., Goldstein, R.: Modelling Tumor-Immune Systems with Cell-DEVS. In: Proceedings of the European Modeling and Simulation Conference 2008, Nicosia, Cyprus (2008)
15. Poliakov, E., Wainer, G., Hayes, J., Jemtrud, M.: A Busy Day at the SAT Building. In: Proceedings of AIS 2007, Artificial Intelligence, Simulation and Planning. Buenos Aires, Argentina (2007)
16. Castonguay, P., Wainer, G.: Aircraft Evacuation DEVS Implementation & Visualization. In: Proceedings of SCS/ACM Springsim 2009 (DEVS Symposium), San Diego, CA, USA (2009)
17. Wang, S., Van Schyndel, M., Wainer, G., Subashini, V., Woodbury, R.: Interactive DEVS-based Building Information Modeling & Simulation for Emergency Evacuation. In: Proceedings of Winter Simulation Conference, Berlin, Germany (2012)
18. Kennedy, R.C., Lane, K.E., Arifin, S.N., Fuentes, A., Hollocher, H., Madey, G.R.: A GIS aware agent-based model of pathogen transmission. International Journal of Intelligent Control and Systems 14(1), 51–61 (2009)

Towards a Comprehensive Understanding
of Multi-state Cellular Automata

Jan M. Baetens* and Bernard De Baets

KERMIT, Department of Mathematical Modelling, Statistics and Bioinformatics,
Ghent University, Coupure links 653, Gent, Belgium
{jan.baetens,bernard.debaets}@ugent.be

Abstract. Motivated by the fact that many cellular automata (CAs) for
describing biological, physical or chemical processes are built upon more
than two states, whereas most the majority of results on the stability
of CAs is restricted to two-state CAs, we show in this paper how non-
directional Lyapunov exponents can be used to assess the stability of
multi-state CAs. Moreover, we pay particular attention to the different
types of defects that may emerge during the evolution of such CAs from
a single initial defect of a given type. Numerical results are presented for
the family of three-state totalistic CAs.

1 Introduction

Even from a superficial inspection of CA literature, it is immediately clear that
most researchers in the domain have devoted their attention to two-state CAs
ever since their formalization by von Neumann [14], whereas profound studies
on the nature and dynamics of their multi-state counterparts are scarce. Indeed,
even though multi-state CAs serve as a basis for models describing biological
competition [12], excitable media [1,7], epidemics [13], reaction-diffusion processes [19] and the immune system [4], only few authors have endeavored a
profound analysis of multi-state CAs. Moreover, these works are often restricted
to one or a few particular rules, as opposed to studies on two-state CAs that
often cover an entire family of rules, most frequently the family of so-called elementary CAs [3,8,15]. Unarguably, the bias of literature towards two-state CAs
is caused by the fact that the number of rules within any given family of multi-
state CAs is huge, which becomes an insurmountable hurdle if one cannot rely
on a method that allows for a relatively rapid analysis of the CAs' dynamics.

Some results on the dynamics of multi-state CAs have nevertheless been reported and should be mentioned in this context. For instance, the properties
of the Potts model [11], which is an extension of the Ising model, have been
well studied and documented [17], while also the Greenberg-Hastings model [7]
has been investigated elaborately [5,6]. Further, Wuensche has investigated the
three-state beehive rule [18], while Peltomaki et al. examined the intriguing
spatio-temporal patterns that can emerge in their three-state model [10]. Yet,

---

* Corresponding author.

J. Wąs, G.C. Sirakoulis, and S. Bandini (Eds.): ACRI 2014, LNCS 8751, pp. 16–24, 2014.
© Springer International Publishing Switzerland 2014

none of these works introduces a generic method of analysis that allows for an in-depth analysis of any kind of multi-state CA. At the same time, the generic approaches that have been established to capture CA dynamics, such as non-directional Lyapunov exponents [3], the Lempel-Ziv complexity [9] and others, are either restricted to CAs with two states or have been introduced only theoretically.

As a first step towards the establishment of a comprehensive theory for grasping the dynamics of multi-state CAs, we investigate in this paper how non-directional Lyapunov exponents can be relied upon to assess the sensitivity of one-dimensional, three-state CAs to directional perturbations of the initial condition.

2   Methods

2.1   Preliminaries

In the framework of this paper, we will restrict ourselves to one-dimensional, three-state totalistic CAs which can be conveniently represented by a quintuple $\mathscr{C} = \langle \mathcal{T}, S, s, N, \Omega \rangle$. Therein, $\mathcal{T}$ denotes a countably infinite tessellation of a 1-dimensional Euclidean space, consisting of consecutive intervals c_i, $i \in \mathbb{N}$, typically referred to as cells, and S is a set of three states, say $\{0, 1, 2\}$. Further, the output function $s : \mathcal{T} \times \mathbb{N} \to S$ gives the state value of cell c_i at the t-th discrete time step, the neighborhood function N is here defined as $N(c_i) = (c_{i-1}, c_i, c_{i+1})$, and finally the transition function $\Omega : \mathbb{N} \to S$ governs the dynamics of each cell c_i, i.e.

$$s(c_i, t+1) = \Omega(\sigma_i),$$

where $\sigma_i = s(c_{i-1}, t) + s(c_i, t) + s(c_{i+1}, t)$.

2.2   Rationale

Just as in the case of two-state CAs, measuring the sensitive dependence on initial conditions of their three-state counterparts should be done by carefully tracking all possible defects in tangent space that arise from an initial perturbation. Yet, upon transgressing from Boolean state sets to, possibly, multi-state sets there are a few issues one has to keep in mind. Firstly, if the multi-state set is endowed with an ordering, defects are no longer necessarily the same. Indeed, in such a setting the 'difference' between 0 and 2 is different from the one between, say, 1 and 2, such that also the magnitude of the emerging defects has to be tracked. Secondly, without an ordering imposed on S, defects have the same magnitude, but one then might need to account for the different types of defects. More specifically, if we consider a k-state CA, at most $\frac{k(k-1)}{2}$ different types of defects can emerge during the course of the CA evolution, one for every possible combination of states, namely $0 - 1$, $0 - 2$, ..., $0 - k$, $1 - 2$, ..., $(k-1) - k$. Distinguishing among them will allow one in the end to get a better insight into the sensitive dependence on the initial conditions. Clearly, if two-state CAs are at stake, there exists only one type of defect, being the one that involves flipping state zero to one, or vice versa, and sensitive dependence on initial conditions traces back unambiguously to that particular type of defect.

2.3 Defect Propagation in Three-State CAs

Here, we endow $S = \{0, 1, 2\}$ with a cyclic ordering, denoted $[0, 1, 2]$, which makes that the distance between any of the states is the same, and we may essentially confine ourselves to tracking only two kinds of defects, being the ones that bring along a right shift of a cell's state, on the one hand, and defects invoking a left shift of a cell's state, on the other hand.

Let s_0 and s_0^* be two initial configurations of a 3-state CA $\mathscr{C}$, such that there is only one $c_i \in \mathcal{T}$ for which it holds that $s_0(c_i) \neq s_0^*(ci)$. Given the fact that the state set is cyclic, the defect invoked by such a perturbation constitutes either a right or left shift of c_i's state, referred to in the remainder as R- and L-defect, respectively. Denoting the number of these defects at the t-th time step as ϵ_t^+ and ϵ_t^-, respectively, the total number of defects at the t-th discrete time step can be written as $\epsilon_t = \epsilon_t^+ + \epsilon_t^-$. Formally, ϵ_t^+ and ϵ_t^- are given by

$$\epsilon_t^+ = \left| \{i \mid s^*(c_i, t) <_{s(c_i, t)} S \setminus \{s(c_i, t), s^*(c_i, t)\}\} \right|, \tag{1}$$

and

$$\epsilon_t^- = \left| \{i \mid s^*(c_i, t) >_{s(c_i, t)} S \setminus \{s(c_i, t), s^*(c_i, t)\}\} \right|, \tag{2}$$

respectively.

At this point, it is important to emphasize that the directionality of the initial perturbation does not imply any directionality of the defects that emerge during the course of the CA's evolution since both L- and R-defects might appear as soon as $t > 0$, irrespective of the type of initial defect. For that reason, the overall maximum Lyapunov exponent (MLE) should be computed from the total number of defects ϵ_t, i.e.

$$\lambda = \lim_{t \to \infty} \frac{1}{t} \log \left(\frac{\epsilon_t}{\epsilon_0} \right), \tag{3}$$

but keeping track of defect direction allows us to compute the exponential rates by which the number of L- and R-defects grows, as

$$\lambda^+ = \lim_{t \to \infty} \frac{1}{t} \log \left(\frac{\epsilon_t^+}{\epsilon_0} \right), \tag{4}$$

and

$$\lambda^- = \lim_{t \to \infty} \frac{1}{t} \log \left(\frac{\epsilon_t^-}{\epsilon_0} \right), \tag{5}$$

respectively. Clearly, if a truly unordered CA is at stake, one might obtain $\frac{k(k-1)}{2}$ such rates. Analyzing these rates will enable a better insight into the nature of the instability of a three-state CA. For instance, it is to be expected that defects will not necessarily have to coexist, such that they might propagate nonuniformly. furthermore, there might exist rules for which one of them will evaluate to $-\infty$, whereas the other might be positive, which means that the rule's overall instability (λ will be positive) can be traced back completely to the emergence of either L- or R-defects.

2.4   Limits on Defect Propagation in Three-State CAs

It is well known that the MLE of one-dimensional, nearest-neighbor, two-state CAs is bounded from above by the size of the neighborhood [3], i.e. by $\log(3)$, as this limits the number of paths along which defects can propagate. Consequently, also the MLE of their three-state counterparts must be bounded from above by the neighborhood size, and likewise for the propagation rates of R- and L-defects. This means that the total number of defects, but even so the number of R- and L-defects, is upper bounded by 3^t, which immediately implies that a maximum increase of the number of L-defects hinders the propagation of any R-defects, and vice versa.

Aside from this overall upper bound on the MLE of three-state CAs, it can be expected that it should be possible to relate it in some way to the so-called sensitivity of a CA to its inputs, as has been shown for two-state CAs [3]. Yet, this is not straightforward as one can no longer rely on a single Jacobian matrix to assess the sensitivity of a CA to its inputs, and therefor tackling this issue is considered to be beyond to scope of this paper presenting preliminary results.

3   Results

3.1   Nonuniform Defect Propagation

In order to exemplify the nonuniform nature of defect propagation in multi-state CAs, Fig. 1 visualizes the defect cone for the three-state totalistic CAs with rule numbers, according to [16], 317 and 1809 which are evolved for 500 time steps, starting from a random initial condition on a system consisting of 1001 elements, upon introduction of both L- and R-defects in the 11 most centrally located cells at $t = 0$. In the case of the former rule, this figure clearly shows that L- and R-defects occur mostly simultaneously in the center of the defect cone, whereas L-defects are dominating in its outer regions where L- and R-defects cannot coexist. These two regions are separated by a zone where R-defects dominate and the defects can still coexist, though coexistence is relatively rare as compared to the inner region.

On the other hand, the defect cone of rule 1809 illustrates that defects can be mutually exclusive across the entire cone. Many other three-state CAs displaying such behavior can be found. Consequently, it should be obvious that the propagation of defects in multi-state CAs deserves careful consideration as their multivaluedness makes that an assessment of their stability will in many cases definitely depend on the type of initial defect, which hence should be accounted for when trying to assess a CA's overall stability.

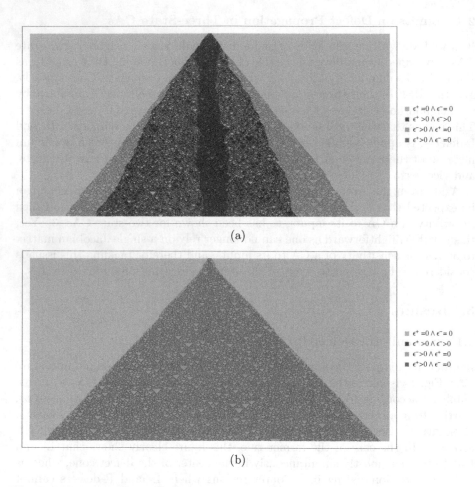

Fig. 1. Defect cone after 500 time steps for rules 317 (a) and 1809 (b) starting from a random initial condition with L- and R-defects in the 11 most centrally located cell of a system consisting of 1001 cells

3.2   Experimental Setup

In the remainder of this paper, the family of one-dimensional, nearest-neighbor, three-state totalistic CAs will be studied more elaborately in the sense that the dynamics of its members will be compared to the one of the well-studied elementary CAs. It encloses 2187 different rules [16]. For each of them, the propagation of R- and L-defects emerging from a single defect was tracked for 5000 time steps in a one-dimensional system consisting of 500 elements and this procedure was repeated over an ensemble E of 30 random initial perturbations, i.e. $E = \{_e s_0^* \mid e = 1, \ldots, 30\}$; half of them originating from the introduction of an L-defect and the other half from introducing an R-defect. As such, the numerical values given in the remainder of this paper represent averages over the members of E, unless stated otherwise.

The ensemble was considered in order to account for the fact that the intrinsic discreteness of a CA sometimes makes its stability assessment dichotomous [2], meaning that some perturbations might invoke instability, while others give rise to stable behavior. This is caused by the fact that, as opposed to continuous dynamical systems, there does not necessarily exist a path between a given configuration and a CA's fixed point(s). In the remainder, we will refer to a CA for which $_e\lambda = -\infty$, respectively $_e\lambda > 0$, for all members of the ensemble E as unconditionally superstable, respectively unconditionally unstable, while a rule will be labeled as conditionally unstable if there exists at least one member in the ensemble E that gives rise to converging phase space trajectories, while at least one other of the same ensemble leads to diverging phase space trajectories. In contrast to the suggestion by Bagnoli et al. [3], we did not swap the states of two randomly chosen pairs of cells at every time step, as the dependence of a CA's stability on its initial configuration just reflects its truly discrete nature.

In order to have a means of comparison, also the MLEs for the 256 two-state, elementary CAs were computed numerically over an ensemble of 30 random initial perturbations.

3.3   The Stability of Three-State Totalistic CAs

Figure 2(a) depicts the relative proportion of rules in each of the three stability regimes for both the 256 elementary CAs and the 2187 totalistic CAs that are considered throughout the remainder of this paper. Apparently, it is especially the share of rules which may invoke stability for some initial perturbations, i.e. the conditionally stable rules, that is significantly larger in case of the latter CA family. This should not come as surprise as it was demonstrated in Section 3.1 that defect propagation in three-state totalistic CAs depends on the type of defect, such that also the type of initial defect will often play a crucial role in whether or not a defect will be able to propagate in the long run.

Aside from the discrepancy that exists between both CA families with respect to the relative importance of the different stability regimes, there are also clear discrepancies between the real-valued MLEs of the (un)conditionally unstable rules within these families as illustrated by means of the box-and-whisker charts depicted in Fig. 2(b). More precisely, these charts indicate that the real-valued MLEs are generally higher among the three-state totalistic CAs. Moreover, the variability among the real-valued MLEs within the class enclosing the conditionally unstable rules is significantly more pronounced in the case of the three-state CAs as opposed to the variability among the ECA that display the same stability regime, and conversely for the class of unconditionally unstable rules. The fact that (un)conditionally unstable three-state totalistic CAs give, on average, rise to a faster divergence of phase space trajectories may be understood by acknowledging that cells can contain different types of defects, as such increasing the likeliness that they will be able to propagate.

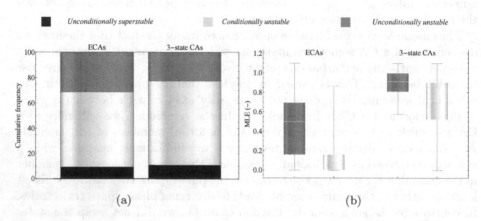

Fig. 2. Relative proportion of rules in each of the three stability regimes for both the 256 elementary CAs and the 2187 totalistic CAs (a) and box-and-whisker charts for the real-valued MLEs of the (un)conditionally unstable rules

3.4   L- Versus R-Defects

As demonstrated by Fig. 1, L- and R-defects might or might not coexist. For that reason, it may be anticipated that discrepancies might also arise between the number of L- and R-defects after only a few iterations for many rules, and that these will persist as the CA evolves through time. This expectation is confirmed by Fig. 3, which depicts histograms of the ratios of the average number of L-defects versus the average number of R-defects at the 5000-th time step for the (un)conditionally unstable rules as a function of the type of initial defect. For the sake of visualization, ratios higher than five were reclassified to five, and similarly for ratios smaller than 0.2. Although the ratios are frequently fairly close to one in the case of unconditionally unstable CAs, the average number of L- and R-defects regularly differs by a factor five or more for the conditionally unstable rules, irrespective of the initial defect type. This indicates that it are especially the rules of which the stability depends on the location of the initial defect, and hence on the initial condition, that exhibit the most pronounced

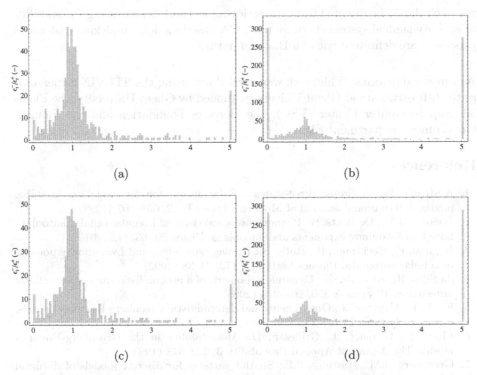

Fig. 3. Ratio of the number of L-defects (ϵ_t^-) versus the number of R-defects (ϵ_t^+) for unconditionally unstable rules (a and c) and conditionally unstable rules (b and d) starting from an initial L-defect (a and b) and R-defect (c and d)

nonuniform defect propagation. These discrepancies become even more patent upon closer inspection of the magnitude of the reclassified ratios. Typically, the number of L-defects can differ up to almost 2000 orders of magnitude from the number of R-defects after 5000 time steps.

From Fig. 3 it can further be inferred that the rules favoring L-defects are more or less balanced by the ones favoring R-defects, though there seems to be a slight imbalance in the case of unconditionally unstable rules as these appear to favor L-defects, irrespective of the initial defect type.

Conclusions

In this paper, we showed how one can assess the stability of three-state CAs by means of a dedicated set of Lyapunov exponents, thereby accounting for the different types of defects that emerge during the evolution of these multi-state counterparts of the widely studies Boolean CAs. As a first step towards a more complete understanding of the dynamics of multi-state CAs, this paper indicates that it might be much more involved to assess their stability than it first seems due to the emergence of several types of defects. Nevertheless, future research should be directed towards retrieving methods for assessing the stability of such dynamical systems because most CA-based models mimicking real-world processes are definitely not of a Boolean nature.

Acknowledgments. This work was carried out using the STEVIN Supercomputer Infrastructure at Ghent University, funded by Ghent University, the Flemish Supercomputer Center (VSC), the Hercules Foundation and the Flemish Government department EWI.

References

1. Andrecut, M.: A simple three-states cellular automaton for modelling excitable media. International Journal of Modern Physics B 12, 601–607 (1998)
2. Baetens, J.M., De Baets, B.: Phenomenological study of irregular cellular automata based on Lyapunov exponents and Jacobians. Chaos 20, 033112 (2010)
3. Bagnoli, F., Rechtman, R., Ruffo, S.: Damage spreading and Lyapunov exponents in cellular automata. Physics Letters A 172, 34–38 (1992)
4. da Silva, R., Alves Jr., N.: Dynamic exponents of a probabilistic three-state cellular automaton. Physica A 350, 263–276 (2005)
5. Fisch, R., Gravner, J.: One-dimensional deterministic Greenberg-Hastings models. Complex Systems 9, 329–348 (1995)
6. Fisch, R., Gravner, J., Griffeath, D.: Metastability in the Greenberg-Hastings model. The Annals of Applied Probability 3, 329–348 (1993)
7. Greenberg, J.M., Hastings, S.P.: Spatial patterns for discrete models of diffusion in excitable media. SIAM Journal on Applied Mathematics 34, 515–523 (1978)
8. Langton, C.: Computation at the edge of chaos. Physica D 42, 12–37 (1990)
9. Lempel, A., Ziv, J.: On the complexity of finite sequences. IEEE Transactions on Information Theory 22, 75–81 (1976)
10. Peltomäki, M., Rost, M., Alava, M.: Characterizing spatiotemporal patterns in three-state lattice models. Journal of Statistical Mechanics: Theory and Experiment P02042 (2009)
11. Potts, R.B.: Some generalized order-disorder transformations. Mathematical Proceedings of the Cambridge Philosophical Society 48, 106–109 (1952)
12. Reichenbach, T., Mobilia, M., Frey, E.: Self-organization of mobile populations in cyclic competition. Journal of Theoretical Biology 254, 368–383 (2008)
13. Sirakoulis, G.C., Karafyllidis, I., Thanailakis, A.: A cellular automaton model for the effects of population movement and vaccination on epidemic propagation. Ecological Modelling 133, 209–223 (2000)
14. von Neumann, J.: The general and logical theory of automata. In: Jeffres, L.A. (ed.) The Hixon Symposium on Cerebral Mechanisms in Behaviour, pp. 1–41. John Wiley & Sons, Pasadena (1951)
15. Wolfram, S.: Universality and complexity in cellular automata. Physica D 10, 1–35 (1984)
16. Wolfram, S.: A New Kind of Science. Wolfram Media, Inc., Champaign (2002)
17. Wu, F.: The Potts model. Reviews of Modern Physics 54, 235–268 (1982)
18. Wuensche, A.: Glider dynamics in 3-value hexagonal cellular automata: the beehive rule. International Journal of Unconventional Computing 1, 375–398 (2005)
19. Zanette, D.H.: Multistate cellular automaton for reaction-diffusion processes. Physical Review A 46, 7573–7577 (1992)

Iterative Arrays with Set Storage

Martin Kutrib and Andreas Malcher

Institut für Informatik, Universität Giessen
Arndtstr. 2, 35392 Giessen, Germany
{kutrib,malcher}@informatik.uni-giessen.de

Abstract. Iterative arrays with set storage (SIA) are one-dimensional arrays of interconnected interacting finite automata. The input is supplied sequentially to the distinguished communication cell at the origin. In addition, the communication cell controls a set storage. To this end, it is equipped with a one-way writing tape where strings for the set operations are assembled, and the data storage *set* where words of arbitrary length can be stored. The computational capacity of (real-time) SIA is investigated. It is shown that such devices are strictly stronger than classical iterative arrays and classical set automata. Moreover, the witness languages reveal that the combination of both principles is strictly stronger than just the union of the single principles. Some basic closure properties are studied. Furthermore, in contrast to the situation for classical set automata, it is shown that any constant number of operations on the set cannot increase the computational capacity of classical iterative arrays. Finally, the decidability of the restriction to a finite number of set operations is addressed, where it turns out that the problem is not even semi-decidable.

1 Introduction

The state changes of the single automata, called cells, of an iterative array are synchronous at discrete time steps. In order to support the modeling of massively parallel systems running systolic algorithms, the input to the entire device is supplied sequentially. To this end, the distinguished cell at the origin, called communication cell, is equipped with a one-way read-only input tape. The data supplied to iterative arrays can be arranged as strings of symbols.

In connection with formal language recognition classical iterative arrays without set storage (IA) have been introduced in [7], where closure properties of sets of patterns accepted in real time are investigated. Furthermore, a technique was developed which allows to show that some sets of patterns cannot be accepted by real-time IA. As a consequence it turned out that the language class accepted by real-time IA is incomparable with the class of context-free languages. However, in [6] it is shown that linear time and two dimensions are sufficient to parse all context-free languages. The ability of real-time IA to recognize rather complicated sets of unary patterns was first shown in [9], where a real-time IA for prime numbers is constructed. Pattern manipulation is the main aspect in [1]. A characterization of various types of IA by restricted Turing machines and several

J. Wąs, G.C. Sirakoulis, and S. Bandini (Eds.): ACRI 2014, LNCS 8751, pp. 25–34, 2014.

results especially speed-up theorems are given in [10–12]. Some further studies concern infinite hierarchies beyond linear time [13] and in between real time and linear time [3], hierarchies depending on the amount of nondeterminism [4] and the number of alternating steps performed by the communication cell [2], as well as descriptional complexity issues [16, 18]. Several more results in connection with formal languages can be found, for example, in [21–23].

Several studies include proofs that some language cannot be accepted by some type of iterative array. In many cases the limitations of iterative arrays to retrieve previously stored information from the array in due time are utilized. An example formalized below is a situation, where a sequence of strings followed by a single string is supplied as input. The task to solve by the IA is to check whether the last single string belongs to the sequence or not. There are several practically relevant applications for such a situation. Suppose for example the sequence are variables declared in some program. Then the check can be seen as verification whether the variable encoded as single string has been declared or not. The reason why real-time iterative arrays fail to solve the task is as follows. The strings of the sequence can be stored in the array. But since their number is arbitrary, they have to be stored also far away from the communication cell. So, there is not enough time to retrieve all of them until the computation is over.

Various generalizations of IA that add additional mechanisms or data structures to the communication cell have been considered as well. In [20], IA are studied in which all cells are additionally connected to the communication cell. It turned out that even this direct central control cannot increase the computational capacity of iterative arrays. Moreover, iterative arrays can simulate any fixed number of pushdown stores [5, 8], queues, or rings [14] without any delay of time. In particular this implies that these data structures cannot help to solve the problem of fast information retrieval.

Here we study iterative arrays where the communication cell is additionally equipped with a set storage (SIA) for strings. Operations on the set are adding, removing, or testing strings. To this end, the communication cell has access to a one-way writing tape where strings for the set operations are assembled. To some extent, the set storage can be seen as cache whose elements are content addressable. So, the information retrieval is independent of the precise location of the information in the storage.

The paper is organized as follows. After the definition of the model and an example in Section 2, we study the computational capacity of (real-time) SIA. It is shown that such devices are strictly stronger than classical iterative arrays and classical set automata. Moreover, the witness languages reveal that the combination of both principles is strictly stronger than just the union of the single principles. Then we turn to some basic closure properties. Section 4 is devoted to the question to what extent the set storage has to be used in order to increase the power of iterative arrays without set storage. It is known that just two set operations strictly increase the power of finite automata [17]. In contrast to this result, any constant number of operations on the set cannot increase the computational capacity of classical IA. Finally, the decidability of the restriction to a finite number of set operations is addressed, where a reduction of the emptiness problem of iterative arrays shows that the problem is not even semi-decidable.

2 Preliminaries and Definitions

We denote the set of natural numbers $\{0, 1, ...\}$ by $\mathbb{N}$. The empty word is denoted by λ, the reversal of a word w by w^R, and for the length of w we write $|w|$. We write $\subseteq$ for set inclusion, and $\subset$ for strict set inclusion. The cardinality of a set M is denoted by $|M|$.

An iterative array with set storage is an infinite linear array of finite automata, sometimes called cells. We identify the cells by natural numbers. Each cell except the origin is connected to its both nearest neighbors (one to the left and one to the right). The input is supplied sequentially to the distinguished communication cell at the origin which is connected to its immediate neighbor to the right only. In addition, the communication cell controls the set storage. To this end, it is equipped with a one-way writing tape where strings for the set operations are assembled, and the data storage *set* where words of arbitrary length can be stored. At each time step, the communication cell may either write a substring to the end of the writing tape, insert or remove the word written on the tape to or from the set, or test whether the word written on the tape belongs to the set. Each time a set operation in, out, or test is performed, the content of the writing tape is erased and its head is reset to the left end. So, altogether we have two different local transition functions. The state transition of all cells but the communication cell depends on the current state of the cell itself and the current states of its both neighbors. The state transition of the communication cell additionally depends on the current input symbol (or if the whole input has been consumed on a special end-of-input symbol). The finite automata work synchronously at discrete time steps. Initially they are in the so-called quiescent state.

Formally, an *iterative array* with set storage (SIA, for short) is a system $\langle S, A, T, F, s_0, \#, \delta, \delta_0 \rangle$, where S is the finite set of *cell states*, A is the finite set of *input symbols*, T is the finite set of *tape symbols*, $F \subseteq S$ is the set of *accepting states*, $s_0 \in S$ is the *quiescent state*, $\# \notin A$ is the *end-of-input symbol*, $\delta : S^3 \to S$ is the partial *local transition function for non-communication cells* satisfying $\delta(s_0, s_0, s_0) = s_0$, $\delta_0 : (A \cup \{\#\}) \times S^2 \to (S \times (T^* \cup \{\text{in}, \text{out}\})) \cup (S \times \{\text{test}\} \times S)$ is the partial *local transition function for the communication cell*, where in is the instruction to add the content of the tape to the set, out is the instruction to remove the content of the tape from the set, and test is the instruction to test whether or not the content of the tape is in the set. In the latter case, the successor state is the first component of the triple if the test is positive, and the third component otherwise.

Let M be an SIA. A *configuration* of M is a description of its global state which is actually a quadruple $(\sigma, v, z, \mathbb{S})$, where $\sigma : \mathbb{N} \to S$ is a mapping that maps the single cells to their current states, $v \in \Sigma^*$ is unread part of the input, $z \in T^*$ is

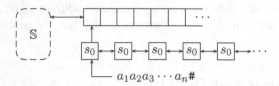

Fig. 1. Initial configuration of an iterative array with set storage

the content of the tape, and $\mathbb{S} \subseteq T^*$ is the finite set of stored words. The *initial configuration* for an input string w is set to $(\sigma_0, w, \lambda, \emptyset)$, where $\sigma_0(i) = s_0$, $i \geq 0$. Subsequent configurations are computed by the *global transition function* Δ. Let $(\sigma, v, z, \mathbb{S})$ be a configuration. Then its successor configuration $(\sigma', v', z', \mathbb{S}') = \Delta(\sigma, v, z, \mathbb{S})$ is as follows: Set $a = \#$, $v' = \lambda$ if $v = \lambda$, and $a = a_1$, $v' = a_2 a_3 \cdots a_n$ if $v = a_1 a_2 \cdots a_n$. For $i \geq 1$, set $\sigma'(i) = \delta(\sigma(i-1), \sigma(i), \sigma(i+1))$. Then

$$\sigma'(0) = s, \ z' = zu, \mathbb{S}' = \mathbb{S} \qquad \text{if } \delta_0(a, \sigma(0), \sigma(1)) = (s, u) \text{ for } u \in T^*,$$
$$\sigma'(0) = s, \ z' = \lambda, \ \ \mathbb{S}' = \mathbb{S} \cup \{z\} \text{ if } \delta_0(a, \sigma(0), \sigma(1)) = (s, \texttt{in}),$$
$$\sigma'(0) = s, \ z' = \lambda, \ \ \mathbb{S}' = \mathbb{S} \setminus \{z\} \text{ if } \delta_0(a, \sigma(0), \sigma(1)) = (s, \texttt{out}),$$
$$\sigma'(0) = s_1, z' = \lambda, \ \mathbb{S}' = \mathbb{S} \qquad \text{if } \delta_0(a, \sigma(0), \sigma(1)) = (s_1, \texttt{test}, s_2) \text{ and } z \in \mathbb{S},$$
$$\sigma'(0) = s_2, z' = \lambda, \ \mathbb{S}' = \mathbb{S} \qquad \text{if } \delta_0(a, \sigma(0), \sigma(1)) = (s_1, \texttt{test}, s_2) \text{ and } z \notin \mathbb{S}.$$

Thus, the global transition function Δ is induced by δ and δ_0.

An input w is accepted by an SIA M if at some time i during its course of computation the communication cell enters an accepting state.

$$L(M) = \{ w \in A^* \mid w \text{ is accepted by } M \}$$

is the *language accepted* by M. Let $t : \mathbb{N} \to \mathbb{N}$ be a mapping. If all $w \in L(M)$ are accepted with at most $t(|w|)$ time steps, then $L(M)$ is said to be of time complexity t. The family of all languages that are accepted by SIA with time complexity t is denoted by $\mathscr{L}_t(\text{IA})$. The index is omitted for arbitrary time. If t is the function $n+1$, acceptance is said to be in *real time* and we write $\mathscr{L}_{rt}(\text{SIA})$. The *linear-time* languages $\mathscr{L}_{lt}(\text{SIA})$ are defined according to $\mathscr{L}_{lt}(\text{SIA}) = \bigcup_{k \in \mathbb{N}} \mathscr{L}_{k \cdot n}(\text{SIA})$.

An SIA that never utilizes its set, that is, never performs an `in`-operation, is a classical iterative array (IA). Since without `in`-operation the set is useless, we simplify the notation by omitting the components T from the system and let the transition function for the communication cell δ_0 be a mapping from $(A \cup \{\#\}) \times S^2$ to S.

In order to clarify the notation we give an example.

Example 1. The language
$L = \{ \$x_1 \$x_2 \$ \cdots \$x_k \& y \mid k \geq 1, x_i, y \in \{a, b\}^* \text{ and } y = x_j \text{ for some } 1 \leq j \leq k \}$
does not belong to $\mathscr{L}_{rt}(\text{IA})$, but is accepted by some real-time SIA.

In contrast to the assertion, assume M is a real-time IA with state set S accepting L. For simplicity, we consider words from L where all subwords x_i have the same length, say n, and $k = n$. When M has processed all input symbols up to &, the remaining computation depends on the last n input symbols and the states of the cells $1, 2, \ldots, n + 2$. For the $n + 2$ states there are at most $|S|^{n+2}$ different possibilities.

On the other hand, for any pair of different prefixes $w = \$x_1\$x_2\$ \cdots \$x_n\&$ and $w' = \$x'_1\$x'_2\$ \cdots \$x'_n\&$ with $|x_i| = |x'_i| = n$, $1 \leq i \leq n$, there exists at least one $1 \leq \ell \leq n$ such that $x_\ell \neq x'_\ell$. This implies $wx_\ell \in L$ and $w'x_\ell \notin L$. There are 2^{n^2} different prefixes of the given form. Since for n large enough, $|S|^{n+2} < 2^{n^2}$, there are two different prefixes that lead to the same situation with respect to the states of the cells $1, 2, \ldots, n + 2$. So, either wx_ℓ and $w'x_\ell$ are both accepted or both rejected. The contradiction implies that L does not belong to $\mathscr{L}_{rt}(\mathrm{IA})$.

Basically, the simple idea for the construction of a real-time SIA

$$M' = \langle \{s_0, s_1, s_2, s_{acc}, s_{rej}\}, \{a, b, \$, \&\}, \{a, b\}, \{s_{acc}\}, s_0, \#, \delta, \delta_0 \rangle$$

accepting L is as follows. The communication cell writes the x_i on the tape. When a \$ or & appears in the input the tape inscription is inserted into the set. When the endmarker is read, a test is performed in order to check whether the tape inscription y matches any x_i.

Formally, the transition function δ is entirely defined by $\delta(s_0, s_0, s_0) = s_0$. The transition function δ_0 is as follows, where $x \in \{a, b\}$.

1. $\delta_0(\$, s_0, s_0) = (s_1, \lambda)$
2. $\delta_0(x, s_1, s_0) = (s_1, x)$
3. $\delta_0(\$, s_1, s_0) = (s_1, \mathtt{in})$
4. $\delta_0(\&, s_1, s_0) = (s_2, \mathtt{in})$
5. $\delta_0(x, s_2, s_0) = (s_2, x)$
6. $\delta_0(\#, s_2, s_0) = (s_{acc}, \mathtt{test}, s_{rej})$

$\square$

Example 1 contains a special case of a technique to disprove that languages are accepted by real-time IA. The general technique has been shown in [7]. It is based on equivalence classes which are induced by formal languages.

As mentioned before, iterative arrays can simulate any fixed number of push-down stores [5, 8], queues, or rings [14] without any delay of time. We will utilize this fact frequently in the sequel.

3   Computational Capacity

Here we turn to study the computational capacity of iterative arrays with set storage. In particular, we compare it with the power of other related computing models. If we consider the construction of the real-time SIA in Example 1 then we notice that the capacity of the iterative array is not used at all. The communication cell does the job single-handedly. So, basically, the example reveals that there is a language that can be accepted by some classical set automaton but cannot be accepted by any real-time iterative array. Taking into account that the mirror language $\{ wcw^R \mid w \in \{a, b\}^* \}$ is accepted by some real-time iterative array [7], but cannot be accepted by any classical set automaton [17], we also have the converse situation. So, we have derived the next theorem.

Theorem 2. *The families of languages accepted by real-time IA and classical set automata are incomparable.*

The previous theorem shows that the combination of iterative arrays and set automata is stronger than each of the single devices for its own.

Corollary 3. *The family of languages accepted by real-time IA as well as the family of languages accepted by classical set automata is strictly included in the family $\mathscr{L}_{rt}(SIA)$.*

The results so far raise immediately the question for the power of SIA that is gained by the *combination* of both computing principles. Is the combination stronger than just the union of the single principles? In other words, is there a language accepted by a real-time SIA that is neither accepted by a classical set automaton nor by a real-time IA. The next theorem answers the question in the affirmative.

Theorem 4. *There is a language not accepted by any real-time IA and not accepted by any classical set automaton, that is accepted by some real-time SIA.*

Proof. The witness language of the theorem is a modification of the language used in Example 1:

$$L = \{\, x_1 \$ x_2 \$ \cdots \$ x_k \& y \mid k \geq 1, x_1, x_2, \ldots, x_k \in \{a,b\}^{\ell}, \ell \geq 0,$$

$$\text{and } y^R = x_j \text{ for some } 1 \leq j \leq k \,\}$$

The main difference is that now all x_i have to have the same length and that the mirror image of the suffix y has to match one of the x_i. The proof that L does not belong to $\mathscr{L}_{rt}(IA)$ is almost textually along the line of Example 1.

Next assume L is accepted by some classical set automaton. Since the family of languages accepted by set automata is closed under intersection with regular sets [17], the language $L \cap \{a,b\}^* \& \{a,b\}^*$ is accepted by a classical set automaton as well. However, the intersection is precisely the mirror language $\{\, w \& w^R \mid w \in \{a,b\}^* \,\}$ that cannot be accepted by classical set automata [17].

It remains to be shown that L is, in fact, accepted by some real-time SIA M. The idea to construct M is as follows. As mentioned before, a real-time IA can simulate any constant number of pushdown stores. So, we assume that the communication cell of M has access to two pushdown stores which are initially empty. When M reads the first subword x_1 it is stored into, say, the first pushdown store, while the second one remains empty. Nothing is written on the tape in this phase. When the first $\$$ appears in the input, M changes its behavior. Now, every input symbol read is pushed into the second pushdown store. Moreover, at every time step one symbol is popped from the first pushdown store and is written to the tape. If the second $\$$ appears this phase is over. The subwords x_1 and x_2 have the same length if the first pushdown store gets empty at exactly that time. At this moment, the second pushdown store contains the mirror image of x_2 and the tape inscription is the mirror image of x_1 which is stored in the set by an **in**-operation. In the next phase, the pushdown stores interchange their roles, subword x_3 is pushed, and the mirror image of x_2 is stored in the set. These phases are repeated until the **&** appears in the input. At that time again the tape inscription is stored in the set. Moreover, it is known whether all subwords x_i have the same length, the set contains exactly the words $x_1^R, x_2^R, \ldots, x_{k-1}^R$, one of the pushdown stores is empty, and the other one contains the mirror image of x_k. In the final phase, at every time step a symbol of y is read and written on the tape, and a symbol from the non-empty pushdown store is popped and compared with input symbol. In this way, the suffix y is compared with x_k^R. Moreover, when the end-of-input symbol is read, the tape inscription is y which is compared with the set content by a **test**-operation. Finally, the input is accepted if the test is positive or y matches x_k^R. $\qquad\square$

Even for linear-time SIA an upper bound is given by the deterministic context-sensitive languages, that is, by DLINSPACE.

Theorem 5. *The family $\mathscr{L}_{lt}(SIA)$ is included in DLINSPACE.*

Next, we turn to derive some basic closure properties of the language families under consideration. Besides the fact that closure properties can shed some light on the structure of a language family they may be used as powerful reduction tools in order to simplify proofs or constructions. Closure under certain operations indicates a certain robustness, while non-closure properties may serve, for example, as a valuable basis for extensions.

For deterministic devices the closure under complementation is often shown by interchanging accepting and non-accepting states. But, in general, this requires halting computations. The proof of the following proposition is similar as for IA [15].

Proposition 6. *The language families $\mathscr{L}_{rt}(SIA)$ and $\mathscr{L}_{lt}(SIA)$ are effectively closed under complementation.*

Proof. Since an input is accepted when the communication cell enters an accepting state at some arbitrary time step, the complementary device cannot be constructed by simply interchanging accepting and non-accepting states. Actually, the communication cell will enter accepting as well as non-accepting states during a computation. To cope with this problem we modify a given linear-time, say $(k \cdot n)$-time SIA M in the following way.

Basically, the modified SIA M' simulates M. In addition, it uses a pushdown store to which the input is pushed. When the end-of-input symbol appears, M' starts to pop one symbol from the pushdown store in every $(k-1)$th time step. In this way, the pushdown store gets empty at time $k \cdot n$. This is the time step at which we wish to make the final decision whether to accept or to reject the input. To this end, the communication cell of M' has to remember if it has entered an accepting state at some time before. So, we use a copy S' of the state set S of M, and modify the local transition function to drive the communication cell of M' into a state of S' when it enters an accepting state. Subsequently, the normal behavior of the communication cell of M is simulated, except that states of S' are used instead of states of S. In this way, M' accepts if and only if the communication cell is in some state of S' at time $k \cdot n$. In order to accept the complement of $L(M)$ it is now sufficient to let the communication cell of M' enter a new accepting state if and only if it is not in some state of S' at time $k \cdot n$.

The construction for real-time SIA is similar. In this case the first appearance of the end-of-input symbol gives the time step to decide. The pushdown store is not used.   □

The closure under union and intersection for IA is often shown with the two-track technique, that is, two tracks of an IA are used to simulate both given IA in parallel. This idea is not applicable for SIA, since it is not clear how to manage with one set the contents of two sets in parallel. However, it is possible to simulate the given IA sequentially, where both simulations use different tape symbols to avoid any interference with possibly set contents left from the first simulation.

Proposition 7. *The language family $\mathscr{L}_{lt}(SIA)$ is closed under union and intersection.*

It is currently unknown whether or not $\mathscr{L}_{rt}(SIA)$ is closed under union and intersection. We conjecture the non-closure of $\mathscr{L}_{rt}(SIA)$ under these operations. Since $\mathscr{L}_{lt}(SIA)$ is closed under union and intersection, we obtain the following result.

Corollary 8. *The union closure as well as the intersection closure of $\mathscr{L}_{rt}(SIA)$ belongs to $\mathscr{L}_{lt}(SIA)$.*

4   Limited Operations on the Set

It is known that the non-regular language $\{\, wcw \mid w \in \{a,b\}^* \,\}$ is accepted by a classical set automaton performing just one **in**- and one **test**-operation [17]. Thus, two set operations are sufficient to increase the computational power of a finite automaton. In iterative arrays we have the situation of many identical finite automata, and the question is how many set operations are necessary here to increase the computational power. The next theorem says that, in contrast to classical set automata, a finite number of set operations, even **in**-operations is not sufficient.

Theorem 9. *Let $k \geq 0$ be an integer and M be a real-time SIA which performs at most k **in**-operations on the set in every accepting computation. Then an equivalent real-time IA can effectively be constructed.*

Finally, we consider the question whether there is an algorithm that decides whether a given (real-time) SIA performs at most a constant number of **in**-operations on the set. It turns out that such an algorithm does not exist. Moreover, the problem is not even semi-decidable.

Theorem 10. *Let $k \geq 0$ be an integer and M be a (real-time) SIA. Then it is neither semi-decidable whether M performs at most k nor whether M performs at all a constant number of in-operations on the set in every accepting computation.*

Proof. It is shown in [18, 19] that it is not semi-decidable whether the language accepted by a given real-time IA is empty. In the following this emptiness problem for real-time IA is reduced to the problem in question.

Any real-time iterative array can effectively be modified so that it enters an accepting state only when the first # appears in the input. To this end, the communication cell just has to remember if it was accepting before. Now, it can decide to enter an accepting state or not when the first # appears. So, let $M = \langle S, A, F, s_0, \#, \delta, \delta_0 \rangle$ be an arbitrary real-time iterative array with this property. We use new symbols $a, b, \hat{\#}$ such that $A \cap \{a, b, \hat{\#}\} = \emptyset$ and construct a real-time SIA $M' = \langle S \cup \{q, q_{rej}\}, A \cup \{a, b, \hat{\#}\}, \{a\}, \{q\}, s_0, \#, \delta', \delta_0' \rangle$ accepting the language $\{ v\hat{\#}w \mid v \in L(M), w \in \{a, b\}^* \}$, where

1. $\delta'(s_1, s_2, s_3) = \delta(s_1, s_2, s_3)$, for $s_1, s_2, s_3 \in S$,
2. $\delta'(q, s_2, s_3) = q$, for $s_2, s_3 \in S \cup \{q\}$,
3. $\delta_0'(x, s_1, s_2) = (\delta_0(x, s_1, s_2), \lambda)$, for $x \in A$, $s_1, s_2 \in S$,
4. $\delta_0'(\hat{\#}, s_1, s_2) = (q, \lambda)$, if $\delta_0(\#, s_1, s_2) \in F$ for $s_1, s_2 \in S$,
5. $\delta_0'(\hat{\#}, s_1, s_2) = (q_{rej}, \lambda)$, if $\delta_0(\#, s_1, s_2) \notin F$ for $s_1, s_2 \in S$,
6. $\delta_0'(a, q, s_2) = (q, a)$, for $s_2 \in S \cup \{q\}$, and
7. $\delta_0'(b, q, s_2) = (q, \mathtt{in})$, for $s_2 \in S \cup \{q\}$.

The idea is that M' simulates M without any set operation until the communication cell of M would enter an accepting state on input symbol #. If this does not happen, M' enters the non-accepting state q_{rej} on input symbol $\hat{\#}$ or blocks the computation and, thus, rejects. Otherwise, M' enters its accepting state q on input symbol $\hat{\#}$ and continues the computation on input symbols a and b. Now, every a-sequence is written on the tape, whereas an input symbol b initiates an in-operation. So, we have that once M accepts some input v, the SIA accepts all words $v\hat{\#}\{a, b\}^*$. In particular, it performs an in-operation for any symbol b from the suffix. Therefore, the number of in-operation of M' cannot be bounded by any constant in this case. However, if $L(M)$ is empty, M' never enters state q and, hence, never performs an in-operation at all. We conclude that M' performs a constant number of in-operations on the set in every accepting computation if and only if $L(M)$ is empty. If we could semi-decide for M' whether k or a finite number of set operations is performed, we could semi-decide the emptiness of M which is a contradiction. □

References

1. Beyer, W.T.: Recognition of topological invariants by iterative arrays. Tech. Rep. TR-66. MIT, Cambridge, Proj. MAC (1969)
2. Buchholz, T., Klein, A., Kutrib, M.: Iterative arrays with a wee bit alternation. In: Ciobanu, G., Păun, G. (eds.) FCT 1999. LNCS, vol. 1684, pp. 173–184. Springer, Heidelberg (1999)

3. Buchholz, T., Klein, A., Kutrib, M.: Iterative arrays with small time bounds. In: Nielsen, M., Rovan, B. (eds.) MFCS 2000. LNCS, vol. 1893, pp. 243–252. Springer, Heidelberg (2000)
4. Buchholz, T., Klein, A., Kutrib, M.: Iterative arrays with limited nondeterministic communication cell. In: Words, Languages and Combinatorics III, pp. 73–87. World Scientific Publishing (2003)
5. Buchholz, T., Kutrib, M.: Some relations between massively parallel arrays. Parallel Comput. 23, 1643–1662 (1997)
6. Chang, J.H., Ibarra, O.H., Palis, M.A.: Parallel parsing on a one-way array of finite-state machines. IEEE Trans. Comput. C-36, 64–75 (1987)
7. Cole, S.N.: Real-time computation by n-dimensional iterative arrays of finite-state machines. IEEE Trans. Comput. C-18(4), 349–365 (1969)
8. Čulik II, K., Yu, S.: Iterative tree automata. Theoret. Comput. Sci. 32, 227–247 (1984)
9. Fischer, P.C.: Generation of primes by a one-dimensional real-time iterative array. J. ACM 12, 388–394 (1965)
10. Ibarra, O.H., Jiang, T.: On one-way cellular arrays. SIAM J. Comput. 16, 1135–1154 (1987)
11. Ibarra, O.H., Palis, M.A.: Some results concerning linear iterative (systolic) arrays. J. Parallel Distributed Comput. 2, 182–218 (1985)
12. Ibarra, O.H., Palis, M.A.: Two-dimensional iterative arrays: Characterizations and applications. Theoret. Comput. Sci. 57, 47–86 (1988)
13. Iwamoto, C., Hatsuyama, T., Morita, K., Imai, K.: On time-constructible functions in one-dimensional cellular automata. In: Ciobanu, G., Păun, G. (eds.) FCT 1999. LNCS, vol. 1684, pp. 316–326. Springer, Heidelberg (1999)
14. Kutrib, M.: Cellular automata – a computational point of view. In: Bel-Enguix, G., Jiménez-López, M.D., Martín-Vide, C. (eds.) New Developments in Formal Languages and Applications. SCI, vol. 113, pp. 183–227. Springer, Heidelberg (2008)
15. Kutrib, M.: Cellular automata and language theory. In: Encyclopedia of Complexity and System Science, pp. 800–823. Springer (2009)
16. Kutrib, M., Malcher, A.: The size impact of little iterative array resources. J. Cellular Automata 7, 489–507 (2012)
17. Kutrib, M., Malcher, A., Wendlandt, M.: Deterministic set automata. In: Shur, A. (ed.) DLT 2014. LNCS, vol. 8633, pp. 303–314. Springer, Heidelberg (2014)
18. Malcher, A.: On the descriptional complexity of iterative arrays. IEICE Trans. Inf. Syst. E87-D, 721–725 (2004)
19. Seidel, S.R.: Language recognition and the synchronization of cellular automata. Tech. Rep. 79-02, Department of Computer Science, University of Iowa (1979)
20. Seiferas, J.I.: Iterative arrays with direct central control. Acta Inform. 8, 177–192 (1977)
21. Seiferas, J.I.: Linear-time computation by nondeterministic multidimensional iterative arrays. SIAM J. Comput. 6, 487–504 (1977)
22. Smith III, A.R.: Real-time language recognition by one-dimensional cellular automata. J. Comput. System Sci. 6, 233–253 (1972)
23. Terrier, V.: On real time one-way cellular array. Theoret. Comput. Sci. 141, 331–335 (1995)

Isotropic Cellular Automaton for Excitable Media with Random Neighbor Selection

Mio Kobayashi

National Institute of Technology, Anan College, 265 Aoki Minobayashi, Anan, Tokushima 774-0017, Japan

Abstract. This paper proposes a new isotropic cellular automaton (CA) model for reproducing the Belousov–Zhabotinsky reaction observed in excitable media. Although several CA models have been proposed that exhibit isotropic patterns of the reaction, most of them need complicated rules, a large number of neighboring cells, and multiple thresholds to decide the excitation condition of cells. The proposed model uses only one threshold and simple time-evolution rules on the basis of states of selected neighboring cells; the selected cells are randomly chosen from eight neighboring cells. It is this randomness in selecting neighboring cells that causes the model to generate isotropic patterns. This study shows that patterns generated by the proposed model are highly isotropic. Furthermore, we use simulation results to elucidate how generated patterns are related to the initial states assigned to central cells.

Keywords: isotropic cellular automaton, Belousov–Zhabotinsky reaction, randomness.

1 Introduction

Studies of reaction-diffusion systems are important to investigate nonlinear phenomena, and many phenomena observed in chemistry, biology, and other disciplines are represented by the reaction-diffusion systems. A typical example of oscillatory phenomena in a reaction-diffusion system is the Belousov–Zhabotinsky (BZ) reaction which is observed in excitable media [1]. Often, the BZ reaction is theoretically modeled through simultaneous differential equations [2], $\partial u/\partial t = f(u,v) + D_u \nabla^2 u$, $\partial v/\partial t = g(u,v) + D_v \nabla^2 v$, where $u(x,y,t)$ and $v(x,y,t)$ are state variables corresponding to the concentrations of two kinds of medium, and D_u and D_v are diffusion coefficients. Typical nullclines $f(u,v) = 0$ and $g(u,v) = 0$, as well as the trajectory are shown in Fig. 1. The intersection of two nullclines indicates the equilibrium point. The state at the equilibrium point is stable when the perturbation is week; however, it becomes unstable and change along with the arrow when the strength of the perturbation exceeds a certain threshold by the effect of the diffusion; the state of the excitable media returns to the equilibrium point again. Thus, the specific patterns of excitable media are reproducible with the simultaneous differential equations.

An alternative approach to study the BZ reaction is to use cellular automata (CA) [3–5], which are dynamic computational systems with discrete time, space,

J. Wąs, G.C. Sirakoulis, and S. Bandini (Eds.): ACRI 2014, LNCS 8751, pp. 35–44, 2014.
© Springer International Publishing Switzerland 2014

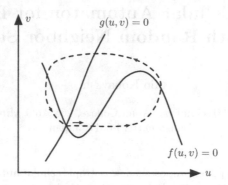

Fig. 1. Typical phase diagram for the BZ reaction.Solid curves indicates nullclines; dashed curve is the trajectory starting from the equilibrium point

and state variables. The behavior of CAs is completely specified by simple rules governing local relationships. This implies that CAs have the advantage of being able to reproduce the various patterns observed in nonlinear phenomena at low computational cost. Nevertheless, even though CAs offer fast calculation speeds, it have some shortcomings, such as the lack of curvature and dispersion effects and unwanted anisotropy in wave front motion [4, 5]. To resolve these issues, revised CA models have been proposed. Such CA models use large neighborhoods to model curvature effects, and they consider dispersion by making the threshold a linear function [6]. These CA models satisfactorily overcome curvature and dispersion effects. However, in excitable media [7], anisotropy of wave propagation has not been completely eliminated in the CA models proposed so far because the cell shape of the periodic lattice propagates to macroscopic scales.

Markus and Hess have proposed an isotropic CA model for excited media [8] that succeeds in excluding anisotropy of wave front motion; however, practical calculations of the model require large computational resources because the model adopts wide-ranging neighboring cells to update the cell state. Nishiyama et al. have proposed an isotropic CA model that uses only a few (four or eight) neighboring cells to eliminate anisotropy of wave propagation [9]. The Nishiyama CA model for excitable media is a simple square lattice that uses two different thresholds for the excitation of cells. The key to isotropy in their CA model is that the two different thresholds distribute with spatial randomness. Using their CA model, they succeeded in representing wave patterns observed in BZ reactions while preserving isotropy in the propagating waves.

However, if we need to select the types of generated wave patterns by adjusting parameter values, such as values of thresholds, then a model with fewer parameters is more manageable because it would allow parameters to be more easily adjusted to proper values. Therefore, in the CA model proposed in this paper, only one threshold is used for excited media. Our proposed CA model generates isotropic patterns on the basis of randomness with which multiple cells are selected from eight neighboring cells to update the state of the central

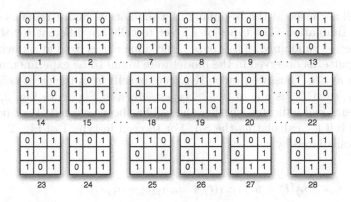

Fig. 2. All 28 possible combinations for selecting six cells from eight neighboring cells

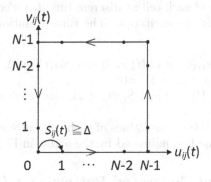

Fig. 3. Phase diagram that gives the time-evolution rules for $u_{ij}(t)$ and $v_{ij}(t)$

cell. This paper presents results from simulations using the proposed isotropic CA model. In addition, we investigate how generated patterns depend on initial states of the central cells. We also discuss the results and future study.

2   Model Description

The CA model proposed in this paper is defined on a two-dimensional square lattice. Each cell on the lattice has two state variables $u_{ij}(t)$ and $v_{ij}(t)$ corresponding to states of activator and inhibitor in excitable media at discrete time t, where i and j stand for column numbers and row numbers of the lattice, respectively. The two state variables $u_{ij}(t)$ and $v_{ij}(t)$ take values from 0 to $N-1$. Each state of the cell is updated by using the value of $S_{ij}(t)$, which is defined by

$$S_{ij}(t) = \sum_{k \in L_{ij}} u_k(t), \tag{1}$$

where L_{ij} denotes a group of d cells randomly selected from the eight neighboring cells. The quantity d is the number of cells, which are labeled from 0 to 8. The L_{ij}

for each cell is chosen at the beginning of a simulation, and it remains constant during the simulation. The types of L_{ij} set to cells are different (or the same) and are selected randomly. In this paper, the value of d is fixed at six because the generated patterns observed in the model were found to be experimentally most isotropic at $d = 6$. Thus, we randomly select six cells from the eight neighboring cells; hence, each L_{ij} is one of the 28 types shown in Fig. 2. In Fig. 2, the one or zero in each cell indicates whether the cell has been selected (1) or not (0) by the central cell for calculating the S_{ij}. For the cell in type 1 of Fig. 2, $S_{ij}(t)$ of the cell is calculated by

$$S_{ij}(t) = u_{i+1j-1}(t) + u_{i-1j}(t) + u_{i+1j}(t)$$
$$+u_{i-1j+1}(t) + u_{ij+1}(t) + u_{i+1j+1}(t). \tag{2}$$

To update the state of each cell at discrete time t, we consider parameter Δ, which is a threshold for the excitation. The time-evolution rules we use are as follows:

(1) For excitation, if $u_{ij}(t) = v_{ij}(t) = 0$ and $S_{ij}(t) \geq \Delta$, then $u_{ij}(t+1) = 1$, while $v_{ij}(t)$ stays at $v_{ij}(t+1) = 0$;
(2) Else, if $u_{ij}(t) = v_{ij}(t) = 0$ and $S_{ij}(t) < \Delta$, then each state stays at $u_{ij}(t+1) = v_{ij}(t+1) = 0$;
(3) If $u_{ij}(t) + v_{ij}(t) \neq 0$ then the values of each cell automatically transit to the next point along the line indicated by the arrow in Fig. 3.

3   Dependence of Generated Patterns on L_{ij} Distributions

To investigate the dependence of generated patterns on L_{ij} distributions, we consider the expected value related to the 3×3 cells at the center of the square lattice. We number those cells from 0 to 8, as shown in shown in Fig. 4(a). The initial conditions are $u_{ij}(0) = 1$ and $v_{ij}(0) = 0$ on the central cell and $u_{ij}(0) = v_{ij}(0) = 0$ on all other cells. Therefore, we consider only the central 3×3 cells. In the proposed model, each cell has one of L_{ij} types shown in Fig. 2. Then, the theoretically expected value E_m for the mth cell in Fig. 4(a) is given by

$$E_m = \alpha M_m, \quad m = 0, 1, \cdots 8, \tag{3}$$

where α is the ratio of the number of selected neighboring cells to the number of all neighboring cells; we randomly select six cells from the eight neighboring cells; hence, $\alpha = 0.75$. In addition, the experimentally expected value E'_m is calculated by

$$E'_m = \sum_{h=0}^{M_m} hP_{hm}, \quad m = 0, 1, \cdots 8, \tag{4}$$

where h is the number of times the mth cell is selected by its eight neighboring cells in calculating their $S_{ij}(t)$. Note that we do not consider the outside cells of

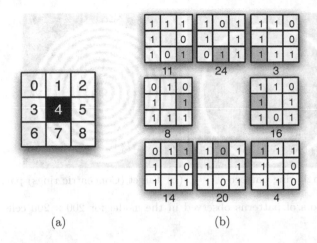

(a)   (b)

Fig. 4. (a) Numerical labels assigned to the central 3×3 cells in a two-dimensional square latticeD(b) Example of a distribution of L_{ij} on central cells. Each cell has one of the L_{ij} types shown in Fig. 2.

central 3×3 cells. In Eqs. (3) and (4), M_m indicates the maximum value of h for the mth cell and is defined by

$$M_m = \begin{cases} 3, & m = 0, 2, 6, 8 \\ 5, & m = 1, 3, 5, 7 \\ 8, & m = 4. \end{cases} \tag{5}$$

where M_m is the number of neighboring cells of the mth cell in Fig. 4(a).

In Eq. (4), P_{hm} is the probability that the mth cell is selected h times by its neighboring cells; it is theoretically defined by

$$P_{hm} = \frac{M_m!}{(M_m - h)!h!} (\alpha)^h (1 - \alpha)^{M_m - h}. \tag{6}$$

For example, assuming that the central 3×3 cells have the distribution L_{ij} shown in Fig. 4 (b). Figure 4 (b) shows that the black cell (labeled $\ddot{4}$) in Fig. 4(a) is selected by seven neighboring cells; that is, it is selected by all neighboring cells except the one that directly lies below it. This excluded cell has the type of L_{ij} appearing in type 20 of Fig. 2. Therefore the probability P_{hm} is calculated by

$$P_{74} = \frac{8!}{(8 - 7)!7!} (0.75)^7 (0.25)^{8-7} = 0.267, \tag{7}$$

where $h = 7$, $m = 4$, $\alpha = 0.75$, and $M_m = 8$.

Using the experimentally expected value E'_m on the basis of P_{hm} determined by simulations, we can clarify relationships between the generated patterns and the distribution of L_{ij} on the central 3×3 cells. On the basis of the analysis results, we can selectively generate patterns by setting the proper distribution of L_{ij} on the central 3×3 cells.

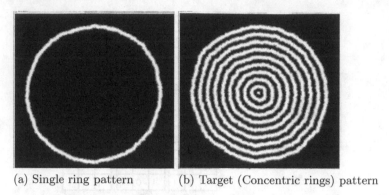

(a) Single ring pattern   (b) Target (Concentric rings) pattern

Fig. 5. Snapshots of patterns observed in the model for 200×200 cells at $t = 150$, $\Delta = 3$, and $N = 5$

4   Results

In this section, results from simulations and a statistical analysis of the model are presented. In the simulations, each cell has one of the L_{ij} types shown in Fig. 2. At the beginning of a simulation, each cell was randomly assigned one of those 28 types, and that assignment remained constant throughout the simulation.

4.1   Result from Simulations

Figure 5 shows snapshots of typical patterns observed in a simulation of the model for 200×200 cells at $t = 150$, $\Delta = 3$, and $N = 5$. The gray scale from black to white corresponds to values of $u_{ij}(t)$ from 0 to $N - 1$. Figures 5(a) and 5(b) show the single ring pattern and the target (the concentric rings) pattern, respectively. These were produced by the initial conditions $u_{ij}(0) = 1$ and $v_{ij}(0) = 0$ at $i = j = 100$ on the central cell and $u_{ij}(0) = v_{ij}(0) = 0$ on all other cells. In the single ring pattern in Fig.5(a), the ring-shaped wave is generated around the central cell by the initial state and the distribution of L_{ij} for the central cell. The wave spreads outward as the number of time steps increases. Figure 5(b) shows the target pattern observed in the model. The initial states of $u_{ij}(0)$ and $v_{ij}(0)$ generating the target pattern are the same as those that generate the single ring pattern. In addition, the ring-shaped wave observed in the target pattern is, at first, similar to the single ring pattern; however, ring-shaped waves are repeatedly generated around the central cell and spread outward. The ring-shaped waves in the target pattern were repeatedly generated with period $4(N - 1)$.

The generations of the target and single ring patterns in the model do not depend on the initial states of $u_{ij}(0)$ and $v_{ij}(0)$ but on the distribution of the L_{ij} from the possibilities shown in Fig. 2. Details of the relationship between the distribution of L_{ij} and the generated patterns are presented in the next section.

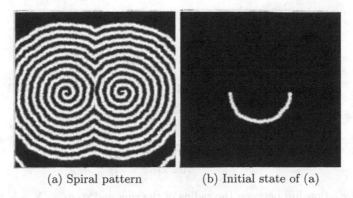

(a) Spiral pattern   (b) Initial state of (a)

Fig. 6. Snapshots of a spiral pattern observed in the model for 200×200 cells at $t = 150$, $\Delta = 3$, $N = 5$ and its initail state at $t = 0$

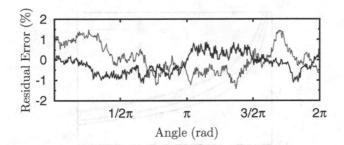

Fig. 7. Plot of the residual error of the ring pattern observed in the proposed model and Nishimaya's model in Ref. [9] at $R = 300$. The residual error is defined as the percentage of deviations from the circle with the radius R which is the average radius value of each ring. The solid line shows the proposed model at $\Delta = 3$, and $N = 5$. The dashed line shows Nishiyama's model at $\Delta_1 = 3$, $\Delta_2 = 7$, and $N = 5$.

Figure 6(a) shows the spiral pattern observed in the model, which was generated by the initial state shown in Fig. 6(b). To prepare the initial state for the spiral pattern, we first generated the single ring pattern shown in Fig. 5(a). Then, we removed the upper (or lower) part of the ring to create a half ring. The remainder was used as the initial state for the spiral pattern.

In Fig. 7, the residual errors in the ring pattern observed from the model are compared with those from the Nishiyama model [9] at $R = 300$ and $N = 5$. Here R is the average radius value of each ring. The solid line shows the proposed model at $\Delta = 3$. The dashed line shows the Nishiyama model at $\Delta_1 = 3$ and $\Delta_2 = 7$. The figure indicates that the residual error in the proposed model is less than one percent at all angles; hence, the ring pattern generated by the proposed model is more isotropic than that generated by the model in [9].

In Fig. 8, the relationship between the radius of the ring pattern and the number of simulation time steps for the proposed model is compared with that from the Nishiyama model at $N = 5$. In the figure, the slope of each line represents the

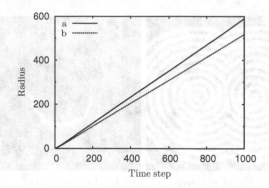

Fig. 8. The relationship between the radius of the ring and steps at $N = 5$. Solid line a indicates proposed model at $\Delta = 3$. Dashed line b indicates Nishiyama's model [9] at $\Delta_1 = 3$ and $\Delta_2 = 7$.

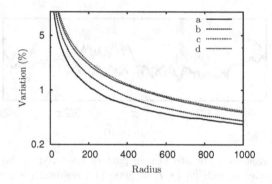

Fig. 9. The relationship between the radius of the ring and the variation of the radius at $\Delta = 3$, a: $N = 5$, b: $N = 7$, c: $N = 10$, and d: Nishiyama's model in Ref.[9], $\Delta_1 = 3$, $\Delta_2 = 7$, $N = 5$

propagation velocity of the wave front. The solid line (a) is from the proposed model with $\Delta = 3$, while the dashed line (b) is the result from the Nishiyama model [9] with $\Delta_1 = 3$ and $\Delta_2 = 7$. Figure 8 indicates that the wave in the proposed model propagates faster than the Nishiyama model.

Figure 9 shows variations from the circle as functions of the radius of the ring pattern. In the figure, lines (a), (b), and (c) were obtained from the proposed model using $\Delta = 3$ with $N = 5$, 7, and 10, respectively. Line (d) is from the Nishiyama model [9] with $\Delta_1 = 3$, $\Delta_2 = 7$, and $N = 5$. The ring patterns from the proposed modele with $\Delta = 3$ grow closer to a complete circle as the radius increases. In addition, the ring patterns observed in the proposed model at $N = 5$ and 7 are more isotropic than the one observed in [9] at any radius.

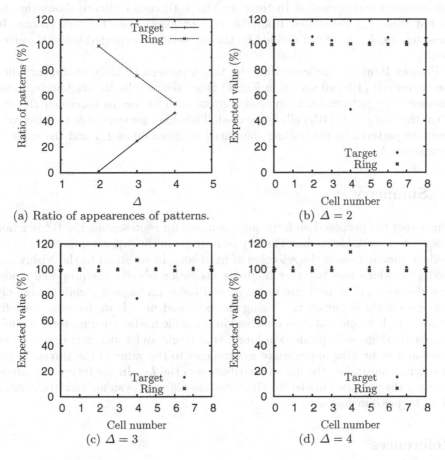

(a) Ratio of appearences of patterns.

(b) $\Delta = 2$

(c) $\Delta = 3$

(d) $\Delta = 4$

Fig. 10. The result of 100,000 times simulation at $N = 5$

4.2   Dependence on Initial Conditions

In this section, we discuss results from a statistical analysis to investigate how generated patterns depend on initial distributions of L_{ij} on central 3×3 cells.

Figures 10(a)–(d) show results obtained from simulations over 100,000 times steps.

Figure 10(a) shows the percentages of appearances of the target pattern and the single ring pattern on varying the threshold parameter Δ. The fraction of appearances of the target (single ring) pattern increases (decreases) as the value of parameter Δ.

Figures 10(b)–(d) show the relationship between the expected value of each cell and each pattern observed in the model. Over the simulations, we measured the probabilities P_{hm}, which are theoretically given by (6), with which the target (single ring) pattern was generated. Then, the expected value E'_m was calculated using the computed P_{hm} in (4). In Figs. 10(b)–(d), each abscissa contains the cell numbers corresponding to those in Fig. 4(a); each ordinate shows the expected value E'_m calculated from the P_{hm} obtained from the simulations. In these figures, E'_m has been divided by the theoretically expected value E_m given by (3).

Figures 10(a)–(d) indicate that the target pattern is likely to appear when the center cell (4th cell shown in Fig. 4) is not selected by its neighboring cells; moreover, the pattern tends to easily appear with increasing threshold Δ, even when the center cell (4th cell) is selected. Therefore, we were able to selectively generate patterns by controlling the initial distribution of L_{ij} and the value of parameter Δ.

5 Summary

This paper has proposed an isotropic CA model for representing the BZ reaction observed in excitable media. The key to isotropy in the proposed model is to introduce randomness in the selection of neighbors. In constrast to the Nishiyama model [9], which uses two thresholds for excitation of cells, the proposed model provides waves that are more isotropic and faster propagating while using only a single threshold parameter. Using the proposed model, we have successfully reproduced isotropic patterns observed in excitable media; such patterns include concentric rings and spirals. We found that single and concentric rings can be generated by making appropriate assignments to the value of the threshold parameter Δ controlling the initial distribution of the L_{ij}. In the future, we intend to apply the proposed model to other reaction-diffusion systems and to CA models of higher dimensions.

References

1. Zaikin, A.N., Zhabotinsky, A.M.: Concentration Wave Propagation in Two-dimensional Liquid-phase Self-oscillating System. Nature 225, 535–537 (1970)
2. Meron, E.: Pattern formation in excitable media. Phys. Rep. 218, 1–66 (1992)
3. Wolfram, S.: A New Kind of Science. Illinois (2002)
4. Madore, B.F., Freedman, W.L.: Computer Simulations of the Belousov-Zhabotinsky Reaction. Science 222, 615–616 (1983)
5. Winfree, A.T., Winfree, E.M., Seifert, H.: Organizing centers in a cellular excitable medium. Physica D 17, 109–115 (1985)
6. Gerhardt, M., Schuster, H., Tyson, J.J.: Cellular automaton model of excitable media II & III. Physica D 46, 392–426 (1990)
7. Barkley, D.: A model for fast computer simulation of waves in excitable media. Physica D 49, 61–70 (1991)
8. Markus, M., Hess, B.: Isotropic cellular automaton for modelling excitable media. Nature 347, 56–58 (1990)
9. Nishiyama, A., Tanaka, H., Tokihiro, T.: An isotropic cellular automaton for excitable media. Physica A 387, 3129–3136 (2008)

Power Spectral Analysis
of the Computation Process by Rule 110

Shigeru Ninagawa[1,3] and Genaro J. Martínez[2,3]

[1] Kanazawa Institute of Technology, Nonoichi, Japan
ninagawa@neptune.kanazawa-it.ac.jp
[2] Escuela Superior de Cómputo, Instituto Politécnico Nacional, México, D. F.
genaro.martinez@uwe.ac.uk
[3] University of the West of England, Bristol, United Kingdom

Abstract. An elementary cellular automaton rule 110 supports universal computation by emulating cyclic tag system and its evolution starting from random initial configurations exhibits $1/f$ noise. In this research we investigate the power spectra of rule 110 during the computation process emulating cyclic tag system. As a result, $1/f$-type power spectra are observed in the most actively interacting area among the whole array, while in the less active area the power spectra exhibit Lorentzian or periodic types. These results suggest the relationship between $1/f$ noise and computability in cellular automata.

Keywords: rule 110, computational universality, 1/f noise, cyclic tag system.

1 Introduction

It is known that elementary cellular automaton (ECA), namely one-dimensional and two-state, three-neighbour CA rule 110 is computationally universal [1] that means any algorithms can be performed by setting appropriate initial conditions. On the other hand, the evolution of rule 110 starting from a random configuration exhibits $1/f$ noise [2]. $1/f$ noise is a random process whose spectrum as a function of the frequency f behaves like $1/f^\beta$ with $\beta \approx 1$ at low frequencies. $1/f$ noise has been observed in various phenomena such as the voltages or currents of vacuum tubes, diodes, and transistors or the frequency of quartz crystal oscillators, but a general explanation of these phenomena has not yet been forthcoming [3]. Moreover the Game of Life (LIFE), a two-dimensional and two-state, nine-neighbour outer semi-totalistic CA, supports universal computation [4] and exhibits $1/f$-type spectrum starting from a random configuration [5]. These results suggest that there is a relationship between computational universality and $1/f$ noise in CAs.

Let us attract attention to the fact that $1/f$ noise in ECA rule 110 and LIFE has been observed in the evolution from random initial configurations in previous works [2,5]. The power spectra of the computation process of ECA rule 110, however, have not been investigated yet. In this paper we study the

J. Wąs, G.C. Sirakoulis, and S. Bandini (Eds.): ACRI 2014, LNCS 8751, pp. 45–54, 2014.

computation process of ECA rule 110 by means of power spectral analysis. In section two we make a brief explanation of cyclic tag system (CTS) emulated by rule 110. The results of spectral analysis are shown in section three. Finally we discuss the implication of the results in section four.

2 Cyclic Tag System Emulated by Rule 110

The transition function of ECA rule 110 is given by:

$$\frac{111}{0}\frac{110}{1}\frac{101}{1}\frac{100}{0}\frac{011}{1}\frac{010}{1}\frac{001}{1}\frac{000}{0}.$$

The upper line represents the state of the neighbourhood and the lower line specifies the state of the center cell at the next time step. There are a lot of stationary or propagating patterns in the evolution of rule 110 and Fig. 1 shows some of them necessary to realize computation on the array of rule 110. Cook proved the computational universality of rule 110 by showing that rule 110 can emulate CTS [1].

A^4 $\qquad\qquad\qquad\qquad\qquad C_2 \qquad\qquad\qquad\qquad\bar{E}\qquad\qquad\qquad\qquad E^4$

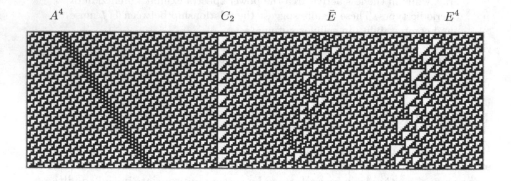

Fig. 1. Space-time configuration of propagating patterns $(A^4,\bar{E},E^4)$ and stationary pattern (C_2) in rule 110. The time goes from the top to the bottom.

A CTS is an abstract machine that has an infinitely long tape divided into cells. Each cell can contain a symbol, 0 or 1. At each step, the CTS removes one symbol from the front of the tape and if that is '1', then it appends the appendant to the end of the tape according to a fixed appendant table that defines the machine, while an '0' causes the appendant to be skipped. An appendant is cyclically chosen from the appendant table. The system halts if the string on the tape is empty. CTSs are proved to be computationally universal.

For example, the transition of the initial word '1' with the appendant table (1, 101) is given as following:

$$
\begin{array}{l}
1 \\
\vdash \quad 1_a \\
\vdash \qquad 1_b \; 0_c \; 1_d \\
\vdash \qquad\quad 0 \;\; 1 \;\; 1_e \\
\vdash \qquad\qquad 1 \;\; 1 \\
\vdash \qquad\qquad\quad 1 \;\; 1_f \\
\vdash \qquad\qquad\quad \cdots
\end{array}
\tag{1}
$$

where indices $a, \cdots, f$ of the symbol '0' or '1' are for use in the explanation of the behaviour of the CTS in Fig. 3.

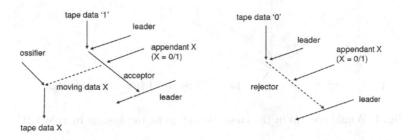

Fig. 2. Fundamental process in the emulation of cyclic tag system by rule 110. Left: tape data '1' is erased and symbol 'X' is appended. Right: tape data '0' is erased and appendant is skipped. The time goes from the top to bottom.

The computing process of CTS can be implemented on the array of rule 110. In this article we limit ourselves to briefly outline the mechanism of CTS emulation by rule 110. A detailed explanation of the emulation of CTS by rule 110 is found in Ref. [6]. The left of Fig. 2 schematically shows the process of erasing the symbol '1' from the front of the tape and appending the first symbol 'X' (X='0' or '1') of the appendant. The time goes from the top to the bottom. The tape symbol '1' is represented by a package of four stationary C_2 gliders (1Ele$\_C_2$). The term in the parenthesis is the one according to the naming convention employed in Ref [6]. The appendant '0' (0Blo$\_\bar{E}$), and '1' (1BloP$\_\bar{E}$, 1BloS$\_\bar{E}$) are represented by a package of 12 $\bar{E}$ gliders in which the phase and distance between each one of them differ between the symbol '0' and '1'. The appendants are separated by a leader (SepInit$\_E\overline{E}$) that consists of two E^4 and six $\bar{E}$ gliders. When the leader collides against the tape data '1', both the leader and the tape data vanish and an acceptor is created. The acceptor converts the appendant 'X' into a moving data 'X' and vanishes at the collision with the next leader. The moving data '0' (0Add$\_\bar{E}$) and '1' (1Add$\_\bar{E}$) are represented by a package of four $\bar{E}$ gliders in which the phase and distance between each one of them differ

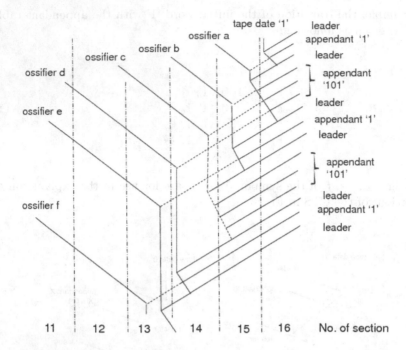

Fig. 3. Whole process in the emulation of cyclic tag system by rule 110

between the symbol '0' and '1'. An ossifier (4_A^4) consists of four A^4 gliders moving to the right and converts moving data '0', or '1' into tape data '0' or '1' respectively when they crisscross. These processes correspond to the transition $1s_1\cdots s_n \vdash s_1\cdots s_n X$, $s_i \in \{0, 1\}$ on the tape of a CTS.

The right of Fig. 2 shows the process of erasing the symbol '0' from the front of the tape and appending nothing to the tape. The tape symbol '0' ($0\mathrm{Ele}\_C_2$) is represented by a package of four stationary C_2 gliders in which the phase and distance between each one of them differ from the symbol '1'. The collision between the leader and the tape data '0' generates a rejector. The rejector removes the appendant 'X' and vanishes at the collision with the next leader. These processes correspond to the transition $0s_1\cdots s_n \vdash s_1\cdots s_n$ on the tape of a CTS.

Figure 3 shows the whole process of the emulation of CTS we deal with in this article. The CTS has the appendant table (1, 101) and its transition with an initial string '1' is described in Eq. (1). The array size is 65,900. The emulation process reaches stationary configuration in which there remain tape data '1' and an acceptor at about $t = 54,500$ (time starts from $t = 0$) because of finite array size. The vertical dashed-dotted lines represent the border between sections mentioned in section three. The vertical broken and solid lines represent tape data '0' and '1' respectively. The broken lines drawn diagonally from the top right to the bottom left represent moving data '0' or '1'. The acceptor and rejector are represented by solid or broken lines drawn diagonally from the top left to the bottom right respectively. The ossifiers labeled a, b, $\cdots$, f correspond to the one in Eq. (1). The initial configuration file can be downloaded at the web site [7].

3   Power Spectra of Cyclic Tag System

Let $s_x(t) \in \{0, 1\}$ denote the value of site x at time step t in an CA. The discrete Fourier transform of a time series of states $s_x(t)$ of the site x for $t = 0, 1, ..., T-1$ is given by

$$\hat{s}_x(f) = \frac{1}{T} \sum_{t=0}^{T-1} s_x(t) \exp(-i\frac{2\pi t f}{T}), \quad f = 0, 1, \cdots, T-1. \tag{2}$$

We define the power spectrum of CA as

$$S(f) = \frac{1}{N} \sum_{x=0}^{N-1} |\hat{s}_x(f)|^2, \tag{3}$$

where N denotes the total number of sites and the summation is taken in all sites. The period of the component at a frequency f in a power spectrum is given by T/f. The least square fitting of power spectrum $S(f)$ by

$$\ln(S) = \alpha + \beta \ln(f), \tag{4}$$

from $f = 1$ to $f = f_b$ gives the exponent β. The residual sum of squares σ^2 is given by

$$\sigma^2 = \frac{1}{f_b} \sum_{f=1}^{f_b} (\ln(S) - \alpha - \beta \ln(f))^2. \tag{5}$$

The whole array is so large that its power spectrum does not inform us about the regional difference among the array. So we divide the whole array into 20 sections (section $0 - 19$ starting from the left) of 3,295 cells and calculate the power spectrum of each section individually. So we set $N = 3,295$ in Eq.(3). The way of dividing the whole array is after the example of [8] in which the computation process of rule 110 is analyzed by means of LZ complexity. The locations of section $11, \cdots, 16$ are depicted in Fig. 3. As the computation process ends at about $t = 54,500$, we set $T = 55,000$ in Eq.(2). Since we are interested in the long term correlation during the computation process, we use $f_b = 100$ in Eq.(4) and Eq.(5) to focus on the power in low frequencies.

The stationary and propagating patterns and the interaction between them are elaborately utilized for implementing CTS in the evolution of rule 110. On the other hand, the periodic background does not seem to play an essential role for performing computation. Therefore we can guess that the essential feature of the evolution of rule 110 as a computing process is not lost by the removal of the periodic background from the space-time pattern and that the power spectrum calculated from the evolution obtained by removing the periodic background

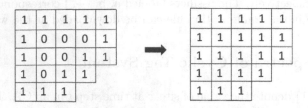

Fig. 4. Template used to remove the periodic background of rule 110

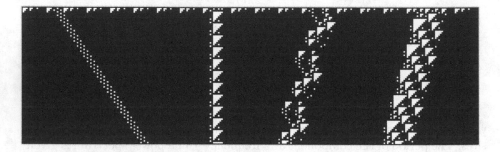

Fig. 5. Filtered space-time pattern of Fig. 1

characterizes more appropriately the dynamics of computation process in rule 110 than the original one. The periodic background has spatial period 14 and temporal period 7 and consists of a template depicted in the left of Fig. 4. To remove the periodic background, we scan the space-time pattern from the upper left to the lower right searching for a pattern coincident with the template in the left of Fig. 4 and change the state zero into the state one in the matched pattern as shown in the right of Fig. 4. We call a space-time pattern obtained by removing the periodic background from the original space-time pattern 'filtered' space-time pattern. Figure 5 is the filtered space-time pattern obtained from the one shown in Fig. 1.

The power spectra of section 10 - 17 are shown in Fig. 6 and in Fig. 7. Both the x and y axes are plotted on a logarithmic scale. Since the evolution on the other sections has only gliders passing through the array without any changes, they are not involved here.

4   Discussions

Figure 8 shows the exponent β (left) and the residual sum of squares σ^2 (right) of each section estimated by Eq.(4) and Eq.(5) in the range of frequencies $f = 1 - 100$. In section 13 - 16, the exponents are in the range between -1 ± 0.2 both in the original and filtered power spectra. So we can conclude that the behaviour in these sections exhibits $1/f$ noise. Since these sections are the most

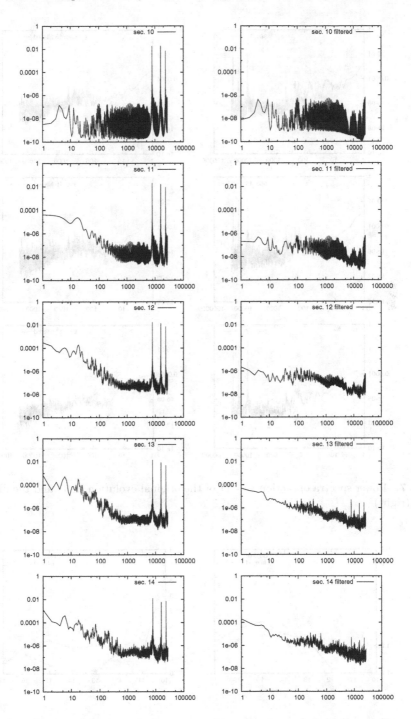

Fig. 6. Power spectra of section 10 - 14 of the original evolution (left) and the filtered one (right)

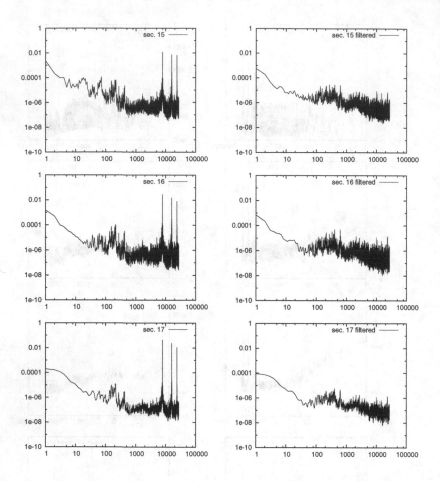

Fig. 7. Power spectra of section 15 - 17 of the original evolution (left) and the filtered one (right)

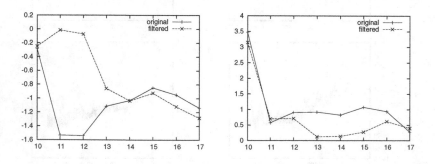

Fig. 8. Exponent β (left) and the residual sum of squares σ^2 (right) the of power spectrum of section $10 - 17$

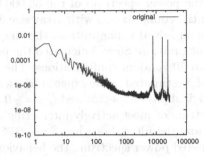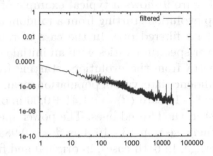

Fig. 9. Power spectra of the evolution starting from a random configuration with array size 3,295 for $T = 55,000$. Left: original evolution ($\beta = -1.444$, $\sigma^2 = 0.304$), Right: filtered one ($\beta = -0.628$, $\sigma^2 = 0.101$). β and σ^2 are estimated in the range of $f = 1 - 100$.

actively interacting area among the array as shown in Fig. 3, these results support the conjecture of the relationship between $1/f$ noise in CAs and computational universality presented in the case of two-dimensional CAs in Ref. [5] and addressed in detail in the case of ECAs in Ref. [2].

One of the main mechanisms to produce $1/f$ noise is intermittency in chaotic dynamical systems [9]. A system with a particular parameter value exhibits periodic behaviour, which is disrupted occasionally and irregularly by a "burst". This burst persists for a finite duration, then it stops and a new periodic behaviour starts. The evolution in section 13 - 16 goes through alternately periodic phases in which gliders are shifting without a collision and bursts caused by collision of the gliders as shown in Fig. 3. It seems likely that the recurrence of the periodic phases and the bursts generates intermittency and causes the $1/f$ noise in rule 110.

The residual sums of squares σ^2 in section 13 - 16 have smaller value in the filtered power spectra than in the original ones. The smaller the residual sum of squares σ^2 is, the more the power spectrum fits into the power law. In other words, by removing periodic background from the space-time pattern, the evolution gets close to $1/f$-type behaviour. This result implies that the origin of $1/f$-type power spectra in the evolution of computation process in rule 110 is the pattern created by the interaction between moving and stationary patterns rather than periodic background.

The exponent of section 17 is in the range between -1 ± 0.2 only in the original power spectrum, not in the filtered one. This is because the power at low frequencies becomes flat as shown in Fig. 7. This kind of power spectrum is called Lorentzian spectrum that is caused by a fluctuation with time constant. In section 17, the gliders are wiped off the array at about $t = 9,900$. That seems to bring a finite relaxation time into the evolution of section 17. The same thing can be said of section 11. The power spectrum of the original evolution in section 10 is characterized by sharp peaks caused by periodic background. The behaviour of section 12 exhibits power law spectrum but the exponent β is far from -1.

Figure 9 shows a typical example of the power spectrum of the 55,000 time step evolution starting from a random initial configuration with array size 3,295 and its filtered one. In the case of random initial configuration, the shape of power spectrum varies with an initial configuration. So we calculated the power spectra from the evolutions starting from 50 random configurations. The 95% confidence intervals of population mean of β estimated in the range of frequencies $f = 1 - 100$ are $\langle\beta\rangle = -1.41 \pm 0.06$ in original power spectra and $\langle\beta\rangle = -0.52 \pm 0.04$ in the filtered ones. The power spectrum of most actively interacting area, namely, section 13 - 16, has $\beta = -0.985$ and the filtered one has $\beta = -0.983$ on average. In both cases, in original and filtered power spectrum, the behaviour of computing process has $1/f$ characteristics more obviously than the one starting from a random configuration. In other words, $1/f$ noise in rule 110 is generated prominently by the combination of the dynamics of the rule and the elaborately designed initial configuration although the dynamics of rule 110 has the property of $1/f$-type fluctuation by itself in some degree.

References

1. Cook, M.: Universality in elementary cellular automata. Complex Systems 15, 1–40 (2004)
2. Ninagawa, S.: Power spectral analysis of elementary cellular automata. Complex Systems 17, 399–411 (2008)
3. Keshner, M.S.: $1/f$ noise. Proc. IEEE 70, 211–218 (1982)
4. Berlekamp, E.R., Conway, J.H., Guy, R.K.: Winning Ways for Your Mathematical Plays, vol. 2. New York Academic Press (1982)
5. Ninagawa, S., Yoneda, M., Hirose, S.: 1/f fluctuation in the "Game of Life". Physica D 118, 49–52 (1998)
6. Martínez, G.J., McIntosh, H.V., Seck-Tuoh-Mora, J.C., Vergara, S.V.C.: Reproducing the cyclic tag system developed by Mattew Cook with rule 110 using the phase f_{i-1}. J. Cellular Automata 6, 121–161 (2011)
7. Martínez, G.J.: Elementary cellular automaton rule 110, http://uncomp.uwe.ac.uk/genaro/rule110/ctsRule110.html
8. Ninagawa, S., Martínez, G.J.: Compression-based analysis of cyclic tag system emulated by rule 110. J. Cellular Automata 9, 23–35 (2014)
9. Manneville, P.: Intermittency, self-similarity and $1/f$ spectrum in dissipative dynamical systems. J. Physique 41, 1235–1243 (1980)

Cellular Automata and Formulae on Monoids

Toshikazu Ishida[1], Shuichi Inokuchi[2], and Yasuo Kawahara[3]

[1] Center for Fundamental Education, Kyushu Sangyo University,
Fukuoka, 813-8503, Japan
tishida@ip.kyusan-u.ac.jp

[2] Faculty of Information Engineering, Fukuoka Institute of Technology,
Fukuoka, 811-0295, Japan
inokuchi@fit.ac.jp

[3] Professor Emeritus, Kyushu University, Fukuoka, Japan
kawahara@i.kyushu-u.ac.jp

Abstract. This paper studies cellular automata with binary states on monoids making use of formulae in propositional logic, instead of local functions. Also we prove that the multiplication of formulae, defined by monoid action, determines the composition of transition functions of CA. This result converts the reversibility of transition functions to the reversibility of formulae. Several examples of reversible formulae are illustrated. Finally, introducing the Stone topology on configuration spaces, we give a neat proof of Hedlund's theorem for CA.

Keywords: Cellular automata, monoids, propositional logic, reversibility, Stone topology, Hedlund's theorem.

1 Introduction

The study of cellular automata (CA) was introduced by von Neumann and Ulam as theoretical models capable of self reproduction and universal computation. Recently CA often mean CA on groups, and mathematical theory of CA has been developed related to theory of groups [2]. The reversibility of CA is one of important properties which should be studied. For example, Kari [6] showed that the reversibility for 2-dimensional CA is undecidable. The reversibility of given CA concerns with the composition [4] of transition functions. However the composition of transition functions of CA seems to behave awkwardly in terms of traditional local rules. On the other hand one may recognise the following analogy [5] between CA and propositional logic.

CA		Logic
set of states $Q = \{0,1\}$	$\leftrightarrow$	set of truth values $Q = \{0,1\}$
cell space G	$\leftrightarrow$	set of propositional variables G
configuration $m \in Q^G$	$\leftrightarrow$	valuation $m \in Q^G$
local rule $f : Q^N \to Q$ $(N \subseteq G)$	$\leftrightarrow$	formula A

The above analogy suggests a new view point on CA from propositional logic.

J. Wąs, G.C. Sirakoulis, and S. Bandini (Eds.): ACRI 2014, LNCS 8751, pp. 55–64, 2014.

This paper studies CA with binary states on monoids making use of formulae in propositional logic, instead of local functions. According to the above analogy we reformulate transition functions of CA making use of shifted configurations and valuation for formulae. Extending the notion of shifted configurations we define the multiplication of formulae on monoids, which consist of substitution of formulae (trees) and shifts (monoid action). In fact the multiplication of formulae gives a direct expression of the composition of transition functions (Cf. [5]). This result converts the reversibility of transition functions to the reversibility of formulae. Moreover, the multiplication tells us many information on the reversibility of binary CA on monoids. Finally, to demonstrate the soundness of our formulation of CA with formulae, we will examine if our CA satisfies a basic theorem of transition functions, due to Hedlund [3] and Richardson [8]. To this end we introduce Stone topology on configuration spaces, which consequently coincides with the prodiscrete topology [2] since the state set Q has just two elements. Fortunately the Stone topology and formulae are good for each other and we show a neat proof of the characterisation theorem for CA.

The paper is organised as follows. In section 2 we recall fundamentals on propositional logic [1]. In section 3 we introduce shifted formulae as monoid action and redefine transition functions of CA using formulae instead of local functions. Also the basic properties of transition functions are described. In section 4 the multiplication of formulae applying monoid action is defined, and we state the basic properties of the multiplication. Also we prove the main result, and give two examples of reversible formulae and a table of iteration rules of formulae with two variables are illustrated. In section 5 we will introduce Stone topology on configuration spaces, and give a neat proof for Hedlund's theorem [3,8] on CA.

2   Propositional Logic

First we recall the fundamentals on propositional logic to emerge an analogy of propositional logic [1] and CA theory [2].

Let X be a set of propositional variables (or atomic propositions) and let $\perp$ and $\to$ be logical symbols. Formulae on X are defined by BNF:

$$A ::= x \mid \perp \mid A \to A \quad (x \in X)$$

Other logical symbols are introduced by the usual abbreviations.

Negation: $\neg A = A \to \perp$,
Verum: $\top = \neg\perp$,
Disjunction: $A \vee B = \neg A \to B$,
Conjunction: $A \wedge B = \neg(A \to \neg B)$,
Equivalence: $A \leftrightarrow B = (A \to B) \wedge (B \to A)$,
Exclusive or: $A + B = \neg(A \leftrightarrow B)$.

In what follows, we assume that $Q = (\{0, 1\}, \wedge, \vee, \neg)$ is a Boolean algebra of truth values. The implication operator $\Rightarrow$ on Q is defined by $a \Rightarrow b = \neg a \vee b$.

Operations $\Leftrightarrow$ (equivalence), $+$ (exclusive or (XOR), addition modulo 2) on Q are defined by the same way as the above abbreviations.

Definition 1. A *valuation* (interpretation) m for a set X is a function $m : X \to Q$. The *truth value* $m[\![A]\!] \in Q$ of a formula $A \in F(X)$ by m is inductively defined as follows.

1. $m[\![x]\!] = m(x)$ for all $x \in X$.
2. $m[\![\bot]\!] = 0$,
3. $m[\![A \to B]\!] = m[\![A]\!] \Rightarrow m[\![B]\!]$ for $A, B \in F(X)$.   □

For two formulae A and B on X we write as $A \equiv B$, if $m[\![A]\!] = m[\![B]\!]$ for all valuations $m : X \to Q$.

Proposition 1. *Let A, B, C be formulae on X. Then the following hold.*

1. $A \vee B \equiv B \vee A$, $(A \vee B) \vee C \equiv A \vee (B \vee C)$, $A \vee A \equiv A$,
2. $A \wedge B \equiv B \wedge A$, $(A \wedge B) \wedge C \equiv A \wedge (B \wedge C)$, $A \wedge A \equiv A$,
3. $A + B \equiv B + A$, $(A + B) + C \equiv A + (B + C)$,
4. $\neg(\neg A) \equiv A$, $\neg(A \vee B) \equiv \neg A \wedge \neg B$, $\neg(A \wedge B) \equiv \neg A \vee \neg B$,
5. $A + A \equiv \bot$, $A + \bot \equiv A$, $\neg A \equiv A + \top$.   □

3 CA on Monoids

In this section we will describe a notion of CA on monoids. First shifted formulae are defined by making use of monoid action. In what follows, we assume that M is a monoid with a unit element e, and the set of all formulae on M will be denoted by $F(M)$.

Definition 2. For a formula $A \in F(M)$ and $x \in M$, the *shifted formula* $xA \in F(M)$ is defined by induction on A:

1. $xy \in M$ (monoid multiplication in M) for $y \in M$,
2. $x\bot = \bot$,
3. $x(A \to B) = xA \to xB$ for formulae A and B on M.   □

The following states the basic properties of shifted formulae.

Proposition 2. *Let A and B be formulae on M and $x, y \in M$. Then the following hold.*

1. $eA = A$,
2. $(xy)A = x(yA)$,
3. $x(\neg A) = \neg(xA)$,
4. $x(A \vee B) = xA \vee xB$,
5. $x(A \wedge B) = xA \wedge xB$,
6. $x(A + B) = xA + xB$.   □

A function (valuation) $m : M \to Q$ is called a *configuration* on M, in a context of CA. We denote by Q^M the set of all configurations $m : M \to Q$. For $q \in Q$ the constant configuration $\hat{q} \in Q^M$ is defined by $\hat{q}(x) = q$ for all $x \in M$. Now we briefly recall traditional definition of transition functions of CA on groups. Given a group G and a local function $f : Q^N \to Q$ (where N is a finite subset of G), the transition function $T_f : Q^G \to Q^G$ is defined as $T_f(m)(x) = f((x^{-1}m)|_N)$ for all $m \in Q^G$ and $x \in G$, where the notation $m|_N$ denotes the restriction of m to a subset N of G. The usage of an inverse element in the last definition is avoidable by considering a shifted local function $x \cdot f : Q^{xN} \to Q$ instead of a shifted configuration $x^{-1}m$. Applying this idea we will give a new formulation for transition functions of CA on monoids as follows.

Definition 3. For a formula $A \in F(M)$ define a function $T_A : Q^M \to Q^M$ by $T_A(m)(x) = m[\![xA]\!]$ for all $m \in Q^M$ and $x \in M$. The function T_A is called the *transition function* (or cellular automaton) defined by A on M. ☐

Since a traditional local rule of CA with binary states is a Boolean function with finite variables, it has a disjunctive normal form. Thus the class of CA defined by logical formulae contains the class of binary CA defined by traditional local rules.

Proposition 3. *Let $x, y \in M, m \in Q^M$ and $A, B \in F(M)$. Then the following hold.*

1. $T_y(m)(x) = m(xy)$. *In particular* $T_e = \mathrm{id}_{Q^M}$ *(identity function on Q^M).*
2. $T_\perp(m) = \hat{0}$,
3. $T_{A \to B}(m)(x) = T_A(m)(x) \Rightarrow T_B(m)(x)$,
4. $T_{\neg A}(m)(x) = \neg(T_A(m)(x))$,
5. $T_{A \vee B}(m)(x) = T_A(m)(x) \vee T_B(m)(x)$,
6. $T_{A \wedge B}(m)(x) = T_A(m)(x) \wedge T_B(m)(x)$,
7. $T_{A+B}(m)(x) = T_A(m)(x) + T_B(m)(x)$,
8. $A \equiv B$ *iff* $T_A = T_B$. ☐

Let $\mathbb{N}$ be the additive monoid of all naturals and $y \in \mathbb{N}$ ($y \neq 0$). Then it is readily checked that the transition function T_y is surjective but not pre-injective. This suggests that GOE theorem fails for CA on $\mathbb{N}$, and CA on monoids form a wider class than CA on groups.

We now formulate shifted configurations using monoid action.

Definition 4. For a configuration $m \in Q^M$ and $x \in M$ the shifted configurations $x^\circ m \in Q^M$ are defined as $(x^\circ m)(y) = m(xy)$ for all $y \in M$. ☐

The following states the basic properties of shifted configurations.

Proposition 4. *Let $x, y \in M, m \in Q^M$ and $A \in F(M)$. Then the following hold.*

1. $e^\circ m = m$,
2. $(xy)^\circ m = y^\circ(x^\circ m)$,
3. $(x^\circ m)[\![A]\!] = m[\![xA]\!]$,
4. $T_A(x^\circ m) = x^\circ(T_A(m))$,
5. $A \equiv B$ *implies* $xA \equiv xB$.

☐

4   Multiplication of Formulae

Using the monoid action the multiplication of formulae can be defined as well as shifted formulae. In the next section it turns out that the multiplication of formulae dominates the composition of transition functions of CA on monoids.

Definition 5. Let A and C be formulae on M and $x \in M$. The multiplication AC of A and C is inductively defined as follows.

1. xC (shifted formula) is already defined for $x \in M$,
2. $\perp C = \perp$,
3. $(A \to B)C = AC \to BC$ for formulae A, B on M. □

The following states the basic properties of the multiplication of formulae.

Proposition 5. *Let A, B, C be formulae on M and $x, y \in M$. Then*

1. *$Ae = A$, $A(xy) = (Ax)y$,*
2. *Either $A\perp = \perp$ or $A\perp = \top$,*
3. *$(\neg A)B = \neg(AB)$,*
4. *$(A \vee B)C = AC \vee BC$,*
5. *$(A \wedge B)C = AC \wedge BC$,*
6. *$(A + B)C = AC + BC$,*
7. *$(AB)C = A(BC)$,*
8. *$T_A(m)[\![B]\!] = m[\![BA]\!]$,*
9. *$A \equiv A'$ and $B \equiv B'$ imply $AB \equiv A'B'$.* □

Remark. $A(B \to C) \equiv AB \to AC$ and $A(B \vee C) \equiv AB \vee AC$ need not hold.

An element x of M is *right cancelable* if $ax = bx$ implies $a = b$ for all $a, b \in M$.

Proposition 6. *Let $x \in M$ be right cancelable and $A \in F(M)$. Then*

1. *If $Ax \equiv \perp$, then $A \equiv \perp$.*
2. *If $Ax \equiv \top$, then $A \equiv \top$.* □

Definition 6. For a formula $A \in F(M)$, the set $V(A)$ of all variables in A is defined as follows:

1. $V(x) = \{x\}$ for $x \in M$,
2. $V(\perp) = \emptyset$,
3. $V(B \to C) = V(B) \cup V(C)$ for formulae B and C. □

The set $V(A)$ is a finite subset of M and serves the neighborhood of a local rule A. It is easily verified that $m|_{V(A)} = m'|_{V(A)}$ implies $m[\![A]\!] = m'[\![A]\!]$, and that $V(AB) = V(A)V(B)$ holds, where $V(A)V(B) = \{ab \in M \mid a \in V(A) \wedge b \in V(B)\}$.

Lemma 1. *Let $A, B \in F(M)$ and $x \in M$. Then the following hold.*

1. *If $A \equiv x$, then $x \in V(A)$.*
2. *If $AB \equiv e$, then there exist $a \in V(A)$ and $b \in V(B)$ such that $ab = e$.*

Proof. (1) Consider a configuration $x^* \in Q^M$ such that $x^*(y) = 1$ if $y = x$ and $x^*(y) = 0$ otherwise. Assume $A \equiv x$ and $x \notin V(A)$. Then $x^*|_{V(A)} = \hat{0}|_{V(A)}$ and so

$$
\begin{aligned}
1 &= x^*(x) \\
&= x^*[\![x]\!] && \{\, x \in M \,\} \\
&= x^*[\![A]\!] && \{\, A \equiv x \,\} \\
&= \hat{0}[\![A]\!] && \{\, x^*|_{V(A)} = \hat{0}|_{V(A)} \,\} \\
&= \hat{0}[\![x]\!] && \{\, A \equiv x \,\} \\
&= \hat{0}(x) && \{\, x \in M \,\} \\
&= 0,
\end{aligned}
$$

which is absurd. Hence $A \equiv x$ implies $x \in V(A)$.

(2) Assume $AB \equiv e$. By the result of (1) we have $e \in V(AB) = V(A)V(B)$ and so there exist $a \in V(A)$ and $b \in V(B)$ such that $ab = e$. □

The composition $S \circ T$ of a function $T : Q^M \to Q^M$ followed by a function $S : Q^M \to Q^M$ is defined as usual: $\forall m \in Q^M. (S \circ T)(m) = S(T(m))$. Although the composition of transition functions of CA seems to behave awkwardly in terms of traditional local rules $f : Q^N \to Q$, the multiplication of formulae directly represents the composition of transition functions.

Theorem 1 ([5]). *For all formulae $A, C \in F(M)$ the identity $T_A \circ T_C = T_{AC}$ holds.*

Proof. We need to show the following:

1. $T_x \circ T_C = T_{xC}$ for $x \in M$,
2. $T_\perp \circ T_C = T_{\perp C}$,
3. $T_{A \to B} \circ T_C = T_{(A \to B)C}$ for $A, B \in F(M)$.

(1) $T_x \circ T_C = T_{xC}$:

$$
\begin{aligned}
(T_x \circ T_C)(m)(y) &= T_x(T_C(m))(y) \\
&= T_C(m)(yx) && \{\, \text{Prop. 3 (1)} \,\} \\
&= m[\![(yx)C]\!] && \{\, \text{Def. 3} \,\} \\
&= m[\![y(xC)]\!] && \{\, \text{Prop. 5 (2)} \,\} \\
&= T_{xC}(m)(y). && \{\, \text{Def. 3} \,\}
\end{aligned}
$$

(2) $T_\perp \circ T_C = T_\perp$:

$$
\begin{aligned}
(T_\perp \circ T_C)(m) &= T_\perp(T_C(m)) \\
&= \hat{0} && \{\, \text{Prop. 3 (2)} \,\} \\
&= T_\perp(m).
\end{aligned}
$$

(3) $T_{A \to B} \circ T_C = T_{(A \to B)C}$:

$$
\begin{aligned}
& (T_{A \to B} \circ T_C)(m)(y) \\
&= T_{A \to B}(T_C(m))(y) \\
&= T_A(T_C(m))(y) \Rightarrow T_B(T_C(m))(y) & \{ \text{ Prop. 3 (4) } \} \\
&= (T_A \circ T_C)(m)(y) \Rightarrow (T_B \circ T_C)(m)(y) & \{ \text{ Def of } \circ \} \\
&= T_{AC}(m)(y) \Rightarrow T_{BC}(m)(y) & \{ \text{ induction hypo. } \} \\
&= T_{AC \to BC}(m)(y) & \{ \text{ Prop. 3 (4) } \} \\
&= T_{(A \to B)C}(m)(y). & \{ \text{ Prop. 3 (9) } \}
\end{aligned}
$$

$\square$

A transition function $T_A : Q^M \to Q^M$ defined by a formula A is *reversible* if it is bijective and $T_A^{-1} = T_B$ for some formula B. A formula A is *reversible* if there exists a formula B on M such that $BA \equiv e$ and $AB \equiv e$. By the virtue of Theorem 1 and Proposition 3 (8), A is reversible iff T_A is reversible.

Proposition 7. *Let A, B and C be formulae on a monoid M. Then*

1. *If $AB \equiv e$ and $CA \equiv e$, then $B \equiv C$.*
2. *A and B are reversible iff so are AB and BA.*
3. *If $AC \equiv \bot$, $C \not\equiv \bot$ and $C \not\equiv \top$, then A is irreversible.*

Proof. (1) and (2) are trivial.
(3) Assume $DA \equiv e$ for some formula D. Then we have $C = eC \equiv (DA)C = D(AC) \equiv D\bot$. Hence $C \equiv \bot$ or $C \equiv \top$ by Prop. 5 (2). This contradicts the assumption. $\square$

Remark. The single condition $AC \equiv \bot$ does not always imply that A is irreversible. $(e\bot = \bot)$

Next, we give examples of reversible formulae. For a formula $A \in F(M)$ and a natural n define the n-th power of A by $A^0 = e$ and $A^{n+1} = A^n A$.

Proposition 8. *Let $m \geq 3$ and $n \geq 1$ be integers, $x \in M$, and G_m the least common multiple of $3, 5, \cdots, 2m+1$. Also for each integer $k \geq 1$ define a formula $p_k(x)$ by $p_k(x) = e + x + x^2 + \cdots + x^{k-1}$. If $x^n = e$ and $n = \pm 1 \pmod{G_m}$, then $p_{2m+1}(x)$ is reversible.* $\square$

The formula $p_3(x) = e + x + x^2$ extends a local rule with Wolfram number 150.

Proposition 9. *Let $x \in M$. If $x^{2n-1} = e$ for an integer $n \geq 2$, then the formula $A = (\neg e \wedge x) + x^2$ is reversible.* $\square$

The formula $A = (\neg e \wedge x) + x^2$ extends a local rule with Wolfram number 166. For the proof of Prop. 9 refer to [7,5]. Next, we show a table of iteration rules of CA within two variables $e, x \in M$.

(e,x)	(1,1)	(1,0)	(0,1)	(0,0)	Formula	Iteration rule
A_0	0	0	0	0	$\bot$	$T_{A_0}(m) = \hat{0}$
A_1	0	0	0	1	$\neg(e \vee x)$	$A_1^{2n+1} = x^n A_1,\ A_1^{2n+2} = x^n A_1^2$
A_2	0	0	1	0	$\neg(x \to e)$	$A_2^{n+1} = x^n A_2$
A_3	0	0	1	1	$\neg e$	$A_3^2 = e$
A_4	0	1	0	0	$\neg(e \to x)$	$A_4^{n+1} = A_4$
A_5	0	1	0	1	$\neg x$	$A_5^n = (\neg e)^n x^n$
A_6	0	1	1	0	$e + x$	$A_6^n = (e + x)^n$
A_7	0	1	1	1	$\neg(e \wedge x)$	$A_7^{2n+1} = x^n A_7,\ A_7^{2n+2} = x^n A_7^2$
A_8	1	0	0	0	$e \wedge x$	$A_8^{n+1} = A_8^n \wedge x^{n+1}$
A_9	1	0	0	1	$\neg(e + x)$	$A_9^n = \neg(e + x)^n$
A_{10}	1	0	1	0	x	$A_{10}^n = x^n$
A_{11}	1	0	1	1	$e \to x$	$A_{11}^{n+1} = x^n A_{11}$
A_{12}	1	1	0	0	e	$A_{12} = \mathrm{id}_Q$
A_{13}	1	1	0	1	$x \to e$	$A_{13}^{n+1} = A_{13}$
A_{14}	1	1	1	0	$e \vee x$	$A_{14}^{n+1} = A_{14}^n \vee x^{n+1}$
A_{15}	1	1	1	1	$\top = \neg\bot$	$T_{A_{15}}(m) = \hat{1}$

5   Stone Topology

In this section, we show the fundamental theorems [3,8] using Stone topology. First we recall Stone topology which consequently coincides with the prodiscrete topology [2], since $Q = \{0,1\}$. For each formula $A \in F(M)$ define a subset U_A of Q^M by

$$U_A = \{m \in Q^M \mid m[\![A]\!] = 1\}.$$

It is clear that $U_\bot = \emptyset$, $U_\top = Q^M$, $U_{A \wedge B} = U_A \cap U_B$, $U_{A \vee B} = U_A \cup U_B$ and $U_{\neg A} = Q^M - U_A$ since $Q = \{0,1\}$. The set $\mathcal{S}_B$ of subsets of Q^M defined by

$$V \in \mathcal{S}_B \leftrightarrow \forall m \in V \exists A \in F(M).\ m \in U_A \subseteq V$$

is a topology on Q^M. Thus the subset $\{U_A \mid A \in F(M)\}$ of $\mathcal{S}_B$ forms a basis of the topology $\mathcal{S}_B$. The topology $\mathcal{S}_B$ is called the *Stone topology* on Q^M. Generally the Stone topology means a topology on the set of all ultra filters in Boolean algebras, but we remark that a configuration, namely a valuation, bijectively corresponds to a ultra filter in the free Boolean algebra $F(M)/\equiv$.

In the Stone topology every U_A is clopen (open and closed), since $U_A = Q^M - U_{\neg A}$. The configuration space Q^M with Stone topology is compact Hausdorff and totally disconnected. The readers can readily verify that the Stone topology coincides with the prodiscrete topology, because the state set Q has just two elements. In what follows we assume that the configuration space Q^M is endowed with the Stone topology.

Proposition 10 ([3,8]). *Every transition function $T_A : Q^M \to Q^M$ of CA on M is continuous.*

Proof. We need to prove $T_A^{-1}(U_C) = U_{CA}$ for all $A, C \in F(M)$:

$$
\begin{aligned}
m \in T_A^{-1}(U_C) &\leftrightarrow T_A(m) \in U_C \\
&\leftrightarrow T_A(m)[\![C]\!] = 1 \\
&\leftrightarrow m[\![CA]\!] = 1 \quad \{ \text{ Prop. 5 (8) } T_A(m)[\![C]\!] = m[\![CA]\!] \} \\
&\leftrightarrow m \in U_{CA}.
\end{aligned}
$$

$\square$

Lemma 2. *For every continuous function* $g : Q^M \to Q$, *there exists a formula* $A \in F(M)$ *such that* $g(m) = m[\![A]\!]$ *for all* $m \in Q^M$.

Proof. The singleton subset $\{1\}$ of Q is clopen, since Q is a discrete space. Also from the continuity of g its inverse image $g^{-1}(\{1\})$ is clopen, and compact since Q^M is compact Hausdorff. Hence there exist a finite number of formulae $A_1, \ldots, A_k$ such that $g^{-1}(\{1\}) = U_{A_1} \cup \cdots \cup U_{A_k}$. Then for all $m \in Q^M$ we have

$$
\begin{aligned}
g(m) = 1 &\leftrightarrow m \in g^{-1}(\{1\}) \\
&\leftrightarrow m \in U_{A_1} \cup \cdots \cup U_{A_k} \\
&\leftrightarrow m \in U_{A_1 \vee \cdots \vee A_k} \\
&\leftrightarrow m[\![A_1 \vee \cdots \vee A_k]\!] = 1,
\end{aligned}
$$

which implies $g(m) = m[\![A_1 \vee \cdots \vee A_k]\!]$, because of $Q = \{0,1\}$. $\square$

A function $T : Q^M \to Q^M$ *commutes with shifts* if $T(x^\circ m) = x^\circ(T(m))$ for all $m \in Q^M$ and $x \in M$.

Corollary 1 ([3,8]). *If a function* $T : Q^M \to Q^M$ *is continuous and commutes with shifts, then there exists a formula* $A \in F(M)$ *such that* $T = T_A$.

Proof. Define a function $g : Q^M \to Q$ by $\forall m \in Q^M . \ g(m) = T(m)(e)$. Then g is continuous since g is the composition of T and the e-th projection $p_e : Q^M \to Q$. By the last lemma 2 there exists a formula $A \in F(M)$ such that $g(m) = m[\![A]\!]$ for all $m \in Q^M$. Hence for all $m \in Q^M$ and $x \in M$ we have

$$
\begin{aligned}
T_A(m)(x) &= m[\![xA]\!] &&\{ \text{ Def. 3} \} \\
&= (x^\circ m)[\![A]\!] &&\{ \text{ Prop. 4 (3) } \} \\
&= T(x^\circ m)(e) &&\{ m[\![A]\!] = g(m) = T(m)(e) \} \\
&= (x^\circ(T(m)))(e) &&\{ T \text{ commutes with shifts } \} \\
&= T(m)(xe) &&\{\text{def of } x^\circ\} \\
&= T(m)(x).
\end{aligned}
$$

which shows $T = T_A$. The proof is completed. $\square$

Corollary 2. *A transition function* T_A *is reversible iff it is bijective.*

Proof. It is trivial from the definition of the reversibility that reversible transition functions are bijective. Assume that T_A is bijective. Then its inverse function

T_A^{-1} is continuous, since Q^M is a compact Hausdorff space. Also T_A^{-1} commutes with shifts:

$$
\begin{aligned}
T_A^{-1}(x^\circ m') &= T_A^{-1}(x^\circ T_A(m)) \ \{ \ m' = T_A(m) \ \} \\
&= T_A^{-1} T_A(x^\circ m) \quad \{ \ x^\circ T_A(m) = T_A(x^\circ m) \ \} \\
&= x^\circ m \\
&= x^\circ (T_A^{-1}(m')). \quad \{ \ m' = T_A(m) \ \}
\end{aligned}
$$

$\square$

6 Conclusion

In the paper we presented a new view point on CA with binary states from an analogy between propositional logic and CA theory, and the reversibility of CA was converted to the reversibility of formulae generated by monoids. Finally we gave a neat proof of Hedlund's theorem making use of Stone topology.

Many questions on CA on monoids remain to research in the future. Firstly we have to develop more computation laws of formulae on monoids. Is the approach adopted here generalisable to non-binary states? It may be partly possible by treating with many valued logic, but we are aware that in non-binary case Stone topology doesn't work. Moreover it may be necessary to reexamine whether well-known theorems and properties of CA on groups also hold in the case of monoids. In particular, it seems to be interesting to seek an analogy of the game of life and universal CA (like CA-110) on monoids.

Acknowledgments. The authors thank unknown referees for their helpful advice and comments.

References

1. Kleine Büning, H., Lettmann, T.: Propositional Logic: Deduction and Algorithms, Cambridge. Cambridge Tracts in Theoretical Computer Science (1999)
2. Ceccherini-Silberstein, T., Coornaert, M.: Cellular Automata and Groups. Springer Monographs in Mathematics. Springer, Berlin (2010)
3. Hedlund, G.A.: Endomorphisms and automorphisms of the shift dynamical system. Mathematical Systems Theory 3(4), 320–375 (1969)
4. Inokuchi, S., Ito, T., Fujio, M., Mizoguchi, Y.: A formulation of composition for cellular automata on groups. IEICE Transactions on Information and Systems E97-D(3), 448–454 (2014)
5. Inokuchi, S., Ishida, T., Kawahara, Y.: Propositional logic and cellular automata, to appear in RIMS Kokyuroku, Research Institute for Mathematical Sciences, Kyoto University
6. Kari, J.: Reversibility of 2D cellular automata is undecidable, Cellular automata: theory and experiment (Los Alamos, NM, 1989). Physica D 45, 379–385 (1990)
7. Nobe, A., Yura, F.: On reversibility of cellular automata with periodic boundary conditions. Journal of Physics A: Mathematical and General 37, 5789–5804 (2004)
8. Richardson, D.: Tessellations with local transformations. J. Computer and System Sciences 6, 373–388 (1972)

A Scalable Method for Constructing Non-linear Cellular Automata with Period $2^n - 1$

Shamit Ghosh, Abhrajit Sengupta,
Dhiman Saha, and Dipanwita Roy Chowdhury

Indian Institute of Technology, Kharagpur

Abstract. Non-linear functions are very essential in different crypto primitives as they increase the security of the cipher designs. On the other hand, maximum length sequences help to prevent repeatability of a pseudorandom generator. Linear functions such as LFSR and linear cellular automata are used to generate maximum length sequences. However linear maximum length sequences are not secure. So there is a necessity of a construction that can provide both non-linearity and maximum length sequence for optimized cipher designs. In this work, we propose an algorithm for synthesizing a maximum length non-linear cellular automata to fulfill the requirement. Extensive experimentation on the proposed scheme shows that the construction achieves high non-linearity. Moreover, we have implemented and tested the design in Xilinx Spartan-3 FPGA platform and the hardware overhead is shown to be nominal.

Keywords: Cellular Automata, Non-linearity, maximum length sequence, pseudo random sequence.

1 Introduction

Cellular Automata (CA) are very powerful computational model which finds applications in different scientific domains. The simple structure of CA along with their hardware friendly nature makes them very attractive to the researchers. Extensive research and analysis have been done till date to study different properties of CA. While the concept of CA was first formulated by *John von Neumann*, the work of *Stephen Wolfram* during 1980s presents an enormous collection of results on CA and introduces some groundbreaking results as well. CA can be broadly categorized into two classes, *Linear CA* and *Non-linear CA*. The linear CA rules only consist of linear operations such as XOR/XNOR while non-linear CA rules can contain linear operations along with other non-linear operations principally AND/OR operations. Another interesting construction is *Hybrid CA* where each cell, unlike *uniform CA*[1],does not need to follow the same rule. The self-evolving nature of CA has numerous applications including the generation of good pseudorandom sequence. These properties along with its high diffusion makes CA a very attractive candidate for crypto primitives.

---

[1] All the cells in uniform CA follow same rule.

J. Wąs, G.C. Sirakoulis, and S. Bandini (Eds.): ACRI 2014, LNCS 8751, pp. 65–74, 2014.
© Springer International Publishing Switzerland 2014

Using an n-cell linear hybrid CA (LHCA), it is possible to generate a maximum length[2] sequence which is proved to be a good pseudorandom number generator. It is known from early literature that for linear feedback shift register (LFSR), every n-degree polynomial has a unique mapping to a corresponding LFSR. Though, in 1996, in a pioneering paper [1], it was reported that the same relation exist for an LHCA, synthesizing an LHCA is non-trivial. If the polynomial is a primitive one, then it generates a maximum length LHCA. Since, randomness is an essential criteria for any crypto primitive, maximum length CA is a good choice. However, a linear CA is not known to be secured. Observing, either a sequence of bits yielded from a particular position of an LHCA (mostly LSB or MSB) or the whole state of the register (if accessible), one can easily derive a set of linear equations. As solving a set of linear equations is an easy problem, the initial seed of the LHCA can be easily retrieved and thus compromising the security of the whole scheme. For this reason, there is a principal requirement of non-linearity in the pseudorandom pattern generation especially in the field of cryptography. Wolfram has proposed the idea of using the rule 30 for CA based non-linear pseudorandom generator. But, this does not guarantee a maximum length cycle. Besides, in [2], it has been shown that this scheme can also be broken using the fact that changing the seed does not guarantee the change of output sequence due to lack of maximum length. This precludes the need of both non-linearity and maximum length in a symmetric cryptosystem. Moreover, we cannot omit the necessity of linear operations completely as it provides us security against different side channel attacks like power attack, timing attack etc. In all standard symmetric key ciphers like AES [3], GRAIN [4], KECCAK [5], both linear and non-linear functions are used to overcome these problems.

In this paper, we propose a scalable construction method to generate a maximum length non-linear hybrid CA (NHCA) from a maximum length LHCA. We also focus on synthesizing NHCA with minimal neighborhood dependency as it would be more hardware optimized. The non-linearity of some constructed NHCA is computed and it is also shown that non-linearity increases significantly with each iteration.

The rest of the paper is organized as follows. Section 2 discusses notions and definitions of some well-known terms which are exercised throughout the paper. This section also briefly presents the existing research works in the related field. The synthesis algorithm and its theoretical basis is furnished in Section 3 and the affect of the non-linearity injection is studied as well. The hardware implementation details and comparative study is given in Section 4. Finally, Section 5 concludes the work.

---

[2] A maximum length CA has a cycle length $2^n - 1$.

2   Preliminaries

In this section we discuss some basic notions that are used throughout the paper. Some definitions and theorems are also discussed here. Based on these theoretical studies, we further proceed to our proposed scheme.

2.1   Notions

Throughout the paper, we have used "$\oplus$" to denote bitwise XOR operation and "$\cdot$" for bitwise AND operation. To represent the complement of a Boolean variable x, we use $\bar{x}$. We have used some common terms related to Boolean functions and cryptography which are defined below.

Definition 1. *Hamming Weight*: *Number of Boolean 1's in a Boolean function's truth table is called the Hamming weight of the function.*

Definition 2. *Affine Function in* $GF(2)$: *A Boolean function which can be expressed as XOR of some or all of its input variables and a Boolean constant is an affine function.*

In this paper the term *Affine Function* simply refers to Affine Function in $GF(2)$.

Definition 3. *Non-linearity*: *Let, f be a Boolean function of variables, $x_1, x_2, \cdots, x_n$ and A be the set of all affine functions in $x_1, x_2, \cdots, x_n$. The minimum of all the Hamming distances between f and the Boolean functions in A is the non-linearity of f.*

Definition 4. *Algebraic Normal Form*: *Any Boolean function can be expressed as XOR of conjunctions and a Boolean constant, True or False. This form of the Boolean function is called its Algebraic Normal Form (ANF).*

2.2   CA Basics

Cellular Automata are studied as mathematical model for self organizing statistical systems. CA can be one-dimensional or multi-dimensional. In this paper, we discuss only about one-dimensional two state CA. They can be considered as an array of cells where each cell is a one bit memory element.

The neighbor set $\mathbf{N}(i)$ is defined as the set of cells on which the i-th cell is dependent on each iteration. The simplest class of CA are *elementary CA* or *three-neighborhood CA* where each cell evolves in every time step based on some combinatorial logic on the cell itself and its two nearest neighbors. More formally, for a three-neighborhood CA, $\mathbf{N}(i) = \{i-1, i, i+1\}$. So, if the value of i-th cell at t-th time step is $q_i(t)$, then

$$q_i(t+1) = f(q_{i-1}(t), q_i(t), q_{i+1}(t))$$

where f denotes some combinatorial logic. We call the set of all feedback functions as ruleset and express as $\mathcal{F}$. The state transition of one iteration of a CA is expressed as $\mathcal{S}_{t+1} = \mathcal{F}(\mathcal{S}_t)$ where $\mathcal{S}_t$ is the set of all cells in the CA at t-th time step.

Since, a three-neighborhood CA having two states (0 or 1) can have $2^3 = 8$ possible binary states, there are total $2^{2^3} = 256$ possible rules. Each rule can be represented as an decimal integer from 0 to 255. If the combinatorial logic for the rules have only Boolean XOR operation, then it is called *linear* or *additive* rule. Some of the three-neighborhood additive CA rules are 0, 60, 90, 102, 150 etc. Moreover, if the combinatorial logic contains AND/OR operations, then it is called *non-linear* rule.

An n cell CA with cells $\{x_0, x_1, \cdots, x_{n-1}\}$ is called *null boundary* CA if $x_n = 0$ and $x_{-1} = 0$. Similarly for a *periodic boundary* CA $x_n = x_0$.

A CA is called *uniform*, if all its cells follow the same rule. Otherwise, it is called *non-uniform* or *hybrid* CA. For a hybrid CA, the sequence of the rules followed by the cells in a particular order (MSB to LSB or vise versa). If all the ruleset of a hybrid CA are linear, then we call the CA a linear one. In Fig. 1, a 4 cell null boundary LHCA is shown.

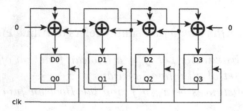

Fig. 1. Null Boundary Max. Length LHCA with Primitive Polynomial $x^4 + x^3 + 1$

2.3 Contemporary Maximum Length Non-linearity

Many previous works have been done to synthesize an NFSR of length 2^n. The sequence generated by this kind of NFSR are called *de Bruijn Sequences*. Different algorithms for generating de Bruijn sequences are discussed in [6]. Using an underlying maximum length LFSR, an NFSR of length $2^n - 1$ can be generated by using the method proposed in [7]. For generating maximum length NHCA, [8] devices an algorithm that manipulates the number of clock cycles based on the input using an underlying LHCA. However, this method varies the number of clock cycle and hence unsynchronized for different inputs. Besides, it needs an additional counter and also a comparator that increases the hardware cost.

3   Synthesizing Non-linear Hybrid Cellular Automata

In this section we first discuss some theoretical aspects that lead us to the construction of a maximum length non-linear CA. We define the term *unique predecessor NHCA* (UPNHCA) for a three neighborhood NHCA, whose every reachable state has only one immediate predecessor. Let, f_i be the feedback function of the i-th cell, then we define an operation called *shifting* as followed.

Definition 5. *The one cell shifting operation, denoted by $f_i \xrightarrow{P} f_{i\pm1}$ moves a set of ANF monomials P from i-th cell of an NHCA to all the cells from $(i-1)$ to $(i+1)$-th cell, according to the dependency of the affected cells upon the i-th cell. Each variables in P is changed by their previous state. Similarly, a k cell shifting is obtained by applying the one cell shifting operation for k times upon the initial NHCA and symbolized as $f_i \xrightarrow{P} f_{i\pm k}$.*

For example, we have a 5-bit 3 neighborhood CA with the following initial ruleset:

$$f_0 = (x_1 \oplus x_0)$$
$$f_1 = (x_2 \oplus x_1 \oplus x_0)$$
$$f_2 = (x_3 \oplus x_2 \oplus x_1) \oplus x_4$$
$$f_3 = (x_4 \oplus x_3 \oplus x_2)$$
$$f_4 = x_3$$

It is clear from the equations that x_3 is the previous state of x_4. Now applying the shifting $f_2 \xrightarrow{x_4} f_{2\pm1}$, the new ruleset becomes:

$$f_0 = x_1 \oplus x_0$$
$$f_1 = (x_2 \oplus x_1 \oplus x_0) \oplus x_3$$
$$f_2 = (x_3 \oplus x_2 \oplus x_1) \oplus x_3$$
$$f_3 = (x_4 \oplus x_3 \oplus x_2) \oplus x_3$$
$$f_4 = x_3$$

The previous state is obtained by the inverse operation of the underlying UPNHCA. As for an UPNHCA has only one unique state, so it is trivial that it is invertible. Here we state a theorem depicting the effect of shifting operation if applied on a UPNHCA.

Theorem 1. *Given an UPNHCA, a shifting $f_i \xrightarrow{P} f_{i\pm k}$, $i + k \leq n - 1$ and $i - k \geq 0$, results an equivalent UPNHCA where P does not contain any terms that belongs to $\mathbf{N}(i)$.*

Proof. Let the length of a sequence generated by a UPNHCA is M and the ruleset of the UPNHCA is $\mathcal{F} = \{f_{n-1}, \cdots, f_0\}$. Again, let $\mathcal{S}^0$ is the initial state of cells where $\mathcal{S}^0 = (x_{n-1}^0, \cdots, x_1^0, x_0^0)$. Now we apply the k cell shifting operation on the i-th cell for a set of monomials whose initial state was P^0, $i+k < M$ and $i - k > 0$. Here, we show the equivalence of the states in time with the shifting operation.

The state at i-th time can be expressed as :

$$P^i = \mathcal{F}^i(P^0)$$

Similarly, for $(i + k)$-th state,

$$
\begin{aligned}
P^{i+k} &= \mathcal{F}^{i+k}(P^0) \\
&= \mathcal{F}^i(\mathcal{F}^k(P^0)) \\
&= \mathcal{F}^i(P^k)
\end{aligned}
$$

We shift the initial state to a new one like $P_{new}^0 = P^k$. As the UPNHCA is invertible, so we take $(k - i)$-th previous state from P_{new}^k.

$$
\mathcal{F}^{-(k-i)}(P_{new}^k) = \mathcal{F}^i(\mathcal{F}^{-k}(P_{new}^k)) = \mathcal{F}^i(P_{new}^0)
$$

This relation shows the affect of applying the shifting operation where $P_{new}^0 = P^k$ is obtained after $f_i \xrightarrow{P} f_{i\pm k}$. The initial state of i-th cell is shifted but the overall set of sequence does not change at all. Hence, the shifting operation results in an equivalent UPNHCA.   ■

Note that, if any of P's variables belongs to $\mathbf{N}(i)$, then after shifting operation, each state may not have a unique predecessor. So, it is necessary that P should not have any term that belongs to $\mathbf{N}(i)$. Before injecting the non-linearity to the required position, a shifting opeartion is applied to the corresponding non-linear function at the required position to retain the maximum length. The procedure to synthesize a maximum length NHCA from a maximum length 90-150 LHCA is depicted in Algorithm 1 followed by an example. The correctness of the algorithm is stated in Theorem 2.

Algorithm 1: NHCA Synthesize Algorithm

Input: A maximum length LHCA with ruleset $\mathcal{F}_L$, A position j to inject non-linearity and the set of cells of the LHCA $\mathcal{S}$
Output: A maximum length NHCA ruleset $\mathcal{F}_N$

1: $\mathcal{F}_N \leftarrow \mathcal{F}_L$
2: Let $\mathcal{F}_N = \{f_{n-1}, \cdots, f_0\}$
3: $\mathcal{X} \subset \mathcal{S} : \forall x \in \mathcal{X}, x \notin \mathbf{N}(j)$ ▷ select a subset from $\mathcal{S}$
4: $P \leftarrow \mathbf{f_N}(\mathcal{X})$ ▷ $\mathbf{f_N}$ is non-linear function
5: $f_j \leftarrow f_j \oplus P$
6: $(f_j \xrightarrow{P} f_{j+1})$ ▷ Apply shifting operation
7: $f_j \leftarrow f_j \oplus P$
8: **return** $\mathcal{F}_N$

Example 1. Let a maximum length three neighborhood LHCA is synthesized from the primitive polynomial $x^5 + x^2 + 1$ to obtain the ruleset $\mathcal{F}_N = \{f_0, \cdots, f_{n-1}\}$ such that:

$$f_0 = x_1 \oplus x_0$$
$$f_1 = x_2 \oplus x_1 \oplus x_0$$
$$f_2 = x_3 \oplus x_2 \oplus x_1$$
$$f_3 = x_4 \oplus x_3 \oplus x_2$$
$$f_4 = x_3$$

We inject the the non-linearity into the bit $j = 2$. Let, $\mathcal{X} = \{0, 4\}$ and $\mathbf{f_N}(a, b) = a \& b$ where a and b are two boolean one bit variables. So, according to Algorithm 1, the function f_j would be updated like $f_j = f_j \oplus \mathbf{f_N}(x_0 \& x_4) = f_j \oplus (x_0 \& x_4)$. Now, applying the shifting operation $f_j \xrightarrow{x_0 \& x_4} f_{j+1}$, the whole ruleset is :

$$f_0 = x_1 \oplus x_0$$
$$f_1 = x_2 \oplus x_1 \oplus x_0 \oplus ((x_0 \oplus x_1) \& x_3)$$
$$f_2 = x_3 \oplus x_2 \oplus x_1 \oplus (x_0 \& x_4) \oplus ((x_0 \oplus x_1) \& x_3)$$
$$f_3 = x_4 \oplus x_3 \oplus x_2 \oplus ((x_0 \oplus x_1) \& x_3)$$
$$f_4 = x_3$$

This ruleset is a maximum length NHCA synthesized using Algorithm 1.   ■

Theorem 2. *The Algorithm 1 generates a maximum length NHCA.*

Proof. Let $\mathcal{L}$ be an n-cell 3 neighborhood periodic boundary LHCA of the following form

$$f_i(x_{i-1}, x_i, x_{i+1}) = x_{i-1} \oplus x_{i+1} \oplus (c_i \cdot x_i) \tag{1}$$

$\forall i \in \{0, \cdots, n-1\}$ where $x_{-1} = 0$, $x_n = 0$, $c_i \in \{0, 1\}$. If $c_i = 0$, then the i-th cell follows rule 90, else it follows rule 150.

Now, for a j, $1 < j < n - 1$, the feedback function is changed like following,

$$f_{j-1}(x_{j-2}, x_{j-1}, x_j) = x_{j-2} \oplus x_j \oplus (c_{j-1} \cdot x_{j-1}) \oplus f_N(x_{j-2}, x_{j+2})$$
$$f_j(x_{j-1}, x_j, x_{j+1}) = x_{j-1} \oplus x_{j+1} \oplus (c_j \cdot x_j) \oplus (c_j \cdot f_N(x_{j-2}, x_{j+2}))$$
$$\oplus f_N(f_{j-2}, f_{j+2}) \tag{2}$$
$$f_{j+1}(x_j, x_{j+1}, x_{j+2}) = x_j \oplus x_{i+2} \oplus (c_{j+1} \cdot x_{j+1}) \oplus f_N(x_{j-2}, x_{j+2})$$

and rest of the states are kept same as $\mathcal{L}$ to obtain a new NHCA $\mathcal{N}$. First, we have to show that, the LHCA $\mathcal{L}$ and the NHCA $\mathcal{N}$ generate the same set of outputs.

In case of the underlying LHCA $\mathcal{L}$, the feedback function for j-th term was,

$$f_j(x_{j-1}, x_j, x_{j+1}) = x_{j-1} \oplus x_{j+1} \oplus (c_j \cdot x_j). \tag{3}$$

As, $F \oplus F = 0$ for any Boolean function F, so we can rewrite the equation (3) as following:

$$f_j(x_{j-1}, x_j, x_{j+1}) = x_{j-1} \oplus x_{j+1} \oplus (c_j \cdot x_j) \oplus F \oplus F.$$

Let's take $F = f_N(x_{j-2}, x_{j+2})$ where f_N is some non-linear function. So the equation now looks like,

$$f_j(x_{j-1}, x_j, x_{j+1}) = x_{j-1} \oplus x_{j+1} \oplus (c_j \cdot x_j) \oplus f_N(x_{j-2}, x_{j+2}) \oplus f_N(x_{j-2}, x_{j+2}). \quad (4)$$

Now, we apply shifting on one of the f_N terms like this, $f_j \xrightarrow{f_N} f_{j+1}$. According to Theorem 1, the new CA would generate same set of sequences as $x_{j-2}, x_{j+2} \notin N(j)$.

In Algorithm 1, we have used a maximum length LHCA. So, the synthesized NHCA will also have a period of $2^n - 1$.   ■

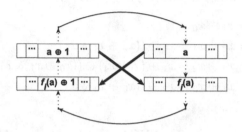

Fig. 2. Effect of Non-linearity on the NHCA cycle

It is trivial that NHCA synthesized according to Algorithm 1 is invertible. It can also be noted that, the effect of the non-linearity can be dispersed as many cells as possible by shifting the non-linear function upto required number of steps. However, this increases the neighborhood dependency as well as the hardware cost. So, we have limited the construction of NHCA upto 5 neighborhood for optimization purpose.

The affect of the non-linearity injection in one bit is shown in Fig. 2. Here, we assume that i-th bit is injected with a non-linear function $\mathbf{f_N}$ and $\mathbf{f_N}(0, 0, \cdots, 0) = 0$. Each non-zero value of the injected non-linear function complements exactly two states of the original LHCA cycle.

We have computed the non-linearity of some of the synthesized NHCA and the results have been depicted in Table 1. The LSB of the NHCA is 0 indexed and only the non-linearity of the MSB is considered. The underlying maximum length LHCA is synthesized from a primitive polynomial [1] and represented as a listing of non-zero coefficients. For example, the set $(8, 6, 5, 1, 0)$ represent the polynomial $x^8 + x^6 + x^5 + x + 1$. The positions of the non-linearity injection are also shown. For each position i, the non-linear function used is of the form $f_N = (x_{i+2} \cdot x_{i-2})$. Finally, the non-linearity with their corresponding iteration is given in the table.

The 12-bit NHCA depicted in Table 1 is used to show the increase of non-linearity with each iteration in Fig. 3.(a). The corresponding graph is shown in Fig. 3.(b) that clearly indicates that the non-linearity increases rapidly after a few numbers of initial iterations.

Table 1. Non-linearity with Iteration for Different NHCA

Polynomial	Non-linearity Position		Iteration						
			1	2	3	4	5	6	7
5, 2, 0	2		0	2	12	12	12	10	10
9, 4, 0	7		0	2	0	12	48	96	176
10, 3, 0	2,7		0	2	4	8	16	128	160
12,7,4,3,0	2,9		0	2	2	16	32	64	128
16, 5, 3, 2, 0	2,11		0	0	0	4	32	192	448

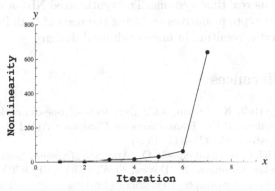

Iteration	Non-linearity Difference
1	0
2	2
3	0
4	14
5	16
6	32
7	64
8	640

(a) Non-linearity Difference   (b) Non-linearity Difference Linegraph

Fig. 3. Change of Non-linearity in 12 bit NHCA

4   Implementation Details

We have implemented and tested the proposed scheme in Xilinx Spartan-3 XC3S1500-4FG676C FPGA platform. The LHCAs are represented same as Table 1.For each underlying LHCA and their corresponding NHCA after non-linearity injection using Algorithm 1, the implementation details are shown in Table 2.

Table 2. Implementation Summary and Comparison in Xilinx XC3S1500 FPGA

Polynomial	Non-linear Positions	Number of Slices			Number of LUTs		
		LHCA	NHCA	Increase	LHCA	NHCA	Increase
8,6,5,1,0	2	6	7	16.67%	11	14	27.27%
16,5,3,2,0	2,11	11	12	9.09%	22	23	4.54%
64,4,3,1,0	2,32,59	36	48	33.33%	72	95	31.94%
128,29,27,2,0	2,32,64,123	98	96	-2.04%	190	185	-2.63%

Table 2 clearly states that Algorithm 1 synthesizes a maximum length NHCA with a very little or no extra hardware. Besides, the positions of non-linearity injections can be chosen suitably to minimize the hardware overhead.

5   Conclusion

In this paper we have presented a scalable method to construct an n-cell NHCA with period $2^n - 1$. The generated NHCA has very less hardware overhead compared to the contemporary methods and the time overhead is negligible as well. This makes the construction suitable for resource constraint environments as well as real time systems. The synthesized NHCA can be efficiently used in various crypto primitives replacing the need of both linear and non-linear modules, thereby, resulting in more optimized designs.

References

1. Cattell, K., Muzio, J.C.: Synthesis of one-dimensional linear hybrid cellular automata. IEEE Transactions on Computer-Aided Design of Integrated Circuits and Systems 15, 325–335 (1996)
2. Meier, W., Staffelbach, O.: Analysis of pseudo random sequences generated by cellular automata. In: Davies, D.W. (ed.) EUROCRYPT 1991. LNCS, vol. 547, pp. 186–199. Springer, Heidelberg (1991)
3. Daemen, J., Rijmen, V.: The Design of Rijndael. Springer (2002)
4. Hell, M., Johansson, T., Meier, W.: Grain: a stream cipher for constrained environments. Int. J. Wire. Mob. Comput. 2, 86–93 (2007)
5. Bertoni, G., Daemen, J., Peeters, M., Assche, G.V.: The keccak sha-3 submission. Submission to NIST (Round 3) (2011)
6. Fredricksen, H.: A survey of full length nonlinear shift register cycle algorithms. SIAM Review 24(2), 195–221 (1982)
7. Dubrova, E.: A scalable method for constructing galois nlfsrs with period $2^n - 1$ using cross-join pairs. IEEE Transactions on Information Theory 59, 703–709 (2013)
8. Das, S., Roy Chowdhury, D.: Generating cryptographically suitable non-linear maximum length cellular automata. In: Bandini, S., Manzoni, S., Umeo, H., Vizzari, G. (eds.) ACRI 2010. LNCS, vol. 6350, pp. 241–250. Springer, Heidelberg (2010)

Systolic Dissemination in the Arrowhead Family

Dominique Désérable

INSA – Institut National des Sciences Appliquées,
20 Avenue des Buttes de Coësmes, 35043 Rennes, France*
deserable@gmail.com

Abstract. Although cellular automata (CA) are usually driven by a local rule, global communications are often needed either to synchronize a
process or to share common data. However, these communications must
be carried out from the nearest-neighbor, local transition. Such disseminations are named "systolic" herein: this metaphor is borrowed from the
eponymous cellular architectures. The core of this study is the topology
of the *"arrowhead"* family underlying the CA network in the hexagonal
tessellation. The graphs of this family, directed or undirected, are Cayley graphs, or graphs of groups and are therefore vertex-transitive. As a
consequence, the local rule is the same within the whole network. Two
types of dissemination are presented: a (one–to–all) broadcasting and a
(all–to–all) gossiping. For each type, a 3–port, directed scheme and a 6–
port, undirected scheme are derived from construction. It is shown that
the complexity of these algorithms is the graph diameter, either directed
or undirected, according to the case study.

Keywords: cellular automata, hexagonal topology, arrowhead and diamond, systolic dissemination, broadcasting, gossiping.

to *Wacław Franciszek Sierpiński*

1 Introduction

Global communications are often needed in cellular automata. A typical example is the Firing Squad Synchronization Problem wherein the "General" gives
an order to all "soldiers" to fire the transition synchronously [1, 2]. Another
example is the propagative mode in a "lattice–grain" CA used to simulate the
void propagation in a granular system and wherein transition and timestep must
be considered at two different time scales [3]: the timestep termination must be
detected at each transition, that involves a perpetual and global communication
within the network to synchronize the timestep. Other examples are related in
complex systems with long-range interactions [4] as well as many others in CA
literature [5].

---

* Until September 2013.

J. Wąs, G.C. Sirakoulis, and S. Bandini (Eds.): ACRI 2014, LNCS 8751, pp. 75–86, 2014.
© Springer International Publishing Switzerland 2014

Global communications in networks are generally classified into: (one–to–all) broadcasting, (all–to–one) gathering, (all–to–all) gossiping, (personalized–one–to–all) scattering, (personalized–all–to–all) scattering–gathering [6]. In a coarse–grain context, these tasks are highly time–consuming and space–consuming. For example, given a message of length L and a network of order N, broadcasting requires a buffer of size L whereas gossiping may require a buffer of size NL. The situation is even "worse" for personalized communications. But the coarse–grain protocols are seldom appropriate for (fine–grain) cellular automata. For this reason, further investigations were derived under a "systolic" form: this metaphor is borrowed from H. T. Kung when introducing the massively parallel, VLSI, pipelined cellular architectures [7]. The gap between systolic and cellular algorithms and architectures is very tight whenever the time evolution is synchronous and controlled by a global clock (the "pulse"). Besides, the "messages" carried within cellular networks are usually short messages. For example, the gossiping scheme in [3] requires only a 1–bit buffer. We focus herein on the most usual types of dissemination: broadcasting and gossiping and their "systolic" pattern involved. For fine-grain systolic dissemination, we can refer in particular to [8–10] and references therein.

The core of this study is the topology of the "*arrowhead*" family underlying the CA network in the *hexagonal* tessellation. A well-known, but different construction is the H_n "honeycomb", a hexagonal torus with n circular rings arranged around a central node [11–13]. On the contrary, the *arrowhead* construction follows a recursive scheme and yields various representations of (directed) digraphs or (undirected) graphs: (Sierpiński–like, hexagonal) *arrowheads* or (lozenged, orthogonal) *diamonds*. The construction of arrowheads and diamonds, not isomorphic as digraphs, is induced by two possible orientations in the hexavalent lattice. In their undirected version, they are isomorphic and merely define four distinct representations of the same graph. It has been shown that their associated networks provide a good framework for routing [14, 15] and other coarse–grain global communications like broadcasting [16] and gossiping [17]. So far, the hexagonal arrowhead underlies a lattice–grain automata network [18–20, 3] whereas the orthogonal diamond, named "T_n" therein, is the subject of several works on cellular multiagent systems [21–23]: performances are compared with another network "S_n", a subnetwork of T_n which is just the 2^n–ary 2–cube [24]; note that another family of "augmented" k–ary 2–cubes was investigated elsewhere [25] for any k but which coincide with T_n only when $k = 2^n$.

The systolic disseminations investigated herein, broadcasting and gossiping, are either "3–port" or "6–port". The 3–port pattern is induced by the outgoing arcs of the vertices in the digraphs whereas the 6–port pattern is induced by the incident edges of the vertices in the graphs. The complexity of the disseminations is just the diameter, either "oriented" for the first pattern or 'non–oriented" for the second pattern. The arrowhead family is presented in Sect. 2 and the systolic dissemination in Sect. 3 before Conclusion.

2 The Arrowhead Family

The genesis of the "arrowhead family" is revealed and then the main properties of its digraphs and graphs are emphasized. The description is short and rather informal and should be underpined from [26] and from [27–29] for tiling, algebraic groups, and graph theory.

2.1 Genesis

Two natural ways (among an infinity) of re–tiling the hexagonal tessellation with a polyhex as new "prototile" are displayed in Fig. 1. In (↑), the H_n "honeycomb" [11–13] can be recognized, with its n circular rings of length $6p$ ($p \leq n$) arranged around a central tile and of order $N = 3n^2 + 3n + 1$ ($n = 1$ for the 7–hex thereon). In (↓), a first step is defined from a "N–SW–SE" 4–hex[1] [26] chosen among the seven existing tetrahexes [27]. In both cases, a torus underlying a CA network with periodic boundaries can be derived and the transformation is straightforward from adjacency[2].

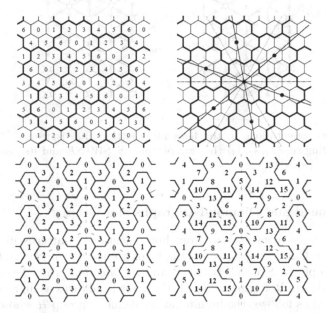

Fig. 1. (↑) 7–hex prototile tiling the hexagonal tessellation: symmetry axes of the prototile and symmetry axes of the elementary tiling do not coincide.
(↓) Step 1 – 4–hex prototile tiling the hexagonal tessellation: both symmetry systems fit. Step 2 – The construction is recursive: 16–hex generated from four 4–hexes, etc...

---

[1] The "propeller" in Wolfram MathWorld.
[2] Incidentally, the undirected hexavalent lattice is the dual of the hexagonal tiling: a center of tile is a vertex in the lattice and there is an edge connecting two vertices *iff* their corresponding tiles are adjacent.

When tiling the plane with H_n prototiles, it can be observed in Fig. 1 that the axes joining the center of these prototiles and the symmetry axes of the elementary tiling do not coincide. On the contrary, the symmetry is stabilized with our 4–hex. A relevant illustration of this discrepancy between prototiles can be found in [30]. Moreover, this construction can reiterate stepwise: a second step generates a 16–hex from four 4–hexes and so forth...

A similar stepwise construction can also be generated from a "S–SW–SE" 4–hex[3]. As a matter of fact, the two valid patterns N–SW–SE and S–SW–SE are induced by the two possible "isotropic" and "anisotropic" orientations in Fig. 2 for the hexavalent lattice.

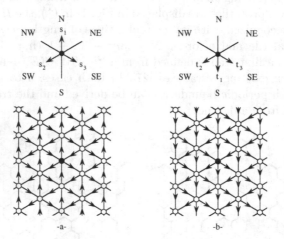

Fig. 2. The two orientations in the hexavalent lattice: (a) "isotropic" N–SW–SE and its generating set (s_1, s_2, s_3) (b) "anisotropic" S–SW–SE and its generating set $(t_1, t_2, t_3) = (s_1^{-1}, s_2, s_3)$

2.2   Arrowhead and Diamond Digraphs and Graphs

The above stepwise construction from both mentioned patterns gives rise to their respective Cayley digraphs, or graphs of groups: the *arrowhead* from the so-called isotropic N–SW–SE pattern[4] and the *diamond* from the anisotropic S–SW–SE pattern. Referring to Fig. 1, the arrowhead torus as digraph of order 4 is constructed as follows: the infinite lattice defines a group $\mathcal{H}$ whose elements are the vertices, the group operation $x \to xs$ connects vertex x to vertex xs and s is one of the three elements of the generating set in Fig. 2a. The subset of vertices "0" is the subgroup $\mathcal{H}_0$ of $\mathcal{H}$ and the subsets of vertices "i" are the four cosets $\mathcal{H}_i$ ($i = 0, 1, 2, 3$). The index $|\mathcal{H} : \mathcal{H}_0|$ of $\mathcal{H}_0$ in $\mathcal{H}$ is 4 and the quotient

---

[3] The "bee" in Wolfram MathWorld: the five remaining tetrahexes, namely *bar*, *pistol*, *worm*, *arch* and *wave* do not fit.

[4] We borrow the term "arrowhead" from Mandelbrot [31] about one of the Sierpiński's fractal constructions [32].

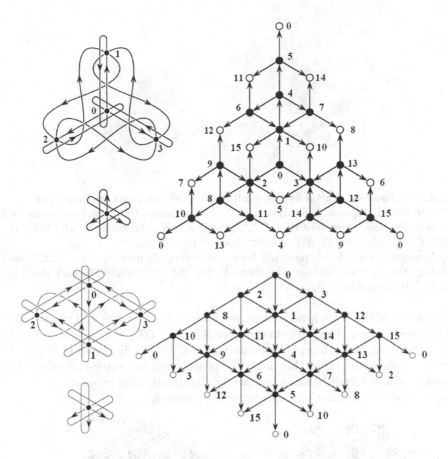

Fig. 3. (↑) Oriented arrowhead $\overrightarrow{\mathcal{AT}}_0$, $\overrightarrow{\mathcal{AT}}_1$, $\overrightarrow{\mathcal{AT}}_2$ and (↓) diamond $\overrightarrow{\mathcal{DT}}_0$, $\overrightarrow{\mathcal{DT}}_1$, $\overrightarrow{\mathcal{DT}}_2$. Some vertices are replicated in white for convenience.

group $\mathcal{H}/\mathcal{H}_0$ is the vertex set (0,1,2,3) of the digraph $\overrightarrow{\mathcal{AT}}_1$ in Fig. 3. Note the correspondence between arcs in digraph $\overrightarrow{\mathcal{AT}}_1$ and adjacency in the 4–hex of Fig. 1 through the N–SW–SE pattern. By the same transformation, the 16–hex in Fig. 1 turns into $\overrightarrow{\mathcal{AT}}_2$ in Fig. 3. In the same way, $\overrightarrow{\mathcal{AT}}_0$ results from a 1–hex prototile as elementary tile.

The diamonds $\overrightarrow{\mathcal{DT}}_n$ displayed in Fig. 3 for $n = 0, 1, 2$ result from a similar construction but now based upon the anisotropic S–SW–SE pattern of Fig. 2b. In the digraph notation, n stands for the step of the stepwise construction and will also denote the "size" of the digraphs.

The (undirected) arrowhead and diamond graphs denoted $\mathcal{AT}_n$ and $\mathcal{DT}_n$ are derived from their respective associated digraph by just releasing the orientation. The order of the graphs (or digraphs) is $N = 4^n$ from construction. The number of arcs, for digraphs, or edges, for graphs, is clearly $3N$. The stepwise

Fig. 4. Sierpiński–like fractal figures, both graph representations are isomorphic.
($\leftarrow$) Arrowhead stepwise generation $n = 7$. Schematically, the arrowhead splits into nine triangles, say: three N–SW–SE "$\triangle$–heads" A_1, A_2, A_3, three S–NE–NW "$\triangle$–tails" A_1', A_2', A_3', three N–SW–SE "$\triangledown$–bodies" B_1, B_2, B_3.
($\rightarrow$) Hexagonal arrowhead, resulting from embedding A_i into A_i' $(i = 1, 2, 3)$ and splitting into six triangles, say: the three N–SW–SE $\triangledown$–triangles B_i and the three S–NE–NW $\triangle$–triangles $A_i \cup A_i'$.

construction of the arrowhead is displayed for $n = 7$ in Fig. 4 as well as its hexagonal representation. The full connection of $\mathcal{AT}_3$ and $\mathcal{DT}_3$ is displayed in Fig. 5. The orthogonal, homeomorphic representation of $\mathcal{DT}_3$ is displayed in Fig. 6. As Cayley graphs or digraphs they have the property to be vertex-transitive, that means that any vertex behaves identically. Practically, this property involves a unique local rule within their associated CA network.

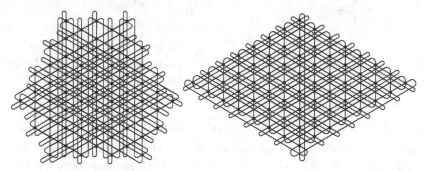

Fig. 5. Arrowhead and diamond $\mathcal{AT}_3$ and $\mathcal{DT}_3$. Undirected graphs are isomorphic.

3   Systolic Dissemination

Broadcasting and gossiping schemes, either 3–port or 6–port are investigated. For convenience, the CA orthogonal representation is considered according to the new cardinal orientation in the inset of Fig. 6. For the 3–port case, an "*arrowhead*" output pattern N–SW–E and a "*diamond*" output pattern N–NE–E are defined. By symmetry, their – CA read–only – input pattern will be S–NE–W (arrowhead) and S–SW–W (diamond) respectively.

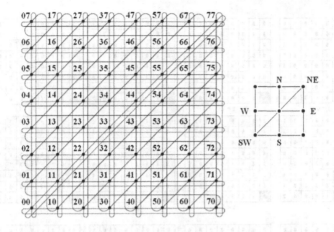

Fig. 6. The orthogonal diamond for $n = 3$, labeled in (i, j) Cartesian coordinates, homeomorphic to the diamond. Inset: new cardinal orientation N–S, E–W, NE–SW.

The complexity of the disseminations is just the diameter, either "oriented" for the two 3–port patterns or "non–oriented" for the unique 6–port pattern. The diameter defines the length of the shortest path between the most distant pair of vertices; such a pair is said to be *antipodal*. The exact value of the diameters is claimed in each case as well as the number of antipodals [33]. Since the graphs are vertex-transitive, the results hold from any vertex.

3.1 Dissemination 3–Port

Oriented Diameters and Antipodals

Claim. Let $\vec{D}_n$ be the oriented diameter of $\vec{\mathcal{AT}}_n$ and $\vec{\mathcal{DT}}_n$. Then

$$\vec{D}_n = \sqrt{N} - 1. \tag{1}$$

Let $\vec{\mathcal{N}}_{A,n}$ (resp. $\vec{\mathcal{N}}_{D,n}$) be the number of antipodals in $\vec{\mathcal{AT}}_n$ (resp. $\vec{\mathcal{DT}}_n$). Then

$$\vec{\mathcal{N}}_{A,1} = 3 \; ; \; \vec{\mathcal{N}}_{A,n} = 6 \; (n > 1) \; ; \; \vec{\mathcal{N}}_{D,n} = 2\sqrt{N} - 1. \tag{2}$$

Broadcasting 3–Port. The algorithm hereafter performs a systolic 3–port broadcasting through the *arrowhead* input pattern S–NE–W from a source ("originator") to the whole cellular network. The source data is a 1–bit signal to broadcast. The systolic broadcasting is achieved after $\vec{D}_n$ two-stage timesteps:

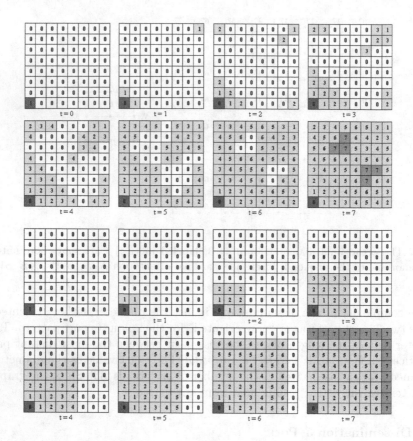

Fig. 7. Systolic broadcasting 3–port. After a full reset ($t = 0$), the 1–bit signal in the source ("originator" which could be everywhere) is set to 1. From $t = 1$, distances from source are displayed. Position and number of antipodals (2) are highlighted from $t = \vec{D}_n - 1$. After $\vec{D}_n$ timesteps, the signal is propagated within the whole network. ($\uparrow$) Broadcasting 3-port in $\vec{\mathcal{AT}}_3$. ($\downarrow$) Broadcasting 3-port in $\vec{\mathcal{DT}}_3$.

Algorithm *B3P–A*

```
Reset all cells: x = 0; Set source cell: x = 1;
From Step 1 to Step Dₙ
  Get 3-uple (xS, xNE, xW);
  Compute x = x or (xS or xNE or xW)
End timestep
```

A similar algorithm performs the same operation, now through the *diamond* input pattern *S–SW–W*:

Algorithm $B3P$–D
  Reset all cells: $x = 0$; Set source cell: $x = 1$;
  From Step 1 to Step $\vec{D}_n$
    Get 3-uple (xS, xSW, xW);
    Compute $x = x$ or $(xS$ or xSW or $xW)$
  End timestep

By the way, the distribution of antipodals is detected from step $\vec{D}_n$ -1. The broadcast is displayed in Fig. 7.

Gossiping 3–Port. A systolic 3–port gossip follows exactly the same 3–uple input scheme. The only difference is the initial state and the internal 1–bit operation. A simple way to check whether the gossip yields the expected result is to assign a N–bit state word x everywhere from the cell's $ID = 2^n i + j$ in Fig. 6 as $x = 2^{ID}$: all N bits are set to 0 except the ID bit set to 1 and to execute an OR operation onto the chosen 3–uple. Upon completion, the gossip result yields a N–bit state as $(111...11)$ everywhere. That is, from the *arrowhead* input 3–uple:

Algorithm $G3P$–A
  Set current cell: $x = 2^{ID}$;
  From Step 1 to Step $\vec{D}_n$
    Get 3-uple (xS, xNE, xW);
    Compute $x = x$ or $(xS$ or xNE or $xW)$
  End timestep

and similarly for the *diamond* input 3–uple. For brevity's sake, gossip snapshots cannot be displayed here.

3.2   Dissemination 6–Port

Non-Oriented Diameter and Antipodals

Claim. The arrowhead $\mathcal{AT}_n$ has a diameter

$$D_n = \frac{2\sqrt{N} - 1}{3} \quad \text{or} \quad D_n = \frac{2(\sqrt{N} - 1)}{3} \tag{3}$$

depending on the odd–even parity of n. Let $\mathcal{N}_{A,n}$ be the number of antipodals in $\mathcal{AT}_n$, then

$$\mathcal{N}_{A,1} = 3 \; ; \quad \mathcal{N}_{A,2} = 9 \; ; \quad \mathcal{N}_{A,n} = \begin{cases} 6 \\ 12 \end{cases} \tag{4}$$

depending on the odd–even parity of $n > 2$. Since $\mathcal{AT}_n$ and $\mathcal{DT}_n$ are isomorphic, the above results hold also for $\mathcal{DT}_n$.

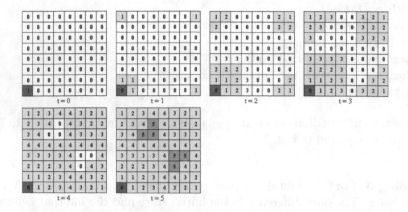

Fig. 8. Systolic broadcasting 6–port. After a full reset ($t = 0$), the 1–bit signal in the source is set to 1. From $t = 1$, distances from source are displayed. Position and number of antipodals (4) are highlighted from $t = D_n - 1$. After D_n timesteps, the signal is propagated within the whole network. Broadcasting 6-port in $\mathcal{AT}_3$ (resp. $\mathcal{DT}_3$).

Broadcasting 6–Port. The only change for a systolic 6–port broadcasting is to operate with two opposite input 3–uples, eg. S–NE–W and N–SW–E. Recall that $\mathcal{AT}_n$ and $\mathcal{DT}_n$ are isomorphic. The systolic broadcasting is achieved after D_n two-stage timesteps:

Algorithm *B6P*
```
Reset all cells: x = 0; Set source cell: x = 1;
From Step 1 to Step Dₙ
  Get 3-uple (xS, xNE, xW); Get 3-uple (xN, xSW, xE);
  Compute x = x or (xS or xNE or xW));
  Compute x = x or (xN or xSW or xE))
End timestep
```

The broadcast is displayed in Fig. 8 and a 6–port gossip would follow a similar suitable scheme.

4   Conclusion

Fine–grain, "systolic" broadcasting and gossiping in the *arrowhead* family were presented herein within its digraphs and graphs and the communication scheme was emphasized for the oriented case. It is worth pointing out that the input pattern depends only upon the initial state, not upon the communication type. The diameters, which define the time complexity and the distribution of antipodals were highlighted in the orthogonal representation. Other global communications as well as their systolic patterns in the hexagonal representation will be investigated elsewhere.

References

1. Moore, E.F.: The firing squad synchronization problem. In: Moore, E.F. (ed.) Sequential Machines, Selected Papers, pp. 213–214. Addison-Wesley, Reading (1964)
2. Umeo, H.: Firing squad synchronization problem in cellular automata. In: Encyclopedia of Complexity and Systems Science, pp. 3537–3574 (2009)
3. Désérable, D.: Propagative mode in a lattice-grain CA: time evolution and timestep synchronization. In: Sirakoulis, G.C., Bandini, S. (eds.) ACRI 2012. LNCS, vol. 7495, pp. 20–31. Springer, Heidelberg (2012)
4. Désérable, D., Dupont, P., Hellou, M., Kamali-Bernard, S.: Cellular automata in complex matter. Complex Systems 20(1), 67–91 (2011)
5. Chopard, B., Droz, M.: Cellular automata modeling of physical systems. Cambridge University Press, Cambridge (1998)
6. Fraigniaud, P., Lazard, E.: Methods and problems of communication in usual networks. Discrete Applied Mathematics 53(1-3), 79–133 (1994)
7. Kung, H.T.: Why systolic architectures? Computer 15(1), 37–46 (1982)
8. Liestman, A.L., Richards, D.: Perpetual gossiping. Par. Proc. Lett. 3(4), 347–355 (1993)
9. Hromkovič, J., Klasing, R., Unger, W., Wagener, H.: The complexity of systolic dissemination of information in interconnection networks. In: Cosnard, M., Ferreira, A., Peters, J. (eds.) CFCP 1994. LNCS, vol. 805, pp. 235–249. Springer, Heidelberg (1994)
10. Flammini, M., Pérennes, S.: Lower bounds on systolic gossip. Information and Computation 196(2), 71–94 (2005)
11. Chen, M.-S., Shin, K.G., Kandlur, D.D.: Addressing, routing and broadcasting in hexagonal mesh multiprocessors. IEEE Trans. Comp. 39(1), 10–18 (1990)
12. Morillo, P., Comellas, F., Fiol, M.A.: Metric problems in triple loop graphs and digraphs associated to an hexagonal tessellation of the plane, TR 05-0286 (1986)
13. Albader, B., Bose, B., Flahive, M.: Efficient communication algorithms in hexagonal mesh interconnection networks. J. LaTeX Class Files 6(1), 1–10 (2007)
14. Désérable, D.: Minimal routing in the triangular grid and in a family of related tori. In: Lengauer, C., Griebl, M., Gorlatch, S. (eds.) Euro-Par 1997. LNCS, vol. 1300, pp. 218–225. Springer, Heidelberg (1997)
15. Désérable, D.: Hexagonal Bravais–Miller routing of shortest path (unpublished)
16. Désérable, D.: Broadcasting in the arrowhead torus. Computers and Artificial Intelligence 16(6), 545–559 (1997)
17. Heydemann, M.-C., Marlin, N., Pérennes, S.: Complete rotations in Cayley graphs. European J. Combinatorics 22(2), 179–196 (2001)
18. Désérable, D.: A versatile two-dimensional cellular automata network for granular flow. SIAM J. Applied Math. 62(4), 1414–1436 (2002)
19. Cottenceau, G., Désérable, D.: Open environment for 2d lattice-grain CA. In: Bandini, S., Manzoni, S., Umeo, H., Vizzari, G. (eds.) ACRI 2010. LNCS, vol. 6350, pp. 12–23. Springer, Heidelberg (2010)
20. Désérable, D., Masson, S., Martinez, J.: Influence of exclusion rules on flow patterns in a lattice-grain model. In: Kishino (ed.) Powders & Grains, pp. 421–424. Balkema (2001)
21. Ediger, P., Hoffmann, R., Désérable, D.: Routing in the triangular grid with evolved agents. J. Cellular Automata 7(1), 47–65 (2012)
22. Ediger, P., Hoffmann, R., Désérable, D.: Rectangular vs triangular routing with evolved agents. J. Cellular Automata 8(1-2), 73–89 (2013)

23. Hoffmann, R., Désérable, D.: All-to-all communication with cellular automata agents in 2D grids: topologies, streets and performances. J. Supercomputing 69(1), 70–80 (2014)
24. Dally, W.J., Seitz, C.L.: The torus routing chip. Dist. Comp. 1, 187–196 (1986)
25. Xiang, Y., Stewart, I.A.: Augmented k–ary n–cubes. Information Sciences 181(1), 239–256 (2011)
26. Désérable, D.: A family of Cayley graphs on the hexavalent grid. Discrete Applied Math. 93, 169–189 (1999)
27. Grünbaum, B., Shephard, G.C.: Tilings and patterns. Freeman & Co., NY (1987)
28. Grossman, I., Magnus, W.: Groups and their graphs. New Mathematical Library, vol. 14. Random House, New-York (1964)
29. Harary, F.: Graph theory. Addison-Wesley, Reading (1969)
30. Désérable, D.: Embedding Kadanoff's scaling picture into the triangular lattice. Acta Phys. Polonica B Proc. Suppl. 4(2), 249–265 (2011)
31. Mandelbrot, B.B.: The fractal geometry of nature. Freeman and Cie (1982)
32. Sierpiński, W.: On a curve every point of which is a point of ramification. Prace Mat.–Fiz. 27, 77–86 (1916), et Acad. Pol. Sci. II, 99–106 (1975)
33. Désérable, D.: Arrowhead and diamond diameters (unpublished)

On the Dynamics of Multi-information in Cellular Automata

Gregor Chliamovitch, Bastien Chopard, and Alexandre Dupuis

Department of Computer Sciences, University of Geneva, Switzerland
Gregor.Chliamovitch@unige.ch

Abstract. After reviewing a few key quantities of information theory, we investigate in this paper the behaviour of multi-information in elementary cellular automata. It will turn out that the usual classification by Wolfram is not well supported in terms of this information measure, or, more likely, that multi-information is blind to the kind of complexity displayed by those automata.

1 Introduction

While for decades information theory did not spread much out of the frontiers of the domain it had been designed for (apart from entropy which originates from thermodynamics and is so deeply grounded into statistical physics [6]), in recent years several attempts have been made to take advantage of the whole information-theoretic toolkit in the study of statistical mechanical systems as well as in the study of complexity in the large [1]. It is nevertheless not clear thus far whether or not information theory has something fundamental to tell us about the nature of complexity at all.

Any attempt to cope with complexity has sooner or later to face one-dimensional cellular automata, since these are among the simplest complex systems one can think of. Moreover, they display a wide range of behaviours, that can be classified according to the complexity of the pattern they unfold over time. While the most famous such classification is due to Wolfram [11], it is regularly challenged and many alternatives have been proposed (see [5] and references therein).

If indeed information theory has deep insights to reveal on the nature of complexity, it is likely that automata which are very different in terms of Wolfram's notion of complexity should also exhibit different behaviours when considered from an information-theoretic viewpoint. Accordingly, our aim in this paper is to investigate the temporal behaviour of multi-information over time in all 256 elementary automata. It will turn out that while observed behaviours fall into a limited number of categories, this classification is definitely at odds with more usual ones.

We start in section 2 with an express review of information theory, putting emphasis on the concept of *multi-information* which, in our view, bears a particular relevance. We consider Wolfram's classification in section 4, but before that

J. Wąs, G.C. Sirakoulis, and S. Bandini (Eds.): ACRI 2014, LNCS 8751, pp. 87–95, 2014.

we will have to pause in order to discuss how those quite abstract information-theoretic concepts may be translated in operational terms. This is the purpose of section 3.

2   Review of Information Theory

The most fundamental building block of information theory is *entropy*. Although the term was introduced first in the context of thermodynamics, it soon received an interpretation as a measure of uncertainty contained in a probability distribution $p(X)$. More precisely, *Shannon entropy* is defined as [9]

$$H(X) := \sum_x p(x) \ln \frac{1}{p(x)}. \tag{1}$$

It provides a characterization of the uncertainty on a variable X which is unique with respect to a set of intuitive axioms [4]. In the same way, *mutual information* provides a unique caracterization of how much the knowledge of one variable X impacts the prediction on another, Y. We simply calculate the reduction of entropy brought by the knowledge of Y, i.e.

$$I(X,Y) := H(X) - H(X|Y). \tag{2}$$

where $H(X|Y)$ denotes the entropy of the conditional density $p(X|Y)$. A simple calculation shows that I can be re-written as

$$I(X,Y) = H(X) + H(Y) - H(X,Y) = \sum_{x,y} p(x,y) \ln \frac{p(x,y)}{p(x)p(y)} \tag{3}$$

and is therefore obviously symmetric. In terms of the so-called *Kullback-Leibler (KL) divergence*, which provides a measure of pseudo-distance in the space of distributions, mutual information can be seen to quantify, in a sense, how far the variables are from being independent of each other [3].

To give an example, if X and Y are both binary variables, and the joint probability is given by $p(0,0) = 0.1, p(0,1) = 0.2, p(1,0) = 0.4$ and $p(1,1) = 0.3$, the marginal probability of X is given by $p_X(0) = p(0,0) + p(0,1) = 0.3$ and $p_X(1) = p(1,0) + p(1,1) = 0.7$, while the marginal probability of Y is given by $p_Y(0) = p(0,0) + p(1,0) = 0.5$ and $p_Y(1) = p(0,1) + p(1,1) = 0.5$. The mutual information can now be calculated to be

$$\begin{aligned}
I(X,Y) &= p(0,0) \ln \frac{p(0,0)}{p_X(0)p_Y(0)} + p(0,1) \ln \frac{p(0,1)}{p_X(0)p_Y(1)} \\
&\quad + p(1,0) \ln \frac{p(1,0)}{p_X(1)p_Y(0)} + p(1,1) \ln \frac{p(1,1)}{p_X(1)p_Y(1)} \\
&= 0.1 \ln \frac{0.1}{0.15} + 0.2 \ln \frac{0.2}{0.15} + 0.4 \ln \frac{0.4}{0.35} + 0.3 \ln \frac{0.3}{0.35} \\
&\simeq 0.024.
\end{aligned} \tag{4}$$

Many generalizations of mutual information to more than two variables have been proposed over time (see, among others, [8]), but since any such generalization is usually crafted in order to find use in a specific domain of research, none has actually met universal consensus yet. In our view the most intuitive one is found in a quantity known as *multi-information* (and sometimes -less properly- *total correlation*). It is defined as [10]

$$M(X_1, ..., X_N) := \sum_{i=1}^{N} H(X_i) - H(X_1, ..., X_N). \tag{5}$$

When expressed directly in terms of probabilities, that is

$$M(X_1, ..., X_N) = \sum_{x_1, ..., x_N} p(x_1, ..., x_N) \log \frac{p(x_1, ..., x_N)}{p(x_1)...p(x_N)}, \tag{6}$$

it becomes obvious that multi-information can be understood as the KL distance to independence between variables, and in this respect plays the same role in the multivariate case that mutual information plays in the bivariate one. This is the key quantity we will be considering in the following sections, since it treats all variables on an equal footing and does not introduce spurious distinctions between variables.

3   The Markovian Framework

An important restriction regarding the use of entropy, mutual or multi-information is that it requires the full knowledge of the probability density of the system under consideration. This knowledge of the density may be lacking sometimes, in which case the formalism breaks down, but nonetheless systems with known distribution represent a wide class on which theoretical and numerical experiments can be carried through.

Things become a bit more tedious when we want to investigate the temporal behaviour of information measures, which requires knowing how the probability density itself changes over time. Often this is done using Monte-Carlo methods, by evolving copies of the system and reconstructing the probabilities by sampling trajectories. This is for instance the approach adopted in [7], where another kind of information-theoretical measure is discussed. It has the drawback that we are then exposed to sampling errors.

An alternative way to proceed would be to determine the evolution rule itself, according to which the density evolves. Could we do that, we could so to speak follow all trajectories at once, even the least probable ones[1]. This amounts to a

---

[1] An illustration is provided by Wolfram's rule 40 which brings *almost* all configurations to the state where all cells take value 0, *except* for a few periodic configurations. While such configurations could well be missed by an inadequate sampling, the alternative method keeps them as long as they are not explicitly assigned a vanishing probability. See section 4 below.

description in terms of Markov chains, where the knowledge of history allows us to predict towards which states the system could evolve. We will restrict ourselves here to the case that the knowledge of a *finite* history is sufficient to predict possible futures. By extending the state space, actually all such processes can be recast in the form of *memoryless Markov chains* (or simply *Markov chains*), by what we mean that the forthcoming states can be predicted knowing the current state of the process only ; previous states do not alter the future in any way.

While this second approach seems to outperform the usual sampling in terms of accuracy, it actually suffers from its numerical cost. Assume for instance we deal with a dynamical system constituted by N agents taking binary values in $\{0, 1\}$. We have in this case 2^N possible configurations, while assuming the system is driven by a dynamics with a k-steps memory we have 2^{kN} possible relevant histories to keep into consideration, which becomes soon untractable even for small values of N and k.

Nonetheless this formalism has some advantages that cannot be given up easily. In particular it allows a more straightforward transition from numerical exploration to theoretical investigation of information measures in complex systems, and therefore seems an approach worth being promoted. Still more importantly, as we already mentioned, this approach does not require to select (arbitrarily) an initial configuration, but handles them all as long as they are not explicitly assigned probability zero[2].

In the following, we will therefore focus on Markovian processes of order $k = 1$ for the sake of tractability. In more mathematical terms, denoting by $W_{SS'}$ the probability of transition from state $S = (s_1, ..., s_N)$ (s_i denoting the i-th node) to state $S' = (s'_1, ..., s'_N)$, the formula ruling the joint density of states considered at two consecutive times is written as

$$p(S', t + 1; S, t) = p(S, t)W_{SS'}. \tag{7}$$

Iterating this formula allows to write

$$p(S', t + \tau; S, t) = p(S, t)(W^\tau)_{SS'}, \tag{8}$$

and starting from this expression we can recover the probability of being in a state S' at a later time by summing on former positions, so as to get

$$p(S', t + \tau) = \sum_S p(S', t + \tau; S, t) = \sum_S p(S', t)(W^\tau)_{SS'}. \tag{9}$$

---

[2] Admittedly there remains some arbitrariness inasmuch as we have to select *some* initial distribution. While the transient phase will be affected by a change of initial density, the conclusions we draw regarding the equilibrium regime are nevertheless independent of the inital distribution as long as the system is ergodic. This is not always the case, but still much less restrictive than assuming that the system tends towards the same configuration whatever its initial configuration - which is certainly wrong in the case of the elementary cellular automata dealt with in this paper.

Given the full density of the system, univariate marginals appearing in the definition of multi-information are calculated by summing on irrelevant nodes. Assuming for instance we need the marginal of, say, node s_1, we have to compute

$$p(s_1, t) = \sum_{s_2,\ldots,s_N} p(S, t). \tag{10}$$

The interplay between nodes and states is a major source of confusion and requires careful attention when coming to implementation.

Since multiplying matrices of size n is a process of order $O(n^3)$, noting that $k = 1$ implies $n = 2^N$ means that the effort required by the calculation of successive probability densities grows exponentially with the number of nodes (not to mention the corresponding memory saturation).

4 Elementary Cellular Automata

In order to check whether or not Wolfram's classification can be recovered by considering the behaviour of multi-information, we scanned all 256 rules (actually only the 88 of them that are non-equivalent) and investigated how, starting from an uniform initial distribution (therefore with $M = 0$), the distribution evolves during 50 steps, which for the small systems investigated here is long enough to reach the stationary regime, and calculated the associated multi-information. Due to lack of space, only eight typical behaviours are displayed here (figure 1).[3]

We may note that while different kinds of patterns are obtained, they fall into a limited number of types, whose figure 1 provides a representative sample. These patterns are essentially characterized by 1) the length of their transient phase 2) the fact they converge either to a stable value or reach a periodic regime 3) the value of M to which they converge 4) the fact that these characteristics are independent of each other.

Rule 154 below offers a good example of a rule whose M vanishes. It is nevertheless not typical in that it stays at $M = 0$ forever and does not go through a correlated phase. Another rule displaying this behaviour is 0, but in this case this is easily understood since it jumps directly from an uncorrelated initial to a density where only the state having all nodes 0 survives. Rule 154, on the other side, displays a non-trival configurational pattern.

Rule 164 (Wolfram class II) provides an example of an automaton reaching a partly correlated phase after two iterations, followed by a decay of M towards some finite value. This behaviour is frequently encountered, with some variations regarding the intensity of the peak and the final value of M, and this for classes I and III as well as II. Rule 40 is an interesting instance of class I automaton displaying this behaviour. This rule converges to the empty configuration for most of the possible initial configurations, but in some scarcer cases it converges

---

[3] The results obtained for all 256 rules can be found on the webpage *http://www.cui.unige.ch/~chopard/Sophocles*. Patterns for mutual information are displayed there as well.

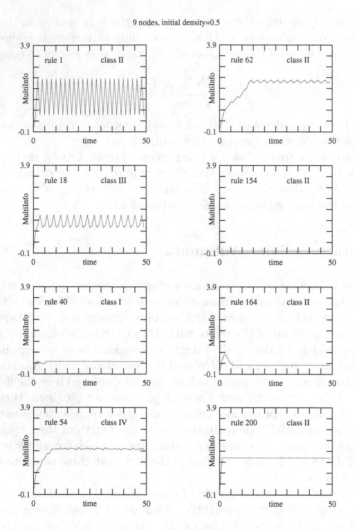

Fig. 1. A catalogue of typical behaviours displayed by multi-information in elementary cellular automata

to other stable configurations. Indeed the multi-information is seen to stabilize at some non-zero value indicating that the stable configuration is not unique when all configurations are initially taken into account.

Rule 200 (class II) shows another frequent behaviour. Here M happens to reach immediately its equilibrium value, but sometimes the transient phase can be longer. This situation is encountered in all first three classes. Note that the equilibrium value of M varies considerably ; see for instance 78 which reaches the highest M we observed.

A striking example of periodic regime is provided by rule 1, belonging to class II. Although its oscillations are unusually strong, it is a nice example of an automaton with period 2. This can be observed by looking at the configurational

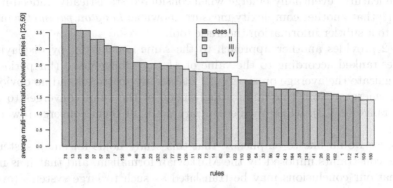

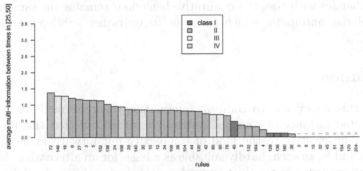

Fig. 2. All 88 elementary automata ranked according to their informational content in the stationary regime

pattern as well. A more intriguing case is 18 (class III), which oscillates with period 3. This could nevertheless not have been expected when looking at the configurational pattern, which displays a chaotic behaviour typical of class III. On the other side, 94 also exhibits oscillations of longer period, but belongs to class II. This is also the case of 62, which shows an unusually long transient phase. Interestingly this oscillatory multi-information is observed in classes II, III and IV but never in class I.

An instance of class IV is provided by rule 54. The period here is particularly long, but other rules form class IV have shorter ones so that it should not be considered as a specific feature of complex rules.

To summarize, it seems that while it is indeed possible to establish a classification of rules based on the behaviour of the multi-information, it appears hazardous to make a link with complexity in the sense of Wolfram since all kinds of patterns discussed above can be found in almost all four classes. The most we can say is that when considering both ends of the complexity spectrum, that is classes I and IV, patterns of multi-information can be safely attributed. It is difficult otherwise to discriminate between classes I and II, II and III and III and IV. Some patterns tend nevertheless to appear more (resp. less) frequently when Wolfram's complexity increases, so that it might be possible that some distinctive features eventually emerge when considered statistically. Indeed it is shown in [2] that another complexity measure known as *Langton parameter* may be linked to a subtler information-theoretic tool.

Figure 2 provides another approach to the same conclusion, by displaying all 88 rules ranked according to the value of M they converge to (for periodic rules we indicate the average on a period). Classes are scattered and no obvious clustering emerges. Note that interestingly none of the rules converges to an M in the range $(2.5, 3)$, while on the contrary many of them converge towards $M \approx 0.9$.

Finally, we would like to emphasize that this study holds for small systems due to the constraints imposed by the Markovian formalism, and that it is not certain that our conclusions may be translated as such to large systems (even if experiments carried through different sizes suggest that while the equilibrium value of M changes with size, the qualitative behaviour remains the same). Size effects in cellular automata, which turn out to be rather subtle, are further adressed in [2].

5   Conclusion

Our goal in this paper was to confront information-theoretic methods with a well-documented instance of complex systems. It turned out that this tool appeared rather unsensitive to the kind of complexity put forward in Wolfram's classification and is, as such, hardly suitable as a basis for an alternative classification of these systems. Some clues suggest nonetheless that a more elaborated treatment might reveal some statistical regularities.

Acknowledgements. The authors acknowledge funding from the European Union Seventh Framework Programme (FP7/2007- 2013) under grant agreement number 317534 (Sophocles project). They also gratefully acknowledge the anonymous reviewers for their valuable comments.

References

[1] Ay, N., Olbrich, E., Bertschinger, N., Jost, J.: A Geometric Approach to Complexity. Chaos 21 (2011)
[2] Chliamovitch, G., Chopard, B., Velasquez, L.: (to appear)
[3] Cover, T., Thomas, J.: Elements of Information Theory. Wiley-Interscience, New York (2006)
[4] Khinchin, A.I.: Mathematical Foundations of Information Theory. Dover, New York (1957)
[5] Martinez, G.: A Note on Elementary Cellular Automata Classification. arXiv, 1306-5577 (2013)
[6] Penrose, O.: Foundations of Statistical Mechanics. Pergamon, Oxford (1969)
[7] Quax, R., Apolloni, A., Sloot, P.M.A.: The Diminishing Role of Hubs in Dynamical Processes on Complex Networks. Journal of the Royal Society Interface 10(88) (2013)

[8] Schreiber, T.: Measuring Information Transfer. Physical Review Letters 85(2), 461–464 (2000)

[9] Shannon, C.: The Mathematical Theory of Communication. Bell System Technical Journal 27, 379–439, 623–656 (1948)

[10] Watanabe, S.: Information Theoretical Analysis of Multivariate Correlation. IBM Journal 14(3), 66–82 (1960)

[11] Wolfram, S.: Statistical Mechanics of Cellular Automata. Reviews of Modern Physics 55(3), 601–644 (1983)

Lyapunov Exponents of One-Dimensional, Binary Stochastic Cellular Automata

Wouter Van der Meeren*, Jan M. Baetens, and Bernard De Baets

KERMIT, Department of Mathematical Modelling, Statistics and Bioinformatics,
Ghent University, Coupure links 653, Gent, Belgium

Abstract. In this paper the stability of elementary cellular automata (ECAs) upon introduction of stochasticity, in the form of an update probability for each cell, is assessed. To do this, Lyapunov exponents, which quantify the rate of divergence between two nearby trajectories in phase space, were used. Furthermore, the number of negative Lyapunov exponents was tracked, in order to gain a more profound insight into the interference between the stability and the update probability, and an upper bound on the Lyapunov exponents of stochastic cellular automata (SCAs) was established.

1   Introduction

Stochastic cellular automata (SCAs) are often used for modelling natural and physical processes, such as the dynamics of forests and the interaction between chemical substances [3,6,7]. For instance, Reichenbach et al. [4] have shown that an SCA can be used to simulate the interaction between microorganisms in such a way that qualitatively similar spatial aggregates of microorganisms emerge in silico as is the case in vitro. Although Lyapunov exponents as a means to determine the stability of cellular automata (CAs) were already established two decades ago within the framework of deterministic CAs, in the works of Wolfram [10], Shereshevsky [5] and Bagnoli [2], the effect of stochasticity on the stability of elementary CAs (ECAs) has not yet been examined. Since SCAs are so often used in practical models, it might be important to assess the influence of stochasticity on the stability of SCAs.

2   Preliminaries

Stochasticity in the context of CAs can be interpreted in several ways. Here, the following definition is adopted.

Definition 1. *A one-dimensional, binary stochastic cellular automaton $\mathcal{C}$ is a sextuple*

$$\mathcal{C} = \langle \mathcal{T}, S, s, N, \phi, \psi \rangle,$$

where

---

* Corresponding author

J. Wąs, G.C. Sirakoulis, and S. Bandini (Eds.): ACRI 2014, LNCS 8751, pp. 96–104, 2014.

(i) $\mathcal{T}$ is a countably infinite array of cells c_i

(ii) $S = \{0, 1\}$

(iii) The output function $s : \mathcal{T} \times \mathbb{N} \to S$ yields the state value of cell c_i at the t-th discrete time step, i.e. $s(c_i, t)$.

(iv) N is the neighborhood function, such that $N(c_i) = \{c_{i-1}, c_i, c_{i+1}\}$

(v) ϕ and ψ are functions,

$$\phi : S^3 \to S,$$

$$\psi : S^3 \to S,$$

each ϕ and ψ governing the dynamics of cell c_i, i.e.,

$$s(c_i, t+1) = \begin{cases} \phi(\tilde{s}(N(c_i), t)), & \text{with probability } p, \\ \psi(\tilde{s}(N(c_i), t)), & \text{with probability } 1 - p, \end{cases}$$

where $p \in [0, 1]$ represents the probability that the transition according to ϕ occurs and where $\tilde{s}(N(c_i), t) = \{s(c_{i-1}), s(c_i), s(c_{i+1})\}$.

In literature one-dimensional, binary CAs are often referred to as elementary CAs (ECAs). In the remainder of this paper, ECAs will be labeled according to Wolfram's nomenclature [9]. Further, the transition function ψ is the so-called identity rule (204), such that with a probability $1-p$ the state of a given cell does not change. Also, since an infinite array is impractical for computer simulations, an approximation was performed, by using a finite array, denoted as $\mathcal{T}^*$, with cyclic boundary conditions.

In order to quantify the interference between an ECA's stability and the update probability p, we resorted to Lyapunov exponents and the related input sensitivity, which were introduced originally by Bagnoli et al. [2] to assess the stability of ECAs. The finite-time Lyapunov exponent, denoted as λ, is defined as follows:

$$\lambda = \frac{1}{T} \log \left(\frac{\epsilon_t}{\epsilon_0} \right), \tag{1}$$

with ϵ_0 and ϵ_t the initial number of defects, usually one, and the number of defects at time step t, respectively, where the latter should be quantified by tracking all possible defects that emerge from the introduction of a single defect at $t = 0$, as well as their multiplicity. A defect in this context is defined as a configurational difference between the configurations evolved by two CAs after the same number of time steps, from initial configurations that differ in only one cell. Negative Lyapunov exponents indicate a decreasing number of defects and are therefore a property of stable CAs, whereas a positive Lyapunov exponent indicates that initially close phase trajectories diverge exponentially, which is a feature of an unstable CA. The input sensitivity, denoted as $\bar{\mu}$, is defined as:

$$\bar{\mu} = \left(\prod_{t=1}^{T} \mu(t) \right)^{1/T}, \tag{2}$$

where T is the number of time steps and

$$\mu(t) = \frac{1}{|\mathcal{T}^*|} \sum_{i=1}^{|\mathcal{T}^*|} \frac{1}{|N(c_i)|} \sum_{j:c_j \in N(c_i)} J_{ij},$$

with J the Boolean Jacobian matrix, whose (i,j)-th element is the Boolean derivative of cell c_i to cell c_j [8]. Mathematically, this Boolean derivative can be expressed as:

$$\frac{\partial s(c_i, t+1)}{\partial s(c_j, t)} = \phi(s(c_1,t), s(c_2,t), \ldots, s(c_i,t), \ldots, s(c_j,t), \ldots)$$

$$\oplus \phi(s(c_1,t), s(c_2,t), \ldots, s(c_i,t), \ldots, \bar{s}(c_j,t), \ldots),$$

where $\bar{s}(c_j, t)$ is the Boolean complement of $s(c_j, t)$ and $\oplus$ is the sum mod 2 operator.

It should be kept in mind that with decreasing values of p fewer cells are updated at a given time step. Therefore, the number of time steps has to be adjusted in order to ensure that more or less an equal number of updates is considered across the entire range of update probabilities. Since only a fraction p of the cells is updated at every consecutive time step, the number of time steps required for an equal number of cell updates has to be divided by p. Furthermore, in order to be able to compare Lyapunov exponents across ECAs with the same transition function ϕ, but different update probabilities, they should be normalized. The normalized Lyapunov exponent, denoted as λ_n, can be defined as the Lyapunov exponent divided by its maximum. Therefore, an upper bound on the Lyapunov exponents of stochastic ECAs (SECAs) must be established. For deterministic ECAs, the upper bound, denoted as λ_m, is given by [1]:

$$\lambda_m(\bar{\mu}) = \log(3\bar{\mu}), \tag{3}$$

where the factor 3 accounts for the connectivity, being the average neighborhood size, of the tessellation or, in this case, the array. Equation (3) can be extended to SECAs, however, it should be noticed that $\bar{\mu}$ will depend on p.

To avoid confusion, two new symbols are introduced: $\bar{\mu}_1$ and $\bar{\mu}_p$. These symbols represent $\bar{\mu}$ in the deterministic case and the stochastic case, respectively. $\bar{\mu}_p$ is the weighted average of $\bar{\mu}_1$ and the inverse of the connectivity, where p acts as a weighing coefficient,

$$\bar{\mu}_p = p\, \bar{\mu}_1 + \frac{1-p}{3} \tag{4}$$

The reasoning behind Eq. (4) is the following. On average, a fraction p of all cells will be updated at every consecutive time step, since every cell has a probability p of being updated. For the updated cells it is expected that the average input sensitivity equals the one obtained in the deterministic case. Further, since only a fraction p of the cells is updated on average, the remaining fraction is not updated. Consequently, the value of the latter cells at the next time step depends only on their current value. Therefore, they are only sensitive to one cell in their neighborhood, being themselves, such that their sensitivity ($\bar{\mu}$) is given by $1/3$. Using Eq. (4), the upper bound on the Lyapunov exponents of SECAs is given by:

$$\lambda_m(\bar{\mu}, p) = \log(3\bar{\mu}_p) = \log(1 - p + 3p\,\bar{\mu}_1).\qquad(5)$$

This upper bound is visualized in Figure 1. The upper bound is only plotted for positive values, because the Lyapunov exponent of a CA must be $-\infty$ as soon as it is negative.

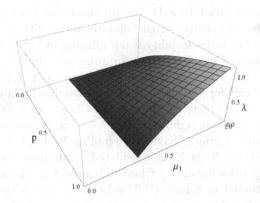

Fig. 1. Upper bound on the Lyapunov exponents of SECAs

3   Results

3.1   Experimental Setup

In the following, the results of the in silico experiments will be discussed and a classification of SECAs will be proposed, on the basis of the interference between their stability and the update probability. The simulation approach used here is the one used by Baetens and De Baets [1] and not the one used by Bagnoli et al. [2], as the latter forces the CA to a more stable configuration, if there exists one, by randomly swapping the states of pairs of cells. Baetens and De Baets [1] use an ensemble of random initial conditions and assess the stability by checking which fraction of the initial conditions leads to a negative Lyapunov exponent. In this paper, an ensemble $\mathcal{E}$ of 30 random initial conditions was assembled. For every member of this ensemble the Lyapunov exponent was computed using Eq. (1) after evolving the SECA for 250,000 cell updates, which equals 500 time steps in the deterministic scenario, after which the numerically obtained values were normalized with respect to the upper bound given by Eq. (5). The grid size was 500 and cyclic boundary conditions were imposed, similar to the setup of Bagnoli in the case of ECAs [2]. Here, three stability classes are distinguished: [1]

Class 1: $\lambda = -\infty$ for all members of the ensemble
Class 2: $\lambda = -\infty$ for some, but not all members of the ensemble
Class 3: $\lambda \geq 0$ for all members of the ensemble

The case where $\lambda = -\infty$ is special, since this occurs if the number of defects becomes zero. This is the case for stable SCA, for they are recognized by converging phase space trajectories.

3.2   Classification of SECAs

Upon classifying the SECAs within the considered SCA family, four clearly distinct and two intermediate classes were found. To avoid confusion with other classification systems, letters instead of numbers are used to designate the stability classes. **Class A** and **Class B** contain rules that belong to Class 1 and Class 3, respectively, irrespective of the update probability p. Hence, they enclose the SECAs for which the stability is not affected by the update probability. **Class C** rules belong to Class 1 for a certain range of values of p and to Class 2 for p values below that range, as well as for p close to 1. **Class D** rules also exhibit Class 2 behavior for p close to 1, but, for smaller update probabilities a shift towards more stable behavior, being either Class 1, or Class 2, with a large number of members of the ensemble having $\lambda = -\infty$, is observed. Since there are several rules that exhibit behavior resembling both Class C and Class D behavior, another class, **Class E**, is considered, containing these intermediary rules. All remaining rules belong to Class 2, irrespective of the update probability and were gathered in **Class F**. The behavior of the rules belonging to this last class is more or less similar across the different members, leaving some minor exceptions aside. Table 1 gives the final classification of the SECAs.

Table 1. Classification of the 88 minimal [8] 1D SECAs

Class	Rule number
A	0, 8, 32, 40, 128, 136, 160, 168
B	51, 54, 57, 60, 105, 108, 150, 156, 204
C	1, 3, 7, 19, 23, 50, 178
D	2, 10, 15, 34, 42, 130, 162, 170
E	5, 14, 24, 56, 138, 142, 152, 184
F	4, 6, 9, 11, 12, 13, 18, 22, 25, 26, 27, 28, 29, 30, 33, 35, 36, 37, 38, 41, 43, 44, 45, 46, 58, 62, 72, 73, 74, 76, 77, 78, 90, 94, 104, 106, 110, 122, 126, 132, 134, 140, 146, 154, 164, 172, 200, 232

3.3   Phenomenology of SECAs

Now that a classification is completed, a few exemplary rules will be examined in more detail, in order to exemplify the different classes. More precisely, we will focus our attention on rules 0, 23, 30, 90, 110, 130, 150, 184 and 204. Rules 0 and 204 exhibit trivial behavior.

Rule 150 is a typical rule for which stochasticity does not influence the stability, because every cell is sensitive to each of its neighboring cells. Therefore, stochasticity slows down defect propagation, but defects can never disappear (Figure 2).

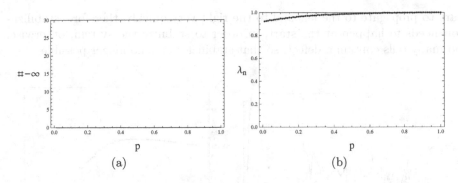

Fig. 2. The number of members in the ensemble $\mathcal{E}$ giving rise to infinite Lyapunov exponents (a) and the average of the finite normalized Lyapunov exponents λ_n (b) as a function of the update probability p, for SECA 150

The behavior of rules belonging to Class D, exemplified here by rule 130 (see Figure 3), is also quite easily understood. The introduction of stochasticity can be seen as a push towards a more stable configuration, similar to the approach used by Bagnoli et al. [2]. However, instead of swapping places of two cells, the state of a cell is kept constant while others change, which also changes the configuration of the entire SECA.

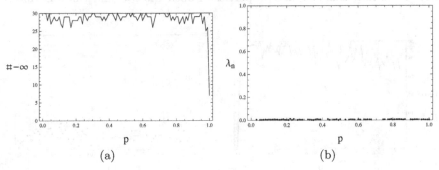

Fig. 3. The number of members in the ensemble $\mathcal{E}$ giving rise to infinite Lyapunov exponents (a) and the average of the finite normalized Lyapunov exponents λ_n (b) as a function of the update probability p, for SECA 130

For rules belonging to Class C, for example rule 23 (Figure 4), a similar reasoning can be followed for values of p close to 1. Yet, for low update probabilities, the stability decreases again. The reason why is not yet fully understood, but, the following observation was made when analyzing the space-time diagrams of rules in this class, as well as the multiplicity of defects. Essentially, it appeared that the initial defect introduced in SECAs belonging to both Class C and Class D stays very localized in the case of the deterministic scenario ($p = 1$). For Class D rules this is still the case when p decreases, meaning that there is no need for an immediate stabilization of the system. In contrast, for Class C rules, defects start to propagate to the left and to the right very quickly, therefore, stabilization needs to happen at the start, in order to stabilize the system, otherwise, too many cells contain a defect, so that stabilization is no longer possible.

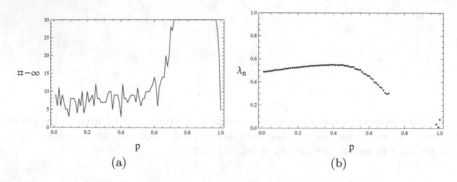

(a)   (b)

Fig. 4. The number of members in the ensemble $\mathcal{E}$ giving rise to infinite Lyapunov exponents (a) and the average of the finite normalized Lyapunov exponents λ_n (b) as a function of the update probability p, for SECA 23

Rule 184, a clear example of a Class E rule, is given in Figure 5. This figure clearly shows that this rule has properties of both Class C and Class D rules.

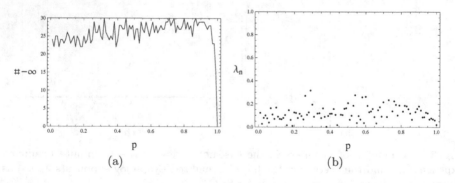

(a)   (b)

Fig. 5. The number of members in the ensemble $\mathcal{E}$ giving rise to infinite Lyapunov exponents (a) and the average of the finite normalized Lyapunov exponents λ_n (b) as a function of the update probability p, for SECA 184

Based on the averages of the finite Lyapunov exponents, a lot of rules belonging to Class F exhibit behavior similar to that of Class B rules. However, some of the ensemble's members lead to $\lambda = -\infty$. This is the case for rule 30 (Figure 6), but also for rules 90 and 110.

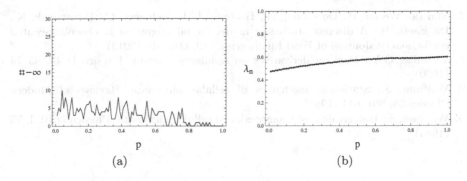

Fig. 6. The number of members in the ensemble $\mathcal{E}$ giving rise to infinite Lyapunov exponents (a) and the average of the finite normalized Lyapunov exponents λ_n (b) as a function of the update probability p, for SECA 30

4   Conclusions and Future Work

The results in this paper indicate that the stability of many ECAs may change abruptly if the cell updates are no longer deterministic. This might have repercussions on the usability of SCAs for mimicking real-world processes. Extending the approach presented in this paper to such models will enable us to verify their nature and steer their development.

Acknowledgments. This work was carried out using the STEVIN Supercomputer Infrastructure at Ghent University, funded by Ghent University, the Flemish Supercomputer Center (VSC), the Hercules Foundation and the Flemish Government – department EWI. Part of this research was supported by the Fund for Scientific Research-Flanders (FWO-V), project G083812N.

References

1. Baetens, J.M., De Baets, B.: Phenomenological study of irregular cellular automata based on Lyapunov exponents and Jacobians. Chaos 20, 033112 (2010)
2. Bagnoli, F., Rechtman, R., Ruffo, S.: Damage spreading and Lyapunov exponents in cellular automata. Physics Letters A 172, 34–38 (1992)
3. Kubo, T.: Forest spatial dynamics with gap expansion: Total gap area and gap size distribution. Journal of Theoretical Biology 180, 229–246 (1996)
4. Reichenbach, T., Mobilia, M., Frey, E.: Mobility promotes and jeopardizes biodiversity in rock-paper-scissors games. Nature 448, 1046–1049 (2007)
5. Shereshevsky, M.A.: Lyapunov exponents for one-dimensional cellular automata. Journal of Nonlinear Science 2, 1–8 (1992)
6. Van der Weeën, P., Baetens, J.M., De Baets, B.: Design and parameterization of a stochastic cellular automaton describing a chemical reaction. Journal of Computational Chemistry 32, 1952–1961 (2011)

7. Van der Weeën, P., De Clercq, N., Baetens, J.M., Delbaere, C., Dewettinck, K., De Baets, B.: A discrete stochastic model for oil migration in chocolate-coated confectionery. Journal of Food Engineering 119, 602–610 (2013)
8. Vichniac, G.Y.: Boolean derivatives on cellular automata. Physica D 45, 63–74 (1990)
9. Wolfram, S.: Statistical mechanics of cellular automata. Reviews of Modern Physics 55, 601–644 (1983)
10. Wolfram, S.: Universality and complexity in cellular automata. Physica D 10, 1–35 (1984)

Synthesis of Non-uniform Cellular Automata Having only Point Attractors

Nazma Naskar[1], Sumit Adak[2], Pradipta Maji[3], and Sukanta Das[2]

[1] Department of Information Technology,
Seacom Engineering College, Howrah, 711302, India
naskar.preeti@gmail.com
[2] Department of Information Technology,
Indian Institute of Engineering Science and Technology, Shibpur
(formerly Bengal Engineering and Science University, Shibpur), 711103, India
maths.sumit@gmail.com, sukanta@it.becs.ac.in
[3] Machine Intelligence Unit, Indian Statistical Institute,
203 B. T. Road, Kolkata, India 700108
pmaji@isical.ac.in

Abstract. This paper studies a special class of non-uniform cellular automata (CAs) that contain only single length cycle (point) attractors in their state space. These CAs always converge to some point attractors. A number of theorems and lemmas are reported in this paper to characterize this class of CAs. *Reachability tree*, a discrete tool for characterizing 1-d CA, has been utilized to develop theories for these types of CAs. We finally report an algorithm that *synthesizes* a non-uniform cellular automaton having only point attractors.

Keywords: Single length cycle attractor (point attractor), multi state attractor, reachability tree, cyclic states.

1   Introduction

Synthesis of a non-uniform cellular automaton (CA) refers to a process that selects individual rules for cells. Aim of this paper is to synthesize a non-uniform CA that always converges to some point attractors. The boundary condition is assumed here as null. This type of CAs attracted the researchers due to their utility in several applications, like pattern classification and recognition [1,6,3], design of associative memory, etc. [4].

However, to ensure that the CA will always converge to point attractors, we have to explore the state space of the CA to see whether it contains any multi-length cycle attractor. To efficiently synthesize our required CA, we first characterize them. An introductory characterization has already been reported in [5]. We use *reachability tree* [2], a mathematical tool, in our characterization. The tool is further utilized to develop synthesis algorithm.

J. Wąs, G.C. Sirakoulis, and S. Bandini (Eds.): ACRI 2014, LNCS 8751, pp. 105–114, 2014.

Table 1. The rules 5, 73, 200 and 80

Present state :	111	110	101	100	011	010	001	000	*Rule*
(*RMT*)	(7)	(6)	(5)	(4)	(3)	(2)	(1)	(0)	
(i) Next state :	0	0	0	0	0	1	0	1	5
(ii) Next state :	0	1	0	0	1	0	0	1	73
(iii) Next state :	1	1	0	0	1	0	0	0	200
(iv) Next state :	0	1	0	1	0	0	0	0	80

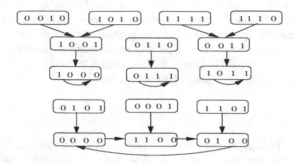

Fig. 1. State Transition Diagram of CA $\langle 5, 73, 200, 80 \rangle$

2　Preliminaries

The cellular automata (CAs) we consider here are the elementary cellular automata that use null boundary condition. The next state functions of these CAs, known as 'rule' [7], are commonly represented through a tabular form (Table 1). The first row of the Table 1 lists the possible 8 combinations of the present states of left, self and right neighbor of a cell. The last four rows indicate the next states of the cell for the rules 5, 73, 200 and 80 respectively.

Traditionally, the cells of an automaton follow same rule. Such a CA is *uniform CA*. In a *non-uniform CA*, the cells may follow different rules. We refer a rule vector $\mathcal{R} = \langle \mathcal{R}_0, \cdots \mathcal{R}_i, \cdots \mathcal{R}_{n-1} \rangle$ for an n-cell non-uniform CA, where the cell i follows $\mathcal{R}_i$. Obviously, uniform CAs are special case of non-uniform CAs.

The first row of Table 1 notes the combinations of the present states of three neighbors. Borrowing vocabulary from *Switching Theory*, we refer each combination as a Rule Min Term (RMT) [2]. Here we introduce a set Z_8^i that contains the valid RMTs of $\mathcal{R}_i$. That is, $Z_8^i = \{k \mid \text{RMT } k \text{ of } \mathcal{R}_i \text{ is valid}\}$. Since we have 8 RMTs (Table 1), generally $|Z_8^i| = 8$.

The state transition diagram (see Fig. 1) of an automaton may contain *cyclic* and *acyclic* states. The states 0000, 1100, 0100, 1000, 0111 and 1011 are the cyclic states, and they form attractors. The 0000, 1100 and 0100 form an attractor of length 3, whereas the rest three states form three attractors of length 1 (point attractors). In this work, we put our attention on those CA which contain only

Table 2. Relationship between i^{th} and $(i+1)^{th}$ RMTs

i^{th} RMT	$(i+1)^{th}$ RMTs
0, 4	0, 1
1, 5	2, 3
2, 6	4, 5
3, 7	6, 7

point attractors. However, the acyclic states can be of two types - *reachable* and *non-reachable*. A state is reachable if it has at least one predecessor. The acyclic states 1001 and 0011 are reachable, whereas the 0010, 1010, 0110, 1111 (Fig. 1) are non-reachable.

A CA state can also be viewed as a sequence of RMTs. For example, the state 1110 in null boundary condition can be viewed as $\langle 3764 \rangle$, where 3, 7, 6 and 4 are corresponding RMTs on which the transition of first, second, third and forth cells can be made. For an n-bit state, we get a sequence of n RMTs. However, two consecutive RMTs in an RMT sequence (RS) are related [2]. The relation is noted in Table 2. We call two RMTs r and s $(r \neq s)$ equivalent to each other if $2r$ (mod 8) $= 2s$ (mod 8). Therefore, RMTs 0 and 4 are equivalent to each other. Similarly, RMTs 1 and 5, RMTs 2 and 6, and RMTs 3 and 7 are equivalent to each other.

3   Reachability Tree (RT) and State Transition

Definition 1. *Reachability tree for an n-cell cellular automaton under null boundary condition is a rooted and edge-labeled binary tree with $n+1$ levels, where $E_{i.2j} = (N_{i.j}, N_{i+1.2j}, l_{i.2j})$ and $E_{i.2j+1} = (N_{i.j}, N_{i+1.2j+1}, l_{i.2j+1})$ are the edges between nodes $N_{i.j} \subseteq Z_8^i$ and $N_{i+1.2j} \subseteq Z_8^{i+1}$ with label $l_{i.2j} \subseteq N_{i.j}$, and between nodes $N_{i.j}$ and $N_{i+1.2j+1} \subseteq Z_8^{i+1}$ with label $l_{i.2j+1} \subseteq N_{i.j}$ respectively $(0 \leq i \leq n-1, 0 \leq j \leq 2^i - 1)$. Following relations are maintained in the tree:*

1. *$l_{i.2j} \cup l_{i.2j+1} = N_{i.j}$*
2. *$\forall r \in l_{i.2j}$ (resp. $\forall r \in l_{i.2j+1}$), RMT r of $\mathcal{R}_i$ is 0 (resp. 1) and RMTs $2r$ (mod 8) and $2r+1$ (mod 8) of $\mathcal{R}_{i+1}$ are in $N_{i+1.2j}$ (resp. $N_{i+1.2j+1}$)*
3. *$\bigcup_{0 \leq j \leq 2^i-1} N_{i.j} = Z_8^i$, $(0 \leq i \leq n-1)$*

Fig. 2 shows the reachability tree for the CA of Fig. 1. Under the null boundary condition, only 4 RMTs are valid for left most and right most cells, and $Z_8^0 = \{0,1,2,3\}$ and $Z_8^3 = \{0,2,4,6\}$. Hence, the root $N_{0.0} = Z_8^0$. The label of edge $E_{0.0}$ is $\{1,3\}$, as RMTs 1 and 3 of rule 5 are 0. We write RMTs of a label on the edge within a bracket. However, the label of edge $E_{2.7}$ is empty, that is $l_{2.7} = \phi$. This edge is non-reachable. Fig. 2 marks such nodes as black. Since $Z_8^n = \phi$ for an n-cell CA, the leaf nodes are empty. Number of leaves (excluding black leaves as they don't exit) is 8, which is the number of reachable states. We call edge $E_{i.2j}$ as 0-edge and $E_{i.2j+1}$ as 1-edge where $0 \leq j \leq 2^i - 1$. A sequence of edges

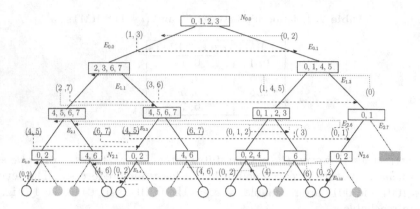

Fig. 2. Reachability Tree of CA $\langle 5, 73, 200, 80 \rangle$. The links are also shown.

from the root to a leaf node represents a reachable state, when 0-edge and 1-edge are replaced by 0 and 1 respectively. For example, 0011 is a reachable state in Fig. 2. On the other hand, the states 1110 and 1111 are non-reachable.

Reachability tree gives us information about reachable states. A sequence of edges $\langle E_{0.j_0} E_{1.j_1} \cdots E_{i.j_i} E_{i+1.j_{i+1}} \cdots E_{n-1.j_{n-1}} \rangle$ from root to a leaf associates a reachable state and at least one RS $\langle r_0 r_1 \cdots r_i r_{i+1} \cdots r_{n-1} \rangle$, where $r_i \in l_{i.j_i}$ and $r_{i+1} \in l_{i+1.j_{i+1}}$ ($0 \le i < n-1$, $0 \le j_i \le 2^i - 1$, and $j_{i+1} = 2j_i$ or $2j_i + 1$). That is, the sequence of edges represents at least two CA states. Note that if RMT r_i is 0 (resp. 1) then $E_{i.j_i}$ is 0-edge (resp. 1-edge). Therefore, the reachable state is the next (resp. present) state of the state (resp. predecessor), represented as RMT sequence. Interestingly, there are 2^n RSs in the tree, but number of reachable states may be less than 2^n. However, a sequence of edges may associate m-number of RSs ($m \ge 1$), which implies, this state is reachable from m-number of different states.

Since the RSs and the states, both of an automaton can be traced in the tree, which RS corresponds to what state can be identified. To identify this correspondence, we form *links* among edges. The links are formed for each RMT $r \in l_{i.j}$, present on edge $E_{i.j}$ ($0 \le i \le n-1$, $0 \le j \le 2^i - 1$). By the processing of reachability tree, we find the links among the edges for each individual RMT on the tree. The links are formed depending on whether the RMTs are self replicating (defined below) or not.

Definition 2. *An RMT x0y (resp. x1y) is said to be self replicating if RMT x0y (resp. x1y) is 0 (resp. 1).*

For example, RMT 2 (010) of rule 5 is self replicating, whereas all the RMTs except RMT 2 of rule 200 are self replicating (see Table 1). If an RMT $r \in l_{i.j}$ is not self replicating, then there is a link from the edge $E_{i.j}$ to $E_{i.k}$ ($j \ne k$). Depending on the values of j and k, we can classify the links in the following way: forward link (when $j < k$), backward link (when $j > k$) and self link (when

$j = k$). The rules, followed to form links in a reachability tree, are noted below:

1) If RMT $r \in l_{0.j}$ is self replicating ($j = 0$ or 1),
   The edge $E_{0.j}$ is self linked for RMT r.
   Otherwise, if $j = 0$,
        there is a forward link from $E_{0.0}$ to $E_{0.1}$ for RMT r;
        else, there is a backward link from $E_{0.1}$ to $E_{0.0}$ for RMT r.

2) If $E_{i-1.j}$ is self linked for RMT $r \in l_{i-1.j}$,
   and if s is self replicating
        where $s \in l_{i.2j}$ (resp. $s \in l_{i.2j+1}$) is $2r$ (mod 8) or $2r + 1$ (mod 8),
        then $E_{i.2j}$ (resp. $E_{i.2j+1}$) is self linked.
   But if s is not self replicating,
        then there is a forward link from $E_{i.2j}$ to $E_{i.2j+1}$ (resp. backward link
from $E_{i.2j+1}$ to $E_{i.2j}$).

3) If there is a link from $E_{i-1.j}$ to $E_{i-1.k}$ ($j \neq k$) for RMT $r \in l_{i-1.j}$,
        and $s \in l_{i.2j}$ (resp. $s \in l_{i.2j+1}$) is $2r$ (mod 8) or $2r + 1$ (mod 8),
        then there is a link from $E_{i.2j}$ (resp. $E_{i.2j+1}$) to $E_{i.2k}$ while $s \in \{0, 1, 4, 5\}$
or to $E_{i.2k+1}$ while $s \in \{2, 3, 6, 7\}$.
        [It is forward link if $j < k$, backward link if $j > k$]

Example 1. We apply the above rules on each RMT of each edge to get the links in the tree. Fig. 2 shows the links of edges caused by RMTs of the CA $\langle 5, 73, 200, 80 \rangle$. There is a (forward) link from $E_{0.0}$ to $E_{0.1}$ for RMT 3 (forming links using rule 5), so a dotted line is drawn from RMT 3 of $E_{0.0}$ to $E_{0.1}$. Now, we get a forward link from $E_{1.1}$ to $E_{1.3}$ for RMT 6 (forming links using rule 73). However, no lines are shown in Fig. 2 for RMTs involved in self links. Now, we can get links from $E_{2.2}$ to $E_{2.6}$ for RMT 4 (forming links using rule 200), and from $E_{3.4}$ to $E_{3.12}$ for RMT 0 (forming links using rule 80). Therefore, for the RS $\langle 3640 \rangle$, we can get a sequence of links, hence a sequence of edges $\langle E_{0.1}E_{1.3}E_{2.6}E_{3.12} \rangle$, which points to 1100. Note that the RS $\langle 3640 \rangle$ corresponds to the state 1100. The sequence $\langle E_{0.0}E_{1.1}E_{2.2}E_{3.4} \rangle$ associates the state 0100, as well as the RS $\langle 3640 \rangle$. The RS $\langle 3640 \rangle$, hence the state 1100, is the predecessor of the state 0100. See Fig. 1 for verification. Therefore, the links establish relationships among the states.

Lemma 1. *There exist only two links to $E_{i.j}$, for any j, from $E_{i.k}$ and from $E_{i.l}$ when $0 \leq i \leq n - 1$, and only one link to $E_{i.j}$ from $E_{i.m}$ when $i = n - 1$ in a reachability tree ($0 \leq k, l, m \leq 2^i - 1$).*

As an example, edge $E_{0.0}$ of Fig. 2 has only two links, one from $E_{0.0}$ for RMT 1 (self link) and another from $E_{0.1}$ for RMT 0 (backward link). Same is true for $E_{0.1}$ for RMTs 2 and 3. In the next level, each edge has two links for two RMTs. To $E_{1.0}$ link from $E_{1.3}$ (for RMT 0) and $E_{1.2}$ (for RMT 1), to $E_{1.1}$ link from $E_{1.0}$ (for RMT 2) and $E_{1.1}$ (for RMT 3). In the leaf, however $E_{3.0}$ has only one link from $E_{3.12}$ for RMT 0.

Cross link: Applying the following rules of links, we can get a forward (or backward) link, like $E_{i.j_1}(r_1) \to E_{i.j_2}(r_2) \to \cdots \to E_{i.j_{q-1}}(r_{q-1}) \to E_{i.j_q}$. Now, for some values of i $(0 \leq i \leq n-1)$, we may find forward links and backward links which combined form a loop. That is, a cycle of links like $E_{i.j_1}(r_1) \to \cdots \to E_{i.j_q}(r_q) \to \cdots \to E_{i.j_m}(r_m) \to E_{i.j_1}$ can be observed. We refer this link as *cross link*. We define the length of a cross link as the number of RMTs involved in the link (here, it is m).

Example 2. Let us consider Fig. 2 for the CA $\langle 5, 73, 200, 80 \rangle$. We get a cross link: $E_{0.0}(2) \to E_{0.1}(1) \to E_{0.0}$. It is noticed that at each level of Fig. 2, a cross link exists. Finally we get a cross link among $E_{3.j}$s: $E_{3.0}(0) \to E_{3.4}(0) \to E_{3.12}(0) \to E_{3.0}$ (Fig. 2). Length of the cross link is 3, and it can be noted that length of multi state attractor of the CA is also 3 (Fig. 1).

From Example 2, we can see that the cross link plays an important role in forming multi state attractors. In this part, we report some characteristics of cross link which affect multi state attractors.

Theorem 1. *An n-cell CA contains multi state attractor, if a cross link among $E_{n-1.k}s$ exists.*

Example 3. There exists a cross link of length 3 in Fig. 2: $E_{0.0}(2) \to E_{0.1}(1) \to E_{0.0}$. Corresponding CA (Fig. 1) has a multi state attractor of length 3.

Theorem 2. *An RMT $r \in l_{i.j}$ can not be a part of a cycle, if the RMT is not involved in a self link or cross link $(0 \leq i \leq n-1, 0 \leq j \leq 2^i - 1)$.*

Corollary 1. *An n-cell CA contains m number of point attractors, if m number of self-linked $E_{n-1.k}s$ exist.*

Example 4. According to Fig. 2, at leaf level there is 3 self linked at $E_{3.7}(6)$, $E_{3.8}(0)$ and $E_{3.11}(6)$, and also from state transition diagram (Fig. 1) we can see that there are three point attractors. Hence, only self links form point attractors at leaf level.

Theorem 3. *An n-cell CA contains at least one multi state attractor, if a set of RMTs form cross link among the edges $E_{i.j_1}, E_{i.j_2}, \cdots, E_{i.j_k}$ where $0 \leq j_k \leq 2^i - 1$, and the edges are not involved in any self link.*

Corollary 2. *An n-cell CA contains at least one multi state attractor if a RMTs $r_1, r_2, \cdots, r_s$ of $\mathcal{R}_i$ form cross link among edges $E_{i.j}s$ and RMTs $2r_1$ (mod 8), $2r_1 + 1$ (mod 8), $2r_2$ (mod 8), $2r_2 + 1$ (mod 8), $\cdots$, $2r_s$ (mod 8), $2r_s + 1$ (mod 8) also participate a cross link among $E_{i+1.k}s$.*

Based on the theories developed, we next report the synthesis of non-uniform CA that always converges to point attractors.

4   Synthesis of CA Having only Point Attractors

In this section, we discuss the procedure of getting a rule vector $\mathcal{R}$ of a non-uniform cellular automaton that contains only point attractors in its state space. According to Theorem 1, Theorem 2 and Corollary 1, we can identify following characteristics of reachability tree of an n-cell CA that contains only point attractors.

1. There exists at least one self-linked edge $E_{n-1.k}$ for any value of k.
2. There is no cross-link among the edges $E_{n-1.k}$s.

In the proposed synthesis scheme what we do is,
1. we first select $\mathcal{R}_0$, from root node of the reachability tree, get edges from the root, identify links between edges following rule 1 of link formation, and get the nodes of level 1,
2. then we select $\mathcal{R}_1$ and get the edges from the nodes and identify the links,
3. next we select $\mathcal{R}_2$ and repeat step 2, and so on. We finally get the tree and then verify if $E_{n-1.k}$s contain only self links and no cross links.

4.1   Dealing with Self Link

It is obvious from the rules 1 and 2 of link formation that to get self linked edge $E_{n-1.k}$ for some k, there has to exist at least one self-linked edge $E_{i.k}$ for any value of k, where $0 \le i \le n - 1$. To get the point attractors from reachability tree, we allow only self link. If we only allow self link, like as *rule* 204, where all the RMTs belongs to self link, then at leaf 2^n nodes (for an n-cell CA) are reachable and form 2^n point attractors.

Generally for a n-cell CA ($n > 2$), we observe that many of the nodes carry same property, as well as all the RMTs of the nodes are in self link. If we get two or more nodes with same property at any level, then we can consider only one for further processing. Two nodes are said to be *sub-node* of each other if all the RMTs of one node are same or equivalent RMTs of another node. As an example, in Fig. 3, $N_{2.0}$ and $N_{2.3}$ are sub-node of each other because the RMTs of $N_{2.0}$ ($N_{2.0} = \{0, 1, 2, 3\}$) are same or equivalent of $N_{2.3}$ ($N_{2.3} = \{4, 5, 6, 7\}$). Therefore, we only take one node for further processing. To maintain the characteristics (1), we use following condition.

Condition 1. *If RMTs $r_1, r_2, \cdots, r_k$ of $\mathcal{R}_i$ participate in self links, then either RMTs $2r_1, 2r_2, \cdots, 2r_k$ (mod 8) or RMTs $2r_1+1, 2r_2+1, \cdots, 2r_k+1$ (mod 8) of $\mathcal{R}_{i+1}$ are self replicating.*

4.2   Dealing with Cross Link

To maintain the characteristics (2), we can deal with only self links and do not allow any cross link at any level. If we do not allow any cross link at intermediate levels, then only self link can exist. Therefore we get the all attractors as a point

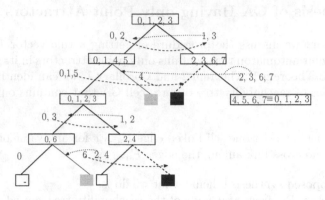

Fig. 3. Reachability tree $\langle 106, 220, 102, 96 \rangle$ with links

attractor, but its a trivial case and then we will get very limited number of CA. So, we allow cross links at intermediate levels. But before the leaf level the cross links have to be disappeared.

Lemma 2. *If there is a cross link at level i of a reachability tree which trigger cross links at level $(i+1)$, level $(i+2)$, level $(i+3)$, then there always exists at least one cross links at level j of the tree where $0 \le i \le n-1$ and $i+3 < j \le n-1$.*

Since we want to synthesize a CA that does not have any multi state attractors, we select $\mathcal{R}_{i+1}$ such a way that the cross link of level i, if any, can not trigger any cross link at level $(i+3)$. To guarantee this, we select $\mathcal{R}_{i+1}$ in such a fashion that the RMTs of the rule follow Condition 2.

Condition 2. *If RMTs r_1 and r_2 of $\mathcal{R}_i$ participate in a cross link at level i, then RMTs $2r_1$ (mod 8) and $2r_2 + 1$ (mod 8) of $\mathcal{R}_{i+1}$ are self replicating (resp. non self replicating), and RMTs $2r_1 + 1$ (mod 8) and $2r_2$ (mod 8) of $\mathcal{R}_{i+1}$ are non self replicating (resp. self replicating).*

4.3 The Weight

A RMT r $(r \in l_{i.j})$ may be involved in more than one link, whether the links are forward or backward (part of cross link) or self. This situation comes, when an edge $l_{i.j} = \{0, 4\}$ where RMT 0 is self linked and RMT 4 makes a forward link to $E_{i.k}$. Then $l_{i+1.2j}$ or $l_{i+1.2j+1}$ contains RMTs 0 and 1 (as per Table 2). So, RMT 0 or 1 comes twice (one from RMT 0 and one from RMT 4), whether the link will be self (follow the link of RMT 0 of $E_{i.j}$) or forward (follow the link of RMT 4 of $E_{i.j}$). As an example, in Fig. 2, the RMT 2 of $E_{2.4}$ and RMT 3 of $E_{2.5}$ has two links.

To handle this situation, We introduce $w_{i.j}^r$ as the weight of RMT $r \in l_{i.j}$. The weight $w_{i.j}^r$ is the total number of links from $E_{i.j}$ to itself or to some other edges for RMT r. If $l_{i.j} = \phi$ (for some j), the edge $E_{i.j}$ is non-reachable. Now, for each $s \in l_{i.k}$, we decrease $w_{i.k}^s$ by 1 if $E_{i.k}(s) \to E_{i.j}$ for any value of k. After this decrement, if the weights of all RMTs of $l_{i.k}$ have become 0, we consider the edge as non-reachable. Note that $w_{i.k}^s$ can never be 0 if RMT s is involved in a self or cross link. In here, we will not consider those RMTs ($s \in l_{i.j}$) which weight is 0 ($w_{i.j}^s = 0$). So, weight of an RMT may be more than one in some cases. As an example, in Fig. 2, weight of all RMTs of $l_{0.j}s$ and $l_{1.j}s$ is 1. But in $l_{2.j}s$, we find the RMTs which weight is 2 ($w_{2.4}^2 = w_{2.5}^3 = 1$), therefore those RMTs have two links.

4.4   Algorithm

According to Theorem 2, only those RMTs can be part of cycle which participate in cross link or make a self link. Therefore, we deal with only those RMTs which either in self link or cross link. The algorithm deals with the labels of edges and we do not form whole tree at a time. Rather we deal with two labels – $\{l_{i.0}, l_{i.1}, \cdots l_{i.2^i-1}\}$ and $\{l_{i+1.0}, l_{i+1.1}, \cdots l_{i+1.2^{i+1}-1}\}$. We proceed with only non-empty labels, l_0, l_1, $\cdots$ and l_0', l_1', $\cdots$. Here, l_j corresponds to the label of $E_{i.j}$ and l_k' correspond to the label of $E_{i+1.k}s$ ($0 \le i \le n-1$). We report the desired CA (rule vector) that only contain point attractors.

Algorithm 1. SynPointStateAttrCA
Input*: n (CA size).*
Output*: $\langle \mathcal{R}_0, \mathcal{R}_1, \cdots, \mathcal{R}_{n-1} \rangle$ (n-cell CA).*
Step 1: *Select $\mathcal{R}_0$ so that at least one RMT is self replicating. Put each valid RMT r of $\mathcal{R}_0$ in l_0 (resp. l_1) if RMT r is 0 (resp. 1).*
Step 2: *For $i = 1$ to $n-1$, repeat Step 3 to Step 11.*
Step 3: *If i equals to $n-1$, then goto Step 9.*
Step 4: *Find and store $2r \pmod 8$ and $2r+1 \pmod 8$ for all RMTs r, that are self linked at $(i-1)^{th}$ level and set RMTs at i^{th} level using Condition 1.*
Step 5:*Check whether a cross link exists for any RMTs of $l_j s$.*
   If exists, goto Step 7.
   Otherwise, goto Step 6.
Step 6: *Set all blank RMTs of $\mathcal{R}_i$ arbitrarily, goto Step 10 and discard all forward and backward links.*
Step 7: *For each cross link at $(i-1)^{th}$ level, set RMTs at i^{th} level using Condition 2 and fill remaining blank RMTs of $\mathcal{R}_i$ arbitrarily.*
Step 8: *Check whether any overlapping situation occur for any RMT of $\mathcal{R}_i$.*
   If exists, goto Step 9.
   Otherwise, goto Step 10.
Step 9: *Find a $\mathcal{R}_i$, that discard all cross link.*
Step 10: *For each non-empty labels l_k*
     Find l_{2k}' and l_{2k+1}' so that, if $r \in l_k$ and $s = 2r \pmod 8$ or $2r+1$ (mod 8), then $s \in l_{2k}'$ (resp. l_{2k+1}') when RMT s of $\mathcal{R}_i$ is 0 (resp. 1).
Step 11:*Assign non-empty and unique l_j' to l_k so that the links among l_j' for each RMT is maintained.*
Step 12:*Report the CA $\langle \mathcal{R}_0, \mathcal{R}_1, \cdots, \mathcal{R}_{n-1} \rangle$.*

Theorem 4. *If cross links does not exist in i^{th} level of Algorithm 1, then at i^{th} level maximum number of self linked edges is 4 $(0 \leq i \leq n - 1)$.*

Corollary 3. *Complexity of Algorithm 1 is $O(n)$.*

Proof. The complexity of the algorithm depends on n only (Step 2). We set rules within Step 4 to Step 8. In Step 4 we set Rule $\mathcal{R}_i$ for i^{th} level depending on self link of $(i-1)^{th}$. Step 5 checks existence of cross link. If cross link does not occur, then according to Theorem 4, there are maximum 4 unique edge. So, at the leaf level we can get maximum 4 unique edge (because in leaf level, there is no cross link). Therefore, complexity of the algorithm is $O(n)$.

Example 5. Let us consider the synthesis of a 4-cell CA. First, we select 102 as $\mathcal{R}_0$ randomly which has at least one self replicating RMT (RMTs 0 and 3 are self replicating). One cross link is formed between $E_{0.0}$ and $E_{0.1}$ $[E_{0.0}(2) \rightarrow E_{0.1}(1) \rightarrow E_{0.0}]$ (See Fig. 3 for verification). Now, using *Step 4* and *Step 7* rule 220 is selected as $\mathcal{R}_1$. In rule 220, most of the equivalent RMTs have same values, therefore, there is no cross link among $E_{1.j}$s. Number of unique nonempty set (node) is reduced to one. We now select rule 102 as $\mathcal{R}_2$ (using *Step 4* and *Step 6*). Finally, we select rule 96 as $\mathcal{R}_3$ (using *Step 9*). Therefore, the CA is $\langle 106, 220, 102, 96 \rangle$, which contains only point attractors (Fig. 3 has no cross link at leaf level).

References

1. Bandini, S., Vanneschi, L., Wuensche, A., Shehata, A.B.: Cellular automata pattern recognition and rule evolution through a neuro-genetic approach. J. Cellular Automata 4(3), 171–181 (2009)
2. Das, S., Sikdar, B.K., Pal Chaudhuri, P.: Characterization of Reachable/Nonreachable Cellular Automata States. In: Sloot, P.M.A., Chopard, B., Hoekstra, A.G. (eds.) ACRI 2004. LNCS, vol. 3305, pp. 813–822. Springer, Heidelberg (2004)
3. Maji, P., Shaw, C., Ganguly, N., Sikdar, B.K., Pal Chaudhuri, P.: Theory and Application of Cellular Automata For Pattern Classification. Special Issue of Fundamenta Informaticae on Cellular Automata 58, 321–354 (2003)
4. Maji, P., Pal Chaudhuri, P.: Non-uniform cellular automata based associative memory: Evolutionary design and basins of attraction. Inf. Sci. 178(10), 2315–2336 (2008)
5. Naskar, N., Adak, S., Das, S.: Identification of non-uniform periodic boundary cellular automata having only point states. In: AUTOMATA 2013: 19th International Workshop on Cellular Automata and Discrete Complex Systems, pp. 67–75 (September 2013)
6. Raghavan, R.: Cellular automata in pattern recognition. Information Sciences 70(12), 145–177 (1993)
7. Wolfram, S.: Theory and Application of Cellular Automata. World Scientific (1986)

Non Uniform Cellular Automata Description of Signed Partition Versions of Ice and Sand Pile Models*

Gianpiero Cattaneo[1], Giampiero Chiaselotti[2], Alberto Dennunzio[1],
Enrico Formenti[3], and Luca Manzoni[3]

[1] Dipartimento Di Informatica, Sistemistica e Comunicazione
Università di Milano – Bicocca, Viale Sarca 336 – U14, I–20126 Milano, Italia
cattang,dennunzio@disco.unimib.it
[2] Dipartimento di Matematica, Università della Calabria,
Via Pietro Bucci, Cubo 30B, 87036 Arcavacata di Rende (CS), Italy
chiaselotti@unical.it
[3] Univ. Nice Sophia Antipolis, CNRS, I3S, UMR 7271
06900 Sophia Antipolis, France
formenti@unice.fr, luca.manzoni@i3s.unice.fr

Abstract. This paper reviews the well-known formalisations for ice and
sand piles, based on a finite sequence of non-negative integers and its
recent extension to signed partitions, i.e. sequences of a non-negative
and a non-positive part of integers, both non increasing.

The ice pile model can be interpreted as a discrete time dynamical
system under the action of a vertical and a horizontal evolution rule,
whereas the sand pile model is characterized by the unique action of the
vertical rule.

The signed partition extension, besides these two dynamical evolution
rules, also takes into account an annihilation rule at the boundary region
between the non-negative and the non-positive regions. We provide an
original physical interpretation of this model as a p-n junction of two
semiconductors.

Moreover, we show how the sand pile extension of the signed partition environment can be formalized by mean of a non-uniform cellular
automaton (CA) since the vertical and the annihilation evolution rules
have the formal description of two CA local rules. Finally, we provide a
similar construction for the ice pile extension.

1 Introduction: From Brylawski Dominance Lattice to Goles-Kiwi Piles Dynamics

Investigations of integer partitions has been treated from a pure algebraic point
of view in the seminal paper of Brylawski in [1], further on developed by Greene

---

* This work has been supported by the French National Research Agency project EMC
(ANR-09-BLAN-0164) and by the Italian MIUR PRIN 2010-2011 grant "Automata
and Formal Languages: Mathematical and Applicative Aspects" H41J12000190001.

J. Wąs, G.C. Sirakoulis, and S. Bandini (Eds.): ACRI 2014, LNCS 8751, pp. 115–124, 2014.

and Kleitman in [11]. Let us recall that an *integer partition* of the non-negative integer $m \geq 0$, also *m-partition*, is a finite non–increasing sequence of m non-negative integers $w = (w_1, w_2, \ldots, w_m)$, such that $w_1 \geq w_2 \geq \ldots \geq w_m \geq 0$, satisfying the condition $m = \sum_{i=1}^{m} w_i$. The collection $P(m)$ of all such m-integer partitions is equipped with the *dominance* or *majorization* partial ordering $\leq$ defined as follows: let $w = (w_1, \ldots, w_m)$ and $w' = (w'_1, \ldots, w'_m)$ be two m-partitions, then

$$w \leq w' \quad \text{iff} \quad \forall i = 1, \ldots, m, \quad \sum_{j=1}^{i} w_i \leq \sum_{j=1}^{i} w'_i \qquad (1.1)$$

The algebraic structure $L_B(m) := (P(m), \leq)$ of all m-integer partitions equipped with the dominance order turns out to be a lattice bounded by the maximum element $\hat{1} = (m, 0, \ldots, 0) = (m)$ and the minimum element $\hat{0} = (1, \ldots, 1) = (1^m)$. For the sake of simplicity, in the sequel we adopt the convention of deleting zeros in any m–partition. With respect to the dominance ordering one can introduce the notion of *covering*: the element w *covers* w', or w' *is covered* by w, iff $w' \leq w$ and there is no element z such that $w' \leq z \leq w$.

In [8] Goles and Kiwi performed a paradigmatic change from the lattice point of view to a dynamical description of $P(m)$ in which the Ferrers diagram of a m-partition describes m vertical columns of ice cubes in an Ice Pile Model (IPM). In this new interpretative context any m-partition $w = (w_1, \ldots, w_m)$ describes a configuration of a discrete dynamical system in which the lattice condition of covering is equivalently expressed by two dynamical *evolution rules*, assumed as primitive, which determine the dynamical evolution of the system in a single time step:

(V-evolution rule). If in the configuration $w = (w_1, \ldots, w_m)$ it is $w_i - w_{i+1} \geq 2$ (for $i = 1, \ldots, m-1$), then the following dynamical transition holds:

$$(w_1, \ldots, w_i, w_{i+1}, \ldots, w_m) \to (w_1, \ldots, w_i - 1, w_{i+1} + 1, \ldots, w_m) \qquad (1.2)$$

(H-evolution rule). If in the configuration $w = (w_1, \ldots, w_m)$ there exist two indexes i, j, with $j > i + 1$, such that $w_i - 1 = w_{i+1} = \ldots = w_{j-1} = w_j + 1$, then the following dynamical transition holds:

$$(\ldots, w_i, \ldots, w_j, \ldots) \to (\ldots, w_i - 1, w_{i+1}, \ldots, w_{j-1}, w_j + 1, \ldots) \qquad (1.3)$$

According to [8]: "The IPM can be physically interpreted as piles of ice cubes which interact from left to right. Whenever two consecutive piles have a height difference of at least 2, a cube tumbles from the left to the right pile [evolution rule V]. Otherwise, when piles i, j have a height difference equal to 2, a cube slides without friction from pile i to pile j [evolution rule H]." Then, the covering condition $w \to w'$ is now interpreted as a dynamical transition from the state w at some time instant t to the update state w' at the successive time instant $t + 1$ under the action of either the evolution rule V or the evolution rule H. In this case w is called the *predecessor* of w' and w' the *successor* of w.

In general a predecessor w may produce more than one successor $w'_1, w'_2, \ldots$ each of which is the result of the application of one of the two evolution rules V or H in a suitable site i of w. From the dynamical point of view, the application to a given configuration $w(t)$ from $P(m)$, considered as the state of some dynamical evolution at time t, of one of the two evolution rules, either V or H, leads to a new configuration $w(t+1)$ as the state at the next time $t+1$. In this way a *trajectory*, or *dynamical path*, from the initial state w_i at time $t = 0$ to the final state w_f reached at time t_f, is a chain of length $l = t_f + 1$ between these two states: $w_i = w(0) \to w(1) \to \ldots \to w(t) \to w(t+1) \to \ldots \to w_f = w(t_f)$.

Any configuration $w \in P(m)$ different from the minimal one $\hat{0} = (1^m)$ is the covering of at least one configuration w'. On the contrary, the configuration (1^m) is not the covering of any other possible configuration and it is the unique configuration such that a trajectory which reaches it cannot have any further dynamical evolution. So, the configuration (1^m) is the unique *equilibrium state* of the ice pile dynamics. Coherently with the general fact that more than one successor can be produced from a predecessor by different applications of the evolution rules, also trajectories with initial state (m) and final state (1^m) can be more than one.

> *Remark 1.* Let us stress that the two rules V and H, which perform the dynamical evolution of the ice pile systems $P(m)$, preserve the total sum m of which any configuration $w \in P(m)$ is an integer partition, determining as well defined a transformation $P(m) \to P(m)$.
>
> From the ice piles interpretation of any w, if one assign to a single ice cube a unit mass then m represents the total mass of the ice system. In this way, the dynamical evolution generated by the action of rules V and H satisfies the principle of "*mass conservation in an isolated system.*"

1.1   The Sand Pile Model (SPM)

Goles and Kiwi in the same paper [8] introduced another model based on the collection $P(m)$ of all m–partitions but in which the dynamical evolution is the result of the application only of the vertical rule V (the H rule is not allowed), with a change of the physical interpretation in the sense that the non-negative integer w_i of a configuration $w \in P(m)$ now is interpreted as the number of sand grains stacked at the column in the site i (sand pile model (SPM)). In this SPM "the dynamics [induced from the V rule] is specified as follows: a grain of sand tumbles from site i to site $i+1$, iff the height difference $w_i - w_{i+1}$ is at least z_c, where $z_c = 2$. Clearly z_c represents a critical slope of the sand pile." [8]. Of course, the mass conservation principle is satisfied also in the SPM.

In the case of SPM, the space $P(m)$ of all configurations can be equipped with a binary relation of *covering* saying that the configuration $w \in P(m)$ "V-*covers*" the configuration $w' \in P(m)$, denoted by $w \to_V w'$, iff w' is obtained from w by the application of the V rule at a site i of w. In this case, w (resp., w') is said to be the V-*predecessor* (resp., V-*successor*) of w' (resp., w). On the basis of this covering relation one can introduce the notion of *trajectory* of initial state

$w(0)$ as a finite sequence of configurations in which at any instant one is the V–successor of the previous: $w(0) \to_V w(1) \to_V \ldots \to_V w(t_f)$. The configuration $w(t_f)$ is its final state reached at time t_f.

A SPM partial ordering $\leq_V$ can be introduced on $P(m)$ according to the following. Let w and w' be two m-partitions, then $w \leq_V w'$ iff there exists a finite sequence of configurations $w(1), \ldots, w(t_f - 1)$ s.t. $w \to_V w(1) \to_V \ldots \to_V w(t_f - 1) \to_V w'$. If the SPM context is clear, from now on we omit the subscript V in the involved notation.

In the SPM dynamics an *equilibrium state*, sometimes also called *fixed point*, is a configuration w^{eq} such that $\forall i = 1, \ldots, m - 1$, $w_i^{eq} - w_{i+1}^{eq} \leq 1$ (the V evolution rule cannot be applied and so the set of all V–successors is empty). The SPM dynamics starting from any initial configuration $w(0) \in P(m)$ converges towards a unique equilibrium (fixed) point, independently of the order in which the sites are updated [8]. Moreover, the ordered SPM of all m-partitions from $P(m)$ obtained starting from the initial m-partition $\hat{1} = (m, 0, \ldots, 0) = (m)$ is a lattice, denoted by $SPM(m) := (P(m), \leq_V)$. Moreover, $SPM(m)$ is a suborder of the IPM lattice $L_B(m) := (P(m), \leq)$, and the SPM dynamical evolution leads to the unique equilibrium point of the form $P_{\hat{1}} = (k, k-1, \ldots, k'+1, k', k', k'-1, \ldots, 1)$.

A characterization of those configurations which belong to $SPM(m)$ is given in [9]. Moreover, for an analysis of the relationship between $SPM(m)$ and $SPM(m+1)$, in particular as $SPM(m+1)$ can be reconstructed from $SPM(m)$, and other interesting results on these arguments see [12].

An interesting result regards the relationship between the IPM and SPM lattices on the same configuration space $P(m)$ of all m-partitions, which can be found in [10] and summarized in the following steps.

First of all one collects in $\Phi(m)$ all SPM fixed points, then for any fixed point $P \in \Phi(m)$ the collection of all configurations whose dynamics, as initial state, converges to P is denoted by $U_{SPM(m)}(P) = \{w \in P(m) : P \leq_V w\}$. Now it is easy to show that the collection of all such $U_{SPM(m)}(P)$ as P ranges in Φ is a partition of $P(m)$.

Let us stress that the collection of all $SPM(m)$ dynamical evolutions starting from the initial state $\hat{1} = (m)$ has the ordering structure of lattice converging to the unique equilibrium point $P_{\hat{1}}$, this lattice behavior in general is not true for $U_{SPM(m)}(P)$, with P a generic SPM equilibrium point.

1.2 The CA Description of SPM and the Mixed Alternate CA–PDP Version of IPM

We have seen that the SPM model is based on the configuration space $P(m)$ of all m-partitions, with a dynamical evolution generated by the evolution rule V. As pointed out by Goles–Kiwi in [8], this rule can be formalized as the *local rule* of a Cellular Automaton (CA) consisting of a one–dimensional lattice of cells, whose state space of any cell is $S = \{0, 1, \ldots, m\}$, the global configuration space S^m, and the local rule of radius 1, $f : S^3 \to S$, has the form:

$$f(a, b, c) = \begin{cases} b+1 & \text{if } b \leq a - 2 \text{ and } b \leq c+1 \\ b-1 & \text{if } b \geq c+2 \text{ and } b \geq a - 1 \\ b & \text{otherwise} \end{cases} \quad (1.4)$$

Note that in CA theory the *global state space*, or *configuration space*, is S^m, i.e., the collection of all m-length sequences $u = (u_1, \ldots, u_m)$ of non-negative integers $u_i \geq 0$, without the requirements that this sequence is non increasing with total sum m. The *global dynamics* induced by a parallel application of this CA local rule to any cell of the automaton is formalized as the *next state function* given by the application $F : S^m \to_f S^m$ assigning to the configuration $u \in S^m$ the new configuration $F(u) \in S^m$ whose i component $[F(u)]_i$, for $i = 2, \ldots, m - 1$, is given by

$$[F(u)]_i = f(u_{i-1}, u_i, u_{i+1}) \quad (1.5)$$

with the *boundary evolutions* $F[(u)]_1 = u_1 - 1$ if $u_1 - u_2 \geq 2$, $= u_1$ otherwise and $[F(u)]_m = u_m$.

This produces a deterministic dynamics with initial state u_0 at time instant $t = 0$, formally $u_0 \to_f u(1) \to_f \ldots \to_f u(t) \to_f u(t+1) \to_f \ldots \to_f u_f$, where the final state u_f is an *equilibrium state*, i.e., *fixed point* $F(u_f) = u_f$, reached at the final time instant t_f, i.e., $u(t_f) := u_f$.

Concretely, any cell of a CA can be considered as a device consisting of two memories: a fixed one which contains the implementation in a suitable language of the local rule (1.4) and a variable one, consisting in three places in which the information of the state of the cell plus the states of the neighboring cells are located. The keywords of CA are *local*, in the sense that the update of the state of any cell takes into account the information of the states of all the cell of its neighborhood, and *uniform*, in the sense that the local rule which performs this update is the same in any cell of the lattice.

But in the present context of SPM we consider the sub-dynamics obtained by the restriction of the global rule F to the collection $P(m)$ of all m-partitions, which is stable under F, i.e., $F(P(m)) \subseteq P(m)$, generating the *next state function* of the dynamics $F : P(m) \to_f P(m)$.

Example 1. The configuration $w = (125111)$ is an element of S^{11}, which does not belong to $P(11)$ since it is not decreasing. In any way, the application of the CA rule (1.4) produces the (deterministic) unique trajectory $(125111) \to_f (124211) \to_f (123311) \to_f (123221)$, with the last as equilibrium configuration.

The equation (1.4) is the formalization in the CA context of the evolution rule V according to the equation presented in [8, section 1.2], reformulated in [4]. Of course, this CA approach cannot be applied to the case of the evolution rule H "since the staircase [i.e, horizontal] update rule allows arbitrary far sites to interact, the IPM is not a cellular automata." [8].

In the case of an IPM, this does not prevent to consider, besides the parallel application of the local rule (1.4) as a CA dynamics, also a parallel distributed processing (PDP) of a non-uniform and non–local formalization of the H rule according to the mappings $f_i : P(m) \to S$, for $i = 1, \ldots, m - 1$:

$$f_i(u_1,\ldots,u_m) = \begin{cases} u_i - 1 & \text{if } u_i = u_{i+1} + 1 \wedge \exists j > i+1 : u_j = u_i - 2 \\ & \qquad \wedge \ \nexists k < i-1 : u_k = u_i + 1 \\ u_i + 1 & \text{if } u_i = u_{i-1} - 1 \wedge \exists k < i-1 : u_k = u_i + 2 \\ & \qquad \wedge \ \nexists j > i+1 : u_j = u_i - 1 \\ u_i & \qquad \text{otherwise} \end{cases} \qquad (1.6)$$

Example 2. An example with application of this parallel rule is given by the configuration $u = (4433222110)$, for which a three times parallel application of rules (1.6) to the adjacent plateaus in places $|2,5|$, $|4,8|$, and $|7,10|$ leads to the new configuration $u' = (4333222111)$.

In any way, it results that the parallel application to the same configuration of both the CA evolution V–rule (1.4) and the PDP evolution H–rule (1.6) in general is not compatible, as the following example shows.

Example 3. Let us consider the configuration $w = (7,3,3,3,2)$, then the single application of the H–rule at site $i = 1$ evolves to the configuration $w' = (6,4,3,3,2)$, whereas the application of the single V-rule at the plateau $|i = 2, j = 5|$ leads to the configuration $w'' = (6,3,3,3,3)$, with a conflict of their parallel application in the site $i = 2$, in which $w'_2 = 4$ and $w''_2 = 3$.

One can avoid this drawback by an alternate application in a parallel way of the two rules, and this should be the argument of some forthcoming papers.

2   The Dominance Lattice of Signed Partitions and Its Equivalent Dynamical Formulation

A natural extension of the above theory of IPM, based on the collection $P(m)$ of all integer (non-increasing) integer partitions of the non-negative integer $m \geq 0$, consists in the enlargement of the basic space to the collection $O(m,n)$ of all *signed partitions* having as sum the (non necessarily positive) integer $m \in \mathbb{Z}$, i.e., those finite sequence of integers $w = (w_1,\ldots,w_n|w_{n+1},\ldots,w_{2n})$ such that $n \geq w_1 \geq \ldots \geq w_n \geq 0 \geq w_{n+1} \geq \ldots \geq w_{2n} \geq -n$, satisfying the condition $w_1 + \ldots + w_n + w_{n+1} + \ldots + w_{2n} = m$. The elements from $O(m,n)$ are also called (m,n)–signed partitions. The finite sequence $w_+ = (w_1,\ldots,w_n)$ is the *positive part* of the signed partition w and the finite sequence $w_- = (w_{n+1},\ldots,w_{2n})$ its negative part, both of length n, and so sometimes we denote by $w = (w_+|w_-)$ the original signed partition of m.

The collection $O(m,n)$ of all equally length signed partitions of the integer m can be equipped by the natural extension of the dominance ordering previously defined on $P(m)$ by equation (1.1) in the following way.

For any pair of (m,n)–signed partitions $w = (w_1,\ldots,w_n|w_{n+1},\ldots,w_{2n})$ and $w = (w'_1,\ldots,w'_n|w'_{n+1},\ldots,w'_{2n})$:

$$w \leq w' \quad \text{iff} \quad \forall i = 1,\ldots,2n, \quad \sum_{j=1}^{i} w_j \leq \sum_{j=1}^{i} w'_j \qquad (2.1)$$

In [3, Theorem 3.1] one can find the following result which is the generalization to the signed partitions context of the analogous result proved by Brylawski in [1].

Theorem 1. *Under the conditions $-n^2 \leq m \leq n^2$, the structure $(O(m,n), \leq)$ is a lattice.*

Moreover, if k and r are the unique non–negative integers such that $n^2 - |m| = kn + r$, with $r < n$, then

$$
\hat{1}^{m,n} = \begin{cases} (n, \ldots, n, r, 0, \ldots, 0| - n, \ldots, -n) & \text{if } m < 0 \\ (n, \ldots, n|0, \ldots, 0, -r, -n, \ldots, -n) & \text{if } m > 0 \\ (n, \ldots, n| - n, \ldots, -n) & \text{if } m = 0 \end{cases} \quad (2.2)
$$

with n (resp., $-n$) repeated exactly k times when $m < 0$ (resp., $m > 0$), is the maximum element of the lattice.

Analogously, if k and r are the unique non–negative integers such that $|m| = kn + r$, with $r < n$, then

$$
\hat{0}^{m,n} = \begin{cases} (0, \ldots, 0| - k, \ldots, -k, -(k+1), \ldots, -(k+1)) & \text{if } m < 0 \\ (k+1, \ldots, k+1, k, \ldots, k|0, \ldots, 0) & \text{if } m > 0 \\ (0, \ldots, 0|0, \ldots, 0) & \text{if } m = 0 \end{cases} \quad (2.3)
$$

with $-(k+1)$ (resp., $k+1$) repeated exactly r times when $m < 0$ (resp., $m > 0$), is the minimum element of the lattice.

Another interesting result is the extension to the lattice $O(m,n)$ of the Brylawski characterization of the covering by dominance ordering inside $L_B(m)$, according to a result proved in [2]. Without entering in formal details, let us denote a signed partition from $O(m,n)$ as $w = (a_1, \ldots, a_n | b_1, \ldots, b_n)$ with $a = (a_1, \ldots, a_n)$ the non–increasing, non-negative part of w and $b = (b_1, \ldots, b_n)$ its non-increasing, non-positive part. Then, the main result obtained in [2, Corollary 4.3] is that the signed partition $w = (a|b)$ covers with respect to the dominance ordering (2.1) the signed partition $w' = (a'|b')$, denoted as usual by $w \to w'$, iff one of the following 5 evolution rules is applied to a suitable site i of w:

Rule 1. Which is the V-evolution rule applied to the positive part a of w. If $d_i(a) = a_i - a_{i+1} \geq 2$ and $i < n$, then (and compare with ¡...¿)

$$
a_1, \ldots, a_i, a_{i+1}, \ldots, a_n \to a_1, \ldots, a_i - 1, a_{i+1} + 1, \ldots, a_n
$$

Rule 2. Which is the H-evolution rule applied to the positive part a of w. If $i + l \leq n$, then

$$
a_1, \ldots, a_{i-1}, p+1, p, \ldots, p, p-1, a_{i+l+1}, \ldots, a_n \to
$$
$$
\to a_1, \ldots, a_{i-1}, p, p, \ldots, p, p, a_{i+l+1}, \ldots, a_n \quad (2.4)
$$

Rule 3. Which is the "dual" V-evolution rule applied to the negative part b of w. If $d_j(b) = b_j - b_{j+1} \geq 2$ and $j < n$, then

$$b_1, \ldots, b_j, b_{j+1}, \ldots, b_n \to b_1, \ldots, b_j - 1, b_{j+1} + 1, \ldots, b_n$$

Rule 4. Which is the "dual" H-evolution rule applied to the negative part b of w. If $j + l \leq n$, then

$$b_1, \ldots, b_{j-1}, -p+1, -p, \ldots, -p, -p-1, b_{j+l+1}, \ldots, b_n \to$$
$$\to b_1, \ldots, b_{j-1}, -p, -p, \ldots, -p, -p, b_{j+l+1}, \ldots, b_n \quad (2.5)$$

Rule 5. Which is the "interaction" rule between the positive and the negative part of w:

(i) boundary double-cliff: if $a_n \neq 0$ and $b_1 \neq 0$, then

$$a_1, \ldots, a_n | b_1, \ldots, b_n \to a_1, \ldots a_n - 1 | b_1 + 1, \ldots, b_n$$

(ii) boundary slippery-cliff: if $a_k = 1, a_{k+1} = \cdots = a_n = 0$, for some $1 \leq k < n$ and $b_1 \neq 0$, then

$$a_1, \ldots, a_{k-1}, 1, 0, \ldots, 0 | b_1, \ldots, b_n \to a_1, \ldots, a_{k-1}, 0, 0, \ldots, 0 | b_1 + 1, \ldots, b_n$$

(iii) boundary cliff-slippery: if $a_n \neq 0$ and $b_l = -1, b_1 = \cdots = b_{l-1} = 0$, for some $1 \leq l < n$, then

$$a_1, \ldots, a_n | 0, \ldots, 0, -1, b_{l+1}, \ldots, b_n \to a_1, \ldots a_n - 1 | 0, \ldots, 0, 0, b_{l+1}, \ldots, b_n$$

(iv) boundary double-slippery: if $a_k = 1, a_{k+1} = \cdots = a_n = 0$, for some $1 \leq k < n$, and $b_l = -1, b_1 = \cdots = b_{l-1} = 0$, for some $1 \leq l < n$, then

$$a_1, \ldots, a_{k-1}, 1, 0, \ldots, 0 | 0, \ldots, 0, -1, b_{l+1}, \ldots, b_n \to$$
$$a_1, \ldots, a_{k-1}, 0, 0, \ldots, 0 | 0, \ldots, 0, 0, b_{l+1}, \ldots, b_n$$

3   The Signed Partition Version of Goles–Kiwi SPM and Its Non Uniform CA Formalization

The signed partitions version of the SPM model is based on the configuration space $O(m, n)$ to which one applies the only vertical Rules 1 (at the non–negative part) and 3 (at the non–positive part), plus the interaction Rule 5 (at the junction $n|n+1$). The V–rule 1 has the same CA version given formally by (1.4), when applied to the non–negative part a of a signed partition $w = (a|b)$ from $O(m, n)$, in this context denoted by $f_+ : S^3 \to S$. The V–rule 3 must be formalized in a "dual" way when applied to the non–positive part b of the configuration $w = (a|b)$, according to the following (and compare with (1.4)):

$$f_-(a, b, c) = \begin{cases} b+1 & \text{if } b \geq a-2 \text{ and } b \geq c+1 \\ b-1 & \text{if } b \leq c-2 \text{ and } b \leq a-1 \\ b & \text{otherwise} \end{cases} \quad (3.1)$$

Moreover, the interaction rule has the form of a local rule whose state space is $S = \{0, \ldots, n\}$ and radius $r = 1$, defined as

$$f_{int}(a, b, c) = \begin{cases} b - 1 & \text{if } b \neq 0 \text{ and } c \neq 0 \\ b + 1 & \text{if } b \neq 0 \text{ and } a \neq 0 \\ b & \text{otherwise} \end{cases} \tag{3.2}$$

The corresponding CA is *non uniform* since the global dynamical evolution rule on the configuration space $O(m, n)$ is the mapping $F : O(m, n) \to O(m, n)$ defined in the following way, for every configuration $w \in O(m, n)$:

$$[F(w)]_i = \begin{cases} f_+(w_{i-1}, w_i, w_{i+1}) & \text{according to (1.4) if } i = 2, \ldots, n-1 \\ f_-(w_{i-1}, w_i, w_{i+1}) & \text{according to (3.1) if } i = n+2, \ldots, 2n-1 \\ f_{int}(w_{i-1}, w_i, w_{i+1}) & \text{according to (3.2) if } i = n, n+1 \end{cases} \tag{3.3}$$

The *non uniformity* of this CA is due to the fact that the dynamical evolution depends "locally" from three radius $r = 1$ different local rules, whose action depends from the particular cell in the site i of the automata: if $i = 2, \ldots, n-1$ it is the local rule (1.4) which updates the cell with non-negative state, if $i = n+2, \ldots, 2n-1$ it is the local rule (3.1) which updates the cell with non-positive state, and if $i = n, n+1$ it is the interaction local rule which updates the p–n junction cells. The updates of the boundary cells are the usual for the sit $i = 1$ and the dual for the site $j = 2n$.

Of course, the mixed CA–PDP description of the signed partition version of IPM can be formulated using local rules (1.4), (3.1), and (3.2) for the parallel CA V-steps and global rule (1.6) for the non-negative part with its dual for the non-positive part of the parallel H-steps.

4   Comments and Further Developments

In this paper the generalization to the case of signed integer partitions of some standard result of the SPM and IPM models is presented. In particular, the IPM equivalent formulation of covering relation induced from the dominance ordering by a V and a H evolution rules is extended to the case of signed partitions in which one needs an interaction rule between the positive-negative boundary. This leads to an interesting description of the dynamics occurring in a p–n junction of two semiconductors, as discussed in [2].

The usual CA description of the SPM is extended to a non uniform parallel application of three local rules, one for the non-negative part, its dual for the non-positive part, and one describing the local interaction at the boundary $n|n+1$ between these two parts. The parallel description of the IPM is given by a mixed alternate application of a CA local rule and a global PDP rule.

Several interesting research directions may originate from this paper. First of all, one can consider the generalisation of signed partition to the Kadanoff sand pile model [7]. Indeed, in [13, 14], a curious phenomenon of wavelets takes place.

It would be interesting to see how these wavelets interact at the junction point between the negative and the positive part of the partition.

Another possibility is to generalise the initial condition to any possible partition with the requirement of being non-increasings like it has been done for the SPM and IPM case in [6, 5].

References

[1] Brylawski, T.: The lattice of integer partitions. Discrete Mathematics 6, 201–219 (1973)
[2] Cattaneo, G., Chiaselotti, G., Gentile, T., Oliverio, P.A.: The lattice structure of equally extended signed partitions (2013), preprint, submitted for publication
[3] Cattaneo, G., Chiaselotti, G., Stumbo, F., Oliverio, P.A.: Signed integer partitions as extension of the Goles–Kiwi ice and sand pile models (2014), preprint, submitted for publication
[4] Cattaneo, G., Comito, M., Bianucci, D.: Sand piles: from physics to cellular automata models. Theor. Comput. Sci. 436, 35–53 (2012)
[5] Formenti, E., Masson, B.: Fixed points of generalized ice pile models. Poster Proceedings of ECCS 2005, Paris (November 2005)
[6] Formenti, E., Masson, B.: A note on fixed points of generalized ice piles models, vol. 2, pp. 183–191 (2006)
[7] Formenti, E., Goles, E., Martin, B.: Computational complexity of avalanches in the kadanoff sandpile model. Fundam. Inform. 115, 107–124 (2012)
[8] Goles, E., Kiwi, M.A.: Games on line graphs and sand piles. Theoret. Comput. Sci. 115, 321–349 (1993)
[9] Goles, E., Morvan, M., Phan, H.D.: Sandpiles and order structure of integer partitions. Discrete Applied Mathematics 117, 51–64 (2002)
[10] Goles, E., Morvan, M., Phan, H.D.: The structure of linear chip firing game and related models. Theoret. Comput. Sci. 270, 827–841 (2002)
[11] Green, C., Kleitman, D.J.: Longest chains in the lattice of integere partitions ordered by majorization. Europ. J. Combinatoric 7, 1–10 (1986)
[12] Latapy, M., Mantaci, R., Morvan, M., Phan, H.D.: Structure of some sand piles models. Theoret. Comput. Sci. 262, 525–556 (2001)
[13] Perrot, K., Rémila, E.: Kadanoff sand pile model. avalanche structure and wave shape. Theor. Comput. Sci. 504, 52–72 (2013)
[14] Perrot, K., Rémila, É.: Emergence of wave patterns on kadanoff sandpiles. In: Pardo, A., Viola, A. (eds.) LATIN 2014. LNCS, vol. 8392, pp. 634–647. Springer, Heidelberg (2014)

Variable Entangling in a Quantum Battle of the Sexes Cellular Automaton

Ramón Alonso-Sanz

Technical University of Madrid, ETSIA (Estadística, GSC)
C.Universitaria, Madrid 28040, Spain
ramon.alonso@upm.es

Abstract. The effect of variable entangling on the dynamics of a spatial quantum formulation of the iterated battle of the sexes game is studied in this work. The game is played in the cellular automata manner, i.e., with local and synchronous interaction. The effect of spatial structure is assessed when allowing the players to adopt quantum and classical strategies, both in the two and three parameter strategy spaces.

1 Introduction

1.1 The Classic Context

The so-called *battle of the sexes* (BOS) is a simple example of a two-person (♀ and ♂) asymmetric game, i.e., a game whose payoff matrices are not coincident after transposition. Thus, $\mathbf{P}_{\sigma} = \begin{pmatrix} R & 0 \\ 0 & r \end{pmatrix}$, and $\mathbf{P}_{\varphi} = \begin{pmatrix} r & 0 \\ 0 & R \end{pmatrix}$. The rewards $R > r > 0$ quantify the preferences in a conventional couple fitting the traditional stereotypes: the male prefers to attend a *Football* match, whereas the female prefers to attend a *Ballet* performance. Both players hope to *coordinate* their choices, but the *conflict* is also present because their preferred activities differ [14].

Using uncorrelated probabilistic strategies $\mathbf{x} = (x, 1-x)'$ and $\mathbf{y} = (y, 1-y)'$, the expected payoffs (p) in the BOS game are:

$$p_{\sigma}(x; y) = \mathbf{x}'\mathbf{P}_{\sigma}\mathbf{y} \quad , \quad p_{\varphi}(y; x) = \mathbf{x}'\mathbf{P}_{\varphi}\mathbf{y}. \tag{1}$$

The pair of strategies $(\mathbf{x}, \mathbf{y})$ are in Nash equilibrium if $\mathbf{x}$ is a best response to $\mathbf{y}$ and $\mathbf{y}$ is a best response to $\mathbf{x}$. The three pairs of strategies in Nash equilibrium in the BOS game are: $x = y = 0$, $x = y = 1$, and $(x = R/(R+r), y = 1 - x)$. Both players get the same payoff if $y = 1-x$, with a maximum $p^+ = (R+r)/4$ for $x = y = 1/2$.

In a different game scenario, the players have not an active role, instead of it a probability distribution $\mathbf{\Pi} = (\pi_{ij})$ assigns probability to every combination of player choices, so $\mathbf{\Pi} = \begin{pmatrix} \pi_{11} & \pi_{12} \\ \pi_{21} & \pi_{22} \end{pmatrix}$ in 2×2 games [14]. Thus, the expected payoffs

J. Wąs, G.C. Sirakoulis, and S. Bandini (Eds.): ACRI 2014, LNCS 8751, pp. 125–135, 2014.
© Springer International Publishing Switzerland 2014

in the BOS are: $\begin{aligned} p_{\sigma} &= \pi_{11}R + \pi_{22}r \\ p_{\varphi} &= \pi_{11}r + \pi_{22}R \end{aligned}$. If $\pi_{11} = \pi_{22} = \pi$, both players get the same payoff $p^= = \pi(R + r)$, which if $\pi > 1/4$ is not accessible in the uncorrelated strategies scenario; with maximum $p^+ = (R + r)/2$ if $\pi = 1/2$.

The quantum approach described in the next subsection, participates of both the independent active players model (1), and the so-called correlated games, where an *external* random device $\mathbf{\Pi}$ determines the players moves.

1.2 Quantum Games

In the quantization scheme introduced by Eisert et al. [8], the classical pure strategies are assigned two basic vectors $|0\rangle$ and $|1\rangle$ respectively, in a Hilbert space of a two level system. The state of the game is a vector in the tensor product space spanned by the basis vectors $|00\rangle$, $|01\rangle$, $|10\rangle$, $|11\rangle$, where the first and second entries in the ket refer to the players A and B respectively.

The quantum game protocol starts with an initial entangled state $|\psi_i\rangle = \hat{J}|00\rangle$, where $\hat{J}$ is a symmetric unitary operator that *entangles* the player's qubits and that is known to both players. To ensure that the classical game is a subset of its quantum version, it is necessary that $\hat{J} = exp(i\frac{\gamma}{2}\hat{D}^{\otimes 2})$, where $\gamma \in [0, \pi/2]$. Thus,

$$\hat{J}|00\rangle = \begin{pmatrix} \cos(\gamma/2) & 0 & 0 & i\sin(\gamma/2) \\ 0 & \cos(\gamma/2) & -i\sin(\gamma/2) & 0 \\ 0 & -i\sin(\gamma/2) & \cos(\gamma/2) & 0 \\ i\sin(\gamma/2) & 0 & 0 & \cos(\gamma/2) \end{pmatrix}\begin{pmatrix} 1 \\ 0 \\ 0 \\ 0 \end{pmatrix} = \begin{pmatrix} \cos(\gamma/2) \\ 0 \\ 0 \\ i\sin(\gamma/2) \end{pmatrix}.$$

The players choose independently their quantum strategies as local unitary operators $(\hat{U})$, $\hat{U}_A$ and $\hat{U}_B$. After the application of these strategies, the state of the game evolves to $|\psi_{f_o}\rangle = (\hat{U}_A \otimes \hat{U}_B)\hat{J}|00\rangle$. Prior to measurement, the $\hat{J}^\dagger$ gate is applied and the state of the game becomes:

$$|\psi_f\rangle = \hat{J}^\dagger(\hat{U}_A \otimes \hat{U}_B)\hat{J}|00\rangle \equiv (\psi_1 \ \psi_2 \ \psi_3 \ \psi_4)' \qquad (2)$$

This follows a pair of Stern-Gerlach type detectors for measurement. As a result, $\mathbf{\Pi} = \begin{pmatrix} |\psi_1|^2 & |\psi_2|^2 \\ |\psi_3|^2 & |\psi_4|^2 \end{pmatrix}$. Consequently, the expected payoffs in the BOS become:

$$p_{\begin{Bmatrix} \sigma \\ \varphi \end{Bmatrix}} = \begin{Bmatrix} R \\ r \end{Bmatrix}|\psi_1|^2 + \begin{Bmatrix} r \\ R \end{Bmatrix}|\psi_4|^2 \qquad (3)$$

We will considerer here the two-parameter subset of the SU(2) space of strategies:

$$\hat{U}(\theta, \alpha) = \begin{pmatrix} e^{i\alpha}\cos(\theta/2) & \sin(\theta/2) \\ -\sin(\theta/2) & e^{-i\alpha}\cos(\theta/2) \end{pmatrix}, \ \begin{matrix} \theta \in [0, \pi] \\ \alpha \in [0, \pi/2] \end{matrix} . \qquad (4)$$

If $\alpha_A = \alpha_B = 0$, or if $\gamma = 0$, it turns out (denoting $\omega \equiv \theta/2$):

$$\mathbf{\Pi} = \begin{pmatrix} \cos^2 \omega_A \cos^2 \omega_B & \cos^2 \omega_A \sin^2 \omega_B \\ \sin^2 \omega_A \cos^2 \omega_B & \sin^2 \omega_A \sin^2 \omega_B \end{pmatrix} = \begin{pmatrix} \cos^2 \omega_A \\ \sin^2 \omega_A \end{pmatrix} \begin{pmatrix} \cos^2 \omega_B & \sin^2 \omega_B \end{pmatrix} . \quad (5)$$

Thus, the joint probabilities factorize as in the *classical* game employing independent strategies (1) with $x = \cos^2 \omega_A$, $y = \cos^2 \omega_B$. So to say, the θ parameters are the *classical* ones. In the classic $\gamma = 0$ context, exactly middle-levels of the θ and α parameters lead to $\mathbf{\Pi} = \begin{pmatrix} 1/4 \ 1/4 \\ 1/4 \ 1/4 \end{pmatrix}$. Thus, in the BOS game:
$p_{\sigma} = p_{\varphi} = (R+r)/4$.

In contrast, with maximal entangling ($\gamma = \pi/2$), if $\theta_A = \theta_B = 0$, it is:
$\mathbf{\Pi} = \begin{pmatrix} \cos^2(\alpha_A + \alpha_B) & 0 \\ 0 & \sin^2(\alpha_A + \alpha_B) \end{pmatrix}$, a non-factorizable probability distribution. With $\gamma = \pi/2$ and equal middle-level election of the parameters by both players, $\mathbf{\Pi}$ degenerates, as $\pi_{22} = 1$. Thus, the two-parameter strategies model (4) is somehow biased towards the female player.

We will consider here also the three-parameter strategies [5] scenario:

$$\hat{U}(\theta, \alpha, \beta) = \begin{pmatrix} e^{i\alpha} \cos(\theta/2) & e^{i\beta} \sin(\theta/2) \\ -e^{-i\beta} \sin(\theta/2) & e^{-i\alpha} \cos(\theta/2) \end{pmatrix}, \quad \begin{matrix} \theta \in [0, \pi] \\ \alpha, \beta \in [0, \pi/2] \end{matrix} . \quad (6)$$

2   The Spatialized QBOS

In the spatial version of the BOS we deal with, each player occupies a site (i, j) in a two-dimensional $N \times N$ lattice. We will consider that *males* and *females* alternate in the site occupation. Thus, both kind of players are arranged in a chessboard form, so that every player is surrounded by four partners (φ-σ, σ-φ), and four mates (φ-φ, σ-σ).

In a cellular automata (CA)-like implementation, in each generation (T) every player plays with his four adjacent partners, so that the payoff $p_{i,j}^{(T)}$ of a given individual is the sum over these four interactions. In the next generation, every player will adopt the parameter choice $(\alpha_{i,j}^{(T)}, \theta_{i,j}^{(T)})$ of his nearest-neighbor mate (including himself) that received the highest payoff. In case of a tie, the player maintains his choice.

Details of the *male-female* site occupation, as well as simple examples of the initial dynamics, are given in [2,3]. Incidentally, an initial study of the spatialized quantum prisoner's dilemma was reported in [1].

All the simulations in this work are run in a $N = 200$ lattice with periodic boundary conditions and initial random assignment of the parameter values. Thus, initially: $\overline{\theta} \simeq \pi/2 = 1.57$, and $\overline{\alpha} \simeq \pi/4 = 0.78$. The computations have been performed by a double precision Fortran code run on a mainframe.

Figure 1 shows the long-term $(T = 200)$ mean payoffs across the lattice $(\overline{p})$ in five simulations of a two-parameter quantum (5,1)-BOS CA with variable entanglement factor γ. The bias towards the female player in the model with maximal entangling (pointed out in the Introduction section) becomes apparent in Fig. 1 for high γ values, specifically for $\gamma > 3\pi/8$. In contrast to this, the initial increase of the entangling factor, from the classic $\gamma = 0$ context, leads to a dramatic bifurcation of the mean payoffs in favor to the male player, reaching a peak close to (5,1) when γ approaches $\pi/8$. Before, but close, this value of γ, both mean payoffs commence a smooth approach as γ increases, reaching fairly equal values by $\gamma \simeq 3\pi/8$.

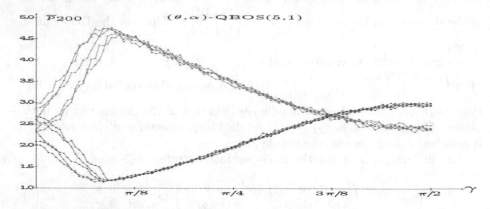

Fig. 1. Long-term mean payoffs in five simulations of a two-parameter quantum (5,1)-BOS CA with entangling factor γ

Figure 2 shows how the main features of the plots in Fig. 1 remain with the (2,1), (4,1) and (6,1) BOS parameters, though in the $R = 2$ case with a fairly flat appearance, and in the $R = 4$ case with the region with low γ rather noisy.

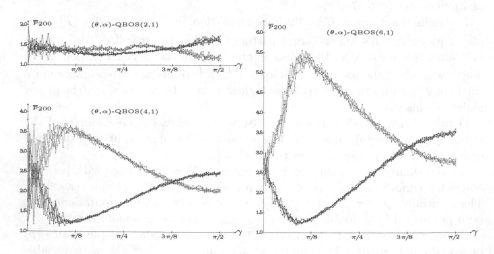

Fig. 2. Long-term mean payoffs in five simulations of two-parameter quantum (2,1), (4,1) and (6,1)-BOS CA with entangling factor γ

Examples of the dynamics and long-term patterns in the scenario of Fig. 1 for particular fairly high γ values may be found in [3]. A further example in shown here in Fig.3, which deals with a very low entanglement factor: $\gamma = \pi/16$. The far left panel of the figure shows the evolution up to $T=200$ of the mean values across the lattice of θ, α as well of the actual ($\overline{p}$) and theoretical mean payoffs. The $\overline{\theta}$ values evolve initially in opposite direction from their mean values, close to $\pi/2 = 1.57$, $\overline{\theta}_{\male}$ decreases up to 0.699, whereas $\overline{\theta}_{\female}$ grows up to 2.411. But the ulterior dynamics depletes this high $\overline{\theta}_{\female}$ value, so that it fairly stabilizes it in a low value, and $T = 200$ it is $\overline{\theta}_{\female} = 0.654$. The $\overline{\theta}_{\male}$ parameter decreases up to 0.364 at $T = 200$. The dynamics of both $\overline{\alpha}$ parameter values is smoother compared to that of $\overline{\theta}$, so from the initial $\overline{\alpha} \simeq \pi/4 = 0.78$, at $T = 200$ it is: $\overline{\alpha}_{\male} = 0.794$ and $\overline{\alpha}_{\female} = 0.661$. The parameter dynamics in Fig.3 quickly drives the $\overline{p}$ mean payoffs to distant values, so that from approximately $T = 10$, the mean female payoff becomes stabilized around $\overline{p}_{\female} = 1.41$, and from approximately $T = 100$ the male payoff is stabilized around $\overline{p}_{\male} = 4.12$. Thus, the dynamics clearly favours the process to the male player, a kind of result contrasting with the bias towards the female player in the Eisert et al. model with full entangling.

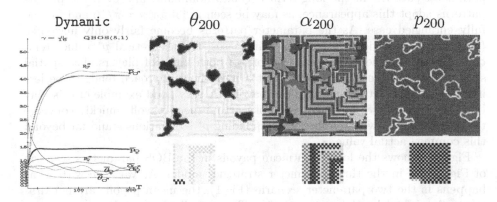

Fig. 3. Simulation of a two-parameter quantum (5,1)-BOS CA with $\gamma = \pi/16$. Far Left: Evolving mean parameters and payoffs. Center: Parameter patterns at $T=200$. Far Right: Payoff patterns at $T=200$. Increasing grey levels indicate increasing parameter pattern values.

The curves labelled p^* in the left panel of Fig. 3 show the *theoretical* (or *mean-field*) payoffs, i.e., the payoffs achieved for both kind of players in a single hypothetical two-person game with players adopting the mean parameters appearing in the spatial dynamic simulation. Namely,

$$
U^*_{\male} = \begin{pmatrix} e^{i\overline{\alpha}_{\male}} \cos \overline{\omega}_{\male} & \sin \overline{\omega}_{\male} \\ \sin \overline{\omega}_{\male} & e^{-i\overline{\alpha}_{\male}} \cos \overline{\omega}_{\male} \end{pmatrix} \quad , \quad U^*_{\female} = \begin{pmatrix} e^{i\overline{\alpha}_{\female}} \cos \overline{\omega}_{\female} & \sin \overline{\omega}_{\female} \\ \sin \overline{\omega}_{\female} & e^{-i\overline{\alpha}_{\female}} \cos \overline{\omega}_{\female} \end{pmatrix} .
$$

As a general rule, due the spatial heterogeneity in the parameter values, the theoretical mean-field estimations of the mean payoffs are different to the actual ones. In the particular case of Fig. 3, the theoretical payoffs $\mathbf{p}^*$ estimate fairly well the trends of the actual mean payoffs $\overline{\mathbf{p}}$, but $\mathbf{p}^*_{\circlearrowleft}$ over-estimates $\overline{\mathbf{p}}_{\circlearrowleft}$ and $\mathbf{p}^*_{\circlearrowleft}$ under-estimates $\overline{\mathbf{p}}_{\circlearrowleft}$.

Figure 3 shows also the snapshots of the parameter and payoff patterns at $T = 200$, both for the full lattice and its zoomed 23×23 central part. Both maze-like structures and coordination clusters may be appreciated at some extent in the parameter patterns. In the θ parameter pattern, the maze-like structure is tenuously visible, whereas the coordination clusters stands up. In the α parameter pattern, the maze-like structure is predominant but also coordination clusters are appreciated. Coordination, favouring the male players, predominates in the payoff pattern, where the disagreement becomes apparent in the form of clear (meaning low payoff) closed narrow zones.

For a given value of γ, e.g., $\gamma = \pi/16$ in Fig.3, the variation of the initial parameter pattern configurations only alters minor details of the evolving dynamics, the main features of the dynamics and of the long-term patterns are preserved. As a general rule, as γ increases the maze-like appearance of the parameter patterns in the long-term becomes dominant, and even the payoffs patterns adopt this appearance, as may be seen in [3] for $\gamma = \pi/16$ and for the fully entangled case. As the parameter patterns become fairly only maze-like (with no coordination clusters) as γ increases, the theoretical p^* values tend to poorly reflect the actual mean payoffs of both kinds of players. The spatial structure marks the difference, so that a mean-field approach tends to be less indicative of the actual spatial mean payoffs. A very good example of this may be that of $\gamma = 3\pi/8$, in which case both actual mean payoffs quickly converge to an equal value, whereas their corresponding p^* estimations stand far beyond this common actual value.

Figure 4 shows the long-term mean payoffs in the BOS parameters scenario of Fig. 1, but in the three-parameter strategies model. At variance with what happens in the two parameter scenario (Fig.1), the mean payoffs are not dramatically altered by the variation of γ. The overall effect of the increase of γ being a moderation in the variation of the $\overline{p}$ values that oscillate nearly over 2.5. Please, note that in the three-parameter strategies model, there is not any bias favoring the female player, so that there is not any tendency to any player over rating the other one. The spatial ordered structure induces a kind of self-organization effect, which allows to achieve fairly soon, approximately at $T = 20$, pairs of mean payoffs that are accessible only with correlated strategies in the two-person game. Recall that the maximum equalitarian payoff in the uncorrelated context is $p^+ = (R+r)/4 = 1.5$, whereas the payoffs in the simulations of Fig. 4 with high entanglement factor reach values over 2.5, not far from the maximum feasible equalitarian payoff $p^= = (R + r)/2 = 3.0$.

The main features of the plots in the Fig. 4 have been checked to be preserved with the BOS parameters $(2,1)$, $(4,1)$ and $(6,1)$. In these three cases, the general form of the $\overline{\mathbf{p}}$ versus γ plots is that shown here for $(5,1)$ in Fig. 4, reaching

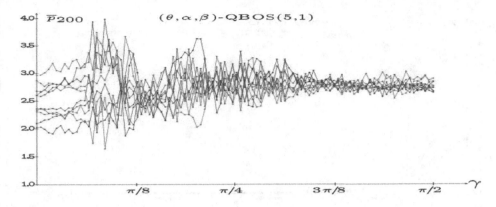

Fig. 4. Long-term mean payoffs in five simulations of a three-parameter quantum (5,1)-BOS CA with entangling factor γ

long-term $\overline{p}$ values not far from $(R + r)/2$. Thus, with $R = 2$ around 1.5, with $R = 4$ around 2.25, and with $R = 6$ around 3.25.

Examples of the dynamics and long-term patterns in the scenario of Fig. 4 with $\gamma = \pi/2$ may be found in [2]. Early patterns in a particular $\gamma = \pi/2$ simulation are also shown in [2]. Accordingly with the absence of bias favouring any of the types of players, in the three-parameter simulations both mean payoffs, and parameter values evolve in a fairly parallel way. The parameter patterns show a rich structure (enclosing both maze-like and nucleation regions) so that the mean-field estimations $\mathbf{p}^*$ do not follow the actual payoffs $\overline{\mathbf{p}}$.

3   Unfair Contest

Let us assume the unfair situation: A type of players is restricted to classical strategies $\tilde{U}(\theta, 0)$, whereas the other type of players may use quantum $\hat{U}(\theta, \alpha)$ ones [9].

Figure 5 shows the long-term mean payoffs in five simulations of an unfair two-parameter quantum male (red) versus classic female (blue) (5,1)-BOS CA with variable entanglement factor γ. The evolution of the mean payoffs of both players is that expected: As soon as γ takes off, the quantum player over rates the classic player. The bifurcation of both $\overline{p}$-values is very rapid, so that by $\pi/4$ the payoff of the classic player is lowered to the stable value 1, whereas that of the quantum player reaches an almost stable value close to 5. With the (4,1) BOS parameters, the plots in the scenario of Fig. 5 do not present a crisp bifurcation-like appearance: They are highly noisy for low γ values, and from nearby $\pi/8$ they change rather abruptly to $p_{\male}$ close to 4, and $p_{\female}$ close to 1. In the same vein, with the (2,1) BOS parameters, the plots are highly noisy, i.e., with no clear advantage for any of the players, up to γ close to $\pi/8$, only beyond this value of the entangling factor, the quantum player over rates the classic one, but in a notable way, e.g., with full entangling: $p_{\male} \simeq 1.5$, $p_{\female} \simeq 1.25$. By contrast, with $(R = 6, r = 1)$, the bifurcation appearance is more defined than

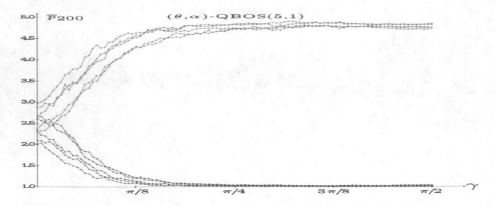

Fig. 5. Long-term mean payoffs in five simulations of an unfair two-parameter quantum (red) versus classic (blue) (5,1)-BOS CA with entanglement factor γ

that shown here for (5,1), with the plots corresponding to the different initial quantum parameter randomizations very close all along their dynamics.

Examples of the dynamics and long-term patterns in the unfair scenario of Fig. 5 with $\gamma = \pi/2$ may be found in [2]. In this scenario, there is a general drift to zero by every parameter, so that the mean-field approach operates properly.

Figure 6 shows the long-term mean payoffs in five simulations of an unfair three-parameter quantum male (red) versus classic female (blue) (5,1)-BOS CA with variable entanglement factor γ. Initially, for low γ, the general appearance of the curves in Fig.6 is the same as that of the Fig.5. But before $\pi/8$, a kind of phase transition rockets the payoff of the male players and plummets that of the female players. Immediately after this episode, both types of payoffs commence to approach, so that by $\gamma = \pi/4$ they equalize at the level $\bar{p} = 3.0$. After this middle-level of γ, the quantum player increasingly over rates the classic player. With very high levels of γ the monotone evolution of the $\bar{p}$-values appears disrupted, so that the (5,1) payoffs are not reached. Even, coordination fails close to maximal entangling so that the payoff of the classic player goes slightly under $r = 1$ close to $\gamma = \pi/2$. The main features of the plots in Fig. 6 are preserved with the BOS parameters (4,1) and (6,1); even the small $\bar{p}_{\male} < 1$-basin with very high γ. With $(R = 2, r = 1)$, i) the classic player does not over rate the quantum one, ii) both players equalize at $\bar{p} = 1.5$ by $\gamma = \pi/4$, iii) the $\bar{p}_{\female} < 1$ region enlarges compared to the scenarios with greater R, as it commences at $\gamma = 3\pi/8$.

Examples of the dynamics and long-term patterns in the scenario of Fig. 6 with maximal entangling may be found in [2]. This article also consider the case of three-parameter quantum versus semi-quantum contests, semi-quantum referring to players that may not implement one of the *quantum* parameters, either α or β, but have access to the other one, β or α respectively (in both cases with the θ parameter operative). The effect of variable entanglement on quantum versus semi-quantum contests is shown in Figs. 7 and 8. The changing predominance in Fig. 7 is highly surprising, and that of the (θ, α)-player in the highest range on γ fully unexpected. This is not the case in Fig. 8, in which case

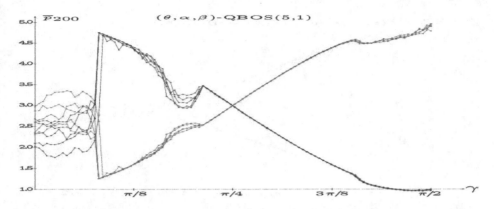

Fig. 6. Long-term mean payoffs in five simulations of an unfair three-parameter quantum (red) versus classic (blue) (5,1)-BOS CA with entanglement factor γ

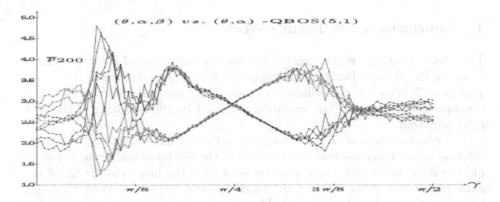

Fig. 7. Long-term mean payoffs in five simulations of a three-parameter quantum (red) versus (θ, α) semi-quantum (blue) (5,1)-BOS CA with entanglement factor γ

what is very notable is the wide range of γ values in which the (θ, β)-player over rates the quantum players, with no equalization at $\gamma = \pi/4$.

Again, it has been checked that the main features of the plots in the scenarios of Figs. 7 and 8 are preserved with the BOS parameters (4,1) and (6,1). Nevertheless, the interval with *indefinite* plot appearance when γ is low varies at some extent: It is wider in the (4,1) model, and narrower with (6,1) BOS parameters. With $(R = 2, r = 1)$, the full quantum player over rates the (θ, α)-player from $\gamma = \pi/4$, whereas in the full quantum versus (θ, β) contest, the (θ, β)-player only slightly over-rates the full quantum player around the $[\pi/4, 3\pi/8]$ interval of γ.

Let us conclude this section by remarking that figures 7 and 8 make apparent that the role of the α and β parameters in the three-parameter model is fairly different.

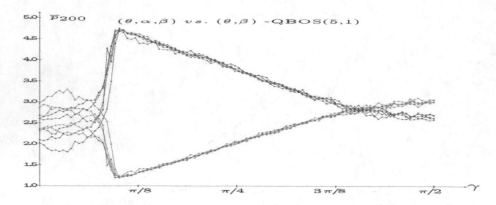

Fig. 8. Long-term mean payoffs in five simulations of a three-parameter quantum (red) versus (θ, β) semi-quantum (blue) (5,1)-BOS CA with entanglement factor γ

4   Conclusions and Future Work

The effect of variable entangling on the dynamics of a spatial quantum formulation of the iterated Battle of the Sexes (BOS) game is studied in this work. The game is played in the cellular automata (CA) manner, i.e., with local and synchronous interaction. The evolution is guided by the imitation of the best paid neighbour.

The effect of increasing the entangling factor (γ) differs notably when considering two or three parameter strategies. In the fair quantum versus quantum players scenario, i) with two-parameter strategies, the mean payoffs ($\bar{p}$) of the male player over rates those of the female players when γ is lower than $3/4$ times its maximum value; beyond this value the female player over rates the male player, ii) with three-parameter strategies, the mean payoffs are not dramatically altered by the increase of γ, the main effect being a moderation in the variation of the $\bar{p}$ values.

In the unfair quantum versus classic scenario, i) with two-parameter strategies, the effect of increasing γ is somehow that expected: It boosts the quantum player to over rate the classic player, ii) with three-parameter strategies, if γ is over its middle value, the quantum player over rates the classic player, but in most of the parameter region below the γ-middle value, unexpectedly, the classic player over rates the quantum player. In unfair three-parameter quantum versus semi-quantum contests, highly surprising effects emerge, as the semi-quantum player over rates the full quantum player in wide γ regions.

The findings just reported apply precisely for the case of the $(R = 5, r = 1)$ BOS parameters. With more separated parameter values, such as $(R = 6, r = 1)$ the simulations that we have run confirm qualitatively the findings reported for (5,1), even in a more definite manner. With closer parameter values, we have tried (4,1), again the findings reported in this study qualitatively remain, albeit the details of the dynamics and the spatial structure of the parameter and payoff patterns may vary notably in some cases. On the contrary, simulations run with close numerical values of the BOS parameters, such as (2,1), have proved to produce less definite dynamics, in particular when dealing with unfair contests. An analytical study of cellular automaton quantum games is due, albeit it appears to be very challenging.

Other quantization schemes [11,12] deserve to be studied in the spatial context. In particular, the scheme introduced by Marinatto and Weber [10,15], a model with no bias favouring to any of the players.

Further study is due on games with asynchronous and probabilistic updating, as well as on the effect of increasing degrees of spatial dismantling, and that of memory [4]. These are deviations from the canonical cellular automata paradigm which may lead to more realistic models.

Acknowledgment. This work was supported by the Spanish grant M2012-39101-C02-01. Part of the computations of this work were performed in EOLO and FISWULF, HPC machines of the International Campus of Excellence of Moncloa, funded by the Spanish Governement and Feder Funds.

References

1. Alonso-Sanz, R.: A quantum prisoner's dilemma cellular automaton. Proc. R. Soc. A 470, 20130793 (2014)
2. Alonso-Sanz, R.: On a three-parameter quantum battle of the sexes cellular automaton. Quantum Information Processing 12(5), 1835–1850 (2013)
3. Alonso-Sanz, R.: A quantum battle of the sexes cellular automaton. Proc. R. Soc. A 468, 3370–3383 (2012)
4. Alonso-Sanz, R.: Dynamical Systems with Memory. World Scientific Pub. (2011)
5. Benjamin, S.C., Hayden, P.M.: Comment on "Quantum games and quantum strategies". Physical Review Letters 87(6), 069801 (2001)
6. Du, J.F., Xu, X.D., Li, H., Zhou, X., Han, R., et al.: Entanglement playing a dominating role in quantum games. Physics Letters A 89(1-2), 9–15 (2001)
7. Du, J.F., Li, H., Xu, X.D., Zhou, X., Han, R.: Phase-transition-like behaviour of quantum games. J. Phys. A: Math. and Gen. 36(23), 6551–6562 (2003)
8. Eisert, J., Wilkens, M., Lewenstein, M.: Quantum games and quantum strategies. Physical Review Letters 83(15), 3077–3080 (1999)
9. Flitney, A.P., Abbott, D.: Advantage of a quantum player over a classical one in 2x2 quantum games. Proc. R. Soc. Lond. A 459(2038), 2463–2474 (2003)
10. Marinatto, L., Weber, T.: A quantum approach to static games of complete information. Physics Letters A 272, 291–303 (2000)
11. Nawaz, A., Toor, A.H.: Dilemma and quantum battle of sexes. J. Phys. A: Math. and General 37(15), 4437 (2004)
12. Nawaz, A., Toor, A.H.: Generalized quantization scheme for two-person non-zero sum games. J. Phys. A: Math. Gen. 37(47), 11457 (2004)
13. Nowak, N.M., May, R.M.: Evolutionary games and spatial chaos. Nature 359, 826–829 (1992)
14. Owen, G.: Game Theory. Academic Press (1995)
15. Situ, H.: A quantum approach to play asymmetric coordination games. Quantum Information Processing 13(3), 591–599 (2013)

Experimental Finitization of Infinite Field-Based Generalized FSSP Solution

Luidnel Maignan[1] and Jean-Baptiste Yunès[2],*

[1] LACL, Universié Paris-Est Créteil, France
luidnel.maignan@u-pec.fr
[2] LIAFA, Université Paris-Diderot, France
Jean-Baptiste.Yunes@univ-paris-diderot.fr

Abstract. In a previous work (see [3]) we presented a general scheme to solve the 1D Generalized Firing Squad Synchronization Problem. We designed it in a modular way using the concept of fields (open CA). The solution was not designed as a finite cellular automaton because we needed unbounded integers as states for distance fields, and the recursive nature of the algorithm leaded to a unbounded number of fields. In this paper, we show as claimed, that this approach does lead to a finite cellular automaton. We exhibit a transformation function from infinite to finite states and write a program that generates the associated finite transition table while checking its validity and the conservation of the input-output behavior of the original cellular automaton.

Keywords: cellular automata, automata minimization, quotient automata, firing squad synchronization problem.

1 Introduction

In this paper we tackle the Generalized Firing Squad Synchronization Problem, GFSSP for short (see [8]). The problem is to design a CA able to synchronize every element of a given infinite family of shapes (in 1D shapes are lines, and in general in 2D shapes are rectangles). The requirements are that the synchronization should be obtained starting from a initial configuration where all cells are quiescent but one that initiates the process and and that the evolution should end in a configuration where all cells are all in the same state that has never been reached before. In [3,4] we presented an algorithm that solves the GFSSP in the 1D and 2D cases. We claimed that this algorithm is interesting because it is well modularized, so that one can clearly understand how the algorithm really works. As a consequence, one can now think about giving a formal proof of correctness for it more easily than for other such attempts (see [5,7,9]), because things are presented in a much more semantical way using simple concepts.

Our solution is built using the very common recursive scheme that splits the space into two equal parts until elementary spaces are detected (see [1,6]).

* This work was partially supported by the french program ANR 12 BS02 007 01.

J. Wąs, G.C. Sirakoulis, and S. Bandini (Eds.): ACRI 2014, LNCS 8751, pp. 136–145, 2014.

But contrary to the common practice, the middles are detected explicitly using integers to represent the appropriate distance information, and the recursivity is also expressed explicitly by stacking up a recursive sequence of "split-at-the-middle" modules. This explicitness is the key of the clarity of this solution. But since the obtained cellular automaton is required to work on arbitrarily big spaces, the integers involved and the number of splittings are both unbounded, leading *a priori* to an infinite number of states. These preliminary results are summarized in Sect. 2.

Of course, arguments are given in [3,4] to show that these two sources of infinity can be eliminated. Nowaday, it is clear that this explicit approach is very fruitful and more and more results are and will be built on top of it, so these arguments need to be made precise and fully checked. So after reminding these arguments, Sect. 3 will expand the main result of this paper: the infinite cellular automaton can indeed be quotiented using an appropriate projection function encoding the arguments. This is checked experimentally by programming the projection function and an automatic extraction of the associated finite transition table which checks that the behavior of the original infinite cellular automaton is preserved. Finally, we summarize the contribution and comment on what remains to be done in this line of work in Sect. 4. Note that for the sake of brevity, without loss of too much generality, we restrict the problem to the simple case of the 1D dimensional case with arbitrary position of the general.

2   The Infinite Cellular Automaton

We remind the reader that FSSP is about synchronizing a line of inactive cells that has been actived in an asynchronous way, and that our solution is based on a recursive splitting of the space in two equal sub-spaces, up to some point where the spaces are elementary and can then be trivially synchronized. We begin by the description of the asynchronous activation process in Sect. 2.2. As more and more cells are active, the initial space is discovered and its middle is detected as described in Sect. 2.3. This leads to two half-spaces, and we apply the same process described in Sect. 2.3 to split these half-spaces into quarter-spaces, and these quarter-spaces into eighth-spaces and so on recursively as described in Sect. 2.4. From this recursive splitting, the synchronization signal is fired by each cell when no further splitting is possible as described in Sect. 2.5. All of this is just a summary of already published results. We conclude this section with a short remark in Sect. 2.6, about the states stored at each cell. This serves as a entry point to the main contribution of this paper which is discussed in Sect. 3.

2.1   Notation

The space is a line of cells denoted S and encoded as an interval $[0, L-1]$ of $\mathbb{Z}$. The neighborhood vectors are $\nu = \{-1, +1\}$, and we denote as $N(c) = \{c+i \in S \mid i \in \nu\}$ the neighbors of a given cell c. We explicitly indicate $N(c) \cup \{c\}$ when the cell c has to be taken into account. The solution is described using the concept of fields. A field is simply an open cellular automaton, *i.e.* a CA that takes inputs from its outside and produces outputs available to its environment. This permits easy composition of such machines. We denote by $f_t(c)$ the value of the field f at timestep t and at cell c. The transition function of the fields are written in the form of field equations $f_{t+1}(x) = \langle expr \rangle$ where $\langle expr \rangle$ may involve values taken from other fields. Intuitively, once all the fields have been introduced, the set of states and transition function of the complete cellular automaton are (in first approximation) a product of the set of values and of the transition function of each field.

2.2   The Input

The classical specification of the FSSP requires all the cells to be inactive at the initial configuration, except one cell called the general. So we first consider the predicate field inp : $\mathbb{N} \times \mathcal{S} \to \mathbf{2}$ which indicates at each timestep $t \in \mathbb{N}$ and each cell $c \in \mathcal{S}$ whether it is inactive ($\neg\,\mathrm{inp}_t(c)$) or active ($\mathrm{inp}_t(c)$). A cell becomes active anytime one of its neighbors is active. Formally, we have:

$$\mathrm{inp}_{t+1}(c) = \exists c' \in \mathrm{N}(c);\ \mathrm{inp}_t(c'). \tag{1}$$

The inactivity of the cells means that all the inactive cell have to be in the same state. The reader can check that all the following field equations ensure this property. This input field represents the asynchronous activation of the cells that we have to transform into a globally synchronous event.

2.3   The Initial Space and Its Splitting

When a cell is active, we want it to participate in splitting of the region of the space it is in. This region will be split into two equal parts and so forth.

First we need to represent this concept of region. In a given space, its middle(s) is(are) the cell(s) which is(are) further from both of its ends, then we need to represent in each cell its distance to its nearest border. For this, we introduce two predicate fields brd and ins. The first, brd, states whether a given cell represents a border of a region or not. The second, ins, states whether a given cell is strictly inside the region or not.

The first region to split being the whole space, we add two predicates brd^0 and ins^0 formally described in the following way:

$$\mathrm{brd}_{t+1}^0(c) = \mathrm{inp}_{t+1}(c) \wedge \exists i \in \nu;\ c + i \notin \mathcal{S}; \tag{2}$$

$$\mathrm{ins}_{t+1}^0(c) = \mathrm{inp}_{t+1}(c) \wedge \forall i \in \nu;\ c + i \in \mathcal{S}. \tag{3}$$

Note that no information is built if the cell is not active, and that the predicate inp is entirely encoded in these two predicates since $\mathrm{inp}_t(c) \Leftrightarrow \mathrm{brd}_t^0(c) \vee \mathrm{ins}_t^0(c)$. From these fields, we can now describe the distance-to-the-nearest-border field, denoted dst, by the following:

$$\mathrm{dst}_{t+1}^l(c) = \begin{cases} \min_{c' \in \mathrm{N}(c)}\{1 + \mathrm{dst}_t^l(c')\} & \text{if } \mathrm{ins}_{t+1}^l(c) \\ 0 & \text{otherwise.} \end{cases} \tag{4}$$

It expresses the fact that if the cell is inside, its distance to the nearest neighbor is exactly one plus the minimum distance among the paths computed by its neighbors, and 0 otherwise. Here, the superscript is l and not just 0 because these distances will be computed in the exact same way for all the following regions (half-spaces, quarters-spaces, etc).

An important remark is that the fields inp, ins, brd and dst are dynamic, they produce different values from time to time. Typically, a cell starts by being inactive, then it determines whether it is strictly inside or on the border of the space, and finally, if it is inside, its distance value will monotonously increase to its final value. It is necessary to identify when these values are the final correct ones, *i.e.* when their values will not evolve anymore because they correspond to the definitive situation.

This can be achieved with the help of a simple argument: an active border is stable (has a correct value) by definition and will forever keep the values $(\text{ins}, \text{brd}, \text{dst}) = (\bot, \top, 0)$ and an active cell which is not a border is stable if its distance value has been computed from a stable distance value in its neighborhood. We encode this into a predicate field denoted sta which is formally defined as in the following:

$$\text{sta}^l_{t+1}(c) = \bigvee \begin{cases} \text{brd}^l_{t+1}(c) \\ \exists c' \in N(c); \ \text{dst}^l_{t+1}(c) = 1 + \text{dst}^l_t(c') \wedge \text{sta}^l_t(c'). \end{cases} \tag{5}$$

At this stage, the middle of the space is easily detected as the stable local maxima of the distance field. A little subtlety remains when the space has an even number of cells, as there are two middle cells in the middle, and that we need them to appear at the same time (if not the synchronization may not appear everywhere at the same time). Taking this into account leads to the following formal definition of the field (see [3]) mid:

$$\text{mid}^l_{t+1}(c) = \bigvee \begin{cases} \text{dst}^l_{t+1}(c) > \max_{c' \in N(c)} \{\text{dst}^l_t(c')\} \\ \quad \wedge \ \forall c' \in N(c), \text{sta}^l_t(c'), \\ \text{dst}^l_{t+1}(c) = \max_{i \in \nu} \{\text{dst}^l_t(c+i)\} \\ \quad \wedge \ \forall c' \in N(c) \cup \{c\}, \text{sta}^l_t(c'). \end{cases} \tag{6}$$

Altogether, the fields dst^0, sta^0 and mid^0 split the space described by brd^0 and ins^0 in two equal parts. They form what we call a **layer**. As many splitting are required to synchronize, they are indexed. This is the purpose of the superscripts l in the former formulas. The evolution of the values of the fields of the layer $l = 0$ are shown in Fig. 1a in the case where the general is the leftmost cell. Cells left blank are inactives and the gray background represents the stable field. Thick cells are those representing the middle(s).

2.4   The Splitting of Regions and Recursion

The previous section describes the splitting of the whole space into half-spaces, that we called the layer $l = 0$. Further splittings are computed by layers $l+1 > 0$,

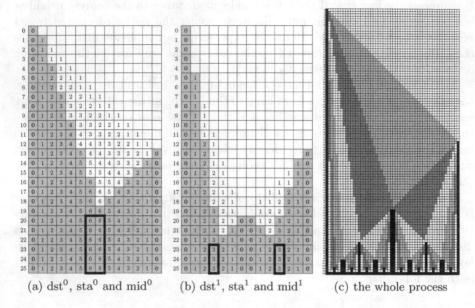

(a) dst^0, sta^0 and mid^0 (b) dst^1, sta^1 and mid^1 (c) the whole process

Fig. 1. Evolutions on a line of cells

each of them taking its inputs in the predicate fields brd^l and mid^l to take into account the splitting computed by the previous layer. This is done by letting the borders of the layer $l + 1 > 0$ be the union of the borders and middles of the layer l.

$$\mathrm{brd}_{t+1}^{l+1}(c) = \mathrm{brd}_{t+1}^l(c) \vee \mathrm{mid}_{t+1}^l(c). \tag{7}$$

One can remark that a cell has $\mathrm{brd} = \top$ only when it is *guaranteed* to be a border of a subdivided region. We need the same property for ins and want this field to be $\top$ if and only if it is guaranteed to never be a middle in the previous layer. Since distance values are only increasing, if a cell holds a stable value and has a value in its neighborhood that is greater, this will be forever the case, preventing it to become a middle. More formally we have:

$$\mathrm{ins}_{t+1}^{l+1}(c) = \bigwedge \begin{cases} \mathrm{ins}_{t+1}^l(c) \wedge \mathrm{sta}_{t+1}^l(c); \\ \exists c' \in \mathrm{N}(c); \ \mathrm{dst}_t^l(c') > \mathrm{dst}_{t+1}^l(c). \end{cases} \tag{8}$$

This definition links all the layers into an unbounded pipeline of splitting processes. Figure 1b shows the evolution of the layer 1. Blank cells are those for which $\neg\,\mathrm{brd}^1$ and $\neg\,\mathrm{ins}^1$. Stacking up all the subsequent layers leads to an evolution which can be summarized as in Fig 1c.

2.5   The Output

The last interesting field to consider is the output field named out. Such a field gives the opportunity to use the automaton as a functional brick of a bigger system. In our context, it is a boolean field that on each cell tells if that cell is synchronized or not, *i.e.* out : $\mathbb{N} \times \mathcal{S} \to \mathbf{2}$. A cell is synchronized when there is a layer where all its neighbors are borders. Of course, we are actually considering a solution to the problem, so that it should be clear that this field has the following properties: $\exists t_s, \forall c, \mathrm{out}_{t_s}(c) = \top$ and $\forall t < t_s, \mathrm{out}_t(c) = \bot$. Formally, the output field is defined as:

$$\mathrm{out}_{t+1}(c) = \exists l \in \mathbb{N}, \forall c \in \mathrm{N}(c) \cup \{c\}; \mathrm{brd}_t^l(c'). \tag{9}$$

2.6   The States of the CA

Let us make an important remark on the information stored at each cell. At first sight, it may seem that it is needed to encode the values of (inp, brd^0, ins^0, dst^0, sta^0, mid^0, brd^1, ins^1, dst^1, sta^1, mid^1, ...). But this is far too much redundant. In fact, the fields brd, ins and mid are only here to ease the description of the algorithm. Their values at time t are not used at time $t+1$, they are like variables local to the transition function. By observing the previous equations, it should be clear that any field value at time $t + 1$ is computed using the values of brd, ins and mid at time $t + 1$ and not those at time t.

One may prefer to observe that the definition of these three fields can be inlined each time they are used. This leads to a much longer definition of dst and sta, but these new definitions respect entirely the cellular automaton constraint that the value at $(t + 1, c)$ is computed based on values at $(t, c - 1)$, (t, c) and $(t, c + 1)$.

So the structure of a state of a cell can be represented as (inp, dst^0, sta^0, dst^1, sta^1, dst^2, sta^2, ...).

3   From an Infinite to a Finite Cellular Automaton

3.1   The Reduction: Principles

There are two crucial points in our discussion, both relative to the finiteness of the cellular automaton. The first one is that the distance fields use integers and the second is that there is *a priori* an unbounded number of layers. But both of these sources of infinity can be eliminated as follows.

First, let us discuss the numbers of layers. Among all the values represented by all the fields in a particular configuration, most of them are stable, will not evolve anymore, and all the information that they provide has been entirely consumed. Indeed, we can safely tell that the value of a layer l is entirely consumed at cell when each neighbor of this cell knows whether it is a border or an inside at level $l + 1$, since the only goal of the layer l is to build this information. As an illustration, Fig. 2 shows all the layer values at time step 50 for a line of 54 cells and a general at position 11. Forgetting about cells corresponding to borders at some level, layer values in gray background are the only whose information has not been entirely consumed, and there is always one and only one such layer at

0	1	2	3	4	5	6	7	8	9	10	11	12	13	14	15	16	17	16	15	14	13	12	11	10	9	8	7	6	5	4	3	2	1	0
0	1	2	3	4	5	6	7	8	8	7	6	5	4	3	2	1	0	1	2	3	4	5	6	7	8	8	7	6	5	4	3	2	1	0
0	1	2	3	4	3	2	1	0	0	1	2	3	4	3	2	1	0	1	2	3	4	3	2	1	0	0	1	2	3	4	3	2	1	0
0	1	2	1	0	0	0	1	0	0	1	0	0	0	0	1	1	0	1	1	0	0	0	0	1	0	0	1	0	0	0	1	1	1	0
0	1	0	0	0	0	0	0	0	0	0	0	0	0	0	0	0	0	0	0	0	0	0	0	0	0	0	0	0	0	0	0	0	0	0
0	0	0	0	0	0	0	0	0	0	0	0	0	0	0	0	0	0	0	0	0	0	0	0	0	0	0	0	0	0	0	0	0	0	0

Fig. 2. All layers (level 0 on top) at time 50 for 54 cells and general at position 11

B	4	3	3	2	2	2	3	B	B	3	2	2	2	2	3	3	B	3	3	2	2	2	2	3	B	B	3	2	2	2	2	3	3	3	B
0	1	2	1	4	3	2	1	0	0	1	2	3	4	3	1	1	0	1	1	3	4	3	2	1	0	0	1	2	3	4	1	1	1	0

Fig. 3. First reduction: the first line is the level of the conserved layer

each cell. Therefore, it should be enough to conserve in each cell only the values of this layer and its level, as in Fig. 3.

This leaves us two integer fields preventing the cellular automaton to have a finite number states, but both of them have a very special property: they are Lipschitz continuous, *i.e.* the absolute value of their derivative are uniformly bounded (here 1). This is a special case of what has been studied in [2], where it is shown that such Lipschitz-continuous integer fields, whose only useful information is the difference between cells (and this is the case here, although it might not be apparent at first), can be transformed into a finite-state field. When the bound on the differences is 1, then only 3 states are required. So we can encode the distances and the number of their level modulo 3 and get back an identically behaving cellular automaton.

These are the two arguments that we want to make precise and check experimentally in the rest of this section.

3.2 The Reduction: Quotient Cellular Automaton

The discussion of Sect. 3.1 suggests that there exists a **finite quotient cellular automaton** that behaves exactly like the original infinite one. If we denote by Q the set of states of our infinite cellular automaton, by $\delta : Q^3 \to Q$ its transition function, and by $o : Q^3 \to \mathbf{2}$ its output function, the previous section states that Q contains too much information, and that a projection function $\pi : Q \to R$ exists which conserves only a finite but sufficient part. The resulting finite cellular automaton (R, γ, p) working on the finite set of states R is the quotient $(Q, \delta, o)/\pi$, *i.e.* the only triplet satisfying:

$$
\begin{array}{ccc}
Q & \xleftarrow{\ \delta\ } & Q^3 \\
\pi \downarrow & \quad \pi^3 \downarrow & \searrow^{o} \\
& & \quad \mathbf{2} \\
R & \xleftarrow{\ \gamma\ } & R^3 \quad \nearrow_{p}
\end{array}
$$

where $\pi^3 : Q^3 \to R^3$ denotes the function $(a, b, c) \mapsto (\pi(a), \pi(b), \pi(c))$. For those used to quotienting by equivalence relation and not by projection function, this triplet (R, γ, p) is isomorphic to the quotient cellular automaton $(Q, \delta, o)/ \sim$ obtained using the equivalence relation $x \sim y \Leftrightarrow \pi(x) = \pi(y)$. In this context, the commutative diagram expresses the fact that the equivalence classes are respected by the transition function δ and the the output function o, thus lifting the equivalence relation at the level of a congruence on the original cellular automaton as required for the quotienting to make sense.

3.3   The Reduction: Automatic Extraction

First let us describe the projection function encoding the arguments discussed in Sect. 3.1. Each state (inp,dst^0,sta^0,dst^1,sta^1,dst^2,sta^2,...) is reduced to a finite part (inp, rbrd, rlvl, rdst, rsta) in the following way:

$$\text{rbrd} = \text{inp} \wedge \exists l \in \mathbb{N};\ dst^l = 0 \wedge sta^l. \tag{10}$$

$$\text{lvl} = \begin{cases} 0 & \text{if rbrd} \vee \neg \text{inp}; \\ \min\{l \in \mathbb{N} \mid dst^{l+1} = 0\} & \text{otherwise.} \end{cases} \tag{11}$$

$$\text{rlvl} = \text{lvl mod 3} \tag{12}$$

$$\text{rdst} = \begin{cases} 0 & \text{if rbrd} \vee \text{inp}; \\ dst^{\text{lvl}} \text{ mod 3} & \text{otherwise.} \end{cases} \tag{13}$$

$$\text{rsta} = sta^{\text{lvl}} \vee \text{rbrd} \tag{14}$$

To produce the transition table for γ, we start with an empty finite transition table and execute the original infinite CA on sufficiently many initial configurations, where the meaning of "sufficiently many" is also determined experimentally as will be discussed below. During these executions, we take each local transition $(a, b, c) \mapsto d$ that occurs and add its reduced counterpart $(\pi(a), \pi(b), \pi(c)) \mapsto \pi(d)$ to the transition table of the finite CA under construction as required by the quotienting commutative diagram. However, in order to make sure that the projection function π does respect the commutative diagram, we check at each adding of a transition that we never have two different $\pi(d) \neq \pi(d')$ for the same $(\pi(a), \pi(b), \pi(c)) = (\pi(a'), \pi(b'), \pi(c'))$. We should do the same for the output function, but here it is so simple that the reduced output function is obvious, provided that the projection function is correct:

$$\text{rout}_{t+1}(c) = \forall c \in \text{N}(c) \cup \{c\};\ \text{rbrd}_t(c'). \tag{15}$$

3.4   The Reduction: Results

The result of the computation is illustrated in Fig. 4. We show an execution of the computed finite CA running on a line of 35 cells where the general is initially located on the twelfth cell. The reduced distance field is represented with numbers 0, 1 and 2. The color of the background represents the index of the level of a cell using three colors white, light gray, dark gray. The borders are represented with bolder surrounding squares.

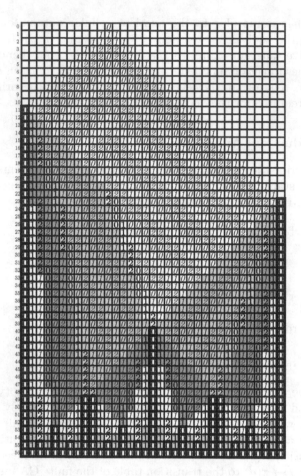

Fig. 4. The finite CA running on a line of length 35

The transition table has been generated using spaces of size up to 100 with all possible positions of the general. Only 69 executions were actually useful to complete the table. After that, the completeness of the transition table has been checked successfully on spaces of size up to 750 with all possible positions of the general again.

The number of states of the CA extracted is 21 and the number of transition rules is 523 in our restricted case where we only consider the generalized FSSP, i.e. only one general at the initial configuration. One can remark that the number of states that anyone naturally uses to obtain a Minsky-like solution is about 15; but such a solution is much simpler than a minimal one. Mazoyer built his first minimal-time solution with the help of 17 states, but it synchronizes only with a general initially located on the leftmost cell.

4   Conclusion

In this paper we detailed how we were able to obtain a FSSP solution from an infinite cellular automaton. That infinite cellular automaton was previously designed in order to model a generic algorithm that solves the FSSP. That algorithm was such designed to ease its understanding and to show that there exists a very general solution to the problem that tackles many variants of the problem. We claimed several times that this infinite cellular automaton could be reduced to a finite one but we only gave informal arguments about this. Here, we showed how it could be easy to verify with the help of a computer and by experimentation that this could be effectively done. Our algorithm produced a 21 states, 523 transitions rules CA which solves the Generalized FSSP on a line in minimal time.

This is surprisingly very near what one could obtained by hand, and our solution is much more clear on how the synchronization is obtained, there is no tricky part in it only a simple reduction of a simple machine implementing a simple algorithm. It could certainly be possible to reduce the number of states using a more efficient projection function or using a kind of minimization algorithm.

This is an interesting future direction of work.

References

1. Balzer, R.: An 8-state minimal time solution to the firing squad synchronization problem. Information and Control 10, 22–42 (1967)
2. Maignan, L., Gruau, F.: Integer gradient for cellular automata: Principle and examples. In: Self-Adaptive and Self-Organizing Systems Workshops, SASOW 2008, pp. 321–325 (2008)
3. Maignan, L., Yunès, J.-B.: A spatio-temporal algorithmic point of view on firing squad synchronisation problem. In: Sirakoulis, G.C., Bandini, S. (eds.) ACRI 2012. LNCS, vol. 7495, pp. 101–110. Springer, Heidelberg (2012)
4. Maignan, L., Yunès, J.B.: Moore and von Neumann neighborhood n-dimensional generalized firing squad solutions using fields. In: AFCA 2013 Workshop. CANDAR 2013 Conference, Matsuyama, Japan, December 4-6 (2013)
5. Mazoyer, J.: A six-state minimal time solution to the firing squad synchronization problem. Theoretical Computer Science 50, 183–238 (1987)
6. Moore, E.E.: Sequential Machines, Selected Papers, pp. 213–214. Addison-Wesley (1964)
7. Noguchi, K.: Simple 8-state minimal time solution to the firing squad synchronization problem. Theoretical Computer Science 314(3), 303–334 (2004)
8. Schmidt, H., Worsch, T.: The firing squad synchronization problem with many generals for one-dimensional CA. In: Levy, J.-J., Mayr, E.W., Mitchell, J.C. (eds.) 3rd IFIP International Conference on Theoretical Computer Science. IFIP, vol. 155, pp. 111–124. Springer, Boston (2004)
9. Yunès, J.B.: An intrinsically non minimal-time Minsky-like 6-states solution to the firing squad synchronization problem. RAIRO-Theor. Inf. Appl. 42, 55–68 (2008)

Cellular Automata (CA) Model for Primality Test

Nirmalya Sundar Maiti, Soumyabrata Ghosh, and Parimal Pal Chaudhuri

Cellular Automata Research Lab (CARL), CARLBio Pvt.Ltd and Alumnus Software Ltd,
Saltlake City, Kolkata 700091, India
nirmalya@carlbio.com

Abstract. Theory and application of Cellular automata (CA) as a global Transform for detecting compositeness of a number is reported. To test an n bit odd valued number N in the range 2^{n-1} to $(2^n\text{-}1)$, a Compositeness Detecting CA (CDCA) set is designed with $N = S$ as a Self Loop Attractor (SLA) State, where $S = S' \times S''$, S' is the largest factor of S, $S'' = 3,5,7,\cdots$. The set has at least one CDCA with the state S' in its attractor basin; the CA initialized with S' reaches the attractor S after S'' time steps. A number is detected as a prime if no CDCA is synthesized.

Keywords: Compositeness Detecting Cellular Automata (CDCA), Rule Vector Graph (RVG), Level Graph (LG), Cellular Automata Transform.

1 Introduction

In last few decades researchers developed many efficient probabilistic and deterministic schemes [1–3]. A significant milestone in this journey is observed in 2004 with the introduction of AKS algorithm [4] - a deterministic algorithm with complexity $O(n)^{12}$, where n is the number of bits necessary to represent N. The complexity was subsequently improved to $O(n)^{7.5}$. It has been also proposed that the complexity can be further reduced to $O(n)^6$ if distribution of Sophie Germain conjecture is true. Finally, Lenstra and Pomerance [5] presented a version of the compositeness test which runs in $O(n)^6$ complexity unconditionally. Improvement over this limit to $O(n)^4$ has been conjectured [6] subject to validity of generalized Riemann Hypothesis. In the above background, we present a Transform Domain analysis for primality testing based on three neighborhood Cellular Automata (CA) rules as Transform Operator.

   Twin goals of this research is - employ the power of CA evolution (i) to address the age of problem of primality test, and (ii) to aim reduction of complexity to a level lesser than $O(n^6)$. This paper reports a scheme to realize the first goal. Next section presents an overview of the basic scheme.

2 Design of Compositeness Detecting n-cell CA (CDCA) to Test an n Bit Odd Number N in the Range 2^{n-1} to 2^n-1

The CA based scheme exploits the power of CA evolution to ensure efficient design of CDCA for which the largest factor $S' \in \{S^*\}$ and the CA initialized with S' reaches

J. Wąs, G.C. Sirakoulis, and S. Bandini (Eds.): ACRI 2014, LNCS 8751, pp. 146–155, 2014.

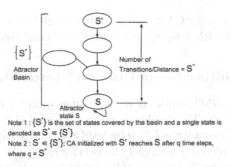

Note 1 : {S'} is the set of states covered by the basin and a single state is denoted as S' ∈ {S'}.

Note 2 : S' ∈ {S'}; CA initialized with S' reaches S after q time steps, where q = S"

Fig. 1. Attractor Basin of a CDCA with $S = (S' \times S'')$ as an Attractor

the attractor after q time steps where $q = S''$ (Figure 1). A CA in the rest of the paper refers to an n cell three neighborhood null boundary two state per cell CA with its Rule Vector (RV) as $< R_0\ R_1\ \cdots\ R_{i-1}\ R_i\ R_{i+1}\ \cdots\ R_{n-1} >$. Further, such a CA has a Single Self Loop Attractor (SLA) and hence also referred to as SSLACA (Single SLA CA). Example 1 illustrate the basic scheme.

Example 1: Figure 2 shows the partial attractor basin of 6 cell CA $< 9\ 165\ 165\ 153\ 177\ 65 >$ designed with 63 as Self Loop Attractor (SLA). It is declared as a non-prime number since its factor 21 reaches the attractor 63 after 3 time steps of CA evolution.

A number N is represented with an n bit string as $< a_0\ a_1\ \cdots\ a_{i-1}\ a_i\ a_{i+1}\ \cdots\ a_{n-1} >$, $a_i = 0$ or 1, $i = 0$ to $(n\text{-}1)$. The binary string is transformed to octal digit string as $N = S = < T^0\ T^1\ \cdots\ T^{i-1}\ T^i\ T^{i+1}\ \cdots\ T^{n-1} >$, where $T^i = < a_{i-1}\ a_i\ a_{i+1} >$ ranges from $T(0) = <000>$ to $T(7) = <111>$, where an octal digit k in the range 0 to 7 is denoted in text as $T(k)$ and simply as k in diagrams. For a valid octal digit string, T^{i+1} is derived

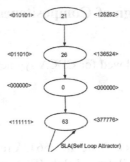

Fig. 2. Partial attractor basin of the CA <9 165 165 153 177 65> with 63 as SLA - it identifies 63 as a composite number

out of $T^i = < a_{i-1}\ a_i\ a_{i+1} >$ by deleting a_{i-1} and appending 0 and 1 as a_{i+2}. It has been shown in [7, 9] that for efficient analysis of CA evolution, it is desirable to process octal digit string rather than its binary counterpart. CA preliminaries along with the associated terminologies, design of Rule Vector Graph (RVG) out of RV (rule vector) of a CA have been detailed in [7–9]. Figure 3 illustrates a RVG for the RV of CA along with state transitions. A new class of graph referred to as Level Graph (LG) used for

CDCA synthesis follows. In the CA paradigm an octal digit 0 to 7 is referred to as Rule Min Term (RMT). A valid RMT string represents a valid octal digit string.

2.1   Generation of LG(i) (i=0,1,$\cdots$ (n-1)) out of ith Level RVG of an n Cell CA

Each node in a LG is a RMT, while its directed edge specifies the destination node reachable from source node. The number of nodes for each LG is 8; while LG(0) and LG(n-1) have 4 nodes. Generation of LG(i) for level i is noted in Algorithm 1. It accepts Rule Vector Sub-graph (RVS) for level (i-1), i, (i+1) for rule triplet $< R_{i-1} R_i R_{i+1} >$. RMT at level i (noted on the ith level edge) is viewed as a node in LG(i). Five LGs are noted in Figure 4 for the RVG of Figure 3(a). Reachability matrix of a LG component denotes reachability of a node from others.

Algorithm 1: Generate LG (i) (for level i of RVG)

Input: RVS (i-1), RVS (i), and RVS (i+1) - the three Rule
    Vector Sub-graph for level (i-1), i, and (i+1) of RVG.
Output: LG (i).
Step 1(a): For each RMT T (a node) at i^{th} level generate the possible
    next state bit triplets $< b_{i-1} b_i b_{i+1} >$ on the edges of
    valid sub-paths in RVS(i-1), RVS(i), and RVS(i+1).
    1(b): Convert it to the decimal number and mark it as the terminating RMT node.
Step 2: Connect the two RMTs with an edge.
Step 3: Repeat Step 1 and 2 for each RMT of the level i.
Step 4: Stop.

3   Rule Analysis for Design of Compositeness Detecting CA (CDCA)

Table 1 reports 28 CA rules employed for CDCA synthesis. A few terminologies are introduced next.

3.1   Terminologies

Definition 1: Balanced Rules (BR): There are 256 CA rules. Out of these rules, there are $8_{C_4} = 70$ rules referred to as Balanced Rule (BR), each having four 0's and four 1's in its 8 bit pattern $< b_7 b_6 b_5 b_4, b_3 b_2 b_1 b_0 >$; b_k ($k = 0(000)$ to $7(111)$) refers to the next state bit for RMT $T(k) = k$. The RMTs can be rearranged as $< < T(7) T(6) T(5) T(3)> <T(4) T(2) T(1) T(0)> >$, where first group covers RMTs having two 1's in their three bit binary pattern, while the second group have two 0's - these are respectively referred to as 1-Major and 0-Major RMTs. The next state bit strings are referred to as 1/0 - Major strings.

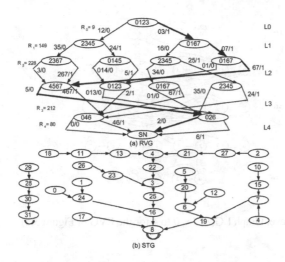

Fig. 3. Rule Vector Graph (RVG) for Rule Vector (RV) <9 149 228 212 80> and its State Transition Graph

Definition 2: (2,2) Rules : The BRs are grouped as - (i) (2,2) rules, each having two $1'$s in next state bits of 1-Major string $< b_7\ b_6\ b_5\ b_3 >$ and 0-Major string $< b_4\ b_2\ b_1\ b_0 >$. On re-arrangement of RMTs, rule 197 = <1100,0101> is a (2,2) rule while 147 = <1000,1011> is a non-(2,2) rule.

Definition 3: PSL RMT of a Rule R_i - Each of the CDCA rules and their binary patterns expressed in 1/0-major string is listed in Table 1 along with Potential Self Loop (PSL) RMTs. A RMT T(k) is a PSL RMT if $b_i = a_i$, where T(k) = $< a_{i-1}\ a_i\ a_{i+1} >$, and b_i is the next bit for the RMT of the rule, T(k) = k varies from 0 <000> to 7 <111>. For a RV $< R_0\ R_1 \cdots R_i \cdots R_{n-1} >$, a state represented as a valid RMT string $< T^0\ T^1 \cdots T^i \cdots T^{n-1} >$ is a self loop state, if each rule R_i has a PSL RMT that is compatible with PSL RMT for the rule R_{i+1}, $i = 0$ to $(n-2)$.

Definition 4: 4RMT Node - A node in the RVG of a CA having only four RMTs is referred to as 4 RMT Node.

Definition 5: CDCA Rule - A rule that generates only 4RMT node is referred to a CDCA rule. Out of the thirty-two (2,2) rules, only 28 are CDCA rules listed in Table 1.

Definition 6: Level Node Group (LNG), Dominating and Dominated LNG - Different 4RMT combinations available in the RVG of a CDCA are referred to as LNG (0 to 9) (Table 2).

Definition 7:(LNG, RT) Vector - Each rule of the RT (Rule Triplet) is one of the CDCA rules listed in Table 1. A LNG transformed by the rule triplet is represented as a vector - $< $ LNG(i-1) R_{i-1} LNG(i) R_i LNG(i+1) R_{i+1} LNG(i+2) $>$, where R_{i-1} transforms LNG(i-1) to LNG(i) which is next transformed to LNG(i+1) by the rule R_i. Finally LNG(i+1) gets transformed to LNG(i+2) by the rule R_{i+1}. Table 3 shows two (LNG,RT) vectors.

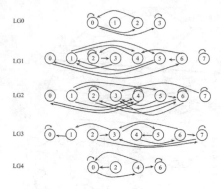

LG0

LG1

LG2

LG3

LG4

Fig. 4. Level Graph LG(i), $i = 0$ to 4 for the RVG of Figure 3(a)

A list of (LNG,RT) vectors for each Rule Triplet (RT) is stored in a data base. The RTs are classified as: (i) Sink RT $< R_{n-3}\ R_{n-2}\ R_{n-1} >$ for which LG(n-1), LG(n-2) are defined along with reachability matrix, (ii) Mid RT $< R_{i-1}\ R_i\ R_{i+1} >$ for which LG(i) is defined similarly, and (iii) Root RT - for which LG(0) and LG(1) are defined. Analysis of reachability matrix for LG(i) specifies the set $\{q_i\}$, where q_i is the time steps necessary to reach T^i from any other node in the LG(i), $q_i = 3, 5, 7, \cdots$.

4 CDCA (Compositeness Detecting CA) Synthesis Algorithm

The synthesis scheme starts with the selection of one Sink RT such that the LG(n-1) and LG(n-2) ensures compatible RMT pair $T^{n-1} = < a_{n-2}a_{n-1}0 >$ and $T^{n-2} = < a_{n-3}a_{n-2}a_{n-1} >$ are PSLRMT along with the set $\{q_{n-1}\}$ and $\{q_{n-2}\}$ specified from respective reachability matrix. Let $T'^{(n-1)}$ reach T^{n-1} after q_{n-1} ($q_{n-1} \in \{q_{n-1}\}$) time steps where $T'^{(n-1)} = < a'_{n-2}a'_{n-1}0 >$; $T'^{(n-2)}$ reach T^{n-2} after q_{n-2} ($q_{n-2} \in \{q_{n-2}\}$) time steps, where $T'^{(n-2)} = < a'_{n-3}a'_{n-2}a'_{n-1} >$. Also the algorithm ensures that $a'_{n-1} \times q_{n-1} = a_{n-1}$ and $a'_{n-2} \times q_{n-2} = a_{n-2}$ through binary multiplication where $q_{n-1} = q_{n-2}$.

Let the traversal of nodes in the path from $T'^{(n-1)}$ to T^{n-1} be noted as $< T'^{(n-1)}$ $p_{n-1}^1\ p_{n-1}^2 \cdots p_{n-1}^{q-1}\ T^{n-1} >$ and from $T'^{(n-2)}$ to T^{n-2} as $< T'^{(n-2)}\ p_{n-2}^1\ p_{n-2}^2 \cdots p_{n-2}^{q-1}\ T^{n-2} >$. The rule pairs R_{n-1} and R_{n-2} of Sink RT are selected in such a manner that p_{n-1}^j and p_{n-2}^j is a compatible RMT pair, where $j = 1$ to $q - 1$. The above discussions in respect of a pair of compatible paths in a pair adjacent LGs has been formalized in the next definition.

Definition 8: Locked LG Path Pair - A pair of paths
(i) T'^i to T^i denoted as $< T'^i p_i^1 p_i^2 \cdots p_i^{q-1} T^i >$ and
(ii) T'^{i-1} to T^{i-1} be noted as $< T'^{i-1} p_{i-1}^1 p_{i-1}^2 \cdots p_{i-1}^{q-1} T^{i-1} >$
is referred to as Locked LG path pair if p_i^j and p_{i-1}^j are compatible RMT pair for all j = 1 to $q - 1$.

Table 1. Twenty-eight CDCA Rules along with PSLRMTs

Rule	8 bit Pattern of the rule $< b_7$ to $b_0 >$	PSL RMT	Rule	8 bit Pattern of the rule $< b_7$ to $b_0 >$	PSL RMT
45	0010,1101	1,2,3,4	57	0011,1001	1,3
58	0011,1010	0,3	60	0011,1100	0,1,2,3
75	0100,1011	3,4,5,6	77	0100,1101	1,2,3,4,5,6
78	0100,1110	0,2,3,4,5,6	89	0101,1001	1,3,5,6
90	0101,1010	0,3,5,6	92	0101,1100	0,1,2,3,5,6
99	0110,0011	4,6	101	0110,0101	1,2,4,6
102	0110,0110	0,2,4,6	114	0111,0010	0,6
141	1000,1101	1,2,3,4,5,7	153	1001,1001	1,3,5,7
154	1001,1010	0,3,5,7	156	1001,1100	0,1,2,3,5,7
163	1010,0011	4,7	165	1010,0101	1,2,4,7
166	1010,0110	0,2,4,7	177	1011,0001	1,7
178	1011,0010	0,7	180	1011,0100	0,1,2,7
195	1100,0011	4,5,6,7	197	1100,0101	1,2,4,5,6,7
198	1100,0110	0,2,4,5,6,7	210	1101,0010	0,5,6,7

Table 2. List of Level Node Group (LNG)

LNG INDEX (x) = 0 to 9	Set of 4RMT Nodes denoted as {LNG(x)}	No of 4RMT	LNG(x) dominated by LNG(y)- (y)
0	{0145},{2367}	2	y = 3,5,6,7,8
1	{0167},{2345}	2	y = 4,5,6,7,8
2	{0123},{4567}	2	y = 4,8
3	{0123},{0145},{2367},{4567}	4	y = 8
4	{0123},{0167},{2345},{4567}	4	y = 8
5	{0145},{0167},{2345},{2367}	4	y = 6,7,8
6	{0145},{0167},{2345},{2367},{4567}	5	y = 8
7	{0123},{0145},{0167},{2345},{2367}	5	y = 8
8	{0123},{0145},{0167},{2345},{2367},{4567}	6	
9	{0123}	1	

Note 1: A {LNG(x)} $\subset$ {LNG(y)}, if the set of 4RMT nodes of {LNG(x)} are covered by those of {LNG(y)} $x, y \in \{0$ to $9\}$

Table 3. Two sample (LNG, RT) vectors for the CDCA <9 165 165 153 177 65> in its RVG shown in Figure 5

(LNG, RT) Vector	Reachability Matrix M	
<LNG(9) 9 LNG(1) 165	$0,7 \to 6,7$	For
LNG(1) 165 LNG(1)>	$1,6 \to 4,5$	LG(1),
RT<9 165 165>	$2,5 \to 2,3, 3,4 \to 0,1$	$R_i = 165$
<LNG(1) 153 LNG(1) 177	$0,7 \to 7, 1,6 \to 4$	For
LNG(4) 65 (Gr)>	$2 \to 0, 3 \to 1$	LG(4),
RT<153 177 65>	$4 \to 3, 5 \to 2$	$R_i = 177$

Thus selection of the RT $< R_{i-1}\ R_i\ R_{i+1} >$ from the RT database is guided by the enforcing the following constraints C1 to C3 for the given input number $N = < T^0\ T^1 \dots T^{i-1}\ T^i\ T^{i+1} \dots T^{n-1} >$; with R_i and R_{i+1} specified in earlier iteration step:

C1: T^{i-1} and T^i are compatible RMT pair and PSLRMTs.

C2: Locked LG path $(i,(i-1))$ exits for a pair of RMTs T'^i and T'^{i-1} reaching respectively to T^i and T^{i-1} after $q_i = q_{i-1}$ time steps where $q_i \in \{q_i\}$ and also $q_{i-1} \in \{q_{i-1}\}$ derived from LG(i) and LG($i - 1$).

C3: Binary multiplication with carry ensures that $a'_i \times q_i = a_i$ where $q_i = q_{i-1}$.

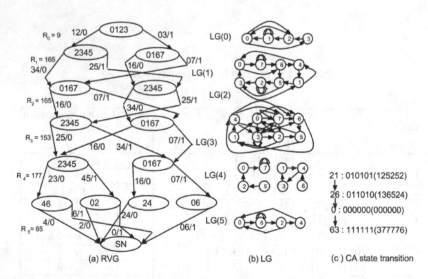

Fig. 5. RVG and LG(i) for 6 cell CA <9 165 165 153 177 65> (Example 1 CA, Section 2) with state 63 = <111111> = <377776> as SLA state

The following example illustrates CDCA synthesis procedure.

Example 2: Figure 5 shows the RVG and LG of Rule Vector < 9 165 165 153 177 65 > (Example 1 CA noted in Section 2). It identifies number 63 as a composite number. Partial STG of the CA (Figure 5(c)) shows that 21 reaches SLA 63 after 3 time steps. The RVG and LG are shown in Figure 5(a) and Figure 5(b). The octal and binary strings for the transition path $21 \to 26 \to 0 \to 63$ are noted in Figure 5(c). The CDCA is synthesized satisfying C1,C2,C3. At first sink triplet $<153\ 177\ 65>$ is picked from the sink triplet set such a way that $T^4 = T(7)$ and $T^5 = T(6)$ are compatible RMT pair and PSLRMTs. In LG(5) T(2) reaches T(6) after 3 time steps through RMT sequence $T(2) \to T(4) \to T(0) \to T(6)$ while in LG(4), T(5) reaches T(7) after same 3 time steps through RMT sequence $T(5) \to T(2) \to T(0) \to T(7)$. Each corresponding RMT pair in the paths (shown with bold edges) LG(4) and LG(5) are compatible & so forms a Locked LG path Pair. Binary multiplication of $1(a_5') \times (11)_2 = 1(a_5)$ with a carry 1 and $0(a_4')$ $\times (11)_2 = 1(a_4)$ after adding the carry. The multiplication constraint, as highlighted in Figure 5(c), ensures that $\{01\}$ (of 21) is the local factor of $\{11\}$ (of 63).

In next step, mid triplets $<165\ 153\ 177>$ and $<165\ 165\ 153>$ are picked satisfying constraints C1, C2, C3.

Finally, root triplet $<9\ 165\ 165>$ is picked. All the Locked LG path pairs picked out of Root Rule Triplet are shown in Figure 6.

Synthesized Rule Vector $<9\ 165\ 165\ 153\ 177\ 65>$ ensures that 63 in non-prime number and the largest factor is 21(010101).

A recursive CDCA synthesis algorithm is next formally introduced.

Algorithm 2: CDCA Synthesis Algorithm(n,N)

Input: (i) Rule Triplet (RT) Database, (ii) List of 8 bit prime numbers.
Output: N is prime or not.
Step 1: (a) (i) Calculate the set $\{q\}$ (odd numbers from 3 to $\sqrt{N}$),
　　　　　　(ii)trial set $\{t\}$=NULL.
Step 1: (b) If $n \leq 8$ try only by the input prime numbers.
Step 2: (a) Pick a sink triplet from sink triplet set satisfying C1,C2,C3
　　　　　　 and with set $\{q'\}$ derived out of LNG(n-1) & LNG(n-2).
Step 2: (b) If no sink triplet left go to Step 8.
Step 2: (c) Else for each q' ($q' \in \{q'\}$) call CDCA Synthesis Algorithm(n',q').
Step 2: (d) If q' is detected as prime go to Step 3.
Step 2: (e) If $\{q'\}$ list exhausted go to Step 2(a) to try with next sink TR.
Step 3: (a) If q' is not in $\{t\}$, Insert q' in set $\{t\}$ and repeat Steps 4 and 5 for (n-4) times.
Step 3: (b) Else go to Step 2(c).
Step 4: Pick a mid triplet from mid triplet set satisfying C1,C2,C3
　　　　　where the LG(i) node T'^i reach T^i after q' time steps.
Step 5: If no such mid triplet found go to Step 2(c) to try with next q'.
Step 6: Pick a root triplet from root triplet set satisfying C1,C2,C3
　　　　　where the LG(0) node T'^0 reach T^0 and LG(1) node T'^1
　　　　　reach T^1 after q' time steps and go to Step 9.
Step 7: If No root triplet found go to Step 2(c) to try with next q'.
Step 8: N is a prime.Stop.
Step 9: N is a Non-prime.Stop.

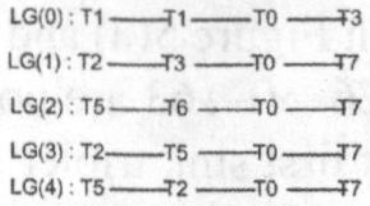

LG(0) : T1 —— T1 —— T0 —— T3
LG(1) : T2 —— T3 —— T0 —— T7
LG(2) : T5 —— T6 —— T0 —— T7
LG(3) : T2 —— T5 —— T0 —— T7
LG(4) : T5 —— T2 —— T0 —— T7

Fig. 6. Locked LG paths in adjacent LGs for $q = 000011$ identifying largest factor 21

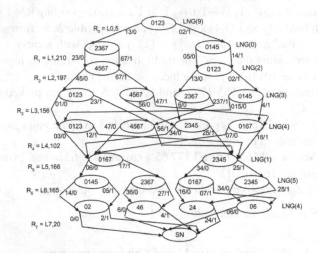

Fig. 7. RVG for the CA <5 210 197 156 102 166 165 20> with state 169 = <1010,1001> = <2525,2412> as SLA state

Recursive calls to CDCA synthesis algorithm is illustrated in the next example.

Example 3: Figure 7 shows the RVG of Rule Vector < 5 210 197 156 102 166 165 20 >. It identifies number 169 as a composite number as state 13(00001101) reaches state 169(10101001) after 13 time steps. Figure 8 shows a few LGs of the RVG.

For $q' = 3, 7, 11$ no sink RT is synthesized due to C3 constraint is not satisfied. After trial with $q' = 3, 7, 11$ the algorithm picks sink triplet <166 165 20> from the sink triplet set such a way that $T^7 = T(2)$ and $T^6 = T(1)$ are compatible RMT pair and PSLRMTs. In LG(7), T(2) reaches T(2) after 13 time steps through RMT sequence T(2) → T(6) → T(0) → T(0) → T(0) → T(4) → T(6) → T(4) → T(6) → T(4) → T(2) → T(2) → T(2) → T(2) while in LG(6), T(5) reaches T(1) after same 13 time steps through RMT sequence T(5) → T(3) → T(4) → T(4) → T(0) → T(2) → T(7) → T(2) → T(7) → T(6) → T(1) → T(1) → T(1) → T(1) Each corresponding RMT pair in LG(6) and LG(7) are compatible as p_6^j & $p_7^j (j= 1$ to 12) are compatible RMT pair. Also $T'^6 = T(5)$ and $T'^7 = T(2)$ are compatible RMT pair. Binary multiplication of $1(a_7') \times (1101)_2 = 1(a_7)$ with a carry 110 and $0(a_6') \times (1101)_2 = 0(a_6)$. The multiplication constraint ensures that {01} is the local factor of {01}. Next, executing Steps 4 & 5 iteratively, mid triplet <102 166 165>, <156 102 166>, <197 156 102>, <210 197 156> are picked in each iteration satisfying constraints C1, C2, C3. In Step 6 root triplet <5 210 197> is picked. Successful execution of the CDCA synthesis Algorithm ensures that 169 is a non-prime number and its largest factor is 13.

The CDCA synthesis algorithm is exhaustively tested for $n \leq 16$ bits. A few 32-bit composite numbers is also successfully tested by CDCA synthesis algorithm. Exhaustive testing with $n > 16$ is in progress.

Reachability Matrix M of LG Nodes

LG(0)	LG(1)	LG(4)	LG(6)	LG(7)
0 -> 2/3	0,5-> 4/5	0,3,4,7 -> 0/1/4/7	0 -> 2	0,6 -> 0/4
1 -> 0	1,4 -> 6/7	1,2,5,6 -> 2/3/6/7	1, -> 1	2,4 -> 2/6
2 -> 2,3	2 -> 0		2 -> 7	
3 -> 1	3 -> 1		3 -> 4	
	6 -> 2		4 -> 0/4	
	7 -> 3		5 -> 3/7	
			6 -> 1/5	
			7 -> 2/4	

Fig. 8. Few LGs of the CA <5 210 197 156 102 166 165 20>

5 Conclusion

This paper introduces CA theory and its application to address the age old problem of testing compositeness of a number.

References

1. Baillie, R., Wagstaff Jr., S.S.: Lucas pseudoprimes. Math. Comp. 35, 1391–1417 (1980)
2. Cohen, H., Lenstra Jr., H.W.: Primality testing and jacobi sums. Math. Comp. 42, 297–330 (1984)
3. Solovay, R.M., Strassen, V.: A fast monte-carlo test for primality. SIAM Journal on Computing 6(1), 84–85
4. Agrawal, M., Kayal, N., Saxena, N.: Primes is in p. Annals of Mathematics 160(2), 781–793 (2004)
5. Lenstra Jr., H.W., Pomerance, C.: Primality testing with gaussian periods (July 2005), Preprint Available as
   http://www.math.dartmouth.edu/~carlp/PDF/complexity072805.pdf
6. Miller, G.L.: Riemann's Hypothesis and Tests for Primality. Journal of Computer and System Sciences 13(3), 300–317 (1976), doi:10.1145/800116.803773
7. Maiti, N.S., Ghosh, S., Munshi, S., Pal Chaudhuri, P.: Linear Time Algorithm for Identifying the Invertibility of Null-Boundary Three Neighborhood Cellular Automata. Complex Systems 19(1) (2010)
8. Maiti, N.S., Ghosh, S., Sikdar, B.K., Pal Chaudhuri, P.: Rule Vector Graph (RVG) to Design Linear Time Algorithm for Identifying the Invertibility of Periodic-Boundary Three Neighborhood Cellular Automata. Journal of Cellular Automata 7(4), 335–362 (2012)
9. Ghosh, S., Maiti, N.S., Sikdar, B.K., Pal Chaudhuri, P.: On Invertible Three Neighborhood Null Boundary Uniform Cellular Automata. Complex Systems 20(1), 47–65 (2011)

Numerical Modelling of Fracture Based on Coupled Cellular Automata Finite Element Approach

Konrad Perzyński[*], Mateusz Sitko, and Łukasz Madej

AGH University of Science and Technology Al. Mickiewicza 30, 30-059, Cracow, Poland
kperzyns@agh.edu.pl

Abstract. Investigation of failure of Dual Phase steels on the basis of the developed concurrent cellular automata finite element model is the subject of the present paper. Physical background of phenomena responsible for failure in these steels is described first. Then details of the developed random cellular automata model are presented. Particular attention is put on proper definition of the transition rules describing initiation and propagation of fractures across the microstructure. Finally combined cellular automata finite element model is established. Examples of obtained results are also presented within the paper.

Keywords: cellular automata, finite element, dual phase steel, failure.

1   Introduction

The most widely used example of Advanced High Strength Steels (AHSS) are dual phase (DP) steels with the tensile strength of 400-1200 MPa. The name dual-phase was firstly reported by Hayami and Furukawa in (Hayami & Furukawa, 1975). The DP steels have been successfully applied in the production of the automobile structural parts because they are characterized by combination of a good formability, high bake hardenability and crash worthiness. These elevated properties are the results of the properly designed microstructure morphologies, which consists mainly of ferrite matrix (around 70-90%) and a hard martensitic phase (around 10-30%) as seen in Fig. 1. However, it has to be mentioned that small amount of bainite, perlite or retained austenite may also be present in the DP microstructure. Properties of DP steels are affected by many factors, including: volume fraction of martensite, average carbon content and carbon distribution in martensite, ductility of martensite, distribution of martensite, ferrite grain size, carbon distribution, alloying elements content in ferrite etc. (Calcagnotto, Adachi, Ponge, & Raabe, 2011). However, due to the combination of two phases with significantly different material properties, the DP steels are endangered by the probability of failure during manufacturing stages.

---

[*] Corresponding author.

J. Wąs, G.C. Sirakoulis, and S. Bandini (Eds.): ACRI 2014, LNCS 8751, pp. 156–165, 2014.

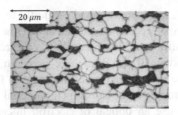

Fig. 1. Dual phase steel, white phase – ferrite, dark phase – martensite; LOM (Light Optical Microscopy)

2   Failure Mechanism in Dual Phases Steel

Failure in dual phase steels has in general ductile character, however influence of brittle failure mechanisms can also be clearly visible. When DP fracture is considered four mechanisms can be distinguished: cracking of martensite, decohesion at ferrite/martensite interface, decohesion between ferrite/ferrite interfaces and finally voids coalescence:

(a) cracking of martensite
Tensile test results demonstrated that cracks in martensite already occur at very low local strain levels.

(b) decohesion at ferrite/martensite interface
It is stated that, a dominant percentage of voids nucleates at higher strain levels at the ferrite/martensite interface by the decohesion.

(c) decohesion between ferrite/ferrite interfaces
Because of differences in hardness of the investigated phases, stress localization perpendicular to loading direction usually occurs leading to delamination of the ferrite grains.

(d) voids coalescence
Voids nucleated on the basis of above mentioned mechanisms starts to coalescence leading to fracture propagation. Voids propagate across the microstructure and elongate in the direction of straining, giving an increase in the void density and total void area fraction.

Conventional numerical approaches used to deal with fracture in steels fail to describe these mechanisms that are directly related to microscale features. Thus, modern numerical models based on the digital material representation are more often used (Asgari, Ghadbeigi, Pinna, & Hodgson, 2012; Vajragupta, et al., 2012; Perzyński & Madej, 2013).

3   Digital Material Representation (DMR)

The DMR is expected to create a possibility of analysing material behaviour in conditions that are difficult or even impossible to be monitored experimentally (Szyndler & Madej, 2013). The main objective of the DMR is creation of the digital representation of microstructure with its features represented explicitly to match real microstructure morphology. A description of recent developments in the DMR concept of single phase polycrystalline metallic materials in various research laboratories across the world is described in (Madej, 2010). While, the problem of generation of reliable representation of dual phase microstructure is presented in (Madej, 2012). One of the most commonly used solutions to obtain digital material representation of a dual phase microstructure is to use an optical or electron microscope picture and apply image processing methods (Rauch & Madej, 2010). This approach provides the possibility to obtain an exact representation of complex shapes of ferritic and martensitic phases, however information on particular grains within these phases is missing. Thus, in this article Authors developed an image processing algorithm capable to distinguish between two phases and subsequent grains. This is of importance during further development of the cellular automata model of DP steel failure.

First, microstructure image (Fig. 2a) is subjected to digital treatment with the threshold function. This step is realized in the GIMP software (GNU Image Manipulation) (the GIMP Documentation, 2013). The thresholding algorithm performs simple binarization procedure. White pixels represent the pixels of the image, which values are below the threshold range, and black pixels represent pixels with values higher than the threshold range. After thresholding, some noise can be observed in the image, which disrupts visual separation of the two phases (Fig. 2b). To remove that noise the filtering algorithm is applied (Fig. 2c). Finally erosion algorithm is applied to remove grain boundaries from the microstructure and leave only martensite islands in ferritic matrix as seen in Fig. 2d.

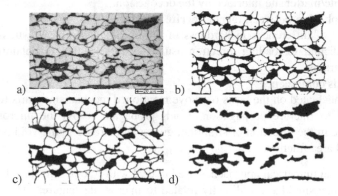

Fig. 2. a) Real microstructure image, and DMR images after b) thresholding c) filtering and d) removing grain boundaries algorithms

The binary form of the microstructure presented Fig. 2c, is an input for the second stage of the algorithm - separation and coloring procedure to identify subsequent ferrite grains. For this purpose the cellular automata (CA) (Sieradzki & Madej, 2013) based algorithm was used within the work. The algorithm involves coloring stage combined with the grain growth model. A single pixel in each grain is selected to represent a grain nuclei. Next, a simple transition rule is applied: when a neighbor of a particular cell in the previous time step is in the state 'already grown', then this particular cell can also change its state. The grains grow with no restrictions until they fill the entire investigated domain. As a result, each grain has the unique color identifier, what is shown in Fig. 3.

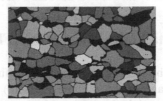

Fig. 3. Image after colorizing procedure

Another stage is required to remove thin grain boundaries and is also based on mentioned grain growth CA model. Main goal of this method is to remove all black cells from the image. The transition rule states that when one or more of the neighbors surrounding cell is black than the cell accepts a color of one of its neighbors. Procedure is repeated until all of the black cells change their color. It has to be emphasize that in the present work different colors of subsequent grains do not represent crystallographic orientations, they are just used to distinguish particular grains. The outcome of the model is presented in Fig. 4.

Fig. 4. Effect of the CA grain growth algorithm

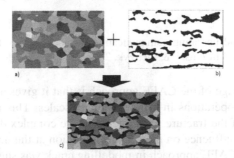

Fig. 5. Subsequent main steps of the developed image processing approach

As a result a temporary DMR without any black regions representing martensite islands is created. The last step of the algorithm is responsible for combining results obtained after simple image processing (Fig. 2d) with the temporary DMR from Fig. 4. Eventually, complex DP microstructure morphology is restored, where both martensite islands as well as subsequent ferrite grains are clearly visible.

Obtained digital material representation is now an input for the developed cellular automata finite element model of failure in Dual Phase steels.

4   Cellular Automata Finite Element (CAFE) Approach

When advantages provided by the CA are combined with the advantages of the FE approach the CAFE (Cellular Automata Finite Element) model is established. The basic assumption of this approach is that each method resolves a single physical problem in different scales. There are two types of multi scale models based on the CA: upscaling and concurrent (Madej, Mrozek, Kuś, Burczyński, & Pietrzyk, 2008) (Fig. 6). Upscaling (hierarchical) exists in the situation when constitutive model from the higher scale (FE) is created on the basis of results received from simulation at lower scale e.g. from a CA model. Concurrent (hybrid), when existing problem is resolved in parallel scales and the results are transferred during each simulation time step between computational domains.

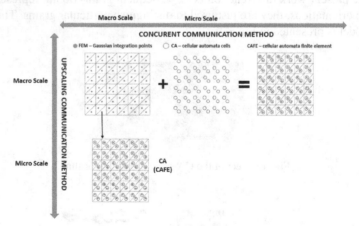

Fig. 6. Concurrent and upscaling communication methods used in the multiscale modelling (Madej, Mrozek, Kuś, Burczyński, & Pietrzyk, 2008)

The main advantage of the CAFE approach is that it gives an opportunity to simulate metal forming operations in different length scales. This is important especially during modelling of the fracture phenomena, where complex deformation state at the macro scale has an influence on the fracture initiation at the microscale and vice versa. First use of the CAFE approach in modelling crack was suggested by Beynon and Das in (Beynon, Das, Howard, Palmier, & Shterenlikht, 2002) and (Shterenlikht & Howard, 2006).

The concurrent cellular automata finite element model was developed in the present work to replicate mentioned above fracture initiation and propagation criteria.

In this approach each integration point is related with a single cellular automata cell. Thus, the random cellular automata approach was used in the investigation.

The first step in development of the cellular automata model is focused on definition of the CA space, internal variables, cells states and transition rules. As mentioned, the random cellular automata space was created that matches the finite element mesh computational domain. Five different kinds of cells internal variables were proposed in the model to reflect the underlying microstructure: *ferrite, martensite, buffer zone, ferrite-ferrite neighbor* and *ferrite-martensite neighbour*. Additionally, two types of cells states were defined: *no fracture* and *fracture*.

Cell states can change according to the defined transition rules, when fracture criteria are reached and local neighborhood gives opportunities for fracture initiation. Due to the fact that random cellular automata approach was selected for the investigation, cells has to define its neighbors at the beginning of each time step based on the predefined neighborhood radius R. All of cells, which are inside the prescribed circle belong to the neighborhood of a particular cell as seen Fig. 7.

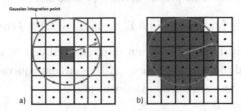

Fig. 7. CA random neighborhood communication method a) before choosing neighbors b) after choosing neighbors

In every time step $(t + 1)$ the CA model receives information from FE integration points about actual equivalent plastic strain and stress values. The information is used by defined transitions rules that designed to replicate mentioned above fracture mechanisms occurring in the DP steels. Transitions rules implemented in the model can change the state of the investigated cell from *not fracture* to *fracture* and are defined as follows:

- **martensite grains brittle fracture initiation rule**

$$Y_{m(martensite)}(t_{i+1}) = \begin{cases} fracture \Leftrightarrow A \\ Y_{m(martensite)}(t_i) \end{cases} \tag{1}$$

where: $Y_{m(martensite)}(t_{i+1})$ – state of the mth cell from the martensite phase at the t_{i+1} time step, A – logical function formulated on the basis of available knowledge about the considered phenomenon:

$$A = (\varepsilon_m \geq \varepsilon_f^{ml})$$

where: ε_m – equivalent plastic strain in considered cell belonging to martensite phase, ε_f^{ml} – critical equivalent plastic strain for fracture initiation in martensite phase.

- **martensite grains brittle fracture propagation rule**
  Part A in the equation (1) is described as:

$$A = (\varepsilon_m \geq \varepsilon_f^{mP}) \wedge Y_{m(martensite)}^l(t_i) = fracture$$

where: ε_m – equivalent plastic strain in considered cell belonging to martensite phase, ε_f^{mP} – critical equivalent plastic strain for fracture propagation in martensite phase, $Y_{m(martensite)}^l(t_i)$ – state of the lth neighbor of the mth cell from the martensite phase.

- **ferrite-martensite border ductile fracture initiation rule**

$$Y_{m(ferrite-martensite)}(t_{i+1}) = \begin{cases} fracture \Leftrightarrow A \\ Y_{m(ferrite-martensite)}(t_i) \end{cases} \qquad (2)$$

where: $Y_{m(ferrite-martensite)}(t_{i+1})$ – state of the mth cell from the border between ferrite and martensite phases at the t_{i+1} time step.

$$A = \left(\varepsilon_m \geq \varepsilon_f^{fmI}\right) \wedge Y_{m(martensite)}^l(t_i) = fracture$$

where: ε_m – equivalent plastic strain in considered cell belonging to border between ferrite and martensite phases, ε_f^{fmI} – critical equivalent plastic strain for fracture initiation between ferrite-martensite phase.

- **ferrite-martensite border ductile fracture propagation rule**
  Part A in the equation (2) is described as:

$$A = (\varepsilon_m \geq \varepsilon_f^{fmP}) \wedge Y_{m(ferrite-martensite)}^l(t_i) = fracture$$

where: ε_f^{fmP} – critical equivalent plastic strain for fracture propagation between ferrite-martensite phase, $Y_{m(ferrite-martensite)}^l(t_i)$ – state of the lth neighbor of the mth cell from the border between ferrite and martensite phases.

- **ferrite-ferrite border ductile fracture initiation rule**

$$Y_{m(ferrite-ferrite)}(t_{i+1}) = \begin{cases} fracture \Leftrightarrow A \\ Y_{m(ferrite-ferrite)}(t_i) \end{cases} \qquad (3)$$

where: $Y_{m(ferrite-ferrite)}(t_{i+1})$ – state of the mth cell from the border between ferrite and ferrite phases at the t_{i+1} time step.

$$A = \left(\varepsilon_m \geq \varepsilon_f^{ffI}\right) \wedge Y_{m(ferrite-martensite)}^l(t_i) = fracture$$

where: : ε_m – equivalent plastic strain in considered cell belonging to border between ferrite and ferrite phases, ε_f^{ffI} – critical equivalent plastic strain for fracture initiation between ferrite phases.

- **ferrite-ferrite border ductile fracture propagation rule**
  Part A in the equation (3) is described as:

$$A = (\varepsilon_m \geq \varepsilon_f^{ffP}) \wedge Y_{m(ferrite-ferrite)}^l(t_i) = fracture$$

where: ε_f^{ffP} – critical equivalent plastic strain for fracture initiation between ferrite-ferrite phase, $Y_{m(ferrite-ferrite)}^l(t_i)$ – state of the lth neighbor of the mth cell from the border between ferrite phases.

- **ferrite grains ductile fracture initiation and propagation rule**

$$Y_{m(ferrite)}(t_{i+1}) = \begin{cases} fracture \Leftrightarrow A \\ Y_{m(ferrite)}(t_i) \end{cases} \tag{4}$$

where: $Y_{m(ferrite)}(t_{i+1})$ – state of the mth cell from the ferrite phase at the t_{i+1} time step,

$$A = (\varepsilon_m \geq \varepsilon_f^{fIP})$$

where: ε_f^{fIP} – critical equivalent plastic strain for fracture initiation and propagation in ferrite phase.

The cellular automata model parameters were identified on the basis of the literature data presented in (Avramovic-Cingaraa, Ososkov, Jain, & Wilkinson, 2009). As a case study, a simple tension test was selected for the present research to show model capabilities. Initial microstructure morphology was obtained on the basis of described image processing algorithm and then it was discretized using 130 000 three node linear plane strain triangle finite elements (CPE3) (Fig. 8). The applied specific mesh was obtained with developed FE mesh generation software (Madej, Krużel, Cybułka, Perzyński, & Banaś, 2012). To ensure the continuity of solutions space, left-right periodic boundary conditions were employed. To enforce periodicity to the DMR authors added a specific buffer zone to create an investigated DMR. Based on simple rule of mixture different material definitions were adopted to surrounding buffer zone for the investigated cases. Finite element model was created in the commercial ABAQUS application. The cellular automata model was incorporated into the solution via subroutine VUMAT written in C++ and Fortran.

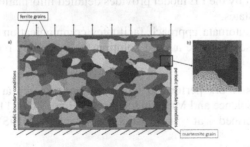

Fig. 8. a) DMR before tension test and b) size of FE discretization density

Example of obtained results from the CAFE model after 0.27 of deformation are presented in Fig. 9.

It can be found that brittle fractures start to initiate from the 0.14 engineering strain.

Full brittle fracture propagation ends when strain is equal to 0.23. In the same

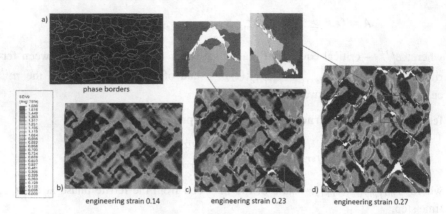

Fig. 9. Microstructure a) before applied deformation and equivalent strain distribution after b) 0.14, c) 0.23 and d) 0.27 of deformation

time decohesion at the borders between ferrite-martensite phases starts to initiate and propagate. When strain value increase to 0.27, fractures starts to grow along the ferrite-ferrite borders and finally coalescence with other cracks leading to complete material failure.

5   Conclusions

Possibility of using the CAFE approach for modeling fracture behaviour in DP steel grades was clearly presented in the paper. Based on the presented research it can be concluded that:

— modified image processing algorithm provides digital material representation of dual phase steel with explicit representation of subsequent grains,
— complicated failure system existing in multiphase materials can be successfully modeled at the microscale with the CA method,
— additional support by the FE model provides detailed information on changes in the strain and stress states,
— random cellular automata approach facilitates communication with the finite element mesh, and seems to be a good solution for modelling phenomena occurring during plastic deformation.

Acknowledgements. Work performed within statute research at the Department of Applied Computer Science and Modeling at the AGH no. 11.11.110.291. The calculations were performed at the ACK Cyfronet: MNiSW/IBM_BC_HS21/ AGH/076/2010.

References

Asgari, A., Ghadbeigi, H., Pinna, C., Hodgson, P.D.: Multiscale modelling of stress and strain partitioning in high strength dual phase steels. Computer Methods in Materials Science (12), 163–174 (2012)

Avramovic-Cingaraa, G., Ososkov, Y., Jain, M.K., Wilkinson, D.S.: Effect of martensite distribution on damage behaviour in DP600 dual phase steels. Materials Science and Engineering A 516, 7–16 (2009)

Beynon, J.H., Das, S., Howard, I.C., Palmier, E.J., Shterenlikht, A.: The combination of cellular automata and finite elements for the study of fracture; the CAFE model of fracture. In: ECF14 - 14th European Conference on Fracture, Krakow, 241–248 (2002)

Calcagnotto, M., Adachi, Y., Ponge, D., Raabe, D.: Deformation and fracture mechanisms in fine- and ultrafine-grained ferrite/martensite dual-phase steels and the effect of aging. Acta Materialia 59, 658–670 (2011)

Hayami, S., Furukawa, T.: A family of high, cold-rolled steels. In: Microalloying Strenght 1975 (1975)

Madej, L.: Digital Material Representation of Polycrystals in Application to Numerical Simulations of Inhomogeneous Deformation. Computer Methods in Materials Science 10, 1–13 (2010)

Madej, L.: Realistic description of dual phase steel morphology on the basis of the Monte Carlo method. Computer Methods in Materials Science 12(3), 197–206 (2012)

Madej, L., Krużel, P., Cybułka, P., Perzyński, K., Banaś, B.: Generation of dedicated finite element meshes for multiscale applications with Delaunay triangulation and adaptive finite element - cellular automata algorithms. Computer Methods in Materials Science 12(2), 85–96 (2012)

Madej, L., Mrozek, A., Kuś, W., Burczyński, T., Pietrzyk, M.: Concurrent and upscaling methods in multi scale modelling - case studies. Computer Methods in Materials Science 8(1), 1–15 (2008)

Perzyński, K., Madej, L.: Numerical analysis of influence of the martensite volume fraction on DP steels behavior during plastic deformation. Archives of Metallurgy and Materials 58(1), 211–215 (2013)

Rauch, L., Madej, L.: Application of the automatic image processing in modelling of the deformation mechanisms based on the digital representation of microstructure. International Journal for Multiscale Computational Engineering 8(3), 343–356 (2010)

Shterenlikht, A., Howard, I.: The CAFE model of fracture - application to a TMCR steel. Fatigue and Fracture of Engineering Materials and Structures 29(9-10), 770–787 (2006)

Sieradzki, L., Madej, L.: A perceptive comparison of the cellular automata and Monte Carlo techniques in application to static recrystallization modeling in polycrystalline materials. Computational Materials Science 67, 156–173 (2013)

Szyndler, J., Madej, L.: Effect of number of grains and boundary conditions on digital material representation deformation under plane strain. Archives of Civil and Mechanical Engineering (2013) (in press)

The GIMP Documentation, GIMP (2013), http://docs.gimp.org/ (retrieved August 14, 2013)

Vajragupta, N., Uthaisangsuk, V., Schmaling, B., Münstermann, S., Hartmaier, A., Bleck, W.: A micromechanical damage simulation of dual phase steels using XFEM. Computational Materials Science (54), 271–279 (2012)

Two-Layer CA Model for Simulating Catalytic Reaction at Dynamically Varying Temperature*

Anastasia Kireeva

The Institute of Computational Mathematics and Mathematical Geophysics, SB RAS
Prospekt Akademika Lavrentieva 6, Novosibirsk, Russia
kireeva@ssd.sscc.ru

Abstract. A two-layer cellular automata (CA) model of carbon monoxide (CO) oxidation reaction on platinum is proposed and investigated. This reaction in non-equilibrium conditions can be accompanied by appearance of surface waves, spirals and turbulences on the catalyst. A two-layer CA is a parallel composition of the two CA: the main CA simulating the oxidation reaction, and the second layer CA simulating spatio-temporal distribution of the catalyst surface temperature. Using the second layer allows us to take into account changes of surface catalytic properties when temperature changes and investigate the oxidation reaction dynamics for different temperature.

Keywords: two-layer cellular automaton, composition of cellular automata, catalytic reaction, surface temperature variation, surface waves, reagents concentration oscillation.

1 Introduction

The catalytic reaction of carbon monoxide (CO) oxidation on the platinum group metals is interesting both from practical and fundamental standpoints. In the catalytic reaction, different self-organization phenomena such as surface waves, spirals and rings may appear. Moreover, the reaction dynamics depends on external factors: reagents partial pressure, surface and gas temperature. Thus, the CO oxidation catalytic reaction is a complex nonlinear system. A powerful method of such a systems investigation is cellular automata simulation. Cellular automata (CA) models of various physical, chemical, social phenomena are described and studied by many researchers [1]-[6].

The CO oxidation reaction over platinum (Pt_{100}) surface is simulated by Monte Carlo method [7]. This model uses constant rates coefficients of reaction stages without allowance for the reaction dynamics at temperature variation. A two-layer CA makes possible simulating CO oxidation reaction allowing for surface temperature variations. The first layer CA simulates the reaction dynamics depending on surface temperature, which is simulated by the second layer CA.

---

* Supported by 1) Russian Fund for Basic Research, Project 14-01-31425-mol-a (2014), 2) Russian Fund for Basic Research, Project 12-03-00766-a, 3) Siberian Branch of Russian Academy of Sciences, Interdisciplinary Project 47.

J. Wąs, G.C. Sirakoulis, and S. Bandini (Eds.): ACRI 2014, LNCS 8751, pp. 166–175, 2014.

The aim of this research is developing the CO oxidation reaction over Pt catalyst CA-model allowing for surface temperature changes and studying the dynamics reaction for different temperature distributions.

This paper consists of Introduction, three sections and Conclusion. The first section includes the description of CO oxidation reaction mechanism and formulas for calculation of the rate coefficients depending on temperature. The second section describes a two-layer CA-model of the reaction: the main CA and the second layer CA. Results of CA simulation are presented in Section 3.

2   The Mechanism of CO Oxidation Reaction over Pt_{100}

In the course of the CO oxidation reaction, moving gas molecules of CO and O_2 strike at the catalyst and adsorb. On the catalyst surface neighbouring adsorbed molecules of CO and O_2 immediately form CO_2, which desorbs from the catalyst to the gas. Experimental and theoretical studies show that in the course of the CO oxidation reaction, the Pt_{100} surface structure is reconstructed from a cubic (1×1) to a hexagonal (hex) structure under the influence of the adsorbed CO [8,9]. In [7], the following mechanism of the reaction is studied:

$$s_1 : CO_{gas} + * \xrightarrow{p_1} CO_{ads} \text{ - CO adsorption from gas;}$$

$$s_2 : CO_{ads}^{hex} \xrightarrow{p_2} CO_{gas} + *_{hex} \text{ - CO desorption from the active center } *_{hex};$$

$$s_3 : CO_{ads}^{1 \times 1} \xrightarrow{p_3} CO_{gas} + *_{1 \times 1} \text{ - CO desorption from the active center } *_{1 \times 1};$$

$$s_4 : 4CO_{ads} \xrightarrow{p_4} 4CO_{ads}^{1 \times 1} \text{ - CO}_{ads} \text{ induced phase transition } hex \to 1 \times 1;$$

$$s_5 : *_{1 \times 1} \xrightarrow{p_5} *_{hex} \text{ - structural phase transition } 1 \times 1 \to hex; \tag{1}$$

$$s_6 : O_{2(gas)} + 2*_{1 \times 1} \xrightarrow{p_6} 2O_{ads}^{1 \times 1} \text{ - O}_2 \text{ adsorption on the neighbouring } *_{1 \times 1};$$

$$s_7 : O_{2(gas)} + 2*_{hex} \xrightarrow{p_7} 2O_{ads}^{hex} \text{ - O}_2 \text{ adsorption on the neighbouring } *_{hex};$$

$$s_8 : CO_{ads} + * \xrightarrow{p_8} * + CO_{ads} \text{ - CO}_{ads} \text{ diffusion over the surface;}$$

$$s_9 : CO_{ads} + O_{ads} \to CO_{2(gas)} + 2 * \text{ - interaction between CO}_{ads} \text{ and O}_{ads}.$$

Here the symbols "$*_{hex}$", "$*_{1 \times 1}$" and "$*$" denote the vacant active center of the surface with hexagonal, cubic and an arbitrary structure (hex or 1×1), respectively. The symbols $s_1 - s_9$ in (1) denote elementary stages of the oxidation reaction.

According to the algorithm proposed in [7], the active centers of a catalyst surface are chosen at random, and one of the above-mentioned stages s_i is chosen with probability p_i calculated by the formula:

$$p_i = k_i / \sum_{l=1}^{8} k_l, i = 1, \ldots, 8, \tag{2}$$

where k_i is a rate coefficient of the i-th stage.

In [7], $k_i, i = 1, \ldots, 7$, are constant values corresponding to the surface temperature $T = 480$ K, whereas in this paper, the rate coefficients depend on the surface temperature and are calculated by the Arrhenius equation:

$$k_i = v_i \cdot exp[-E_i/(R \cdot T)], \; i = 2, 3, 4, 5, 8, \qquad (3)$$

where v_i is a pre-exponential factor determined by the frequency of molecules collisions, E_i is the activation energy equal to the minimum energy required to start a chemical reaction, $R = 1.985875 \cdot 10^{-3}$ [kcal $\cdot$ K^{-1} $\cdot$ mol^{-1}] is the Universal gas constant and T is the absolute temperature on the Kelvin scale.

The values of v_i and E_i for the stages s_i, $i = 2, 3, 4, 5, 8$, of CO oxidation reaction are specified in [10]: $v_2 = 4 \cdot 10^{13}$ [s^{-1}], $v_3 = 3 \cdot 10^{15}$ [s^{-1}], $v_4 = 10^{15}$ [s^{-1}], $v_5 = 5 \cdot 10^{11}$ [s^{-1}], $v_8 = 0.68$ [cm^2/s], $E_2 = 28.5$ [kcal/mol], $E_3 = 37.3$ [kcal/mol], $E_4 = 31.9$ [kcal/mol], $E_5 = 25$ [kcal/mol], $E_8 = 7$ [kcal/mol].

A pre-exponential factor of diffusion v_8 is specified in [10] as 0.68 [cm$^2 \cdot$ s^{-1}]. To compare v_8 with other pre-exponential factors, it should be evaluated in the s^{-1} units. In this paper, the pre-exponential factor of diffusion v_8 is taken about $6 \cdot 10^6$ [s^{-1}]. The oscillations of reagents concentrations, coinciding with [7], are obtained by computing experiments for this value of v_8.

The rate coefficients k_1, k_6 and $k_7 = k_6 \cdot 10^{-3}$ are determined by the partial pressure and do not depend on the surface temperature. The stage s_9 is realized immediately after CO and O$_2$ adsorption or after diffusion if CO$_{ads}$ and O$_{ads}$ appear in the nearest neighbor.

3 The Two-Layer CA Model of CO Oxidation Reaction over Pt$_{100}$

For simulating the CO oxidation reaction dynamics with the temperature influence, a two-layer CA is used. The two-layer CA is a parallel composition [11] of two cellular automata: the main CA ($\aleph_{CO}$) simulating the oxidation reaction and the CA of second layer ($\aleph_T$) simulating a temperature spatio-temporal distribution on the catalyst surface:

$$\aleph_S = \varUpsilon(\aleph_{CO}, \aleph_T). \qquad (4)$$

In the general case, a CA is defined by the four concepts [3,11]: $\aleph = \langle A, X, \Theta, \mu \rangle$, where A is a cells *state alphabet*, X is a *set of names*, Θ is a *local operator*, μ is a *operation mode*. A *cell* is represented by a pair $(u, (i, j))$, where $u \in A$ is a cell state, $(i, j) \in X$ is a cell name. Alphabet A represents possible states of the investigated system. A set of names X is a set of integer coordinates of cells in the discrete space corresponding to the system space. The local operator Θ defines the cells states updating rules according to the system behavior. The operation mode μ defines the order of the local operator Θ application to the cells $(i, j) \in X$.

3.1 The Main CA Simulating the CO Oxidation Reaction over Pt

A CA simulating the CO oxidation reaction is defined as follows.

$$\aleph_{CO} = \langle A_{CO}, X_{CO}, \Theta_{CO}, \alpha \rangle. \tag{5}$$

The state alphabet A_{CO} is chosen according to the reagents participating in reaction (1): $A = \{*_{1\times1}, *_{hex}, CO_{ads}^{1\times1}, CO_{ads}^{hex}, O_{ads}^{1\times1}, O_{ads}^{hex}\}$, where $*_{1\times1}$ and $*_{hex}$ denote the vacant active center of the surface with hexagonal and cubic structures, $CO_{ads}^{1\times1}$ and CO_{ads}^{hex} are carbon monoxide adsorbed on 1×1 and hex centers, $O_{ads}^{1\times1}$ and O_{ads}^{hex} are oxygen adsorbed on 1×1 and hex centers, respectively.

The set of names is $X_{CO} = \{(i,j) : i = 1, \ldots, M_i, j = 1, \ldots, M_j\}$. On X_{CO}, naming functions $\varphi(i,j) : X_{CO} \to X_{CO}$ are introduced. A naming function determines one of the neighbors for a cell with the name (i,j). A set of naming functions determines an underlying template $T(i,j)$, defining the nearest neighbors of the cell (i,j). In the CA model $\aleph_{CO}$, the templates shown in Fig. 1 are used.

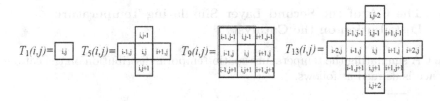

Fig. 1. Underlying templates used in the CA-model of oxidation reaction

The local operator $\Theta_{CO}(i,j)$ defines the rules of cells states updating according to the stages of oxidation reaction (1), $\Theta_{CO}(i,j)$ is a system of substitutions $\theta_l, l \in \{2,3,4,5\}$, and their superpositions $\theta_{(l,9)} = \theta_9(\theta_l)$, $l \in \{1,6,7,8\}$:

$$\Theta_{CO}(i,j) = \{\theta_{(1,9)}, \theta_2, \theta_3, \theta_4, \theta_5, \theta_{(6,9)}, \theta_{(7,9)}, \theta_{(8,9)}\}. \tag{6}$$

Each substitution $\theta_l \in \Theta_{CO}(i,j)$ corresponds to the elementary stage s_l. The application of $\Theta_{CO}(i,j)$ to the cell (i,j) consists in the choice of one of the substitutions either θ_l or $\theta_{(l,9)}$ with probability p_l (2) and calculation of the new states of cells in $T(i,j)$.

The substitutions θ_l, $l \in \{2,3,4,5\}$, are applied to a single cell, hence the template $T_1(i,j)$ is used. The substitution θ_4 is applied to a block consisting of four neighboring cells. The block is chosen at random out of the template $T_9(i,j)$. For application of θ_l, $l \in \{6,7,8,9\}$, two cells are required: (i,j) and one of its four neighbors $\varphi_k(i,j) \in T_5(i,j)$, $k = 1,2,3,4$, is chosen with probability 0.25.

The application of $\theta_{(l,9)} = \theta_9(\theta_l)$, $l = 6,7,8$, is performed as follows. At first, θ_l is applied to the cell (i,j). Immediately after that, θ_9 is applied to both cells: (i,j) and $\varphi_k(i,j)$, using four neighbors of (i,j) and four neighbors of

$\varphi_k(i,j) \in T_5(i,j)$. Thus, the application of $\theta_{(l,9)} = \theta_9(\theta_l)$, $l = 6, 7, 8$, requires to use the template $T_{13}(i,j) = \bigcup_{k=1}^{4} T_5(\varphi_k(i,j))$.

The application of superposition $\theta_{(1,9)} = \theta_9(\theta_1)$ requires the template $T_5(i,j)$ since the substitution θ_1 is applied to the cell (i,j), then the substitution θ_9 is applied to this cell, using one of four neighboring cells $\varphi_k(i,j) \in T_5(i,j)$.

The operation mode of $\aleph_{CO}$ is asynchronous. This mode prescribes the local operator to be applied to a randomly chosen cell, changing its state immediately. The simulation process is divided into *iterations*. An iteration of $\aleph_{CO}$ is $| X_{CO} |$ $\cdot M_{diff}$ application of the substitutions $\theta_l \in \Theta_{CO}(i,j)$ to randomly chosen cells $(i,j) \in X_{CO}$, M_{diff} being a parameter of CO diffusion intensity. The diffusion in the oxidation reaction occurs M_{diff} times more often than other chemical processes, therefore iteration of $\aleph_{CO}$ is M_{diff} times increased. According to [7,8], M_{diff} is selected in the range $50 \div 100$.

An iteration transfers the cellular array $\Omega(t)$ into $\Omega(t+1)$, where t is an iteration number. The sequence $\sum(\Omega) = \Omega(0), \ldots, \Omega(t), \Omega(t+1), \ldots, \Omega(t_{fin})$ is named *evolution*.

3.2   The CA of the Second Layer Simulating Temperature Distribution on the Catalyst

The CA simulating the temperature spatio-temporal distribution on the catalyst surface is defined as follows:

$$\aleph_T = \langle A_T, X_T, \Theta_T, \alpha \rangle. \tag{7}$$

The state alphabet $A_T = \{u \in \mathbb{R}\}$ corresponds to values of the catalyst surface temperature. The set of names $X_T = \{(i,j) : i = 1, \ldots, M_i, j = 1, \ldots, M_j\}$ corresponds to coordinates on the catalyst surface. The underlying template of $\aleph_T$ is $T_5(i,j)$.

The temperature spatio-temporal evolution on the catalyst surface is simulated by the multi-particle CA model for diffusion simulation [12], except for one feature. In $\aleph_T$, the cells states are real numbers as opposed to those in the multi-particle CA model, where cells states are integer numbers. The main idea of this CA model is as follows. A cell state is divided into two parts according to the value of γ: $u = (1 - \gamma) \cdot u + \gamma \cdot u$, where γ is a parameter determining the model diffusion rate, the neighboring cells exchanging values of their second parts.

The local operator Θ_T is determined on the basis of [12] as follows:

$$\Theta_T(i,j) = \{(u, (i,j))(u_k, \varphi_k(i,j))\} \rightarrow \{(u\prime, (i,j))(u_k\prime, \varphi_k(i,j))\}, \tag{8}$$
$$u\prime = (1 - \gamma) \cdot u + \gamma \cdot u_k, \quad u_k\prime = (1 - \gamma) \cdot u_k + \gamma \cdot u, \quad k = 1, 2, 3, 4.$$

The operation mode of $\aleph_T$ is asynchronous. An iteration of $\aleph_T$ is $| X_T |$ applications of the local operator Θ_T to randomly chosen cells $(i,j) \in X_T$.

3.3   A Parallel Composition of $\aleph_{CO}$ and $\aleph_T$

In the course of the CO oxidation reaction a cooling down or heating of some parts of the surface proceeds which cause a change in the reaction properties of the catalyst. Hence, a inhomogeneous distribution of temperature over the catalyst produces different reaction rates for different parts of the surface. A two-layer CA enables one to simulate the reaction dynamics under such inhomogeneous changes in the catalyst properties.

As mentioned above, the two-layer CA $\aleph_S$ is a parallel composition of the main CA $\aleph_{CO}$ (5) and CA of the second layer $\aleph_T$ (7). According to [11], the parallel composition is defined as follows. Between the names sets of $\aleph_{CO}$ and $\aleph_T$ there exists a one-to-one correspondence: $X_{CO} = \gamma(X_T)$. The cells states of $\aleph_{CO}$ depend on the cells states of $\aleph_T$ in the following way. The probability of $\theta_l \in \Theta_{CO}(i,j)$, $l = 1, \ldots, 8$, application to the cell $(i,j) \in X_{CO}$ is a function of state of the second layer cell $(i,j) \in X_T$.

Thus, the simulation algorithm is as follows. The cell $(i,j) \in X_{CO}$ is randomly selected. For this, the cell corresponding to that of the second layer $(i,j) \in X_T$ is selected. New values of the rate coefficient k_l, $l = 1, \ldots, 8$, are calculated by (3) for the cell state $(i,j) \in X_T$. Then the new values of probabilities p_l, $l = 1, \ldots, 8$, are calculated by (2) and one of the substitutions $\theta_l \in \Theta_{CO}(i,j)$, $l = 1, \ldots, 8$, is chosen with probability p_l and applied to the cell $(i,j) \in X_{CO}$. Each iteration of the two-layer CA $\aleph_S$ includes one iteration of $\aleph_{CO}$ and one iteration of $\aleph_T$.

4   The Results of the CA Simulation of CO Oxidation Reaction over Pt

The CO oxidation reaction is simulated by means of the two-layer CA $\aleph_S$ with the cellular array size $M_i \times M_j = 400 \times 400$ cells for different values of k_1 and k_6. The diffusion intensity value is $M_{\text{diff}} = 50$. The temperature diffusion rate γ is equal to 0.8. At the initial moment, all the cells states of the main CA $\aleph_{CO}$ are $*_{\text{hex}}$, corresponding to a free catalyst surface with a hexagonal structure. Initial cellular array of the second layer CA $\aleph_T$ is different for different computing experiments, it is the model parameter. For annihilation of boundary effects, the periodic boundary conditions are used.

In the course of the simulation, the following characteristics are obtained: concentrations of reagents adsorbed on the catalytic surface per one cell: $n(O_{\text{ads}})$ and $n(CO_{\text{ads}})$, intensity of CO_2 formation per one cell: $v(CO_2)$, a portion of the surface with cubic and hexagonal structure per one cell: $n(1 \times 1)$ and $n(hex)$.

The computing experiment is carried out with the same parameters as in [7]: $k_1 = 14.7$ and $k_6 = 56$. The initial state of $\aleph_T$ is taken as follows:

$$(u,(i,j)) : \quad u = \begin{cases} T_c = 480\ K, & \text{if } i \in [50; 350]\ \&\ j \in [50; 350], \\ T_b = 200\ K, & \text{otherwise.} \end{cases} \tag{9}$$

Thus, at $t = 0$, the catalyst surface has a high temperature of $480\ K$ in the central 300×300 square and a low temperature $200\ K$ on the borders (Fig. 2 a).

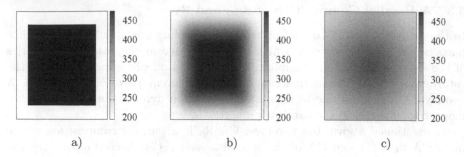

a)   b)   c)

Fig. 2. The spatio-temporal distribution of temperature over the catalyst surface: a) at the initial time; b) at the 1,000-th iteration; c) at the 8,000-th iteration

Then temperature is gradually equalized on the whole catalyst surface owing to a heat transfer from the heated central part to cold borders. Heat transfer obtained by $\aleph_T$ evolution is presented in Fig. 2 b, c. Here, the black color represents heat, the white color representing cold.

As a result of the CA simulation with the two-layer CA $\aleph_S$, the following dynamics of CO oxidation reaction is observed (Fig. 3). In the beginning, the platinum surface is in the *hex* state (Fig. 3 a) with temperature distribution

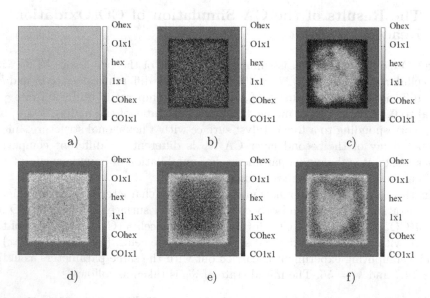

a)   b)   c)

d)   e)   f)

Fig. 3. Changes in adsorbed reagents coverages $CO_{ads} \leftrightarrow O_{ads}$ during the reaction: a) the surface in the *hex* state (the initial time); b) the surface covered with CO_{ads} (the 30-th iteration); c) O_2 adsorption (the 40-th iteration); d) the surface covered with O_{ads} (the 55-th iteration); e) the central part of surface covered with CO_{ads} (the 105-th iteration); f) the central part of surface covered with O_{ads} (the 120-th iteration)

shown in Fig. 2 a. The rate coefficients values are greater for the heated surface. Hence, the oxidation reaction occurs only on the heated central square, whereas on the borders with a low temperature reaction does not occur. Since the probability of the CO adsorption at the hexagonal active centers is greater than that of the O_2 adsorption, CO_{ads} accumulates on the surface (Fig. 3 b). Simultaneously with CO_{ads} accumulation, due to the phase reconstruction of the surface (stage s_4), 1×1 surface portion increases. Since probability of O_2 adsorption on 1×1 surface exceeds that of CO adsorption, oxygen is adsorbed on the catalyst surface (Fig. 3 c) and interacts with CO_{ads}. Due to this interaction, a portion of the vacant active centres $*_{1 \times 1}$ increases. However, a free 1×1 surface is unstable, $*_{1 \times 1}$ centers are reconstructed in $*_{hex}$ owing to spontaneous phase transition (stage s_5). An increase of hex surface portion again creates favourable conditions for CO adsorption.

Meanwhile, by this time the temperature of initially heated square borders decreases owing to the heat transfer and, consequently, the rate coefficients values

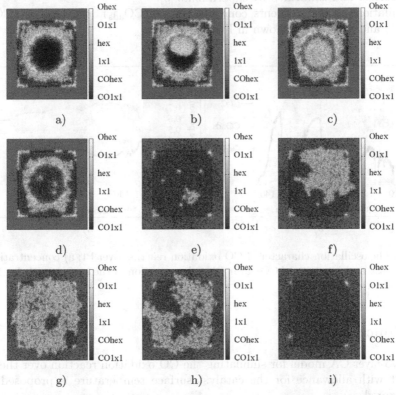

Fig. 4. Changes in coverages $CO_{ads} \leftrightarrow O_{ads}$ at surface temperature equalizing: a) CO_{ads} circle inside O_{ads} ring; b) formation of O_{ads} wave inside CO_{ads} circle; c) O_{ads} circle in the catalyst center, d) CO_{ads} coverage inside O_{ads} ring; e) CO_{ads} coverage of the catalyst surface; f) propagation of O_{ads} starting from separate islands; g) O_{ads} coverage of the surface; h) propagation of CO_{ads}; i) CO_{ads} coverage of the surface

decrease for these active centers. Therefore, on the surface borders reconstruction of $*_{1 \times 1}$ into $*_{hex}$ centers does not occur. Thus, on the initially heated square borders, O_{ads} accumulates and does not desorb (Fig. 3 d). Whereas on the heated central square alternating CO and O_2 adsorption again occurs (Fig. 3 e, f). In result, oscillations of adsorbed reagents coverages are observed.

When the surface temperature is equalizing over the catalyst (Fig. 2 c), O_{ads} circle appears in the initially heated square. Then, changes in the reagents coverage of CO_{ads} into O_{ads} and vice versa occur only inside this oxygen circle at the catalyst center (Fig. 4 a - d).

Further, at temperature equalization, CO_{ads} and O_{ads} islands are being spread over the whole surface. However, complete surface coverage by one reagent is not formed. For example, Fig. 4 e - f shows one cycle of the changes in coverages $CO_{ads} \leftrightarrow O_{ads}$. There are O_{ads} islands on the surface mainly covered by CO_{ads}. Oxygen islands are propagated by the surface, CO_{ads} islands continually staying on the catalyst and growing slowly. Gradually CO_{ads} again covers the whole surface except several small O_{ads} islands. Such behaviour of the reaction is physically correct and confirmed by experiments [9].

Oscillations of the reagents concentrations $n(CO_{ads})$, $n(O_{ads})$, $n(v(CO_2))$, $n(1 \times 1)$ and $n(hex)$ are shown in Fig. 5.

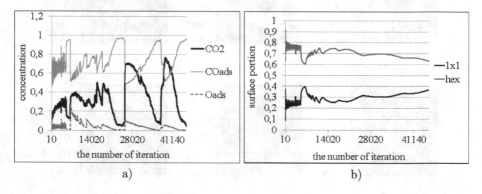

Fig. 5. The oscillation character of CO oxidation reaction over Pt: a) concentration of CO_{ads}, O_{ads} and intensity of CO_2 formation; b) a portion of the surface with 1×1 and hex structures

5   Conclusion

The two-layer CA model for simulating the CO oxidation reaction over the surface Pt with allowance for the catalyst surface temperature is proposed and investigated.

It was found that CA $\aleph_S$ demonstrates oscillations of adsorbed reagents concentrations, CO_2 formation intensity, and a portion with 1×1 and hex surface structures. The oscillations are accompanied by different chemical waves on the modeling surface. The oxidation reaction dynamics changes with variation of the surface temperature at the heat transfer. The two-layer CA makes possible to simulate and study the reaction behavior for a variable catalyst temperature.

References

1. Wolfram, S.: Cellular Automata as Simple Self-Organizing Systems. Caltech preprint CALT-68-938 (1982), http://www.stephenwolfram.com/publications/articles/ca/82-cellular/index.html
2. Young, D.A.: A local activator-inhibitor model of vertebrate skin patterns. In: Wolfram, S. (ed.) Theory and Applications of Cellular Automata. Advanced series on complex systems, vol. 1, pp. 320–327. World Scientific Publishing (1986)
3. Bandman, O.L.: Cellular Automatic Models of Spatial Dynamics. System Informatics - Methods and Models of Modern Programming 10, 59–113 (2006) (in Russian)
4. Vanag, V.K.: Dissipative structures in reaction-diffusion systems. In: Izhevsk, M. (ed.) Regular and Chaotic Dynamics, p. 300. Institute of computer researches (2008) (in Russian)
5. Sirakoulis, G.C., Karafyllidis, I., Soudris, D., Georgoulas, N., Thanailakis, A.: A new simulator for the oxidation process in integrated circuit fabrication based on cellular automata. Modelling and Simulation in Materials Science and Engineering 7(4), 631–640 (1999)
6. Sirakoulis, G.C., Karafyllidis, I., Thanailakis, A.: A Cellular Automaton Methodology for the Simulation of Integrated Circuit Fabrication Processes. Future Generation Computer Systems 18(5), 639–657 (2002)
7. Matveev, A.V., Latkin, E.I., Elokhin, V.I., Gorodetskii, V.V.: Monte Carlo model of oscillatory CO oxidation having regard to the change of catalytic properties due to the adsorbate-induced Pt(100) structural transformation. Journal of Molecular Catalysis A. Chemical 166, 23–30 (2001)
8. Matveev, A.V., Latkin, E.I., Elokhin, V.I., Gorodetskii, V.V.: Application of statistical lattice models to the analysis of oscillatory and autowave processes in the reaction of carbon monoxide oxidation over platinum and palladium surfaces. Kinetics and Catalysis 44(5), 692–700 (2003)
9. Gorodetskii, V.V., Elokhin, V.I., Bakker, J.W., Nieuwenhuys, B.E.: Field electron and field ion microscopy studies of chemical wave propagation in oscillatory reactions on platinum group metals. Catalysis Today 105, 183–205 (2005)
10. Imbihl, R., Cox, M.P., Ertl, G.: Kinetic oscillations in the catalytic CO oxidation on Pt(100): Theory. Journal of Chemical Physics 83(4), 1578–1587 (1985)
11. Bandman, O.: Using Multi core computers for implementing cellular automata systems. In: Malyshkin, V. (ed.) PaCT 2011. LNCS, vol. 6873, pp. 140–151. Springer, Heidelberg (2011)
12. Medvedev, Y.: Multi-particle Cellular-Automata Models for Diffusion Simulation. In: Hsu, C.-H., Malyshkin, V. (eds.) MTPP 2010. LNCS, vol. 6083, pp. 204–211. Springer, Heidelberg (2010)

Modelling Ordered Nanopourous Structures by Anodization via Cellular Automata

Bartosik Łukasz[1], Stafiej Janusz[1], and Di Caprio Dung[2]

[1] Institute of Physical Chemistry Kasprzaka 44/52 , Warsaw, Poland
[2] Institut de Recherche de Chimie Paris, CNRS – Chimie ParisTech,
11 rue P. et M. Curie, 75005 Paris, France

Abstract. A cellular automata model to simulate nanostructured alu-
mina creation via anodization is proposed. The model mimics the Field
Assisted Dissolution theoretical approach of the anodization process. The
key parameters influencing the structures of the layer are identified and
an attempt to recreate the two step anodization procedure in simulation
conditions is made. The effect of dissolution rate and surface diffusion are
considered. Simulation have been run on NVIDIA Tesla cards using the
techniques of parallel programming to increase speed of the simulations.

Keywords: Anodization, Cellular Automata, Parallel programing, aluminum oxide growth.

1 Introduction

Anodization is an electrochemical process of coating a metal with a layer of its
oxide. The process is known since the 1920's and has been used in metal protection, staining and decoration. Anodization is a simple and versatile process
than can be performed for many valve metals including titanium [1], aluminum
[2] and hafnium [3]. To conduct the process one needs to apply voltage to a
piece of metal submerged in a proper electrolyte. In 1953 Keller, *et. al.* [4] have
first revealed the structure of anodic aluminum oxide using transition electron
microscopy. In place of an expected barrier layer hexagonally ordered pores were
discovered. At the time the discovery went rather unnoticed and little work
was done to continue the research. However with the advent of nanotechnology
ordered layers of oxides have found new applications, namely they are perfect
scaffolds in synthesis of nanostructures [5]. In 1995 Matsuda *et. al.* [6] discovered the experimental conditions sufficient for synthesis of nanoporous anodic
aluminum oxide. Additional work soon followed with papers by Li [7], Jessensky
[8] and Matsuda [9]. A common problem in anodization is that the initial layer is
very disorganized due to surface defects of the metal. Various procedures such as
polishing, electropolishing and etching are used to pretreat the metal, one of the
most common ones is the so called two step anodization suggested by Matsuda
[10]. In two step anodization the metal layer undergoes two separate anodiza-
tions. The first anodization removes defects from the surface and establishes a

J. Wąs, G.C. Sirakoulis, and S. Bandini (Eds.): ACRI 2014, LNCS 8751, pp. 176–186, 2014.

pore network, the oxide layer is then washed away and the second anodization takes place upon the already cleaned and organized metal surface.

Despite the huge amount of experimental work on the subject fairly little theoretical work to explain the mechanism of pore formation has been done. Among proposed theories two are most widely considered: Field Assisted Dissolution (FAD) [11] and Field Assisted Flow (FAF) [12]. In this work we follow the FAD using the cellular automata approach.

2   Model

We employ a probabilistic, asynchronous cellular automaton on a cubic lattice with Moore connectivity. Furthermore we assume that the difference in distance between the facet neighbor sites and the corner neighbor sites is negligible. Additionally we use periodic boundary conditions along two of lattice axes and fixed boundary conditions along the remaining axis. There are a total of six states in the model and eight rules for updating lattice site states. In order to make simulation times more manageable we decided to use the computational power of GPU. The simulation program is designed to take advantage of multiple cores available on NVIDIA Tesla cards. In a CUDA setup the workload is divided between threads organized in blocks. Upon creation these blocks cannot interact with one another other than through updating the global memory on the card. Our goal was to statistically allow every site to have one chance of undergoing an update per one time step. The amount of information necessary to determine if a site update is to occur is equivalent to knowing exactly what are the states of the extended neighborhood of a given site. The extended neighborhood is 2 sites in each directions netting a 5x5x5 cube. All the sites in this cube have to remain in their states unless the central site fulfills the conditions for an update of states. This also means two adjacent cubes contain sites that do not influence each other in that particular step in any way. This allows us to organize threads to work on such cubes in parallel and thus improve efficiency over a conventional program. One iteration of this procedure however covers only 0.8% of sites, to account for this we repeat the update procedures 125 times per time step each time randomly choosing a central point for the starting cube and subsequently partitioning the whole space into appropriate cubes. This approach allows to combine parallelization with efficient information flow through the system.

The states in our model are labeled and their physical meaning discussed as follows. Let us label M the state corresponding to the metal, OX - to the oxide, EF - to the walker for electric field in the oxide, A - to anion vacancy in the oxide S - to solvent. The *metal*, *oxide* and *solvent* states represent what their names suggest while the *anion* and especially *electric field* states require further explanation. These three states have one feature in common. They are all *oxide-like* sites containing specific additional molecules or information. The *anion* states represents a portion of the oxide layer that contains anions formed during the dissociation of the solvent at the solvent-oxide layer interface. The *electric field* particles or rather their flux represent the information on the electric field at a given location. It is common to refer to the states as species or particles that occupy lattice sites.

Another element of the CA approach are the rules to update the states of the lattice sites in the time step basing on the states of the sites in the preceding time step. In the following we explain the rules, how we write them and what they actually mean. The rules of reaction or diffusion follow the same scheme as presented below:

$$Particle1(position\ A) + Particle2(position\ B) \rightarrow$$
$$Particle3(position\ A) + Particle4(position\ B)$$

Position A and B are a pair of nearest neighbor sites for a given lattice connectivity. Let us note here that the position in the equation is important and related to the actual position in the grid, so reaction:

$$M + OX \rightarrow M + EF \tag{1}$$

is not the same as

$$M + OX \rightarrow EF + M \tag{2}$$

because the states of sites after each of these reaction would be different. The difference comes from the fact that in the case of the second reaction the *metal* particle moves from site A to site B while in the first one it stays at the same site. The rules to change the states are as follows:

Reaction-type rules:

$$M + S \rightarrow OX + OX \tag{3}$$
$$M + OX \rightarrow M + EF \tag{4}$$
$$EF + S \rightarrow S + S \tag{5}$$
$$EF + S \rightarrow A + S \tag{6}$$
$$M + A \rightarrow OX + OX \tag{7}$$

Diffusion-type rules:

$$EF + OX \rightarrow OX + EF \tag{8}$$
$$EF + A \rightarrow A + EF \tag{9}$$

Each one of these rules is probabilistic with its probability given in a data file at the start of the simulation. Rule (3) describes the passivation of a metal surface in a corrosive environment. Rule (4) creates *electric field* walkers that simulate the presence of electric field. The sequence of rules (5), (6) give us the possible outcomes of what happens under influence of the electric field. Rules (5) and (6) mimic two possible processes occurring on the interface. The later rule describes water dissolution and inserting an anion into the oxide layer, while the former describes dissolving of the oxide layer itself. It is important to note that reactions (5) and (6) are checked in sequence during the execution of the simulation program. It is therefore of critical importance to properly adjust the data file probabilities to match the desired values. Typically this is achieved by setting the probability of reaction (6) to 1. In such a case reaction (5) occurs with probability P set in the data file and reaction (6) occurs with probability 1-P due to the sequencial nature of the code. There is only one rule governing the shape change of the metal-oxide interface, rule (7) which mimics the formation of metal oxide in a reaction of anions and the metal itself. The evolution of the porous oxide layer is thus essentially ruled by a subtle balance between its growth at the metal-oxide interface and its dissolution at the oxide-solvent interface controlled by the distribution of the electric field.

The process described by the following equations:

$$S + OX \rightarrow OX + S \tag{10}$$
$$S + A \rightarrow A + S \tag{11}$$

mimics surface diffusion and it is governed by a different mechanism than the previously described processes. Such a swap is always allowed if the number of pairs of *oxide-like* neighbors (bonds) increases or stays the same. *Oxide-like* neighbors are *oxides*, *electric field* and *anions*, all of which can exist within the oxide layer. If number of bond decreases the probability of the swap is given by $\exp(-E_b \Delta N_b)$ where E_b is bond energy and N_b is the decrease in number of bonds (metropolis Monte Carlo algorithm [13]). Surface diffusion hence is described by two parameters: the number of surface diffusion steps per reaction step and the probability of a swap that decreases bond number by one (P_{bond}). The latter scales with the power of the number of neighbors missing. In our CA model E_b is given as a probability of a particle to go to a site that has 1 bond less. The number of bonds is the number of non-*solvent* particles in the neares neighborhood of a given particle *oxide-like* particle. In the case of counting neighbors for the site containing a *solvent* the number of bonds is decreased by 1 to account for the fact that in the case of a swap a site that previously held an *anion* or an *oxide* will now hold a *solvent* and thus form no bonds.

We assume that the system is in a steady state and that the oxide layer is a conductor. To determine the electric field at a given point we use the Poisson equation:

$$\Delta \varphi = \frac{\rho_f}{\epsilon} \tag{12}$$

Inside the conductor the number of charges is $\rho_f = 0$ and the Poisson equation is reduced to a Laplace equation

$$\Delta \varphi = 0 \tag{13}$$

This equation has identical form as the diffusion equation in steady state:

$$\Delta c = 0 \tag{14}$$

Hence the same methodology can be used to solve both problems. It is well known that the diffusion equation can be solved via Random Walk. We use the Random Walk approach to solve the Laplace equation and find the potential and electric field distribution on the oxide-solvent interface. The Random Walk is solved via swapping sites that are neighbors according to the diffusion rules.

The simulation program has three main kernels: the reaction kernel, the diffusion kernel and the surface diffusion kernel. These kernels correspond to the rule types stated above. In each of the 125 iterations that make one full time step each kernels receives its own starting point on the lattice, the kernels are then executed in the order given previously. The reasons for such an organization are flexibility and computational effectivness. The main goal of designing this cellular automaton was to simulate various models of nanostructure creation. Hence the main design features were easy incorporation of new particles and new CA rules thus the separation into the three kernels by the kind of rules. This sepration also carries computational consequences since diffusion rules all have a probability of 1, so the step of generating a random number and checking if a given process should occur is redundant and can be omitted in order to increase simulation speed. In much the same manor only in surface diffusion explicit knowledge of all the extended neigbourhood in a given direction is required while for reaction and diffusion processes knowledge of the states of two cells per cube would be sufficient. Iteration of the three kernels also intermixes steps of diffusion, reaction and surface diffusion thus negating any artificial global order of the processes. Additional kernels include the initial condition kernel which gives the starting states of all the cells in the system, a termination kernel that ends a simulation once a given type of particles appears in the vicinity of one of the fixed boundaries of the system.

In this paper we discuss the influence of two parameters on the resulting interface. These are the dissolution probability described by rule (5) and the number of surface diffusion steps per reaction step.

3   Results and Discussion

Presented below are the results for simulations:

Table 1. Parameters used in the simulations

Simulation parameters		Reaction probabilities	
X-axis size	100	$M + S \rightarrow OX + OX$	1
Y-axis size	100	$M + OX \rightarrow M + EF$	0.005
Z-axis size	200	$EF + S \rightarrow S + S$	P_{dis}
Surface steps	1	$EF + S \rightarrow A + S$	$1 - P_{dis}$
Diffusion steps	1	$M + A \rightarrow OX + OX$	1

The parameter P_{bond} is found to have far less influence than the number of diffusion steps and its value was fixed at 0.02.

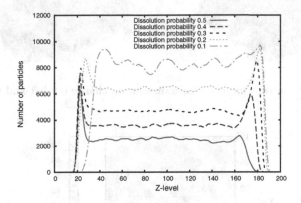

Fig. 1. Oxide layer distribution with respect to dissolution chance

The plots for various dissolution values share common features. From bottom to top in the system (left to right on figure 1) one can see an initial peak which corresponds to the pore bottoms, then a nearly flat layer at a given level which corresponds to the pore walls and a peak at the top of the system which corresponds to remnants of the initial interface and beginning of pore formation. The smallest dissolution probability corresponds to the situation when oxide growth exceeds the rate of dissolution due to oxygen anion creation and thus no pores are formed. In figure 2 one can see that for a dissolution rate of 0.5 the amount of material is insufficient to form a regular porous structure. The pores are interconnected and full of side holes. In contrast a well defined porous structure can be seen for a dissolution chance of 0.3. Further evidence of a porous structure of the material can be seen in the cross section of the layer in figure 3, the Fourier transform of this cross section reveals hexagonal symmetry in the system.

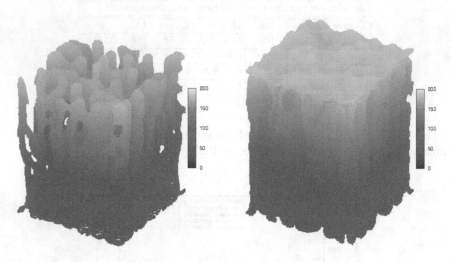

Fig. 2. Oxide solvent interface for a dissolution chance 0.5 left and 0.3 right

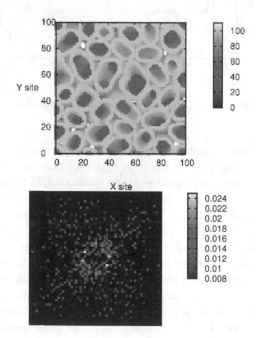

Fig. 3. Left cross section at the 102 level, right Fourier transform of the interface

We also mimic the process of surface diffusion at the oxide layer surface with the solvent. The oxide sites "prefer" sites on the lattice that have many oxide neighbors and will move towards sites with more neighbors if they get a chance. The parameter we use to control this process is the number of times per reaction step that oxide particles search for another location to which they could move. If a site with more neighbors is found then a swap of particles takes place. Results of changing the rate of surface diffusion are presented in figures 4-7.

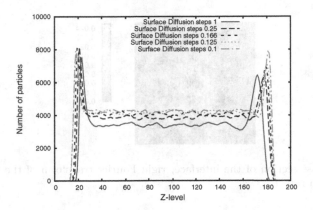

Fig. 4. Oxide layer distribution with respect to surface diffusion rates

Fig. 5. Oxide solvent interface for surface diffusion rate 1 left and 0.1 right

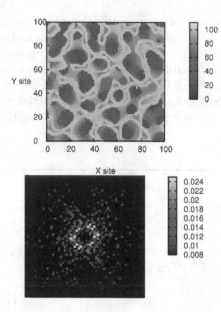

Fig. 6. Left cross section of the interface, right Fourier transform of the interface for surface diffusion rate 1

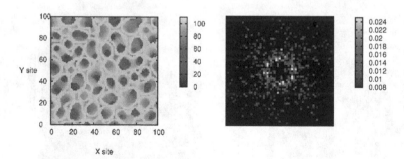

Fig. 7. Left cross section of the interface, right Fourier transform of the interface for surface diffusion rate 0.1

All the profiles have a similar outline with only the fastest surface diffusion rate simulation having a porosity vastly different from the other results. The reason for this behavior is over liquefaction of a layer making oxide particles amass in regions where there is already many of them. This causes the peak at the "top"of the system to broaden noticeably.

The side views of the layer do not reveal at first site the profound change in structure that has actually taken place. However the cross sections leave little room for doubt.

The cross sections reveal that surface diffusion plays a crucial role in the formation of nanopores. In the case of a lower surface diffusion rate the pores have a noticeably smaller diameter, there are more of them and they are not interconnected as much as in the case of a higher surface diffusion rate. On the Fourier transform figures 6 and 7 it is visible that the hexagonal symmetry of the pores is retained when changing the surface diffusion rate.

4 Conclusions

We succeed to create a relatively simple cellular automata model that mimics nanostructured oxide formation on aluminum. Our simulation results are in qualitative agreement with experimental data. The resulting structures show hexagonal symmetry which brakes the quadratic symmetry imposed on the system via the choice of the Moore neighborhood on a cubic lattice. We identified key parameters influencing the porosity of the layer, pore size and distribution and managed to successfully replicate the two step anodization procedure in our simulations.

Acknowledgments. The authors would like to acknowledge the Foundation for Polish Science for financial support of the research.

References

1. Wang, J., Zhao, L., Lyn, V.Y.-S., Lin, Z.: Journal of Material Chemistry 19, 3682–3687 (2009)
2. Rezazadeh, H., Ebrahimzadeh, M., Yam, M.R.Z.: World Academy of Science. Engineering and Technology 70, 30–32 (2012)
3. Garcia-Vergara, S.J., et al.: Electrochimica Acta 54, 3662–3670 (2009)
4. Keller, F., Hunter, M.S., Robinson, D.L.: Journal of the Electrochemical Society 100, 411–419 (1953)
5. Mutalib Jani, A., Losic, D., Voelcker, N.: Progress. Mater. Sci. 58, 636–704 (2013)
6. Masuda, H., Fukuda, K.: Science 268, 1466–1468 (1995)
7. Li, A.P., et al.: Journal of Applied Physics 84, 6023–6026 (1998)

8. Jessensky, O., Muller, F., Gosele, U.: Journal of the Electrochemical Society 145, 3735–3740 (1998)
9. Masuda, H., Yada, K., Osaka, A.: Japanese Journal of Applied Physics Part 2 - Letters 37, L1340–L1342 (1998)
10. Matsuda, H., Satoh, M.: Japanese Journal of Applied Physics Part 2 - Letters 35, L126–L129 (1996)
11. Hoar, T.P., Mott, N.F.: Journal of Physics and Chemistry of Solids 9, 97–99 (1959)
12. Garcia-Vergara, S.J., Iglesias-Rubianes, L., Blanco-Pinzon, C.E., Skeldon, P., Thompson, G.E., Campestrini, P.: Proc. R. Soc. A 462, 2345–2358 (2006)
13. Landau, R.H., Paez, M.J., Bordeianu, C.C.: Computational Physics. NACE International, Houston (2005)

Overview of Cellular Automaton Models for Corrosion

Cristian Felipe Pérez-Brokate[1], Dung di Caprio[2], Damien Féron[1,3], Jacques De Lamare[1], and Annie Chaussé[3]

[1] CEA, DEN, DANS, DPC, Service de Corrosion et du Comportement des Matériaux dans leur Environnement, 91 191 Gif sur Yvette Cedex, France
cristianfelipe.perezbrokate@cea.fr
[2] Institut de Recherche de Chimie Paris, CNRS – Chimie ParisTech, 11 rue Pierre et Marie Curie, 75005 Paris, France
[3] Laboratoire Analyse et Modélisation pour la Biologie et l'Environnement, UMR 8587, CNRS-CEA-Université d'Evry Val d'Essonne, Bd F. Mitterrand 91 025 Evry, France

Abstract. A review of corrosion process modeling using cellular automata methods is presented. This relatively new and growing approach takes into account the stochastic nature of the phenomena and uses physico-chemical rules to make predictions at a mesoscopic scale. Milestone models are analyzed and perspectives are established.

Keywords: Cellular Automaton, Corrosion, Pitting, Model, Mesoscopic.

1 Introduction

Corrosion affects every economic sector in the world with a cost estimated as 4% of the gross national product [1]. This phenomenon concerns mainly metals, which undergo a progressive change because of their physico-chemical interactions with their environment, possibly leading to functional degradations. Metal ions often precipitate on the surface, forming an oxide layer that may significantly reduce the corrosion rate (passivation phenomenon) [2]. Many studies have focused on understanding the breakdown mechanism and the protective effect of the corrosion induced oxide layer, whose rupture can lead to localized forms of corrosion. Some examples are pitting and cracking, that can propagate through the metal leading to dramatic consequences [3].

Creating a predictive model for corrosion processes is a real challenge, since they generally correspond to multiphase (most of the time gas-liquid-solid), multidimensional problems, involving coupled phenomena (electrochemical reactions, species diffusion, mechanical stress) and requiring a precise knowledge of the elements that interact. Experimentation is complicated to perform and may not be reliable for long time extrapolation [4]. As far as numerical modeling is concerned, partial differential equation (PDE) based deterministic models have been continuously developed [5–7]. The weak point of these models lies in

J. Wąs, G.C. Sirakoulis, and S. Bandini (Eds.): ACRI 2014, LNCS 8751, pp. 187–196, 2014.
© Springer International Publishing Switzerland 2014

their inability to take into account the stochastic nature of the corrosion phenomena [8].

Alternative models using Monte Carlo methods [9–12] allow the consideration of this stochastic behavior, but are not appropriate to describe some macroscopic phenomena, as they start from the microscopic scale. Cellular automaton (CA) models are based on a discretized description of time, space and state contrary to PDE models in which the three domains are continuous. Their main advantage is their ability to treat large domains, using simplified rules and taking into account the phenomenon's stochastic character [13]. As an example, they may be appropriate to simulate the initiation of localized corrosion or passivation and depassivation processes [14].

2   Evolution of Cellular Automaton Corrosion Models

In this section we propose a classification of the basic models that involve simple corrosion rules, which have been used for later models. Then we sort specialized models for specific cases, like the study of the oxide layer between the electrolyte and the metal or the influence of the properties of the electrolyte. Each discretized cell represents a species that evolves in time following a set rule. The Brownian motion is represented by a random walk over the lattice.

2.1   First Corrosion Models

Historically, the first developed CA models for corrosion have been used to study the evolution of the surface morphology in metal samples. In the following, we name the model by the author of the publication in which it appeared for the first time.

Before the appearance of the first CA numerical simulations, the main focus of the research was on the electrochemical and chemical aspects of corrosion. The first CA models were based on the study of the morphology of the pit, Meakin [15] related the transition from metastable to stable pit growth with the balance between the passivation and dissolution rate. The effects of the chloride ions were simulated as corrosive elements in the fluid, and the passivation and depassivation were simulated as random effects on the corrosion front controlled by a probability coefficient. This model is represented in Fig.1 a). There are four kind of cells: two solution sites (corrosive and non-corrosive) and two metal sites (reactive and non-reactive). The corrosion effect is modeled by the dissolution of the reactive sites in contact with corrosive sites of the fluid.

Making simulations in only two space dimensions does not allow a complete study of the pit morphology and evolution. Balázs [16] used an approach based on a top view, considering the pit growth as a spreading phenomenon, because it was easily comparable with experiments. In this model, the aggressiveness of the electrolyte and the restriction of the pit growth are accounted through the incorporation of a probability coefficient on the cathodic reactions. There are four kinds of sites, the empty sites that represent the sample surface, the active and occupied sites that represent the places where the dissolution is taking place and the candidate sites that are adjacent to the active sites. The transformation rules are a progression from a candidate stage to active, then all the adjacent cells become candidate and finally the active site becomes occupied so it will not change its state any more. This is schematically shown in Fig.1 b).

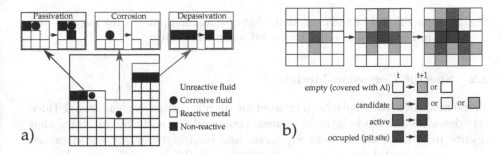

Fig. 1. a) Corrosive fluid dissolves reactive metal. Random passivation and depassivation on metal [15] b) Pit growth spreading on active and occupied sites [16].

Morphological details like roughness were studied by Córdoba-Torres [17–19] using a localized corrosion approach. The anodic and cathodic reactions are realized in different sites of the corrosion front to obtain an electrochemical balance. The dissolution is represented by an intermediate adsorbate for the reaction expressed as:

$$M \rightleftharpoons M(I)_{ads} + e^- \tag{1}$$

$$M(I)_{ads} \rightarrow M(II)_{sol} + e^-. \tag{2}$$

The cathodic counterpart involves an intermediate cation bound to the metal, which is modeled by a blockage on the reactivity of the site. The electrochemical equations are:

$$C^+ + e^- \rightarrow C_{ads} \tag{3}$$

$$C^+ + C_{ads} + e^- \rightarrow C_{2,sol}. \tag{4}$$

This approach allows corrosion in horizontal directions and consequently the detachment of metal from the corrosion front. This is illustrated in Fig.2 a) as well as the modeling of (1)–(4). This author was mainly interested in the simulation of a simple electrochemical model, composed by generic reactions, since in reality, following thermodynamics [20] reaction (1) is complete from left to right and does not lead to a balance.

The electrolyte corrosive effects are studied by Malki [10]. This is one of the first models of pitting corrosion. In this approach the corrosive cells dissolve the reactive metal, the concentration in the electrolyte is balanced by the creation of non-corrosive sites and the metal dissolution rate is controlled via a probability coefficient that depends on the pit length due to the ohmic resistance. This is illustrated in Fig.2 b).

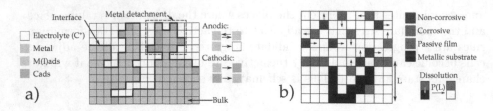

Fig. 2. a) Anodic and cathodic reactions that dissolves and protects the metal respectively [17] b) Dissolution of metal controlled by pit length [10]

2.2   Specific Corrosion Models

These kinds of models have been created for specific corrosion phenomena. Taleb [21] describes the oxide layer in a mesoscopic scale as a cluster of atoms that results from the reaction between metal and electrolyte, where the detached species of the metal can move by self diffusion. In this model the oxide layer is porous. When pitting corrosion starts propagating, the growth rate depends on the balance between oxide layer repassivation, the local environment inside the pit and the ohmic resistance between the anode and the cathode of the corrosion reaction. Di Caprio [22] have modeled this theory adding the passivation and depassivation events with a probability that depends on the depth of the pit.

Other improvements of these models have been performed, like for instance: the use of the Pilling-Bedworth ratio in the reaction of the electrolyte and metal to obtain a chemical balance on the density of the reactants and products [23,24]; the effect of the oxygen in the diffusion of species [25]; the erosion effects represented in a dissolution probability [26] or the insertion of protective chromium elements inside the metal [27]. Fig.3 a) shows an improved model that considers metal sites that detach from the bulk, walk randomly through the oxide layer and then react when they touch the electrolyte. The dissolution probability depends on the metal neighbors to simulate the erosion effects.

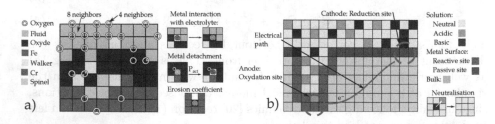

Fig. 3. a) Detached metal walks to the oxide layer, reacts when touches the electrolyte. [25] b) Spatially separated reactions for a pH depend model [28].

With the objective of making a more realistic model, Vautrin [28] has proposed a representation of the anodic and cathodic reactions spatially separated. Fig.3 b) shows cathodic and anodic site randomly chosen over the corrosion front: the anodic site is inside the pit while the cathodic site is outside, then depending on the local pH of each site, the reaction is different. The diffusion phenomena in the solution are represented by a random walk [29]. When an acidic and a basic site move to the same cell, neutralization occurs. In a modified model, a simplification has been added with the anodic and cathodic reaction on a same site, as it is possible on a mesoscopic scale [30]. This last model became very robust with the incorporation of the influence of local pH [31] and the dissolution of the passive layer.

Focused on the electrolyte properties, Li [32,33] has modeled the precipitation of metallic ions of the solution into a salt film by adding a species that decreases locally the pH of the solution. Wang [34, 35] adopted the salt film species in their model but also added a mechanical effect by coupling a finite element model to the CA model that gives a corrosion probability as a function of the local stress. This model is represented in Fig.4 a). Other authors studied the inter-granular corrosion by changing the dissolution probability for species on the grain boundaries [36, 37].

Using 3D simulations, Van der Weeën [38] has developed a model where the actions of the corrosive chloride ions in solution are taken into account. They modeled the concentration and potential gradient as a probability that ions prefer to move inside pits, the cathodic protection by a probability that pit initiation does not occur near an active pit and the ohmic resistance variation as a dissolution probability that depends on the depth of the pit. This model is schematically shown on Fig.4 b). One important aspect of the research is the experimental comparison of the number of pits, average pit depth and affected surface.

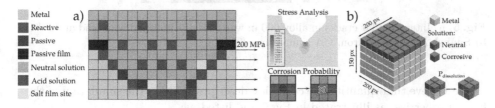

Fig. 4. a) Electrochemical simulation coupled with mechanical analysis [34] b) 3D simulations with dissolution probability controlled by pit length and cathodic protection [38]

Pidaparti [39] developed a model using two progressive states: the initiation state and the pit propagation state. The first one is given to all cells that are not corroded and it increases randomly at each time step. When it reaches a given value, the cell becomes corroded and starts propagating with the second state rule. This rule takes into account the state of the local neighborhood and a mathematical expression accounting for the pH of the solution, the temperature, the dissolution parameter and the potential difference between the metal and the solution. A complex sensibility analysis needs to be made to calibrate these parameters.

3   Results

Numerical results have to be compared with reality. Fig.5 a) shows a typical corrosion crack found in a metal alloy 600 (Nickel base alloy) at high temperature that has been reproduced by the model of Di Caprio [22] as shown on Fig.5 b). It is seen that the same probability parameters can lead to different results. This is due to the stochastic aspect of the model. Other models like the one of Stafiej et al. [4, 40] have shown the influence of the spatially separated anodic and cathodic reaction on the appearance of the auto catalytic environment and roughness properties inside the pit.

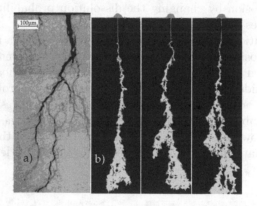

Fig. 5. a) Intergranular cracks in alloy 600 in water circuit polluted with lead at 360 °C b) Snapshots obtained from CA simulations [22]

We believe that quantitative corrosion description lies in the simulation of the basic properties, as illustrated in Fig.6 and listed as:

1. The oxidation and reduction reactions are represented as two simultaneous events which occur in separate electrically connected locations. This event is driven by the potential difference, which is a function of the ohmic drop [1, 41]. This is represented as a choice of the position of each site depending on the localization inside the pit. The result of each reaction depends on the local pH of the electrolyte.
2. The precipitation of chloride ions inside the pit that blocks the anodic reaction, according to experimental results [42]. This explains that from a certain pit depth, the propagation of the pit occurs laterally.
3. The passive layer is represented as a continuous layer covering the metal, which can depassivate with a given probability [43].

4. The dissolution of the metal ions is represented as the transformation of metal sites to solution sites [44].

5. The diffusion of the species is simulated as a Brownian motion, according to $< r^2 >= 2dD\Delta t$, where r is the distance between two adjacent cells, d is the dimensionality, D is the diffusion coefficient and Δt is the time step [29].

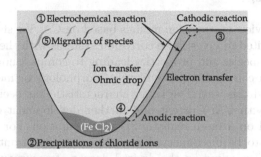

Fig. 6. Representation of the physico-chemical parameters used in the proposed model

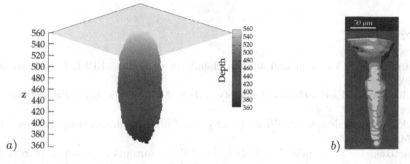

Fig. 7. a) 3D model of pit morphology b) X-ray microtomography of a pit in 304 rod [42]

The above statements have been used to create a model with six states: metal cells that can be reactive or inert, passive layer cells that can be formed at the metal-solution interface and solution cells that can be acidic, basic or neutral. Electrochemical and chemical reactions drive the evolution of the metal reactive cells, the development of the passive layer as well as the dynamics in the solution. The evolution of the cells is based on a asynchronous algorithm where cells are further organized into cubic blocks of cells. The objective is to update a cell and its neighbors avoiding possible simultaneous updates of an identical cell in a parallel implementation of the code. The CUDA environment has been adapted for graphic processing units (GPU) [45]. For each kernel call, in a regular array of non adjacent blocks, a randomly chosen cell is chosen in order to avoid spurious correlations. The cell evolves according to rules reflecting the physicochemical properties mentionned in the five points above.

Fig. 7 a) shows first results of our 3D simulation in a simplified model that only takes into account the corrosion effects of chloride ions in the electrolyte and a passivation-depassivation effect. These results can be compared experimentally with recent progresses on pitting imagery, as shown in Fig. 7 b), taken from a X-ray microtomography.

4   Conclusions

We have given a review of corrosion models based on CA. We show that the CA approach is well suited to investigate corrosion systems with their large number of electrochemical species and properties leading to complex non linear dynamics. Indeed, certain corrosion aspects like pit morphology or metal detachment are better described this way. The latter characteristic has been found only by corrosion models with CA. Current and further development of these models have to be focused on a more realistic 3D representation. For instance, metal parts that appear to be disconnected from the corrosion front in 2D may be connected in 3D. Depending on the desired degree of accuracy, the model can be improved with the inclusion of other specific evolution rules and parameters in the simulation.

References

1. Landolt, D.: Corrosion and surface chemistry of metals. EPFL Press, Lausanne (2007)
2. Ailor, W.H., Electrochemical Society (eds.): Atmospheric corrosion. Wiley, New York (1982)
3. Szklarska-Smialowska, Z.: Pitting corrosion of aluminum. Corrosion Science 41(9), 1743–1767 (1999)
4. Bartosik, L., Di Caprio, D., Stafiej, J.: Cellular automata approach to corrosion and passivity phenomena. Pure and Applied Chemistry 85(1), 247–256 (2013)
5. Okada, T.: A theory of perturbation initiated pitting. Journal of the Electrochemical Society 132(3), 537–544 (1985)
6. Beck, T.R., Grens, E.A.: An electrochemical mass transport kinetic model for stress corrosion cracking of titanium. Journal of the Electrochemical Society 116(2), 177–184 (1969)
7. Bataillon, C., Bouchon, F., Chainais-Hillairet, C., Fuhrmann, J., Hoarau, E., Touzani, R.: Numerical methods for the simulation of a corrosion model with moving oxide layer. Journal of Computational Physics 231(18), 6213–6231 (2012)
8. Frankel, G.S.: Pitting corrosion of metals a review of the critical factors. Journal of the Electrochemical Society 145(6), 2186–2198 (1998)
9. Caleyo, F., Velázquez, J., Valor, A., Hallen, J.: Probability distribution of pitting corrosion depth and rate in underground pipelines: A monte carlo study. Corrosion Science 51(9), 1925–1934 (2009)
10. Malki, B., Baroux, B.: Computer simulation of the corrosion pit growth. Corrosion Science 47(1), 171–182 (2005)
11. Reigada, R., Sagués, F., Costa, J.M.: A monte carlo simulation of localized corrosion. The Journal of Chemical Physics 101(3), 2329–2337 (1994)

12. Murer, N., Buchheit, R.G.: Stochastic modeling of pitting corrosion in aluminum alloys. Corrosion Science 69, 139–148 (2013)
13. Toffoli, T.: Cellular automata as an alternative to (rather than an approximation of) differential equations in modeling physics. Physica D: Nonlinear Phenomena 10(1-2), 117–127 (1984)
14. Marcus, P., Maurice, V., Strehblow, H.H.: Localized corrosion (pitting): A model of passivity breakdown including the role of the oxide layer nanostructure. Corrosion Science 50(9), 2698–2704 (2008)
15. Meakin, P., Jøssang, T., Feder, J.: Simple passivation and depassivation model for pitting corrosion. Physical Review E 48(4), 2906–2916 (1993)
16. Balázs, L., Gouyet, J.F.: Two-dimensional pitting corrosion of aluminium thin layers. Physica A: Statistical Mechanics and its Applications 217(3-4), 319–338 (1995)
17. Córdoba-Torres, P., Nogueira, R.P., de Miranda, L., Brenig, L., Wallenborn, J., Fairén, V.: Cellular automaton simulation of a simple corrosion mechanism: mesoscopic heterogeneity versus macroscopic homogeneity. Electrochimica Acta 46(19), 2975–2989 (2001)
18. Córdoba-Torres, P., Nogueira, R.P., Fairén, V.: Forecasting interface roughness from kinetic parameters of corrosion mechanisms. Journal of Electroanalytical Chemistry 529(2), 109–123 (2002)
19. Córdoba-Torres, P., Nogueira, R.P., Fairén, V.: Fractional reaction order kinetics in electrochemical systems involving single-reactant, bimolecular desorption reactions. Journal of Electroanalytical Chemistry 560(1), 25–33 (2003)
20. Pourbaix, M., Staehle, R.W., Pourbaix, M., Pourbaix, M.: Lectures on electrochemical corrosion, vol. 870. Springer (1973)
21. Taleb, A., Stafiej, J., Chaussé, A., Messina, R., Badiali, J.: Simulations of film growth and diffusion during the corrosion process. Journal of Electroanalytical Chemistry 500(1-2), 554–561 (2001)
22. Di Caprio, D., Vautrin-Ul, C., Stafiej, J., Saunier, J., Chaussé, A., Féron, D., Badiali, J.P.: Morphology of corroded surfaces: Contribution of cellular automaton modelling. Corrosion Science 53(1), 418–425 (2011)
23. Saunier, J., Dymitrowska, M., Chaussé, A., Stafiej, J., Badiali, J.: Diffusion, interactions and universal behavior in a corrosion growth model. Journal of Electroanalytical Chemistry 582(1-2), 267–273 (2005)
24. Di Caprio, D., Vautrin-Ul, C., Stafiej, J., Chaussé, A., Féron, D., Badiali, J.P.: Cellular automata approach for morphological evolution of localised corrosion. Corrosion Engineering, Science and Technology 46(2), 223–227 (2011)
25. Lan, K.C., Chen, Y., Yeh, T.K., Hung, T.C., Liu, M.L., Yu, G.P.: Scale removal oxidation behavior of metal in supercritical water modeled by cellular automaton. Progress in Nuclear Energy 53(7), 1034–1038 (2011)
26. Tan, T., Chen, Y.: Scale removal cellular automaton oxidation models of metals in lead bismuth eutectic. Journal of Electroanalytical Chemistry 626(1-2), 89–97 (2009)
27. Lan, K.C., Chen, Y., Hung, T.C., Tung, H.M., Yu, G.P.: Simulation of the growth of oxide layer of stainless steels with chromium using cellular automaton model: Verification and parameter study. Computational Materials Science 77, 139–144 (2013)
28. Vautrin-Ul, C., Chausse, A., Stafiej, J., Badiali, J.: Simulations of corrosion processes with spontaneous separation of cathodic and anodic reaction zones. Polish Journal of Chemistry 78(9), 1795–1810 (2004)

29. Chopard, B., Droz, M.: Cellular automata modeling of physical systems. Cambridge University Press, Cambridge (2005)
30. Vautrin-Ul, C., Taleb, A., Stafiej, J., Chaussé, A., Badiali, J.: Mesoscopic modelling of corrosion phenomena: Coupling between electrochemical and mechanical processes, analysis of the deviation from the faraday law. Electrochimica Acta 52(17), 5368–5376 (2007)
31. Aarão Reis, F.D.A., Stafiej, J., Badiali, J.P.: Scaling theory in a model of corrosion and passivation. The Journal of Physical Chemistry B 110(35), 17554–17562 (2006)
32. Li, L., Li, X.G., Dong, C.F., Cheng, Y.F.: Cellular automaton model for simulation of metastable pitting. Corrosion Engineering, Science and Technology 46(4), 340–345 (2011)
33. Li, L., Li, X., Dong, C., Huang, Y.: Computational simulation of metastable pitting of stainless steel. Electrochimica Acta 54(26), 6389–6395 (2009)
34. Wang, H., Han, E.H.: Mesoscopic simulation of diffusion characteristics in the corrosion film. Journal of Materials Science & Technology 28(5), 427–432 (2012)
35. Wang, H., Han, E.H.: Simulation of metastable corrosion pit development under mechanical stress. Electrochimica Acta 90, 128–134 (2013)
36. Lishchuk, S.V., Akid, R., Worden, K., Michalski, J.: A cellular automaton model for predicting intergranular corrosion. Corrosion Science 53(8), 2518–2526 (2011)
37. Taleb, A., Stafiej, J.: Numerical simulation of the effect of grain size on corrosion processes: Surface roughness oscillation and cluster detachment. Corrosion Science 53(8), 2508–2513 (2011)
38. Van der Weën, P., Zimer, A.M., Pereira, E.C., Mascaro, L.H., Bruno, O.M., De Baets, B.: Modeling pitting corrosion by means of a 3D discrete stochastic model. Corrosion Science 82, 133–144 (2014)
39. Pidaparti, R.M., Fang, L., Palakal, M.J.: Computational simulation of multi-pit corrosion process in materials. Computational Materials Science 41(3), 255–265 (2008)
40. Stafiej, J., Di Caprio, D., Bartosik, L.: Corrosion passivation processes in a cellular automata based simulation study. The Journal of Supercomputing 65(2), 697–709 (2013)
41. Marcus, P.: Corrosion Mechanisms in Theory and Practice, 3rd edn. CRC Press, Boca Raton (2011)
42. Ghahari, S.M., Davenport, A.J., Rayment, T., Suter, T., Tinnes, J.P., Padovani, C., Hammons, J.A., Stampanoni, M., Marone, F., Mokso, R.: In situ synchrotron x-ray microtomography study of pitting corrosion in stainless steel. Corrosion Science 53(9), 2684–2687 (2011)
43. Macdonald, D.D.: The history of the point defect model for the passive state: A brief review of film growth aspects. Electrochimica Acta 56(4), 1761–1772 (2011)
44. Vautrin-Ul, C., Mendy, H., Taleb, A., Chaussé, A., Stafiej, J., Badiali, J.: Numerical simulations of spatial heterogeneity formation in metal corrosion. Corrosion Science 50(8), 2149–2158 (2008)
45. CUDA: http://www.nvidia.com/object/cuda_home_new.html

Cellular Automata Finite Element Approach for Modelling Microstructure Evolution under Thermo-Mechanical Processing Conditions

Rafal Golab, Mateusz Sitko, Joanna Szyndler, and Łukasz Madej

AGH University of Science and Technology Al. Mickiewicza 30, 30-059, Cracow, Poland
rgolab@agh.edu.pl

Abstract. The concurrent cellular automata finite element (CAFE) approach for modelling microstructure evolution under thermo-mechanical processing conditions is the subject of the present work. Particular attention is put on modelling two phenomena, static recrystallization after deformation and phase transformation during heating. Details of the developed models are presented within the paper. Both models are implemented based on the CA Framework, which is also described in the work. Finally cellular automata approaches are combined with the finite element model based on the digital material representation idea. The numerical modelling of complex multistage hot deformation process was selected as a case study to show capabilities of the developed cellular automata finite element model.

Keywords: cellular automata, finite element, static recrystallization, phase transformation, framework.

1 Introduction

Final exploitation properties of polycrystalline metallic materials are the result of specifically designed combination of the thermo-mechanical processing operations. Processing conditions during manufacturing stages directly influence morphology of the final microstructure (e.g. size, shape or dimensions of microstructural features), which is then related to the obtained in-use mechanical properties. The major mechanism controlling the microstructure evolution during or after deformation comes from the recrystallization and phase transformation processes. These temperature activated phenomena are composed of two subsequent mechanisms: nucleation and grain/phase growth, that lead to significant changes in the microstructure. However, finding the correlation between these phenomena and obtained material properties is quite difficult. An extensive experimental investigation is usually required, which unfortunately is time consuming and expensive at the same time.

Increasing computational power of modern computers and mentioned economic aspects make the numerical simulation a very powerful investigation tool that can be used to support mentioned experimental research. The simulation of recrystallization and phase transformation phenomena can be performed with various numerical ap-

J. Wąs, G.C. Sirakoulis, and S. Bandini (Eds.): ACRI 2014, LNCS 8751, pp. 197–207, 2014.

proaches based on the conventional continuum as well as on discrete models. One of them is a discrete Cellular Automata (CA) method [1] that can provide detailed information about microstructure changes during thermal processing conditions. In recent years a lot of microstructure evolution models in metallic materials based on cellular automata method were created [2-5]. Unfortunately, developed models were designed as in-house codes capable to solve only a specific problem e.g. the simulation of dynamic or static recrystallization. If a new model e.g. austenite to ferrite phase transformation was required, the algorithmic and programming work had to be started from scratch, which significantly increases model development time.

To solve this problem authors decided to develop an universal framework for cellular automata method, in which the basic cellular automata algorithmic solutions are available to each user. This allows focusing the main burden of work on developing the appropriate transition rules that replicate physical phenomena and not on implementation aspects. As a result, the use of such a framework to develop of the numerical model will be possible for material scientists without extensive knowledge of programming and algorithmic solutions.

The framework capabilities can additionally be extended when joined with the continuum Finite Element (FE) model. In that case the combined Cellular Automata Finite Element (CAFE) model can be established and can be used to model both thermal and mechanical processing conditions. To properly join the finite element model with the cellular automata approach the Digital Material Representation (DMR) idea is used in the paper. Both, the basis of the digital material representation idea as well as fundamentals of the developed CA framework are presented in the following part of the paper.

2   Finite Element Model Based on Digital Material Representation Approach

The concept of the DMR was recently proposed and is dynamically evolving [6-8]. The main objective of the DMR is creation of the digital representation of microstructure with an explicit representation of its features. The more precisely the DMR is applied, the more realistic are the results of calculations regarding material behaviour. Various methods can be used to create statistical (e.g., cellular automata, Monte Carlo, sphere growth, inverse analysis) or exact representation of microstructure [9].

In the present work to ensure a detailed transfer of the real microstructure into the digital material representation model, authors decided to use an image processing algorithm [10]. However, due to the complexity of the microstructure morphology additional manual corrections of the obtained results were necessary. As a result, the exact replication of complex shapes of particular grains was obtained as seen in Fig. 1.

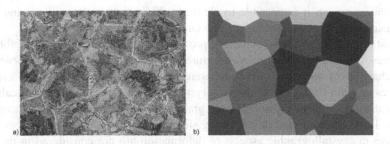

Fig. 1. a) LOM image of initial austenite microstructure morphology, b) digital form of the microstructure

To incorporate the obtained digital material representation into the finite element solution and to properly capture material behaviour along the grain boundaries, specific nonuniform FE meshes that are refined along the grain boundaries have to be generated. To obtain continuity of the solution space at the micro scale level, the periodic boundary conditions have to be applied. In the case of periodic boundary conditions, there must be the same number of FE mesh nodes on both sides of the sample. Nodes from one side of material are then connected with appropriate nodes on the opposite side. Thus, the morphology of the digital microstructure should have a periodic character as well. Equations which were introduced to deal with periodic boundary conditions are described as:

$$u_x^{LeftNode} - u_x^{RightNode} - \Delta U_x = 0$$
$$u_y^{LeftNode} - u_y^{RightNode} - \Delta U_y = 0$$

(1)

where: $u_{x,y}^{LeftNode,RightNode}$ - displacements calculated in the particular nodes, $\Delta U_{x,y}$ - difference of displacement in both directions.

However, morphologies of digital microstructures obtained from image processing algorithms do not have a periodic character. To solve this issue the digital material representation can be surrounded by a homogeneous buffer zone [11], and then periodic boundary conditions are applied as schematically presented in Fig. 2.

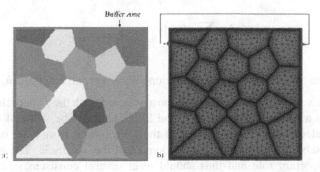

Fig. 2. A Digital Material Representation with a) buffer zone and b) periodic boundary conditions

With this approach it is possible to eliminate the impact of free edges, and such digital material behaves as a small part of a larger real specimen.

The last stage of model development is providing material properties in the form of flow curves to the investigated microstructure morphology. Selected flow curves describe behaviour of austenite phase and were identified experimentally. To capture differences in grain flows due to various crystallographic orientations in the reality, a diversification of the flow curves for each grain is introduced using the Gaussian distribution. Thus, each grain is described by slightly different flow stress values [12]. Differences in crystallographic aspects of deformation are not considered in the present model as conventional finite element model is applied. The obtained digital material representation model is presented in Fig. 3. Such model is used to apply plane strain compression conditions that are present in the channel die test, which is investigated in the work.

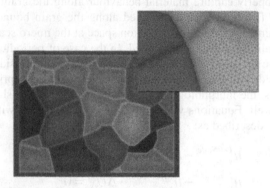

Fig. 3. Digital material representation of the investigated austenite microstructure

The data transfer from the FE model into the CA code is based on the SPH (Smoothed Particle Hydrodynamic) interpolation method.

The concept of an integral representation of function $f(x)$ at location x in the SPH method is given by an integral of multiplication of the product of the function and an appropriate kernel function W_{ij}. If the value of the $f(x)$ function is known only in a finite set of discrete points, it can be written as:

$$\langle f(x) \rangle \cong \sum_{j=1}^{N} f(x_j) W_{ij}(x - x_j, h_{sm}) V_j, \qquad (2)$$

where: the $\langle \; \rangle$ – kernel approximation, W_{ij} – kernel function, h_{sm} – smoothing length of the support domain, V_j – volume associated with the jth particle.

Eq. (2) is a basic equation used in the SPH method. The value of the function at point x is calculated by a summation of the contribution from a set of neighbouring particles (j subscript) from the support domain of the x particle. The Kernel function plays an important role and thus should meet several consistency conditions to be applicable in the SPH method. The quintic spline Kernel is used in the present work:

$$W(R, h_{sm}) = \alpha_d \begin{cases} (3-R)^5 - 6(2-R)^5 + 15(1-R)^5 & 0 \le R < 1 \\ (3-R)^5 - 6(2-R)^5 & 1 \le R < 2 \\ (3-R)^5 & 2 \le R < 3 \\ 0 & R > 3 \end{cases} \quad (3)$$

with $\alpha_d = 7/478\pi \, h_{sm}^2$.

The strain values calculated at every Gaussian integration point are interpolated by the SPH interpolation into the discrete regular CA space and are used as initial conditions for further microstructure evolution modeling on the basis of the cellular automata framework.

3   Cellular Automata Framework

Cellular automata approach is a discrete mathematical model consisting of a regular cell grid, where each cell can have one of a finite number of states. Idea of the cellular automata has its origins in the work of von Neumann [13]. The major assumption of the CA approach is to describe the system using a set of relatively simple rules and interactions between the components of the system (cell) instead of describing a complex system with differential equations. Cellular automata model in most applications is composed of the following components:

grid - usually build of identical cells whose states can be described using both variables: discrete and continuous,

neighborhood relations-used to define logical connections between the cells,

a set of transition rules-used to replicate physical mechanisms leading to investigated phenomenon. As a results transition rules control changes between states of the cells.

The most important part of the cellular automata model is the above-mentioned set of transition rules as the dynamics of the system is introduced into the model by these rules. Changes in the cell state are made based on the state of the cell and the state of cells belonging to the neighborhood in the previous time step. Additionally, stochastic properties of the system, mainly through the introduction of non-deterministic transition rules and the definition of the neighborhood can be easily incorporated into the microstructure evolution models. However, as mentioned, each newly formed microstructure evolution model based on the cellular automata method that could find practical application had to be implemented from scratch. This required knowledge of the author, not only in his field of expertise such as metallurgy and materials science, but also detailed knowledge in the field of computer programming.

Due to the fact that all models based on cellular automata method, have some common elements e.g. solution space, type of neighborhood, strictly defined state boundary conditions or general transition rules, encapsulation of those elements is possible in the form of a universal software - framework developed by the authors [14]. Such an application provides a possibility to easily define the parameters common to each material model, as well as to define particular transition rules releasing the end-user from implementation issues. As a result this approach allows modeling of microstructure development by scientists across material science community.

List of basic assumptions of the framework is summarized as follows:

framework is to serve primarily the construction of complex physical models,
framework should be efficient and effective,
framework has to be easy to use for people who don't know programming,
initially, CA Framework should work properly on Linux, but ultimately CAF should be completely portable between platforms.

Technologies like C++ for main functionality and MPI for Message Passing Interface and OpenGl for visualization purposes were mainly used to create the CA framework. Details of the model can be found in earlier work [14]. Two microstructure evolution models were implemented on the basis of the framework and combined with the DMR finite element model.

4   Austenite – Ferrite Phase Transformation Model

The first developed CA model is designed to simulate austenite – ferrite transformation during cooling in the 2D space. Each CA cell is described by several state and internal variables: the cell can be in three different states: ferrite (α), austenite (γ) and ferrite-austenite (α/γ). Additionally, internal variables are defined to describe other necessary microstructure features. Cells contain information e.g. how many ferrite phase is in a particular cell $F_{i,j}$, what is the carbon concentration in each cell $C_{i,j}$, the growth length $l_{i,j}$ of the ferrite-austenite cell into the austenite cell or the growth velocity $v_{i,j}$ of the interface cell. These internal variables are used in the transition rules to replicate mechanisms of phase transformation. Details on this approach can be found in [15].

Two major parts of the model are defined to describe nucleation and growth of the ferrite grains in the austenitic matrix. Nucleation is stochastic in nature, thus in the present model, to replicate the stochastic character of nucleation, a number of nuclei n is calculated in a probabilistic manner at the beginning of each time step:

$$n = N\left(T_i\right)\left(\frac{B_i}{B_0}\right)^3 P\left(\tau\right) \tag{4}$$

where: B_0, B_i - mean amount of γ cells at the beginning and i-th time step, respectively, N – total number of α nuclei, P – probability, τ – time step.

Locations of grain nuclei are generated randomly along austenite grain boundaries. When a cell is selected as a nuclei, the state of this cell changes from austenite (γ) to ferrite (α).

Ferrite growth is controlled by the carbon diffusion, thus the carbon distribution across the microstructure is evaluated by the solution of the diffusion equation on the basis of the finite difference (FD) method. The transition rules describing growth of ferrite grains during phase transformation are designed to replicate experimental observations of mechanisms responsible for this process [15]. The velocity of the α/γ interface is assumed to be a product of the mobility M and the driving force for interface migration F:

$$v = MF \tag{5}$$

The driving force for the phase transformation F is due to the differences in the carbon concentration in equilibrium conditions and in particular cell:

$$F = \beta(C_{eq}(T_i) - C_{i,j}^{\gamma}) \tag{6}$$

where: β – model coefficient, C_{eq} – equilibrium carbon concentration calculated using Thermocalc software, $C_{i,j}$ – carbon concentration in the (i,j) CA cell.

The following transition rules are proposed in the model to replicate the phenomena occurring at the austenite-ferrite boundary. When the ferrite phase is present in the material, the CA ferrite cells grow into the austenite phase. In the current time step t the growth length of the austenite-ferrite cell with indexes (i,j) towards an austenite neighbouring cell with indexes (k,l) is described as:

$$l_{i,j}^t = \int_{t_0}^t v_{i,j} \, \mathrm{d}t \tag{7}$$

where: t_0 – time when the CA cell (i,j) changed into the ferrite state, $v_{i,j}$ – the growth velocity of the CA cell (i,j).

The growth velocity v is obtained from (5) and then the ferrite volume fraction in the CA cell (k,l) is calculated as a results of the ferrite growth:

$$F_{k,l} = \sum_1^{N_{neigh}} \frac{l_{i,j}^t}{L_{CA}} \tag{8}$$

where: $F_{k,l}$ – total ferrite volume fraction in the CA cell (k,l), as a contribution from all the neighbouring austenite-ferrite CA cells, L_{CA} – dimension of the CA cell in the CA space, t – time step.

When the ferrite volume fraction reaches value of one, the cell changes its state to ferrite (α).

5   Static Recrystallization (SRX) Model

The SRX is another model implemented within the cellular automata framework for the purposes of the present work and major assumptions are gathered below. In this model, only two state variables have been created – a CA cell can either be in the unrecrystallized or recrystallized state. Each CA cell in the unrecrystallized state can become the nucleus with the probability determined by:

$$p = N S t \tag{9}$$

where: S – volume in which nucleation can appear, t – time, N – coefficient computed by:

$$N = M_N \exp\left(-\frac{Q_a}{RT}\right)$$ (10)

where: Q_a – activation energy for nucleation, R – universal gas constant, T – temperature, M_N – coefficient.

After the CA cell becomes a nucleus of a new recrystallized grain, the grain growth process is simulated. The velocity of a moving grain boundary is again calculated according to (5), however different driving force is applied, namely stored energy:

$$F = 0.5 G b_g^2 \rho$$ (11)

where: G - shear modulus, b_g - Burger's vector, ρ - mean dislocation density in the material.

Finally, the cell coverage by the recrystallization front or another grain is calculated by:

$$RX_{i,t}^{fraction} = RX_{t,t-1}^{fraction} + \sum_{j=1}^{rx}\left(\frac{v_j t_{step}}{c_s}\right)$$ (12)

where: $RX_{i,t-1}^{fraction}$ – the level of coverage of the i–th cell in the previous (t-1) time step, rx – number of recrystallized neighbours (stored energy driving force) or number of neighbouring cells that belong to recrystallized grains (grain boundary curvature driving force), v_j – velocity of the recrystallization front or recrystallized grain boundary, t_{step} – length of time step, c_s – cellular automata cell size.

Again when the recrystallized volume fraction reaches value of one, the cell changes its state to recrystallized. More details on the model are available in [8].

6   Numerical Examples – Case Study

The numerical modelling of complex multistep hot deformation process was selected as a case study to show capabilities of the developed cellular automata finite element model approaches. The process involves four passes of plastic deformation in channel die followed by static recrystallization after each pass to restore the deformed microstructure. After the last deformation pass the sample was cooled down to room temperature and the phase transformation occurred in the investigated microstructure. Schematic investigated thermo-mechanical cycle is presented in Fig. 4.

Results obtained after each stage of the investigated deformation cycle are presented in Fig. 5. Subsequent stages of phase transformation during heating are shown in Fig. 6.

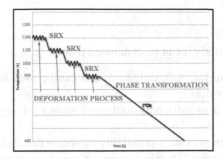

Fig. 4. Thermo – mechanical cycles applied during the research

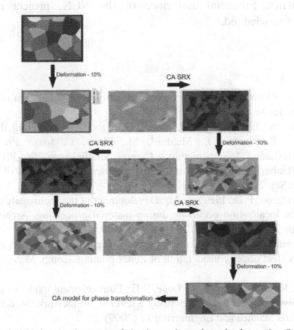

Fig. 5. Results obtained after each stage of the investigated cycle from the finite element and cellular automata SRX models

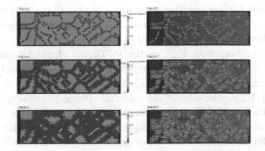

Fig. 6. Microstructure (left) and carbon distribution (right) after the phase transformation

7   Conclusions

Based on the presented study it can be concluded that:

- Developed framework is a flexible tool, that can be used to create complex microstructure evolution models.
- CA framework is a user-friendly tools and allows adding new microstructure evolution models.
- CAFE approach can provide a possibility to obtain detailed information on state of the material for subsequent CA calculations e.g. precise value of stored energy.

Acknowledgements. Financial assistance of the NCN, project no. 2011/01/D/ST8/01681, is acknowledged.

References

1. Davies, C.H.J.: Growth of nuclei in a cellular automaton simulation of recrystalization. Scripta Materialia 36, 35–40 (1997)
2. Das, S., Palmiere, E.J., Howard, I.C.: CAFE: a tool for modelling thermomechanical processes. In: Palmiere, E.J., Mahfouf, M., Pinna, C. (eds.) Proc. Thermomech. Processing: Mechanics, Microstructure & Control, Sheffield, pp. 296–301 (2002)
3. Rollett, A., Raabe, D.: A hybrid model for mesoscopic simulation of recrystallization. Comp. Mater. Sci. 21, 69–78 (2001)
4. Madej, L., Hodgson, P.D., Pietrzyk, M.: Development of the multi-scale analysis model to simulate strain localization occurring during material processing. Archives of Computational Methods in Engineering 16, 287–318 (2009)
5. Raabe, D., Hantcherli, L.: 2D cellular automaton simulation of the recrystallization texture of an IF sheet steel under consideration of Zener pinning. Comp. Mater. Sci. 34, 299–313 (2009)
6. Bemacki, M., Resk, H., Coupez, T., Loge, R.E.: Finite element model of primary recrystallization in polycrystalline aggregates using a level set framework. Modelling and Simulation in Materials Science and Engineering 17 (2009)
7. Li, W., Zabaras, N.: A virtual environment or the interrogation of 3D polycrystalline microstructures including grain size effect. Computational Material Science 44, 1163–1177 (2009)
8. Sieradzki, L., Madej, L.: A perceptive comparison of the cellular automata and Monte Carlo techniques in application to static recrystallization modeling in polycrystalline materials. Computational Materials Science 67, 156–173 (2013)
9. Madej, L., Rauch, L., Perzynski, K., Cybulka, P.: Digital Material Representation as an efficient tool for strain inhomogeneities analysis at the micro scale level. Archives of Civil and Mechanical Engineering 11, 661–679 (2011)
10. Rauch, L., Madej, L.: Application of the automatic image processing in modelling of the deformation mechanisms based on the digital representation of microstructure. International Journal for Multiscale Computational Engineering 8, 343–356 (2010)
11. Szyndler, J., Madej, L.: Effect of number of grains and boundary conditions on digital material representatioin deformation under plain strain. Archives of Civil and Mechanical Engineering, http://dx.doi.org/10.1016/j.acme.2013.09.001

12. Madej, L., Sieradzki, L., Sitko, M., Perzynski, K., Radwański, K., Kuziak, R.: Multi scale cellular automata and finite element based model for cold deformation and annealing of a ferritic-pearlitic microstructure. Computational Materials Science 77, 172–181 (2013)
13. Von Neumann, J.: Theory of self reproducing automata. University of Illinois, Urbana (1966), Bamk, A.W. (ed.)
14. Spytkowski, P., Klimek, T., Rauch, Ł., Madej, L.: Implementation of cellular automata framework dedicated to digital material representation. Computer Methods in Materials Science 9, 283–288 (2009)
15. Golab, R., Bachniak, D., Bzowski, K., Madej, L.: Sensitivity Analysis of the Cellular Automata Model for Austenite-Ferrite Phase Transformation in Steels. Applied Mathematics 4(11), 1531–1536 (2013)

A Preliminary Cellular Model for Secondary Lahars and Simulation of 2005 Case of Vascún Valley, Ecuador

Guillermo Machado[1,2], Valeria Lupiano[3],
Maria Vittoria Avolio[2], and Salvatore Di Gregorio[2]

[1] National University of Chimborazo, Faculty of Engineering, Riobamba, Ecuador
gmachado@unach.edu.ec
[2] University of Calabria, Dept. of Mathematics and Computer Science, 87036 Rende (CS), Italy
machado@mat.unical.it, {avoliomv,salvatore.digregorio}@unical.it
[3] University of Calabria, Dept. of Biology, Ecology, Earth Sciences, 87036 Rende (CS), Italy
valeria.lupiano@unical.it

Abstract. Lahars represent one of the most destructive natural disasters as number of casualties in the world. Secondary lahars are very complex surface flows, which originate from the mobilization of pyroclastic deposits by exceptional heavy rainfalls. Simulation of secondary lahars could be an important tool for risk management in threatened regions. Multicomponent (macroscopic) Cellular Automata (CA) characterize a methodological approach for modelling large scale (extended for kilometers) complex phenomena, that evolve on the basis of local interactions. A preliminary three dimension CA model was developed and partially applied on a real event: the 2005 secondary lahar of Vascún Valley, Ecuador. Simulations are satisfying, a comparison is performed with the previous successful two dimensions model Titan2D, based on PDE, together with simulation results of the same event.

Keywords: Cellular Automata, Lahar, Modelling, Simulation, Natural Hazard.

1 Introduction

Lahars are mixtures of water and volcanic sediments with consistency, viscosity and approximate density of concrete: they are fluid, when sloping moving up to 100 km/h as far as an extreme distance of 300 Km, solid at rest in the flat terminal zone [10].

Primary lahars originate by direct volcanic eruptive activity: lava or pyroclastic flows melt snow and glacier and/or mix with wet soil; another cause during an eruption could be a glacier, lake breakout, where water, combined with volcanic material, generates a flood [11].

Secondary lahars originate along thick volcanic deposits when a largest amount of water becomes available by heavy rainfalls or typhoons and mobilizes sediments of previous volcanic activity. Both the types of lahar can grow by soil erosion and/or incorporation of water, along watercourses [11]. Main mechanisms, related to secondary lahars, are percolation of an adequate water quantity on abundant unconsolidated sediment in order to trigger a mobilization process, flood formation and evolution

J. Wąs, G.C. Sirakoulis, and S. Bandini (Eds.): ACRI 2014, LNCS 8751, pp. 208–217, 2014.
© Springer International Publishing Switzerland 2014

along the volcano steep slopes with high gravitational potential energy, contemporary possible soil erosion and water inclusion along watercourses or lakes, water extrusion and solidification process in flat zones of the final phase.

Lahar modelling involved different types of approaches [11]: empirical models based on smart correlations of phenomenon observables (e.g., LAHARZ [13]), simple rheological and hydrological models, that assume acceptable simplifications as composition-independent flow behavior or Newtonian flow behavior (e.g., [5]), PDE numerical methods approximating PDE of complex physical behavior of lahar [12]; lack of precise information (that is a normal condition) about the real events of lahar can generate various problems for applying these methods to simulation.

The previous listed mechanisms were modelled according to the methodological approach of Multicomponent (or Macroscopic) Cellular Automata (CA) [7] for computer simulation of surface flows [5]: water percolation (model SOIL [7] and model SCAVATU [6]); soil detachments evolving in debris, mud, granular flows (family of models SCIDDICA [7], [4], [2]); furthermore solidification could be described as viscosity variation by water loss in similar equational way as viscosity variation of lava flows by cooling (SCIARA model [7], [1]).

Intuitively a CA can be seen as a space, partitioned in cells, each one embedding an identical input/output computing unit. Each cell is characterized by its state. S is the finite set of the states. Input for each cell is local and is given by the states of m neighboring cells, where the neighborhood conditions are given by a pattern invariant in time and space. At time 0, cells are in arbitrary states (initial conditions) and the CA evolves changing simultaneously the state at discrete times, according to (local, depending on the input) rules, that are invariant in time and space.

CA approach is based on the definition of "simple", but fundamental local rules, that have to observe conservation physical laws in the context of space and time discretization. Such rules have to capture the significant interacting processes. The phenomenon evolution "emerges" by local interactions: "simplest" rules can generate very complex realistic behaviors.

We developed **LLUNPIY** (Lahar modelling by Local rules based on an UNderlying PIck of Yoked processes, from the Quechua word llunp'iy meaning flood) a three dimensions deterministic CA model for simulation of secondary lahars, taking into account experience and solutions matured in the elaboration of previous models.

Other models were used for lahar computer simulations: the two dimensions model Titan2D [4] was developed for simulating granular, mud, debris flows and lahars; it is based upon a depth-averaged model for an incompressible Coulomb continuum, a "shallow-water" granular flow. The conservation equations for mass and momentum are solved with a Coulomb-type friction term both for the internal interactions of flow components and external interactions flow components and basal surface. An optimal simulation of part of the 2005 secondary lahar of Vascún Valley, Ecuador was performed by Titan2D [14]; such a simulation represents a touchstone for our research.

The second section introduces the CA model of lahar LLUNPIY, and then the third one is dedicated to the 2005 secondary lahar of Vascún Valley, Ecuador. Results of LLUNPIY simulation of the Vascún Valley are reported in the fourth section; some conclusions close the paper in the fifth section.

2   The CA Model LLUNPIY for Lahar Simulation

CA modelling and simulation of real complex "macroscopic" systems implies that a time-space correspondence must be explicitly established between the model and the real world in order to compare phenomenon development with simulation progress; the cell has to correspond to a precise space portion, the transition step has to correspond to a time interval; moreover cell state must account for components, that are related to various characteristics of the space portion and transition function must account for a complexity of interrelating processes of similar or different nature.

Multicomponent Cellular Automata, (MCA, also known as Macroscopic Cellular Automata) characterize such a methodological approach for modeling complex systems, especially macroscopic phenomena, that need many components both for the states (sub-states) in order to account for different properties of the cell and for the transition function ("elementary" processes) in order to account for various different interacting dynamics.

Sub-states permit to operate in three effective dimensions by two-dimensional MCA, if all the quantities concerning the third dimension may be expressed as substates (LLUNPIY case); furthermore a MCA step is an ordered sequence of applied elementary processes, every elementary process implies the MCA state updating.

Sometimes, the investigated phenomenon involves external influence which cannot be described in terms of local rules (e.g. the rain), so a kind of input from the "external world" for some cells has to be introduced in MCA approach [7], [6].

2.1   LLUNPIY Main Specifications

LLUNPIY considers secondary lahars from the first mobilization phase by rainfall to the final phase in flat areas, when the lahar, that reduces heavily its load and velocity by water loss, can solidify and can partially "be diluted" and "disappear" into a water-course with a water flow, sufficiently high to englobe the lahar matter.

Two interacting fluids must be considered in the cell: free water and lahar fluid phase in order to implement the following cell mechanisms. When water from the rainfall percolates, accumulates on the bottom of erodible soil and overcomes a fixed threshold, the detachment occurs in the cell; surface water, erodible soil and water content of soil mix develop the lahar flow; afterwards maximum water content in lahar is depending on its kinetic energy, water surplus is released as free water in surface, while fluid lahar viscosity grows.

The fluid lahar inside a cell is modelled as a "cylinder" tangent the next edge of the hexagonal cell with mass, velocity and barycenter co-ordinates. Three cases are possible for outflows toward adjacent cells: internal flows (cylinder shift is all inside the cell), external flows (cylinder shift is all outside the cell) and mixed case.

The hexagonal CA model LLUNPIY is the septuple: $<R, G, X, S, P, \tau, \gamma>$ where :

- $R = \{(x, y)/ \ x,y \in \mathbb{N}, \ 0 \le x \le l_x, \ 0 \le y \le l_y\}$ is the set of points with integer co-ordinates, that individuate the regular hexagonal cells, covering the finite region, where the phenomenon evolves. $\mathbb{N}$ is the set of natural numbers.

- $G \subseteq R$ is the set of cells, where the raining "influence" is active.
- $X = \{(0, 0), (1, 0), (0, 1), (-1, 1), (-1, 0), (0,-1), (-1,-1)\}$, the neighborhood index, identifies the geometrical pattern of cells, which influence state change of the central cell: the central cell (index 0) itself and the six adjacent cells (indexes 1,..,6).
- S is the finite set of states of the finite automaton, embedded in the cell; it is equal to the Cartesian product of the sets of the considered sub-states (Table 1).
- P is the set of the global physical and empirical parameters, which account for the general frame of the model and the physical characteristics of the phenomenon (Table 2), the choice of some parameters is imposed by the desired precision of simulation where possible, e.g., cell dimension; the value of some parameters is deduced by physical features of the phenomenon, e.g., turbulence dissipation, even if an acceptable value is fixed by the simulation quality by attempts, triggered by comparison of discrepancies between real event knowledge and simulation results;
- τ: $S^7 \to S$ is the cell deterministic state transition, it accounts for the following main components of the phenomenon: water percolation, water inclusion and extrusion, water flow, lahar flow, lahar solidification, soil mobilization and erosion.
- γ: $\mathbb{N} \times G \to S$ expresses the raining water quantity to be added for G cells at each CA step. $\mathbb{N}$ is here referred to the step number.

Table 1. Sub-states

SUB-STATES	DESCRIPTION
A, LT, D,	cell Altitude, Lahar Thickness, erodible soil Depth
WL, WKE, WO	Water Level, Water Kinetic Energy, Water Outflows (6 components normalized to a thickness)
SR, SWC, LWC	Soil Receptivity, Soil Water Content, Lahar Water Content
X, Y	the co-ordinates X and Y of the lahar barycenter inside the cell
MX, MY,	the components x and y of the lahar Momentum inside the cell
E, EX, EY, KHE (6 components)	External flow normalized to a thickness, External flow co-ordinates X and Y, Kinetic Head of External flow
I, IX. IY, KHI (6 components)	Internal flow normalized to a thickness, Internal flow co-ordinates X and Y, Kinetic Head of Internal flow

Table 2. Physical and empirical parameters

PARAMETERS	DESCRIPTION
a, t	cell apothem (m), temporal correspondence of a CA step (s)
fc	friction coefficient parameter (°)
td, ed, pe, mt	lahar parameters: turbulence dissipation (-) and erosion dissipation (-) of energy; lahar parameter of progressive erosion (-), mobilization threshold (m, because KH is normalized to a length)
hc, ir	detrital cover hydraulic conductivity (m/s), infiltration rate (m/s)
wrr, mst, khl	water flow parameters: relaxation rate (-); maximum sediment transport (%), kinetic head loss (m)
st, ct, adh	solidification threshold (%), critical thickness (m), adherence (m)

2.2   Outline of LLUNPIY Transition Function

Many parts of LLUNPIY transition function are borrowed by other CA models with opportune changes. More explanations can be found in the references. In the formulae, neighborhood index for sub-states is specified between square brackets, if it is not referred to central cell; ΔQ means Q value variation, multiplication is explicitly "·".

Fluid Lahar and Water Outflows. Outflows computation is performed in two steps: determination of the outflows by the Algorithm for the Minimization of Differences (AMD [7], [3]) applied to "heights" of the cell neighborhood and determination of the shift of the outflows [4], [2]. Free water can transport sediments according to the same transition function in [6].

Terms of AMD are the height (h) of cells in the neighborhood , to be minimized by flows (f), whose sum is equal to the quantity $q=LT[0]-still(LWC[0],st,ct,adh)$ to be distributed from the central cell. *still* is the function that determines the *still* part of the fluid lahar (normalized to a thickness). $h[0]=A[0]+KH[0]+still(LWC[0],st,ct,adh)$ for the central cell, while $h[i]=A[i]+LT[i]+corr(MX[0],MY[0])$ $1 \leq i \leq 6$ for the other neighborhood cells. The "correcting" function *corr* account for directional effects concerning momentum by an alteration of height values [2]. *still* and *corr* are not used for water flow computation [6].

The outflow path from the central cell to a neighboring cell i follows an ideal direction between two points: the fluid lahar barycenter of central cell and the center of the adjacent cell i accounting the slope $\theta[i]$ (Fig. 1).

The $f[i]$ shift "sh" is computed according to the following simple formula, that averages the movement of all the mass as the barycenter movement of a body on a constant slope with a constant friction coefficient: $sh = v \cdot t + g \cdot (\sin\theta - fc \cdot \cos\theta) \cdot t^2/2$ with "g" gravity acceleration and initial velocity $v=\sqrt{(2 \cdot g \cdot KH[0])}$ [4]; the outflow could be represented as a cylinder whose barycenter corresponds to the barycenter of lahar matter inside the central cell and following the above-mentioned direction.

A turbulence effect is modelled by a proportional kinetic head loss at each LLUNPIY step: $-\Delta KH=td \cdot KH$. This formula involves that a velocity limit is asymptotically imposed de facto, for a maximum value of slope.

Erodible layer ⟶

Bedrock ⟶

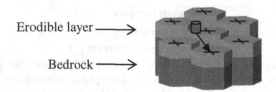

Fig. 1. Outflow direction from central cell to the center of an adjacent cell in 3-dimensions

Water Percolation and Soil Mobilization. The surface water loss by absorption is computed according to empirical considerations: a maximum infiltration rate ir is determined according to the physical characteristics of the erodible soil. *SWC* is computed according the erodible soil depth D. When SWC implies saturation of the erodible soil, all the erodible soil comes off and develops in fluid lahar ($\Delta LT=WL+D$, $\Delta WL=0$, $\Delta D=0$). Viscosity is depending on SWC by parameters st, ct, adh.

Soil Erosion. When the kinetic head value overcomes an opportune threshold ($KH>mt$) depending on the soil features then a mobilization of the detrital cover occurs proportionally to the quantity overcoming the threshold $pe\cdot(KH-mt)=\Delta LT =-\Delta D$ (the detrital cover depth diminishes as the debris thickness increases), the kinetic head loss is: $-\Delta KH = ed\cdot(KH-mt)$. The mixing of the eroded detrital cover with the earlier debris involves that the earlier debris kinetic energy becomes the kinetic energy of all the mass of debris, it implicates trivially a further kinetic head reduction; momentum variation follows from velocity reduction and increasing of moving mass.

Water Extrusion and Viscosity Increase. Viscosity is modelled as the part of lahar thickness that cannot be movable according to some rules, similar to [1] and depending on LWC. Furthermore a relation is defined among maximum LWC and KH, a water extrusion occurs when KH diminishes and maximum possible LWC is exceeded, a threshold determines fluid lahar turns into erodible soil ($\Delta D=LWC$; $LWC=0$).

3   The 2005 Secondary Lahar of Vascún Valley, Ecuador

The Vascún valley is a deep gorge, set to the northern flank of Tungurahua stratovolcano (Fig. 2) crossed by the Rio Vascún. The thermal structure "El Salado Baths" lies along the banks of the river, while the town of Baños is located in the depositional area. Volcano hazards are produced by tephra falls, lava flows, pyroclastic flows, and lahars; someone reached populated areas at the base of the volcano, threatening about 25,000 people. Also Baños was affected more times by lahars [8, 9].

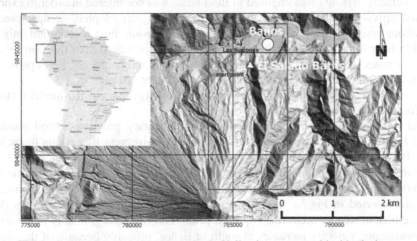

Fig. 2. Tungurahua Volcano. The Vascún Valley is represented inside the box.

On February 12th, 2005, heavy rainfalls have caused the remobilization of ashfall deposits, giving rise to a lahar in the Rio Vascún valley. The mean velocities of flows were estimated on the base of records of alert instrumentations. They vary between 7 m/s and 3 m/s, depending on the cross sections [14]. The lahar volume, measured by Acoustic Flow Monitor, was approximately estimated 70.000 m³, while a subsequent investigation, carried out by Instituto Geofisico Ecuatoriano, estimates it 55.000 m³. The lahar ran through the valley approximately for 10 km and flooded El Salado Baths during the passage of the flows, then reached Pastaza River.

Note that chronicle of the event, above described, is taken from the work of Williams et al., 2008 [14]. These authors performed simulations of part of the event (about 2 km) with Titan2D with start point at 2005 m a.s.l. and final point approximately at the end of Las Illusiones. We refer to their data and simulations for comparison with our simulation because they were able to collect data while the documentation of the other real event is scarce.

4   Simulations of the 2005 Lahar of Vascún Valley

We referred for event simulation to the DEM with 1m cell size (supplied to us by Dr. Gustavo Cordoba). It was integrated (in QGIS software) for the last 500m by a DEM with 5m cell size (supplied to us by Eng. Patricia Mothes). Also, a uniform thickness of 5m was imposed for detrital cover, because detailed surveys were not available. All this introduces a series of approximations, that affects certainly simulations, but do not detract from the effectiveness of the model.

First simulations were limited by the partial information on the 2005 Lahar of Vascún Valley. We worked on a set of data, that didn't include all the lahar extension: we consider a stretch of about 2,3 km, from elevation 2150 m a.s.l. (about 850m upstream of el Salado Bath) to elevation 1900 m a.s.l. (in correspondence of Pastaza river). The area, where our simulation starts, does not concern the detachment phase: the primary detachment phase occurs 8 Km upriver. A kind of detachment, where an initial velocity of 7 m/s was imposed to fluid lahar, was considered in order to express the first arrival of lahar. An equivalent fluid approach was adopted, because precise data about water flows are not available. Therefore, erosion must account not only for erodible layer, but for water inclusion. The total mass is inclusive of the water mass. This generates a discrepancy between lahar volume, measured on the deposit and fluid lahar volume including water to be loss in the event last part.

It was important in such conditions to start with only a part of the model that can be a future base for usage of other parts.

The transition function was applied to the elementary processes: "soil erosion" "fluid lahar outflows" and accounts for fluid lahar movement that wants to include implicitly the water contribution.

Figure 3 shows the simulation of part of 2005 lahar with LLUNPIY. In particular, the maximum debris thickness values, that were reached by the fluid lahar in simulation, are reported in Fig.3a. Maximum velocities, reached by simulated flows (Fig. 3b), are high in steeper areas (the expected result) and decrease gradually at the outlet in downstream. Velocity increases at south of Baños, probably because of the higher gradient of the river bed. Erosion has a trend similar to that of the velocity (Fig. 3c).

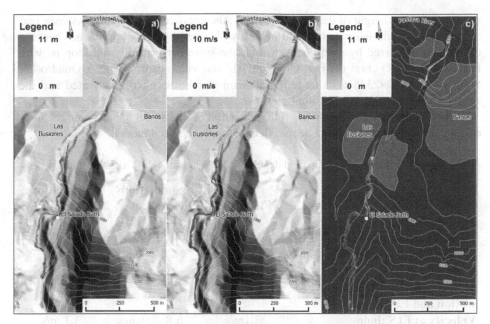

Fig. 3. a) Maximum thickness, b) Maximum velocity, and c) eroded regolith, in simulated event

Table 3 synthetizes values of Figure 3 and compares such data with field data of Instituto Geofisico Ecuatoriano reported in [14]. Such field data are obviously partial for the complete development of catastrophic phenomenon, but extremely precious by comparison with our simulations. Observation data are not sufficient to a precise comparison with the simulation paths that are partial because of the limited field data. Furthermore. lahar starts with null velocity in the simulation of Williams et al. [14], while LLUNPIY simulations start with 7 m/s velocities. The difference for total eroded mass rises from the lost water volume that cannot be considered in measurements.

5   Conclusions

We applied partially LLUNPIY because the available data of real event regard only a part of 2005 lahar of Vascún Valley. We consider ourselves lucky for obtaining such data for such a catastrophic event. An accurate analysis was performed in order to compare data of different sources and to obtain the most faithful reconstruction for a part of the event and extended the zone under study in [14]. We are confident to improve our reconstruction by a deeper study and further contributions.

Simulation results demonstrate that the applied part of LLUNPIY is working well if we consider the partial, sometime rough data concerning the event, pre-event, post-event more the unavoidable errors in event records. This part of model is reliable for starting an extension, where further specifications must be considered and tested. The simulations were satisfying in terms of reproducing the global dynamic of the events, such as velocity, height of detrital flow, times; the good correspondence between real and simulated fluid lahar path would be easily obtained by many approaches because the flow is canalized by steep faces. Simulation were performed by desktop pc with Processor Intel(R) corel (TM)i7, CPU 2.8GHz and video card: NVIDIA Quadro FX 580, CA is 1570×2345 cells large. Parallelism was not explicitly activated and the simulation average time was 15 minutes.

Future research will concern the full application of the model for this case and other ones; its validation implies a deep reflection on the devised model.

Table 3. Comparison among field data, TITAN2D and LLUNPIY simulation data

	Field data	Simulations output TITAN2D	Simulation output LLUNPIY
Mean Velocity between Retu Seismic Station and AFM station	7 m/s	-	-
Mean Velocity between AFM station and El Salado	3.10 m/s	-	-
Velocity at El Salado	3.1m/s	5.8–8.9. m/s	3.1 m/s
Velocity at final Las Ilusiones		1.1–2.6 m/s	3 m/s
Time between AFM station and El Salado	16 minutes	-	-
Time between start point and El Salado	-	-	6-7 minutes
Time between El Salado and final Las Ilusiones	-	-	14 minutes
Total time between start point and Las Ilusiones	-	~8-14 minutes	20 minutes
Eroded debris between start point and El Salado	-	-	38000 m^3
Eroded debris between El Salado and Las Ilusiones	-	-	71000m^3
Total eroded layer between start point and final point Las Ilusiones	55000/70000m^3	50000/70000m^3	109000 m^3

Acknowledgments. The authors are grateful to many scientists for obtaining precious data concerning the 2005 Lahar of Vascún Valley, useful information, advices and comments. We remember just Dr. Gustavo Cordoba Guerrero, Professor at the University of Narinno, Colombia, Eng. Patricia Mothes, Researcher at Instituto Geofisico de Ecuador, Dr. Michel Sheridan, Professor Emeritus at the University of Buffalo, USA.

References

1. Avolio, M.V., Crisci, G.M., Di Gregorio, S., Rongo, R., Spataro, W., Trunfio, G.A.: SCIARA γ2: an improved Cellular Automata model for Lava Flows and Applications to the 2002 Etnean crisis. Computers & Geosciences 32, 897–911 (2006)
2. Avolio, M.V., Di Gregorio, S., Lupiano, V., Mazzanti, P.: SCIDDICA-SS3: A New Version of Cellular Automata Model for Simulating Fast Moving Landslides. The Journal of Supercomputing (2013), doi:10.1007/s11227-013-0948-1, ISSN 0920-8542
3. Avolio, M.V., Di Gregorio, S., Spataro, W., Trunfio, G.A.: A Theorem about the Algorithm of Minimization of Differences for Multicomponent Cellular Automata. In: Sirakoulis, G.C., Bandini, S. (eds.) ACRI 2012. LNCS, vol. 7495, pp. 289–298. Springer, Heidelberg (2012)
4. Avolio, M.V., Lupiano, V., Mazzanti, P., Di Gregorio, S.: Modelling combined subaerial-subaqueous flow-like landslides by Cellular Automata. In: Umeo, H., Morishita, S., Nishinari, K., Komatsuzaki, T., Bandini, S. (eds.) ACRI 2008. LNCS, vol. 5191, pp. 329–336. Springer, Heidelberg (2008)
5. Costa, J.E.: Hydraulic modeling for lahar hazards at Cascades volcanoes. Environmental and Engineering Geosciences £, 21–30 (2004)
6. D'Ambrosio, D., Di Gregorio, S., Gabriele, S., Gaudio, R.: A Cellular Automata Model for Soil Erosion by Water. Physics and Chemistry of the Earth, EGS, Part B 26(1), 33–39 (2001)
7. Di Gregorio, S., Serra, R.: An empirical method for modelling and simulating some complex macroscopic phenomena by cellular automata. Future Generation Computer Systems 16(2/3), 259–271 (1999)
8. Egred, J.: Historia de las erupciones del volcán Tungurahua. Instituto Geofísico, unpub. rep., Escuela Politécnica Nacional, Quito, 70 p. (1999)
9. Hall, M.L., Robin, C., Beate, B., Mothes, P., Monzier, M.: Tungurahua Volcano, Ecuador: structure, eruptive history and hazards. Journal of Volcanology and Geothermal Research 91, 1–21 (1999)
10. Hoblitt, R.P., Miller, C.D., Scott, W.E.: Volcanic Hazards with Regard to Siting Nuclear-Power Plants in the Pacific Northwest. U.S. Geological Survey Open-File Report. 87-297 (1987)
11. Manville, V., Major, J.J., Fagents, S.A.: Modeling lahar behavior and hazards. In: Modeling Volcanic Processes The Physics and Mathematics of Volcanism, ch. 14, pp. 300–330 (2013), http://dx.doi.org/10.1017/CBO9781139021562.014
12. Pitman, E.B., Nichita, C.C., Patra, A.K., Bauer, A.C., Sheridan, M.F., Bursik, M.: Computing Granular Avalanches and Landslides. Physics of Fluids 15(12) (2003)
13. Schilling, S.P.: LAHARZ: GIS Programs for Automated Mapping of Lahar-inundation Hazard Zones: U.S. Geological Survey Open-File Report 98-638 (1998)
14. Williams, R., Stinton, A.J., Sheridan, M.F.: Evaluation of the Titan2D two-phase flow model using an actual event: Case study of the 2005 Vazcún Valley Lahar. Journal of Volcanology and Geothermal Research 177, 760–766 (2008)

Vulnerability and Protector Control: Cellular Automata Approach

Omar Jellouli[1], Abdessamed Bernoussi[1],
Mina Amharref[1], and Samira El Yacoubi[2]

[1] Faculty of Sciences and Techniques, B.P. 416, Tangier, Morocco
[2] Department of mathematics and computer science, University of Perpignan, France

Abstract. In this work we consider the protector control problem using cellular automata approach. We give some definitions and characterizations of vulnerable zones and protector control for a cellular automaton model. We illustrate this notion through a fire forest example using a developed application with JAVA environment.

1   Introduction

Understanding of complex environmental systems which involve a large number of interacting components and exhibit important features at multiple spatial and temporal scales, remains an important issue on which several researchers are focused . In connection with the theory of complex systems, the study of the behavior of these systems will help to predict and/or control their evolution.

For the study of distributed parameters systems, the classical approach was based on Partial Differential Equations (PDEs) and a large literature has been devoted to this approach. However, the complexity of real systems ranging from biology and ecology to medicine and species abundance, leads to serious difficulties both in control theory and in the model implementation.

In this context and with the growing interest in spatial modeling, the investigation of more and more efficient modeling tools is necessary. The adopted methods should ensure the persistence of the main properties of these systems, such as their symmetries and conservation laws and their global dynamics.

Among the problems related to systems analysis, we consider the concept of vulnerability which characterizes the response of a distributed parameters system subject to an expanding spatial disturbance. For such problem, we consider an approach based on cellular automata (CA) models and investigate the possibility of protecting the region which is vulnerable to the effects of a given disturbance. The notions of vulnerability and protector control have been recently introduced and studied by means of PDEs in both linear and nonlinear cases [1,2]. Their practical use which generally needs a hard implementation of PDEs, particularly in the case of controlled processes, is still limited. The purpose of this paper is to consider CA models, which are often described as a counterpart to PDEs, as tools for modelling and simulating vulnerability and risk for some real phenomena such as pollution, flood, forest fire, etc.). The reason behind the choice of

J. Wąs, G.C. Sirakoulis, and S. Bandini (Eds.): ACRI 2014, LNCS 8751, pp. 218–227, 2014.

CA models is their capability to provide a powerful framework for investigating spatial expanding behaviours in part due to their explicit representation of space.

Despite the apparent simplicity of CA models, they are able to describe the complexity of real world systems by means of local transition rules which will be directly expressed as algorithms and then easily implemented as computer programs [3,12,15]. They will be used in this paper to illustrate a theoretical aspect of systems and control theory through a simple example. It consists of modelling and simulating a fire spread, considered as a disturbance of a system described by a vegetation dynamics. The control will be also introduced in order to protect a prescribed vulnerable area from the fire spreading. The concept of spreadability have been already studied by means of CA models [5,11] where a characterization of spreadable zones has been established. The control which is defined for distributed parameters systems as an external excitation which may steer the system to a given objective, has been also introduced for CA models [6]. For the studied example, several models for vegetation or fire dynamics can be considered among the large literature devoted to these systems [8,9,13,14]. The investigated model in this paper which has been used only to illustrate the notions of vulnerability and protector control, has to be simplified for a more general study.

This paper is organized as follows. In the next section, after recalling the basic definition of CA models, the study of vulnerability and protector control by means of CA models will be given. Section 3 is focused on the example of a forest fire dynamics. Simulation results will be given to illustrate the considered phenomenon using a developed simulator. Some concluding remarks are given in section 4.

2   Vulnerability and Protector Control with Cellular Automata Approach

In this paper we consider the protector control problem with cellular automata approach. We recall the CA principle.

2.1   Cellular Automata

Cellular automata are discrete models for systems that vary in space and time. First introduced by von Neumann in the 1950s when studying self-reproducing machines, they have been used in several settings and provided models for a wide range of complex phenomena, including fluid dynamics, traffic model, excitable media, forest fire or pattern formation. This has led to a large body of literature, e.g. [3,4,7,16,17] and the references therein.

A standard CA consists of a regular infinite uniform lattice with a discrete variable at each site, named cell. The state of each cell is updated based on the previous states of its immediate neighboring cells according to a set of local rules.

In what follows, the time variable is given in $I = \{0, 1, 2, \cdots\}$.

Definition 1. *A cellular automaton is usually specified by the quadruple $\mathcal{A} = (\mathcal{L}, \mathcal{S}, N, f)$ where :*

- *$\mathcal{L}$ is a lattice defined by a regular grid of cells denoted by $c_{i_1 i_2 \cdots i_d}$, on a d-dimensional domain Ω. In a two-dimensional domain, a cell will be denoted by $c_{i,j}$,*
- *$\mathcal{S}$ a finite set of states given as a commutative ring $\mathcal{S} = \{0, 1, \cdots, k-1\}$ in which modular arithmetic will be used,*
- *a finite neighborhood $\mathbf{N}(c)$ of size n which summarizes the effects of the surrounding cells on the state evolution of cell c,*
- *a set of local transition rules which update the state of cell c depending on the neighborhood of cell c ($N(c)$). It can be given by a transition function :*

$$f : \begin{array}{c} \mathcal{S}^{N(c)} \longrightarrow \mathcal{S} \\ s_t(N(c)) \longrightarrow s_{t+1}(c) \end{array}$$

In this section we consider the concept of vulnerability and protector control as it was introduced in [1,2,10] using PDEs, through cellular automata approach.

2.2   Vulnerability and Protector Control: Cellular Automata Approach

Let us consider a dynamical system which evolves in a domain $\Omega \subset \mathbb{R}^n$.

We will consider in what follows, a disturbed controlled system described by a cellular automaton. Denote by $\mathcal{A} = (\mathcal{L}, \mathcal{S}, N, f)$, $\mathcal{A}' = (\mathcal{L}, \mathcal{S}', N, f')$ and $\mathcal{A}'' = (\mathcal{L}, \mathcal{S}'', N, f'')$ the considered cellular automata in the autonomous, disturbed not controlled and disturbed-controlled cases respectively.

Spreadability and Vulnerability

Let $\mathcal{P}$ be a given property specifying the spatial disturbance defined by:

$$\mathcal{P}s'_{t_i}(c) \Leftrightarrow s'_{t_i}(c) = s' \tag{1}$$

where $s' \in \mathcal{S}'$ is a given state and $s'_{t_i}(c)$ denotes the state of cell c in the disturbed case, at time $t_i \in I$ where I is a given time interval. Consider the following set :

$$\omega_{t_i} = \left\{ c \in \mathcal{L} | \ \mathcal{P}s'_{t_i}(c) \right\} = \left\{ c \in \mathcal{L} | s'_{t_i}(c) = s' \right\} \tag{2}$$

Let σ be a nonempty subset of $\mathcal{L}$ consisting of n_σ cells.

Definition 2.   – *We say that the property $\mathcal{P}$ is spreadable from ω_{t_0} if :*

$$\omega_{t_i} \subset \omega_{t_{i+1}} \quad \forall i \in I \tag{3}$$

– *We say that a given region σ is $\mathcal{P}$-vulnerable if there exist an instant $t \in \ ]t_0, T[$ such that :*

$$\sigma \cap \omega_t \neq \emptyset \tag{4}$$

Considering $\tau_{t_N} = \bigcup_{t_s \in]t_0, t_N[} \omega_{t_s}$ where $\omega_{t_s} = \{c \in \mathcal{L} | \mathcal{P} s'_{t_s}(c)\}$, the trajectory of the property $\mathcal{P}$. We have the characterization of the vulnerable zones.

Proposition 1. *The zone σ is vulnerable if and only if :* $\sigma \cap \tau_{t_N} \neq \emptyset$

The fact that $\sigma \cap \tau_{t_N} \neq \emptyset$ means that σ is in the trajectory of the property $\mathcal{P}$ and consequently the property $\mathcal{P}$ will reach σ.

Protector control

Let us now consider the protector control problem using a CA approach.

For a given area $\sigma \subset \mathcal{L}$, denote by $S^\sigma = \{s : \sigma \to S\}$ the set of mappings consisting of the restriction to σ of a CA configuration. Assume that σ is vulnerable, so there exists a time t_i such that : $s'_{t_i} \neq s_{t_i}$
Consider now a dynamical control denoted by u which aims to protect the zone σ. The control domain is assumed to be variable and it is given at time t by $D_t = \{c \in \mathcal{L} | u_t(c) \neq 0\}$ where u_t denotes the control variable. The problem consists in finding the family of domains D_t such that $\sigma \cap \tau^u_{t_N} = \emptyset$ where $\tau^u_{t_N}$ is the new trajectory of $\mathcal{P}$ for the controlled system.

The new obtained transition rule for the controlled CA is defined as follows :

$$s''_{t_{i+1}}(c) = f''\left(s''_{t_i}(N(c)), u_{t_i}(c)\chi_\sigma\right) \tag{5}$$

where $f''(s''_t(N(c)), u) = s_{t+1}$. It means that for cells in σ, the state value s_t evolves normally without disturbance when a control u is applied. Otherwise, $f''(s''_t(N(c)), 0) = s'_t$ and the disturbance is expanding in the absence of control.

We give the following definitions.

Definition 3. *If a given zone σ is vulnerable then:*

- *The zone σ is said to be exactly protectable from time t_1 if there exists a control u such that at every time $t_i \geq t_1$:*

$$s_{t_i} = s''_{t_i} \tag{6}$$

where $s_{t_i} \in S^\sigma$ and $s''_{t_i} \in S''^\sigma$ are the configuration at the time t_i of the autonomous and the disturbed-controlled system respectively .
In this case u is said to be an exact protector control.

- *The zone σ is said to be weakly protectable if there exists a control u such that $\forall \varepsilon > 0$:*

$$\frac{Card\left(\sigma \cap \tau^u_{t_N}\right)}{Card\left(\sigma\right)} \leq \varepsilon \tag{7}$$

where $\dfrac{Card\left(\sigma \cap \tau^u_{t_N}\right)}{Card\left(\sigma\right)}$ represents the proportion of cells in the region σ that are reached by the property P at a given time. We say that u is a weak protector control.

Proposition 2. *The zone σ is protectable, if there exists a protector control u such that:*

$$\tau_{t_N}^u \cap \sigma = \emptyset \tag{8}$$

where $\tau_{t_N}^u$ is the controlled trajectory of the disturbance.

To illustrate our approach, we consider the following example.

3   Forest fire Dynamics Example

3.1   Model Description

Consider a two dimensional CA defined on a regular lattice $\mathcal{L}$ where cells are denoted by c_{ij} and $N(c_{ij})$ a Von Neumann neighborhood of radius 1. The fundamental dynamical properties of a CA model are the definition of the cell state and the local rules that update this state from one time step to the next. We consider a CA model in three situation: autonomous, disturbed not controlled and disturbed-controlled systems, defined on the same lattice L with the same type of neighborhood but each CA has its own set of states and transition function.

Autonomous case: CA for a vegetation dynamics

<u>The states set</u> $\mathcal{S} = \{0, 1, 2, 3, 4\}$ where values 1 to 4 describe successive vegetation stages from a seed to adult plant. Value 0 is for a vacant cell.

State 0 : vacant cell   ,   or   **State 1 : seed**

 or   **State 2 : germination** ,   or   **State 3 : young plant**

or   **State 4 : adult plant**   ,

<u>The transition rules</u> f. Defined by the following updating rules :

– A vacant cell will be occupied by a seed if at least one of its neighbours is an adult plant.

$$\text{if } s_{t_i}(c_{ij}) = 0 \text{ then } s_{t_{i+1}}(c_{ij}) = \begin{cases} 1 & \text{if } \exists k, l \mid c_{kl} \in N(c_{ij}) \text{ and } s_{t_i}(c_{kl}) = 4 \\ 0 & \text{otherwise} \end{cases}$$

– A seed will evolve to a germination state at the next time step.

$$\text{if } s_{t_i}(c_{ij}) = 1 \text{ then } s_{t_{i+1}}(c_{ij}) = 2$$

– The transition from germination to young vegetation is given by :

$$\text{if } s_{t_i}(c_{ij}) = 2 \text{ then } s_{t_{i+1}}(c_{ij}) = \begin{cases} 0 & \text{if } \forall k, l \mid c_{kl} \in N(c_{ij}) \mid s_{t_i}(c_{kl}) = 4 \\ 3 & \text{otherwise} \end{cases}$$

– The young state goes to the adult state in the next time step

$$\text{if } s_{t_i}(c_{ij}) = 3 \text{ then } s_{t_{i+1}}(c_{ij}) = 4$$

– In adult state, the growth of the vegetation slowed down. However the plant can die (in an arbitrary way) before reaching the maximal age at time T_{dead} (where T_{dead} is a random selection for every cell).

$$\text{if } s_{t_i}(c_{ij}) = 4 \text{ then } s_{t_{i+1}}(c_{ij}) = \begin{cases} 4 \text{ if } \begin{array}{l} s_{t_i - T_{dead}}(c_{ij}) = s_{t_i - T_{dead}+1}(c_{ij}) \\ = \cdots = s_{t_i}(c_{ij}) = 4 \end{array} \\ 0 \text{ if } t_i = T_{dead} \end{cases}$$

Disturbed system: CA with Fire

The set of states $\mathcal{S}' = \{0, 1, 2, 3, 4\}$ where :

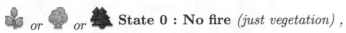 **State 0 : No fire** *(just vegetation)* ,

State 1 : Excitement by fire ,   **State 2 : Fire**

State 3 : Ash

State 4 : Empty cell *(nothing at all)*

The transition rules f':

– The distribution of fire is made in a plant cover. We give then the following transition rules :

$$\text{if } s'_{t_i}(c_{ij}) = 0 \text{ then } s'_{t_{i+1}}(c_{ij}) = \begin{cases} 1 \text{ if } \begin{array}{l} s_{t_i}(c_{ij}) \in \{2, 3, 4\} \text{ and} \\ \exists kl \mid c_{kl} \in N(c_{ij}) \text{ and } s'_{t_i}(c_{kl}) = 1 \end{array} \\ 0 \quad \text{otherwise} \end{cases}$$

– if $s'_{t_i}(c_{ij}) = 1$ then $s'_{t_{i+1}}(c_{ij}) = 2$
– In the burned-out state, the fire remains stable during a period of combustion T_{fire}. This parameter which depends on the vegetation stage, environment, wind, etc, will be in this study, randomly selected for every cell. After this time, the fire goes out and the cells will be occupied by ash. That is the transition from fire to ash.

$$\text{if } s'_{t_i}(c_{ij}) = 2 \text{ then } s'_{t_{i+1}}(c_{ij}) = \begin{cases} 2 \text{ if } \begin{array}{l} s'_{t_i - T_{fire}}(c_{ij}) = s'_{t_i - T_{fire}+1}(c_{ij}) \\ = \cdots = s'_{t_i}(c_{ij}) = 2 \end{array} \\ 3 \text{ if } t_i = T_{fire} \end{cases}$$

– The total dispersion of ash: cells become empty.

$$\text{if } s'_{t_i}(c_{ij}) = 3 \text{ then } s'_{t_{i+1}}(c_{ij}) = 4$$

– When the cell becomes empty, it always remains empty and obviously it can be occupied by a new seed if we start again the simulation of vegetation.

$$\text{if } s'_{t_i}(c_{ij}) = 4 \text{ then } s'_{t_{i+1}}(c_{ij}) = 4$$

Remark 1. (i) There are several factors that may affect the spread of fire. Slope which has a considerable influence on the rate of spread, especially in the initial stages of fire, wind power and direction, type of vegetation, humidity, etc. In the CA rules, these parameters can play an important role and have to be taken into account.

(ii) It should be noted that we are not dealing in this paper with modelling of vegetation dynamics or fire. These are just examples of dynamics considered in order to illustrate the notions of vulnerability and protector control. A more rigourous study is should be done in this direction for which a good formalism of these aspects have to be defined.

Controlled CA

We introduce the protector control in order to protect a chosen (vulnerable) zone σ. The effect of the control consists in changing the transition rule of fire spread introducing a control term u.

-Transition rules f'':

A given cell c_{ij}, with some vegetation, can be burned if there is a fire in its neighborhood. So to protect the zone σ we have to determine a domain of the control variable u_{t_i} denoted by D, such that for each $c_{ij} \in D$, and $t_i \in I$ $u_{t_i}(c_{ij}) = u$. The effect of the control u is to stop the fire spread toward the region σ.

$$\text{if } s''_{t_i}(c_{ij}) = 0 \text{ then } s''_{t_{i+1}}(c_{ij}) = \begin{cases} 1 & \text{if} & \begin{matrix} s_{t_i} \in \{2,3,4\} \text{ and} \\ \exists kl \mid c_{kl} \in N(c_{ij}) \text{ and } s''_{t_i}(c_{kl}) = 1 \\ c_{ij} \in D \end{matrix} \\ u & \text{if} \\ 0 & \text{otherwise} \end{cases}$$

 or **State 0 : No fire (just vegetation)**

 State 1 : Excitement by fire , **: Control u**

3.2   Simulation Results

The given simulations for the considered CA were performed using a developed application with JAVA environment. The CA is based on a regular grid of cells representing the domain Ω. The obtained lattice is $L = \{c_{ij} \mid 1 \leq i \leq M, \ 1 \leq j \leq M\}$ with $M \times M$ representing the total total number of cells in L.

The states of cells on the boundaries of the grid are set to zero value which means the choice of adiabatic boundary conditions.

Autonomous CA

The simulation starts with an initial state consisting of empty cells except for some isolated seeds.

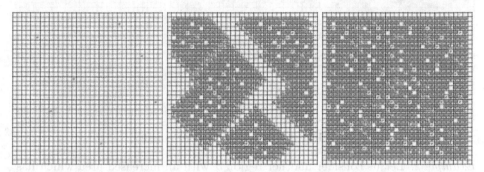

Fig.1. Evolution of a plant cover with M=33

Disturbed System with Fire

The simulation starts with an initial condition at $t' = 1$ when the fire starts at the cell $c_{5,15}$.

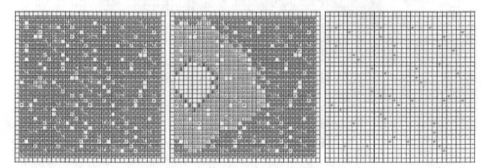

Fig.2. Spreadable fire and vulnerable area

Remark 2. The fire is spreading over the whole area. We can then deduce the vulnerable area which has to be protected.

Controlled Case

According to the simulation of fire spreading, the vulnerable zone is the area located in the right of cell $c_{5,15}$ which is excited with fire. Therefore, the region σ to be protected, must be set in this area.

Let $\sigma \subset \mathcal{L}$ be a region defined by: $\sigma = \{c_{ij} \mid 18 \leq i \leq 25 \,,\, 12 \leq j \leq 22\}$

Example 1. In this particular case, we can notice that the region σ can be protected from fire spreading when the control domain consists of a rectangular zone $D = \{c_{ij} \mid 16 \leq i \leq 27 \,,\, 10 \leq j \leq 24\}$.

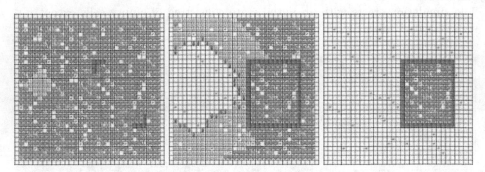

Fig.3. The zone σ is protected

Example 2. Let us consider another region σ with an increased area which has to be protected. Let D be the following new domain of the control action :

$$D = \{c_{ij} \mid 14 \le i \le 28 \,,\, 8 \le j \le 26\}$$

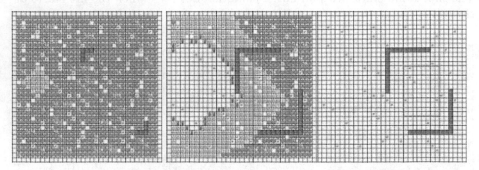

Fig.4. The zone σ is not protected

In the two examples, we illustrate the possibility of protecting a given region against the fire spread with a 'good' choice of the domain D in example 1, Fig. 3. As the control value u has been fixed for all controlled cells, the size and location of the domain D remains for the moment, the only way to control the propagation of fire toward the vulnerable area.

4   Conclusion

In this paper we attempt to investigate the protector control problem using cellular automata approach. The protector control consists to protect a given zone faced to a spreadable disturbance. We consider the case of a control with dynamic support and we illustrate this aspect through a simple example of forest fire.

The modelling of the vegetation and fire dynamics is not the main objective of this work. These dynamics have been considered only to illustrate the protector control concept and vulnerability through cellular automata approach. Furthermore, the concept of protector control has to be rigourously defined and characterized in relation with vulnerability and spreadability concepts. Such problems are under investigation.

References

1. Bernoussi, A.: Spreadability and vulnerability of distributed parameter systems. International Journal of Systems Science 38(4), 305–317 (2007)
2. Bernoussi, A.: Spreadability, vulnerability and protector control. Mathematical Modelling of Natural Phenomena 5(7), 145–150 (2010)
3. Chopard, B., Droz, M.: Cellular automata Modelling of Physical Systems. Cambridge University Press, Cambridge (1998)
4. Deutsch, A., Dormann, S.: Cellular automaton modeling of biological pattern formation (2005)
5. El Yacoubi, S., El Jai, A.: Cellular automata and spreadability. International Journal of Mathematical and Computer Modelling 36, 1059–1074 (2002)
6. El Yacoubi, S.: A Mathematical method for control problems on Cellular Automata models. International Journal of Systems Sciences 39(5), 529–538 (2008)
7. Greenberg, M.J., Hastings, S.P.: Spatial patterns for discrete models of diffusion in excitable media. SIAM Journal on Applied Mathematics 34(3), 515–523 (1978)
8. Karafyllidis, I., Thanailakis, A.: A model for predicting forest fire spreading using cellular automata. Ecological Modelling 99, 87–97 (1997)
9. Progias, P., Sirakoulis, G.C.: An FPGA Processor for Modelling Wildfire Spread. Mathematical and Computer Modeling 57(5-6), 1436–1452 (2013)
10. Qaraai, Y., Bernoussi, A.: Protector control: Extension to a class of nonlinear distributed systems. International Journal of Applied Mathematics and Computer Science 20(3), 427–443 (2010)
11. Slimi, R., El Yacoubi, S.: Spreadable Cellular Automata: Modelling and Simulation. International Journal of Systems Sciences 40(5), 507–520 (2009)
12. Toffoli, T.: Cellular automata as an alternative to (rather than an approximation of) differential equations in modeling physics. Physica D: Nonlinear Phenomena 10(1), 117–127 (1984)
13. Trunfio, G.A.: Predicting Wildfire Spreading Through a Hexagonal Cellular Automata Model. In: Sloot, P.M.A., Chopard, B., Hoekstra, A.G. (eds.) ACRI 2004. LNCS, vol. 3305, pp. 385–394. Springer, Heidelberg (2004)
14. Trunfio, G.A., D'Ambrosio, D., Rongo, R., Spataro, W., Di Gregorio, S.: A New Algorithm for Simulating Wildfire Spread Through Cellular Automata. ACM Transactions on Modeling and Computer Simulation 22, 6:1–6:26 (2011) ISSN: 1049-3301
15. Vichniac, G.Y.: Simulating physics with cellular automata. Physica D: Nonlinear Phenomena 10(1), 96–116 (1984)
16. Wolfram, S.: Cellular automata and complexity: collected papers, vol. 1. Addison-Wesley, Reading (1994)
17. Zapp, M.L., Green, M.R.: Sequence-specific RNA binding by the HIV-1 Rev protein. Nature 342(6250), 714–716 (1989)

UNDATA: A Preliminary Cellular Automata Model for Tsunami Simulation

Francesco Gullace[1], Maria Vittoria Avolio[2], and Salvatore Di Gregorio[2]

[1] University of Calabria, Dept. of Physics, 87036 Rende (CS), Italy
gllfnc87104i725g@studenti.unical.it
[2] University of Calabria,
Dept. of Mathematics and Computer Science, 87036 Rende (CS), Italy
{avoliomv,salvatore.digregorio}@unical.it

Abstract. The Cellular Automata (CA) model UNDATA for tsunami simulation is here presented. UNDATA was developed in order to be coupled to SCIDDICA, a CA efficient model for subaerial/subaqueous flow type landslides for cases when a displacement in water of a significant volume could generate a tsunami. This model works also for different generating causes. Applications to theoretic and real cases are satisfying.

Keywords: Cellular Automata, Modelling and Simulation, Tsunami.

1 Introduction

Cellular Automata (CA) represent a versatile computational paradigm, introduced by von Neumann for a self-reproduction theory.

CA may be described intuitively as a space partitioned in cells (a regular space tessellation or alternatively the corresponding lattice), each one embedding an identical input/output computing unit: a Finite Automaton (FA). Each cell is characterised by its state. S is the finite set of the FA states. Input for each cell is given by the states of m neighbouring cells, where the neighbourhood conditions are given by a pattern, invariant in time and space.

At time $t = 0$, cells are in arbitrary states (initial conditions) and the CA evolves changing simultaneously the states at discrete times, according to a same FA transition function $\tau : S^m \rightarrow S$, that is invariant in time and space.

Complex Dynamical Systems, evolving mainly on the base of local interactions [7][28] can be modelled by CA. CA methodology is sometime alternative to classic PDE approaches [26].

MCA (Macroscopic CA), a CA definition extension [10], was developed for modelling and simulating large scale natural phenomena and was applied especially to surface flows [2]. Such MCA are defined within a limited tessellation (corresponding to the space where the phenomenon evolves) of hexagonal cells. A cell state (decomposed in sub-states is defined for each cell and describes the characteristics (e.g., the sub-state water depth) of the corresponding portion of space. When sub-states capture completely the third dimension as in surface flows, two dimensions MCA suffice for really three-dimensions simulations.

J. Wąs, G.C. Sirakoulis, and S. Bandini (Eds.): ACRI 2014, LNCS 8751, pp. 228–237, 2014.

The phenomenon can involve, from a macroscopic viewpoint, a complexity of interacting processes of similar or different nature. The transition function τ may be decomposed into elementary processes, $\tau_1, \tau_2, ...$, each of which involves the update of the state of each cell.

Tsunami characteristics are adequate for a MCA modelling, because such a phenomenon may be efficaciously described by local interactions. A tsunami is a series of water waves (the so-called wave train) caused by the displacement of a large volume of a body of water, generally an ocean or a lake, generated by earthquakes, volcanic eruptions, landslides, etc.; waves periods range from minutes to hours; wave heights of tens of meters can be generated by large events [21]. Tsunami generated by subaerial and/or subaqueous landslides are an impending hazard for Mediterranean sea [22]. Friedrics [12], Aida [1], Hammak [14] conducted important theoretical studies; PDE Approximate Numerical Methods were afterwards developed, e.g., by Tinti [23].

Applications to many different real cases were performed, e.g., by Harbitz [15] and by Tinti [24][25].

SCIDDICA (Simulation through Computational Innovative methods for the Detection of Debris flow path using Interactive Cellular Automata) is a MCA model for landslides [5], whose features are prevalently fluid dynamical. Versions SCIDDICA-SS2 [3][4][18] and SCIDDICA-SS3 [6] were successfully developed for subaerial and/or subaqueous landslides.

Developing a MCA model for tsunami simulation permits to couple it efficiently and efficaciously to SCIDDICA in order to simulate the overall phenomenon landslide + tsunami; furthermore the tsunami generation can be advantageously calculated according to the precise progress of the landslide into the water.

UNDATA (UNDulance Auxiliary model for Tsunami simulation by cellular Automata) is a first MCA model [13]. The double coupled model SCIDDICA-UNDATA was applied on a well-known real event: the subaerial-subaqueous debris flow of Albano lake (1997) in Italy [17], that generated tsunami waves, few meters high. Results agree satisfactorily with the surveys despite of the smallness of the event.

Methods of type Lattice Boltzmann (LB), particular types of CA, were used for tsunami simulations. Janßen, Grilli and Krafczyk [16] developed a LB model for the solution of the non-linear shallow water equations, including a simple model for the treatment of the wet-dry interface, an efficient GPGPU implementation was performed; Frandsen [11] explores LB methods for free-surface modeling in single phase flows in order to compute carefully the tsunami-generated runup onto beaches. Other 2-dimensional CA models for tsunami simulation were developed by Mohamed and Rajasekaran [20], based on Huygens principle; they consider extended neighbourhoods in square and hexagonal tessellations for increasing precision in wave propagation. The model aim is to simulate the wave front for a tsunami warning system.

The next section defines the model UNDATA and its coupling to SCIDDICA, while the simulation results of tsunami in Albano lake are shown in the third section; comments and conclusions are at the end.

2 UNDATA: A CA Model for Simulating Tsunami Propagation

The CA model UNDATA is partly based on a numerical method for simulating electromagnetic fields, nominally TLM (Transmission Line Matrix or Transmission Line Modelling) [8][9]; TLM is translated in terms of CA. Therefore a TLM short introduction, that highlights its particular application to UNDATA, follows. Furthermore an outline of SCIDDICA-SS2, that was coupled to UNDATA, must be preliminary to its presentation, in order to specify the interaction mechanisms landslide-tsunami.

2.1 TLM Method for UNDATA

TLM (Transmission Line Matrix or Transmission Line Modelling) is a numerical method for simulating electromagnetic fields in a context of discrete time and space (a regular lattice), where pulses propagate. At each time step the lattice nodes receive the incident pulses and send the scattered ones [22].

A scattering matrix, determined by TLM gives the reflection and transmission coefficients for the pulses according the telegrapher's equation. It can be seen that every node turns into a secondary source of spherical wave. These waves combine to form the overall waveform (Huygens principle)[9].

Changes of tension in the equivalent circuit in the lumped model for transmission line are described by the so called telegrapher's equation,

$$\frac{\partial^2 V}{\partial x^2} = L_{\mathrm{d}} C_{\mathrm{d}} \frac{\partial^2 V}{\partial t^2} + R_{\mathrm{d}} C_{\mathrm{d}} \frac{\partial V}{\partial t} \ . \tag{1}$$

For a lossless transmission line (R_d is negligible) we have

$$\frac{\partial^2 V}{\partial x^2} = L_{\mathrm{d}} C_{\mathrm{d}} \frac{\partial^2 V}{\partial t^2} \tag{2}$$

which is a wave equation for V describing a pulse propagating with speed

$$v = \frac{\Delta x}{\Delta t} = \sqrt{\frac{1}{L_{\mathrm{d}} C_{\mathrm{d}}}} \ . \tag{3}$$

In a hexagonal network made of transmission line with the same impedance, a pulse that reaches a node sees five transmission line connected in parallel, with a total impedance $Z_{\mathrm{T}} = Z/5$. Part of the pulse is reflected (the reflection coefficient being $\rho = -2/3$). The scattered pulse toward the ith next node ($^S V_i$),

$1 \leq i \leq 6$, is the sum of the reflected and transmitted part of the incident one (^IV_j) where $1 \leq j \leq 6 \wedge i \neq j$:

$$^SV_i = -\frac{2}{3}{}^IV_i + \frac{1}{3} \sum_{\substack{i \neq j \\ 1 \leq j \leq 6}} {}^IV_j \ . \tag{4}$$

The entire scattering process can be expressed in matrix form as

$$\begin{bmatrix} ^SV_1 \\ ^SV_2 \\ ^SV_3 \\ ^SV_4 \\ ^SV_5 \\ ^SV_6 \end{bmatrix}_{k+1} = -\frac{1}{3} \begin{bmatrix} -2 & 1 & 1 & 1 & 1 & 1 \\ 1 & -2 & 1 & 1 & 1 & 1 \\ 1 & 1 & -2 & 1 & 1 & 1 \\ 1 & 1 & 1 & -2 & 1 & 1 \\ 1 & 1 & 1 & 1 & -2 & 1 \\ 1 & 1 & 1 & 1 & 1 & -2 \end{bmatrix} \begin{bmatrix} ^IV_1 \\ ^IV_2 \\ ^IV_3 \\ ^IV_4 \\ ^IV_5 \\ ^IV_6 \end{bmatrix}_k \tag{5}$$

where k and $k+1$ are successive time steps.

2.2 Outline of SCIDDICA-SS2

SCIDDICA-SS2 [3][4][18] is a deterministic two dimensional CA with regular hexagonal cells for simulating subaerial-subaqueous flow-type landslides with large blocks inside. It includes progressive detachment for primary and secondary sources, surface erosion, matter loss and rheological changes in the water transition. It is specified by the quintuple:

$$SCIDDICA - SS2 = \langle R_S, X_S, S_S, P_S, \tau_S \rangle$$

– R_S is the set of regular hexagons, that cover the region, where the phenomenon evolves.
– $X_S = (0,0), (0,1), (0,-1), (1,0), (1,-1), (-1,0), (-1,1)$ defines the neighbourhood of the cell, it identifies the geometrical pattern of cells, which influence any state change of the generic cell, includes the central cell itself (index 0) and the six adjacent cells (indexes 1, ... ,6). Note that the sum of indexes of opposite hexagons is always 7.
– S_S is the set of states, they are specified by soil sub-states and flows sub-states.
    Soil sub-states: A is the cell altitude, D is the depth of soil erodible stratum, that could be transformed by erosion in landslide matter; TH is the average thickness of landslide matter of the cell, X and Y are the co-ordinates of its barycentre with reference to the cell centre, KH is its kinetic head. Flow sub-states: E is the part of flow, the so called external flow (normalised to a thickness), that penetrates the adjacent cell from central cell, XE and YE are the co-ordinates of its barycentre with reference to the adjacent cell centre, KHE is its kinetic head (six components for each sub-state); I is the part of flow toward the adjacent cell, the so called internal flow (normalised to a thickness), that remains inside the central cell; XI and YI are the co-ordinates of its barycentre with reference to the central cell centre, KHI is its kinetic head (six components for all the sub-states).

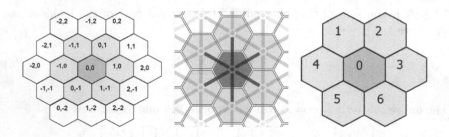

Fig. 1. From left to right: a piece of hexagonal tessellation with the neighbourhood of cell $(0,0)$; the corresponding triangular lattice; index values for a generic neighbourhood

- P_S is the set of the global physical and empirical parameters of the phenomenon: a is the cell apothem; t is the temporal correspondence of a CA step; adh_w, adh_a are the water/air adhesion values, i.e. the landslide matter thickness, that may not be removed; fc_w, fc_a are the water/air friction coefficient for the landslide matter outflows; td_w, td_a, ed_w, ed_a are water/air parameters for energy dissipation by turbulence, water/air parameters for energy dissipation by erosion; ml is the matter loss in percentage when the landslide matter enters into water; mt_w, mt_a are the water/air activation thresholds of the mobilisation; er_w, er_a are the water/air progressive erosion parameters; wr is the water resistance parameter.
- $\tau_S : S_S^7 \to S_S$ is the deterministic state transition for the cells in R_S, with $card(X_S) = 7$. It is split in four consecutively applied functions, that compute:
  - altitude, kinetic head and debris thickness variation by detrital cover mobilisation;
  - kinetic head variation by turbulence dissipation;
  - debris outflows (thickness, barycentre co-ordinates, kinetic head) determination and their shift deduced by the motion equations;
  - composition of debris inside the cell (remaining debris more inflows) and determination of new thickness, barycentre co-ordinates, kinetic head.

At the beginning of the simulation, the states of the cells in R_S are specified by defining the initial CA configuration. The initial values of the sub-states are accordingly initialised. In particular, A assumes the morphology values except for the detachment area, where the thickness of the landslide mass is subtracted from the morphology value; TH is zero everywhere except for the detachment area, where the thickness of landslide mass is specified; D assumes initial values corresponding to the maximum depth of the mantle of soil cover, which can be eroded. All the values related to the remaining sub-states are zero everywhere. At each next step, the function τ_S is applied to all the cells in R_S, so that the configuration changes in time and the CA evolution is obtained.

2.3 UNDATA

$$\text{UNDATA} = \langle R_U, X_U, S_U, P_U, \tau_U \rangle$$

- $R_U = R_S$ is the set of regular hexagons, that cover the region, where the phenomenon evolves.
- $X_U = X_S$ identifies the geometrical pattern of cells, which influence any state change of the generic cell, includes the central cell itself (index 0) and the six adjacent cells (indexes 1, ... ,6).
- S_U is the set of states, they are specified by the following sub-states: W is the water depth; $^{I}P^6$, $^{S}P^6$ are respectively the six incident and scattered pulses.
- P_U is the set of the global physical and empirical parameters of the phenomenon: a , the cell apothem, and t , the temporal correspondence of a CA step, are the same as in SCIDDICA-SS2, then ρ, the reflection coefficient, and tc, the transmission coefficient.
- $\tau_U : S_U^7 \rightarrow S_U$ is the deterministic state transition for the cells in R_U, with $card(X_U) = 7$. It is expressed by the following elementary processes, according to TLM formulae and SCIDDICA inputs:
  - computation of incident pulses generated by sinking and movement of matter in water and their propagation; input is determined by the SCIDDICA–SS2 transition function for subaqueous cells;
  - computation of scattered and reflected pulses from incident ones inside the cell;
  - pulses composition for computation of incident pulses and water depth updating;
  - land inundation computation for determining water depth for tsunami effect.

At the beginning of the simulation, the states of the cells in R_U are specified by defining the initial CA configuration. The initial values of W are initialised accordingly to the morphology values of A. All the values related to the remaining sub-states are zero everywhere.

At each next step, the function τ_U is applied to all the cells in R_U, so that the configuration changes in time and the CA evolution is obtained. Of course, there is no change until debris flows reach the subaqueous cells. Applications to theoretic cases work very well; e.g., constant depth water with an obstacle with two symmetric slits to the initial perturbation point (fig. 2).

Fig. 2. Phases of propagation of waves in a classic case, using UNDATA

3   The 1997 Albano Tsunami Generated by Debris Flows

The double coupled model SCIDDICA-UNDATA was applied on the real event the subaerial-subaqueous debris flow of Albano lake (1997) in Italy.

This landslide occurred in the eastern slope of the Albano lake on the 7th of November 1997 after an intense rainfall event (128 mm in 24 hours), and it began as a soil slide, mobilizing about 300 m^3 of eluvial material. The mobilized mass was channeled within a steeply dipping impluvium (about 40°) and thus evolved as a debris flow which entrained a large amount of debris material along the bottom of the channel and reached an estimated volume of some thousands of cubic meters at the coastline. A few amount of material was deposited at the coastline while a greater quantity entered in water generating a little tsunami wave [17].

SCIDDICA-SS2 simulations were advantaged by the detailed subaerial and submerged topographic data, acquired in 2005 and 2006 through aerial LiDAR and sonar multibeam swath bathymetric surveys [17].

The function $\sqrt{(R \bigcap S)/(R \bigcup S)}$ is used for evaluating the fitness of landslide simulation, where R is the set of cells involved in the real event, S is the set of cells involved in simulated event; a value greater than 0.70 is considered acceptable. Lake Albano simulation overcomes 0.85 (fig. 3). Such a result is good in comparison with results obtained by other methodologies [18].

Of course, coupling of SCIDDICA with UNDATA doesn't affect such good results, because SCIDDICA is the input for UNDATA and accounts independently for energy balance.

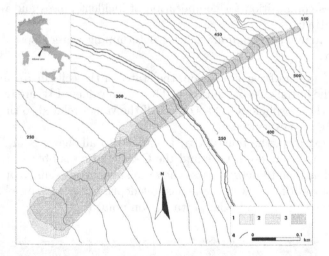

Fig. 3. The 1997 Albano lake subaerial-subaqueous debris flow. Key: (1) real event, (2) simulated event, (3) intersection between real and simulated event, (4) water level.

Effects of tsunami were detected by examining villas overlooking the lake, their walls carried clearly traces of the waves, therefore the maximum water-level was accurately deduced at many points on the coast [19].

First simulations have shown encouraging results regarding the general behaviour of the model, unpublished notes of Mazzanti were consulted [19], tsunami
invasion maximum levels were satisfactorily compared with the simulation results (fig. 4).

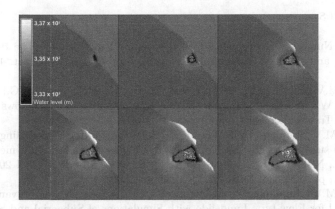

Fig. 4. The 1997 Albano lake tsunami simulation, from the initial landslide entering in
water (top left) to the maximum landslide subaqueous extension (bottom right). 335
m is the water level.

Even if UNDATA shows very acceptable results (just as in the case of Albano
lake), a manifest approximation exists, that could result non-negligible especially
in uniform 2D cases. The error is due to the discretization of the effective displacements. The solution adopted to solve the problem of this approximation
is to consider an inhomogeneous cellular automata model in which the pulses
propagate into the cell for a distance depending on the water depth in that cell,
before they reach the neighbours.

4   Comments and Conclusions

The double coupled model SCIDDICA-UNDATA was applied on the real event
the subaerial-subaqueous debris flow of Albano lake (1997) in Italy. First simulations have shown encouraging results regarding the general behaviour of the
model, but have also highlighted the necessity to improve approximations of the
new MCA. One of the possible future improvements of the model will concern
the UNDATA reduction of such errors.

The model was implemented in C++ on a dual core and spent less than 1
hour for a simulation involving a matrix of 800×600 cells;

Furthermore, UNDATA, even if in its precision limits, may be opportunely
enclosed in a more complex CA model for sandy shore erosion in order to simulate
wave generations and propagations. It implies to improve modelling interactions
with the sea bed in shallow waters.

Acknowledgements. This research was partially funded by PON (Operational National Plan) 2007 2013 from MIUR (Italian Research Ministry of Research) project SIGIEC: Integrated management system for Coastal erosion ID: PON01 02651.

References

1. Aida, I.: Numerical Experiments for the Tsunami Propagation – The 1964 Niigata Tsunami and the 1968 Tokachi-oki Tsunami. Bull. Earthq. Res. Inst. 47, 673–700 (1969)
2. Avolio, M.V., Crisci, G.M., D'Ambrosio, D., Di Gregorio, S., Iovine, G., Rongo, R., Spataro, W.: An extended notion of Cellular Automata for surface flows modelling. WSEAS Transactions on Computers 2(4), 1080–1085 (2003)
3. Avolio, M.V., Lupiano, V., Mazzanti, P., Di Gregorio, S.: Modelling combined subaerial-subaqueous flow-like landslides by Cellular Automata. In: Umeo, H., Morishita, S., Nishinari, K., Komatsuzaki, T., Bandini, S. (eds.) ACRI 2008. LNCS, vol. 5191, pp. 329–336. Springer, Heidelberg (2008)
4. Avolio, M.V., Lupiano, V., Mazzanti, P., Di Gregorio, S.: An advanced Cellular Model for Flow-type Landslide with Simulations of Subaerial and Subaqueous cases. In: Wohlgemuth, V., Page, B., Voigt, K. (eds.) EnviroInfo 2009, Environmental Informatics and Industrial Environmenal Protection: Concepts, Methods and Tools, Proc. of the 23rd International Conference on Informatics for Environmental Protection, September 09-11, vol. 1, pp. 131–140. HTW Berlin, University of Applied Sciences, Germany (2009) ISBN 978-3-8322-8397-1
5. Avolio, M.V., Di Gregorio, S., Lupiano, V., Mazzanti, P., Spataro, W.: Application context of the SCIDDICA model family for simulations of flow-like landslides. In: Proceedings of the 2010 International Conference on Scientific Computing, Las Vegas, Nevada, USA, July 12-15, pp. 40–46. CSREA Press (2010) ISBN 1-60132-137
6. Avolio, M.V., Di Gregorio, S., Lupiano, V., Mazzanti, P.: SCIDDICA-SS3: A New Version of Cellular Automata Model for Simulating Fast Moving Landslides. The Journal of Supercomputing (2013), doi:10.1007/s11227-013-0948-1, ISSN 0920-8542
7. Chopard, B., Droz, M.: Cellular automata modeling of physical systems. Cambrige University Press Collection Alea (1998)
8. Christopoulos, C.: The Transmission Line Modeling Method: TLM. IEEE Press, Piscataway (1995)
9. de Cogan, D., O'Connor, W.J., Pulko, S.: Transmission Line Matrix in Computational Mechanics. CRC Press (2006)
10. Di Gregorio, S., Serra, R.: An empirical method for modelling and simulating some complex macroscopic phenomena by cellular automata. Future Generation Computer Systems 16(2/3), 259–271 (1999)
11. Frandsen, J.B.: Free-surface lattice Boltzmann modeling in single phase flows. Advances in Coastal and Ocean Engineering 10, 163–219 (2008)
12. Friedrichs, K.O.: On the Derivation of Shallow Water Theory (Appendix to The Formation of Breakers and Bores, by J. J. Stoker). Comm. Pure Applied Math. 1, 81–85 (1948)
13. Gullace, F.: Verifica di alcune ipotesi per l'introduzione della fenomenologia dello tsunami in un modello ad automi cellulari per frane subaeree/subacquee. "Laurea thesis" in Italian, Dept of Physics, Univ. of Calabria (2011)

14. Hammack, J.L.: A Note on Tsunamis: Their Generation and Propagation in an Ocean of Uniform Depth. J. Fluid Mech. 60, 769–799 (1973)
15. Harbitz, C.B.: Model Simulation of Tsunamis Generated by Storegga Slides. Marine Geology 104, 1–21 (1992)
16. Janßen, C.F., Grilli, S.T., Krafczyk, M.: Efficient simulations of long wave propagation and runup using a LBM approach on GPGPU hardware. In: Proc. 22nd Offshore and Polar Engng. Conf. (ISOPE 2012), Rodos, Greece, June 17-22, pp. 145–152 (2012)
17. Mazzanti, P., Bozzano, F., Esposito, C.: Submerged landslides morphologies in the Albano lake (Rome, Italy). In: Lykousis, V., Sakellariou, J.L.D. (eds.) Proc. of 3rd Intern. Symp. Submarine Mass Movements and Their Consequences, Lugano, Switzerland. Advances in Natural and Technological Hazards Research, vol. 27, pp. 243–250. Springer, Heidelberg (2007)
18. Mazzanti, P., Bozzano, F., Avolio, M.V., Lupiano, V., Di Gregorio, S.: 3D numerical modelling of submerged and coastal landslides propagation. In: Mosher, D.C., Shipp, C., Moscardelli, L., Chaytor, J., Baxter, C., Lee, H., Urgeles, R. (eds.) Submarine Mass Movements and Their Consequences IV. Fourth International Symposium on Submarine Mass Movements and their Consequences, Austin, Texas, November 8-11. Advances in Natural and Technological Hazards Research, vol. 28, pp. 127–138. Springer, Netherlands (2009)
19. Mazzanti, P.: Personal communication (2011)
20. Mohamed, E.S., Rajasekaran, S.: Propagation of Tsunami Waves Multi-Factor Spread Simulation Based on CA Model. COMPUSOFT, An International Journal of Advanced Computer Technology 2(8) (2013)
21. Nelson, S.A.: Tsunami, Natural Disasters (October 2010), www.tulane.edu/~sanelson/geol204/tsunami.htm
22. Papadopoulos, G.A., Daskalaki, E., Fokaefs, A.: Tsunamis Generated by Coastal and Submarine Landslides in the Mediterranean Sea. In: Submarine Mass Movements and Their Consequences. Advances in Natural and Technological Hazards Research, vol. 27, pp. 415–422 (2007)
23. Tinti, S., Bortolucci, E., Chiavettieri, C.: Tsunami Excitation by Submarine Slides in Shallow-water Approximation. Pure and Applied Geophysics. Birkhäuser Verlag, Basel (2001)
24. Tinti, S., Pagnoni, G., Zaniboni, F.: The landslides and tsunamis of the 30th of December 2002 in Stromboli analysed through numerical simulation. Springer (2005)
25. Tinti, S., Pagnoni, G., Zaniboni, F., Manucci, A.: Stromboli Island (Italy): Scenarios of Tsunamis Generated by Submarine Landslides. Pure and Applied Geophysics. Birkhäuser Verlag, Basel (2008)
26. Toffoli, T.: Cellular Automata as an alternative to (rather than an approximation of) differential equations in modeling physics. Physica 10D, 117–127 (1984)
27. von Neumann, J.: Theory of self reproducing automata. University of Illinois Press (1966)
28. Wolfram, S.: A new kind of science. Wolfram media Inc. (2001)

Modeling Rainfall Features Dynamics in a DEM Satellite Image with Cellular Automata

Moisés Espínola[1], José Antonio Piedra-Fernández[1], Rosa Ayala[1],
Luis Iribarne[1], and Saturnino Leguizamón[2]

[1] Applied Computing Group, University of Almería, Spain
[2] Regional Faculty, National Technological University, Mendoza, Argentina

Abstract. Cellular automata have been widely used in the field of remote sensing for simulating natural phenomena over two-dimensional
satellite images. Simulations on DEM (Digital Elevation Model), three-
dimensional satellite images, are very rare. This paper presents a study
of modeling and simulation of the weather phenomenon of precipitation
over DEM satellite images through a new algorithm, RACA (RAinfall
with Cellular Automata). The aim of RACA is to obtain, from the simulation, numerical and 3D results related to the water level that allow us
to make decisions on important issues such as avoiding the destruction of
human life and property from future natural disasters, establishing future
urbanized areas away from locations with high probability of flooding or
estimating the future water supply for arid regions.

1 Introduction

The physical characteristics of weather phenomena have been modeled extensively and simulated by the worldwide scientific community. A deep investigation
into the nature of these processes allows us to know and, above all, to predict
the effects they have on the Earth's surface. Such predictions allow us to antici-
pate the effects of weather events before they occur. For example, at the present
time we know about many future consequences of climate change, or we can
save lives by warning the population before a hurricane hits. One of the most
studied weather phenomena is the process of rainfall, and its virtual modeling is
a key factor in the estimation of various environmental changes caused by this
phenomenon: variation of the amount of water remaining in a swamp, formation
of new rivers, soil erosion, etc. The phenomenon of rainfall has been investigated
from various scientific perspectives, using diverse methods. Mathematical modeling of physical properties is a fairly complex process with many variables to
consider.

Remote sensing [17] is the most relevant perspective that allows us to acquire
information about the surface of the land and environmental information values
[2] without having actual contact with the area being observed [5]. Examples
of remotely sensed applications include searching for water resources, ascertain-
ing soil quality, addressing environmental protection, and creating meteorology
simulations, among others [10].

J. Wąs, G.C. Sirakoulis, and S. Bandini (Eds.): ACRI 2014, LNCS 8751, pp. 238–247, 2014.

Cellular automata [20][11] have been widely used during the last decades for environmental simulations like modeling land features dynamics [13], simulating snow-cover dynamics [14], characterization of natural textures [12], modeling vegetation systems dynamics [1], detecting Vibrio cholerae by indirect measurement [15], simulating forest fire spread [16], modeling lava flows [19], understanding of urban growth [3], projecting population percentages infected by periodic plague [9] or modeling species competition and evolution [4].

This paper presents research applying the methodology of cellular automata to model and simulate the meteorological process of rainfall to a DEM satellite image provided by NASA, showing hydrological results in both numerical and three-dimensional of flow remaining water. There exist several previous studies related to this subject: a cellular automata model for soil erosion by water [7], a cellular automata algorithm for simulation of surface flows in large plains [18], cellular automata algorithms for drainage network extraction and rainfall data assimilation [6] or developments of a flood inundation model based on the cellular automata approach [8]. All these research works obtain very realistic results because they use a large number of states and rules in the cellular automata. However, they have the drawback that it is necessary to know a priori a large number of parameters to configure the performance of cellular automata, and therefore, it is necessary to perform a preliminary study of the simulation region. In many cases there is no such information to perform a simulation, or it is hard to get it in terms of time. However, RACA uses very few states and rules of cellular automata in order to simplify the simulation process, implementing only the gravity and providing numerical and 3D quick view results on the final water level. Therefore, RACA does not need to perform a preliminary study of the simulation area and, although RACA will not be 100% accurate, it will be very approximate, and with a very low computational cost. The results obtained by RACA can be used for natural disaster prevention in urban areas with probability of flood, projection of future construction projects and urban planning or estimation of future water supply for arid regions, among other things.

2   Simulating Rainfall with Cellular Automata

This project presents the work of modeling and simulation of swamps and river flow, based on cellular automata, considering a volume of rainfall in a given time interval. To accomplish that goal, elevation data provided by the Shuttle Radar Topographic Mission (SRTM) were used. The DEM satellite image, named S32W070 by NASA, corresponds to a part of Argentina, with the geographical coordinates South 32° and West 70°. The original DEM satellite image was degraded in spatial resolution and corrected for some voids appearing on it. Each pixel of the DEM image degraded has a spatial resolution of 1 m^2 and an altitude ranging from 20 to 100 m. The spatial degradation process has been performed to accentuate the difference between the results obtained by various types of climates. The resulting image (600 x 600 pixels) can be seen in Figure 1 (a). A 3D view of the DEM image can also be observed in Figure 1 (b).

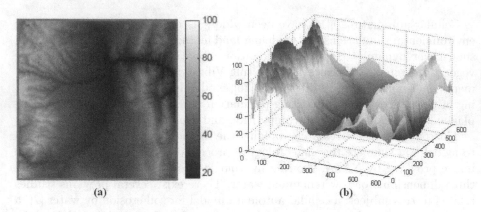

Fig. 1. NASA DEM image S32W070: (a) Plan view (b) 3D view

Each pixel of the DEM satellite image corresponds to a square shaped cell with bare earth as type of ground and size of 1 m². Each cell of cellular automaton has two states, the original altitude of the corresponding DEM pixel (state #1) and the level reached by the water volume (state #2). The total height of a pixel will be the sum of both states.

Before the simulation process, RACA loads the DEM satellite image and the initial conditions, and takes as input arguments the samples of rainfall measured in liters per square meter of different times, which may be days, weeks, months, years, etc. The configuration of the cellular automaton is also loaded before the simulation process. Then, RACA applies the rules of its cellular automaton on the DEM satellite image performing a complete simulation for each of the samples of rainfall, using as many iterations as necessary in each simulation for water to fall and accumulate in the lower levels image. As boundary conditions, RACA simulates a vertical wall on the borders of the image. The results are presented not only at the end of the whole simulation process, but also after each iteration of the cellular automaton. So, RACA has the following input-output components:

- **DEM image loading.** The state #1 of RACA is the terrain altitude obtained from the DEM image. The value of this state in the cells does not vary along the simulation process.
- **Initial conditions loading.** Before applying the 3D simulation, we start with initial conditions: existing water level in the swamp/river. These values are stored in state #2 of RACA and its values vary along the simulation process.
- **Precipitation graphs.** To carry out the simulation, the volume of precipitation must be measured in liters per square meter for each corresponding time-step (day, week, month, year, etc.).
- **Configuration of cellular automata.** The transition function, neighborhood and maximum iterations number of RACA must be established before starting the simulation.

- **RACA: rainfall with cellular automata.** Each input argument (precipitation graph samples) that falls over each image pixel DEM will be used to calculate the volume of liters per square meter, and a full simulation of the water addition and outflows in the image will be established. The transition function f, through cellular automaton rules, will pass the corresponding volume of water from each cell to its neighbor with lower elevation height considering the total height (state #1 + state #2), as the water goes down. When the water is reaching lower pixels that have neighboring cells with elevation greater than or equal to their own, the flow will increase on that surface: the pixel altitude (state #1) plus volume of water level accumulated on it (state #2). This step will be repeated in each iteration of the cellular automaton until all water of the image stagnates and stops moving between cells or until the maximum number of iterations. At that moment, the simulation of the current input argument ends, and the simulation of the next sample of precipitation graph begins.

- **Results.** Finally, RACA shows the accumulated flow after each iteration of cellular automaton as well as the total water level after the complete process simulation. The quantity of water that exists on a given DEM image pixel is calculated by multiplying the state #2 of the each cell (level of water above the pixel) by 1000 because, as each DEM image pixel has a spatial resolution of 1 m^2, then each three-dimensional cube of virtual representation has a resolution of 1 m^3, and each cubic meter has a volume of 1000 liters. To calculate the total flow of the geographical area, we add the flow stored on each of the pixels of the DEM image. This flow is shown both numerically and in 3D virtual view. Figure 2 shows the general RACA architecture with all the input-output components.

The synchronous and homogeneous cellular automaton of RACA can be defined mathematically by the following expression:

$$RACA = (d, r, Q, \#, V, f) =$$ (1)

$$(3, \{4|8\}, [q_{terrain\_alt}, q_{water\_level}], [DEM\_alt, initial\_water], V, f)$$

where:

- $d = 3$: the spatial dimension of the RACA cellular automaton is 3, so cells are distributed in 3D form.
- $r = \{4|8\}$: the neighborhood dimension may consist of the von Neumann or Moore neighborhood.
- $Q = [q_{terrain\_alt}, q_{water\_level}]$: each cell has a set of two states, the terrain altitude and the water level.
- $\# = [DEM\_alt, initial\_water]$: the quiescent state, or initial value. This value is DEM_alt for $q_{terrain\_alt}$ and $initial\_water$ for q_{water_level}.
- V: the neighborhood vector is configurable to 4 or 8 surrounding neighbours of each one of the cells.

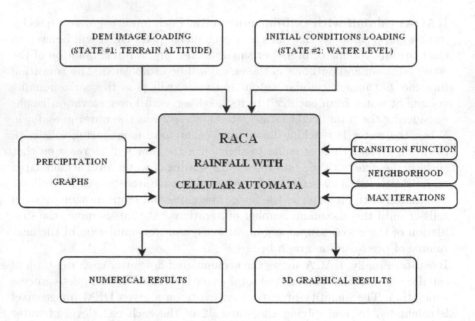

Fig. 2. General RACA architecture

- f: the transition function applies the rules to each one of the cells along the different iterations in order to change their states taking into account the neighborhood chosen, as shown in the following expression:

$$f : Q^{\{4|8\}+1} \rightarrow Q \tag{2}$$

The transition function of RACA applies the following rules:

- Rule #1. If $water\_flow < q_{(i)water\_level}$:
  $q_{(i)water\_level} = q_{(i)water\_level}\text{-}water\_flow$
  $q_{(j)water\_level} = q_{(j)water\_level}\text{+}water\_flow$

- Rule #2. If $water\_flow \geq q_{(i)water\_level}$:
  $q_{(i)water\_level} = 0$
  $q_{(j)water\_level} = q_{(j)water\_level}\text{+}q_{(i)water\_level}$

where $q_{(i)}$ is the current cell, $q_{(j)}$ is the neighboring cell with lower height (if there are several neighboring cells with the same height, we take a random one) and $water\_flow$ is defined by the following expression:

$$water\_flow = \frac{(q_{(i)terrain\_alt} + q_{(i)water\_level}) - (q_{(j)terrain\_alt} + q_{(j)water\_level})}{2} \tag{3}$$

With the results obtained from RACA, several objectives can be achieved, from which we have highlighted the top three:

- **Objective #1:** Natural disaster prevention in urban areas with probability of flood. With the assistance of cellular automata, we can calculate the index ratio of flood disasters and streams in urban areas using the graphs of rainfall recorded historically in that region. In the visual results provided by the algorithm, we can clearly see which regions of the 3D DEM image will be covered by water after performing the corresponding simulations. Therefore, if an urbanized area appears to have a very high flood risk, then appropriate authorities can act to avoid loss of human life.
- **Objective #2:** Projection of future construction projects and urban planning. We can identify safe regions for development around geographical areas at risk of flooding. Given all the graphs of rainfall recorded historically in a particular region, we can calculate the maximum height reached by the water at different points of the three-dimensional satellite image. Taking into account the results, we must never create urban areas at altitudes lower than the height risk for certain areas with probability of flood in order to prevent further loss of life.
- **Objective #3:** Estimation of future water supply of a population. Taking into account the rainfall charts for the type of climate of a particular area, we can make very rough estimates of the approximate cumulative water flow in a region that has a constructed wetland. Our algorithm also considers the initial amount of water that the swamp could have (initial conditions before simulation). In addition, we can calculate the most appropriate areas for the construction of a dam to optimize the process of accumulation of water with a minimum wall built.

3   Results and Conclusions

In order to compare the results provided by different types of climate, the rainfall simulation with RACA on the DEM satellite image has been carried out using four different annual precipitation graphs, each one corresponding to a different climate. As the DEM satellite image belongs to a region of Argentina, we have taken four types of climates characteristic from different parts of the country: arid climate of mountain range and bolsones (La Rioja), cold damp climate (Ushuaia, Tierra de Fuego), temperate humid pampas climate (Buenos Aires) and subtropical climate with no dry season (Posadas, Misiones). Figure 3 shows the graphs of annual precipitation for the four different types of climates that have been taken from the great variety found in Argentina. As can be seen, the annual precipitation graphs are arranged in growing order, taking as reference the total number of liters per square meter per year.

The first graph corresponds to the drier climate, where precipitation is recorded only during the summer months, and the last graph corresponds to the wetter climate in which precipitation is recorded during all months of the year. For each graph of annual precipitation, 12 simulations have been made (one for each month of the year). Therefore, the results given in this paper were obtained after making a total of 48 simulations.

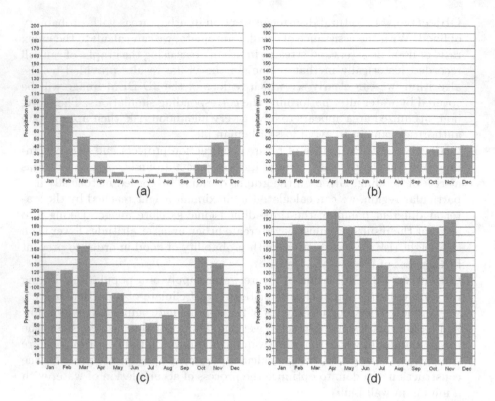

Fig. 3. Graphs of annual precipitation for 4 types of climate: (a) Arid climate of mountain range and bolsones (b) Cold damp climate (c) Temperate humid pampas climate (d) Subtropical climate with no dry season

For each simulation, we used as many iterations of cellular automata as necessary until the water stopped moving. In the first few months, in which water levels are lower, the number of iterations of the cellular automata has been greater than in the subsequent months in which water levels are higher, consequently the water has less height to descend the mountain in those early months.

To simplify the huge number of results offered by the 48 simulations, we used as a reference only the annual final result of each type of climate after the simulation of all the months of the year, rejecting the individual results of each month of the year.

After performing the simulations, the arid climate of mountain range and bolsones records a total annual precipitation of 392 liters per square meter. With that amount of annual rainfall, the water reaches a maximum height level of 33.19 meters above sea level, or in other words, 13.19 meters above the minimum level of DEM image (20 meters). The total cumulative flow in this type of climate is 141 million liters.

In the second place, the cold damp climate records a total annual precipitation of 539 liters per square meter, with the water reaching a maximum height of 34.35

meters above sea level, 14.35 on the minimum level of DEM image. The total cumulative flow is 194 million liters.

In the third place, the temperate humid pampas climate records a total annual precipitation of 1231 liters per square meter (more than double the previous climate), reaching a maximum water level height of 38.03 meters above sea level, 18.03 over the minimum level of the DEM image. The total cumulative flow is 443 million liters. Note that, although the flow is more than double the previous climate, the maximum headroom barely varies more than 4 meters. With the greatest height in the DEM image, there are fewer mountains occupying the space, and thus there is more free volume to be occupied by water.

Finally, the subtropical climate with no dry season records a total annual precipitation of 1926 liters per square meter, reaching the maximum water level height of 40.50 meters above sea level, 20.50 minimum on DEM image. The cumulative flow is 693 million liters. Table 1 shows a summary of the numerical annual results obtained after conducting simulations of the four climate types.

Table 1. Numerical results obtained in the 4 types of weather (where ATP=Annual Total Precipitation, MLW=Maximum Level of Water and TCF=Total Cumulative Flow)

Type of weather	ATP	MLW	TCF
(a) Arid climate of mountain range and bolsones	392 liters/m^2	13.19 m	141x10^6 liters
(b) Cold damp climate	539 liters/m^2	14.35 m	194x10^6 liters
(c) Temperate humid pampas climate	1231 liters/m^2	18.03 m	443x10^6 liters
(d) Subtropical climate with no dry season	1926 liters/m^2	20.50 m	693x10^6 liters

The simulation also provides 3D graphic results that facilitate the analysis of the values obtained. These 3D graphic results can be configured to provide the best possible view by changing the position of the camera through the keyboard, not only to view the image from the desired perspective but also to navigate freely across the surface of the DEM satellite image with the objective of seeing the most interesting details up close. We can see the visual difference between accumulated flow of the arid climate of mountain range and bolsones, the driest of the four, and the subtropical climate with no dry season, which is the wettest. This technique offers a multitude of practical applications, such as locating the most appropriate place to put a dam wall in order to maximize the accumulated water flow, or checking the flood risk in villages near wetlands depending on the amount of rainfall in a year in that geographic region. In these images, the water is represented by dark blue, the lower areas with light colors (blue or light green), and the higher areas with darker colors (like orange or dark red). Figure 4 shows the results in annual 3D graphics obtained in four climate types studied from the same approach perspective view of the camera.

4   Future Work

Future application opportunities of cellular automata are diverse and pragmatic. For example, we could add to the simulation by accounting for the evaporation

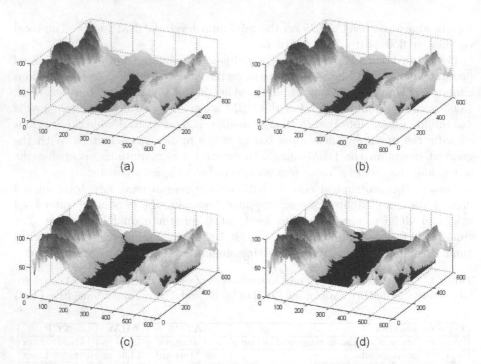

Fig. 4. 3D annual graphics results obtained in 4 types of climates: (a) Arid climate of mountain range and bolsones (b) Cold damp climate (c) Temperate humid pampas climate (d) Subtropical climate with no dry season.

process of water stored in the swamp, taking into account different variables that influence the evaporation process. Additionally, cellular automata could be used to simulate the process of soil erosion after the fall of rain for a long period of time to see how the passage of water modifies the appearance of the landscape. A third application is to create a system of optimal positioning of the wall of a dam to maximize the accumulated water flow after rain.

Acknowledgment. This work was funded by the EU ERDF and the Spanish Ministry of Economy and Competitiveness (MINECO) under Project TIN2010-15588, and the Andalusian Regional Government (Spain) under Project P10-TIC-6114. This work was also supported by the CEiA3 and CEIMAR consortiums.

References

1. Balzter, H., Braun, P., Kühler, W.: Cellular automata models for vegetation dynamics. Ecological Modelling 107, 113–125 (1998)
2. Barret, E.C., Curtis, L.F.: Introduction to environmental remote sensing. Cheltenham Stanley Thornes Publishers Ltd. (1999)

3. Cheng, J., Masser, I.: Cellular automata based temporal process understanding of urban growth. In: Bandini, S., Chopard, B., Tomassini, M. (eds.) ACRI 2002. LNCS, vol. 2493, pp. 325–336. Springer, Heidelberg (2002)
4. Chopard, B., Lagrava, D.: A cellular automata model for species competition and evolution. In: El Yacoubi, S., Chopard, B., Bandini, S. (eds.) ACRI 2006. LNCS, vol. 4173, pp. 277–286. Springer, Heidelberg (2006)
5. Chuvieco, E., Huete, A.: Fundamentals of satellite remote sensing. CRC Press (2010)
6. Coppola, E., Tomassetti, B., Mariotti, L., Verdecchia, M., Visconti, G.: Cellular automata algorithms for drainage network extraction and rainfall data assimilation. Hydrological Sciences-Journal-des Sciences Hydrologiques 52(3), 579–592 (2007)
7. D'Ambrosio, D., Di Gregorio, S., Gabriele, S., Gaudio, R.: A cellular automata model for soil erosion by water. Physics and Chemistry of the Earth (B) 26(1), 33–39 (2001)
8. Dottori, F., Todini, E.: Developments of a flood inundation model based on the cellular automata approach: testing different methods to improve model performance. Physics and Chemistry of the Earth 36, 266–280 (2011)
9. Dzwinel, W.: A cellular automata model of population infected by periodic plague. In: Sloot, P.M.A., Chopard, B., Hoekstra, A.G. (eds.) ACRI 2004. LNCS, vol. 3305, pp. 464–473. Springer, Heidelberg (2004)
10. Guzman, O.F., Gómez, I.D.: Fundamentos físicos de teledetección. Instituto Geográfico Agustin Codazzi IGAC (2007)
11. Kari, J.: Theory of cellular automata: a survey. Theoretical Computer Science 334, 3–33 (2005)
12. Leguizamón, S., Espínola, M., Ayala, R., Iribarne, L., Menenti, M.: Characterization of texture in images by using a cellular automata approach. In: Lytras, M.D., Ordonez de Pablos, P., Ziderman, A., Roulstone, A., Maurer, H., Imber, J.B. (eds.) WSKS 2010, Part II. CCIS, vol. 112, pp. 522–533. Springer, Heidelberg (2010)
13. Leguizamón, S.: Modelling land features dynamics by using cellular automata techniques. In: Proceedings of the ISPR Technical Comission 7 Mid-Term Symposium "From Pixels to Processes", pp. 497–501 (2006)
14. Leguizamón, S.: Simulation of snow-cover dynamics using the cellular automata approach. In: Proc. of the 8th Int. Symposium on High Mountain Remote Sensing Cartography, pp. 87–91 (2005)
15. Lobitz, B., Beck, L., Huq, A., Woods, B., Fuchs, G., Faruque, A., Colwell, R.: Climate and infectious disease: use of remote sensing for detection of Vibrio cholerae by indirect measurement. Proc. National Academic Sci. USA 97(4), 1438–1443 (2000)
16. Muzy, A., Innocenti, E., Aiello, A., Santucci, J.F., Santonio, P.A., Hill, D.: Modelling and simulation of ecological propagation processes: application to fire spread. Environmental Modelling and Software 20, 827–842 (2005)
17. Rees, W.G.: Physical principles of remote sensing, 2nd edn. Cambridge University Press (2001)
18. Rinaldi, P., Dalponte, D., Vénere, M., Clausse, A.: Cellular automata algorithm for simulation of surface flows in large plains. Simulation Modelling Practice and Theory 15, 315–327 (2007)
19. Spataro, W., D'Ambrosio, D., Rongo, R., Trunfio, G.A.: An evolutionary approach for modelling lava flows through cellular automata. In: Sloot, P.M.A., Chopard, B., Hoekstra, A.G. (eds.) ACRI 2004. LNCS, vol. 3305, pp. 725–734. Springer, Heidelberg (2004)
20. Wolfram, S.: A new kind of science. Wolfram Media Inc. (2002)

Cellular Automata Model with Game Theory for Power Management of Hybrid Renewable Energy Smart Grids

Prodromos Chatziagorakis[1], Constantinos Elmasides[2], Georgios Ch. Sirakoulis[1], Ioannis Karafyllidis[1], Ioannis Andreadis[1], Nikolaos Georgoulas[1], Damianos Giaouris[3], Athanasios I. Papadopoulos[3], Chrysovalantou Ziogou[3], Dimitris Ipsakis[3], Simira Papadopoulou[3], Panos Seferlis[3], Fotis Stergiopoulos[3], and Paris Voutetakis[3]

[1] Department of Electrical and Computer Engineering,
Democritus University of Thrace, Xanthi, Greece
[2] Systems Sunlight S.A., Xanthi, Greece
[3] Chemical Process Engineering Research Institute,
Centre for Research and Technology Hellas, Thermi-Thessaloniki, Greece
gsirak@ee.duth.gr

Abstract. In recent years, control of smart grids that match electricity demand in different sites and forms with supply has been considered as one of the most difficult aspect of smart energy grids design. In this paper we present a Cellular Automata (CA) based approach combined with Game Theory for the enhancement of Power Management Strategies (PMSs) of multiple Hybrid Renewable Energy Systems (HYRES) that form a smart grid for the exchange of energy. More specifically, taking advantage of the local interactions of HYRES we coupled CA principles with Public Goods Game (PGG) for modeling. The presented CA model focuses on providing valuable feedback for PMSs of the understudy HYRES connected in a grid. In this manner, a flexible network based HYRES design is considered and applied to specific HYRESs located in Olvio, near Xanthi, Greece, part of SYSTEMS SUNLIGHT facilities. The proposed model can be applied to the understudy HYRESs grid management to enhance and optimize its PMS based on the provided energy prediction scenarios.

Keywords: Cellular Automata, Game Theory, Modeling, Power Management Strategy, Hybrid Renewable Energy System, Smart Energy Grids.

1   Introduction

The applying control of smart grids that match electricity demand in different sites and forms with supply has been considered as one of the most difficult aspects of smart energy grids design [1]. On the other hand, a new type of Renewable Energy Systems (RES) is becoming all the more popular as a response to the continuously growing need for green energy [2]. That is the *Hybrid Renewable Energy Systems* (HYRES). Such a hybrid energy system usually consists of two or more renewable energy sources used together to provide increased system efficiency as well as greater balance in energy supply. This combination offers the advantage of exploiting

J. Wąs, G.C. Sirakoulis, and S. Bandini (Eds.): ACRI 2014, LNCS 8751, pp. 248–257, 2014.

different types of green energy without completely depending on the availability of a single one. Therefore, hybrid systems present a better balance in energy production than the conventional systems, which make use of a single technology and tend to be more inconsistent. However, despite the advantages that the adoption of HYRES may have, there are still some weak spots. Research and development efforts are required for: improving their performance, establishing techniques for accurately predicting their output reliably and integrating them with other conventional generating sources. Moreover, the cooperation between the different discrete systems does not often occur in the most efficient way. For example, storage of the excess energy supply does not always occur in the most effective way and thus the system usually depends on conventional fuels. The optimized management of the various co-operating subsystems is the key point towards achieving the best possible green energy utilization and system efficiency.

In this context, the term "cooperation" is leading to game theory, which is defined as the analysis of mathematical prototypes of collaboration and antagonism between intelligent rational decision-makers [3]. Moreover, taking into consideration the technological advances in smart grids design, *Cellular Automata* (CA) concept can be considered as a wise choice to model them. More specifically, smart energy grids are designed with greater number of HYRESs, which are found in a more mesh or grid-like regular structure and the resulting distribution of the electricity produced and stored is becoming more complex. In regards to the aforementioned Game Theory, one of the most suitable for our case study examples is the *Public Goods Game* (PGG) [4-8], because there are systems that compete for the overall produced energy, which are affected by the decisions made and the resulting consumption.

As a result, a model was produced using game theory concepts, and more specifically PGG, on CA lattice, to simulate the impact of the conflict of many nodes of a smart energy grid demanding electricity. Additionally, this model will also be easily coupled with an autonomous HYRES, where its estimations can be used by a central control unit in order to create in real time the proper Power Management Strategies (PMSs) for the efficient smart energy grid utilization that can lead to the overall optimization. For doing so, a generic network model is also described for the representation of the hybrid power generation systems taken into consideration in this work. In order to test the efficiency of the proposed model an already implemented HYRES which locate at premises of Systems SUNLIGHT at Xanthi Greece is considered. The architecture of the smart grid into consideration and the systems which are connected to the smart grid are illustrated in Fig. 1. Each system serves its own AC load (1kW), the power is produced using a PV rated at 2.7kW, 5.4kW and 15kW respectively. Lead-acid battery (BAT) arrays of 2000Ah, 2000Ah and 3000Ah are also utilized to provide the necessary power to the systems during night time and when the available renewable power is not enough to serve the demanded loads. As a backup option each system has a diesel generator (DG) of 1.1kW. Furthermore two of them (System 2, System 3) are equipped with wind generators (WG), 3kWp each. At System 3 there is a 4kW Polymer Electrolyte Membrane (PEM) electrolyser (EL) that generates hydrogen from the excess of energy and stores it at 30bar pressure cylinders. Finally System 3 has a 4kW PEM Fuel Cell (FC) system that produces power when required using the stored hydrogen. Within each standalone system DC and AC busses are established where each device is connected to them through appropriate power converters (Fig. 1). The specific system combines different renewable technologies, has some storing capabilities and also includes a conventional energy generator as a backup unit. The current HYRES system supplies a part of SYSTEMS SUNLIGHT facilities with electricity, without the interference of any other power plant.

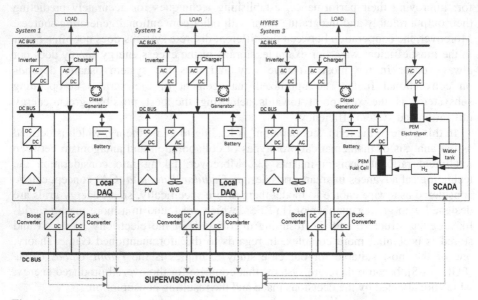

Fig. 1. System topology, architecture of the smart grid node and information flow among the systems, the converters and the supervisory station

2   The Proposed Cellular Automaton Model Using Public Goods Game Concepts

In order to apprehend the dynamics between cooperation and competition for power management and electricity demand in the context of smart grids, mathematical tools are needed as mentioned in Section 1. Game theory provides mathematical tools to model, structure and analyze interactive scenarios. It can be defined as the study of mathematical models of conflict and cooperation between intelligent rational decision-makers. Among other well-known game theory paradigms we will focus on the Public Goods Game (PGG) [4], which presents the interactions of individuals constituting a group. For instance, some individuals are awarded with an equal amount of money. Afterwards, the individuals are facing a challenge; to invest in total or a part of the initial amount awarded into a common pot, being aware that the common pot raised, will be multiplied and divided equally to all of them, regardless the contribution each one made. In the case that everyone invests the entire initial amount, everyone will get a greater amount of the money invested. Still, each one is tempted to "free-ride" on the investments made by other members of the group, since this way there is no risk for his initial capital. Assuming that all players follow this "rational" strategy, the initial capital will remain static [5].

From a theoretical point of view, players participate in a PGG in groups of n players. The game is elapsed t rounds. On every round of the game, a player i obtains an award w and faces the dilemma on how to divide it. He must choose between an investment c_i, to a public good, the common pot, and private utilization, $w - c_i$. The total amount invested by the n members of a society is multiplied by β, $\beta < n$, and equally distributed to the n members [4]. Denoting $m = \beta / n$, $m < 1$, the payoff of player i at each round as a function of the contribution to the public good is illustrated by equation (1). Finally, at the beginning of the next round, the obtained award w for a player i, will be equal to the payoff π_i gained by the player at the previous round.

$$\pi_i = w - c_i + m \sum_{i=1}^{n} c_i \tag{1}$$

In PGG, the public good or environment is depicted by the multiplication factor β, that in the case of remaining constant during the game, the public good cannot be totally consumed by players that adopt "wrong" strategies. The amounts that are chosen by the players for investment have an impact on the production of the common good that will be equally divided among them [7].

Common sense dictates that in a society that is donating itself with a public good, every individual constituting it will be highly tempted to become a free rider, meaning to give in little or nothing at all, with consequences to the welfare of the community and at the same time receiving the rewards everyone else receives. The fact that the phenomenon of free riders will cause the community to provide its members with less rewards, is also predicted by economic theory [6]. Moreover, supremacy of asocial, defecting strategies is prognosticated by traditional and evolutionary game theory. On the other hand, a permanent and strong willingness to cooperate in societies is significant [5]. It becomes impressive to differentiate from theoretical prognostications, granted the significant obstacles to establish and maintain cooperative behavior in large groups. However, the progress in theory and experiments has demonstrated some methods that are capable of encouraging cooperation. Many modifications of the classic PGG have been proposed, including spatial PGG, and PGG in which the players are separated in groups [8]. In spatially extended systems cooperators can have great advantages when they form clusters that reduce exploitation through defectors [5]. As a result the use of Cellular Automata (CA) comes into hand, taking advantage of their ability to successfully depict local interactions and incorporate inhomogeneities in their local rule.

CA can be considered models of physical systems, where space and time are discrete and interactions are local. In general, a CA requires:

1. A regular lattice of cells covering a portion of a d–dimensional space;

2. A set $C\left(\vec{r}, t\right) = \left\{ C_1\left(\vec{r}, t\right), C_2\left(\vec{r}, t\right) ..., C_m\left(\vec{r}, t\right) \right\}$ of variables attached to each site $\vec{r}$ of the lattice, giving the local state of each cell at the specific time value t;

3. A rule $R = \{R_1, R_2, ...,R_m\}$ which specifies the time evolution of the states $C\left(\vec{r}, t\right)$ in the following way: $C_j\left(\vec{r}, t+1\right) = R_j\left(C\left(\vec{r}, t\right), ..., C\left(\vec{r} + \vec{\delta}_q, t\right)\right)$, where $\vec{r} + \vec{\delta}_k$ designate the cells which belong to a given neighbourhood of cell $\vec{r}$.

In the above definition, the rule R is identical for all sites and it is applied simultaneously to each of them, leading to synchronous dynamics. However, spatial (or even temporal) inhomogeneities can be introduced. Furthermore, in the above definition, the new state of a particular cell r at time $t+1$ is only a function of the previous state of the specific cell and of the cells which belong to its designated neighbourhood. The neighbourhood of cell $\overset{-}{r}$ is the spatial region in which a cell needs to search in its vicinity. For 2–d CA, two types of neighbourhood are usually considered: namely, von Neumann neighbourhood, which consists of a central cell (the one which is to be updated) and its four geographical neighbours north, west, south and east and Moore neighbourhood which contains, in addition, second nearest neighbours northeast, northwest, southeast and southwest, i.e. a total of nine cells, whereas the von Neumann neighbourhood comprises of only five cells. CA have sufficient expressive dynamics to represent phenomena of arbitrary complexity [9] and at the same time can be simulated exactly by digital computers, because of their intrinsic discreteness, i.e. the topology of the simulated object is reproduced in the simulating device [10]. The CA approach is consistent with the modern notion of unified space–time. In computer science, space corresponds to memory and time to processing unit. In CA, memory (CA cell state) and processing unit (CA local rule) are inseparably related to a CA cell. Furthermore, they can easily handle complicated boundary and initial conditions, inhomogeneities and anisotropies [11].

As mentioned above, a hot ongoing research topic is the conflict and the cooperation for the shared power resources between different or same Hybrid Renewable Energy Systems (HYRESs) of a smart energy grid. Consequently, a model is proposed here, to simulate the conflict between autonomous HYRESs and to estimate its impact over the entire smart grid's performance. The CA rules that will apply on that situation are considered to be in accordance with the PGG described earlier. The CA cells are regarded as the HYRESs of a smart energy grid and it is assumed, for sake of simplicity that they are identical, thus they are represented as PGG players placed in CA cells in a square grid. The HYRESs are, usually consisting of Photovoltaic Arrays, Wind Generators, Polymer Electrolyte Membrane (PEM) Fuel Cells, Battery Arrays, Diesel Generators, etc. In a real energy grid system, each HYRES could be different depending on the varying electricity priorities of the corresponding buildings that serve like households, schools, medical clinics, etc. As a result, the reward of every CA cell will simulate the accessibility to "pool of power/ produced and stored electricity" of the smart grid for approximately the same period of time for an HYRES according to its needs for electricity demand. That means that the public good will be assumed to be the total amount of electricity produced by all available HYRESs for a time period. Moreover, the investment of a player placed in a CA cell in every round will correspond to the amount of electricity resources that the HYRES does not need and can be stored by fuel cell and used from other HYRESs. As the amount of "pool of power/ produced and stored electricity" accessibility by a HYRES is modeled as the payoff of every player, the available common good through time depends on the payoffs of the players.

The players/cells of the proposed model are placed in a square CA grid. Each CA cell will interact with his neighbors, as they constitute a community of a PGG. Furthermore, the type of the neighborhood and the boundary conditions can be altered in order to depict different smart energy networking grids. Without loss of generality, the neighborhood type selected was Moore, the boundary conditions are selected to be periodic, for sake of clarity, and the grid is 5×5, in order to simulate a system of 25 players competing over a "pool of power/ produced and stored electricity". However, the model is not restricted by these options. As mentioned before, other smart grids can be easily simulated by using a larger grid and different neighborhood's radius.

Another parameter of the CA model is the time steps, namely the game rounds, here empirically chosen equal to 100. Furthermore, the multiplication factor β is set to 10, a value lower than the amount of HYRESs connected to the grid, $n=25$, in order to keep the "social dilemma". The multiplication factor can be altered to a constant or dependent by time value to simulate different system circumstances. The gain of every player (i,j) on round t for the configuration described above is given by Equation (2).

$$
\begin{aligned}
\text{sd}Gain_{(i,j)}^{t} = \frac{\beta}{n} \big(&Investment_{(i-1,j)} + Investment_{(i,j-1)} + \\
&Investment_{(i+1,j)} + Investment_{(i,j+1)} + \\
&Investment_{(i-1,j-1)} + Investment_{(i-1,j+1)} + \\
&Investment_{(i+1,j-1)} + Investment_{(i+1,j+1)} + \\
&Investment_{(i,j)} \big)
\end{aligned}
\tag{2}
$$

Moreover, the payoff of every player i on round t, is given by Equation (3).

$$
Payoff_{(i,j)}^{t} = Payoff_{(i,j)}^{t-1} - Investment_{(i,j)} + \text{sd}Gain_{(i,j)}^{t}
\tag{3}
$$

where $Investment_{(i,j)} = (produced\_power)_{(i,j)} - (power\_consumption)_{(i,j)}$

Furthermore, the amount of the investment of every player is determined by the strategy it adopts. Players with investment value 0 are defectors and represent HYRESs that need an excessive amount of energy due to increased electricity demands. Also, players choosing investment value 1, namely cooperators, represent HYRESs that need a very small amount of energy and do not interfere significantly with the others' needs. Moreover, every player can choose intermediate values to invest, simulating the proportional need of energy.

Finally, the total payoff of a single HYRES at the end of the last round will be the sum of the rewards obtained for all previous rounds. As the payoff of each player on one round represents the ability to access the same amount of produced and stored electricity of the system for a period of time, the total payoff of the group will represent the available utilization of the produced and stored electricity that is corresponding to the energy performance in terms of electricity demand and service of the smart energy grid.

3   Efficient Representation of Energy Management Strategies

In this section we will review the representation of PMSs as described in [12] where the microgrid was seen as a graph and the flow of power and hydrogen within was described through flowsheets. More specifically, each device in the microgrid is seen as a node of a graph and its connection as an edge in Fig. 2.

Table 1. Microgrid parameters

PV (66.64W rated power)	217
WG (1kW rated power)	3
BAT	3000Ah
EL	5000W
BF	8bar, ~1m3
FT	20bar, ~220m3

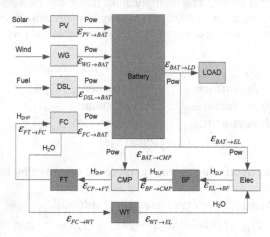

Fig. 2. Network diagram of the standalone microgrid [1]. The parameters of the system are given in Table 1.

In our system the flows between the nodes can be in various states like electrical energy (POW) or hydrogen in high pressure (H2P) and hence the input to each node for each state j is given by:

$$F_n^{In,j}(t) = SF_n^j(t) + \sum_{l=1}^{N} \varepsilon_{l \to n}(t) F_{l \to n}^{Out,j}(t) \qquad (4)$$

where $F_n^{In,j}(t)$ is the input to node n at the instant t, $SF_n^j(t)$ are external inputs, $F_{l \to n}^{Out,j}$ are the outputs of the other nodes, $\varepsilon_{l \to n}(t)$ are binary variables that determine the connection of a specific edge and N is the number of nodes in the graph. For example in the case of the battery, equation (4) can be written as:

$$F_{BAT}^{In,POW}(t) = \sum_{l=1}^{N} \left(\varepsilon_{l \to BAT}(t) F_{l \to BAT}^{Out,POW}(t) \right)$$
$$= \varepsilon_{FC \to BAT}(t) F_{FC \to BAT}^{Out,POW}(t) + \varepsilon_{RES \to BAT}(t) F_{RES \to BAT}^{Out,POW}(t) + \varepsilon_{DSL \to BAT}(t) F_{DSL \to BAT}^{Out,POW}(t) \qquad (5)$$

where $F_{RES \to BAT}^{Out,POW} = F_{PV \to BAT}^{Out,POW} + F_{WG \to BAT}^{Out,POW}$.

The binary variables that determine the connection can be defined as

$$\varepsilon_{l \to n}(t) = L\left(\varepsilon_{l \to n}^{Avl}(t), \varepsilon_{l \to n}^{Req}(t), \varepsilon_{l \to n}^{Gen}(t)\right) \tag{6}$$

where L is a logical operator (like AND, OR, ...) and $\varepsilon_{l \to n}^{Avl}(t), \varepsilon_{l \to n}^{Req}(t), \varepsilon_{l \to n}^{Gen}(t)$ are three binary variables that determine the availability, the requirement and other general conditions necessary to activate the connection l to n. In general the activation of a connection (from node l to n) depends on logical propositions c_i that can be described by binary variables ρ_i. For example, for the activation of the FC in order to supply power to the battery we have $c_{FC \to BAT}$. There is a requirement for energy to be delivered to the battery which it terms of the ρ variables can be written as:

$$\rho_{FC \to BAT}^{SOC(t)} = \left[SOC(t) < Str_{FC \to BAT}^{SOC(t)}(t)\right] \tag{7}$$

where the numerical variable $Str_{FC \to BAT}^{SOC(t)}(t)$ defines the lack of available energy in the battery and SOC is the state of charge. In case there is a hysteresis zone (as it is usually the case in such systems) then (7) can be written as:

$$\rho_{FC \to BAT}^{SOC(t)} = \left[SOC(t) < Lo_{FC \to BAT}^{SOC(t)}(t)\right] \vee$$
$$\left[\left[Str_{FC \to BAT}^{SOC(t)}(t) < SOC(t) < Stp_{FC \to BAT}^{SOC(t)}(t)\right] \wedge \left[\varepsilon_{FC \to BAT}(t^-) = 1\right]\right] \tag{8}$$

where $Stp_{FC \to BAT}^{SOC(t)}(t)$ is the upper limit of the hysteresis zone and t^- is the previous observation instant.

Using this approach it is possible to systematically represent any PMS for a microgrid and to create many other PMSs by simple altering some variables in these tables. Also the aforementioned approach can be easily extended to a networked environment where each node will be an autonomous station. The objective is to optimally exchange energy between the involved nodes and to avoid the utilization of diesel generator while protecting the accumulators within each node. In order to implement such approach a new set of zones are defined, the request and surplus zones, that are modelled using the same principles as the hysteresis zones of each subsystem.

4   Flexible PMS Representation

In the following we use the energy scenarios presented in Section 2 and combine it with the PMS representation of Section 3. The objective is to study the SOC of the systems in the case of isolated operation and in the case of energy exchange. A three days period of time is selected during July. The request and the surplus zones are set between 50V to 52V and 54V to 56V respectively. The response of the systems is shown at Fig. 3.

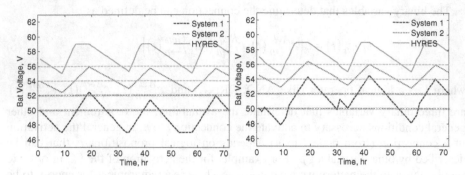

Fig. 3. (a) Battery voltage when systems are isolated. (b) Battery voltage response when systems exchange energy.

In the first case (Fig. 3a) we can observe that System 1 needs power and when the battery voltage drops below 47V the diesel generator is enabled at the nighttime of the 3rd day (between 52nd -58th hour). At the same time it is observed that system HYRES has an excess of energy which is transformed into hydrogen since the exchange of energy is not allowed. On the second case (Fig. 3b), where energy is allowed to be exchanged between the system, it is observed that HYRES provides energy to System 1 and thus, the use of energy is avoided. When the systems operated isolated, System 3 requests power for 64 sampling periods whereas in case of energy exchange System 3 requests power for 17 sampling periods. This clearly shows that the available energy is used in a better way and that the diesel generator is not used. Also it is observed that the depth of discharged of System 3 is reduced, which signifies that the overall lifetime of its accumulators is protected. Finally the amount of energy that cannot be absorbed by the network is also reduced from 38KWh to 24KWh which is also beneficial for the overall network performance. As far as the hydrogen storage is concerned in the first case the electrolyzer operates for 23hrs whereas in the second cease for 16 hrs. Although energy is distributed to the network, a smaller amount of hydrogen continues to be produced and stored at the final tanks for future usage.

5   Conclusions

In this paper, a Cellular Automata (CA) based approach combined with Game Theory for the enhancement of Power Management Strategies (PMSs) of multiple Hybrid Renewable Energy Systems (HYRES) that form a smart grid for the exchange of energy was presented. The presented CA model focuses on providing valuable feedback for PMSs of the understudy HYRES connected in a grid. In this manner, a flexible network based HYRES design is considered and applied to a specific HYRES located in Olvio, near Xanthi, Greece, part of SYSTEMS SUNLIGHT facilities. The proposed model can be applied to the understudy HYRES grid managing to enhance and optimize its PMS based on the provided energy prediction scenarios.

Acknowledgments. This work is co-financed by National Strategic Reference Framework (NSRF) 2007-2013 of Greece and the European Union, research program "SYNERGASIA" (SUPERMICRO – 09ΣYN-32-594).

References

1. Nordman, B., Christensen, K., Meier, A.: Think Globally, Distribute Power Locally. Computer, 89–90 (2012)
2. Deshmukha, M.K., Deshmukh, S.S.: Modeling of hybrid renewable energy systems. Renewable and Sustainable Energy Reviews 12(1), 235–249 (2008)
3. Myerson, R.B.: Game theory: Analysis of conflict. Harvard University Press (1991)
4. Brañas-Garza, P., Espinosa, M.P.: Unraveling Public Good Games. Games 2(4), 434–451 (2011)
5. Hauert, C., Szabó, G.: Prisoner's dilemma and public goods games in different geometries: compulsory versus voluntary interactions. Complexity 8(4), 31–38 (2003)
6. Kim, O., Walker, M.: The free rider problem: Experimental evidence. Public Choice 43, 3–24 (1984)
7. Sirakoulis, G.C., Karafyllidis, I.: Cooperation in a Power-Aware Embedded System Changing Environment: Public Goods Games with Variable Multiplication Factors. IEEE Transactions on Systems, Man, and Cybernetics–Part A: Systems and Humans 42(3), 596–603 (2012)
8. Janssen, M.A., Goldstone, R.L.: Dynamic-persistence of cooperation in public goods game when group size is dynamic. Theoretical Biology 243(1), 134–142 (2006)
9. Sirakoulis, G.C., Bandini, S. (eds.): ACRI 2012. LNCS, vol. 7495. Springer, Heidelberg (2012)
10. Sirakoulis, G.C., Karafyllidis, I.: Cellular Automata and Power Consumption. Journal of Cellular Automata 7(1), 67–80 (2012)
11. Tsompanas, M.-A.I., Kachris, C., Sirakoulis, G.C.: Evaluating conflicts impact over shared last-level cache using public goods game on cellular automata. In: HPCS 2012, pp. 326–332 (2012)
12. Giaouris, D., Papadopoulos, A.I., Ziogou, C., Ipsakis, D., Voutetakis, S., Papadopoulou, S., Seferlis, P., Stergiopoulos, F., Elmasides, C.: Performance investigation of a hybrid renewable power generation and storage system using systemic power management models. Energy 61, 621–635 (2013)

A Novel Algorithm for Coarse-Graining
of Cellular Automata

Krzysztof Magiera[*] and Witold Dzwinel

AGH University of Science and Technology, Department of Computer Science,
Al.Mickiewicza 30, 30-059 Kraków, Poland
{kmagiera,dzwinel}@agh.edu.pl

Abstract. The coarse-graining is an approximation procedure widely used for simplification of mathematical and numerical models of multiscale systems. It reduces superfluous – microscopic – degrees of freedom. Israeli and Goldenfeld demonstrated in [1,2] that the coarse-graining can be employed for elementary cellular automata (CA), producing interesting interdependences between them. However, extending their investigation on more complex CA rules appeared to be impossible due to the high computational complexity of the coarse-graining algorithm. We demonstrate here that this complexity can be substantially decreased. It allows for scrutinizing much broader class of cellular automata in terms of their coarse graining. By using our algorithm we found out that the ratio of the numbers of elementary CAs having coarse grained representation to "degenerate" – irreducible – cellular automata, strongly increases with increasing the "grain" size of the approximation procedure. This rises principal questions about the formal limits in modeling of realistic multiscale systems.

Keywords: multiscale systems, coarse graining, cellular automata.

1   Introduction

The current challenges in modeling and computer simulation (e.g. in systems biology) involve searching for new modeling paradigms, which would allow for simulating multiscale complex systems. Preferably, we are looking for a unified computational framework, which could be matched to the following spatio-temporal scales of interest through out the process of successive coarse-graining of finer scales. The "coarse graining" (CG) can be understood as a numerical equivalent of some renormalization procedures used from many years in physics for simplification of formal mathematical models. In terms of computational modeling it can be defined as an approximation process, which limits the number of microscopic degrees of freedom (DOF) and the frequency of their motion starting from the smallest to the largest scales of interest. The primary challenge is to develop a CG model that is significantly easier to simulate but that reproduces the same physical behavior as a reference microscopic model.

---

[*] Corresponding author.

J. Wąs, G.C. Sirakoulis, and S. Bandini (Eds.): ACRI 2014, LNCS 8751, pp. 258–267, 2014.
© Springer International Publishing Switzerland 2014

Signal decomposition and signal multiresolution are the good metaphors of the notions of coarse graining and multiscaling. Every signal can be decomposed onto its approximations and details on successive resolution levels by using a set of basis functions with compact support (such as wavelets, RBFs etc.). Finally, the signal can be represented as the sum of the approximation on a given resolution level and all the details from finer scales. By cutting off the the least important details, i.e. all of them having the weights below a certain threshold, the signal can be reconstructed by using the approximation and only a fraction of the most important details. This rises the following question. Does a similar decomposition exist in the context of simulation of multiscale systems? To find the analogies between signal and multiscale systems decomposition let us consider elementary 1-D cellular automata as the most simplistic model of computations. In the scope of this conceptual framework we can try to answer the elementary question. Can be the elementary CA systems approximated? Does exist a general and efficient coarse-graining procedure for cellular automata?

In this paper we stick to the concept of coarse-graining, which has been introduced to 1-D cellular automata by Israeli and Goldenfeld in [1,2]. First, we briefly present the idea. Then we demonstrate the CG algorithm of much lower computational complexity than the original one [1]. This allows for scrutinizing much broader class of automata in the context of coarse-graining than in [2]. Consequently, we estimate the number of CA's with CG ability for grain sizes $N>2$. Finally, we sketch the analogy between coarse-graining of cellular automata and more realistic modeling paradigm, namely, the particle method.

2 Coarse Graining of Cellular Automata

Let us define the original cellular automata CA as $A=(a(t),\Sigma_A,f_A)$ and its coarse-grained equivalent $B=(b(T),\Sigma_B,f_B)$. The states of A and B are labeled by finite alphabets Σ_A and Σ_B of sizes $|\Sigma_A|$ and $|\Sigma_B|$, respectively. The update rules, defined as $f_i:\{\Sigma_i\}^\Theta \to \Sigma_i$. where Θ stands for the neighborhood size (i.e., $\Theta=3$ for 1-D basic CA) and $i \in \{A,B\}$, consist of a complete number $R_i=|\Sigma_i|^{\wedge}|\Sigma_i|^\Theta$ of CA rules and govern the evolution of lattices of CA states $a(t)$ and $b(T)$ in discrete times t and $T=N\cdot t$, respectively. The projection function $P: \Sigma_A{}^N \to \Sigma_B$ is used to map the block of N cells from A (i.e. A^N grain (*supercell*)) into a single cell of B. This projection has to satisfy the following CG condition [1]:

$$P \cdot \underbrace{f_A \cdot ... \cdot f_A}_{N} \cdot a = f_B \cdot P \cdot a. \tag{1}$$

The expression $f_A(...)$ means, that we apply the update rules f_A of automata A to every cell in the lattice $a(t)$, while $P(...)$ denotes the CG procedure. The equation (1) says, that by running N times the cellular automata A and then coarse-graining it by using $P(.)$, we obtain the same configuration as applying $P(.)$ at first (i.e. coarse graining of A to B), and then running automata B only once. The Eq.(1) has to be satisfied for any starting configurations $a(0)$ of A. Israeli and Goldenfeld [1,2] developed a brute-force procedure for finding coarse grained configuration of a given automata A, which can be sketched as follows. Let us define a *supercell* automata:

$$A_N = \left(a^N(t), \Sigma_A^N, f_{A^N} \right) \tag{2}$$

which operates over blocks of N cells from $a(t)$ lattice. For 1-D automata with neighborhood of size $\Theta = 3$ the local function f_{A^N} is then $f_{A^N} : \{\Sigma^N\}^3 \to \Sigma^N$. We can compute easily the value of f_{A^N} for some $x = (x_1; x_2; x_3)$ where $x_i \in \{\Sigma^N\}$ and $i = 1, 2, 3..$ This could be done by converting x into $3N$-element lattice of automata A, and by running A exactly N times:

$$y = \underbrace{f_A \cdot \ldots \cdot f_A}_{N} \cdot x. \tag{3}$$

Now we can choose the alphabet of coarse grained automata B, which fits into the alphabet of A_N, i.e.,

$$\Sigma_B \subseteq \Sigma_A, \tag{4}$$

because for $\Sigma_B \equiv \Sigma_{A^N}$ mapping function $P(.)$ is injective, and we would not have any benefits from coarse-graining. By employing all these definitions, we can rewrite Eq.(1) as follows:

$$f_B \left[P(x_1); P(x_2); P(x_3) \right] = P \left(f_{A^N} [x_1; x_2; x_3] \right). \tag{5}$$

We need to keep in mind, that $P(.)$ has not to be injective thus exists a possibility that $(P(x'_1); P(x'_2); P(x'_3)) = (P(x_1); P(x_2); P(x_3))$ for different triples of N-element blocks, i.e., $(x'_1; x'_2; x'_3) \, \square \, (x_1; x_2; x_3)$. In that case for both triples:

$$f_B[P(x_1); P(x_2); P(x_3)] = f_B[P(x'_1); P(x'_2); P(x'_3)].$$

Hence, in general:

$$\forall (x', x; P(x_i) = P(x'_i)) : P \left(f_{A^N} [x'_1; x'_2; x'_3] \right) = P \left(f_{A^N} [x_1; x_2; x_3] \right). \tag{6}$$

The CG process eliminates degrees of freedom of local processes without loosing the global features of CA evolution. For example, as shown in Figs.1a,b, the rule 128 is the coarse grained version of the rule 146. In [2], the full diagram of of all coarse-grained basic 1-D automata is presented. It is worth to mention that the cellular automata of complexity from class IV (such as rule 110) can be coarse grained only to trivial rules, i.e., 0 and 255.

The mapping function $P(.)$ is responsible for information loss. As shown in Fig.2 (upper panel), only when $\Sigma_B \equiv \Sigma_{A^N}$ no information is being lost, since $P(.)$ is injective. For such the alphabet Σ_B, the coarse-graining of A is trivial and it always exists. Therefore, it is reasonable to consider much smaller Σ_B than Σ_{A^N} (see Fig.2b (lower panel)). On the other hand, as shown in Fig.1c, by increasing the alphabet Σ_A (i.e. assuming that $\Sigma_A \subset \Sigma_B \subset \Sigma_{A^N}$) the fine-scale information can be partially reconstructed.

The main conclusions can be summarized as follows:

1. By applying to the most of elementary 1-D cellular automata the coarse graining procedure described above, it is possible to obtain their simpler (but not trivial) approximations.

2. Many coarse-grained CA can be simple and predictable.
3. A few irreducible CA may have trivial CG representations.
4. Finer, physically important DOF, can be incorporated to the CG model by increasing the alphabet $\Sigma_B \supset \Sigma_A$ and changing the rule set.

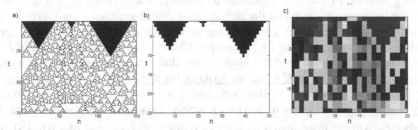

Fig. 1. The effect of coarse graining of rule 146 a) the original rule 146 b) its CG version – rule 128, c) CG version of the rule 146 using larger alphabet Σ_B [1,2,3]

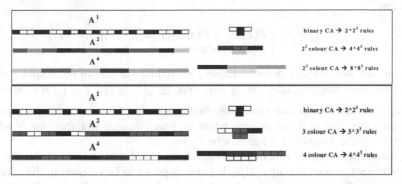

Fig. 2. The diagram demonstrating the process of coarse graining of CA. Information about finer scales can be preserved in new rules, which are created from a greater alphabet Σ_B than the original one Σ_A [3].

3   Fast Coarse Graining

The simple brute-force algorithm for finding projection $P(.)$ described in [1,2] is very computationally demanding. We need to consider all possible cellular automata for being likely the result of coarse graining of A. For each CA we need to loop over all mapping functions $P(.)$ and finally for each mapping $P(.)$ we have to process all possible starting configurations for N'th block version of CA. For CA automata with neighborhood of size Θ, alphabet Σ and block size N, the computational complexity of this method is as follows:

$$O\left(|\Sigma|^{|\Sigma|^N} + |\Sigma|^{|\Sigma|^\Theta} + |\Sigma|^{N\Theta} \right) \tag{7}$$

The number of operations required to find coarse grained representation of A grows really fast especially with the neighborhood size Θ. For example, in case of 1-D binary automata A with two neighbors on right, and two neighbors on left side ($\Theta=5$), the number of operations required to find coarse graining of A is proportional to

$7 \cdot 10^{13}$. When we consider $\Theta=7$, the number of operations reaches $8 \cdot 10^{40}$. In this section we present the algorithm of much lower computational complexity of order $O\left(|\Sigma|^{N\Theta}\right)$.

For a given cellular automata A over alphabet Σ and a block size N, we write that a mapping function $P(.)$ over Σ^N generates a correct coarse graining of A if there exists a cellular automata A^N such that the definition of coarse graining from Eq.(6) is satisfied with respect to A^N and $P(.)$. In that case we say that A^N is *generated* by a mapping function $P(.)$ and that mapping $P(.)$ is *correct*. Clearly, the size of co-domain of $P(.)$ is equal to the size of alphabet of A^N. Now we see that <u>instead of searching for a coarse grained version of a given CA we are looking for a *correct* mapping function.</u> The idea behind our algorithm is that we start from some basic mapping function $P : \Sigma_A^N \rightarrow \Sigma_P$, which gives us a *correct* coarse-graining of cellular automata A to alphabet Σ_P. After that we search for a set of states $X=\{x_1, x_2,...x_N\}$ of a size $k>1$, such that it produces a *correct* derivative mapping function $P'(.)$ by assigning arguments of $P(.)$, which return values from $\{P(x_1), P(x_2), ...P(x_N)\}$ to the same value of $P(x_1)$. It means that:

$$P'(z) = \begin{cases} P(x_1) & \text{if } P(z) \in \{P(x_1), P(x_2)..., P(x_k)\} \\ P(z) & \text{otherwise} \end{cases} \qquad (8)$$

It is clear that with the step described above we reduce the size of the output alphabet Σ'_P of the new mapping function by $k-1$, thus $|\Sigma'_P| = |\Sigma_P| - k + 1$. We can repeat that step several times in order to obtain better mapping functions with even smaller output alphabet. We stop that process when we reach desired alphabet size or when a *correct* derivative mapping $P'(.)$ cannot be found.

For an initial mapping function we can chose any function with arbitrarily large output alphabet, since the output alphabet size is going to be reduced in the course of the algorithm. For an integer N and alphabet Σ of size $s=|\Sigma|$, let us define identity function $Id_{s,N}$ over alphabet Σ^N, such as it assigns a unique value for each sequence of symbols from Σ of size N. For example, for binary CA and $N=2$ an identity mapping function looks as follows: $Id_{2,2}=\{(\square\square)\rightarrow 0, (\square\blacksquare)\rightarrow 1, (\blacksquare\square)\rightarrow 2, (\blacksquare\blacksquare)\rightarrow 3\}$. For a given cellular automata A over alphabet Σ and grain size N we see that the corresponding Id mapping produces a valid coarse-grained automata over alphabet of size $|\Sigma|^N$. Thus we can use Id mapping as an entry point to the algorithm.

Let us focus now on a way of finding X, that will produce *correct* derivative mapping $P'(.)$ from the starting *correct* mapping $P(.)$. We start from a simplified version of that task. We want to find a set X of size 2. For a cellular automata A with neighborhood Θ, grain size N and a *correct* mapping function $P:\Sigma^N \rightarrow \Sigma_P$ over A, the simplified version of the problem defined above is equivalent to the problem of finding a pair of states x,y such that $P(x)\neq P(y)$. We assume also that the mapping $P'(.)$ defined as follows is *correct*:

$$P'(z) = \begin{cases} P(x) & \text{if } P(z) = P(x) \text{ or } P(z) = P(y) \\ P(z) & \text{otherwise} \end{cases} \qquad (9)$$

From now on we will refer to the procedure of creating new mapping function $P'(.)$ from the pair of states $x, y \in \Sigma^N$ as *merging* of states x and y. Let $r^{t=N}$ be a CA configuration obtained by running N steps of cellular automata A starting from configuration $r \in \Sigma^{N\Theta}$ (consisting of Θ N-grains). Let $e(r)$ be the middle block of of size N of the configuration r. Now assume we choose some arbitrary states $x, y \in \Sigma^N$ we want to *merge* in order to obtain mapping $P'(.)$. If the mapping $P(.)$ is not *correct*, then there exists a pair of CA configurations $r_1, r_2 \in \Sigma^{N\Theta}$ such that $P'(.)$ maps $e(r_1)$ and $e(r_2)$ to the same value, but the mapping of $e\left(r_1^{t=N}\right)$ and $e\left(r_2^{t=N}\right)$ differs. This follows directly from the definition of coarse graining from Eq.(6). However, if $P'(.)$ mapped $e\left(r_1^{t=N}\right)$ and $e\left(r_2^{t=N}\right)$ to the same value, then $P'(.)$ might still be a *correct* mapping. Therefore we write that the pair of states x,y *enforces* pair of states $e\left(r_1^{t=N}\right), e\left(r_2^{t=N}\right)$. In other words, *enforcing* is a relation defined over two pairs of states from Σ^N. We say that a pair of states (u_1,u_2) *enforces* another pair (v_1,v_2) if mapping function obtained by *merging* states u_1 and u_2 is not *correct* until we *merge* states v_1 and v_2. As we can see above, *enforcement* can be easily computed for all the possible two pairs of states from Σ^N. In that way we can create an *enforcement graph* (EG), where nodes corresponds to a pair of states from Σ^N and there exists directed edge between the nodes only when starting node *enforces* the succeeding one. The EG for elementary rule 29 with $N=2$ is presented in Fig.3.

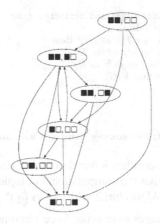

Fig. 3. Enforcement graph for elementary rule CA 29 with $N=2$

This EG graph contains exactly 6 nodes. Each one represents different pair of binary automata states (there are exactly 4 such the states). The pseudo-code for finding an *enforcement graph* a one-dimensional CA is presented in Algorithm.2 panel. For a given 1-D cellular automata A over alphabet Σ with neighborhood size Θ and grain size N, the computational complexity of Algorithm.2 is $O\left(|\Sigma|^{N\Theta}\right)$.

By using EG graph it is easy to find a solution for the problem of finding set of states X of size 2 that will produce *correct* derivative mapping $P'(.)$. Clearly, when there is a node with no outgoing edges in EG, then the pair of states representing that node is the answer. Otherwise, when does not exist such the node, it is impossible to find such the set X. However, thanks to that observation, it is clear that in order to find a solution to the main problem, when size of X is not restricted, we need to find a component in EG graph (subset of nodes), such that there are no outgoing edges from the component's nodes to the nodes outside of it. To find such a component in enforcement graph it is sufficient to use any algorithm for determining strongly connected components. Since the graph of strongly connected components is acyclic, we can always find at least one component satisfying our condition (in directed acyclic graph it will be the closing node under topological order). We may try to join states represented by nodes from that component as long as we will not join all of the states at the same time producing a primitive mapping.

```
G ← generate enforcement graph for A with block size N;
P ← Id ; // Start from identity mapping
Σ ← alphabet of A;
Loop
    C ← find topologically last strongly-connected component of G;
    P' ← P;
    foreach v ∈ C do
    |   join P'(state₁(v)) and P'(state₂(v))
    end
    if #P' < #Σ then
    |   break ;      /* after joining states from C, there are to
    |   few elements left in the alphabet */
    end
    P ← P';
    // Remove joined edges and verticies from G
    foreach v ∈ V(G) do
    |   if P(state₁(v)) = P(state₂(v)) then
    |   |   remove (·, v) edges from E(G);
    |   |   remove (v, ·) edges from E(G);
    |   |   remove v from V(G);
    |   end
    end
EndLoop
return P
```
Algorithm 1: Find coarse-graining of A with block size N

The pseudo-code from Algorithm.1 panel contains detailed description of all the steps from above. It is clear that the computational complexity of Algorithm.1 can be bound by the complexity of Algorithm.2 which is $O\left(|\Sigma|^{N\Theta}\right)$. The fast coarse graining algorithm has several advantages over brute force approach [1]. The main advantage is, of course, computational complexity. In all presented methods the complexity is exponential. Although, considering relatively small values of CA attributes (small neighborhood size and the grain size N), it still plays a significant role.

As shown in Table 2, the "Fast" algorithm is 2^N times faster than "Brute-Force" algorithm. This gives us the possibility to find some of CA coarse graining which are computationally unreachable by the original algorithm from [1]. The second advantage of the fast algorithm is that it can produce coarse graining to CA automata with various sizes of alphabet. This property is very intriguing since not every CA could be coarse grained to automata within the same alphabet. In particular, 6 elementary CA rules have coarse-graining representation with 3-element alphabet which cannot be coarse grained within binary alphabet. These specific CA's are the rules: 29,71,72 (and three symmetric rules: 237, 184 and 226).

Table 1. The number of operations of coarse graining algorithms for grain size $N=3$

N	Algorithm	$\Theta = 3$	$\Theta = 5$	$\Theta = 7$	$\Theta = 9$
3	Brute-Force	33554432	$36028797 \cdot 10^9$	$18268770 \cdot 10^{40}$	$46068877 \cdot 10^{157}$
	Fast CG	512	32768	2097152	134217728

```
Σ ← alphabet of 𝒜;
Θ ← neighbourhood size of 𝒜;
G ← create empty graph;
M ← empty map;
// Examine all starting states for N'th version of 𝒜
foreach {s_NΘ} ∈ Σ^NΘ do
    {m_Θ} ← (Id(s_1,...,s_N),...,Id(s_{NΘ−N},...,s_{NΘ}));
    {s_N^t} ← run 𝒜 on {s_NΘ} N times;
    m^t ← Id(s_1^t,...,s_N^t);
    M[{m_Θ}] ← m^t;
end
foreach {X_Θ} ∈ {1,...,N}^Θ do
    foreach i ∈ 1,...,Θ do
        foreach S_1,S_2 ∈ {1,...,N} and S_1 ≠ S_2 do
            /* Look for 2 starting states that has only one
               different element                          */
            {X_Θ^1} ← {X_Θ};
            X_i^1 ← S_1;
            {X_Θ^2} ← {X_Θ};
            X_i^2 ← S_2;
            if M[{X_Θ^1}] ≠ M[{X_Θ^2}] then
                V_1 ← vertex({S_1,S_2});
                V_2 ← vertex({M[{X_Θ^1}],M[{X_Θ^1}]});
                add vertices V_1,V_2 to V(G);
                add edge(V_1,V_2) to E(G);
            end
        end
    end
end
```
Algorithm 2: Generate Enforcement Graph for 𝒜 with block size N

4   Preliminary Results

Classification of cellular automata that have their CG representations is very difficult and time consuming [1,2]. Here we estimate only the number of CA's with coarse-graining ability for various grain size N. For each CA the fast CG algorithm has been used. We have checked one by one all the members of the elementary CA set, searching for their CG representations with increasing N, until its coarse grained equivalent will be found. The results obtained are presented in Fig.4. On the x-axis of the plot from the left panel of Fig.4 a single bar shows at the bottom (in red) the number of cellular automata that have CG representations for various grain sizes N ($|\Sigma|=2$). Whereas, at the top of each bar, we show the number of cellular automata without significant (i.e., the CA within the alphabet of size $2N$) CG equivalent. As one can see, for $N=3$ more than a half of cellular automata have the ability of coarse-graining within the binary alphabet. This ratio increases with increasing N, and for $N=6$ reaches 75%. The right panel plot from Fig.4, shows the percentage of elementary CA without CG representation. It means that randomly chosen elementary automata cannot be coarse grained with probability less then 0.06, assuming that the grain size $N<=7$. The plot has asymptotic character. For $N>7$ one can expect that the most of the automata would have CG equivalent. However, we anticipate that the CA rules belonging to the class IV will remain computationally irreducible.

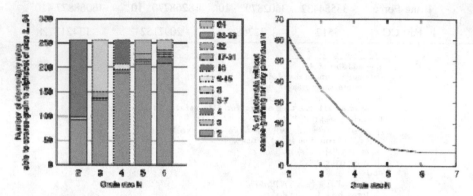

Fig. 4. a) Number of elementary automata having CG representations with various alphabet size and for grain size $N = 2$; 3; 4; 5; 6. b) Percentage of elementary rules, which cannot be coarse-grained for the grain size $n<=N$ and $|\Sigma|=2$

5   Concluding Remarks and Discussion

We present a new algorithm for coarse graining of cellular automata. Its computational complexity is $O\left(|\Sigma|^{N\Theta}\right)$ comparing to $O\left(|\Sigma|^{|\Sigma|^N} + |\Sigma|^{|\Sigma|^{\Theta}} + |\Sigma|^{N\Theta}\right)$ of the original method [1]. Additionally, unlike the brute force approach, our algorithm can find the coarse-grained cellular automata B, which has different alphabet than the source one (A). This allows for exploring much coarser approximations of elementary CA with larger number of neighbors. We have demonstrated that with increasing N more and more automata become reducible, i.e., they can have simpler coarse-grained equivalents (excluding trivial ones). The interesting questions remain still opened. What is the common property of CA systems, which cannot be coarse grained within $|\Sigma|<2N$ for large N. What does "coarse graining ability" mean in the context of CA complexity classes?

The results of CA approximation may have direct relationship with modeling of multiscale real-life systems. Let us consider the model of interacting particles called particle method (PM) (e.g. [3,4]). The particle method is a discrete, off-grid and very general paradigm of modeling, which has its roots in N-body problem and well known molecular dynamics (MD) method. PM is broadly used for simulation of many physical, chemical, biological and social phenomena (e.g. [3,4]). Its scope of application was described, e.g., in [3,4]. Unlike cellular automata, the particle method is a discrete-continuum paradigm in which discrete particles evolve in continuous space and time. The coarse graining methods of PM remain very similar to those applied for CA. Particularly:

1. Both paradigms, CA and PM, are homogeneous, i.e., their principles remain the same in every spatio-temporal scale.

2. The "grain" of CA consists of N finer automata, while the fluid particle is a coarse grained representation of N interacting MD atoms [4,5].
3. The projection operator $P(.)$ in CA corresponds to the averaging rule in PM.
4. The f_B transition function corresponds to a coarse grained collision operator between fluid particles and particle motion scheme.
5. Similarly as f_B (macroscopic CA rule) comparing to f_A (microscopic CA rule), the collision operator Ω between fluid particles can be more complicated than the respective interaction force between MD atoms. For example, the collision operator Ω may consists not only of conservative interactions but dissipative and Brownian tensor interactions as well [4,5]. They represent averaged degrees of freedom from atomistic scale. Moreover, the ordinary differential equation of the Newtonian motion can be coarse grained by more demanding stochastic differential equations.

Summarizing, the problem of coarse graining of a realistic physical model - such as the method of interacting particles - from microscopic (MD) to macroscopic formulation (fluid particles), looks conceptually similar to that applied for CA systems. Of course, the terms such as the "projection function" and "alphabet" are very different for the two and have rather metaphoric character. Nevertheless, one can expect that many of conclusions drawn from coarse-graining of CA systems can be directly transferred to more realistic multiscale models of interacting particles. Particularly, it is interesting if correspondingly to irreducible local CA rules there exist similar setups in particle systems, for which any coarse graining procedure fails. This may impose formal limits on the usage of coarse graining in modeling and simulation of multiscale systems by employing interacting particles.

Acknowledgments. This research is financed by the Polish National Center of Science (NCN), project UMO – 2013/10/M/ST6/00531 and partially by AGH grant No.11.11.120.777. KM is the inventor of the fast coarse-graining algorithm and he wrote some parts of the paper; WD is supervisor and advisor of KM. He composed this paper and wrote some of its parts including: the introduction, the first section and the conclusions.

References

1. Israeli, N., Goldenfeld, N.: Coarse-graining of cellular automata, emergence, and the predictability of complex systems. Phys. Rev. E. 73(2), 026203 (2006)
2. Israeli, N., Goldenfeld, N.: Computational irreducibility and the predictability of complex physical systems. Physical Review Letters 92(7), 074105 (2004)
3. Dzwinel, W.: Complex automata as a novel conceptual framework for modeling biomedical phenomena. In: Byrski, A., Oplatková, Z., Carvalho, M., Dorohnicki, M.K. (eds.) Advances in Intelligent Modelling and Simulation. SCI, vol. 416, pp. 269–298. Springer, Heidelberg (2012)
4. Dzwinel, W., Yuen, D.A., Boryczko, K.: Bridging diverse physical scales with the discrete-particle paradigm in modeling colloidal dynamics with mesoscopic features. Chemical Engineering Sci. 61, 2169–2185 (2006)
5. Espanõl, P.: Fluid particle model. Phys. Rev. E 57, 2930–2948 (1998)

Cellular Automata Model for Protein Structure Synthesis (PSS)

Soumyabrata Ghosh, Nirmalya S. Maiti, and Parimal Pal Chaudhuri

CARLBio Pvt Ltd, Alumnus Software Limited,
Kolkata, India, 700091
soumya@carlbio.com
http://carlbio.com

Abstract. This paper is a refinement and extension of the Protein modelling Cellular Automata Machine (PCAM) reported in [1] for prediction of protein structure. An efficient organization of Knowledge Base (KB) is reported in the current paper. The KB is reorganized with emphasis on the residues in the Transition Regions (TRs) between structural regions like alpha helices or beta strands and an unstructured or loop regions. The meta-knowledge derived out of the KB analysis is employed for synthesis of protein structure from the primary chain of amino acid residues. Design of synthesis algorithm ensures incorporation of probable orientation of structural parameters of residues in the TR. A few structures are finally selected based on the computation of exposed surface area and core size. The algorithm is tested for the challenging protein targets from [9] to synthesize structures with reasonable accuracy and low execution time.

Keywords: Protein Structure Synthesis (PSS), Protein modelling Cellular Automata Machine (PCAM).

1 Introduction

Experimental determination of a protein structure from its sequence is labour intensive, time consuming, and expensive. Building a robust model for protein structure prediction has received considerable attention in last few decades [3,4,5,6,7]. Clear winner in this race is the Molecular Dynamic Simulation tools [6]. It works based on the energy minimization of the forces experienced by thousands of atoms of different amino acids in a protein chain. It aims to address the Multi-Body problem of exponential complexity. Naturally, it demands the support of large computing power with high execution time. An alternative model based on evolutionary coupling of amino acid residues is reported in [7].

We reported a novel approach [1] for protein structure prediction based on the knowledge derived out of CA model operated on more than 13,000 unique proteins available in Protein Data Bank (PDB). Unlike any homology model, our Knowledge Base (KB) is created out of a CA cell modelling an amino acid irrespective of the protein chain it may belong to. Further, the proposed CA framework models the biological process of protein synthesis from codon string with tRNA molecule. The physical domain data of amino acid chain of a protein get transformed to binary bit pattern of CA rules. We next

J. Wąs, G.C. Sirakoulis, and S. Bandini (Eds.): ACRI 2014, LNCS 8751, pp. 268–277, 2014.

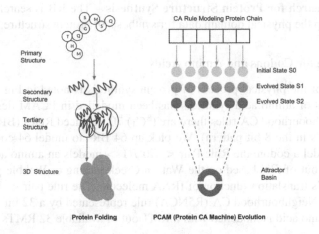

Fig. 1. PCAM evolution modelling folding of protein chain to minimum energy configuration

design a PCAM (Protein modeling CA Machine)from the input Amino Acid sequence. The PCAM evolution to Attracter Basin models the Minimum Energy conformation in physical domain.The details of this approach is reported in [1]. A brief overview of PCAM design is presented in the next section.The Knowledge Base (KB) for mapping model parameters to physical domain parameters is covered in Section 3. The meta-knowledge derived from the KB guides the synthesis algorithm reported in Section 4.

2   Protein Modelling Cellular Automata Machine (PCAM) — An Overview

An overview of the model reported in [1] is noted below.

Step 1: Physical Domain (PD) to Transform Domain(TD) – Three neighbourhood CA rules are used to model codons, while five neighbourhood CA rules are employed to model twenty amino acids. Physical domain characteristics of codons, anti-codons, and amino acids are mapped to binary bit patterns of CA rules. A protein gets transformed to a CA Rule Vector (RV) $< R_0\ R_1\ ...\ R_i\ ...\ R_{n-1} >$ where i^{th} ($i = 0$ to $n-1$) amino acid is modelled by i^{th} cell of the CA. In the process, a protein chain gets modelled as a PCAM (Protein modelling Cellular Automata Machine).

Step 2: PCAM Evolution – PCAM evolution to its Attractor Basin, as shown in Fig 1, models protein evolution to its minimum energy conformation. PCAM evolution generates Transform Domain Parameters (TDP).

Step 3: Creation of a Knowledge Base (KB) – TDP generated out of PCAM evolution are mapped to physical domain data of a protein chain. The KB is derived out of the available protein structures in PDB by running the PCAM for each protein chain.

Step 4: KB Search for Protein Structure Synthesis – The KB is searched with the TDP to pick up the physical domain data for synthesis of protein structure.

2.1 CA Rule for Codons and Amino Acids

An overview of the physical process of protein synthesis is noted in Fig 2. This biological process of amino acid synthesis has been modelled in PCAM design. Out of 256 three neighbourhood CA rules there are ($^{8}C_{4}$) 70 Balanced Rules (BR) (with four 1's and four 0's in the 8 bit pattern). We pick up 64 BRs to model 64 codons. While a rule $R0'$ model a codon, the Rule Pair $< R0\ R1 >$ models an amino acid; the rule $R0$ is derived out of $R0'$ based on the Watson-Creek pairing or Wobble pairing. The rule $R1$ models translation function of tRNA molecule. The rule pair $< R0\ R1 >$ is a Restricted 5 Neighbourhood CA (R5NCA) rule represented by a 32 bit string. Each atom of an amino acid is modelled with a RMT out of available 32 RMTs 0(00000) to 31(11111).

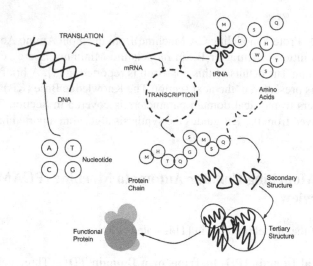

Fig. 2. Protein Synthesis out of codon string, commonly known as Central Dogma of Biology

The chiral and aliphatic carbons with the hydrogen atoms are represented as a component of an amino acid. Such entities are marked in the CA model as Functional Components (FCs). RMT assigned to an atom is shown adjacent to the atom in Fig 3(c). For example, in the case of amino acid Valine, RMTs 19 and 12 are assigned respectively to Cα carbon and H atom covalently bonded. FCs (CH,CH$_3$, OH, NH$_3$, COO etc.) of these two amino acids are marked in the figure.

The Functional Components (FCs) can be grouped as: (a) Non-Polar (NP), (b) Polar Uncharged (PU), (c) Polar Positive (PP), (d) Polar Negative (PN),and (e) Aromatic Ring (AR) denoted respectively as $\widetilde{a}, \widetilde{b}, \widetilde{c}, \widetilde{d}, \widetilde{e}$. The FCs representing atom groups of an amino acid play a key role in the CA model detailed in next section.

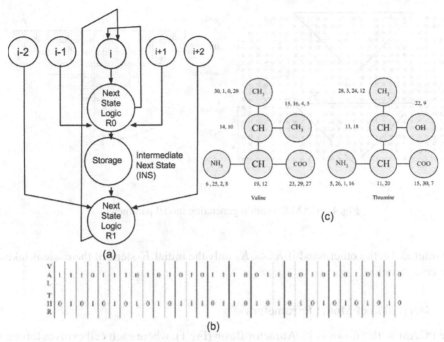

Fig. 3. (a) A R5NCA (Restricted 5 Neighbourhood CA) i^{th} cell operated with rule $R = <R_i0 \ R_i1>$ Note : sequential execution of R_i0 followed by R_i1 generates its next state b_k for RMT $k = <a_{i-2} \ a_{i-1} \ a_i \ a_{i+1} \ a_{i+2}>$, (b) 32 Bit Rule (shown as 0 to 31 from left to right) for amino acid Valine (VAL) and Threonine (THR) (c)Mapping of two amino acids to two 32 bit parameters (shown in Fig 4(b)) of 5 neighbourhood CA rules. Functional Components (FCs) are shown in circle

3   PCAM Evolution to Generate Model Parameters

The n cell PCAM (for n length amino acid sequence) is operated with an n bit initial state (0 for non-polar and 1 for polar amino acid) in successive time steps till it reaches an attractor basin. Each CA cell generates cyclic states in the attractor basin (Fig 4). Prior to evolution in a cycle, a cell traverses through transitory path. Each cell of R5NCA modelling an amino acid generates binary output 0 or 1. However, the state of a cell is evaluated in the context of its two left and right neighbours,. The state of ith cell is evaluated as five bit pattern $< b_{i-2} \ b_{i-1} \ b_i \ b_{i+1} \ b_{i+2} >$ where b_{i-2}, b_{i-1}, b_i, b_{i+1}, b_{i+2} are the binary outputs of $(i-2)^{th}$, $(i-1)^{th}$, i^{th}, $(i+1)^{th}$, and $(i+2)^{th}$ cells . This five bit pattern refers to a RMT (Rule Min Term) of ith cell. The RMT has been mapped to an atom of the amino acid as noted in Fig 3(c). Further, this atom belongs to a specific Functional Component (FC) as explained earlier. In its attractor basin, each CA cell runs through a cycle generating a set of its FCs. In order to synthesize the 3D structure, we concentrate on K step evolution in a cycle. If a cycle length is (say) K' where $K' < K$, then $(K-K')$ number of last transitory step evolution is

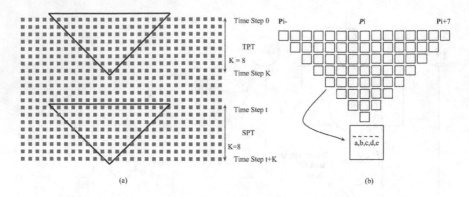

Fig. 4. PCAM Evolution generating model parameters

considered. On the other hand if $K' > K$, only the initial K steps of the cycle is taken into consideration.

3.1 Derivation of Model Parameters

The PCAM settles down in its Attractor Basin (Fig 1), where each cell evolves through its cycle generating one of the five FCs $(\tilde{a}, \tilde{b}, \tilde{c}, \tilde{d}, \tilde{e})$ in each step. The cyclic status of CA cell models the stable state of the amino acid in the 3D conformation where the cycle models the vibration of the amino acid molecule. Hence cyclic path of a CA cell is marked as Stable Path (SP). Prior to settling in cyclic path the CA cell evolves in Transitory non-cyclic Path (TP). A K length path is a string of K number of FCs generated by a cell in K successive steps. Evolution of ith cell for K time steps generating K length path is affected by $(K-1)$ left and right neighbours in (say) time step t, $(k-2)$ left and right neighbours in time step $(t+1)$ and so on. Finally, at the triangle tip the cell generates its FC after $(t+K)$ time steps. In each successive evolution step, a CA cell generates one or more of FCs $(\tilde{a}, \tilde{b}, \tilde{c}, \tilde{d}, \tilde{e})$, as indicated in Fig 4(b). Sum of individual parameters evolved by each cell over K time steps generates CA model Parameter Vector $P = < A \; B \; C \; D \; E >$, where $\sum \tilde{a} = A$, $\sum \tilde{b} = B$, $\sum \tilde{c} = C$, $\sum \tilde{d} = D$, and $\sum \tilde{e} = E$, summation taken for evolution of each cell over the entire triangle (Fig 4(b)). For the current version of Protein Structure Prediction (PSS) module, the value of $K = 8$.

4   Knowledge Base (KB)

The architecture of KB is presented in Fig 5. It is based on the data extracted from only 13000 unique protein chains from Protein Data Bank after exclusion of structurally similar chains.These proteins with known tertiary (3D) and secondary structures are analysed. Three types of physical domain data are extracted - (a) Amino Acid sequence, (b) α Torsion Angle Data, and (c) Secondary Structural Data. Transform Domain parameters derived out of PCAM evolution are used to create Tertiary Structural Knowledge

Base, while two more knowledge bases are generated from the meta data derived from the secondary structural data.

4.1 Knowledge Base for Tertiary Structure

The physical domain parameters for Tertiary structure are derived with a Transform applied on the 3D coordinate value of C_α atom of an amino acid residue backbone. The Transform generates three distance parameters $d1$, $d2$, $d3$ and a torsion angle α for alpha carbon atom as shown in Fig 6. Distances are the linear distances from $C_{\alpha(i)}$ to $C_{\alpha(i-1)}$, $C_{\alpha(i-2)}$, $C_{\alpha(i-3)}$ respectively. While, angle is the dihedral angle between planes $D_1(C_{\alpha(i)}, C_{\alpha(i-1)}, C_{\alpha(i-2)})$ and $D_2(C_{\alpha(i-1)}, C_{\alpha(i-2)}, C_{\alpha(i-3)})$; the intersection line between two planes passes through points $C_{\alpha(i-1)}$ and $C_{\alpha(i-2)}$.

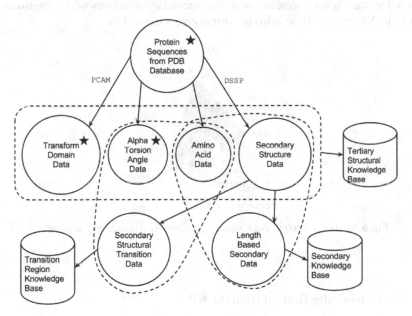

Fig. 5. Knowledge Base (KB) architecture for Protein Structure Synthesis. (Note: Star marked blocks were available in the earlier version of KB reported in [1]).

Thus the 3D coordinate values of the alpha carbon atom of ith amino acid is represented as $F_i =< \alpha_i \ d1_i \ d2_i \ d3_i >$. As shown in Fig 6, the model parameter vector P_i for the ith cell is derived from four consecutive $C_{\alpha(i)}$ position - $(i - 2)$, $(i - 1)$, (i), and $(i + 1)$. In the current version of the KB, amino acid sequence $< aa_{i-2} \ aa_{i-1} \ aa_i \ aa_{i+1} >$ and secondary structural type (helices, strand or unstructured) $< ss_{i-2} \ ss_{i-1} \ ss_i \ ss_{i+1} >$ of this four consecutive positions are also stored along with P_i. The model parameter vectors of this four positions $< P_{i-2}P_{i-1}P_iP_{i+1} >$ are mapped to physical domain parameter vector F_i as noted below.

Model Parameter for i^{th} Cell

$$< P_{i-2}\ P_{i-1}\ P_i\ P_{i+1} >$$

Physical Parameter for i^{th} residue

$$< F_{i-2}\ F_{i-1}\ F_i\ F_{i+1} >$$
$$< aa_{i-2}\ aa_{i-1}\ aa_i\ aa_{i+1} >$$
$$< ss_{i-2}\ ss_{i-1}\ ss_i\ ss_{i+1} >$$

4.2   Knowledge Base for Secondary Structure and Transition Region (TR)

Secondary structures derived from PDB database by DSSP algorithm are used to create two separate Knowledge Bases illustrated in Fig 7. In the first one, Amino Acid data and secondary structure data (Helices, Strands and Loops) are classified on the basis of length and adjacent structures. This data is stored in Secondary Knowledge Base. Further, all Transition Regions (TR) between secondary structures (for example - Helix to Loop) are studied with reference to associated amino acids and observed α torsion angle. This data is stored in another database - Transition Knowledge Base. Secondary Knowledge Base is used to select probable secondary structures while Transition Regions (TR) Knowledge Base helps to correct errors in the TRs.

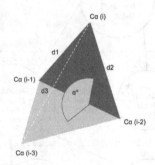

Fig. 6. Sequence Protein Backbone $C_{\alpha(i)}$ showing $d1$, $d2$, $d3$, and angle α

4.3   Meta Knowledge Derived from the KB

The current version of Knowledge Base (KB) is designed to capture observed deformities in intrinsically unstructured regions (Turn, Bend, Coil etc) of proteins and also the Transition Regions (TRs). The meta knowledge derived from the observed deformities enables synthesis of artificial torsion angle sequence for the residues in unstructured region covering loop, turn etc and also in the TRs.

All three modules of the Knowledge Base are stored in a high speed non-relational Redis database. Close to 13,000 thousands unique protein structures from PDB are used to derive the KB that covers approximately 38 million instances of different amino acid residues.

5 Protein Structure Synthesis (PSS)

The synthesis algorithm for a candidate protein executes the following steps on the amino acid chain of primary structure.

Step 1: PCAM for the candidate chain is designed and operated to derive model parameters.

Step 2: Secondary structures (Helix(H), Strand(E), unstructured regions(L) including turn, bend and coil) of the candidate chain is predicted by using [10].

Step 3: An error correcting algorithm developed with the help of Secondary Structural KB is implemented on the secondary structure predicted in Step 2.

Step 4: For each residue in secondary structures predicted in Step 2 (and corrected in Step3),the parameter $F = < \alpha, d1, d2, d3 >$ are derived from the Tertiary Structural KB.

Step 5: Transition Regions (TRs) are selected and $\alpha, d1, d2, d3$ are modified with help of Transition Knowledge Base

Step 6: All combinations are locally superimposed to cluster similar structures synthesized. One representative structure is selected for each region and concatenated recursively to produce complete structures of the candidate protein chain

Step 7: Finally, synthesized structures are analysed on the basis of exposed surface area and core size to select the most desirable option(s). Stop.

The quality of PSS output is next analysed for a number of proteins for which identification of structure is a challenging task.

6 Results and Discussions

Detailed analysis of a protein with PDB id 2LR8 is discussed. A brief summery of two others proteins are noted for space constraint.

6.1 Result of CASP8-Associated Protein 2 from Homo Sapiens (2LR8)

The tertiary structure of CASP8-associated protein 2 from Homo sapiens is CASP8 taget HR8150A from Northeast Structural Genomics Consortium (NESG) [8]. It has no similar structure in PDB, so folding of its structure is hard to predict. The 70 amino acid long chain is modelled with our PCAM as discussed in Step 1 of the Protein Structure Synthesis (PSS) Algorithm reported in Section 5. The error correcting algorithm in Step 3 replaces the wrongly predicted Strand (E) with a helix and also corrects length of another helix. Further, the Transition Regions (TRs) are marked to allow possible modification of $\alpha, d1, d3, d3$ data.

Based on the transform domain parameters, amino acid and predicted secondary structure, $\alpha, d1, d2, d3$ are selected from the Tertiary Knowledge Base in Step 4. Without the modification in TRs, this tertiary structure predicted shows differences in folding of secondary structures leading to Root Mean Square Deviation (RMSD) of 16.20. After the modification of $\alpha, d1, d2, d3$ discussed in Step 5 with help of the Transition Region Knowledge Base, the folding of the predicted structure becomes closer to the native folding with RMSD 3.32 (Fig 8).The total execution time of the PSS process for the target 2LR8 is 45.2 minutes on a Dual core Desktop with 32 GB memory.

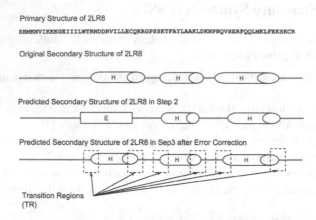

Primary Structure of 2LR8

SHMKNVIKKKGEIIILWTRNDDRVILLECQKRGPSSKTFAYLAAKLDKNPNQVSERFQQLMKLFEKSKCR

Original Secondary Structure of 2LR8

Predicted Secondary Structure of 2LR8 in Step 2

Predicted Secondary Structure of 2LR8 in Sep3 after Error Correction

Transition Regions
(TR)

Fig. 7. Secondary Structure Prediction and Correction of target protein 2LR8

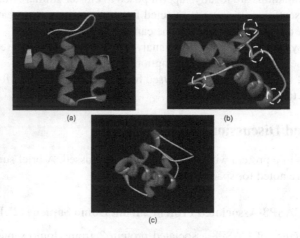

(a)

(b)

(c)

Fig. 8. Secondary Structure Prediction and Correction of target protein 2LR8. (a) Original or Native Structure; (b) Synthesized Structure without TR Correction. TRs are marked with dotted circle;(c) Final synthesized structure with modification of TR regions.

6.2   Result of Yeast Tyrosine Phosphatase (LTP1) and Azotobacter Vinelandii Ferredoxin I Mutant

Tyrosine phosphatase is a low-molecular weight protein having important cellular functions. We have predicted the tertiary structure of this sequence with RMSD value 2.767. The cluster of Azotobacter vinelandii ferredoxin I (FdI) has an unusually low reduction potential relative to other structurally similar ferredoxins . The 3D structure of such low reduction potential ferredoxins are studied with mutagenesis. We have studied one of such mutant (PDB ID 1B0V) proteins containing four chains of 106 residues each. We have predicted the tertiary structure of this sequence with RMSD value 3.651.

7 Conclusion

Rather than prediction of protein structure, we have concentrated in this paper to synthesize the structure from its primary chain. The steps of synthesis algorithm have been illustrated for 3 target proteins with RMSD value between 2.7 to 3.7. Synthesis of structures for a large number of target proteins are on progress.

References

1. Ghosh, S., Maiti, N.S., Chaudhuri, P.P.: Theory and Application of Restricted Five Neighborhood Cellular Automata (R5NCA) for Protein Structure Prediction. In: Sirakoulis, G.C., Bandini, S. (eds.) ACRI 2012. LNCS, vol. 7495, pp. 360–369. Springer, Heidelberg (2012)
2. Moult, J., et al.: A large-scale experiment to assess protein structure prediction methods. Proteins 23(3) (1995)
3. Yue, K., Dill, K.A.: Sequence-structure relationships in proteins and copolymers. Phys. Rev. E 48, 2267–2278 (1993)
4. Lamont, G.B., Merkie, L.D.: Toward effective polypeptide chain prediction with parallel fast messy genetic algorithms. In: Fogel, G., Corne, D. (eds.) Evolutionary Computation in Bioinformatics, pp. 137–161 (2004)
5. Dill, K.A., Bromberg, S., Yue, K., Fiebig, K.M., Yee, D.P., Thomas, P.D., Chan, H.S.: Principles of protein folding — A perspective from simple exact models. Protein Science 4, 561–602 (1995)
6. Rohl, C.A., Baker, D.: De novo determination of protein backbone structure from residual dipolar couplings using Rosetta. J. Am. Chem. Soc. 124(11), 2723–2729 (2002)
7. Marks, D.S., Hopf, T.A., Sander, C.: Protein structure prediction from sequence variation. Nature Biotech. 30(11) (2012)
8. Pulavarti, S., Sathyamoorthy, B.: Northeast Structural Genomics Consortium (NESG). Solution NMR Structure of CASP8-associated protein 2 from Homo sapiens, http://www.rcsb.org/pdb/explore.do?structureId=2lr8
9. Moult, J., et al.: Critical assessment of methods of protein structure prediction (CASP): round III. Proteins: Structure, Function, and Bioinformatics 37(S3), 2–6 (1999)
10. Rost, B., Sander, C.: Prediction of protein secondary structure at better than 70% accuracy. J. Mol. Biol. 232, 584–599 (1993)

The Basic Reproduction Number for Chagas Disease Transmission Using Cellular Automata

Baki Cissé, Samira El Yacoubi, and Sébastien Gourbière

Institute of Modelling, Analysis in Geo-Environment and Health,
IMAGES - University of Perpignan, France

Abstract. This paper presents mathematical and numerical results for a cellular automaton model describing the transmission dynamics of Chagas disease in both homogeneous and heterogeneous environments. The basic reproduction number R_0 which integrates factors that determine whether the pathogen can establish or not will be computed using the next-generation matrix approach. The simulation results show the effect of landscape heterogeneity in the vector transmission.

Keywords: vector-borne disease, spatial dynamics, transmission, basic reproduction number.

1   Introduction

Chagas disease is a major public health problem in Latin or south America. It kills 40 thousand people per year, affecting 10 million, and more than 50 million people live in areas at risk. Chagas disease is caused by infection with the parasite *Trypanosoma cruzi* which is transmitted by many species of bugs of the triatominae sub-family who feed on a large diversity of vertebrate hosts, a fraction of which only being able to transmit the parasite [14].The study of ecological dynamics of this disease requires strong potential in mathematical modelling which will help to understand the key of parasite transmission and to suggest efficient control strategies. The most predominant models are described by a set of differential equations which have been successfully used for studying several diseases such as SARS, Influenza A, Superbug, Malaria, Chagas and Dengue, see for example [1,5,15,19]. However, theses models do not take into account spatial factors and are not density dependent. They usually neglect the local character of the spreading process. In this context, cellular automata (CA) approach offers more realistic models which incorporate spatial parameters to reflect the heterogeneous real environment [7,10,11,20]. Several works dealing with epidemic CA models have been developped [2,4,11,20]. In [6], a deterministic CA model involving host and vector populations has been developed. In this paper, we use the basic reproduction number R_0 computed with the next generation method, in order to investigate the impact of some environmental factors on the transmission dynamics. This will help to determine on which parameter we can act in order to prevent or control the parasite transmission. Furthermore, in collaboration with several partners in Latin America, optimal strategies will be investigated and tested in study villages.

J. Wąs, G.C. Sirakoulis, and S. Bandini (Eds.): ACRI 2014, LNCS 8751, pp. 278–287, 2014.
© Springer International Publishing Switzerland 2014

2   Model Formulation

The proposed model consists of a SIR-SI at which the hosts and vectors populations are partitionned into subclasses. Hosts population is formed by healthy
individuals who are susceptible to infection (S), infected individuals (I), that can
transmit the disease by contact to the susceptibles vectors and recovered individuals (R), that are either not or much less able to transmit the disease than they
are infectious. We assumed also that the hosts can be competent (high ability to
spread the parasite) or non competent, can not spread the disease. The vectors
population is composed by susceptibles (S) and infected (I) individuals. Vectors
are assumed not to have an immune class. This compartmental approach of CA
have been successfully used to describe disease spreading [6,15]. The model is
defined as follows:

1. Space is represented by a square lattice $\mathcal{L}$ where a cell is given by its coordinates (i, j) and can be occupied by hosts or/and vectors.
2. The state of cell (i, j) at time t will be characterized by the 3-tuple
   $(s_t^H(i, j), s_t^h(i, j), s_t^V(i, j))$ given by :
   - $s_t^H(i, j) = (S_t^H(i, j), I_t^H(i, j), R_t^H(i, j))$ denotes the competent host H
     state. It gives the number of susceptible, infectious or recovered hosts in
     cell (i, j) at time t.
   - $s_t^h(i, j) = (S_t^h(i, j), 0, 0)$ represents the non competent host h state. It
     gives the number of susceptible h in cell (i, j) at time t. Non competent
     host can not be infected nor recovered.
   - $s_t^V(i, j) = (S_t^V(i, j), I_t^V(i, j))$ denotes the vector state which gives the
     number of susceptible and infectious vectors in cell (i, j) at time t.
   The state set is then $\mathcal{S} = \{0, 1, ..., M_H\}^3 \times \{0, 1, ..., M_h\}^3 \times \{0, 1, ..., M_V\}^2$
   where M_H, M_h and M_V are the maximum number of competent hosts, non
   competent hosts and vectors respectively, inside the cell.
3. The neighborhood $\mathcal{N}$ of size n will be defined as the set of coordinates (α, β):
   $\mathcal{N} = \{(\alpha_k, \beta_k), 1 \le k \le n\} \in Z \times Z$ and the neighborhood of cell (i, j) which
   will be denoted by $\mathcal{N}_{ij}$, is given by the set $\{(i+\alpha_1, j+\beta_1), ..., (i+\alpha_n, j+\beta_n)\}$,
4. The transition function f will give the state of cell (i, j) at time $(t + 1)$ in
   terms of the states of its neighbouring cells at time t. The changes in $s_t^H(i, j)$,
   $s_t^h(i, j)$ and $s_t^V(i, j)$ are computed according to the dynamics of the disease
   transmission.

The CA rules will describe the epidemiological dynamics incorporating demographic parameters such as birth and death rates. For the competent hosts,
the model integrate the number of susceptible competent hosts which have been
infected by the infected vectors at a given time. This will take into account two
factors; the vector search rate denoted by C and assumed to be constant in this
study, and the preference parameter denoted by Pv and given at each cell (i, j)
by the following formula: $Pv(i, j) = \dfrac{p_H}{p_H N_t^H(i, j) + p_h N_t^h(i, j)}$ where $p_{H/h}$ is the
vector feeding preference for competent/non competent hosts and $N^{H/h}$ is the

total population of competent/non competent hosts. We assume that only susceptible competent host may be infected from the bite of an infectious vector with a per contact probability of transmission β_{HV}. The competent/non competent host natural death rate and the vector natural mortality rate are denoted by $d_{H/h}$ and d_V respectively which may be spatially depentent. Moreover, disease-induced mortality of infectious and recovered competent hosts will also occur with the associated pathogen virulences α_{IH} and α_{RH}. In addition, a loss of immunity is assumed in the proposed general model, for recovered hosts which will become susceptible with a rate l_H. The birth flow of vectors and competent/non competent hosts are given by B_V and $B_{H/h}$ respectively. Finally, we assume that infection occurs only for competent hosts with two phases (acuate and chronic) considered with a transmission rate r_H. Non competent hosts can not transmit the disease. No infected nor recovered compartments are considered in this case.

The epidemiological dynamics under the above assumptions is governed by equations (1), (2) and (3) for competent hosts and equation (4) for non competent hosts.

$$
\begin{align}
S_{t+1}^H(i,j) &= S_t^H(i,j) + B_H(i,j) - d_H(i,j)S_t^H(i,j) + l_H R_t^H(i,j) \notag \\
&\quad - CI_t^V(i,j)Pv(i,j)\beta_{HV}S_t^H(i,j) \tag{1} \\
I_{t+1}^H(i,j) &= I_t^H(i,j) - (d_H(i,j) + \alpha_{IH} + r_H)I_t^H(i,j) \notag \\
&\quad + CI_t^V(i,j)Pv(i,j)S_t^H(i,j)\beta_{HV} \tag{2} \\
R_{t+1}^H(i,j) &= R_t^H(i,j) - (d_H(i,j) + \alpha_{RH} + l_H)R_t^H(i,j) + r_H I_t^H(i,j) \tag{3}
\end{align}
$$

$$
S_{t+1}^h(i,j) = S_t^h(i,j) + B_h(i,j) - d_h(i,j)S_t^h(i,j) \tag{4}
$$

The vector dynamics will integrate geographical parameters which give the vector spatial distribution that match the environmental characteristics. The migration phenomenon between different cells among a specified CA neighbourhood denoted by $\mathcal{N}^*$ (star denotes $\mathcal{N}$ without the central cell), will be considered with a given dispersal rate μ_V which is supposed to be spatially dependent in the general model.

$$
\begin{align}
S_{t+1}^V(i,j) &= S_t^V(i,j) + B_V(i,j) - (d_V(i,j) + \mu_V(i,j))S_t^V(i,j) \notag \\
&\quad + \mu_V(i,j) \sum_{(\alpha_k,\beta_k)\in\mathcal{N}^*} d^{(\alpha_k,\beta_k)}(i,j)S_t^V(i+\alpha_k,j+\beta_k) \notag \\
&\quad - CS_t^V(i,j)Pv(i,j)\left(I_t^H(i,j)\beta_{VI_H} + R_t^H(i,j)\beta_{VR_H}\right) \tag{5} \\
I_{t+1}^V(i,j) &= I_t^V(i,j) - (d_V(i,j) + \mu_V(i,j))I_t^V(i,j) \notag \\
&\quad + \mu_V(i,j) \sum_{(\alpha_k,\beta_k)\in\mathcal{N}^*} d^{(\alpha_k,\beta_k)}(i,j)I_t^V(i+\alpha_k,j+\beta_k) \notag \\
&\quad + CS_t^V(i,j)Pv(i,j)\left(I_t^H(i,j)\beta_{VI_H} + R_t^H(i,j)\beta_{VR_H}\right) \tag{6}
\end{align}
$$

where β_{VI_H} and β_{VR_H} are the per contact probabilities of pathogen transmission to vector from infectious and recovered competent host H respectively.

The parameter $d^{\alpha_k, \beta_k}(i,j) = \dfrac{1}{\| (i,j) - (i+\alpha_k, j+\beta_k) \|_2} = \dfrac{1}{\sqrt{\alpha_k^2 + \beta_k^2}}$ is a weight coefficient associated to the number of sucseptible vectors in the neighbouring cell $(i+\alpha_k, j+\beta_k)$ moving to the cell (i,j) with a probability $\mu_V(i,j)$, $\| \cdot \|_2$ representing the Euclidean norm. This parameter may be defined also for competent/non competent hosts when migration is involved in hosts dynamics. All the involved parameters in the model are given in Table 1.

Table 1. Estimates of the parameter of the model for Chagas disease

Parameter definition	Symbol	Dimension	Estimate
Vector demography and feeding			
Vector birth flow	B_V	$week^{-1}$	6500/52
Vector natural mortality rate	d_V	$week^{-1}$	1/52
Vectors dispersal rate	μ_V	-	0.05
Vector search rate	C	-	0.5
Vector feeding preference for competent host H	p_H	-	0.55
Vector feeding preference for non competent host h	p_h	-	0.45
Host demography			
Competent host H birth flow	B_H	$week^{-1}$	$1000/(3*52)$
Non competent host H birth flow	B_h	$week^{-1}$	$1000/(3*52)$
Competent host H natural death rate	d_H	$week^{-1}$	$1/(3*52)$
Non competent host h natural death rate	d_h	$week^{-1}$	$1/(3*52)$
Pathogen transmission			
Per contact probability of transmission from vector to competent host H	β_{HV}	-	0.005
Per contact probability of transmission from Infectious competent host H to vector	β_{VI_H}	-	0.9
Per contact probability of transmission from Recovered competent host H to vector	β_{VR_H}	-	0.15
Pathogen within-host dynamics			
Pathogen virulence to Infectious competent host H	α_{I_H}	$week^{-1}$	0.0001
Pathogen virulence to Recovered competent host H	α_{R_H}	$week^{-1}$	0.00005
Transmission rate from the acute to the chronic phases of infection	r_H	$week^{-1}$	1/6

3 Basic Reproductive Number R_0

We use the Next Generation Matrix (NGM) approach to compute a certain epidemiological threshold known as the basic reproduction number R_0. This key parameter is intended to quantify the spread of disease by estimating the average number of secondary infectious in a wholly susceptible population. It is primarily used as a threshold parameter to determine the stability of the disease free equilibrim (DFE). If $R_0 > 1$ the disease will persist and become endemic to the population but if $R_0 < 1$ the disease will fade out of the population [1].

The NGM method is based on the construction of two matrices denoted by F and V [8], which describe the new occurences of infection and the transition from one state of infection to another.

Assuming the system is at the DFE $E_0 = (S_0^H, I_0^H, R_0^H, S_0^h, S_0^V, I_0^V)$, the transmission matrix F includes all rate at which new infections occur:

$$
F = \begin{bmatrix}
0 & 0 & \dfrac{C_{P_H} S_0^H}{(p_H N_0^H + p_h N_0^h)}\beta_{HV} \\
0 & 0 & 0 \\
\dfrac{S_0^V C_{P_H}}{(p_H N_0^H + p_h N_0^h)}\beta_{V I_H} & \dfrac{S_0^V C_{P_H}}{(p_H N_0^H + p_h N_0^h)}\beta_{V R_H} & 0
\end{bmatrix}
$$

where $N^{H/h/V}$ is the total population size of competent/non-competent hosts and vectors respectively. The transition matrix V is built from the rates at which already infected individuals move from one category to another:

$$
V = \begin{bmatrix}
d_H + \alpha_{I_H} + r_H & 0 & 0 \\
-r_H & d_H + \alpha_{R_H} + l_H & 0 \\
0 & 0 & d_V
\end{bmatrix}
$$

which is invertible. Thus, $R_0 = \sigma(FV^{-1})$ is obtained with the spectral radius operator $\sigma(.)$ calculated as the dominant eigenvalue of matrix FV^{-1} :

$$
R_0 = \frac{C_{P_H}}{(p_H N_H^* + p_h N_h^*)} \sqrt{\left| \frac{S_H^* S_V^* \beta_{HV}}{d_V(d_H + \alpha_{I_H} + r_H)} \left(\frac{r_H \beta_{V R_H}}{(d_H + \alpha_{R_H} + l_H)} - \beta_{V I_H} \right) \right|}
$$

The DFE for our vector-borne disease model corresponds to :
$S_0^H = \dfrac{B_H}{d_H}, \ I_0^H = 0, \ R_0^H = 0, \ S_0^h = \dfrac{B_h}{d_h}, \ S_0^V = \dfrac{B_V}{d_V} \ and \ I_0^V = 0$, so that the reproductive number can be expressed with respect to the eco-epidemiological parameters of the model:

$$
R_0 = \frac{C_{P_H}}{d_V \left(p_H \frac{B_H}{d_H} + p_h \frac{B_h}{d_h}\right)} \sqrt{\left| \frac{B_H B_V \beta_{HV}}{d_H(d_H + \alpha_{I_H} + r_H)} \left(\frac{r_H \beta_{V R_H}}{(d_H + \alpha_{R_H} + l_H)} - \beta_{V I_H} \right) \right|} \tag{7}
$$

Some parameters in the expression of R_0 are assumed to be constant in time whereas other parameters will vary over space or with time. When $R_0 > 1$ the disease tends to emerge from the cell where it lives and spread throughout the lattice. To better understand this process of propagation, it is proposed to determine the conditions on the abundance of the vector N_V and the transmission rate 'C'.

3.1   Influence of Vector's Abundance on R_0

To study the influence of the vector's abundance on the emergence of the disease, we are interested in the impact of B_V and d_V on the basic reproduction number R_0.

Influence of vector birth flow (B_V) on the disease emergence. The condition $R_0 > 1$ implies, by algebraic manipulation :

$$B_V > \left(\frac{d_V(p_H B_H/d_H + p_h B_h/d_h)}{Cp_H}\right)^2 \frac{d_H(d_H + \alpha_{I_H} + r_H)}{\left|\frac{r_H \beta_V R_H}{(d_H + \alpha_{R_H} + l_H)} - \beta_{V I_H}\right| B_H \beta_{HV}} = B_{V_l}$$

Using the parameters of Chagas disease, the simulations were performed on two-dimensional array where infection starts within a single central cell.

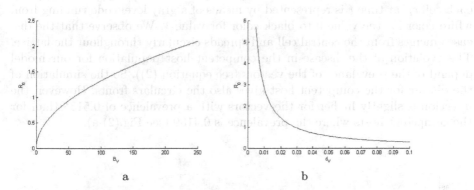

a   b

Fig. 1. Evolution of the basic reproductive number according to the vector birth flow B_V (a) and the vector mortality rate d_v (b)

Influence of vector mortality rate(d_V) on the disease emergence. $R_0 > 1$ implies:

$$d_V < \frac{Cp_H}{(p_H B_H/d_H + p_h B_h/d_h)} \times$$

$$\sqrt{\left|\frac{B_H B_V \beta_{HV}}{d_H(d_H + \alpha_{I_H} + r_H)}\left(\frac{r_H \beta_V R_H}{(d_H + \alpha_{R_H} + l_H)} - \beta_{V I_H}\right)\right|} = d_{V_l}$$

Figure (1)-a shows that R_0 grows rapidly with B_V. This could be explained by the fact that in a 'good' environment for vectors reproduction, the number of bites on the relevant host vectors will increase, thereby increasing the rate of infection. The limit value B_V beyond which the disease will emerge $B_{V_l} = 57.0320$.

Figure (1)-b shows that R_0 decreases rapidly when d_V increases. The epidemic therefore evolves inversely to mortality vectors. It is quite intuitive in the sense that less vectors lead to less potential bites on competent hosts and therefore to fewer infections. The use of control strategies such as insecticide which allow to exceed the limit mortality value $d_{V_l} = 0.0285$ could help limiting the spread of the epidemic.

4   Disease Spreading

To study the spatial evolution of our vector-born disease model, we look at two types of scenarii considering both a homogeneous and heterogeneous environments. In the second case, we assume that landscape is divided on 'good' and 'bad' cells.

4.1   Homogeneous Environment

We consider a landscape consisting of identical cells and study the spatial evolution of Chagas disease in the vector. The proportion of infected vectors (I_t^V) in each cell c_{ij} at time t is represented by means of a gray level code running from white color for the value 0 to black color for value 1. We observe that the disease emerges from the central cell and spreads circularly throughout the lattice. The evolution of the disease in the competent host population for our model depend of the prevalance of the vectors (see equation (2)). So the simulation of the disease for the competent host gives also the circulars fronts. However, the infection is slightly higher for the vectors with a prevalence of 0.5138 than for the competent hosts where the prevalence is 0.4159 (see Fig.(2)-a).

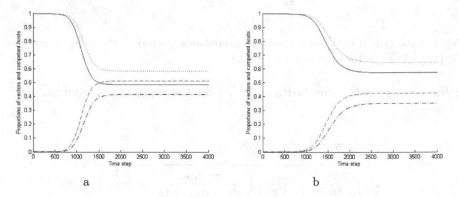

a   b

Fig. 2. Global dynamics of vector and competent host infection in the homogeneous (a) and heterogeneous (b) environments. Solid and dashed lines: number of susceptibles and infected vectors in the lanscape. Dotted and dash-dot lines: number of susceptibles and infected (infectious and recovered) competent host in the landscape.

4.2   Heterogeneous Environment

In order to study the effect of environment structure on the reproduction of hosts and vectors, we consider a landscape composed of cells refered to 'good' or 'bad' habitats. The host and vector species adaptation are modelled by setting each species death rate (d_s) for the susceptibles s where $s = H, h, V$ and $d_H + \alpha_{p^H}$ with $p = I, R$ at different levels in the two habitats [6]. These demographic parameters are given 'good' values in the habitat that species is adapted to, and 'bad' values in the other habitat:

For the simulations, the landscape was set up by randomly distributing 'good' and 'bad' cells that occurs in equal frequency with $E_s^+ = 1.5$ and $E_s^- = 0.5$. We give in Fig.(2)-b, the global evolution of the infection in a vector and competent host population and in Fig.(3), the spatial evolution in the vector.

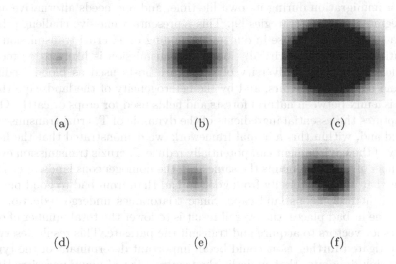

(a)   (b)   (c)

(d)   (e)   (f)

Fig. 3. Spreading of the disease with Moore neighborhood in homogeneous (a-c) and heterogeneous (d-f) environments for vector species at times t=400, t=600 and t=800 respectively

Fig. (3) shows a uniform spread of the infection in the heterogeneous environment. The propagation follows non circular fronts and will probably depends on the density of 'good' and 'bad' cells in the landscape.

Similar results have been obtained for competent hosts. We notice that the infection is slightly higher in the vector population with a prevalence of 0.4252 than in the competent hosts with a prevalence of 0.3512 (see Fig.(2)-b). Furthermore, camparing the two considered environments, it seems that the prevalence of infection in vectors and competent hosts is more important in the homogeneous case.

5   Discussion

In Latin America, vector transmission remains the main source of T. cruzi infections in human. The life-long exposition to vectors makes the number of contacts so high that, despite a very low probability of transmission per contact [17], the prevalence of infection can be substantially higher than 50%. Accordingly, vector control initiatives have been launched that are based on domestic and peri-domestic insecticide spraying. These strategies target key vector species that are able to heavily infest houses, but there is an emerging awareness that non-domiciliated triatomines, that are not adapted to the human habitat, also represent a serious public health concern. Typically, T. dimidiata in Mexico fly into houses from the peridomestic and forest habitats [3,16], especially at the periphery of the villages where sylvatic insects are attracted by artificial lights [18]. In such case, insecticide spraying is of limited efficacy, as it can only control vector immigration during its own life-time, and one needs alternative and more integrated control strategies [9]. This represents a massive challenge that requires a substantial increase in our understanding of T. cruzi transmission in the sylvatic environment. Critically, parasite transmission is likely to be modulated there by the large diversity of vertebrate hosts used as blood feeding sources and parasite reservoirs, and by the heterogeneity of the landscape that typically is a mix between natural forests and fields used for crops or cattle. Our model captures the essential ingredients of the dynamic of T. cruzi transmission in the wild and, within this minimal framework, we demonstrated that the heterogeneity of the environment can potentially reduce T. cruzis transmission even if the number of vectors remains the same as in the homogeneous landscape. The rational is that more vectors fly from good to bad than from bad to good places in a typical heterogeneous landscape. Since triatomines undergo reduction in their life-time in bad places, the overall result is to lower the total number of opportunities for vectors to acquire and transmit the parasite. This result deserves to be investigated further as it could be an important determinant of the typical source-sink dynamics that underlie the transmission of many parasites [19]. Finally, spatial heterogeneity and random temporal variations are two central tenets of the ecology and evolution of many organisms that interact and show conceptual analogies [12,13]. The conclusions drawn from our model are thus likely to hold for temporal (and not only spatial) variability, whose impact on pathogens transmission has not been consistently studied so far. This new model thus provides opportunities to investigate key emerging issues about the transmission of T. cruzi and could easily be adapted to work on other vector-borne diseases.

References

1. Annan, K., Fisher, M.: Stability Conditions of Chagas-HIV Co-infection Disease Model Using the Next Generation Method. Applied Mathematical Sciences 7(57), 2815–2832 (2013)
2. Mikler, A.R., Venkatachalam, S.: Modeling Infectious Diseases using Global Stochastic Cellular Automata. Journal of Biological Systems 4, 421–439 (2005)
3. Barbu, C., Dumonteil, E., Gourbière, S.: Characterization of the dispersal of non-domiciliated Triatoma dimidiata through the selection of spatially explicit models. PLoS Negl. Trop. Dis. 4(8), e777 (2010)
4. Batty, M.: Cities and Complexity: Understanding Cities with Cellular Automata, Agent-Based Models, and Fractals. The MIT Press (2007)
5. Beauchemin, C., Samuel, J., Tuszynski, J.: Some simple epidemic models. Theoretical Biology 232, 223–234 (2005)

6. Cissé, B., El Yacoubi, S., Gourbière, S.: A cellular automaton model for the transmission of Chagas disease in heterogeneous landscape and host community. Submitted to Int. Journal of Applied Mathematical Modelling
7. Chopard, B., Droz, M.: Lattice-Gas Cellular Automata and Lattice Boltzmann Models: an Introduction. Cambridge University Press (1998)
8. Diekmann, O., Heesterbeek, J.A.P., Roberts, M.G.: The construction of next-generation matrices for compartmental epidemic models. Royal Society Interface 7, 873–885 (2010)
9. Dumonteil, E., Nouvellet, P., Rosecrans, K., Ramirez-Sierra, M.J., Gamboa-León, R., Cruz-Chan, V., Rosado-Vallado, M., Gourbière, S.: Eco-bio-social determinants for house infestation by non-domiciliated Triatoma dimidiata in the Yucatan Peninsula, Mexico. PLoS Negl. Trop. Dis. 26:7(9), e2466 (2013)
10. El Yacoubi, S.: A Mathematical method for control problems on Cellular Automata models. International Journal of Systems Sciences 39(5), 529–538 (2008)
11. Gagliardi, H.F., Alves, D.: Small-World Effect in Epidemics Using Cellular Automata. Journal of Mathematical Population Studies 17, 79–90 (2010)
12. Gourbière, S., Gourbière, F.: Competition between unit-restricted fungi: a metapopulation model. J. Theor. Biol. 217(3), 351–368 (2002)
13. Gourbière, S., Menu, F.: Adaptive dynamics of dormancy duration variability: evolutionary trade-off and priority effect lead to sub-optimal adaptation. Evolution 63(7), 1879–1892 (2009)
14. Gourbière, S., Dorn, P., Triplet, F., Dumonteil, E.: Genetics and evolution of triatomines: from phylogeny to vector control. Heredity 108, 190–202 (2012)
15. de Castro Medeiros, L.C., Castilho, C.A.R., Barga, C., de Souza, W.V., Regis, L., et al.: Modeling the Dynamic Transmission of Dengue Fever: Investigating Disease Persistence. PLoS Negl. Trop. Dis. 5(1), e942 (2011), doi:10.1371/journal.pntd.0000942
16. Nouvellet, P., Dumonteil, E., Gourbière, S.: Effects of genetic factors and infection status on wing morphology of Triatoma dimidiata species complex in the Yucatan Peninsula, Mexico. Infection, Genetics and Evolution 11(6), 1243–1249 (2011)
17. Nouvellet, P., Dumonteil, E., Gourbière, S.: The Improbable Transmission of Trypanosoma cruzi to Human: The Missing Link in the Dynamics and Control of Chagas Disease. PLoS Negl. Trop. Dis. 7(11), e2505 (2013)
18. Pacheco-Tucuch, F.S., Ramirez-Sierra, M.J., Gourbière, S., Dumonteil, E.: Public street lights increase house infestation by Triatoma dimidiata, vector of Chagas disease in the Yucatan Peninsula. PLoS One 7(4), e36207 (2012)
19. Rascalou, G., Pontier, D., Menu, F., Gourbière, S.: Emergence and prevalence of human vector-borne diseases in sink vector populations. PLoS ONE 7(5), e36858 (2012), doi:10.1371/journal.pone.0036858
20. Schimit, P.H.T., Monteiro, L.H.A.: On the reproduction number and the topological properties of the contact network: An epidemiological study in mainly locally connected cellular automata. Ecological Modeling 220, 1034–1042 (2009)
21. Sirakoulis, G.C., Karafyllidis, I.: A cellular automaton model for the effects of population movement and vaccination on epidemic propagation. Ecological Modeling 133, 209–223 (2000)
22. Slimi, R., Yacoubi, S.E., Dumonteil, E., Gourbière, S.: A cellular automata model for chagas disease. International Journal of Applied Mathematical Modelling 33, 1072–1085 (2009)
23. Hoja White, S., Martin del Rey, A., Rodriguez Sanchez, G.: Modeling epidemics using cellular automata. Applied Mathematics and Computation 186, 193–202 (2007)

Modelling Spatial Distribution
of the Barents Sea Cod Fishery*

Arne Eide

Nofima and University of Tromsø, Norway
arne.eide@uit.no

Abstract. The paper presents a cellular automata (CA) model for the growth and spatially distribution of the Northeast Arctic cod including a harvest model based on economical rational behaviour. Rules and range of the CA model are estimated from observations and biological theory, and the environmental conditions are assumed to be in accordance with the IPCC A1B scenario for the following 45 years. The aim of the model developed is to study fleet behaviour based on available management decisions, resource information and economic performance. This paper presents fleet performance in the model under open access conditions, considering two different types of vessels (small and large) placed in four different homeports. Fleet smartness is a key parameter controlling the fish finding ability of each fleet. The study shows that increasing smartness reveals increasing differences between small and large vessels placed in different homeports. While homeport clusters vessels at low levels of smartness, vessel size and range clusters vessels at higher levels of smartness.

Keywords: Economics, Open access fisheries, NEA cod, Climate change.

1 Introduction

The Northeast Arctic (NEA) cod stock carries out long distance annual migrations and possesses a number of other buffering capacities enabling the stock to adapt to fluctuating environmental conditions. Climate change may cause these environmental fluctuations to exceed their normal boundaries in the years to come, making the adapting capacities of the cod stock even more important.

Previous studies suggest that management constraints may have a greater impact than climate change on the highly fluctuating Northern marine ecosystems [1], [2]. Studies also indicate that possible changes in the spatial distribution of cod and other marine organisms in the Barents Sea may be the most significant impact from climate changes.

This paper aims to set up and parameterise a spatially distributed bioeconomic model of the Barents Sea cod fishery as a test bed for different management regimes and fishing strategies, including temporal and spatial variation in the fishing activities.

---

* The research leading to these results has received funding from the European Union's Seventh Framework Programme within the Ocean of Tomorrow call – ACCESS.

J. Wąs, G.C. Sirakoulis, and S. Bandini (Eds.): ACRI 2014, LNCS 8751, pp. 288–299, 2014.
© Springer International Publishing Switzerland 2014

2   Model Structure and Climate Scenario

We assume the climatic conditions to follow the SRES A1B scenario published by the Intergovernmental Panel on Climate Change (IPCC) in Assessment Report 4 (AR4) and downscaled to the Barents region by the REMO5.1 model [3]. The model outputs define the border conditions of simulations performed by the *SinMod* model [4], providing the presented model with spatial and temporal distribution of physical and biological variables.

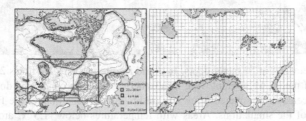

Fig. 1. Available geographical resolutions in the *SinMod* model (left panel) and the 80 km x 80 km grid which is used in the ecosystem model (right panel)

The time unit is one month and the spatial resolution provides a lattice of homogeneous 80 km x 80 km cells (as shown in the right panel in Fig. 1). Both temporal and spatial units are aggregated from the *SinMod* model, the latter illustrated in the left panel of Fig. 1. According to the findings of [5] cod may have a range of 210 to 720 km over a period of 30 days, indicating that 3 cells in all direction from a given cell in the grid represents a reasonable range of a cod individual during a period of one month, corresponding to the CA range 2.

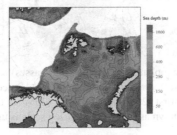

Fig. 2. Bathymetric map of the model region, the shallow water area of the Barents Sea. The white area represents ocean depths of more than 1000 meter. Source: *SinMod*.

The *SinMod* modelling project has by the courtesy of project leader Dag Slagstad provided ocean depth information (Fig. 2) and time series of spatially distributed ocean temperatures and zooplankton biomasses (Fig. 3 and 4). The time series are obtained from simulations based on the downscaled IPCC A1B scenario [6] and covers the 45 year period 2012-2057 with monthly intervals. In this study the *SinMod* data have been converted from a grid resolution of 20 km times 20 km to the model resolution (80 km times 80 km).

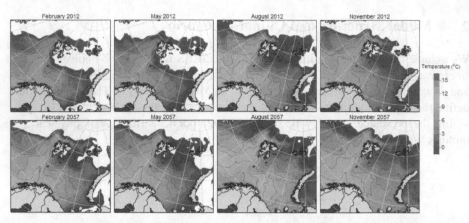

Fig. 3. Sea temperatures at 50 meter depts. In a grid resolution of 20 km times 20 km, obtained from the *SinMod* model when employing atmospheric bordering conditions downscaled from the IPCC A1B scenario. The panels show the mid-month of each quarter the first (2012) and last year (2057) of the simulations. Areas with temperatures below -1.5 °C are left out (indicated by white area).

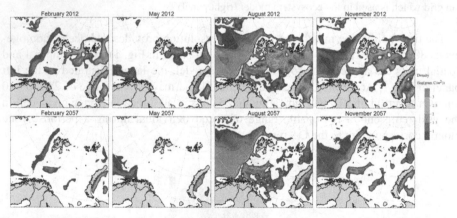

Fig. 4. Spatial distribution of zooplankton densities (biomasses) calculated by *SinMod* simulations while running the downscaled version of the IPCC A1B scenario. The panels show the mid-month of each quarter the first (2012) and last year (2057) of the simulations. Zooplankton densities below 2 g C/m^2 are shown as white areas. A log scale is used in the figure.

Temperatures considered are average monthly values at depths of 50 meter. Zooplankton biomasses are aggregated biomasses including several species, all characterised by being spatially determined by physical processes and nutrients availability, in contrast to living organisms at higher trophic levels where individual behaviour of the species significantly influence the spatial distribution.

The carrying capacity in terms of potential cod biomass each cell can hold in each month throughout the considered period is assumed to depend on biological and physical environmental conditions within the cell, represented by the A1B scenario through inputs from the *SinMod* model (Figures 2, 3 and 4).

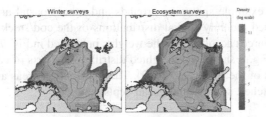

Fig. 5. Normalised spatial distributions of NEA cod as it appears in winter- and ecosystem surveys aggregated over the years 2004-2010. The distributional charts are obtained by interpolating and integrating *FishExChange* data. A logarithmic scale is used.

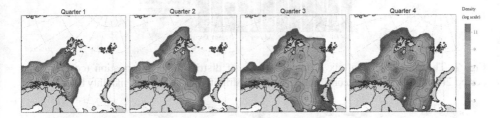

Fig. 6. Normalised quarterly spatial distributions of NEA cod catches aggregated over 2004-2009. The distributional charts are obtained by interpolating and integrating *FishExChange* data. A logarithmic scale is used.

Information on spatial distribution of NEA cod for the period 2004-2010 is provided by the *FishExChange*[1] project. Catches are registered on a quarterly basis while the surveys take place once a year, winter surveys in April/May and ecosystem surveys in August/September. Age structured data has been aggregated for the purpose of this study. Registered catches are interpolated spatially by Radial Basis Function (RBF) interpolation [7] and the interpolated surface is integrated and distributed on an equal size geographic grid as shown in Fig. 1 based on equal size projection (Lambert Azimuthal, corresponding to the projection used in the *SinMod* model, coordinates origin in 60N, 58E). Resulting spatially distributed biomasses and catches are shown in Fig. 5 and 6.

3   Temporal and Spatial Distribution of Carrying Capacities

The different sources providing information about the spatial distribution of cod represent different sampling methods and different aims. The catch information obviously gives a biased overall distribution since the most profitable areas are expected to be overrepresented. Further are surveyed areas constrained and may exclude cod

---

[1] The *FishExchange* database at http://www.imr.no/fishexchange/fishexchangedatabase/nb-no has been made available for this project by the courtesy of project leader Jan Erik Stiansen, database developer Trond Westgård, Geir Odd Johansen, Cecilie Kvamme, Sigbjørn Mehl, Silje Seim, Åge Fotland, Bjørn Ådlandsvik and Sigrid Lind Johansen.

dense areas, as for example spawning grounds and other coastal areas in the winter surveys. The assumed monthly spatial distributions of the cod stock are estimated by the different data sources according to the weights presented in Fig. 7.

The top row of Fig. 8 shows the weighted distribution charts of carrying capacities for selected months of the first year (2012). The distribution areas are directly drawn from normalised catches, surveys and ocean depts.

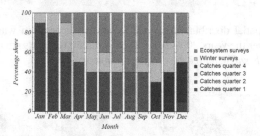

Fig. 7. The composition of six different sources of distributional information (covering the period 2004-2009/2010) for constructing overall distributional charts on a monthly basis

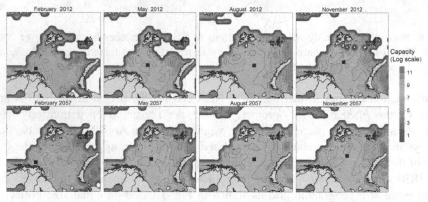

Fig. 8. Spatial distribution of environmental carrying capacities for NEA cod the first (2012) and last (2062) or the performed simulations. The distribution is based on different sources of spatial distribution of NEA cod during the period 2004-2010, ocean temperatures and zooplankton biomasses from *SinMod* (A1B scenario runs) and ocean depths. The monthly centres of gravity for the levels of carrying capacities are shown as black squares. The size of each square corresponds to the grid resolution (80 km times 80 km, see right hand panel of Fig. 1).

The bottom row of Fig. 8 is based on assumed changes in the distributional pattern (carrying capacity levels) caused by changes in temperatures (Fig. 3) and zooplankton production patterns (Fig. 4). Together with ocean depths (Fig. 2) and the initial migration pattern (Fig. 10), these are essential factors for the distribution of cod.

The following assumptions have been implemented in the calculation of changing carrying capacities: NEA cod distribution is constrained to ocean depths less than 1000 meter (Fig. 2) and ocean temperatures (average at 50 meter depth) higher than -1.5 °C (Fig. 3). In addition, environmental carrying capacities are reduced by 80% when zooplankton densities fall below 2 g carbon per square meter (Fig. 4).

Centres of gravity of the potential spatially distributed biomass of NEA cod (the black squares shown in Fig. 8) indicate insignificant changes in spatial distribution of cod over the 45-year period (2012-2057). Centres of gravity only move one cell (80 km) sideways (to the right, indicating eastward and slightly northward movement) the first and last quarters of the year when comparing the situations in 2012 and 2057 (Fig. 8). A more careful look on the monthly centres of gravity confirms this. Fig. 12 shows monthly distributions of centres of gravity placed into the model lattice in selected years. The changes over the 45-year period are insignificant and the intra-annual variation is always constrained by the same rectangular limiting borders.

Spatially aggregated monthly carrying capacities (summing up cell capacities in the distribution area) over the 45-year period indicate a slight decline by about 2017-2018, thereafter normalising to 2012-level in the end of the 2020s before increasing in the mid-2030s. The high values remain towards the end of the period (Fig. 9).

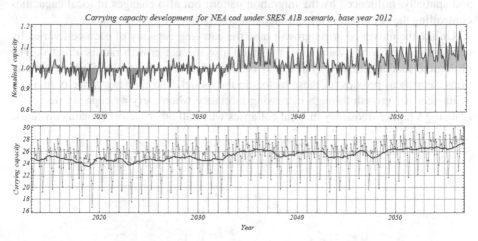

Fig. 9. The upper panel shows monthly aggregates of normalised (base year 2012) carrying capacities for NEA cod based on *SinMod* A1B simulations and initial distribution data from the *FishExChange* project (2004-2010). The anomalies show percentage deviation from corresponding month in 2012. The lower panel shows the monthly changes in terms of total carrying capacities of all cells (in million tons cod biomass). The red curve gives the monthly variation while the blue curve is the 12-month moving average of these numbers.

4   CA Model of Cod Growth and Biomass Distribution

A cellular automata (CA) model following the set up in [8] is implemented for the NEA cod stock, based on historical growth and spatial distribution pattern represented by the current climatic conditions. The CA rules utilise Moore neighbourhoods of range 2, a spatial resolution of 80 x 80 km and a temporal resolution of one month.

Distribution rules are identified by fitting modelled migratory pattern to the current capacity data, representing the annual variation in the NEA Cod stock distribution. The biological CA rules (which could be interpreted as migration matrices) are found by an algorithm minimising sum of squared distances between actual (Fig. 8, upper row) and modelled centres of gravity of spatial distribution of cod under current climate conditions. Fig. 10 shows the observed migration pattern (in blue) and the modelled pattern (in red). Fig. 12 displays monthly centres of gravity in different years as obtained by the estimated CA rules (Fig. 11) after implementing the A1B scenario.

The procedure described above is first carried out for a growth rate believed to be within the range of the actual growth. Then the growth rate was calibrated on the basis of assumed maximum biomass level (in its natural state, without fishing, this level is assumed to be twice the observed maximum level of 4 million tons [9], and growth; before repeating the procedure until estimated *universal gross growth rates* converge to 11% per month. This growth rate is not to be confused with the marginal growth of individuals (e.g. the growth rate of a von Bertalanffy equation) or the intrinsic growth rate of a surplus production function. Adjusted by local collapses [8] the net growth also has a spatial dimension as the net growth varies both temporally and spatially, influenced by the migration pattern but also changes in local capacities controlling the occurrence of local biomass collapses.

Unlike the universal gross growth rate, the carrying capacity of each cell varies by temperature and food availability, by which also the net growth rate is affected. The biological model utilises physical and biological data provided by *SinMod* simulations, serving as proxies for these factors in the model. The carrying capacity of a cell influences net growth through increasing mortality when carrying capacity decreases (causing a higher frequency in local collapses when all other factors remain constant).

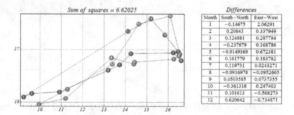

Month	South–North	East–West
1	−0.14675	2.06291
2	0.20643	0.337949
3	0.124881	0.287784
4	−0.237679	0.168786
5	−0.0149369	0.672381
6	0.161779	0.183782
7	0.119731	0.0243271
8	−0.0916978	−0.0952665
9	0.0503585	0.0737355
10	−0.361316	0.247403
11	0.101613	−0.568273
12	0.620642	−0.734871

Fig. 10. Estimated (blue) and modelled (red) centres of gravity of the spatial distribution of cod. The modelled centres of gravity are obtained by numerically minimising the sum of square distances between actual and modelled centres of gravity. The final distances are shown as differences (in cell units) in the table.

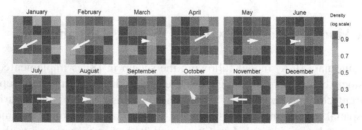

Fig. 11. CA rules (migration patterns) when assuming Moore neighbourhoods with a range of 2 (cells). The figures indicate monthly diffusion into neighbouring cells from the centre cell and the arrows (vectors) show the average direction and intensity of the migration.

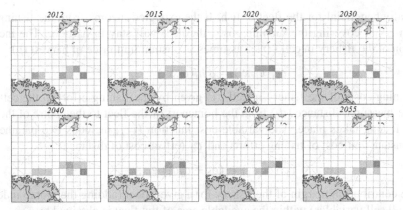

Fig. 12. Monthly centres of gravity in the cod stock distribution for selected years 2012 – 2055 based on the A1B scenario capacity data for an unexploited cod stock. Darker cell colour indicates that the cell is centre of gravity in two or more months the selected year. Grid size and geographical orientation is extracted from the right hand panel in Fig. 1.

It is already possible to make an important conclusion from the model, illustrated by Fig. 12 in which monthly centres of gravity of cod biomass are pictured for selected years up to 2055. There are no signs of significant climate driven changes in cod distribution over this period of 45 years.

5   Open Access Fishery

The fishery is assumed to largely follow the model presented in [8]. Monthly vessel catches (h) are distributed on different cells according to available biomass in each cell (x), a fleet specific catchability coefficient (q), fleet specific stock-output elasticity (β) and the fishing effort produced by the fleet in the actual cell during a period of one month (e). A Cobb-Douglas harvest function is assumed [10], the harvest in cell i is then given by

$$h_i(e_i, x_i) = q \, e_i \, x_i^{\beta} \; . \tag{1}$$

Let E_t be the total fishing effort of all cells at month t, summing up each effort within each cell in a total of n cells:

$$E_t = \sum_{i=1}^{n} e_{i,t} \; . \tag{2}$$

While E_t is the total fishing effort produced by the fishing fleet during month t, the fleets total capacity of producing effort could be higher. Let the theoretical maximum level of effort production be F_t. The produced fishing effort is then constrained by

$$0 \le E_t \le F_t \; . \tag{3}$$

Capacity utilisation (E/F) is determined by expected economic performance and, if existing, constraining regulations. Without regulations, the fleet will fish if it is economically beneficial for the fleet to fish. If the expected income from the fishing operation is not covering the running costs, the fleet will stay in harbour. The income function of the fishery in cell i (re_i) assumes a constant unit price of harvest (p):

$$re_i(e_i, x_i) = p\, h_i(e_i, x_i) \ . \tag{4}$$

Running costs of the fishery in cell i is given by the fishing effort in the cell (e_i) and the measured distance (d_i) from the homeport of the fleet to the centre of the cell where fishing takes place. The variable cost function (vc_i) includes two parameters: c_e (constant unit cost of fishing effort) and c_d (effort cost of distance):

$$vc_i(e_i, d_i) = (c_e + c_d d_i)\, e_i \ . \tag{5}$$

The contribution margin of the fishery for a given fleet (adding the month indexes, m, for all cell variables) within the available area of the fleet is obtained by

$$cm(e, x, d) = \sum_{m=1}^{12} \sum_{i=1}^{n} \{re_{m,i}(e_{m,i}, x_{m,i}) - vc_{m,i}(e_{m,i}, d_{m,i})\} \tag{6}$$

when the variables (e, x, d) represent the matrices $(e_{m,i}, x_{m,i}, d_{m,i})$ respectively for $i \in [1, n]$ and $m \in [1, 12]$. Annual net revenue in the same fishery is

$$\pi(e, x, d) = cm(e, x, d) - fc \tag{7}$$

when fc is the fixed cost per vessel.

While the fleet economy in the short run will determine fleet utilisation (E/F), previous economic performance also influences future effort producing capacity of the fleet (F), which will increase or decline depending on economic performance in a speed determined by the assumed entry/exit rates of the fleet. In this model entry and exit rates (fg and fd respectively) are independently given as exogenous parameters.

When including the opportunity costs of labour and capital in c_e, c_d and fc, normal profit is embedded as a cost component. Equation (7) therefore represents economic rent or abnormal profit in the fishery. In an open access fishery then the sign of $\pi(e, x, d)$ determines growth and decline in the fleet size (F, the capacity of effort production) over time according to the following rules:

$$\begin{aligned} If \quad \pi(e, x, d) &< 0 \quad then \quad F_{t+1} = (1 - fd)F_t \\ If \quad \pi(e, x, d) &> 0 \quad then \quad F_{t+1} = (1 + fg)F_t \end{aligned} \tag{8}$$

Because of temporal and spatial variation of fish biomasses, also revenues and costs of fishing in different areas (cells) varies in time and by area. Fishers are assumed to target the cells of the highest revenue-cost ratios given the available information. Without any prior knowledge about costs and revenues, it may be argued that it is rational to have a uniform distribution of effort in the area within range of the fleet. $e_{i,t}$ is the fishing effort of cell i at time t. With n available cells, uniform distribution of effort gives a fishing effort of $e_t = \frac{E_t}{n}$ in all available cells in month t.

This relates to the assumed revenue-cost ratio by the introduction of a smartness (or effort distribution) parameter $s = 0$. s reflects increasing knowledge on costs and revenues potentials (including fish finding abilities) by increasing value of s. Assume the distribution of effort within the lattice to be given by

$$e_{j,t} = \frac{\left(\frac{re_{j,t}}{vc_{j,t}}\right)^s}{\sum_{i=1}^{n}\left(\frac{re_{i,t}}{vc_{i,t}}\right)^s} E_t \; . \tag{9}$$

6   Results

Obviously uniform distribution of effort is obtained by $s = 0$ in equation (9), while $s = 1$ gives an effort distribution perfectly reflecting the distribution of revenue-cost ratios. Increasing s-values reflect increasing ability to identify the most profitable cells. As s approaches infinity all effort moves into the single cell with marginal higher ratio than any other cell.

Monthly changing biological CA rules (Fig. 11) and the dynamic interaction between biological processes and open access fleet dynamics lead to pseudo-random patterns causing fluctuating quantities of quasi rent in the fleet over time. [1], [2] show that the flow of quasi rent in open access fisheries may even exceed the abnormal profit obtained in a regulated fishery. The following example indicates how climate change may affect the fishery on the equally shared Russian and Norwegian NEA cod stock, in a situation of pure open access dynamics.

The fleet dynamics of the Norwegian cod fishery is modelled in larger details while a corresponding catch quantity is assumed obtained by Russian vessels in the area available for the Russian fleet. The assumed distribution of Russian catches follow the distribution of cod biomasses in the relevant area.

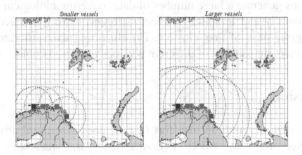

Fig. 13. The maps shows four Norwegian fishing ports: Svolvær (blue), Tromsø (magenta), Hammerfest (green) and Vardø (red); and monthly ranges of two fleets (smaller and larger vessels) placed in each port. The fleet range from the centre of the homeport cell is four squares (cells) for the smaller vessels and eight squares for the larger vessels.

The Norwegian fleet consists of two different vessel types (small and large vessels) placed in four different homeports: Svolvær, Tromsø, Hammerfest and Vardø (Fig. 13). The initial number of vessels is identical in each port, with the same number of small and large vessels. Each type of vessels (small and large) has the same technological efficiency, price on harvest and cost functions independent of homeport (for more details please contact the author).

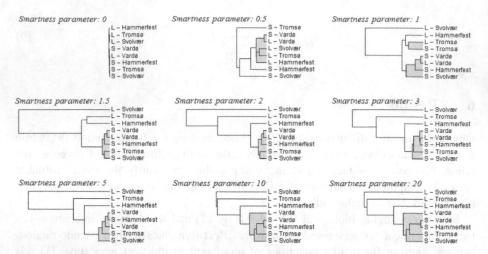

Fig. 14. Dendrogram plots of performance relations between small (*S*) and large (*L*) fishing vessels operating from four different North-Norwegian homeports (Svolvær, Tromsø, Hammerfest and Vardø) for different values of the smartness-parameter *s*. Clustering level 5 is shaded.

Simulations covering the 45-year period (2012-2057) where performed for nine different smartness parameter (*s* in equation 9). The selected values of *s* were 0, 0.5, 1, 1.5, 2, 3, 5, 10 and 20. A priori *s*-values below 1 is rather unlikely. The upper limit of *s* is more difficult to identify, but it seems reasonable to expect the value to be within the interval of 1 and 10, representing a wide range of possible outcomes.

The simulations generate a large number of data, covering biological and economic performance, spatially and temporally. Fleet differences are illustrated in Fig.14 in terms of dendrogram plots of fleet clusters. The clustering scales (horizontal axes) are fixed, e.g. the clustering patterns of different *s*-values are comparable.

7   Conclusion

As expected uniform distribution of effort (*s* = 0) does not reveal any performance differences between the vessels (Fig. 14). At *s* = 0.5 large vessels in all homeports cluster slightly and clearly more than the smaller vessels. However, as the *s*-value increases beyond one, the tendency of clustering among small vessel also increases, while this is not the case for the large-scale vessels.

Another pattern displayed in Fig. 14 is a clustering tendency on homeport rather than vessel type at low *s*-values (particularly strong for the Vardø-fleet) while type of vessel (small and large) seems to be an increasingly more important clustering factor as the *s*-value becomes higher. This seems reasonable, since increased smartness (e.g. fish-finding capacity) to some extent may compensate for geographical disadvantages. It is however surprising that this effect tends to be stronger for the smaller vessels than for the larger.

Test simulations without climate change show a large degree of correspondence with the results presented above, even though measured cluster differences are less pronounced than those shown in Fig. 14. This indicates that today's marginal differences between fleet segments could increase because of changing climatic conditions. The most important conclusion is however, that technological development and changes in fleet performance, in addition to choice of management regime, could potentially have a stronger impact on the economic performance of Northern fisheries than climate change may have.

References

1. Eide, A.: Economic impacts of global warming. The case of the Barents Sea fisheries. Natural Resource Modeling 20(2), 199–221 (2007)
2. Eide, A.: An integrated study of economic effects of and vulnerabilities to global warming on the Barents Sea cod fisheries. Climatic Change 87(1), 251–262 (2008)
3. Jacob, D., Andrae, U., Elgered, G., Fortelius, C., Graham, L.P., Jackson, S.D., Karstens, U., Koepken, C., Lindau, R., Podzun, R., Rockel, B., Rubel, F., Sass, H.B., Smith, R.N.D., van den Hurk, B.J.J.M., Yang, X.: A comprehensive model intercomparison study investigating the water budget during the BALTEXPIDCAP Period. Meteorol. Atmos. Phys. 77, 19–43 (2001)
4. Slagstad, D., McClimans, T.A.: Modeling the ecosystem dynamics of the Barents sea including the marginal ice zone: I. Physical and chemical oceanography. Journal of Marine Systems 58(1), 1–18 (2005)
5. Rose, G.A., deYoung, B., Colbourne, E.B.: Cod (*Gadus morhua*) migration speeds and transport relative to currents on the North-East Newfoundland Shelf. ICES J. Mar. Sci. 52, 903–914 (1995)
6. Nakícenovíc, N., Alcamo, J., Davis, G., de Vries, B., Fenhann, J., Gaffin, S., Gregory, K., Grübler, A., Jung, T.Y., Kram, T., Emilio la Rovere, E., Michaelis, L., Mori, S., Morita, T., Pepper, W., Pitcher, H., Price, L., Riahi, K., Roehrl, A., Rogner, H.-H., Sankovski, A., Schlesinger, M.E., Shukla, P.R., Smith, S., Swart, R.J., van Rooyen, S., Victor, N., Dadi, Z.: Special report on emissions scenarios, 599 pages. Cambridge University Press, Cambridge (2000)
7. Myers, D.E.: Spatial interpolation: an overview. Geoderma 62(1), 17–28 (1994)
8. Eide, A.: On the limits of improved fish finding capacity and its contribution to resource conservation. In: Chan, F., Marinova, D., Anderssen, R.S. (eds.) 19th International Congress on Modelling and Simulation. Modelling and Simulation Society of Australia and New Zealand, MODSIM 2011, pp. 2493–2499 (December 2011), http://www.mssanz.org.au/modsim2011/E16/eide.pdf, ISBN: 978-0-9872143-1-7
9. Lilly, G.R., Wieland, K., Rothschild, B.J., Sundby, S., Drinkwater, K., Brander, K., Ottersen, G., Carscadden, J.E., Stenson, G.B., Chouinard, G.A.: Decline and recovery of Atlantic cod (*Gadus morhua*) stocks throughout the North Atlantic. In: Kruse, G.H., Drinkwater, K.F., Ianelli, J.N., Link, J.S., Stram, D.L., Wespestad, V., Woodby, D. (eds.) Resiliency of Gadic Stocks to Fishing and Climate Change, pp. 39–66. Alaska Sea Grant, University of Alaska, Fairbanks (2008)
10. Eide, A., Skjold, F., Olsen, F., Flaaten, O.: Harvest Functions: The Norwegian Bottom Trawl Cod Fisheries. Marine Resource Economics 18, 81–93 (2003)

Training Cellular Automata to Simulate Urban Dynamics: A Computational Study Based on GPGPU and Swarm Intelligence

Ivan Blecic, Arnaldo Cecchini, and Giuseppe A. Trunfio

Department of Architecture, Planning and Design, University of Sassari, Italy
{ivan,cecchini,trunfio}@uniss.it

Abstract. We present some results of a computational study aimed at investigating the relationship between the spatio-temporal data used in the calibration phase and the consequent predictive ability of a Cellular Automata (CA) model. Our experiments concern a CA model for the simulation of urban dynamics which is typically used for predicting spatial scenarios of land-use. Since the model depends on a large number of parameters, we calibrate the CA using Cooperative Coevolutionary Particle Swarms, which is an effective approach for large-scale optimizations. Moreover, to cope with the relevant computational cost related to the high number of CA simulations required by our study, we exploits the computing power of Graphics Processing Units.

Keywords: Cellular Automata, Urban Models, Cooperative Coevolution, GPU.

1 Introduction

Cellular Automata (CA) models for the simulation of urban dynamics can provide to decision-makers and urban planners accurate information on the growth of cities, including the types, location and amount of land-use conversions . For this reason, they have been used in several ways to support land use planning, policy evaluation, and analysis of future scenarios of urban growth [1–3]

Among the open research challenges in the field of CA-based modelling of urban systems, a recurrent issue is represented by *calibration*, which consists of adapting the parameter-dependent transition rules to make the modelled urban phenomena matching the reality. CA calibration is often challenging because it involves high-dimensional search spaces. To cope with this problem, the current research trend in the field suggests the use of automated optimisation procedures [4–6]. The latter, are based on the availability of historical maps of the area under study, which are used, together with an appropriate metric of agreement, to guide the search of the values of model parameters. In this regard, an important issue concerns the relationship between the predictive ability of the calibrated model and the historical maps used in the optimization process. For example, for a CA modeller is relevant to be aware of the possible calibration error, with the related

J. Wąs, G.C. Sirakoulis, and S. Bandini (Eds.): ACRI 2014, LNCS 8751, pp. 300–309, 2014.

loss of model accuracy, that can be expected when very few historical maps are available to support the optimization process. To our knowledge, this issue was not addressed by systematic studies in the literature.

In this paper we present some results of a broader computational study on the calibration of a constrained CA for simulating urban dynamics. Our main objective was to investigate the extent to which the availability of historical maps and the way in which they are used, may affect the quality of the calibration process, as well as the predictive power of the resulting model. Our experiments take advantage of a parallel CA model already presented in [7], which is based on general-purpose computing on graphics processing units (GPGPU). This allowed us to perform an empirical investigation based on the execution of several millions of CA simulations in a reasonable time. Moreover, in order to cope with the high number of parameters involved in the calibration, we use a state-of-the-art metaheuristic, namely the Cooperative Coevolutionary Particle Swarm optimization (CCPSO) [8], which is a variation of the standard Particle Swarm Optimization (PSO) algorithm [9] specifically designed to deal with optimizations in spaces with a high number of dimensions.

2   The CA Urban Model and Its Calibration Problem

We use a CA representing the geographical space of interest and evolved in order to mimic its land-use dynamics over time. The model was parallelized for the GPGPU platform provided by nVidia, as explained in [7]. In order to obtain high efficiency, we formulated the parallelization so as to avoid significant memory transfers between the CPU and GPU during the simulation. As a result, our GPGPU approach leads to speedups that can easily exceed the value of 100, compared to the corresponding sequential implementation on a standard workstation [7]. This was key factor to allow the presented investigation.

In our CA model, the relevant component of the state of each cell represents its land-use class (such as residential, industrial, commercial, agriculture). Cells may also hold other information relevant to the simulation, such as their distance from the main transportation networks, constraints related to zoning regulations and cells' physical features (slope, elevation, etc.). During the simulation of such a CA, each cell can change its land use depending on its neighbouring cells and its internal state. However, the cell's state transition also depends on some global constraints on the total amount of each land use that is allowed at each time step. The model, as proposed in [1], includes three categories of land uses: *(i)* *static*, which cannot change during the simulation (e.g. transportation network, public services and facilities). A static land-use can however influence the other uses within its neighbourhood by exerting attractive or repulsive effects on them; *(ii)* *active* uses, for which there is an explicit demand (e.g. in terms of area) at each time step; *(iii)* *passive* uses, representing land available to be transformed into active uses during the simulation.

In the adopted model, the CA neighbourhood is defined as the square region around the cell with a sufficient size to allow local-scale spatial processes to be captured in the CA transition rules. At the beginning of each CA step, the so-called transition potentials P_j [1, 10] are computed for each cell and each active land use. This is done with the following equation:

$$P_j = I_i + \gamma S_j Z_j N_j \tag{1}$$

where:

- i is the current cells land use and $I_i \geq 0$ represents an inertia due to the transformation costs of transition from the use i to a different use;
- $\gamma_j = 1 + (-\ln \psi)^{\alpha_j}$, where ψ is a random number between 0 and 1 and α_j is a parameter that provides a degree of randomness;
- $S_j \in [0, 1]$ is the *suitability* factor for the active land use j, which is expressed as a logistic function of n_f local predictors x_k (e.g. the cell's distance from the street network or the terrain slope) as follows:

$$S_j = \frac{exp(\sum_{k=1}^{n_f} b_{kj} x_k)}{1 + exp(\sum_{k=1}^{n_f} b_{kj} x_k)} \tag{2}$$

where the parameters b_{kj} are estimated through the calibration process.
- $Z_j \in [0, 1]$ defines the degree of legal or planning permissibility of the j-th land use (for example due to zoning regulations by the planning authority);
- N_j is the so called *neighbourhood effect* computed as:

$$N_j = \nu + \sum_{c \in V} \phi(a_{i,j}, b_{i,j}, c_{i,j}, d_{i,j}; \delta_c) \tag{3}$$

where the summation is extended over all the cells of the cell's neighbourhood V and: i denotes the current land use of the cell $c \in V$, δ_c is the distance from the neighbouring cell c, and $\phi(a_{i,j}, b_{i,j}, c_{i,j}, d_{i,j}; \delta)$ is a piecewise linear function, depending on the four scalar parameters, $a_{i,j}, b_{i,j}, c_{i,j}$ and expressing the influence of the i-th land-use at the distance δ on the potential land use j. The term ν is a constant value computed before the beginning of the simulation so that $N_j \geq 0$.

Once the cell's P_j have been computed, the CA evolution is consists of transforming each cell into the state with the highest potential, given the exogenous constraint on the overall number of cells in each state imposed for that step [1].

The dynamics of the CA model described above depends on many scalar parameters that must be adapted to the specific application context. In particular, if the model includes n_s static land uses, n_p passive uses and n_a actively modelled uses, it depends on: (i) n_a parameters I_i defining the inertial contribution to the transition potentials; (ii) $n_f n_a$ parameters involved in the logistic suitability defined by Eq. (2); (iii) $4(n_s + n_a + n_p) n_a$ parameters $a_{ij}, b_{ij}, c_{ij}, d_{ij}$ involved in the piecewise functions $\phi_{i,j}$ of Eq. (3); (iv) n_a parameters α_j defining the degree of randomness. All the above parameters can be collected in a vector $\mathbf{p}$ belonging to a D-dimensional search space. With respect to $\mathbf{p}$, the model can be optimised to maximise the fitting between the simulated and real patterns.

In the following we indicate with $\bar{\mathcal{V}}$ a *training set* collecting some maps $\bar{\omega}^{(t)}$, which correspond to historical land-use data on the area under study. Starting from a known configuration $\omega^{(0)}$, and given a vector $\mathbf{p}$ of parameters, the CA can be executed for the computation of a set $\mathcal{V}$ of automaton configurations $\omega^{(t)}$ corresponding to the training maps $\bar{\omega}^{(t)}$.

The agreement between the real spatio-temporal sequence and the simulated one should be quantified through a suitable measures of fitness $\Theta(\bar{\mathcal{V}}, \mathcal{V})$, which is computed for each value of $\mathbf{p}$. Given the fitness function, in our view the automatic calibration consists of maximising $\Theta(\bar{\mathcal{V}}, \mathcal{V})$, with respect to $\mathbf{p}$, through a suitable search algorithm. To this purpose, we use a variation of the standard Particle Swarm Optimization (PSO) algorithm [9], which was specifically designed to deal with optimizations in spaces with a high number of dimensions, namely the Cooperative Coevolutionary PSO (CCPSO) approach [8]. The latter was already successfully tested for urban CA calibrations in [11], where the details on its formalization and implementation can be found.

3   Computational Study

3.1   Experimental Setup

We applied the model to the area of the city of Heraklion, Crete. The CA representing the urban area was composed of 277×151 cells each with the side of 50 meters and the initial configuration was initialized with the urbanization map of the year 1980, labelled as $\omega^{(0)}$ in Fig. 1. In the model, we included seven land uses, four of which actively modelled. The latter were *residential dense, residential sparse, industrial areas*, and *commercial areas*. The *undeveloped land*, which essentially represents agricultural and natural land cover classes, was considered as the only passive land use. The only static land use was *green urban areas and facilities*. Also, we used a square neighbourhood with side of 20 cells. For determining the suitabilities given by Eq. (2) we used six driving factors, namely: *distance from main roads, distance from secondary roads, terrain slope, altitude, distance from the sea* and *distance from the city center*. In order to reduce the number of unknown model parameters, we adopted the value of 0.01 for all the α_i that define the simulation randomness. Given the above characteristics, the model depends on $D = 140$ unknown parameters.

To measure the agreement between maps during calibration, we use a modified version of the standard Kappa statistic, namely the so called Kappa Simulation K_s [12]. The standard Kappa measures the agreement between two categorical datasets relative to the expected agreement by chance (i.e. when the given sizes of classes are reallocated randomly). In the modified K_s version, the agreement between the two maps is corrected accounting for the sizes of class transitions, which are computed taking as a reference the initial map. We defined the fitness function as follows:

$$\Theta(\bar{\mathcal{V}}, \mathcal{V}) = \frac{1}{|\bar{\mathcal{V}}|} \sum_{\bar{\mathcal{V}}, \mathcal{V}} K_s(\omega^{(0)}, \bar{\omega}^{(\tau_i)}, \omega^{(\tau_i)}) \qquad \bar{\omega}^{(\tau_i)} \in \bar{\mathcal{V}}, \ \omega^{(\tau_i)} \in \mathcal{V} \qquad (4)$$

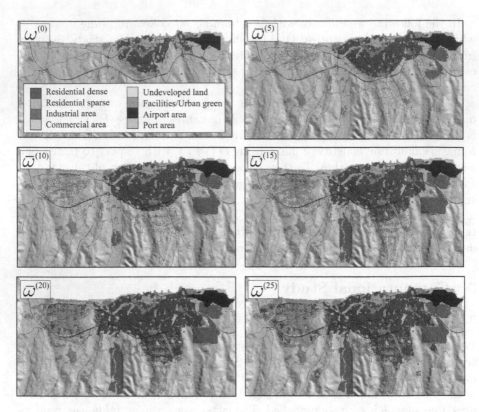

Fig. 1. Some CA configurations produced through the randomly drawn model parameters and used in the calibration study

where the τ_i indicates the time step in which the configurations are known. In other words, we defined the fitness as the arithmetic mean of all the K_s computed on the corresponding training and simulated maps.

In a preliminary stage of our numerical experimentation, we produced a training set through the CA itself. This guaranteed the existence of a zero-error solution of the calibration problem, thus allowing for an unbiased evaluation of the results obtained through the calibration procedures. To such purpose, we randomly generated the 140 unknown parameters of the model within plausible ranges, trying to achieve a fairly realistic land-use dynamics. Using such parameters, the CA simulation was then performed for 25 steps obtaining the dynamics shown in Fig. 1 and a set of CA configurations

$$\bar{\mathcal{V}} = \left\{ \omega^{(t)} \mid t = 1 \ldots 25 \right\} \tag{5}$$

It is important to note that for our purposes would not be useful to derive a vector of parameters by means of a calibration process based on a real map. Indeed, this would introduce a bias in the sense that new calibrations would tend to provide vectors of parameters that better reproduce the configurations used for the original calibration. This does not apply if the parameters are randomly drawn, though within predetermined intervals.

The computational experiments discussed in the following essentially consist of using training sets composed of some of the maps in $\bar{\mathcal{V}}$ with the aim of reproducing the correct dynamics after model calibration.

As for the constraints, for the 15th CA step we used the actual amount of land for each land-use taken from a 2010 map of the area. Then, we adopted a scenario of linear increment in land-use demand between steps 0 and 25.

We assigned to each calibration a budget of 20000 CA evaluations and we carried out 10 independent runs for each experiment, averaging the results in terms of achieved fitness. Moreover, we ran the optimization algorithms on a workstation equipped with two different GPUs: the nVidia Tesla K40 and a nVidia Geforce GTX 680 graphic card. In order to exploit both GPUs, we developed a multi-GPU program using the C++/CUDA languages and a multi-threads approach according to a master-slaves paradigm.

3.2   Results and Discussion

In the study we considered a number of different training sets composed of one or more maps taken from the set $\bar{\mathcal{V}}$ defined in Eq. 5. However, due to space limitations only some results will be discussed here. In the following, we indicate with $\bar{\mathcal{V}}_i$ a training set including only $\bar{\omega}^{(i)}$, with $\bar{\mathcal{V}}_{i,j}$ a training set including $\bar{\omega}^{(i)}$, $\bar{\omega}^{(j)}$ and so on. In Fig. 2 we show the averaged convergence plots of the optimizations for some experiments. The statistics on the attained fitnesses are shown in Table 1.

As expected, a calibration point after only five CA steps gave rise to a relatively easy optimization problem. This is due to the small differences between the two configurations $\omega^{(0)}$ and $\bar{\omega}^{(5)}$. More in details, according to Table 1 in this case the optimization algorithm was able to achieve the average fitness $\Theta = 0.980$. Note that because of the probabilistic nature of the optimization algorithm, given a training set, a lower standard deviation implies a lower number of optimization runs that are needed to obtain a reliable calibration. As shown by Fig. 2 and Table 1, including calibration points in more advanced time steps, produced a reduction of the speed of convergence with decreased fitness value and increase of the variability of the calibration results. In most calibration configurations a t-test on the results showed that the achieved fitness values were essentially equivalent. Note however that such an equivalence only refers to the achieved fitness considered as a casual variable given by a probabilistic calibration process. As shown later, the used training sets can indeed lead to very different simulation qualities.

Table 1 also shows the average computation time which was necessary for an optimization: Thanks to the GPGPU acceleration, the average time took by a 25-steps CA simulation was 0.2 s.

Our experimental setup allows to examine the quality of calibration with respect to all reference configurations included in $\bar{\mathcal{V}}$ (see Eq. 5). To this end, we used the best parameter vectors obtained in the calibrations and we ran the

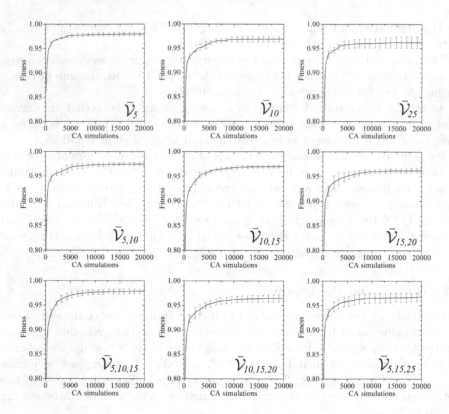

Fig. 2. Convergence plots of the average fitness Θ and its standard deviation for some calibration tests. The statistics were computed over 10 independent runs on each test.

Table 1. Statistics on the achieved fitness Θ and elapsed time in seconds over 10 independent runs for some calibration tests

Training set	$\bar{\mathcal{V}}_5$	$\bar{\mathcal{V}}_{10}$	$\bar{\mathcal{V}}_{25}$	$\bar{\mathcal{V}}_{5,10}$	$\bar{\mathcal{V}}_{10,15}$	$\bar{\mathcal{V}}_{15,20}$	$\bar{\mathcal{V}}_{5,10,15}$	$\bar{\mathcal{V}}_{10,15,20}$	$\bar{\mathcal{V}}_{5,15,25}$
Avg	0.980	0.969	0.963	0.975	0.970	0.962	0.979	0.965	0.967
Std. Dev.	0.004	0.006	0.012	0.003	0.003	0.005	0.005	0.007	0.009
Min	0.975	0.964	0.952	0.970	0.967	0.955	0.974	0.955	0.956
Max	0.983	0.977	0.975	0.977	0.973	0.966	0.984	0.972	0.976
Avg. Time	1171	2099	4647	2104	3305	3686	3007	3772	4763

corresponding CA simulation by calculating the adopted measure of agreement K_s between $\bar{\omega}^{(t)}$ and $\omega^{(t)}$ at each step t. The objective was to obtain a quantification of the accuracy that can be achieved along the simulation. Some validation results are summarized in Table 2. It is also interesting to examine in details the values of K_s along the simulation for the different training sets, which are depicted in Fig. 3. According to the results, the actual quality of calibrations in the

Table 2. Validation results for some of the calibration tests. The statistics were computed on the validation set (composed of 25 maps) in terms of K_s.

	$\bar{V}_5$	$\bar{V}_{10}$	$\bar{V}_{15}$	$\bar{V}_{5,10}$	$\bar{V}_{5,15}$	$\bar{V}_{10,15}$	$\bar{V}_{15,20}$	$\bar{V}_{5,10,15}$	$\bar{V}_{10,15,20}$
Average K_s	0.958	0.971	0.960	0.970	0.983	0.971	0.967	0.983	0.972
Worst K_s	0.934	0.957	0.952	0.959	0.977	0.957	0.962	0.972	0.967

considered range of 25 CA steps, was significantly different for the used training sets. In general, there was a good K_s in a neighbourhood of the calibration point (note that in correspondence to the latter, for the single point calibration, the K_s value corresponds to the fitness Θ achieved during calibration). However, the deterioration of the simulation quality greatly depended on where the calibration occurred. For example, from Fig. 3 it is clear that the easiest calibration at the step 5, in spite of the high value of the achieved fitness (i.e. $\Theta = 0.980$), did not provide a suitable vector of model parameters, leading to the low average agreement of 0.958 in terms of K_s (see Table 2). This is not surprising, given that the map produced by a single CA step does not contain enough information on the system's dynamics. Also, looking at the other extreme, the calibration at the farthest point from the origin (i.e. using $\bar{V}_{25}$) produced a good agreement only in the immediate vicinity of the initial and final configurations, with an average of 0.957. However, with a single calibration-point in an intermediate position (e.g. for $\bar{V}_{10}$ and $\bar{V}_{15}$) the evolution of agreement during the simulation showed a low variability and an average value quite close to that obtained in the calibration phase. Interestingly, in our case study, we can achieve a reasonable quality of the calibrated model using a single historical map, as long as it does not refer to a point which is too close or too far from the beginning of the simulation.

Better results were obtained using more than one calibration point. In particular, using $\bar{V}_{5,15}$ led to a good agreement with the validation set along the whole simulation, characterized by an average K_s of 0.983 with a minimum of 0.977. According to the results in Fig. 3, it seems that using only two calibration points, provided they are well spaced and not too close to the beginning of the simulation, can lead to a suitable CA model optimization. The validation of calibration based on the training set $\bar{V}_{5,10,15}$ showed a quite stable K_s during the simulation, with an average value of 0.983 and a worst value of 0.972. However, these value are substantially equivalent to those obtained using the smaller training set $\bar{V}_{5,15}$ (see Table 2). Therefore, increasing the training set $\bar{V}_{5,15}$ with an intermediate map proved essentially useless. Clearly, this is because, in our case study, the map $\bar{\omega}^{(10)}$ did not provide any supplementary informational contribution. It is important to highlight that the insights that can be drawn from the experiments described above refer to a case in which the rules that determine the urban dynamics (i.e. the parameters) are constant over time. However, this can be, at least approximately, the case for many historical periods and urban areas in the world.

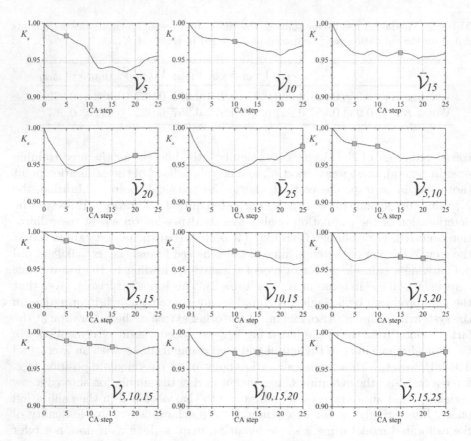

Fig. 3. Agreement, in terms of K_s, with the validation set during the simulation. Calibration points are highlighted.

The results can also be examined from a forecasting perspective. For example, supposing that some maps corresponding to CA steps between 0 and 15 (i.e. the hypothetical current time) are available, we can estimate the influence of calibration error in forecasting the CA configuration at the 25th step (the hypothetical future time). As can be seen from Fig. 3, the best forecasting ability was achieved through a model calibrated using $\bar{\mathcal{V}}_{5,15}$ (final K_s of 0.982) and $\bar{\mathcal{V}}_{5,10,15}$ (final K_s of 0.980). Using a single calibration point led to poor predictive performance of the model: the values of K_s at the 25th CA step were, 0.956, 0.970 and 0.959 for $\bar{\mathcal{V}}_5$, $\bar{\mathcal{V}}_{10}$ and $\bar{\mathcal{V}}_{15}$, respectively.

4   Conclusions and Future Work

Constrained CA for land use change simulations often depends on many parameters that must be determined through a calibration process. The latter usually requires the availability of a training set containing an adequate number of historical maps of the area under study. Using a suitable experimental setup and some advanced computational techniques, we investigated the influence of the composition of the training set on the quality of the resulting calibration. We presented and discussed in this paper only some experiments. However, the whole study required the execution of more than 5 million simulations. In return, it provided numerous insights and allowed us to quantify in various conditions the calibration and validation errors, as well as their implications in the case of land-use change forecasting. Future work will investigate the effect of the different training sets using a multi-objective metaheuristics [13], in which the fitness function is based on various landscape metrics.

References

1. White, R., Engelen, G.: High-resolution integrated modelling of the spatial dynamics of urban and regional systems. Computer, Environment and Urban Systems 24, 383–400 (2000)
2. Barredo, J.I., Kasanko, M., McCormick, N., Lavalle, C.: Modelling dynamic spatial processes: simulation of urban future scenarios through cellular automata. Landscape and Urban Planning 64, 145–160 (2003)
3. Blecic, I., Cecchini, A., Falk, M., Marras, S., Pyles, D.R., Spano, D., Trunfio, G.A.: Urban metabolism and climate change: A planning support system. Int. J. Applied Earth Observation and Geoinformation 26, 447–457 (2014)
4. Feng, Y., Liu, Y., Tong, X., Liu, M., Deng, S.: Modeling dynamic urban growth using cellular automata and particle swarm optimization rules. Landscape and Urban Planning 102, 188–196 (2011)
5. Rabbani, A., Aghababaee, H., Rajabi, M.A.: Modeling dynamic urban growth using hybrid cellular automata and particle swarm optimization. Journal of Applied Remote Sensing 6 (2012)
6. Blecic, I., Cecchini, A., Trunfio, G.A.: A comparison of evolutionary algorithms for automatic calibration of constrained cellular automata. In: Taniar, D., Gervasi, O., Murgante, B., Pardede, E., Apduhan, B.O. (eds.) ICCSA 2010, Part I. LNCS, vol. 6016, pp. 166–181. Springer, Heidelberg (2010)
7. Blecic, I., Cecchini, A., Trunfio, G.A.: Cellular automata simulation of urban dynamics through GPGPU. The Journal of Supercomputing 65, 614–629 (2013)
8. van den Bergh, F., Engelbrecht, A.P.: A cooperative approach to particle swarm optimization. IEEE Trans. Evolutionary Computation 8, 225–239 (2004)
9. Kennedy, J., Eberhart, R.: Particle swarm optimization. In: Proceedings of the IEEE International Conference on Neural Networks, vol. 4, pp. 1942–1948 (1995)
10. Wu, F.: SimLand: A prototype to simulate land conversion through the integrated GIS and ca with ahp-derived transition rules. International Journal of Geographical Information Science 12, 63–82 (1998)
11. Blecic, I., Cecchini, A., Trunfio, G.A.: Fast and accurate optimization of a GPU-accelerated CA urban model through cooperative coevolutionary particle swarms. Procedia Computer Science 29, 1631–1643 (2014)
12. van Vliet, J., Bregt, A.K., Hagen-Zanker, A.: Revisiting Kappa to account for change in the accuracy assessment of land-use change models. Ecological Modelling 222, 1367–1375 (2011)
13. Blecic, I., Cecchini, A., Trunfio, G.A.: A decision support tool coupling a causal model and a multi-objective genetic algorithm. Appl. Intell. 26, 125–137 (2007)

Cellular Automaton Approach to Arching in Two-Dimensional Granular Media

Takumi Masuda[1], Katsuhiro Nishinari[1], and Andreas Schadschneider[2]

[1] Department of Aeronautics and Astronautics, Faculty of Engineering,
University of Tokyo, Hongo, Bunkyo-ku, Tokyo 113-8656, Japan
msdtakumi@gmail.com, tknishi@mail.ecc.u-tokyo.ac.jp
[2] Institut für Theoretische Physik, Universität zu Köln, 50937 Köln, Germany
as@thp.uni-koeln.de

Abstract. Clogging of granular materials and jamming of pedestrian crowds occur because of the formation of arches at bottlenecks. We propose a simple microscopic model that is able to reproduce oscillation phenomena due to formation and destabilization of arches in 2-dimensional flows. The dynamics of particles in front of a bottleneck is described by a one-dimensional stochastic cellular automaton on a semicircular geometry. The model predicts the existence of a critical bottleneck size for jamless particle flows and allows to determine the dependence of the jamming probability on the system size. The model can also be studied analytically and the results are in good agreement with simulations.

Keywords: Granular matter, Evacuation process, Bottleneck flow, Arching effect.

1 Introduction

Granular materials are defined as assemblies of particles, which include powders, sand grains and seeds. Hence they are used in many industrial processes, e.g. in the pharmaceutical industry which treats powers and pills and agriculture industry which processes seeds and grains. Furthermore, dense pedestrian crowds exhibit behavior similar to those of granular materials in some situations, e.g., lane formation [1] in groups of oppositely moving pedestrians and clogging in evacuation flows near bottlenecks [2, 3].

One of the most undesirable situations of granular materials is clogging, which is costly and annoying but ubiquitous in the industries relying on storing and transporting granular materials and even in pedestrian evacuations. Clogging is usually called *jamming* in the context of pedestrian crowd dynamics.

A remarkable observation made by To, Lai and Pak [4] in experiments is the existence of a critical bottleneck size above which no jamming occurs. They concluded that vaulted structures of particles (*arches*) are not stable for bottlenecks wider than the critical size. Janda et al. [5] have investigated granular flows through a bottleneck and obtained an empirical law which relates the jamming probability with the bottleneck size. Their result is represented by a sigmoid function similar to the Gompertz function.

J. Wąs, G.C. Sirakoulis, and S. Bandini (Eds.): ACRI 2014, LNCS 8751, pp. 310–319, 2014.
© Springer International Publishing Switzerland 2014

One focus of recent studies on granular flows has been on bottleneck flows with external perturbations. It has been reported that vibrations improve bottleneck flows by suppressing the arching effect [6]. Additionally, because of formation and destabilization of arches, vibrated granular materials display intermittent flows which switch between jamming and unjamming states. Although granular materials require external perturbations to resume flow, pedestrian crowds rapidly resolve clogging by self-adjustment [3]. The two states of the intermittent flows randomly alternate and distributions of their lifetime have been investigated. The avalanche size, defined as the number of particles passing through a bottleneck during a single unjamming state, follows an exponential law [5, 7–9]. On the other hand, the duration of a jamming state obeys power law [9].

2 Model

In the following we propose a simple model [10] that captures the essence of the observed behavior of many-particle systems near a bottleneck, e.g. oscillation phenomena. Although particle flows usually are three-dimensional, we focus here on two-dimensional realizations which are relevant for pedestrian dynamics, but have also been studied for granular materials. For simplicity, we ignore fluctuations that occur in the bulk of granular assemblies. Instead, we focus on properties of intermittent behavior which stem from the *arch effect*. The precise structure of the arches is irrelevant for the properties of the flow. This assumption allows us to formulate the dynamics of the particles by a one-dimensional stochastic cellular automaton. Its sites are arranged in a semicircular shape which reflects the typical form of arches (Fig. 1). Here we have assumed that no arches appear in the area nearer to the bottleneck than the semicircle which implies that its size is of the order of the bottleneck width. If the site size is chosen as the typical size of the particles (grains), each site can be occupied by at most one particle. Hence, each site j can be in two different states, empty ($s_j = 0$) or occupied ($s_j = 1$). The configuration $(1, \ldots, 1)$ where all sites are occupied represents arch formation. If $P(C)$ denotes the probability of finding a configuration $C = (s_1, \ldots, s_L)$ in the steady state, the arching probability is given by $P_{\mathrm{arch}} = P(1, \ldots, 1)$.

In order to define the dynamics of the model we assume that the bulk of the granular assembly acts as a particle bath which supplies particles to the system at constant rate α. Then empty sites become occupied with probability α which can be interpreted as the probability that a particle finds an available gap. It is called *inflow* in the following. The *outflow* is represented by the annihilation of a particle. The probability of this process depends on the occupancy of the two neighboring sites. If both are occupied, then the particle is annihilated with probability γ. For the other cases the outflow probability is β. At the boundary sites, the outflow depends only on a single neighboring site. It occurs with probability δ when the site is occupied and with β for an empty neighbor site. In the physical regime, γ and δ are smaller than β, since these parameters capture the effects of friction among grains and walls. Hence γ and δ decrease as friction

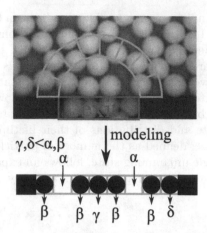

Fig. 1. Definition of the model. Top: A semicircle which is slightly larger than the width of the exit is divided into discrete sites which can contain at most one particle. Bottom: Definition of a one-dimensional stochastic cellular automaton characterized by four parameters α, β, γ and δ. An arch corresponds to the configuration where all sites are occupied. The arrow into a site represents a particle inflow corresponding to particle creation at a rate α. The arrows pointing out of sites indicate the outflow which is defined by 3-site interactions. In the bulk it occurs with rates β or γ and at the boundaries with rate β or δ.

becomes stronger. In each step, these update rules are applied to a randomly chosen site (random-sequential update), which is an approximate realization of a stochastic process in continuous time.

A flow rate $Q(C)$ for a configuration C can be defined as the probability that an outflow event occurs. In particular, the flow rate for the arching configuration $Q(1, \ldots, 1) = (2\delta + (L-2)\gamma)/L =: Q_{\text{arch}}$ indicates the probability that an arch breaks.

For simplicity, we restrict our attention to the cases where $\alpha = \beta \neq 0$ and $\gamma = \delta$. The first condition implies that inflow and outflow rates are identical when no friction acts. The second identity implies that the friction between particles and between particles and walls are identical. In this situation, $Q_{\text{arch}} = \gamma$ is independent of the system size L. We introduce a new parameter $\varepsilon = \gamma/\beta$ so that $0 \leq \varepsilon \leq 1$ in the physical regime.

3   Intermittent Flow

In this section, we investigate the time evolution of the model. In simulations we observe intermittent flows, in good qualitative agreement with experiments on granular materials. The dynamical behavior of the model indicates the presence of two states: jamming and continuous flow. Jamming is represented in the graph (Fig. 2) by horizontal regions, where due to the existence of an arch no particles are annihilated. The other parts show non-vanishing particle flows. A similar intermittent behavior with random alternation between two such states can be observed in granular flows and escaping stampedes [3, 9].

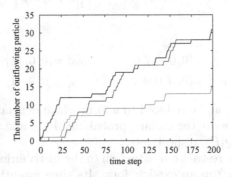

Fig. 2. The dynamical behavior of the model for $\alpha = \beta = 0.9, \gamma = \delta = 0.1, L = 3$ and different realizations of the stochastic dynamics. It is shown that jamming and unjamming states randomly alternate.

4   Properties of the Model in the Stationary State

Here, we consider the arching probability P_{arch} and the mean flow rate, which is given by the weighted average (over the probability distribution of the configurations) of flow rates.

We first study the two limiting cases $\varepsilon = 0, 1$ that can be easily considered. In the case $\varepsilon = 0$, flow cannot resume once an arch has formed. Consequently, the arching probability is 1 and the mean flow rate is 0. This situation corresponds to an absorbing state where the system attains a trivial stationary state without dynamics. Similar behavior is observed when granular materials flow through a narrow hopper without vibration. In the case $\varepsilon = 1$, all configurations appear uniformly in the steady state since inflow and outflow occur at the same rate. Therefore the probability for each configuration is $1/2^L$. In addition, the mean flow rate is $\beta/2$ since each site is occupied by a single particle with a probability of $1/2$ and a particle can flow at the rate β.

Next, we calculate the interval between the two limiting cases by introducing the 2^L-dimensional vectors $|P\rangle$ and $\langle Q|$ such that

$$|P\rangle = \sum_{(s_1,\ldots,s_L)} P(s_1,\ldots,s_L)|s_1,\ldots,s_L\rangle, \tag{1}$$

$$\langle Q| = \sum_{(s_1,\ldots,s_L)} Q(s_1,\ldots,s_L)\langle s_1,\ldots,s_L| \tag{2}$$

where $\langle s_1,\cdots,s_L| = \langle s_1| \otimes \cdots \otimes \langle s_L|, \quad \langle 0| = (1,0), \quad \langle 1| = (0,1). \tag{3}$

$P(C)$ and $Q(C)$ have been defined in Sec. 2. The summation $\sum_{(s_1,\ldots,s_L)}$ is over all configurations. From the definition of the flow rate, $\langle Q|$ is obtained as

$$\langle Q| = \langle q_l| \otimes \langle a|^{\otimes L-2} + \sum_{j=2}^{L-1} \langle a|^{\otimes(j-2)} \otimes \langle q_b| \otimes \langle a|^{\otimes(L-j-1)} + \langle a|^{\otimes(L-2)} \otimes \langle q_r| \quad (4)$$

where
$$\langle q_l| = (0,0,\beta,\delta), \qquad \langle q_b| = (0,0,\beta,\beta,0,0,\beta,\gamma),$$
$$\langle q_r| = (0,\beta,0,\delta), \qquad \langle a| = \langle 0| + \langle 1| = (1,1). \quad (5)$$

It is clear that $\langle Q|/\beta$ can be reduced to a form which depends only on ε. Using this notation, we can write the arching probability P_{arch} and the mean flow rate as $\langle 1,\ldots,1|P\rangle$ and $\langle Q|P\rangle$, respectively.

In the following, we restrict our attention to the distribution of configurations in the steady state $|P\rangle$ in an explicit form. Its time evolution is given by the master equation. Using the quantum formalism (see e.g. [11, 12]), it can be cast in the form of a Schrödinger equation with some stochastic "Hamiltonian" $\mathcal{H}$ defined by the transition rates. In the stationary state it takes the form

$$\mathcal{H}|P\rangle = 0. \quad (6)$$

The Hamiltonian is readily constructed from the update rule of the model [13–15]. Because of the 3-site interaction the Hamiltonian of our model is more complicated than e.g. the asymmetric exclusion process:

$$\mathcal{H} = h_l \otimes I_2^{\otimes(L-2)} + \sum_{j=2}^{L-1} I_2^{\otimes(j-2)} \otimes h_b \otimes I_2^{\otimes(L-j-1)} + I_2^{\otimes(L-2)} \otimes h_r. \quad (7)$$

where I_2 means the 2×2 identity matrix. h_l, h_r are $2^2 \times 2^2$ matrices defining boundary terms, and h_{int} is the $2^3 \times 2^3$ matrix describing a three-site interaction in the bulk. Explicitly they are given by

$$h_b = \begin{pmatrix} -\alpha & 0 & \alpha & 0 & 0 & 0 & 0 & 0 \\ 0 & -\beta & 0 & \beta & 0 & 0 & 0 & 0 \\ \alpha & 0 & -\alpha & 0 & 0 & 0 & 0 & 0 \\ 0 & \beta & 0 & -\beta & 0 & 0 & 0 & 0 \\ 0 & 0 & 0 & 0 & -\alpha & 0 & \beta & 0 \\ 0 & 0 & 0 & 0 & 0 & \beta & 0 & \gamma \\ 0 & 0 & 0 & 0 & \alpha & 0 & -\beta & 0 \\ 0 & 0 & 0 & 0 & 0 & \beta & 0 & -\gamma \end{pmatrix},$$

$$h_r = \begin{pmatrix} -\alpha & 0 & \alpha & 0 \\ 0 & -\beta & 0 & \delta \\ \alpha & 0 & -\alpha & 0 \\ 0 & \beta & 0 & -\delta \end{pmatrix}, \quad h_l = \begin{pmatrix} -\alpha & \beta & 0 & 0 \\ \alpha & -\beta & 0 & 0 \\ 0 & 0 & -\alpha & \delta \\ 0 & 0 & \alpha & -\delta \end{pmatrix}. \quad (8)$$

The master equation (6) implies that $|P\rangle$ depends on the parameters of the model only through ε since $(\mathcal{H}/\beta)|P\rangle = 0$ holds and $\mathcal{H}/\beta$ can be reduced to a form independent from $\alpha, \beta, \gamma, \delta$.

The arching probability $P_{\text{arch}} = \langle 1, \ldots, 1|P\rangle$ and the mean flow rate $\langle Q|P\rangle$ can be calculated with the following formula[10]:

$$\langle w|P\rangle = \frac{\det[\, H + |V\rangle\langle w|\,]}{\det[\, H + |V\rangle\langle V|\,]} \qquad \text{where} \qquad \langle V| = (1, \ldots, 1). \tag{9}$$

P_{arch} and $\langle Q|P\rangle/\beta$ for the system size $L = 2, 3$ are given by

$$P_{\text{arch}}\big|_{L=2} = \frac{1}{3\varepsilon + 1}, \qquad P_{\text{arch}}\big|_{L=3} = \frac{\varepsilon + 23}{39\varepsilon^2 + 130\varepsilon + 23}, \tag{10}$$

$$\frac{\langle Q|P\rangle}{\beta}\bigg|_{L=2} = \frac{2\varepsilon}{3\varepsilon + 1}, \qquad \frac{\langle Q|P\rangle}{\beta}\bigg|_{L=3} = \frac{4(7\varepsilon^2 + 17\varepsilon)}{39\varepsilon^2 + 130\varepsilon + 23}. \tag{11}$$

For larger L the expressions become too complicated to be given here. However, their explicit form can in principle be obtained by simple algebraic procedures from the explicit formula (9).

The arching probabilities and the mean flow rates are shown in Fig. 3 and Fig. 4, respectively. They perfectly coincide with simulation results. It is found that the arching probabilities (resp. the mean flow rate) monotonically decrease (resp. increase) with respect to ε and the system size L. This agrees with the observation that large arches become unstable.

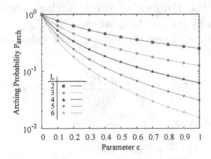
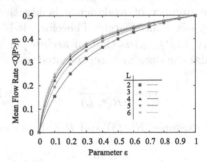

Fig. 3. Arching probabilities for various system sizes L. Dots indicate the simulation results. The lines show the theoretical results deduced from (9).

Fig. 4. Mean flow rates for various system sizes L. Dots indicate the simulation results. The lines show the theoretical results deduced from (9).

It is conjectured that the parameter $\varepsilon = \gamma/\beta$ can be interpreted as an indicator for the magnitude of jam suppression. Indeed, for increasing ε the system properties are more similar to the unjamming state and, as we have considered above, the conditions $\varepsilon = 0$ and $\varepsilon = 1$ correspond to the limiting cases of jamming and continuous flow, respectively. Therefore, ε reflects the magnitude of vibration in granular flows or the self-adjustment by pedestrians. In pedestrian dynamics, ε can be viewed as an indicator for the pedestrian's discipline near the exit. Let us consider a situation where arches are formed during a rush through a bottleneck. Because of the high velocity of the pedestrians and the large friction between them this situation is described by large values of α and β and small values of γ and δ. This means that ε is small. As a consequence, ε reflects the self-adjustment by pedestrians.

5   Avalanche Size

Let us now focus on the avalanche size m. In our model, the avalanche size is defined as the number of outflowing particles between two successive jamming states. From the update rules of our model it is readily deduced that arches are not stable in the sense that they have an infinite lifetime, except for the case $\varepsilon = 0$. We therefore consider all arches with lifetimes larger than a stability threshold N as "stable" and regard jamming states as durations where stable arches prevent flows. The probability that an arch is stable is given by $S :=$ $1 - Q_{arch} \sum_{t=1}^{N} (1 - Q_{arch})^{t-1} = (1 - Q_{arch})^N$ since the lifetime distribution of arches is $Q_{arch}(1 - Q_{arch})^{t-1}$ which has the expectation value $1/Q_{arch}$. The lifetime distribution of stable arches $(t > N)$ is given by $Q_{arch}(1 - Q_{arch})^{t-(N+1)}$ which has the expectation value $1/Q_{arch} + N$.

Presuming that avalanche sizes are distributed exponentially as observed in experiments, we are interested in their expectation value. It is obtained by dividing the mean flow rate $\langle Q|P \rangle$ by the number of avalanches per unit time. The number of avalanches is identical to the number of stable arches since they occur alternately. Therefore, it is given by $SP_{arch}Q_{arch}$ where $P_{arch}Q_{arch} =$ $P_{arch}/(1/Q_{arch})$ is that of arches per unit time. Thus the expectation value of avalanche sizes m is represented as

$$m = \frac{1}{SR(\varepsilon, L)} \qquad \text{where} \qquad R(\varepsilon, L) = \frac{Q_{arch}P_{arch}}{\langle Q|P \rangle}. \tag{12}$$

For example, $R(\varepsilon, 3)$ and $R(\varepsilon, 4)$ are calculated as

$$R(\varepsilon, 3) = \frac{\varepsilon + 23}{4(7\varepsilon + 17)}, \qquad R(\varepsilon, 4) = \frac{11\varepsilon^2 + 78\varepsilon + 103}{2(24\varepsilon^3 + 181\varepsilon^2 + 366\varepsilon + 197)}. \tag{13}$$

The form of (12) implies that the variables $(\gamma, \varepsilon, L, N)$ of m are separated so that $R(\varepsilon, L)$ depends only on physical properties of the system and S contains parameters (γ, N) which do not have a simple interpretation in real systems. Since (γ, N) depend on the length of the time step they have to be determined empirically for each experiment.

As shown in Fig. 5, the simulation results coincide well with the exponential distribution, which has also been observed in experiments and other simulations of granular flow [5, 9]. This fact agrees with the presumption that avalanche sizes in our model distributed exponentially. Hence the analytical results are in good agreement with the simulation results.

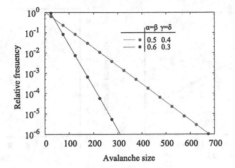

Fig. 5. Histogram of avalanche sizes. The lines are calculated with (12) under the presumption that the distribution is exponential. Dots indicate simulation results for $N = 5$, $L = 3$.

6   Jamming Probability

Let us now consider the jamming probability J. It is interpreted in our model as the probability that an avalanche size is less than a threshold M. Hence, it is obtained by integrating the avalanche size distribution from 0 to M:

$$J = 1 - \exp(-M/m) = 1 - \exp[-SMR(\varepsilon, L)]. \qquad (14)$$

Although the dependence of $R(\varepsilon, L)$ on ε has a rational form as implied from (9), the dependence on L is nontrivial. This fact motivates us to approximate $R(\varepsilon, L)$ by an analytical function. Fig. 6 shows that $R(\varepsilon, L)$ is represented by an exponential function of the form $A(\varepsilon)B(\varepsilon)^{-L}$ for $\varepsilon \geq 0.4$. This assumption can be justified for the case $\varepsilon = 1$. In fact, $R(1, L) = Q_{\mathrm{arch}} P_{\mathrm{arch}} / \langle Q | P \rangle = \gamma(1/2^L)/(\beta/2) = 2^{-L+1}$.

Identifying $A(\varepsilon)$ and $B(\varepsilon)$ with $R(\varepsilon, 3)$ and $R(\varepsilon, 4)$, we can write the jamming probability with the Gompertz function as

$$J(\varepsilon, L) = 1 - \exp[-A(\varepsilon)SMB(\varepsilon)^{-L}], \qquad (15)$$

$$\text{where} \quad A(\varepsilon) = \frac{[R(\varepsilon, 3)]^4}{[R(\varepsilon, 4)]^3}, \quad B(\varepsilon) = \frac{R(\varepsilon, 3)}{R(\varepsilon, 4)}. \qquad (16)$$

The simulation results shown in Fig. 7 agree well with our previous assumptions that the avalanche size distribution and $R(\varepsilon, L)$ are exponential.

The jamming probability J converges to 1 for any system size L in the limit $M \to \infty$ in principle, as deduced from (15). However, at a finite M the jamming probability becomes 0 at a finite system size L in practice. In experiments, this fact corresponds to the existence of a critical outlet size above which no arches appear [4, 5].

A typical value of ε may be estimated from experimental results. Mankoc et al. [6] introduced a bivariate model characterized by p and q, which indicate the probability that a particle passes through the outlet without forming an arch

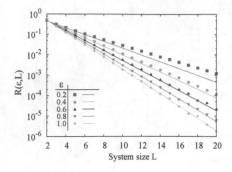

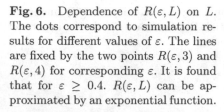

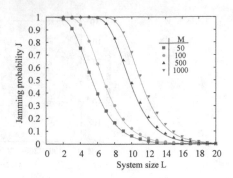

Fig. 6. Dependence of $R(\varepsilon, L)$ on L. The dots correspond to simulation results for different values of ε. The lines are fixed by the two points $R(\varepsilon, 3)$ and $R(\varepsilon, 4)$ for corresponding ε. It is found that for $\varepsilon \geq 0.4$. $R(\varepsilon, L)$ can be approximated by an exponential function.

Fig. 7. Jamming probability as function of system size L for $\alpha = \beta = 0.6$, $\gamma = \delta = 0.3$ and $N = 5$. The plots are simulation results and the lines are defined by (15). The jamming probabilities gradually decrease with increasing L. They practically become zero already for relatively small system sizes.

and the probability that a particle is delivered from an arch, respectively. The parameters have been estimated experimentally as $p = 0.981$, $q = 0.836$ for an outlet of 3.02 grain diameters width. Although their experiments are in three dimensions, we assume that the results are appropriate for our model. From the definition, q can be interpreted in our model as $S = 1 - q$. Comparing the expectation values of avalanche sizes deduced by both models, we obtain that $R(\varepsilon, L) = (1 - p)/(p + q - pq)$. Additionally, we use $L \simeq 6.9$ which is reported from experiments in [16] as the number of particles involved in an arch for the outlet of 3.03 grains diameter width. Then we obtain $\varepsilon \simeq 0.92$.

7 Conclusion

We have interpreted the dynamical behavior of particles in front of a bottleneck as a cellular automaton model with 3-site interactions arranged in a semicircular shape. From the simulations and the analytical results we can conclude that the model reproduces the generic behavior which characterizes bottleneck flows in many-particle systems. The resulting dynamics exhibits two clear regions: jamming and continuous flow. The model parameter ε has a physical interpretation: in granular flows it reflects the magnitude of applied vibrations and in pedestrian streams it its related to the pedestrian's discipline near the exit. The avalanche size distribution is exponential and the jamming probability is well approximated by the Gompertz function. The expectation value of avalanche sizes and the coefficients of the Gompertz function can be determined analytically. The model reveals the existence of a critical outlet size above which no arches appear in practice. The parameter ε, which characterizes the physical properties of the model, can be estimated by methods which have been used in previous studies.

The model can be extended to be more compatible with actual particle flows. Although we focus on two-dimensional flows for simplicity, the model can be extended to three-dimensional flows in a straightforward way. Moreover, we have formulated the model assuming that an arch appears only in a single semicircular layer. Again the model can be made more realistic by considering multiple layers to take account the effects of the upstream and allow for variations in arch size.

References

1. Visser, T., Wysocki, A., Rex, M., Löwen, H., Royall, C.P., Imhof, A., van Blaaderen, A.: Lane formation in driven mixtures of oppositely charged colloids. Soft Matter 7, 2352 (2011)
2. Helbing, D., Farkas, I., Vicsek, T.: Simulating dynamical features of escape panic. Nature (London), 407, 487 (2000)
3. Helbing, D., Buzna, L., Johansson, A., Werner, T.: Self-Organized Pedestrian Crowd Dynamics: Experiments, Simulations, and Design Solutions. Transp. Sci. 39, 1 (2005)
4. To, K., Lai, P.-Y., Pak, H.K.: Jamming of Granular Flow in a Two-Dimensional Hopper. Phys. Rev. Lett. 86, 71 (2001)
5. Janda, A., Zuriguel, I., Garcimartín, A., Pugnaloni, L.A., Maza, D.: Jamming and critical outlet size in the discharge of a two-dimensional silo. Europhys. Lett. 84, 44002 (2008)
6. Mankoc, C., Garcimartin, A., Zuriguel, I., Maza, D., Pugnaloni, L.A.: Role of vibrations in the jamming and unjamming of grains discharging from a silo. Phys. Rev. E 80, 011309 (2009)
7. Zuriguel, I., Garcimartín, A., Maza, D., Pugnaloni, L.A., Pastor, J.M.: Jamming during the discharge of granular matter from a silo. Phys. Rev. E 71, 051303 (2005)
8. Helbing, D., Johansson, A., Mathiesen, J., Jensen, M.H., Hansen, A.: Jamming of Granular Flow in a Two-Dimensional Hopper. Phys. Rev. Lett. 97, 168001 (2006)
9. Janda, A., Maza, D., Garcimartín, A., Kolb, E., Lanuza, J., Clément, E.: Unjamming a granular hopper by vibration. Europhys. Lett. 87, 24002 (2009)
10. Masuda, T., Nishinari, K., Schadschneider, A.: Critical Bottleneck Size for Jamless Particle Flows in Two Dimension. Phys. Rev. Lett. 112, 138701 (2014)
11. Schütz, G.M.: Exactly Sovable Models for Many-Body Systems. In: Domb, C., Lebowitz, J.L. (eds.) Phase Transitions and Critical Phenomena, vol. 19. Academic Press (2001)
12. Schadschneider, A., Chowdhury, D., Nishinari, K.: Stochastic Transport in Complex Systems: From Molecules to Vehicles. Elsevier, Amsterdam (2010)
13. Derrida, B., Evans, M.R., Hakim, V., Pasquier, V.: Exact solution of a 1d asymmetric exclusion model using a matrix formulation. J. Phys. A26, 1493 (1993)
14. Krebs, K., Sandow, S.: Matrix product eigenstates for one-dimensional stochastic models and quantum spin chains. J. Phys. A30, 3165 (1997)
15. Klauck, K., Schadschneider, A.: On the ubiquity of matrix-product states in one-dimensional stochastic processes with boundary interactions. Physica A271, 102 (1999)
16. Garcimartín, A., Zuriguel, I., Pugnaloni, L.A., Janda, A.: Shape of jamming arches in two-dimensional deposits of granular materials. Phys. Rev. E 82, 031306 (2010)

Modeling of Friction Dynamic Motion
by Cellular Automata

Seiya Yamagishi[1] and Shin Morishita[2]

[1] Graduate Student, Yokohama National University, Japan
[2] Graduate School of Environment and Information Sciences, Yokohama National University,
79-7 Tokiwadai, Hodogaya-ku, Yokohama, 240-8501, Japan
mshin@ynu.ac.jp

Abstract. Friction vibration in a dynamic system composed of a slider supported by a spring on a belt was modeled and simulated by Cellular Automata (CA). Friction vibration in mechanical systems has been studied for a long time and various models have been proposed to understand its physical phenomena, but dynamical behavior of an elastic body on friction surface has not been revealed yet. This may be caused by the complexity of friction between two surfaces, and CA can be used as a strong tool of modeling physical phenomena introducing local neighbor and transition rules based on observation of phenomena. It may not be easy to derive the governing equation of motion including friction. In this study, a modeling procedure of friction dynamics by CA was discussed. The new model was based on a spring–block model proposed by Burridge and Knopoff, but an additional layer of internal surface was introduced to consider the contact area of sliding surfaces. The self-excited vibration, including the stick-slip vibration and the divergent phenomena could be simulated in the proposed CA model.

Keywords: Cellular Automata, Simulation, Friction, Friction vibration, Stick-slip, Self-excited vibration.

1 Introduction

Theory of Newtonian dynamics helps us to understand or predict the movement of objects in natural world, and we have designed various tools, machines or structures based on Newtonian dynamics. Friction force is defined as resistance force produced between two surfaces when they have some amount of relative velocity. As known well, Newtonian dynamics describes almost nothing about the detail of friction force. The friction force is said to have been defined by G. Amontons and C. A. de Coulomb.

In spite of the fact that we usually make use of friction force in daily life, and sometimes try to remove it, the friction force always exists in this real world. From the viewpoint of vibration, it tends to decrease the vibration amplitude as a function of damping of the system. At the same time, it is known that it works as a source of exciter of the system when the equivalent damping is negative.

J. Wąs, G.C. Sirakoulis, and S. Bandini (Eds.): ACRI 2014, LNCS 8751, pp. 320–329, 2014.
© Springer International Publishing Switzerland 2014

The friction dynamics have been of much interest and concern to a number of researchers for hundreds of years. After the age of mass production which is the result of the industrial revolution, the friction has been studied as an important problem in machine components. Today, this problem is being studied such diverse fields as seismology, physics, tribology, metallurgy, and fracture. The mechanism of frictional motion is, however, not understood in detail [1].

Friction force is always produced between two surfaces of contacting objects, and the precise surface state cannot be observed in general. This is why the cause of friction has not been revealed. There are irregularities or roughness on the surface of objects even if it is carefully prepared and seems perfectly flat. Two surfaces which seem to keep in touch with each other are supported by the highest peak of the roughness, and accordingly the real contact area between surfaces may be very small. The real contact area is almost independent to the size of the surfaces, and it is determined by the applied load through the contact surfaces. In the real contact area, plastic deformation occurs to support the load. As a result, adhesion occurs in these areas and it needs friction force to shear these junctions. Recently, real-time visualization of contact point was carried out to clarify the transient process from stick to slip. Rubinstein et al. performed real-time visualization of the contact area between two polymethyl methacrylate blocks [2]. And Muller et al. proposed Cellular Automata (CA) model focusing on the topography and the wear of the surface of the braking system under the condition that the relative velocity is set to be constant [3].

In mechanical engineering field, there has been a considerable number of studies which create heuristic models by repeating the experiment and correcting some base model to reproduce the behavior. These models reproduce the result of experiment accurately, but it is difficult to respond to the changes of mechanical properties, for example, surfaces roughness of materials, Young's modulus, or shear strength. It falls into the results the database is required before simulating a frictional motion. In this study, we modeled the friction dynamics by introducing local dynamics between solid surfaces and taking into account the inertial force. This paper first explains the physical model of friction surfaces, and then suggests CA model and result of simulation.

2   Modeling of Friction Surface

2.1   Physical Model

First, this paper explains the physical model of friction surfaces between two materials. This was composed of two plates and some blocks which were connected by springs to each other as shown in Fig.1. This model was based on spring-block model proposed by Burridge and Knopoff (BK model) [4], and a new additional layer of internal surface was introduced to consider the contact area of sliding surfaces. Several CA models of spring-block model (e.g., Olami et al. [5]) have been reported in the seismology field.

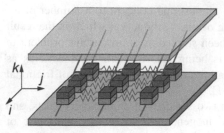

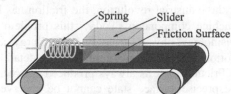

Fig. 2. Physical model of friction surface. Upper and lower plates were the main body of the materials, and blocks placed between these plates were the contacting points between two surfaces. Springs connected among blocks represented the elasticity of the blocks, and elastic beams represented that of sliding surface.

Fig. 1. Slider on moving belt. The slider was connected to the wall by a spring and it was placed on the belt moving at a constant speed.

This new model had three special features. The plates expressing the main body of material were divided into upper and lower ones to simulate sliding motion of two surfaces, and a large number of blocks were introduced between two plates. The blocks were connected to each other by springs which represented elasticity of connecting surface. When one block moved to some extent, adjacent blocks might receive a certain force from the shifted block. The blocks were divided into upper and lower parts, which contributed to simulate "touch and detach" state of surfaces. The upper and lower blocks were also supported by elastic beams attached to the corresponding plates. Introducing two layers of blocks, and representing real contact behavior of sliding surfaces were new idea in this paper and were different from BK model in seismology field. Though there were various sizes of contact points between two surfaces, the blocks which represented the contact sections were divided into the same areas of rectangles in this CA model. This model was applied to the system that a slider with attached spring fixed at one end placed on a belt moved at a constant speed as shown in Fig. 2. So, the upper plate represented the main body of the slider and the lower plate that of the belt. When shear force was applied, the sliding state of local contact points was expressed as the state where the upper and lower blocks were detached. And the state whose convex portions of solid surface were in contact with the opposite could be represented as the state where the upper and lower blocks came to the same position. Springs binding between the blocks represented elasticity of the blocks, and the force was transmitted through the spring to the blocks around when a block displaced. This represented a state where the stress was generated when the deforming force was applied to the contact point. The spring connecting the upper and lower plates with the blocks represented a state where shear force was applied to each contact point when the shear force worked between two objects. The mass of the blocks were ignored as was minute each contact points, and it was assumed that only the plate representing the main body had a mass.

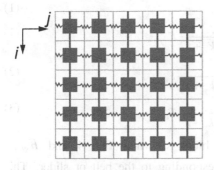

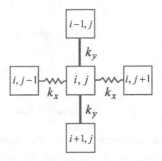

Fig. 3. Blocks on the cell surface. The size of blocks were equal to the cells, but blocks were drawn smaller than actual in this figure for the description of the model.

Fig. 4. Assigned numbers of cells. The springs connecting the blocks in the horizontal direction and the vertical direction had the same spring constant respectively.

2.2   CA Model

CA was applied to the physical model of friction surface. In case of modeling of physical phenomena, the governing equations are needed to understand the phenomena. This method may be applied to general phenomena, so far has yielded a lot of results, but it is not an effective method for the phenomenon that the behavior of the whole is determined by local interactions between the elements constituting the phenomenon. Friction has been introduced into dynamics using the experimental parameters represented by "friction coefficient", and it is obvious that the friction coefficient itself does not represent the phenomenon. Friction may be regarded as a phenomenon in which the behavior of the entire system is emergent by local interactions between the contact points distributed on the contact surface.

Figure 3 shows just one side of the friction surface. The friction surface was modeled by placing the blocks on the contact surface discretized in cell. Blocks might move in the lateral direction on the cell plane. The size of the blocks was equal to those of the cells. In this model, the state variables of cells were the state of "block" or "void". When the state was "block", "position coordinates", "acting force", the state of "touch" or "detach", and "displacement" from the equilibrium position were added as state variables. Blocks were bound to the upper surface of the belt or the lower surface of the slider. The forces acting from the spring to the blocks were considered to act only in the horizontal direction which coincided to moving direction of the belt or slider. This surface constituted a friction surface by facing the other surface. Springs connecting to blocks in the moving direction transmitted only the axial forces, on the other hand, springs connecting the belt or the slider to blocks and spring connecting the blocks to each other in the direction perpendicular to the direction of travel transmitted the shear force. The position of the blocks was expressed symbolically as shown in Fig. 4. When the respective block (i, j) moved to the equilibrium position, the force acting on the block (i, j) changed as follows;

$$F_{i,j} \to 0 \tag{1}$$

$$F_{i,j\pm1} \to F_{i,j\pm1} + \frac{k_x}{2k_x + 2k_y + k_z} F_{i,j} \tag{1}$$

$$F_{i\pm1,j} \to F_{i\pm1,j} + \frac{k_y}{2k_x + 2k_y + k_z} F_{i,j} \tag{2}$$

$$F_{Slider} \to F_{Slider} + \frac{k_z}{2k_x + 2k_y + k_z} F_{i,j} \tag{3}$$

where, the subscript of F is the number of block shown in Fig. 4, and F_{Slider} represents the force acting on the plate corresponding to the belt or slider. This process should be applied at the same time for all blocks, so the forces acting on each block were updated together after they were calculated once. On the other hand, the blocks in "touch" state moved together and force acting on the upper and the lower blocks changed as follows;

$$F_A \to F_A - \frac{K_{SA}(F_A + F_B)}{K_{SA} + K_{SB}} \tag{4}$$

$$F_B \to F_B - \frac{K_{SB}(F_A + F_B)}{K_{SA} + K_{SB}} \tag{5}$$

where, F_A is the force acting on the upper block, F_B is the force acting on the lower block, K_{SA} is the sum of the spring constants surrounding the upper block and K_{SB} is that of the lower block.

Force acting on the slider and the surrounding blocks might change in the following process: Assuming that a spring constant of the spring connecting between the blocks was k.

$$F \to F + k\,dx = F + \frac{k(F_A + F_B)}{K_{SA} + K_{SB}} \tag{6}$$

In addition, if the slider moved dx, the force acting on main body of slider changed, if the number of blocks of the slider was $L_x \times L_y$.

$$F_{Slider} \to F_{Slider} - \left(\sum_{i=1}^{L_y} \sum_{j=1}^{L_x} k_z + k_p \right) dx \tag{7}$$

Then the force acting on the upper surface blocks changed as;

$$F_{i,j} \to F_{i,j} + k_z\,dx \tag{8}$$

With these local neighborhood rules, the transition rules about how to move the slider and the block were determined as follows.

Movement of Blocks to the Balanced Position

Block moved to a position where the force acting on it was balanced and the force acting on the blocks and the main body of slider were calculated. Blocks fixed in upper and lower moved in a direction that balance the forces acting on them in the same manner as one block.

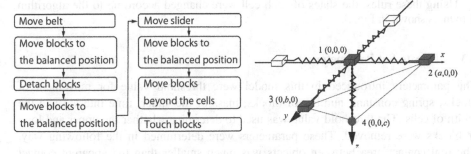

Fig. 5. Algorithm of the CA model

Fig. 6. Tetrahedral element. The node 1, 2, 3 were the blocks adjacent to each other, and the node 4 was the point in the object.

Movement of Blocks beyond Cells

Blocks were moved over a cell in accordance with the movement of the main body of the slider or the belt. In the case that some blocks were in "touch" state, all blocks including the belt side moved together to give priority to the movement of the blocks in the slider side. On the other hand, if there was not any block in "touch" state, the blocks on the slider side moved with the main body of slider and blocks on the side of belt moved with the main body of belt.

Movement of Sliders

Force was applied to the slider body from the springs that connected to the block. If the block moved to a position where the force was balanced, this force became equal to the sum of forces acting between the upper and lower blocks and was deemed to be equal to the force which worked between the belt and the slider. When this force was F, the mass of slider was m and the position of slider was x, the equation of motion of the slider shown in Fig. 2 was

$$m\ddot{x} + k\,x = F \tag{10}$$

and the position and the speed of the slider in each time step was calculated by using numerical integration scheme such as Runge-Kutta method.

Detachment of Blocks

After the belt and blocks were displaced and the force acting on the blocks were balanced, the shearing force acting from the spring on one block and the shear force acting between the blocks lower and upper were balanced. Therefore, it was assumed that the fixation of the upper and lower blocks was removed when the force acting on the block exceeded a threshold value.

Movement of Belt

The belt was forced to move at constant speed in a step and a force was applied to the lower blocks from the springs connecting the lower blocks to the main body of the belt.

Using these rules, the states of each cell were changed according to the algorithm shown as shown in Fig. 5.

2.3   How to Set Parameters

The parameters introduced in this model were threshold value for movement of blocks, spring constant, number of blocks, mass of the slider, time interval and the width of cells. The threshold value was used to determine whether the upper and lower blocks were removed. These parameters were determined in the following way. The real contact area between objects was much smaller than the apparent contact area, therefore the pressure generated in each contact points reached plastic flow pressure. Assuming that they were deviated when the shear stress generated in them exceeded the shear strength, and then the threshold value was proportional to the contact area. Furthermore, if each convex was assumed to be hemispherical and contacting points was only at the top of them, the contact area might be proportional to the height of the protrusion. Then, the threshold was proportional to the sum of the height of the convex portion in contact. The maximum value of the contact area of each block was equal to the area of a rectangle division. The maximum value of the threshold was equal to the maximum shear strength calculated from this area.

To determine the spring constant, the relationship of the affected force and the displacement of the center block were calculated from the rigidity of the tetrahedral element consisting of the central points of the blocks neighboring and a point in the object inside [6]. The surface of the object was assumed to be smooth, and the origin of coordinate system was the position of the center block. The forces acting on each block for the x-axis direction while the center block was moved by u_1 to the x-axis direction were:

$$X_1 = \left(\frac{1}{a^2} + \frac{1}{b^2}\frac{1-2\mu}{2(1-\mu)} + \frac{1}{c^2}\frac{1-2\mu}{2(1-\mu)} \right) \left(\frac{E(1-\mu)}{(1+\mu)(1-2\mu)} \right) V u_1 \tag{9}$$

$$X_2 = -\frac{1}{a^2}\frac{E(1-\mu)V}{(1+\mu)(1-2\mu)}u_1 \tag{10}$$

$$X_3 = -\frac{1}{b^2}\frac{EV}{2(1+\mu)}u_1 \tag{11}$$

$$X_4 = -\frac{1}{c^2}\frac{EV}{2(1+\mu)}u_1 \tag{12}$$

Here, the force and displacement are considered only in x-axis, X_1, X_2, X_3, X_4 are the force acting on each points. a and b are the distance between the blocks next to each other, and c is the depth to consider the deformation of the surface. V is the volume of the tetrahedral element. The spring constants from this element were obtained from the coefficient of these equations, and by overlaying the values obtained from the other elements, the spring constants were determined.

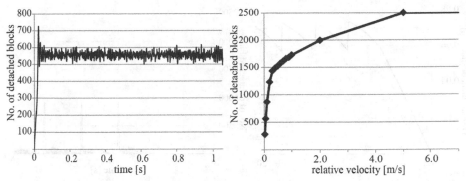

Fig. 7. No. of detached blocks in each time step

Fig. 8. No. of detached blocks in each belt speed

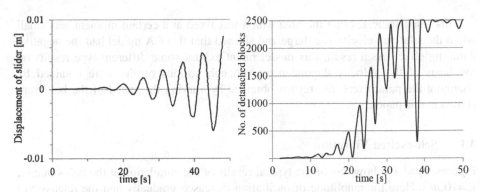

Fig. 9. Displacement of slider in each time step when the amplitude increased gradually ($v_b = 10.0 \ m/s$)

Fig. 10. No. of detached blocks in each time step when the slider moved as shown in Fig. 9

3   Results and Discussions

By using CA model described above, the state and the position of blocks and position and speed of the slider were simulated. In order to investigate the relationship between the number of blocks to be detached at each step and the relative speed of the belt and the slider, the simulation was performed under the condition that the slider was stationary. Figure 7 shows the typical result in this condition. At the first step, all blocks touched to the opposite blocks and force was not applied to the blocks. When the belt moved to the right in Fig. 2, the applied shearing force between the belt and the slider caused a local slip. Thereafter, the number of detached blocks became constant. The number of detached blocks for each relative speed was shown in Fig. 8. Blocks were easily detached with the increase of the belt velocity. The force acting between the upper and the lower blocks was reduced with decreasing of the number of blocks in contact, so the force acting on the slider was decreased with an increase in the relative speed of the belt and the slider.

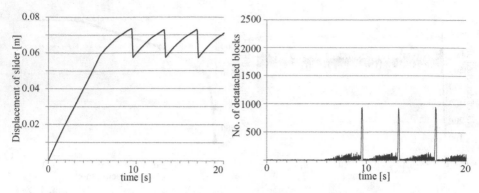

Fig. 11. Displacement of slider in each step when the stick-slip occurred (=0.01m/s)

Fig. 12. No. of detached blocks in each time step when the slider moves as shown in Fig.11

This result indicates that the area which was fixed at a certain moment was small when the relative velocity was large and showed that this CA model had the negative damping effect. As a result, this model might exhibit some different type results on the basis of the velocity dependence. Although various results were obtained by changing the parameters, the results obtained by varying the speed of the belt were shown in this paper.

3.1   Self-excited Vibration

Figures 9 and 10 show one of the typical results of the simulation at the belt velocity, v_b=10 m/s. Here the amplitude of oscillation increased gradually and the relative velocity was also increased. Almost all blocks slipped and just small shear force was applied between the belt and the slider when the amplitude was large. But when the amplitude was large, there existed some interval when the relative velocity was small because the blocks were connected to each other by springs and there still existed a small number of blocks in "touch" state. Under this condition, the amplitude continued to increase, and the movement of slider grew into a self-excited vibration.

3.2   Stick-Slip Vibration

Figures 11 and 12 show other type of vibration when the speed of the belt was changed to 0.01 m/s. There was almost no detached block and the slider moved to the right along with the belt for a few seconds from the beginning. When the belt moved, shear force was applied between the belt and the slider, which caused a decrease of contact area due to local slip. Then the number of detached blocks increased gradually, and many blocks disconnected and slider moved to the left suddenly, thereafter the belt and slider contacted again and began to move to the right together. This phenomenon is called "stick-slip" vibration. Blocks were linked each other, so slips of the blocks were took place in a chain reaction, and this was consistent with the actual phenomenon, and consequently the relationship of slip and increase or decrease of the contact area in the friction surface was reproduced.

4 Conclusions

CA model for friction vibration of a slider on a moving belt was proposed and simulation was performed to reproduce the friction vibration due to the state change of the friction surfaces between solids. As a result, we developed a new CA model which could reproduce the different type of friction vibration; stick-slip vibration and self-excited vibration.

- Stick-slip vibration: When the speed of belt was small, the slider was fixed to the belt by friction force produced at the contact area, and as the force through spring attached to the slider was increased due to displacement of the slider, the contact area was reduced. When the shear force exceeded over a certain threshold value caused by the sum of contact force at contacted blocks, rapid decrease of the contact area was took place and sliding of the entire surface was generated. After the slider slipped on the belt, the shear force decreased and the slider moved again with the belt. The CA model could simulate increase/decrease of the contact area according to the displacement of a slider.
- Self-excited vibration: When the belt speed was large enough, the slider slipped on the belt from the beginning, and small amount of shear force was transmitted from the belt. Even under this condition, several blocks were attached to each other and the belt dragged the slider in the same direction. This drag force caused the growth of amplitude and followed by a self-excited vibration.

Although the present CA model was able to reproduce the variation of contact area between the slider and belt, we will have to present the relation between the contact area variation and the equivalent damping coefficient which has been introduced to describe the phenomenon of self-excited vibration.

References

1. Bowden, F.P., Tabor, D.: The Friction and Lubrication of Solids. Oxford University Press, London (1950)
2. Rubinstein, S.M., Cohen, G., Fineberg, J.: Detachment fronts and the onset of dynamic friction. Naure 430(26), 1005–1009 (2004)
3. Muller, M., Ostermeyer, G.P.: A Cellular Automaton model to describe the three-dimensional friction and wear mechanism of brake systems. Wear 263, 1175–1188 (2007)
4. Burridge, R., Knopoff, L.: Model and Theoretical Seismicity. Bulletin of the Seismoligical Society of America (1967)
5. Olami, Z., Feder, H.J., Chrinstensen, K.: Self-Organized Criticality in a Continuous, Non-conservative Cellular Automaton Modeling Earthquakes. Physical Review Letters 68, 1244–1247 (1992)
6. Seferlind, L.J.: Applied Finit Element Analysis, 2nd edn. John Wiley & Sons (1984)
7. Yamagishi, S., Morishita, S.: Modeling of Stick-Slip Dynamic Behavior by Cellualr Automata. In: Computing and Networking (CANDAR), pp. 540–544 (2013)
8. Nakano, K., Maegawa, S.: Stick-Slip in sliding systems with tangential contact compliance. Tribology International 42, 1771–1780 (2009)

Agent Based Simulation of Spreading in Social-Systems of Temporarily Active Actors

Gergely Kocsis and Imre Varga

University of Debrecen, Faculty of Informatics,
Department of Informatics Systems and Networks,
Kassai Str. 26. H-4028 Debrecen, Hungary
{kocsis.gergely,varga.imre}@inf.unideb.hu
http://www.inf.unideb.hu

Abstract. In this work a novel model of information spreading processes in systems of dynamic active-inactive actors is presented. In our model information can flow only through those actors of the system that are currently active. Based on this model we carried out computer simulations showing how the activity of agents affect the process. We also carried out some basic investigation of the effect of inhomogeneous activity. The results of the work can be used to qualitatively predict what would be the effect if the activity of agents would change in a social system.

Keywords: ABM, spreading, active nodes.

1 Introduction

The investigation of social spreading phenomena is in the focus of research for a couple of decades and the importance of it is still increasing. The main reason of this is that however the fundamentals of the field have been invented at the beginning of the XXth century [1, 2], the importance of it again increased with the appearance of novel social systems of the information society such as online social networks. Information diffusion – and more generally social diffusion phenomena – have been investigated in a huge number of works [3–5]. However in these works the actors of the social system are modeled as always active entities or the activity of them is only marginally mentioned. This assumption however does not represent the real properties of these actors. Contrary to the above works here we investigate the effect of inactivity of agents on spreading phenomena e.g. on the spreading of information on a social network. To be able to focus on the effect of the temporal change of activity of agents itself, we extend a previously introduced model of information spreading and study the resulting differences. We examine homogeneous activity on different types of networks from regular lattices to scale-free networks. At the end we also analyze the effect of inhomogeneous activity based on realistic data. One final goal of ours is to find an answer to the question: ,,How inactivity of actors of a social system affect spreading phenomena in it and what can we do to make this spreading faster?".

J. Wąs, G.C. Sirakoulis, and S. Bandini (Eds.): ACRI 2014, LNCS 8751, pp. 330–338, 2014.
© Springer International Publishing Switzerland 2014

Though the exact validation of the answer of such a question is far from being trivial, based on our results one can get an idea e.g. how to make an advertising campaign more effective, by making some actors more active than others. Then later the results of these actions can be measured by advertising effectiveness measuring indicators such as number of visitors of a homepage, or number of downloads of a given paper.

2   Model

In our model the actors of the social system are represented by interacting agents put on a given network topology. All agents have the following properties to describe them: $S_i \in \{0, 1\}$ tells if agent i is informed or not. $R_i \in \{0, 1\}$ describes whether an agent inactive or active. There are 3 system wide properties as well. These properties describe the agents, but we set the values of them to be equal for all of them so that analytical investigation of the model becomes more easy. α shows how sensitive an agent is for information coming from its neighbors. β shows the sensitivity of agents for outer information. These two parameters were presented in a previous model in [6]. Finally the probabilistic value γ tells how often agents go inactive. For all three values $\alpha, \beta, \gamma \in [0, 1] \in \mathbb{R}$. Larger values are for more sensitivity and more probability of being inactive respectively.

Since α, β and γ are equal for all agents, and do not change during the evolution of the model agents can be at four different states that are the following:

σ_0	active-uninformed	$R = 1, S = 1$
σ_1	inactive-uninformed	$R = 0, S = 1$
σ_2	active-informed	$R = 1, S = 0$
σ_3	inactive-informed	$R = 0, S = 0$

Led by the states of their neighbors and their environment, agents can stochastically change their own states at discrete points of time following the below described state change rules.

Active-uninformed (σ_0) agents can go to *inactive-uninformed* state σ_1 with possibility γ. They can get informed – meaning that they switch to active-informed σ_2 state with probability $(1 - \gamma)A$, where A tells the probability of getting informed based on the current state of the agent, its neighbors, and the environment. The meaning of A is described in details below. From the previous 2 rules it comes clearly, that agents at state σ_0 can also stay in the same state with probability $(1 - \gamma)(1 - A)$. *Inactive-uninformed* (σ_1) agents can change their state to *active-uninformed* (σ_0) with probability $(1 - \gamma)$ while with probability γ they can also stay at the same state (σ_1). In our model *informed* agents can not go uninformed, thus *active-informed* (σ_2) agents can choose only between two possibilities at each timestep: With probability γ they can turn *inactive-informed* (σ_3) and with probability $(1 - \gamma)$ they can stay *active*. Finally *inactive-informed* (σ_3) agents also stay *inactive-informed* with probability γ and change to *active-informed* with probability $(1 - \gamma)$. Summarizing the above rules we can say that agents go or stay *inactive* with probability γ and go or stay active with probability $(1 - \gamma)$. Only active agents can affect and be affected by other agents. And only *active-uninformed* can turn informed with probability $(1 - \gamma)A$, where A is presented later in eq. 1. On Fig. 1 one can follow these rules more easily.

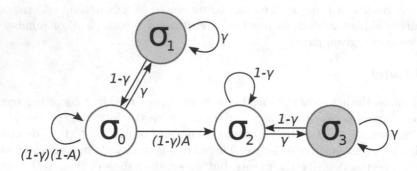

Fig. 1. State-change rules of agents of our model. Red circles are for uninformed agents while green ones are for informed agents. Grey filled circles are for inactive states. With probability γ agents go/stay inactive and with probability $1 - \gamma$ they go/stay active. The information of active-uninformed agents follow the rule presented in [6].

The most crucial state change in our model is the change from uninformed (σ_0) state to informed (σ_2). This rule is motivated by the model presented in a previous work [6]. This model describes information spreading as the consequence of the competition of two separate information channels. Namely agents get information from an outer channel, and from their neighbors. As it was written above in our model α and β tells how sensitive agents are to the information sources. Based on these parameters and the new ones catching the activity of agents, the probability that an active agent goes informed is again $(1 - \gamma)A$, where A is

$$A = 1 - exp(\alpha S_i R_i \sum_{j=1}^{n_i} ((1 - S_j)R_j) + \beta S_i R_i),\qquad(1)$$

where n_i is the number of neighbors of agent i. It is important to emphasize again that in our case however all agents have the same values for α and β only active agents can spread and receive information. This phenomenon is also caught in eq. 1, where in the $exp()$ function we describe the incoming information to an agent as the following: If an agent is not informed and active it can receive information from their active informed neighbors. The amount of information coming from them is multiplied by the respective sensitivity α. After this if again the agent is *active-uninformed* it receives information from the outside. This amount is again multiplied by the sensitivity to it β.

3   Results of Computer Simulations

To investigate the time evolution of our model for different parameters on different network topologies, we carried out computer simulations. In all our simulations the system size was set to $N = 10^6$. the sensitivity values, based on previous studies of ours [6] were $\alpha = 10^{-2}$ and $\beta = 10^{-4}$.

3.1 Results on Square Lattice

At first we sit our agents on a square lattice topology with periodic boundary condition. This makes visualization of the system very easy so we can get a look into the evolution of the system through snapshots of it. Fig. 2 shows snapshots of the system at three different points of time. It can be seen clearly that the evolution of the system shows much similarity to the referred model. At first some random agents get informed due to the outer information channel. After a time these agents serve as nucleation points of growing clusters while as time passes the whole system tends to arrive to a homogeneous informed state. The effect of the activity property of agents comes visible if we take a look at the time needed for the system to arrive to its final state. It can be seen at the first sight that the dynamic activity of agents dramatically slows down spreading however the evolution of the system does not show other qualitative changes.

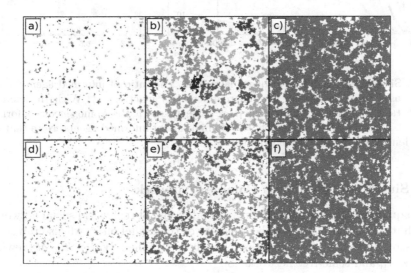

Fig. 2. Snapshots of the system on a square lattice taken at different points of time. a, b and c) shows the case of 0 inactivity. d, e and f) are for non zero inactivity ($\gamma = 0.5$). $t = 100, 250, 375$ respectively for a, b and c while $t = 350, 800, 1250$ respectively for d, e and f. Note that while the qualitative behavior of the system does not change with the raised level of inactivity, the evolution of it dramatically slows down.

In order to get a better insight of this slowing we analyzed the amount of informed agents in the system during its evolution. The results of plotting the percentage of informed agents in the system ($\sigma_2 + \sigma_3$) as a function of time are presented on Fig. 3. The first important information of this figure is that the shape of the curves on Fig. 3 a) follows the well known logistic form that usually appears in the case of diffusion processes. It can also be seen clearly that however the spreading process shows the same fashion regardless of the value of γ the time needed to reach the state where 95% the agents are informed $t_{\langle S \rangle = 0.95}$ is not a linear function of γ. Even, from the semi-logarithmic scale of Fig 3 b) it can be seen that this dependence is faster than exponential. The reason why we chose to examine $t_{\langle S \rangle = 0.95}$ instead of $t_{\langle S \rangle = 1}$ is that the spreading slows down so much close to the homogeneous state that $t_{\langle S \rangle = 1} \to \infty$, however $t_{\langle S \rangle = 0.95}$ still fits our needs while the respective value can be reached in a reasonable time.

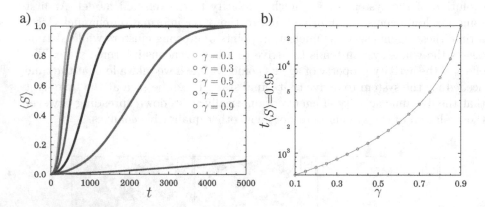

Fig. 3. Simulation results on a square lattice. a) The ratio of informed agents in the system as a function of time for different levels of inactivity γ. With the increase of γ it takes non-linearly more and more time to reach the homogeneous informed state. b) The time needed to reach 95% domination of informed agents. Note that the dependence on γ is faster than exponential.

3.2   Simulation Results on Complex Networks

Since square lattice is far from being a good model of real world social networks, now that we got an insight to the behavior of the model on it, we also ran simulations on more complex networks. Namely we applied *Watts-Strogatz* rewired lattices [7], and scale-free networks [8].

The rewired lattices generated by the method invented by Watts and Strogatz are still pretty far from real social network topologies however they have two very important properties. *i*.) These are one of the most simple networks known to have small-world property that is a fundamental property of real social network topologies as well. *ii*.) By tuning the rewiring probability between two extreme cases of p ($p = 0$ and $p = 1$) we can map the behavior of our model continuously from regular lattices to networks much closer to the real form of social network topologies.

Since the most crucial parameter of rewired lattices is the rewiring probability p we carried out simulations for different values of γ while we ran p continuously between 0 and 1. Fig. 4 a) clearly shows that the domination time $t_{\langle S \rangle = 0.95}$

decreases with the growing of p and this is independent of the actual value of γ. One can even possibly say that this dependence follows a power law at least at the first half of the interval $[0, 1]$. However because of the short range of values and the obvious differences at the very beginning and at the end we more likely state that these curves are just close to follow a power law. Comparing Fig. 3 b) and Fig. 4 b) shows that the qualitative time evolution of the model does not change if we switch from a regular square lattice to a rewired lattice (on the figure rewiring probability $p = 0.9$, however we found similar pictures for other values of p as well).

As it is well-known in the literature that realistic social networks have scale-fee property, we also performed simulations on these types of networks. Namely we used the model invented by Varga et. al. to generate networks with the proper parameters [9, 10]. To get realistic results, these networks are similar to the topology of Facebook (based on the Facebook sample of Koblenz Network Collection [11]). Our results showed hardly any difference between the case of a scale-free network and rewired lattices. This means that while rewiring probability p has some effect on the spreading (see Fig. 4 a)), other topological properties do not affect its nature. The result of these simulations are presented on Fig. 4 b).

3.3   The Effect of Inhomogeneous Activity

In all the previous cases we assumed that however the probability of being inactive γ can be set between 0 and 1 continuously, the chosen value is system wide. This mean that we handle all the agents of the system as if they were similar. It is easy to see that this assumption is far from being realistic. However previous

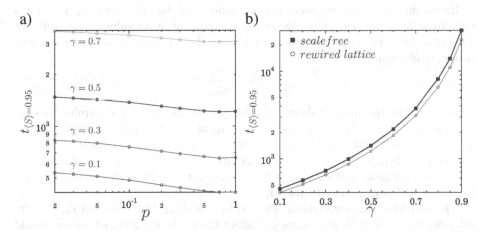

Fig. 4. Simulation results on complex networks. a) The time needed by the system to evolve to a state where 95% of the agents are informed $t_{\langle S \rangle = 0.95}$ as a function of the rewiring probability p. $t_{\langle S \rangle = 0.95}$ is decreasing almost following a power law. b) The information time of the system increases faster than exponential with the increase of γ for rewired lattice and for scale-free networks as well.

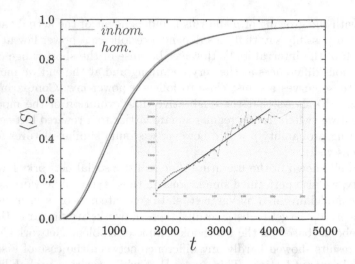

Fig. 5. Time evolution of the system in cases of homogeneous and inhomogeneous activity. Note that there is even quantitatively hardly any difference between the two curves. This means that the increased activity of high degree nodes does not make the spreading much faster without increasing activity of law degree nodes. *inset*: The activity of nodes depends linearly on their degree [12].

studies showed that the activity of agents of a social system depends linearly on the number of contacts. More precisely on a social network if we draw the amount of posts of agents as a function of the number of their connections we see an almost linear trend [12] (see inset of Fig. 5).

Based on this result we modified our model, so that the value of γ is not a system-wide parameter anymore, but it can change of its value γ_i for different i agents. To catch the above mentioned linear dependence we set the inactivity property of agents to:

$$\gamma_i = \gamma(1 - \frac{n_i}{n_{max}}), \tag{2}$$

where n_{max} is the highest degree in the system and n_i is the number of connections of agent i. As a result of this the agent with the highest degree will be almost always active and the agents with low degree go/stay inactive in each timestep with a probability $\gamma_i \to \gamma$. Or more simply, we make higher degree nodes linearly more active, so that the system gets closer to the real case, while it can be still parametrized through γ.

The results of our simulations showed that making the agents of the system inhomogeneous in this sense does not affect the evolution as much as one would expect (see Fig. 5). Based on our previous knowledge that emphasize the importance of high degree nodes of the system it would not be surprising if we would find that making these nodes more active makes the spreading dramatically faster. In contrary however according to our simulations this speeding up does not happen. The reason of this is that however high degree nodes are connected to many low degree nodes, because the inactivity of these latter ones information can not be sent or received. The result of this is that however high degree nodes try to be much more active than before, they find no agents to interact with. From the above results it comes clearly that if one wants to increase the speed of spreading on a social network he has to take care to increase or at least do not decrease the activity of low degree nodes as well.

This statement also has a practical meaning for example advertisers on social networks. It tells us that if one would like to improve the effectiveness of an advertising campaign it is not enough to focus on central nodes. The increasing of the activity of marginal parts of the network is also essential.

4 Discussion

In this paper we introduced a novel model of spreading phenomena on social systems where the actors are active only in a given part of their time. Based on computer simulations we showed that the increased inactivity of agents slows down the spreading however this change does not have a qualitative effect. We ran our simulations on systems with different network topologies (square lattice, rewired lattice, scale-free network). In all cases we found that the time needed for the system to reach an almost homogeneous informed state depends on the probability of an agent to be inactive as a faster than exponential function. In the most realistic case, where the network topology was a scale-free network, we also examined the effect of inhomogeneous inactivity. We found that the increased activity of central nodes can not make the spreading faster if in the same time the activity of peripheral actors is not increased. Based on these results, in the future we would like to investigate the system using different sensitivity of actors. In our later plans we would also like to test our model on more dynamic networks. We would also like to apply our model outside social networks e.g. in the case of wireless sensor networks.

Acknowledgments. The publication was supported by the TÁMOP-4.2.2. C-11/1/KONV-2012-0001 project. The project has been supported by the European Union, co-financed by the European Social Fund.

References

1. Rogers, E.M.: Diffusion of Innovations, 5th edn. Free Press, New York (2003), ISBN: 0-7432-2209-1
2. Weidlich, W.: Sociodynamics: A systematic approach to mathematical modelling in the social sciences, pp. 113–187. Dover Publications, Mineola (2000)
3. Newman, M.E.J.: Networks - An introduction, University of Michigan and Santa Fe Institute, pp. 627–675. Oxford University Press (2010)
4. Couzin, I.D., Ioannou, C.C., Demirel, G., Gross, T., Torney, C.J., Hartnett, A., Conradt, L., Levin, S.A., Leonard, N.E.: Uninformed individuals promote democratic consensus in animal groups. Science 332(6062), 1578–1580 (2011)

5. Apolloni, A., Channakeshava, K., Durbeck, L., Khan, M., Kuhlman, C., Lewis, B., Swarup, S.: A Study of Information Diffusion over a Realistic Social Network Model. In: Proceedings of CSE 2009, Vancouver, Canada, August 29-31 (2009)
6. Kocsis, G., Kun, F.: Competition of information channels in the spreading of innovations. Physical Review E 84, 2 (2011)
7. Watts, D.J., Strogatz, S.H.: Collective dynamics of "small-world" networks. Nature 393, 440–442 (1998)
8. Barabási, A., Albert, R.: Emergence of scaling in random networks. Science 286, 509–512 (1999)
9. Varga, I., Németh, A., Kocsis, G.: A novel method of generating tunable underlying network topologies for social simulation. In: Proceedings of 4th IEEE International Conference on Cognitive Infocommunicaitons, pp. 71–74 (2013)
10. Varga, I., Kocsis, G.: Generating network topologies with clustering similar to online social networks. Submitted as pre-proceedings to SMSEC 2014 (2014)
11. Gjoka, M., Kurant, M., Butts, C.T., Markopoulou, A.: Walking in Facebook: A Case Study of Unbiased Sampling of OSNs. In: Proceedings of IEEE INFOCOM 2010, San Diego, CA (2010)
12. Huberman, B.A., Romero, D.M., Wu, F.: Social networks that matter: Twitter under the microscope. First Monday 14 1 (2009)

Cellular Automata for Modeling Language Change

William A. Kretzschmar[1] and Ilkka Juuso[2]

[1] Department of English, Park 317, University of Georgia, Athens, GA 30602, USA
[2] Department of Computer Science and Engineering, Erkki Koiso-Kanttilan Katu 3,
FIN-90014 University of Oulu, Finland
kretzsch@uga.edu, ilkka.juuso@ee.oulu.fi

Abstract. This paper describes the use of cellular automata to model dialect feature diffusion as the adaptive aspect of the complex system of speech. We show how a feature, once established, can spread across an area, and how the distribution of a dialect feature as it stands in Linguistic Atlas data could either spread or diminish. Throughout hundreds of iterations, we can watch regional and social distribution patterns emerge as a consequence of update rules. We validate patterns with respect to the linguistic distributions known to occur in the Linguistic Atlas Project.

Keywords: Cellular automata, complex systems, language variation, simulation.

1   Introduction

There are many uses to which a cellular automaton (CA) may be put, but to date language change has not been very prominent in the list. We are aware of only three earlier descriptions of CAs in language variation studies, none of them very extensive. Thus our use of a CA is the first that we know about that builds a comprehensive, GIS-aware framework for analysis and that uses real survey data from the American Linguistic Atlas Project. Moreover, our CA is designed explicitly to model language change within the framework of complexity science. We model dialect feature diffusion as the adaptive aspect of the complex system of speech. We show how a feature, once established, can spread across an area, and how the distribution of a dialect feature as it stands in Linguistic Atlas data could either spread or diminish. Throughout hundreds of iterations, we can watch regional and social distribution patterns emerge as a consequence of update rules. Finally, we validate patterns with respect to the linguistic distributions known to occur in the Linguistic Atlas Project.

In the three earlier discussions of CAs to represent language change, Kretzschmar 1992 described the operation of a CA for the purpose of language diffusion studies, Keller 1994 reported unpublished work on an early cellular automaton that he compared to linguistic distributions, and Grieve, Speelman, and Geeraerts 2010 implemented a CA for presentation at a linguistics conference but without specific discussion of how its operation illustrated language interaction. Kretzschmar 1992 described the rule-based process from CAs but his experiments were not automated. Keller (1994: 100-101) reports the work of Jules Levin from an otherwise unpublished

J. Wąs, G.C. Sirakoulis, and S. Bandini (Eds.): ACRI 2014, LNCS 8751, pp. 339–348, 2014.

1988 mimeograph from the University of California-Riverside. Levin had created a small (55 x 55 cells) CA, in which he randomly seeded black and white cells. Keller reports Levin's rules as having the target cell stay the same if all of its neighbors had the same status, and that a white cell had a 51% chance of staying white if four of its neighbors were white and four were black; this process produced clustered results when run over many iterations. Keller quotes Levin (1994: 101) as saying that "I regard this as only a very primitive and abstract preliminary model that hopefully mimics linguistic interaction." None of these discussions implement a CA that follows the principles of GIS, including geocoding locations, allowing for boundary effects, and following principles such as the inverse square rule for the effects of distance on influence. Moreover, none of the earlier discussions specifies a theoretical framework for using the CA as a model, as we do with complex systems. We believe, therefore, that we are breaking new ground with our CA, both in its technical development and in its theoretical motivation.

1.1   Language Change and Diffusion

Language change is usually considered from the point of view of the language as a system. Linguistics as a science began in the nineteenth century when an academic movement known as the Neogrammarians promoted the idea that language operates mechanically, in contrast to earlier spiritual and prescriptive notions. Since that time linguists, and members of the public as well, uphold the idea of language as a static, hierarchical system, beginning with elementary education in language arts where children are taught that language has a grammar and that they should observe its rules. Subsequently, language change has been considered as a regular, mechanical process. The two variations on this process most often cited are NeoGrammarian change and lexical diffusion (see Kerswill 2002: 188). In either NeoGrammarian change or lexical diffusion, the outcome of change is that the pronunciation of a segment within a word class has a new value when compared to the pronunciation of the same segment at a previous time. When a number of such changes are grouped together using the classic method of comparative and historical linguistics, the result is differentiation of languages over time as represented in the standard stemma of the Indo-European language family. More recently, John Nerbonne has used advanced statistical methods to measure the effects of the wave theory and the gravity model on linguistic diffusion (2010). Nerbonne applies the technique of Levenshtein distance (or edit distance) to aggregated data as a dialectometric measure of how different the locations in a geographic area might be. Nerbonne found that, while the gravity model based on different population sizes might account for about 6% of the variance in the aggregated data, geography accounted for 16% to 37% of the variation (2010: 11). Here, too, the emphasis is on the system, the binary difference between an original state and a changed state at different locations in the aggregated data. Whether we consider NeoGrammarian change or lexical diffusion, and however we measure diffusion, according to the usual view we see that change is binary -- one state of a phoneme becomes another state, an individual adopts a feature or does not -- and the binary change is considered to mark the status of two different linguistic systems.

1.2   Complex Systems

In opposition to the usual view of change, it is possible to see that the process of diffusion certainly occurs as a result of cultural interaction -- massive numbers of people talking (and more recently writing) to each other. As opposed to the traditional approaches to linguistic diffusion within linguistic systems, we can choose to consider what all of the people say, rather than just consider that one element in a grammar becomes different over time. The scientific model that best fits this process is called complex systems, or complex adaptive systems.

Complex systems, as described in physics, evolutionary biology, and many other sciences, are made up of massive numbers of components continually interacting with one another, and this results in self-organization and emergent order. For speech (as described in Kretzschmar 2009, 2010), the randomly interacting components correspond to all of the different variant realizations of linguistic features as they are deployed by human agents, speakers. These variants might be different pronunciations, or different words for the same thing, or different ways of saying or writing the same thing, i.e. any aspect of speech that is recognizable for itself and therefore countable. The activity in the system consists of all of our conversations and writing. The exchange of information is not the same as sharing the meaningful content of what we say and write (which is exchange in a different sense), but instead our implicit comparison of the use of different components by different speakers and writers, as they use them in different kinds of conversations and writings. Such a comparison involves the exchange of information between speakers on a different level, but not less significantly, than the linguistic message: we speakers are always measuring ourselves against one another with language and with other aspects of culture like clothing styles, foodways, or social expectations for interpersonal behavior, in order to negotiate our membership in all of the different regional and social populations in which we participate. Our feedback from the exchange of information in conjunction with different populations causes reinforcement, in that speakers and writers are more likely to employ particular components in future occurrences of particular circumstances for conversations and writing. We learn what works best for us in our different context groups, and we make choices between linguistic variants, or other aspects of communication culture, that suit our particular situation at any moment. So, if we are in New York, we should not think that the language is bad because it does not sound like London. Similarly, we talk and write differently in the different situations of our lives, whether we are within the family or in a classroom or in a courtroom. It is thus evident that every individual must command different variant realizations of any feature, and groups of speakers must maintain an inventory of different variants of any feature, in order to allow different choices for different situations. Human agents can think about and choose how to deploy linguistic variants, but that does not change the basic operation of feedback and reinforcement; we all make choices inside of the complex system of speech, in relation to current circumstances.

The order that emerges in speech when considered as a complex system is not grammar as we usually think of it, but instead the frequency profile of different possible variants, whether particular words, pronunciations, or constructions, that come to occur in particular situations. When we consider the evidence from a linguistic survey such as the American Linguistic Atlas Project, a great many more variants per linguistic feature than we might imagine are in competition, often fifty or one hundred or even more choices. Just a few of these are very common, while most are rare, which creates a nonlinear profile. An additional property of emergence is scaling: the nonlinear shape of the frequency pattern is about the same at every scale and for every group (see Kretzschmar, Kretzschmar, and Brockman 2013 for differences in curves at different scales), but different variants have different relative frequencies at different scales. These frequency differences, the result of feedback in the complex system, differentiate the speech of different groups of people.

Consideration of the complex system of speech, then, differs essentially from work on traditional models of diffusion. Rather than any hierarchical system of linguistic types in which entries change over time, what changes in a complex system is the frequency of individual variants in the nonlinear profile. Rather than having a single value for a linguistic feature change from one state to another in any traditional model of diffusion, a binary change, the complex system of speech always has large numbers of competing variants which all change in frequency over time. Moreover, the scaling factor of complex systems accounts for the simultaneous coexistence of many varieties of the same language because the patterns of frequencies for different variants will be different for different populations, at the same time that we can describe the pattern of frequencies for a population as a whole.

We therefore require an environment for modeling linguistic change within a complex system. Our CA is an ideal tool for this. As described by Wolfram (2002), CAs are known to produce patterns over the course of many iterations of the right simple rules. Many rule sets quickly turn all locations in a grid on or off, or resolve quickly into fixed patterns. Some rule sets create ever-changing, chaotic behavior. However, a few rule sets create complex behavior, such as the emergence of stable clusters, and this is what we attempt to achieve in our CA.

2   A Linguistically Motivated Cellular Automaton

In this paper we investigate the possibility of using a CA as an environment for modeling linguistic change according to concepts adapted from linguistics and the theory of complex systems. To facilitate the work we have developed a versatile CA in Javascript for use inside HTML5-capable browsers such as Google Chrome. The CA supports the use of geocoded data from linguistic surveys to run a range of simulations to both better understand linguistic phenomena captured by the original data and, as we do in this paper, create plausible models of linguistic change over time. In the work described here we use linguistic data and social metadata obtained from the Linguistic Atlas of the Middle and South Atlantic States (LAMSAS) for 1162 speakers surveyed across the eastern seaboard of the United States.

2.1   Working with Survey Data

In order to ground our investigations in real linguistic data, we seed the CA with data on the occurrence of linguistic features and the social characteristics of the speakers employing each feature as obtained from the Linguistic Atlas of the Middle and South Atlantic States (LAMSAS). The LAMSAS data consists of 1162 interviews conducted from the 1930s onwards across the eastern seaboard of the United States, from northern Florida to upstate New York and inland to Georgia and West Virginia. The dataset contains short speaker biographies, a set of key social metadata for each speaker and the responses each speaker gave to a range of survey questions designed to elicit lexical, grammatical and phonetic features of language use.

The CA is designed as a square matrix of user-definable proportions that forms a grid of geocoded cells to cover the whole survey area. For working with the LAMSAS data we have set the CA to a size of 151 x 151, which gives us a grid of 22801 geocoded cells, out of which 8600 cells fall within the survey area. The geocoded survey data is projected onto this grid yielding 1162 cells, or 13.5% of all cells, with real data on the linguistic features elicited at these locations and the social characteristics of the speakers from whom the features were elicited. Figure 1 shows the seeded CA.

Fig. 1. All survey locations. Black cells represent locations where one or more features were elicited from a speaker in the survey, white cells represent locations in-between survey locations, and grey cells represent locations outside the survey region. Note that some padding is introduced around the edges of the survey area.

Each of the 1162 cells represents a single speaker from the original survey data and has information on the social characteristics of the speaker and the responses they gave to each of the survey questions. The social characteristics include for each speaker the sex (male/female), age (in years), education level (a 7-step classification), occupation type (a 13-type classification), residence type (urban/rural) and the aggregate informant type (a 3-step classification) as assigned by the survey. The linguistic data is organized by survey question so that, for example, loading in question L6#2 of the survey seeds the CA with all 109 different terms used for *thunderstorm* by the speakers. In the current implementation of the CA we can load in all of the social data and all of the responses for a selected question and then run simulations using rules addressing both the pure proximity and the social similarity of adjacent cells.

Only 13.5% of the operational cells have social metadata. The lack of social metadata is not an issue for simulations using proximity-only rules, but for investigating the impact of different social contexts it is a pronounced issue. To generate social metadata for the remaining 7438 cells within the survey area we developed an interpolation mechanism that considers both the local context and the overall global context when assigning social characteristics to new cells. The interpolation process is integrated into the running of the CA so that social metadata is only created when a new cell is activated (i.e. gains a linguistic feature for the first time) and is then retained for the remainder of the simulation. It is also possible to run the interpolation as a pre-processing step where a set of relaxed birth and survival rules are used to grow the pattern from existing cells until all of the artificial cells have social metadata and then this metadata is saved for later use. Using the CA mechanism to interpolate social metadata ensures that for each interpolation we have a neighborhood of a certain size around the cell to base the calculations on. This way the assigned metadata values both adhere to their original global proportions but are also appropriate in their local context, e.g. we get mostly rural cells in rural areas and mostly urban cells is urban areas.

The process of assigning social metadata for newborn cells is based on the extended neighborhood ($N=10$) around each cell and the global proportions of each social feature value in the original seed. The local neighborhood is tallied using inverse square weighting by neighborhood order, and the resulting local proportion (L) for each value is then adjusted towards the corresponding global proportion of that value among all the possible values (G) by a set level of influence ($i=0.02$) using Equation 1. Those values that are not found in the local neighborhood receive a base proportion (L_b) based on Equation 2, indicating that the values could be found just outside the local neighborhood. These combined proportions (S) are then interpreted as scores for each feature value and used to set up a lottery space, where each value has a likelihood of being assigned for a given social feature that is proportionate to how common the value is in both the local and the global context. Finally, a single value is selected for each social feature by drawing a random number inside the lottery space and assigning the corresponding value.

$$S = (L + i(L-G))/(1+i) \tag{1}$$

$$L_b = 1/(N+1)^2 \tag{2}$$

The CA provides tools to evaluate the appropriateness of each outcome produced by the social feature lottery. Firstly, it is possible to compare how the proportions of each value for each feature have changed as a result of the lottery using a combined chart display. Secondly, the CA provides color-coded views over the grid showing both the old and the new locations for each value of a selected feature. Using these tools to verify the outcomes we created a test set of three different seeds, marked as seeds A, B and C, for our investigations here. Each seed has social characteristics (sex, age, education, occupation, urban/rural residence, and informant type) in the same proportions for both the original seed cells, representing real survey speakers, and for the in-between cells, representing new artificial speakers.

2.2   Rule Processing

The CA supports running simulations with rules addressing both the pure proximity and the social similarity of adjacent cells. The proximity-based rules address eight neighbors in the immediate neighborhood of each cell. Similarly, the socially-motivated rules choose eight socially similar neighbors from an extended neighborhood of cells up to two orders away (N=2). The CA supports elaborate recipes for social similarity consisting of weights and allowable differences in values for one or more selected social features. For the work presented in this paper we consider the social influence as a second-order phenomenon (25%), and therefore combine the proximity and social neighborhood votes applying a 75/25 ratio. In other words, a neighboring cell will get a 0.75 vote based on proximity and may get an extra vote of up to 0.25 if it meets the criteria for social similarity.

3   Observing Emergence

Emergence is the defining property of complex systems, the appearance of order out of interactions. The most important question for our work on the CA is what emergence looks like on a map.

3.1   Proximity

In order to observe emergence, we apply a rule in which 2, 3, or 4 neighbors in the first-order neighborhood are needed to turn a location on, and 5, 6, 7, or 8 neighbors are needed to keep a location on. We often use all 1162 locations of the survey speakers as a starting position; we have also used a seed with a small number of locations turned on for at least one location. Running the CA always fills the matrix with live cells, given at least one sufficiently dense group of live locations at the start. We know that the CA has produced a successful simulation if it produces dense, stable clusters of the kind we always observe in the real data. Figure 2 illustrates the comparison. The left side of Figure 2 shows a map of the dialect feature *lounge* (a variant name for a sofa) prepared with the statistical technique of density estimation (DE; see Kretzschmar and Light 1996), which estimates the likelihood of elicitation of a dialect feature at 3000 locations in the survey area. The right side of the figure shows the display of a state from the CA which shows similar dense clusters in a background of constantly changing locations.

Stable clusters emerge from the general interaction at between 500 and 1000 iterations. Introduction of a small random element that changes the decision for a location (eg. 0.01% to 0.05%) slows down the formation and changes the location of stable clusters; random elements over 0.06% throw the CA from a complex state into a chaotic state where no clusters are produced. Clusters do not appear where we expect them (e.g. a cluster for squall may appear in the mountains rather than along the coast where we expect it), because we have not built contingency into the model. Contingencies such as demographic shifts and movements (e.g., westward migration in America) help to shape actual locations of variant distributions.

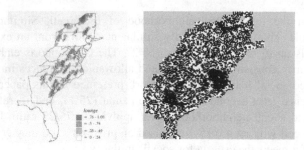

Fig. 2. A DE display of real data (left) and the CA state at 500 iterations (right)

In order to see the clusters better, we use two different visualizations as shown in Figure 3. The right-side map in Figure 2 shows the standard view CA after 500 iterations, starting from the locations of the 1162 LAMSAS speakers. The left-side map in Figure 3 shows a view which fades the color of locations that have only been on for one iteration (i.e. new born cells). Since the CA generates a nonlinear model of cell ages, this view fades a very large number of live cells. The remaining clusters show up clearly, whether small or large ones. The right-side map in Figure 3 shows the age view, which shows active cells at levels of darkness corresponding to their age, the oldest cells being the darkest. This view indicates that many of the clusters in the fade new born view are temporary, and that longer-term stable clusters do emerge from the CA.

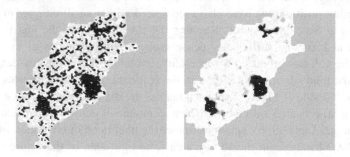

Fig. 3. Fade new born view (left) and Age view (right)

If the CA is run for 5000 iterations using the described rules, the large stable clusters eventually fill the matrix. Thus the CA may be seen to operate in stages, an initial period where the starting position expands to fill the matrix at approximately 50% density of active cells (c. 200 iterations), a period in which stable clusters begin to form (from 200 to 1000 iterations), and a final extended period where the stable clusters expand to fill the matrix at a high density of active cells.

3.2   Social Similarity Weighting

We have also used social metadata to influence decisions at locations. Clusters regularly emerge when we select socially similar locations from among the second order neighbors (24 possible locations instead of 8), and weight the social influence as a second-order phenomenon (25%). We have created multiple separate interpolations of social metadata to the cells of the matrix not occupied by any of the original 1162 speakers. Each interpolation creates a starting position with social metadata in the same proportion across the matrix as the proportions among the original survey speakers, but with different metadata for different particular locations. These different starting positions work equivalently to produce clusters, but create the clusters at different locations. Figure 4 illustrates the differences between three starting positions, labeled A, B, and C. Figure 5a shows the age view of the state of the CA after 500 iterations, when the evaluation process using the 2,3,4/5,6,7,8 rule set is weighted by the age of the speakers, where speakers were considered to be similar if their age was within plus or minus ten years, and where the impact of the social metadata was considered to be 25%. Similar age is thus considered to be a second-order factor, less important than immediate proximity and equivalent to a neighbor two units away. Clusters have clearly formed, similar to those in Figure 3b. Figures 4b and 4c also show the age view after 500 iterations with similar weighting by age, only for two different starting positions. We see that clusters have emerged from these starting positions as well, only in different parts of the matrix.

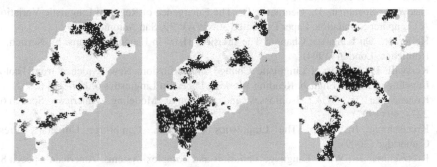

Fig. 4. Three different seeds for *age* as a criterion of social similarity: Seed A (left),   Seed   B (middle) and Seed C (right). Any cells within ±10 years are considered socially equal. All states have been captured using the Age view at 1000 iterations.

Thus social similarity interacts with proximity and operates in the CA model according to the same kind of simple interactional rules, not according to complicated psychological conditioning sometimes described in sociolinguistics.

4   Future Work and Conclusion

Finally, we have now set up the CA to run multiple variants simultaneously, and to process both immediate proximity and six different social tracks at the same time. Initial testing shows that all variants that survive the first few iterations, typically 10% to 15% of the hundred or more variants for many items, all rise to a saturation of about 50% in the matrix and then slowly build stable clusters. Processing so many variants and so many social tracks all at the same time comes at the cost of much slower processing times. Still, we believe that multidimensional processing of this kind may help us to produce the nonlinear distributional patterns we expect to see in real sample data, as the output of a complex system. So far, we do see a nonlinear frequency profile in the ages of different live locations on the matrix, and we hope to be able to generate a similar nonlinear profile among the many variants for any item we process.

We are pleased at this point to have created a CA that does allow us to observe the emergence of clusters for single features, both on the basis of immediate proximity in the Moore neighborhood and with weighting for social characteristics. In other work we have also shown that the CA can be used to make generalizations based immediately on the original survey data. Combining these two aspects, we believe it is now possible to model speech with a CA, in much the same way that CAs can model behavior in many other disciplines.

References

1. Abrams, D., Strogatz, S.: Linguistics: Modelling the Dynamics of Language Death. Nature 424(6951), 900 (2003)
2. Grieve, J., Speelman, D., Geeraerts, D.: The Emergence of Regional Linguistic Variation: A Computer Simulation. Paper Presented at NWAV 39, San Antonio (2010)
3. Keller, R.: On Language Change: The Invisible Hand in Language, Trans. by Nerlich, B. Routledge, London (1994)
4. Kerswill, P.: Models of Linguistic Change and Diffusion: New Evidence from Dialect Leveling in British English. Reading Working Papers in Linguistics 6, 187–216 (2002)
5. Kretzschmar Jr., W.A.: Isoglosses and Predictive Modeling. American Speech 67, 227–249 (1992)
6. Kretzschmar Jr., W.A.: The Linguistics of speech. Cambridge University Press, Cambridge (2009)
7. Kretzschmar Jr., W.A.: Language variation and complex systems. American Speech 85, 263–286 (2010)
8. Kretzschmar Jr., W.A., Kretzschmar, B., Brockman, I.: Scaled measurement of geographic and social speech data. Literary and Linguistic Computing 28, 173–187 (2013)
9. Kretzschmar Jr., W.A., Light, D.: Mapping with Numbers. Journal of English Linguistics 24, 343–357 (1996)
10. Nerbonne, J.: Measuring the diffusion of linguistic change. Philosophical Transactions of the Royal Society B: Biological Sciences, vol. 365, pp. 3821–3828 (2010)

Sznajd Model with Memory

Norbert Sendra[1] and Tomasz M. Gwizdałła[2]

[1] Gtech Poland Sp. z o.o.
Al. Jerozolimskie 92, 00-807 Warszawa, Poland
nsendra@uni.lodz.pl
[2] Dept. of Solid State Physics, University of Łódź,
Pomorska 149/153, 90-236 Łódź, Poland

Abstract. Modification of the classical Sznajd model, by introducing a probability factor representing persuasibility of the cell on the social pressure has been presented. Two different variants of the factor as a function of the previous cell's opinion have been investigated. The new model exhibits different and in this context more realistic time of stabilization and probability of the achieved stable points.

1 Introduction

The classical Sznajd model [1–3] used for sociological simulation of opinion formation has shown that even a simple evolution rule can invoke complex system behaviour. A simply, idealistic model seems to be a helpful tool for scientists allowing to effectively simulates not complicated sociological behaviour without dedicated power of supercomputers, but at the same time provides material for further research.

In the following paper we would like to present modification of the classical Sznajd model which incorporates memory of the single cell. The modification slightly changes system behaviour, thereby leading to more realistic observations. Technically, we change Sznajd Model evolution rule by introducing a probability parameter representing ability of the cell to change internal state in the preceding time step. The parameter in analogy to the real observation will not be constant but will change dynamically while the system evolutes.

Here, we consider one dimensional model, however there are known generalizations on the square lattice [4, 5] or even 3d system [6] . An idea of introducing probability factor to the model is not new [7], nevertheless subordinate evolution rule to the previous cell states and therefore to the system memory has not been proposed yet.

2 Sznajd Model

The starting point of our investigation is the classical Sznajd model, built on the 1-dimensional lattice containing N elements. Each element, in analogy to the Ising model, can be either occupied ($s_i^t = +1$) or unoccupied ($s_i^t = -1$). In

J. Wąs, G.C. Sirakoulis, and S. Bandini (Eds.): ACRI 2014, LNCS 8751, pp. 349–356, 2014.

the reminder, s_i^t will denote state of the i-th element in t-th time step. We will also refer to the set of states as to the $\{A, B\}$ what simplifies the representation. The evolution rule of the system corresponds to the popular sociological sentence 'united we stand, divided we fall' [1]. In the classical Sznajd model, if two adjoining cells in the same step share the same opinion (their states are identical), they spread the opinion on the closest neighborhood. In mathematical form the rule presents Eq. 1.

$$if \quad s_i^t = s_{i+1}^t \quad then \quad s_{i-1}^{t+1} = s_i^t \quad and \quad s_{i+2}^{t+2} = s_t \tag{1}$$

On the contrary, if two consecutive cells do not share the same 'opinion', they strengthen local opinion disproportion what can be presented by the rule Eq. 2.

$$if \quad s_i^t \neq s_{i+1}^t \quad then \quad s_{i-1}^{t+1} = s_{i+1}^t \quad and \quad s_{i+2}^{t+1} = s_i^t \tag{2}$$

Essentialy, Eq. 2 is sufficient to describe both types of behaviour.

In the contrary to the typical cellular automata system, Sznajd Model evolutes randomly i.e. in a time step the rule is applied only to the one randomly chossen i-th element of the lattice.

For the sake of compatibility with the original approach we present the basic formulation with two cases. The crucial idea of the original approach is to consider the dynamics as the outward process ie. the process where the information flows outside the subsystem taken onto account. This is significantly different approach as compared with the majority methods related to the single state/spin modification in various simulation methods where the considered spin is influenced by its neighborhood. As the typical case we can mention here for example the well-known Glauber approach [8].

In the end, applying Eq. 2 iteratively leads to the one of the tree stable points:

1. all cells are occupied/all cells up: ($AAAAAA...$),
2. all cells are unoccupied/all cells down: ($BBBBBB...$),
3. alternate cells are occupied and unoccupied/up and down ($ABABAB...$),

The first two stable points are reached each with probability 0.25 and the third one with probability 0.50 for simulations with a totally random initial state, i.e. when each cell is initially assumed occupied with probability 0.50 ($p_0 = 0.50$).

One can easily find the physical analogs of presented configurations. While the first two correspond to a ferromagnetic system, the last one can be interpreted as the antiferromagnetic one. That is why it is common to use the notion of total magnetization m^t in time step t (see Eq. 3) as a second order statistics, and we will rely on that one throughout the study. For simplicity we assign zero to an unoccupied site ($s_i^t = 0$) instead of -1. This assumption make it certainly impossible to use the defined above value of magnetization. By using the presented set of states $\{0, 1\}$ we can however easily calculate the density of occupied cells ρ^t and the relation connecting both values is obviously simple and linear (see Eq. 4).

$$m^t = \frac{1}{N} \sum_{i=1}^{N} s_i^t \tag{3}$$

$$\rho^t = \frac{m^t + 1}{2} \tag{4}$$

The typical relaxation time for the system containing $N = 1000$ cells is about 10^4 Monte Carlo Sweeps (MCS). One MCS corresponds to the N spin-flip attempts (Monte-Carlo Steps), where N denotes system size.

As it has been mentioned earlier, the Sznajd model is a very rough generalization of the sociological opinion simulation and does not cover all details of the realistic concept. In spite of its simplicity it produces quite reasonable results and manifests very interesting behaviour what renders it a valuable basis for further investigation.

The main idea of our paper is to extend the presented model by taking into the consideration the fact that people are generally conservative in their opinions. They do not change opinion easily, therefore the assumption that it is equally possible to change opinion at the beginning of the simulation and after the stable point has been reached may be unrealistic. Sociological research in that matter does not reveal all aspects of the phenomenon. That is why we propose that for a typical agent/person the probability of changing the opinion depends on the number of times the person adjusted his opinion in the past. It means that it is relatively easily to change the opinion of the individual whose view on the particular subject is yet not mature. When the opinion is already built and stable it becomes more difficult to convince him to change it. Obviously, the assumption that people are conservative can be still considered as a generalization and we can find exceptions from such behaviour but in general people are rather reluctant to change the opinions, especially if we're talking about political inclinations.

3   Sznajd Model with Memory

The classical Sznajd model assumes that the parameter describing how difficult it is to convince a person is constant and equals 1.0, whereas we propose it to be a function of opinion change history of that person. Let n represent the number of opinion changes for a particular cell in Sznajd model and p_i^t represents the probability of changing state for i-th cell in t-th step. If we are talking about a person without developed opinion for particular subject, we can assume that the parameter describing probability of changing opinion is equal 1.0. On the contrary, if person changed his opinion quite often in the past, then each time it will be more difficult to convince him for the different opinion, so we can express it as the probability factor approaching 0.0 if n goes to infinity.

We should mention that this second property is the crucial one for our model. As a candidate function to fulfil these requirements we select two functions of power-law character shown in Eq. 5 and 6.

$$p_i^t = \frac{1}{n} \tag{5}$$

$$q_i^t = \frac{1}{\sqrt{n}} \tag{6}$$

3.1 Model with $p_i^t = \frac{1}{n}$

A new factor p_i^t transforms the evolution rule to the new form Eq. 7.

$$if \quad s_i^t \neq s_{i+1}^t \quad then \quad s_{i-1}^{t+1} = s_{i+1}^t \quad and \quad s_{i+2}^{t+1} = s_i^t$$
$$with \quad probability \quad p_{i-1}^t \quad and \quad p_{i+2}^t \tag{7}$$

Simulating this model shows that freezing time does not depend on the system size or initial state, moreover, the system stabilizes always in 4-5 MCS. Such a short freezing time suggests that stabilization in this model can not be connected with specific configuration of the cells but is rather an effect of the quickly decreasing probability. It's obvious, as one Monte Carlo Sweep (MCS) includes N spin flips. N spin flips on average spread full system, i.e. in theory we can assume that in one MCS, each system cell evolves once. In 4-5 steps, on average each system cell evolves 4-5 times therefore probability factors for each cell p_i^t equals $\frac{1}{4}$ or $\frac{1}{5}$. This observation confirms that the probability that the cell will change its state in the one of later steps is relatively small and diminishes very quickly. In order to prevent such a quick stabilization we add the memory reset process (when performed the n variable is for all cells set to 0). Such a reset is performed after every 20 MCS. The evolution of such a dynamical system is presented in the Fig. 1. The plot clearly discloses the stepwise character. It can be explained as the series of permanent fast stabilizations and resets which breaks these stabilizations.

Although the assumed p_i^t dependence with the reset added leads to a evaluation scheme which does not stabilize in the long time we have to underline that this is the effect of a little artificial procedure of resetting the memory of whole population. It seems that we can generally assume that the behaviour of the model $p_i^t = \frac{1}{n}$ is not interesting and not valuable for sociological simulation purposes, albeit there are places where similar process takes place and the model would be used. We are referring to a closed community, where interaction between the cells undergoes periodical changes (e.g. the prison environment with a regular prisoners interchange - mixing of prisoners prevents escapes).

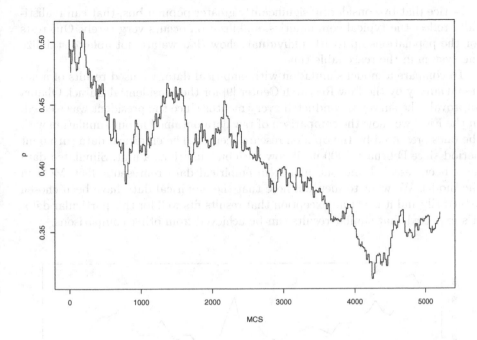

Fig. 1. An evolution diagram for the $p_i^t = \frac{1}{n}$ model with memory reset every 20 MCS

3.2 Model with $q_i^t = \frac{1}{\sqrt{n}}$

A new factor q_i^t transforms the evolution rule to the new form Eq. 8.

$$if \quad s_i^t \neq s_{i+1}^t \quad then \quad s_{i-1}^{t+1} = s_{i+1}^t \quad and \quad s_{i+2}^{t+1} = s_i^t$$
$$with \quad probability \quad q_{i-1}^t \quad and \quad q_{i+2}^t \tag{8}$$

This function, on the contrary to the first one, evinces mildly monotonic behaviour. It is expected, as in this model we will not observe quick quasi-stabilization. We have performed 1000 simulations of systems with 1000 cells from random initial state and it has been observed that the system features tree stable points, exactly the same like in the classical Sznajd Model. The difference is the probability of occurrence of such states. Every of the two configurations with the ferromagnetic ordering (all cells with the same state) is reached each with probability 0.12 while the configuration with alternate states is reached with probability 0.76. The difference of stable states distribution seems to be more likely caused by the longer stabilization time. When the system evolves longer,it is more probable that it will be caught in the point where the states are alternating.

The very important observation is that the typical relaxation time for the system at stake is about 10^6 MCS, therefore significantly longer (two orders of magnitude) than for the classical model.

Notice that by considering significantly greater populations, that can realistically reflect the typical communities, stabilization occurs very rarely. Our tests for the populations up to 10^5 individuals show that we are not able to stabilize the system in the reasonable time.

To compare a model simulation with empirical data, we used results of a national survey by the Pew Research Center [9] for the presidential Barack Obama approval. The survey is conducted every months since the president was elected. In the Fig.2 we show the comparison of raw data obtained in our simulation with the ones presented by the opinion research center. The empirical data surmount period since February 2009 until now with one month as a unit. Simulated data have been rescaled and one month in empirical data represents 4550 MCS in the model. We want to mention here that the empirical data have been chosen arbitrarily and it is not an exception that results fits well for this particular data. It's expected that similar results can be achieved from other comparisons.

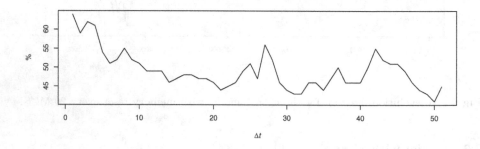

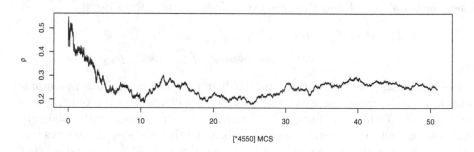

Fig. 2. Empirical data of the public acceptance for the president Barack Obama [9] (upper) and simulation of the model q_i^t from random initial state (lower) with $N = 1000$

In the Fig.3 we show the dependence of the autocorrelation function on the time used in the calculations. The choice of plot is typical for the presented type of study and can be found for instance in the Sznajd's paper [1]. Time correlation in the model seems to mimic empirical data behaviour very well.

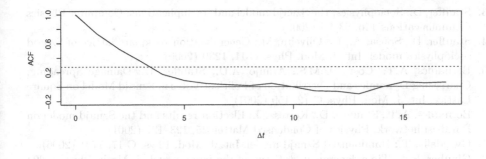

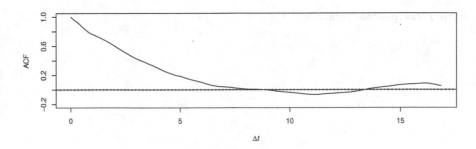

Fig. 3. Autocorrelation for empirical data (upper) and simulation (lower)

4   Summary

The two proposed probability factors p_i^t and q_i^t, significantly change classical Sznajd model behaviour. The first one effects on very fast system stabilization. It is not the effect of reaching the configuration stable point but the consequence of strong dependency of the cell change probability on the number of the previous states. This problem is reduced in second factor. Evolution of the q_i^t model, presents much longer stabilization time, what is crucial in simulations; they are longer and reach same stable points as the seminal model. The homogeneous configurations are however obtained more rarely. It is interesting and promising observation, especially when the results of the simulation quite good represents empirical data.

The inclusion of memory reset process as applied to the first model does not have equivalent in reality, but in further investigation it can be circumstanced to use it for simulation of the crucial changes in a sociological context like e.g. a revolution.

References

1. Sznajd-Weron, K., Sznajd, J.: Opinion evolution in closed community. Int. J. Mod. Phys. C 11, 1157 (2000)
2. Sznajd-Weron, K.: Sznajd model and its applications. Acta Physica Polonica B 36, 2537 (2005)

3. Stauffer, D.: Sociophysics: the Sznajd model and its applications. Computer Physics Communications 146, 93–98 (2002)
4. Stauffer, D., Sousa, A., De Oliveira, M.: Generalization to square lattice of Sznajd sociophysics model. Int. J. Mod. Phys. C 11, 1239 (2000)
5. Bernardes, A.T., Costa, U.M.S., Araujo, A.D., Stauffer, D.: Damage Spreading, Coarsening Dynamics and Distribution of Political Votes in Sznajd Model on Square Lattice. Int. J. Mod. Phys. C 12, 159 (2001)
6. Bernardes, A.T., Stauffer, D., Kertesz, J.: Election results and the Sznajd model on Barabasi network. Physics of Condensed Matter 25, 123–127 (2001)
7. Gwizdalla, T.: Randomized Sznajd model. Int. J. Mod. Phys. C 17, 1791 (2006)
8. Glauber, R.J.: Time-dependent statistics of the Ising model. J. Math. Phys. 4, 294 (1963)
9. http://www.pewresearch.org

Detecting Emergent Phenomena in Cellular Automata Using Temporal Description Logics*

Stathis Delivorias[1], Haralampos Hatzikirou[2],
Rafael Peñaloza[1,2], and Dirk Walther[1,2]

[1] TU Dresden, Theoretical Computer Science, Germany
[2] Center for Advancing Electronics Dresden, Germany
{Stathis.Delivorias,Haralampos.Hatzikirou,
Rafael.Penaloza,Dirk.Walther}@tu-dresden.de

Abstract. Cellular automata are discrete mathematical models that have been proven useful as representations of a wide variety of systems exhibiting emergent behavior. Detection of emergent behavior is typically computationally expensive as it relies on computer simulations. We propose to specify cellular automata using a suitable Temporal Description Logic and we show that we can formulate queries about the evolution of a cellular automaton as reasoning tasks in this logic.

1 Introduction

Cellular automata are discrete mathematical models that have been proven useful as representations of a wide variety of systems that feature non-linear dynamics. Initially cellular automata were introduced by John von Neumann as a formal model for cellular growth and replication. These automata have been successfully applied to model complex systems in physics, biology and many other scientific disciplines. Applications can be found in fluid dynamics, biological pattern formation, neural networks, cooperative systems, etc. Cellular automata have also been intensively studied in dynamical systems theory and computation theory, and they have been considered as discrete dynamical systems as well as a model for parallel computation [9,4,7].

We focus on complex systems exhibiting emergent behavior, where the properties at the larger scale are qualitatively different from those at the smaller scale. New functionalities may emerge when small components (like cells) are aggregated into larger entities (tissues and organs). We understand emergence as a property of a composite system (i.e., not just a component of the system) that arises through the interaction of the components and that persists over a period of time. Examples of emergence are plentiful and varied, and they typically involve some form of oscillation and pattern formation. Detection of emergent phenomena is typically computationally expensive as it involves the exploration of possible parameter settings and the corresponding phase space of the system.

* This work was partially supported by the German Research Foundation (DFG) within the Cluster of Excellence 'Center for Advancing Electronics Dresden'.

J. Wąs, G.C. Sirakoulis, and S. Bandini (Eds.): ACRI 2014, LNCS 8751, pp. 357–366, 2014.

The challenge we encounter is the description of interesting temporal system properties and their verification in an automated way. The general aim of this work is to develop a logic-based modeling language that is suited for describing such phenomena but that still allows effective reasoning. Our method of specifying properties of the evolution of cellular automata is using a suitable Temporal Description Logic. Queries about the evolution of a cellular automaton can then be formulated as reasoning tasks in this logic.

Description Logics (DLs) are a well-known family of logic-based knowledge representation formalisms [2]. They are designed to describe and reason about static aspects of an application domain. DLs form the logical basis of the web ontology language OWL 2, which is the current recommendation of the World Wide Web Consortium (W3C) [8]. Ontology languages based on DLs have been widely adopted for modeling a large class of domains, and an increasing number of ontologies is made available in dedicated repositories. To represent dynamical patterns, combinations of DLs and temporal logics have been proposed resulting in Temporal Description Logics [1,5]. In this paper, we describe cellular automata using the Temporal DL $\text{LTL}_{\mathcal{ALCO}}$, which is a combination of Linear-time Temporal Logic (LTL) [6] and the basic DL $\mathcal{ALC}$ extended with nominals [2]. The idea is to use the standard reasoning tasks in this logic such as subsumption and satisfiability checking w.r.t. a knowledge base to derive properties of the evolution of the cellular automaton. In particular, we aim at describing and verifying emergent properties such as oscillation and drift.

Expressive Temporal DLs tend to exhibit high worst-case reasoning complexity [5]. However, it remains to be seen whether reasoning in practice is actually unfeasible. An alternative to using expressive logics is to design a Temporal DL that is expressive enough to enable us to specify interesting queries on cellular automata while, at the same time, allowing for efficient reasoning. Finding the right balance between expressivity and computational complexity is at the core of research in DL.

2 Cellular Automata

We consider two-dimensional synchronous cellular automata that are based on a regular rectangular finite lattice.

Definition 1. *A 2-D finite regular cellular automaton is a tuple* $\Lambda = \langle S, n, f \rangle$ *where S is a finite set of states, $n \in \mathbb{N}$ is the diameter of the automaton, and* $f : S^{k \times k} \to S$ *is the local transition function, where $k \leq n$ is an odd number.* ⊣

We refer to 2-D finite regular cellular automata simply as CA, and we refer to matrix coordinates as *cells*.

Definition 2. *A configuration of the CA Λ is a matrix $C \in S^{n \times n}$. Let $m = \frac{k-1}{2}$ and $\ell = n + 2m$. A boundary condition for Λ is an operator* $* : S^{n \times n} \to S^{\ell \times \ell}$ *such that for all $C \in S^{n \times n}$ and all $(i,j) \in \{1, ..., n\}^2$, $C^*[i+m, j+m] = C[i,j]$.*

Fig. 1. The temporal realization for the execution triplet $(\Lambda_1, *, C_0)$

Given a boundary condition $*$, a configuration C and a cell $(x, y) \in \{1, ..., n\}^2$, the neighborhood *of (x, y) w.r.t. (Λ, C^*) is $\mathbf{N}_{(x,y),C^*} \in S^{k \times k}$ with*

$$\mathbf{N}_{(x,y),C^*}[i, j] = C^*[i + (x - 1), j + (y - 1)].$$

A function $F : S^{n \times n} \to S^{n \times n}$ is the global transition function *of Λ w.r.t. $*$ if for all $C \in S^{n \times n}$ it holds that $F(C)[i, j] = f(\mathbf{N}_{(i,j),C^*})$. The infinite sequence $\mathbf{C} = (C_0, C_1, C_2, ...)$ where $C_i \in S^{n \times n}$ and $C_i = F(C_{i-1})$ for all $i \in \mathbb{N}$ is the* temporal realization *of the automaton, with C_0 as its* initial configuration. $\dashv$

Since a temporal realization is uniquely determined by a cellular automaton Λ, a boundary condition $*$ and an initial configuration C_0, we denote it with $\mathbf{C}(\Lambda, *, C_0)$. Moreover, we refer to $(\Lambda, *, C_0)$ as *execution triplet*.

Example 3. Let $\mathcal{R} = \mathcal{R}_1 \cup \mathcal{R}_2$, where

$$\mathcal{R}_1 = \left\{ \begin{pmatrix} x_1 & x_2 & x_3 \\ 0 & 1 & 0 \\ x_4 & x_5 & x_6 \end{pmatrix} \middle| x_i \in \mathbb{Z}_2 \text{ for } i \in \{1, ..., 6\} \right\}, \text{ and}$$

$$\mathcal{R}_2 = \left\{ \begin{pmatrix} x_1 & x_2 & x_3 \\ x_4 & 0 & x_5 \\ x_6 & x_7 & x_8 \end{pmatrix} \middle| x_i \in \mathbb{Z}_2 \text{ for } i \in \{1, ..., 8\}, x_2 = 1 \text{ or } x_7 = 1 \right\}.$$

Consider $\Lambda_1 = \langle \mathbb{Z}_2, 4, f \rangle$ with $f : \mathbb{Z}_2^{3 \times 3} \to \mathbb{Z}_2$ given by

$$f(N) = \begin{cases} 1 & \text{if } N \in \mathcal{R} \\ 0 & \text{if } N \notin \mathcal{R}, \end{cases}$$

the boundary condition $* : \mathbb{Z}_2^{4 \times 4} \to \mathbb{Z}_2^{6 \times 6}$ where $C^*[i, j] = 0$ holds for every $(i, j) \in \{1, ..., 6\}^2 \setminus \{2, 3, 4, 5\}^2$, and the initial configuration

$$C_0 = \begin{pmatrix} 0 & 0 & 0 & 0 \\ 1 & 0 & 1 & 0 \\ 0 & 0 & 0 & 0 \\ 0 & 1 & 0 & 1 \end{pmatrix}.$$

Figure 1 provides a graphical representation of the temporal realization of this CA. After the fourth step, the configuration cycles back to the third configuration, i.e. $C_4 = C_3$. This means that the remainder of the temporal realization cycles between two global states. This property is called a *global oscillation* (of period 2). $\lhd$

We formally define some characteristic emergent properties of cellular automata.

Definition 4. *Let Λ be a CA. The temporal realization $\mathbf{C}(\Lambda, *, C_0)$ results in a global oscillation of period $\tau > 0$ if there exists a $t_0 \in \mathbb{N}$ such that for every $t_1 \geq t_0$, $C_{t_1} = C_{t_1+\tau}$. We call the smallest such t_0 the starting moment of the global oscillation.* ⊣

Every temporal realization of a CA Λ results in a global oscillation of some period. The total number of configurations of $\Lambda = \langle S, n, f \rangle$ is $|S|^{n^2}$. Since every configuration of Λ has a unique successor, the starting moment t_0 of the global oscillation of a temporal realization satisfies $t_0 < |S|^{n^2}$.

Definition 5. *Let Λ be a CA. The temporal realization $\mathbf{C}(\Lambda, *, C_0)$ leads to a fixed point if it results in a global oscillation of period 1. $\mathbf{C}(\Lambda, *, C_0)$ yields a phase transition if it leads to a fixed point with starting moment t_0, where $C_{t_0}[i,j] = C_{t_0}[i',j']$ for all $(i,j), (i',j') \in \{1, ..., n\}^2$.* ⊣

We now discuss oscillating patterns that appear only at a part of the grid. We use the notion of a *block element* of a matrix, which is a connected submatrix. Let M be an $n \times n$ matrix. An $s_1 \times s_2$ matrix M_0, for $s_1, s_2 \leq n$, is a *block element* of M if there is a tuple $(x, y, s_1, s_2) \in \{1, ..., n\}^4$ such that $M_0[i,j] = M[x-1+i, y-1+j]$ for all $(i,j) \in \{1, ..., s_1\} \times \{1, ..., s_2\}$. The tuple (x, y, s_1, s_2) denotes the *block coordinates* of M_0 in M, and $C(x, y, s_1, s_2)$ denotes the block element of the matrix C with block coordinates (x, y, s_1, s_2). Note that x and y describe the position of the block element, while s_1 and s_2 refer to the size of the block element. We also represent the tuple (x, y, s_1, s_2) with two vectors $\boldsymbol{x} = \langle x, y \rangle$, $\boldsymbol{s} = \langle s_1, s_2 \rangle$, and we write $C(\boldsymbol{x}, \boldsymbol{s})$.

Definition 6. *The temporal realization $\mathbf{C}(\Lambda, *, C_0)$ results in a localized oscillation of period τ if there exist a $t_0 \in \mathbb{N}$ and block coordinates (x, y, s_1, s_2) such that for every $t_1 \geq t_0$, it holds that $C_{t_1}(x, y, s_1, s_2) = C_{t_1+\tau}(x, y, s_1, s_2)$.* ⊣

We also consider the drifting of a *particle* during a temporal realization of a CA, where by particle we mean a structure of oscillating size and shape. To this end, we require the additional notions of velocity, trajectory and size oscillation. A *velocity function* with *period* τ is a function $\mathbf{v} : \mathbb{N} \to \mathbb{Z}^2$ such that $\mathbf{v}(t+\tau) = \mathbf{v}(t)$ for all $t \in \mathbb{N}$. If $\mathbf{v}$ is a velocity function of period τ, given an *initial position* $\boldsymbol{x}_0 \in \mathbb{N}^2$, a function $\boldsymbol{g} : \mathbb{N} \to \mathbb{Z}^2$ with $\boldsymbol{g}(0) = \boldsymbol{x}_0$ and $\boldsymbol{g}(t) = \boldsymbol{x}_0 + \sum_{\kappa=0}^{t-1} \mathbf{v}(\kappa)$ for $t > 0$, is called a *drifting trajectory*. A *size oscillation* of *period* τ is a function $\boldsymbol{s} : \mathbb{N} \to \mathbb{N}^2$ such that $\boldsymbol{s}(t + \tau) = \boldsymbol{s}(t)$ for all $t \in \mathbb{N}$.

Definition 7. *Let Λ be a CA. The temporal realization $\mathbf{C}(\Lambda, *, C_0)$ exhibits a drift of period τ for $t \geq \tau$ time steps if there exist a $t_0 \in \mathbb{N}$, a drifting trajectory $\boldsymbol{g}$ and a size oscillation $\boldsymbol{s}$ such that for every $t_1 \in \mathbb{N}$ with $t_0 \leq t_1 < t_0 + t - \tau$, it holds that $C_{t_1}^*(\boldsymbol{g}(t_1 - t_0), \boldsymbol{s}(t_1 - t_0)) = C_{t_1+\tau}^*(\boldsymbol{g}(t_1 - t_0 + \tau), \boldsymbol{s}(t_1 - t_0 + \tau))$.* ⊣

3   Temporal Description Logic

We use $\text{LTL}_{\mathcal{ALCO}}$ to describe CA. As we will see, there is a clear and strong correlation between a certain class of knowledge bases defined in this language, and the cellular automata described in the previous section.

Let N_C, N_R and N_I be mutually disjoint sets of *concept-*, *role-* and *individual names*, respectively. Concepts C in $\text{LTL}_{\mathcal{ALCO}}$ are built using the grammar rule:

$$C ::= \top \mid A \mid \{a\} \mid \neg C \mid C \sqcap C \mid \exists r.C \mid \bigcirc C \mid C\,\mathcal{U}\,C$$

where $A \in N_C$, $r \in N_R$, and $a \in N_I$. The symbols $\top$ ("truth"), $\{a\}$ ("nominal"), $\neg$ ("negation"), $\sqcap$ ("conjunction") and $\exists$ ("existential restriction") are logical operators of the Description Logic $\mathcal{ALCO}$, whereas $\bigcirc$ ("next") and $\mathcal{U}$ ("until") are temporal operators of the Temporal Logic LTL. We use the usual abbreviations $\bot = \neg\top$ ("falsehood"), $C \sqcup D = \neg(\neg C \sqcap \neg D)$ ("disjunction"), $\forall r.C = \neg\exists r.\neg C$ ("universal restriction"), $\Diamond C = \top\,\mathcal{U}\,C$ ("eventually"), and $\Box C = \neg\Diamond\neg C$ ("always").

An expression of the form $C \sqsubseteq D$, where C and D are concepts, is called a *concept inclusion*. A finite set of concept inclusions is a *TBox*. An expression of the form $C(a)$, where C is a concept and $a \in N_I$, is called a *concept assertion*. For $r \in N_R$ and $a, b \in N_I$, an expression of the form $r(a, b)$ is called a *role assertion*, and $\Box r(a, b)$ is a *rigid role assertion*. A finite set of concept and role assertions is called an *ABox*. A pair $\mathcal{K} = (\mathcal{T}, \mathcal{A})$ consisting of an TBox $\mathcal{T}$ and an ABox $\mathcal{A}$ is called a *knowledge base*.

We are interested in describing the evolution of a CA. In particular, we want to describe how the states of its cells evolve over time. $\text{LTL}_{\mathcal{ALCO}}$ can naturally express relevant properties of CAs, as it is illustrated by the following example.

Example 8. The fact that every cell eventually reaches a fixed point can be expressed in $\text{LTL}_{\mathcal{ALCO}}$ using the concept inclusion

$$\top \sqsubseteq \Diamond\Box B \sqcup \Diamond\Box\neg B,$$

stating that every cell ($\top$) is either ($\sqcup$) at some point in the future ($\Diamond$) going to stay forever ($\Box$) black, or it will eventually remain forever white ($\neg B$). On the other hand, the property that no cell reaches a fixed point can be expressed as

$$\top \sqsubseteq \Box\Diamond B \sqcap \Box\Diamond\neg B.$$

To express that after t transitions, every cell has at least one neighbor that is black we use

$$\top \sqsubseteq \bigcirc^t \exists r_n.B,$$

where $\bigcirc^t$ indicates t steps and $\exists r_n.B$ the existence of a black neighbor.   ◁

We want to use individual names to refer to the cells of a CA. As the set of cells does not change over time, we use a fixed-domain semantics for $\text{LTL}_{\mathcal{ALCO}}$. A *temporal interpretation* is a pair $\mathcal{I} = (\Delta, \cdot^{\mathcal{I}})$, where Δ is a non-empty *domain* and $\cdot^{\mathcal{I}}$ is a function that maps every $a \in N_I$ to $a^{\mathcal{I}} \in \Delta$, under the unique name assumption (i.e., no two individual names are mapped to the same domain element); every $A \in N_C$ to $A^{\mathcal{I}} \subseteq \mathbb{N} \times \Delta$, and every $r \in N_R$ to $r^{\mathcal{I}} \subseteq \mathbb{N} \times \Delta \times \Delta$. Then $\cdot^{\mathcal{I}}$ is extended to concepts by setting $\top^{\mathcal{I}} = \mathbb{N} \times \Delta$, $(\neg C)^{\mathcal{I}} = (\mathbb{N} \times \Delta) \setminus C^{\mathcal{I}}$, $(C \sqcap D)^{\mathcal{I}} = C^{\mathcal{I}} \cap D^{\mathcal{I}}$, $\{a\}^{\mathcal{I}} = \mathbb{N} \times \{a^{\mathcal{I}}\}$,

$$(\exists r.C)^{\mathcal{I}} = \{(t, x) \in \mathbb{N} \times \Delta \mid \exists y \in \Delta. (t, x, y) \in r^{\mathcal{I}} \wedge (t, y) \in C^{\mathcal{I}}\},$$

$$(\bigcirc C)^{\mathcal{I}} = \{(t, x) \in \mathbb{N} \times \Delta \mid (t+1, x) \in C^{\mathcal{I}}\}, \text{ and}$$

$$(C \mathcal{U} D)^{\mathcal{I}} = \{(t, x) \mid \exists t_0 > t. (t_0, x) \in D^{\mathcal{I}} \wedge \forall t' : t \leq t' < t_0. (t', x) \in C^{\mathcal{I}}\}.$$

A temporal interpretation $\mathcal{I}$ *satisfies* a concept C if $C^{\mathcal{I}} \neq \emptyset$; $\mathcal{I}$ *satisfies* a concept inclusion $C \sqsubseteq D$ if $C^{\mathcal{I}} \subseteq D^{\mathcal{I}}$; $\mathcal{I}$ *satisfies* a concept assertion $C(a)$ if $(0, a^{\mathcal{I}}) \in C^{\mathcal{I}}$, a role assertion $r(a, b)$ if $(0, a^{\mathcal{I}}, b^{\mathcal{I}}) \in r^{\mathcal{I}}$ and a rigid role assertion $\Box r(a, b)$ if $(t, a^{\mathcal{I}}, b^{\mathcal{I}}) \in r^{\mathcal{I}}$, for every $t \in \mathbb{N}$. We say that $\mathcal{I}$ is a *model* of a TBox $\mathcal{T}$ or an ABox $\mathcal{A}$ if it satisfies every concept inclusion in $\mathcal{T}$ or every assertion in $\mathcal{A}$, respectively; and $\mathcal{I}$ is a model of a KB $\mathcal{K} = (\mathcal{T}, \mathcal{A})$ if $\mathcal{I}$ is a model of both, $\mathcal{T}$ and $\mathcal{A}$. If there is a model of a KB $\mathcal{K}$ that satisfies C, then C is *satisfiable* w.r.t. $\mathcal{K}$. If every model of $\mathcal{K}$ satisfies $C \sqsubseteq D$, then C is *subsumed* by D w.r.t. $\mathcal{K}$.

In the next section, we show a correspondence between CA as defined in Section 2 and $\mathrm{LTL}_{\mathcal{ALCO}}$ KBs describing them. To this end, we require the following notion of isomorphism.

Definition 9. *Two temporal interpretations* $\mathcal{I} = (\Delta^{\mathcal{I}}, \cdot^{\mathcal{I}})$, $\mathcal{J} = (\Delta^{\mathcal{J}}, \cdot^{\mathcal{J}})$ *are* isomorphic *if there is a bijection* $h : \Delta^{\mathcal{I}} \to \Delta^{\mathcal{J}}$, *called* isomorphism, *such that* $h(a^{\mathcal{I}}) = a^{\mathcal{J}}$ *for every* $a \in N_I$, *and for all* $x, y \in \Delta^{\mathcal{I}}$, *and* $t \in \mathbb{N}$, *it holds that:*

(a) $(t, x) \in A^{\mathcal{I}}$ *iff* $(t, h(x)) \in A^{\mathcal{J}}$, *for every* $A \in N_C$; *and*
(b) $(t, x, y) \in r^{\mathcal{I}}$ *iff* $(t, h(x), h(y)) \in r^{\mathcal{J}}$, *for every* $r \in N_R$. $\dashv$

Lemma 10. *If* $\mathcal{I}$ *and* $\mathcal{J}$ *are two isomorphic temporal interpretations, then:*

(i) *A concept* C *is satisfied by* $\mathcal{I}$ *iff* C *is satisfied by* $\mathcal{J}$;
(ii) $\mathcal{I}$ *satisfies* $C \sqsubseteq D$ *iff* $\mathcal{J}$ *satisfies* $C \sqsubseteq D$; *and*
(iii) $\mathcal{I}$ *is a model for a TBox* $\mathcal{T}$, *an ABox* $\mathcal{A}$ *or a KB* $\mathcal{K}$ *iff* $\mathcal{J}$ *is a model for* $\mathcal{T}$, $\mathcal{A}$ *or* $\mathcal{K}$, *respectively.* $\dashv$

4   Reasoning about CA with TDL

In the following, we focus on a specific class of CA. We use $\mathbb{Z}_2$ as the set of states and a neighborhood of size 3×3. The boundary condition $*$ is such that for all configurations C, $C^*[i, j] = 0$ for every $(i, j) \in \{1, ..., n+2\}^2 \setminus \{2, ..., n+1\}^2$, where n is the diameter of the automaton. Hence, from now on, when referring to a CA Λ we mean a tuple of the form $\langle \mathbb{Z}_2, n, f \rangle$, where $f : \mathbb{Z}_2^{3 \times 3} \to \mathbb{Z}_2$. We use the following signature to describe such a CA Λ:

$$N_I = \{a_{xy} \mid x, y \in \{1, ..., \ell\}\},$$

$$N_C = \{B\},$$
$$N_R = \{r_r, r_l, r_d, r_u\},$$

where $\ell = n+2$ is a parameter that depends on the diameter n of Λ. The intended meaning of these symbols is as follows. The individual names in N_I represent the cells of the automaton, the concept name B states that a cell is black (formally, its state is $1 \in \mathbb{Z}_2$) and the four role names in N_R represent the right, left, up and down neighbors, respectively, as they are found in the neighborhood matrix. We use a symbol for the bijection between $\mathbb{Z}_2$ and $\{B, \neg B\}$. Let $\chi \colon \{B, \neg B\} \to \mathbb{Z}_2$ with $\chi(B) = 1$ and $\chi(\neg B) = 0$.

A *neighborhood concept* is a complex concept of the form, where X_i, for $1 \le i \le 9$, ranges over $\{B, \neg B\}$:

$$\exists r_l.\exists r_u.X_1 \sqcap \exists r_u.X_2 \sqcap \exists r_r.\exists r_u.X_3 \sqcap \exists r_l.X_4 \sqcap X_5 \sqcap$$
$$\sqcap \exists r_r.X_6 \sqcap \exists r_l.\exists r_d.X_7 \sqcap \exists r_d.X_8 \sqcap \exists r_r.\exists r_d.X_9.$$

We denote such concepts as $N(M)$ where $M = \begin{pmatrix} \chi(X_1) & \chi(X_2) & \chi(X_3) \\ \chi(X_4) & \chi(X_5) & \chi(X_6) \\ \chi(X_7) & \chi(X_8) & \chi(X_9) \end{pmatrix}$.

Definition 11. *Let* $(\Lambda, *, C_0)$ *be an execution triplet. The knowledge base for* $(\Lambda, *, C_0)$ *is defined as* $\mathcal{K}_{(\Lambda,*,C_0)} = (\mathcal{T}_{(\Lambda,*,C_0)}, \mathcal{A}_{(\Lambda,*,C_0)})$, *where*

$$\mathcal{T}_{(\Lambda,*,C_0)} = \{N(M) \sqsubseteq \bigcirc X \mid M \in \mathbb{Z}_2^{3\times3}, X = \chi^{-1}(f(M))\} \cup$$
$$\{\top \sqsubseteq \{a_{ij} \mid i,j \in \{1,\ldots,\ell\}\}\},$$
$$\mathcal{A}_{(\Lambda,*,C_0)} = \{\Box r_r(a_{xy}, a_{zw}) \mid x,y,z,w \in \{1,\ldots,\ell\}, x = z, w = y+1\} \cup$$
$$\{\Box r_l(a_{xy}, a_{zw}) \mid x,y,z,w \in \{1,\ldots,\ell\}, x = z, w = y-1\} \cup$$
$$\{\Box r_d(a_{xy}, a_{zw}) \mid x,y,z,w \in \{1,\ldots,\ell\}, y = w, z = x+1\} \cup$$
$$\{\Box r_u(a_{xy}, a_{zw}) \mid x,y,z,w \in \{1,\ldots,\ell\}, y = w, z = x-1\} \cup$$
$$\{(\Box\forall r.\bot)(a) \mid r \in N_R, \Box r(a,b) \notin \mathcal{A}_1, a,b \in N_I\} \cup$$
$$\{X(a_{ij}) \mid i,j \in \{2,\ldots,\ell-1\}, X = \chi^{-1}(C_0[i-1,j-1])\} \cup$$
$$\{\Box\neg B(a_{ij}) \mid (i,j) \in \{1,\ldots,\ell\}^2 \setminus \{2,\ldots,\ell-1\}^2\}. \qquad \dashv$$

We show below that there is a one-to-one correspondence between the knowledge base for $(\Lambda, *, C_0)$ and the temporal realization of this execution triplet. To this end, we employ the notion of a canonical interpretation defined as follows.

Definition 12. *The* canonical interpretation *for the execution triplet* $(\Lambda, *, C_0)$ *is defined as* $\mathcal{J} = (\Delta^{\mathcal{J}}, \cdot^{\mathcal{J}})$, *where* $\Delta^{\mathcal{J}} = \{1,\ldots,\ell\}^2$, $B^{\mathcal{J}} = \{(t, (i,j)) \mid C_t^*[i,j] = 1\}$, $a_{ij}^{\mathcal{J}} = (i,j)$ *for every* $a_{ij} \in N_I$, *and*

$$r_r^{\mathcal{J}} = \{(t, (x,y), (z,w)) \mid t \in \mathbb{N}, x = z, w = y+1\},$$
$$r_l^{\mathcal{J}} = \{(t, (x,y), (z,w)) \mid t \in \mathbb{N}, x = z, w = y-1\},$$
$$r_d^{\mathcal{J}} = \{(t, (x,y), (z,w)) \mid t \in \mathbb{N}, y = w, z = x+1\},$$
$$r_u^{\mathcal{J}} = \{(t, (x,y), (z,w)) \mid t \in \mathbb{N}, y = w, z = x-1\}. \qquad \dashv$$

First we show that this canonical interpretation is the unique model of $\mathcal{K}_{(\Lambda,*,C_0)}$, up to isomorphism.

Lemma 13. *Let $(\Lambda, *, C_0)$ be an execution triplet. The canonical interpretation $\mathcal{J}$ is a model of $\mathcal{K}_{(\Lambda,*,C_0)}$, and every model of $\mathcal{K}_{(\Lambda,*,C_0)}$ is isomorphic to $\mathcal{J}$.* ⊣

We now show how to decide the existence of emergent properties in CA through standard reasoning in LTL$_{\mathcal{ALCO}}$. We use the following notation: $\bigcirc^1 := \bigcirc$ and $\bigcirc^{n+1} := \bigcirc\bigcirc^n$, $(\exists r)^1 := \exists r$ and $(\exists r)^{n+1} := \exists r.(\exists r)^n$, for all $n \in \mathbb{N}$. In addition, for any concept C, we set $(\exists r)^0.C := C$ and $\bigcirc^0 C := C$.

Proposition 14. *Let Λ be a CA. The temporal realization $\mathbf{C}(\Lambda, *, C_0)$ results in a global oscillation of period τ iff $\top$ is subsumed by $\Diamond\Box((B \sqcap \bigcirc^\tau B) \sqcup (\neg B \sqcap \bigcirc^\tau \neg B))$ w.r.t. $\mathcal{K}_{(\Lambda,*,C_0)}$.* ⊣

Corollary 15. *The temporal realization $\mathbf{C}(\Lambda, *, C_0)$ yields a fixed point iff $\top$ is subsumed by $\Diamond\Box((B \sqcap \bigcirc B) \sqcup (\neg B \sqcap \bigcirc \neg B))$ w.r.t. $\mathcal{K}_{(\Lambda,*,C_0)}$. $\mathbf{C}(\Lambda, *, C_0)$ yields a phase transition iff $\top$ is subsumed by either $\Diamond\Box(B \sqcap \bigcirc B)$ or by $\Diamond\Box(\neg B \sqcap \bigcirc \neg B)$ w.r.t. $\mathcal{K}_{(\Lambda,*,C_0)}$.* ⊣

The complex concept $D_\tau = ((B \sqcap \bigcirc^\tau B) \sqcup (\neg B \sqcap \bigcirc^\tau \neg B))$ for arbitrary $\tau \in \mathbb{N}$ will be used to model local oscillation. We call it *individual τ-repetition*. We can then define the concept of *(i,j)-sized τ-repetition* inductively: $D_\tau^{1\times 1} = D_\tau$, $D_\tau^{(i+1)\times 1} = D_\tau^{i\times 1} \sqcap (\exists r_d)^i.D_\tau$ and $D_\tau^{i\times(j+1)} = D_\tau^{i\times j} \sqcap (\exists r_r)^j.D_\tau^{i\times 1}$.

Proposition 16. *Let Λ be a CA and $\mathbf{C}(\Lambda, *, C_0)$ be a temporal realization. $\mathbf{C}(\Lambda, *, C_0)$ results in local oscillation of period τ iff $\mathcal{K}_{(\Lambda,*,C_0)}$ satisfies*

$$\Diamond \bigsqcup_{(i,j)\in\{1,\ldots,n\}^2} \Box D_\tau^{i\times j}$$

⊣

Let $\mathfrak{r} = (r_1, r_2, \ldots, r_n)$ be a finite sequence of role symbols. We call $\mathfrak{r}$ a *composite role* and we abbreviate with $\exists\mathfrak{r}$ the syntactic entity of the form $\exists r_1.\exists r_2 \ldots \exists r_n$. Let $n = |\mathfrak{r}|$ be the *length* of $\mathfrak{r}$. We consider the empty sequence as a composite role of length 0. To model the drift property we use the complex concept $D_{\tau,\mathfrak{r}} = ((B \sqcap \bigcirc^\tau \exists\mathfrak{r}.B) \sqcup (\neg B \sqcap \bigcirc^\tau \exists\mathfrak{r}.\neg B))$ where $\mathfrak{r}$ is a composite role and $\tau \in \mathbb{N}$. We call it *individual $\mathfrak{r}$-drifting τ-repetition*. The concept of *(i,j)-sized $\mathfrak{r}$-drifting τ-repetition* is then defined inductively: $D_{\tau,\mathfrak{r}}^{1\times 1} = D_{\tau,\mathfrak{r}}$, $D_{\tau,\mathfrak{r}}^{(i+1)\times 1} = D_{\tau,\mathfrak{r}}^{i\times 1} \sqcap (\exists r_d)^i.D_{\tau,\mathfrak{r}}^{1\times 1}$ and $D_{\tau,\mathfrak{r}}^{i\times(j+1)} = D_{\tau,\mathfrak{r}}^{i\times j} \sqcap (\exists r_r)^j.D_{\tau,\mathfrak{r}}^{i\times 1}$.

Proposition 17. *Let Λ be a CA. The temporal realization $\mathbf{C}(\Lambda, *, C_0)$ exhibits a drift of period τ for t time steps iff $\mathcal{K}_{(\Lambda,*,C_0)}$ satisfies*

$$\Diamond \bigsqcup_{|\mathfrak{r}|<n^2} \bigsqcap_{t_1=0}^{\tau-1} \bigsqcup_{|\mathfrak{p}|<n^2} \left(\bigsqcup_{(i,j)\in\{1,\ldots,n\}^2} \left(\bigsqcap_{t_2=0}^{\mu} \bigcirc^{t_1+t_2\tau}(\exists\mathfrak{r})^{t_2}.\exists\mathfrak{p}.D_{\tau,\mathfrak{r}}^{i\times j} \right) \right)$$

where $\mathfrak{p}$ and $\mathfrak{r}$ are composite roles and $\mu = \lfloor \frac{t-t_1}{\tau} \rfloor$. ⊣

The study of combinations of Temporal Logics and Description Logics has a long history. In particular, the combination of the basic DL $\mathcal{ALC}$ with LTL, and some of their extensions, has been studied in [3,10]. For these logics, it has been shown that all the standard reasoning problems, such as satisfiability and subsumption between concepts, are ExpSpace-complete. For our reductions, we have included two kinds of additional expressivity into our temporal DL: nominals and rigid role assertions.

At first sight, the use of rigid role assertions may seem problematic. Indeed, it is known that reasoning in LTL$_{\mathcal{ALC}}$ w.r.t. TBoxes is undecidable whenever rigid roles are allowed; even if no TBox is used, the problem is still non-elementary [3]. However, in our case, the *rigidness* of a role is limited to the few named individuals that describe the cells of the automaton. Indeed, the rigid role assertion $\Box r(a, b)$ is merely a syntactic variant of the concept inclusion $\{a\} \sqsubseteq \exists r.\{b\}$. The only remaining question is the cost of including nominals into our formalism.

To the best of our knowledge, the precise complexity of reasoning in LTL$_{\mathcal{ALCO}}$ has never been settled. While we provide no formal proof for this, we conjecture that reasoning in LTL$_{\mathcal{ALCO}}$ should not be harder than for LTL$_{\mathcal{ALC}}$, i.e., it should remain ExpSpace-complete. This conjecture is supported by the fact that typically nominals do not increase the complexity of reasoning in description logics. Moreover, at this high complexity, it is possible to guess exponentially large structures without leaving the complexity class. Unfortunately, for practical matters, the efficiency of reasoning algorithms is typically negatively affected by the amount of nominals used. Whether this is indeed an issue in our case and whether it can be improved upon remains a topic for future work.

5   Conclusions

We have proposed to describe cellular automata using a Temporal Description Logic. Queries about the temporal evolution of a cellular automaton can then be formulated as reasoning tasks in this logic. In particular, we have described the emergent properties of global oscillation, local oscillation, and drift in the Temporal DL LTL$_{\mathcal{ALCO}}$. We have shown that verifying these properties w.r.t. a cellular automaton can be formulated as subsumption and satisfiability checking problems in that logic (cf. Propositions 14, 16 and 17).

There are also other relevant properties of a cellular automaton that would be interesting to describe and verify, which require to define different reasoning tasks for the Temporal DL. For instance, properties of the local transition rules that hold for all initial conditions, or derive the set of initial conditions that lead to a given configuration.

The study of computational complexity of the reasoning tasks can possibly help to further classify cellular automata in terms of the types of queries that can be answered within certain resource bounds. For future work, it would be interesting to analyze in detail the computational complexity of LTL$_{\mathcal{ALCO}}$, and also to find other logics that possibly offer a better compromise between expressivity and computational complexity. It is also important to check whether the full expressivity of $LTL_{\mathcal{ALCO}}$ is needed for expressing the class of CA that we consider, and whether the same results can be achieved using fewer or different logical operators.

An interesting potential application could be the prediction of catastrophic events, here regarded as emergent behavior, in multi-component dynamic systems. To illustrate our perspective, electronic malfunctions can emerge from micro-circuit interactions. Typically, CA can be used to model such systems. Monitoring is the golden standard for identifying potential malfunctions. Our envisaged logic-based language, combined with system monitoring, could identify signatures in the CA rules and improve the predictability of such catastrophic events.

Another prospective application motivated by Temporal DL reasoning on cellular automata could be in clinical praxis. In particular, cardiograms or encephalograms provide a short-time observation of hearts or brains, respectively. Extensions of our methodology could potentially extract essential properties of that system and the reasoner could provide a prediction of dangerous emergent behaviour such as heart attacks or epileptic seizures.

References

1. Artale, A., Kontchakov, R., Lutz, C., Wolter, F., Zakharyaschev, M.: Temporalising tractable description logics. In: Proc. of TIME 2007: the 14th International Symposium on Temporal Representation and Reasoning, pp. 11–22. IEEE Computer Society Press (2007)
2. Baader, F., Calvanese, D., McGuinness, D.L., Nardi, D., Patel-Schneider, P.F. (eds.): The description logic handbook: theory, implementation, and applications. Cambridge University Press (2007)
3. Gabbay, D., Kurusz, A., Wolter, F., Zakharyaschev, M.: Many-Dimensional Modal Logics: Theory and Applications. Elsevier (2003)
4. Lena, P.D., Margara, L.: Computational complexity of dynamical systems: The case of cellular automata. Information and Computation 206(9-10), 1104–1116 (2008)
5. Lutz, C., Wolter, F., Zakharyaschev, M.: Temporal description logics: A survey. In: Proc. of TIME 2008: the 15th International Symposium on Temporal Representation and Reasoning, pp. 3–14. IEEE Computer Society Press (2008)
6. Pnueli, A.: The temporal logic of programs. In: Proc. of SFCS 1977: the 18th Annual Symposium on Foundations of Computer Science, pp. 46–57. IEEE Computer Society Press (1977)
7. Sutner, K.: Computational classification of cellular automata. Int. J. General Systems 41(6), 595–607 (2012)
8. W3C OWL Working Group. OWL 2 Web Ontology Language: Document Overview (2009), http://www.w3.org/TR/owl2-overview/
9. Wolfram, S.: A New Kind of Science. Wolfram Media (2002)
10. Wolter, F., Zakharyaschev, M.: Temporalizing description logics. In: Proc. of FroCoS 1998: the 2nd International Symposium on Frontiers of Combining Systems, pp. 379–402. Kluwer Academic Publishers (2000)

Direction-Reversible Self-Timed Cellular Automata for Delay-Insensitive Circuits

Daniel Morrison and Irek Ulidowski

Department of Computer Science, University of Leicester, England

Abstract. We introduce a new Self-Timed Cellular Automaton capable of simulating *reversible delay-insensitive* (DI) circuits. In addition to a number of reversibility and determinism properties, our STCA exhibits *direction-reversibility*, where reversing the direction of a signal and running a circuit forwards is equivalent to running the circuit in reverse. We define also several extensions of the STCA which allow us to realise three larger classes of DI circuits, including *parallel* circuits. We then show which of the reversibility, determinism and direction-reversibility properties hold for these classes of circuits.

1 Introduction

Delay-insensitive (DI) circuits are a category of asynchronous circuits which make no assumption about delays within modules and lines (wires) connecting the modules, and have no global clock. It is argued in [10] that typical logical gates such as NAND and XOR are not Turing-complete when operated in a DI environment. Therefore implementations of DI modules and circuits in alternative technologies, such as cellular automata ([6]) and RSFQ circuits ([18]), are researched actively in recent years. DI circuits were introduced by Keller ([3]) who characterised the conditions required for correct DI operation and gave various universal sets of modules. Subsequent work by Patra and Fussell ([17]) went into finding more efficient universal sets of modules.

Reversible modules were originally studied by Fredkin and Toffoli ([2]) who proposed a number of synchronous universal logic gates. More recently, Morita, Lee, Peper and Adachi carried out research into finding efficient universal sets of reversible *serial* DI modules (where only one signal travels around a circuit) with memory, such as *Rotary Element* ([12]), and *Reading Toggle* and *Inverse Reading Toggle* ([8]). The sets of all possible 2-state reversible serial modules with two, three and four pairs of input/output lines were enumerated in [13]. Implementations of reversible serial DI modules in *Self-Timed Cellular Automata* (STCAs) ([19]), a special type of asynchronous cellular automata, are shown in several papers including [8], [9] and [7]. How these various concepts relate to each other was discussed by Morita in [11]. Further investigations by Morrison and Ulidowski into combining reversibility with parallelism in the context of DI modules, and the resulting limitations of such modules, can be found in [15,16].

In this paper we introduce novel STCAs for non-arbitrating parallel DI circuits, including STCAs for the reversible versions of such circuits. Our STCAs

J. Wąs, G.C. Sirakoulis, and S. Bandini (Eds.): ACRI 2014, LNCS 8751, pp. 367–377, 2014.

have several very useful properties, most notably they support what we call direction-reversibility.

Section 2 introduces DI modules and some universality results and Section 3 introduces STCAs. In Section 4 we define two new STCAs for the simulation of reversible serial and serial modules. We then show how to extend our STCAs to support two subclasses of parallel modules in Section 5. Section 6 concludes the paper. All constructions in this paper were verified using a STCA simulator. The software, as well as the constructions in this paper, can be found at [14].

2   Delay-Insensitive Modules

We present delay-insensitive modules using a high-level notation developed in [15], which naturally describes external concurrent behaviour of modules. The notation defines a module as a mapping between sets of concurrent input signals and output signals, rather than in the sequential machine style of Keller ([3]). Details how this high-level notation is derived from the sequential machine notation can be found in [15].

A module is a 4-tuple $\{Q, I, O, T\}$, where Q is a finite set of states ranged over with q, $q' \ldots$ or $S, S' \ldots$, I is a set of input lines and O is a set of output lines both ranged over with a, $b \ldots$. The map $T \subseteq Q \times (P(I) \setminus \emptyset) \to Q \times (P(O) \setminus \emptyset)$ is called the *transition map* and it assigns an input set in a given state to an output set and a new state. This describes the effects of a concurrent set of input signals to a module. The environment is required to signal the set of lines corresponding to one defined input set. Upon receiving the full input set, the module produces signals on lines corresponding to the output set and changes the state, according to T. The environment may then begin signalling a new input set. If an input set is undefined in a given state, it is assumed that this input set is never signalled in the given state.

The *inverse* of $\{Q, I, O, T\}$ is the module $\{Q, O, I, T^{-1}\}$ where T^{-1} is the inverse of T. If T is a bijection then both T and T^{-1} are functions, and the module is *reversible*. A module is called *irreversible* if it is not reversible. We call a module *serial* if all input and output sets are singletons, and no two input sets are equal in any given state. Modules which are not serial are called *parallel*.

A *network* or *circuit* of modules is a collection of instances of modules, such that the output of a module is connected to at most one input of another module. We say that a network of modules is *delay-insensitive* if the network operates correctly regardless of delays in any of the lines or modules. We call a network a *realisation* of a module if the input/output behaviour of a network simulates correctly the input/output behaviour of the module. A network is reversible if all modules within the network are reversible, otherwise it is irreversible. A network is serial if all modules within the network are serial, otherwise it is parallel. We say that a set of modules is *universal* for a class of modules, if any module within the class can be realised using only modules from the set.

To improve readability, we present a module as a set of equations of the form $q = (A, B).q' + \cdots + (A', B').q''$, where q is a state of the module and $(A, B).q'$ is an *action* which means the input set A in state q results in the output set B and a change to state q'. For example, $(\{a, b, c\}, \{d, e\}).S_1$ of S_0 says that in state S_0, the environment may signal the lines a, b and c exactly once each, concurrently in any order or at the same time, and this will result in a signal on d, a signal on e, and a new state S_1. Set brackets are omitted for singleton sets.

Figure 1 shows the modules Reading Toggle (RT) and Inverse Reading Toggle (IRT) ([8]), which are both reversible serial, and are each other's inverses. We use A, B as states and R, T, T_A, T_B as inputs and outputs to be consistent with the notation in [8]. The set $\{RT, IRT\}$ is universal for reversible computation ([8]), and a network of RT and IRT modules can realise any reversible serial module. Hence $\{RT, IRT\}$ is universal for the class of reversible serial modules.

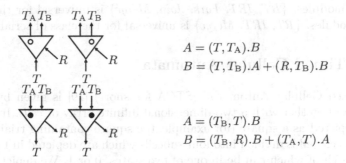

$$A = (T, T_A).B$$
$$B = (T, T_B).A + (R, T_B).B$$

$$A = (T_B, T).B$$
$$B = (T_B, R).B + (T_A, T).A$$

Fig. 1. Reading Toggle (top) and Inverse Reading Toggle (bottom)

Figure 2 shows several other common DI modules. For consistency with the original definitions, F, J and M denote states. *Fork* and *Join* are parallel modules and are reversible. *Merge* is a serial module and is irreversible.

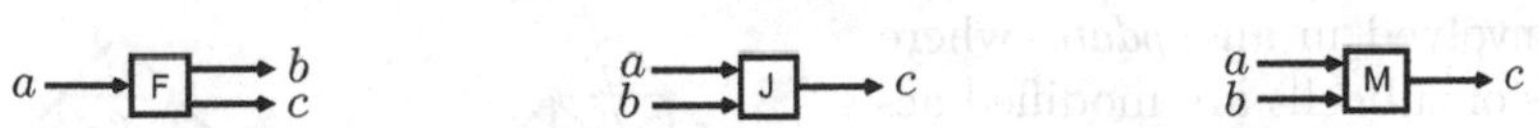

$$F = (a, \{b, c\}).F \qquad J = (\{a, b\}, c).J \qquad M = (a, c).M + (b, c).M$$

Fig. 2. *Fork*, *Join* and *Merge* modules

We call a module *arbitrating* (*arb* for short) if there is a state with different actions $(A, B).q'$ and $(A', B').q''$ such that either $A \subseteq A'$ or $A' \subseteq A$. We say that a module is *non-arbitrating* (*non-arb*) if it is not arbitrating. Informally, arbitration corresponds to a form of non-determinism. As each possible input set in a given state corresponds to a set of signals arriving, for a module to be deterministic in a delay-insensitive environment, no input set cannot be a subset of another input set in the same state, and no input set can lead to two different output sets or different states. All modules defined so far are non-arb. It is clear that all serial modules are non-arb. Keller's ATS module ([3]) is arb.

Correspondingly, we call a module *backwards-arbitrating* (*b-arb* for short) if for all actions in all states, there are two different actions $(A, B).q'$ and $(A', B').q''$ such that $q' = q''$ and either $B \subseteq B'$ or $B' \subseteq B$. We say that a module is *non-backwards-arbitrating* (*non-b-arb*) if it is not b-arb. *Merge* is an example of a b-arb module.

In [15] it is shown, through illustrating the general construction, that the set {*DM, Fork, Join*} is universal for the class of non-arb non-b-arb modules, {*DM, Fork, Join, Merge*} is universal for the class of non-arb modules and {*DM, Merge*} is universal for the class of serial modules, where *DM* is a reversible serial module defined in [16]. As {*RT, IRT*} is universal for any reversible serial module, it can realise *DM*. This gives us several new universal sets.

Proposition 1. {*RT, IRT, Fork, Join*} is universal for the class of non-arb non-b-arb modules. {*RT, IRT, Fork, Join, Merge*} is universal for the class of non-arb modules. {*RT, IRT, Merge*} is universal for the class of serial modules.

3   Self-Timed Cellular Automata

A Self-Timed Cellular Automaton (STCA for short) [19] is given by a set of *update rules* together with a two-dimensional infinite array of *cells*. In Figure 3 a cell is depicted as a square (for example, the square containing triangles with a, b, c, d). Each cell is divided into four subcells which are depicted in Figure 3 as triangles, each of which can be in one of two states, 0 or 1. We depict the state 0 with a clear triangle, and the state 1 with a black triangle. The default state of subcells is 0 and is known as the *quiescent* state. The state of all cells and their subcells in the two-dimensional array is known as a *configuration*, and the state of cells and subcells in the initial array is called the *initial configuration*. Configurations are ranged over by $C, C' \ldots$ and $D, D' \ldots$. In this paper we identify an STCA with the set of update rules R, simply by R.

A set of subcells in a configuration may be involved in an *update*, where the states of subcells are modified according to one of the *update rules*. An update involves a full cell (comprised of its four subcells) together with the cell's four adjacent neighbouring subcells on the two-dimensional plane.

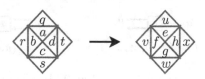

Fig. 3. Depiction of an update rule

Figure 3 shows how a general update rule is depicted (image taken from [7]), where $a, b, c, d, e, f, g, h, q, r, s, t, u, v, w, x \in \{0, 1\}$. This means that subcells a, b, c, d, q, r, s, t of a configuration are updated to e, f, g, h, u, v, w, x, respectively, giving a new configuration. Following [19], an update of a set of subcells may only occur if an update rule is defined for the current state of the given subcells.

Subcells are assumed to update instantaneously and randomly at any time if a corresponding update rule is defined. However, as two adjacent cells share subcells in their update codomain, we assume, following [20], that no two adjacent cells may update simultaneously.

We say that a set of update rules is *locally reversible*, if no two update rules have identical right-hand sides. Similarly, we say that a set of update rules is *locally deterministic* if no two update rules have identical left-hand sides.

An update causes the current configuration to change to a new configuration. We define an *execution* of a configuration C as a sequence of configurations $C \to C' \to C'' \ldots$, where $\to$ represents that one or more updates have occurred simultaneously. The reflexive and transitive closure of $\to$ is denoted by $\to^*$. We say that C' is *reachable* from C if $C \to^* C'$, and we call C' a *derivative* of C.

In this paper we assume that configurations give rise only to those executions that satisfy *weak fairness* ([4]). An execution $C_1 \to C_2 \to \ldots$, with $C = C_1$, is weakly fair whenever if (a) there are different C_k, C_l in the execution with $k < l$ such that $C_{l+1} = C_k$ (a "loop" containing C_k and C_l is reachable from C) and (b) there is $D \neq C_i$, for $k \leq i \leq l$, such that $C_j \to D$, for some $k \leq j \leq l$, (D is not one of the configurations of this loop and the execution can leave the loop by updating to D), then $C_m = D$ for some $m > l$ (the execution leaves the loop eventually). Informally, once an execution reaches a loop and if it is possible to break from the loop by updating to a configuration outside the loop, then the configuration will be reached eventually. Weak fairness allows us to achieve the effect of Keller's ([3]) *finite-blocking* property which requires that signals are assimilated eventually by modules.

Next we define two important properties of STCAs. We say that a configuration C is *globally deterministic* if there exist a configuration D such that, for all C', if $C \to^* C'$, then $C' \to^* D$. Informally, D is the configuration that all executions from C must reach eventually. Moreover, we say that a configuration C is *globally reversible* if there exist a configuration D such that, for all C', if $C' \to^* C$, then $D \to^* C'$. Informally, all executions to C originate from D. This is a modification of global reversibility defined in [7], and is made here to accommodate for parallel signals and looping execution sequences.

For the purposes of this paper, we assume that the configurations are finite two-dimensional arrays, such that the four "edges" of the grid contain a row of cells which are not involved in updates.

Examples of STCAs developed for the simulation of reversible serial DI circuits can be seen in [9], [8] and [7]. [9] and [7] contain locally reversible and locally deterministic rules.

4 Direction-Reversible STCA for Serial DI Modules

In this section we define a new STCA intended for the simulation of serial DI modules, including reversible modules.

In Fig. 4, we give four different rules along with their multiple of 90 degrees rotations. Hence each line in Fig. 4 represents an equivalence class of rules. In the context of DI circuits, a signal is represented by a single subcell in state 1, with the subcell adjacent to its longest side in the quiescent state. Signals are considered to "point" in the direction perpendicular to the subcell's longest side. We refer to this set of rules, (and the STCA defined by this set) as *RS*.

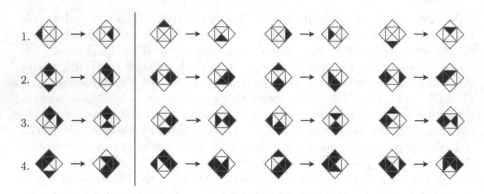

Fig. 4. The set of rules RS for reversible serial modules. Each class 1-4 consists of a single rule (on the left) together with three of its rotations (on the right). The classes represent the following behaviours: 1) Signal movement; 2) Right turn; 3) Left turn (direction-reversal of class 2); 4) Memory toggle.

Given an update rule r, consider an operation δ on r where $\delta(r)$ is defined by (a) *inverting* r, namely swapping the left and right-hand sides, and then (b) *inverting the direction of the signal* in the resulting rule, namely swapping the states of subcells inside the squares given by the following pairs (q, a), (c, s), (r, b), (d, t), (u, e), (g, w), (v, f), (h, x) as depicted in Fig. 3. We call $\delta(r)$ the *direction-reversal* (rule) of r. Given the set of rules R, $\delta(R)$ is the set of direction-reversal rules of the rules in R. For example, the direction-reversal of rule 2 in Fig. 4 is rule 3, namely $\delta(2) = 3$, and vice-versa. Also, $\delta(1)$ is the third rule in class 1 and $\delta(4)$ is the third rule in class 4.

Proposition 2. For each rule r in RS, $\delta(r) \in RS$. Hence, $\delta(RS) = RS$.

This implies that for each construction in RS which performs an operation on a single signal, inverting the direction of the signal in the rules has the same effect as using the inverses of rules. Moreover, we have:

Proposition 3. All rules of RS are locally reversible and locally deterministic.

Figure 5 shows a single construction which acts as either RT or IRT, depending which lines are used as inputs. This is a consequence of the direction-reversal nature of RS. We say that such constructions are *direction-reversible*. This implies that RS can be used to perform universal computation, and to simulate any reversible serial module (see Section 1). Furthermore, as both RT and IRT are simulated by a single construction separate constructions are not required to realise the inverse of a reversible serial circuit. Inverting a circuit in RS simply requires changing the direction of the signal. This bidirectional nature implies a potential advantage when considering physical implementation.

The properties of global reversibility and global determinism hold for all configurations which simulate reversible serial modules since the local reversibility

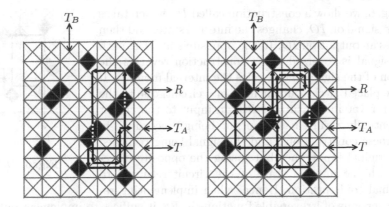

Fig. 5. Left: RT/IRT in state A. Right: RT/IRT in state B. When R and T are used as inputs, the construction acts as RT with T_A and T_B as outputs, and vice-versa for IRT. The images show the path of the signal T when the construction is utilised as RT. A white line through a memory structure indicates that the memory's state is toggled and the signal continues in the same direction. We note that, as can be seen here, the first and third rotations of the memory toggle rule (class 4) in RS are not required to realise RT/IRT, but are included to increase the design flexibility when implementing larger circuits.

and local determinism of the rules, together with the presence of a single signal, result in unique execution sequences.

Proposition 4. Any reversible serial module can be realised by a configuration in RS. Such configurations, and their derivatives, are globally deterministic, globally reversible, and direction-reversible.

The STCA in [8] supports direction-reversal, but the rules are not locally reversible or locally deterministic. We are not aware of any other STCA which allows direction-reversal. Furthermore, the STCA in [8] requires five classes of rules which are rotational-symmetric and reflective-symmetric. Our STCA RS uses only four classes of rotation-symmetric rules. The smallest STCA for simulating reversible serial circuits that we are aware of appears in [9]. It uses four classes of rotation-symmetric rules, but direction-reversal is not supported.

We now demonstrate a useful construction in RS. In [1] it is shown that any irreversible (forwards-deterministic) function (which we call I) of the form $(Input \rightarrow Output)$ can be converted to a reversible function which simulates the former. In order to be left with a garbage-less result, this requires a complex series of functions A, B, C where: A is a reversible version of the original irreversible function I, which performs the function of I while recording the computation history; B is a function which copies the output (excluding the computation history); and C is the inverse of A which removes the computation history and the first copy of the output, while reproducing the original input. This results in a new function of the form $(Input \rightarrow Input + Output)$ which simulates I.

In Fig. 6, we show a construction called *DR* which takes
an input signal on *IO*, changes the internal state, and then
produces an output on *IO*. In the opposite state, the path
of the signal is reversed. This construction reverses the
direction of the signal and toggles the internal memory. If
*DR*s are placed at the output lines of a circuit, due to the
direction-reversible nature of *RS*, an input to the circuit
will eventually result in the output being "recorded" in
one of these constructions, and the signal being returned
to the original input line (but facing the opposite direction), with the internal state of the circuit returned to
its original configuration. Hence, when implementing re-

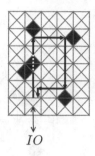

IO

Fig. 6. *DR*

versible versions of irreversible functions in *RS*, it suffices to implement only the
function *A*. *DR* can also be possibly utilised in scenarios where a computation
may need to be "aborted" and have the effects reversed.

In Fig. 7, we give the set of rules *M* for realising *Merge*. Informally, the new
rules extend the left/right-turn structure so that a signal approaching from the
previously unused side is (irreversibly) forwarded to the opposite side. Hence the
left/right turn structure can now operate as *Merge*. The rules in *M* are locally
deterministic but not locally reversible.

Fig. 7. The set of rules *M* to implement *Merge*. The rotation-symmetric equivalences
are included for ease of implementation, but are not required if turns (classes 2 and 3
in *RS*) are utilised.

Our second STCA is $S = RS \cup M$. *S* supports the reversible constructions
demonstrated in this section. Interestingly, direction-reversal is maintained for
all of these constructions. However, attempting to perform a direction-reversal
on constructions which utilise *Merge* may result in unexpected behaviours.

Theorem 5. All rules in *S* are locally deterministic. Any serial module can
be realised by a configuration in *S*. Such configurations, and their derivatives,
are globally deterministic. Configurations which realise reversible serial modules,
and their derivatives, are direction-reversible.

5   Extending to Parallel DI Modules

We now show how *RS* and *S* can be extended to cover parallel circuits. Recall
that {*RT, IRT, Fork, Join*} is universal for the class of non-arb non-b-arb modules (Proposition 1). Hence it suffices to add the rules for *Fork* and *Join*: these
are given in Figure 8.

Fig. 8. The set of rules P for parallel non-arb non-b-arb circuits. The rules represent: p1 *Fork* to *Join* evolution; p2 *Join* to *Fork* evolution; p3 (p4) *Fork* to *Join* (*Join* to *Fork*) evolution while producing outputs.

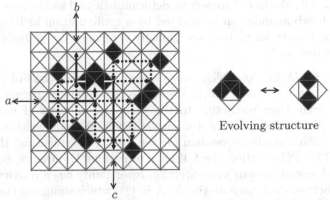

Evolving structure

Fig. 9. *Fork* and *Join*. The central structure evolves between *Fork* and *Join* patterns according to p1 and p2 in Fig. 8. When a (b, c) is used as an input, the construction acts as *Fork* (*Join*) with b and c (a) as outputs. The image shows the path of signals when used as a *Fork*. Signals loop along the dotted lines until they encounter the evolving structure in the correct state. This will eventually happen due to the weak fairness assumption in Section 3.

Fig. 10. The set of rules C to implement the crossing of intersecting signals

In order to maintain local reversibility and local determinism, rotation equivalent rules are not permitted. This imposes a design constraint on the layout of such circuits, and implies that *Fork* and *Join* constructions must be oriented appropriately in order to function correctly. This is trivially overcome by utilising left/right turn constructions when designing circuits. We note that the direction-reversal version of each rule in P is also in P, thus $\delta(P) = P$

Figure 9 shows a *Fork* and *Join* construction. As *Fork* and *Join* are each other's inverses, they can be realised with a single direction-reversible construction. This is achieved by two simple structures that evolve constantly, one into the other. The central structure is an *evolving structure* (as opposed to previously seen *static structures*), as updates can occur continuously even when no signals are present. It can be verified that the construction is globally deterministic and globally reversible when signals are applied as intended.

Figure 10 contains rules for crossing of signals. Note that $\delta(C) = C$.

We now define our third STCA $RP = RS \cup P \cup C$. As the construction for *Fork/Join* (Fig. 9) is direction-reversible, globally deterministic and globally reversible when operated with appropriately placed signals, it is easy to see that when combining the construction with that of RT/IRT and connecting lines appropriately as in DI circuits, the resulting configuration is also direction-reversible, globally deterministic and globally reversible.

Theorem 6. All rules in RP are locally deterministic and locally reversible. Any non-arb non-b-arb module can be realised by a configuration in RP. Such configurations, and their derivatives, are globally deterministic, globally reversible and direction-reversible.

We note the STCA in [20] which can implement the full class of parallel DI modules, but not with rules which are locally reversible or permit direction-reversibility, even when restricting to the reversible subclass of modules. We also note the *Partitioned Cellular Automaton* (PCA) from [5] which is similar to a STCA but with a smaller codomain for the update function, and three states per subcell. This PCA realises the full class of parallel DI circuits, but like [20] not with local reversibility or with direction-reversibility when restricting to the reversible subclass. And, we note the ACA in [21] which simulates the universal NAND gate via the use of parallel arbitrating DI modules.

Finally, we define our last STCA $NAP = RS \cup P \cup C \cup M$ for non-arbitrating parallel modules and, correspondingly to Theorems 5 and 6, we have:

Theorem 7. All rules in NAP are locally deterministic. Any non-arb module can be realised by a configuration in NAP. Such configurations, and their derivatives, are globally deterministic. Configurations which realise non-arb non-b-arb modules, and their derivatives, are direction-reversible.

6   Conclusion

In this paper we have introduced a new Self-Timed Cellular Automaton for reversible serial DI circuits. This STCA is locally reversible and locally deterministic. The STCA allows circuits to be inverted by reversing the direction of the signal. We have discussed the potential advantages of such a property, and shown how it can be used to realise efficiently garbage-less reversible functions. We have then shown how to extend the STCA to all serial modules, non-arb non-b-arb modules, and finally all non-arb modules while retaining local determinism and global determinism. We have shown that in the case of non-arb non-b-arb modules, global determinism and direction-reversibility are preserved.

References

1. Bennett, C.H.: Logical reversibility of computation. IBM Journal of Research and Development 17(6), 525–532 (1973)
2. Fredkin, E.F., Toffoli, T.: Conservative logic. International Journal of Theoretical Physics 21(3/4), 219–253 (1982)

3. Keller, R.M.: Towards a theory of universal speed-independent modules. IEEE Transactions on Computers 23(1), 21–33 (1974)
4. Kwiatkowska, M.Z.: Defining process fairness for non-interleaving concurrency. In: Veni Madhavan, C.E., Nori, K.V. (eds.) FSTTCS 1990. LNCS, vol. 472, pp. 286–300. Springer, Heidelberg (1990)
5. Lee, J., Adachi, S., Peper, F.: A partitioned cellular automaton approach for efficient implementation of asynchronous circuits. Comp. J. 54(7), 1211–1220 (2011)
6. Lee, J., Adachi, S., Peper, F., Morita, K.: Embedding universal delay-insensitive circuits in asynchronous cellular spaces. Fundam. Inf. 58(3-4), 295–320 (2003)
7. Lee, J., Huang, X., Zhu, Q.: Embedding simple reversed-twin elements into self-timed reversible cellular automata. J. Converg. Info. Tech. 6(1) (2011)
8. Lee, J., Peper, F., Adachi, S., Morita, K.: An asynchronous cellular automaton implementing 2-state 2-input 2-output reversed-twin reversible elements. In: Umeo, H., Morishita, S., Nishinari, K., Komatsuzaki, T., Bandini, S. (eds.) ACRI 2008. LNCS, vol. 5191, pp. 67–76. Springer, Heidelberg (2008)
9. Lee, J., Peper, F., Adachi, S., Morita, K., Mashiko, S.: Reversible computation in asynchronous cellular automata. In: Calude, C.S., Dinneen, M.J., Peper, F. (eds.) UMC 2002. LNCS, vol. 2509, pp. 220–229. Springer, Heidelberg (2002)
10. Martin, A.J.: The limitations to delay-insensitivity in asynchronous circuits. In: Procs. of AUSCRIPT 1990, pp. 263–278. MIT Press (1990)
11. Morita, K.: Reversible computing systems, logic circuits, and cellular automata. In: ICNC 2012, pp. 1–8. IEEE Computer Society (2012)
12. Morita, K.: A simple universal logic element and cellular automata for reversible computing. In: Margenstern, M., Rogozhin, Y. (eds.) MCU 2001. LNCS, vol. 2055, pp. 102–113. Springer, Heidelberg (2001)
13. Morita, K., Ogiro, T., Tanaka, K., Kato, H.: Classification and universality of reversible logic elements with one-bit memory. In: Margenstern, M. (ed.) MCU 2004. LNCS, vol. 3354, pp. 245–256. Springer, Heidelberg (2005)
14. Morrison, D.: Homepage, Department of Computer Science, University of Leicester (2014), http://www.cs.le.ac.uk/people/dm181
15. Morrison, D., Ulidowski, I.: Arbitration and reversibility of parallel delay-insensitive modules. In: Yamashita, S., Minato, S.-I. (eds.) RC 2014. LNCS, vol. 8507, pp. 67–81. Springer, Heidelberg (2014)
16. Morrison, D., Ulidowski, I.: Reversible delay-insensitive distributed memory modules. In: Dueck, G.W., Miller, D.M. (eds.) RC 2013. LNCS, vol. 7948, pp. 11–24. Springer, Heidelberg (2013)
17. Patra, P., Fussell, D.S.: Efficient building blocks for delay insensitive circuits. In: Procs. of Async 1994, pp. 196–205. Society Press (1994)
18. Patra, P., Fussell, D.S.: Efficient delay-insensitive RSFQ circuits. In: Procs. of ICCD 1996, pp. 413–418. IEEE Computer Society (1996)
19. Peper, F., Isokawa, T., Kouda, N., Matsui, N.: Self-timed cellular automata and their computational ability. Future Gener. Comput. Syst. 18(7), 893–904 (2002)
20. Peper, F., Lee, J., Adachi, S., Mashiko, S.: Laying out circuits on asynchronous cellular arrays: a step towards feasible nanocomputers? Nanotechnology 14(4), 469 (2003)
21. Schneider, O., Worsch, T.: A 3-state asynchronous CA for the simulation of delay-insensitive circuits. In: Sirakoulis, G.C., Bandini, S. (eds.) ACRI 2012. LNCS, vol. 7495, pp. 565–574. Springer, Heidelberg (2012)

Implementation of a Cellular Automaton with Globally Switchable Rules

Václav Šimek, Richard Růžička, Adam Crha, and Radek Tesař

Faculty of Information Technology, Brno University of Technology,
Bozetechova 2, 612 66 Brno, Czech Republic
{simekv,ruzicka,itesar,icrha}@fit.vutbr.cz

Abstract. Cellular automata represent a discrete model of a computational machine with the inherent concept of totally distributed state transitional function. Previous studies have indicated that well-devised type of a global influence turns out to be an important factor in terms of improving the overall efficiency of a computation process within automata. In this context, polymorphic electronics is an approach that introduces a specific way of a global control to the circuit, not by means of using a dedicated global signal but through employing an inherent environmental variable. In our case the global information is uniformly propagated through the existing voltage supply rail, which is naturally available to all individual cells of a given automaton. It seems that the suggested approach may be very useful for the implementation of enhanced cellular automata. In this paper, the real hardware implementation of a cellular automaton using polymorphic chip and the obtained experimental results are presented together with a subsequent discussion.

Keywords: Cellular automata, polymorphic electronics, globally controlled reconfiguration.

1 Introduction

Reconfiguration of digital circuits is a widely accepted method how to deal with certain classes of problems in an efficient way. In addition, recent advancements within the field of design techniques and components for digital circuits outline yet another perspective, where the aptly chosen set of components is deployed with the purpose of executing several different (intended) functions [1]. Such type of circuit is typically designed as a compact structure including multifunctional, as well as conventional elements. The physical layout of the circuit alone remains untouched and only behaviour of the explicitly selected components changes.

Polymorphic circuits [2] closely adhere to the suggested multifunctional operation scheme where the function change is subjected to the actual state of the operating environments; it may be triggered by various parameters with direct influence on the electronic structures power supply voltage level, voltage level of a signal, temperature, etc. Most importantly, the change of the polymorphic circuit function comes right away (without any eminent delay perceived) and sensitivity to the environments is naturally embedded to the circuit itself [3].

J. Wąs, G.C. Sirakoulis, and S. Bandini (Eds.): ACRI 2014, LNCS 8751, pp. 378–387, 2014.

Cellular automaton (CA) notion as a sequential circuit with distributed (local) transition function, where the implementation of the transition function was carried out with a multifunctional (polymorphic) circuit, is proposed in [10]. The main idea in this case is that globally controlled change of local transition function may help to notably improve computation efficiency and, in the same time, obtain new patterns during an evolution of CA, which would be unreachable with a conventional approach [16]. The theoretical conception proposed in [10] is now used for a physical creation of a 1D CA with globally switchable local transition function using real polymorphic gates.

The structure of this paper is organized as follows: section 2 contains brief summary of CA principles useful for the subsequent experiments. Section 3 introduces general features and relevant technical aspects of polymorphic electronics. The configuration of the actual experimental workbench is described in section 4 and section 5 presents discussion on the obtained results. Finally, section 6 concludes the paper.

2 Cellular Automata

A group of certain types of physical models depicting real situation, where the model can be represented by a software algorithm or even in the form of a fabricated device, is referred to as cellular automata [11]. Cellular automata are also recognized as dynamic, synchronous systems, which typically operate in a discrete time and space, i.e. the value of individual model variables is subjected to a swift transition between the specified states depending on the time step.

The space in which the CA performs required calculation may potentially contain an infinite number of cells. However, in real applications it is obviously far more convenient to adopt a finite range of the underlying abstraction. This observation is especially true in conjunction with digital systems and circuits modelling. The actual computational space is mostly represented through a grid-like structure that can have up to n-dimensions. At a given moment each cell may be assigned one particular state out of q possible variants, where q is size of state set. If $q = 2$ (size of state set), then CA is called binary CA.

The updated values (states) of cells within a given system model are obtained through the application of a local transition function, which is the same for the whole automaton. The local transition function calculates new state of a given cell using its current state and also the immediate state of relevant neighbours from its vicinity. The local transition function is also called a transition rule.

The selected rule can be further decomposed into a finite set of partial rewriting steps. Resulting size of this set clearly depends on the exact number of cell allowable neighbours. In case of a simple 1D CA its surroundings may consist of just two nearest neighbours, 1 cell on each side. Furthermore, the entire rule set is made up of the following collection based on 3-bit combinations: (111, 110, 101, 100, 011, 010, 001, 000). A certain rule set determines what will be the upcoming cell state, e.g. $(111, ..., 000) \Rightarrow 0, 0, 0, 1, 1, 1, 1, 0$. If we carefully look at the new states of all combinations, we can perceive it as a number represented in a binary domain. This number is then converted into the decimal representation, which in fact specifies the rule's name. In this case the rule is called Rule 30.

All the experimental work carried out within the scope of this contribution is proposed around 1D CA with two possible cell states and with two specific rules, in particular Rule 232 and Rule 150. There can be identified many different parameters as the evaluation of CA characteristics. With respect to the specific rules mentioned above and feasibility of the expected implementation comprising polymorphic hardware building blocks, the most important features are following:

1. **Parallelism** - evaluation of all cells running in parallel,
2. **Locality** - new state of a cell depends on its current value and neighbours,
3. **Homogenity** - all cells use the same local transition function.

3   Polymorphic Electronics

Generally, polymorphic circuits can be used in various situations where the adaptation of a given circuit may take place with respect to the potentially variable operating conditions or as a direct response to the explicit need for a smart and fast reconfiguration process [4]. Such behaviour is obviously useful in case of circuits that must adapt themselves to unfriendly or harsh environments, e.g. by restriction of power consumption [5] or heat dissipation [6], while simultaneously keeping the essential functional or operational characteristics within a safety range. The notion of polymorphic electronics is also useful in case of applications that are basically mono-functional, but still exhibit a strong need for some peculiar add-on features. This is attractive e.g. for embedded diagnostics [7], security applications [2], etc.

It is possible to recognize two different methods how to create polymorphic sequential circuits. The first one is based just on the utilization of polymorphic flip-flops [8]. Another approach [4], proposed by Ruzicka, simply combines ordinary flip-flops and polymorphic gates in the next-state logic. Examples of polymorphic sequential circuits, possible synthesis techniques and purpose of such circuits in dependable applications were published in [4], [5], [6], [9]. There also exist several techniques which facilitate the synthesis of polymorphic combinational circuits (see section 4). The characteristic features of polymorphic electronics are obviously useful for both combinational and sequential circuits.

Plenty of diverse types of polymorphic circuits were proposed by means of using various evolutionary design methods. In this perspective special attention was given above all to so-called Cartesian Genetic Programming (CGP) [17]. But even non-evolutionary (conventional) design methods were introduced. However, the practical utilization also depends on the availability of suitable polymorphic components (gates). Polymorphic circuits could be obviously used with an advantage in a number if applications that assume adaptation of the circuit to the unfriendly environment or as a means of smart and fast reconfiguration [4].

Under the main objective of this contribution, multifunctional nature of polymorphic circuitry is exploited for a globally controlled reconfiguration process of the local transition function, thus, influencing state of cells in a given CA. This approach brings a kind of global information to the system, which is otherwise characterised by locality, in order to increase the effectiveness of computation.

The implementation of a global control scheme involves relatively modest difficulty when the cellular automata are modelled purely in software, because each cell is accessible in a constant time. However, as a physical fabrication of cellular automata-based hardware truly utilizes the concept of locality (only neighbouring cells are physically connected) there is a highly constrained or no way at all how to manage an access to each particular cell from boundary cells [10]. However, polymorphic electronics with its intrinsic global control capabilities of logic functions opens a feasible way towards physical circuit implementation.

4   Implementation of Global Control Scheme

The principle of locality is one of the key building elements behind the traditional concept of a cellular automaton. However, the complete lack of global influence within the structure of CA may impose significant disadvantages, for example, in terms of a bit cumbersome evolution toward expected solution. It was demonstrated in [10] that the introduction of certain procedures enabling global control mechanism can lead to a significant increase of computation effectiveness. Another benefits of a global control are closely associated with the necessity to initialize a CA based model of a given system or computation problem into a required state. For example, the authors in [18] have addressed an efficient method of CA global initialization based on FPGA technology.

4.1   Constraints of Physical Fabrication

The implementation of necessary resources enabling global control within CA doesnt bring any serious difficulty on a software level. The notable point is that all the instantiated cells are accessible in a constant time and therefore no shortcomings associated with information or data exchange are observed. Due to the fact that hardware version of such system model closely follows the concept of locality, where only the adjacent or closely neighbouring cells are connected together, a very difficult way, if any at all, how to gain an access to a particular cell placed well beyond the edge is available.

A fundamental problem with the on-chip realization of a CA-like system, where the global control means are requested, typically lies in the fact that an invaluable chip estate area would have to be also designated for global control wires routing purpose. If we consider a potentially tremendous number of cells, which may be populated in case of a very complex system representation, such approach would be more than cost prohibitive. Therefore, no additional wires attached to all the cells within a given CA, except the fundamental power supply delivery rail, should be tolerated. Such restricted design conditions makes the whole matter a bit complicated task to accomplish.

4.2   Solution with Polymorphic Gates

The main objective here is to demonstrate an approach leading towards the efficient and transparent means how to globally change the local transition function associated with each cell. The presented solution is based on the adoption of so called polymorphic gates. If the transition function is handled as a digital circuitry with the polymorphic gates sensitive to V_{dd} supply level, its possible to achieve a dynamic parallel reconfiguration of these functions, which takes place just in an instant upon the V_{dd} change, for all the cells in a desired way.

Polymorphic experimental chip REPOMO32 [13], previously developed at our institution, will be used for the hardware implementation of CA transition function. REPOMO32 chip contains up to 32 digital logic blocks where each of them may work in a conventional way or as the polymorphic gate. The active mode of each block and the interaction with its surroundings can be easily adjusted by means of downloading configuration bitstream. Moreover, the interconnection structure inside REPOMO32 chip allows their combination into larger functional units, regardless of the configured behaviour.

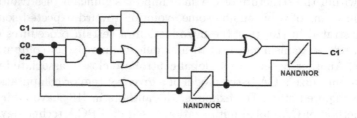

Fig. 1. Circuit level view of polymorphic based solution for 3-bit parity/3-bit majority function (rule 150/232)

Typical hardware structure of a transition function within CA includes two important parts – combinatorial cell state transition logic and a synchronous sequential block typically composed of a flip-flop. The proposed internal organization of next state combinatorial portion of a transition function based on the polymorphic gates is depicted for 1D cellular automaton on a Fig. 1 above.

Because the transition function has a certain number of polymorphic gates used for its implementation, the impact of V_{dd} changes on the overall CA performance and its subsequent evolution will be demonstrated. Basically, the active operation mode of the transition function will alternate between Rule 150 (which is 3-bit parity function) and Rule 232 (which is 3-bit majority function) with respect to the actual level of V_{dd} level. In fact, the automaton uses Rule 150 when V_{dd} enters the range of $3.9 - 5V$. On the other hand, drop of V_{dd} value below approximately $3.8V$ threshold will immediately notify the automaton to use the Rule 232.

Due to the fact that just a single rail is available for the purpose of supply voltage delivery to the configurable logic blocks inside REPOMO32 chip, all of them are simultaneously exposed to voltage transitions mentioned above. However, it is going to have an decisive effect only on those with the polymorphic mode turned on. In the same time, the remaining configurable logic blocks, where the conventional digital operation was intentionally selected, exhibit a stable behaviour, completely free of any side effect or unexpected fluctuations, even under the varying supply voltage level within the specified ranges.

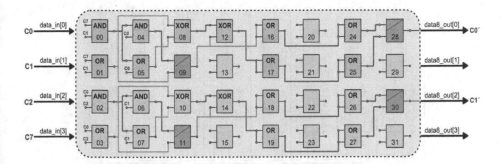

Fig. 2. Internal configuration of REPOMO32 chip depicting the rule 150/232 behavior within 2 cells of CA

Fig. 2 above provides a detailed circuit level view on the REPOMO32 internal configuration, which is using conventional and polymorphic gates altogether. It shows the implementation of a transition function for 2 cells (cell C0 and C1) of CA. The actual circuitry includes two polymorphic gates with NAND/NOR mode, two XOR gates, two OR gates and finally two AND gates. Of course, the resulting circuit solution within REPOMO32 chip could be even more compact. But due to relatively limited resources, e.g. the constrains imposed on the input/output signals and their routing among the available digital blocks, it was necessary to use, for example, the block number 16 and 24 switched into OR mode just in order to get the resulting value of a combinatorial stage, which implements the transition function, safely out of the chip.

With the conventional CMOS digital gates it would be necessary to employ some sort of multiplexing scheme coupled with dedicated global control signals for switching between the two different physical circuits (3-bit parity and 3-bit majority). It is obvious that two two-input XOR gates are necessary for the parity function. On the other hand, majority function requires four two-input gates. Finally, multiplexing stage would be based on three two-input gates. Therefore we arrive at 9 gates in total so the conventional solution appears to be more costly in terms of consumed two-input gates than the polymorphic counterpart.

The complete structure of CA involves 8 cells in our case. If we consider the fact that its possible to place two local transition functions within single REPOMO32 chip, its evident that 4 of these chips will be needed for a full-scale implementation. Besides the essential platform with a matrix of configurable logic elements, including the polymorphic ones, additional external flip-flops were used in order to establish necessary register functionality. A closer look at Fig. 3 below unveils the logic behind the mutual interconnection of the individual cells. In fact, each cell has a direct contact with its immediate neighbours, e.g. cell denoted as C5 is placed among C4 and C6.

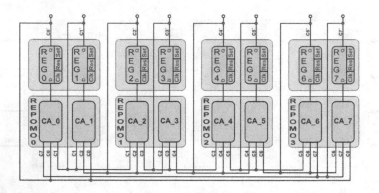

Fig. 3. Block diagram that shows the high level structure of the CA implementation

5   Experimental Results and Discussion

The proposed variant of a CA with a global control scheme was successfully implemented using the physically fabricated REPOMO32 chip. However, in order to demonstrate the validity of this claim, it was very important to investigate at first if the CA function remains stable even without supply voltage change and, in the same time, if the behaviour corresponds to the prescribed rule as well. Finally, its operation was carefully verified within the two allowable V_{dd} ranges, as explained earlier. All the following results were obtained during the actual workbench measurements, where the digital scope Agilent DSA90254A and the logic analyser Agilent 16823A were used as the main instruments.

Polymorphic gates were initially switched into NAND mode, where the behaviour of CA transition function strictly adhered to Rule 150. Binary sequence of 10111101 was used as the input stimulus. Zero value observed at NAND/NOR signal indicates that the power supply is switched into NAND mode. Moreover, the rising edge of EN signal was used just for the synchronization and triggering purposes during the measurement. CLK signal then governed the operation of flip-flops attached to the output stage of each CA cell state combinatorial transition function, see Fig. 4 below.

Now, it is important to find out if the same evidence holds for V_{dd} level periodically alternating within a range of $3.3 - 5V$. If one closely follows the

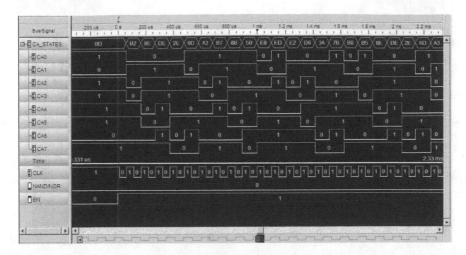

Fig. 4. Cellular automaton operation with selected NAND mode of polymorphic gates due to 5V supply voltage. Rule 150 is therefore executed with binary 10111101 input pattern. The signal waveform was captured by the logic analyser Agilent 16823A.

voltage trace on Fig. 5 below it is possible to distinguish the NAND and NOR operation modes i.e. 5V level for NAND mode (Rule 150) and 3.3V for NOR mode (Rule 232). Because the circuit layout of REPOMO32 chip is quite rugged, so to say, small glitches visible on the voltage trace do not trigger the unwanted change of the polymorphic gate operation mode. After all, its not a difficult to recognize that the digital waveform within Fig. 5 corresponds to the expected behaviour when Rules 150 and 232 are being repeatedly applied.

5.1   Future Research Activities

The vivid field of digital circuits is continuously exposed to the emergence of a new and highly perspective materials for physical fabrication of elementary structures. In this context, the future work could be devoted to the possible exploitation of these materials for a new generation of multifunctional digital building blocks (i.e. gates) and, thus, their application within cellular automata domain. One can imagine digital gates based on materials like graphene or even organic electronics. For example, pentacene based transistors with ambipolar properties could potentially lead to even more compact solution [14], [15].

The point is that digital logic elements created with contemporary CMOS process are built upon set of complementary pairs of n-channel and p-channel transistors. On the other hand, the notion of ambipolarity principle refers to the situation when a single transistor structure, once fabricated from suitable materials, may behave like p-channel or n-channel device with respect to the operating conditions at a given moment. This observation clearly opens a path towards space-efficient circuit structures due to the fact, that only one type of transistor, with ambipolar or multifunctional nature, is actually deployed.

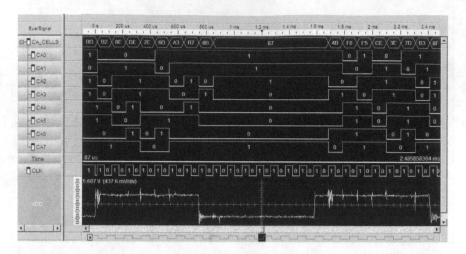

Fig. 5. Cellular automaton operation is continuously alternating between NAND/NOR mode due to variable level of V_{dd} supply voltage. Rules 150/232 are executed here with the binary input pattern 10111101. The resulting combined signal waveform is showing the traces from logic analyser in the upper portion, whereas the runtime behaviour of V_{dd} captured by the digital scope Agilent DSA90254A is depicted at the bottom.

6   Conclusions

It has been successfully demonstrated that a local transition function can be globally adjusted when exploiting a suitable approach. Instead of adhering to the conventional methods, our solution is based on a direct exploitation of the polymorphic gates embedded within the physical circuit structure, which is responsible for the behaviour of a local transition function. In this way, just an ordinary change of V_{dd} level, which is naturally available to all configurable gates inside REPOMO32 chip, allows a local transition function to be selected accordingly (alternation of Rule 150 and Rule 232 in our case). Thanks to the introduction of an intrinsic global control scheme it was possible to obtain the patterns that it would not be feasible to produce with just a single CA. Finally, in case of 1D cellular automaton the resulting solution is even cheaper in terms of the actual gates count than the one based on a conventional circuit solution.

Acknowledgments. This work was supported by the grant Unconventional Design Techniques for Intrinsic Reconfiguration of Digital Circuits: From Materials to Implementation (LD14055) and by the IT4Innovations Centre of Excellence (CZ.1.05/1.1.00/02.0070).

References

1. Ruzicka, R.: On Bifunctional Polymorphic Gates Controlled by a Special Signal. WSEAS Transactions on Circuits 7(3), 96–101 (2008) ISSN 1109-2734

2. Stoica, A., Zebulum, R.S., Keymeulen, D.: Polymorphic electronics. In: Liu, Y., Tanaka, K., Iwata, M., Higuchi, T., Yasunaga, M. (eds.) ICES 2001. LNCS, vol. 2210, pp. 291–302. Springer, Heidelberg (2001)
3. Ruzicka, R., Sekanina, L., Prokop, R.: Physical demonstration of Polymorphic Self-checking Circuits. In: Proc. of the 14th IEEE On-Line Testing Symposium, pp. 31–36. IEEE CS (2008)
4. Ruzicka, R.: Dependable Controller Design using Polymorphic Counters. In: Proc. of 12th Euromicro Conference on Digital System Design, pp. 355–362. IEEE CS, Los Alamitos (2009)
5. Ruzicka, R.: Gracefully Degrading Circuit Controllers Based on Polytronics. In: Proc. of 13th Euromicro Conference on Digital System Design, pp. 809–812. IEEE CS, Los Alamitos (2010)
6. Ruzicka, R., Simek, V.: Chip Temperature Selfregulation for Digital Circuits Using Polymorphic Electronics Principles. In: Proceedings of 14th Euromicro Conference on Digital System Design, pp. 205–212. ICSP, Los Alamitos (2011)
7. Sekanina, L., Starecek, L., Kotásek, Z., Gajda, Z.: Polymorphic Gates in Design and Test of Digital Circuits. International Journal of Unconventional Computing 4(2), 125–142 (2008) ISSN 1548-7199
8. Zebulum, R.S., Stoica, A.: Ripple Counters Controlled by Analog Voltage. NASA Tech. Briefs 30(3), 2 (2006)
9. Ruzicka, R.: New Polymorphic NAND/XOR Gate. In: Proceedings of 7th WSEAS International Conference on Applied Computer Science, pp. 192–196. WSEAS, Venice (2007)
10. Sekanina, L., Komenda, T.: Global Control in Polymorphic Cellular Automata. Journal of Cellular Automata 6(4-5), 301–321 (2011)
11. Wolfram, S.: A New Kind of Science, 1197 p. Wolfram Media, Champaign (2002)
12. Kari, J.J.: Basic Concepts of Cellular Automata. In: Rozenberg, G., et al. (eds.) Handbook of Natural Computing, pp. 3–24. Springer, Heidelberg (2012)
13. Sekanina, L., Rika, R., Vaek, Z., Prokop, R., Fujcik, L.: REPOMO32 - New Reconfigurable Polymorphic Integrated Circuit for Adaptive Hardware. In: Proc. of the 2009 IEEE Symposium Series on Computational Intelligence - Workshop on Evolvable and Adaptive Hardware, pp. 39–46. IEEE CIS, Nashville (2009)
14. Paasch, G., Lindner, T., Rost-Bietsch, C.: Operation and Properties of Ambipolar Organic Field-effect Transistors. Journal of Applied Physics 98(8), 084505-1–084505-13 (2005)
15. Wang, S.D., Kanai, K., Ouchi, Y., Seki, K.: Bottom contact ambipolar organic thin film transistor and organic inverter based on C60/pentacene heterostructure. Organic Electronics 7(6), 457–464 (2006)
16. Chandler, S.J.: Cellular Automata with Global Control from The Wolfram Demonstrations Project (2009),
   http://demonstrations.wolfram.com/CellularAutomataWithGlobalControl
17. Miller, J.F., Thomson, P.: Cartesian Genetic Programming. In: Poli, R., Banzhaf, W., Langdon, W.B., Miller, J., Nordin, P., Fogarty, T.C. (eds.) EuroGP 2000. LNCS, vol. 1802, pp. 121–132. Springer, Heidelberg (2000)
18. Vourkas, I., Sirakoulis, G.C.: FPGA based cellular automata for environmental modeling. In: 19th IEEE Int. Conf. Electronics, Circ. and Syst (ICECS), Seville, Spain, December 9-12, pp. 93–96 (2012)

Highly Compact Automated Implementation of Linear CA on FPGAs

Ayan Palchaudhuri, Rajat Subhra Chakraborty, Mohammad Salman,
Sreemukh Kardas, and Debdeep Mukhopadhyay

Department of Computer Science and Engineering,
Indian Institute of Technology Kharagpur,
Kharagpur, West Bengal, India – 721302
{ayan,rschakraborty,md.salman,sai.sreemukh,debdeep}@cse.iitkgp.ernet.in

Abstract. The current literature on cellular automata (CA) mostly overlooks the fact that the perceived regularity and locality of interconnects in a CA are often *logical* rather than *physical*, and difficult to achieve in practical implementations. Optimized mapping, placement and routing of circuits are especially challenging for *Field Programmable Gate Array* (FPGA) platforms, which often result in low-performance implementations. We develop a design methodology for the automated implementation of low-resource, high-performance CA circuits, by optimal usage of the underlying FPGA architecture, direct primitive instantiation, and constrained placement. Case study for an 1-D CA circuit reveal higher performance, lower hardware resource requirement (by a factor of 0.5 X), acceptable power-delay product (PDP), and superior design scalability, in comparison to implementations derived by standard FPGA CAD tool design flow.

Keywords: Cellular Automata, FPGA, Look-Up Table, Placement.

1 Introduction

The regular, modular and cascadable structure of cellular automata (CA) with only local neighbourhood dependence of the cells are the attractive features that makes it suitable for VLSI implementation [1,2]. Although theoretically, CAs are attractive enough, in practice, their implementation on FPGAs often turn out to be inefficient, because usually the user has limited control on the inference of logic elements, along with their placement and routing. Moreover, the CAD algorithms that perform these steps in an FPGA, typically have some probabilistic metaheuristic components (e.g. *simulated annealing*) [3], which makes the performance of a given design somewhat unpredictable when implemented on a given FPGA platform. Hence, it cannot be guaranteed that connected CA cells in logical proximity would actually have a very short length of interconnect between them, when implemented physically.

With significant increase in circuit complexity for FPGA-based designs, even the most sophisticated CAD tools often result in circuit implementations with

J. Wąs, G.C. Sirakoulis, and S. Bandini (Eds.): ACRI 2014, LNCS 8751, pp. 388–397, 2014.

unsatisfactory performance and resource requirements, owing to their inability to optimally exploit the underlying FPGA architecture and routing fabric. Hence, implementations derived through the standard automatic logic synthesis based design flow starting with the Behavioral or Register Transfer Level (RTL) Hardware Description Language (HDL) describing the circuit, can be outperformed by more *custom* design techniques. If the implementation has a sufficiently regular structure, it becomes possible to automate the generation of their HDL description and placement constraint files.

Direct *primitive instantiation* is an effective approach for optimization of designs on the Xilinx FPGA platform [4], and is often the only approach, or is simpler than rewriting the RTL code to coax the logic synthesis tool to infer the desired architectural components. Placement steps also need to be constrained and controlled, as the CAD placement tools, if allowed to perform unconstrained placement and routing, often result in large routing delays. This happens because the technology-mapped logic elements, both inferred and instantiated, can get unevenly and randomly distributed across the FPGA fabric, resulting in greater routing and interconnect delays, thereby contributing to the critical path delay.

The only disadvantage of using a design methodology involving direct primitive instantiation and constrained placement is that the design becomes less portable and harder to maintain. In spite of this, the methodology is very effective in practice, considering the facts that (a) often the target FPGA platform is known before the circuit is designed, and, (b) FPGAs from a related family from the same vendor are often backward compatible regarding the design elements (primitives and macros) supported. For example, newer versions of FPGAs of the Virtex family from Xilinx are expected to support primitives supported in some older Virtex versions. Thus, the HDL code for instantiating primitives targeting the older versions, and the constraints to control the placement, can be reused in the newer version after small modifications, if necessary.

In practice, CA circuits are useful for test pattern generation and construction of Built In Self Test (BIST) structures within VLSI chips [2]. Since the structures are based on simple rules and amenable to fast designs, high performance hardware implementation of CA algorithms has always been an important research topic over the years. Previously, when the advanced FPGA families were not available, FPGA architecture supporting 5-input 3-output AND-XOR based logic blocks along with an efficient multi-level AND-XOR logic minimization scheme was proposed for efficient implementation of CA array [5]. In [6], authors demonstrated faster implementation of CA on FPGA hardware, compared to optimized software implementation by achieving a speed-up in the range of 14 to 19. A methodology for VLSI implementation of CA algorithms, where an automatic translation scheme from CA algorithms to the corresponding VHDL, was proposed in [7]. FPGA based CA implementation was also reported in [8]. However, to the best of our knowledge, there has been no reported work regarding the principles, design philosophy and CAD techniques for efficient low-level implementation of CA on modern families of actual FPGAs, aiming to map the CA structures optimally to the native architecture of the FPGA.

To summarize, the following are the main contributions of our work:

- We develop a methodology to design high performance CA circuits, following a *bit-sliced* philosophy for Xilinx Virtex-6 FPGAs, by making optimal use of the native hardware resources on the target platform. We perform constrained placement of the hardware primitives, so that the logically related slices are juxtaposed as much as possible.
- We develop a CAD tool to automate the design descriptions of 1-D CA circuits by prompting the user to enter the following fields: CA rule numbers and their corresponding encoding, hybrid CA rule string and the starting coordinates to map the circuit on the FPGA fabric. The tool can also examine the feasibility of placement of the CA circuits by ensuring that the area spanned by it on the FPGA fabric is not occupied by any other logic.
- We establish the superiority of the proposed methodology by designing and implementing 1-D CA circuits as a case study. In comparison to the circuits derived from RTL descriptions by logic synthesis using the standard FPGA CAD tools, those designed following the proposed design technique demonstrate higher performance, lower area, acceptable power delay product (PDP), and superior design scalability.

The rest of the paper is organized as follows. In Section 2, we discuss the architecture of Xilinx Virtex-6 slices. In Section 3, we describe the proposed design methodology for realization of efficient high-performance CA circuits on FPGA. The associated design automation tool has been described in Section 4. The implementation results to establish the superiority of the proposed design methodology have been tabulated and interpreted in Section 5. We conclude in Section 6.

2   Virtex-6 Architecture

Each *Configurable Logic Block* (CLB) of Virtex-6 architecture supports two *slices*, where each slice comprises of four look-up tables (LUTs), a single length-4 carry chain, wide function multiplexers, and eight flip-flops (FFs) [9], as shown in Fig. 1. The LUTs or function generators in Virtex-6 FPGAs can implement any arbitrary six-input, one-output logic function, but can also be configured to realize a five (or lower)-input, two-output (using the O_6 and O_5 terminals) logic function. Out of the eight FFs per slice, four FFs can accept inputs either from the O_5 outputs of the LUTs, or external bypass inputs to the slice. The combination of four LUTs with eight registers provides both performance advantages and resource reduction over previous architectures, for example, Virtex-5, that supports four FFs in each slice [10].

In the next section, we describe the proposed design methodology based on optimal use of hardware primitives available on the target FPGA platform.

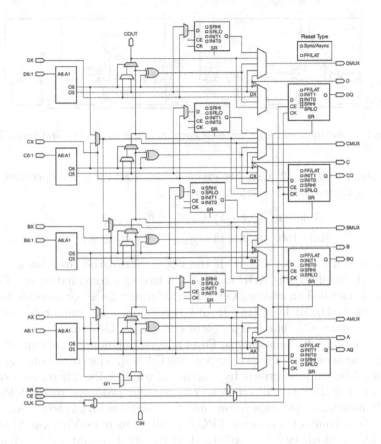

Fig. 1. Virtex-6 Slice Architecture [9]

3   Design Methodology

3.1   Adapting CA to the Native FPGA Architecture

To demonstrate the design philosophy, consider a *null boundary*, maximal length linear CA [11]. Such a circuit usually is a collection of a discrete lattice of cells, where each cell has a storage element in the form of a D-FF and associated combinational logic. The state of a n-bit CA is denoted by the n-bit tuple obtained by concatenating the values held by the D-FFs at that instant of time. Thus, if the CA has n cells, then the state at any instant may be expressed as $Y_t = \{q_0(t), q_1(t), ..., q_{n-1}(t)\}$, where $q_i(t)$ denotes the state of the ith cell at the tth instant of time. The state of the ith cell at the $(t+1)^{th}$ instant of time is denoted by $q_i(t+1)$, where $q_i(t+1) = f\left(q_{i-1}(t), q_i(t), q_{i+1}(t)\right)$, and determines the combinational logic for each stage. Here, the next state logic function '$f()$', is known as the *rule of the CA* [11]. By convention, if the next state function of a cell is expressed in the form of a truth-table, then the equivalent decimal output is called *rule number of the CA*. For example, the next state logic equations for

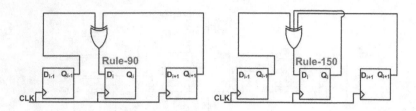

Fig. 2. Combinational logic for cells corresponding to *rule-90* and *rule-150*

rule-90 and *rule-150* [12] CAs are given in Eq. 1 and Eq. 2 respectively, with their circuit representations depicted in Fig. 2.

$$\text{Rule-90:} \quad q_i(t+1) = q_{i-1}(t) \oplus q_{i+1}(t) \tag{1}$$

$$\text{Rule-150:} \quad q_i(t+1) = q_{i-1}(t) \oplus q_i(t) \oplus q_{i+1}(t) \tag{2}$$

where $q_i = 0$ if $i < 0$ or $i \geq n$. If the CA is *linear*, the combinational logic functions $f()$ involves only XOR logic. A CA having a combination of XOR and XNOR logic is called an *additive* CA, whereas for *non-linear* or *non-additive* CA, $f()$ involves AND/OR logic [13]. If all CA cells obey the same rule, then it is termed as *uniform* CA, else it is a *hybrid* CA. *Linear* CAs can also be described by their *characteristic polynomials*. From a given polynomial, we can efficiently determine the structure of the corresponding CA [14]. The corresponding CA by convention is usually described by a string of 0's and 1's, where, for example, '1' refers to rule-150 and '0' refers to rule-90. Our proposed methodology can efficiently implement two-rule *linear*, *additive*, *uniform* and *hybrid* CAs.

With the advent of advanced FPGA families such as Virtex-6, that have 6-input LUTs which can be configured in the dual output mode, significant hardware reduction can be achieved which has been used to our advantage in our proposed design philosophy. *Packing* is a key step in the FPGA tool flow that is tightly integrated with the boundaries between *logic synthesis, technology mapping* and *placement* [15]. For Virtex-5 FPGAs, the packing technique targets the dual-output LUTs to achieve area efficiency by exploring the feasibility of packing two logic functions into a single LUT [15]. This is possible whenever the two logic functions have no more than five distinct input variables. In such cases, a more efficient mapping of the design is expected, culminating into shorter interconnect wirelength, which in turn results in lesser critical path delay. However, our implementation results for Virtex-6 family of FPGAs, which is an advanced and modified version of Virtex-5, clearly show that in spite of the methodology adopted by the common FPGA CAD tools, the packing behavior is highly unpredictable and the tool fails to configure the LUTs in the dual output mode. This doubles the overall LUT requirement and consequently the number of slices. By detailed experimentation with the *Xilinx ISE* CAD tool for FPGAs, we observed that for certain combinational circuits (e.g. comparators), the packing step is efficiently carried out, whereas for certain sequential circuits or any pipelined implementations, the packing step continues to remain to be an inefficient one.

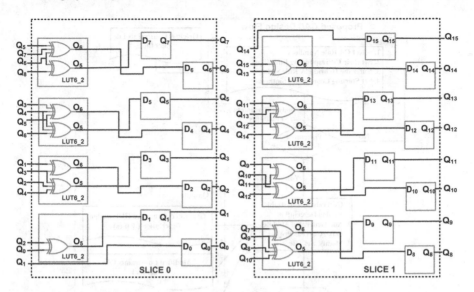

Fig. 3. Optimized architecture for a high-performance 16-bit 1-D linear CA for the (primitive) polynomial $x^{16} + x^5 + x^3 + x^2 + 1$ (or the equivalent hybrid rule $< 0001111001001000 >$) mapped on Xilinx Virtex-6 FPGAs

Consider an 1-D CA where the next state of a particular cell depends only on itself or on one or both of its two immediate neighbours. It is easy to deduce that in such cases, any two adjacent cells can have a maximum of four distinct inputs. In such a situation, it is possible to pack the next state logic for any two adjacent cells of a CA in a single LUT. Since Virtex-6 architectures facilitate registering of both the LUT outputs using two FFs present in the same slice as that of the LUT, we can achieve a compact FPGA realization of the architecture. The architecture for a 16 cell 1-D linear maximal length CA for the (primitive) polynomial $x^{16} + x^5 + x^3 + x^2 + 1$ (or the equivalent *hybrid* rule $< 0001111001001000 >$) [16] is shown in Fig. 3. Thus, in this process, for an n-cell maximal length CA architecture, $\lceil n/8 \rceil$ Virtex-6 FPGA slices are required.

3.2 Constrained Placement for Improved Performance

When no placement constraints are provided, the Xilinx Place and Route (P&R) CAD software tool performs an unoptimized floorplanning by apparently random placement of logic elements into arbitrary vacant slices, leading to inefficient routing and decreased speed of operation. The speed degradation becomes even more evident in larger circuits. To mitigate this effect and to have a regular and compact placement, we provide placement constraints for mapping the logically related LUTs, carry-chain and flip-flops into a single slice and placing logically related slices in the closest proximity possible, during design synthesis and technology mapping. This can be done by listing the constraints in the Xilinx proprietary "User Constraints File" (.ucf) format for the top-level design.

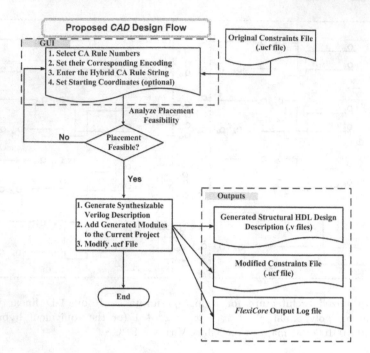

Fig. 4. The *CAD* design flow

4   Design Automation for CA

The design of the circuits described in Sect. 3 can be automated using a CAD
tool developed by us. The tool is developed in Java, includes a simple GUI,
and currently supports two-rule linear, additive, uniform and hybrid CAs. The
CAD software can be invoked from the TCL command-prompt in-built in Xilinx
ISE, using a top-level TCL script. Fig. 4 shows the CAD tool based design
methodology. The top-level script invokes a GUI, which displays the list of rules
corresponding to which equivalent CA circuits can be generated, and prompts the
user to enter the following fields: the two CA rule numbers, their corresponding
encoding of 0 and 1, and the hybrid CA rule comprising of a string of 0's and 1's.
The CAD tool interprets the string by reading two bits at a time, calculates the
truth table of the dual output LUTs appropriately for realizing the next state
logic for the CA cells, and instantiates the required FPGA logic elements in the
HDL. The user can also optionally enter the starting coordinate of the FPGA
slice for the entire constrained placement exercise. If this is not provided by the
user, the CAD tool determines the feasible starting coordinate from the existing
project constraint (.ucf) file.

After the user enters the options, the CAD tool examines the feasibility of
the regular, constrained placement of the circuit on the FPGA fabric, with the
starting coordinates as entered by the user, or the one deduced automatically. It
takes into consideration the existing placement constraints, if any, in the existing

Table 1. CA Implementations

Polynomial	Mode of Implementation	Freq (MHz)	Power-Delay Product (μJ)	#FF	#LUT	#Slice
32, 28, 27, 1, 0	RTL design	1014.20	31.61	32	30	8
	Proposed design	1103.75	31.15	32	16	4
48, 28, 27, 1, 0	RTL design	320.41	37.36	48	46	12
	Proposed design	1089.32	40.26	48	24	6
64, 4, 3, 1, 0	RTL design	361.40	43.80	64	64	16
	Proposed design	1083.42	52.92	64	32	8
80, 38, 37, 1, 0	RTL design	414.08	64.05	80	78	20
	Proposed design	976.56	59.08	80	40	10
96, 49, 47, 2, 0	RTL design	361.79	70.92	96	96	24
	Proposed design	908.27	62.59	96	48	12

project constraints file. If the placement is deemed feasible, it generates synthesizable Verilog descriptions for the selected circuits, and adds the files to the current project. The .ucf file is modified by addition of the relevant placement constraints for the newly generated circuits. In addition, a log file is created to provide the user with all the necessary information about the generated modules. If the tool fails to find a feasible placement configuration, it reports it to the user and again prompts to enter a different starting coordinate. Note that the situation where a feasible placement cannot be found rarely arises, given the large availability of resources on a Virtex-6 family FPGA.

5   Results and Discussions

The circuits described in Sect. 3 were implemented on Xilinx Virtex-6 FPGA, device family XC6VLX550T, package FF1760 and speed grade -2 using the *Xilinx ISE* (v 12.4). CAs with polynomials of the order 32, 48, 64, 80 and 96, were implemented using two different techniques – RTL coding followed by unconstrained automatic logic synthesis by ISE and the custom design technique using the proposed design methodology. For RTL based design, the Xilinx Post P&R results indicate that double the FPGA area gets consumed than what a compact realization should have taken. The operating speed for the CA circuits also drastically reduces as the order of the polynomial is steadily increased. The implementation results were compared with respect to their frequency of operation, PDP, and hardware resource requirement (FFs, LUTs and slices), and are tabulated in Table-1. PDP was calculated as the product of the power dissipation and the (minimum) clock-period supported by the circuit, as reported by ISE. The polynomials are from [17] and, for example, the entry in the polynomial field of Table-1, 32 28 27 1 0, represents the polynomial $x^{32} + x^{28} + x^{27} + x + 1$.

As observed from the partial floorplan (physical) view of the mapped CA circuits in Fig. 5, the inferred logic elements (shown using dark shades) for the RTL design are not compactly packed into each slice and placed distant apart in a random, haphazard fashion throughout a large FPGA area. The floorplan for the proposed design, however, shows a very compact realization with the circuit elements placed in adjacent locations. We can thus conclude that FPGA CAD

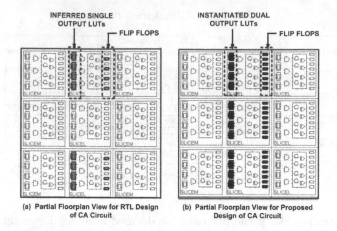

(a) Partial Floorplan View for RTL Design (b) Partial Floorplan View for Proposed
of CA Circuit Design of CA Circuit

Fig. 5. Partial Floorplan Views for the CA Circuits mapped onto the Virtex-6 FPGA fabric

tools, for designs derived from RTL descriptions, cannot exploit the local neighborhood property of CAs, and ultimately result in long interconnects leading to serious performance degradation. This is undesirable as speed is critical from the hardware accelerator point of view in building high performance cryptographic cores [2]. The higher resource requirement also shows that the mapping of the circuit on the FPGA fabric is not optimal for the RTL based implementations. No amount of changes in the option settings of the Xilinx ISE tool for optimization goal and effort, placer extra effort, global optimization and other additional synthesis and timing constraints for the RTL implementation can infer or match up the high speed and reduced area of our proposed architecture.

6   Conclusion

We have proposed and implemented an automated design methodology for high performance 1-D CA circuits on Xilinx FPGAs, by utilizing hardware as economically as possible. We have shown that constraining the placement of the circuit building blocks is crucial in improving the speed, and the regularity of the proposed designs enables automating the design descriptions and related constraints. Compared to synthesized circuits obtained from RTL based design, our designs occupy lower FPGA area (by a factor of 0.5 X) and shows superior performance and operand width scalability, with acceptable PDP. Our future research would be directed towards realizing more complex CA such as 2-D CA using the same philosophy.

References

1. Chowdhury, D.R., Chaudhuri, P.P.: Architecture for VLSI Design of CA Based Byte Error Correcting Code Decoders. In: Proceedings of the 7th International Conference on VLSI Design, pp. 283–286 (1994)

2. Sarkar, P.: A Brief History of Cellular Automata. ACM Computing Surveys (CSUR) 32(1), 80–107 (2000)
3. Areibi, S., Grewal, G., Banerji, D., Du, P.: Hierarchical FPGA Placement. Canadian Journal of Electrical and Computer Engineering 32(1), 53–64 (2007)
4. Ehliar, A.: Optimizing Xilinx designs through primitive instantiation. In: Proceedings of the 7th FPGAworld Conference, FPGAworld 2010, pp. 20–27. ACM, New York (2010)
5. Chattopadhyay, S., Roy, S., Chaudhuri, P.P.: Technology Mapping on a Multi-Output Logic Module built around Cellular Automata Array for a new FPGA Architecture. In: Proceedings of the 8th International Conference on VLSI Design, pp. 57–62 (1995)
6. Halbach, M., Hoffmann, R., Röder, P.: FPGA Implementation of Cellular Automata Compared to Software Implementation. In: ARCS Workshops, vol. 41, pp. 309–317 (2004)
7. Sirakoulis, G.C., Karafyllidis, I., Thanailakis, A., Mardiris, V.: A methodology for VLSI implementation of Cellular Automata algorithms using VHDL. Advances in Engineering Software 32(3), 189–202 (2000)
8. Torres-Huitzil, C., Delgadillo-Escobar, M., Nuno-Maganda, M.: Comparison between 2D cellular automata based pseudorandom number generators. IEICE Electronics Express 9(17), 1391–1396 (2012)
9. Xilinx Inc., Virtex-6 FPGA Configurable Logic Block User Guide UG364 (v1.2) (February 3, 2012),
   http://www.xilinx.com/support/documentation/user_guides/ug364.pdf
10. Xilinx Inc., Virtex-5 FPGA User Guide UG190 (v5.4) (March 16, 2012),
    http://www.xilinx.com/support/documentation/user_guides/ug190.pdf
11. Das, A.K., Ganguly, A., Dasgupta, A., Bhawmik, S., Chaudhuri, P.P.: Efficient Characterization of Cellular Automata. IEE Proceedings E Computers and Digital Techniques 137(1), 81–87 (1990)
12. Chaudhuri, P.P., Chowdhury, D.R., Nandi, S., Chattopadhyay, S.: Additive Cellular Automata Theory and its Application, vol. 1. IEEE Computer Society Press (1997)
13. Mukhopadhyay, D.: Group Properties of Non-linear Cellular Automata. Journal of Cellular Automata 5(1-2), 139–155 (2010)
14. Cattell, K., Muzio, J.C.: Synthesis of One-Dimensional Linear Hybrid Cellular Automata. IEEE Transactions on Computer-Aided Design of Integrated Circuits and Systems 15(3) (1996)
15. Ahmed, T., Kundarewich, P.D., Anderson, J.H.: Packing Techniques for Virtex-5 FPGAs. ACM Transactions on Reconfigurable Technology and Systems (TRETS) 2(3), Article 18, 18:1–18:24 (2009)
16. Cattell, K., Muzio, J.: Technical Report: Tables of linear cellular automata for minimal weight primitive polynomials of degrees up to 300. Issue: 163. University of Victoria (B.C.), Department of Computer Science (1991)
17. Bardell, P.H., McAnney, W.H., Savir, J.: Built-In Test for VLSI: Pseudorandom Techniques. John Wiley & Sons (1987)

Shortest Path Computing Using Memristor-Based Circuits and Cellular Automata

Dimitrios Stathis, Ioannis Vourkas, and Georgios Ch. Sirakoulis

Department of Electrical & Computer Engineering,
Democritus University of Thrace (DUTh), Xanthi, Greece
{dstathis,ivourkas,gsirak}@ee.duth.gr

Abstract. This paper addresses Cellular Automata (CA) based algorithm implementations using circuits with memory resistors (memristors). Memristors are two-terminal passive nonvolatile resistance switching devices whose unique adaptive properties are suitable for massively parallel computational purposes. The sparse nature of computations using network configurations of memristors resembles certain operational features and computing capabilities of CA. Here a memristive CA capable of detecting the shortest path between given nodes of a mesh with weighted edges is proposed. Simulation results are in absolute agreement with the solutions given by the corresponding CA-based algorithmic approach. The proposed memristive CA circuit structure is also used for the effective solution of the traveling salesman problem.

Keywords: Cellular Automata, memristor, memristive computing, parallel algorithms, shortest path problem, traveling salesman problem.

1   Introduction

Solution of the shortest path problem (SPP) has always been a hot topic in graph theory because of its wide application field. There are three well-known alterations of this problem: (a) the single source shortest path; i.e. the shortest path from a given vertex of a graph to all others, (b) the all pairs shortest path; i.e. the shortest path between all possible pairs of the vertices, and (c) the single source single destination shortest path.

Cellular automata (CA), an inherently parallel computing paradigm able to capture globally emerging behavior from collective interaction of simple and local components, have been successfully applied to a range of computational problems including path planning and SPP [1]-[3]. CA-based models are straightforward to implement in hardware (HW); CA-based circuit design reduces to the design of a single, relatively simple cell, and the total layout is uniform [4]. In CA-based HW realizations the algorithms are executed fast especially when implemented on Field Programmable Gate Arrays (FPGAs) where the parallelism of the CA structure is well exploited.

However, the recent discovery of memristor, i.e. a two-terminal passive nonvolatile resistance switching device, has so far shown abilities that could revolutionize HW

J. Wąs, G.C. Sirakoulis, and S. Bandini (Eds.): ACRI 2014, LNCS 8751, pp. 398–407, 2014.

computing architectures [5]-[7]. The unique adaptive properties of memristors are ideal for computational purposes and certainly open new pathways for the exploration of advanced computing paradigms. Reported properties of network configurations of memristors in [8] showed that composite memristive systems significantly improve the efficiency of logic operations via massive parallelism [9]-[10]; it is the dynamical behavior of a memristor's resistance (memristance) that is used for computational purposes, and calculation consists in the evolution of the memristances of all involved devices. The sparse nature of such computations resembles certain operational features and computing capabilities of CA, whereas it also leads to scalable HW architectures with very high device densities.

In this paper we exploit the computing capabilities of memristive networks to propose a circuit-level approach to CA structures using memristors. Our work is based upon [11] where Itoh and Chua first discussed simulation of CA in networks of memristors. Here we describe a fundamental memristive cell which can implement the desired CA rule and then employ it to create two-dimensional structurally-dynamic (also called topological) CA able to compute the shortest path between given nodes of a mesh with weighted edges. The main contributions of this paper are: (a) a memristor-based CA capable of detecting the nodes of a given mesh belonging to the shortest path from one source-node of the mesh to one or multiple destination-nodes; (b) the application of the proposed memristive CA for the solution of the traveling salesman problem.

2   Memory Resistors (Memristors) *in Brief*

Memristor (concatenation of "memory resistor"), the fundamental circuit component (joining the resistor, the capacitor, and the inductor) predicted by Chua in 1971 represents one of today's latest technological achievements [12]. Although there had been experimental clues to the memristor's existence all along the last two centuries, memristive properties of various materials had always been shadowed by other effects that were of primary interest [13]. It was not until 2008 when Chua's theory of memristor was successfully linked to its first *modern* practical implementation by Williams' group at Hewlett Packard Laboratories [5]. This discovery originated intense research activity in this novel scientific field and generated unprecedented worldwide interest for its potential applications.

Memristor (here used to describe both an *ideal* memristor as well as a generalized memristive system [14]) is a passive two-terminal electronic device whose behavior is described by a nonlinear constitutive relation:

$$v = R(x, i)i \tag{1}$$

between the voltage drop at its terminals v and the current flowing through the device i, where:

$$\dot{x} = f(x, i) . \tag{2}$$

$x = (x_1, x_2, ..., x_n)$ denotes n state-variables $x_1, x_2, ... x_n$, which do not depend on any external voltages or currents, whereas the nonlinear function $R(x,i)$ is called memory resistance (memristance) and has the unit of Ohms (Ω); it varies between two limiting values: the less resistive (R_{ON}) and the high resistive (R_{OFF}) state. The reason why memristors are substantially different from the other fundamental circuit elements is that, when the applied voltage is turned off, they still remember how much voltage was applied before and for how long; thus presenting *memory of their past*. That's an effect that can't be duplicated by any circuit combination of resistors, capacitors, and inductors. The nonvolatile memory property of memristors is a direct consequence of the state-dependent Ohm's law in Eq. 1.

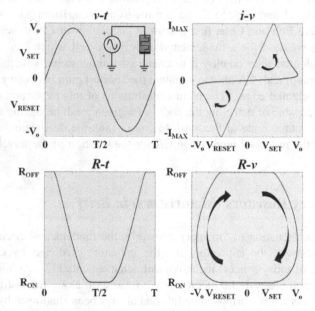

Fig. 1. Simulation results from the response of a memristor to a $\{V_o, f\} = \{$ 2V, 5Hz $\}$ sinusoidal ac applied voltage. The provided graphs include the applied voltage signal (v-t), the hysteretic current-voltage (i-v) characteristic, and the corresponding change of the memristance with time (R-t) and with the applied voltage (R-v), respectively.

Throughout this work all conducted simulations employ a published model of a voltage-controlled memristor which attributes its behavior to quantum tunneling [15]. Its definition is generally given by the following equations:

$$i = G(L)v \tag{3}$$

$$\dot{L} = f(v). \tag{4}$$

Here L defines the tunnel barrier width, which is the single state variable of the system, and G is the conductance of the device (memductance). This model is based on the assumption that the switching rate of L is small below/fast above a voltage threshold (namely V_{SET} or V_{RESET}), which is viewed as the minimum voltage required to impose a change on the physical structure of the device. The time derivative of the state variable in Eq. 4 is interpreted as the speed of movement of the tunnel barrier due to the applied voltage, whereas function f captures the highly nonlinear response of the memristor.

The simulation results from the response of a single memristor under ac voltage bias according to the used model are shown in Fig. 1. The values given to the parameters of the model are $\{a, b, c, m, f_o, L_o, V_{SET}, V_{RESET}\}=\{5\times10^3, 10, 0.1, 82, 310, 5, 1V, -1V\}$ and the resulting resistance ratio between the two boundary resistive states is $R_{OFF}/R_{ON} \approx 10^2$ with $R_{OFF} \approx 200K\Omega$ and $R_{ON} \approx 2K\Omega$. L_o is the maximum value that L can attain, whereas $\{a, b, c, m, f_o\}$ are constant fitting parameters which determine the tunneling distance change-rate and provide the capability of simulating memristive devices with different physical structures and geometries [15]. We note here that when $\{a, b\} > 0$ then a positive/negative voltage applied to the top terminal with respect to the bottom terminal (denoted by the black thick line) always tends to decrease/increase the memristance. Throughout this work all simulations are conducted using Easy Java Simulations (EJS) environment and all differential equations are numerically solved using a 4th order Runge-Kutta integration method [16].

3   Memristive Cell

The basic memristive CA cell is schematically shown in Fig. 2. It includes five memristors: a reversely polarized memristor (RPM) holding the state of the cell (state-memristor), and four forward polarized memristors (FPMs) which are driven by four inputs corresponding to the connections of a von Neumann neighborhood (input memristors). The input memristors are identical and have maximum memristance $R_{OFF} \approx 20K\Omega$, whereas $R_{OFF} \approx 1M\Omega$ is used for the state-memristor. These anti-serially connected memristors form a voltage divider circuit and the aforementioned memristance boundary values were chosen so that the state-memristor, after switching to R_{OFF}, would effectively prevent any induced change in the state of the input memristors which are still in the OFF state. Moreover, the cell comprises two switches, a dc voltage source, a current pulse generator (PG), and a set of four variable resistors which are used for programming the intercellular connections.

All input memristors are initialized in R_{OFF} whereas the state-memristor is initialized in R_{ON}. Switch S_1 is initially open and the current pulse generator is driving switch S_2. In this particular configuration the cell only receives input signals from its neighbors but does not send any signal back to them. This way we take into account *structural dynamics* of CA; i.e. when links between cells can be activated or deactivated depending on the states of the cells that these links connect. The variable resistors are used to facilitate mapping of directed graphs on the CA-based HW platform; resistors are given a low/high enough value so as to practically allow/prevent particular directed connections corresponding to directed edges of a graph.

PG drives switch S_2 and provides a pulse wave I_p to the state-memristor in order to read its state. I_p consists of positive-negative paired current pulses of appropriate amplitude and duration and switch S_2 is set to position '2' only when a positive current pulse is applied. The negative pulse sets switch S_2 to position '1' so the cell updates its state taking into account the incoming signals (if any) and the previous stored state.

Whenever a cell receives at least one input signal from its neighbors then the corresponding input memristor(s) change their state from OFF to ON and subsequently the state-memristor switches from ON to OFF state due to the increasing voltage drop on its terminals. This change prevents any subsequent change to the rest of the input memristors since voltage drop on their terminals will always be below the voltage threshold; the majority of the applied voltage will drop on the state-memristor. Next, when the state-memristor is being read by a short positive pulse I_p, if it is found in the OFF state then switch S_1 closes and the output ports are activated, thus allowing the cell to transmit dc voltage signals to its neighbors. Afterwards, regardless of the received inputs, the state of the state-memristor cannot be further changed. In short, all cells have two possible states and whenever they receive an excitation input from anyone of their neighbors then they switch to a different but constant state. Taking into account the selected boundary memristance values for the state and the input memristors, the output dc signal in simulations is set to 20V for all cells regardless of the size of the CA.

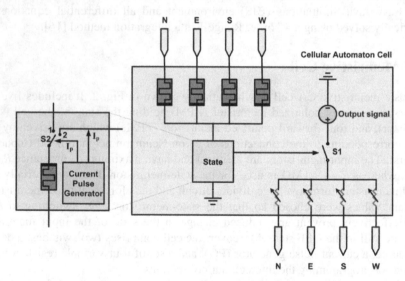

Fig. 2. A memristive CA cell with four inputs and one output connecting with the nearest cells belonging to the von Neumann neighborhood. N, E, S, and W denote the four geographical neighbors, namely north, east, south and west.

In the following section we describe how a two-dimensional array comprising such memristive cells can be used for various scenarios of shortest path computations.

4   Memristive Cellular Automaton for Shortest Path Computing

In this work we consider mesh grids of n vertices arranged on a discrete lattice where any vertex is connected to its closest neighbors by links of nonnegative weights. The memristive cellular automaton which we propose consists of an $M \times N$ rectangular array of memristive cells $C_M(i, j)$ with Cartesian coordinates (i, j) where $i = 1, 2, \ldots$,

M, and $j = 1, 2, \ldots, N$. All cells are assumed to be identical as described in the previous section.

When searching for the shortest path between two given vertices of a mesh (single source, single destination), the given graph is first mapped onto the CA. Connections between the cells are configured as unidirectional, bidirectional, or completely closed, by using the variable resistors, thus facilitating the mapping of any kind of directed graph whose edges are of equal weight. Computation is initiated by triggering the source cell and then a wave of stimulation propagates in all directions and modifies accordingly the states of the cells. Since all neighbor connections are considered to be of equal weight, the aggregate weight of a particular path is here identified by the total number of "hops" in-between source and destination nodes. Computation is assumed finished when the state-memristor of the destination cell switches to the OFF state or if the computation steps have exceeded the total number of nodes; the later means that there is no path connecting the two given cells.

The source cell is the only one which is initialized with its state-memristor in OFF state so as to be able to transmit output signal to its neighbors from the very beginning. In each step switch S_2 is maintained in position '1' for $\Delta t = 0.5$s, which is enough time for the memristors of the cell to complete their state transition if they are biased with an input signal. Then switch S_2 returns to position '2' for the state-memristor to be read. As explained earlier, after receiving the very first input(s), any cell afterwards remains unaffected by the rest of its neighbors during computation.

When computation is completed, the shortest path is found by reading the state of the input memristors of the cells. Those found in the ON state indicate the exact neighbor(s) from where the input signal was received; these neighboring cells belong to the shortest path solution. If more than one of the input memristors is found in the ON state, it means that there are multiple paths reaching simultaneously a particular cell. In this case all options are by default of equal total weight (hop count), so only one of the available paths is randomly selected to be included in the final result. This way, all nodes forming the shortest path(s) can be located by searching backwards from the destination cell until the source cell is reached. The proposed memristive CA is also suitable for the computation of shortest paths between one source and multiple destination cells. The following pseudo-code describes the entire evolution of the memristive CA during shortest path computations:

```
initialize CA and define source and destination(s);
steps = 0;
while (no path is found) {
  t=0;
  for all cells do {
    calculate voltage drop on memristors;
    update memristance values according to the model;
    increase t;
  } while (t <= Δt);
  for all cells {
    if (state-memristor is OFF) {
```

```
      close switch S1;
   }
 }
 increase steps;
 if (state-memristor of destination cell(s) is OFF) {
   shortest path found;
 }
 If (steps > total cells) {
   no path was found;
   exit;
 }
}
calculate backwards the shortest path(s);
```

The effectiveness of the proposed memristive CA is proved through a series of simulations with different types of two-dimensional mesh grids. In all conducted simulations the parameters of the memristor model [15] were set to the following values $\{a, b, c, m, f_o, L_o, V_{SET}, V_{RESET}\} = \{5 \times 10^4, 10, 0.1, 310, 5, -1.5, 1.5\}$. In each step, wherever input signals are applied to a cell, the voltage drop on each memristor inside the cell is calculated using Kirchhoff's current law. The states of the memristors are updated according to the equations of the employed model during time $t = \Delta t$, i.e. while the input signal (voltage) is applied. Afterwards, the state-memristor is being read; if its memristance is found higher than the predefined threshold defining the OFF state, then switch S_1 closes, otherwise S_1 remains open.

Fig. 3 shows a given directed graph where we wish to find the shortest path from the left upper vertex to the right lower vertex. This particular graph is the same with the one in [3] where Adamatzky tested one of the first proposed CA-based algorithms for shortest path computations. Fig. 4 presents the solution of the problem for this specific scenario and also the visualization of the memristive CA when computation is over. Boundary conditions apply to the outmost cells by using the variable resistors of the cells.

In Fig. 4b the CA cells are the blue square nodes. Edge directivity is indicated as follows: the four adjacent neighboring squares of a specific cell can be either filled red to denote that there is no incoming connection from the opposite cell in this direction, or have no color to denote a normal incoming connection. After computation is over, some of the aforementioned adjacent squares of the cells which belong to the shortest path solution are filled green to indicate the direction of the input signal received from the previous cell of the shortest path. Hence, starting from the destination cell, the source cell can be reached by step-by-step moving to the next cells that are found in the direction indicated by the green marks. The number of necessary computation steps for the proposed CA is equal to the number of hops within the shortest path. The presented simulation results are in absolute agreement with those in [3].

Fig. 5 shows the simulation results of shortest path computations on a graph different from that of Fig. 3. More specifically, Fig. 5a concerns a single source single destination scenario, whereas in Fig. 5b the proposed memristive CA is used for a single source with multiple destinations shortest path search. In the last case, computation

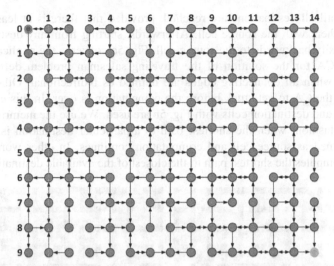

Fig. 3. A directed graph. Arrows indicate direction of the edges. In this example the *red vertex* with coordinates (0, 0) is source and the *green vertex* with coordinates (9, 14) is destination.

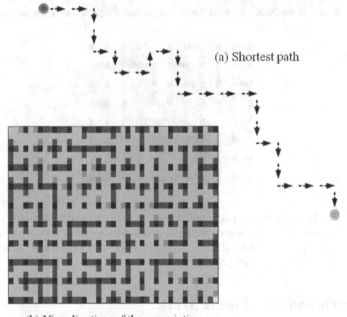

(a) Shortest path

(b) Visualization of the memristive
Cellular Automaton

Fig. 4. Shortest path computation for the directed graph of Fig. 3. (a) macroscopically shows the solution to the problem where each arrow indicates the direction of every subsequent move. (b) shows the visualization of the memristive CA when computation is complete.

continues until all destinations are reached, provided that there is at least one path connecting them with the source cell. Afterwards, starting from any destination one navigates easily backwards to the source cell. Fig. 5c concerns the application of the memristive CA for the solution of the traveling salesman problem defined on the same graph when all connecting edges are defined as bidirectional. Otherwise it is possible for the CA to get stuck before the computation is over. In this example the same source and destination cells with Fig. 5b are used. We use the memristive CA in an iterative fashion; when the shortest path to a particular destination is found, the latter is defined as source cell and computation continues. In other words, the CA each time computes the shortest path to the closest of the available destinations.

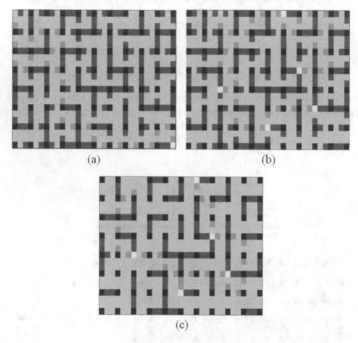

Fig. 5. Different shortest path computation scenarios on the same graph. (a) single source single destination solution, (b) single source multiple destination solution, and (c) solution of the traveling salesman problem when all cell connections are set bidirectional. *Source vertex* is orange and *destination vertices* are yellow.

5   Conclusions and Future Work

In this work we designed a two-dimensional memristor-based structurally dynamic cellular automaton capable of detecting the nodes of a given mesh belonging to a shortest path solution. Simulations confirm the effectiveness of the proposed CA for both single source single destination and also multiple destination scenarios of the problem. Iterative application of the CA provides a solution for the traveling salesman problem as well. The proposed CA cell can be easily modified to consider different types of local neighborhoods even in three-dimensional mesh grids. It is expected that experimental implementation of memristive CA structures could be done in massively parallel processors or neuromorphic computing architectures of the near future.

Acknowledgement. This work was supported in part by the BODOSSAKI Foundation in Greece.

References

1. Ioannidis, K., Sirakoulis, G.C., Andreadis, I.: A path planning method based on Cellular Automata for Cooperative Robots. Applied Artificial Intelligence 25(8), 721–745 (2011)
2. Golzari, S., Meybodi, M.R.: A Maze Routing Algorithm Based on Two Dimensional Cellular Automata. In: El Yacoubi, S., Chopard, B., Bandini, S. (eds.) ACRI 2006. LNCS, vol. 4173, pp. 564–570. Springer, Heidelberg (2006)
3. Adamatzky, A.I.: Computation of shortest path in cellular automata. Math. Comput. Modelling 23(4), 105–113 (1996)
4. Vourkas, I., Sirakoulis, G.C.: FPGA based cellular automata for environmental modeling. In: 19th IEEE Int. Conf. Electronics, Circuits, and Systems (ICECS 2012), pp. 93–96. IEEE Press, Seville (2012)
5. Strukov, D.B., Snider, G.S., Stewart, D.R., Williams, R.S.: The missing memristor found. Nature 453, 80–83 (2008)
6. Vourkas, I., Sirakoulis, G.C.: Recent progress and patents on computational structures and methods with memristive devices. Recent Patents on Electrical & Electronic Engineering 6(2), 101–116 (2013)
7. Yang, J.J., Strukov, D.B., Stewart, D.R.: Memristive devices for computing. Nat. Nano 8, 13–24 (2013)
8. Adamatzky, A., Chua, L. (eds.): Memristor Networks. Springer International Publishing, Switzerland (2014)
9. Pershin, Y., Di Ventra, M.: Solving mazes with memristors: A massively parallel approach. Phys. Rev. E 84, 046703 (2011)
10. Ye, Z., Wu, S.H.M., Prodromakis, T.: Computing shortest paths in 2D and 3D memristive networks. arXiv:1303.3927 (2013)
11. Itoh, M., Chua, L.O.: Memristor cellular automata and memristor discrete-time cellular neural networks. Int. J. Bifurcation Chaos 19(11), 3605–3656 (2009)
12. Chua, L.O.: Memristor - The missing circuit element. IEEE Trans. Circuit Theory 18(5), 507–519 (1971)
13. Prodromakis, T., Toumazou, C., Chua, L.: Two centuries of memristors. Nature Materials 11, 478–481 (2012)
14. Chua, L.O., Kang, S.M.: Memristive devices and systems. Proc. IEEE 64(2), 209–223 (1976)
15. Vourkas, I., Sirakoulis, G.C.: A novel design and modeling paradigm for memristor-based crossbar circuits. IEEE Trans. Nanotechnol. 11(6), 1151–1159 (2012)
16. Easy Java Simulations (EJS), http://fem.um.es/Ejs/

Generation of TPMACA
for Pattern Classification*

Sung-Jin Cho[1], Han-Doo Kim[2], Un-Sook Choi[3], Seok-Tae Kim[4],
Jin-Gyoung Kim[1], Sook-Hee Kwon[1], and Gil-Tak Gong[1]

[1] Department of Applied Mathematics, Pukyong National University,
Busan 608-737, Korea
sjcho@pknu.ac.kr
[2] Institute of Basic Sciences and Department of Applied Mathematics,
Inje University, Gimhae 621-749, Korea
mathkhd@inje.ac.kr
[3] Department of Information and Communications Engineering,
Tongmyoung University, Busan 608-711, Korea
choies@tu.ac.kr
[4] Department of Information and Communications Engineering,
Pukyong National University, Busan 608-737, Korea
setakim@pknu.ac.kr

Abstract. The important prerequisites of designing pattern classifier
are high throughput and low cost hardware implementation. The simple, regular, modular and cascadable local neighborhood sparse network
of Cellular Automata (CA) suits ideally for low cost VLSI implementation. Thus the multiple attractor CA is adapted for use as a pattern
classifier. By concatenating two predecessor multiple attractor CA (TP-
MACA) we can construct a pattern classifier. In this paper we propose
a method for finding dependency vector by using a 0-basic path. Also
we propose various methods for generating TPMACA corresponding to
a given dependency vector.

1 Introduction

Cellular Automata (CA) was first introduced by Von Neumann for modeling biological self-reproduction [1]. Das et al. developed a matrix algebraic tool capable
of characterizing CA [2]. We use a simple two-state 3-neighborhood CA with cells
arranged linearly in one dimension. The cells evolve in discrete time steps according to some deterministic rule that depends only on a logical neighborhood.
Each cell is essentially comprised of a memory element and a combinatorial logic
that generates the next-state of the cell from the present-state of its neighboring
cells (left, right, and self) [3]. A CA that generates only cyclic states during its
state transitions is known as *group* CA, whereas a CA generating both cyclic
and non-cyclic states is *nongroup* CA. For a group CA, each state has a unique

---

* This work was supported by the National Research Foundation of Korea Grant
funded by the Korean Government (NRF-2013S1A5B6053791).

J. Wąs, G.C. Sirakoulis, and S. Bandini (Eds.): ACRI 2014, LNCS 8751, pp. 408–416, 2014.

immediate predecessor. CA have been used for diverse applications such as modeling biological self-reproduction, modeling problems of number theory, parallel processing computation, test pattern generation, pseudorandom number generation, cryptography, error correcting codes and signature analysis etc. ([4] $\sim$ [7]). Pattern classification is the process of identifying common properties among a set of patterns in a database. A sample test pattern set from the database, each pattern belonging to one of the predefined classes, is used to train the pattern classifier. Subsequent to training, the pattern classifier performs the task of prediction. The important prerequisites of designing pattern classifier are high throughput and low cost hardware implementation. The simple, regular, modular and cascadable local neighborhood sparse network of CA suits ideally for low cost VLSI implementation. Thus multiple attractor CA (MACA) is adapted for use as a pattern classifier. Many researchers ([8] $\sim$ [14]) showed that MACA trees form natural clusters which can be employed to the task of pattern classification and associative memory. For this reason, Ganguly et al. proposed the pattern classifier by concatenating TPMACAs [13]. And Maji et al. showed that the pattern classifier reduces the complexity of the classification algorithm from $O(n^3)$ to $O(n)$ by using dependency vector (DV) and dependency string (DS) consisting of DVs [11]. To obtain the DV they needed to solve the linear system of $2^{n-1} - 1$ equations with n-variables. Moreover they didn't mention how to construct a TPMACA corresponding to the given DV. In this paper we propose a method for finding the DV by using a 0-basic path. Also we propose various methods for generating TPMACA corresponding to a given DV.

2 Background

A CA consists of a number of cells. In a 3-neighborhood dependency, the next state $q_i(t+1)$ of a cell is assumed to depend only on itself and on its two neighbors (left and right), and is denoted as $q_i(t+1) = f(q_{i-1}(t), q_i(t), q_{i+1}(t))$ where $q_i(t)$ represents the state of the ith cell at the tth instant of time and f is the next state function and referred to as the rule of the CA. Since f is a function of 3 variables, there are 2^{2^3} possible next state functions. The cells evolve in discrete time steps according to some deterministic rule that depends only on logical neighborhood.

$$rule\ 60\ \ : q_i(t+1) = q_{i-1}(t) \oplus q_i(t)$$
$$rule\ 90\ \ : q_i(t+1) = q_{i-1}(t) \oplus q_{i+1}(t)$$
$$rule\ 102: q_i(t+1) = q_i(t) \oplus q_{i+1}(t)$$
$$rule\ 150: q_i(t+1) = q_{i-1}(t) \oplus q_i(t) \oplus q_{i+1}(t)$$
$$rule\ 170: q_i(t+1) = q_{i+1}(t)$$
$$rule\ 240: q_i(t+1) = q_{i-1}(t)$$

If the next-state generating logic employs only XOR logic, then the CA is called a *linear* CA. An n-cell linear CA is characterized by an $n \times n$ matrix T. T is referred to as the *state transition matrix* of the CA. The state transition matrix T is a tridiagonal matrix.

Definition 2.1. [3] (i) Nongroup CA: A CA generating both cyclic and non-cyclic states is called a nongroup CA.

(ii) Attractor : A state having a self-loop is referred to as an attractor. An attractor can be viewed as a cyclic state with unit cycle length.

(iii) MACA : The nongroup CA for which the state transition diagram consists of a set of disjoint components forming (inverted) tree-like structures rooted at attractors is referred to as multiple attractor CA (MACA). In case the number of attractors is one, we call the CA single-attractor CA (SACA).

(iv) TPMACA : TPMACA is a MACA such that every reachable state in the state transition diagram has only two immediate predecessors. TPSACA is a SACA such that every reachable state in the state transition diagram has only two immediate predecessors. If T is the state transition matrix of the n-cell TP-SACA, then the rank of T is $n - 1$.

(v) Characteristic polynomial : The characteristic polynomial $c_T(x)$ of an n-cell CA is defined by $c_T(x) = |T \oplus xI|$ where x is an indeterminate, I is the $n \times n$ identity matrix, and T is the CA state transition matrix.

(vi) Minimal polynomial : The minimal polynomial $m_T(x)$ of the state transition matrix T of an n-cell CA is the monic polynomial over $GF(2) = \{0, 1\}$ of least degree such that $m_T(T) = 0$. The minimal polynomial of an n-cell TPSACA is x^n.

Since $rank(A) + dimN(A) = n$ for any $m \times n$ matrix A, where $dimN(A)$ is the dimension of the nullspace of A [15], if $rank(T \oplus I) = r$ in an n-cell MACA with the state transition matrix T, then the number of attractors is 2^{n-r}, where I is the $n \times n$ identity matrix. Let V be a subspace of a vector space S. DV represents each individual linear dependency relationship of the variables supported by all the elements in V. DS represents the multiple linear dependency, if it exists in V [10]. Since the 0-tree of the state transition diagram of a given TPMACA is a subspace, $DV \cdot x = 0$ for all states x in the 0-tree.

We use $\mathbf{C}_M^n$ to denote the n-cell TPMACA with $c_{T_{M_n}}(x) = m_{T_{M_n}}(x) = x^{n-1}(x+1)$. A CA based pattern classifier T can be constructed by concatenating m TPMACAs as follows.

$$T = \begin{pmatrix} [T_1] & & & & \\ & [T_2] & & & 0 \\ & & \ddots & & \\ & & & [T_i] & \\ & 0 & & & \ddots \\ & & & & & [T_m] \end{pmatrix}$$

Thus T is the state transition matrix of the MACA $\mathbf{C}_T$ arranged in block diagonal form from m number of TPMACA $\mathbf{C}_{T_{M_i}}^n$'s $(i = 1, 2, \cdots, m)$. Here $c_{T_{M_i}}(x) = x^{n_i-1}(x+1)(i = 1, 2, \cdots, m)$ and $n_1 + n_2 + \cdots + n_m = n$.

DV_i corresponds to the state transition matrix T_{M_i} of an n_i-cell TPMACA $\mathbf{C}_M^{n_i}$. And $DS =< DV_1|DV_2|\cdots|DV_m >$ corresponds to the pattern classifier T.

3   Properties of TPMACA with Two Attractors

Hereafter we use n-cell TPMACA $\mathbf{C}_M^n$ with the state transition matrix T_{M_n} such that $c_{T_M}(x) = m_{T_M}(x) = x^{n-1}(x+1)$ satisfying

(i) $rank(T_{M_n}) = n - 1$,
(ii) The number of attractors is 2,
(iii) The number of states in the 0-tree is 2^{n-1}.

Since $m_{T_M}(x) = x^{n-1}(x+1)$, the depth of $\mathbf{C}_M^n$ is $n-1$. In this section we analyze $\mathbf{C}_M^n$.

The following theorem is an important criterion for generating TPMACA corresponding to a given DV.

Theorem 3.1. In an n-cell TPMACA $\mathbf{C}_M^n$, the number of 1's of the diagonal elements in the state transition matrix T_{M_n} of $\mathbf{C}_M^n$ is odd.

Proof. The sum of eigenvalues of T_{M_n} is the sum of the diagonal elements of T_{M_n}[15]. Since $c_{T_{M_n}}(x) = x^{n-1}(x+1)$, the sum of eigenvalues is 1. Hence the number of 1's of the diagonal elements of T_{M_n} is odd.

Theorem 3.2. Let $\mathbf{C}_M^n$ be an n-cell TPMACA with the state transition matrix T_{M_n}. Then $c_{T_{M_n}}^{n-1}(x) = c_{T_{M_n}}(x)$.

Proof. If α is an attractor of T_{M_n}, then $T_{M_n}\alpha = \alpha$ and $T_{M_n}^{n-1}\alpha = \alpha$. Thus the eigenvalues of $T_{M_n}^{n-1}$ and T_{M_n} are the same. Hence $c_{T_{M_n}}^{n-1}(x) = c_{T_{M_n}}(x)$.

Let $\mathbf{C}$ be a nongroup CA with depth d and let T be the state transition matrix of $\mathbf{C}$. Then we call $\mathbf{x} \to T\mathbf{x} \to \cdots \to T^d\mathbf{x}(= \alpha)$ an α-*basic path* of the α-tree in $\mathbf{C}$, where $\mathbf{x}$ is a nonreachable state of the α-tree in $\mathbf{C}$ [16]. Fig. 1 shows the 0-basic path of 3-cell TPMACA $\mathbf{C}_M^3$.

By Theorem 3.3, we can easily find the DV of $\mathbf{C}_M^n$.

Theorem 3.3. Let $\mathbf{C}_M^n$ be an n-cell TPMACA with the state transition matrix T_{M_n}. And let $\mathbf{x} \to T_{M_n}\mathbf{x} \to \cdots \to T_{M_n}^{n-1}\mathbf{x}(= 0)$ be a 0-basic path of the 0-tree in $\mathbf{C}_M^n$, where $\mathbf{x}$ is a nonreachable state of the 0-tree in $\mathbf{C}_M^n$. Then the DV of $\mathbf{C}_M^n$ is the unique basis vector of the nullspace $N(B_0)$,

where $B_0 = \begin{pmatrix} \mathbf{x} \\ T_{M_n}\mathbf{x} \\ \vdots \\ T_{M_n}^{n-2}\mathbf{x} \end{pmatrix}$.

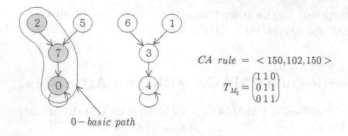

$$CA\ rule\ = \ <150,102,150>$$

$$T_{M_3} = \begin{pmatrix} 1\ 1\ 0 \\ 0\ 1\ 1 \\ 0\ 1\ 1 \end{pmatrix}$$

0 − basic path

Fig. 1. The 0-basic path

Proof. Since $\{\mathbf{x}, T_{M_n}\mathbf{x}, \cdots, T_{M_n}^{n-2}\mathbf{x}\}$ is a basis of the 0-tree in $\mathbf{C}_M^n$, each state $\mathbf{y}$ in the 0-tree can be written by $\mathbf{y} = a_1\mathbf{x} \oplus a_2 T_{M_n}\mathbf{x} \oplus \cdots \oplus a_{n-1}T_{M_n}^{n-2}\mathbf{x}$, $a_i \in \{0,1\}$. Since

$$0 = DV \cdot (a_1\mathbf{x} \oplus a_2 T_{M_n}\mathbf{x} \oplus \cdots \oplus a_{n-1}T_{M_n}^{n-2}\mathbf{x})$$
$$= a_1 DV \cdot \mathbf{x} \oplus a_2 DV \cdot T_{M_n}\mathbf{x} \oplus \cdots \oplus a_{n-1}DV \cdot T_{M_n}^{n-2}\mathbf{x}$$

for all $a_i(i = 1, 2, \cdots, n-1)$, we get $DV \cdot \mathbf{x} = 0, DV \cdot T_{M_n}\mathbf{x} = 0, \cdots, DV \cdot T_{M_n}^{n-2}\mathbf{x} = 0$. This means that $B_0 DV^t = \mathbf{0}$, i.e., $DV \in N(B_0)$. Since $rank(B_0) = n-1, dim N(B_0) = 1$. Hence the DV of $\mathbf{C}_M^n$ is unique.

In Fig.1, $B_0 = \begin{pmatrix} 0 & 1 & 0 \\ 1 & 1 & 1 \end{pmatrix}$ and $N(B_0) = \{000, 101\}$. Hence DV is (101).

For the state transition matrix T_M of $\mathbf{C}_M^n$ the following hold [12]:
(i) $T_{M_n}^n = T_{M_n}^{n-1}$.
(ii) The nonzero rows of $T_{M_n}^{n-1}$ are all the same and the nonzero row is the DV of $\mathbf{C}_M^n$.

By using the above results we analyze the relationship between $T_{M_n}^{n-1}$ and the nonzero attractor of $\mathbf{C}_M^n$ as follows. Let $T_{M_n}^{n-1} = (\mathbf{r_1}, \mathbf{r_2}, \cdots, \mathbf{r_n})^t$ and $\alpha = (a_1, a_2, \cdots, a_n)^t$ be a nonzero attractor of $\mathbf{C}_M^n$. Since α is an attractor, $T_{M_n}^{n-1}\alpha = T_{M_n}^{n-2}\alpha = \cdots = \alpha$. Thus

$$(\mathbf{r_1}\alpha, \cdots, \mathbf{r_i}\alpha, \cdots, \mathbf{r_n}\alpha)^t = T_{M_n}^{n-1}\alpha = \alpha = (a_1, \cdots, a_i, \cdots, a_n)^t.$$

If $a_i = 1$, then $\mathbf{r_i}\alpha = 1$ and thus $\mathbf{r_i} \neq \mathbf{0}$. Hence by (ii) $\mathbf{r_i}$ is a DV of $\mathbf{C}_M^n$. Therefore we can see nonzero rows of $T_{M_n}^{n-1}$ from the nonzero attractor of $\mathbf{C}_M^n$. Moreover if T_{M_n} is a state transition matrix of a 90/150 TPMACA $\mathbf{C}$ which is a TPMACA with rules 90 and 150, then T_{M_n} is symmetric and thus $T_{M_n}^{n-1}$ is symmetric. So the DV of $\mathbf{C}$ is the nonzero attractor of $\mathbf{C}$.

For example if

$$T = \begin{pmatrix} 1 & 1 & 0 & 0 & 0 \\ 1 & 1 & 1 & 0 & 0 \\ 0 & 1 & 1 & 1 & 0 \\ 0 & 0 & 1 & 1 & 1 \\ 0 & 0 & 0 & 1 & 1 \end{pmatrix}$$

, then $\alpha = (10101)$. Since T is symmetric, T^4 is also symmetric and thus

$$T^4 = \begin{pmatrix} 1 & 0 & 1 & 0 & 1 \\ 0 & 0 & 0 & 0 & 0 \\ 1 & 0 & 1 & 0 & 1 \\ 0 & 0 & 0 & 0 & 0 \\ 1 & 0 & 1 & 0 & 1 \end{pmatrix}.$$

Hence $DV = \alpha = (10101)$.

For a given TPMACA $\mathbf{C}_M^n$ the DV of $\mathbf{C}_M^n$ always exists. But every binary vector need not be a DV of $\mathbf{C}_M^n$. Ganguly showed the vector of the form $(v_1 \cdots v_i \underbrace{0 \cdots 0}_{(k \geq 2)} v_{i+k+1} \cdots v_n)(v_i = v_{i+k+1} = 1)$ is not a DV for any TPMACA [12].

The following theorem shows that the vector of the form $(0 * \cdots * 0)$ is also not a DV for any TPMACA.

Theorem 3.4. For an n-cell TPMACA $\mathbf{C}_M^n$ there does not exist an n-bit DV of the form $(0 * \cdots * 0)$.

Proof. Let $DV = (0v_2 \cdots v_{n-1} 0)$. Without loss of generality we may assume that $v_2 = v_{n-1} = 1$.

The state transition matrix T_{M_n} of $\mathbf{C}_M^n$ is of the following form.

$$T_{M_n} = \begin{pmatrix} t_{11} & t_{12} & 0 & \cdots & 0 & 0 & 0 \\ t_{21} & t_{22} & t_{23} & \cdots & 0 & 0 & 0 \\ 0 & t_{32} & t_{33} & \cdots & 0 & 0 & 0 \\ \vdots & \vdots & \vdots & \ddots & \vdots & \vdots & \vdots \\ 0 & 0 & 0 & \cdots & t_{n-2,n-2} & t_{n-2,n-1} & 0 \\ 0 & 0 & 0 & \cdots & t_{n-1,n-2} & t_{n-1,n-1} & t_{n-1,n} \\ 0 & 0 & 0 & \cdots & 0 & t_{n,n-1} & t_{nn} \end{pmatrix}.$$

Since $T_{M_n}^n = T_{M_n}^{n-1}$, $DV \cdot T_{M_n} = DV$. In this case, $DV = (0 * \cdots * 0)$ and thus the first(resp. last) element of $DV \cdot T_{M_n}$ is t_{21}(resp. $t_{n-1,n}$). Therefore $t_{21} = t_{n-1,n} = 0$. Suppose $t_{11} = 1$. Then the first row of $T_{M_n}^{n-1}$ is $(1 * \cdots *)$. Since $(1 * \cdots *)$ is a nonzero vector, $(1 * \cdots *)$ must be the DV. Since DV is $DV = (01 * \cdots * 10)$, $(1 * \cdots *)$ can not be the DV. Thus $t_{11} = 0$. Similarly $t_{nn} = 0$. So the first column and the last column are zero vectors. Consequently $rank(T_{M_n}) \leq n - 2$. But $rank(T_{M_n}) = n - 1$. This is a contradiction. Hence DV of the form $(0 * \cdots * 0)$ does not exist.

4   Generation of TPMACA Corresponding to the Given DV

In this section we propose various methods for generating TPMACA $\mathbf{C}_M^n$ corresponding to the given n-bit DV by using TPMACA $\mathbf{C}_M^{n-1}$ with the $(n-1)$-bit DV.

Theorem 4.1. Let $T_{M_{n-1}}$ be the state transition matrix of a TPMACA $\mathbf{C}_M^{n-1}$. And let $(v_1 \cdots v_{n-1})$ be the DV of $\mathbf{C}_M^{n-1}$ and let $\mathbf{e}_i$ be the standard ith unit vector. Then the following hold.

(i) If $DV = (v_1 \cdots v_{n-1}0)$, then $T = \begin{pmatrix} T_{M_{n-1}} & \mathbf{0} \\ \mathbf{e}_{n-1}^t & 0 \end{pmatrix}$ is the state transition matrix of $\mathbf{C}_M^n$.

(ii) If $DV = (0v_1 \cdots v_{n-1})$, then $T = \begin{pmatrix} 0 & \mathbf{e}_1^t \\ \mathbf{0} & T_{M_{n-1}} \end{pmatrix}$ is the state transition matrix of $\mathbf{C}_M^n$.

(iii) If $DV = (v_1 \cdots v_{n-1}v_{n-1})$, then $T = \begin{pmatrix} T_{M_{n-1}} & \mathbf{e}_{n-1} \\ \mathbf{0} & 0 \end{pmatrix}$ is the state transition matrix of $\mathbf{C}_M^n$.

(iv) If $DV = (v_1v_1 \cdots v_{n-1})$, then $T = \begin{pmatrix} 0 & \mathbf{0} \\ \mathbf{e}_1 & T_{M_{n-1}} \end{pmatrix}$ is the state transition matrix of $\mathbf{C}_M^n$.

The TPMACA $\mathbf{C}_M^5$ with $DV = (10101)$ can not be obtained from Theorem 4.1. So we need the following theorem.

Theorem 4.2. Let $(10101 \cdots 101)$ be a $(2n+1)$-bit DV. Then the rule of TPMACA $\mathbf{C}_M^{2n+1}$ corresponding to the DV is $< r_1, r_2, \cdots, r_{2n+1} >$, where

$$r_i = \begin{cases} 150 & , i: \text{odd} \\ 102 & , i: \text{even}. \end{cases}$$

Table 1 shows 3-cell TPMACA $\mathbf{C}_M^3$ corresponding to DV. We can generate the n-cell TPMACA $\mathbf{C}_M^n$ for the given n-bit DV by using results of Table 1, Theorems 4.1 and 4.2.

In Table 1, we can change rule corresponding to $DV = (101)$ as $< 150, 60, 150 >$ if necessary.

Table 1. 3-cell TPMACA $\mathbf{C}_M^3$ corresponding to DV

DV	T of $\mathbf{C}_M^3$	rule
001	$\begin{pmatrix} 0 & 1 & 0 \\ 0 & 0 & 1 \\ 0 & 0 & 1 \end{pmatrix}$	$< 90, 170, 102 >$
100	$\begin{pmatrix} 1 & 0 & 0 \\ 1 & 0 & 0 \\ 0 & 1 & 0 \end{pmatrix}$	$< 60, 240, 90 >$
101	$\begin{pmatrix} 1 & 1 & 0 \\ 0 & 1 & 1 \\ 0 & 1 & 1 \end{pmatrix}$	$< 150, 102, 150 >$
111	$\begin{pmatrix} 0 & 0 & 0 \\ 1 & 0 & 0 \\ 0 & 1 & 1 \end{pmatrix}$	$< 240, 240, 150 >$

Example 4.3. Let (0101011) be a 7-bit DV. Then the TPMACA $\mathbf{C}_M^7$ corresponding to the DV is obtained by Theorems 4.1 and 4.2 as the following.

$$T = \begin{pmatrix} 0 & \mathbf{e}_1^t & 0 \\ 0 & \mathbf{T}_{M_5} & \mathbf{e}_5 \\ 0 & \mathbf{0} & 0 \end{pmatrix}$$

is the state transition matrix of $\mathbf{C}_M^7$, where $\mathbf{e}_1^t = (10000)$ and

$$T_{M_5} = \begin{pmatrix} 1 & 1 & 0 & 0 & 0 \\ 0 & 1 & 1 & 0 & 0 \\ 0 & 1 & 1 & 1 & 0 \\ 0 & 0 & 0 & 1 & 1 \\ 0 & 0 & 0 & 1 & 1 \end{pmatrix}.$$

5   Conclusion

In this paper we proposed a method for finding DV by using a 0-basic path of TPMACA $\mathbf{C}_M^n$. And we analyzed the relationship between DV and attractor. Also we gave various methods for generating TPMACA corresponding to the given DV.

References

1. Von Neumann, J.: The theory of self-reproducing automata. University of Illinois Press, Urban (1966), Burks, A.W. (ed.)
2. Das, A.K., Pal Chaudhuri, P.: Vector space theoretic analysis of additive cellular automata and its application for pseudo-exhaustive test pattern generation. IEEE Trans. Comput. 42, 340–352 (1993)
3. Pal Chaudhuri, P., Chowdhury, D.R., Nandy, S., Chattopadhyay, C.: Additive cellular automata theory and applications, vol. 1. IEEE Computer Society Press, California (1997)
4. Cho, S.J., Choi, U.S., Kim, H.D., Hwang, Y.H., Kim, J.G., Heo, S.H.: New synthesis of one-dimensional 90/150 linear hybrid group cellular automata. IEEE Trans. Comput.-Aided Des. Integr. Circuits Syst. 26(9), 1720–1724 (2007)
5. Ponkaew, J., Wongthanavasu, S., Lursinsap, C.: A nonlinear classifier using an evolution of Cellular Automata. In: International Symposium on ISPACS, pp. 1–5 (2011)
6. Ponkaew, J., Wongthanavasu, S., Lursinsap, C.: Two-class classifier cellular automata. In: IEEE Symposium on ISIEA, pp. 354–359 (2011)
7. Bandini, S., Vanneschi, L., Wuensche, A., Shehata, A.B.: Cellular automata pattern recognition and rule evolution through a neuro-genetic approach. Journal of Cellular Automata 4(3), 171–181 (2009)
8. Das, S., Mukherjee, S., Naskar, N., Sikdar, B.: Characterization of single cycle CA and its application in pattern classification. Electronic Notes in Theoretical Computer Science 252, 181–203 (2009)
9. Naskar, N., Das, S., Sikdar, B.: Characterization of nonlinear cellular automata having only single length cycle attractors. Journal of Cellular Automata 7, 431–453 (2013)
10. Maji, P., Pal Chaudhuri, P.: Theory and application of cellular automata for pattern classification. Fundamenta Informaticae 58, 321–353 (2003)
11. Maji, P., Shaw, C., Ganguly, N., Sikdar, B.K., Pal Chaudhuri, P.: Theory and application of cellular automata for pattern classification. Fundamenta Informaticae 58, 321–354 (2003)
12. Ganguly, N.: Cellular Automata Evolution: Theory and Applications in Pattern Recognition and Classification, Ph. D. thesis CST Dept. BECDU India (2003)
13. Ganguly, N., Maji, P., Dhar, S., Sikdar, B.K., Pal Chaudhuri, P.: Evolving cellular automata as pattern classifier. In: Bandini, S., Chopard, B., Tomassini, M. (eds.) ACRI 2002. LNCS, vol. 2493, pp. 56–68. Springer, Heidelberg (2002)
14. Ganguly, N., Maji, P., Sikdar, B.K., Pal Chaudhuri, P.: Design and characterization of cellular automata based associative memory for pattern recognition. IEEE Trans. on Systems, Man, and Cybernetics - Part B: Cybernetics 34(1), 672–679 (2004)
15. Horn, R.A., Johnson, C.R.: Matrix analysis. Cambridge University Press (1985)
16. Cho, S.J., Choi, U.S., Kim, H.D.: Analysis of complemented CA derived from a linear TPMACA. Computers and Mathematics with Applications 45, 680–698 (2003)

Sharing Secrets by Computing Preimages of Bipermutive Cellular Automata

Luca Mariot and Alberto Leporati

Dipartimento di Informatica, Sistemistica e Comunicazione,
Università degli Studi Milano, Bicocca,
Viale Sarca 336/14, 20124 Milano, Italy
l.mariot@campus.unimib.it, alberto.leporati@unimib.it

Abstract. A secret sharing scheme based on one-dimensional bipermutive cellular automata is discussed in this paper. The underlying idea is to represent the secret as a configuration of a bipermutive CA and to iteratively apply a preimage computation algorithm until a sufficiently long configuration to be splitted among the participants is obtained. The scheme is proved to be both perfect and ideal, and a simple extension is shown to induce a sequential access structure which eventually becomes cyclic, where the upper bound on the length of the cycles depends on the radius of the adopted local rule.

Keywords: Cellular automata, cryptography, secret sharing schemes, bipermutivity, preimage computation, cyclic access structure.

1   Introduction

Secret sharing schemes (SSS) were originally introduced by Shamir [8] and Blakley [1] as a method to securely share a *secret* among a set $\mathcal{P}$ of n participants, in such a way that only the members belonging to some *authorized subsets* of $\mathcal{P}$, specified through an *access structure*, can recover the secret by pooling their shares.

During the last few years some SSS based on *cellular automata* (CA) have been proposed in the literature, the first of which can be traced back to del Rey, Mateus and Sánchez [2]. Specifically, the scheme described in [2] exploits the reversibility of *linear memory cellular automata* (LMCA). The secret is represented as one of the k initial conditions in a k-th order LMCA which is then evolved for n iterations. Each player then receives one of the n resulting CA configurations as a share. The access structure generated by this scheme can be defined as a (k, n) *sequential threshold*, since at least k consecutive shares are required in order to evolve backwards the LMCA and recover the secret, meaning that there are in total $n - k + 1$ minimal authorized subsets. Most of the later CA-based SSS [6,4,3] use the same LMCA principle of del Rey, Mateus and Sánchez's scheme, and thus feature similar access structures.

In this paper, we propose a secret sharing scheme designed upon a different CA primitive, namely *bipermutive* cellular automata (BCA), which is less complex (since BCA are memoryless) and which generates a more flexible access structure than LMCA-based schemes. We initially show a basic version of our scheme where all participants are required to combine their shares to recover the secret, which is set by the dealer as

J. Wąs, G.C. Sirakoulis, and S. Bandini (Eds.): ACRI 2014, LNCS 8751, pp. 417–426, 2014.

an m-bit configuration of a one-dimensional BCA. The automaton is then evolved backwards by iteratively applying a preimage computation algorithm until a configuration of length $k \cdot m$ is obtained, which is finally splitted among the k players. To recover the secret, the players just have to juxtapose their shares and evolve the CA forwards.

We prove that the scheme is *perfect*, meaning that an attacker knowing fewer than k shares cannot determine anything about the secret in an information-theoretic sense, and *ideal*, since the size of the shares equals the size of the secret. We finally introduce an extension to the scheme, called *secret juxtaposition*, which induces a (k,n) *sequential* threshold access structure that eventually becomes *cyclic*, thus yielding n minimal authorized subsets where n is bounded by 2^{2r}, being r the radius of the local rule.

The rest of the paper is structured as follows. Section 2 covers the basic notions and terminology about cellular automata and secret sharing schemes used throughout the paper. Section 3 shows the algorithm PREIMAGE-CONSTRUCTION, used to compute the preimage of a CA configuration under a bipermutive rule. Section 4 describes the basic version of our SSS, where all the k shares are required to recover the secret. Section 5 analyses the security properties of the basic scheme, proving that it is both perfect and ideal. In Section 6, the extended scheme is introduced and shown to generate an eventually cyclic access structure. Finally, Section 7 recaps the key features of the proposed scheme and its advantages over del Rey, Mateus and Sánchez's scheme, and sketches some possible developments for future research.

2   Preliminary Definitions

2.1   Cellular Automata

In this work we focus on the model of *one-dimensional finite boolean cellular automata*, which we define as a triple $\langle C, r, f \rangle$ where C is a finite one-dimensional array of *cells*, $r \in \mathbb{N}$ is the *radius* and $f : \mathbb{F}_2^{2r+1} \to \mathbb{F}_2$ is a boolean function specifying the *local rule*. We denote by $|C| = m$ the size of the array. During a single time step, each of the central cells $i \in \{r+1, \cdots, m-r\}$ in C updates its binary *state* by computing in parallel the local rule f on the neighbourhood formed by itself, the r cells at its left and the r cells at its right. We do not deal with any *boundary condition*, since the leftmost and rightmost r cells are not updated. Consequently, the *global rule* of a CA can be considered as a vectorial boolean function $F : \mathbb{F}_2^m \to \mathbb{F}_2^{m-2r}$, and thus the size of the cell array shrinks by $2r$ cells from one time step to the next. Clearly, this means that the global rule can be applied only a limited number of times, as long as $m \geq 2r + 1$.

Given the radius r, there exist $2^{2^{2r+1}}$ local rules. Each rule f can be compactly indexed by its corresponding *Wolfram code*, which is the decimal representation of the truth table of f. A local rule $f : \mathbb{F}_2^{2r+1} \to \mathbb{F}_2$ is *leftmost permutive* if there exists a *generating function* $g_L : \mathbb{F}_2^{2r} \to \mathbb{F}_2$ such that $f(x) = x_1 \oplus g_L(x_2, \cdots, x_{2r+1})$ for all $x = (x_1, \cdots, x_{2r+1}) \in \mathbb{F}_2^{2r+1}$. Similarly, f is called *rightmost permutive* if there is $g_R : \mathbb{F}_2^{2r} \to \mathbb{F}_2$ such that $f(x) = g_R(x_1, \cdots, x_{2r}) \oplus x_{2r+1}$. Rule f is called *bipermutive* if it is both leftmost and rightmost permutive. In this case, g_L is itself rightmost permutive with a certain generating function $g : \mathbb{F}_2^{2r-1} \to \mathbb{F}_2$ (equivalently, g_R is leftmost permutive with the same g). Hence, f can be written as $f(x) = x_1 \oplus g(x_2, \cdots, x_{2r}) \oplus x_{2r+1}$.

2.2 Secret Sharing Schemes

Generally speaking, a *secret sharing scheme* is a procedure which enables a *dealer D* to share a *secret S* (for instance, a cryptographic key) among a set $\mathcal{P} = \{P_1, P_2, \cdots, P_n\}$ of participants or *players*. Each player P_i receives a *share* B_i from the dealer, and a subset $A \subseteq \mathcal{P}$ is *authorized* if its members can reconstruct S by combining their shares. Authorized subsets are specified through an *access structure* $\Gamma \subseteq 2^{\mathcal{P}}$. Usually, Γ is required to be *monotone*, that is, if $A_1 \in \Gamma$ and $A_1 \subseteq A_2$ then $A_2 \in \Gamma$. An authorized subset $M \in \Gamma$ is called *minimal* if $N \notin \Gamma$ for all $N \subset M$. A monotone access structure Γ can thus be defined as the union-closure of the *basis* Γ_0, which is the family of all minimal authorized subsets. In (k, n) *threshold schemes*, such as Shamir's scheme [8], the basis is defined as $\Gamma_0 = \{A \subseteq \mathcal{P} : |A| = k\}$, meaning that all subsets of k or more players can recover the secret. The CA-based secret sharing scheme proposed by del Rey, Mateus and Sánchez [2] can be defined as a *sequential* (k, n) threshold scheme, since at least k *consecutive* shares are required to recover the secret. The minimal authorized subsets are thus of the form $A = \{P_i, P_{i+1}, \cdots, P_{i+k-1}\}$, with $1 \leq i \leq n - k + 1$.

The security model adopted for the study of secret sharing schemes considers the information an attacker can obtain about the secret S by having the shares of a generic unauthorized subset. In particular, schemes which do not leak any information on S by knowing the shares of any unauthorized subset $U \notin \Gamma$ are called *perfect*. To formalise this notion in a probabilistic framework, we follow the approach laid out by Stinson [9].

Let $\mathcal{S}$ be the space of secrets and $\mathcal{B}$ the space of possible shares. We define a *distribution rule* as a function $\varphi : \mathcal{P} \to \mathcal{B}$ which assigns to each player in $\mathcal{P}$ a share from $\mathcal{B}$. Given a secret $S \in \mathcal{S}$, the set $\mathcal{F}_S$ denotes the family of all distribution rules induced by S. The dealer selects both the secret and the corresponding distribution rule according to two probability distributions, which we respectively denote by $Pr(S)$ and $Pr(\varphi)$. These probability distributions and the set $\mathcal{F} = \bigcup_{S \in \mathcal{S}} \mathcal{F}_S$ are assumed to be public, hence known to an attacker. Considering a generic subset of players $G \subseteq \mathcal{P}$, a *shares distribution* δ_G is a possible assignment of shares to the members of G. Given a distribution rule φ, the corresponding shares distribution δ_G is thus the image of the restriction $\varphi|_G$. By $\mathcal{B}_G(S) = \{\varphi|_G : \varphi \in \mathcal{F}_S\}$ we denote the set of all possible shares distributions to G induced by the secret S. The probability distribution on all possible values of δ_G is obtained as follows:

$$Pr(\delta_G) = \sum_{S \in \mathcal{S}} \left(Pr(S) \cdot \sum_{\varphi \in \mathcal{B}_G(S)} Pr(\varphi) \right) . \tag{1}$$

We can now give the formal definition of *perfect* secret sharing scheme.

Definition 1. *A set of distribution rules* $\mathcal{F} = \bigcup_{S \in \mathcal{S}} \mathcal{F}_S$ *is a* perfect secret sharing scheme *having access structure* $\Gamma \subseteq 2^{\mathcal{P}}$ *if for all unauthorized subsets* $U \notin \Gamma$ *and for all shares distributions* δ_U *it results that* $Pr(S|\delta_U) = Pr(S)$.

Assuming that a suitable notion of *size* is defined on both the secrets and the shares (for example, the number of bits used to encode them), a perfect secret sharing scheme is called *ideal* if for all $S \in \mathcal{S}$ the sizes of the shares generated by any distribution rule $\varphi \in \mathcal{F}_S$ equal the size of S.

3   Building Preimages of Bipermutive CA

In this section we describe a procedure to reconstruct a preimage of a CA configuration under a bipermutive rule, which is the basic primitive used in our secret sharing scheme.

Let us suppose that $f : \mathbb{F}_2^{2r+1} \to \mathbb{F}_2$ is bipermutive. Denoting by g the generating function of f on the central $2r-1$ variables and by y the value of $f(x_1, \cdots, x_{2r+1})$, the following equalities hold:

$$y = x_1 \oplus g(x_2, \cdots, x_{2r}) \oplus x_{2r+1}$$
$$x_{2r+1} = x_1 \oplus g(x_2, \cdots, x_{2r}) \oplus y$$
$$x_{2r+1} = f(x_1, x_2, \cdots, x_{2r}, y) \ .$$

Hence, the value of the rightmost input bit can be recovered by computing f on the vector $(x_1, x_2, \cdots, x_{2r}, y)$. Clearly, a symmetrical result holds when knowing y and the rightmost $2r$ bits of the input, which give the value of x_1. This property of bipermutive rules allows one to determine a preimage $p \in \mathbb{F}_2^{m+2r}$ of a configuration $c \in \mathbb{F}_2^m$ using the following procedure:

PREIMAGE-CONSTRUCTION
  1. Set in a random position of p a block of $2r$ random bits $(p_i, p_{i+1}, \cdots, p_{i+2r-1})$.
  2. Determine the value of p_{i+2r} by computing $f(p_i, \cdots, p_{i+2r-1}, c_i)$.
  3. Shift the window of $2r$ bits one place to the *right*, and compute the value of p_{i+2r+1} by evaluating $f(p_{i+1}, \cdots, p_{i+2r}, c_{i+1})$. Continue to apply this step until the rightmost bit p_{m+2r} has been computed.
  4. Determine the value of p_{i-1} by computing $f(c_{i-1}, p_i, \cdots, p_{i+2r-1})$.
  5. Shift the window of $2r$ bits one place to the *left*, and compute the value of p_{i-2} by evaluating $f(c_{i-2}, p_{i-1}, \cdots, p_{i+2r-2})$. Continue to apply this step until the leftmost bit p_1 has been computed.

Thus, the preimage is uniquely determined by the value of configuration c and by the initial $2r$-bit random block. This implies that every CA configuration has exactly 2^{2r} preimages under a bipermutive rule; the fact that the initial block can be placed in any position does not influence the total number of preimages. Figure 1 reports an example of preimage computation using the elementary (i.e. with radius $r = 1$) rule 150.

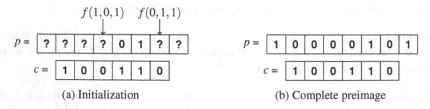

(a) Initialization   (b) Complete preimage

Fig. 1. Example of preimage computation for $c = (1, 0, 0, 1, 1, 0) \in \mathbb{F}_2^6$ using the elementary bipermutive rule 150, defined as $f(x_{i-1}, x_i, x_{i+1}) = x_{i-1} \oplus x_i \oplus x_{i+1}$

Gutowitz [5] originally proposed to use the algorithm PREIMAGE-CONSTRUCTION to implement a CA-based symmetric cryptosystem, using local rules which are either leftmost or rightmost permutive, so that the initial block can be placed only to the leftmost and rightmost position of the preimage, respectively. The secret key is the permutive rule employed to build the preimages of the CA. Oliveira, Coelho and Monteiro [7] refined Gutowitz's cryptosystem by using bipermutive rules, since in this case the differences in the ciphertexts obtained starting from slightly different plaintexts propagate in both directions, and thus make differential cryptanalysis more difficult.

4   A (k,k) Secret Sharing Scheme

We now describe the basic version of our secret sharing scheme, in which all participants must pool their shares in order to recover the secret by using the properties of bipermutive rules explained in Section 3.

First, we observe that by iterating the procedure PREIMAGE-CONSTRUCTION, at each time step the size of the preimage grows by $2r$ bits. Hence, starting from a configuration c having length m, after t iterations we obtain a preimage of length $L(t) = 2rt + m$. Thus, given $k \in \mathbb{N}$, the number of iterations necessary to obtain a preimage of size $k \cdot m$ is $t = m(k-1)/2r$. Since t has to be an integer number, $2r$ must divide $m(k-1)$. However, in order to prove the security properties of our scheme in the next section, we assume the additional constraint that $2r$ divides m. Denoting by $\mathcal{P} = \{P_1, P_2, \cdots, P_k\}$ the set of k players, we also assume that an order on $\mathcal{P}$ has already been mutually established by the dealer and the players, and that each player knows its index $i \in \{1, \cdots, k\}$.

Our secret sharing scheme can be described as follows.

Setup Phase
1. The *dealer D* sets the secret S to be shared (having length $|S| = m$ bits) as a configuration of a cellular automaton, and it chooses at random a bipermutive local rule of radius r, where r is such that $2r|m$.
2. D applies PREIMAGE-CONSTRUCTION for $T = m(k-1)/2r$ iterations, randomly choosing at each step the value and the position of the initial $2r$-bit block to start the construction of the preimage.
3. After T iterations, D obtains a preimage having length $k \cdot m$ which contains a sequence of $2r$ random adjacent bits starting at a random position. The preimage depends in general on $2rT = m(k-1)$ random bits. The dealer splits the preimage in k blocks of m bits, and securely sends one block to each player according to the order defined on $\mathcal{P}$ (hence block B_1 goes to P_1, B_2 to P_2, etc. up to P_k). Finally, D publishes the bipermutive rule used to evolve the CA backwards.

Recovery Phase
1. All the k players pool their shares in the correct order to get the complete preimage of the CA.
2. After having determined the preimage, the players evolve the CA forward for $T = m(k-1)/2r$ iterations, using the local rule published by the dealer. Notice that the players can compute by themselves T, since they know m, k and r.
3. The configuration obtained after T iterations is the original secret S.

Figure 2 depicts the setup phase.

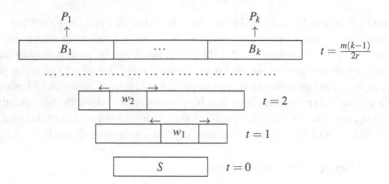

Fig. 2. Setup phase of the (k,k) secret sharing scheme. The randomly placed blocks w_i represent the initial $2r$ random adjacent bits used to reconstruct each preimage.

5   Security Properties of the Basic Scheme

The access structure of the basic scheme shown in Section 4 is trivially composed by one set, which is the set of all players $\mathcal{P}$. In order to investigate the security properties of the scheme, we thus have to analyse the information an attacker can gain about the secret by knowing a subset of $k-1$ or fewer shares. We begin with the following preliminary results.

Lemma 1. *Let* $F : \mathbb{F}_2^{m+2r} \to \mathbb{F}_2^m$ *be the global rule of a CA defined by a bipermutive local rule* $f : \mathbb{F}_2^{2r+1} \to \mathbb{F}_2$. *Then, by fixing a block* $\tilde{x} \in \mathbb{F}_2^{2r}$ *of $2r$ adjacent coordinates in* $x \in \mathbb{F}_2^{m+2r}$, *the resulting restriction* $F|_{\tilde{x}} : \mathbb{F}_2^m \to \mathbb{F}_2^m$ *is a permutation on* $\mathbb{F}_2^m$.

Proof. Let us denote by $x \in \mathbb{F}_2^{m+2r}$ the CA configuration and by $y \in \mathbb{F}_2^m$ the image of F. Assuming that the first component of the block $\tilde{x} \in \mathbb{F}_2^{2r}$ is placed at position i of x, with $1 \le i \le m-2r+1$, we have to prove that the function $F|_{\tilde{x}}$ which maps the remaining vector $\hat{x} = (x_1, \cdots, x_{i-1}, x_{i+2r}, \cdots, x_m) \in \mathbb{F}_2^m$ to y is bijective. Given $y \in \mathbb{F}_2^m$ and a block of $2r$ consecutive bits in the preimage, the remaining ones are uniquely determined by the application of the algorithm PREIMAGE-CONSTRUCTION. Consequently, each output $y \in \mathbb{F}_2^m$ has a unique preimage under $F|_{\tilde{x}}$, and thus $F|_{\tilde{x}}$ is bijective.   □

In the next Lemma we denote by $x(t)$ the configuration obtained by evolving the CA forward for t steps, with $x(0)$ being the first preimage resulting from the juxtaposition of the k shares in the correct order. We also use the notation $(x_u, \cdots, x_v)(t)$ to represent the subvector of the configuration $x(t)$ included between the indices $u < v$.

Lemma 2. *Let* B_l, *with* $1 \le l \le k$, *be the only unknown share among* $B_1, \cdots, B_k$. *Then, there exists a permutation* $\Pi : \mathbb{F}_2^m \to \mathbb{F}_2^m$ *between B_l and the secret S.*

Proof. We first consider the case where $l = 1$, in which the unknown block of m bits is $B_1 = (x_1, \cdots, x_m)(0)$. By evolving the CA forward, at each time step t the block $(x_1, \cdots, x_m)(t)$ remains unknown. Indeed, since the application of the global rule shrinks the configuration by $2r$ bits, after t iterations only the rightmost $m(k-1) - 2rt$ bits of $x(t)$ are determined. In particular, the block $(x_{m+1}, \cdots, x_{m+1+2r})(t)$ of $2r$ bits is known.

Hence, for all $t \in \{1, \cdots, T\}$ where $T = m(k-1)/2r$, by Lemma 1 there is a permutation $\pi_1(t) : \mathbb{F}_2^m \to \mathbb{F}_2^m$ which maps the block $(x_1, \cdots, x_m)(t-1)$ in the block $(x_1, \cdots, x_m)(t)$. By observing that $(x_1, \cdots, x_m)(T) = S$, the permutation Π between B_1 and S can thus be defined as $\Pi = \pi_1(T) \circ \pi_1(T-1) \circ \cdots \circ \pi_1(1)$.

If the missing share is B_k, a symmetric reasoning stands by considering for all t the block $(x_{m(k-1)+1}, \cdots, x_{mk})(t)$ containing the rightmost m unknown bits.

We now prove the generic case where $1 < l < k$. This means that the unknown m-bit block is $(x_{(l-1)m+1}, \cdots, x_{lm})(0)$. Similarly to the case $l = 1$, by evolving the CA forward the block $(x_{(l-1)m+1-2rt}, \cdots, x_{lm-2rt})(t)$ is undetermined, and by Lemma 1 there is a permutation $\pi_l(t)$ between this block and $(x_{(l-1)m+1-2r(t-1)}, \cdots, x_{lm-2r(t-1)})(t-1)$. In particular, the 2r-bit block which fixes $\pi_l(t)$ is the one placed to the left of the cell $x_{(l-1)m+1-2r(t-1)}$. Clearly, t does not range in the set $\{1, \cdots, T\}$. In fact, at a certain step $\hat{t} < T$ the index of the first cell in the unknown m-bit block will be less than 2r. Recall that in Section 4 we required that $2r|m$, i.e. $m = 2rb$ for some $b \in \mathbb{N}$. Thus, at time $\hat{t} = 1 + (l-1)b$ the vector $(x_1, \cdots, x_m)(\hat{t})$ is undetermined. But we know from the case $l = 1$ that there is a series of permutations $\pi_1(t)$ for $\hat{t} < t \leq T$ which maps this block to the secret S. Hence, the permutation Π between B_l and S can be defined as $\Pi = \pi_1(T) \circ \cdots \circ \pi_1(\hat{t}+1) \circ \pi_l(\hat{t}) \circ \cdots \circ \pi_l(1)$.   □

In what follows, we denote by $S = \mathbb{F}_2^m$ the space of secrets, which coincides with the space of shares $\mathcal{B}$. Let us assume that the uniform probability distribution is defined on S, that is $Pr(S) = 1/2^m$ for all $S \in S$. Given a secret S, the distribution rule $\varphi \in \mathcal{F}_S$ assigning to each of the k players a share from $\mathcal{B}$ is determined by the 2r-bit blocks used to build the CA preimages, thus by a total of $m(k-1)$ bits. Assuming that the dealer chooses uniformly at random these bits, for all $\varphi \in \mathcal{F}_S$ it follows that $Pr(\varphi) = 1/2^{m(k-1)}$.

Let us suppose that $U \subseteq \mathcal{P}$ is a subset of participants such that $|U| = |\mathcal{P}| - 1 = k - 1$. The probability that a particular share distribution δ_U occurs given a secret S can be computed as

$$Pr(\delta_U|S) = \sum_{\varphi \subset B_U(S)} Pr(\varphi) \ . \tag{2}$$

Given $S \in S$, by Lemma 2 we know that for all distributions of $k - 1$ shares δ_U there is only a single additional share B_l that, joined to those of U, uniquely determines the secret S, since there is a permutation Π between B_l and S. Consequently, $|B_U(S)| = 1$ and Equation (2) becomes

$$Pr(\delta_U|S) = \sum_{\varphi \in B_U(S)} Pr(\varphi) = \frac{1}{2^{m(k-1)}} \ . \tag{3}$$

Computing the probability of a particular share distribution δ_U over all possible secrets $S \in S$ is now straightforward:

$$Pr(\delta_U) = \sum_{S \in S} \left(P(S) \cdot \sum_{\varphi \in B_U(S)} Pr(\varphi) \right) . \tag{4}$$

Since $Pr(S) = 1/2^m$ for all $S \in \mathcal{S}$ and $|\mathcal{S}| = 2^m$, Equation (4) can be rewritten as

$$Pr(\delta_U) = 2^m \cdot \frac{1}{2^m} \cdot \frac{1}{2^{m(k-1)}} = \frac{1}{2^{m(k-1)}} \quad . \tag{5}$$

We have thus concluded that, for all $S \in \mathcal{S}$,

$$Pr(\delta_U) = Pr(\delta_U | S) \quad , \tag{6}$$

that is, the occurrence of the share distribution δ_U to the subset U is independent from the occurrence of the secret S. Clearly, we can make the same reasoning for all subsets $U \subseteq \mathcal{P}$ such that $|U| < |\mathcal{P}| = k$; the only quantity which changes is the cardinality of the set $B_U(S)$, but this is irrelevant in order to get Equation (6).

We can now prove the following result.

Theorem 1. *The (k,k) secret sharing scheme described in Section 4 is perfect.*

Proof. Let U be a generic unauthourized subset of players having cardinality $|U| < k$, and let δ_U be a share distribution to the members of U. Using Bayes' theorem, we have

$$Pr(S | \delta_U) = \frac{Pr(\delta_U | S) \cdot Pr(S)}{Pr(\delta_U)} \quad . \tag{7}$$

By Equation (6), we know that $Pr(\delta_U) = Pr(\delta_U | S)$. Hence, $Pr(S | \delta_U) = Pr(S)$. □

Thus, by knowing $k - 1$ or fewer shares the attacker gains no information about the secret. Finally, it is also easy to see that the scheme is ideal, since the CA is iterated the number of times necessary to get a preimage having length $k \cdot m$. Hence, the size of each of the k shares equals the size of the secret.

6   An Extension to the Basic Scheme

The secret sharing scheme described in Section 4 can be trivially employed to implement any access structure $\Gamma \subseteq \mathcal{P}$: for each authorized subset $A \in \Gamma$, it simply suffices to re-run the setup phase and create a new (independent) set of shares to be distributed to the members of A. However, as the size of $\mathcal{P}$ grows, this method quickly becomes impractical, since each player must hold a different share for every authorized subset he belongs to. We now introduce an extension to the basic scheme called *secret juxtaposition*, which allows one to reuse the same shares thus creating more authorized subsets with a single setup phase.

Let us assume that a set of k shares has been created by following the basic setup procedure, and distributed to a set of k participants. In order to add an additional player without having to recompute all the shares, we can append another copy of the secret S to the right of the existing one (respectively, to the left). Then, we run the algorithm PREIMAGE-CONSTRUCTION for each preimage towards the right (respectively, towards the left) to compute the additional share of $m = |S|$ bits. Note that in this case it is not necessary to pick random bits, since in each preimage more than $2r$ bits are already determined.

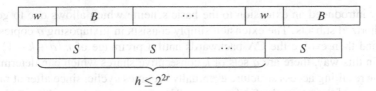

Fig. 3. After at most $h \leq 2^{2r}$ juxtaposed copies of S, the algorithm PREIMAGE-CONSTRUCTION repeats the $2r$-bit block w at the end of the preimage. At this point, the subsequent m-bit block in the preimage will be a copy of B, since the part of the image which is relevant for PREIMAGE-CONSTRUCTION is always S.

Thus, by juxtaposing q copies of the secret S and by evolving the CA backwards for $T = m(k-1)/2r$ steps, we get $q+k-1$ shares of m bits, and each of the q subsets of k consecutive shares can recover the secret, since the corresponding space-time cone collapses on a copy of S. The resulting access structure is however more flexible than the sequential threshold induced by del Rey, Mateus and Sánchez's scheme [2]. In fact, in our scheme by continuing to append copies of the secret the shares obtained will eventually repeat. This happens because after at most 2^{2r} juxtapositions of S, the last $2r$-bit block in the first preimage will be already occurred at another index corresponding to the end of a copy of S and the beginning of the next one (see Figure 3).

As a consequence, after a certain number of juxtapositions the access structure of our scheme becomes *cyclic*, meaning that the sets of k consecutive shares which can recover the secret are the ones that can be formed by considering the CA preimage at time T as a ring. The minimal authorized subsets $M \in \Gamma_0$ of a generic (k,n) cyclic access structure are defined for all $i \in \{1, \cdots, n\}$ as $M = \{P_{j(i)}, P_{j(i+1)}, \cdots, P_{j(i+k-1)}\}$, where $j(z) = 1 + [(z-1) \mod n]$ for all $z \in \{i, \cdots, i+k-1\}$. It is easy to see that in a (k,n) cyclic access structure there are n minimal authorized subsets, in contrast to the $n-k+1$ yielded by a sequential threshold scheme. Thus, assuming that the first preimage of the CA repeats itself after n juxtapositions of the secret S, with $n \leq 2^{2r}$, the extended scheme can be used to implement a cyclic access structure for a set of n players, by evolving the CA backwards for T steps starting from a configuration composed by n copies of S. We note that Theorem 1 still holds for the extended scheme, under the assumption that the attacker knows fewer than k consecutive shares.

7   Conclusions

We presented a new secret sharing scheme which employs bipermutive cellular automata as a primitive, differently from the LMCA-based approach schemes usually proposed in the literature. The main idea of our scheme is to set the secret S as a configuration of a bipermutive CA and to evolve it backwards using the algorithm PREIMAGE-CONSTRUCTION until a preimage of length $k \cdot m$ is obtained, which is subsequently splitted among the k players. We proved that this basic version of the scheme in which all the k players have to pool their shares to recover the secret is perfect, meaning that an attacker who knows fewer than k shares gains no information about S. Moreover, we showed that the scheme is ideal, since the shares have the same size of the secret.

We finally introduced an extension to the basic scheme which allows one to generate more authorized subsets. The extension simply consists in juxtaposing q copies of the secret S and then evolve the CA backwards until a preimage of $m(q + k - 1)$ bits is reached. In this way, there are q sets of k consecutive shares which can determine the secret. The resulting access structure eventually becomes cyclic, since after at most 2^{2r} juxtapositions of the secret the final shares will begin to repeat themselves.

The main advantages of our scheme compared to del Rey, Mateus and Sánchez's LMCA-based model [2] can be synthesised as follows. First, bipermutive CAs have a simpler structure than k-th order linear memory CA, since the next states of the cells depend only on the current configuration. Hence, our scheme is possibly amenable to more efficient and cost-effective hardware implementations. Moreover, the cyclic access structure induced by our scheme is more flexible, since it eventually generates n minimal authorized subsets rather than the $n - k + 1$ produced by the scheme of del Rey, Mateus and Sánchez [2].

There are several possibilities for further research and improvements on this subject. From a practical point of view, it would be useful to investigate if there exists a general method to determine *exactly* after how many juxtapositions of the secret the shares begin to repeat themselves, without having to simulate the CA backwards. This is equivalent to the following problem: given a bipermutive rule f and a CA configuration having spatial period m, find the periods of its preimages under the application of f. Another interesting direction of research would be to generalise the secret sharing scheme to the case of d-dimensional cellular automata, with $d \geq 2$, and to consider the resulting access structures: clearly, the number of authorized subsets would be greater than in the one-dimensional case, since each share would be adjacent to more shares.

Acknowledgements. The authors wish to thank the anonymous referees for their comments to improve the paper. This work was partially supported by Consorzio Milano Ricerche and International Analytics Ltd.

References

1. Blakley, G.: Safeguarding cryptographic keys. In: Proceedings of the 1979 AFIPS National Computer Conference, pp. 313–317. AFIPS Press, Monval (1979)
2. del Rey, Á.M., Mateus, J.P., Sánchez, G.R.: A secret sharing scheme based on cellular automata. Appl. Math. Comput. 170(2), 1356–1364 (2005)
3. Eslami, Z., Ahmadabadi, J.Z.: A verifiable multi-secret sharing scheme based on cellular automata. Inf. Sci. 180(15), 2889–2894 (2010)
4. Eslami, Z., Razzaghi, S.H., Ahmadabadi, J.Z.: Secret image sharing based on cellular automata and steganography. Pattern Recogn. 43(1), 397–404 (2010)
5. Gutowitz, H.: Cryptography with dynamical systems. In: Goles, E., Boccara, N. (eds.) Cellular Automata and Cooperative Phenomena, pp. 237–274. Kluwer Academic Press (1993)
6. Marañón, G.Á., Encinas, L.H., del Rey, Á.M.: A multisecret sharing scheme for color images based on cellular automata. Inf. Sci. 178(22), 4382–4395 (2008)
7. Oliveira, G., Coelho, A., Monteiro, L.: Cellular automata cryptographic model based on bi-directional toggle rules. Int. J. Mod. Phys. C 15(8), 1061–1068 (2004)
8. Shamir, A.: How to share a secret. Commun. ACM 22(11), 612–613 (1979)
9. Stinson, D.R.: Cryptography: theory and practice, 3rd edn. CRC Press, Boca Raton (2006)

Inapplicability of Fault Attacks against Trivium on a Cellular Automata Based Stream Cipher

Jimmy Jose[1], Sourav Das[2], and Dipanwita Roy Chowdhury[1]

[1] Department of Computer Science and Engineering,
Indian Institute of Technology Kharagpur, India
{jimmy,drc}@cse.iitkgp.ernet.in
[2] Infinera India Pvt Ltd
sourav10101976@gmail.com

Abstract. The current work analyses fault attacks on Trivium. These attacks exploit the slow pace of non-linearisation and reversibility of the encryption function. Cellular Automata can be effectively deployed to circumvent these shortcomings. CASTREAM, a CA based stream cipher, is difficult to reverse as well as highly non-linear and the non-linearity is attained very fast. In this paper, we show that CASTREAM is strong against fault attacks for which Trivium is vulnerable.

Keywords: Fault Analysis, Trivium, Stream Cipher, CASTREAM, Cellular Automata.

1 Introduction

Stream ciphers are an important branch in symmetric key-cryptography and used as a fast encryption mechanism for communication channels. Stream ciphers have gained a lot of attention in recent years and provide fast encryption. In stream ciphers, a pseudo-random keystream sequence is generated from a secret key. The plain-text is simply XORed with the keystream to encrypt the message at the encryption site. At the decryption site, the same keystream is generated with the same secret key. The cipher-text is XORed with the keystream to get back the plain-text. The eStream project [15] had been launched to search for good stream ciphers that can provide advantage in performance over block ciphers.

The eStream project has divided the stream ciphers into two categories, namely, software oriented stream ciphers that provide fast encryption in software and hardware oriented stream ciphers that provide fast encryption with easy hardware implementation. Traditionally, the hardware oriented stream ciphers used LFSRs (Linear Feedback Shift Registers) filtered with a non-linear function. Later, stream ciphers started using NFSRs, which are LFSRs with non-linear feedback. The NFSRs are linearly combined to produce the keystreams. Trivium [5] is an example of such stream ciphers.

Trivium is one of the finalists in the eStream project. Its strongest features are simplicity in operation, high throughput, and low hardware requirement. Like other eStream finalists, Trivium has gained a lot of attention from cryptanalysts.

J. Wąs, G.C. Sirakoulis, and S. Bandini (Eds.): ACRI 2014, LNCS 8751, pp. 427–436, 2014.

Some of the attacks that are proposed on initialization modes are Cube attacks [4,6], Cube testers [3], and Conditional Differential Cryptanalysis [11,12].

Recently, fault analysis [7] gets a lot of attention due to the ease of its practical implementation. In this attack, it is assumed that the attacker can introduce a fault on a particular state bit and then track the fault to deduce the key bits or the initial state bits. The attacker has only partial control over the exact position and the timing of the fault. There has been some success by inducing faults and then performing differential analysis on the keystream bits [8,9]. This attack was later improved in [13] by using advanced algebraic techniques. It was shown in [10] that on a random fault, it is possible to determine the exact position and the time of the fault. They also performed differential analysis to determine the state bits.

The stream cipher, CASTREAM [1], was proposed in ACRI 2012 using Cellular Automata. CASTREAM is a Trivium-like cipher where non-linear state bits and linear state bits employing Cellular Automata are combined linearly to produce keystreams. CASTREAM has the main advantage of getting high-throughput. This was possible since Cellular Automata, being a parallel transformation, enable us to extract multiple bits at a time as keystream.

In this paper, we show that the fault attacks applied on Trivium are not really applicable to Cellular Automata based stream cipher CASTREAM. Cellular Automata diffuse the state bits very fast as all the bits undergo XOR transformations in every cycle. This makes a fault which is introduced in the state, spread very fast and makes it very difficult to track. LFSRs, on the other hand, diffuse the state bits very slowly as only the last bit undergo XOR transformation at every cycle. Thus, a Cellular Automata based stream cipher naturally tends to resist fault attacks.

We take up each of the fault attacks reported against the NFSR based cipher Trivium and show that the fault attack is not applicable to the Cellular Automata based stream cipher CASTREAM. This work can be extended by taking other Cellular Automata based cipher as an example. For example, CAR30 [14] is another Cellular Automata based cipher with very strong security properties and is based on classical Rule 30 of Cellular Automata along with a maximum length CA. It has been shown that the fault attacks will not be applicable for CAR30. Extending this work, it can be shown concretely that the specific fault attacks against Trivium are not applicable to CAR30 as well.

This paper is organised as follows. We begin with Preliminaries in Section 2 and give a description of Trivium and CASTREAM. Section 3 describes the fault attacks that were mounted on Trivium. We put a rigorous analysis on each of the attacks to show that they are not applicable to CA based stream cipher CASTREAM. We conclude by Section 4.

2   Preliminaries

A number of attacks have been reported against LFSR based stream ciphers. Trivium [5] is an eStream [15] finalist which is LFSR based and so vulnerable to these attacks. Among these reported attacks, fault attack is one of the most effective and practical attack on Trivium. Cellular automata can be used as a good cryptographic primitive against fault attack. CASTREAM is a Cellular Automata based stream cipher and we investigate how this cipher prevents fault attack for which Trivium is vulnerable. A brief description of Trivium and CASTREAM is provided in the following subsections.

2.1   Trivium Description

Trivium has 3 NFSRs. Let us denote the 288 state bits of Trivium as $S = (s_1, \cdots, s_{288})$, key bits as $K = (k_1, \cdots, k_{80})$ and IV bits as $V = (v_1, \cdots, v_{80})$. The keystream and feedback functions of these NFSRs are:

$$KS \leftarrow s_{66} \oplus s_{93} \oplus s_{162} \oplus s_{177} \oplus s_{243} \oplus s_{288}$$
$$t_1 \leftarrow s_{66} \oplus s_{91} \cdot s_{92} \oplus s_{93} \oplus s_{171}$$
$$t_2 \leftarrow s_{162} \oplus s_{175} \cdot s_{176} \oplus s_{177} \oplus s_{264}$$
$$t_3 \leftarrow s_{243} \oplus s_{286} \cdot s_{287} \oplus s_{288} \oplus s_{69}$$
$$(s_1, \cdots, s_{93}) \leftarrow (t_3, s_1, \cdots, s_{92})$$
$$(s_{94}, \cdots, s_{177}) \leftarrow (t_1, s_{94}, \cdots, s_{176})$$
$$(s_{178}, \cdots, s_{288}) \leftarrow (t_2, s_{178}, \cdots, s_{287})$$

At initialisation, the system is iterated for 1152 cycles without producing any keystreams. The Key-IV loading takes place as follows:

$$(s_1, \cdots, s_{93}) \leftarrow (k_1, \cdots, k_{80}, 0, \cdots, 0)$$
$$(s_{94}, \cdots, s_{177}) \leftarrow (v_1, \cdots, v_{80}, 0, 0, 0, 0, 0)$$
$$(s_{178}, \cdots, s_{288}) \leftarrow (0, \cdots, 0, 1, 1, 1)$$

Trivium is broken if one of its inner states is known since we can use *algorithm 1* to reach the initial state from a given state thereby revealing the secret key.

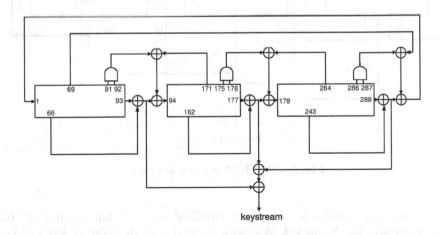

Fig. 1. Trivium block diagram

Algorithm 1. Trivium Key Recovery

input: Trivium inner state $(s_1, \cdots, s_{288})$ at some time instant and IV $(v_1, \cdots, v_{288})$

output: Key $(k_1, \cdots, k_{80})$

1: **while** $(s_{81}, \cdots, s_{93}, s_{174}, \cdots, s_{288}) \neq (0, \cdots, 0, 1, 1, 1)$ **and** $(s_{94}, \cdots, s_{173}) \neq$ $(v_1, \cdots, v_{80})$ **do**

2:     $(t_3, s_1, \cdots, s_{92}) \leftarrow (s_1, s_2, \cdots, s_{93})$

3:     $(t_1, s_{94}, \cdots, s_{176}) \leftarrow (s_{94}, s_{95}, \cdots, s_{177})$

4:     $(t_2, s_{178}, \cdots, s_{287}) \leftarrow (s_{178}, s_{179}, \cdots, s_{288})$

5:     $s_{93} \leftarrow t_1 \oplus s_{66} \oplus s_{91} \cdot s_{92} \oplus s_{171}$

6:     $s_{177} \leftarrow t_2 \oplus s_{162} \oplus s_{175} \cdot s_{176} \oplus s_{264}$

7:     $s_{288} \leftarrow t_3 \oplus s_{243} \oplus s_{286} \cdot s_{287} \oplus s_{69}$

8: **end while**

9: $(k_1, \cdots, k_{80}) \leftarrow (s_1, \cdots, s_{80})$

2.2   A Brief Description of CASTREAM

CASTREAM [1] is a stream cipher suitable for both hardware and software. In Trivium, the nonlinearisation process is very slow. CASTREAM makes it faster. Cellular Automata (CA) prevent correlation attacks and the small s-boxes prevent algebraic attacks. There are two non-linear blocks and one linear block (linear block guarantees the period) combined linearly to produce 128 keystream bits at a time. Each of the three blocks are of length 128. Non-linear blocks contain three layers, a 128-bit maximum length CA sandwiched between two layers containing multiple variable length small s-boxes.

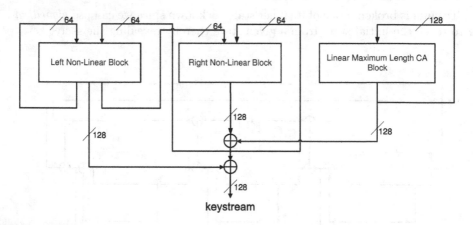

Fig. 2. CASTREAM block diagram

Left and right non-linear blocks are intialised with 128-bit key and 128-bit IV respectively. The linear CA block is initialised with the XOR of key and IV. Cipher is iterated six times in the initialisation phase without generating any output. In each iteration, the XOR of the three blocks is fed back to linear CA block. Let L_i, R_i, and C_i denote the ith bit of left non-linear, right-non linear, and linear CA blocks respectively. $L_1 \cdots L_{16}, R_1 \oplus C_1 \cdots R_{16} \oplus C_{16}, L_{17} \cdots L_{32}$, $\cdots, L_{49} \cdots L_{64}, R_{49} \oplus C_{49} \cdots R_{64} \oplus C_{64}$ fed back to the first non-linear block and $L_{65} \cdots L_{80}, R_{65} \oplus C_{65} \cdots R_{80} \oplus C_{80}, L_{81} \cdots L_{96}, \cdots, L_{113} \cdots L_{128}, R_{113} \oplus C_{113} \cdots$ $R_{128} \oplus C_{128}$ fed back to the second non-linear block. From seventh iteration onwards, the XOR of the bits of all the three blocks is taken out as the keystream and linear maximum length CA block feedbacks itself. In CASTREAM, each state bit depends on all the key bits and IV bits after initial six iterations.

3   Fault Prevention Using Cellular Automata

Side Channel Attacks (SCA) are attacks that exploit the pitfalls in the implementation of the cryptosystem. The attack can be active or passive. Active attacks disturb the proper functioning of the system whereas passive do not. Fault attack is a type of active SCA where internal state of the system is revealed by injecting faults thereby making the key open. Trivium is vulnerable against a number of fault attacks [8–10, 13] reported in literature. We analyse each of these fault attacks and thus identify the weak part of the construction of the cipher which is responsible for the fault attack to be successful. CASTREAM [1] is one Trivium-like cipher that employs Cellular Automata unlike the LFSR of Trivium. In this section, we show that the fault attacks which are successful on Trivium are ineffective against CASTREAM. This is due to the parallel transformation of the Cellular Automata that spreads the fault very quickly into the state which makes it difficult to track.

3.1   Differential Fault Analysis of Trivium

Differential Fault Analysis (DFA) is an active side channel attack where an attacker inserts a fault into the enciphering/deciphering process or she inserts a fault into the cipher state. The paper [8] focusses on the latter technique.

The fault model is based on the following assumptions.

1. attacker can alter only one random bit.
2. this can be done multiple times on the same inner state.
3. attacker is able to obtain the keystreams with and without fault injections from the same inner state.

In Trivium, the keystream is generated by taking XOR of two inner state bits from each of the three registers. Because of the structure of the cipher, 66 linear and 82 quadratic equations can be deduced. The distance between the two state bits which contribute to keystream generation is different in each of the three registers. This provides a mechanism to find out the random bit position e where the fault was injected.

For the sake of clear understanding, we briefly restate the two attacks presented in [8]. In the attack using linear equations, first of all, for each fault position e, $1 \le e \le 288$, the keystream difference bits d_i are represented as follows.

$d_i = z_i \oplus z_i'$, where z_i is the ith keystream bit and z_i' is the ith keystream bit after fault injection.

The linear equations are represented by a matrix M with 289 columns representing the 288 state variables plus one for the RHS of the equation. All the 66 linear equations are added to M first. Sufficient number of faults are introduced to form keystream difference equations and added to M so that M is capable enough to solve the required number of inner state bits. The algorithm performs well when some of the inner state bits are guessed than computed. When all the inner state bits of the cipher are available, Trivium function, which is reversible, is run backwards until the cipher reaches the intial state. First 80 bits of the intial state is the required key (*algorithm 1*).

In the second attack, pair-quadratic equations are also used. They are equations containing linear terms and quadratic terms of the form $s_j.s_{j+1}$. The matrix M contains $288+287+1$ columns representing 288 state variables, 287 pair-quadratic terms and 1 representing RHS of the equation. All the 148 equations (66 linear and 82 quadratic) are added to M. Faults are introduced and corresponding equations are added to M as was done in the first attack. Whenever some previously unknown variable is found, M is scanned so that some quadratic terms may be converted to linear. This along with classic algebraic techniques are repeated in tandem until all state bits are computed. Like the first attack, Trivium is run backwards to find the key.

Attack Prevention in CASTREAM. In [8], two attacks, viz. linear and quadratic, are proposed. In both the attacks, the reversibilility of Trivium (*algorithm 1*) is exploited. In CASTREAM [1], s-boxes are implemented using Cellular Automata. The use of multiple variable length s-boxes make the function difficult to reverse.

In CA based s-box, if n represents the seed, m the input (number of cycles), T the characteristic matrix corresponding to the CA, and y the output, then
$$y = T^m * (n).$$

If m is varied keeping n constant, output y varies exponentially with respect to the input m. If we take a 4–cell maximum length CA having rule vector $< 90, 150, 90, 150 >$, then the characteristic matrix is given as follows.

$$T = \begin{pmatrix} 0 & 1 & 0 & 0 \\ 1 & 1 & 1 & 0 \\ 0 & 1 & 0 & 1 \\ 0 & 0 & 1 & 1 \end{pmatrix}$$

If the generator polynomial is X^4+X+1 and the seed is $< 1,0,1,0 >$, then the evolution of CA is governed by the following functions

$y_0 = x_0 \oplus x_1 \oplus x_2 \oplus x_1x_2 \oplus x_0x_1x_2 \oplus x_3 \oplus x_0x_3 \oplus x_0x_2x_3$

$y_1 = x_1 \oplus x_2 \oplus x_0x_3 \oplus x_1x_3 \oplus x_0x_1x_3 \oplus x_0x_2x_3 \oplus x_1x_2x_3$

$y_2 = x_0x_1 \oplus x_1x_2 \oplus x_0x_1x_2 \oplus x_0x_3 \oplus x_0x_1x_3 \oplus x_2x_3 \oplus x_0x_2x_3 \oplus x_1x_2x_3$

$y_3 = x_2 \oplus x_0x_2 \oplus x_1x_2 \oplus x_3 \oplus x_0x_3 \oplus x_2x_3 \oplus x_1x_2x_3$

where (x_0, x_1, x_2, x_3) and (y_0, y_1, y_2, y_3) are input and output vectors respectively [2].

These equations show that each output bit depends on all the input bits and the algebraic degree of the output bits is three. It can be shown that these two conditions will remain for different seeds. This is the case of a 4x4 s-box. It can be similarly shown that the algebraic degree of 5x5 and 6x6 s-boxes are 4 and 5 respectively.

We have tried to investigate how CASTREAM will respond to DFA. Our analysis show that actual algebraic degree in CASTREAM will be nine as we have two layers of s-boxes. The attack in [8] uses 66 linear and 88 quadratic equations against TRIVIUM which is not possible in CASTREAM as the algebraic degree is higher.

Now, we show how fault position determination is not possible in CASTREAM as opposed to Trivium. In Trivium, each keystream bit at any iteration is generated by XORing the specific inner state bits s_{66}, s_{93}, s_{162}, s_{177}, s_{243}, and s_{288}. That is, two bits each from the three registers take part in keystream generation. The distance between these bits in each register is unique; 27, 15, and 45 respectively for the first, second, and third registers. The fault position is determined by exploiting this uniqueness. However, this technique will not work in CASTREAM. The keystream bits generated in each iteration of CASTREAM depends on all the 128 bits in each of the three CA blocks. So unlike Trivium, it does not provide unique distances between the state bits. This is one reason why fault position determination is not possible in CASTREAM. Next we show how the tables that are used in [8] to find fault positions cannot be constructed in the case of CASTREAM.

If $L_{1,j}$, $R_{1,j}$, and $C_{1,j}$ represent the first bit of each of the three 128 bit blocks of CASTREAM in iteration j, then

$$KS_{1,j+1} = L_{1,j+1} \oplus R_{1,j+1} \oplus C_{1,j+1},$$

where $KS_{1,j+1}$ represents the first keystream bit in iteration j+1. $L_{1,j+1}$, $R_{1,j+1}$, and $C_{1,j+1}$ depend on 30, 30, and 17 inner state bits respectively in j^{th} iteration. So a single keystream bit in $(j+1)^{th}$ iteration depends on 77 bits of iteration j. This dependence prevents the precomputation of the tables.

3.2 Floating Fault Analysis of Trivium

Floating Fault Analysis (FFA) [9] follows the principles from DFA. The major difference from DFA is that it treats each new inner state bit as a new variable. Since the attack uses 800 iterations and each iteration generates three new inner state bits, the total number of variables are 800*3+288=2688, including the 288 initial inner state bits. This method needs only 3.2 fault injections on average to break the cipher. The Trivium inner state at time t is represented as

$$IS_t = (x_{t-1}, \cdots, x_{t-93}, y_{t-1}, \cdots, y_{t-84}, z_{t-1}, \cdots, z_{t-111}),$$

where $\{x_n\}$, $\{y_n\}$, and $\{z_n\}$ represent the sequences produced by the three registers of Trivium. IS_0 represents the intial state where key and IV are used for initialisation. Another sequence $\{o_n\}$ represents the keystream sequence. *Delta sequences* are sequences which represent the difference between the sequences with and without fault injection. They are denoted by $\{\delta x_n\}$, $\{\delta y_n\}$, $\{\delta z_n\}$, and $\{\delta o_n\}$.

The attack strategy is on the same line as in DFA. Since the representation is different and the number of variables is higher in comparison with DFA attack, more number of variables are revealed in each fault injection. These are substituted in higher degree equations to reduce their degree. Let IS_t be an unknown fixed inner state of Trivium. Corresponding to 800 consecutive keystream bits o_n, 800 linear equations are added. Corresponding to x_n, y_n, and z_n, 3*800=2400 quadratic equations are added. Faults are injected as in DFA so that the number of delta keystream equations generated are sufficient enough to reveal all the bits of IS_t. Then, Trivium is run backwards until it reaches the intial state to reveal the key.

Attack Prevention in CASTREAM. In FFA, 800 linear equations are added corresponding to 800 consecutive Trivium keystream bits. In addition, 2400 quadratic equations are added corresponding to the new variables generated in 800 iterations. As the smallest s-box in a layer of multiple variable length s-boxes has a degree three and a CASTREAM non-linear block has two layers of this kind, CASTREAM will not generate linear or quadratic equations. As already mentioned, the overall algebraic degree will be nine. The fault position determination technique in FFA is the same as that of DFA. We have already shown that this is not possible in CASTREAM. This will prevent the attacker from finding out IS_t, the inner state at some time t. Even if IS_t is known, since CASTREAM function is difficult to reverse, we may not be able to run it backwards from this known state to reach the initial inner state to find out the secret key.

3.3   Hu et al. Fault Attack

In this attack [10], weaker assumptions are used in comparison with FFA. They are

1. Fault injection can be done at random time in place of fixed time.
2. Instead of changing exactly one random bit, fault injection can be done in a random area within eight consecutive bits. The area will not span more than one register out of the three Trivium registers.

A method known as Checking Method is used to find out fault injection time and fault position. The original keystream and and fault injected keystream are taken as input. Each of the three Trivium registers are divided into three regions for a total of nine, and each region is separately analysed to find out the time and the position. If the fault injection time t varies uniformly in the range $0 \le t \le 32$, then we need only the original keystream and 16 fault injected keystreams of 195 bits length to break Trivium.

Attack Prevention in CASTREAM. To break Trivium in this fault model, enough linear equations at known time are generated by injecting faults several times. At least 200 additional linear equations are generated using fault injections in addition to the 66 linear equations generated without fault injections. Some pair-quadratic equations that are generated other than the linear equations are also used since they may be converted later to linear when some bits become known. But the CASTREAM model with non-linear blocks having a maximum length CA sandwiched between two layers of variable length multiple s-boxes prevent generation of linear and quadratic equations as the smallest s-box is having an algebraic degree of three. Since we have two layers of s-boxes, the algebraic degree of CASTREAM is nine.

Checking Method in the fault model performs the analysis by dividing the Trivium registers into different regions according to the bit positions which contribute to the modification of inner state bits and keystream generation. This is not applicable to CASTREAM as all the current inner state bits take part in the modification of inner state bits and keystream generation in each iteration. Fault Floating Method also will not work as explained under Floating Fault Analysis.

3.4   Mohamed et al. Attack

This attack [13] improves the FFA [9] by

1. improving the equation preprocessing part
2. using SAT solver to speed up the solving part

IN FFA, during the equation preprocessing phase, solved variables are substituted only in higher degree polynomials. In the improved method, substitution is done in all the linear and quadratic polynomials which provides more linear equations, thereby speeding up the attack. The elimination process used in the former technique is not used here.

The polynomials thus generated using the improved technique, which are in Algebraic Normal Form (ANF), are converted to Conjunctive Normal Form (CNF) so that the resulting satisfiability (SAT) problem can be solved using a SAT solver and the inner state values are extracted. After this, Trivium is run backwards to reach the initial state, thereby revealing the secret key. When FFA attack takes 3.2 fault injections on average with a keystream sequence of 800 bits to break the cipher, the improved one needs only two fault injections with a 420 bit length keystream sequence.

Experimental results with two fault injections showed that more lower degree polynomials are generated when the injections occured in the middle register out of the three Trivium registers.

Attack Prevention in CASTREAM. SAT solver takes linear and quadratic equations represented in CNF as input. This is not possible in CASTREAM as its algebraic degree is nine. As stated earlier, even with a known inner state at any instant, we may not be able to find the secret key as CASTREAM is difficult to reverse.

4   Conclusion

The present work concentrated on analysing the strength of Cellular Automata based stream cipher CASTREAM against fault attacks. We studied and analysed fault attacks on Trivium, the LFSR based stream cipher and mounted them against CASTREAM. We have shown how CASTREAM prevents the fault attacks reported against Trivium by exploiting the inherent properties of Cellular Automata.

Other than fault attacks, there are a few other attacks reported in literature against Trivium. It is of great research interest whether the CA based stream cipher can prevent those attacks also.

References

1. Das, S., Roy Chowdhury, D.: *CASTREAM*: A New Stream Cipher Suitable for Both Hardware and Software. In: Sirakoulis, G.C., Bandini, S. (eds.) ACRI 2012. LNCS, vol. 7495, pp. 601–610. Springer, Heidelberg (2012)
2. Das, S., Roy Chowdhury, D.: Generating Cryptographically Suitable Non-linear Maximum Length Cellular Automata. In: Bandini, S., Manzoni, S., Umeo, H., Vizzari, G. (eds.) ACRI 2010. LNCS, vol. 6350, pp. 241–250. Springer, Heidelberg (2010)
3. Aumasson, J.-P., Dinur, I., Meier, W., Shamir, A.: Cube Testers and Key Recovery Attacks on Reduced-Round MD6 and Trivium. In: Dunkelman, O. (ed.) FSE 2009. LNCS, vol. 5665, pp. 1–22. Springer, Heidelberg (2009)
4. Dinur, I., Shamir, A.: Cube Attacks on Tweakable Black Box Polynomials. In: Joux, A. (ed.) EUROCRYPT 2009. LNCS, vol. 5479, pp. 278–299. Springer, Heidelberg (2009)
5. De Canniere, C., Preneel, B.: Trivium Specifcation,
   http://www.ecrypt.eu.org/stream/triviump3.html (accessed February 25, 2014)
6. Fouque, P.A., Vannet, T.: Improving Key Recovery to 784 and 799 rounds of Trivium using Optimized Cube Attacks. In: Moriai, S. (ed.) FSE 2013. LNCS, vol. 8424, pp. 502–517. Springer, Heidelberg (2014)
7. Hoch, J.J., Shamir, A.: Fault Analysis of Stream Ciphers. In: Joye, M., Quisquater, J.-J. (eds.) CHES 2004. LNCS, vol. 3156, pp. 240–253. Springer, Heidelberg (2004)
8. Hojsík, M., Rudolf, B.: Differential Fault Analysis of Trivium. In: Nyberg, K. (ed.) FSE 2008. LNCS, vol. 5086, pp. 158–172. Springer, Heidelberg (2008)
9. Hojsík, M., Rudolf, B.: Floating Fault Analysis of Trivium. In: Chowdhury, D.R., Rijmen, V., Das, A. (eds.) INDOCRYPT 2008. LNCS, vol. 5365, pp. 239–250. Springer, Heidelberg (2008)
10. Hu, Y., Gao, J., Liu, Q., Zhang, Y.: Fault analysis of Trivium. Design Code and Cryptograpy 62, 289–311 (2011), doi:10.1007/s10623-011-9518-9
11. Knellwolf, S., Meier, W., Naya-Plasencia, M.: Conditional Differential Cryptanalysis of NLFSR-Based Cryptosystems. In: Abe, M. (ed.) ASIACRYPT 2010. LNCS, vol. 6477, pp. 130–145. Springer, Heidelberg (2010)
12. Knellwolf, S., Meier, W., Naya-Plasencia, M.: Conditional Differential Cryptanalysis of Trivium and KATAN. In: Miri, A., Vaudenay, S. (eds.) SAC 2011. LNCS, vol. 7118, pp. 200–212. Springer, Heidelberg (2012)
13. Mohamed, M.S.E., Bulygin, S., Buchmann, J.: Improved Differential Fault Analysis of Trivium. In: COSADE 2011, pp. 147–158 (2011)
14. Das, S., RoyChoudhury, D.: CAR30: A new scalable stream cipher with rule 30. Cryptography and Communications 5(2), 137–162 (2013)
15. The Estream Project, http://www.ecrypt.eu.org/stream/ (accessed February 25, 2014)

Cellular Automata Approach to Maximum Lifetime Coverage Problem in Wireless Sensor Networks

Antonina Tretyakova[1], Franciszek Seredynski[1], and Pascal Bouvry[2]

[1] Cardinal Stefan Wyszynski University in Warsaw,
Dep. of Mathematics and Natural Sciences,
Woycickiego 1/3, 01-938 Warsaw, Poland
[2] University of Luxembourg, CSC Research Unit,
6, rue Richard Coudenhoven-Kalergi, L-1359 Luxembourg

Abstract. In this paper, we propose a novel distributed algorithm based on Graph Cellular Automata (GCA) concept to solve Maximum Lifetime Coverage Problem (MLCP) in Wireless Sensor Networks (WSNs). The proposed algorithm possesses all advantages of localized algorithm, i.e. using only some knowledge about the neighbors, WSN is able to self-organize in such a way to prolong its lifetime preserving at the same time required coverage ratio of a target field. The paper presents results of experimental study of the proposed algorithm and comparison of them with a centralized genetic algorithm.

Keywords: Coverage control, maximum lifetime coverage problem, cellular automata, wireless sensor networks.

1 Introduction

WSN is a set of huge number of small devices enabling to monitor surroundings, gather information about environment and perform many other tasks. For many missions, sensors are randomly distributed over the target field, where human access is limited or impossible, therefore batteries of sensors cannot be usually rechargeable or renewable. Exhaustion of battery charge implies the change in topology of WSN, quality of its work and reduction of its lifetime.

There are well-known optimization problems in the literature [1], [9], [4], [3] related to WSNs, among which MLC Problem, which will be the subject of this paper. The main issue related to this problem is minimizing energy consumption in order to prolong the lifetime of WSN.

In this paper, we propose a novel distributed algorithm based on Graph Cellular Automata (GCA) concept to solve MLCP in WSNs. In the proposed algorithm, a GCA is constructed on the base of sensor network, its parameters and target field parameters. Our approach was inspired by works concerning application of Cellular Automata to scheduling sensor's activity [2] and a concept of GCA [6], [7].

J. Wąs, G.C. Sirakoulis, and S. Bandini (Eds.): ACRI 2014, LNCS 8751, pp. 437–446, 2014.
© Springer International Publishing Switzerland 2014

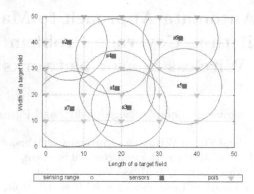

Fig. 1. An example of sensor network deployed over the target field divided on POIs

The remainder of the paper is organized as follows. The next section outlines MLCP. In Section 3, we introduce Graph - based Cellular Automata (GCA). Section 4 presents our proposed GCA-based approach to solve MLCP. Section 5 contains some results of experimental study of our approach. Last section contains conclusion.

2 Maximum Lifetime Coverage Problem Statement

Let us consider a homogeneous sensor network $S = \{s_1, \ldots, s_N\}$ consisting of N sensor nodes randomly distributed over a given *target field F*, a two-dimensional rectangular area of $W \times H \; m^2$. The target field F is uniformly divided on points of interest (POIs) with a step g (see Figure 1).

A sensor is defined as a point of coordinates (x_s, y_s). All sensor nodes have the same sensing range R_s, communication range R_c and battery capacity b. The coverage model of a sensor node is assumed a disk model [9].

It is assumed that each sensor can work in three modes: *active, sleeping* and *dead*. We denote a mode of i–th sensor s_i as $mode(s_i)$, and "1" corresponds to an active mode, while "0" corresponds to a sleeping mode of a sensor. In the active mode a sensor observes an area within its sensing range and can transmit or receive a signal.

Below we give some definitions concerning the problem statement.

Definition 1. A sensor $s(x_s, y_s)$ covers a POI $p(x, y)$ denoted as POI_{obs}, iff the Euclidian distance $d(s, p)$ between them is less than the sensing range R_s.

Definition 2. Coverage of a target field F at $j - th$ time period t_j denoted as $cov(j)$ is defined as a ratio of observed $POIs_{obs}$ by an active sensor network S to all $POIs$, i.e.

$$cov(j) = \frac{|POIs|_{obs}}{|POIs|} \tag{1}$$

A schedule of WSN work is associated with a sequence of numbers called a *coverage string*. These numbers represent a coverage of the target field during a corresponding time interval.

It is assumed that a sensor consumes energy to monitor an area within its sensing range R_s, and energy consumption depends on the time duration, during which a sensor is on. We consider a homogeneous sensor network, where all sensors have the same sensing range, the energy consumption per time interval is constant.

In this paper, we consider Maximum Lifetime Coverage Problem as a scheduling problem applied to WSN solving the point coverage problem regarding to prolongation the lifetime of WSN.

MLCP has an objective to maximize lifetime of WSN by minimizing a number of redundant sensors during each time interval in order to minimize energy consumption. Lifetime of WSN is defined as a sum of m consecutive time intervals' duration, during which the coverage requirement is met, i.e.

$$Lifetime(q) = max\{m|(\forall j)j < m \quad cov(j) \geq q\} \tag{2}$$

Coverage requirement is given by a coverage degree k and a coverage ratio q, which means that at least q-th part of all targets is covered by at least k sensors. Further, we assume k to be equal to 1.

Maximum Lifetime Coverage Problem can be stated as follows:

- *An instance:* Given a set of numbers $POIs = \{1, 2, ..., P\}$, each element represents an ordinal number of a POI (a target), given a family of N subsets $S = \{S_1, S_2, ..., S_N\}$, where each element $S_i \subseteq POIs$, $i = 1, 2, ..., N$, is related to covered POIs by i-th sensor, and given integer number b.
- *Objective:* Find a maximal number m of subsets $\{S'_1, S'_2, ..., S'_m\}$, where $S'_j \subseteq S$, such that the number of covered elements $|\cup_{S_i \in S'_j} S_i|$ meets the coverage ratio (Eq. 3) and each element S_i of the family S is included in b subsets $\{S'_{j_1}, S'_{j_2}, ..., S'_{j_b}\}$ (Eq. 4), i.e.

$$(\forall j)_{j=1,...,m} \frac{|\cup_{S_i \subseteq S'_j} S_i|}{|POIs|} \geq q \tag{3}$$

$$(\forall i)_{i=1,...,N}(\exists j_1, ..., j_b)_{(\forall k)_{k=1,...,b}|1 \leq j_k \leq m}|S_i \in S'_{j_1}, ..., S_i \in S'_{j_m} \tag{4}$$

An objective of searching a maximal number m of subsets satisfying the equation (3) is equivalent to lifetime maximization and corresponds to scheduling activities of sensor nodes. The equation (4) corresponds to the battery capacity restriction.

3   GCA – Based Approach to MLC Problem

3.1   Graph – Based Cellular Automata Concept

Elementary Cellular Automata is a triple, defined by a set of cells, a specification of cell's neighborhood and a state transition function ψ. Each cell i at time t has a state q_i^t. At the next time $t + 1$ the cell's state depends only on the states of neighboring cells and is defined by a transion rule ψ, i.e. $q_i^{t+1} = \psi(q_{i_1}^t, ..., q_{i_k}^t)$, where $i_1, ..., i_k$ are numbers of i-th cell's neighbors.

Graph - based Cellular Automata (GCA) [6], [7], unlike standard Cellular Automata (CA), is presented by a graph, where cells correspond to nodes of a given graph. A neighborhood of radius 1, labeled as $1 - neighborhood$, of a cell is defined as nodes connecting to this cell by one edge. A transition rule updates states of graph's nodes.

3.2   GCA and MLC Problem

Let us consider a graph $< S, E >$, where S is a set of sensors, while E is a set of edges. Two nodes are connected, iff they have at least one common POI within their sensing range.

A state of a sensor cell is defined by one of three numbers: 0, 1 and 2. State "0" is related to the sleeping mode of the sensor, state "1" corresponds to the active state of the sensor and state "2" concerns to a dead sensor, i.e.

$$q_i^t = \begin{cases} 0, & if\, i-th\, sensor\, is\, in\, sleeping\, state\, at\, time\, t, \\ 1, & if\, i-th\, sensor\, is\, in\, active\, state\, at\, time\, t, \\ 2, & otherwise. \end{cases} \quad (5)$$

Two cells are neighbors, if the related to them nodes in the graph are connected by one edge. Let us denote $neigh_s(i)$ a neighborhood of i-th element of coordinates (x_i, y_i) consisting of sensor neighbors, i.e., $neigh_s(i) = \{s_j \in S \mid d(s_i, s_j) \le R_c \}$.

During evolving GCA cell's states are changed according to an internal transition function, determined for each cell. In this work, we consider a set of transition functions called $R - rules$ which are defined as follows. If a i-th sensor cell has R-rule as a transition function, i.e., $\psi(i, t) = R$, the state of the sensor cell in the next time slot will be active, if no more than R neighboring sensors are active and the battery is charged, and becomes sleeping otherwise, i.e.,

$$q_i^{t+1} = \begin{cases} 1, if\, (\exists l)(\forall m)_{m \le l \le R} q_{j_m}^t = 1\, \&\, s_{j_m} \in neigh_s(i)\, \& b_i(t+1) > 0 \\ 0, otherwise. \end{cases} \quad (6)$$

4   Cellular Automata-Based Algorithm to Solve Maximum Lifetime Coverage Problem

In this Section, we present distributed algorithm, based on GCA, which is executed on all sensor nodes in WSN.

In *active* state (see, Section II) a sensor observes a circle area within its sensing range R_s, while in *sleeping* state sensor's sensing unit is off. Independently of the *active* or *sleeping* state a sensor can broadcast and receive data during the certain time intervals, called *exchange STATE messages*. A sensor passes to *dead* state, when its battery is exhausted. A round before this moment the sensor broadcasts this information in the $STATE$ message and its neighbors remove it from their neighbors' list.

GCA Algorithm to solve MLCP consists of two phases. The first phase is configuration of network process. During the configuration process, sensors gather information about their neighbors via broadcasting short $HELLO$ messages and creating a list of neighbors. $HELLO$ message contains information about localization of the sender. A list of neighbors contains identifiers of the neighbors and a list of common POIs with the given sensor.

The second executable phase (see, Algorithm 1) is divided into rounds. During each round, a charged sensor can be in one of three states: *active, sleeping* or *dead*. During the lifetime of whole sensor network, each sensor can be in *active* state no more than b times, where a parameter b corresponds to sensor's battery capacity. After one round of activity a battery charge is decreased by one.

Algorithm 1. GCA Algorithm for MLC Problem in WSN

---

   for each evolution step **do**
      information available: neighbors' states, sensor's transition function
      send STATE message to neighbors
      receive STATE messages from neighbors
      compute state
      update state
      update battery
   end for

At the beginning, all sensor nodes dependently on an initial GCA state can be in active state or in sleeping state. In the experimental part, we examine five initial configurations, denoted by a number $N_{init} = p$ with $p \in \{0, 0.25, 0.5, 0.75, 1\}$. These configurations are the following: all sensors are in sleeping state ($N_{init} = 0$), all nodes are in active state ($N_{init} = 1$) and each sensor is active with probability p, where $p \in \{0.25, 0.5, 0.75\}$.

Each round has a sensing phase, when according to GCA algorithm sensors are scheduled to be activated or deactivated. Before the end, a round has an exchange $STATE$ messages phase, when sensors broadcast $STATE$ messages for the next round. In each time round, active nodes perform sensing and sleeping nodes will turn off their sensing units to save energy. $STATE$ message contains state (active, sleep or dead) information of the sensor.

5 Experimental Results

5.1 Experimental Setup

In this section, we present some results of experimental study of the proposed algorithm. The experimental study was conducted in two steps. Firstly, several number of experiments was made in order to estimate the best values for parameters of the algorithm. The purpose of the next step was to compare the GCA algorithm with the other algorithms recently proposed in the literature.

All the results in this section are based on averaging of five runs for different initial GCA's states for three different random sensors deployment, called Instance1, Instance2 and Instance3. Sensors are deployed over the target field F of dimensions $(L \times L)m^2$, where in all experiments we assume $L = 100$. POIs are uniformly distributed over the target field F in every g m, where $g = 5$. WSN consists of 100 sensors, sensing range R_s is equal to 20 m, communication range R_c is equal to 50 m in order conserve connectivity requirement.

5.2   Experiment 1

The first experiment is devoted to study behavior of a sensor network with fixed distribution of different R-rules over sensor cells and the same initial state (N_{init} = 0) of GCA. We consider a homogeneous GCA with several R-rules.

Coverage string obtained by GCA for constant R-Rules with $R \in \{1, 2, 3, 4, 5, 7, 9, 11, 13, 15\}$, the initial state $N_{init}=0$ and battery capacity $b=10$ for the fixed rule distribution is presented in Figure 2. As one can see, there exist a dependence of a coverage level on a R-rule. WSN can live longer with lower R-rules for lower coverage ratio q requirement. For example, Lifetime(0.65) is equal to 50 for 2-rule, Lifetime(0.7) is equal to 43 for 3-rule, while for the same R-rules ($R < 5$), Lifetime(0.9) is equal to 0. Only for R greater than 5, GCA provides a good quality lifetime for high coverage ratio q, i.e. $q \geq 0.9$.

The next figure shows a dependence of Lifetime(q) on q obtained for Instance 1 with fixed R-Rules distribution with $R \in \{1, 2, 3, 4, 5, 7, 9, 11, 13, 15\}$, the initial state $N_{init}=0$ and battery capacity $b=10$. As one can see from Figure 3, for each coverage ratio q requirement, a R-rule can be outlined, such that GCA provides the best Lifetime(q). For example, for coverage ratio q equal to 0.95, 0.9, 0.85 and 0.8, the best rules are 11-rule, 9-rule, 5-rule and 4-rule, respectively.

In Figure 4, we see ten curves for ten different values of coverage ratio q which represent dependence of Lifetime(q) on a number R. As we can observe, all curves have the same structure, at the beginning with growing R, Lifetime(q) also increases achieving its maximum, afterwards it decreases. At the maximum point, we obtain the best Lifetime(q) value for the given coverage ratio q with the certain R-rule. Therefore, this figure shows the similar results as the previous one, but with more precisely defined R-rule.

The average and maximal values of Lifetime(0.9) for the random initial states with $N_{init} \in \{0.25, 0.5, 0.75\}$ and one value for the deterministic initial states with $N_{init} \in \{0, 1\}$ for the three Instances, three battery capacities setup: $b \in \{10, 20, 30\}$ and four R-rules ($R \in \{5, 9, 13, 17\}$) are presented in Table 1. As one can observe the values in the columns corresponding to $N_{init}=0$ and $N_{init}=1$ are the same. If, at the beginning all the sensors are switched off, i.e. initial state of GCA is described by $N_{init}=0$, each sensor has all neighbors in the sleeping state, therefore, according to the R-Rule with a positive R, at the next time slot

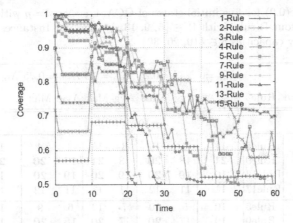

Fig. 2. Coverage string obtained by GCA for Instance 1 with fixed R-rules distribution with $R \in \{1, 2, 3, 4, 5, 7, 9, 11, 13, 15\}$, the initial state $N_{init}=0$ and battery capacity $b=10$

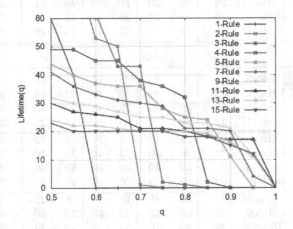

Fig. 3. Dependence of Lifetime(q) on q obtained for Instance 1 with fixed R-Rules distribution with $R \in \{1, 2, 3, 4, 5, 7, 9, 11, 13, 15\}$, the initial state $N_{init}=0$ and battery capacity $b=10$

it changes its state to the active one. This statement is fullfilled for all sensors, hence, GCA transforms to the state corresponding to $N_{init}=1$.

As one can see from the table, for all three instances of WSN independently of a battery capacity the best Lifetime(0.9) is achieved by GCA with 9-rule. The initial state of GCA has a slight impact on the Lifetime(0.9) values. For random initial states Lifetime(0.9) varies, while for zero and one initial states for the best 9-rule, GCA provides the highest results or the results higher than the average over the ones provided by GCA with the same 9-rule and all initial states.

The GCA initial state has small impact on the quality of GCA. Therefore, in the next experiment, we compare lifetime of WSN obtained by GCA algorithm

Table 1. Lifetime(0.9) for five initial states of GCA, i. e. $N_{init} = p$ with $p \in \{0, 0.25, 0.5, 0.75, 1\}$, for four R-rules with R $\in \{5, 9, 13, 17\}$ and for Instances 1, 2 and 3 of WSN with battery capacities $b \in \{10, 20, 30\}$

Instance	Rule	$N_{init}=0$	$N_{init}=0.25$		$N_{init}=0.5$		$N_{init}=0.75$		$N_{init}=1$
			Avg	Max	Avg	Max	Avg	Max	
				b=10					
1	Rule5	11	6	10	3	15	2	4	11
	Rule9	**21**	18	**20**	18	**21**	17	**20**	**21**
	Rule13	16	**19**	20	19	20	19	20	16
	Rule17	11	11	12	11	13	11	12	11
2	Rule5	10	5	10	7	12	6	9	10
	Rule9	19	17	**20**	17	**20**	18	**20**	19
	Rule13	12	**18**	19	**18**	20	**18**	**20**	12
	Rule17	10	10	12	10	11	10	11	10
3	Rule5	2	10	12	6	12	8	12	2
	Rule9	20	**20**	**20**	19	**20**	20	21	20
	Rule13	19	19	20	18	19	18	19	19
	Rule17	18	12	18	13	19	14	19	18
				b=20					
1	Rule5	21	4	13	5	17	5	17	21
	Rule9	**43**	36	40	40	40	39	40	**43**
	Rule13	36	39	39	39	40	39	40	36
	Rule17	21	21	22	20	21	21	23	21
2	Rule5	20	21	40	19	39	15	39	20
	Rule9	39	36	**40**	33	**40**	35	**40**	39
	Rule13	22	**39**	40	**38**	39	**38**	39	22
	Rule17	20	20	20	20	20	20	21	20
3	Rule5	2	10	21	18	24	18	22	2
	Rule9	**40**	**39**	40	40	40	**39**	**40**	40
	Rule13	39	**39**	40	38	39	**39**	39	39
	Rule17	38	28	40	24	38	31	39	38
				b=30					
1	Rule5	31	12	30	15	25	20	25	31
	Rule9	**63**	60	60	60	60	59	60	**63**
	Rule13	56	59	60	53	60	59	59	56
	Rule17	31	31	32	31	31	30	31	31
2	Rule5	30	29	59	23	59	27	28	30
	Rule9	59	**54**	**60**	**58**	**60**	**54**	**60**	59
	Rule13	32	**54**	**60**	53	**60**	52	59	32
	Rule17	30	30	31	30	31	30	30	30
3	Rule5	2	29	56	18	30	25	32	2
	Rule9	60	**60**	**61**	**60**	60	**59**	60	60
	Rule13	59	59	60	59	60	59	60	59
	Rule17	58	48	60	53	59	47	59	58

Table 2. Average and maximum values of Lifetime(0.9) of WSN consisting of 100 sensors obtained by GCA algorithm and GA with battery capacity $b \in \{10, 20$ and $30\}$

b	Lifetime(0.9)	Instance1	Instance 2	Instance 3
	GCA: $N_{init}=0$, 9-rule	21	19	20
10	GA-10	22 (23)	18 (20)	23 (24)
	GA-50	23 (25)	19 (21)	24 (25)
	GCA: $N_{init}=0$, 9-rule	43	39	40
20	GA-10	47 (50)	46 (48)	50 (53)
	GA-50	49 (51)	49 (50)	53 (55)
	GCA: $N_{init}=0$, 9-rule	63	59	60
30	GA-10	69 (76)	70 (73)	79 (85)
	GA-50	75 (76)	74 (75)	79 (80)

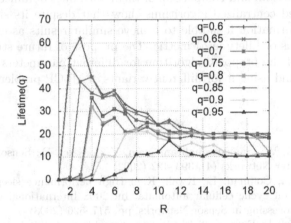

Fig. 4. Dependence of Lifetime(q) on a number R in R-Rule for different $q \in \{0.6, 0.65, 0.7, 0.75, 0.8, 0.85, 0.9, 0.95\}$ obtained for Instance 1 with fixed rule distribution, the initial state $N_{init}=0$ and battery capacity $b=10$

with 9-rule, assuming zero initial state of GCA ($N_{init} = 0$), and results provided by centralized GA.

5.3   Experiment 2

In the second experiment, we compare our proposed distributed algorithm with the centralized genetic algorithm (GA) recently presented in [8]. Experiments were conducted with use of three randomly generated instances of a sensor distribution. Coverage ratio is required to be 90%.

Table 2 contains the average and maximal (in brackets) values of Lifetime(0.9) obtained by GCA with zero initial state, 9-rule as state transition function and by standard GA with population size 10 (GA-10) and 50 (GA-50) [8]. As one can see from Table 2 Lifetime(0.9) values obtained by GA varies due to its stochasticity. Comparing average values of GA with those provided by GCA, it can be stated that GA-10 outperforms slightly GCA for $b=10$ and for some instances provides the similar results as it is seen for Instance 2. For $b=20$ and $b=30$, GA-10, in average, outperformes GCA by 20% and 17%, respectevely.

6   Conclusion

In this paper, we have proposed a novel localized algorithm based on GCA concept to solve MLCP in WSN. The proposed algorithm possesses all advantages of localized algorithm, i.e. it uses only some knowledge about the neighboring sensors of WSN and it is able to self-reorganize in such a way to preserve a required coverage ratio and prolong lifetime of the WSN. Results of experimental study of the algorithm and comparison of them with ones obtained by applying recently proposed centralized algorithms show that despite its simplicity and limited local information it is able to achieve similar results as centralized algorithms in terms of Lifetime(q) metric. The purpose of future studies is more detailed study of the proposed algorithm for different parameters of GCA and WSN densities and using it for different variants of MLCP problem.

References

1. Akyildiz, I., Su, W., Sankarasumbramaniam, Y., Cayirci, E.: Sensor networks: A survey. Computer Networks (4), 393–422 (2002)
2. Baryshnikov, Y., Coffman, E., Kwak, K.J.: High performance sleep-wake sensor systems based on cyclic cellular automata. In: 2008 International Conference on Information Processing in Sensor Networks, pp. 517–526 (2008)
3. Cardei, M., Wu, J.: Energy-efficient coverage problems in wireless ad-hoc sensor networks. Comput. Commun. 29(4), 413–420 (2006), http://dx.doi.org/10.1016/j.comcom.2004.12.025
4. Jones, C.E., Sivalingam, K.M., Agrawal, P., Chen, J.C.: A survey of energy efficient network protocol. Wireless Networks (7), 343–358 (2001)
5. Katsumata, Y., Ishida, Y.: On a membrane formation in a spatio-temporally generalized prisoner's dilemma. In: Umeo, H., Morishita, S., Nishinari, K., Komatsuzaki, T., Bandini, S. (eds.) ACRI 2008. LNCS, vol. 5191, pp. 60–66. Springer, Heidelberg (2008)
6. O'Sullivan, D.: Graph-cellular automata: a generalised discrete urban and regional model. Environment and Planning B: Planning and Design 28(5), 687–705 (2001)
7. Rinaldi, P.R., Dalponte, D.D., Venero, M.J., Clausse, A.: Graph-based cellular automata for simulation of surface flows in large plains. Asian Journal of Applied Sciences 5(4), 224–231 (2012)
8. Tretyakova, A., Seredynski, F.: Application of evolutionary algorithms to maximum lifetime coverage problem in wireless sensor networks. In: 2013 IEEE 27th International Symposium on Parallel and Distributed Processing Workshops and PhD Forum, pp. 445–453 (2013)
9. Wang, B.: Coverage control in sensor network. Springer (2010)

Application of NIST Technical Note 1822 to CA Crowd Dynamics Models Verification and Validation

Jakub Porzycki, Robert Lubaś, Marcin Mycek, and Jarosław Wąs

AGH University of Science and Technology,
Department of Applied Computer Science,
al. Mickiewicza 30, 30-059 Kraków, Poland
{porzycki,rlubas,mycek,jarek}@agh.edu.pl
http://kis.agh.edu.pl/en/start

Abstract. This paper addresses the issue of application of methodology included in NIST technical note 1822: *The Process of Verification and Validation of Building Fire Evacuation Models* [1] in terms of CA crowd dynamics models. The note is a recently released document (November 2013), that proposes a set of verification and validation (V&V) tests as well as methods for an uncertainty analysis. The main aim of this paper is to investigate these tests and methods applied to CA models by showing results of sample tests and discussing CA specific issues.

Keywords: Validation and verification, crowd dynamics, CA.

1 Introduction

One can easily notice a significant lack of well defined, comprehensive and commonly accepted V&V procedures for pedestrian dynamics models. Currently, in most cases, models are tested by their authors using arbitrary chosen criteria.

It is a general agreement that models should be able to reproduce different phenomena like jamming, lanes formation, density waves, patterns at intersections, bottleneck oscillations [2]. On the other hand, fundamental diagrams (speed/density or flow/density relationships) are important elements of quantitative verification. Models should also satisfy basic verification requirements: pedestrians ability to maintain assigned walking speed, not crossing boundaries etc.

Hitherto, the most popular and comprehensive guidance for models V&V was given by two documents released by International Maritime Organization - MSC/Circ.1033 [3] and MSC/Circ.1238 [4]. Regardless of the fact that these documents are designed for ships' evacuation, they are broadly used to V&V of general crowd dynamics models. Improvement suggestions and validation data set for MSC/Circ.1238 are also provided by SAFEGUARD project [5]. Whilst, RiMEA project [6] attempts to adjust this guidelines for building evacuation, however it is mostly focused on verification tests.

J. Wąs, G.C. Sirakoulis, and S. Bandini (Eds.): ACRI 2014, LNCS 8751, pp. 447–452, 2014.
© Springer International Publishing Switzerland 2014

In terms of V&V methodology it is worth to mention efforts of C. Rogsch et al. [7][8]. They executed a number of comparison tests between different models and proposed standard test cases with well defined expected results.

However, none of above documents can be understood as comprehensive methodology guidance. In order to address this issue National Institute of Standards and Technology (NIST) released a Technical Note 1822: *The Process of Verification and Validation of Building Fire Evacuation Models* [1]. The note summarizes current knowledge of building evacuation models V&V, proposes a set of 17 verification tests, includes recommendations for validation data-sets and suggests a procedure of model uncertainty analysis.

The note strongly emphasizes that: *this document is aimed at opening discussion on the topic, rather than being definitive guidance.* Motivation of this paper is to contribute to V&V discussion in terms of CA crowd dynamics modeling. Authors have decided to verify and discuss how the test included in the note works for CA models, especially the Social Distances Model(SDM) [9].

2 Verification Tests

Verification tests cover: pedestrian pre-evacuation times, movement and navigation, exit choice, route availability and flow constraints.

1.1 Pre-evacuation time distribution test verifies model ability to assign to population pre-evacuation times from a given distribution.

2.1 Speed in corridor and **2.2 Speed on stairs** examine pedestrian ability to maintain designed speed $(1\frac{m}{s})$ in 40 m corridor and 100 m stairs. Models with fine grid should be tested for $0\,^{\circ}$ and $45\,^{\circ}$ orientation of corridor with regard to grid. As most crowd dynamics models use different method to deal with possible systematic errors caused by grid size and orientation, we propose that the test should be conducted for more detailed spectrum of angles.

2.3 Movement around a corners - in this test pedestrians should navigate around a corner without penetrating boundaries. Movement rules in CA models are based on allowed/forbidden states, thus boundary penetration is impossible due to this core mechanism. Authors believe that this test could be extended to verify space usage of the pedestrians, as it for example can vary vastly for preference of fastest rather than shortest path (see Fig.: 2).

2.4 Assigned occupant demographics verifies model ability to assign demographic parameters. This test is very similar to test **1.1**.

2.5 Reduced visibility vs. walking speed and **2.6 Occupant incapacitation** are designed to verify influence of smoke on pedestrian movement. It should be stressed that such a functionality is available in CA-based models through the use of specific transition functions, e.g. in [11] . Analogically **2.7 Elevator usage** can be implemented in terms of CA.

2.8 Horizontal counter-flows (rooms) verifies if a model is able to simulate counter-flow and its influence on a evacuation time. In the note the only requirement is that passage time should decrease when number of people in counter-flow increase. We propose to extend expected results to include lane formation phenomena and more detailed passage time changes expectations (e.g. based on a research of T. Kretz et al. [10]).

2.9 Group Behaviors checks if model implements group behavior, namely if a small group is able to wait for one significantly slower member. The whole group has to leave the room, with difference between first and last smaller than a given threshold.

Verification of model's ability to simulate influence of disabled people is covered by **2.10 People with movement disabilities** test. In this test pedestrian should move from one room to another, with and without occurrence of one disabled person directly in front of the exit. Due to a discrete nature of CA models representation of disabled persons using wheelchairs can be problematic, as such person either would occupy a number of cells or be represented by a too small cell.

3.1 Exit choice/usage is suggested to verify deterministic assignment of exits. Pedestrians should leave simulation area with the allocated exit. It should be noted that many simulation models calculate exit assignment (according to distance, density, travel speed etc.), rather than use deterministic assignment - an example assignment generated by SDM is shown in Fig.: 3.

3.2 Social influence verifies if pedestrian is more likely to follow others i.e. choose the same exit. Very often exit choice is separated from movement algorithm, therefore leaving the same exit may by completely uncorrelated with social influence. In case of CA models results of this test may be dependent on details of movement algorithm e.g. dynamic floor field presented in Nishinari et al. [11] may enforce pedestrians to follow others, while dynamic floor field in SDM model [9] will encourage pedestrian to avoid following other in the closest neighborhood (due to finer representation of the space).

3.3 Affiliation tests if a model implements pedestrian affiliation to the chosen exit. Authors believe that such feature coming from cognitive approach is valuable, however whether it should be not in the basic set of tests is debatable.

4.1 Dynamic availability of exits checks if pedestrian is able to change exit choice when one exit becomes unavailable (closed). Pedestrian is expected to not try to leave by the closed doors.

5.1. Congestion verifies whether model is able to reproduce expected congestion, using staircase example. The congestion is expected at the exit from the room and at the base of the stairs. Exemplary results of this experiment are shown at Fig.: 4.

In **5.2. Maximum flow rates** pedestrians should leave a room with one 1 m wide exit to verify if simulated flow do not exceed a given threshold (recommended: 1.33 person per meter per second). This raises a following question: why only maximum flow is tested? We suggest verifying rather more complex parameters like fundamental diagrams as they describe in a more detailed way pedestrian motion.

3   Uncertainty in Evacuation Modeling

One of the aspects very often not dealt with in an evacuation modeling is detailed analysis of uncertainty. The authors of the note propose a very thorough methodology to deal with it. The proposed procedure concentrates on convergence of five types of measures - first two focusing on the evacuation process as a whole and the last three coming from functional analysis dealing with the details of the process i.e. a curve composed from evacuation times of all pedestrians:

1. TET - Total Evacuation Time - evacuation time of the last pedestrian
2. SD - Standard Deviation of the TET
3. ERD - Euclidean Relative Difference - normalized Euclidean distance between evacuation curves, overall agreement between two vectors
4. EPC - Euclidean Projection Coefficient - a factor describing the best possible fit of the two curves
5. SC - Secant Cosine - compares shape of two curves based on their derivatives

Exact definitions of the convergence measures can be found in the note [1]. For each measure a threshold criteria should be chosen i.e. a maximal value of measure and a number of consecutive runs that should meet the criteria. The end of such series is a point where a measure converges.

For the detailed analysis in this paper a verification test 5.2 was chosen. The exact same threshold values as proposed by the note were chosen as well as smoothing constant for SC measure. The detailed results for each measure can be found in Fig. 1.

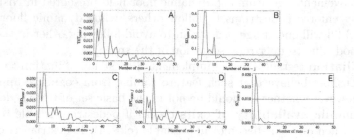

Fig. 1. Total Evacuation Time (A), Standard Deviation (B), Euclidean Relative Difference (C), Euclidean Projection Coefficient (D) and Secant Cosine (E) convergence measures for verification test 5.2. For thresholds proposed by the note (red line) 31 (A), 20 (B), 22 (C), 31 (D) and 13 (E) runs were needed for respective measures to converge.

The procedure of uncertainty analysis can be used both for uncertainty analysis in given evacuation scenario and for identification of minumum number of simulation runs to acheive stable results.

4   Summary

It should be stressed that due to application of non-homogeneous and asynchronous CA to crowd dynamics modeling, it is possible to meet the requirements of basic V&V tests from the note. However, some requirements like taking into account persons using wheelchairs is not possible in classical CA representation and it requires different approach (for instance applying SDM with different geometries of pedestrians). We believe that including the concept of an agent-based modeling facilitates the creation of complex simulations taking into account: demographic data, group behavior, individual response to the threat, etc.

From our point of view the NIST Technical Note 1822 is a valuable initiative in terms of V&V, however it requires several extensions. We propose to take into account: detailed and extended specification of expected results and more tests to verify fundamental diagram and different phenomena. Due to lack of extensive validation datasets, data collection methods in pedestrian dynamics should also be specified. Tests can be divided into generic test and specialized test for different simulation types (eg.: continues/ discrete). We believe that V&V process should be executed by third party, but to achieve this, functionalities required to execute tests have to be well defined.

References

1. Ronchi, E., Kuligowski, E., Reneke, P., Peacock, R., Nilsson, D.: The Process of Verification and Validation of Building Fire Evacuation Models, NIST Technical Note 1822 (2013)
2. Schadschneider, A., Klingsch, W., Kluepfel, H., Kretz, H., Rogsch, C., Seyfried, A.: Evacuation Dynamics: Empirical Results, Modeling and Applications. In: Encyclopedia of Complexity and Systems Science, pp. 3142–3176 (2009)
3. International Maritime Organization, Interim guidelines for evacuation analysis for new and existing passenger ships, MSC.1/Circ.1033 (2002)
4. International Maritime Organization, Guidelines for evacuation analysis for new and existing passenger ships, MSC.1/Circ.1238 (2007)
5. Galea, E.R., Deere, S., Brown, R., Nicholls, I., Hifi, Y., Bresnard, N.: The SAFE-GUARD validation data-set and recommendations to IMO to update MSC Circ 1238, pp. 41–60. The Royal Institution of Naval Architects, London (2012)
6. RiMEA, Richtlinie für Mikroskopische Entfluchtungsanalysen, Ver: 2.2.1 (2009)
7. Rogsch, C., Klingsch, W., Seyfried, A., Weigel, H.: Prediction Accuracy of Evacuation Times for High-Rise Buildings and Simple Geometries by Using Different Software-Tools. In: TGF 2007, pp. 395–400 (2009)
8. Rogsch, C., Klingsch, W., Weigel, H.: Hand-Calculation Methods for Evacuation Calculation - Last Chance for an Old-Fashioned Approach or a Real Alternative to Microscopic Simulation Tools. In: PED 2008, pp. 523-528 (2010)
9. Wąs, J., Lubaś, R.: Adapting Social Distances Model for Mass Evacuation Simulation. Journal of Cellular Automata 8(5/6), 395–405 (2013)
10. Kretz, T., Grünebohm, A., Kaufman, M., Mazur, F., Schreckenberg, M.: Experimental study of pedestrian counterflow in a corridor. JSM: Theory and Experiment (2006)
11. Nishinari, K., Kirchner, A., Namazi, A., Schadschneider, A.: Extended floor field CA model for evacuation dynamics. IEICE Transactions 87-D, 726–732 (2008)

Appendix

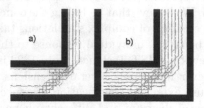

Fig. 2. The **2.3. Movement around a corner** test. The trajectories of twenty occupants showing no penetration of the boundaries. Space usage vary according to pedestrian preference of shortest vs. fastest paths.

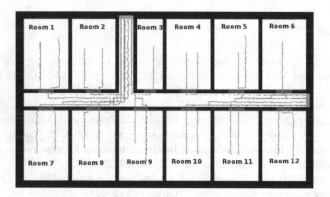

Fig. 3. The **3.1. Exit Route Allocation** test. Exit choice determined in SDM, one can notice that calculated (shortest distance) exit choice from rooms 4 and 10 differs from the note expected results.

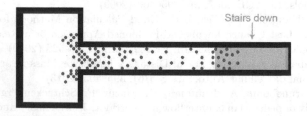

Fig. 4. The **5.1. Congestion** test. A staircase test architecture. Pedestrians are initially located in a room, during simulation they pass through corridor to a staircase. One should expect congestion at the exit from the room and at the base of the stairs.

Effect of Group Behavior on Crowd Dynamics

Wei Xiaoge[1], Song Weiguo[1], Xu Xuan[2], Fang Zhiming[3], and Li Xiaolian[1]

[1] State Key Laboratory of Fire Science, University of Science and Technology of China,
Hefei 230026, P.R. China
[2] China Academy of Safety Science and Technology, Beijing 100029, P.R. China
[3] Shanghai Research Institute of Building Science, Shanghai 200032, P.R. China
wgsong@ustc.edu.cn

Abstract. In recent years, the research on group movement has been drew pedestrian and evacuation dynamicists' attention. In this paper, we explored to build a group model in a simple way. The group model considered two drift parameters, D and d. Thereinto, D expresses the destination's attraction and d stands for group leader's attraction and d is simplified to direct towards the group leader. Meantime, a method of generating groups is proposed. The simulation results show that with the increase of group size, the negative effect of group on crowd becomes greater. And group walking has more obvious effect on group owning large velocity. Besides the increase of group attraction intensity makes the negative effect distinct. In addition, it is found that with the increase of group disperse degree, the negative impact of group walking becomes obvious. What's more, the effect of group disperse degree will not increase without limitation. The findings in this paper help researchers understand the impact of the presence of groups on crowd.

Keywords: group model, movement drift, group leader, group attraction intensity, group disperse degree.

Introduction

In our daily life, the phenomenon of pedestrian walking in group is quite common in the public places, such as the subway station, fairground, sidewalk, market, school, railway station and so on. The previous research also shows that up to 70% of people in a crowd are actually moving in groups, such as friends, couples, or families walking together [1]. The situation of pedestrians walking in group is different from the case that several isolated pedestrians walk together occasionally. The social relationship among the group members makes group cohesion and guarantees group members do not separate from the group. Thus the group members will adopt some actions to maintain the group stability, such as following a companion, rescue behavior during a disaster, waiting other relatives when catching a train and so on. How this phenomenon affects pedestrian movement is a challenge problem. Therefore group research is necessary and meaningful.

Actually the sociologists and psychologists have studied group research since 1950. However they emphasized the influence of social factors on group movement,

J. Wąs, G.C. Sirakoulis, and S. Bandini (Eds.): ACRI 2014, LNCS 8751, pp. 453–461, 2014.
© Springer International Publishing Switzerland 2014

such as dominance, attraction, age, gender [2], similarity [3], power, status [4], cross-cultural [5], personality determinants [6], culture background ,the city size [7] and so on. However, for pedestrian and evacuation dynamicists, they are more inclined to focus on group movement itself and its influence on the crowd movement.

Recently many pedestrian dynamic researchers have focused on group movement. Moussaïd et al. [1] analyze the motion of approximately 1500 pedestrian groups under natural condition, and obtained typical group walking patterns in different crowd density. On the basis of the statistic data, they improved the social force model by considering pedestrian group effect, which is able to simulate local movement behavior of one group.   Qiu et al. [8] focused on modeling group structure by considering both intra-group structure and inter-group relationships. Furthermore Qiu [9] continued to develop a framework for group modeling in agent-based pedestrian crowd simulations. Fridman [10] et al. carried out the observed experiments in different countries and obtained the characteristics of group walking in different culture background, like gender group formations, group speed, avoidance side and personal spaces. Wei [11] carried out an observed experiment and found that the velocity and step frequency of group member are smaller than that of individuals under the same scenario. Meantime, movement consistency of the group members is also verified. In order to properly set initial configurations for pedestrian simulations starting from plausible scenarios which consider the presence of groups in the crowd, Stefania et al. [12] put forward a model based on a stochastic cellular automata to generate granulometric distribution of pedestrian groups in structured spaces. Köster et al. [13] developed a mathematical model for group formation within crowds based on a few simple characteristics. And they get a good quantitative match with a small experiment after calibrating the supposed desire to communicate while walking. Vizzari et al. [14] extracted the characteristics of pedestrians walking in group and proposed the overall utility function considering these characteristics, like the cohesion of groups, to extend the floor field model. Because the way pedestrians walk in group is more complex that the pattern of several isolated pedestrians walking together, the previous group model contains plenty of parameters, and the values of these parameters play an important role in the simulation results.

In this manuscript, we wanted to build a CA group evacuation model in a simple way, which brings only very few parameters, meantime is able to reflect movement characteristics of group. In the following, a brief description of the CA group evacuation model is presented first, followed by the results and discussions. Finally, summary of this manuscript is given.

Group Model Design

Some current group models are indeed able to simulate some characteristics of group walking, such as keeping group formation, group split, group remerge and so on. However, so many parameters in these models are hard to decide. Therefore, we want to build a group model in a simple way, which meantime is able to capture the characteristics of group walking.

Group Model Description

It is well accepted that the group members will try to reach the desired destination meantime they will also try to preserve a limited distance from the other group members [15]. This common cognition shows that when pedestrians walk in group, group members have not only the trend of walking towards the destination but also the tendency to move towards the group so as not to separate from the group. That is to say, there are two drifts for group members in movement process.

Inspired by this idea and refer to [16], two drift parameters, D and d, are defined. The both two reflect direction attraction. Here we assume that each group owns a group leader. Thereinto, D expresses the destination's attraction and d stands for group leader's attraction. Here d is simplified to direct towards the group leader, described in Fig.1(a). For group leaders, their movement is only affected by the destination. In the model, each pedestrian could select one of the eight possible directions with different transition probabilities and move to one of the neighboring cells. We define P_{ij} as the transition probability that a pedestrian moves to the direction (i, j) and its value is given by

$$P_{ij} = \begin{cases} N \times V_{ij} \times \exp(VD_{ij} \times D_{ij}) & leader \\ N \times V_{ij} \times \exp(VD_{ij} \times D_{ij} + Vd_{ij} \times d_{ij}) & else \end{cases} \tag{1}$$

Here V_{ij} denotes the possibility whether the pedestrian can move to the direction (i, j), i.e., $V_{ij}=1$ if the direction is available and $V_{ij}=0$ if it is unavailable. N is a normalization factor to ensure $\sum_{ij} P_{ij} = 1$. The drift D_{ij} here represents the intensity that a pedestrian rushes to the destination. The D_{ij}'s value is calculated by formula (2). θ_{ij} is the intersection angle between D and cell (i,j). Because there are eight possible moving directions of pedestrians, the preferential movement direction may deviate from any of the eight directions. Therefore, the preferential movement direction, i.e. D, is projected into three closest directions. If the cell (i, j) is D's preferential direction, then VD_{ij} is equal to 1, otherwise VD_{ij} is equal to 0, shown in Fig.1(b) And the drift d_{ij} stands for the desire that a group member moves towards the group. The calculation of d_{ij} and Vd_{ij} are similar with the methods obtaining D_{ij} and VD_{ij}.

$$D_{ij} = D \times \cos\theta_{ij} \tag{2}$$

$$d_{ij} = d \times \cos\alpha_{ij} \tag{3}$$

$$VD_{ij} = \begin{cases} 1 & D's \quad preferential \quad direction \\ 0 & else \end{cases} \tag{4}$$

$$Vd_{ij} = \begin{cases} 1 & d's \quad preferential \quad direction \\ 0 & else \end{cases} \tag{5}$$

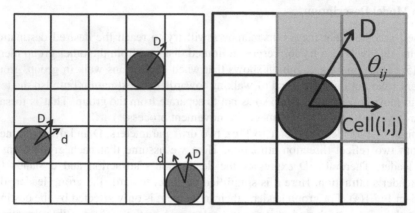

Fig. 1. (left) Description of group model. The red circle is the group leader, and the two pink circles are non-leader group members. D directs to the destination and d points at group leader. (right) Projection of preferential movement direction. The cells covered by blue color are D's preferential movement direction.

Here we adopt sequential update rules. Both the group leaders and group members use the same update rules and the detailed update rules of the model are shown as follows.

- Calculate P_{ij} for each pedestrian.
- According to the value of P_{ij} in eight directions, a most possible movement direction is selected for each pedestrian.
- Update the state of each pedestrian.

Group Generation

The previous research concentrates on the movement of isolated pedestrian, thus the pattern of pedestrian generation adopts stochastic way. However, here we focus on group movement, the group generation needs redefined.

- Firstly, M persons are randomly distributed in the space, and M=N1*N2.
- Secondly, N1 persons are randomly chosen to be "virtual leader".
- The third step is to obtain group members. For one "virtual leader", its location is set to be the searching center, so N2 group members including the "virtual leader" can be obtained from the smaller layer to the larger layer in sequence. Here a parameter R is given, and it means the layer index, which the group members are chosen from. Different R results in different group formations. On the other hand, R is able to reflect the internal distance of a group to some extent. The larger R is, the larger the internal distance is.
- The last is resetting group leader. For one group, each group member's distance to the destination is easily got. The group member owning the smallest distance for the destination is regarded to be the group leader.

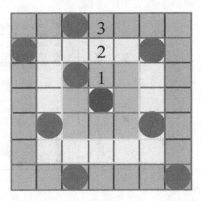

Fig. 2. The grids covered by the blue color, yellow color and green color form the layer 1, the layer 2 and layer 3 respectively. The circle covered by the red color stands for a "virtual leader". If R=2, the persons locate the layer 1 are not chosen to be this virtual leader's group member.

Results and Discussions

The scenario of simulation is 300 pedestrians attempting to leave a one-door square room. The room size is 20m*20m and the exit door size is W=2.4m. The cell size is 0.4m*0.4m. For different desired walk velocities, we set that the walker spends the same walk time of 0.4 s at a time step, which means the desired walk velocities of 0.4, 0.8. 1.2, 1.6 and 2.0 m/s corresponding to 1, 2, 3, 4 and 5 small grids at a time step, respectively. Using the group generation method we proposed, the distribution of groups is easy to obtain in the initialization phase. Other parameters are set as different values to study their impact on evacuation. The position of each pedestrian is updated with update rules. For each simulation scenario, we had done 100 times and got the average results.

The Effect of Group on Crowd

In our model, the parameter d is directed to group leader. To some extent, the value of d stands for group attraction intensity. In order to explore the effect of group on crowd, we had done many simulations with different group attraction intensities, different group sizes and different pedestrian velocities. For each scenario, the simulation results of the crowd only containing isolated pedestrians, can be regarded as reference. The difference between group walking and isolated pedestrian walking can be repressed by formula (3). The larger the value is, the deeper the effect of group on crowd is. Fig.3 describes the simulation results.

$$\text{Error rate} = (ET(group)-ET(single))/ \ ET(single)\% \qquad (6)$$

Where ET(group) means groups' evacuation time, and ET(single) means non-groups' evacuation   time, i.e. the crowd only contains isolated pedestrians without the presence of groups. In the simulation of this section, R is set 1.

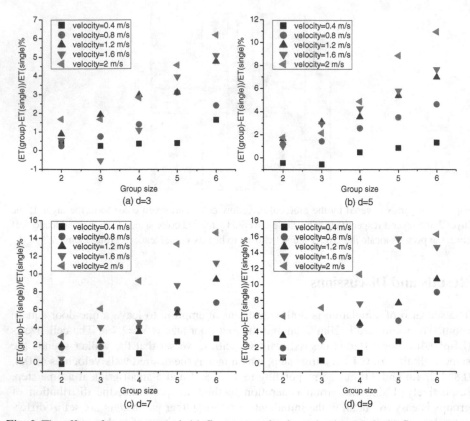

Fig. 3. The effect of group on crowd. (a) Group attraction intensity, i.e. d is 3. (b) Group attraction intensity is 5. (c) Group attraction intensity is 7. (d) Group attraction intensity is 9.

As displayed in Fig.3, most of data are larger than 0, which illustrates that the evacuation time of group walking is larger than that of non-group walking and group walking has a negative effect on pedestrian evacuation. Moreover, the larger the value is, the worse this effect is. In each sub-graph of Fig.3, it is obvious that with the increase of group size, the effect of group on crowd becomes greater. It is harder for large groups to have a good trade-off between moving towards destination and keeping group cohesion. What's more, such effect is more serious for the situation of group owning large velocity. The results indicate that keeping group cohesion brings pedestrians' velocity reduced. Besides, from Fig.3(a)-(d), with the group attraction intensity's increasing, the difference becomes more distinct, especially for group with large velocity. However, when d is set 9, i.e. the ratio of d to D is 9, the maximum value is about 17%. That is to say, when group members gravely concern group cohesion, it will bring at most 20% negative effect. That is to say, when the evacuation time of non-groups is T, the product of groups probably will be 1.2T. Of course, this estimate is not very accuracy. Only we find more accurate evidence, i.e. experiment data, can we quantify the effect of group on crowd dynamics.

The Effect of Group Disperse Degree on Crowd

In the initialization phase, different R will produce different group formations. R is able to reflect group disperse degree to some extent. Small R results in good group cohesion. However, larger R causes one group disperser. In the simulation of this section, d is set 7.

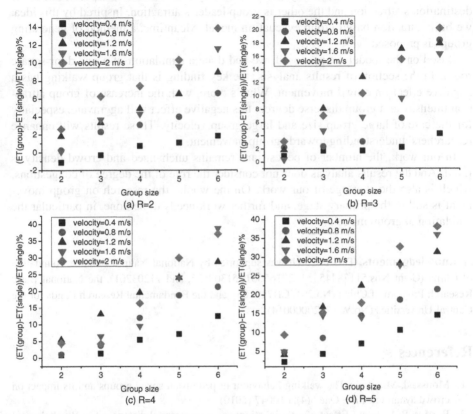

Fig. 4. The effect of group disperse degree on crowd. (a) Group disperse degree, i.e. R is 2. (b) Group disperse degree is 3. (c) Group disperse degree is 4. (d) Group disperse degree is 5.

As described in Fig.4, the impact of group size and velocity on crowd is in line with the products of the above section. From Fig.4(a)-(d), with the increase of R, i.e. the group disperse degree becomes larger, the impact of group walking becomes obvious. When R=3, only a little part of simulation data are larger than 10%, which means the effect of group disperse degree is not heavy at this time. However, when R=4, most simulation data are larger than 10% and some are up to larger than 30%. Such results show that effect of group disperse degree becomes distinct. The disperser the locations of group members is, the bigger the cost of keeping group cohesion is. Besides the situation of R=5 is similar with the case of R=4. This indicates that the effect of group disperse degree increases without limitation.

Summary

Group movement is so common phenomenon in daily life that it should not be ignored in the pedestrian evacuation model. However, there are still many unknown characteristics in group movement. Therefore, in this paper we tried to build a group evacuation model in a simple way. Here we mainly focused on two aspects, one is the destination's attraction and the other is group leader's attraction. Inspired by this idea, we built attraction-based group evacuation model. Meantime, a method of generating groups is proposed.

Based on the model we proposed, we had done a simulation of a one-door square room. In the section of results analysis, the key finding is that group walking has a negative effect on crowd movement. What's more, with the increase of group attraction intensity and group disperse degree, this negative effect will aggravate, especially for the case of large group size and large group velocity. These results will enhance researchers' understanding towards group movement.

In our work, the number of pedestrians remains unchanged and crowd density is fixed. And the results analysis does not consider the role of the degree of congestions, which is also the shortage of our work. On the whole, the research on group movement is still in the primary stage, and further work needs to be done, in particular the validation of group model.

Acknowledgements. This research was supported by National Natural Science Foundation of China (Grant Nos.51178445, 51120165001, 51308526, and 71203201), the National Basic Research Program of China (No.2012CB719705), and the Fundamental Research Funds for the Central Universities (No.WK2320000014).

References

1. Moussaïd, M., et al.: The walking behaviour of pedestrian social groups and its impact on crowd dynamics. PloS One 5(4), e10047 (2010)
2. Barrios, B.A., et al.: Effect of a social stigma on interpersonal distance. The Psychological Record (1976)
3. Bell, P., et al.: High density and crowding. Environmental psychology, 5th edn., pp. 293–332. Thomson Wadsworth, Belmont (2001)
4. Hall, J.A., Coats, E.J., LeBeau, L.S.: Nonverbal behavior and the vertical dimension of social relations: A meta-analysis. Psychological Bulletin 131(6), 898 (2005)
5. Hall, E.: Distances in man: The hidden dimension. Double Day, Garden City (1966)
6. Cook, M.: Experiments on orientation and proxemics. Human Relations 23(1), 61–76 (1970)
7. Wirtz, P., Ries, G.: The pace of life-reanalysed: Why does walking speed of pedestrians correlate with city size? Behaviour 123(1-2), 1–2 (1992)
8. Qiu, F., Hu, X.: Modeling group structures in pedestrian crowd simulation. Simulation Modelling Practice and Theory 18(2), 190–205 (2010)

9. Qiu, F., Hu, X.: A Framework for Modeling Social Groups in Agent-Based Pedestrian Crowd Simulations. International Journal of Agent Technologies and Systems (IJATS) 4(1), 39–58 (2012)
10. Fridman, N., Zilka, A., Kaminka, G.A.: The impact of cultural differences on crowd dynamics in pedestrian and evacuation domains (2011)
11. Wei, X.G., Mai, X., Lv, W., Song, W.G.: Microscopic character and Movement Consistency of Pedestrian Group: An Experimental Study in Campus. In: The 11th IAFSS Symposium (2014)
12. Bandini, S., Manenti, L., Manzoni, S.: Generation of Pedestrian Groups Distributions with Probabilistic Cellular Automata. In: Sirakoulis, G.C., Bandini, S. (eds.) ACRI 2012. LNCS, vol. 7495, pp. 299–308. Springer, Heidelberg (2012)
13. Köster, G., et al.: On modelling the influence of group formations in a crowd. Contemporary Social Science 6(3), 397–414 (2011)
14. Vizzari, G., et al.: An agent-based approach to pedestrian and group dynamics: experimental and real world scenarios. In: Proceedings of the 7th International Workshop on Agents in Traffic and Transportation (2012)
15. Vizzari, G., Manenti, L., Crociani, L.: Adaptive pedestrian behaviour for the preservation of group cohesion. Complex Adaptive Systems Modeling 1(1), 7 (2013)
16. Song, W.G., et al.: Simulation of evacuation processes using a multi-grid model for pedestrian dynamics. Physica A-Statistical Mechanics and Its Applications 363(2), 492–500 (2006)

Effects of Boundary Conditions
on Single-File Pedestrian Flow

Jun Zhang[1], Antoine Tordeux[1], and Armin Seyfried[1,2]

[1] Jülich Supercomputing Centre, Forschungszentrum Jülich GmbH, Germany
[2] Computer Simulation for Fire Safety and Pedestrian Traffic, Bergische Universität
Wuppertal, Germany
{ju.zhang,a.tordeux,a.seyfried}@fz-juelich.de

Abstract. In this paper we investigate effects of boundary conditions
on one dimensional pedestrian flow which involves purely longitudinal
interactions. Qualitatively, stop-and-go waves are observed under closed
boundary condition and dissolve when the boundary is open. To get more
detailed information the fundamental diagrams of the open and closed
systems are compared using Voronoi-based measurement method. Higher
maximal specific flow is observed from the pedestrian movement at open
boundary condition.

Keywords: Single-file flow, Pedestrian experiment, Fundamental diagram, Boundary condition.

1 Introduction

Understanding and predicting the dynamical properties of large crowds is of great
importance to improve the safety and the capacity of pedestrian facilities [1,2].
Even for the basic fundamental diagram, however, large discrepancies are shown
in previous studies [3,4] and is influenced by several factors including pedestrian
motivation, facility geometry, culture differences etc.

The single-file pedestrian flow involves purely longitudinal interactions. The
possible influences on the flow have been studied from various aspects in recent
years. Seyfried et al. measured the fundamental diagram of single file flow for
densities up to 2 m^{-1} [5]. The same experiments were carried out in India by
Chattaraj et al. [6] and in China by Liu et al. [7] to investigate the culture difference on the fundamental diagram. Jelić et al. conducted the similar experiment
inside a ring formed by inner and outer round walls to study the properties
of pedestrians moving in line [8,9]. The density in their experiment reaches 3
m^{-1} and the stepping behavior and fundamental diagrams are studied. From
this study, three regimes (free regime, weakly constrained regime and strongly
constrained regime) are distinguished by analyzing the velocity-spatial headway
relationship. In this way, the pedestrian flow with higher velocity (free flow state)
is divided into two different regimes but the flow for the velocity $v < 0.8\ m/s$,
which belongs to congested states, is not distinguished. Stop-and-go wave [10]

J. Wąs, G.C. Sirakoulis, and S. Bandini (Eds.): ACRI 2014, LNCS 8751, pp. 462–469, 2014.

is a special phenomenon of congested flow. However, the influences of boundary conditions, open or closed, on the fundamental diagram are still need studying.

In this paper, we present new experimental results with higher density range to study the prosperities of single file pedestrian flow. The fundamental diagrams will be analyzed and the influence of different boundary conditions on it will be studied.

2   Experiment Setup

The experiment was performed in an oval corridor in the wardroom of Bergische Kaserne Düsseldorf in Germany in 2006. The circumference of the corridor was about $C = 26\ m$. The participants were female and male soldiers. Pasteboards with high contrast markers were put on the head of each soldier for trajectory extraction. To get different ranges of global density in the corridor, 12 runs were performed with the number of test persons N = 14, 17, 20, 22, 25, 28, 34, 39, 45, 56, 62, 70. This means that the global density ($\rho_g = N/C$) ranges from 0.54 to 2.69 m^{-1} in this experiment.

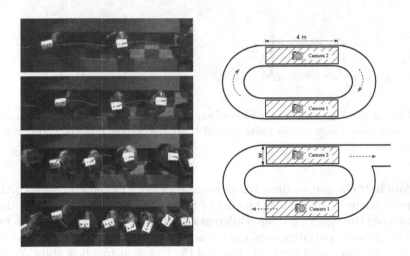

Fig. 1. Snapshots and setup of the single file movement experiment. Two cameras are used to record the movement at different parts of the corridor. Camera 2 is close to the exit.

Fig. 1 shows the sketches and snapshots of the experiment. Two cameras (Camera 1 and 2) were used to record the pedestrian movement in the two 4 m length areas with a frame rate of 25 fps. At the beginning of each run, the pedestrians were arranged in the corridor uniformly. Then they were asked to move three to four rounds in the circuit in normal speed without overtaking. After that an exit near Camera 2 was made and pedestrian went outside the closed corridor. As a result, the movements both in closed and open situations were recorded from the experiment. Pedestrian trajectories were extracted from these video recordings using the software PeTrack [11]. Detailed information about the experiment can be found in [10].

3   Time-Space Diagram

In this section we qualitatively discuss characteristics given by the space-time structure of the trajectories extracted from the video recordings. Fig. 2 shows the time-space diagrams for the runs with N = 25 and 62, which represents the global density 0.96 and 2.38 m^{-1}. In these graphs, instantaneous velocities $v_i(t)$, which is calculated according to the equation(2) with $\Delta t' = 10\ frames$, of each pedestrian are also exhibited.

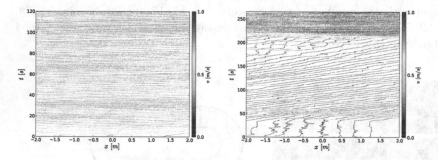

Fig. 2. Time-space diagram for four runs of experiment under both closed and open corridor conditions. There are 25 (left) and 62 (right) pedestrians in the corridor respectively.

The data in these graphs show the movement in both closed and open corridor. Approximatively, the last 20 percent of the observation corresponds to the situations when the system is open. Different states of the pedestrian flow can be observed from these spatiotemporal diagrams. When there are 25 pedestrians in the corridor, the density is relatively low and the flow is at free flow state. With the increase of the number of pedestrians in the corridor, jamming states can be observed obviously and stop-and-go waves start to appear. In the right figure for the run N = 62, the wave is obvious and lasts for a long time. When the exit is opened, the pedestrian flow transfer from congested to free flow states. This transition is related to a rarefaction wave in traffic flow [12,13]. The velocities of pedestrian can increase from smaller than 0.05 m/s to more than 1 m/s rapidly.

4   Analysis and Results

In this section, the fundamental diagram, the basic relationship in traffic engineering, will be investigated using a precise measurement method.

4.1   Measurement Method

According to our previous studies on two dimensional pedestrian flow, the Voronoi-based method has the advantage of high resolution and small fluctuation of measured densities compared to other methods [14, 15]. At a macro level, we therefore use the concept of Voronoi method to calculate the mean values of density and velocity over space in this study.

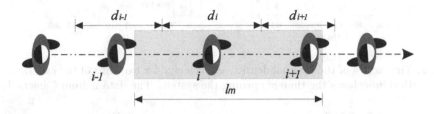

Fig. 3. Illustration of the Voronoi method in one dimensional space. The gray region shows the measurement area.

In two dimension, the Voronoi cell of a pedestrian is obtained based on the locations of his or her neighbors. Similarly, in one dimensional case we calculate the Voronoi space d_i of each pedestrian i base on the positions of his two neighbors $i-1$ and $i+1$. Actually, the length of d_i is half the distance between the two neighbors (see Fig. 3). In this method, a measurement area with the length l_m is selected to calculate the Voronoi density $\rho(t)$ and velocity $v(t)$ at time t:

$$\rho(t) = \frac{\sum_{i=1}^{n} \Theta_i(t)}{l_m} \quad and \quad v(t) = \frac{\sum_{i=1}^{n} \Theta_i(t) \cdot v_i(t)}{l_m} \tag{1}$$

where n is the number of pedestrians whose Voronoi space includes the measurement area (assuming the overlapping length is d_{oi} for pedestrian i). $\Theta_i(t) = d_{oi}/d_i$ represents the contribution of pedestrian i to the density of the measurement area. $v_i(t)$ is the instantaneous velocity of pedestrian i at time t. It is calculated by using his displacement in a small time interval $\Delta t'$ around t, that is

$$v_i(t) = \frac{x_i(t + \Delta t'/2) - x_i(t - \Delta t'/2))}{\Delta t'} \tag{2}$$

In this study, a 3 m measurement area from $x = -1.5\ m$ to $x = 1.5\ m$ is selected. With such selection, it means that at most 7 pedestrians can exist in the area at the same time according to the average size of a standing pedestrian [16]. The time interval $\Delta t' = 0.4\ s$ (corresponding to 10 frames) is used to calculate the velocity. We calculate the densities and velocities every frame.

We select manually the start and end times of the measurement to obtain "stationary" performances for the fundamental diagram. Fig. 4 and 5 show the time series for two runs of the experiment from the two cameras. The green

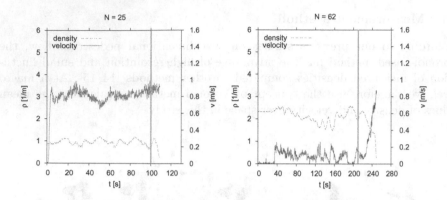

Fig. 4. Time series of the Voronoi density and velocity for two runs of the experiment. The vertical line shows the time of opening the system. The data is from Camera 1.

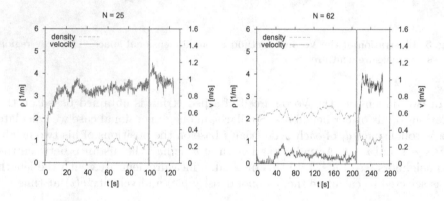

Fig. 5. Time series of the Voronoi density and velocity for two runs of the experiment. The vertical line shows the time of opening the system. The data is from Camera 2.

vertical lines in the graphs show the time for opening the exits. For the run with N = 25, the measured values of the variables do not show significant differences between open and closed systems (the flow is at free flow state). Instead, the values change obviously at high density situation when the system is at jammed state . For the run with N = 62 the effects are so clear that sudden drop of density and sharp rise of velocity (from 0.1 to 1 m/s) are observed. No large differences are found between the data from different cameras. However, the Camera 2 recorded relatively more data under open boundary condition and thus we mainly analyze the data from it in the following.

4.2   Fundamental Diagram

Fig. 6 shows the Voronoi-based fundamental diagram for the pedestrian movement under closed boundary condition. We plot the results from various runs in

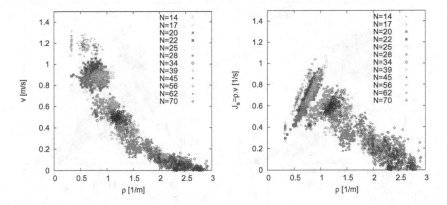

Fig. 6. The fundamental diagram (density-velocity (left) and density-specific flow (right) relationships) of single file pedestrian movement in closed corridor

different symbols to see the changes in more detail. The free velocity is around 1.2 m/s and is obtained from the run with N = 14. For the four runs with N = 17, 20, 22 and 25, the measure densities range from 0.5 to 1 $1/m$ and the free velocity reduces to 0.9 m/s. The maximum specific flow is about 1 s^{-1} around $\rho = 1$ m^{-1}. Whereas, after N = 28 the changes become apparent with the increase of the number of pedestrians inside the corridor. From this graph, it seems that the fundamental diagram could be divided into three parts for density ρ belonging to [0, 1.0], [1.0, 1.7] and [1.7, 3.0]. These should be responding to the three states of pedestrian movement. When the density is smaller than 1.0 m^{-1}, it is free flow state and pedestrian can move smoothly. In the second part, it is congestion state and the specific flow begins to decrease. In this state, the decelerations of pedestrian can be observed sometimes but are not the main property of the movement. The data for $\rho > 1.7$ m^{-1} are mainly from the runs with N =56, 62 and 70. In this state, the stop-and-go waves dominate the pedestrian movement. Especially for the density around 1.7 m^{-1}, the velocity seems to remain constant or increase in a small range. Reflected in the density-specific flow relationship, the specific flow has a transition around this density. Here another point worths noticing is that the change from free flow state to congestion state is not continuous. A gap appears in the density-velocity relationship around $v = 0.7$ m/s.

Next, we study the influence of boundary conditions on the fundamental diagram of single-file pedestrian flow. For open boundary condition only data at free flow state can be observed. The maximal density obtained from this situation is less than 1.3 m^{-1}, as shown in Fig. 7. The free velocities maintain for higher densities in open corridor case. Correspondingly the maximal specific flow increase from 1.0 s^{-1} at closed boundary to 1.3 s^{-1} at open boundary.

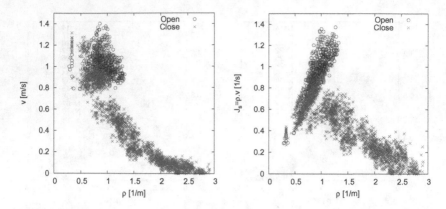

Fig. 7. Comparison of the fundamental diagram (density-velocity (left) and density-specific flow (right) relationships) of single file pedestrian movement under different boundary conditions

5   Summary

In this paper, we study the properties of single file pedestrian movement in oval corridor by means of an experiment performed under laboratory conditions. We investigate the influence of boundary conditions on the flow both quantitatively and qualitatively.

From the time-space diagram, the characteristics of different flow states can be observed qualitatively. Congested density levels with stop-and-go waves can be reached within closed system. If the system is open only free states are observed. When the closed congested system is opened, the flow transfer from jamming state to free one quickly. This is related to a rarefaction phenomenon.

From the analysis it is found that the boundary condition does have influence on the fundamental diagram of the single file pedestrian flow. The free velocities of pedestrians subsist for higher densities under open boundary condition. As a consequence, the measured maximal specific flow is about $1.3 \, s^{-1}$, which is obviously larger than that under closed boundary condition ($1.0 \, s^{-1}$). Further empirical data in this situation is still necessary to confirm this observation.

References

1. Schadschneider, A., Klüpfel, H., Kretz, T., Rogsch, C., Seyfried, A.: Fundamentals of pedestrian and evacuation dynamics. In: Bazzan, A., Klügl, F. (eds.) Multi-Agent Systems for Traffic and Transportation Engineering, ch. 6, pp. 124–154. IGI Global, Hershey (2009)
2. Schadschneider, A., Klingsch, W., Kluepfel, H., Kretz, T., Rogsch, C., Seyfried, A.: Evacuation Dynamics: Empirical Results, Modeling and Applications. In: Encyclopedia of Complexity and System Science, vol. 5, pp. 3142–3176. Springer, Heidelberg (2009)

3. Seyfried, A., Boltes, M., Kähler, J., Klingsch, W., Portz, A., Rupprecht, T., Schad-schneider, A., Steffen, B., Winkens, A.: Enhanced empirical data for the fundamental diagram and the flow through bottlenecks. In: Klingsch, W.W.F., Rogsch, C., Schadschneider, A., Schreckenber, M. (eds.) Pedestrian and Evacuation Dynamics 2008, pp. 145–156. Springer, Heidelberg (2010)
4. Zhang, J., Klingsch, W., Schadschneider, A., Seyfried, A.: Ordering in bidirectional pedestrian flows and its influence on the fundamental diagram. Journal of Statistical Mechanics: Theory and Experiment 2012(02), P02002 (2012)
5. Seyfried, A., Steffen, B., Klingsch, W., Boltes, M.: The fundamental diagram of pedestrian movement revisited. J. Stat. Mech. P10002 (2005)
6. Chattaraj, U., Seyfried, A., Chakroborty, P.: Comparison of pedestrian fundamental diagram across cultures. Advances in Complex Systems 12(3), 393–405 (2009)
7. Liu, X., Song, W., Zhang, J.: Extraction and quantitative analysis of microscopic evacuation characteristics based on digital image processing. Physica A: Statistical Mechanics and its Applications 388(13), 2717–2726 (2009)
8. Jelic, A., Appert-Rolland, C., Lemercier, S., Pettré, J.: Properties of pedestrians walking in line: Fundamental diagrams. Physical Review E E 85(85), 9 (2012)
9. Jelic, A., Appert-Rolland, C., Lemercier, S., Pettré, J.: Properties of pedestrians walking in line: Stepping behavior. Physical Review E E 86, 046111 (2012)
10. Seyfried, A., Portz, A., Schadschneider, A.: Phase coexistence in congested states of pedestrian dynamics. In: Bandini, S., Manzoni, S., Umeo, H., Vizzari, G. (eds.) ACRI 2010. LNCS, vol. 6350, pp. 496–505. Springer, Heidelberg (2010)
11. Boltes, M., Seyfried, A., Steffen, B., Schadschneider, A.: Automatic extraction of pedestrian trajectories from video recordings. In: Klingsch, W.W.F., Rogsch, C., Schadschneider, A., Schreckenberg, M. (eds.) Pedestrian and Evacuation Dynamics 2008, pp. 43–54. Springer, Heidelberg (2010)
12. Lighthill, M.H., Whitham, G.B.: On kinematic waves II: A theory of traffic flow on long crowded roads. Proceedings of the Royal Society of London A, Mathematical and Physical Sciences 229(1178), 317–345 (1955)
13. Richards, P.I.: Shock-waves on the highway. Operations Research 4(1), 42–51 (1956)
14. Steffen, B., Seyfried, A.: Methods for measuring pedestrian density, flow, speed and direction with minimal scatter. Physica A 389(9), 1902–1910 (2010)
15. Zhang, J., Klingsch, W., Schadschneider, A., Seyfried, A.: Transitions in pedestrian fundamental diagrams of straight corridors and t-junctions. Journal of Statistical Mechanics: Theory and Experiment P06004 (2011)
16. Fruin, J.J.: Pedestrian Planning and Design. Elevator World, New York (1971)

Simulation Study of the Spiral Motion of Pedestrians: A Cellular Automata Approach

Kenichiro Shimura[1], Stefania Bandini[2], and Katuhiro Nishinari[1]

[1] Research Center for Advanced Science and Technology, The University of Tokyo,
4-6-1, Komaba, Meguro-ku, Tokyo, 153-8904, Japan
[2] Department of Informatics Systems and Communication,
The University of Milano Bicocca, Viale Sarca 336 - U14, 20126 Milano, Italy
shimura@tokai.t.u-tokyo.ac.jp

Abstract. When the pedestrians share the same objectives moving toward the same direction, huge congestion is often created in some regions. The pedestrians lose mobility in the congestion and subsequently create a deadlock phenomenon. This study considers an event that pedestrians rotate around and moves toward a central object. The pedestrian motion is modelled by use of Cellular Automata (CA) to analyse how the congestion at centre region is developed. The model is implemented in hexagonal lattice with static floor fields in polar coordinate. Interaction of rotational and centripetal mobility generates the spiral motions of the pedestrian. In this study, various simulations are carried out to investigate the effect of model parameters and macroscopic properties. The pedestrian motion creates high density area at centre region and the density gradually decreases toward outside. The radial distribution of the circumferential density characterises the pedestrian flow, such that a deadlock occurs at the inner region and a free flow occurs at the outer region. Moreover a possible solution for easing the deadlock is also suggested in this paper.

Keywords: Cellular Automata, pedestrian, crowd dynamics, rotational flow, floor field, polar coordinate.

1 Introduction

In some custom or religious event, pedestrians share the same objectives. The pedestrian behaviour is driven by a strong intension to accomplish the common targets. In such a situation massive congestion may occur. The pedestrians lose mobility and strong pressure force on pedestrians may cause a devastating accident. The deadlock is the phenomenon that the pedestrians dramatically lose mobility in severe congestion. This study considers an event that pedestrians rotate around and moves toward a central object and is aimed to understand the deadlock mechanism at the rotational centre. Such an event is particularly seen in one of the Islamic rituals so called Tawaf which is performed during the Hajj, a pilgrimage of Muslims to Mecca. In Tawaf, pilgrims circumambulate the Kaaba in counter clockwise for seven times at Masjid Al-Haram mosque. The pilgrims also try to leach as near as possible to the

J. Wąs, G.C. Sirakoulis, and S. Bandini (Eds.): ACRI 2014, LNCS 8751, pp. 470–480, 2014.
© Springer International Publishing Switzerland 2014

Kaaba at the rotational centre. Combination of these two movements results in the outward spiral followed by inward spiral pedestrian trajectory. While mass number of pedestrians shares this characteristic behaviour, the outward trajectories must cross the inward trajectories. The crossing of the pedestrian trajectory causes a clogging of those who are already moved inside while more and more pedestrians flow into the centre region. The issue is how those pedestrians at centre region to escape outwards efficiently. Despite various solutions may be available, those approaches fairly limited due to the environmental limitation such that more inside to the centre then the available space is lesser. One can see that if the density of pedestrians at the centre region is reduced by controlling the inward flow then outward flow can be increased because of more mobility is gained. Thus it is of great importance to understand how the deadlock is created. The simulation based study is carried out by introducing a Cellular Automata (CA) model describing a rotational and centripetal motion.

Various study on pedestrian dynamics has been performed aiming for many social applications such as Evacuation, Crowd control, etc. [1-3]. Despite CA is a rule based model in discrete time and space, the Social Force Model [4,5] describes the interactional force between pedestrians by differential equations in continuous space. Regarding to rotational pedestrian behaviour, an existing model [6,7] reproduces the rotational motion by pre-giving a desired circular pathway for every pedestrian. The pedestrian motion is then defined in the way that to reduce the deviation of current position and the desired pathway. In Social Force model, the direction of pedestrian movement is defined by the difference between the desired direction to a goal and actual direction that the pedestrian moved. This definition gives the pedestrian to move along the shortest path to a desired goal. When pedestrians have strong intention to detour as in rotational motion, it is necessary to set sub-goals continuously aligned along the circular pathway. The commonality of these two approaches is that preliminary given pathway is required to reproduce the rotational motion. The method of successive adjustment of pedestrian position from the desired pathway includes a regulator mechanism and is not an autonomous approach. The issue is to model the pedestrian motion as self-organised system which requires the autonomy in the model. This paper introduces a CA model which reproduces the spiral pedestrian motion employing the floor field method [6-11]. The floor field in polar coordinate is newly introduced and corresponding transition rules and probabilities are also designed to fit these purposes. Then various simulations are carried out to investigate how the parameters affect the deadlock phenomenon.

2   Modelling

For the case of the circular motion, the Polar coordinate is more convenient than use of the Cartesian coordinate since the dynamics is constrained within rotational system. The orthogonal coordination in x and y are transformed in radial r and angular θ elements. The first step is to create radial and angular floor fields. Fig. 1(a) and (b) illustrates the Radial and Angular static floor fields and are calculated by Eq. 1.

$$R_k = \sqrt{x_k^2 + y_k^2} \qquad , \qquad A_k = \tan^{-1}(y_k / x_k) \qquad (1)$$

Where, $\{k : \text{hexagonal lattice}\}$ x, y denotes the distance of cell k from the rotational centre in Cartesian coordinate.

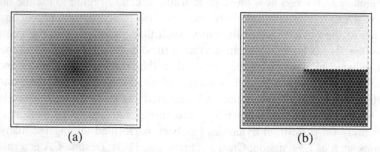

(a)   (b)

Fig. 1. The static floor field pattern of (a) Radial floor field R_k, and (b) Angular floor field A_k

In the floor field lattice, the values R_k and A_k are stored in each cells and configured in the descending order giving the geometrical information to the particles. In Fig.1, smaller value is expressed with darker colour and the pedestrians are directed to smaller floor field value. Despite square lattice is often used for CA models the hexagonal lattice is chosen here, since its compatibility with closely packed circular particles. When pedestrians are packed in a crowd, the geometrical configuration such that a pedestrian is surrounded by other six pedestrians is seen. The pedestrian motion is therefore defined by the interaction of six neighbourhood cells whilst either four or eight neighbourhood cells are considered in the square lattice. The advantage of employing the hexagonal lattice is that more directional elements are implemented in the equidistance neighbourhood cells compared to the square lattice.

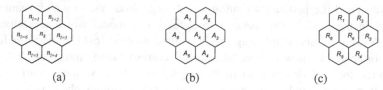

(a)   (b)   (c)

Fig. 2. The neighbourhood configuration. (a) The particle , (b) Angular floor field (c) Radial Floor field.

Secondary, the transition rule of the model is expressed as Eq. 2. As shown in the neighbourhood configuration in Fig 2 (a), n denotes the occurrence probability that the cell is occupied, p denotes the transition probability, index k denotes the current cell of interest, l denotes the neighbourhood cells, and t denotes the time step.

$$n_l^{t+1} = n_k^t \, p_l (1 - n_l^t) \qquad (2)$$

Fig 2 (b) and (c) illustrates the configuration of the neighbourhood cells l for each of the floor field. Where $(A_l)_{l=1,2,3,4,5,6}$ and $(R_l)_{l=1,2,3,4,5,6}$ denotes the values of angular and rotational floor field in the neighbourhood, respectively. The preference q_l of the particle moves to cell l form its neighbourhood cells k is defined as Eq. (3).

$$q_l = \alpha a_l + \beta r_l \quad , \qquad \text{Where,} \quad a_l = \frac{A_l}{\sum A_l} \, , \, r_l = \frac{R_l}{\sum R_l} \qquad (3)$$

Where the factors α and β denote the tendency factors which define the strength of the motional tendencies in angular and radial directions where α and β is normalised as $\alpha + \beta = 1$. The preference q_l contains the factors which defines the possibility of the particle moves to all the directions. In order to constrain the motion within the counter clockwise, we further introduce the directional Boolean expressions such as u_l and v_l which exclusively operates on the a_l and r_l, respectively. The lth component of u_l is 1 if the value of a_l is below certain threshold and 0 elsewhere. Similarly to this the lth component of v_l has 1 if the value of r_l is below certain threshold and 0 elsewhere. Since the floor field is defined in descending order this threshold is taken as ith and jth smallest values of A_l and R_l respectively. By this way the direction of the particle can be limited to the desired angular and radial directions. Thus the transition probability p_l of a particle in cell k moves to cell l is given as Eq. 4.

$$p_l = \frac{q_l}{\sum q_l} \qquad , \text{ where } q_l = \alpha a_l u_l + \beta r_l v_l \qquad (4)$$

$$u_l = \begin{cases} 1, & \text{if } A_l < A_{(i)} \\ 0, & \text{otherwise} \end{cases} \quad \text{and} \quad v_l = \begin{cases} 1, & \text{if } R_l < R_{(j)} \\ 0, & \text{otherwise} \end{cases}$$

The transition rule defined in Eq. (2) and the corresponding transition probability shown in Eq. (4) is parallelly applied to all the cells in the lattice for each time step. The updating cell is selected by random order but each cell is updated only ones at each time step.

3   Results and Discussions

The simulations are carried out for various initial densities, the values of i and j. The results are illustrated in Fig. 3. For the initial condition, the desired numbers of particles defined as the initial density are randomly placed in the circular area within radius 25. Despite the density is usually defined with respect to the lattice size here in this paper the "initial density" is defined by the number of particles with respect to the circular area at the centre of the lattice. This is due to avoid the avoidance of the wall effect. Starting from these initial conditions as shown in Fig. 3 (a1), (b1), (c1), and (d1), the simulations are performed till the steady state Fig. 3 (a3), (b3), (c3), and (d3). Fig. 3 (a2), (b2), (c2), and (d2) illustrates the image of transient dynamics of the particles. In the figure, the current positions of the particles are marked as dark black. And the traces of the particles for previous five consecutive steps are shown in descending grey colour scale. Then the dynamics can be represented as the afterimage of the moving particles.

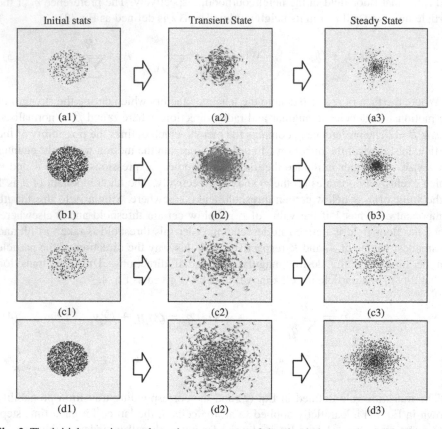

Fig. 3. The initial, transient, and steady state pattern of the simulation results, where (a) Initial density = 0.15 and $i=j=2$, (b) Initial density = 0.5 and $i=j=2$, (c) Initial density = 0.15 and $i=j$ =3, (d) Initial density = 0.5 and $i=j$ =3. Moreover, the transient state is illustrated with the afterimage of 5 consecutive steps.

It is seen from the figure that the particles are making a spiral movement for every cases. In this dynamics, the rotational movement is governed by the angular element and the tendency towards the rotational centre is governed by the radial element. Where the former is subjected by the static angular floor field shown in Fig.1 (b) and the latter is subjected by that of radial floor field as seen in Fig. 2(a). The combination of these two dynamics creates the particle movement such that spirally moving towards the rotational centre. Although in depth analysis is necessary for understanding the dynamics in terms of angular velocity and circumferential velocity, the spiral dynamics is qualitatively expressed with this model. In Fig. 3 (a3) and (b3) dark black area around the rotational centre is seen. Within this region the particles are closely packed and the density is almost a unity thus the particles have no mobility. This deadlock phenomenon depends on the initial density such that, the higher initial density is, the larger the deadlock area. The deadlock occurs because inward flow is higher than outer flow. Those particles first leached to the centre are locked-in at the vicinity of the rotational centre and simultaneously more particle are rushing in from the outer area, thus the probability that those particles come outside from this area is substantially low.

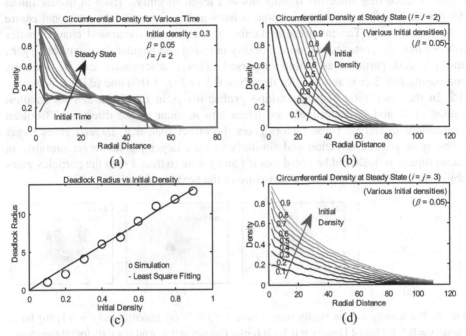

Fig. 4. (a) Circumferential density for various times. (b) Circumferential density at the steady state for initial densities of 0.1 to 0.9. And $\beta = 0.05$ and $i=j=2$. (c) Radial distance of the deadlock area. (d) The same condition of that for Fig.4 (b) except $i=j=3$.

To analyse the mechanism of the deadlock, Fig.4 (a) illustrates the circumferential densities at each radial distance plotted for various time steps between the initial to the steady state. The circumferential density is calculated by counting the number of occupied cells in equidistance cells from the centre. Initially, the particles are uniformly placed on the equidistant circumferential cells of the radius up to 50. The circumferential density is set to 0.25 for every radial distance. The figure shows that the inbound flow characterises the macroscopic dynamics. The density at near centre area increases and simultaneously decreases at outer area with respect to time. At the steady state, the radial density profile shows gradual decrease toward outside giving more mobility to pedestrians. Fig.4 (b) illustrates the circumferential density at the steady state for various initial densities. The part where the density is unity in the figure reflects the dead lock region. The density profile in general exhibits gradual decrease toward outside. For the case of initial density = 0.1, the deadlock only occurs at the most inner part and the area of the deadlock increases as initial density increases. Fig.4 (c) shows the deadlock radius with respect to the initial densities. In the figure, the result of the simulation is plotted with circle, while the straight line is a least square fitting on the simulated result. The fitted results suggest that the deadlock radius has linear relationship with initial density. Fig. 4 (d) illustrates the circumferential density at the steady state for various initial densities when $i=j=3$ whereas Fig. 4 (b) is the case that for $i=j=2$. As seen from the figure that there is no deadlock occurring since the density doesn't leach to unity. Even at higher initial density such as 0.9, the circumferential density at the vicinity of the rotational centre is less than unity. The influence of factors i and j to the dynamical characteristics follows that, the particles has more mobility in radial and angular direction for larger i and j , thus particles are more dispersed. This characteristics can be seen by comparing Fig. 3 (a3) and (c3) for density = 0.1 or Fig. 3 (b3) and (d3) for density = 0.5. In the calculation of the transition probability p_i in Eq. 4, ith and jth smallest values of A_l and R_l respectively are taken into account as the directional Boolean expressions u_l and v_l. These factors gives the effect such that, larger i gives larger mobility in angular direction and similarly to this, larger j gives larger mobility in radial direction. It should be noted that if i and j is more than 4 then the particles gains ability to move backward due to the nature of the hexagonal lattice.

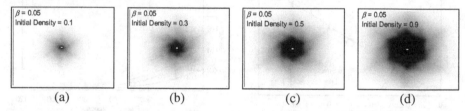

Fig. 5. The density map at steady state, where $i = j = 2$. (a) Initial Density = 0.1, (b) Initial Density = 0.3, (c) Initial Density = 0.5, (d) Initial Density = 0.9. And $\beta = 0.05$ for all the cases.

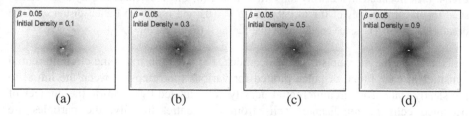

Fig. 6. The density map at steady state, where $i = j = 3$. (a) Initial Density = 0.1, (b) Initial Density = 0.3, (c) Initial Density = 0.5, (d) Initial Density = 0.9. And $\beta = 0.05$ for all the cases.

These characteristics can be seen in the density map. Fig. 5 and Fig. 6 illustrates the density map at the steady state for the cases of $i=j=2$ and $i=j=3$, respectively. These are calculated by cumulating the occupation of each cell during the simulation repeated for 100 randomly selected initial conditions. These density maps represent the occupation probability of the cells in the lattice and thus the cell with darker black has higher possibility of being occupied. In the case of $i=j=2$, By comparison of Fig. 5 (a), (b), (c), and (d), the deadlock area is increasing together with initial density increment. Despite substantial deadlock area is seen when $i=j=2$, the particles are widely dispersed throughout the lattice when $i=j=3$ whilst all other parameters are remaining the same. However this is one of the characteristic of CA where locally defined microscopic rules affect largely on the macroscopic dynamics. This fact further suggests that to crate the adequate model for real world applications, it is a great importance of verifying the consistency of the model by comparing the simulation results with real data or experiments. Visually comparing the results with publically available images of Tawaf, the parameters used for Fig. 5 favourably shows the qualitative agreement.

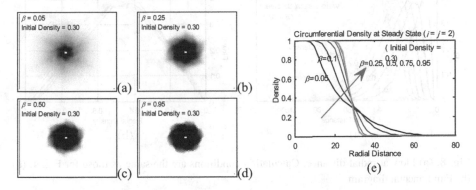

Fig. 7. The density map at steady state, (a) $\beta = 0.05$, (b) $\beta = 0.25$, (c) $\beta = 0.50$, (d) $\beta = 0.95$. And Initial Density = 0.3 for all the cases. (e) Circumferential density for various β.

Series of simulations are further performed to see how radial tendency factor β affects to the steady state. The value of β in Eq. 4 affects the inbound or outbound radial motions where larger the value of β, higher the radial mobility. Fig. 7(a), (b), (c), and (d) illustrate the density map at the steady state where the initial density is taken as 0.3. It is seen that almost all the particles are rushing inward as β increases. Strong tendency towards the centre restricts the outbound and rotational mobility, and thus the large area around the centre is significantly crowded. Fig. 7(e) illustrates this feature. It is seen that larger value of β causes the steeper density gradient. As result substantial deadlocked area is produced around the rotational centre then no mobility can be gained for the most of the pedestrians since the density remains unity. This is the extreme case but if all of the pedestrians share the one particular aim trying to leach the centre as quickly as possible with competition.

Moreover, flow analysis is carried out to understand the dynamic behaviour. Fig.8(a) shows the flow at radial distance for various initial densities and corresponding fundamental diagram is illustrated in Fig.8(b).The flow is defined within the equidistance ring at given radial distance. It is calculated by sum of the pedestrians made circular movement inside the ring and the pedestrians moved from the adjacent rings. Besides, those who moved out from the ring are included as moved in particles of its adjacent rings. There are several characteristics in the flow at the steady state. At the near centre region the flow is zero where no mobility is gained for all pedestrians considered as deadlock region. The region outside of deadlock, the area is fairly congested thus low mobility for pedestrians. The density decreases towards the outside thus the flow increases. At the region where the density nearly equals to 0.5 the flow leaches the maximum. Thereafter in the outer region, the pedestrians are under free flow where the density dominants the flow that is flow decreases as number of pedestrian decreases. These characteristics are also seen in the fundamental diagrams as shown in Fig. 8(b). Where in the figure, right half part illustrates the deadlock area and left half part illustrates the free flow area.

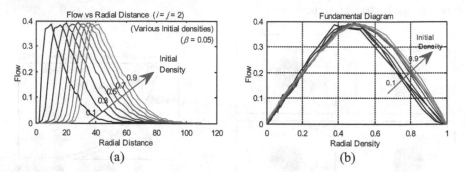

Fig. 8. (a) Flow at radial distance. Calculation conditions are the same as those for Fig. 4. (b). (b) Fundamental diagram.

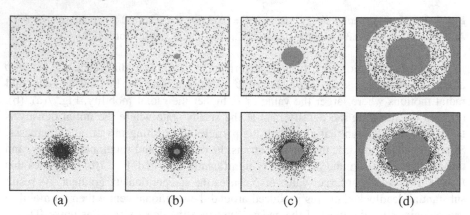

Fig. 9. The effect of inaccessible area shown as grey circle at the centre for various radius R_I, (a) $R_I = 0$, (b) $R_I = 8$, (c) $R_I = 28$, (d) $R_I = 56$ with ring like pedestrian walkway. In each subfigures, top and bottom figure shows the initial and steady state conditions, respectively.

Further investigation is carried out for the possibility of deadlock elimination. One possible way is to make the circular area at the centre region where the pedestrians' access is restricted. Fig. 9 illustrates the simulation results carried out for various radiuses R_I of the restricted circle. The total number of pedestrians equivalent to the initial density = 0.5 as defined in Fig. 3(b) are randomly placed in the unrestricted area. The figure shows the initial conditions and resulting steady states. It is seen that the deadlock at the most inward circumference is eased when the radius R_I is larger. It is because the pedestrians gain more mobility as a result of increase in the available space. While the radial distance of the maximum flow is 28 in Fig. 8(a) at the density=0.5, Fig. 9(c) illustrates the case that the pedestrian motion is constrained at outside of this radial distance. Series of simulations show that the deadlock is not observed and the flow increases when the restricted area is larger than this maximum flow radius. These results suggest that the minimum radius of rotation and pedestrian density are the major factors to control the deadlock. Fig. 9(d) is the case that the pedestrians are constrained in the ring like walkway. Such configuration is partly implemented to Masjid Al-Haram. Although the pedestrians have to walk longer distance to circumambulate but it is an effective solution to ease the congestion as well as increase the pedestrian flow.

4   Conclusion

In this study, the spiral motion of pedestrians is modelled in CA. The model is constructed on the hexagonal lattice with static floor field in polar coordinate. The effect on the dynamics by model parameters are investigated. The results suggests that $i=j=2$ is favourable selection to simulate the spiral motion while α and β are the parameters to describe the level of rotational or centripetence intension of pedestrians. For the application of real situation the values of α and β should be carefully evaluated and heterogeneously applied to individual pedestrians. As for the general characteristics of the spiral motion, the pedestrian density decreases gradually form the centre to the outer region at the steady state. The deadlock phenomena at the centre region is highly affected by the circumambulate radius and pedestrian density. In terms of the pedestrian flow, it is characterised as the deadlock, maximum flow then free flow region in outward direction from the centre zone. Based on these characteristics, this study further suggests the possible solution to ease the congestion at the centre region by increasing the minimum circumambulate radius.

References

1. Song, W., Xu, X., Wang, B.H., Ni, S.: Simulation of evacuation processes using a multigrid model for pedestrian dynamics. Physica A 363, 492–500 (2006)
2. Jiang, R., Wu, Q.S.: The moving behavior of a large object in the crowds in a narrow channel. Physica A 364, 457–463 (2006)
3. Weng, W.G., Chen, T., Yuan, H.Y., Fan, W.C.: Cellular automaton simulation of pedestrian counter flow with different walk velocities. Phys. Rev. E 74, 036102 (2006)
4. Helbing, D., Farkas, I., Vicsek, T.: Simulating dynamical features of escape panic. Nature 407, 487 (2000)
5. Helbing, D., Molnar, P.: Social force model for pedestrian dynamics. Phys. Rev. E 51, 4282 (1995)
6. Sarmady, S., Haron, F., Talib, A.Z.H.: A cellular automata model for circular movements of pedestrians during Tawaf. Simulation Modelling Practice and Theory 19, 969–985 (2011)

7. Sarmady, S., Haron, F., Talib, A.Z.H.: Multi-Agent Simulation of Circular Pedestrian Movements Using Cellular Automata. In: Second Asia International Conference on Modelling & Simulation, AICMS 2008, pp. 654–659 (2008)
8. Burstedde, C., Klauck, K., Schadschneider, A., Zittartz, J.: Simulation of pedestrian dynamics using a two dimensional cellular automaton. Physica A 295, 507 (2001)
9. Kirchner, A., Schadschneider, A.: Simulation of evacuation processes using a bionics-inspired cellular automaton model for pedestrian dynamics. Physica A 312, 260 (2002)
10. Kirchner, A., Klupfel, H., Nishinari, K., Schadschneider, A., Schreckenberg, M.: Simulation of competitive egress behavior: comparison with aircraft evacuation data. Physica A 324, 689 (2003)
11. Yanagisawa, D., Nishinari, K.: Mean-field theory for pedestrian outflow through an exit. Physical Review E 76, 061117 (2007)

CA Crowd Modeling for a Retirement House Evacuation with Guidance

Eleftherios Spartalis, Ioakeim G. Georgoudas[*], and Georgios Ch. Sirakoulis

Democritus University of Thrace, Department of Electrical & Computer Engineering,
Laboratory of Electronics, GR-67100 Xanthi, Greece
{esparta,igeorg,gsirak}@ee.duth.gr

Abstract. This paper studies the impact of guidance on evacuation processes. A Cellular Automata (CA) based model has been, therefore, elaborated in order to introduce group categorization and guidance attributes. The crowd is categorized according to motional skills and a special group is assigned leadership features. The presented scenario includes the evacuation of a retirement house with the help of the nursing staff. Simulation results prove the significance of proper guidance. The latter optimizes the response of the model by activating alternative routes that decrease congestion levels in front of exits.

Keywords: Cellular automata, Crowd movement, Distribution, Guidance.

1 Introduction

Massive shifting of people constitutes a phenomenon of great scientific interest, especially in cases of emergent evacuation. The outer scope of such studies is to ensure safe evacuation under various circumstances. Different methodologies have been developed in order to simulate crowd behavior. Brogan and Hodgins have used systems of particles and potentials to describe the motion of special groups of people [1], whereas Braun et al. extended the social force model by introducing the notion of individualism [2]. Anticipation models utilize Markov chains in order to describe the way that people move from one node of the network to the other one [3]. Finally, gas models describe crowd flow and density changes with time, in respect to principles of liquid or gas dynamics, making use of partial derivatives' equations [4]. Among other microscopic and macroscopic models, like for example social force models and agent based models [5], Cellular Automata (CA) models can be considered as one of the most pronounced and suitable ones for modeling crowd dynamics [6-9]. In particular, there are CA models where each cell is assigned a specific weight, which is related to human psychology and behavior, location and width of exits, position of the obstacles etc. All cells comprise the ground field. There are two kinds of such fields; static and dynamic. Static fields do not evolve with time and they are not modified due to the presence of individuals. Nishinari et al. [10] have introduced methods of determining

---

[*] Corresponding author.

J. Wąs, G.C. Sirakoulis, and S. Bandini (Eds.): ACRI 2014, LNCS 8751, pp. 481–491, 2014.

the weight of a cell. An Euclidean system of measurement is suitable for rooms without obstacles, whereas Manhattan and Dijkstra measurements are used when obstacles exist. Dijkstra algorithm defines the shortest route and individuals' movements are represented more realistic. Varas et al [11] have introduced a system of measurement that responds in accordance to the Dijkstra algorithm, presenting additionally better time performance. Dynamic fields vary with time and presence of people. In contrast to static fields, human psychology and behavior as well as the spatial distribution of individuals change the weight of a cell during a time step. Furthermore, the movement of pedestrians is affected by the weight of the cells as well as the rules of interaction among them.

In the presented work, pedestrian dynamics are simulated with the use of CA, which successfully combines microscopic as well as macroscopic attributes. Most of the proposed realizations assume that individuals are uniformly distributed and their formation is only commented around exits. In the proposed model, the spatial distribution of the crowd dominantly affects the response of the model by changing the weight of the cells during each time step. The crowd consists of independent particles and its behavior is technically configured, according to the response of each particle to the transition rule of the CA.

Furthermore, the proposed model has been efficiently applied to simulate the evacuation of a retirement house by older people aided by the nursing staff. To do so, there has been also developed a graphical interface in order various scenarios of crowd movement to be simulated and prominent features of crowd dynamics to be investigated. The user is enabled to define distinct characteristics of the venue, incorporating both spatial and crowd forming features. Particularly, there are options regarding the population, the behavior of the crowd, the speed and the existence of different types of individuals (such as middle-aged, nursing staff and older people). Multi-parameterization enhances the perspectives of an efficient study of crowd behavior in respect to the attributes of the venue. Collective phenomena are prominent to the simulated crowd behavior. A static model has also been applied and its response has been utilized as a state of reference for all simulation measurements. The parameterization of the model results in interesting findings associated with the role of the guiding personnel. Moreover, the consequences of the existence of obstacles and the distribution of the crowd in an evacuation process are considered aiming at minimizing related injuries and casualties. It is drawn that distribution varying values of the potential field optimize the response of the model by activating alternative routes and thus alleviating congestion. Simultaneously, this study aims at deriving information that could be applied to the design of frequent crowded sites and at assessing the time that is demanded in order a venue to be abandoned safely.

2   Model Description

The proposed model is a heterogeneous CA model that includes individuals with different walking speeds. Literature describes discrete models allowing pedestrians to move more than a single cell per time step [12-13]. The modelling of different speed profiles is done by increasing individuals' movement capabilities rather than by modifying the current time scale [13]. The underlying driving mechanism stems from a dynamic potential field that principally directs crowd movement according to the minimum distance from the exits. Each cell is assigned a particular "weight" that is a registered potential value, which represents the distance from the closer exit. In static models, these values remain constant. Furthermore, diagonal directions are permitted. The adopted Moore neighbourhood allows diagonal motion in expense of a $\sqrt{2}$ spatial burden. Moreover, grouping and guidance of moving particles is enabled by introducing the follow-the-leader effect within the motion driving mechanism [14]. Thus, the model further extends the applicability of the one proposed by Varas et al. [11] aiming at minimizing the calculating cost and outline the different characteristics of the crowd during evacuation with maximum accuracy.

More particularly, the model is defined as follows:

•   Space is divided into an orthogonal grid and the exit is assigned value 0.
•   All neighbour cells are assigned a value according to the following rules:
1) provided that the corresponding cell is assigned value N, then all horizontal and vertical neighbours are assigned value $N+1$, whereas diagonal neighbours are assigned value $N+3/2$. This is an attempt to compromise the fact that the distance between two diagonal neighbours is greater than the distance between two horizontal (vertical) ones.
2) Each cell is assigned the minimum from all the possible values.

•   Then all cells that are adjacent to the close neighbourhood of the corresponding cell are elaborated.
•   The process takes place in parallel for each different cell.
•   Walls are also taken into consideration and cells adjacent to them are assigned very high values. Thus, pedestrians will never try to occupy these cells.
•   Each individual attempts to occupy the cell of its closest neighbourhood that is assigned the minimum value.
•   In case that more than one individuals target the same cell, then the choice takes place randomly. Each individual shares the same probability to occupy the target cell.
•   Each individual is assigned a small probability to remain to its present position, even if its next movement is realisable.

The weight of each cell depends on the location of the cell, the exits as well as the obstacles. Provided that these parameters are stable then the corresponding field does not vary with time and it is characterised as static. Nevertheless, in the case that the unique criterion of evacuation mechanism is the distance from the exits, then it is possible congestion to arise in front of one exit, whereas there are others, alternative ones around wider and not congested. A number of individuals could, therefore, abandon the congested exit, and start moving towards another exit. In order to approach this kind of crowd behavior, it is incorporated a dynamic approach. Each individual tries to move towards the neighboring cell with the smaller potential field. However, the values of the field at each cell are updated during every time step, according to the distance from the exit, the width of each exit, as well as the density of the crowd. The introduction of time-varying parameters within the generation of the virtual potential fields results in a remarkable decrease of the evacuation time as well as to a more realistic simulation process.

Thus, the model incorporates dynamic features, by varying its response according to the allocation of the crowd members during each time step. The following two parameters have been assumed, in order to calculate the weight $W_x^A(t)$ of cell x in regard to an exit A, during time step t:

$W_{x,static}^A$: the distance from exit A is defined according to the static system of measurement that is applied.

$T_x^A(t)$: the number of individuals that exist near exit A during time step t

Hence:

$$W_x^A(t) = W_{x,static}^A + \alpha T_x^A(t): \tag{1}$$

where

$$T_x^A(t) \frac{|T_x^A(t)| + \frac{1}{2}|E_x^A(t)|}{d_A} \tag{2}$$

$V(t) = \{y|y \text{ occupied cell during time step } t\}$

$$P_x^A(t) = \{y|W_{y,static}^A < W_{x,static}^A\} \text{ and } y \epsilon V_i \tag{3}$$

$$E_x^A(t) = \{y|W_{y,static}^A = W_{x,static}^A \text{ and } y \epsilon V_i\} \tag{4}$$

and d_a the width of exit A. $|P_x^A(t)|$ and $|E_x^A(t)|$ indicate the number of individuals $P_x^A(t)$ and $E_x^A(t)$ respectively. Moreover, the values of matrix $W_{x,static}^A$ can be derived from a system of measurement, such as Euclidean, Manhattan, Dijkstra. Constant α depends on the individuals and the conditions of the surroundings. It is called crowd avoiding coefficient. The greater its value the more impact it has on parameter $T_x^A(t)$ (impact of distribution), thus indicating less interest to crowded exits. For $\alpha=0$, $W_x^A(t) = W_{x,static}^A$, hence the dynamic model is trivialized to the corresponding static one. Finally, the weight of cell x at time step t appears at $W_x(t)$ and it is calculated according to the following formula:

$$W_x(t) = min\{W_x^A(t) \mid A \text{ exit}\}. \tag{5}$$

To avoid conflicts, in the case that more than one individuals try to approach the same cell then all candidate individuals are randomly assigned a probability value. The one with the greater probability is chosen

The parameters that determine the morphology of the field, such as its dimensions, the number, location and width of the exits, the number and location of the obstacles, the positioning of the crowd and its categorization into groups that behave differently, is adjustable by the user.

3   Pedestrian Evacuation without Guidance

Various scenarios of pedestrian evacuation are examined. The ground truth for all measurements is realized by a static field formation, which simulates the evacuation of a group of pedestrians without any guidance, where all individuals move with the same speed and all members try to move to the neighboring cell that is closer to the exits. In the following, it is examined how factors that do not vary with time affect the evacuation time, as for instance, the presence of groups of people with different velocities, the width of the exits, as well as the location of the obstacles [15]. Finally, an example that incorporates dynamic features is provided.

According to the first scenario, each pedestrian moves without guidance towards the closest exit, meaning that the only criterion of movement is distance. Provided that the density of the crowd within the room is low, the model responds adequately. The room has a dimension of 50×50 cells and there are three exits with the same width. The spread of the pedestrians in the field is even, which means that there is approximately the same number of people near each exit. The total population amounts to 77 individuals. Each pedestrian chooses to move towards the closest exit and this decision does not change. The duration of the evacuation from the room is 34 time steps. Then the following question arises: How does the evacuation time change with respect to the presence of obstacles in front of each of the exits? In such a case, the number of time steps increase up to 44 time steps.

Then, a more complex version of evacuation with an increased density of pedestrians is analyzed. The room includes now three exits of different width, various obstacles and two rooms with a common exit. Provided that the crowd consists of 175 individuals, the evacuation time equals to 73 time steps. Moreover, in a public place, it is possible each individual to have different speed. For example, an adult moves faster than an old man. Then evacuation time rationally increases. The proposed model can verify this assumption. In case that half of the 175 individuals are moving with a speed of a cell per time step and the rest of them with a speed of a cell per two time steps, then 83 time steps are required for the evacuation of the floor field, that is 10 additional time steps. This difference increases as the density of the crowd increases. A second example for the same venue examines the evacuation times with the presence of about 370 individuals. The required time is now 149 time steps, when the crowd moves with two different speed groups, that is 50 more time steps.

In the view of the foregoing, factors that affect evacuation time are further elaborated in the simulation process and the corresponding results are presented. The first parameter that is examined is the width of each exit. More particularly, in the scenery of previous example, the first exit has the width of a cell, the second of two cells and finally the third of three cells. With presence of two groups moving with different speeds and a total population of 370 individuals, widening the exits up to 3 cells the expected decrease in the evacuation time equals to 88 steps (Fig. 1(a)). This corresponds to a decrease of almost 40%.

The introduction of time-varying parameters within the generation of the virtual potential fields results in a remarkable decrease of the evacuation time as well as to a more realistic simulation process. Hence, the distribution of the crowd in the room is taken into consideration. An individual is considered as an obstacle for all the others that try to reach the same exit. Such an obstacle is dynamically formed, since people tend to huddle as they approach the exit. Under such conditions, it is may be preferable for a pedestrian to move to another exit that is further but requires less time to get out of the room, since the additional time needed to overcome the crowd-formed obstacles is long.

Two different groups of a total 370 individuals evacuated the area in 115 time steps, whereas the adoption of the static field resulted in an evacuation within 194 time steps. In the diagram of Fig.1(b), it can be noticed that the blue line that corresponds to the dynamic simulation process, has almost the same leaning along its entire route, whereas the leaning of the red line in the static model changes and becomes less abrupt at about 70 time steps. This happens because people in the static model choose a single exit and their choice does not change during the whole simulation. Obviously, in the dynamic model the crowd is continuously re-distributed to the exits depending on the current conditions. Thereby, the value which the pedestrians abandon the field with, remains constant, thus accomplishing more realistic simulation and optimized evacuation time.

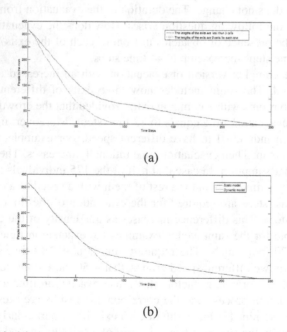

(a)

(b)

Fig. 1. (a) Evacuation times for exits with different width in each case. (b) Evacuation times for the floor field in Fig. 3 both for the static (red color) and the dynamic model (blue color).

4   Pedestrian Evacuation with Guidance

In the following another crucial factor that decisively affects evacuation process is taken into consideration. According to the simulation scenery, groups of people with different speeds are defined, each one representing a different skilled category. One such group takes over guidance responsibilities, thus realizing the tendency of weak people to follow others in emergent circumstances. The latter behavioral symptom derives from psychological reasons. The psychology of the crowd plays a significant role in the selection of an exit. Especially, in cases of emergency and for people that belong to special categories, e.g. elderly, such a selection is a tough decision. Under such circumstances, the presence of trained personnel may be proven lifesaving. They must be in a position to lead the crowd in case of an emergency fast and secure out of the building. The examples that are studied in the following scenarios, refer to a retirement home, where a small number of trained individuals (nurses) leads a numerous crowd (elderly) towards the exits, in order to achieve the fastest possible evacuation time. For this purpose, the dynamic simulation model has been further elaborated.

According to the adopted scenario, the dimension of a retirement home equals to 50x75 cells. The side of each cell corresponds to 40cm [16]. So, the entire area of the floor field is $(50 \times 0.4) \times (75 \times 0.4) = 600m^2$. There are three exits with different widths (the two exits occupy two cells, while the third one occupies three cells) and different rooms that may have a common exit. There are three groups of people. Yellow cells indicate the location of the nurses. Brown and red colors represent two groups of elderly people, each one moving with a different speed. The speed of an adult who is running is approximately 8km/h or 2.2m/s. Nurses are assumed to move with this speed. Elderly move approximately with half of this speed. The first group that consists of the red-colored pedestrians is moving with a speed of 4km/h or 1.1m/s and the second, brown-colored group moves with a speed of 5.3km/h or 1.4m/s.

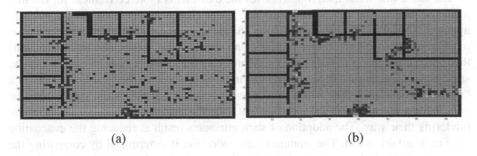

(a)   (b)

Fig. 2. (a) Dynamic simulation model for the evacuation of a retirement home. The nurses (yellow color) lead the elderly (brown and red color) to the exits. (b) A snapshot of the simulation for the same example in a different temporal moment.

According to the adopted scenario (Fig. 2), nurses try to lead the elderly to the exits. In order to achieve their goal, they have to decide which exit is more convenient for this purpose. Each one of the elderly decides to follow the nurse that is closer to him/her. The distances between elderly and nurses vary according to their location at each moment, as depicted in the colored representation of the corresponding potential field (Fig. 3). This means that, if at the beginning an elderly was following nurse A and after t time steps a nurse B is closer, she/he can stop following nurse A and start heading towards nurse B. Moreover, if an elderly is in the first place close to one of the exits, she/he can move towards to that exit without any guidance. As a result, each nurse acts as a leader of a group of elderly, which she/he must lead to an exit. The nurse chooses the exit on the basis of the same criteria that apply to the previously described dynamic model that is according to the distance from the exit, the density of the on-going crowd around the exit and the width of the exits.

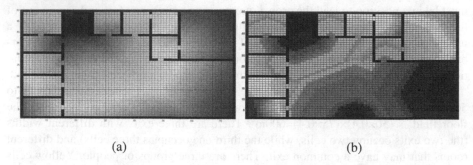

(a)   (b)

Fig. 3. (a) Colored representation of the potential values of cells for a specific nurse. The elderly in the blue area will follow the nurse. (b) Potential values of each cell for the snapshot of Fig.2 (b). The colored areas near the dark blue imply that a pedestrian needs a little time to reach the exit, while for the colored areas near red this time is considerably longer. Potential values of cells change in every time step.

The nurse that leads the group chooses the exit that is more convenient for the majority of people that follow her/him. The route choice of the nurse is dynamically updated, Thus, provided that conditions change during simulation and another exit is more convenient for the majority of the members of the group then the nurse leads this part of the group to the new exit. Moreover, if a nurse is near an exit and at the same time a couple of old people are still moving towards it, then she/he will get in a "waiting state". So, she/he will wait in a predetermined position in the area around the exit, waiting all elderly to abandon the area, simultaneously ensuring that she/he is not hindering their way. The adoption of such attributes result at reducing the evacuation time to a certain extent. The amount of the reduction is determined by comparing the above results with the corresponding ones that are produced by the static model without guidance (Fig. 4(a)). The initial population is in both cases is 315 individuals.

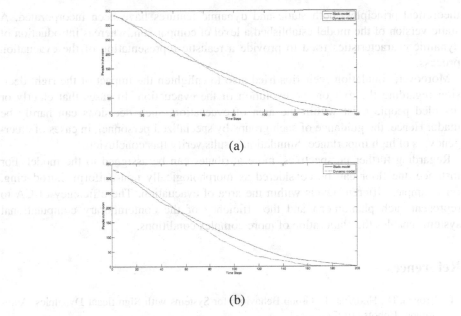

(a)

(b)

Fig. 4. (a) The number of the individuals in relation to the time for the static (blue) and dynamic (red) model. (b) Evacuation times from the floor field of Fig. (a) having moving obstacles and different width exits for the static and the dynamic model, respectively.

Static model responds in 28 seconds (159 time steps), whereas the dynamic one responds in 26 seconds (143 time steps). Furthermore, a more complex scenario is also examined. Within the area exist obstacles and the width of an exit is reduced to one cell. This toughens the decision for the choice of the appropriate exit in comparison to the previous example. Indeed, the static model requires 33 seconds (182 time steps), whereas the corresponding dynamic model responds in 28 seconds (157 time steps). Corresponding diagrams are depicted in Fig. 4(b). In case that the width of the other exit decreases, then the response gap between the two models, static and dynamic, further broadens. According to the results, the evacuation time for the static model is 58 seconds (278 time steps), whereas for the dynamic model, only 29 seconds (162 time steps). This is explained by the fact that the lower exit is easier accessible due to its position. Taking into account the lack of guidance, a greater number of pedestrians is moving towards this exit. As a consequence, the potential values of individuals that abandon the area is now slowing down to the half. Correspondingly, the congestion caused is greater and the evacuation time increases extensively.

5   Conclusions and Future Work

The scope of this work is to indicate the efficient optimization of the response of a CA based model that simulates crowd behavior, when dynamic parameterization features are incorporated as well as group guidance is applied. To this direction, the evacuation of a retirement house has been thoroughly studied. Regarding the theoretical principles, both static and dynamic features have been incorporated. A static version of the model established a level of comparison, whereas introduction of dynamic characteristics tried to provide a realistic representation of the evacuation process.

Moreover, simulation scenarios tried also to enlighten the impact of the right decision regarding the exit on the evolution of the evacuation. In cases that elderly or disabled people exist within the area of evacuation, such decisions can hardly be made. Hence, the guidance of such groups by specialized personnel, in cases of emergency, is of high importance. Simulation results verify this conclusion.

Regarding further perspectives, more attributes can be assigned to the model. For instance, the floor can be considered as morphologically non-uniform, introducing, for example, different levels within the area of evacuation. The efficiency of CA to represent such phenomena and the efficiency of the contemporary computational systems enables the elaboration of more complex conditions.

References

1. Brogan, D., Hodgins, J.: Group Behaviors for Systems with Significant Dynamics. Autonomous Robots (1997)
2. Braun, A., Musse, S.R., de Oliveira, L.P.L., Bodmann, B.E.J.: Modeling Individual Behaviors in Crowd Simulation. In: Proc. Computer Animation and Social Agents (CASA). IEEE Computer Society, Washington, DC (2003)
3. Lovas, G.C.: Modeling and Simulation of Pedestrian Traffic Flow. Transportation Research (1994)
4. Henderson, L.F.: The Statistics of Crowd Fluids. Nature (1971)
5. Helbing, D., Farkas, I., Vicsek, T.: Simulating Dynamical Features of Escape Panic. Nature (2000)
6. Bandini, S., Manzoni, S., Umeo, H., Vizzari, G. (eds.): ACRI 2010. LNCS, vol. 6350. Springer, Heidelberg (2010)
7. Sirakoulis, G.C., Bandini, S. (eds.): ACRI 2012. LNCS, vol. 7495. Springer, Heidelberg (2012)
8. Wąs, J., Lubaś, R., Myśliwiec, W.: Proxemics in discrete simulation of evacuation. In: Sirakoulis, G.C., Bandini, S. (eds.) ACRI 2012. LNCS, vol. 7495, pp. 768–775. Springer, Heidelberg (2012)
9. Bandini, S., Manzoni, S., Mauri, G., Redaelli, S.: Emergent pattern interpretation in vegetable population dynamics. J. Cellular Automata 2(2), 103–110 (2007)
10. Nishinari, K., Kirchner, A., Namazi, A., Schadschneider, A.: Extended floor field CA model for evacuation dynamics. IEICE Trans. Inf. & Syst. E87-D, 726–732 (2004)
11. Varas, A., Cornejo, M.D., Mainemer, D., Toledo, B., Rogan, J., Muñoz, V., Valdivia, J.A.: Cellular automaton model for evacuation process with obstacles. Physica A 382(2), 631–642 (2007)
12. Kirchner, A., Klupfel, H., Nishinari, K., Schadschneider, A., Schreckenberg, M.: Discretization effects and the influence of walking speed in cellular automata models for pedestrian dynamics. Journal of Statistical Mechanics: Theory and Experiment (10), P10011 (2004)

13. Bandini, S., Crociani, L., Vizzari, G.: Heterogeneous Speed Profiles in Discrete Models for Pedestrian Simulation. In: 93rd Transportation Research Board Annual Meeting, Committee number AHB45 - TRB Committee on Traffic Flow Theory and Characteristics, Washington (January 2014)
14. Vihas, C., Georgoudas, I.G., Sirakoulis, G.C.: Cellular Automata Incorporating Fol-low-the-Leader Principles to Model Crowd Dynamics. J. Cellular Automata 8(5-6), 333–346 (2013)
15. Yanagisawa, D., Tanaka, Y., Jiang, P., Tomoeda, A., Ohtsuka, K., Suma, Y., Nishinari, K.: Theoretical and Experimental Study on Excluded Volume Effect in Pedestrian Queue. In: SICE Annual Conference 2010, August 18-21, pp. 559–562. IEEE Xplore (2010)
16. Burstedde, C., Klauck, K., Schadschneider, A., Zittartz, J.: Simulation of pedestrian dynamics using a twodimensional cellular automaton. Phys. A 295(3-4), 507–525 (2001)

Multiscale Simulation of Pedestrians for Faster Than Real Time Modeling in Large Events

Bernhard Steffen and Mohcine Chraibi

Jülich Supercomputing Centre – Forschungszentrum Jülich GmbH
52425 Jülich, Germany
{b.steffen,m.chraibi}@fz-juelich.de
http://www.fz-juelich.de/ias/jsc/cst

Abstract. The Hermes project [1] demonstrated the usefulness of on site faster than real time simulations of probable evacuation scenarios for security personnel. However, the hardware needed was prohibitively expensive [2]. The present paper shows that a multiscale approach can perform the simulation in a fraction of time without loss of useful information. The main problem is the correct passing of agents from a coarse scale model to a fine scale model, here from a CA model to a force based model. This will be achieved by inserting agents into the force based model at positions and speeds optimized for smooth walking either by a priori information or using Voronoi cells. Connecting a Queue model to a continuous model has already been done successfully [3].

We also show that a slightly modified CA method can address the problem, too, at even less computational cost, with some possible loss of accuracy.

Keywords: Cellular automata, modeling, pedestrian dynamics.

1 Introduction

The last century has seen a tremendous growth of the worlds population, together with an increasing concentration of the population in big cities. Therefore, the safe and effective organization of pedestrian facilities has gained in importance, as the crowds gathering in one place (for ceremonies, entertainment, work or education) get more frequent and larger. Basic rules for planning of pedestrian facilities were already known to Greeks and Romans, as the quality of the egress routes e.g. at the theater in Ephesus or the Coliseum in Rome proves. Modern systematic planning began in the late 19th century and was motivated by some catastrophic fires in theaters and ballrooms and aimed exclusively at safe emergency egress [4–6]. The planning tools were mostly defining required width of exits, stairs, and corridors for buildings holding a number of persons. For the planning of buildings accommodating very many people or of mass events, the modeling of the egress has been standard since about 1990.

This can be (and is) done on different scales. The coarsest scale uses a tree or network of pathways that take time, but have no active capacity restriction, and

J. Wąs, G.C. Sirakoulis, and S. Bandini (Eds.): ACRI 2014, LNCS 8751, pp. 492–500, 2014.

nodes (doors, junction of floors etc), that do have active capacity restrictions [7]. An intermediate scale is handled by a cellular automata (CA) model where space and time are discrete and agents are moving from one space element to another according to some transition rules [8–10]. The finest scale uses models in continuous space and time where agents are moved usually according to Newton's laws, by forces generated mostly internally as a reaction to the desired momentary destination and the local environment. Examples of this Ansatz are [11, 12].

The Hermes project demonstrated that on the site faster than real time simulations of probable crowd movement are feasible and useful for crowd management. However, the requirements in specific hardware were higher than facilities are willing to pay by a large margin. One problem was the price of monitoring of the present situation, another one the required graphic hardware, and the third one, which we will address here, is the hardware requirements of the simulations. The users formulated a goal of 2 min for the simulation time, such that they would have enough time to view the results and still be able to react precociously to potential oncoming problems.

In this paper we show how the hardware requirements of the simulation can be drastically reduced by some novel hybrid approach without loosing useful information. With this, and progress in the fields of graphic display and crowd monitoring, the hardware cost of an on site simulation can be reduced to an amount that may be in reach for large-scale facilities.

2   Which Scale for Which Purpose

All the details we give are taken from the Esprit Arena in Düsseldorf, Germany. However, stadiums of similar size all over the world are constructed along the same lines. The dimensions and numbers of seating areas, stairs, corridors and doors differ, but this changes just details of the modeling. We consider only the clearing of a stadium. The filling can be treated similarly. The positions of persons within the rows need not be known for a queue model.

There are basically five different areas in the stadium, which we consider in order of passage. See Fig.1.

The persons start in the seating area. Here are rows of about 20 seats with a narrow pass-way leading to stairs, usually on both sides, occasionally only to one side, but then the row is only short. Overtaking is almost not possible. It is certainly enough to model each row as a queue emptying into the stairs model.

The next area is the stairs leading up or down within the grandstand. These are wide enough for two persons aside. They collect ≈ 15 persons per row from a number of rows and bring them to the level of the exit. On the stairs, the movement is restricted in direction and step length, so the dynamics in this region is better described by a CA. It may even be sufficient for some purposes to model the stairs with the adjacent rows as just one queue, but then all information about the shape of the plume of waiting persons is lost.

The stairs end at a small and curved landing connecting three stairs with the passage to the corridor in the back of the grandstand starts.

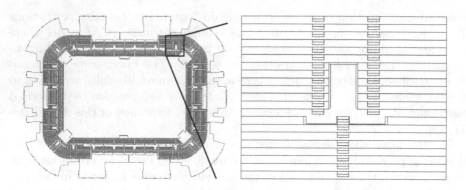

Fig. 1. Plan of the arena (left), Abstraction of a block around a vomitory(right)

For this landing and the passage, standard CA methods give no satisfactory results, since the geometry hardly fits in a predefined grid.

We simulate the dynamics in these areas with the generalized centrifugal force model (GCF) [12], which is a space continuous model that was used in the final test of the Hermes project.

In an emergency clearing, it can be expected that everybody takes the fastest way out, which means traversing the corridor on a short route and choosing one of the doors approximately opposite to the exit from the grandstand for the final egress. In this mode, the corridor offers ample space and can be modeled simply as a delay line. In front of the doors, plumes of persons trying to get out may accumulate, which can be modeled by CA. From observation and and modeling [2] in the Hermes project we know that these plumes do not fill the corridor, i.e. there is always some space behind where persons can move more or less freely. This is valid for both corridors. For the stairs from the second floor to the ground, the CA model as described below is sufficient [10].

All together, the largest part of the area can be modeled by CA or even network models, and only a small part, holding maybe 5% of the people in the stadium, may require a more elaborate and costly model, under the assumption that the coupling of the models does not introduce serious problems. Coupling of models has rarely been investigated before [3]. In this paper the requirements and details of a CA-continuous transition are given. In the Hermes project, such a coupling was not available, and the simulation used exclusively the GCF model throughout. From this we estimate that with a queue model for about half the persons in the stadium, CA models for almost all the others, and GCF for less than 10%, we can reduce the hardware requirements to a small fraction. The additional workload resulting from the transfer of agents between the models is negligible.

2.1 A Modified CA Model for the Exits from the Grandstand to the Outer Stairs

The principles of CA for simulating pedestrians are explained in detail in the literature, e.g. [8, 9]. We give a short sketch following [9]. The floor geometry is discretised into tiles, usually of 0.4 m². An initial distribution of agents on the tiles is defined. In every time step each agent can move to another tile (or stay were it is) according to a probability depending on:

- The availability of free space (only one person per tile at any time).
- A floor field describing the intended directions.
- Personal properties, describing e.g. handicaps, motivation.

With a time step of 0.3 s this gives a reasonable speed of free movement of about 1.3 m/s. The static floor field S is usually derived from the gradient of the distance to the destination (exit) in some metric, the Manhattan metric being the most common one because it is extremely simple to implement even in complex geometries.

Geometries not fitting the grid can be handled by locally changing the movement probabilties. The distance based floor field makes the persons cut corners, which introduces an artificial bottleneck at each bend, as only the innermost lane is effectively utilized. Space continuous models with simple shortest path routing experience similar problems. By introducing a floor field that keeps the distance to the inner wall of a bend, we can overcome this problem and utilize the full width of the bend [10]. See Fig. 2.

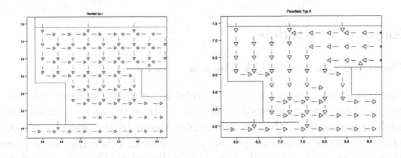

Fig. 2. Standard floor field (left) and improved floor field (right) of the critical section on the landing

Fig. 3 shows the two versions of the flow field in the critical area and the utilization of the tiles, that is the number of persons passing through this tile during a clearing of the Grandstand.

Unfortunately at the moment the improved floor field has to be generated manually. The decision where an inner wall has to be considered is obvious in the present problem, but in general it may not be so. Some problems of CA remain – the stairs are ≈ 1 m wide, so two cells are not enough to map the geometry and three cells are too much, and in reality a sharp turn slows people down, in CA it does not. Furthermore, the passage from stairs to the final exit has some angle slightly different from 90°. Therefore, the approach will need calibration to be accurate. Other approaches to improve the treatment of bends with CA [9, 15] by dynamic floor field and inertia, have been proposed.

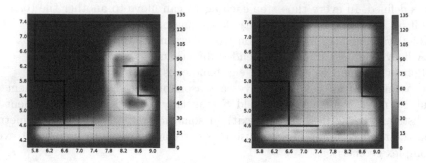

Fig. 3. Utilisation of cells (persons passing through during evacuation) with standard floor field (left) and with improved Floor field(right)

For the stairs leading down from the second floor, which are ≈ 2.4 m wide with a 180° turn at every landing, this CA model is sufficient to realistically describe the dynamics in this kind of geometry.

3 Coupling of Models

3.1 Coupling Queues to CA Models

The transition from a queue to a CA model is quite straightforward. We give every row in the geometry one cell to the side of the stairs at the proper position. After each update-step, if this agent has moved out to the stairs, the next one will be taken from the queue and placed in the system. When the queue is empty, the cell will be treated as a wall. The reverse direction is not used in our case, but the principle is similar. A small number of cells serves as entrance to the queue. If the queue is not filled up yet, agents from these cells are just taken out of the CA model after the update step. Otherwise they stay, so that a full queue blocks the exiting from the CA model.

For this method to work properly, it is necessary to place the transfer cells not directly into a door or other bottleneck, but a few steps behind in an area where capacity is more than usually needed [13].

3.2 Coupling a CA Model to a Continuous Model

A Simple Coupling for Use in Corridors. The transfer area has to be in a region where the pedestrian stream is not sensitive to variation of conditions, notably well before any active bottleneck. Otherwise, the nonlinear effects of both models (and reality) may give unwanted behavior of the models. It is also important that any agent placed in the force model is equipped with a position and speed that is locally adapted to the other agents, so that all forces are in the normal range for the situation in the transfer zone.

If agents are placed at random, there may be spurious jams, just like a car on a freeway making some sudden maneuver will cause a jam even with moderate traffic density. With the placement of agents entering the GCF model from the CA model we try to mimic an oncoming stream of persons in the transition region as well as we can.

For the present situation, where the transfer is at the end of the stairs in a corridor, we can use a simple method. For this, every agent has to carry an identification. We define a transit zone two cells long and as wide as the stairs in the CA model. Any agent that has made it there is eligible for transfer to the GCF model and flagged accordingly. The transfer process is started after completion of each CA update and organized as follows:

First, all agents in the CA model flagged for transfer are tested, whether the corresponding person in the GCF model has left the transfer zone. In this case, the person is removed from the CA process. Then we calculate a few factors that influence the insertion into the GCF model. One is the CA density in the transfer zone. If it is very high, ρ is reduced to a value where increasing density increases flow. Using the fundamental diagram [14] the speed v and the distance d for 1D walking are calculated from ρ.

For the insertion, we use the fact that in narrow corridors walkers have a tendency to form lanes at least 0.3 m wide. Persons in adjacent lines usually walk with at least half a step distance in forward direction. Accordingly, persons are inserted. See Fig. 4

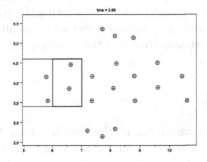

Fig. 4. Positions in front of the central stairs. The transfer zone is indicated. the leftmost two agents have been placed in the last step. Three agents each on top and bottom come from the other stairs.

After calculating the position of the lanes in the corridor, we find for every lane the most backward position of a person in the GCF model. We then place the agents that have entered the transfer zone in the last time step of the CA model successively in the lane where there is the most headway, at a position in walking direction at least d behind the agent in front, $d/3$ behind the agents in neighboring lanes, and 5 cm behind the trailing agent. The last requirement is just to break possible symmetries in the positions. The agents start with speed v. The test for the success of this arrangement is that speed and relative position of persons in the GCF model will not change rapidly after insertion. As people walk forward, the density usually increases towards the bottleneck.

A General Approach Using a Voronoi Tessellation. In a more complex geometry, there is no formation of lanes and therefore no a priori given positions. Here we use a Voronoi tessellation of the end of the GCF model. This approach has been tried successfully for coupling a network model to a force model [3]. The corners of the Voronoi cells within the cluster of GCF walkers and the edges of those cells extending far behind into the area not modeled with GCF can be suitable positions for insertion.

The corner points can be used only if the distance to the neighboring agents is sufficient. Placing a agent there will increase the local density and change all forces in the neighborhood, it should be done only if there is ample space. The edges behind run far out, possibly to infinity. The position on the edge we choose is $d/2$ from the agents defining the adjacent Voronoi cells.

As the computation of a Voronoi tessellation is costly, the area of tessellation should be cropped in front as much as possible.

3.3   Coupling a Force Model to a CA Model

Care has to be taken that the capacity of the cross section in the CA model exceeds the actual flux of the GCF model, so that people can be transferred freely as soon as they have crossed some line starting the transfer zone. To avoid artifacts in the GCF model, we consider a virtual room annexed to the original geometry such that pedestrians that exit the building still have influence on the pedestrians behind them.

4   Results

With this approach, we have simulated the clearing of one block of the stadium, holding about 600 seats, into the circumferential corridor. The complete clearing in combined queue and CA mode takes 0.031 s on a quadcore i5 compiled with gfortran in release mode, but without code optimization.

Fig. 5 left shows a screenshot of a hybrid-simulation. Green points are agents coming from the queue waiting to be inserted in the CA system. Blue points are CA agents moving in the two stairs towards the three transition areas (filled rectangles with red, blue and green). After reaching a transition area the CA-agents transpose in GCF-agents (red points) and move in space continuously towards the exit of the block.

For the CA model, the flux out of the exit was 15% higher than the result in Hermes with 3 cells stair width and about 20% lower with 2 cells. The full hybrid model had a flux close to the Hermes simulations of the same block. The GCF model needs 30 time steps per time step of CA, and each time step is more

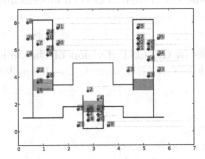
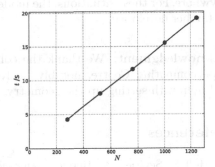

Fig. 5. Left: Screenshot of a simulation showing different types of agents. Right: Execution times with respect to the number of simulated agents.

costly per agent. This explains the total time of 8 s for 522 persons on an i7. Fig. 5 right shows that the computing time grows linearly with the number of agents in the block. This is easy to explain if one considers the fact that the run time is dominated by the GCF calculations, which handles an almost constant number of persons in the area of calculation for most of the clearing time. Only right at the start and at the end the area will not be filled with agents.

The implementation is not yet optimized for speed, there is hope that it can be made considerably faster. As the blocks are geometrically separated, they can be treated sequentially. The CA method for the egress from the corridor is expected to need not more time than the clearing of the blocks because the space involved is smaller. This means that the user requirement of less than 2 min for simulation of an entire stadium is within reach on a high end office computer.

5   Conclusions and Outlook

For events where people come, stay and leave, the simulation is possible on standard office hardware up to quite large events. Because the prices of graphic equipment have declined - a 40" monitor is consumer hardware now − , the hardware costs are dominated by the sensors or cameras for finding the distribution of persons in the event. While these are declining, too, they may still be considerable.

Future work will have to go in two directions. One is to make the modeling user-friendlier. Setting up the geometries for the model and defining the regions of transfer from one to another is still a task for an expert requiring much time and therefore costly. There are usually architectural plans of the facility available, but these do not translate easily into the geometry description needed for modeling. Further, defining the floor field or any other method of choosing the local preferred direction is not an automatic task yet, either.

The second direction is to the treatments of events where people walk around or come and go freely any time, such that bidirectional traffic is present almost anywhere. For these situations, the models and the transfer between models must be further developed.

Acknowledgment. We thank the colleges in the CST division of the Jülich Supercomputing Centre, notably U. Kemloh and G. Lämmel, for discussions and help with setting up the geometry.

References

1. Holl, S., Seyfried, A.: Hermes - An evacuation assistant for mass events. inSiDe 7, 60–61 (2009)
2. Kemloh, U., Steffen, B., Seyfried, A., Chraibi, M.: Parallel Real Time Computation of Large Scale Pedestrian Evacuations. Advances in Engineering Software, 60–61, 98–103 (2013)
3. Lämmel, G., Steffen, B.: A Fast Simulation Approach for Urban Areas. Transportation Research Board 93, 84–98 (2014)
4. Dieckmann, D.: Die Feuersicherheit in Theatern. Jung München (1911)
5. Fruin, J.J.: Pedestrian Planning and Design. Elevator World, New York (1971)
6. Predtetschenski, W.M., Milinski, A.I.: Personenströme in Gebäuden - Berechnungsmethoden für die Projektierung. Verlagsgesellschaft Rudolf Müller, Köln-Braunsfeld (1971)
7. Lämmel, G., Grether, D., Nagel, K.: The Representation and Implementation of Time-Dependent Inundation in Large-Scale Microscopic Evacuation Simulations. Transport. Res. C. 18, 84–98 (2010)
8. Blue, V.J., Adler, J.L.: Cellular Automata Microsimulation of Bi-Directional Pedestrian Flows. J. Transp. Res. B. 1678, 135–141 (2000)
9. Kirchner, A., Schadschneider, A.: Simulation of Evacuation Processes Using a Bionics-Inspired Cellular Automaton Model for Pedestrian Dynamics. Physica A 312, 260–276 (2002)
10. Steffen, B., Seyfried, A.: Modelling of Pedestrian Movement Around 90° and 180° Bends. In: Advanced Research Workshop "Fire Protection and Life Safety in Buildings and Transportation Systems", pp. 243–253 (2009)
11. Molnár, P.: Modellierung und Simulation der Dynamik von Fußgängerströmen. Shaker, Aachen (1996)
12. Chraibi, M., Seyfried, A., Schadschneider, A.: Generalized Centrifugal-Force Model for Pedestrian Dynamics. Phys. Rev. E 82, 046111 (2010)
13. Rogsch, C., Klingsch, W., Seyfried, A., Weigel, H.: Prediction Accuracy of Evacuation Times for High-Rise Buildings and Simple Geometries by Using Different Software-Tools. In: Traffic and Granular Flow, pp. 395–400. Springer (2007)
14. Seyfried, A., Boltes, M., Kähler, J., Klingsch, W., Portz, A., Rupprecht, T., Schadschneider, A., Steffen, B., Winkens, A.: Enhanced Empirical Data for the Fundamental Diagram and the Flow Through Bottlenecks. In: Pedestrian and Evacuation Dynamics, pp. 145–156. Springer, Heidelberg (2010)
15. Schadschneider, A., Eilhardt, C., Nowak, S., Will, R.: Towards a Calibration of the Floor Field Cellular Automaton. In: Pedestrian and Evacuation Dynamics, pp. 557–566. Springer, Heidelberg (2010)

Cellular Automata Pedestrian Movement Model SIgMA.CA: Model Parameters as an Instrument to Regulate Movement Regimes

Ekaterina Kirik[1,2] and Tat'yana Vitova[1]

[1] Institute of Computational Modelling SB RAS,
Krasnoyarsk, Akademgorodok, Russia, 660036
kirik@icm.krasn.ru
[2] Siberian Federal University, Krasnoyarsk, Russia

Abstract. In the paper a connection of model parameters with movement regimes in different geometrical conditions are considered for the cellular automata floor field pedestrian movement model SIgMA.CA. Evacuation time is considered as measure of influence.

Keywords: (specific) flow rate, pedestrian dynamics, cellular automata, transition probabilities, movement strategies.

1 Introduction

This article deals with one Cellular automata (CA) pedestrian dynamics model and follows the papers [4,6,7] that presented investigation of this model – the SIgMA.CA pedestrian movement model. The model is the stochastic discrete floor field CA model and supposes short-term decisions made by the pedestrians [3,5]. A possibility to move according the shortest path and the shortest time strategies are implemented to the model. Previously the influencing of a space geometry on models' dynamics [4], the validation with fundamental diagrams [6] and bottleneck flows were presented [7].

The validation with fundamental diagram under periodic boundary conditions in straight corridor gives increasing of the specific flow rate with increasing density up to $3 - 3, 5 \, [pers/m^2]$; and then it goes down. Such behavior coincide with experimental data [8].

Diffusion of the model flow was checked in the experiment under open boundary conditions for a set of corridors 50 m, 100 m, 150 m in length. It was shown that the model maintains initial density up to $0, 5 - 0, 75 \, [pers/m^2]$ (it agrees with natural data [2]) and then diffusion is realized.

The specific flow rate, [pers/m/sec], versus densities was investigated under periodic boundary conditions for straight corridor and corridor with four 90-degree turns. It was shown that dynamics of the model is very sensitive to the shape of way starting with the lowest densities. Only for $\rho < 0, 75 \, [pers/m^2]$ flows in both pathes approximately coincide. Then for $\rho > 0, 75 \, [pers/m^2]$ presence of turns results in a slowing down of the velocities and flows (approximately in half).

J. Wąs, G.C. Sirakoulis, and S. Bandini (Eds.): ACRI 2014, LNCS 8751, pp. 501–507, 2014.

It was shown that models' specific flow rate, [pers/m/sec], behaves more or less permanent with increasing bottleneck width b that quantitatively agrees with natural data [8].

Here we are aimed to present influence of model parameters on movement regimes (using of the shortest path and/or the shortest time strategies).

In the next section the model is presented. Section 3 contains description of the case study and results obtained. We conclude with a summary.

2   Description of the Model

2.1   Space and Initial Conditions

A space (plane) is known and sampled into cells $40cm \times 40cm$ in size which can either be empty or occupied by one pedestrian (particle) only (index $f_{ij} = \{0,1\}$). Cells may be occupied by walls (index $w_{ij} = \{0,1\}$) and other nonmovable obstacles[1].

The model imports idea of a map (static floor field S) from floor field (FF) CA model [1,9] that provides pedestrians with information about ways to exits. Our field S increases radially from exit cells. It doesn't evolve with time and isn't changed by the presence of the particles.

A target point for each pedestrian is the nearest exit. Each particle can move to one of four its next-neighbor cells or to stay in present cell (the von Neumann neighborhood) at each discrete time step $t \to t+1$; i.e., $v_{max} = 1[step]$.

A direction of the movement of each particle at each time step is random and determined in accordance with the distribution of transition probabilities and transition rules.

2.2   Update Rules and Transition Probability

A scheme typical of the stochastic CA models is used. At the first stage, some preliminary calculations are made. Then, at each time step the transition probabilities are calculated, and the directions are selected. In the case, when there are more than one candidate to occupy a cell, a conflict resolution procedure is applied. Finally, a simultaneous transition of all the particles is made.

In our case, the *preliminary step* includes the calculation of FF S. Each cell $S_{i,j}$ stores the information on the shortest discrete distance to the nearest exit. The probabilities of movement from cell (i,j) to, e.g., up neighbor is[2]

$$p_{i-1,j} = \frac{\tilde{p}_{i-1,j}}{N_{i,j}} = N_{i,j}^{-1} \exp\left[k_S \triangle S_{i-1,j} - k_P F_{i-1,j}(r^*_{i-1,j}) - \right.$$

$$\left. - k_W\left(1 - \frac{r^*_{i-1,j}}{r}\right)\tilde{1}(\triangle S_{i-1,j} - \max \triangle S_{i,j})\right](1 - w_{i-1,j}); \quad (1)$$

---

[1] Here and below under "obstacle" we mean only nonmovable obstacles (walls, furniture). People are never called "obstacle".

[2] Probabilities $p_{i,j+1}, p_{i+1,j}, p_{i,j-1}$ are calculated similarly. $p_{i,j} = 0$: the probability of retaining the current position is not calculated directly. Nevertheless, the decision rules are organized so that such opportunity could be taken.

where
- $N_{i,j} = \tilde{p}_{i-1,j} + \tilde{p}_{i,j+1} + \tilde{p}_{i+1,j} + \tilde{p}_{i,j-1}$;
- $\triangle S_{i-1,j} = S_{i,j} - S_{i-1,j}$, $k_S \geq 0$ is the (model) field S sensitive parameter (the higher k_S, the better directed the movement);
- $\max \triangle S_{i,j} = \max \triangle S_{i-1,j}, \triangle S_{i,j+1}, \triangle S_{i+1,j}, \triangle S_{i,j-1}$;
- $r > 0$ is the visibility radius (model parameter) representing the maximum distance (number of cells) at which the people density and obstacles influence on the probability in the given direction;
- $r^*_{i-1,j}$ is the distance to the nearest obstacle in the given direction ($r^*_{i-1,j} \leq r$);
- $F_{i-1,j}$ is people (dimensionless) density in this direction which lies within $[0,1]$, see [5];
- k_P is the (model) people sensitivity parameter which determines the effect of the people density, the higher parameter k_P, the more pronounced the shortest time strategy;
- $k_W \geq k_S$ is the (model) wall sensitivity parameter which determines the effect of walls and obstacles.

The decisions rules are the following:

1. If $N_{i,j} = 0$, motion is forbidden.
2. If $N_{i,j} \neq 0$, target cell $(l,m)^*$, $(l,m)^* \in I = \{(i-1,j),(i,j+1),(i+1,j),(i,j-1),(i,j)\}$ is chosen randomly using the transition probabilities.
3. (a) If $N_{i,j} \neq 0$ and $(1 - f^*_{l,m}) = 1$, then target cell $(l,m)^*$ is fixed.
   (b) If $N_{i,j} \neq 0$ and $(1 - f^*_{l,m}) = 0$, then the cell $(l,m)^*$ is not available as it is occupied by other particle. In such case $p_{i,j} = \sum_{(y,z) \in I:(1-f_{y,z})=0} p_{y,z}$
   and $p_{y,z} = 0 \forall (y,z) \in I : (1 - f_{y,z}) = 0$. Again, the target cell is chosen randomly using the transformed probability distribution.
4. Whenever two or more pedestrians have the same target cell, movement of all the involved pedestrians is denied with probability μ. One of the candidates moves to the desired cell with the probability $1 - \mu$. The pedestrian allowed to move is chosen randomly.
5. The pedestrians that are allowed to move perform motion to the target cell.
6. The pedestrians that appear in the exit cells leave the room.

The above rules are applied to all the particles at the same time; i.e., parallel update is used.

3   Numerical Experiments

3.1   Discussion on the Model Parameters

The simplest shape of the way, the strait corridor, supposes that strategy of the shortest path coincides with the shortest time strategy for the whole way. Geometry of the way does not influence on the movement, and the shape of the flow and velocity are only determined by the density. To realize only the shortest path strategy the model density sensitive parameter k_P has to be low ($k_P < k_S$).

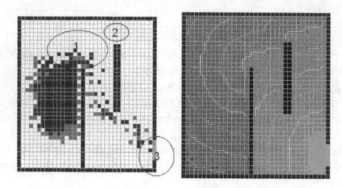

Fig. 1. Left: a complex space and screenshot of the evacuation in accordance with the shortest path strategy, "narrow" points 1, 2, 3 are denoted. Right: field S with isolines.

If there are turns on the way, congestions appear before turns (depending on density), and some people start to use detours facilities (that means to follow the shortest time strategy) and not to wait when the shortest path will free. In the model the shortest time strategy is pronounced under $k_P \gg k_S$. The mechanism is the following. If the shortest path direction has a high density, $F(r^\star) \approx 1$, the probability of this direction goes down. At the same time, the probability $(F(r^\star) \ll 1)$ of direction that is more favorable for movement rises. In this case detours around high-density regions has the largest probability. One can say that the model is density adjustable.

Low visibility radius r may be interpreted like a moving in dark or smoke conditions. The higher r the more sensitive model to the nearest people density and obstacles.

3.2   Case Study 1

Here we will consider two geometries: a straight corridor $50\,m \times 2\,m$ in size and a complex space which is presented in figure 1. This complex space is chosen due to turn (point 1) and possibility to take detours (point 2). We will consider an evacuation time as a criterion and investigate model dynamics under different model parameters which provide different movement regimes. In simple space (straight corridor) two strategies coincide. The complex space supposes realization of both strategies in order to provide realistic movement. Otherwise a slight regard to an avoidance of congestions is supposed: a small (unrealistic) turn radius (point 1) that results in congestion before turn, detours facilities are not used (point 2), an ineffective use of the exit width (point 3), Figure 1.

To realize different strategies and regulate movement regime we fixed the field S-sensitive parameter $k_S = 4$ (remember that probabilities are density adaptive; the low people density lowers the effect of people density component in 1, and the probability of the shortest path strategy increases automatically). And dependence of evacuation time (T_{cp}, [step]) in open boundary conditions versus initial density for different pairs of parameters k_P and r are presented in

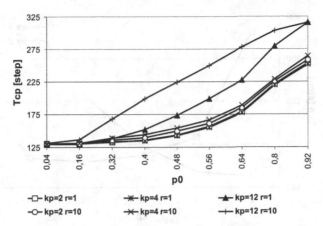

a) Evacuation time for the straight corridor for different pairs k_P and r;

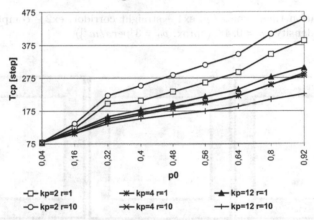

b) Evacuation time for the complex geometry corridor for different pairs k_P and r.

Fig. 2. Evacuation time for different geometries

figure 2 (initial density is given dimensionlessly here). One can see in figure 2 that the pair $k_P = 12$ and $r = 10$ is the best for the complex geometry (it gives the fastest evacuation time) and provides the slowest evacuation from the straight corridor. So the parameter k_P regulates movement regimes from only the shortest path strategy ($k_P \leq k_S$) to combinations of strategies ($k_P > k_S$). Nevertheless there is a limit for k_P value, figure 3 shows it for geometries when using of two strategies are supposed.

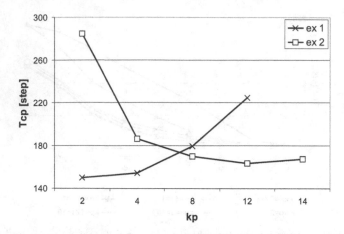

Fig. 3. Evacuation time versus k_P: ex1 – straight corridor, ex2 – complex geometry. $r = 10$, initial density $\rho_0 = 0,48$. (aprox. $\rho_0 = 3\,[pers/m^2]$).

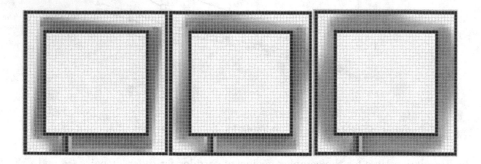

Fig. 4. Utilizing of space for different parameters k_P from left to right – $k_P = 2$, $k_P = 4$ and $k_P = 12$, other parameters were equal for all cases – $r = 1$, $k_S = k_W = 4$. Black cells are walls, grey cells – cells which were visited by particles during simulation. Brightness of the gray depends on number of visits.

3.3 Case Study 2

In this case study we considered clockwise movement in a corridor with four 90-degree turns. And the matter of the investigation was an utilizing of geometry space under different model parameters and initial density $\approx \rho_0 = 3\,[pers/m^2]$.

In real life turns assume that flow before turn should adjust for changing a movement direction. And it depends on density of the flow. So while turning people may use only the shortest path strategy in low densities, and they use combinations of the strategies in higher densities.

We consider utilizing of the space available for movement as measure of realizing the shortest time strategy that means making detours around the congested areas. Figure 4 shows that the best space utilizing is provided by $k_P = 12$ (when both strategies may be realized), and it provides the best evacuation time.

Summary

To conclude note that model parameters provide an instrument to tune movement regimes from the shortest path strategies to combinations of the shortest path and the shortest time strategies. It is an important point because different geometries suppose different movement regimes (remember here we considered not emergent movement) and parameters should be in agreement with geometry. The next step is to create methods for automatic adaptation of parameters in accordance with local density and geometrical situation.

Acknowledgment. This work is supported by the Integration project of SB RAS, number 49/2012.

References

1. Burstedde, V., Klauck, K., Schadschneider, A., Zittartz, J.: Simulation of pedestrian dynamics using a 2-dimensional cellular automaton. Physica A 295, 507–525 (2001)
2. Kholshevnikov, V.: Forecast of human behavior during fire evacuation. In: Proceedings of the International Conference "Emergency Evacuation of People from Buildings - EMEVAC", pp. 139–153. Belstudio, Warsaw (2011)
3. Kirik, E., Yurgel'yan, T., Krouglov, D.: The Shortest Time and/or the Shortest Path Strategies in a CA FF Pedestrian Dynamics Model. Journal of Siberian Federal University, Mathematics and Physics 2(3), 271–278 (2009)
4. Kirik, E., Yurgel'yan, T., Krouglov, D.: On Influencing of a Space Geometry on Dynamics of Some CA Pedestrian Movement Model. In: Bandini, S., Manzoni, S., Umeo, H., Vizzari, G. (eds.) ACRI 2010. LNCS, vol. 6350, pp. 474–479. Springer, Heidelberg (2010)
5. Kirik, E., Yurgel'yan, T., Krouglov, D.: On realizing the shortest time strategy in a CA FF pedestrian dynamics model. Cybernetics and Systems 42(1), 1–15 (2011)
6. Kirik, E., Yurgel'yan, T., Krouglov, D.: On Time Scaling and Validation of a Stochastic CA Pedestrian Dynamics Model. In: Peacock, R.D., Kuligowski, E.D., Averill, J.D. (eds.) Proceedings of the International Conference on "Pedestrian and Evacuation Dynamics' 2010", pp. 819–822 (2011)
7. Kirik, E., Vitova, T.: On validation of the SIgMA.CA pedestrian dynamics model with bottleneck flow. In: Sirakoulis, G.C., Bandini, S. (eds.) ACRI 2012. LNCS, vol. 7495, pp. 719–727. Springer, Heidelberg (2012)
8. Schadschneider, A., Klingsch, W., Kluepfel, H., Kretz, T., Rogsch, C., Seyfried, A.: Evacuation Dynamics: Empirical Results, Modeling and Applications. In: Encyclopedia of Complexity and System Science, vol. 3, pp. 3142–3192. Springer (2009)
9. Schadschneider, A., Seyfried, A.: Validation of CA models of pedestrian dynamics with fundamental diagrams. Cybernetics and Systems 40(5), 367–389 (2009)

Case Study of Phase Transition
in Cellular Models of Pedestrian Flow

Marek Bukáček[1,*] and Pavel Hrabák[1,2]

[1] Faculty of Nuclear Sciences and Physical Engineering
Czech Technical University in Prague
Trojanova 13, 120 00 Prague, Czech Republic
{bukacma2,pavel.hrabak}@fjfi.cvut.cz
[2] Institute of Information Theory and Automation
Academy of Sciences of the Czech Republic
Pod Vodarenskou vezi 4, 182 08 Prague, Czech Republic
hrabak@utia.cas.cz

Abstract. One room with one exit and one multiple entrance is modelled using 32 different settings and modifications of floor field model. The influence of following aspects are investigated in the scope of the transition from free flow to congestion phase with respect to the inflow rate: Heterogeneity/Homogeneity; With/Without bounds; Moore/von Neumann neighbourhood; Synchronous/Asynchronous update; High/Low friction. Considering the average travel time through the room and average room occupancy the settings incorporating the bounds and synchronous update seems to match the experimental data from the qualitative point of view.

Keywords: Floor field model, phase transition, travel time, bounds principle, asynchronous update.

1 Introduction

Cellular automata models are very useful tool for real time simulations of egress or evacuation of large and complex facilities [12]. Such network consists of several connected segments with exits and entrances.

Cellular models investigated in this article are based on the floor field model described in [8]. Our aim is to investigate the influence of several aspects that modify the FF model. Basic overview of floor field model modifications can be found in [9], [10], [11]. We focus on the modifications leading to real microscopic behaviour as line formation or heterogeneity of agents as mentioned in [1] or [6].

Different approaches are compared within the scope of phase transition in simple design of one room with one exit and one multiple entrance, which could be considered as one segment of larger network. In [4] or [5] the transition from low to high density with respect to inflow parameter α has been studied for simple floor field model.

---

* Corresponding author.

J. Wąs, G.C. Sirakoulis, and S. Bandini (Eds.): ACRI 2014, LNCS 8751, pp. 508–517, 2014.
© Springer International Publishing Switzerland 2014

The inflow rate α determines the number of pedestrians willing to enter the room during 1 s. General feature of similar hopping particle systems with open boundaries is an existence of a critical (saturation) inflow α_S indicating phase transition. Similarly to [4], we aim to study the boundary induces phase transition between the free flow phase (characterized by the low density) and the congested phase (high density) in the dependence on inflow α. Considered modification of FF model are investigated in the steady state.

2   Considered Models

As mentioned above, we focus on the simulation of passing through a room with the entrance on one side and the exit on the opposite side. To match the experiments described in [1] and [2], the room was equipped with one exit of the width corresponding to one cell and three entrances placed on the opposite wall to the exit, as illustrated in Figure 1. The inflow is controlled by the inflow parameter α, which determines the number of pedestrians coming to the entrance per one second (i.e., if the room capacity is reached, agents are accumulated in front of the entrance). For purposes of the simulation, the room 7.2 m long and 4.4 m wide has been chosen. The cellular model used for the simulation is described below.

Commonly, the space is divided into square cells by rectangular lattice $\mathbb{L}$ with lattice constant equal to 0.4 m. Every cell is denoted by the position of it's center $x = (x_1, x_2)$, the scale of axes x_i corresponds to the lattice constant. The exit is placed to the origin $E = (0,0)$. As we consider a simple rectangular room, the "playground" is given by cells $x \in \{-w, -w+1, \ldots, w-1, w\} \times \{1, 2, \ldots, l\} \cup \{E, I_{-1}, I_0, I_1\}$, where $2w+1$ is the width and l is the length of the room in cells, i.e., $w = 5$ and $l = 18$ for above described setting; $I_j = (j, l+1)$ are the cells of the entrances, as illustrated in Figure 1.

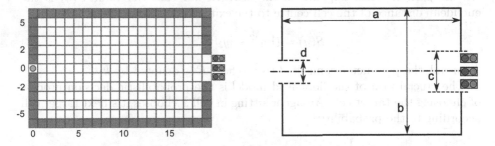

Fig. 1. The room with parameters $a = 7.2$ m, $b = 4.4$ m, $c = 1.3$ m, $d = 0.5$ m is modelled by the rectangular lattice 11×18 cells, i.e., $w = 5$, $l = 18$

Every cell can be either occupied by one agent (representing the pedestrian) or empty. In the following, this is captured by the occupation identifier O, i.e., $O(y) = 1$ for occupied cell and $O(y) = 0$ for the empty cell, $y \in \mathbb{L}$. As we will often evaluate the occupancy of the cells from the point of view of the agent sitting in cell x, it is beneficial to use the "personal" occupancy identifier $O_x(y)$ with $O_x(x) = 0$ and $O_x(y) = O(y)$ for $y \neq x$. This is useful for the agent not to block it's actual cell during the decision process.

To simulate and control the randomized inflow of pedestrians into the room, geometric distribution was used. The number of steps between the input of two consecutive agents to one entrance I_j is given stochastically by the geometric distribution, i.e., the probability of another agent coming to the row in front of the entrance I_j is

$$p(k) = (\alpha h/3)(1 - \alpha h/3)^{k-1}, \tag{1}$$

where h is the length of the algorithm step, which depends on the used updating scheme, as described below.

2.1 Decision Process

Agents (pedestrians) are moving along the lattice by hopping from one cell to another. For purposes of this article the nearest-neighbour interaction has been chosen, i.e., the agent is choosing only cells in the nearest neighbourhood. More precisely, an agent in the cell x can choose to jump to the cell $y \in N(x)$, where

$$N(x) = \left\{ y \in \mathbb{L}; \ \max_{j=1,2} |x_j - y_j| \leq 1 \right\} \tag{2}$$

is the Moore neighbourhood of the cell x. To distinguish the diagonal and non diagonal motion the diagonal direction indicator D is used in this article, i.e., $D_x(y) = 1$ if $(x_1 - y_1) \cdot (x_2 - y_2) \neq 0$ and $D_x(y) = 0$ otherwise.

The main advantage of the floor-field model is the incorporation of the static field S that is closely related to the distance of the cell to the exit and therefore indicates the cell atractivity (shorter distance to the exit means grater benefit for the particle when hopping to the cell). In our case the value $S(y)$ is the euclidean distance of the cell centre to the exit

$$S(y) = \left(|y_1|^2 + |y_2|^2 \right)^{1/2} . \tag{3}$$

As usual, the parameter connected to the field F is denoted by k_F.

The crucial idea of the floor-field model is the probabilistic decision process of choosing the target cell. An agent sitting in cell x chooses it's next target cell according to the probability

$$P(x \to y) = \frac{1}{\mathcal{N}} \exp \left\{ -k_S S(y) \right\} \left(1 - k_O O_x(y) \right) \left(1 - k_D D_x(y) \right) . \tag{4}$$

The normalization $\mathcal{N}$ assures that $\sum_{y \in N(x)} P(x \to y) = 1$, parameters k_O and k_D are used to distinguish different settings of this general model. The parameter k_S has been set to the value $k_S = 3.5$ to balance the deterministic motion in free flow and stochastic behaviour in the congested cluster (see [1] or [6]). As will be explained in detail below, for purposes of this article two values of k_O

have been chosen: $k_O = 1$ corresponding to the situation that occupied cells are excluded from the decision process and $k_O = 0$ incorporating the possibility of choosing an occupied cell, which is closely related to the principle of bounds. Analogically, $k_D = 1$ corresponds to the von Neumann neighbourhood and $k_D = 0.7$ corresponds to the Moore neighbourhood with certain diagonal movement penalisation [6].

2.2 Asynchronous Update

Aside the decision process, the case study focuses on the influence of updating scheme. Updating schemes presented in this article are inspired by the asynchronous cellular automata schemes presented in [3]. We use similar approach to the *clocked* scheme, i.e., every agent has assigned it's own timer which ticks at different rates for different agents. Furthermore, when the principle of bounds is incorporated ($k_O = 1$), the timer is influenced by the motion of other agents, as will be mentioned below and is discussed in [1].

If we denote by τ_α own period of the agent $\alpha \in A$, the time of agent's next activation is calculated as $t_{\text{next}} = t_{\text{actual}} + \tau_\alpha$. For the study here two cases are distinguished: homogeneous and heterogeneous. In the homogeneous case, all agents have the same own period $\tau = 0.3$ s (1.33 ms^{-1} in free flow); in heterogeneous case two kinds of agents are considered: faster agents with $\tau_1 = 0.3$ s and slower agents with $\tau_2 = 0.4$ s (1.00 ms^{-1} in free flow) with the ratio of occurrence 50 %.

To distinguish the synchronous and asynchronous update within the heterogeneous case, the time-line has been divided into isochronous intervals of the length $h > 0$. Within the k-th step of the algorithm, such agents are activated, whose time of next activation t_{next} belongs to the interval $\langle kh; (k+1)h \rangle$. The value of $h = 0.3$ s corresponds to the synchronous update (slower agents "miss" one of four steps) and $h = 0.05$ corresponds to the asynchronous update.

To compensate the length of the diagonal step in the case of Moore neighbourhood, which is $\sqrt{2}$-times longer, the next activation time after such step is calculated as $t_{\text{next}} = t_{\text{actual}} + \tau_\alpha \cdot q$, where q is a rational approximation of $\sqrt{2}$ in this article chosen to be $q = 3/2$. This is together with the bounds principle called *adaptive time span* [1].

2.3 Bounds and Conflicts

The bounds principle is closely related to the possibility of choosing an occupied cell ($k_O \neq 1$). If an agent chooses as his target cell an occupied cell then the *bound* to the blocking agent is created. The bound holds until the blocker moves or until the blocked agent is activated. In the case of the earlier movement of the blocker (i.e., if the blocker moves within the algorithm step before the activation of the blocked agent), the blocked agent follows the blocking agent immediately outside his activation step. This principal supports the motion in lines and is further discussed in [1] or [6].

In this article simple solution of conflicts using the friction parameter μ investigated in [7] is used. If more agents try to enter the unoccupied cell, with probability μ none of the agents moves; with probability $1 - \mu$, of the agents is chosen at random to enter the cell. Other agents remain in their original cells. Analogically is the conflict solved in the case, when more then one agent is bounded to common blocking agent.

3   Phase Transition in Simulations

In [4] the transition from low density to high density phase in dependence on inflow parameter α has been investigated with respect to the friction function parameter ζ. In this article we focus on such dependence on the model type classified according to Table 1. The investigation is far from complete parameter investigation or validation. We aim above all to point out characteristic features and mechanism of the transition.

As we aim to investigate the system in the steady state, we have let the model to evolve for a long period. By the free flow setting we understand such set of parameters under which the room does not become overfilled by the agents. The congested setting is characterized by the creation of stable cluster in front of the exit, which size grows to the capacity of the room. By the transition from the free flow to the congestion phase we understand the change from free flow to congestion setting by increasing inflow parameter α.

We distinguish 32 combinations of different representative settings according to Heterogeneity/Homogeneity; With/Without bounds; Moore/von Neumann neighbourhood; Synchronous/Asynchronous update; High/Low friction. The numbering of given settings together with specific values of parameters is given in Table 1.

Table 1. Numbering of specific settings and given parameters. In the following figures, the setting is identified by the corresponding position as shown in the right part of the table, odd numbers represent high friction. Therefore, setting 11 means heterogeneity, bounds, asynchronous update, Moore neighbourhood, and high friction.

Heterogenous	Homogenous
HET: $\tau_1 = 0.3$ s	HOM: $\tau = 0.3$ s
$\tau_2 = 0.4$ s	
No bounds	Bounds
F: $k_D = 1.0$	O: $k_D = 0.0$
Moore	von Neumann
M: $k_O = 0.7$	N: $k_D = 1.0$
Synchronous	Asynchronous
S: $h = 0.3$	A: $h = 0.05$
High friction	Low friction
H: $\mu = 0.7$	L: $\mu = 0.2$

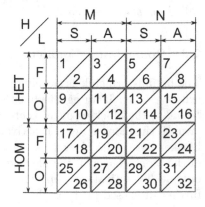

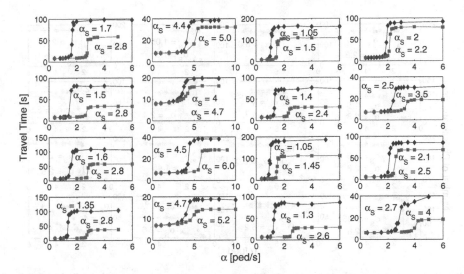

Fig. 2. Travel time with respect to α. The graph position corresponds to Table 1. Blue diamonds represent $\mu = 0.7$ and red squares $\mu = 0.2$.

For each of the 32 settings, simulations with variety of inflow parameters α have been performed. Three basic characteristics have been measured in the steady state: travel time, room occupancy, and real inflow into the room. By the travel time we understand the time an agent spent in the room, i.e., from the time of the entrance (which is different from the time of coming to the row in front of the exit) to the time of leaving the room through the exit; room occupancy denotes the average number of agents inside the room, and the real inflow stands for the number of pedestrians entering the room per second. This quantity corresponds in the steady state to the average flow. Simulation results for dependency of stated quantities are plotted in Figures 2 – 3.

From the Graphs several conclusions can be made:

3.1 Saturation

In Figures 2 – 3, appropriate values of saturation inflow α_S are added to the graphs. From the graphs we can read that the "capacity" of the room is not necessarily close to the number of cells $11 \times 18 = 198$. When the bounds principle is implemented (row 2 and 4, numbers 9-16 and 26-32), the maximal number of pedestrians is significantly lower. This can be explained by the possibility of choosing an occupied cell. Agents partially stand in lines and only several of them are trying to run over the crowd.

3.2 Smooth Transition vs. Sharp Jump

Another important aspect is the shape of the curves near the saturation point. In the majority of the settings the average travel time levels before the saturation

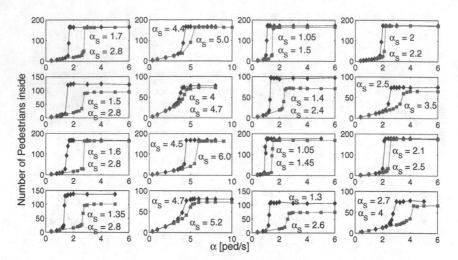

Fig. 3. Occupancy with respect to α. The graph position corresponds to Table 1. Blue diamonds represent $\mu = 0.7$ and red squares $\mu = 0.2$.

point (number of pedestrians increases linearly). The change of the curves towards the saturation value is sharp, jump-like. In settings with bounds and asynchronous updates (numbers 11/12, 15/16, 27/28, and 31/32) is the transition much smoother with respect to inflow α. The Travel time increases slightly before the saturation point and smoothly reaches the maximum corresponding to the saturation. This phenomenon is more obvious in the case of Moore neighbourhood (columns 1 and 2), as expected. the smooth shape of the travel time curve in the case of bounds can be explained by the motion in lines which is supported by this principle. Agents are rather waiting in lines then walk around each other. In the higher inflow case ($2.0 < \alpha < 4.0$) leads to slight increase of the travel time, but suppresses the overall delay caused by the friction.

3.3 Heterogeneous vs. Homogeneous

From the observations it follows that the heterogeneity of the system does not qualitatively nor quantitatively influence the system on the macroscopic bases captured by the travel time, occupancy, or saturation point. This is mainly caused by two aspects. Firstly, the macroscopic quantities are compared by means of aggregated data, which suppresses the heterogeneity nature. Secondly, the heterogeneity in the setting is given by the 50-50 distribution of velocities τ_1 and τ_2 keeping the decision process intact (there are no aggressive pedestrians etc.). Nevertheless, in microscopic point of view does the heterogeneity influence the histograms of travel time in the free flow with $\alpha \ll \alpha_S$ as shown in Figure 4.

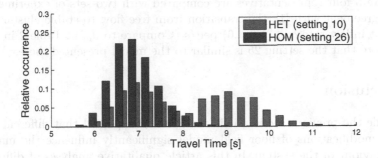

Fig. 4. Travel time histograms for free flow $\alpha = 0.4$ ped/s

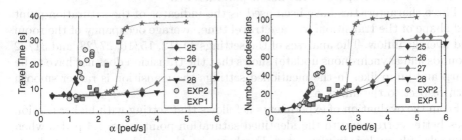

Fig. 5. Comparison of selected settings with experiments (yellow circles and orange squares)

3.4   The Friction Parameter μ

The friction parameter influences mainly the behaviour of the system with synchronous updates. Although the value $\mu = 0.7$ seems to be unrealistic (values between 0.2 and 0.3 are commonly used as e.g. in [7]), in the settings incorporating bounds and/or asynchronous update the number of conflicts is suppressed, therefore it is important to increase the friction to maintain the ratio of conflicts per time unit.

3.5   Comparison with Experiments

Our research group organized several experiments with similar setting to the simulations described in this article. Those experiments were designed to observe the phase transition by means of stability of the cluster in front of the exit. The discussion concerning mentioned experiment can (or will) be found in [1] and [2]. Additional experiment was organized in 29th April 2014. Similarly to previous experiments, 80 volunteers from FNSPE CTU were walking through the experimental room. As the number of volunteers did not reach the capacity of the room, the numbers of pedestrians in the room as well as the average travel time measured was lower then in appropriate steady state. Therefore, the congestion phase was recognized by means of growing number of pedestrians in the room.

In Figure 5 four representatives are compared with two sets of experimental data. In agreement with [1], the transition from free flow to stable cluster was observed at inflow rate $\alpha \in (1.3, 1.6)$ ped/s (Compare to J_{in} of Table 2 in [1]). Here we note that the setting 25 is similar to the model presented there.

4   Conclusion

To conclude the previous section, it is obvious and expected that different settings and modifications of floor field model significantly influence the macroscopic behaviour of the system. In this article qualitative analyses of different approaches has been performed by means of the phase transition from low to high density with respect to the inflow parameter α.

Three characteristics have been used as the indicator of the saturation point and shape of the transition: average travel time, average occupancy of the room and average inflow. The analyses of the settings 11/12, 15/16, 27/28, and 31/32 (bounds and asynchronous update) shows that the transition does not have to be sharp and jump-like. In the mentioned settings the transition is rather smooth with respect to the inflow α.

From the evaluation of experiments it follows that setting with higher friction does better correspond to the identified saturation point $\alpha_S \approx 1.4$ ped/s when principle of bounds is implemented. Furthermore, the synchronous update leads to better correspondence as well, as can be shown in Figure 5, where synchronous settings 25/26 are compared to asynchronous settings 27/28. The asynchronous update significantly suppresses the conflicts and therefore increases the maximal outflow from the room which leads to unrealistic high value of the saturation $\alpha \approx 4$ ped/s.

From the above mentioned analysis supported by the simple observation of the microscopic motion we conclude that the synchronous update with bounds, high friction, and Moore neighbourhood is in the best correspondence with performed experiments.

Acknowledgements. This work was supported by the grant SGS12/197/ OHK4/3T/14 and by the Czech Science Foundation under the grant 13-13502S. We would like to thank Mr. Milan Krbálek and his students for assistance in mentioned experiments.

References

1. Bukáček, M., Hrabák, P., Krbálek, M.: Cellular model of pedestrian dynamics with adaptive time span. In: Wyrzykowski, R., Dongarra, J., Karczewski, K., Waśniewski, J. (eds.) PPAM 2013, Part II. LNCS, vol. 8385, pp. 669–678. Springer, Heidelberg (2014)
2. Bukáček, M., Hrabák, P., Krbálek, M.: Experimental analysis of two-dimensional pedestrian flow in front of the bottleneck. In: Traffic and Granular Flow 2013. Springer, Heidelberg (to be published, 2014)

3. Cornforth, D., Green, D.G., Newth, D.: Ordered asynchronous processes in multi-agent systems. Physica D 204(1-2), 70–82 (2005)
4. Ezaki, T., Yanagisawa, D., Nishinari, K.: Analysis on a single segment of evacuation network. Journal of Cellular Automata 8(5-6), 347–359 (2013)
5. Ezaki, T., Yanagisawa, D., Ohtsuka, K., Nishinari, K.: Simulation of space acquisition process of pedestrians using proxemic floor field model. Physica A 391(1-2), 291–299 (2012)
6. Hrabák, P., Bukáček, M., Krbálek, M.: Cellular model of room evacuation based on occupancy and movement prediction: Comparison with experimental study. Journal of Cellular Automata 8(5-6), 383–393 (2013)
7. Kirchner, A., Nishinari, K., Schadschneider, A.: Friction effects and clogging in a cellular automaton model for pedestrian dynamics. Physical Review E 67(5 2), 056122/1–056122/10 (2003)
8. Kirchner, A., Schadschneider, A.: Simulation of evacuation processes using a bionics-inspired cellular automaton model for pedestrian dynamics. Physica A: Statistical Mechanics and its Applications 312(1-2), 260–276 (2002)
9. Nishinari, K., Kirchner, A., Namazi, A., Schadschneider, A.: Simulations of evacuation by an extended floor field ca model. In: Hoogendoorn, S., Luding, S., Bovy, P., Schreckenberg, M., Wolf, D. (eds.) Traffic and Granular Flow 2003, pp. 405–410. Springer, Heidelberg (2005)
10. Schadschneider, A., Chowdhury, D., Nishinari, K.: Stochastic Transport in Complex Systems: From Molecules to Vehicles. Elsevier Science B. V., Amsterdam (2010)
11. Schadschneider, A., Seyfried, A.: Empirical results for pedestrian dynamics and their implications for cellular automata models. In: Timmermans, H. (ed.) Pedestrian Behavior - Models, Data Collection and Applications, pp. 27–43. Emerald Group, Bingley (2009)
12. Was, J., Lubaś, R.: Adapting social distances model for mass evacuation simulation. Journal of Cellular Automata 8(5-6), 395–405 (2013)

Simulation of Public Opinion
with Ideas of Cellular Automata

Terpil Ievgen and Makarenko Alexander

Institute for Applied System Analysis at National Technical University of Ukraine "KPI",
Peremogy Avenue 37, 03056, Kiev-56, Ukraine
terpiljenya@gmail.com, makalex@i.com.ua

Abstract. Cellular automata approach for public opinion modeling is considered. Aiming the possibility of a practical use, we extend standard peer effects model by introducing the idea of states dependence and irregular lattice into it. The applicability of proposed approach was examined by modeling the parliamentary elections in Ukraine.

Keywords: Public opinion, cellular automata, electoral fields, predicting elections, mentality change, modeling, applications.

1   Introduction

Studying behavior of active agents in large communities (e.g. movement of pedestrians, the evolution of social systems, and collective psychology of society) requires the consideration of multiple factors [1-4]. Among those is the accounting for the mentality of the behavior of a community of agents [5], which includes the study of social interactions between the agents.

The public opinion modeling is important for understanding social processes, whereas the study of voting, elections and prediction of their results is the imminent part of it.

Many approaches have been proposed for elections modeling: methods of mathematical statistics including spatial statistics; system dynamics; differential equations; neural networks; game theory; Markov chains and many others.

Each of the approaches above has its achievements as well as shortcomings, which are due to the objective hurdles in the study of elections. First, we deal with the large distributed volumes of data. Second, there is need to account for the nature of opinion spreading among the collection of agents by different mechanisms.

One of the possible modeling methods is the cellular automata (CA), which have some very useful properties: ease of programming, local nature of rules, flexibility of improving and changing the rules during CA evolution.

The application of cellular automata to the public opinion modeling has quite a history starting from [6] till more recent works (see for example [7]). However till now many research problems lack the adequate solutions. Our previous experience with cellular automata leads us to some new ideas about applications of CA to election

J. Wąs, G.C. Sirakoulis, and S. Bandini (Eds.): ACRI 2014, LNCS 8751, pp. 518–525, 2014.
© Springer International Publishing Switzerland 2014

modeling. One idea is to use non-regular cells for representation of the non-homogenous electoral fields and data. Another one is to account for the dependences between electoral choices. The third idea is to combine CA with the geoinformational systems.

Section 2 of the paper describes the principles of using cellular automata to election modeling. Section 3 details the CA model and applies it to prediction of election outcomes in Ukraine. The final section explores possible further developments of the proposed approach.

2   Peer Effect Model

In the base of the peer effects model is a hypothesis, that electoral preferences of an individual are determined by the preferences of his/her immediate environment.

Consider an individual who decides to vote for one of the n candidates at the time $t+1$. Take Moore neighborhood as voter's environment. In this case the transition function of the cellular automata would be described by the equation

$$y^{i,j}(t+1) = argmax_{v=1..n}C(v,O(i,j),t), \qquad (1)$$

where $y^{i,j}(t)$ - candidate, which is chosen by the individual from the cell i,j in time t

$O(i,j)$ – neighborhood of cells with indices i,j

$C(v,O(i,j),t)$ – the number of cells with a value v in the neighborhood $O(i,j)$

So, the voter chooses the alternative the most of his neighbors have chosen. However, instead of using *argmax* function we can calculate the weight of each of the options as $\dfrac{C(v,O(i,j),t)}{\sum_v C(v,O(i,j),t)}$, and use this weight as probability of selecting corresponding option

$$P\{y^{i,j}(t+1)=v\} = \frac{C(v,O(i,j),t)}{\sum_v C(v,O(i,j),t)}, \qquad (2)$$

A typical configuration of the automata is shown in Figure 1.

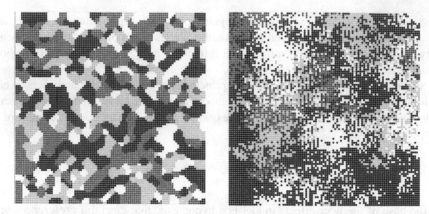

Fig. 1. An example of typical calculated configuration after 20-30 cycles of peer effects model by using classical automata (left) and probabilistic automata (right)

Classical peer effects automata are determined by transition function (1). They are characterized by fast convergence (20-30 cycles) and form stable group of voters with clear and sufficiently smooth boundaries. In contrast, the stochastic model (2) does not converge and form complex evolutions (see Fig. 2), which are also characterized by the voter groups formation, however, these groups are not as clear as in the classical model.

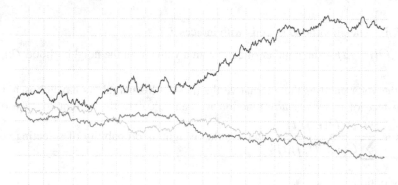

Fig. 2. Dynamics of the political party's supporters number for each candidate in model with probability. Axis OX – time steps, axis OY – rate of candidate.

Besides peer effects models, which were described above, there are numerous extensions that take into account uneven initial distribution, "weak ties", influence of external factors and allocation of "neutral alternatives." However, they are rather abstract and it is difficult to apply them for practical modeling. Although, cellular automata (1) and (2) can serve as a basis for construction of a usable model of public opinion. In the next section, we extend the model (1) including dependences between options.

3   Generalized Model of Public Opinion

In real life, the electoral choices in different time moments cannot be completely independent. Thus we propose to introduce the dependences between states. Recall that the formal definition of cellular automata needs a triple-set

$$\langle Z_n, S, Q \rangle,$$ (3)

where Z_n - lattice of cells;
S - set of states of the automata cells;
Q - transition function of cellular automata.

We can build an automata lattice in different ways. For theoretical studies it can be Moore neighborhood, but for practical problems with real data we can consider non regular lattice.

For instance, in Ukrainian elections, the Central Election Commission gives the results by each of the 33 thousand of polling station and by each of the 225 electoral districts. We select the later to be the automata cells in our model. However, the construction of a regular lattice using these data is not a trivial task (see Fig. 3). We can say that we are dealing with an irregular grid.

To build such grid it is necessary to define a set of cells and a neighborhood for each of them. Specifying electoral territorial units, we can determine the geographic coordinates of the centers and their boundaries. Thus we can define a neighborhood as all territorial units which have a common border with a set. However, in practice, this approach may be insufficient. Since correct setting of a neighborhood is critical to describe the influence of the environment, it is reasonable to take into account public transportation infrastructure and the terrain. This means, for example, that districts, which are separated by a wide river with no bridges have a very little contact with each other. On the other hand districts that are connected by many roads show high mutual dependence.

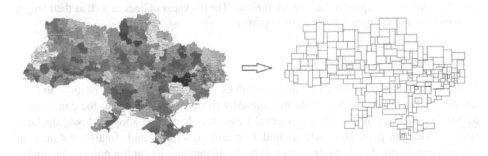

Fig. 3. Building an irregular lattice by using a map of electoral districts in Ukraine

So, to set a grid of automata we need to define a neighborhood of each territorial election unit on the basis of infrastructure and topography data or use Moore neighborhood for theoretical studies.

3.1   Dependence of Electoral Options

The states of the automata cells are electoral options. If a cell is in the i state at the time t, it supports the i-th option (candidate, party). So if there is an election at the time t the cell votes for the option i.

Suppose we want to characterize dependence between options. This can be done by an expert, who can evaluate the dependence between options by placing a certain weight. Thus we get a matrix of electoral options' relationships.

$$M = \begin{pmatrix} 1 & ... & w_{1,n} \\ ... & ... & ... \\ w_{n,1} & ... & 1 \end{pmatrix} \tag{4}$$

where $i, j = 1..n$, n – number of electoral options

$w_{i,j}$ - the weight of dependence between two options as probability of voter transition from one state to another.

This matrix can be represented by a graph (see Fig. 4), where the distance between nodes is proportional to the weight between relevant options.

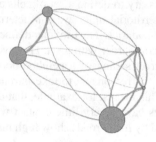

Fig. 4. Graph of the dependences between options. The thickness of lines as well as their length is proportional to the weight between two options.

3.2   Transition Function

It should be noted that till now our model does not include the direct attitude to candidates by the voters. This is done intentionally to make the attitude to the candidate's actions outside the model as an external influence. It can be adopted laws, declarations of election programs, actions under certain conditions and, finally, defamation about a candidate. These parameters can be evaluated using opinion polls or by analysis of media publications.

We assume that in today's world of mass media, conclusions regarding to the candidate's actions would be the same way for each cell. Thus, define a general support of i-th party as $R_i(t)$ at the time $t \in \{1,..T\}$

Consider an electoral district $k \in K$, where $K = \{k_1 ... k_m\}$ is a set of districts (set of automata's cells). Thus, the evolution of i-th candidate's rate in district k at the times $t \in \{1,..T\}$ can be described as follows

$$y_i(t+1) = y_i(t) + \varphi(y_i)\Delta_i(t+1) \tag{5}$$

where $y_i(t)$ - rating of candidate i in time t

$\Delta_i(t+1)$ - change in the number of voters, which is caused by external factors (external influence and the influence of the neighborhood, which will also be external to the k- th district);

$\varphi(y_i)$ - adoption rate of external influence on candidate i in k- th district;

External factors can be formalized as

$$\Delta_i(t+1) = f_i(t+1) + o_i(t) \tag{6}$$

where $f_i(t+1) = R_i(t+1) - R_i(t)$ - change in the national support of i- th party

   $o_i(t)$ - peer effects;

If we know the population size of each district, we can consider the peer effects as weighted average of candidates' rates in neighboring cells

$$o_i(t) = \frac{\sum\limits_{i \in O(k)} w_i y_i(t)}{\sum\limits_{j \in O(k)} w_j} \tag{7}$$

where $O(k)$ - set of cells in the k-th neighborhood

Let us consider now the coefficient of external influence. It refers to how the changes of general rating are accepted in a cell. For example, if a certain political party is gaining national popularity, but the voters of a district prefer some opposite electoral option, that party will get less support in this district. This can be described by the following rules

$$\varphi^+(y_i) = \sum_{j=1}^{n} w_{ij} y_j$$
$$\varphi^-(y_i) = \sum_{j=1}^{n} w_{ji}(1 - y_j) \tag{8}$$

which are aggregated according to the nature of external influence

$$\varphi = \begin{cases} \varphi^+(y_i), \Delta_i(t+1) > 0 \\ \varphi^-(y_i), \Delta_i(t+1) < 0 \end{cases} \tag{9}$$

These adoption rates of external influence can be explained as the number of voters in certain district that may approve i-th candidate or disapprove it respectively. (See Fig. 5)

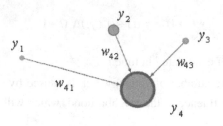

Fig. 5. Electoral "reserve" of alternative

3.3   Numerical Simulation

To verify correctness of the described above approach, we made a numerical simulation of evolution of electoral opinion polls during elections to Ukrainian Parliament for the last 6 years.

Initial distribution of cells is based on the election results to the Verkhovna Rada of Ukraine in 2006. An expert-defined matrix represents dependencies between the main political forces existing in Ukraine for the last 8 years. These parties were taken as electoral options. Let's take the nationwide political party support rate which is based on quarterly polls as an input to the model. Moreover, there was additional early parliamentary election in 2007. Their results were used for configuration the parameters of the model.

Figure 6 shows the model prediction of results of the regular election to the Verkhovna Rada of Ukraine in 2012.

Fig. 6. Simulated (left) and real distribution (right) of electoral field in 2012: dark gray - Party of Regions and Communist Party of Ukraine, gray - Batkivshchyna and Ukrainian Democratic Alliance for Reform (UDAR), light gray - All-Ukrainian Union "Svoboda"

Picture demonstrates correspondence between the simulated results and the real electoral distribution in Ukraine in 2012. Special attention should be paid to the fact that during 2007 – 2012 two new parties (All-Ukrainian Union "Svoboda" and UDAR) appeared in the Ukrainian political life. And model correctly predicted regions of its emergence and distribution of its electorate. It was possible due to taking into account the dependences between electoral options.

However, it should be noted that in certain districts there was observed a significant difference between model prediction and official election results, particularly where the later had abnormally high support for a certain party. This difference can be interpreted as the indicator of potential voting irregularities (fraudulent misrepresentation of results and voter fraud).

4   Conclusion

The paper describes the cellular automata approach to the public opinion modeling using the concept of non-homogeneous cells. Numerical experiments with the real data of parliament election in Ukraine confirm the usefulness of proposed approach. The approach can be improved by using cellular description of mentality including internal dynamic models for mental states evolution.

References

1. Makarenko, A., Musienko, A., Popova, A., Poveshenko, G., Samorodov, E., Trofimenko, A.: Cellular Automata, Agents with Mobility and GIS for Practical Problems. In: Sirakoulis, G.C., Bandini, S. (eds.) ACRI 2012. LNCS, vol. 7495, pp. 738–742. Springer, Heidelberg (2012)
2. Makarenko, A., Krushinski, D., Musienko, A., Goldengorin, B.: Towards Cellular Automata Football Models with Mentality Accounting. In: Bandini, S., Manzoni, S., Umeo, H., Vizzari, G. (eds.) ACRI 2010. LNCS, vol. 6350, pp. 149–152. Springer, Heidelberg (2010)
3. Krushinski, D., Makarenko, A.: Cellular automata with anticipation: examples and presumable applications. In: Dubois, D. (ed.) Computing Anticipatory Systems. AIP Conf. Proceed. Series, vol. 1303, pp. 246–254. AIP N.- Y. (2010)
4. Lande, D., Furashev, V.: Fundamentals of information and social-legal modeling, LLC "PanTot" (2012) (in Russian)
5. Castellano, C., Fortunato, S., Loreto, V.: Statistical physics of social dynamics. ArXiv: 0710.3256v2 [physics-soc-ph], 58 p. (2009)
6. Kasperski, K., Holist, J.A.: Phase Transitions and Hysteresis in a Cellular Automata-Bsased Model of Opinion Formation. J. of Statistical Physics 84(1.2), 169–189 (1996)
7. Alves, S.G., Oliveira Neto, N.M., Martins, M.L.: Electoral surveys influence on the voting processes: a cellular automata model. Arxiv: cond-mat/020413v1, 16 p. (2013)

Estimating Speeds of Pedestrians
in Real-World Using Computer Vision

Sultan Daud Khan, Fabio Porta, Giuseppe Vizzari, and Stefania Bandini

Complex Systems Artificial Intelligence Research Center
University of Milano-Bicocca, Italy

Abstract. This paper proposes a novel approach to a computer vision based automatic system for the estimation of pedestrian velocity in real world traffic systems in which a fixed camera is available. The paper will introduce the adopted framework, which includes a preprocessing phase, an identification and tracking phase, and a speed estimation final phase. Speed estimation, implying a conversion from image to real world coordinates, can be carried out with two different techniques that will be discussed in details and evaluated with reference to achieved results.

Keywords: Computer vision, Pedestrian behaviour analysis.

1 Introduction

Pedestrian injuries and fatalities are one of the most significant problem related to travel and road safety: due to the significant difference in speed and mass, when compared to vehicles like cars and trucks, pedestrians and cyclists (for this reason also called vulnerable road users) often undergo serious accidents. Studies have shown that more than one fifth of the casualties related to road traffic is represented by pedestrians crossing a road [1]. Pedestrians, however, have very different characteristics in terms of age, gender and socioeconomic status; studies have showed that crashes involving pedestrians are related to specific risk factors and road geometrical factors [4], and in particular: (i) age and gender (ii) pedestrian crossing time, (iii) pedestrian crossing speed, (iv) crossing the street with red or green traffic light. Pedestrian crashes affect people from different age groups; however, studies have shown that in United States in 2009, the fatality rate for pedestrians older than 75 years is higher than the fatality rate of any other age group [1]; there are many reasons concurring in determining such a high fatality rate for pedestrian older than 65 years and mainly deficits in (i) their physical abilities, (ii) sensory and perceptual abilities, (iii) cognitive abilities. The importance of this issue is even increased by the global trend of ageing of the population. The rate of elderlies in the population is expected to increase by about 20% by year 2031 [9]. The detection of elder pedestrians and their characterisation is therefore important for at least two types of application: (i) pedestrian modeling and simulation, to gather relevant and precise data for sake of calibration and validation, (ii) monitoring and control systems in the

J. Wąs, G.C. Sirakoulis, and S. Bandini (Eds.): ACRI 2014, LNCS 8751, pp. 526–535, 2014.
© Springer International Publishing Switzerland 2014

Intelligent Transportation Systems context, both at infrastructural level (i.e. fixed cameras influencing semaphores) but also for driving aids and autonomous vehicles. The main aim of this paper is to report preliminary results of an ongoing initiative trying to put together computer vision techniques and competences, on one hand, and awareness of requirements, desiderata and contextual conditions related to pedestrian simulation studies, in an attempt to set up a virtuous cicle including both *analysis* and *synthesis* of pedestrian and crowd dynamics [15]. In particular, this paper proposes a novel approach to a computer vision based automatic system for the estimation of pedestrian velocity in real world traffic systems in which a fixed camera is available.

Previous research on traffic signal control was mainly focused on vehicle monitoring, and very little literature can be found on pedestrians side. An approach to detect and count pedestrians at an intersection using fixed camera is proposed in [3]. The problem of object tracking in an uncontrolled urban environment is discussed in [14]. A single camera looking at an intersection point is used in [5]: the authors focused on motion tracking, and motion segmentation is performed using an adaptive background model that can gain robustness with respect to the changes in illumination while tracking of objects is performed by computing the overlap between bounding boxes. On the side of pedestrian movement automated analysis [2] describe successful techniques that however require either (i) a controlled situation in which pedestrians bear a detectable marker on their heads or (ii) a stereo camera to be adopted in a quasi-zenithal observation position. These conditions are hardly met in real world traffic system, so their work is very useful but mostly for gathering data in controlled situations. The closest related work is reported in [11]. The paper presented a system that accurately estimates speed of individual pedestrians with constant walking speeds. The authors extract foreground objects (blobs) from each image and track each blob using foreground blob tracker. For estimating speed in real world coordinates, they perform camera calibration using Tsai's coplaner calibration method [13]. Our proposed approach is different in some aspects as we adopted Lucas-Kanade Tracker (KLT) for tracking blobs in frame. For estimating speed in real coordinates, we proposed two different approaches 1) Scale factor conversion and 2) Homography matrix conversion.

The following Section will introduce the framework, which includes a preprocessing phase, an identification and tracking phase, and a speed estimation final phase. Speed estimation, implying a conversion from image to real world coordinates, can be carried out with two different techniques that will be discussed in details and evaluated with reference to achieved results. Conclusions and future developments will end the paper.

2 Proposed Framework

Our proposed framework is composed of five processing phases. Frame enhancement, forground segmentation, blob analysis, tracking using Lucas Kanade point tracker (KLT), and velocity estimation. The key objective of our proposed approach is the conversion of image coordinates (pixels/second) to the world coordinates (meter/second). In this section, we will discuss each phase in detail.

2.1 Frame Enhancement

The first step for estimating the actual speed of pedestrians within a sequence of video is improving the quality of each input frame. In fact, with low contrast video frame, it becomes difficult to detect and track all moving objects in the scene. In order to solve this problem, we use Contrast limited adaptive histogram equalization (CLAHE) in [8] to improve the contrast of input image.

2.2 Foreground Segmentation

Identifying moving objects in video sequence is a fundamental and critical task in video surveillance and gesture recognition in human-machine interface. Foreground segmentation is an important pre-processing step for detecting moving objects from the video. Traditionally, background subtraction method is used for extracting moving objects from the video frame where pixels in the currents frame that deviate significantly from the background are considered as part of moving objects. Such kinds of methods are usually prone to errors due to unpredicted and changing behavior of the pixels. In addition, this method can not accurately detect fast moving or slow moving as well as multiple objects. Also these methods are affected by change in illumination in the video frame.

Such errors and noise must be removed from the foreground objects before applying blob analysis and tracking.In order to extract valid and accurate foreground objects, we employed both Gaussian mixture model and Lucas Kanade optical flow as in [7]. As shown in Figure 1, two foreground masks are generated, one by Lucas Kanade optical flow and other by GMM. Foregound mask generated by LK optical flow contains noise and removed by applying median filter. Later on, we apply Morphological processes like morphological opening and closing on the binary image generated by logical product of LK optical flow and GMM. The output image from Morphological processing block contains accurate foreground objects while will applied to Blob analysis block for detecting moving objects.

2.3 Blob Analysis

Blobs are the connected regions in the binary image. The purpose of blob analysis is to detect those points or regions in binary image that are different from other part of image in terms of brightness or area etc. Following are the steps for finding connected components in the binary image: (i) search for unlabeled pixel p, (ii) label all the pixels in connected region containing p by flood fill algorithm, (iii) repeat step 1 and step 2 until all pixels are labeled. In the next step, we measure the area of each connected component. Area of connected component is the number of pixels in the region. There may be different moving objects in

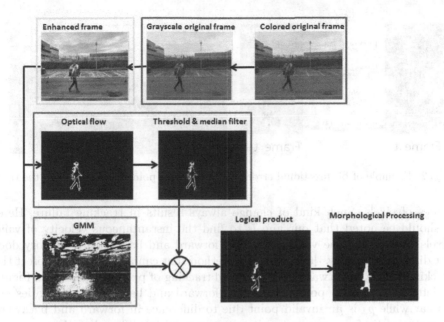

Fig. 1. Foreground segmentation framework

the video frame with different area sizes. In Transportation surveillance system, video frame contains multiple objects like pedestrians, vehicles of different sizes. In this paper, we are interested only in pedestrians whom we want to detect and track over multiple frames. The area of pedestrians is normally contains less number of pixels than vehicles and trucks in other words the size of pedestrian is less than vehicle and trucks. On the basis of this assumption, we set the upper and lower bound of blobs area. The upper and lower bound of blobs area can be found experimentally. The size of blob also depends on the resolution of frame. In this paper, we use videos of resolution 576 x 768 pixels and lower and upper bound of blobs area is [1000 2500] pixels. The connected component (object) will be classified as pedestrian if its area lies within the upper and lower bound otherwise it will be discarded.

2.4 Feature Extraction and Tracking Using KLT

In order to track objects detected in blob analysis step, we use KLT feature tracker [12] where motion is detected by using pyramidal Lucas- Kanade optical flow method, using Shi and Tomasi feature detection algorithm [10]. Pyramidal implementation of Lucas-Kanade gives more robustness against huge movement with different speeds. We detect corner points of each bounding box using Shi and Tomasi corner detector. But through our experiments we realize that points detected in the first frame may not be tracked over multiple frames. This is due to dramatically change in the appearance of the objects and change in intensity

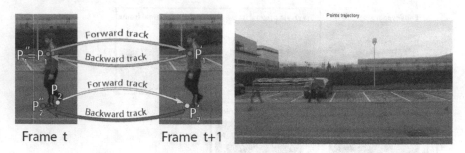

Fig. 2. Example of bi-directional error, on the left, and point trajectories, on the right

values of pixels. Such kind of change always results in tracking failure. Here, it should be noted that our aim is to find the instantaneous velocity of valid pixels. A pixel will be valid pixel if its forward and backward trajectory does not differ significantly. [6] proposed a method that can automatically detect the tracking failure by forward and backward tracking of pixels. As shown in Figure 2 (left), p_1 is a valid point because its forward and backward trajectories are similar while p_2 is an invalid point due to difference in forward and backward trajectories. So for accurate result, we remove all invalid and static pixels and consider only valid pixels. Figure 2 (right) shows the trajectories of valid points in green while trajectories of invalid points in red.

3   Conversion of Image Coordinates to Metric System

In this section, we will present two techniques that, can effectively convert estimates expressed in pixels per second to a real world metric system.

3.1   Scale Factor Conversion

The first conversion approach was defined considering situations in which (i) the direction of the camera is perpendicular to the most frequent paths followed by the tracked pedestrians, (ii) pedestrians mostly move in nearly straight lines, not necessarily having the same minimal distance from the camera. This situation essentially provides a sort of multi lane corridor in which pedestrians rarely change lane. Within this framework, we may be able to associate every tracked pedestrian to a given lane and then we can employ a given *scale factor* (associated to the lane) to convert a distance expressed in pixels to an actual one expressed in meters.

The problem we are facing with this approach is the fact that different lanes have the same length in terms of pixels, that is, image coordinates, whereas in the real world the related trajectories have a very different length due to the distinct distance between the lane and the camera. For instance, distances in the frame domain (on the right) are such that $\overline{ab}_f = \overline{cd}_f = \overline{ef}_f$ while distances in the real world (on the left) have very different relationships, i.e. $\overline{ab}_w < \overline{cd}_w < \overline{ef}_w$.

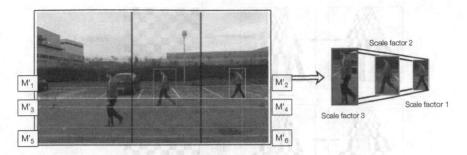

Fig. 3. Sample experimental setting for the scale factor conversion approach

Let us consider the situation highlighted in Figure 3: we have three lanes, respectively associated to segments $\overline{M'_1, M'_2}$, $\overline{M'_3, M'_4}$, $\overline{M'_5, M'_6}$, and they need to associated to three different scale factors. These segments have a specific length expressed in pixels and, in particular, we can define $m'_i = \overline{M'_i, M'_{i+1}}$. Similarly, we can also consider the *actual* segments $\overline{M_i, M_{i+1}}$, whose length m_i in instead expressed in meters. The scale factors, representing how many pixels correspond to a meter in the real world, can therefore be easily computed as $\lambda_i = m'_i/m_i$. Thanks to the tracking phase we have available the distance ΔP_j between the position of one of the valid points j of the tracked pedestrian in two subsequent frames expressed in pixels; the actual distance ΔD_j is computed as $\Delta D_j = \Delta P_j/\lambda_i$ when the tracked pedestrian is moving in lane $\overline{M_i, M_{i+1}}$.

In order to associate a tracked pedestrian to a given lane we exploit the height in pixels of the related bounding box; the rationale of the approach is that the larger the height, the closer to the camera the pedestrian will be. Therefore, we set a number of threshold values $th_1, th_2, \ldots, th_l$ such that l is equal to the number of lanes minus one and $th_i < th_j$ for $i < j$. Whenever the height of the bounding box of a pedestrian is below th_1 it will be associated to the closest lane ($\overline{M'_5, M'_6}$ in our example), whenever the height is between th_i and th_{i+1} it will be associated to lane i, and when it is higher than th_l it is associated to lane l. The values of the thresholds are of course crucial in associating the pedestrian to the correct lane and they must be achieved by manual calibration on experimental videos in the analyzed environment. Moreover, we assume that most pedestrians have an average height, since very short or tall pedestrians might be associated to incorrect lanes.

3.2 Homography Matrix Conversion

The second proposed method to convert pixel coordinates to real world ones employs a projective transformation to carry out at the same time (i) the correction of distortions due to perspective and (ii) the conversion from dimensions expressed in pixels to meters. This method essentially requires the construction of an homography, a projective mapping between two vector spaces, in our case

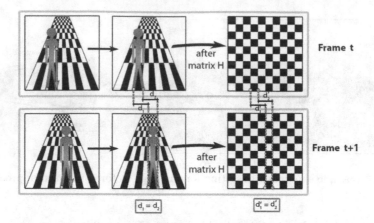

Fig. 4. Example of coordinates conversion through the homography approach: notice how the higher valid point is projected to the line of the lower one

the *image plane* associated to the captured frame and the actual 3D representation of the environment.

Let us consider a point $\bar{x}$ in world coordinates: it corresponds to a vector $\langle x, y, z \rangle$; nonetheless, for the image plane, we are dealing with points for which one of the coordinates is fixed. In particular, we consider an image plane $IP \subset \mathbb{R}^3$ such that $\bar{x} \in IP, \bar{x} = \langle x, y, 1 \rangle$ with $x, y \in \mathbb{R}$. The mapping h from real world to this image plane coordinates generally takes this form $h(\bar{x}) = H \cdot \bar{x}$, where H is a 3×3 non singular matrix. In particular:

$$\begin{pmatrix} x_1' \\ x_2' \\ x_3' \end{pmatrix} = \begin{bmatrix} h_{11} & h_{12} & h_{13} \\ h_{21} & h_{22} & h_{23} \\ h_{31} & h_{32} & h_{33} \end{bmatrix} \cdot \begin{pmatrix} x_1 \\ x_2 \\ x_3 \end{pmatrix} \qquad (1)$$

To set values for the elements of the matrix H we need some actual mappings between known real world coordinates and their related coordinates in the image plane. In particular, we need 4 or more of such mappings. In the experimental setting, therefore, we selected 4 distinct markers lying on a floor in the region of interest of the analyzed area (so with fixed z coordinate, equal to 1 in our case for sake of simplicity in the calculus) for which we gathered the real world coordinates, considering a reference system in which one of the markers is the origin (for sake of simplicity in the measurement). For each mapping between real world and image plane coordinates we can generate two equations for elements of H:

$$x' = \frac{x_1'}{x_3'} = \frac{h_{11}x + h_{12}y + h_{13}}{h_{31}x + h_{32}y + h_{33}} \qquad y' = \frac{x_2'}{x_3'} = \frac{h_{21}x + h_{22}y + h_{23}}{h_{31}x + h_{32}y + h_{33}} \qquad (2)$$

The availability of 4 markers and mappings leads us to having 8 linear equations that are sufficient to solve the system (since one of the coordinates in the image plane is fixed) and therefore compute the values for the elements of H.

Finally, we can compute H^{-1} that can be employed to convert coordinates in the image plane to real world ones.

The above transformation, however, does not preserve the distance between valid points detected on a pedestrian in the frame: for instance, let us consider a moving pedestrian generating valid points respectively for a point of the lower part and higher part of the body. The two points, in the real world, might have the same distance but the above transformation causes their mapped counterparts to have a changing distance unless they are actually on the same line in the image plane. To avoid this error in the mapping we decided to project the upper valid point to the same line of the lower one, as shown in Figure 4.

3.3 Estimation of Actual Speed of Pedestrian

In this section we discuss how to estimate the actual speed of a tracked pedestrian. To find the accurate speed of pedestrian, we calculate the instantaneous velocity of each valid point and the final velocity of the pedestrian is the mean of instantaneous velocities of all valid points. Lets assume that n valid points are detected during tracking for pedestrian and let vi represents the instantaneous velocity of point i. where $i = 1....n$. By using those instantaneous velocity vectors, we can find the average velocity of pedestrian by the equation $Viv(t) = \sum_{i=1}^{n} vi(t)$
where Viv is the average velocity of a pedestrian at time t.

4 Experimental Results

This section presents the quantitative analysis of the results obtained from experiments. We carried out experiments on a PC of 2.6 GHz (Core i5) with 4.0 GB memory. We recorded a video in outdoor environment where a pedestrian moves through lanes with varing speeds. The first column in Table 1a, shows the pedestrian moves through different lanes $\overline{M'_1, M'_2}$, $\overline{M'_3, M'_4}$, $\overline{M'_5, M'_6}$. The second column of Table 1a shows the real speeds of pedestrian calculated at the time of experiment. The remaining columns of Table 1a show the speed calculated using scale factor conversion. We calculate speed at different frame rate. With increasing frame rate, the number of valid points decreases and tracking is stop when no further valid point is detected. From the experiments it is obvious that change in frame rate does not have significant effect on the results, therefore, we keep the normal frame rate which is 1 f/s. From the Table, it can be seen that over all accuray is above 97 % when using scale factor measurement. It is matter of the fact that scale factor conversion rely more on the ground truth data. Table 1b shows the results of homography matrix conversion method. In the same way, first column of Table 1b shows the different lanes and proceeding columns shows the real speeds and speed of pedestrian calculated by our proposed method. We compute different homography matrices by considering different points on image plane near to markers and check the accuracy of each homography matrix. As obvious from Table 1b, homography matrix H2 gives more accurate results than others. It is matter of the fact that homography matrix H2 is computed by considering points on the image plan more closer to markers. Farther the points on image plane from markers, the lesser will be the accuracy. Homography matrix conversion is less dependent on the ground truth and gives us good results.

	Real	1 F.	2 F.	3 F.	4 F.
(M1',M2')	1.52	1.45	1.54	1.52	1.57
(M1',M2')	1.51	1.47	1.5	1.48	1.53
(M1',M2')	1.9	1.93	1.98	1.97	1.93
(M1',M2')	1.28	1.22	1.28	1.26	1.29
(M3',M4')	1.26	1.21	1.25	1.26	1.26
(M3',M4')	1.47	1.4	1.45	1.47	1.42
(M3',M4')	1.78	1.75	1.78	1.81	1.78
(M5',M6')	1.19	1.2	1.22	1.21	1.21
(M5',M6')	1.43	1.45	1.48	1.47	1.45
(M5',M6')	1.77	1.79	1.78	1.77	1.85
Error (%)		2.7%	1.5%	1.3%	1.8%

(a) Mean velocity using different scale factors

	Real	H1	H2	H3	H4
(M1',M2')	1.52	1.48	1.46	1.46	1.48
(M1',M2')	1.51	1.49	1.48	1.46	1.49
(M1',M2')	1.9	1.95	1.92	1.92	1.95
(M1',M2')	1.28	1.21	1.21	1.2	1.21
(M3',M4')	1.26	1.39	1.38	1.34	1.39
(M3',M4')	1.47	1.61	1.62	1.6	1.6
(M3',M4')	1.78	1.96	1.9	1.95	1.97
(M5',M6')	1.19	1.27	1.17	1.27	1.27
(M5',M6')	1.43	1.59	1.49	1.58	1.58
(M5',M6')	1.77	1.84	1.72	1.84	1.84
Error (%)		6.5%	4.8%	6.1%	6.3%

(b) Mean Velocity using Homography Matrix (1/2 fps)

5   Conclusions and Future Works

This paper has presented the first steps and results in an approach towards the development of a computer vision based automatic system for the estimation of pedestrian velocity in real world traffic systems. Data acquired through this system can be useful for both simulation and control systems. In particular, we aim at applying the introduced techniques in studies about the behaviour of pedestrians and drivers in intersections to improve the safety of vulnerable road users. Future works are mainly aimed at, first of all, extending the range of experiments to evaluate the adequacy of the approach to a wider set of situations, and then we also intend to improve the adopted tracking techniques, an extremely challenging task in real world settings: in particular, we are currently testing the adoption of the GMCP-Teacker [16] with encouraging preliminary results.

Acknowledgements. This work was partly supported by the ALIAS project ("Higher education and internationalization for the Ageing Society"), funded by Fondazione CARIPLO.

References

1. Pedestrian safety: A road safety manual for decision-makers and practitioners. Tech. rep., World Health Organization (2013)
2. Boltes, M., Seyfried, A.: Collecting pedestrian trajectories. Neurocomputing 100, 127–133 (2013)

3. Conde, C., Serrano, A., Rodríguez-Aragón, L., Pérez, J., Cabello, E.: An experimental approach to a real-time controlled traffic light multi-agent application. In: Proceedings of AAMAS 2004 Workshop on Agents in Traffic and Transportation, pp. 8–13 (2004)

4. Dernellis, A., Ashworth, R.: Pedestrian subways in urban areas: some observations concerning their use. Traffic Engineering & Control 35(1), 14–18 (1994)

5. Fascioli, A., Fedriga, R.I., Ghidoni, S.: Vision-based monitoring of pedestrian crossings. In: 14th International Conference on Image Analysis and Processing, ICIAP 2007, pp. 566–574. IEEE (2007)

6. Kalal, Z., Mikolajczyk, K., Matas, J.: Forward-backward error: Automatic detection of tracking failures. In: 2010 20th International Conference on Pattern Recognition (ICPR), pp. 2756–2759. IEEE (2010)

7. Li, W., Wu, X., Matsumoto, K., Zhao, H.A.: Crowd foreground detection and density estimation based on moment. In: 2010 International Conference on Wavelet Analysis and Pattern Recognition (ICWAPR), pp. 130–135. IEEE (2010)

8. Reza, A.M.: Realization of the contrast limited adaptive histogram equalization (clahe) for real-time image enhancement. Journal of VLSI Signal Processing Systems for Signal, Image and Video Technology 38(1), 35–44 (2004)

9. Safety for Seniors Working Group (WA): Safety for Seniors: Final Report on Pedestrian Safety (1988)

10. Shi, J., Tomasi, C.: Good features to track. In: Proceedings of 1994 IEEE Computer Society Conference on Computer Vision and Pattern Recognition, CVPR 1994, pp. 593–600. IEEE (1994)

11. Sourtzinos, P., Makris, D., Remagnino, P.: Highly accurate estimation of pedestrian speed profiles from video sequences. In: Remagnino, P., Monekosso, D.N., Jain, L.C. (eds.) Innovations in Defence Support Systems – 3. SCI, vol. 336, pp. 71–81. Springer, Heidelberg (2011)

12. Tomasi, C., Kanade, T.: Detection and tracking of point features. School of Computer Science, Carnegie Mellon Univ. (1991)

13. Tsai, R.Y.: A versatile camera calibration technique for high-accuracy 3D machine vision metrology using off-the-shelf tv cameras and lenses. IEEE Journal of Robotics and Automation 3(4), 323–344 (1987)

14. Vceraraghavan, H., Masoud, O., Papanikolopoulos, N.: Vision-based monitoring of intersections. In: Proceedings of the IEEE 5th International Conference on Intelligent Transportation Systems, pp. 7–12. IEEE (2002)

15. Vizzari, G., Bandini, S.: Studying pedestrian and crowd dynamics through integrated analysis and synthesis. IEEE Intelligent Systems 28(5), 56–60 (2013)

16. Zamir, A.R., Dehghan, A., Shah, M.: GMCP-tracker: Global multi-object tracking using generalized minimum clique graphs. In: Fitzgibbon, A., Lazebnik, S., Perona, P., Sato, Y., Schmid, C. (eds.) ECCV 2012, Part II. LNCS, vol. 7573, pp. 343–356. Springer, Heidelberg (2012)

Geometric Characterization
of Hereditarily Bijective Boolean Networks

Paul Ruet

CNRS, Laboratoire Preuves, Programmes et Systèmes
Université Paris Diderot - Paris 7
Case 7014, 75205 Paris Cedex 13, France
ruet@pps.univ-paris-diderot.fr

Abstract. The study of relationships between structure and dynamics of asynchronous Boolean networks has recently led to the introduction of hereditarily bijective maps and even or odd self-dual networks. We show here that these two notions can be simply characterized geometrically: through orthogonality between certain affine subspaces. We also use this characterization to provide a construction of the class of hereditarily bijective maps, and to study its stability properties.

1 Introduction

Boolean networks represent the dynamic interaction of components which can take two values, 0 and 1. Introduced by von Neumann [17], they have been extensively used to model various biological networks, especially genetic regulatory networks, since the early works of S. Kauffman and R. Thomas [5,6,13]. They are a discrete alternative to differential equations models, in which sufficently precise quantitative data often lack to accurately define the parameters. Regulatory interactions also exhibit strong thresholds effects (sigmoids), so that differential models are often conveniently approximated by piecewise linear equations [12], or one step further discretized into Boolean (or more generally multivalued) networks. See [2,1] for recent surveys.

An increasingly active field of research is the study of asynchronous Boolean networks [15]. An asynchronous Boolean network with n components may be presented by its phase space, which is a partial orientation of the lattice $\{0,1\}^n$, *i.e.*, a directed graph whose vertex set is $\{0,1\}^n$ and whose edges only relate vertices which are 1-distant from each other for the Hamming distance. Asynchronous networks are thus nondeterministic dynamical systems, in which the value of at most one component may be updated at a time.

Although other update schemes of Boolean networks are studied as models of biological networks (in particular random [5] and synchronous networks [6,3], as well as comparisons between update schemes [4]), asynchrony provides a simple mathematical framework in which all possible trajectories are considered. In the context of genetic networks, one may observe that trajectories of piecewise linear models almost surely (in the sense of measure theory) cross only one threshold

J. Wąs, G.C. Sirakoulis, and S. Bandini (Eds.): ACRI 2014, LNCS 8751, pp. 536–545, 2014.

hyperplane at a time, so that only the value of the corresponding component is updated in the discretized Boolean network, which thus follows the asynchronous update scheme.

The asymptotic dynamical properties of asynchronous Boolean networks (nature and number of attractors, e.g., existence and unicity of fixed points or attractive cycles) depend on their structure (the directed graph of interactions between components), but precise relationships between dynamics and structure are very difficult to characterize in general. In [14,16], R. Thomas conjectures rules relating positive or negative cycles in the interaction graphs to non-unicity of fixed points (related to cellular differentiation) or sustained oscillations (related to homeostasis). It is possible to give a precise mathematical status to these rules in the framework of asynchronous networks, by identifying sustained oscillations with *cyclic attractors* and by defining *local interaction graphs* in a way similar to Jacobian matrices (Section 2 recalls the useful definitions). In this framework, while the positive rule is well understood [7], the rule relating (local) negative cycles to the existence of a cyclic attractor is unproved in general. In [9], the special case of and-or nets is partly solved, and in [10] the special case of *antipodal* attractive cycles for and-or nets is fully proved.

In the course of better understanding these relationships, two opposite notions have been independently introduced recently: *even or odd self-dual* networks in [8], and *hereditarily bijective* maps in [10]. They seem particularly relevant to the study of asynchronous Boolean networks which have a non trivial dynamics: indeed, the dynamics of a hereditarily bijective map is weakly terminating to a unique fixed point, hence particularly "simple", while even or odd self-dual subnetworks are necessary for the emergence of a "complex" dynamical behaviour.

In this article, we develop the theory of these classes of networks. We show that hereditary bijectivity, and hence even or odd self-duality, can be simply characterized geometrically: through orthogonality between certain affine subspaces (Section 4). We use this characterization to provide a construction of the class of hereditarily bijective maps (Section 5), and to study its stability properties, in particular to prove that it is stable under inverse. We also study the relationship between the invertibility of a Boolean map and of its Jacobian matrices: we show that if a map from $\{0,1\}^n$ to itself has all its Jacobian matrices hereditarily invertible, then it is hereditarily bijective (while the same statement without heredity is known to be false).

2   Asynchronous Boolean Networks

We need some preliminary definitions and notations. $\mathbb{B}$ denotes the set $\{0,1\}$. Boolean sum $(+)$ and product $(\cdot)$ equip $\mathbb{B}$ with the structure of the field $\mathbb{F}_2$.

Let $\{e_1,\ldots,e_n\}$ be the canonical basis of the vector space $\mathbb{B}^n$, and for each $I \subseteq \{1,\ldots,n\}$, $e_I = \sum_{i\in I} e_i$. For $x,y \in \mathbb{B}^n$, $v(x,y)$ denotes the subset $I \subseteq \{1,\ldots,n\}$ such that $x + y = e_I$, and the Hamming distance $d(x,y)$ is defined as the cardinality of $v(x,y)$.

$$f_1(x) = (x_2 + 1)x_3$$
$$f_2(x) = (x_3 + 1)x_1$$
$$f_3(x) = (x_1 + 1)x_2$$

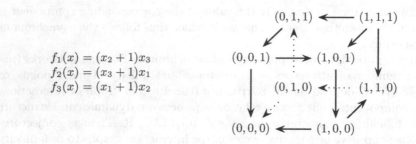

Fig. 1. A Boolean map $f : \mathbb{B}^3 \to \mathbb{B}^3$ and the asynchronous dynamics $\Gamma(f)$ associated to it. For instance, the point $x = (1,0,0)$ in $\Gamma(f)$ has two outgoing edges to $x + e_1 = (0,0,0)$ and $x + e_2 = (1,1,0)$ because $f(x) = (0,1,0) = x + e_1 + e_2$.

Asynchronous Boolean networks can be equivalently presented in terms of directed graphs or in terms of Boolean maps. An *asynchronous Boolean network* can be defined:

1. either as a directed graph whose vertex set is $\mathbb{B}^n$ and whose edges only relate vertices which are 1-distant from each other (for any edge from x to y, $d(x, y) = 1$);
2. or as a map from $\mathbb{B}^n$ to $\mathbb{B}^n$.

The two presentations indeed carry the same information (see Figure 1):

1. To a directed graph γ as above, we may associate a map $\Phi(\gamma) : \mathbb{B}^n \to \mathbb{B}^n$ by $\Phi(\gamma)(x) = x + e_I$, where $\{(x, x + e_i), i \in I\}$ is the set of edges going from x in γ.
2. Conversely, given a map $f : \mathbb{B}^n \to \mathbb{B}^n$ we may define a directed graph $\Gamma(f)$ with vertex set $\mathbb{B}^n$ and an edge from x to y when for some i, $y = x + e_i$ and $f_i(x) \neq x_i$. Here, f_i is defined by $f_i(x) = f(x)_i$. In that case, $d(x, y) = 1$, and clearly, Γ and Φ are inverses of each other.

We call $\Gamma(f)$ the *asynchronous dynamics* associated to f. As we shall consider asynchronous Boolean networks as dynamical systems, the coordinates i such that $f_i(x) \neq x_i$ may naturally be considered as the *degrees of freedom* of x.

2.1   Dynamical Properties

We shall be interested in the following asymptotic dynamical properties of asynchronous Boolean networks.

Let $f : \mathbb{B}^n \to \mathbb{B}^n$. A *trajectory* is a path in $\Gamma(f)$, and an *attractor* a terminal strongly connected component of $\Gamma(f)$. An attractor which is not a singleton (*i.e.*, which does not consist in a fixed point) is called a *cyclic attractor*. *Attractive cycles*, *i.e.*, cyclic trajectories θ such that for each point $x \in \theta$, $d(x, f(x)) = 1$, are examples of cyclic attractors. Observe that attractive cycles are deterministic, since any point in θ has a unique degree of freedom.

Recall that f is *weakly terminating* when for any $x \in \mathbb{B}^n$, some trajectory leaving x leads to a fixed point. Therefore, f has a cyclic attractor if and only if it is not weakly terminating. A stronger form of weak termination may be defined as follows. Given $f : \mathbb{B}^n \to \mathbb{B}^n$, a path from $x \in \mathbb{B}^n$ to $y \in \mathbb{B}^n$ in $\Gamma(f)$ is called a *direct trajectory* when its length is minimal, *i.e.*, equals $d(x, y)$. And $\Gamma(f)$ is said to be *directly terminating* when for any point $x \in \mathbb{B}^n$ there exists a direct trajectory from x to some fixed point.

For instance, the network f defined in Figure 1 has a (non-attractive) cyclic trajectory $(1, 0, 0) \to (1, 1, 0) \to (0, 1, 0) \to (0, 1, 1) \to (0, 0, 1) \to (1, 0, 1) \to (1, 0, 0)$, but it is directly terminating to a unique fixed point. We shall see in Section 3 that this property of direct termination is actually a consequence of the fact that $f + \mathrm{id}$ is hereditarily bijective (Theorem 3).

2.2 Subcubes and Subnetworks

Given $x \in \mathbb{B}^n$ and $I \subseteq \{1, \ldots, n\}$, the subset $x[I]$ consists in all points y such that $y_i = x_i$ for each $i \notin I$; subsets of the form $x[I]$ are called *I-subcubes*, or simply *subcubes* of $\mathbb{B}^n$. If $y = x + e_I$, the subcube $x[I]$ is also denoted by $[x, y]$.

Subcubes of $\mathbb{B}^n$ are affine subspaces: indeed, the vector space $0[I] = \{e_J | J \subseteq I\}$ acts faithfully and transitively on $x[I]$. However, not every affine subspace is a subcube: the subset $\{(0, 0), (1, 1)\}$ is an affine subspace because $(1, 1) + (1, 1) = (0, 0)$, but it is clearly not a subcube.

For any subcube κ, let $\pi_\kappa : \mathbb{B}^n \to \kappa$ be the projection onto κ, defined as follows: if $\kappa = x[I]$,

$$(\pi_\kappa(y))_i = \begin{cases} y_i & \text{if } i \in I \\ x_i & \text{otherwise.} \end{cases}$$

Let also $\iota_\kappa : \kappa \to \mathbb{B}^n$ be the inclusion map. It is then immediate that $\pi_\kappa \circ \iota_\kappa$ is the identity. For any $f : \mathbb{B}^n \to \mathbb{B}^n$, let

$$f\!\restriction_\kappa = \pi_\kappa \circ f \circ \iota_\kappa : \kappa \to \kappa.$$

A *subnetwork* of f is a map $f\!\restriction_\kappa$ for some subcube κ. The asynchronous dynamics $\Gamma(f\!\restriction_\kappa)$ is easily shown to be the subgraph of $\Gamma(f)$ induced by vertices in κ, a characterization which may be taken as an alternative, more intuitive, definition of subnetworks.

We shall need the following lemmas.

Lemma 1. *The projection onto any I-subcube is an affine map, with associated linear transformation the projection $\pi_{0[I]}$ from $\mathbb{B}^n$ onto the linear subspace $0[I]$.*

Proof. If κ is an I-subcube, then:

$$\pi_\kappa(x) = \pi_\kappa(0) + \pi_{0[I]}(x). \tag{1}$$

Indeed, for any $i \notin I$, $(\pi_\kappa(x))_i = (\pi_\kappa(0))_i$ and $(\pi_{0[I]}(x))_i = 0$. And for any $i \in I$, $(\pi_\kappa(x))_i = (\pi_{0[I]}(x))_i = x_i$ and $(\pi_\kappa(0))_i = 0$.   □

Lemma 2. *Let $\kappa = x[I]$ and $\lambda = y[J]$ be any two subcubes of $\mathbb{B}^n$. The image of λ under π_κ is the subcube $\pi_\kappa(y)[I \cap J]$. In other terms, $\pi_\kappa(y[J]) = \pi_\kappa(y)[J] \cap \kappa$.*

Proof. A point of λ is of the form $y + e_K$ for some $K \subseteq J$. By Equation (1), for any $K \subseteq J$:

$$\pi_\kappa(y + e_K) = \pi_\kappa(y) + \pi_{0[I]}(e_K) = \pi_\kappa(y) + e_{I \cap K}.$$

When K varies among all subsets of J, $I \cap K$ varies among all subsets of $I \cap J$. Therefore the image of λ under π_κ equals $\pi_\kappa(y)[I \cap J]$.

Now, observe that $z[I \cap J] = z[I] \cap z[J]$ for any z. Since $\pi_\kappa(y)[I] = x[I] = \kappa$, we conclude that $\pi_\kappa(y)[I \cap J] = \pi_\kappa(y)[J] \cap \kappa$. □

Corollary 1. *If $x, y \in \mathbb{B}^n$ and κ is any subcube, then $\pi_\kappa([x, y]) = [\pi_\kappa(x), \pi_\kappa(y)]$.*

3   Hereditarily Bijective Maps and Even or Odd Self-Dual Networks

A map $f : \mathbb{B}^n \to \mathbb{B}^n$ is said to be *hereditarily bijective* (resp. *hereditarily ufp*) [10] when for any subcube κ, $f\restriction_\kappa$ is bijective (resp. has a unique fixed point). A pair $(x, y) \in \mathbb{B}^n \times \mathbb{B}^n$ called a *mirror pair* of $f : \mathbb{B}^n \to \mathbb{B}^n$ when $(f + \mathrm{id})\restriction_{[x,y]}(x) = (f + \mathrm{id})\restriction_{[x,y]}(y)$, *i.e.*, when x and y have the same degrees of freedom for the projected map $f\restriction_{[x,y]}$.

For any $x \in \mathbb{B}^n$, the translation t_x maps $y \in \mathbb{B}^n$ to $x + y$. The following proposition establishes some immediate stability properties of the class of hereditarily bijective maps.

Proposition 1. *The class of hereditarily bijective maps is stable under:*

1. *composition with translations: if $f : \mathbb{B}^n \to \mathbb{B}^n$ is hereditarily bijective and $x, y \in \mathbb{B}^n$, then so is $t_x \circ f \circ t_y$;*
2. *permutation of coordinates: if $f : \mathbb{B}^n \to \mathbb{B}^n$ is hereditarily bijective and $\sigma \in \mathfrak{S}_n$, then so is $f^\sigma = \sigma \circ f \circ \sigma^{-1}$, where σ acts on $\mathbb{B}^n$ by permuting coordinates.*

Proof. The first property follows from the fact that translations are (hereditarily) bijective and stable under projection on subcubes. The second property follows from the fact that $f^\sigma\restriction_\kappa = (f\restriction_{\sigma(\kappa)})^\sigma$. □

We shall use the results of Section 4 to give another stability property in Corollary 3. Let now id denote the identity map from $\mathbb{B}^n$ to itself. The following theorem relates the above three definitions.

Theorem 1 (Ruet [10]). *For any $f : \mathbb{B}^n \to \mathbb{B}^n$, the following are equivalent:*

1. *$f + \mathrm{id}$ is hereditarily bijective;*
2. *f is hereditarily ufp;*
3. *f has no mirror pair.*

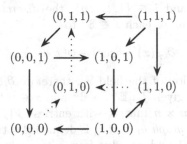

Fig. 2. A network $g : \mathbb{B}^3 \to \mathbb{B}^3$ such that $g + \mathrm{id}$ is not (hereditarily) bijective

A point $x \in \mathbb{B}^n$ is said to be *even* (resp. *odd*) [8] when $\sum_{i=1}^{n} x_i = 0$ (resp. 1). The sum here is again addition in the field $\mathbb{F}_2$. A map $f : \mathbb{B}^n \to \mathbb{B}^n$ is *even* (resp. *odd*) when the image of $f + \mathrm{id}$ is the set of even (resp. odd) points of $\mathbb{B}^n$. Let $\overline{x}$ denote the antipode $x + e_1 + \cdots + e_n$ of $x \in \mathbb{B}^n$. Now, a map f is *self-dual* when for any $x \in \mathbb{B}^n$, $f(\overline{x}) = \overline{f(x)}$, i.e., $(x, \overline{x})$ is a mirror pair.

Point 2 of the following theorem essentially asserts that if $f + \mathrm{id}$ is not hereditarily bijective, not only has f a mirror pair, but it has an even or odd self-dual subnetwork.

Theorem 2 (Richard [8]). *Let $f : \mathbb{B}^n \to \mathbb{B}^n$.*

1. *If for any $i \in \{1, \ldots, n\}$ and $\{1, \ldots, n\} \setminus \{i\}$-subcube κ, $(f + \mathrm{id})\!\restriction_\kappa$ is bijective, and if $f + \mathrm{id}$ is not bijective, then f is even or odd, and self-dual.*
2. *$f + \mathrm{id}$ is hereditarily bijective if and only if f has no even or odd self-dual subnetwork.*

The asynchronous dynamics of hereditarily bijective maps can then be characterized as follows.

Theorem 3 (Richard [8], Ruet [10]). *If $f + \mathrm{id}$ is hereditarily bijective, then $\Gamma(f)$ has a unique attractor, this attractor is a fixed point and $\Gamma(f)$ is directly terminating (in particular, it is weakly terminating).*

As we have already observed, for the network f of Figure 1, $f + \mathrm{id}$ is hereditarily bijective and indeed, f is directly terminating to a unique fixed point. On the other hand, flipping the arrow from $(0, 1, 0)$ to $(0, 0, 0)$ in f gives rise to the network g of Figure 2 without fixed point: $g + \mathrm{id}$ is not bijective (hence not hereditarily bijective) as it never takes value 0, and for $\kappa = (0, 0, 0)[2, 3] = [(0, 0, 0), (0, 1, 1)]$, $g\!\restriction_\kappa$ is an odd self-dual subnetwork.

3.1 Dynamics and Structure

The above definitions are used in [8,10] to understand the relationships between the dynamics of an asynchronous Boolean network f and the structure of its Jacobian matrices $\mathscr{J}(f)(x)$ and interaction graphs $\mathscr{G}(f)(x)$. Let us recall the definitions of $\mathscr{J}(f)(x)$ and $\mathscr{G}(f)(x)$.

Given $\varphi : \mathbb{B}^n \to \mathbb{B}$ and $i \in \{1, \ldots, n\}$, the *discrete i^{th} partial derivative* $\partial\varphi/\partial x_i = \partial_i\varphi : \mathbb{B}^n \to \mathbb{B}$ maps each $x \in \mathbb{B}^n$ to

$$\partial_i\varphi(x) = \varphi(x) + \varphi(x + e_i).$$

The $+$ here is the addition of the field $\mathbb{F}_2$, therefore $\partial_i\varphi(x) = 1$ if and only if $\varphi(x) \neq \varphi(x + e_i)$. Now, given $f : \mathbb{B}^n \to \mathbb{B}^n$ and $x \in \mathbb{B}^n$, the *discrete Jacobian matrix* $\mathscr{J}(f)(x)$ is the $n \times n$ matrix with entries $\mathscr{J}(f)(x)_{i,j} = \partial_j f_i(x)$. And $\mathscr{G}(f)(x)$, the *interaction graph of f at x*, is defined [11] to be the directed graph with vertex set $\{1, \ldots, n\}$ and an edge from j to i when $\mathscr{J}(f)(x)_{i,j} = 1$. The Jacobian matrix $\mathscr{J}(f)(x)$ is therefore simply the transpose of the adjacency matrix of $\mathscr{G}(f)(x)$, and $\mathscr{G}(f)(x)$ is the graph underlying the signed interaction graph defined in [7].

In [8,10], a theorem of Shih and Dong on unicity of fixed points is improved as follows.

Theorem 4. *Let $f : \mathbb{B}^n \to \mathbb{B}^n$.*

1. *If for any $x \in \mathbb{B}^n$, $\mathscr{G}(f)(x)$ has no cycle, then f has a unique fixed point (Shih and Dong [11]).*
2. *If $f + \mathrm{id}$ is not hereditarily bijective, then there exist two points $x, y \in \mathbb{B}^n$ such that $\mathscr{G}(f)(x)$ and $\mathscr{G}(f)(y)$ have a cycle (Ruet [10]).*
3. *If $f + \mathrm{id}$ is not bijective, then for some $k \in \{1, \ldots, n\}$, there exist 2^k points $x \in \mathbb{B}^n$ such that $\mathscr{G}(f)(x)$ has a cycle of length at most k (Richard [8]).*

In [10], it is also shown that the invertibility of all Jacobian matrices $\mathscr{J}(f)(x)$ does not entail invertibility of $f : \mathbb{B}^n \to \mathbb{B}^n$. We prove here that the stronger condition of hereditary invertibility does.

Definition 1 (Hereditary invertibility, nilpotence). *An $n \times n$ matrix with entries in $\mathbb{B}$ is said to be hereditarily invertible (resp. hereditarily nilpotent) when all its principal minors are.*

Lemma 3. *Let M be an $n \times n$ matrix with entries in $\mathbb{B}$. The following are equivalent:*

1. *the graph associated to M has no cycle;*
2. *M is hereditarily nilpotent;*
3. *$\mathscr{I} + M$ is hereditarily invertible, where $\mathscr{I}$ denotes the identity matrix.*

Proof. It is proved in [10] that (1) implies M is nilpotent, hence hereditarily nilpotent because induced subgraphs of M have no cycle either. Therefore, (1) implies (2). Clearly, (2) implies (3).

It remains to prove that (3) implies (1). If $\mathscr{I} + M$ is hereditarily invertible, its diagonal is necessarily $(1, \ldots, 1)$. Assume for a contradiction that the graph associated to M has a cycle: let C be a minimal cycle, *i.e.*, one without chord, and $|C|$ be its vertex set. Then the principal minor $(\mathscr{I} + M)_{|C|}$ is the sum of $\mathscr{I}_{|C|}$ with the matrix of a cyclic permutation: it is therefore not invertible, contradicting the hypothesis. $\square$

Theorem 5. *Let* $f : \mathbb{B}^n \to \mathbb{B}^n$. *If* $\mathscr{J}(f)(x)$ *is hereditarily invertible for each* $x \in \mathbb{B}^n$, *then* f *is hereditarily bijective.*

Proof. By Lemma 3, the condition of the theorem implies that, for any $x \in \mathbb{B}^n$, $\mathscr{I} + \mathscr{J}(f)(x) = \mathscr{J}(f + \mathrm{id})(x)$ has no cycle. By Theorem 4, f is then hereditarily bijective. □

4 Hereditary Bijectivity and Orthogonality

We now turn to the main topic of this paper. A symmetric and nondegenerate bilinear form $\langle \cdot, \cdot \rangle : \mathbb{B}^n \times \mathbb{B}^n \to \mathbb{B}$ is defined on the vector space $\mathbb{B}^n = \mathbb{F}_2^n$ by $\langle x, y \rangle = \sum_{i=1}^n x_i y_i$, with sum and product in $\mathbb{F}_2$. As usual, two vectors x, y are orthogonal when $\langle x, y \rangle = 0$, a symmetric relation denoted by $x \perp y$. Let A and B be two affine subspaces of $\mathbb{B}^n$, with underlying vector spaces V and W respectively: A and B are said to be orthogonal (denoted by $A \perp B$) when for any two vectors $v \in V$ and $w \in W$, $v \perp w$.

We shall use orthogonality of subcubes to characterize hereditary bijectivity.

Theorem 6. *For any* $f : \mathbb{B}^n \to \mathbb{B}^n$, f *is hereditarily bijective if and only if for any* $x, y \in \mathbb{B}^n$ *such that* $x \neq y$, $[x, y] \not\perp [f(x), f(y)]$.

We first need the following lemmas.

Lemma 4. *Two subcubes* $x[I], y[J]$ *of* $\mathbb{B}^n$ *are orthogonal if and only if* $I \cap J = \varnothing$.

Proof. The vector spaces underlying $x[I]$ and $y[J]$ are spanned by the sets $\{e_i | i \in I\}$ and $\{e_j | j \in J\}$ respectively. Therefore $x[I]$ and $y[J]$ are orthogonal if and only if any two spanning vectors e_i, e_j, with $(i, j) \in I \times J$, are orthogonal. As $\langle e_i, e_j \rangle = \delta_{i,j}$, this happens exactly when $i \neq j$ for any $(i, j) \in I \times J$, *i.e.*, $I \cap J = \varnothing$. □

Lemma 5. *Projections onto subcubes are orthogonal projections.*

Proof. By Lemma 1, it suffices to prove that the linear projection onto any linear subspace $0[I]$, with $I \subseteq \{1, \ldots, n\}$, is an orthogonal projection. The null space of $\pi_{0[I]}$ is clearly the subspace $0[J]$, where $J = \{1, \ldots, n\} \setminus I$. By Lemma 4, we may then conclude that the null space $0[J]$ and the range $0[I]$ of $\pi_{0[I]}$ are orthogonal, as expected. □

We now turn to the proof of Theorem 6.

Let us first prove that if f is hereditarily bijective, then for any $x, y \in \mathbb{B}^n$ such that $x \neq y$, $[x, y] \not\perp [f(x), f(y)]$. Assume for a contradiction that for some $x \neq y$, $[x, y] \perp [f(x), f(y)]$. Let $\kappa = [x, y]$ and $\lambda = [f(x), f(y)]$, so that $\kappa \perp \lambda$. By Lemma 5, π_κ maps the whole subcube λ to a single point. Hence in particular, the two points $f(x)$ and $f(y)$ are mapped by π_κ to the same point $\pi_\kappa(f(x)) = \pi_\kappa(f(y))$. Therefore the two points $x, y \in \kappa$ are mapped by $f\restriction_\kappa = \pi_\kappa \circ f \circ \iota_\kappa$ to the same point, and $f\restriction_\kappa$ is not bijective: contradiction.

Conversely, if f is not hereditarily bijective, then $f\!\restriction_\kappa$ is not bijective for some subcube κ: there exist $x, y \in \kappa$ such that $x \neq y$ and $f\!\restriction_\kappa (x) = f\!\restriction_\kappa (y)$. In particular, we have:

$$\pi_{[x,y]}(f(x)) = f\!\restriction_{[x,y]} (x) = f\!\restriction_{[x,y]} (y) = \pi_{[x,y]}(f(y)),$$

and $\pi_{[x,y]}$ maps $f(x)$ and $f(y)$ to the same point. By Corollary 1, $\pi_{[x,y]}$ thus maps the subcube $[f(x), f(y)]$ to a single point. This implies that $[x, y] \perp [f(x), f(y)]$ by Lemma 5. This completes the proof of Theorem 6, and we may summarize the above characterizations as follows.

Corollary 2. *The following are equivalent:*

1. $f + \mathrm{id}$ *is hereditarily bijective;*
2. f *is hereditarily ufp;*
3. f *has no mirror pair;*
4. f *has no even or odd self-dual subnetwork;*
5. *for any* $x \neq y$, $[x, y] \not\perp [f(x) + x, f(y) + y]$.

Another consequence of Theorem 6 is the following stability property of the class of hereditarily bijective maps.

Corollary 3. *Inverses of hereditarily bijective maps are hereditarily bijective.*

Proof. By Theorem 6, we have to prove that if f is hereditarily bijective, then for any $x \neq y$, $[x, y] \not\perp [f^{-1}(x), f^{-1}(y)]$. When $x \neq y$, $f^{-1}(x) \neq f^{-1}(y)$, hence, again by Theorem 6, $[f^{-1}(x), f^{-1}(y)] \perp [f(f^{-1}(x)), f(f^{-1}(y))] = [x, y]$.   □

This property is especially interesting in view of the fact that hereditarily bijective maps do not form a category: $f : (x_1, x_2) \mapsto (x_1, x_1 + x_2)$ and $g : (x_1, x_2) \mapsto (x_1 + x_2, x_2)$ are hereditarily bijective, but their composite $g \circ f : (x_1, x_2) \mapsto (x_2, x_1 + x_2)$ is not.

5   Constructions of Even or Odd Self-dual Networks and Hereditarily Bijective Maps

Even self-dual networks may be constructed in full generality as follows. Given $\sigma \in \mathfrak{S}_n$, let $f : \mathbb{B}^{n+1} \to \mathbb{B}^{n+1}$ be the self-dual network defined on the subcube $0[\{1, \ldots, n\}]$ by $f(x, 0) = (\sigma(x), 0)$ if $\sigma(x)$ is even, $(\sigma(x), 1)$ otherwise (and self-duality determines $f(x, 1)$): then f is clearly even, and any even self-dual network can be constructed in this way. Replacing even by odd in the above definition provides arbitrary odd self-dual networks.

Constructing all hereditarily bijective maps is less immediate. Starting from hereditarily bijective maps $\sigma, \tau : \mathbb{B}^n \to \mathbb{B}^n$, let $f : \mathbb{B}^{n+1} \to \mathbb{B}^{n+1}$ be defined by $f(x, 0) = (\sigma(x), 0)$ and $f(x, 1) = (\tau(x), 1)$. Then f is clearly hereditarily bijective. But in general, there exist other hereditarily bijective maps projecting to σ and τ. Let S be a subset of $\mathbb{B}^n$ which is stable under the action of $\tau^{-1}\sigma$, and let g be defined by $f(x, 0) = (\sigma(x), 0)$ if $x \in S$, $(\sigma(x), 1)$ otherwise, and

$f(x, 1) = (\tau(x), 1)$ if $x \in S$, $(\tau(x), 0)$ otherwise: then g is bijective because, w.r.t. f, the roles of $(x, 0)$ and $(y, 1)$ are permuted exactly when $\sigma(x) = \tau(y)$, i.e., $y = \tau^{-1}\sigma(x)$. For it to be hereditarily bijective (and not merely bijective), one needs to take S stable under the actions of $(\tau\lceil_\kappa)^{-1}\sigma\lceil_\kappa$ for any subcube κ.

These stable sets S may further be characterized as follows, through the orthogonality relation defined in Section 4. Consider the binary relation $x \smile y$ on $\mathbb{B}^n$ defined by $[x, y] \perp [\sigma(x), \tau(y)]$: by Lemma 4, if $x + y = e_I$ and $\sigma(x) + \tau(y) = e_J$, $x \smile y$ is equivalently defined by $I \cap J = \varnothing$. This relation generates an equivalence relation, whose equivalence classes are the required sets.

References

1. Chaouiya, C., Remy, E.: Logical modelling of regulatory networks, methods and applications. Bulletin of Mathematical Biology 75, 891–895 (2013)
2. de Jong, H.: Modeling and simulation of genetic regulatory systems: A literature review. Journal of Computational Biology 9(1), 67–103 (2002)
3. Demongeot, J., Elena, A., Sené, S.: Robustness in regulatory networks: a multidisciplinary approach. Acta Biotheoretica 56(1-2), 27–49 (2008)
4. Goles, E., Salinas, L.: Comparison between parallel and serial dynamics of Boolean networks. Theoretical Computer Science 396, 247–253 (2008)
5. Kauffman, S.A.: Metabolic stability and epigenesis in randomly constructed genetic nets. Journal of Theoretical Biology 22, 437–467 (1969)
6. Kauffman, S.A.: The origins of order: Self-organization and selection in evolution. Oxford University Press (1993)
7. Remy, E., Ruet, P., Thieffry, D.: Graphic requirements for multistability and attractive cycles in a Boolean dynamical framework. Advances in Applied Mathematics 41(3), 335–350 (2008)
8. Richard, A.: A fixed point theorem for Boolean networks expressed in terms of forbidden subnetworks. In: Cellular Automata and Discrete Complex Systems, DMTCS Proceedings (2012)
9. Richard, A., Ruet, P.: From kernels in directed graphs to fixed points and negative cycles in Boolean networks. Discrete Applied Math. 161, 1106–1117 (2013)
10. Ruet, P.: Local cycles and dynamical properties of Boolean networks. To appear in Mathematical Structures in Computer Science (2014)
11. Shih, M.-H., Dong, J.-L.: A combinatorial analogue of the Jacobian problem in automata networks. Advances in Applied Mathematics 34(1), 30–46 (2005)
12. Snoussi, E.H.: Qualitative dynamics of piecewise-linear differential equations: a discrete mapping approach. Dynamics and Stability of Systems 4(3-4) (1989)
13. Thomas, R.: Boolean formalization of genetic control circuits. Journal of Theoretical Biology 42, 563–585 (1973)
14. Thomas, R.: On the relation between the logical structure of systems and their ability to generate multiple steady states and sustained oscillations. Series in Synergetics, vol. 9, pp. 180–193. Springer (1981)
15. Thomas, R.: Regulatory networks seen as asynchronous automata: a logical description. Journal of Theoretical Biology 153, 1–23 (1991)
16. Thomas, R., Kaufman, M.: Multistationarity, the basis of cell differentiation and memory. I. Structural conditions of multistationarity and other non-trivial behaviour. Chaos 11, 170–179 (2001)
17. von Neumann, J.: Theory of self-reproducing automata. University of Illinois Press (1966)

Inner-Independent Radius-Dependent Totalistic Rule of Universal Asynchronous Cellular Automaton

Susumu Adachi

Department of Information and Computer Science, Faculty of Engineering,
Kanazawa Institute of Technology, Japan
adch@neptune.kanazawa-it.ac.jp

Abstract. We propose a model of a 2-dimensional 2-state asynchronous updating cellular automaton with inner-independent radius-dependent totalistic rule. An inner-independent rule is such that the cell's updating does not depend on the state of the center cell. A radius-dependent totalistic rule is a totalistic rule which the neighborhood is an extended Moore neighborhood that consists of cells at orthogonal or diagonal distances 1, 2, 3, 4 and 5 from the center cell, taking summations of the living cells in their domain individually. The rule set designed in this paper is universal for computation, that is, any delay-insensitive circuit can be constructed. We also show the algorithm to prove the correct operations.

1 Introduction

Cellular Automata (CA) [13,5] are dynamic systems in which the space is organized in discrete units called cells that assume one of a finite set of states. These cells are updated in discrete time steps according to a transition function, which determines the subsequent state of each cell from the state of the cells inside a certain neighborhood of the cell.

Asynchronous Cellular Automata (ACA) [7] are CA in which each cell is updated at random times. Though ACA are mostly applied to simulations of natural phenomena, there have been efforts to use them for computation, as the lack of a central clock has rich potential for implementation by nanotechnology. The most recent among these models—and the most efficient in terms of hardware and time resources—use so-called *Delay-Insensitive (DI)* circuits that are embedded on the cell space to implement computation. DI circuits are asynchronous circuits that are robust to delays of signals [6,15,9,1,2].

The number of cell states required for achieving computational universality is an important measure of the complexity of a CA model, and it is especially relevant for implementations by nanotechnology. Researchers aim to minimize this number as much as possible, with various degrees of success: one ACA model with a traditional von Neumann neighborhood requires four cell states [10], whereas the model with Moore neighborhood in [1] and the hexagonal model in

J. Wąs, G.C. Sirakoulis, and S. Bandini (Eds.): ACRI 2014, LNCS 8751, pp. 546–555, 2014.

[2] both require six states. The model in [12] has cells with three states, whereby the neighborhood is von Neumann, but it requires a special type of transition function in which more than one cell needs to be updated at a time in each transition. The more recent model in [3,4] has cells with only two states, with von Neumann neighborhood, but the neighborhood radius is larger.

From a point of view in physical implementation, 2-state inner-dependent totalistic rule is the feasible model that is sufficient for the physical requirement. Moreover, asynchronous updating implies that the model is at the thermal equilibrium, and each cell updates independently from others.

In this paper we use a square lattice CA with inner-independent totalistic rule, that has a larger neighborhood than the model in [3,4]. However, in order to reduce the number of transitions, we adopt a *radius-dependent* totalistic rule. The arguments of the transition function are given by the summations of the living cells in the same domain where each cell is in the same outer-frame in extended Moore neighborhood. Computational universality of the model is proved through formulating three primitive modules for DI circuits, and mapping them on the cell space. The set of the modules, the *Fork*, the *P-Merge*, and the *R-Counter*, is a universal set for the class of DI circuits, meaning that any arbitrary DI circuit can be constructed from them. The transition function of this model can be described by 285 totalistic transitions, in which the cell can update asynchronously if the condition matches.

This paper is organized as follows. Section 2 describes the three primitive modules for DI circuits in more detail. In Section 3, these modules and the signal are implemented on the ACA cell space, and the validity check algorithms for the correct operations are shown. This paper finishes with conclusions.

2 Delay Insensitive Circuits

A DI circuit is an asynchronous circuit in which signals may be subject to arbitrary delays, without these being an obstacle to the circuit's correct operation [8]. Composed of interconnection lines and modules, a DI circuit uses signals—encoded as the change of a line's state—to transfer information from the output side of a module to the input side of another module. The speed of signals is not fixed.

A set of primitive modules from which any DI circuit can be constructed is proposed in Patra [14]. This set, consisting of the so-called *Fork*, *Merge* and *Tria*, is universal, but it suffers from the problem that the Tria requires a large number (six) of input and output lines, which is hard to implement on a CA using cells with only four neighbors each. One way around this problem is to relax some of the conditions on DI circuits, like in [16,11], where lines are allowed to carry more than one signal at a time. The advantage of such *buffering lines* is more design freedom, and this translates into simpler structures of circuits and simpler primitive modules. This paper will employ this concept, allowing the use of primitive modules with at most four input or output lines (Fig. 1):

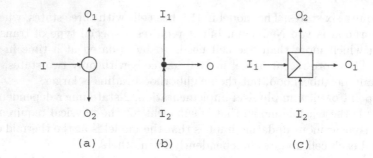

Fig. 1. Primitive modules for DI circuits. (a) Fork, (b) P-Merge, and (c) R-Counter.

1. **Fork**: A signal on input line I in Fig.1(a) is assimilated and duplicated on both output lines O_1 and O_2.
2. **P-Merge (Parallel Merge)**: A signal on input line I_1 (I_2) in Fig.1(b) is assimilated and output on O. Simultaneous signals on I_1 and I_2 are assimilated as well, and will be output as two subsequent signals on O.
3. **R-Counter (Resettable Mod-2 Counter)**: Two subsequent signals on I_1 in Fig.1(c) are assimilated and they give rise to one output signal on O_1. This is called *Mod-2 Counter* functionality, because of the double signal required at I_1 to reinstate the initial "zero" state of the module. Alternatively, when two signals input on both I_1 and I_2, the module outputs a signal on O_2 after assimilating its inputs; this accounts for the *Reset* operation. A signal on only the input line I_1 keeps pending until a signal on either I_1 or I_2 is received. A signal on only the input line I_2 keeps pending until a signal on I_1 is received.

In the next section these modules will be implemented on the cell space, such that DI circuits can be constructed.

3   Delay Insensitive Circuits on Asynchronous Cellular Automata

3.1   Implementation of Signals

The ACA model consists of a 2-dimensional square array of cells, each of which can be in either of the states, 0 and 1. We adopt the extended Moore neighborhood, that consists of the 120 cells at orthogonal and diagonal distances $r = 1, 2, 3, 4$ and 5 from center cell $c_{i,j}$. Moreover, the neighborhood is divided into five domains depending on the radius r (Fig.2), and the center cell is not included in the neighborhood, that is *inner-independent* model.

The transition rule is given as a rule table, in which each rule consists of the numbers of living cells in each radius n_1, n_2, n_3, n_4, n_5, and the state of center cell c' at next time. Therefore, the transition function can be expressed in the form of $c' = f(n_1, n_2, n_3, n_4, n_5)$. The transition rules for a signal propagation are listed as Table 1.

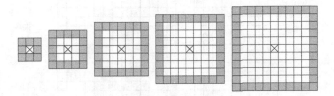

Fig. 2. Extended Moore neighborhood indicated by gray cells ($r = 1, 2, 3, 4$ and 5)

A signal consists of eight living cells as shown in the top-left figure of Fig.3. The signal will transform through the rules via intermediate configurations into the configuration at the bottom-right in the figure, which is the same configuration as the left one, but then shifted one cell to the right. The numbers on the arrays in the figure denote the applied rule numbers in Table 1.

Table 1. Transition table for signal propagation. n_r denotes the number of living cells in r ($r = 1, 2, 3, 4, 5$) domain. c' denotes the next state.

No	n_1	n_2	n_3	n_4	n_5	c'	No	n_1	n_2	n_3	n_4	n_5	c'	No	n_1	n_2	n_3	n_4	n_5	c'	No	n_1	n_2	n_3	n_4	n_5	c'
1	3	3	2	0	0	1	2	3	4	2	0	0	1	3	3	5	2	0	0	1	4	7	3	0	0	0	0
5	1	5	3	0	0	0	6	1	4	3	0	0	0														

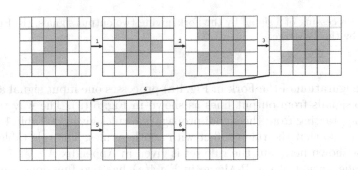

Fig. 3. The basic configuration of a signal (top-left figure) propagates in cellular space by asynchronous updating of transition rules 1 to 6. Through the updating steps, the same configuration (bottom-right figure) shifts one cell to the right.

3.2 Implementation of Modules

The three modules introduced in section 2 are represented on the cell space by the configurations in Fig. 4. The different point of these implementations of the modules from that in our previous work [3,4] is that both Fork and P-Merge have the same configurations as shown in the figure (a).

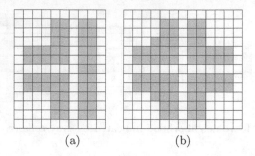

Fig. 4. Configurations of the primitive modules. (a) Fork and P-Merge, and (b) R-Counter.

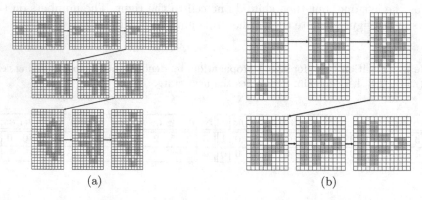

Fig. 5. (a) Processing of a signal by the Fork, giving two output signals. (b) Processing of a signal by the P-Merge.

The configuration of the Fork in Fig.4(a) processes one input signal and generates two signals from output lines as shown in Fig. 5 (a). The way to search rules is that starting from the signal propagation rules given in Table 1, we add each rule not so that the rule conflict with another rules. The rule table for the Fork is not shown here, but the rule set is given in Appendix A.

The configuration of the P-Merge in Fig.4(a) has two functions, one is the Merge, and the other is Parallel Merge. The Merge processes one input signals as shown in Fig. 5 (b), and the P-Merge processes two signals. The way to search rules is also that starting from the signal propagation rules and the added rules for the Fork, we add each rule not so that the rule conflict with another rules. The rule table for the P-Merge is not shown here, but the rule set is given in Appendix A.

The configuration of the R-Counter in Fig.4(b) processes two signals as shown in Fig.6, giving one output signal. The way to search rules is also that starting from the signal propagation rules and the added rules for the Fork and the P-Merge, we add each rule not so that the rule conflict with another rules. The rule table is not shown here, but the final rule function is given by Appendix A.

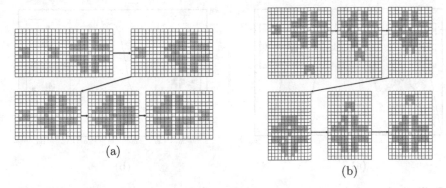

Fig. 6. Processing of signals by the R-Counter. (a) Mod-2 Counter functionality: two signals from the left input line result in a signal output to the right line. (b) Reset functionality: a signal from the left line and a signal from the bottom line result in a signal output to the top line.

If a single signal is input to the left line of the R-Counter, this signal will remain stuck in the R-Counter, that is called *pending*, while no further processing takes place until one more signal is received.

When one more signal is received from the same input line (Fig. 6(a)) an output signal is produced (at the right), whereby the R-Counter reverts to its initial configuration (Mod-2 Counter functionality).

When a reset signal is input to the R-Counter in which a signal is pending (Fig. 6(b)), an output signal is produced from the line at the top, whereby the R-Counter reverts to its initial configuration (Reset functionality).

When there are signals at both input lines, while a signal input from the left is already pending, then the R-Counter has the choice to produce either of the outputs, i.e., the output at the right line or the output at the top line, that is called *arbitration*. One signal remains pending in both cases, but the line at which it remains pending depends on the choice made by the R-Counter.

3.3 Validity Check Algorithm

The signal processing should be checked for the correct operations. The algorithm used in this paper is based on the full search as follows,

- Prepare an initial pattern and a final pattern.
- Add the initial pattern into the `ArrayList` at time $t = 0$.
- List all possible patterns generated from each pattern at time $t - 1$. If each of them does not exist in any `ArrayList`, add it into the `ArrayList` at time t. If the number of possible patterns generated from a pattern is 0, add the pattern into the `ArrayList` at time t.
- Repeat above updating $t \rightarrow t + 1$ until the number of possible patterns is 1 and the pattern coincides with the final pattern.

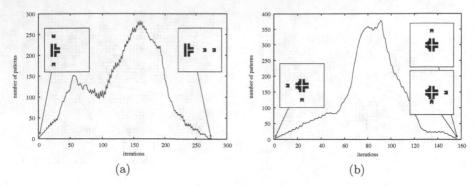

Fig. 7. Typical examples of the time evolution of the number of possible patterns for (a) P-Merge and (b) arbitration. They converge with 1 and 2, respectively.

where, `ArrayList` is one of a java class to store objects, which has a dynamical length, and is used as an array with a fixed length in the time domain, like `ArrayList<cell[][]>[t]`. The result is that the number of patterns is 1 in the end for the the signal propagation and the signal processing through the Fork, the Merge, the P-Merge (Fig. 7(a)), the Mod-2 Counter, and the Reset. Moreover, each converged pattern coincides with the prepared final pattern, respectively.

Next, we have to also check the signal processing for the arbitration. If the R-Counter receives two signals on the left line and one signal on the bottom line, the number of possible final patterns is 2. Therefore the algorithm should be changed as follows,

- Prepare an initial pattern and two final patterns.
- Add the initial pattern into the `ArrayList` at time $t = 0$.
- List all possible patterns generated from each pattern at time $t - 1$. If each of them does not exist in any `ArrayList`, add it into the `ArrayList` at time t. If the number of possible patterns generated from a pattern is 0, add the pattern into the `ArrayList` at time t.
- Repeat above updating $t \to t + 1$ until the number of possible patterns is 2 and the set of patterns coincide with the set of final patterns.

We get the result that the number of patterns is 2 in the end for the patterns of arbitration (Fig. 7(b)). Moreover, the set of converged patterns coincides with the set of final patterns.

4   Conclusions and Discussion

This paper proposed a 2-dimensional 2-state ACA with inner-independent radius-dependent totalistic rule, meaning that a cell's update does not depend on its own state but on the summations of the states of the neighboring cells in which each cell belong to the same extended Moore neighborhood. The model is proved computational universal by showing how a universal set of three primitive modules can be embedded on the cell space. Since the primitive modules have at most four input or output lines each, this embedding fits well into the square lattice topology of the cell space.

We designed one signal pattern, two kinds of module patterns, and 285 transition rules sequentially. The transition rules consist of 6 rules for the signal, 87 rules for the Fork, 52 rules for the P-Merge, and 140 rules for the R-Counter. The number of the rules is smaller than that of our previous ACA models. We also developed the validity check algorithm that proves a given rule set and a given pattern generate a desired final pattern within finite steps. The result is that the algorithm can work well, and the designed rule set and the designed patterns are proved to be correct for the DI circuit operations.

References

1. Adachi, S., Peper, F., Lee, J.: Computation by asynchronously updating cellular automata. J. Stat. Phys. 114(1/2), 261–289 (2004)
2. Adachi, S., Peper, F., Lee, J.: Universality of Hexagonal Asynchronous Totalistic Cellular Automata. In: Sloot, P.M.A., Chopard, B., Hoekstra, A.G. (eds.) ACRI 2004. LNCS, vol. 3305, pp. 91–100. Springer, Heidelberg (2004)
3. Adachi, S., Lee, J., Peper, F.: Universal 2-State Asynchronous Cellular Automaton with Inner-Independent Transitions. In: Proc. of 4th International Workshop on Natural Computing (IWNC 2009). Proceedings in Information and Communications Technology (PICT 2), pp. 107–116. Springer-Japan (2009)
4. Adachi, S., Lee, J., Peper, F.: Universality of 2-State Asynchronous Cellular Automaton with Inner-Independent Totalistic Transitions. In: 16th International Workshop on Cellular Automata and Discrete Complex Systems, pp. 153–172 (2010)
5. Berlekamp, E.R., Conway, J.H., Guy, R.K.: Wining Ways for Your Mathematical Plays, vol. 2. Academic Press, New York (1982)
6. Hauck, S.: Asynchronous design methodologies: an overview. Proc. IEEE 83(1), 69–93 (1995)
7. Ingerson, T.E., Buvel, R.L.: Structures in asynchronous cellular automata. Physica D 10, 59–68 (1984)
8. Keller, R.M.: Towards a theory of universal speed-independent modules. IEEE Trans. Comput. C-23(1), 21–33 (1974)
9. Lee, J., Adachi, S., Peper, F., Morita, K.: Embedding universal delay-insensitive circuits in asynchronous cellular spaces. Fund. Inform. 58(3/4), 295–320 (2003)
10. Lee, J., Adachi, S., Peper, F., Mashiko, S.: Delay-insensitive computation in asynchronous cellular automata. Journal of Computer and System Sciences 70, 201–220 (2005)
11. Lee, J., Peper, F., Adachi, S., Mashiko, S.: Universal Delay-Insensitive Systems With Buffering Lines. IEEE Trans. Circuits and Systems 52(4), 742–754 (2005)
12. Lee, J., Peper, F.: On brownian cellular automata. In: Proc. of Automata 2008, pp. 278–291. Luniver Press, UK (2008)
13. von Neumann, J.: The Theory of Self-Reproducing Automata, edited and completed by A. W. Burks. University of Illinois Press (1966)
14. Patra, P., Fussell, D.S.: Efficient building blocks for delay insensitive circuits. In: Proceedings of the International Symposium on Advanced Research in Asynchronous Circuits and Systems, pp. 196–205. IEEE Computer Society Press, Silver Spring (1994)

15. Peper, F., Lee, J., Adachi, S., Mashiko, S.: Laying out circuits on asynchronous cellular arrays: a step towards feasible nanocomputers? Nanotechnology 14(4), 469–485 (2003)
16. Peper, F., Lee, J., Abo, F., Isokawa, T., Adachi, S., Matsui, N., Mashiko, S.: Fault-Tolerance in Nanocomputers: A Cellular Array Approach. IEEE Trans. Nanotech. 3(1), 187–201 (2004)

A   Transition Rule

A set of transition rules is listed as following table Table 2 and Table 3, except for the signal propagation rules (Table 1).

Table 2. Transition table for the Fork $(7 - 93)$. n_r denotes the number of living cells in r $(r = 1, 2, 3, 4, 5)$ domain. c' denotes the next state.

No	n_1	n_2	n_3	n_4	n_5	c'	No	n_1	n_2	n_3	n_4	n_5	c'	No	n_1	n_2	n_3	n_4	n_5	c'	No	n_1	n_2	n_3	n_4	n_5	c'
7	1	4	3	0	3	0	8	1	4	3	0	4	0	9	1	4	3	4	4	0	10	1	4	3	5	5	0
11	1	4	5	5	5	0	12	1	4	6	5	10	0	13	1	4	7	4	4	0	14	1	4	7	4	5	0
15	1	5	3	0	4	0	16	1	5	3	4	4	0	17	1	5	3	5	5	0	18	1	5	5	5	5	0
19	1	5	6	5	10	0	20	1	5	7	4	4	0	21	1	5	7	4	5	0	22	1	7	8	4	7	0
23	1	7	8	5	7	0	24	1	8	8	4	6	0	25	1	8	8	5	6	0	26	2	4	6	8	10	0
27	2	5	6	8	10	0	28	3	3	2	0	4	1	29	3	3	2	4	4	1	30	3	3	4	4	5	1
31	3	3	6	4	4	1	32	3	4	2	0	4	1	33	3	4	2	4	4	1	34	3	4	4	4	5	1
35	3	4	6	4	4	1	36	3	5	2	0	4	1	37	3	5	2	4	4	1	38	3	5	4	4	5	1
39	3	5	4	4	7	1	40	3	5	5	4	6	1	41	3	5	6	4	4	1	42	3	6	5	4	7	1
43	3	7	4	6	8	1	44	3	7	6	4	10	1	45	3	7	7	4	9	1	46	3	8	7	4	9	1
47	3	8	9	7	7	0	48	3	9	9	5	7	0	49	4	5	6	5	7	1	50	4	6	6	7	7	1
51	5	9	6	8	6	1	52	5	9	6	8	12	1	53	5	11	9	12	4	1	54	5	14	18	13	10	1
55	6	9	9	8	10	1	56	6	10	9	8	10	1	57	6	14	6	10	13	0	58	6	14	7	9	11	0
59	6	14	7	11	10	1	60	6	14	7	11	13	1	61	6	14	7	11	14	0	62	6	14	8	12	11	1
63	6	14	8	12	14	1	64	6	14	13	13	8	1	65	6	14	14	14	9	0	66	6	15	7	11	13	0
67	6	15	13	13	8	1	68	6	15	14	14	9	0	69	6	15	19	14	12	0	70	7	3	0	0	4	0
71	7	3	0	4	4	0	72	7	3	4	4	4	0	73	7	3	5	5	5	0	74	7	5	5	5	10	0
75	7	7	4	5	7	0	76	7	7	5	8	12	0	77	7	9	5	6	8	0	78	7	11	5	7	4	0
79	7	11	7	6	10	1	80	7	11	7	11	4	0	81	7	11	11	7	17	1	82	7	11	16	17	10	1
83	7	13	6	4	9	0	84	7	13	9	8	15	0	85	7	13	12	9	9	0	86	7	13	12	10	9	0
87	7	14	13	10	8	1	88	7	14	13	11	8	1	89	7	14	17	19	10	0	90	7	15	4	8	10	0
91	7	15	5	16	20	1	92	7	15	7	9	11	1	93	7	15	12	13	17	0							

Table 3. Transition table for the P-Merge (94 – 145) and the R-Counter (146 – 285). n_r denotes the number of living cells in r domain. c' denotes the next state.

No	n_1	n_2	n_3	n_4	n_5	c'	No	n_1	n_2	n_3	n_4	n_5	c'	No	n_1	n_2	n_3	n_4	n_5	c'	No	n_1	n_2	n_3	n_4	n_5	c'
94	1	4	6	5	8	0	95	1	5	6	5	7	0	96	1	7	8	4	9	0	97	1	7	8	4	10	0
98	1	8	8	4	9	0	99	2	4	6	7	7	0	100	2	5	6	5	7	0	101	3	5	4	4	10	1
102	3	5	5	5	9	1	103	3	6	5	5	9	1	104	3	7	4	8	12	1	105	3	7	6	4	7	1
106	3	7	7	4	6	1	107	3	8	7	4	7	1	108	3	8	7	4	8	1	109	3	8	9	8	10	0
110	3	9	9	8	10	0	111	4	5	6	8	10	1	112	4	6	6	8	10	1	113	5	9	6	6	8	1
114	5	9	7	10	7	1	115	6	9	5	8	12	0	116	6	9	9	6	7	1	117	6	10	9	8	7	1
118	6	11	9	7	11	1	119	6	11	9	8	11	0	120	6	11	16	16	9	1	121	6	11	16	17	9	1
122	6	12	9	9	4	1	123	6	12	9	9	8	1	124	6	13	11	10	11	1	125	6	13	11	10	12	0
126	6	13	12	12	9	0	127	6	14	6	15	20	0	128	6	15	7	14	17	1	129	7	4	4	4	10	1
130	7	5	5	5	8	0	131	7	7	4	4	10	0	132	7	7	4	5	10	0	133	7	7	5	7	8	0
134	7	11	6	7	5	0	135	7	11	6	7	8	0	136	7	11	8	7	15	1	137	7	11	16	15	8	0
138	7	12	6	10	4	0	139	7	13	6	7	10	0	140	7	13	8	4	15	0	141	7	14	6	14	17	1
142	7	14	8	9	11	0	143	7	15	4	13	17	0	144	8	4	4	5	10	0	145	8	14	5	11	13	1
146	1	4	3	1	4	0	147	1	4	3	3	5	0	148	1	4	3	5	4	0	149	1	4	5	5	7	0
150	1	4	5	6	9	0	151	1	4	5	7	10	0	152	1	4	6	7	9	0	153	1	5	3	1	4	0
154	1	5	3	3	5	0	155	1	5	3	5	4	0	156	1	5	5	5	7	0	157	1	5	5	6	9	0
158	1	5	5	7	10	0	159	1	5	6	7	9	0	160	2	4	7	7	10	0	161	2	4	7	9	10	0
162	2	4	8	9	10	0	163	2	5	7	9	10	0	164	2	5	8	9	10	0	165	2	9	8	10	12	1
166	2	9	9	10	12	1	167	2	9	9	10	13	0	168	2	9	10	10	12	1	169	3	3	6	4	5	1
170	3	3	6	4	6	1	171	3	3	6	4	7	1	172	3	4	6	4	5	1	173	3	4	6	4	6	1
174	3	4	6	4	7	1	175	3	5	4	5	10	1	176	3	5	6	4	5	1	177	3	5	6	4	6	1
178	3	5	6	4	7	1	179	3	7	6	8	13	1	180	3	7	11	11	10	1	181	3	8	10	8	10	0
182	3	8	11	11	10	1	183	3	10	9	9	10	0	184	4	5	8	8	11	1	185	4	6	6	8	9	1
186	4	6	7	9	11	1	187	4	7	6	5	10	1	188	4	7	6	6	10	1	189	4	7	7	5	9	1
190	4	7	7	6	9	1	191	4	8	7	5	8	1	192	4	8	7	5	9	1	193	4	8	7	6	9	1
194	4	10	16	16	11	0	195	4	12	18	17	15	0	196	4	12	19	16	16	0	197	5	8	9	7	10	1
198	5	8	9	8	10	0	199	5	9	7	7	9	1	200	5	9	7	11	5	1	201	5	9	8	8	10	1
202	5	9	8	8	11	1	203	5	9	8	9	11	0	204	5	9	8	10	6	1	205	5	9	17	19	14	0
206	5	9	17	19	15	1	207	5	10	7	7	9	1	208	5	10	13	11	15	0	209	5	10	13	11	16	1
210	5	10	16	16	11	1	211	5	10	16	18	12	1	212	5	10	16	18	13	1	213	5	11	11	12	4	1
214	5	11	17	16	17	0	215	5	12	18	18	15	0	216	5	12	19	17	15	0	217	5	12	19	18	15	1
218	5	12	20	17	17	1	219	5	13	17	19	13	1	220	5	13	18	17	15	1	221	5	13	19	17	16	1
222	6	8	6	7	10	1	223	6	9	10	9	10	1	224	6	10	5	8	12	0	225	6	10	10	9	10	1
226	6	11	7	11	5	0	227	6	11	17	14	14	1	228	6	13	5	14	19	0	229	6	13	13	14	18	0
230	6	13	13	14	21	0	231	6	14	6	14	19	0	232	6	14	17	19	12	0	233	6	14	19	19	13	1
234	6	15	8	13	15	1	235	6	15	8	13	16	1	236	6	15	8	15	16	1	237	7	3	1	4	4	0
238	7	3	3	5	5	0	239	7	3	5	4	5	0	240	7	3	5	5	7	0	241	7	4	5	5	10	1
242	7	5	5	5	9	0	243	7	5	5	7	10	0	244	7	5	5	7	11	0	245	7	5	15	14	12	1
246	7	7	6	8	13	0	247	7	7	7	8	12	0	248	7	7	7	9	13	0	249	7	7	7	12	11	1
250	7	9	11	13	6	1	251	7	9	11	15	10	0	252	7	10	11	7	17	0	253	7	10	16	17	14	0
254	7	10	17	17	15	1	255	7	11	8	10	4	0	256	7	11	9	5	15	1	257	7	11	9	6	15	1
258	7	11	9	11	4	0	259	7	11	9	12	5	1	260	7	11	12	7	14	0	261	7	11	13	7	16	1
262	7	11	15	15	15	1	263	7	11	17	17	12	0	264	7	12	6	10	5	0	265	7	12	10	4	14	0
266	7	12	12	7	14	1	267	7	12	15	14	14	0	268	7	13	8	5	14	0	269	7	13	10	5	14	0
270	7	13	13	5	15	0	271	7	14	7	13	16	1	272	7	14	8	13	17	0	273	7	14	9	14	16	1
274	7	15	5	12	15	0	275	7	15	5	12	16	0	276	7	15	5	13	16	1	277	7	15	7	15	19	1
278	7	15	9	13	17	0	279	7	16	9	12	15	0	280	8	4	16	13	8	1	281	8	5	15	14	12	0
282	8	5	15	16	13	1	283	8	12	12	5	15	0	284	8	12	16	13	13	0	285	8	14	14	7	17	1

Bifurcations of Local Structure Maps as Predictors of Phase Transitions in Asynchronous Cellular Automata

Henryk Fukś[1] and Nazim Fatès[2]

[1] Department of Mathematics and Statistics, Brock University, St. Catharines,
Ontario L2S 3A1, Canada
hfuks@brocku.ca
[2] INRIA, F-54 600 Villers-lès-Nancy, France
nazim.fates@loria.fr

Abstract. We show that the local structure approximation of sufficiently high order can predict the existence of second order phase transitions belonging to the directed percolation university class in α-asynchronous cellular automata.

Probabilistic cellular automata (PCA) rules known as α-*asynchronous rules* are obtained by a random perturbation of the deterministic updating rule: instead of updating all cells simultaneously, we update each cell independently with probability α, the *synchrony rate*, and leave its state unchanged with probability $1 - \alpha$.

The systematic exploration of the properties of α-asynchronous Elementary Cellular Automata by numerical simulations [2] identified rules which exhibited a qualitative change of behaviour for a continuous variation of the synchrony rate: there exists a critical value of α_c which separates an *active phase* in which the system fluctuates around an equilibrium and an *absorbing phase* where the system is rapidly attracted towards a fixed point where all cells are in the same state.

Using the techniques from statistical physics, this abrupt change of behaviour was then identified as a second order phase transitions which belong to the directed percolation (DP) universality class [1]. This identification was conducted by taking as an order parameter the density, that is the average number of cells in state 1, and, up to symmetries, nine rules were found to exhibit such DP behaviour. Their Wolfram numbers are 6, 18, 26, 38, 50, 58, 106, 134, and 146.

The aim of this paper is to study to which extent this second order phase transition can be predicted with analytical techniques. We are in particular interested in answering two questions: (a) Can we explain the existence of the two active and absorbing phases? (b) Can we propose an approximation of the value of the critical synchrony rate α_c that separates the two phases?

Our approach is based on so-called *local structure theory*, proposed in 1987 by H. A. Gutowitz *et al.* [5] as a generalization of the mean-field theory for cellular automata. The basic idea of this theory is to consider probabilities of blocks

J. Wąs, G.C. Sirakoulis, and S. Bandini (Eds.): ACRI 2014, LNCS 8751, pp. 556–560, 2014.

(words) of length k and to construct a map on these block probabilities, which, when iterated, approximates probabilities of occurrence of the same blocks in the actual orbit of a given cellular automaton. In the case of nearest-neighbour binary rule, the aforementioned map is 2^k-dimensional, where k is called the *level* of local structure approximation. However, using the method proposed in [3], it can be reduced to equivalent, but somewhat simpler 2^{k-1} dimensional map.

We will assume that the dynamics takes place on a one-dimensional lattice. Let $s_i(t) \in \{0,1\}$ denotes the state of the lattice site i at time t, where $i \in \mathbb{Z}$, $t \in \mathbb{N}$. We will say that the site i is occupied (empty) at time t if $s_i(t) = 1$ (resp., $s_i(t) = 0$). A *Deterministic elementary cellular automaton* is a dynamical system governed by the local function $f : \{0,1\}^3 \to \{0,1\}$ such that

$$s_i(t+1) = f(s_{i-1}(t), s_i(t), s_{i+1}(t)),$$

for all $i \in \mathbb{Z}$ and for all $t \in \mathbb{N}$. Function f is to be called a *rule* of CA.

In a probabilistic cellular automaton, lattice sites simultaneously change states from 0 to 1 or from 1 to 0 with probabilities depending on states of local neighbours. A common method for defining PCA is to specify a set of local transition probabilities. For example, in order to define a nearest-neighbour PCA one has to specify the probability $w(s_i(t+1))|s_{i-1}(t), s_i(t), s_{i+1}(t))$ that the site $s_i(t)$ with nearest neighbors $s_{i-1}(t), s_{i+1}(t)$ changes its state to $s_i(t+1)$ in a single time step.

We will now define α-*asynchronous elementary cellular automata*. Let $\alpha \in [0,1]$ and let f be a local function of some deterministic CA with Wolfram number $W(f)$. Corresponding α-asynchronous elementary cellular automaton with rule number $W(f)$ is a probabilistic CA for which transition probabilities are

$$w(1|x_1 x_2 x_3) = \alpha f(x_1, x_2, x_3) + (1 - \alpha)x_2. \tag{1}$$

Let us denote by $P_t(\mathbf{b})$ the probability of occurrences of blocks $\mathbf{b} = b_1 b_2 \ldots b_n$ after t iterations of the PCA rule, where $\mathbf{b} \in \{0,1\}^*$. These probabilities, to be called block probabilities, form an infinite hierarchy that we can arrange by defining $\mathbf{P}_t^{(k)}$ as a column vector that holds all the k-block probabilities sorted in lexical order.

Let us now suppose that a PCA is given, and we know its transition probabilities w. Local structure map associated with that PCA is then given by

$$P_{t+1}(a_1 \ldots a_k) = \sum_{b \in \{0,1\}^{k+2}} \prod_{i=1}^{k} w(a_i|b_i b_{i+1} b_{i+2})$$

$$\times \frac{P_t(b_1 \ldots b_k) P_t(b_2 \ldots b_{k+1}) P_t(b_3 \ldots b_{k+2})}{\left(P_t(b_2 \ldots b_k 0) + P_t(b_2 \ldots b_k 1)\right)\left(P_t(b_3 \ldots b_{k+1} 0) + P_t(b_3 \ldots b_{k+1} 1)\right)}. \tag{2}$$

We refer the reader to [3] for details of its construction. It should be understood that the above is a system of 2^k equations, so that we have a separate equation for each $(a_1 \ldots a_k) \in \{0,1\}^k$. In vector form we will write

$$\mathbf{P}_{t+1}^{(k)} = \Lambda^{(k)}\left(\mathbf{P}_t^{(k)}\right), \tag{3}$$

where $\Lambda^{(k)}$, defined by eq. (2), will be called *local structure map* of level k.

Not all components of the block probability vector $\mathbf{P}_t^{(k)}$ are independent. This is due to so-called consistency conditions, that is, equations of the type $P_t(a_1 \ldots a_{k-1}0) + P_t(a_1 \ldots a_{k-1}1) = P_t(a_1 \ldots a_k)$. By exploiting these conditions, 2^k-dimensional local structure map of level k can be reduced to equivalent, but somewhat simpler, 2^{k-1} dimensional map [3].

Detailed analysis of reduced local structure maps for α asynchronous PCA belonging to DP universality class reveals that these maps exhibit transcritical bifurcations as α changes. The bifurcation does not necessarily happens for all k, but rather appears when k is sufficiently high. For rules 6, 18, 38, 50, 106, and 134, we were able to compute fixed points of local structure maps of level 3 directly, by solving equations $\mathbf{P}^{(3)} = \Lambda^{(3)}\left(\mathbf{P}^{(3)}\right)$ with he help of computer algebra software (the maps were transformed to reduced form first). We were also able to determine the stability of these fixed points. Details of these calculations can be found in [4]. Here we only present graphs of typical bifurcation diagrams obtained that way, as shown in Figure 1. Vertical axis in these diagrams corresponds to $P(1)$, which can be obtained from $\mathbf{P}^{(3)}$ by using consistency conditions, as $P(1) = P(100) + P(101) + P(110) + P(111)$. In all three diagrams, the absorbing fixed point $P(1) = 0$ is present, shown as the horizontal line. The active fixed point is represented by the smooth curve, partially solid (stable) and partially dashed (unstable). Exchange of stability takes place at the bifurcation point (circled).

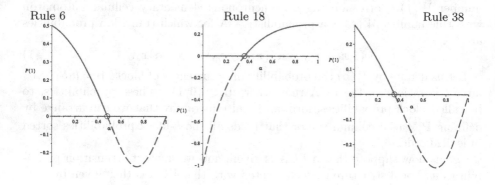

Fig. 1. Bifurcation diagram for local structure equations of level three for rules 6, 18, and 38

For the three remaining rules, 26, 58, and 146, the local structure map $\Lambda^{(3)}$ does not exhibit a transcritical bifurcation, so it is necessary to consider higher order maps, of level four (for rules 26 and 146) and five (for rule 58). Absorbing fixed points of these maps have the same structure as previously described, with $P(1) = 0$. Unfortunately, equations for their active fixed points cannot be solved even with the help of symbolic algebra software, due to the size of relevant equations. It is, however, possible to find the stable branch of the bifurcation diagram by iterating these maps many times, so they converge sufficiently close to the stable fixed point. We performed such iterations for all three cases, and the results are shown in Figure 2. Even though the unstable branch of the active fixed point is missing, it is evident that the active phase appears abruptly as α increases, which provides a strong evidence for transcritical bifurcation.

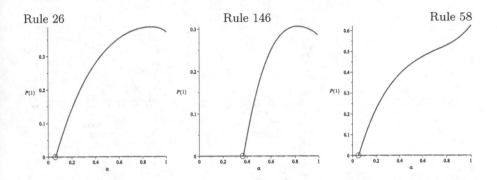

Fig. 2. Partial bifurcation diagrams for local structure equations of level 4 rules 26 and 146, and level 5 for rule 58. Diagrams were obtained numerically with 10^5 iterations.

In summary, we can say that the local structure approximation of order 3 to 5 can predict existence of the phase transition for all DP rules. The local structure map for each of these rules exhibits a transcritical bifurcations, and the direction of the bifurcation agrees with the direction of the phase transition observed experimentally, that is, if the active phase appears (disappears) as α increases, then the non-zero fixed point of the local structure map becomes stable (unstable) as α increases. The point at which the transcritical bifurcation occurs is, however, rather far from the critical point observed experimentally.

Can this be improved by increasing the order of the local structure approximation? The answer is indeed yes, although we cannot expect to be able to find explicit symbolic expressions for fixed points of eq. (2) when k is large. One can, however, iterate $\Lambda^{(k)}$ many times, starting from some generic initial condition, and when this is done, the orbit of $\Lambda^{(k)}$ indeed converges to a stable fixed point, which, depending on the value of α, can be zero or non-zero.

We performed iterations of $\Lambda^{(k)}$ maps for $k = 2 \ldots 9$ for all DP rules, and plotted $P_t(1)$ as a function of α after $t = 10^4$ iterations. Results are shown in Figure 3, together with curves obtained "experimentally" by iterating a given rule for 10^5 steps, using randomly generated initial configurations with $4 \cdot 10^4$ sites and periodic boundary conditions. One can clearly see that local structure maps not only predict existence of phase transitions, but also seem to approximate behaviour of $P_t(1)$ vs. α curves with increasing accuracy as the order of the approximation increases.

Based on the evidence presented in this paper, we suspect that the same may be true for other probabilistic CA rules belonging to DP universality class. It

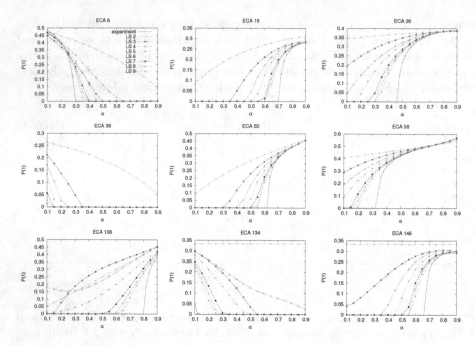

Fig. 3. Experimental results together with local structure approximations up to level 9

is already known to be true for the probabilistic mixture of rules 182 and 200 studied by Mendonça and de Oliveira [6]. We plan to investigate this conjecture for other PCA rules.

References

1. Fatès, N.: Asynchronism induces second order phase transitions in elementary cellular automata. Journal of Cellular Automata 4(1), 21–38 (2009), http://hal.inria.fr/inria-00138051
2. Fatès, N., Morvan, M.: An experimental study of robustness to asynchronism for elementary cellular automata. Complex Systems 16, 1–27 (2005)
3. Fukś, H.: Construction of local structure maps for cellular automata. J. of Cellular Automata 7, 455–488 (2013)
4. Fukś, H., Fatès, N.: Local structure approximation as a predictor of second order phase transitions in asynchronous cellular automata, arxiv.org/abs/1312.5244 (2013)
5. Gutowitz, H.A., Victor, J.D., Knight, B.W.: Local structure theory for cellular automata. Physica D 28, 18–48 (1987)
6. Mendonça, J.R.G., de Oliveira, M.J.: An extinction-survival-type phase transition in the probabilistic cellular automaton p 182–q 200. J. of Phys. A: Math. and Theor. 44(15), art. no. 155001 (2011)

Computing Symbolic Steady States
of Boolean Networks

Hannes Klarner, Alexander Bockmayr, and Heike Siebert

Freie Universität Berlin, FB Mathematik und Informatik,
Arnimallee 6, 14195 Berlin, Germany
Hannes.Klarner@FU-Berlin.de

Abstract. Asymptotic behavior is often of particular interest when analyzing asynchronous Boolean networks representing biological systems
such as signal transduction or gene regulatory networks. Methods based
on a generalization of the steady state notion, the so-called symbolic
steady states, can be exploited to investigate attractor properties as well
as for model reduction techniques conserving attractors. In this paper, we
propose a novel optimization-based method for computing all maximal
symbolic steady states and motivate their use. In particular, we add a
new result yielding a lower bound for the number of cyclic attractors and
illustrate the methods with a short study of a MAPK pathway model.

1 Introduction

Boolean network models have long since proved their worth in the context of
modeling complex biological systems [1]. Of particular interest are number and
size of attractors as well as their location in state space since these properties often relate well to important biological behavior. Different approaches are
available to solve several variations of this problem (see e. g. [2] and references
therein).

In this paper, we utilize the notion of symbolic steady state [3] and a generalization called seeds which represent dynamically closed subspaces of state
space, i.e., subspaces that no trajectory can leave. This property can clearly be
exploited for model reduction and attractor analysis as has been illustrated in
[3]. However, related methods can only be useful in practice if identification of
such symbolic steady states is not based on comprehensive state space analysis.

After providing the relevant terminology, we motivate our research by presenting some theoretical results concerning model reduction and number of attractors. We then introduce the *prime implicant graph* as an object capturing the
essential dynamical information of a network and a related optimization-based
approach allowing for efficient computation of maximal symbolic steady states.
Lastly, we provide a short illustration using a MAPK pathway model.

1.1 Background

We consider variables from the Boolean domain $\mathbb{B} = \{0, 1\}$ where 1 and 0 represent the truth values *true* and *false*. A Boolean *expression* f over the variables

J. Wąs, G.C. Sirakoulis, and S. Bandini (Eds.): ACRI 2014, LNCS 8751, pp. 561–570, 2014.
© Springer International Publishing Switzerland 2014

$V = \{v_1, \dots, v_n\}$ is defined by a formula over the grammar

$$f ::= 0 \mid 1 \mid v \mid \overline{f} \mid f_1 \cdot f_2 \mid f_1 + f_2$$

where $v \in V$ signifies a variable, $\overline{f}$ the negation, $f_1 \cdot f_2$ the conjunction and $f_1 + f_2$ the (inclusive) disjunction of the expressions f, f_1 and f_2. Given an *assignment* $s : V \to \mathbb{B}$, an expression f can be evaluated to a value $f(s) \in \mathbb{B}$ by substituting the values $s(v)$ for the variables $v \in V$. If $f(s) = f(t)$ for all assignments $s, t : V \to \mathbb{B}$, we say f is *constant* and write $f = c$, with $c \in \mathbb{B}$ being the constant value. A *Boolean network* (V, F) consists of n variables $V = \{v_1, \dots, v_n\}$ and n corresponding Boolean expressions $F = \{f_1, \dots, f_n\}$ over V. In this context, an assignment $s : V \to \mathbb{B}$ is also called a *state* of the network and the *state space* $S = S(V)$ consists of all possible 2^n states. The expressions F can be thought of as a function $F : S \to S$ governing the network behavior. The *image* $F(s)$ of a state s under F is defined to be the state t that satisfies $t(v_i) = f_i(s)$. The *steady states* or *fixpoints* $\mathcal{S} = \mathcal{S}(V, F)$ of a Boolean network (V, F) are all states $s \in S$ that satisfy $F(s) = s$. To illustrate these concepts we introduce a running example in Fig. 1.

$$
\begin{array}{lll}
f_1 = v_1 + v_2 & f_1(1101) = 1 + 1 = 1 & F(1101) = 1101 \\
f_2 = v_1 \cdot v_4 & f_2(1101) = 1 \cdot 1 = 1 & F(0000) = 0001 \\
f_3 = \overline{v_1} \cdot v_4 & f_3(1101) = \overline{1} \cdot 1 = 0 & \mathcal{S} = \{1101\} \\
f_4 = \overline{v_3} & f_4(1101) = \overline{0} = 1 &
\end{array}
$$

Fig. 1. (left) An example Boolean network with 4 variables. (middle) An example for how the Boolean expressions are evaluated for a given state $s = 1101$. We specify states by a sequence of n values that correspond to the variables in the order given in V, i.e., $s = 1101$ should be read as $s(v_1) = 1, s(v_2) = 1, s(v_3) = 0$ and $s(v_4) = 1$. (right) An example of the image $F(s)$ of two states 1101 and 0000 where the first is a steady state and the second is not.

2   Methods

2.1   Symbolic Steady States and Seeds

A *partial* or *symbolic state* of the network (V, F) is an assignment $p : U \to \mathbb{B}$ where $U \subseteq V$ is a subset of variables. The set $PS = PS(V, F)$ denotes all possible 3^n partial states of V. We denote the *domain* U of a partial state p by U_p. The partial state $p \in PS$ with $U_p = \varnothing$ is called the *empty partial state* and denoted by $p = \varnothing$. A partial state p references the *subspace* $S[p] := \{s \in S \mid \forall v \in U_p : s(v) = p(v)\}$ of S. The *size* $|p|$ of a partial state p is defined to be $|p| := |U_p|$. Two partial states $p, q \in PS$ are said to be *consistent* if for all $v \in U_p \cap U_q : p(v) = q(v)$. With the *ordering* $p \leq q$ iff p, q are consistent and

$U_p \subseteq U_q$, PS becomes a partially ordered set. We define the *union* $p \sqcup q$ of two consistent partial states p, q by $U_{p \sqcup q} := U_p \cup U_q$ and $p \sqcup q(v) := p(v)$, if $v \in U_p$, and $p \sqcup q(v) := q(v)$, otherwise. Every $\varnothing \neq p \in PS$ has a unique decomposition into $|p|$ partial states of size 1.

Analogous to the evaluation $f(s)$ of an expression f at a state s we define the *expression* $f[p]$ obtained by substituting the values $p(v)$ for the variables $v \in U_p$ in f. The *image* $F[p]$ of a partial state under $F = \{f_1, \ldots, f_n\}$ is the partial state $q : U_q \to \mathbb{B}$ defined by $U_q := \{v_i \in V \mid f_i[p] \text{ is constant}\}$ and $q(v_i) := f_i[p]$, for all $v_i \in U_q$. If $U_q = \varnothing$, we have $F[p] = \varnothing$.

Like in [3], a *symbolic steady state* is a partial state p that satisfies $F[p] = p$, and a *seed* is a partial state p that satisfies $F[p] \geq p$. As we will see, these conditions ensure that the network components that belong to U_p stay fixed when regarding the network dynamics in the subspace $S[p]$. We write $Seeds = Seeds(V, F) := \{p \in PS \mid F[p] \geq p\}$ and $SymS = SymS(V, F) := \{p \in PS \mid F[p] = p\}$. For our running example, these concepts are illustrated in Fig. 2. Note that seeds are a relaxation of symbolic steady states and $\mathcal{S} \subseteq SymS \subseteq Seeds$ holds, i.e., every steady state is a symbolic steady state and every symbolic steady state is a seed. The terminology *seed* is motivated by the observation that for every seed p there is a unique corresponding symbolic steady state q obtained by repeatedly applying $F[\cdot]$ until $F^k[p] = F^{k+1}[p] =: q$. This process is also called *percolation*. Note that if p is a seed, then $F[p]$ is also a seed (since for any $r \in PS$ with $r \geq p$ and any expression f, if $f[p] = c$ then $f[r] = c$).

$$
\begin{array}{llll}
p := 1_1 & q := 0_1 0_2 & r := 1_3 1_4 & s := 0_2 1_4 \\
f_1[p] = 1 & f_1[q] = 0 & f_1[r] = v_1 + v_2 & f_1[s] = v_1 + 0 \\
f_2[p] = 1 \cdot v_4 & f_2[q] = 0 & f_2[r] = v_1 \cdot 1 & f_2[s] = v_1 \cdot 1 \\
f_3[p] = 0 & f_3[q] = \overline{0} \cdot v_4 & f_3[r] = \overline{v_1} \cdot 1 & f_3[s] = \overline{v_1} \cdot 1 \\
f_4[p] = \overline{v_3} & f_4[q] = \overline{v_3} & f_4[r] = 0 & f_4[s] = \overline{v_3} \\
F[p] = 1_1 0_3 > p & F[q] = 0_1 0_2 = q & F[r] = 0_4 \not\geq r & F[s] = \varnothing
\end{array}
$$

Fig. 2. We specify partial states by a sequence of $|p|$ values whose subscript corresponds to the index of the variable, i.e., $1_1 0_3$ means $U_p = \{v_1, v_3\}$ and $p(v_1) = 1, p(v_3) = 0$. Here, p is a seed but not a symbolic steady state because $F[p] > p$, whereas q is a symbolic steady state because $F[q] = q$ and r and s are neither seeds nor symbolic steady states. The example network has 4 seeds and 3 symbolic steady states, namely $Seeds = \{\varnothing, 1_1, 0_1 0_2, 1101\}$ and $SymS = \{\varnothing, 0_1 0_2, 1101\}$.

2.2   Applications

The *state transition graph* of a Boolean network (V, F) is the directed graph $(S, \to)$ where S is the state space of (V, F) and the transitions $\to \subseteq S \times S$ are obtained from F via a given update rule. We mention two update rules here, the *synchronous rule* and its transition relation $\to_F \subseteq S \times S$, and the *asynchronous rule* and its transition relation $\hookrightarrow_F \subseteq S \times S$. The former is defined by $s \rightarrow_F t$ iff $F(s) = t$. To define $\hookrightarrow_F$ we need the Hamming distance $\Delta : S \times S \rightarrow \{1, \ldots, n\}$ between states which is given by $\Delta(s,t) := |\{v \in V \mid s(v) \neq t(v)\}|$. We define $s \hookrightarrow_F t$ iff either $s = t$ and $F(s) = s$ or $\Delta(s,t) = 1$ and $\Delta(t, F(s)) < \Delta(s, F(s))$.

Since $(S, \rightarrow)$ is a directed graph, the standard digraph terminology applies. A path in $(S, \rightarrow)$ is a sequence of states $(s_1, \ldots, s_{l+1})$ with $s_i \rightarrow s_{i+1}$, for $1 \leq i \leq l$. When Boolean networks are used to model the dynamics of a system, paths are also called *trajectories*. An non-empty set $R \subseteq S$ is a *trap set* if for every $r \in R$ and $s \in S$ with $r \rightarrow s$ it holds that $s \in R$. An inclusion-wise minimal trap set is also called an *attractor* of (V, F). Note that every trap set contains at least one minimal trap set and therefore at least one attractor. We distinguish two types of attractors depending on their size. If $X \subseteq S$ is an attractor and $|X| = 1$ then X is a steady state and if $|X| > 1$ we call it a *cyclic attractor*. As mentioned before, a symbolic state p references the subspace $S[p]$. A central idea for various applications is given in the next result, which immediately follows from the properties of p and the definition of $\hookrightarrow_F$ and $\rightarrow_F$.

Theorem 1. *If $p \in Seeds$, then $S[p]$ is a trap set in $(S, \hookrightarrow_F)$ and in $(S, \rightarrow_F)$.*

Proof. Assume $p \in Seeds$ but $S[p]$ is not a trap set. Then there is a $r \rightarrow s$ such that $r \in S[p]$ and $s \notin S[p]$. But then $\exists v_i \in U_p : f_i(r) \neq p(v_i)$ which contradicts $p \leq r$ and $f_i[p] = p(v_i)$.

Application 1: Model Reduction. Let $R \subseteq S$ be a trap set. The partial state $p := stab(R) \in PS$ obtained from R by $U_p := \{v \in V \mid \forall s, t \in R : s(v) = t(v)\}$ and $p(v) := s(v)$, for $v \in U_p$ and $s \in R$ arbitrary, is called the *induced stable state* of R. Note that, in general, the induced stable state of a trap set references a superset of R, i.e., $S[stab(R)] \supseteq R$. A natural model reduction technique is based on the observation that for any trap set $R \subseteq S$, the transitions of any trajectory with an initial state $s_1 \in R$ are governed by the reduced system (V_p, F_p) with $p := stab(R)$ and

$$V_p := \{v \in V \mid v \notin U_p\}, \quad F_p := \{f_i[p] \mid f_i \in F, v_i \in V_p\}.$$

Intuitively speaking, the network (V_p, F_p) is obtained by "dividing out" the partial state p that describes the steady variables in R, see [3] for more details and Fig. 3 for an application to the running example.

Since seeds reference trap sets and since $p \in Seeds$ implies that $stab(S[p]) = p$, they naturally lend themselves for the above mentioned model reduction technique. The largest reduction in terms of state space cardinality is then obtained by considering those symbolic steady states that are maximal w.r.t. the partial order $\leq$, since they yield the smallest subspaces $S[p]$.

Application 2: Cyclic Attractors. The set $\max(Sym\mathcal{S})$ of maximal symbolic steady states w.r.t. $\leq$ has the property that every $p \in \max(Sym\mathcal{S})$ with $|p| < n$ is such that $S[p]$ contains only cyclic attractors.

$f_3 = v_4$
$f_4 = \overline{v_3}$

(a) Reduction by $p = 0_1 0_2$

$f_2 = v_4$
$f_3 = 0$
$f_4 = \overline{v_3}$

(b) Reduction by $q = 1_1$

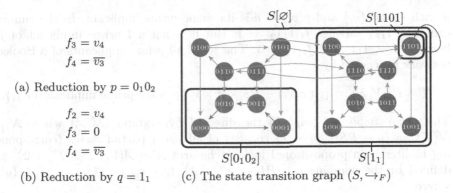

(c) The state transition graph $(S, \hookrightarrow_F)$

Fig. 3. (a,b) The *trap set reduction* applied to the 2 seeds $p = 0_1 0_2$ and $q = 1_1$ of the running example. (c) The asynchronous state transition graph $(S, \hookrightarrow_F)$. The 2 attractors are highlighted with red states and transitions. Rounded rectangles indicate the 4 trap sets that correspond to the 4 seeds of (V, F). Note that each trap set contains an attractor and that $p = 0_1 0_2$, which is maximal w.r.t. $\leq$ and satisfies $|p| = 2 < n$, is such that $S[p]$ contains only cyclic attractors. $q = 1_1$ on the other hand is not maximal and so $S[q]$ may, as is the case here, not contain a cyclic attractor.

Theorem 2. $|\{p \in \max(Sym\mathcal{S}) \mid |p| < n\}|$ *is a lower bound on the number of cyclic attractors of* (V, F).

Proof. Let $p \in \max(Sym\mathcal{S})$ and $|p| < n$. By Theorem 1, $S[p]$ is a trap set and therefore contains an attractor X. If $X = \{x\}$ then x is a steady state such that $p < x$, which contradicts the maximality of p.

Furthermore, since $stab(S[p]) = p$ for $p \in Sym\mathcal{S}$, we may conclude that some $v \in V \setminus U_{stab(S[p])}$ must be involved in the cyclic behavior. In our running example, the partial state $p = 0_1 0_2$ is a maximal symbolic steady state and therefore contains only cyclic attractors, see Fig. 3.

Note that $\mathcal{S} \subseteq \max(Seeds) = \max(Sym\mathcal{S}) \subseteq Sym\mathcal{S}$. Calculating all maximal symbolic steady states thus yields, in addition to the information on cyclic attractors, also all steady states.

2.3   The Prime Implicant Graph

In this section we propose a method for computing the seeds of (V, F). The idea is to translate the task into a hypergraph problem in which every seed is represented by a set of arcs that satisfy certain constraints. As we will show, those arc sets can be computed with existing solvers for integer linear programs.

We consider a directed hypergraph in which each arc corresponds to a minimal size implicant of f_i or $\overline{f_i}$, for some $v_i \in V$. Minimal size implicants are also called prime implicants, see e.g. [4]. We define the following slight variation: For $c \in \mathbb{B}$, a *c-prime implicant* of a non-constant f is a partial state $p \in PS$ satisfying $f[p] = c$, and $f[q] \neq c$ for all $q < p$. For a constant $f_i = c$ we define that

p with $U_p := \{v_i\}$ and $p(v_i) = c$ is its single prime implicant. In the running example, $1_1 1_2$ satisfies $f_1[1_1 1_2] = 1$. But it is not a 1-prime implicant of f_1, because $1_1 < 1_1 1_2$ and $f_1[1_1] = 1$. The set of all prime implicants of a Boolean network is denoted by

$$PI = PI(V, F) := \{(p, c, v_i) \in PS \times \mathbb{B} \times V \mid p \text{ is a } c\text{-prime implicant of } f_i\}.$$

The *prime implicant graph* is the directed hypergraph $(\mathcal{N}, \mathcal{A})$ where $\mathcal{N} = \mathcal{N}(V) := \{p \in PS \mid |p| = 1\}$ consists of all size 1 partial states (corresponding to literals in propositional logic). The arcs $\mathcal{A} = \mathcal{A}(V, F) \subset 2^{\mathcal{N}} \times 2^{\mathcal{N}}$ are defined by the mapping $\alpha : PI \to 2^{\mathcal{N}} \times 2^{\mathcal{N}}, (p, c, v_i) \mapsto (\{p_1, \ldots, p_{|p|}\}, \{q\})$, where

(1) $p = p_1 \sqcup \cdots \sqcup p_{|p|}$ is the unique decomposition of p into size 1 partial states,
(2) $q \in PS$ is defined by $U_q := \{v_i\}$ and $q(v_i) := c$.

The prime implicant graph has exactly one arc for every prime implicant, i.e., $\mathcal{A} := \{\alpha(p, c, v_i) \mid (p, c, v_i) \in PI\}$. The *head* of an arc $a = (\{p_1, \ldots, p_k\}, \{q\})$ is denoted by $H(a) := q$, and its *tail* by $T(a) = p_1 \sqcup \cdots \sqcup p_k$. The prime implicant graph of the running example is given in Fig. 4.

2.4   Prime Implicants and Seeds

Now we establish a relationship between subsets $A \subseteq \mathcal{A}$ and the seeds of a network (V, F). To do so we need the notions of *consistency* and *stability*. A subset $A \subseteq \mathcal{A}$ is *consistent* if for all $a_1, a_2 \in A$ the partial states $H(a_1)$ and $H(a_2)$ are consistent. If $A = \{a_1, \ldots, a_m\} \subseteq \mathcal{A}$ is consistent, the union $H(a_1) \sqcup \cdots \sqcup H(a_m)$ is called the *induced partial state* of A and denoted by $H(A)$. For the special case $A = \varnothing$ we define $H(A) := \varnothing$. A subset $A \subseteq \mathcal{A}$ is *stable* if for every $a \in A$ there is a consistent subset $B_a \subseteq A$ such that $T(a) \leq H(B_a)$. Intuitively, in this case the requirement $T(a)$ for each implication $a \in A$ to become effective is met by some assumptions B_a. The stable and consistent subsets of $\mathcal{A}$ for the running example and their induced partial states are given in Fig. 4. The central idea for the computation of *Seeds* is given in the next result:

Theorem 3. $p \in Seeds$ *if and only if there is a stable and consistent $A \subseteq \mathcal{A}$ such that $H(A) = p$.*

Proof. The statement of the theorem is trivially true for $p = \varnothing$ and $A = \varnothing$.

Hence, assume $\varnothing \neq p$. Let $v_i \in U_p$. Since $F[p] \geq p$ it follows that $f_i[p] = p(v_i)$ and hence that there is a $p(v_i)$-prime implicant q_i of f_i that satisfies $q_i \leq p$. The set $A := \{\alpha(q_i, p(v_i), v_i) \mid v_i \in U_p\}$ is, by definition, consistent and satisfies $H(A) = p$. But it is also stable because $\forall a \in A : T(a) \leq p$. Let $\varnothing \neq A \subseteq \mathcal{A}$ be stable and consistent. Then $\forall v_i \in U_{H(A)} : \exists a \in A : H(a) = H(A)(v_i)$. Hence $F[H(A)] \geq H(A)$ and $H(A) \in Seeds$.

Corollary 1. *Inclusion-wise maximal stable and consistent arc sets induce maximal seeds and therefore maximal symbolic steady states.*

PI $\mathcal{A}$

$(1_1, 1, v_1)$ a_1

$(1_2, 1, v_1)$ a_2

$(0_1 0_2, 0, v_1)$ a_3

$(1_1 1_4, 1, v_2)$ a_4

$(0_1, 0, v_2)$ a_5

$(0_4, 0, v_2)$ a_6

$(0_1 1_4, 1, v_3)$ a_7

$(1_1, 0, v_3)$ a_8

$(0_4, 0, v_3)$ a_9

$(0_3, 1, v_4)$ a_{10}

$(1_3, 0, v_4)$ a_{11}

(a)

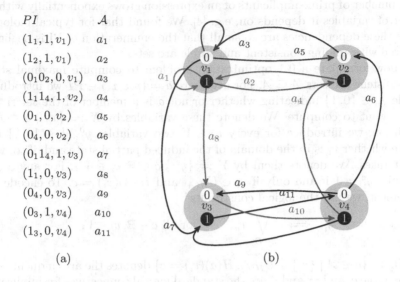

(b)

$$A = \varnothing, \quad B = \{a_3, a_5\}, \quad C = \{a_1\}, \quad
\begin{aligned}
D_1 &= \{a_1, a_4, a_8, a_{10}\} \\
D_2 &= \{a_2, a_4, a_8, a_{10}\} \\
D_3 &= \{a_1, a_2, a_4, a_8, a_{10}\}
\end{aligned}$$ (c)

Fig. 4. (a) The complete set PI of prime implicants of the example network, given in (p, c, v_i) notation. (b) The prime implicant graph $(\mathcal{N}, \mathcal{A})$ of the running example. The 8 nodes are grouped into 4 pairs $0_i, 1_i$ that belong to the same variable v_i. Gray discs represent the groups and are not elements of $\mathcal{N}$. Nodes that correspond to positive literals are drawn in black and negated literals in white. Hyperarcs are represented by several arcs having a common arrowhead. The colors indicate 3 different stable and consistent arc sets. (c) The stable and consistent arc sets induce the following seeds: $H(A) = \varnothing, H(B) = 0_1 0_2, H(C) = 1_1$ and for $i = 1, 2, 3 : H(D_i) = 1101$.

A special case of seeds was first studied in [5,6], where the authors describe *self-freezing circuits* that rely on *canalizing effects*. They occur if, in our terminology, there is a stable and consistent arc set $\varnothing \neq A$ that contains exclusively size 1 prime implicants, i.e., for all $a \in A$ we have $|T(a)| = 1$.

2.5 Computation of the Stable and Consistent Arc Sets

We propose an optimization-based method for finding all maximal stable and consistent arc sets in $(\mathcal{N}, \mathcal{A})$. Integer linear programming (ILP) has previously been suggested as a method for solving problems arising in the study of Boolean networks, see e.g. [7] and references therein. As a preliminary step, the prime implicants PI have to be enumerated. This can be achieved with any implementation of the Quine-McCluskey algorithm, see e.g. [8].

The number of prime implicants of an expression grows exponentially with the number of variables it depends on, e.g. [4]. We found that for typical biological models these dependencies are so small that the enumeration of PI is negligible compared with finding consistent and stable arc sets.

We now formulate a 0-1 optimization problem to compute maximal stable and consistent arc sets $A \subseteq \mathcal{A}$. For every arc $a = (p, c, v_i) \in PI$ we introduce a variable $x_a \in \{0, 1\}$ indicating whether or not a is a member of the set $A \subseteq \mathcal{A}$ that we want to compute. We denote these variables by $X := \{x_a \mid a \in PI\}$. In addition, we introduce for every $v_i \in V$ two variables $y_i^0, y_i^1 \in \{0, 1\}$ that indicate whether v_i is in the domain of the induced partial state and, if so, what value it takes. We denote them by $Y := \{y_i^c \mid c \in \mathbb{B}, v_i \in V\}$. For any $c \in \mathbb{B}$, we require $y_i^c = 1$ if and only if $v_i \in U_{H(A)}$ and $H(A)(v_i) = c$. To encode this requirement, we use the logical constraints

$$y_i^c \iff \bigvee_{a \in B_i^c} x_a, \qquad \text{for all } c \in \mathbb{B}, v_i \in V. \tag{C1}$$

Here, $B_i^c := \{a \in \mathcal{A} \mid \{v_i\} = U_{H(a)}, H(a)(v_i) = c\}$ denotes the arcs inducing v_i to take the value c, and $\Rightarrow$ and $\vee$ are the standard logical connectives for implication and disjunction. Next, we want to enforce the set $A := \{a \in \mathcal{A} \mid x_a = 1\}$ to be stable and consistent. To achieve this, we add the following constraints $(C2)$ resp. $(C3)$:

$$x_a \Rightarrow y_i^{T(a)(v_i)}, \qquad \text{for all } a \in \mathcal{A}, v_i \in U_{T(a)}, \tag{C2}$$

$$\overline{y_i^0} \vee \overline{y_i^1}, \qquad \text{for all } v_i \in V. \tag{C3}$$

To find a first maximal stable and consistent set $A \subseteq \mathcal{A}$, we solve the 0-1 optimization problem (here $\sum$ denotes addition)

$$\text{maximize} \sum_{x_a \in X} x_a, \quad \text{such that (C1), (C2), (C3).} \tag{0-1}$$

All maximal seeds can be enumerated by iteratively solving problem (0-1). Whenever a new solution $z : X \cup Y \to \{0, 1\}$ is found, we add a so-called *no-good cut*, which prevents this solution from being computed again. For example, we can use the constraint

$$\bigvee_{x_a \in G(z)} x_a, \quad \text{where } G(z) := \{x_a \in X \mid z(x_a) = 0\}. \tag{C4}$$

To solve problem (0-1) in practice, we reformulated the constraints (C1)-(C4) as linear 0-1 inequalities. A Python implementation using the integer programming solver `Gurobi` [9] is available at `http://sourceforge.net/projects/boolnetfixpoints`.

3 Application to a MAPK Pathway Model

We computed $\max(Sym\mathcal{S})$ for a network that models the influence of the MAPK pathway on cancer cell fate decisions, published in [10]. It consists of 53 variables that represent signaling proteins, genes and phenomenological components like *proliferation* or *apoptosis*. We found that there are 18 maximal symbolic steady states, 12 of which are steady states. Hence, following Application 2 in Sect. 2.2, there are at least 6 cyclic attractors whose properties can be comprehensively investigated using the 6 corresponding reduced models. An illustration of the largest maximal symbolic steady state, and therefore the smallest corresponding sub-model, is given in Fig. 3.

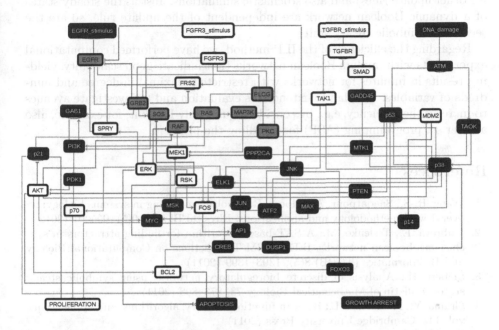

Fig. 5. A representation of the largest of the 6 maximal symbolic steady states p that satisfy $|p| < n$. Here, $|p| = 45$ and the remaining sub-model (V_p, F_p) contains therefore $53 - 45 = 8 = |V_p|$ variables. The underlying *interaction graph* is taken from [10]. Black and white components belong to U_p, with the values 1 and 0 respectively. Red components belong to the remaining sub-model.

4   Discussion

In this paper we propose a way of determining seeds and symbolic steady states of interest, e.g., in the context of model reduction and for estimating the number of cyclic attractors. We provide an optimization-based method for computing seeds exploiting the prime implicant graph. This graph captures properties of fundamental importance for the network behavior allowing to analyze certain aspects of asymptotic dynamics without having to calculate the state transition graph. Here, we focused on maximal seeds and symbolic steady states, however, we find that minimal seeds also carry interesting information. We currently work on extending our methods exploiting this potential of the prime implicant graph and seeds in general, particularly for studying questions related to reachability and to decision making.

The optimization-based method for finding maximal symbolic steady states can be extended from Boolean to multi-valued networks by generalizing the notion of prime implicants from Boolean to multi-valued expressions. Theorem 1 holds not only for synchronous or asynchronous but for *any* update rule (see [11] for other update rules) and also stochastic simulations. Just as the steady states of a dynamic Boolean network are independent of the update rule, so are the seeds and symbolic steady states.

Regarding the efficiency of the ILP method, we have performed computational experiments with random Boolean networks that indicate good scalability, yielding results in minutes for networks with restricted maximal in-degree and hundreds of variables. We plan to extend this evaluation and to investigate avenues to increase the efficiency, e.g., by considering not only ILP but, for example, also answer set programming (ASP) for handling the problem.

References

1. Wang, R.-S., Saadatpour, A., Albert, R.: Boolean modeling in systems biology: an overview of methodology and applications. Physical Biology 9(5), 055001 (2012)
2. Dubrova, E., Teslenko, M.: A SAT-based algorithm for finding attractors in synchronous boolean networks. IEEE/ACM Transactions on Computational Biology and Bioinformatics (TCBB) 8(5), 1393–1399 (2011)
3. Siebert, H.: Analysis of discrete bioregulatory networks using symbolic steady states. Bulletin of Mathematical Biology 73, 873–898 (2011)
4. Crama, Y., Hammer, P.L.: Boolean functions: theory, algorithms, and applications, vol. 142. Cambridge University Press (2011)
5. Fogelman-Soulie, F.: Parallel and sequential computation on boolean networks. Theoretical Computer Science 40, 275–300 (1985)
6. Kauffman, S.A.: The origins of order: Self organization and selection in evolution. Oxford University Press, USA (1993)
7. Akutsu, T., Yang, Z., Hayashida, M., Tamura, T.: Integer programming-based approach to attractor detection and control of boolean networks. IEICE Transactions on Information and Systems 95(12), 2960–2970 (2012)
8. Dick, R.: Quine-McCluskey two-level logic minimization method (2008), http://pypi.python.org/pypi/qm/0.2 (accessed in April 2014)
9. Gurobi Optimization, Inc.: Gurobi optimizer reference manual (2014)
10. Grieco, L., Calzone, L., Bernard-Pierrot, I., Radvanyi, F., Kahn-Perlès, B., Thieffry, D.: Integrative modelling of the influence of mapk network on cancer cell fate decision. PLoS Computational Biology 9(10), e1003286 (2013)
11. Gershenson, C.: Updating schemes in random boolean networks: Do they really matter. In: Artificial Life IX Proceedings of the Ninth International Conference on the Simulation and Synthesis of Living Systems, pp. 238–243. MIT Press (2004)

Equivalences in Multi-valued Asynchronous Models of Regulatory Networks

Adam Streck and Heike Siebert

Freie Universität Berlin
adam.streck@fu-berlin.de

Abstract Multi-valued network models can be described by their topology and a set of parameters capturing the effects of the regulators for each component. Dynamics can then be derived and represented as state transition systems. Different network models may lead to the same transition system, meaning dynamics analysis of a representative model covers a larger class of models. While rather clear in the Boolean case, the properties contributing to this effect become more involved for multi-valued models. We analyze these properties and present a mathematical description of the resulting model equivalence classes.

1 Introduction

Boolean and multi-valued network models have long since shown their worth in providing insights into complex systems, e.g., in the context of molecular networks [1]. System components are represented as variables with a finite value range, e.g., Boolean variables, and component interactions are captured in a directed (multi-)graph. Logical parameters then determine the value evolution of each component over time depending on the values of its regulators. Utilizing some update strategy leads to a transition system describing the evolution of the system state. We focus on the (unitary) asynchronous update allowing only one component value change per transition and only by absolute value one [2]. In particular for describing biological systems, this yields realistic trajectories.

Analysis of such transition systems can be hard due to non-determinism of the dynamics. In biological applications, one often has to compare transition systems of many models since data uncertainty may result in several models consistent with the data. In this context, it is an interesting observation that different models may give rise to the same state transition system. For Boolean networks this phenomenon has been investigated and is directly related to superfluous edges, meaning edges without detectable dynamical effect, in the graph capturing the network topology (see e.g. [3]). In the multi-valued setting however, not only existence but also strength of a regulatory effect can be captured in the model. This allows for models differing both in topology and parametrization to generate the same transition system, even if only functional edges are considered.

In this paper, we clarify the reasons leading to different models exhibiting the same dynamics, creating an equivalence relation on the set of models. We also determine a representative for each class and show a formal method for deciding whether two models belong to a same class.

J. Wąs, G.C. Sirakoulis, and S. Bandini (Eds.): ACRI 2014, LNCS 8751, pp. 571–575, 2014.
© Springer International Publishing Switzerland 2014

2   Background

We start by introducing the relevant notions, with an example given in Fig. 1.
A multi-valued regulatory multi-graph is a triple $G = (V, E, \rho)$ where:

- $V = \{1, \ldots, n\}$ with $n \in \mathbb{N}^+$ is a set of *components*,
- $\rho : V \to \mathbb{N}^+$ assigns a maximal *activity level* to each component,
- $E \subseteq V \times \mathbb{N}^+ \times V$, $n \leq \rho(u)$ for all $(u, n, v) \in E$, is a set of *regulations*.

We denote $\mathcal{G}$ the set of multi-valued regulatory graphs.

The function $\theta : V \times V \to 2^{\mathbb{N}^+}$ giving the *thresholds* of all edges between two
vertices is defined as $\theta(u, v) = \{n \mid (u, n, v) \in E\}$ where $u, v \in V$. Note that
$\theta(u, v) = \emptyset$ if there is no edge from u to v.

2.1   Discrete Kinetic Parameters

As the range of values for each component is finite, we can describe the set of all
possible configurations of the system, called *state space*, $S = \prod_{v \in V}[0, \rho(v)]$. Note
that the state space is shared among the graphs that have the same function ρ
and thus also the same V. We will use $\mathcal{G}_\rho = \{(V, E, \rho') \mid \rho = \rho'\}$ to refer to the
class of graphs that share the same state space.

The set S represents all the qualitatively different configurations of a system.
However, each component is dependent only on the values of its regulators. An
equivalence class on S w.r.t. regulation of a component $v \in V$ is called the
regulatory context. To define the relevant notions we first describe the *activity
interval* of a regulator. For formal reasons we consider an extended threshold
function $\tilde{\theta}$ with $\tilde{\theta}(u, v) = \theta(u, v) \cup \{0, \rho(u) + 1\}$ for all $u, v \in V$. Then

$$I_v^u = \{[j, k) \mid j, k \in \tilde{\theta}(u, v), j < k, \neg(\exists l \in \tilde{\theta}(u, v)(j < l < k))\} \qquad (1)$$

is the set of activity intervals of u in regulation of v. Here, the intuition is that
the regulatory effect of u on v is constant in each of the intervals of I_v^u. Note
that $\bigcup I_v^u = [0, \rho(u)]$, even in the case that there is no edge from u to v.

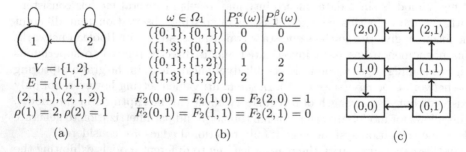

$V = \{1, 2\}$
$E = \{(1, 1, 1),$
$(2, 1, 1), (2, 1, 2)\}$
$\rho(1) = 2, \rho(2) = 1$

$\omega \in \Omega_1$	$P_1^\alpha(\omega)$	$P_1^\beta(\omega)$
$(\{0, 1\}, \{0, 1\})$	0	0
$(\{1, 3\}, \{0, 1\})$	0	0
$(\{0, 1\}, \{1, 2\})$	1	2
$(\{1, 3\}, \{1, 2\})$	2	2

$F_2(0, 0) = F_2(1, 0) = F_2(2, 0) = 1$
$F_2(0, 1) = F_2(1, 1) = F_2(2, 1) = 0$

(a)   (b)   (c)

Fig. 1. (a) A two-node regulatory network. (b) Dynamics of the network, captured
through two parametrizations function for the component 1 and an update function
for the component 2. (c) A transition system shared for both α and β.

The set of regulatory contexts of v is then denoted and defined $\Omega_v = \prod_{u \in V} I_v^u$. For each $v \in V$, a regulatory context $\omega \in \Omega_v$ is a $|V|$-tuple where ω_u is an activity interval I_v^u for each $u \in V$.

The dynamics of the regulatory graph are given via integer values, called *logical parameter*, assigned to each context. We use a *parametrization function* $P_v : \Omega_v \to [0, \rho(v)]$ for each $v \in V$. The parametrization of a regulatory network $G \in \mathcal{G}$ is then a tuple $P = (P_1, \ldots, P_{|V|})$. Lastly, we denote $\mathcal{P}_G$ the set of all parametrizations of the regulatory graph G, called the *parametrization space*.

2.2   Asynchronous Transition Systems

Having a regulatory graph $G = (V, E, \rho)$ and a parametrization $P \in \mathcal{P}_G$ we can fully describe its dynamical behavior as a *transition system* over its state space S. This is a directed graph $(S, \to)$ where $\to \subset S \times S$ is the *transition relation*. As mentioned, we are interested in asynchronous dynamics which means that the transition relation is non-deterministic.

First P is converted into a so-called *update function* $F^P = (F_v^P)_{v \in V}$ where $F_v^P : S \to [0, \rho(v)]$ for all $v \in V$. Here we exploit the fact that for each $s \in S$ and for each $v \in V$ there exists a context $\omega \in \Omega_v$ such that $s \in \prod_{u \in V} \omega_u$. To simplify the notation we will further write $s \in \omega$ instead of $s \in \prod_{u \in V} \omega_u$. For every $v \in V$ we obtain the function $F^P : S \to S$ from a parametrization P_v as

$$F_v^P(s) = \begin{cases} s_v + 1, & \text{if } s_v < P_v(\omega), s \in \omega, \\ s_v, & \text{if } s_v = P_v(\omega), s \in \omega, \\ s_v - 1, & \text{if } s_v > P_v(\omega), s \in \omega. \end{cases} \qquad (2)$$

Having F^P, we now assign each parametrized regulatory graph a transition system via the function $T_G : \mathcal{P}_G \to \{(S, \to)\}$ where $T_G(P) = (S, \to)$ such that

$$\forall v \in V, \forall s \in S(s \to s[v/n] \iff (F_v^P(s) = n \land F_v^P(s) \neq s_v)), \qquad (3)$$

with $x[i/k]$ denoting that in the vector x, the i-th value is substituted for k.

In the following, we will compare the transitions systems generated by regulatory graphs with the same state space, i.e., those in $\mathcal{G}_\rho$ for some ρ. We denote this set of transition systems $\mathcal{T}_\rho = \{(S, \to) \mid T_G(P) = (S, \to), G \in \mathcal{G}_\rho, P \in \mathcal{P}_G\}$.

3   Equivalence Classes of Parametrizations

We now investigate the cases where different parametrized regulatory graphs generate the same transition system. From (3) it is clear that two functions $F^{P_1} \neq F^{P_2}$ will lead to distinct transition systems, while coinciding functions F^{P_1}, F^{P_2} lead to the same dynamics. Thus we focus on the situation where $F^{P_1} = F^{P_2}$ for $P_1 \neq P_2$. Formal proofs are omitted due to page restrictions but can be found at http://nbn-resolving.de/urn:nbn:de:0296-matheon-12946.

Considering the simple example in Fig. 1b, we see that the two different parametrizations lead to the same dynamics. We observe that, other than in the first parametrization, the value $P^{\beta}(\{0,1\}, \{1,2\})$ lies beyond the boundary of the respective activity interval of component 1. To reach this value we thus need to enter a new context. We now define the notion of a *canonical* parametrization that prohibits such effects. Observe that a value change in v can cause the change of context only if v regulates itself. Therefore we say that $P \in \mathcal{P}_G$ is *canonical* if and only if

$$\forall v \in V, \forall \omega \in \Omega_v, \omega_v = [j, k)((P_v(\omega) \geq j - 1) \wedge (P_v(\omega) \leq k)). \tag{4}$$

We also denote $\dot{\mathcal{P}}_G \subseteq \mathcal{P}_G$ the subset of canonical parametrizations in $\mathcal{P}_G$.

We can obtain a clear correspondence between P and F^P if all the contexts contain just a single state, so that no ambiguities are introduced in (2). This partition is achieved when only considering *complete* graphs. Here, $(V, E, \rho) \in \mathcal{G}$ is called complete if and only if for all $u, v \in V$ and every $n \in [1, \rho(u)]$ the edge (u, n, v) is in E.

Theorem 1. *For each $G = (V, E, \rho) \in \mathcal{G}$ it holds that if G is complete then T_G defines a bijection between $\dot{\mathcal{P}}_G$ and $\mathcal{T}_\rho$.*

Based on this theorem, we can consider a complete graph with canonical parametrization as a representative of a class of models with the same behavior. We now show that we can extend a regulatory graph to a complete graph without changing the dynamics by adding *non-functional edges*. Intuitively, in Fig. 1b, the edge $(1, 1, 1)$ is non-functional in P_1^{β}, since there is no influence of the first component on itself detectable in the dynamics, which is not the case for P_1^{α}.

First, we focus on the *canonization* function $Can : \{(G, P) \mid G \in \mathcal{G}, P \in \mathcal{P}_G\} \to \{(G, \dot{P}) \mid G \in \mathcal{G}, \dot{P} \in \dot{\mathcal{P}}_G\}$. For each component $v \in V$ and for each regulatory context $\omega \in \Omega_v$ with $\omega_v = [j, k)$ we construct $\dot{P}$ as follows:

$$\dot{P}_v(\omega) = \begin{cases} j - 1, & \text{if } P_v(\omega) < j - 1 \\ k, & \text{if } P_v(\omega) > k \\ P_v(\omega), & \text{otherwise} \end{cases}.$$

The goal is to ensure that the parameter value can be reached in one transition from any state in the context, thus avoiding the effects illustrated in Fig. 1.

Second, we extend the topology of a graph using the *completion* function $Comp : \{(G, P) \mid G \in \mathcal{G}, P \in \mathcal{P}_G\} \to \{(\hat{G}, \hat{P}) \mid \hat{G} \in \mathcal{G}, \hat{P} \in \mathcal{P}_G\}$. If G is complete, we map (G, P) to itself. For an incomplete $G = (V, E, \rho)$ and some $P \in \mathcal{P}_G$ we consider the non-empty set of missing edges $\hat{E} = \{(u, n, v) \mid u, v \in V, n \in [1, u], (u, n, v) \notin E\}$. Assume that the set of all possible edges has some total ordering. We extend the graph G to $\hat{G}$ such that $\hat{G} = (V, E \cup \{min(\hat{E})\}, \rho)$.

To extended the parametrization $\hat{P}$ to the new topology we observe that $\hat{G}$ gives rise to new contexts that were obtained by partitioning some context of G into two. To preserve the dynamical behavior we simply assign the parameter value of the original context to both resulting new contexts. Formally, we define two assisting variables $n_-, n_+ \in \tilde{\theta}(\hat{u}, \hat{v})$ that denote the closest lower and higher thresholds to $\hat{n}$ that is already in E, i.e.,

$$\neg(\exists m \in \theta(\hat{u}, \hat{v})(n_- < m < n)) \wedge \neg(\exists m \in \theta(\hat{u}, \hat{v})(n < m < n_+)).$$

For each $v \in V$ and for each $\hat{\omega} \in \hat{\Omega}_v$ we then create $\hat{P}$ as

$$\hat{P}_v(\hat{\omega}) = \begin{cases} P_v(\hat{\omega}) & \text{if } v \neq \hat{v} \vee (\omega_{\hat{u}} = [j, k) \wedge (j \neq n_- \vee k \neq n_+)) \\ P_v(\hat{\omega}[\hat{u}/[n_-, n_+)]) & \text{otherwise} \end{cases}.$$

By construction it is clear that the recursive use of $Comp$ on (G, P) results in a fixpoint $Comp^*(G, P)$ signifying a complete graph. Since application of $Comp$ and Can preserve the dynamical behavior, a parameterized graph and its image under these functions give rise to the same update function and thus the same transition system. We can therefore draw the following conclusion:

Theorem 2. *Let $G, G' \in \mathcal{G}$, $P \in \mathcal{P}_G$, and $P' \in \mathcal{P}_{G'}$. Then $T_G(P) = T'_G(P')$ if and only if $Can(Comp^*(G, P)) = Can(Comp^*(G', P'))$.*

4 Conclusion

In the setting of multi-valued networks, both different topologies and different parametrizations do not necessarily lead to distinct dynamics. We have shown how such networks can be grouped into equivalence classes according to their transition systems, provided an explicit description of a representative of such a class and a procedure to identify this representative for an arbitrary network. The procedure highlights two key aspects, namely the resolution of the state space via the regulatory contexts and the parameter values related to self-regulation.

Our method for identifying the classes is not efficient in application, since it relies on construction of a complete graph. In future work, we would like to be able to identify, for each class of models that share the transition system, a representative that is minimal in some sense, and to provide the respective reduction. In the boolean case one does so by removing non-functional edges. However, as illustrated in our example, two models with different numbers of functional edges can generate the same dynamics. As discussed, this effect is closely tied to self loops and parameter values lying beyond the boundaries of the respective activity intervals. To resolve this issue, elimination of such loops would need to be tied to changes in parameter values corresponding to effects of other regulators. Here, one needs to consider the question whether it might not be desirable to have a representative with canonical parametrization and thus a clear relation to the state transitions instead of just focusing on minimizing the number of functional edges.

References

1. Kauffman, S.: Metabolic stability and epigenesis in randomly constructed genetic nets. Journal of Theoretical Biology 22(3), 437–467 (1969)
2. Chaouiya, C., Remy, E., Mossé, B., Thieffry, D.: Qualitative analysis of regulatory graphs: a computational tool based on a discrete formal framework. In: Benvenuti, L., De Santis, A., Farina, L. (eds.) Positive Systems. LNCIS, vol. 294, pp. 119–126. Springer, Heidelberg (2003)
3. Siebert, H.: Local structure and behavior of boolean bioregulatory networks. In: Horimoto, K., Regensburger, G., Rosenkranz, M., Yoshida, H. (eds.) AB 2008. LNCS, vol. 5147, pp. 185–199. Springer, Heidelberg (2008)

Effective Parallelism Rate
by Reversible PCA Dynamics

Pierre-Yves Louis

Laboratoire de Mathématiques et Applications,
UMR 7348, Université de Poitiers & CNRS,
Téléport 2 – BP 30179,
Boulevard Marie et Pierre Curie,
86962 Technopole du Futuroscope de Poitiers, Chasseneuil Cedex, France
Pierre-Yves.Louis@math.univ-poitiers.fr

Abstract. Probabilistic Cellular Automata generalise CA by implementing an updating rule defined through a probability. It means a *synchronous* updating of the constituting cells/sites' states is possible. PCA differ from the *interacting particle systems* where in general at most one site is possibly updated at a time. For a family of reversible (in a stochastic sense) PCA dynamics, we study through numerical simulations the effective flips occurring. When infinitely many sites are considered, there are two regime: an ergodic one and a phase transition regime. When finitely many interacting sites are considered, these regimes corresponds to very different effective parallelism rate. We quantify these changes. When phase transition holds, PCA dynamics is in fact an α-asynchronous one.

Probabilistic Cellular Automata (PCA) are Cellular Automata (CA) where the updating rule is defined through a probability. Like their deterministic version, PCA are a very useful class of models for simulation and analysis of complex systems [1, 2]. They constitute a large family of discrete-time Markov stochastic processes where the transition probability has a product form (*synchronous updating*). Each constituting site or elementary cell may have its state updated between two steps of time. Yet a different family of stochastic processes is more amenable to a theoretical analysis in the framework of probability theory. These are called *interacting particle systems* (IPS) [3]. As well as PCA, they are Markov stochastic processes on a state space which has a product form. They are in general *continuous*-time Markov processes defined through an updating *rate*. There are few general results and detailed analysis is developed for more particular categories of models. Most of the IPS for which detailed theoretical results are available have a kind of *sequential* updating procedure: at most one site may be updated when an exponentially distributed clock rings. An analogous discrete time version of this mechanism is possible. Briefly, these continuous-time stochastic processes allow a small updating infinitely often contrary to the PCA where *all* sites may be updated at discrete time step. These updating may *effectively* not happen so often according to the associated probability which strongly

J. Wąs, G.C. Sirakoulis, and S. Bandini (Eds.): ACRI 2014, LNCS 8751, pp. 576–585, 2014.
© Springer International Publishing Switzerland 2014

depends on the state of the site's neighbourhood. A third category of these processes is asynschronous (P)CA, as investigated for instance in [4–6]. They are CA/PCA where the parallel updating is relaxed and where only a given proportion of sites are submitted to the updating procedure and whose value is then potentially modified.

To be specific, we consider a parameterised PCA family suggested by Derrida [7] which is the parallel version of the Gibbs sampler associated to the famous Ising interaction potential (with nearest neighbour interaction or *finite range*). Under some light assumptions, these PCA are reversible stochastic processes, meaning a kind of "dynamical equilibrium" holds (aka *detailed balance condition*).

For this family, more precise theoretical results were proven. In a non exhaustive way, let us mention the following ones. The form of the time-asymptotic distribution is explicitly known [8] both for a finite collection of interacting cells and for an infinite collection (countable, $\mathbb{Z}^d$ lattice case). Ergodicity versus phase transition/loss of ergodicity region were proven in the $\mathbb{Z}^2$ case [8]. Metastability results hold, giving insight on escape times [9, 10] in the *finitely many interacting sites* case. Through a mean field approximation the parameters' role is more precisely understood [11]. A very nice generalisation of this family was studied in order to sample from a Gibbs measure by tuning the application of the updating rule in a similar way as in the α-asynchronous case [12] and a very interesting non reversible variation was considered in [13].

Due to the detailed balance, a sort of energy potential is naturally associated to this PCA family. This potential is much more complicated than the nearest-neighbour Ising case [11]. This family can be considered as a *gradient dynamics* aiming at minimising this potential. From the perspective of understanding relationships between synchronous/asynchronous updating scheme, a natural question to address on this PCA family is the behaviour of the effective flipping rate (case with finite number of interacting cells) when the parameters are in a region where, for the infinite $\mathbb{Z}^d$ case, loss of ergodicity holds. In this region, the transition probability becomes very small and the effective change of a cell's state becomes rare. The PCA dynamics becomes *de facto* quasi a sequential one or an α-sync one. In this contribution, we aim at precise and quantifying this fact through numerical simulations.

The contribution is organised as follows: we first introduce the general framework from a probabilistic point of view. We precise the meaning of the reversibility property. We then present the previously mentioned parameterised reversible PCA dynamics family. New numerical results concerning the effective updating rate are then summarised. The last section give some conclusions and further forthcoming investigations.

1   General Framework from a Probabilistic Perspective

Consider a collection of sites indexed by a network G. Each site $k \in G$ has an associated value σ_k in a finite space S. Typically, $S = \{0, 1\}$ or $S = \{-1, +1\}$.

The association of a value in S to each site is called a *configuration* and is denoted by $\sigma = (\sigma_k)_{k \in G}$. A *probabilistic* CA dynamics is defined through the synchronous use of an updating rule $p_k(\cdot|\eta)$ where, given the configuration η at the previous time step, $p_k(\cdot|\eta)$ is a probability on S. The global probability to jump towards a configuration σ, starting from a configuration η, is defined as

$$P(\sigma|\eta) = \prod_{k \in G} p_k(\sigma_k|\eta).$$

Given an initial condition, possibly sampled from a starting distribution, the PCA dynamics becomes a discrete-time Markov stochastic process on the state space S^G whose transition matrix is P. It means, knowing what happened up to time $(n-1)$ –more precisely the last state η (markovianity)–, each site is updated independently. In general, the updating rule is assumed to be *translation invariant*, meaning $p_k(\cdot|\eta) = p_0(\cdot|\theta_k\eta)$ where $\theta_k\eta$ denotes the configuration $(\theta_k \eta)_j := \eta_{j+k}$. Just as for CA, the local rule is assumed to be *finite range*: there exists a finite neighbourhood V_k on the graph G such that $p_k(\cdot|\eta) = p_k(\cdot|\eta_{V_k})$ where η_{V_k} denotes $(\eta_j)_{j \in V_k}$. In particular, when G is infinite, this condition ensures the existence of such a stochastic process. It is unique (in distribution) as soon as a starting distribution is fixed. When $p_k(\cdot|\eta)$ is positive, the PCA dynamics is called *positive rates*.

An *interacting particle system* is a continuous-time Markov stochastic process defined on S^G. The infinitesimal local updating *rate* $c_k(\cdot|\eta)$ is the analogous of p_k, requiring only to be positive. The global updating procedure is defined through a *generator* L defined, for any f continuous function on S^G, as

$$Lf(\eta) = \sum_{k \in G} \left(f(\eta^{k,s}) - f(\eta)\right) c_k(\eta^{k,s}|\eta)$$

where $\eta^{k,s}$ is the configuration equal to η on $\{k\}^c$ and taking the value s at site k. Similarly, $c_k(\cdot|\eta)$ only depends on η_{V_k} where V_k is a finite neighbourhood of k. In this form, there is a sequential updating procedure: when the process jumps, it goes from a configuration η to a configuration σ which is a modification in one site of η. At most one site is updated during an infinitesimally small amount of time. Remark, the general definition allows to update when a jump occurs, a *finite* collection of sites. See [3].

The specificity of PCA dynamics as Markov stochastic processes is more blatant when G is infinite since it allows infinitely many local changes. In the G finite case, these PCA processes have the particularity to allow more potential jumps on S^G, especially when it has positive rates.

2   What Does *Reversibility* Mean for a Stochastic Process?

A Markov process is said to be *reversible* if it admits at least one reversible distribution. It means, it exists a probability measure μ on S^G such that

$$\forall \sigma, \eta, \quad \mu(\eta)P(\sigma|\eta) = \mu(\sigma)P(\eta|\sigma).$$

For a continuous-time process, the similar relation is

$$\forall f \text{ continuous on } S^G, \quad \int f\, Lg\, d\mu = \int g\, Lf\, d\mu.$$

Both mean the stochastic process's distribution, with starting distribution μ, is invariant by time inversion $t \mapsto -t$. Despite this definition, this property is related only to the dynamics. Let us recall the following statement proved by Kolmogorov: consider an irreducible Markov chain on a finite state space with transition probability P, the (unique) stationary probability measure is reversible (w.r.t P) if and only if

$$P(\sigma_2|\sigma_1)P(\sigma_3|\sigma_2)\cdots P(\sigma_1|\sigma_k) = P(\sigma_k|\sigma_1)\cdots P(\sigma_2|\sigma_3)P(\sigma_1|\sigma_2)$$

for any finite sequence of states $\sigma_1, \cdots, \sigma_k$.

Reversible probability measures are in particular stationary measures, which means distributions invariant w.r.t. the stochastic dynamics. Equivalently, if the process $(\sigma_n)_{n\in\mathbb{N}}$ starts with a stationary probability measure μ then, for all time n, the distribution of σ_n is equal to μ. Under some assumptions, there is a unique stationary measure, possibly reversible too, and this distribution is the time asymptotic of any Markov chain whose transition probability is $P(\cdot, \cdot)$. Any starting distribution, even deterministic ones, converges thus in distribution towards this unique distribution (*ergodic* behaviour). This situation occurs for positive rates PCA dynamics when G is finite. Nevertheless this statement gives no information concerning the *speed of convergence*.

3 A Family of Reversible Positive Rates PCA Dynamics

We choose $S = \{-1, 1\}$ and $G = \mathbb{Z}^d$ or $G = \Lambda_L := [0, L]^d \cap \mathbb{Z}^d$ for any $L > 0$. Consider a function $\mathcal{K} : \mathbb{Z}^d \to \mathbb{R}$ of finite range: there exists $R > 0$ such that $\mathcal{K}(i) = 0$ for $|i| > R$, and symmetric $\mathcal{K}(i) = \mathcal{K}(-i)$ for every $i \in \mathbb{Z}^d$. This last assumption is necessary and sufficient to ensure the reversibility of the PCA dynamics. Moreover, let $\tau \in \{-1, 1\}^{\mathbb{Z}^d}$ be a fixed configuration. It plays the role of *boundary condition*. For $\Lambda \subset \mathbb{Z}^d$, we define the transition probability $P_\Lambda^\tau(\sigma|\eta) = \otimes_{k\in\Lambda}P_k^\tau(\sigma_k|\eta)$ by

$$P_k^\tau(\sigma_k = s|\eta) = p_k(s|\tilde{\eta}) = \frac{1}{2}\Big[1 + s\tanh(\beta\sum_{k\in\mathbb{Z}^d}\mathcal{K}(k-j)\tilde{\eta}_j + \beta h)\Big], \quad (1)$$

where $\tilde{\eta} = \eta_\Lambda\tau_{\Lambda^c}$; $h \in \mathbb{R}$, $\beta > 0$ are given parameters. The usual notation $\eta_\Lambda\tau_{\Lambda^c}$ denotes the configuration equal to η (resp. τ) for sites in Λ (resp. Λ^c). As stated in [14] (see section 4.1.1 in [15]), this particular form of p_k is indeed the most general one for a shift invariant positive rate PCA on $\{-1, 1\}^{\mathbb{Z}^d}$. Moreover, this updating rule is the parallel version of the Gibbs sampler associated to the famous Ising interaction potential (with nearest neighbour interaction).

Precise theoretical results were proven for this family of positive rates PCA, parameterised by β and h. The form of the time-asymptotic distribution is explicitly known (Prop. 3.1 in [8]) both when G is finite and when $G = \mathbb{Z}^d$. In the $\mathbb{Z}^2$ case, ergodicity versus phase transition/loss of ergodicity region were proven [8, 16] using probabilistic and statistical mechanics techniques. There is indeed an interaction potential φ associated to the PCA dynamics on $\mathbb{Z}^d$:

$$
\begin{aligned}
\varphi_{\{k\}}(\sigma_k) &= -\beta h \sigma_k \\
\varphi_{V_k}(\sigma_{V_k}) &= -\log \cosh\left[\beta \sum_j \mathcal{K}(k-j)\sigma_j + \beta h\right] \\
\varphi_\Lambda(\sigma_\Lambda) &= 0 \;\; \text{otherwise},
\end{aligned}
\tag{2}
$$

This potential is much more complicated than the nearest neighbour Ising model. The aim of the Gibbs sampler procedure is to write down a stochastic dynamics admitting as time-asymptotic an *a priori* prescribed distribution. Starting from the Ising Gibbs measure and implementing the Gibbs sampler updating rule in a *fully* parallel way leads to a different time-asymptotic, now characterised as Gibbs measures w.r.t. this new potential φ.

When $d = 1$, $G = \mathbb{Z}$, since reversible probability measures are Gibbs measures w.r.t φ, the dynamics admits a unique reversible measure. On $\mathbb{Z}$, for finite range potentials, there is no phase transition, meaning it exists a unique Gibbs measure [17].

Let us consider from now on the cases $d = 2$, $\mathcal{K}(0) \geq 0$, $\mathcal{K}(\pm e_i) = 1$ ($i \in \{1, 2\}$ with (e_1, e_2) canonical basis), $h = 0$. This is the *Von Neumann neighbourhood*. In the infinite case $G = \mathbb{Z}^2$, there exists a critical value β_c such that for $\beta < \beta_c$, the PCA dynamics is ergodic, converging in distribution towards the unique Gibbs measure associated to the potential φ. For $\beta > \beta_c$, the PCA dynamics is not ergodic anymore, it exists many reversible distributions, characterised as Gibbs measures w.r.t φ. When $\mathcal{K}(0) = 0$, β_c is exactly the Ising critical value $\log(1 + \sqrt{2})/2 \sim 0.44$. In the corresponding $G = \Lambda_L$ cases, two analogous regimes are observed numerically and characterised by a drastic change in the speed of convergence towards the unique stationary distribution. Theoretically it was stated in [16] that the convergence holds exponentially fast when $\beta < \beta_c$. When $\mathcal{K}(0) = 1$, $\beta_c \in [0.3; 0.35]$ was numerically estimated [15]. Finally, remark when $\mathcal{K}(0) = 1$, for β large, the PCA dynamics becomes a CA with *majority*-voting updating rule over the four nearest neighbours and the site itself.

4   Effective Updating Rate

From now on for simplicity we consider only *periodic boundary conditions*. These are convenient to insure a strict shift-invariant situation for a *finite* number of interacting sites. We use numerical simulation through programs written in R and make use of the "vectorisation" possibilities in order to improve the running time. Since the probabilistic updating rule depends on the state of the neighbourhood η_{V_k}, the global jump probability, given the past, has a product form of elements like $p_0(\cdot|\xi)$ where $\xi \in S_{V_0}$. When the system evolves towards an ordered configuration, the modification of the sites' states may become very unlikely. We want to quantify this loss of effectiveness in the parallel updating.

On $S = \{-1, +1\}$, we call a *flip*, the change of a site's state. Rewrite the updating rule $p_k(\cdot|\eta)$ as a flipping probability $\tilde{p}_k(\eta)$ which is the probability, conditionally to the past, that η_k jumps to $-\eta_k$

$$\tilde{p}_k(\eta) = p_k(+1|\eta)\mathbb{1}_{\eta_k=-1} + p_k(-1|\eta)\mathbb{1}_{\eta_k=+1}$$

where $\mathbb{1}_{\eta_k=-1}$ is short notation for $\mathbb{1}_{\{\eta:\eta_k=-1\}}$ with, for any subset A, $\mathbb{1}_A(x) = 1$ if $x \in A$, and 0 otherwise. We define an *effective flipping rate* ($d = 2$ case)

$$\lambda_{n+1} = \frac{\sum_{k\in\Lambda_L} \mathbb{1}_{\sigma_k(n+1)\neq\sigma_k(n)}}{L^2}. \tag{3}$$

Denoting by $\mathcal{F}_n$ the filtration generated by the process up to time n, we get immediately

$$\mathbb{E}_{\mathcal{F}_n}(\lambda_{n+1}) = \sum_{\xi\in S^{V_0}} \frac{\sharp\{k \in \Lambda_L : V_k = \xi\}}{L^2} \, \tilde{p}_0(\xi).$$

$\sharp$ denotes the cardinality. We then want to compute the different probabilities $\tilde{p}_0(\xi)$ and the proportion of different local configurations. We want to record another quantity's trajectory: the number of nearest neighbours bonds really flipped at the same time

$$q_{n+1} = \frac{\sum_{j\sim k} \mathbb{1}_{\sigma_k(n+1)\neq\sigma_k(n)} \mathbb{1}_{\sigma_j(n+1)\neq\sigma_j(n)}}{2L^2},$$

where $j \sim k$ denotes neighbouring sites. It is indeed interesting to notice, when the nearest-neighbour Ising associated Gibbs sampler is partly synchronised, alternatively on even/odd sites, meaning no pair of neighbouring sites is updated at the same time, then the stationary measure remains the Gibbs measure w.r.t. Ising potential. The potential's modification is then induced by the possible updating of two even/odd neighbouring sites simultaneously.

5   Numerical Results, Case $d = 2$

5.1   Typical Parameters' Values Chosen

We choose to consider here the results when $\mathcal{K}(\pm e_i) = 1$ ($i \in \{1,2\}$), $\mathcal{K}(0) = 1$ and with $h = 0$. Similar results hold modifying the $\mathcal{K}(\cdot)$ function. $\mathcal{K}(\cdot)$ not positive should not modify the main question we address here. When $h \neq 0$, there is a drift toward one value of S. It is more interesting to consider a symmetrical situation. Periodic boundary conditions are chosen for the same reason. We consider $G = \Lambda_L$ with $L = 60$ (3600 sites). Since G is finite in these simulations, the PCA dynamics is *always* ergodic and as explained, there is, for any parameters value of β, h, convergence in distribution towards a unique stationary probability measure μ_β. As stated by theoretical results, and confirmed by these simulations, for β close to 0, μ_β looks like the uniform measure (independent product of 0.5-Bernoulli distributions). For large β, μ_β is concentrated on configurations close to $\underline{+1}$ and $\underline{-1}$ where $\sigma = \underline{+1}$ means $\forall k \in G$, $\sigma_k = +1$. On Fig. 1 results from two typical samples in the cases $\beta = 0.1$ and $\beta = 0.5$ are presented.

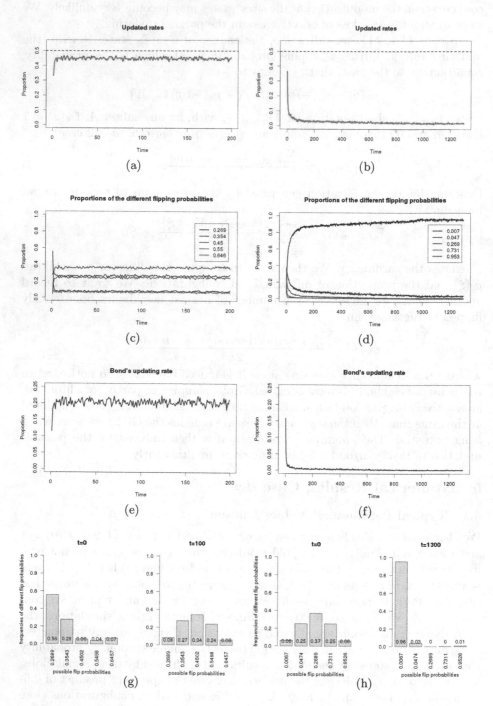

Fig. 1. One sample Simulation's results, case $\beta = 0.1$ left, case $\beta = 0.5$ right

5.2 Non Phase Transition Regime

When $\beta < \beta_c$ the PCA dynamics on $G = \mathbb{Z}^2$ is ergodic with exponential speed of convergence. This corresponds to the non phase transition regime for the associated potential φ. Consider $\beta = 0.1$ for illustration. Running the algorithm up to final time $T = 200$ shows the stationary states is reached. We check for instance the stabilisation of the magnetisation $\sum_{k \in G} \sigma_k / \sharp G$. Notice, one step time is one step of the PCA dynamics, which means $\sharp G$ potential flips. Since ergodicity holds, the starting distribution does not matter. Nevertheless, the phenomenon is more interesting starting with a random configuration distributed according to independent distributions giving weight 0.9 to +1 (see left bar-chart Fig. 1 (g)). One sample of the evolution of λ_n (red curve) and $\mathbb{E}_{\mathcal{F}_n}(\lambda_{n+1})$ (in green) is shown in Fig. 1 (a). This sample, in the stationary regime, gives a constant effective updating rate around 0.44 for both the indicators λ_n and $\mathbb{E}_{\mathcal{F}_n}(\lambda_{n+1})$. On Fig. 3 (a), at $\beta = 0.1$ a mean value on independent trials is coherent with this one sample value of λ_n. Figure 1 (c)) illustrates the time evolution of the different possible flipping probabilities. The symmetries imply that different values of σ_{V_k} give rise to the same flipping probability $\tilde{p}_k(\sigma_{V_k})$. In this example, only 5 different flipping probabilities are associated to the 2^5 values of σ_{V_k}. The associated colour goes from blue to red, blue denotes the configurations less favourable to flip and red the more likely to flip. Figure 1 (e) is the plot of the time evolution of the bond updating rate q_n. Figure 1 (g) represents the bar-chart of the flipping probability. At $T = 100$, this sampled configuration shows a large proportion of local configurations σ_{V_k} with a moderate flipping probability. This match with previous knowledge about the equilibrium distribution μ this configuration is sampled from (up to the finite simulation time bias). Figure 2 (a) shows the bar-plot of the flipping probabilities on a sample from size 100 both at the starting time and at $T = 500$ confirming the previous one sample observations.

5.3 Phase Transition Regime

When $\beta > \beta_c$, the PCA dynamics on $G = \mathbb{Z}^2$ is non ergodic (phase transition regime for the associated potential φ). Consider $\beta = 0.5$. Running the algorithm up to final time $T = 1300$, stationarity is reached for this sample at $T = 1000$. This is slightly observable on Fig. 1 (d) and Fig. 1 (b). *For this sample*, the configuration reached is close to -1. In order to emphasise the polarisation phenomenon occurring, the starting condition was chosen w.r.t the uniform probability on S^{Λ_L}. The effective flipping rate is, in this regime, very quickly lower than 0.1, non increasing, stabilising around $1.6 \ 10^{-2}$. Fig. 1 (d) shows the tiny proportion of local configurations very likely to flip and the large proportion of sites whose neighbourhood make them very unlikely to flip. The bar-plot associated to this sample's flipping distribution illustrates it on Fig. 1 (h), and on Fig. 2 (b) for an i.i.d. sample with size 100.

On Fig. 3 (a) the effective flipping rate is observed for a sample at a large enough time in order to be close to equilibrium. These measures' mean is plotted against β. As expected from the theoretical results, there is a drastic change when

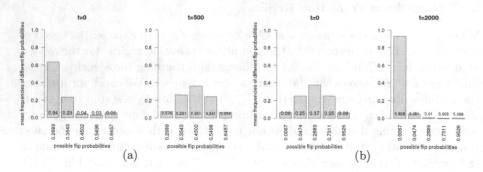

Fig. 2. Simulation's results: average on an i.i.d. sample, case $\beta = 0.1$ left, case $\beta = 0.5$ right

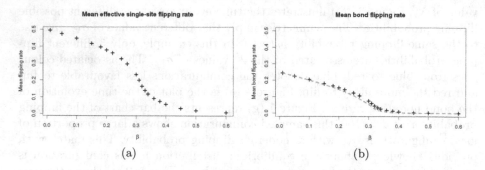

Fig. 3. Simulation's results: average on an i.i.d. sample

approaching β_c and for $\beta > \beta_c$ it is small. The same phenomenon occurs for the effective bond updating rate q_n. It is evident to expect a value close (but not equal) to the square of the single site updating rate. This is plotted on Fig. 3 (b) as dashed green line. Indeed, for small and large value of β, neighbouring local configurations σ_{V_k} and σ_{V_j} (with $j \sim k$) tends to be the same or similar.

6   Conclusion and Further Investigations

This contribution introduce a family of positive rates PCA dynamics from a probabilistic point of view. This family is representative of the reversible PCA dynamics. In conformity with theoretical results concerning the case $G = \mathbb{Z}^2$, the effective flipping rate decreases dramatically close to 0 when the parameters are in a phase transition regime (for $G = \mathbb{Z}^2$). Another motivation of this paper was to quantify this phenomenon. In the challenge to understand advantages/drawbacks between fully parallel and α-asynchronous PCA, it intends to advocate to consider this effective flipping rate indicator. As perspective, other

PCA dynamics, not with positive rates, like Stavskaja model or majority North-East-Center model, and α-asynchronous versions will be considered.

References

1. Kari, J.: Theory of cellular automata: a survey. Theoret. Comput. Sci. 334(1-3), 3–33 (2005)
2. Cervelle, J., Dennunzio, A., Formenti, E., Skowron, A.: Cellular Automata and Models of Computation. Fundamenta Informaticae 126(2-3) (2013)
3. Liggett, T.M.: Interacting particle systems. Springer, New York (1985)
4. Fatès, N.: Asynchronism induces second-order phase transitions in elementary cellular automata. J. Cell. Autom. 4(1), 21–38 (2009)
5. Fatés, N., Morvan, M., Schabanel, N., Thierry, É.: Fully asynchronous behavior of double-quiescent elementary cellular automata. In: Jedrzejowicz, J., Szepietowski, A. (eds.) MFCS 2005. LNCS, vol. 3618, pp. 316–327. Springer, Heidelberg (2005)
6. Regnault, D., Schabanel, N., Thierry, C.: Progresses in the analysis of stochastic 2D cellular automata: a study of asynchronous 2D minority. Theoret. Comput. Sci. 410(47-49), 4844–4855 (2009)
7. Derrida, B.: Dynamical phase transitions in spin models and automata. In: Fundamental Problems in Statistical Mechanics VII (Altenberg, 1989), pp. 273–309. North-Holland, Amsterdam (1990)
8. Dai Pra, P., Louis, P.Y., Roelly, S.: Stationary measures and phase transition for a class of Probabilistic Cellular Automata. ESAIM: Probability & Statistics 6, 89–104 (2002)
9. Cirillo, E.N., Nardi, F.R., Spitoni, C.: Metastability for Reversible Probabilistic Cellular Automata with Self-Interaction. J. Statist. Phys. 132(3), 431–471 (2008)
10. Nardi, F.R., Spitoni, C.: Sharp Asymptotics for Stochastic Dynamics with Parallel Updating Rule with self-interaction. Journ. Stat. Phys. 4(146), 701–718 (2012)
11. Cirillo, E.N., Louis, P.Y., Ruszel, W.M., Spitoni, C.: Effect of self-interaction on the phase diagram of a Gibbs-like measure derived by a reversible Probabilistic Cellular Automata. Chaos, Solitons & Fractals (December 2013)
12. Dai Pra, P., Scoppola, B., Scoppola, E.: Sampling from a Gibbs Measure with Pair Interaction by Means of PCA. Journal of Statistical Physics 149(4), 722–737 (2012)
13. Lancia, C., Scoppola, B.: Equilibrium and Non-equilibrium Ising Models by Means of PCA. Journal of Statistical Physics 153(4), 641–653 (2013)
14. Kozlov, O., Vasilyev, N.: Reversible Markov chains with local interaction. In: Multicomponent Random Systems, pp. 451–469. Dekker, New York (1980)
15. Louis, P.Y.: Automates Cellulaires Probabilistes: mesures stationnaires, mesures de Gibbs associées et ergodicité. PhD thesis, Politecnico di Milano, Italy and Université Lille 1, France (September 2002)
16. Louis, P.Y.: Ergodicity of PCA: Equivalence between Spatial and Temporal Mixing Conditions. Electronic Communications in Probability 9, 119–131 (2004)
17. Georgii, H.O.: Gibbs Measures and Phase Transitions. De Gruyter, Berlin (2011)

Quick Convergence to a Fixed Point: A Note on Asynchronous Elementary Cellular Automata

Nazim Fatès

Inria Nancy Grand-Est, LORIA UMR 7503,
F-54 600, Villers-lès-Nancy, France
nazim.fates@loria.fr

Abstract. This note describes a small step in the analysis of the fully asynchronous cellular automata (i.e., the cells are updated uniformly at random at each time step). We establish the rapid convergence of fifteen minimal Elementary Cellular Automata, showing that their average convergence time to a fixed point scales logarithmically with the size of the automaton. Techniques involve the use of Markov chain analysis and the construction of adequate potential functions. The problem is however left open for twelve other minimal rules, which shows the need to develop this analysis further.

Keywords: Asynchronous cellular automata, stochastic process, Markov chain analysis, fast convergence.

1   Introduction

This note describes a work-in-progress research on simple asynchronous cellular automata (CA). We study the 256 Elementary Cellular Automata submitted to a fully asynchronous updating scheme: at each time step, only one cell is updated, chosen uniformly at random. We ask which are the rules which converge "rapidly" to a fixed point. Formally, the expected time needed to attain a fixed point should scale as a *logarithmic* function of the size of the automaton.

The study of asynchronous cellular automata concerns various fields such as computability [7], dynamical systems [1,5], modelling of natural complex systems, etc. We refer to our recent survey for a presentation of this wide topic of research [2].

The question of the classification of asynchronous cellular automata is still widely open [3]. One way to classify the rules analytically is to study the average time needed to reach a fixed point. Indeed, as experiments show, the dynamical behaviour of the system is strongly related to this convergence time. Moreover, this time falls into well-defined classes [4].

The problem of estimating the convergence time of these rules has recently been tackled with an experimental approach [6]. On the analytical side, only two elementary rules are known to have a logarithmic convergence [4]. But what about the other rules? Can we transpose the analysis carried out for these specific two cases to a wider set of rules?

J. Wąs, G.C. Sirakoulis, and S. Bandini (Eds.): ACRI 2014, LNCS 8751, pp. 586–595, 2014.

We here propose to process in three steps. (a) We first study the rules where the logarithmic convergence can be established simply by counting the number of active cells (see definitions below). (b) Next, we generalise our arguments to the case where a potential function indicates a monotonous convergence. (c) We then use potential functions that describe a fast convergence *on average*.

2 Definitions and Candidates

2.1 Elementary Cellular Automata

An Elementary Cellular Automaton (ECA) is a one-dimensional binary CA with nearest-neighbour interactions. We here tackle the *finite* case where cells are arranged in a ring and we denote by $\mathcal{L} = \mathbb{Z}/n\mathbb{Z}$ the set of cells. The evolution of an ECA is governed by its local function $f : \{0, 1\}^3 \to \{0, 1\}$. This function defines how a cell updates its state according to its own state and the states of its left and right neighbours.

A *transition* is an association of a triplet (x, y, z) with $f(x, y, z)$. We say that a transition is *active* if its application changes the state of a cell, that is, if $f(x, y, z) \neq y$. Eight transitions are needed to define an ECA and the 256 rules will be identified with two different notations. The first one is the classical decimal notation introduced by Wolfram. The second one, called the *t-code*, consists in assigning to an ECA the *labels* of the active transitions of the rule. These labels are presented in the following table:

(x,y,z)	000	001	100	101	010	011	110	111
t-code	A	B	C	D	E	F	G	H

As an illustration, take the majority rule. It has only two active transitions, $(1, 0, 1) \to 1$ and $(0, 1, 0) \to 0$. Its t-code is thus DE and we will denote by 232 − DE this rule when we want to indicate both codes. For the sake of simplicity, instead of studying the 256 ECAs, we will restrict our examination to the 88 so-called *minimal representative* rules. They are the rules which have the smallest decimal code when applying the symmetries of reflexion (left-right exchange) and conjugation (0-1 exchange) and when combining both operations.

2.2 Fully Asynchronous Updating

The state of the automaton at given time is called a *configuration*; the set of configurations is denoted by $\mathcal{E}_n = \{0, 1\}^{\mathcal{L}}$. Recall that we here consider that the updating of the automaton is stochastic. We denote by $(U_t)_{t \in \mathbb{N}} \in \mathcal{L}^{\mathbb{N}}$ the sequence of cells that are selected for update. Let (U_t) be a sequence of such updates and x an initial condition. The evolution of the fully asynchronous ECA is represented by the stochastic process $(x^t)_{t \in \mathbb{N}}$ and defined recursively with: $x^0 = x$ and $x^{t+1} = F(x, U_t)$, with:

$$\forall i \in \mathcal{L}, \ x_i^{t+1} = \begin{cases} f(x_{i-1}^t, x_i^t, x_{i+1}^t) & \text{if } i = U_t \\ x_i^t & \text{otherwise.} \end{cases} \tag{1}$$

For the sake of brevity, the sequence of random updates (U_t) is always implicit and we simply write $F(x)$ for *the random variable* that describes the configuration obtained by a uniform random update on x.

A configuration $x \in \mathcal{E}_n$ is called a *fixed point* if we have $F(x) = x$ with probability 1 (all cells are in a stable state). We denote by $\mathcal{FP}$ the set of fixed points. A cell $i \in \mathcal{L}$ of x is called *active* if the transition that applies in i is active, that is, if $f(x_{i-1}, x_i, x_{i+1}) \neq x_i$. Clearly, a configuration is a fixed point if and only if it contains no active cell. This property is independent of the updating scheme, which implies that both synchronous and asynchronous updating induce the same set of fixed points.

Starting from a configuration x, the convergence time $T(x)$ is the random variable that corresponds to the time required to reach a fixed point. Formally, $T(x) = \min\{t \in \mathbb{N}, x^t \in \mathcal{FP}\}$. For a fixed ring size n, we define the *rescaled* worst expect convergence time as: $\tau(n) = \max_{x \in \mathcal{E}_n} \mathbb{E}\{T(x)\}/n$.

We are now in position to formally define our problem. We want to know what is the class of ECAs which verify: $\tau(n) = \Theta(\log n)$; we will call this a *logarithmic convergence* for short.

2.3 Candidates

Among the 88 minimal rules, we previously identified a subset of rules which appear to converge rapidly to a fixed point [3]. We divided this set into two classes the RCH and RCN classes (see Tab. 1). The RCH and RCN classes respectively contain the rules which rapidly converge to a *homogeneous* fixed point or to a (possibly) *non-homogeneous* fixed point.

The case of 74-BEH, which is now excluded from the list of candidates, is discussed at the end of this note.

Figure 1 shows examples of the space-time diagrams produced by these rules. Remark that, contrary to the usual practice, the initial configuration is not random: it is made of a half-segment of cells in state 1. This condition allows us to observe more easily the fragmentation processes involved in the rapid convergence of these rules.

Table 1. List of the candidates rules in the RCH (top) and RCN (bottom) classes

RCH	0-EFGH	2-BEFGH	8-EGH	10-BEGH
	18-BCEFGH	24-CEGH	26-BCEGH	32-DEFGH
	34-BDEFGH	40-DEGH	42-BDEGH	50-BCDEFGH
	56-CDEGH	58-BCDEGH	74-BEH	106-BDEH
RCN	4-FGH	5-AFGH	12-GH	13-AGH
	36-DFGH	44-DGH	72-EH	76-H
	77-AH	104-DEH	200-E	232-DE

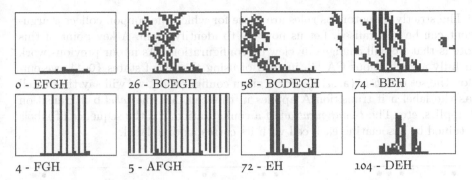

0 - EFGH	26 - BCEGH	58 - BCDEGH	74 - BEH
4 - FGH	5 - AFGH	72 - EH	104 - DEH

Fig. 1. Examples of space time diagrams of the RCH (top) and RCN (bottom) rules. Time goes from bottom to top. Cells with states 0 and 1are respectively reprsented with blue(or dark) and white squares. The time scale is rescaled by a factor $1/n$: the transition from one line to the other is obtained after n updates. The ring size is fixed to $n = 50$ and the random evolution is represented over 30 time steps.

3   Strictly Monotonous Rules

Let us first study the *lower* bound on the convergence time.

Lemma 1. *A rule that has at least one active transition has a convergence time that is at least logarithmic in the size of the automaton.*

Proof. To see why, let t be one active transition of the rule and let the *pattern* $p \in \{0, 1\}^3$ be the sequence of 3 states that generates t. (For instance, for the rule DE, if we choose transition E, we take $p = 010$.) The configuration x obtained by repeating k times the pattern p has a length $n = 3k$ and we call *targets* the k cells at the centre of each pattern (that is, with an index i such that $i \bmod 3 = 1$).

These targets are unstable and a *necessary* condition for the convergence of the system is that they are all stabilised. Clearly, the updating of a target can not stabilise another target and a target is stabilised either if it is updated, or if its right or left neighbour is updated. (This point is further clarified below). The stabilisation time of the target cells can thus be *lower-bounded* by the time needed to update at least one cell in each pattern. This time corresponds to a *coupon collector process*: take k elements that are randomly and uniformly selected at each time step, the average time needed to select each element at least once is equivalent to $k \log k$ for a large k. The convergence time is thus lower-bounded by: $f(n) \leq \tau(n)$ with $f(n) \sim \frac{1}{n} k \log k \sim \frac{1}{3} \log n$. □

Definition 1. *A rule is strictly monotonous if the number of active cells decreases each time an active cell is updated.*

As an example, consider the case of ECA 76-H. This rule has only one active transition and: a) only cells with label h are active and b) an h that is updated is turned into a d and c) no h can be created by updating an h.

The strictly monotonous rules are those for which the coupon collector argument can be generalised. Let us now try to identify them. A key point of this note is that we will change our view on configurations. As in our previous work on fully asynchronous CA [4], instead of using the set of states $\{0, 1\}$, we employ the set of *labels* $\{a, \ldots h\}$. For a given configuration, we will say that a cell has the label a if transition A applies in this cell, has the *label* b if transition B applies, etc. The *t-configuration* of a configuration x is the sequence of labels obtained by associating each cell with its corresponding label.

•• •••		•• ••		••
0 0 1 1 0 0 0 1 1 1 0		0 0 1 1 0 0 0 0 1 1 0		0 0 0 1 0 0 0 0 1 1 0
a b f g c a b f h g c	$\rightarrow$	a b f g c a a b f g c	$\rightarrow$	a a b e c a a b f g c
△		△		

Fig. 2. Example of an evolution of a configuration with rule 4-FGH. In the first line, the presence of a dot indicates the active cells. The second and third lines show the configuration and the associated t-configuration, respectively. In the fourth line, the triangle indicates the cell that is updated.

Figure 2 shows an example of how a configuration evolves with rule 4-FGH and how the t-configurations are modified by the sequential updates. We remark that in t-configurations, when a cell is updated, up to *three* cells may modify their labels: the updated cell, but also its left and right neighbours. In order to find out all the transformations than can occur when a cell is updated, we thus need to consider all the possible triplets of t-labels. There are 32 such possible triplets, which correspond to the possible sequences of five state cells.

These transitions are represented on Table 2; we call this table the *rewriting table*. It can be verified that the triplets correspond to the sequences of five cells $(\alpha, x, y, z, \beta) \in \{0, 1\}^5$ ordered with the following presentation: each column corresponds to a fixed value of (x, y, z), the first to fourth lines correspond to the "border" values (α, β) equal to $(0, 0)$, $(0, 1)$, $(1, 0)$ and $(1, 1)$, respectively. We say that a transition of the table is *active* if the column to which it belongs corresponds to an active transition. For instance, if we take the majority rule $232 - DE$, only the 8 transitions of columns D and E will be active.

We are now in position to list all the strictly monotonous rules.

Theorem 1. *The (minimal) rules that are strictly monotonous are:* 0-EFGH, 4-FGH, 12-GH, 76-H, 77-AH, 200-E, 232-DE.

Proof. Clearly, a rule is strictly monotonous if and only if all the *active* transitions of the rewriting table lead to a negative difference in the number of active cells. In other words, for each active entry of the table, the number of active cells before updating is strictly higher than the number of active cells after updating. We call this condition the *decrease* condition.

For a given rule, let us assign a value 1 or 0 to the eight variables $\omega_a \ldots, \omega_h$, depending on whether the t-code of the rule considered contains or does not

Table 2. Table of the 32 possible re-writing triplets of t-codes. The column corresponds to the 8 possible states of the central cell and the lines corresponds to the 4 possible states of the left and right cells.

	A	B	C	D	E	F	G	H
1	aaa	abe	eca	ede	bec	bfg	fgc	fhg
	bec	bfg	fgc	fhg	aaa	abe	eca	ede
2	aab	abf	ecb	edf	bed	bfh	fgd	fhh
	bed	bfh	fgd	fhh	aab	abf	ecb	edf
3	caa	cbe	gca	gde	dec	dfg	hgc	hhg
	dec	dfg	hgc	hhg	caa	cbe	gca	gde
4	cab	cbf	gcb	gdf	ded	dfh	hgd	hhh
	ded	dfh	hgd	hhh	cab	cbf	gcb	gdf

contain the transitions $A, \ldots, H$, respectively. For instance, for the rule FGH, we have $\omega_a = 0, \ldots, \omega_e = 0$ and $\omega_f = 1, \omega_g = 1, \omega_h = 1$.

We can now discuss the application of the decrease condition. We denote by $\Delta(ij)$ the *variation* of the number active cells in the transition of the column $i \in A, \ldots, H$ and line $j \in \{1, \ldots, 4\}$ of the rewriting table.

First case : we assume that H is active, that is, $\omega_h = 1$. Looking at the entry (D4) of the rewriting table, we have $\Delta(D4) = 3 - (\omega_g + \omega_d + \omega_f)$, which implies that the decrease condition can not be fulfilled by this entry, and thus that transition D is not active: $\omega_d = 0$.

By looking at (B2), we have $\Delta(B2) = 1 - \omega_a$. Again, as this quantity can not be made negative, we have that B is inactive: $\omega_b = 0$. By symmetry, looking at (C3) gives $\omega_c = 0$. We now discuss the value of ω_a.

- If $\omega_a = 1$, the application of the decrease condition on (E1), (F2), (G3), leads to $\omega_e = 0$, $\omega_f = 0$ and $\omega_g = 0$, respectively. As the values of the eight transitions are fixed, we thus find rule $\boxed{AH}$. (The box indicates the minimal representative rules.)
- If $\omega_a = 0$, from (H1) we deduce $\omega_e = 1 \implies \omega_f = 1$ and $\omega_g = 1$. One solution is thus $\boxed{EFGH}$. The case $\omega_e = 0$ gives: $\boxed{FGH}$,FH,$\boxed{GH}$,$\boxed{H}$. (It can be checked these are all valid solutions.)

Second case : we assume that H is inactive, that is, $\omega_h = 0$. By (F2) and (G3), we obtain: $\omega_f = 0$ and $\omega_g = 0$. We now discuss the value of ω_e.

- If $\omega_e = 1$, entries (E1), (B2) and (C2) give: $\omega_a = 0$, $\omega_b = 0$ and $\omega_c = 0$, respectively. We thus obtain rules $\boxed{E}$ and $\boxed{DE}$.
- If $\omega_e = 0$, it can be observed that the possible candidates are all rules whose active transitions are A, B, C and D. These rules can be reduced to previously examined cases by the 0/1-exchange symmetry, as the active transitions of the symmetric rules will contain only E, F, G and H.

$\square$

4   Rules with a Monotonous Potential

The question is now to determine if the previous argument can be generalised to other rules. As an illustration, let us turn our attention to the rule EH. By examining the rewriting table, it can be seen that this rule is "almost" strictly monotonous, but if we look at the entry (H1), we see that one h can produce two e. A simple way to solve the problem is to use the convention that an h counts as much as *three* e. In this case, a transition of type (H1) would still continue to decrease the number of "weighted" active cells.

However, a difficulty appears at this point as, even with this "weighted" active cells, it is no longer possible to reconduct the previous arguments we had on the coupon collector process. Indeed, we have now lost the proportionality that existed between the "activity" and the probability to decrease. We are thus unable to conveniently compare the two processes.

For a particular configuration $x \in \mathcal{E}_n$, we denote by $a(x), \ldots, h(x)$ the number of occurrences of the labels a, $\ldots$, h in x. The argument x will often be omitted for brevity.

Definition 2. *A potential function W is p-linear if it is a positive linear combination of the number of labels of a given configuration, that is, it can be written:* $W(x) = \omega_a a(x) + \cdots + \omega_h h(x)$ *with* $\omega_a, \ldots, \omega_h \in \mathbb{N}$.

Let $\Delta W(x) = W(F(x)) - W(x)$ denote the (random) change in potential from configuration x.

Definition 3. *A rule R is monotonous if there exists a p-linear potential W such that $\forall x \in \mathcal{E}_n$:*

$$W(x) = 0 \implies x \in \mathcal{FP}, \tag{C1}$$

and

$$F(x) \neq x \implies \Delta W(x) < 0. \tag{C2}$$

Lemma 2 (Monotonous convergence). *Let R be a monotonous rule with a potential W that is bounded by $k \in \mathbb{N}$. If there exists a constant $\alpha > 0$ such that:*

$$\forall x \in \mathcal{E}_n, \ \mathbb{E}\{\Delta W(x)\} \leq -\alpha W(x), \tag{C3}$$

then the rescaled worst expected convergence time of R is bounded by $\log k/\alpha$.

In words, three ingredients are needed for a monotonous convergence:
(C1) There exists a non-negative potential W that cancels only on fixed points.
(C2) The potential decreases when a configuration updated on an unstable cell.
(C3) The decrease of W is (at least) proportional to W.

The proof is omitted for the sake of brevity. It mainly relies on the "step forward" method: the average convergence time of the state of a Markov chain is a function of the convergence time of the states that are reachable from this state. It is also necessary to group configurations into the equivalence classes of "isopotential" and to conveniently estimate the average transition time between these sets of configurations.

Theorem 2. *Among the RCN and RCH class, rules 5-AFGH, 8-EGH, 13-AGH, 72-EH are the only (non-strictly) monotonous rules; their convergence time is logarithmic.*

Proof. To show this, we examine the "candidates" for monotony. First, we remark that if the t-code of a rule contains two letters in one of these couples: $A - E$, $B - F$, $C - G$ or $D - H$, then the rule is *not* monotonous. Indeed, if a rule has two of such "opposed" active transitions, a configuration which is updated twice on a cell with such a transition comes back to the initial state. This contradicts the hypothesis of monotony. Second, if we also suppress from our list of candidates the strictly monotonous rules, the only candidates left are: EH, EGH, BEGH, AFGH, and AGH.

We can also rule out BEGH with a specific example. If we start from the configuration 0110, and update the third cell, we obtain the configuration 0100. If we then update the first cell, we obtain 1100, which is equivalent to the initial state, up to a shift. This contradicts the monotony of the rule.

Before presenting suitable potential functions for the remaining rules, we introduce some useful definitions.

Definition 4. *A potential W is tight if it is p-linear and the positive coefficients all correspond to active transitions. W is balanced if the difference of potential brought by the update of a cell is only a function of the label of this cell.*

Claim. W is balanced if and only if: $\omega_a + \omega_d = \omega_b + \omega_c$ and $\omega_e + \omega_h = \omega_f + \omega_g$.

We have no intuitive explanation of this fact, which was discovered empirically. It can be checked that if the two conditions are verified, the entries of each line of the transition table are equal, which guarantees that the rule is balanced. For a given potential function, being balanced is equivalent to having the same values of decrease in potential for a particular column of the rewriting table. In that case, we denote by δ_t the decrease of potential of a cell having a label t.

Case of EGH. We take $W = e + 2g + h$. This potential verifies C1 as it is tight. It verifies C2 as it is balanced with: $\delta_E = \delta_G = \delta_H = -1$. It thus also directly verifies C3 with $\alpha = 1/n$.

Case of AFGH. Similarly, we take $W = a + f + g + 2h$. This potential is tight, which implies that it verifies C1 . The potential is not balanced. However, it can be checked that it decreases by at least 1, when an A, an F, or a G is updated and that it decreases by 4 when an H is updated. Condition C2 is thus verified and we have:

$$\mathbb{E}\{\Delta W\} \leq \frac{1}{n}(-a - f - g - 4h) \tag{2}$$

$$\leq -\frac{1}{n}(a + f + g + 2h) \tag{3}$$

Condition C3 is thus verified with $\alpha = 1/n$.

Due to the lack of space, we omit the similar proofs for AGH and EH.   □

5 Rules with an Average Decrease of Potential

Our efforts to generalise the first argument allowed us to deal with "only" four more rules. The reason why this attempt had a limited success is not so difficult to guess: by requiring that the potential always decreases when an active cell was updated, we were demanding too much.

We now present a lemma that allows us to extend one step further the domain of application of the analysis: in this new step, we will only require that the decrease happens *on average*. The logarithmic convergence time is obtained when the decrease of the potential is proportional to the current value of the potential.

Lemma 3. *Let* $(X_t)_{t\in\mathbb{N}}$ *be a stochastic process whose values are in* $\{0,\ldots,k\}$ *and* $(\mathcal{F}_t)_{t\in\mathbb{N}}$ *a filtration adapted to it. If there exists a constant* $0 < \epsilon < 1$ *such that:*

$$\forall t \in \mathbb{N}, \ \mathbb{E}\{X_{t+1} - X_t \mid \mathcal{F}_t\} \leq -\epsilon X_t$$

then the average time for reaching 0 *is upper-bounded by* $-\frac{\log k+1}{\log 1-\epsilon}$.

The proof is omitted for the sake of brevity. The technical part is to show that the process $Y_t = (1 + X_t)\lambda^t$ is a supermartingale for $\lambda = \frac{1}{1-\epsilon}$. Note that the application of Doob's optional stopping theorem is not straightforward: as the hitting time (to zero) T appears in an exponent in $\mathbb{E}\{Y_T\}$, the calculus of $\mathbb{E}\{T\}$ is not direct. We use Jensen's inequality to solve this difficulty[1].

Theorem 3. *Rules* 2-BEFGH, 32-DEFGH, 34-BDEFGH, 40-DEGH *have a logarithmic worst expected convergence time.*

The proof is omitted due to lack of space. As an exercise, readers can study BEFGH and verify that $W = 3e + 5f + 2h$ is suitable for applying Lemma 3. The proof also relies on a simple fact:

Claim. A rule has a logarithmic convergence if there exists a positive integer m, a p-linear function W such that for every ring size $n \in \mathbb{N}$: $W(x) = 0 \implies x \in \mathcal{FP}$ and

$$\forall x \in \mathcal{E}_n \setminus \mathcal{FP}, \ \mathbb{E}\{\Delta W(x)\} \leq -\frac{1}{m \cdot n}W(x), \tag{4}$$

This fact simply represents an application of Lemma 3 in our context. It is obtained by taking $\epsilon = \frac{1}{mn}$ and with the equivalence: $-\ln(1 - \epsilon) \sim \epsilon$ for $\epsilon \to 0$.

To conclude, we indicate that contrarily to what we first thought, rule 74-BEH does *not* have a logarithmic convergence. Indeed, if we take the fixed point $(011)^k$ for a large k and change one cell state, a "cascade" propagates from right to left and makes the system progressively converge to $\mathbf{0}$. The construction can be made for all ring sizes: repeat pattern 001 and then "complete" with something. This observation underlines the need to distinguish the average and the worst case in our approach of the asynchronous dynamics.

---

[1] The author is grateful to B. Scherrer for this suggestion.

6   Conclusion

This note described a small step in the study of the dynamics of asynchronous cellular automata. We asked what are the rules that display fast convergence to a fixed point. Only two rules were known to display this type of convergence and to date, little progress had been done on identifying other rules.

We clarified the status of 16 (minimal) rules: seven of them were shown to be strictly monotonous and four other were shown to be monotonous, but not strictly. Four non-monotonous rules were analysed with a specific lemma. One ECA was also ruled out of the list of candidates.

The question is now to extend the analysis to the 12 remaining rules. Our intuition is that their logarithmic convergence can not be obtained with the same analytical tools. We however see two ways to advance. First, one could consider state correlations of higher order (the labels only consider an order 3). Second, we may couple the dynamics of the more complex rules with a process that is not a cellular automaton. Indeed, as mentioned earlier, it appears that the origin of the fast convergence is the fragmentation process involved in the dynamics of all these rules. We are thus interested in studying a process where each fragment (that is, a consecutive block of cells in state 1) could "live" separately on a distinct "layer", without interfering with other fragments. The analysis of this process could be simplified by the absence of interaction between fragments. The difficulty though would be to show that its convergence time is logarithmic and still dominates the convergence time of the remaining candidate rules.

References

1. Dennunzio, A., Formenti, E., Manzoni, L.: Computing issues of asynchronous CA. Fundamenta Informaticae 120(2), 165–180 (2012)
2. Fatès, N.: A guided tour of asynchronous cellular automata. In: Kari, J., Kutrib, M., Malcher, A. (eds.) AUTOMATA 2013. LNCS, vol. 8155, pp. 15–30. Springer, Heidelberg (2013)
3. Fatès, N.: A note on the classification of the most simple asynchronous cellular automata. In: Kari, J., Kutrib, M., Malcher, A. (eds.) AUTOMATA 2013. LNCS, vol. 8155, pp. 31–45. Springer, Heidelberg (2013)
4. Fatès, N., Morvan, M., Schabanel, N., Thierry, E.: Fully asynchronous behavior of double-quiescent elementary cellular automata. Theoretical Computer Science 362, 1–16 (2006)
5. Sethi, B., Fatès, N., Das, S.: Reversibility of elementary cellular automata under fully asynchronous update. In: Gopal, T.V., Agrawal, M., Li, A., Cooper, S.B. (eds.) TAMC 2014. LNCS, vol. 8402, pp. 39–49. Springer, Heidelberg (2014)
6. Sethi, B., Roy, S., Das, S.: Experimental study on convergence time of elementary cellular automata under asynchronous update. In: Kari, J., Kutrib, M., Malcher, A. (eds.) Proceedings of AUTOMATA 2013 - Exploratory Papers. Giessen University - IFIG Research Report 1302 (2013)
7. Worsch, T.: (Intrinsically?) universal asynchronous CA. In: Sirakoulis, G.C., Bandini, S. (eds.) ACRI 2012. LNCS, vol. 7495, pp. 689–698. Springer, Heidelberg (2012)

A Study of Aggregated Speed in Road Networks Using Cellular Automata

Lele Zhang, Somayeh Shiri, and Timothy M. Garoni

School of Mathematical Sciences, Monash University, Victoria, Australia
{lele.zhang,tim.garoni,somayeh.shiri}@monash.edu

Abstract. Several recent works have focused on studying the relationship between the aggregated flow and density in arterial road networks. Analogous studies involving aggregated speed appear not to have been yet undertaken, however. Here we study and compare such relations for arterial road networks controlled by different types of adaptive traffic signal systems, under various boundary conditions. To study such systems we simulate stochastic cellular automaton models. Our simulation results suggest that network speed could be used as a surrogate for density, due to a strong anticorrelation between these two network observables. Since speed estimates can be more easily obtained than density estimates, e.g. from probe vehicle data, this suggests that Macroscopic Fundamental Diagrams relating aggregated flow with speed might be a practically useful alternative to those relating flow to density.

Keywords: Macroscopic fundamental diagram, aggregated speed, traffic signal systems, cellular automata, simulation.

1 Introduction

Several recent studies have investigated the relationship between the aggregated flow and density (known as the Macroscopic Fundamental Diagram, or MFD), in urban road networks. Although the basic idea of an MFD dates back at least to [9], convincing empirical evidence for their existence was only recently provided in [2, 3]. These articles spawned a huge amount of research considering conditions under which MFDs should be observed, [8, 11, 18], existence of hysteresis loops [1, 5, 7, 20], and the importance and behavior of spatial heterogeneity [1, 5, 7, 20]. More recently, in addition to being used for characterizing traffic congestion [3, 11, 18, 20], MFDs have been utilized for developing traffic control strategies [6, 10, 15].

Most existing papers discussing MFDs focus on relations between flow and density. In practice however, one generally does not have a mechanism for measuring network density, and some form of surrogate has to be used. One natural surrogate for density is the occupancy of in-road detectors. However, on many networks these detectors are located only very close to intersections and may therefore give a rather inaccurate prediction of the actual link density. By contrast, the availability of probe vehicle data is now making it feasible to obtain reliable estimates of the mean vehicle speeds on each link in an urban network, in real time [12-14, 16, 17]. The availability

J. Wąs, G.C. Sirakoulis, and S. Bandini (Eds.): ACRI 2014, LNCS 8751, pp. 596–604, 2014.

of this data suggests a motivation for extending previous studies of MFDs to a study of the relationship between network-aggregated speed and flow. The current article is a first step in this direction, and explores this relationship by simulating the *NetNaSch* model, a stochastic cellular automata (CA) model introduced in [4].

In [20], two of the present authors compared MFDs of networks governed by three different signal systems and several different choices of boundary conditions. The present article extends this study by investigating the relationship between aggregated speed with the flow and density.

The remainder of this paper is organized as follows. In the Section 2 we describe the NetNaSch model and the network parameters used in our simulations. The simulation results are described in Section 3. We conclude in Section 4 with a discussion.

2   CA Model

We briefly outline the cellular automata model used in our simulations and the corresponding network. The NetNaSch model [4] is a stochastic CA model of traffic flow on arbitrary road networks. Each lane in the model is (a slight generalization of) the *NaSch* model [19]. The model prescribes simple lane-changing rules to allow vehicles to move between neighboring lanes. In addition, it is designed to allow any choice of rules (i.e. traffic signal system) to be applied to traffic traversing intersections. Readers may refer to [4, 20] for a detailed description of the model.

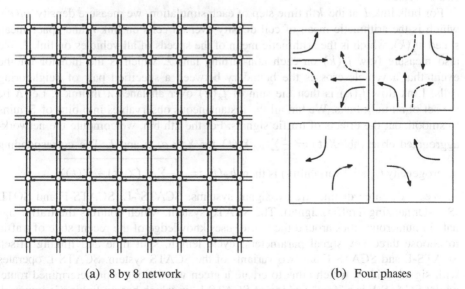

(a) 8 by 8 network   (b) Four phases

Fig. 1. (a) An 8 by 8 square lattice network. (b) Four phases used at each node of the simulated network. Dashed paths are required to give way to continuous paths.

In this study, we consider an 8 by 8 square lattice network, as shown in Fig. 1(a). Each adjacent pair of intersections, or *nodes*, is connected by two oppositely-oriented directed streets, or *links*. In turn, each such link consists of two main lanes, each consisting of 100 cells, plus an additional right-turning lane of 16 cells[1]. Along individual lanes, vehicles move according to the NaSch dynamics with maximum velocity $v_{max} = 3$ cells/second. The deceleration rate is tuned so that the free-flow speed is approximately 60km/hr. Links for which both endpoints belong to the network are referred to as *bulk* links, whereas links for which only one endpoint belongs to the network are referred to as *boundary* links.

To mimic origin-destination behavior, each vehicle makes a random decision about which link it wishes to turn into at the approaching intersection when it first arrives at a link. In the simulation, we assigned each link with the same turning probability $p_T = 0.1$ for left and right turns, implying a probability of $1 - 2p_T = 0.8$ for continuing straight ahead.

We consider two types of boundary conditions: boundary loading and uniform loading. For boundary loading, vehicles are inserted at the start of each *boundary in-link* with an inflow probability α, and are allowed to exit from the end of each *boundary out-link* with an outflow probability β. For uniform loading, in addition to boundary inflows and outflows, we allow vehicles to enter and leave the network via *bulk links* in the network with probabilities γ and δ. We consider isotropic networks, so that the same values of α and β (γ and δ) are applied to all boundary (bulk) links. We consider both time-independent and time-dependent α, β, γ and δ. The cases of boundary and uniform loading can be considered two extreme cases – in a real network we expect the boundary conditions will be intermediate between these two extremes.

For bulk link l at the kth time step of each simulation, we measure density $\rho_l(k)$, which is the arithmetic mean of cell density over all cells on link l, and space mean speed $v_l(k)$, which is the arithmetic mean of the speeds of all vehicles on link l. We also measure flow $J_\lambda(k)$ on each non-turning lane λ, which is the indictor for the event that a vehicle crosses the boundary between a specified pair of neighboring cells. Link flow $J_l(k)$ is then the sum of $J_\lambda(k)$ over all lanes λ in link l. Let Λ be the set of all bulk links. We bin all the instantaneous observables into bins of 5 mins to smooth out the effects of traffic signals. For the tth bin, we compute the network-aggregated observable $X(t) := \frac{1}{\Lambda}\sum_{l \in \Lambda} X_l(t)$ for $X = \rho$, v and J. The corresponding heterogeneity (spatial variability) is then $h_X(t) := \sqrt{\frac{1}{\Lambda}\sum_{l \in \Lambda}(X_l(t) - X(t))^2}$.

We study three distinct traffic signal systems: SCATS[2]-L, SCATS-F and SOTL (Self-Organizing Traffic Lights). The SCATS system, which controls the traffic signals in numerous cities around the world, uses knowledge of the recent state of traffic to choose three key signal parameters: cycle length, split time and linking offset. SCATS-L and SCATS-F are two variants of the SCATS system. SCATS-L operates with signal linking, which aims to create a green wave along a predetermined route, whilst SCATS-F is a "free" version of SCATS-L, in which has no linking is imposed. Both variants of SCATS are cyclic signal systems, in the sense that at each node they consecutively run the four phases shown in Fig. 1(b). By contrast, SOTL is an acyclic

---

[1] As in Australia, vehicles drive on the left side of the road in our CA model.

[2] Sydney Coordinated Adaptive Traffic System.

system, and is designed so that at each phase change the phase with the highest demand is selected [4, 20]. In this paper, the demand of a phase is defined as the product of its idle time and the total number of vehicles on all its in-links. For SOTL, no direct signal coordination is enforced among neighboring nodes. All the three signal systems are adaptive. Compared to the SCATS-like systems, SOTL is less constrained, and it strives to adaptively minimize the network's density heterogeneity as it uses density as the demand metric.

3   Simulations

3.1   Time-Independent Boundary Conditions

For time independent boundary conditions, we fix $\delta = \gamma = 0$, and run the network with a number of different time-invariant values of α, β for 6 (simulated) hours. We find empirically that the system has relaxed to a stationary state by this time (e.g. Fig. 2). We then examine the relation among network-aggregated observables for different signal systems.

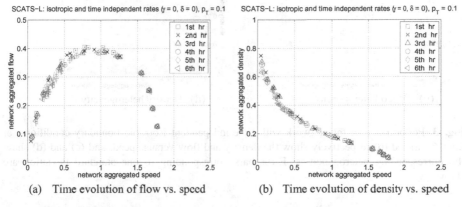

(a) Time evolution of flow vs. speed   (b) Time evolution of density vs. speed

Fig. 2. The speed-flow and speed-density diagrams at hours 1, 2, ..., 6 for network governed by SCATS-L, with time-independent isotropic boundary conditions. Error bars corresponding to one standard deviation are shown.

Figs. 3(a) and (b) show a comparison of the stationary speed-density and speed-flow diagrams, respectively, for the three signal systems, SCATS-F, SCATS-L, and SOTL. The most obvious feature in Fig. 3(a) is that the curves are monotonically decreasing for each signal system. This shows a strong anticorrelation between speed and density. Furthermore, the network governed by SOTL leads to higher speed at the same density in all regimes. This is consistent with our observations reported in [20], that the network controlled by SOTL showed better performance in terms of flow at a given density than the two SCATS systems. In addition, from Fig. 3(b) we see that although at very low speeds ($v < 0.2$) the performance of the three signal systems are very similar, at higher speeds the SOTL curve is located well above the corresponding curves for SCATS, allowing the system to reach higher capacity.

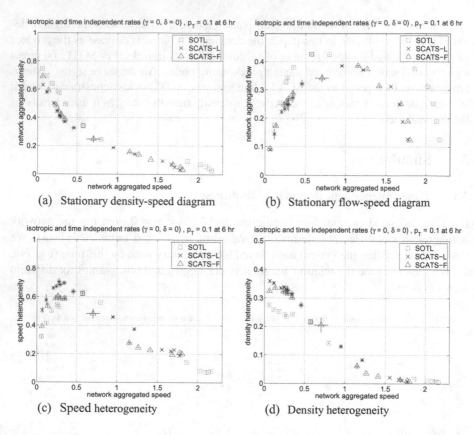

Fig. 3. Performance of the network with time-independent isotropic boundary conditions, at hour 6. (a) and (b) respectively show the density and flow versus speed, and (c) and (d) show the corresponding heterogeneities. Error bars corresponding to one standard deviation are shown.

In order to better understand the role of speed as a surrogate of density, we consider how the corresponding heterogeneity varies. In Fig. 3(c) we observe that for low and high speeds, the network governed by SOTL produces smaller speed heterogeneity, however this does not appear to be the case at intermediate speeds. Comparing with Fig. 3(b) we see that this is despite the fact that the flow is much high for SOTL. This suggests that speed heterogeneity may not be as accurate as density heterogeneity as a predictor of flow breakdown; see Fig. 3(d) for comparison. Comparing Figs. 3(c) and (d) in more detail, we note that while the speed heterogeneity plot has a peak, the density heterogeneity plot appears monotonically decreasing. This is simply because the density does not reach the extremely highly congested regime ($\rho \gtrsim 0.8$) when simulating with boundary loading. If we push the system up to higher densities by loading more uniformly we also observe a unimodal shape emerge in the density heterogeneity curve.

3.2   Time-Dependent Boundary Conditions

For the simulations of time dependent boundary conditions, we fine-tuned α, β, γ and δ so that the resulting network density follows a typical weekday profile with AM and PM peaks. For boundary loading $\gamma = \delta = 0$, whereas $\gamma = \alpha$, and $\gamma = \beta$ for uniform loading.

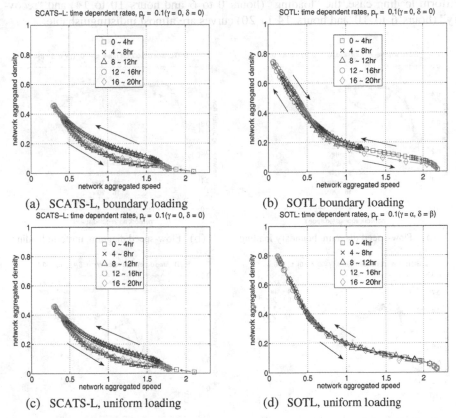

(a) SCATS-L, boundary loading

(b) SOTL boundary loading

(c) SCATS-L, uniform loading

(d) SOTL, uniform loading

Fig. 4. Performance of the network under time-dependent boundary conditions. Left column: SCATS-L; Right column: SOTL. Top row: boundary loading; Bottom row: uniform loading. Error bars corresponding to one standard deviation are shown.

In [20], we studied in detail the hysteresis patterns observed for both of these choices of boundary conditions. For uniform loading we observed clockwise hysteresis loops in the MFD, corresponding to the loading and recovery processes. For the case of boundary loading by contrast, we observed that both clockwise and anticlockwise hysteresis loops could occur in the MFD. In both cases however, the hysteresis loops observed in the MFD coincided with oppositely oriented hysteresis loops in the density heterogeneity plots. This suggests that the hysteresis in flow was being caused by heterogeneously distributed density.

Fig. 4 shows the time evolution of the density-speed diagram for SCATS-L and SOTL in the case of boundary loading, Figs. 4(a) and (b), and uniform loading, Figs 4(c) and (d). The analogous plots for SCAT-F reveal similar behavior with slightly larger loops. In general, v decreases (increases) as ρ increases (decreases) with time. We observe hysteresis loops in the v vs. ρ curves, coinciding with those seen in [20] in the J vs. ρ curves, however they are significantly smaller. In particular, for the uniform loading case, the "loading" (hours 0 to 6 and hours 10 to 14) and "recovery" (hours 6 to 10 and hours 14 to 20) curves are almost indistinguishable.

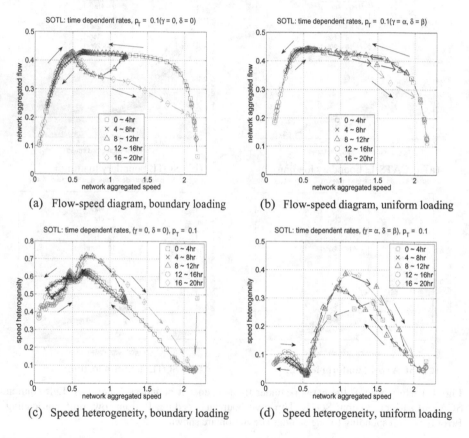

(a) Flow-speed diagram, boundary loading   (b) Flow-speed diagram, uniform loading

(c) Speed heterogeneity, boundary loading   (d) Speed heterogeneity, uniform loading

Fig. 5. Performance of the under time-dependent boundary conditions, using SOTL. Left column: Boundary loading; Right column: Uniform loading. Top row: the flow-speed relation. Bottom row: speed-heterogeneity relation. Error bars corresponding to one standard deviation are shown.

Figs. 5(a) and (b) show the evolution of the aggregated flow-speed diagrams for time dependent boundary conditions, for the system using SOTL. We clearly observe hysteresis loops. Given the monotonically decreasing relationship between density and speed, one would expect these hysteresis loops to be oriented oppositely to those observed in the MFD plots presented in [20]. This is indeed the case. For instance, let us compare the flow-speed plot in Fig. 5(a) with the corresponding MFD in our previous work (refer to Fig. 12(e) in [20]). From hour 8 to hour 12, in the speed-flow plot we observe an anticlockwise hysteresis loop, whereas in [20] the loop was clockwise. For SCATS-L and SCATS-F we also observe hysteresis patterns in the flow-speed plots which coincide precisely with what one would expect from the MFD plots presented in [20]. Note that here the size of the loops for boundary loading (Fig. 5(a)) are larger than those for uniform loading (Fig. 5(b)).

In Figs. 5(c) and (d) we present the speed heterogeneity plots, under boundary and uniform loading, respectively, for the system governed by SOTL. Here we should again expect the opposite behavior to that observed for density heterogeneity in [20], due to the strong anticorrelation between speed and density, and positive correlation between speed heterogeneity and density heterogeneity. This is indeed what we observe. The networks governed by SCATS show similar behavior.

4   Conclusion

In this work we have extended our previous study [20] of MFDs on networks governed by different signal systems, by studying the relations between network-aggregated speed and other network observables including flow, density and speed heterogeneity. For all the three signal systems that we have studied in this article, we found that network speed is strongly negatively correlated with density. Consequently, aggregated speed-flow plots display entirely analogous behavior to MFDs constructed using aggregated density and flow. This suggests aggregated flow may be used as a useful surrogate for aggregated density. This may have practical consequences, since while aggregated density is typically difficult to accurately estimate in a real network, aggregated speed can be provided by probe vehicle data. A validation of the results presented in this paper using practical data is referred to future work.

Comparing the three traffic signal systems, SCATS-F, SCATS-L and SOTL, we found the idealized control scheme SOTL always results in better network performance in terms of producing a higher flow at the same speed and a higher speed at the same density. These results are consistent with the observations made in [20].

References

1. Buisson, C., Ladier, C.: Exploring the impact of homogeneity of traffic measurements on the existence of macroscopic fundamental diagrams. Transportation Research Record 2124, 127–136 (2009)
2. Daganzo, C.F.: Urban gridlock: macroscopic modeling and mitigation approaches. Transportation Research Part B 41(1), 49–62 (2007)
3. Daganzo, C., Geroliminis, N.: An analytical approximation for the macroscopic fundamental diagram of urban traffic. Transportation Research Part B 42(9), 771–781 (2008)
4. de Gier, J., Garoni, T.M., Rojas, O.: Traffic flow on realistic road networks with adaptive traffic lights. Journal of Statistical Mechanics: Theory and Experiment 2011, P04008 (2011)

5. Gayah, V.V., Daganzo, C.F.: Clockwise hysteresis loops in the macroscopic fundamental diagram: an effect of network instability. Transportation Research Part B 45(4), 643–655 (2011)
6. Geroliminis, N., Haddad, J., Ramezani, M.: Optimal perimeter control for two urban regions with macroscopic fundamental diagrams: A model predictive approach. IEEE Transactions on Intelligent Transportation Systems, 1–12 (2012)
7. Geroliminis, N., Sun, J.: Hysteresis phenomena of a macroscopic fundamental diagram in freeway networks. Transportation Research Part A 45(9), 966–979 (2011)
8. Geroliminis, N., Sun, J.: Properties of a well-defined macroscopic fundamental diagram for urban traffic. Transportation Research Part B 45(3), 605–617 (2011)
9. Godfrey, J.: The mechanism of a road network. Traffic Engineering and Control 11(7), 323–327 (1969)
10. Haddad, J., Geroliminis, N.: On the stability of traffic perimeter control in two-region urban cities. Transportation Research Part B 46(9), 1159–1176 (2012)
11. Helbing, D.: Derivation of a fundamental diagram for urban traffic flow. The European Physical Journal B 70(2), 229–241 (2009)
12. Hellinga, B.R., Fu, L.: Assessing expected accuracy of probe vehicle travel time reports. Journal of Transportation Engineering 125(6), 524–530 (1999)
13. Hellinga, B.R., Fu, L.: Reducing bias in probe-based arterial link travel time estimates. Transportation Research Part C 10(4), 257–273 (2002)
14. Jenelius, E., Koutsopoulos, H.N.: Travel time estimation for urban road networks using low frequency probe vehicle data. Transportation Research Part B 53, 64–81 (2013)
15. Knoop, V.L., Hoogendoorn, S.P., Lint, J.W.C.V.: Routing strategies based on macroscopic fundamental diagram. Transportation Research Record: Journal of the Transportation Research Board 2315, 1–10 (2012)
16. Lin, I., Rong, H., Kornhauser, A.L.: Estimating nationwide link speed distribution using probe position data. Journal of Intelligent Transportation Systems 12(1), 29–37 (2008)
17. Liu, H., Ma, W.: A virtual vehicle probe model for time-dependent travel time estimation on signalized arterials. Transportation Research Part C 17(1), 11–26 (2009)
18. Mazloumian, A., Geroliminis, N., Helbing, D.: The spatial variability of vehicle densities as determinant of urban network capacity. Philosophical Transactions of the Royal Society A: Mathematical, Physical and Engineering Sciences 368(1928), 4627–4647 (2010)
19. Nagel, K., Schreckenberg, M.: A cellular automaton model for freeway traffic. Journal de Physique I 2(12), 2221–2229 (1992)
20. Zhang, L., Garoni, T.M., de Gier, J.: A comparative study of macroscopic fundamental diagrams of arterial road networks governed by adaptive traffic signal systems. Transportation Research Part B 40(3), 1–23 (2013)

A New Cellular Automaton Model with Spatiotemporal Process of Lane Changing Execution

Hui-xuan Li[1], Chun-fu Shao[1], Hao-ling Wu[1], Jun-fang Tian[2], and Xun Ji[1]

[1] MOE Key Laboratory for Urban Transportation Complex Systems Theory
and Technology, Beijing Jiaotong University, Beijing, 100044, China
{11114228,cfshao}@bjtu.edu.cn
[2] Institute of systems engineering, College of Management and Economics,
Tianjin University, No. 92 Weijin Road, Nankai District, Tianjin 300072, China

Abstract. In this paper, the spatiotemporal process of lane changing is considered in the cellular automaton models for traffic flow. The lane-changing time and the space required depend on the instantaneous velocity of the vehicle and following vehicle in the destination lane. The simulation is carried out in a two-lane homogeneous system. The speed change of the lane changing vehicle accords with the fundamental diagram and a 2D region is found in the lane changing frequency-velocity plane.

Keywords: Cellular automaton, traffic flow, lane changing.

1 Introduction

Lane changing (LC) and Car following (CF) are two primary driving tasks observed in traffic flow, and are thus vital components of traffic flow theories. Compared to CF which has been widely studied for many years, LC is still needed to receive more attention to explain from the whole process. The whole process of LC consists of decision-making and execution. While the existing models mostly emphasize the decision-making process or the LC's impact on the surrounding traffic during or after the execution process[1], not the execution itself. Lots of research and field observation [2,3] show that the duration of LC ranges from 1.0s to 16.5s, which suggests that it may have a significant impact to the traffic simulation process if we despise the LC execution. And it can be seen that the LC space required varies in different situations in the real traffic. Thus, it is important to investigate the execution of LC from the spatiotemporal process.

There are lots of cellular automaton models have been proposed [4,5]to model the LC, but only few focus on the execution, for instance, a new model considering the effect of LC time presented by Li et al [6]. Among those models, the basic one is symmetric two-lane cellular automaton (STCA) model which assumed a symmetric rule set where vehicles change lanes if the motivation and safe criteria are fulfilled. And the update step is usually divided into two sub-steps: In the

J. Wąs, G.C. Sirakoulis, and S. Bandini (Eds.): ACRI 2014, LNCS 8751, pp. 605–609, 2014.

first sub-step, vehicles may change lanes in parallel according to LC rules and in the second sub-step the lanes are considered as independent single-lane NaSch models [7]. It can be seen that the LC execution is treated as an instantaneous action, which might not suitable for the real traffic.

Thus, in this paper an assumption is proposed: for a LC vehicle, LC time decreases with increasing of vehicle's velocity while the space LC required increases with increasing of following vehicle's velocity in the destination lane.

This paper is organized as follows: We will investigate a new cellular automaton model considered with spatiotemporal process of LC execution in Section 2. In Section 3, simulation results are analyzed in detail. At last, the conclusion is given in Section 4.

2   The New Model

Before we introduce the new model, some points have to be elaborated. According to the assumption, we assume that the LC time and space required depend on the instantaneous velocity when vehicle decides to change lane. More specifically, the time a LC needs decreases with velocity and the safe criteria depends on the following vehicle's speed in the destination lane. We also denote the vehicle takes up the cell(s) which it holds and some ones in front of that vehicle (the number depends on its speed) when it is moving on the single lane, and the LC vehicle takes up the original lane and the destination lane simultaneously, and its region is not "open" for other vehicles until it uses up its LC time. So the parallel update rules of the new model are presented as follows:

Sub-step 1. Determination of the lane changing
    if($flag = 0$)
        if ($d_n < \min(v_{n+1}(t), v_{max})$ and $d_{n,other} > d_n$ and $d_{n,back} > d_{safe}$)
        then $flag = 1$
    else($flag = 1$)
        if($t_{lc} < T_{lc}$)
        then $t_{lc} = t_{lc} + 1$
        else
            $flag = 0$
Sub-step 2. Update of velocity and position for each lane
    Acceleration:
    $v_n(t + 1) = \min(v_n(t) + 1, v_{max})$
    Deceleration:
    $v_n(t + 1) = \min(v_n(t + 1), d_n)$
    Randomization with probability p:
    $v_n(t + 1) = \max(v_n(t + 1) - 1, 0)$
    Car Motion
    $x_n(t + 1) = x_n(t) + v_n(t + 1)$

Here, $flag = 1(0)$ denotes a mark variable to present vehicle being LC (or not), $v_n(t)$ is the velocity of vehicle n at time step t, v_{max} is the maximum velocity. d_n is the gap between vehicle n and its preceding vehicle $n + 1$, $d_n = x_{n+1}(t) - x_n(t) - l$, $x_n(t)$ is the position of vehicle n, l is the length of the vehicle, for LC vehicle $d_n = \min(d_n^l, d_n^r)$, $d_n^l(d_n^r)$ is the number of free cells in front of vehicle n on left (right) lane. $d_{n,other}$ and $d_{n,back}$ denote the number of free cells between the vehicle n and its two neighbor vehicles on the current lane and the other lane at time t, respectively. $d_{safe} = \min(v_{n,back} + 1, v_{max})$ is the safe gap,

$$T_{lc} = \begin{cases} v_{max} - v_n(t) + 1; & v_n(t) > 0 \\ v_{max} + rand(1, v_{max}); & v_n(t) = 0 \end{cases}$$

is the LC time required depending on the velocity when the $flag = 1$, when vehicle is standing, a random LC time is considered to simulate the LC after the vehicle restarting. t_{lc} records the number of time step using for LC currently, p is the randomization probability. If there is another vehicle on the destination lane driving side by side with the vehicle n, then for each one $d_{n,back} = -1$.

The following vehicle of LC vehicle should not change lane because $d_n = d_{n,other}$. For LC vehicle, although it is conservative to take the minimum of d_n^l and d_n^r when it is in the LC process, it could choose a better driving condition on which it finishes the LC, i.e., change to the lane whose $d_n = \max(d_n^l, d_n^r)$, no matter whether it is the destination lane or not. So it can simulate some cases of canceled LC. The two-lane system considering spatiotemporal process of LC time is referred as STCA-ST model.

3 Simulations

We carry out the simulations under the periodic boundary condition, i.e. a circuit road with 2×1000 cells. Only the homogenous system with one type of vehicle is considered. Both cell and vehicle have the length of 7.5m, i.e. $l = 1$. The model parameters $v_{max} = 5$ and $p = 0.3$ are used, the velocity of each vehicle is an integer, ranges from 0 to v_{max}. One time step corresponds to 1s.

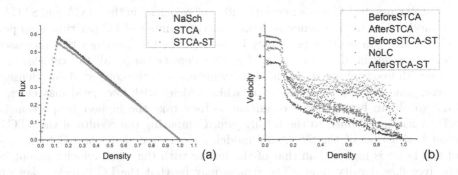

Fig. 1. Comparison result of NaSch, STCA, STCA-ST model. (a) the fundamental diagrams for three models, (b) the speed change of no lane changing, before and after lane changing of STCA model and STCA-ST model.

Fig.1(a) shows the fundamental diagrams. As one can see that the flux per lane in the STCA model is almost the same as that of the single lane model (NaSch). As to the STCA-ST model, the flux in the intermediate density range is lower than that of the STCA model and NaSch model, it can be explained that the LC in the STCA-ST model occupies more spatiotemporal resource. Fig.1(b) shows the speed of LC vehicles before and after LC in the STCA and STCA-ST, and the case without LC. One can see that with density increasing, the velocity decreases in all cases to varying degrees. Compared with the case without LC, both velocities are improved by LC. Before and after LC the speed in the STCA almost keeps steady in the intermediate density range but that in the STCA-ST is decreasing deeply, which is in accordance with the tendency in Fig.1(a). As the density increases to the totally jam [0.8-1.0), LC in STCA-ST could even improve the speed higher than that before LC, which is not seen in the STCA model. It indicates that LC considering spatiotemporal process can obtain better traffic condition for LC vehicle relatively.

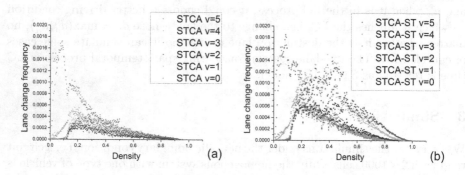

Fig. 2. Lane changing frequency of the vehicles with different velocity. (a) in STCA model, (b) in STCA-ST model.

Fig.2 shows the LC frequency with different velocities in the STCA and STCA-ST model. The LC frequency is defined as the number of LC per time step per vehicle. One can see that as density increasing, the LC frequency first increases then decreases in all cases. In the free flow density range, all the vehicles can drive with free flow speed. As the density increases to the congested flow density range, jams will appear on the road, while vehicles with low speed may change lane to obtain better traffic condition so they take the highest proportion in STCA-ST model until to the totally jam. Comparing the results of the STCA model with that of the STCA-ST model, one can see that, the LC frequency of the latter is higher than that of the former with the same velocity except in the free flow density range. The reason may be that the LC vehicle takes up the two lanes in the execution until it uses up the LC time, the occupancy of the two-lane road becomes higher and the traffic condition becomes worse so that more vehicles are willing to change lane to improve the traffic condition.

In addition, Fig.2(b) shows a phenomenon that LC vehicle in the STCA-ST model takes up a 2-Dimension region in the intermediate density range as more obvious as lower of LC vehicle speed. It can be explained that in the free flow density range, the interaction of vehicle is small enough for LC freely, and in the jam density range, the interaction is huge enough to lead to low LC frequency, but in the intermediate density range, the interaction is oscillating because a leading vehicle changing lane will restrict the LC of following vehicle owe to the spatiotemporal assumption in the STCT-ST model.

4 Conclusion

In this paper, the spatiotemporal process of LC is taken into account in the CA models, which assumes the LC time and space is related to the velocity of the vehicle and following vehicle in the destination lane. The simulation results show that the speed change of LC vehicle in the new CA model accords with the fundamental diagram and the LC frequency-velocity plane is occupied by a 2D region. Finally, we should mention that only the idealized simulation results are presented here. The heterogeneous condition and empirical data need to be considered to verify our model, and these will be done in our future work.

Acknowledgments. This work is supported by the National Basic Research Program of China(No. 2012CB725403).

References

1. Zheng, Z.: Recent developments and research needs in modeling lane changing. J. Transportation Research Part B: Methodological 60, 16–32 (2014)
2. Toledo, T., Zohar, D.: Modeling duration of lane changes. Transportation Research Record, 71–78 (2007)
3. Cao, X., Young, W., et al.: Exploring Duration of Lane Change Execution. 36th Australasian Transport Research Forum (ATRF), Brisbane, Queensland, Australia (2013)
4. Chowdhury, D., Wolf, D.E., Schreckenberg, M.: Particle hopping models for two-lane traffic with two kinds of vehicles: Effects of lane-changing rules. Physica A: Statistical Mechanics and its Applications 235(3), 417–439 (1997)
5. Jia, B., Jiang, R., et al.: Honk effect in the two-lane cellular automaton model for traffic flow. Physica A: Statistical Mechanics and its Applications 348, 544–552 (2005)
6. Li, X.-G., Jia, B., Jiang, R.: The Effect of Lane-Changing Time on the Dynamics of Traffic Flow. In: Zhou, J. (ed.) Complex 2009, Part I. LNICST, vol. 4, pp. 589–598. Springer, Heidelberg (2009)
7. Nagel, K., Schreckenberg, M.: A cellular automaton model for freeway traffic. J. Phys. I France 2, 2221–2229 (1992)

Cellular Automaton Model with Non-hypothetical Congested Steady State Reproducing the Three-Phase Traffic Flow Theory

Junfang Tian[1], Martin Treiber[2], Chenqiang Zhu[1] Bin Jia[3], and HuiXuan Li[3]

[1] Institute of Systems Engineering, College of Management and Economics, Tianjin University, No. 92 Weijin Road, Nankai District, Tianjin 300072, China
jftian@tju.edu.cn
[2] Technische Universität Dresden, Institute for Transport & Economics, Würzburger Str. 35, D-01062 Dresden, Germany
[3] MOE Key Laboratory for Urban Transportation Complex Systems Theory and Technology, Beijing Jiaotong University, Beijing, 100044, China

Abstract. A new assumption is assumed to explain the mechanisms of traffic flow that in the noiseless limit, vehicles' space gap will oscillate around the desired space gap, rather than keep the desired space gap, in the homogeneous congested traffic flow. It means there are no steady states of congested traffic and contradicts with the fundamental diagram approach and three-phase traffic flow theory both of which admit the existence of steady states of congested traffic. In order to verify this assumption, a cellular automaton model with non-hypothetical congested steady state is proposed, which is based on the Nagel-Schreckenberg model with additional slow-to-start and the effective desired space gap. Simulations show that this new model can produce the synchronized flow, the transitions from free flow to synchronized flow to wide moving jams, and multiple congested patterns observed by the three-phase theory.

Keywords: Cellular automaton, three-phase traffic flow, fundamental diagram.

1 Introduction

In order to understand the mechanism of traffic congestion, many models and analysis have been carried out to explain the empirical findings [1–5]. Generally speaking, these models can be classified into the fundamental diagram approach or the three-phase theory. The fundamental diagram is the idealized form of the flow-density curve in traffic flow, which goes through the origin with at least one maximum. It describes the theoretical relationship between density and flow in the stationary homogeneous traffic, i.e., the steady state of identical driver-vehicle units[5]. In the last century, almost all traffic flow models belong to the fundamental diagram approach. In microscopic models, the fundamental

J. Wąs, G.C. Sirakoulis, and S. Bandini (Eds.): ACRI 2014, LNCS 8751, pp. 610–619, 2014.

diagram is linked to the steady states of car-following (CF) or cellular automaton (CA) models. For example, in the Optimal Velocity Model (OV model) [6], the fundamental diagram corresponds to the optimal velocity function itself. In the Nagel-Schreckenberg cellular automaton model (NaSch model), it could be derived in terms of the steady state in the deterministic limit [7]. In the macroscopic or mesoscopic models, it has been directly applied (e.g. the LWR theory [8, 9]) or incorporated into the momentum equation (e.g. the PW theory [10]).

The majority of models in fundamental diagram approach belongs to the two-phase models [6–13], which refers to the free flow phase (F) and the jammed phase (J). The phase transitions involved are the transition from free flow to jams (F→J transition) and the transition from jam to free flow (J→F transition). The fundamental diagram approach explains the jam formation mainly by excess demand, i.e., the traffic inflow exceeds the static capacity defined by the maximum of the fundamental diagram. Additionally, instabilities of traffic flow, which are caused by finite speed adaption time (due to finite accelerations) or reaction time, can lead to jam formation even before static capacity is reached. For the detailed discussion of stability, one can refer to [5, 14].

Based on the long-term empirical analysis, Kerner [3, 4] argues that two-phase models could not reproduce the empirical features of traffic breakdown as well as the further development of the related congested region properly. Then the three-phase theory is introduced, in which there are (1) free traffic flow (2) synchronized flow and (3) wide moving jams. The fundamental hypothesis of the three-phase theory is that the hypothetical steady states of the synchronized flow cover a two-dimensional region in the flow-density plane[1] , in other words there is no fundamental diagram of traffic flow. Over the time, many models within the framework of three-phase theory are proposed [15–25].

In three-phase traffic theory, traffic breakdown is a phase transition from free flow to synchronized flow (F→S transition). Wide moving jams can occur spontaneously in synchronized flow only (S→J transition), i.e. due to a sequence of F→S→J transitions. Empirical observations show that General Patterns (GPs) and Synchronized Patterns (SPs) are two main types of congested patterns at an isolated bottleneck. After the synchronized flow occurs upstream of the bottleneck, the wide moving jams continuously emerge in that synchronized flow and propagate upstream, and then this congested pattern is often called as the General Patterns (GP). However, if the wide moving jams discontinuously emerge on the road, there will just have one or few wide moving jams appearing in that synchronized flow, then this congested pattern is often called as the dissolving General Patterns (DGP). If there is only synchronized flow upstream of the bottleneck, no wide moving jams emerge in the synchronized flow, then this congested pattern is often called as the Synchronized Patterns. And as a result of the F→S transition, various synchronized flow patterns can occur at the bot-

---

[1] Two-dimensional steady states refer to a two-dimensional manifold of steady states parameterized by the associated flow and density. In the flow-density diagram, this is represented by a two-dimensional area of possible states, hence the name.

tleneck, such as the widening synchronized pattern (WSP), local synchronized pattern (LSP), and moving synchronized pattern (MSP).

In this paper, another assumption is conceived to explain the mechanisms of traffic flow that in the noiseless limit, vehicles' space gap will oscillate around the desired space gap, rather than keep the desired space gap, in the homogeneous congested traffic flow, which means there are no steady states of congested traffic. In order to validate this assumption, a new cellular automation model is established in section 2. Empirical findings of three-phase theory are simulated and discussed in section 3. Finally, the conclusion is given in section 4.

2   The New Model

In the fundamental diagram approach, the unique relationship between the equilibrium space gap and speed is assumed in the stationary homogeneous traffic: if the equilibrium space gap is smaller than the actual gap, vehicles tend to accelerate; if the equilibrium space gap is greater than the actual gap, vehicles tend to decelerate; otherwise vehicles tend to keep the uniform speed. However in the three-phase traffic theory, there is no unique relationship between the equilibrium space gap and speed in the stationary homogeneous traffic: if the actual gap is greater than the synchronized gap, vehicles tend to accelerate; if the actual gap is smaller than the safe gap, vehicles tend to decelerate; otherwise vehicles tend to adjust their speed according to the speed of their formers. Although three-phase traffic theory denies the fundamental diagram, both admit the existence of stationary homogeneous traffic in the congested traffic.

Comparing with taking the unique relationship between the equilibrium space gap and speed into the models within the fundamental diagram approach, models in the framework of the three-phase traffic theory are often complicated due to the two-dimensional region, which makes them less practical. We wonder whether there is another assumption that considers more reality than the fundamental diagram approach but less complicated than the three-phase traffic theory. Since there is seldom any evidence confirming the existence of stationary homogeneous traffic in the congested traffic that tends to keep oscillating in reality, the following assumption is proposed: **in the noiseless limit, vehicles' space gap will oscillate around the desired space gap, rather than keep the desired space gap, in the homogeneous congested traffic flow, which means there are no steady states of congested traffic.**

In order to validate this assumption, the following cellular automaton model is proposed whose main mechanisms incorporating this assumption are embodied in the randomization process of vehicles. The parallel update rules are as follows.

1. Determination of the randomization parameter $p_n(t+1)$ and deceleration extent Δv:

$$p_n(t+1) = \begin{cases} p_a : & \text{if } d_n^{\text{eff}}(t) < d_n^*(t) \\ p_b : & \text{if } v_n(t) = 0 \text{ and } t_n^{\text{st}}(t) \geq t_c \\ p_c : & \text{in all other cases} \end{cases} \tag{1}$$

$$\Delta v(t+1) = \begin{cases} b_{\text{defens}} : & \text{if } d_n^{\text{eff}}(t) < d_n^*(t) \\ 1 : & \text{in all other cases} \end{cases} \qquad (2)$$

2. Acceleration:
$v_n(t+1) = \min(v_n(t) + 1, v_{\max})$

3. Deceleration:
$v_n(t+1) = \min(d_n^{\text{eff}}(t), v_n(t+1))$

4. Randomization with probability:
if$(rand() < p_n(t+1))$ then $v_n(t+1) = \max(v_n(t+1) - \Delta v(t+1), 0)$

5. The determination of $t_n^{\text{st}}(t+1)$:
if$(v_n(t+1) = 0)$ then $t_n^{\text{st}}(t+1) = t_n^{\text{st}}(t) + 1$
if$(v_n(t+1) > 0)$ then $t_n^{\text{st}}(t+1) = 0$

6. Car motion:
$x_n(t+1) = x_n(t) + v_n(t+1)$

where $d_n(t)$ is the space gap between vehicle and its preceding vehicle $n + 1$, $d_n(t) = x_{n+1}(t) - x_n(t) - L_{\text{veh}}$, $x_n(t)$ is the position of vehicle n (here vehicle $n + 1$ precedes vehicle n) and L_{veh} is the length of the vehicle. $v_n(t)$ is the speed of the vehicle n, and $v_{\max}$ is the maximum speed. $d_n^*(t) = T v_n(t)$ is the effective desired space gap between vehicle n and $n + 1$, and T is the effective safe time gap between vehicle n and $n+1$ at the steady state. $d_n^{\text{eff}}(t)$ is the effective gap, $d_n^{\text{eff}}(t) = d_n(t) + max(v_{\text{anti}}(t) - g_{\text{safety}}, 0)$, where $v_{\text{anti}} = \min(d_{n+1}(t), v_{n+1}(t) + 1, v_{\max})$ is the expected speed of the preceding vehicle in the next time step. g_{safety} is the parameter to control the effectiveness of the anticipation. Accidents are avoided only if the constraint $g_{\text{safety}} \geq b_{\text{defens}}$ is satisfied. The speed anticipation effect is considered in order to reproduce the real time headway distribution, which has a cut off at the small time headway less than one second [22]. $t_n^{\text{st}}(t)$ denotes the time since the last stop for standing vehicles, while $t_n^{\text{st}}(t) = 0$ for moving vehicles.

The basis of the new model is the rules of the NaSch model with randomization parameter p_c to which a slow-to-start rule and the effective desired space gap $d_n^*(t)$ has been added. The slow-to-start effect is characterized by an increase of the randomization parameter from p_c to $p_b (> p_c)$, which is the element to realize the transition from synchronized flow to wide moving jams. The new model assumes the driver tends to keep the effective gap no smaller than $d_n^*(t)$, otherwise the driver will become defensive. The actual behavioral change is characterized by increasing the spontaneous braking probability from p_c to p_a. Moreover, the associated deceleration will change from 1 to $b_{\text{defens}} (\geq 1)$. This effect is the factor to reproduce the transition from free flow to synchronized flow in the new model.

In the following, the steady states of the new model are analyzed in the unperturbed, noiseless limit. For microscopic traffic flow models, the steady state requires that the model parameters are the same for all drivers and vehicles. In that case, the steady state is characterized by the following two conditions [5]:

1) Homogeneous traffic: All vehicles move at the same speed and keep the same gap behind their respective leaders.

2) No accelerations: all vehicles keep a constant speed.

Since the mechanisms associated with the hypothetical congested steady state analysis are all embodied in the randomization process, the noiseless limit should be taken as $p_a = 1, p_b = 0, p_b = 1$ or $p_a = 1, p_b = 1, p_c = 1$. However, all vehicles will keep a constant speed no matter how long distance between vehicles is in the latter case, which is obviously unrealistic. Thus, we consider the former. According to the model rules, if $d^{\text{eff}}/T \geq v_{\max}$, all vehicles will move with $v_{\max}$; if $d^{\text{eff}}/T < v_{\max}$, all vehicles' speed will take turns to change simultaneously over time between $\max(v - b_{\text{defens}}, 0)$ and v, where $v \in [d^{\text{eff}}/T, \min(v_{\max}, d^{\text{eff}})]$ and $\max(v - 1, 0) < d^{\text{eff}}/T$. It means there are no steady states of congested traffic in the new model. Vehicles space gaps oscillate around the desired gap, i.e., deviations from the steady state are caused by local instabilities (representing the inability of the drivers to keep the desired gap), not by the driver heterogeneity [2], which is consistent with the empirical findings by [27]. Therefore, this model is named the cellular automaton model with non-hypothetical congested steady state (NH model).

3   Simulation Investigation

In this section, simulations are carried out on a road with the length $L_{\text{road}} = 1000L_{\text{cell}}$. Both the cell length and vehicle length are set as $7.5m$, i.e. $L_{\text{cell}} = 7.5m$ and $L_{\text{veh}} = 1L_{\text{cell}} = 7.5m$. One time step corresponds to $1s$. During the simulations, the first 50000 time steps are discarded to let the transients die out. The parameters are shown in Tab.1.

Table 1. Model parameters of NH model

Parameters	L_{cell}	L_{veh}	$v_{\max}$	T	b_{defens}	p_a	p_b	p_c	g_{safety}	t_c
Units	m	L_{cell}	L_{cell}/s	s	L_{cell}/s^2	-	-	-	L_{cell}	s
Value	7.5	1	5	1.8	1	0.95	0.55	0.1	2	8

Traffic patterns that emerge near an on-ramp are studied under open boundary condition. The vehicles drive from left to right. The left-most cell corresponds to $x = 1$. The position of the left-most vehicle is x_{last} and that of the right-most vehicle is x_{lead}. At each time step, if $x_{\text{last}} > v_{\max}$, a new vehicle with speed $v_{\max}$ will be injected to the position $\min(x_{\text{last}} - v_{\max}, v_{\max})$ with probability $q_{\text{in}}/3600$ and q_{in} is the traffic flow entering the main road. At the right boundary, the leading vehicle moves without any hindrance. If $x_{\text{lead}} > L_{\text{road}}$, the leading vehicle will be removed and the following vehicle becomes the leader.

---

[2] Driver heterogeneity, or, more specifically, inter-driver heterogeneity, refers to different parameterizations of every vehicle representing variations of the individual driving style and vehicle performances. If there is no inter-driver heterogeneity (identical drivers and vehicles), all deviations from a steady state are either due to intrinsic randomness (a random term in the accelerations as in the NaSch Model with the randomization probability p $\neq$ 1 or zero), or dynamic instabilities. In the deterministic case of our model, we have only the latter, i.e. "no" internal/intrinsic randomness.

We adopt a simple method to model the on-ramp, which is similar to that of [26]. Assuming the position of the on-ramp is x_{on}, a region $[x_{on}, x_{on} + L_{ramp}]$ is selected as the inserting area of the vehicle from on-ramp. At each time step, we find out the longest gap in this region. If the gap is large enough for a vehicle, then a new vehicle will be inserted at the cell in the middle of the gap with probability $q_{on}/3600$ and q_{on} is the traffic flow from the on-ramp. The speed of the inserted vehicle is set as the speed of its preceding vehicle, and the stop time is set to zero. In this paper, the parameters are set as $x_{on} = 0.8L_{road}$ and $L_{ramp} = 10L_{cell}$.

In Fig.1(a), the reproduced spatial-temporal features of the congested pattern named moving synchronized flow (MSP) are shown (see the empirical figure 7.6 in [4]). In this pattern, synchronized traffic flow spontaneously emerges in the free flow. Fig.1(b) exhibits the widening synchronized flow (WSP, see the empirical figure 7.4 in [4]). For this pattern, wide moving jams do not emerge in synchronized flow. The downstream front of WSP is fixed at the on-ramp and the upstream front of WSP propagates upstream continuously over time. In Fig.1(c), both the downstream and the upstream front of synchronized flow are fixed at the on-ramp, thus, it belongs to the local synchronized pattern (LSP). Moreover, the width of LSP in the longitudinal direction changes over time, which is in accordance with empirical observations (see the empirical figure 7.2 in [4]). Fig.1(d) shows the dissolving General Patterns (DGP) in which just one wide moving jam emerges in the synchronized flow. Fig.1(e) shows the spatial-temporal features of General Pattern (GP).

In order to emphasize the significance of the two-dimensional steady states of synchronized flow, Kerner and Klenov (2006) proposed the Speed Adaption Models (SAMs) in the framework of fundamental diagram approach. The basic hypothesis of SAMs is the double Z-characteristic for the sequence of phase transitions from free flow to synchronized flow to wide moving jams (F→S→J transitions). Based on this hypothesis, SAMs can reproduce both the traffic breakdown and the emergence of wide moving jams in synchronized flow as found in empirical observations. However, SAMs are not able to reproduce the local synchronized patterns (LSPs) consistent with empirical results as well as some of empirical features of synchronized flow between wide moving jams within general patterns (GPs). Kerner et al. attribute these drawbacks of SAMs to the lacking of the two-dimensional steady states of synchronized flow.

Although only free outflow exists in the downstream of wide moving jams in GP of the NH model, it can be easily improved if we decrease the slow-to-start probability p_b or adjust the values of T and b_{defens}, see Fig.1(f),(g). Thus, all the above simulation results are well consistent with the well-known results of the three-phase traffic theory. Therefore it is reasonable to conclude that the two-dimensional steady states of synchronized flow are not an essential requirement for the spatiotemporal dynamics.

Moreover, in Fig.1(a) and (d), one could obtain the propagation velocity of the downstream MSP front is nearly -26.8km/h and the propagation velocity of the downstream jam front is nearly -13km/h which is about half that of

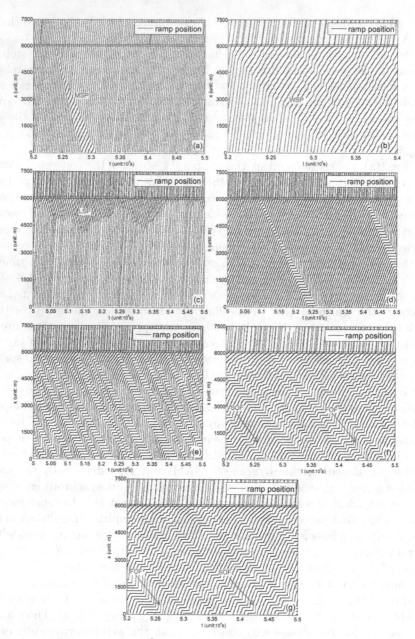

Fig. 1. Trajectories of every 20th vehicle of the NH model. (a) $q_{in} = 2339, q_{on} = 19$ (MSP), (b) $q_{in} = 1728, q_{on} = 968$ (WSP), (c) $q_{in} = 1440, q_{on} = 823$ (LSP), (d) $q_{in} = 1134, q_{on} = 1123$ (DGP), (e) $q_{in} = 920, q_{on} = 1304$ (GP), (f) $q_{in} = 931, q_{on} = 1304$ (GP), (g) $q_{in} = 933, q_{on} = 1011$ (GP) (unit: veh/h). The horizontal direction (from left to right) is time and the vertical direction (from down to up) is space. (f) $P_b = 0.5$, (g) $P_b = 0.55, T = 1.6, g_{safety} = b_{defens} = 2$. 'SOF' and 'FOF' represent the synchronized outflow and free outflow of wide moving jams, respectively.

the downstream MSP front. This is better than the results in most three-phase models which often have propagation velocities as negative as -40km/h or even more negative.

4   Conclusion

The fundamental diagram approach and three-phase traffic flow theory were established to explore the mechanisms of traffic flow. The fundamental diagram approach assumes the existence of the unique space-gap-speed relationship, while the three-phase theory presumes drivers can make arbitrary choice of the space gap within some gap range. One of the most important similarities between both theories is that they both admit the existence of stationary homogeneous traffic in the congested traffic.

In this paper, another assumption is assumed to explain the mechanisms of road traffic flow that in the noiseless limit, vehicles' space gap will oscillate around the desired space gap, rather than keep the desired space gap, in the homogeneous congested traffic flow. It means there are no steady states of congested traffic. In order to verify this assumption, a new model named as the cellular automaton model with non-hypothetical congested steady state (NH model) is proposed. Simulations obtained from an open road with an on-ramp show that NH model can produce the synchronized flow, two kinds of phase transitions i.e. F→S transition and S→J transition, and multiple congested patterns observed by the three-phase theory.

In summary, the NH model produces the same spatiotemporal dynamics as many of the more complex three-phase models. Besides many aspects that are consistent with traffic data, it also includes a feature that is at variance with observations: the propagation velocity of MSP is twice than that of the downstream jam front, while observations indicate that both velocities are of the same order (with values between -20 and -15km/h). It illustrates that the two-dimensional steady states of synchronized flow are not an essential requirement for the spatiotemporal dynamics.

Acknowledgements. This work is supported by the National Natural Science Foundation of China (Grant Nos. 71271150, 71222101) and the 973 Program (No. 2012CB725400).

References

1. Chowdhury, D., Santen, L., Schadschneider, A.: Statistical physics of vehicular traffic and some related systems. Physics Reports 329(4), 199–329 (2000)
2. Helbing, D.: Traffic and related self-driven many-particle systems. Reviews of Modern Physics 73(4), 1067 (2001)

3. Kerner, B.S.: The physics of traffic: empirical freeway pattern features, engineering applications, and theory. Springer (2004)
4. Kerner, B.S.: Introduction to modern traffic flow theory and control: the long road to three-phase traffic theory. Springer (2009)
5. Treiber, M., Kesting, A.: Traffic Flow Dynamics. Springer (2013)
6. Bando, M., Hasebe, K., Nakayama, A., Shibata, A., Sugiyama, Y.: Dynamical model of traffic congestion and numerical simulation. Physical Review E 51, 1035–1042 (1995)
7. Nagel, K., Schreckenberg, M.: A cellular automaton model for freeway traffic. Journal de Physique I 2(12), 2221–2229 (1992)
8. Lighthill, M.J., Whitham, G.B.: On kinematic waves. II. A theory of traffic flow on long crowded roads. Proceedings of the Royal Society of London. Series A. Mathematical and Physical Sciences 229(1178), 317–345 (1955)
9. Richards, P.I.: Shock waves on the highway. Operations Research 4(1), 42–51 (1956)
10. Payne, H.J.: FREFLO: A macroscopic simulation model of freeway traffic. Transportation Research Record 722 (1979)
11. Herman, R., Montroll, E.W., Potts, R.B., Rothery, R.W.: Traffic dynamics: analysis of stability in car following. Operations Research 7(1), 86–106 (1959)
12. Treiber, M., Hennecke, A., Helbing, D.: Congested traffic states in empirical observations and microscopic simulations. Physical Review E 62(2), 1805 (2000)
13. Knospe, W., Santen, L., Schadschneider, A., Schreckenberg, M.: Towards a realistic microscopic description of highway traffic. Journal of Physics A: Mathematical and General 33(48), L477–L485 (2000)
14. Kesting, A., Treiber, M.: How reaction time, update time, and adaptation time influence the stability of traffic flow. Computer - Aided Civil and Infrastructure Engineering 23(2), 125–137 (2008)
15. Kerner, B.S., Klenov, S.L.: A microscopic model for phase transitions in traffic flow. Journal of Physics A: Mathematical and General 35(3), L31 (2002)
16. Kerner, B.S., Klenov, S.L.: Microscopic theory of spatial-temporal congested traffic patterns at highway bottlenecks. Physical Review E 68(3), 036130 (2003)
17. Kerner, B.S., Klenov, S.L.: Deterministic microscopic three-phase traffic flow models. Journal of Physics A: Mathematical and General 39(8), 1775 (2006)
18. Kerner, B.S., Klenov, S.L., Schreckenberg, M.: Simple cellular automaton model for traffic breakdown, highway capacity, and synchronized flow. Physical Review E 84(4), 046110 (2011)
19. Kerner, B.S., Klenov, S.L., Schreckenberg, M.: Simple cellular automaton model for traffic breakdown, highway capacity, and synchronized flow. Physical Review E 84(4), 046110 (2011)
20. Kerner, B.S., Klenov, S.L., Wolf, D.E.: Cellular automata approach to three-phase traffic theory. Journal of Physics A: Mathematical and General 35(47), 9971 (2002)
21. Lee, H.K., Barlovic, R., Schreckenberg, M., Kim, D.: Mechanical restriction versus human overreaction triggering congested traffic states. Physical Review Letters 92(23), 238702 (2004)
22. Neubert, L., Santen, L., Schadschneider, A., Schreckenberg, M.: Single-vehicle data of highway traffic: A statistical analysis. Physical Review E 60(6), 6480 (1999)
23. Tian, J.-F., Jia, B., Li, X.-G., Jiang, R., Zhao, X.-M., Gao, Z.-Y.: Synchronized traffic flow simulating with cellular automata model. Physica A: Statistical Mechanics and its Applications 388(23), 4827–4837 (2009)

24. Gao, K., Jiang, R., Hu, S.-X., Wang, B.-H., Wu, Q.-S.: Cellular-automaton model with velocity adaptation in the framework of Kerners three-phase traffic theory. Physical Review E 76(2), 026105 (2007)
25. Jiang, R., Wu, Q.-S.: Cellular automata models for synchronized traffic flow. Journal of Physics A: Mathematical and General 36(2), 381 (2003)
26. Treiber, M., Kesting, A., Helbing, D.: Understanding widely scattered traffic flows, the capacity drop, and platoons as effects of variance-driven time gaps. Physical Review E 74(1), 016123 (2006)
27. Wagner, P.: Analyzing fluctuations in car-following. Transportation Research Part B: Methodological 46(10), 1384–1392 (2012)

Asymmetric Lane Change Rules
for a Microscopic Highway Traffic Model

Lars Habel and Michael Schreckenberg

Physik von Transport und Verkehr, Universität Duisburg-Essen, Duisburg, Germany
{lars.habel,michael.schreckenberg}@uni-due.de

Abstract. For simulating multi-lane highway traffic with cellular automata (CA) traffic models, realistic lane change rules are required. In many countries, legal regulations distinguish between driving lanes and overtaking lanes. Therefore, asymmetric lane change rules are needed. In this contribution, the CA traffic model by Lee *et al* (Phys. Rev. Lett. **92**(23) (2004) 238702) is extended with those rules. The presented ruleset is then studied in simulations of two-lane and three-lane highways.

Keywords: Microscopic traffic models, Vehicular traffic, Highway traffic, Modelling of lane changing.

1 Introduction

In many countries, vehicles have to drive on the outer lanes of multi-lane highways, when they are not overtaking slower vehicles. This "asymmetric" driving behaviour leads to different values of observables like traffic flow, velocity distribution and time headway distribution on the different lanes compared to multi-lane roads without overtaking restrictions. Empirical research regarding these observations has been performed in Germany and France for two-lane [1], three-lane [2, 3, 4] and four-lane [5] highways.

Since the development of the Nagel-Schreckenberg model [6], much research has been done to make use of realistic CA-based traffic models in traffic information systems. Traffic models like the CDM [7] or the model by Lee *et al* [8] have been presented, which are able to reproduce many empirical findings of the three-phase traffic theory [9].

From a perspective of microscopic modelling, asymmetric lane change rules should be used for simulations, whenever it is empirically necessary. In simulations with real-time empirical data, it is interesting to achieve good results not only by road cross-section, but also by lane. Those results then can be used for lane-specific services, like traffic information for trucks. The operation of a live simulation, where vehicles have to be inserted into/removed from the running system, becomes easier as well, when the distribution of vehicles on the lanes corresponds well to empirical data.

This contribution is organised as follows. In Sec. 2, we briefly introduce the underlying Lee model. In Sec. 3, we present a detailed explanation of asymmetric

J. Wąs, G.C. Sirakoulis, and S. Bandini (Eds.): ACRI 2014, LNCS 8751, pp. 620–629, 2014.
© Springer International Publishing Switzerland 2014

lane change rules for the Lee model, which we recently have introduced in a short way in [10]. Thereafter, we provide simulation results for two-lane (Sec. 4) and three-lane highways (Sec. 5).

2   The Underlying CA Traffic Model

Vehicular motion is simulated using the CA traffic model by Lee *et al* [8], which contains strategies like a velocity-dependent randomisation step, that are known from other previously introduced CA traffic models (e.g. the CDM [7]). In the following, we very shortly introduce the steps of the model, which are necessary to understand our model additions in Sec. 3. A detailed analysis of the Lee model can be found in [11].

In contrast to many other CA traffic models, each vehicle n in the Lee model does not have unlimited braking capabilities, but is only allowed to brake $D = 2$ cells/s in each time step $\Delta t = 1$ s. The cell size is $\Delta x = 1.5$ m. With respect to D, the calculation of the next velocity $v_n^{(t+1)}$ of vehicle n requires to determine a maximum safe velocity $\tilde{c}_n^{(t+1)}$ first. This is the maximum $c_n^{(t+1)}$ that fulfills

$$x_n^{(t)} + \Delta_n^{(t)} + \sum_{i=0}^{\tau_f(c_n^{(t+1)},D)} \left(c_n^{(t+1)} - Di \right) \leq x_{n+1}^{(t)} + \sum_{i=1}^{\tau_l(v_{n+1}^{(t)},D)} \left(v_{n+1}^{(t)} - Di \right) . \quad (1)$$

For the calculation of $\tau_f(c_n^{(t+1)}, D)$ and $\tau_l(v_{n+1}^{(t)}, D)$, it has to be determined, if the vehicle is "optimistic" or "pessimistic". Pessimistic vehicles await a traffic breakdown and maintain a safe distance to their preceding vehicles. Optimistic vehicles only maintain a small gap, that can only compensate small disturbances. Generally, this can lead to dangerous situations [12], but those occur only seldom with the presented rules. The definitions of τ_f, τ_l and the safety gap $\Delta_n^{(t)}$ between vehicles n and $n + 1$ can be found in [8].

After $\tilde{c}_n^{(t+1)}$ is calculated, a velocity $\tilde{v}_n^{(t+1)}$ is obtained by cutting $\tilde{c}_n^{(t+1)}$, so that D is respected. Then, $v_n^{(t+1)}$ is obtained by applying the randomisation step on $\tilde{v}_n^{(t+1)}$.

3   Additional Asymmetric Lane Change Rules

The ruleset consists of four components: Rules for guaranteeing safety of a lane change, decision-making rules for lane changes to the right as well as to the left and an optional right lane overtaking ban. The notation of vehicles can be obtained from Fig. 1. In the following, we assume that vehicles drive on the right side of the road and overtake on the left side.

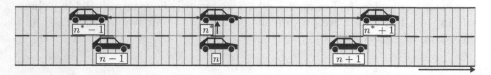

Fig. 1. Situation of vehicles during a lane change: Vehicle n attempts to change the lane. On the new lane, it is labelled as n^*.

Safety. The safety of a lane change of vehicle n with length l_n is checked using the conditions

$$x_{n^*}^{(t)} - x_{n^*-1}^{(t)} > l_{n^*} \tag{2a}$$

$$x_{n^*+1}^{(t)} - x_{n^*}^{(t)} > l_{n^*+1} \tag{2b}$$

$$v_n^{(t)} - D \leq \tilde{c}_{n^*}^{(t+1)} \tag{2c}$$

$$v_{n^*-1}^{(t)} - \beta \leq \tilde{c}_{n^*-1}^{(t+1)} \ , \tag{2d}$$

which have been adopted from the symmetric ruleset presented in [13].

In simulations with more than two lanes, an additional security check has to be performed for lane changes to the central lane(s), because a vehicle from the left and a vehicle from the right could attempt to lane change into the same gap in the same update step. In our simulations, all vehicles that decide to change to the central lane(s) are provisionally moved onto the desired lane. Then, the safety rules (2) are applied on all vehicles on that lane, beginning at the downstream side. If (2) are not fulfilled for a specific lane changing vehicle, this vehicle is moved back onto its origin lane.

Lane Change to the Left. A vehicle changes to a lane further to the left, when it can drive faster there compared to staying on the present lane. As in the symmetric ruleset, this can be modelled with

$$\tilde{v}_{n^*}^{(t+1)} > \tilde{v}_n^{(t+1)} \ . \tag{3}$$

Lane Change to the Right. A vehicle changes back to a lane further to the right, when its overtaking manoeuvre shall end. This is the case, when staying on the present lane is not advantageous any longer compared to a lane change to the right. On the other hand, the vehicle is not allowed to gain an advantage through a lane change to the right, because it then would offend against the right lane overtaking ban. As a consequence, a lane change to the right is only allowed, if

$$\tilde{v}_{n^*}^{(t+1)} = \tilde{v}_n^{(t+1)} \ . \tag{4}$$

Generally, this rule conforms with legal regulations. But as empirically observed [1], vehicles do only change to the right, when there is free space in front of them on new and old lane, because otherwise they eventually would be forced to change back soon. Therefore, other lane changing rules require a minimum distance gap [14, 15] or a minimum time headway [7, 14] for changing back to the right. In the given CA model, $\tilde{v}_{n^*}^{(t+1)}$ and $\tilde{v}_n^{(t+1)}$ implicitly define a time gap in (4), but it depends on the optimism of the lane changing vehicle. Hence, the implicit gap can be very small in free flow. To compensate for this, we demand an additional time gap t_{hlc}, which is ensured through

$$x_{n+1}^{(t)} - x_n^{(t)} - l_{n+1} \geq v_n^{(t)} t_{\text{hlc}} \tag{5a}$$

$$x_{n^*+1}^{(t)} - x_{n^*}^{(t)} - l_{n^*+1} \geq v_n^{(t)} t_{\text{hlc}} . \tag{5b}$$

Below a velocity v_{sym}, we allow lane changing according to the symmetric rules, so that vehicles can change to a faster lane on a congested road section.

Right Lane Overtaking Ban. With the so-far presented ruleset and some trucks on the road, most of the faster vehicles drive on the left lane(s) in free flow. With rising density, disturbances evolve and the vehicles have to reduce their speed, so that vehicles on the right lane begin to overtake them on the "wrong" side. In special circumstances, the velocity differences between the lanes can become very high – e.g. 40 km/h on the left vs. v_{max} on the right lane. This driving behavior can not be found empirically and should be averted in the model. Generally, this problem is not limited to the given CA model. Other CA models mostly have coped with this task only indirectly or not at all. For example, a rule could – in analogy to [14] – force a vehicle n to change to the left even if it would have to break immediately, i.e. if

$$\tilde{v}_{n^*}^{(t+1)} < \tilde{v}_n^{(t+1)} . \tag{6}$$

Then, a vehicle on the left must exist that otherwise would be overtaken on the right by vehicle n in one of the next time steps. Unfortunately, the implementation of (6) leads to a massive increase of lane changes. Therefore, [14] and related CA models have introduced a lane change probability, which makes lane changing a more or less randomised decision. In the CDM [7], vehicles are allowed to change to the right and overtake there, if they would have to break on the left lane. In [15], overtaking on the right is usually prohibited, but allowed with a small probability.

In the present contribution, we prevent overtaking on the right with a speed adaption rule. The implementation idea is depicted in Fig. 2. The position of vehicle $n^* + 1$ on the left lane defines a moving area on the right lane, in which vehicle n should adapt its velocity to that of vehicle $n^* + 1$. Vehicle n is driving inside the area, if

$$x_{n^*+1}^{(t)} - x_n^{(t)} - l_{n^*+1} < v_n^{(t)} . \tag{7}$$

In contrast to CA traffic models with unlimited braking capabilities, the speed adaption can take more than one time step in the given CA model. With respect

Fig. 2. Illustration of the right lane overtaking ban. If vehicle n moves into the coloured area, its maximum velocity is adapted to the current velocity of vehicle $n^* + 1$.

to this, it is more appropriate to influence the maximum velocity instead of the current one, so that the limited deceleration is maintained. Hence, if vehicle n moves into the area, its maximum velocity $v_{\mathrm{max},n}$ is reduced with

$$\min\{v_{\mathrm{ovt}}; v_{n^*+1} + 2\} \;, \tag{8}$$

if $v_{n^*+1} < v_{\mathrm{ovt}}$. With this formula, overtaking on the right is tolerated, when the velocity difference is small and v_{ovt} is not exceeded. The effective maximum velocity can then be calculated with

$$v_{\mathrm{eff},n} = \min\{v_{\mathrm{max},n}; v_{\mathrm{ov}}\} \;, \tag{9}$$

where

$$v_{\mathrm{ov}} = \begin{cases} \min\{v_{\mathrm{ovt}}; v_{n^*+1} + 2\} & \text{if } v_{n^*+1} < v_{\mathrm{ovt}} \text{ and (7) fulfilled} \\ v_{n^*+1} & \text{if } v_{n^*+1} \geq v_{\mathrm{ovt}} \text{ and (7) fulfilled} \\ v_{\mathrm{max},n} & \text{if (7) not fulfilled} \end{cases} \;. \tag{10}$$

$v_{\mathrm{eff},n}$ is used for all calculations regarding vehicle n in the current time step. Thereafter, it expires and has to be calculated again.

Table 1 summarises default values for all parameters of the presented lane change rules. Parameters that are not shown in Table 1 remain unchanged, their default values can be found in [8, 13].

4   Results for Two-Lane Highways

In Fig. 3, we present simulation results of traffic on a two-lane highway with the asymmetric lane change rules, using the parameter values from Table 1. To allow for a comparision with empirical data [1], 10 % of the vehicles were assumed to be trucks, which are not allowed to leave the right lane. The simulations were performed on a 15 km long system with periodic boundary conditions.

Fig. 3(a) shows the distribution of vehicles on the two lanes depending on the cumulative traffic flow. As this relationship is not unique for all densities, only values of the free flow branch have been used. In Fig. 3(b), the relationship between lane usage and density is depicted. Both figures show that the presented lane change rules are able to cause an asymmetric distribution of vehicles on the lanes. At very low densities, most of the vehicles drive on the right lane and only

Table 1. Default values for parameters of the asymmetric lane change rules

Parameter Explanation		Default value
Global parameters		
v_{car}	maximum velocity for cars	25 cells/s
v_{truck}	maximum velocity for trucks	16 cells/s
l_{car}	length of cars	5 cells/s
l_{truck}	length of trucks	10 cells/s
t_{safe}	look-ahead time for optimistic drivers	4 s
v_{ovt}	maximum velocity for overtaking on right lane	16 cells/s
v_{sym}	maximum velocity for symmetric rules	6 cells/s
β	maximum hindrance of follower	1 cells/s
Lane change on two-lane road: left $\rightarrow$ right		
t_{hlc}	minimum time headway	1.8 s
Lane change on three-lane road: left $\rightarrow$ central		
t_{hlc}	minimum time headway	1.5 s
Lane change on three-lane road: central $\rightarrow$ right		
t_{hlc}	minimum time headway	3 s

change to left, when they want to overtake a truck. With rising density, usage of the left lane rises as well. At a flow of about 1450 vehicles/h on both lanes and a density of 7 vehicles/km, the number of vehicles on both lanes is equal. The highest usage of the left lane can be found at a density of 12 vehicles/km, where about 80 % of all vehicles drive on the left lane. In this situation, a cumulated flow of about 3000 vehicles/h can be measured. At further rising densities, the lane usage rates start to approach each other. In synchronised flow between 23 vehicles/km and 40 vehicles/km, about 55 % of all vehicles drive on the left lane. This ratio remains almost constant even for very high densities, as trucks need twice as much space on the lane as cars.

The empirical observations by [1] are reproduced well with the presented lane change rules. This applies not only to the specific flow, at which the left lane is more utilised than the right lane, but also on the lane usage inversion at higher flows. On the downside, the distinct lane usage maximum of 80 % is higher than the empirically found value of 65 %. This divergence mainly results from the presence of only two vehicle classes in the simulation.

The strength of the lane usage inversion and the location of the inversion maximum can be controlled by adjusting t_{hlc}. The parameter influences both criteria at the same time. High values for t_{hlc} lead to a distinct lane usage

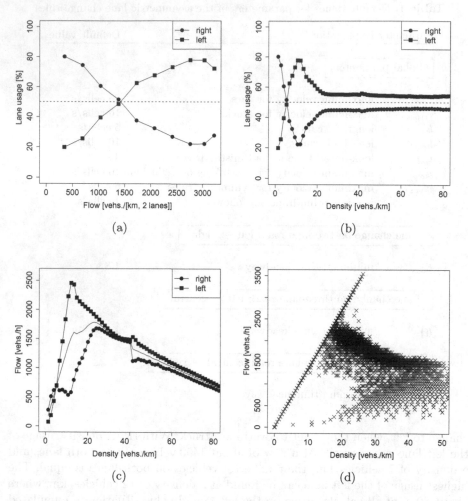

Fig. 3. Results of two-lane simulations. (a): Distribution of vehicles on the two lanes depending on the cumulative traffic flow. (b): Lane usage depending on the density. (c): Global flow-density relationship. The solid line illustrates the average flow. (d): Local flow-density relationship. All 1-minute data points from all simulated densities are depicted.

inversion, that occurs at lower densities. For small values of t_{hlc}, the lane usage inversion only occurs at higher densities and is very small or vanishes at all.

The truck percentage has only a small influence on the strength of the lane usage inversion. Especially the inversion maximum proves to be quite stable, even for small truck percentages. Qualitatively, the rules are able to cause a lane usage inversion even without trucks in the system.

Fig. 3(c) shows the global relationship between flow and density. Here, the different lane usage can be observed as well. In contrast to simulations with symmetric lane change rules, traffic on the left lane contributes much more to the global flow than that on the right lane. It is interesting to note, that the Lee model allows for much higher flows on the left lane than the CDM (2500 vehicles/h vs. 1900 vehicles/h in [7]).

In Fig. 3(d), the locally measured relationship between flow and density is depicted. Between 10 and 15 vehicles/km, distinct high-flow traffic states with maximum flows up to 3500 vehicles/h can be observed. Those states have recently been analysed empirically in [16].

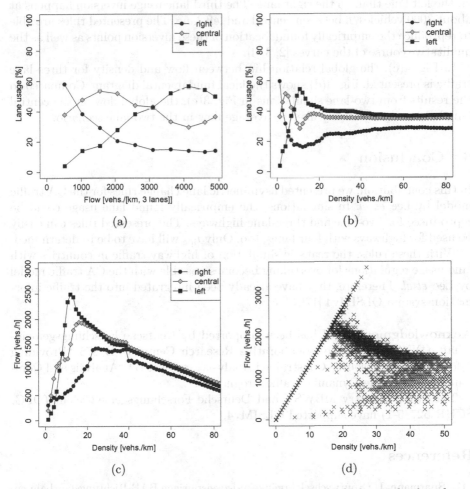

(a)

(b)

(c)

(d)

Fig. 4. Results of three-lane simulations. (a): Distribution of vehicles on the three lanes depending on the cumulative traffic flow. (b): Lane usage depending on the density. (c): Global flow-density relationship. (d): Local flow-density relationship. All 1-minute data points from all simulated densities are depicted.

5   Results for Three-Lane Highways

In Fig. 4, results for three-lane simulations are presented. Those have been performed in the same way as for two-lane highways, again using the parameter values from Table 1. As the lane change rules allow for an arbitrary number of lanes, the implementation of this scenario is simple.

Fig. 4(a) and 4(b) show the distribution of vehicles on the three lanes depending on flow and density. Fig. 4(a) now contains three characteristic points, where the lane usage curves intersect each other. At low flows of about 500 vehicles/h, almost all vehicles drive on the right lane or on the central lane. At about 1000 vehicles/h, the first lane usage inversion occurs between these lanes. Then, the left lane is used by about 20 % of the vehicles as well. At about 2000 vehicles/h, more vehicles drive on the left lane than on the right lane. The third lane usage inversion happens at about 3000 vehicles/h between central and left lane. The presented rules are able to reproduce the empirically found location of these inversion points as well as the qualitative course of the curves [2, 3, 4].

In Fig. 4(c), the global relationship between flow and density for three-lane traffic is presented. Fig. 4(d) shows the local fundamental diagram. Compared to the results from two-lane simulations in Fig. 3(c), the global flow on the central lane behaves qualitatively like the average flow in the two-lane scenario.

6   Conclusion

In this contribution, we presented asymmetric lane change rules for the CA traffic model by Lee *et al.* In simulations, the empirically found lane usage could be reproduced for two-lane and three-lane highways. The presented rules can easily be used for highways with four lanes, too. Only t_{hlc} will have to be re-determined.

With these rules, the realistic simulation of highway traffic in countries with lane usage regulations for overtaking becomes possible with the CA traffic model by Lee *et al.* Therefore, they have already been integrated into the traffic information system OLSIMv4 [17].

Acknowledgments. LH has been supported by Deutsche Forschungsgemeinschaft (DFG) within the Collaborative Research Center SFB 876 "Providing Information by Resource-Constrained Analysis", project B4 "Analysis and Communication for the Dynamic Traffic Prognosis".

The NRW ministry MBWSV and Deutsche Forschungsgemeinschaft (DFG, SCHR 527/5-1) have supported OLSIMv4.

References

[1] Sparmann, U.: Spurwechselvorgänge auf zweispurigen BAB-Richtungsfahrbahnen. Forschung Straßenbau und Straßenverkehrstechnik, vol. 263 (1978)

[2] Leutzbach, W., Busch, F.: Spurwechselvorgänge auf dreispurigen BAB-Richtungsfahrbahnen, Institut für Verkehrswesen, Universität Karlsruhe (1984)

[3] Knospe, W., Santen, L., Schadschneider, A., Schreckenberg, M.: Single-vehicle data of highway traffic: Microscopic description of traffic phases. Phys. Rev. E 65(5), 056133 (2002)

[4] Duret, A., Ahn, S., Buisson, C.: Lane flow distribution on a three-lane freeway: General features and the effects of traffic controls. Transport. Res. C 24, 157–167 (2012)

[5] Geistefeldt, J.: Verkehrsablauf und Verkehrssicherheit auf Autobahnen mit vier-streifigen Richtungsfahrbahnen. PhD thesis, Ruhr-Universität Bochum (2007)

[6] Nagel, K., Schreckenberg, M.: A cellular automaton model for freeway traffic. J. Phys. I France 2(12), 2221–2229 (1992)

[7] Knospe, W., Santen, L., Schadschneider, A., Schreckenberg, M.: A realistic two-lane traffic model for highway traffic. J. Phys. A: Math. Gen. 35(15), 3369 (2002)

[8] Lee, H.K., Barlovic, R., Schreckenberg, M., Kim, D.: Mechanical restriction versus human overreaction triggering congested traffic states. Phys. Rev. Lett. 92(23), 238702 (2004)

[9] Kerner, B.S.: Introduction to Modern Traffic Flow Theory and Control: The Long Road to Three-Phase Traffic Theory. Springer (2009)

[10] Habel, L., Ide, C., Knaup, T., Wietfeld, C., Schreckenberg, M.: Improving a Microscopic Traffic Simulation using Real-Time Information on Environmental Conditions (submitted)

[11] Pottmeier, A.: Realistic Cellular Automaton Model for Synchronized Two-Lane Traffic - Simulation, Validation, and Applications. PhD thesis, University of Duisburg-Essen (2007)

[12] Schadschneider, A.: Cellular Automaton Approach to Highway Traffic: What do we Know? In: Appert-Rolland, C., Chevoir, F., Gondret, P., Lassarre, S., Lebacque, J.P., Schreckenberg, M. (eds.) Traffic and Granular Flow 2007, pp. 19–34. Springer (2009)

[13] Pottmeier, A., Thiemann, C., Schadschneider, A., Schreckenberg, M.: Mechanical Restriction Versus Human Overreaction: Accident Avoidance and Two-Lane Traffic Simulations. In: Schadschneider, A., Pöschel, T., Kühne, R., Schreckenberg, M., Wolf, D.E. (eds.) Traffic and Granular Flow 2005, pp. 503–508. Springer (2007)

[14] Nagel, K., Wolf, D.E., Wagner, P., Simon, P.: Two-lane traffic rules for cellular automata: A systematic approach. Phys. Rev. E 58(2), 1425–1437 (1998)

[15] Wagner, P., Nagel, K., Wolf, D.E.: Realistic multi-lane traffic rules for cellular automata. Physica A 234(3-4), 687–698 (1997)

[16] Knorr, F., Zaksek, T., Brügmann, J., Schreckenberg, M.: Statistical Analysis of High-Flow Traffic States. In: Traffic and Granular Flow 2013 (2013) (to be published)

[17] Brügmann, J., Schreckenberg, M., Luther, W.: Real-Time Traffic Information System Using Microscopic Traffic Simulation. In: Al Begain, K., Al Dabass, D., Orsoni, A., Cant, R., Zobel, R. (eds.) EUROSIM 2013 – 8th EUROSIM Congress on Modelling and Simulation, pp. 448–453. IEEE (2013)

Interactions between Multiple Junctions

Takahiro Tannai[1] and Katsuhiro Nishinari[2]

[1] Department of Advanced Interdisciplinary Studies, School of Engineering,
The University of Tokyo, 4-6-1, Komaba, Meguro-ku, Tokyo 153-8904, Japan
`tannai@jamology.rcast.u-tokyo.ac.jp`
[2] Research Center for Advanced Science and Technology, The University of Tokyo,
4-6-1, Komaba, Meguro-ku, Tokyo 153-8904, Japan

Abstract. We consider a simple TASEP (Totally Asymmetric Simple Exclusion Process) network model with an aggregation point and a branching point. Generally speaking, the aggregation point behaves as a bottleneck and the branching point enables particles to encourage their velocity. However, the correlation among multiple junctions in TASEP network is not known so much. In order to investigate the correlation, we consider a simple TASEP network which including two junctions and discuss the network with an aggregation point and a branching point. From our theoretical analysis and numerical results, it is shown that aggregations become bottlenecks in TASEP networks and that branches enable flow of particles to be larger in many cases.

Keywords: TASEP network, interactions among multiple junctions, effects of junctions in TASEP network.

1 Introduction

Generally in many manufacturing factories, many robots or productions move on some determined networks and stop at the decided place in order to deal with given tasks. According to [1], [2], controls of motions of robots or productions in a manufacturing factory is usually discussed in the sense of optimization control theory or scheduling theory. There are many experimental investigations in both ways. When considering the effectivity of manufactures, either approach is not so useful in some cases, especially dynamic cases. In many approaches, it is assumed that the system is steady, so it is difficult to approach transient systems.

Considering either motions of robots or those of productions, we can regard those as the motions of 'self-driven' particles. Networks of particles in the manufacturing factory have junctions which are aggregations or branchings. It is known that congestions of particles occur at junctions espcially at aggregations and that the expansions of congestions worsen its effectivity. In order to approach the behavior of these particles in the network, we modeled the motions of robots in networks as a stochastic cellular automaton model called the totally asymmetric simple exclusion process (TASEP).

The asymmetric simple exclusion processes (ASEPs) are important physical models of self-driven particles used for research of non-equilibrium phenomena

J. Wąs, G.C. Sirakoulis, and S. Bandini (Eds.): ACRI 2014, LNCS 8751, pp. 630–639, 2014.

[3] and traffic dynamics [4], [5]. The same concept is discussed in biology [6] and mathematics [7]. The development of researches of ASEPs has now played a pivotal role widely in physics, chemistry and biology. ASEPs are one-dimensional stochastic models with discrete time of self-driven particles which move at a discrete lattice. In the model called 'TASEPs', a particle may move to only one direction in the lattice. We will assume that the particle move from left to right. If the left boundary is empty, a particle can enter with probability α. In the bulk, a particle can hop to the next cell with probability u only if the next cell of the particle is empty. When a particle is in the right boundary, it can exit with probability β.

The most important investigation of TASEPs with a double-chain aggregation are introduced by E. Pronina and A. B. Kolomeisky [8]. According to their paper, there are unexpected steady-states which do not occur in the single-chain TASEPs. TASEPs with a branching point where a single-chain lattice diverges into two lattice branches are studied by X. Wang et al [9].

In this paper, the correlation and the interaction between the two types of junctions: dual-input-single-output (aggregation) and dual-output-single-input (branching) are discussed.

2 Model Descriptions

In order to study the interdependence between a double-chain aggregation and a double-chain branching points, we use the discrete time, random update TASEPs connecting two junctions in the way of the figure 1. Let α_1, α_2 be two nonnegative parameters no more than $1/2$ and let p, s be two nonnegative parameters no more than 1. These four parameters are independent of time. A route named Route 1 is the upper route of the Figure 1 which has a branching point. Another route named Route 2 is the lower route of the Figure 1 which is parallel to Route 1 and is including an aggregation point.

In order to explain the model, we introduce some notations (see the figure 1). At first, we consider the steady state of the model because the model is considered to reach the steady state after enough long time passed when particles move. ρ_i is the time average of the density of site i. We also name two sites A and B, which are the aggregation point and the branching point. Near the branching point, the next site to B onto the segment Path is called the site P, and the next site to B on route 1 is called the site $B + 1$. On the other hand, near the merging point, the site just before A on the route 2 is $A - 1$ and the site just before A on the Path is Q.

  – basic rules :
    The model is based on the discrete time, random update TASEPs. We choose a cell randomly and the update obeys the following rules.
  – entrance rules :
    At the left boundaries of route 1 and route 2, with probability α_1, α_2, if the left site is vacant, a particle will enter.

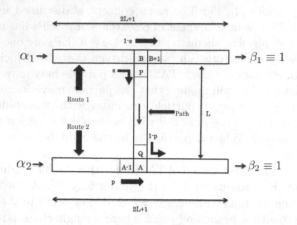

Fig. 1. The Routes of Motions of Particles

- exit rules :
  At the right boundaries of route 1 and route 2, with probability β_1, β_2, if the right site is occupied, a particle will exit. In this paper, we assume that $\beta_1 = \beta_2 = 1$.
- bulk hop rules except junctions :
  At the bulk of three lattices except junction cells, a particle will move to the next cell if the next cell is empty. The hopping probability is 1.
- aggregation rule :
  At the nearest two cells named $A - 1$ or Q, if the cell $A - 1$ is selected and the cell A is empty, then a particle at the cell $A - 1$ hops to the cell A with probability (abbreviated 'w.p.') p, and if the other cell Q is selected and the cell A is empty, then one hops to A w.p. $1 - p$.
- branching rule :
  A particle at the branching cell B hops to one nearest cell named $B + 1$ w.p. $1 - s$ if the upper route (of the figure 1) is chosen and the cell $B + 1$ is empty, or a particle at the cell B hops to the other nearest cell P w.p. s if the other route (of the figure 1) is chosen and the cell P is empty.

3   Theoretical Analysis

In the steady state, based on the mean-field approach similarly to Pronina and Kolomeisky [8], this model can be treated as the total system of separated five TASEP segments given in the figure 2.

We name these sublattices 1-bef, 1-af, 2-bef, 2-af and Path. (The word "af" stands for "after," and the word "bef" stands for "before.") These lattices are characterized as 10 parameters: entrance probabilities and exit probabilities (see the table 1). In the table, elements except $\alpha_1, \alpha_2, \beta_1, \beta_2, 1$ are 'effective probabilities' which means each lattice is looked at as an independent TASEP with these

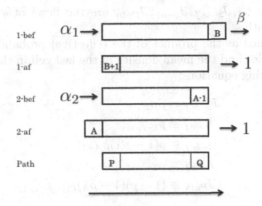

Fig. 2. Decomposition of the Routes of motions of particles : Particles enter from the left side and exit from the right side for each segments

input probabilities and output probabilities. The effective probability is the same concept as the 'effective rate' introduced in [8]. We have to define parameters as follows:

$$\beta \equiv (1 - s)(1 - \rho_{B+1}) + s(1 - \rho_P), \tag{1}$$
$$\alpha'' \equiv p\rho_{A-1} + (1 - p)\rho_Q = \rho_A. \tag{2}$$

According to the table 1 , check the fact that the sublattice 2-af is at Low Density (LD) phase (if $\alpha'' < 1/2$) or at Maximum Current (MC) phase (if $\alpha'' = 1/2$). In either case, the (time average) density of the 2-af is ρ_A.

Table 1. Input / Output Probabilities of Decomposed Segments

sublattice	input probability	output probability
1-bef	α_1	β
1-af	$(1 - s)\rho_B$	1
2-bef	α_2	$p(1 - \rho_A)$
2-af	α''	1
Path	$\alpha'(:= s\rho_B)$	$(1 - p)(1 - \rho_A)$

3.1   Flows of Decomposed Segments and Conservation Laws of Flows

Note that the flow conservation laws through two junction sites are satisfied at the steady state.

$$J_{1-bef} = J_{1-af} + J_{Path}, \tag{3}$$
$$J_{2-bef} + J_{Path} = J_{2-af}, \tag{4}$$

where $J_{1-bef}, J_{1-af}, J_{2-bef}, J_{2-af}, J_{Path}$ are the flows of sublattices 1-bef, 1-af, 2-bef, 2-af, Path.

The flow is defined as the product of the (effective) probability of exit from the considered lattice and the mean density of the last cell in the lattice, so it is given by the following equations:

$$J_{1-bef} \equiv \beta \rho_B, \tag{5}$$

$$J_{1-af} \equiv \rho_{1-last}, \tag{6}$$

$$J_{2-bef} \equiv p(1 - \rho_A)\rho_{A-1}, \tag{7}$$

$$J_{2-af} \equiv \rho_{2-last}, \tag{8}$$

$$J_{Path} \equiv (1 - p)(1 - \rho_A)\rho_Q. \tag{9}$$

where the cells called '1-last' and '2-last' are the right end cells of Route 1 and Route 2, respectively. This definition of flow is called 'throughput' in the scheduling theory and the queuing theory. This means the amount of products at time unit. Using the relations of the finite effects [10], this definition is equivalent to the usual definition of the flow of ASEPs. Thus, we can also write

$$J_{1-af} = (1 - s)\rho_B[1 - (1 - s)\rho_B], \tag{10}$$

$$J_{2-af} = \rho_A(1 - \rho_A). \tag{11}$$

3.2   The Behaviors of the System

In order to explain the behavior of the system, we introduce a notation (1-bef : (2-bef, Path)), for example, (HD : (HD, LD)) means that 1-bef is HD, 2-bef is HD and Path is LD. The phase 'HD' means the high density phase of ASEPs. All the cases of the model and the other segments are as follows: (Lately, we can show the fact that some of these do not exist.)

- (LD : (LD, LD))
- (LD : (HD, LD))
- (LD : (LD, HD))
- (LD : (HD, HD))
- (HD : (LD, LD)) : does not exist
- (HD : (HD, LD)) : does not exist
- (HD : (LD, HD))
- (HD : (HD, HD))

Firstly, we concentrate on the phases of two segments (2-bef and Path), and the following relations are satisfied by using the analogy of the phases of ASEPs. (We denote (2-bef, Path) as the phases of 2-bef, Path.)

1. (LD, LD) : $\alpha_2 < p(1 - \rho_A), \alpha' < (1 - p)(1 - \rho_A)$
2. (LD, HD) : $\alpha_2 < p(1 - \rho_A), \alpha' > (1 - p)(1 - \rho_A)$
3. (HD, LD) : $\alpha_2 > p(1 - \rho_A), \alpha' < (1 - p)(1 - \rho_A)$
4. (HD, HD) : $\alpha_2 > p(1 - \rho_A), \alpha' > (1 - p)(1 - \rho_A)$

Now, we will confirm the case 2 and the case 3 gives us a fact that $\alpha_2 + \alpha' > 1/2$. In the case 2, from the conditions that

$$\alpha_2 < p(1 - \rho_A) \, , \alpha' > (1 - p)(1 - \rho_A) \;\Rightarrow\; \rho_A < 1 - \frac{\alpha_2}{p} \, , \; \rho_A > 1 - \frac{\alpha'}{1 - p}, \quad (12)$$

we derive ρ_A as follows:

$$1 - \frac{\alpha'}{1 - p} < \rho_A < 1 - \frac{\alpha_2}{p}. \quad (13)$$

This inequality and the condition $\alpha' > (1 - p)(1 - \rho_A)$ give us a derivation of p,

$$p < \frac{\alpha_2}{\alpha_2 + \alpha'} \, , p > 1 - 2\alpha' \;\Rightarrow\; 1 - 2\alpha' < \frac{\alpha_2}{\alpha_2 + \alpha'}, \quad (14)$$

which gives us the fact $\alpha_2 + \alpha' > 1/2$. Similarly, in the case 3, from

$$\alpha_2 > p(1 - \rho_A) \, , \alpha' < (1 - p)(1 - \rho_A) \;\Rightarrow\; \rho_A \geq 1 - \frac{\alpha_2}{p} \, , \; \rho_A < 1 - \frac{\alpha'}{1 - p}, \quad (15)$$

we will show the facts that

$$1 - \frac{\alpha_2}{p} < \rho_A < 1 - \frac{\alpha'}{1 - p} \, , \; \frac{\alpha'}{\alpha_2 + \alpha'} < p < 2\alpha_2, \quad (16)$$

which also give us the fact $\alpha_2 + \alpha' > 1/2$.

From the case 4, we can easily show $\alpha_2 + \alpha' \geq 1/2$ since $\alpha_2 \geq p/2, \alpha' \geq (1 - p)/2$.

From these calculation, we can show the following parameter religions:

1. (LD, LD) : $\alpha_2 + \alpha' < \frac{1}{2}$
2. (LD, HD) : $\alpha_2 + \alpha' > \frac{1}{2}$, $\alpha' > \frac{1-p}{2}$
3. (HD, LD) : $\alpha_2 + \alpha' > \frac{1}{2}$, $\alpha_2 > \frac{p}{2}$
4. (HD, HD) : $\alpha_2 > \frac{p}{2}$, $\alpha' > \frac{1-p}{2}$

Also, co-existence lines are obviously shown as follows:

− (LD, LD) & (HD, LD) ($\alpha_2 + \alpha' = \frac{1}{2}$, $\alpha_2 > \frac{p}{2}$)
− (LD, LD) & (LD, HD) ($\alpha_2 + \alpha' = \frac{1}{2}$, $\alpha' > \frac{1-p}{2}$)
− (HD, LD) & (HD, HD) ($\alpha_2 > \frac{p}{2}$, $\alpha' = \frac{1-p}{2}$)
− (LD, HD) & (HD, HD) ($\alpha_2 = \frac{p}{2}$, $\alpha' > \frac{1-p}{2}$)
− (LD, LD) & (HD, LD) & (HD, LD) & (HD, HD) ($\alpha_2 = \frac{p}{2}$, $\alpha' = \frac{1-p}{2}$)

Secondly, using the flow conservation through the branching (3), it is obvious to show that if the Path is the LD phase, then the 1-bef segment is the LD phase. In this case, from (3),

$$\alpha_1(1 - \alpha_1) = (1 - s)\rho_B[1 - (1 - s)\rho_B] + s\rho_B(1 - s\rho_B), \quad (17)$$

$$\rho_B = \frac{1 - \sqrt{1 - 4[s^2 + (1 - s)^2]\alpha_1(1 - \alpha_1)}}{2[s^2 + (1 - s)^2]}. \quad (18)$$

From this, we calculate the output probability of 1-bef,

$$\beta = 1 - [s^2 + (1-s)^2]\rho_B \geq \frac{1}{2},\qquad(19)$$

and the equality is satisfied if and only if $s = 0, 1$.

If the Path is LD and LD/HD co-existence phase, α' is approximately equal to $s\alpha_1(1 - \alpha_1)$. From this approximation, we can define the value

$$s_* := \frac{1 - 2\alpha_2}{2\alpha_1(1 - \alpha_1)},\qquad(20)$$

(from $\alpha' \leq (1-p)/2$), and if $0 \leq s < s_*$, then the LD/LD phase from the above discussion.

Finally, It is need to check the co-existence of the phases LD and HD in the 1-bef. To find this critical value, for simplicity we assume that the density of the branching point approximately equals to the bulk density of the Path. If 1-bef is HD or LD/HD co-existence, from (1),

$$\beta = 1 - (1-s)\rho_B - s[1 - \frac{\rho_B(1 - \rho_B)}{s\rho_B}] = s(2-s)\frac{1+p}{2},\qquad(21)$$

Thus, from the fact that $\beta \leq \alpha_1$,

$$s \geq \frac{1 - 2\alpha_1 + \sqrt{(1 - 2\alpha_1)^2 + (1 - p^2)}}{2(1 - \alpha_1)}.\qquad(22)$$

This critical value is effective if and only if the Path is HD. We note that this critical value is a part of an ellipse in the $p - s$ Diagram 3, so we call the ellipse 'Critical Ellipse.' If $\alpha_1 = 0.5$, this ellipse is a circle.

Now, we summarize this calculation and this discussion as the following diagrams (see the figures 3 and 4). In the figure 4, the critical value is the case when $p = 0.6$ and $s = 0.8$. We call the (theoretical) critical line $2p + s = 2$ is the co-existence line of the two phases (LD, HD) and (HD, LD).

4   Numerical Simulations

In the numerical simulations, we set the model as each route is 101 cells and the length of the Path is 50 cells. Each junction cell is in the middle of each route as the figure 1. In order to observe the effects of the four parameters, we simplify the situation that $\alpha_1 = \alpha_2 = 1/2$. The figure 3 gives us an observation that the effect of changes of α_1 and α_2 is a similar effect of changes of p and s.

The numerical result shown in the figure 4 is the case when $\alpha_1 = \alpha_2 = 1/2$. We change two parameters p and s in order to illustrate the effect of the two junctions.

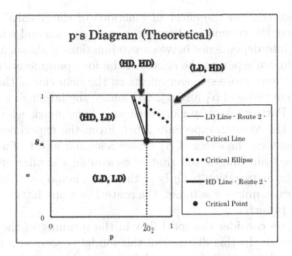

Fig. 3. The $p - s$ Diagram: General Case

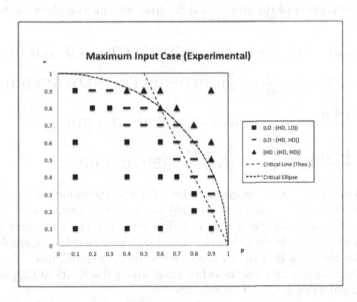

Fig. 4. The $p-s$ Diagram: The case when $\alpha_1 = \alpha_2 = 0.5$ (Comparison with Theoretical Results and Experimental Results). The critical line is an approximation and we will try to find more accurate curves as a future work.

5   Conclusions and Discussions

In this paper, we confirm the effect of junctions of the TASEP networks. We succeed to observe the correlation between an aggregation and a branching, and the effect of the interdependence between two junctions is shown at the behavior of the Path. Also, we separate the effects of the four parameters and those of p and s (mainly p) have more stronger effects on the behavior of the whole model and the Path than those of α_1 and α_2. Obviously, the larger p or s is, the lower the flow of the Path is. Also, p can serve as a benchmark which can predict the behavior of the route 2, especially 2-bef. From the experiment of changing two input parameters, the effect of α_1 brings a similar effect of a change of the parameter of the branching s and that of α_2 causes a similar effect of that of the priority of the aggregation p. Only in the case when $\alpha_2 = 0.5$, the (LD, LD) phase does not exist unless $s = 0$, i.e., the route 1 is a one-lattice TASEP which does not have a branch.

Additionally, we consider the total flow in the meaning of the total productivity of this system. In this discussion, this model is seen as a manufacturing system where products enter from the left side of this system and exit to the right side. The total productivity through this system is quantified as the total flow of this system.

$$J_{Total} := J_{1-af} + J_{2-af} = J_{1-bef} + J_{2-bef}. \tag{23}$$

Using the discussion of the theoretical analysis, we can calculate the total flow as follows:

$$J_{Total} = \alpha_1(1 - \alpha_1) + \alpha_2(1 - \alpha_2) \quad ((LD : (LD, LD))\text{or}(LD : (LD, HD))), \tag{24}$$

$$J_{Total} = \alpha_1(1 - \alpha_1) + \frac{p}{2}(1 - \frac{p}{2}) \quad ((LD : (HD, LD))\text{or}(LD : (HD, HD))), \tag{25}$$

$$J_{Total} = \frac{1+p}{2}(1 - \frac{1+p}{2}) + \alpha_2(1 - \alpha_2) \quad ((HD : (LD, HD))), \tag{26}$$

$$J_{Total} = \frac{1+p}{2}(1 - \frac{1+p}{2}) + \frac{p}{2}(1 - \frac{p}{2}) \quad ((HD : (HD, HD))). \tag{27}$$

The equation (23) is a decresing function of p and the equation (24) is an increasing functions of p. The equation (25) has a maximal value at $p = 1/2$ and is a decreasing function when $p > 1/2$. The fact that the total flow does not depend on s bring us the fact that the (LD, LD) phase enables the whole system to maximize the total flow in any case. Below the 'Critical Ellipse,' J_{Total} has a maximal value at $p = 2\alpha_2$, on the other hand, above the 'Critical Ellipse,' J_{Total} has a maximal value on the 'Critical Line.'

Acknowledgments. T.Tannai acknowleges the support of Graduate School of Engineering, The University of Tokyo, Doctoral Student Special Incentives Program (SEUT RA). We are grateful to the anonymous refrees for constructive comments, helpful suggestions, and informing us of the paper [16].

References

1. Conway, R.W., Maxwell, W.L., Miller, L.W.: Theory of Scheduling. Dover Publications, Inc., Minesota
2. Ghrist, R.: Configuration Spaces and Braid Groups on Graphs in Robotics. In: Braids, Links, and Mapping Class Groups: the Proceedings of Joan Birman's 70th Birthday. AMS/IP Studies in Mathematics, vol. 24, pp. 29–40 (2001)
3. Rajewsky, N., Santen, L., Schadschneider, A., Schreckenberg, M.: The Asymmetric Exclusion Process: Comparison of Update Procedures. Journal of Physics 92(1/2), 151–194 (1998)
4. Huang, D.-W.: Ramp-induced transitions in traffic dynamics. Physical Review E 73, 016123 (2006)
5. Huang, D.-W.: Analytical results of asymmetric exclusion processes with ramps. Physical Review E 72, 016102 (2005)
6. MacDonald, C.T., Gibbs, J.H.: Kinetics of Biopolymerization on Nucleic Acid Templates. Biopolymers 6, 1–25 (1968)
7. Spitzer, F.: Interaction of Markov Process. Advances in Mathematics 5, 246–290 (1970)
8. Pronina, E., Kolomeisky, A.B.: Theoretical investigation of totally asymmetric exclusion processes with on lattices with junctions. J. Stat. Mech., P07010 (2005)
9. Wang, X., Jiang, R., Hu, M.-B., Nishinari, K., Wu, Q.-S.: Totally Asymmetric Exclusion Process on Lattices with a Branching Point. International Journal of Modern Physics C 20(12), 1999–2012 (2009)
10. Derrida, B., Evans, M.R., Hakim, V., Pasquier, V.: Exact solution of a 1D asymmetric exclusion model using a matrix formulation. J. Phys. A: Math. Gen. 26, 1493–1517 (1993)
11. Wang, X., Jiang, R., Nishinari, K., Hu, M.-B., Wu, Q.-S.: Asymmetric Exclusion Processes on Lattices with a Junction: The Effect of Unequal Injection Rates. International Journal of Modern Physics C 20(6), 967–978 (2009)
12. Parmeggiani, A., Franosch, T., Frey, E.: The Totally Asymmetric Simple Exclusion Process with Langmuir Kinetics. Physical Review E 70, 046101 (2004)
13. Kolomeisky, A.B., Schütz, G.M., Kolomeisky, E.B., Straley, J.P.: Phase diagram of one-dimensional driven lattice gases with open boundaries. J. Phys. A: Math. Gen. 31, 6911–6919 (1998)
14. Embley, B., Parmeggiani, A., Kern, N.: Understanding Totally Asymmetric Simple-exclusion-process Transport on Networks: Generic Analysis via Effective Rates and Explicit Vertices. Physical Review E 80, 041128 (2009)
15. Raguin, A., Parmeggiani, A., Kern, N.: Role of Network Junctions for the Totally Asymmetric Simple Exclusion Process. Physical Review E 88, 042104 (2013)
16. Lebacque, J.-P.: First-order Macroscopic Traffic Flow Models: Intersection Modeling, Network Modeling. In: Mahmassani, H.S. (ed.) Transportation and Traffic Theory Flow, Dynamics, and Human Interaction, Proceeding of 16th International Symposium on Transportation and Traffic Theory, pp. 365–386 (2005)

Modeling Disruption and Recovery of Traffic in Road Networks

Lele Zhang and Timothy M. Garoni

School of Mathematical Sciences, Monash University, Victoria, Australia
{lele.zhang,tim.garoni}@monash.edu

Abstract. We study the impact of disruptions on traffic networks, and the relaxation of the system after the removal of the disruption. We model the steady-state density along the disrupted route using a simple phenomenological model. We then combine this model with domain wall theory to analyze the transient behavior of the system. We compare the predictions produced by these macroscopic models with simulations of a stochastic cellular automaton model.

Keywords: Cellular automata, traffic, network, domain wall theory.

1 Introduction

The study of the impact of traffic bottlenecks, or *defects*, on road network performance is of interest, within both traffic engineers and statistical physicists. *Slowdown* bottlenecks, such as ramps, slopes or bad weathers, have been rather extensively studied for one-dimensional systems such as freeway networks [1,4,5,11,12,15] and the asymmetric simple exclusion process (ASEP) [6,7,9]. In addition, bottlenecks caused by lane reductions, due to vehicle breakdown, illegal parking or road work for example, have been studied in [2,8,16]. Such studies have tended to focus on stationary, rather than transient behavior however.

In our previous work [17], we studied an extended domain wall (DW) model [10,14], in which multiple domain walls exist in the system simultaneously. We then used the extended DW model to study the transient behavior of traffic in both one-dimensional and two-dimensional road networks, subject to the imposition and subsequent removal of a lane-reduction defect. It was demonstrated that the macroscopic DW model could predict the transient behavior observed in simulations of a mesoscopic stochastic cellular automaton (CA).

For the two-dimensional system, the DW model requires as input the perturbed stationary density of each link along the route containing the defect. In [17], this input was obtained from simulations of the stationary state of the perturbed CA; i.e. the macroscopic model of the transient behavior required as input simulated results of the stationary behavior. In the current article, we instead introduce a simple phenomenological model, which we refer to as the *link model*, of the perturbed stationary densities. This model is proposed to study the defect-induced heterogeneity in density. As a result, the DW model can use the

J. Wąs, G.C. Sirakoulis, and S. Bandini (Eds.): ACRI 2014, LNCS 8751, pp. 640–649, 2014.
© Springer International Publishing Switzerland 2014

perturbed stationary densities obtained from the link model to reproduce the transient behavior of the defect route. We focus on two-dimensional networks, and find excellent agreement between the joint DW-link model and simulations of a stochastic CA.

2   Models

In this section, we briefly outline three distinct models: the NetNaSch model, the link model and the DW model. The NetNaSch model is a stochastic CA model of traffic networks. To model lane reduction defects using the NetNaSch model, we introduce a single defect cell on one lane of one link. The link model is introduced to describe the perturbed stationary state of the defect route. The DW model, which utilizes the results of the link model at perturbed stationarity, is then used to model the transient regime of the disruption and recovery processes.

2.1   CA Model

The NetNaSch model [3] is a stochastic CA model of traffic flow on arbitrary road networks. Each lane in the NetNaSch model is (a slight generalization of) the NaSch model [13]. In addition, the NetNaSch model prescribes simple rules of lane changing, and allows essentially any desired choice of rules (i.e. traffic signal system) to be applied to traffic traversing intersections. In the present study, we consider a regular 8×8 square grid, as shown in Fig. 1(a). Each adjacent pair of *nodes* (intersections) is connected by two oppositely-oriented directed *links* (roads). In turn, each such link consists of two main lanes, each consisting of 100 cells, plus an additional right-turning lane of 12 cells [1]. Along individual lanes, vehicles move according to the NaSch dynamics with maximum velocity $v_{max} = 3$ cells/sec and deceleration rate $p_{noise} = 0.5$. Vehicles are inserted with an input probability α at the upstream end of each *boundary inlink*. At the downstream end of each *boundary outlink*, a vehicle that wishes to leave the system is allowed to exit with an output probability β. The same values of α and β were applied to all boundary inlinks and outlinks respectively. The boundary links simply act as input/output buffers in the model, and are not considered part of the network for the purposes of measuring observables. Each link was assigned the same turning probability p_T for left and right turns, implying a probability $1 - 2p_T$ for continuing straight ahead. p_T was set to 0.05. Simulating the square-grid network shown in Fig. 1(a) using the NetNaSch model is easily within reach computationally (e.g. less than 10 mins (Processor 3.1 GHz, Intel Core i5, 4GB RAM) for simulating 6 hours of traffic.

We refer to the sequence of the seven adjacent east-bound links in the fifth row in Fig. 1(a) as the *defect route*. When the network has reached stationarity, a defect is inserted into a single cell in the middle of the left lane of the sixth link in the defect route, and is kept there for a duration of $D = 90$ mins. Vehicles

---

[1] As in Australia, vehicles drive on the left side of the road in our CA model.

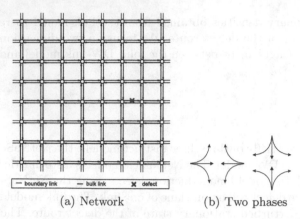

(a) Network   (b) Two phases

Fig. 1. (a) An 8 by 8 square-lattice network with a defect on an eastbound link. (b) Phases used at each node of the simulated network.

cannot move into or hop over the defect site. Simple lane changing rules are included in the model so that vehicles on the defect lane can navigate around the defect.

Our focus in the current article is to understand the stationary and transient behaviors of the flow and density along the defect route. On each link l along the defect route, we measured the density $\rho_l(t)$, which is the arithmetic mean of the cell density $\rho(i, t)$ over all cells i on link l, and flow $J_l(t)$, which is measured at a single point close to the start of link l.

The traffic signals used in the current study essentially correspond to a four-way stop intersection: each node alternately runs the two signal phases shown in Fig. 1(b), each for a single time step. For simplicity, we allow right-turners to filter through the opposing traffic during their green phase without giving way [2]. This system is an idealized model. It is designed to act as an intermediary between realistic signal systems and one dimensional systems. The capacity of such a system is close to that of a one-dimensional system, but its behavior is otherwise inherently two-dimensional.

2.2   Link Model

In this section we introduce an idealized model of the density on the links in a network, based on the flow transfer at each node. Let $F_{k\to l}$ be a function describing the flow from link k to l The dynamics on link l is given by

$$L\frac{d\rho_l}{dt} = \sum_{k \succ l} F_{k\to l} - \sum_{j \prec l} F_{l\to j},   \tag{1}$$

where $k \succ l$ and $j \prec l$ refer to links immediately upstream and downstream of link l respectively, and L denote the length of link l.

---

[2] This system corresponds to the *overpass* network studied in [17].

To understand the *flow transfer function* $F_{k\rightarrow l}$, we look at the flow transfer when the flow out of link k entirely moves into link l. Let $f_{k\rightarrow l}$ denote the flow transfer in this case. We consider a node as a type of buffer and view the process of a vehicle traversing a node as occurring in two stages. Firstly the vehicle arrives at the buffer from the approaching link k, and then it moves into the next link l. The probability that a vehicle arrives at the buffer is approximated by the bulk flow J_k of link k. Whether the vehicle can move into link l at this instant depends on its local density in the neighborhood of the given node, and the vehicle's speed. We find that the simple form $f_{k\rightarrow l} = J_k(1 - \rho_l)^2$ works well in practice. We note that the exponent 2 is approximately the average speed in free flow. From now on, we may write the function $f_{k\rightarrow l}$ as $f(J_k, \rho_l)$.

Let $p_{k\rightarrow l}$ be the turning probability from link k to l. If we assume that the flow from link k to l is independent of other flows out of link k, then $F_{k\rightarrow l} = p_{k\rightarrow l}f_{k\rightarrow l}$. In reality however, the flows are dependent. Consider for example a three-way intersection with inlink k and outlinks l and s and assume $\rho_l \geq \rho_s$. If $\rho_l = 1$ so that $F_{k\rightarrow l} = 0$, then $F_{k\rightarrow s}$ will eventually reduce to zero, since vehicles that wish to move into link s are blocked by those that wish to move into link l (but cannot). More generally, if $\rho_l \gg \rho_s$, then this effect of vehicles wishing to turn into link s being blocked by vehicles wishing to turn into link l will constitute the dominant bottleneck for the flow leaving link k. It follows that $F_{k\rightarrow l} \in p_{k\rightarrow l}[\min\{f_{k\rightarrow s}, f_{k\rightarrow l}\}, f_{k\rightarrow l}]$ and $F_{k\rightarrow s} \in p_{k\rightarrow l}[\min\{f_{k\rightarrow s}, f_{k\rightarrow l}\}, f_{k\rightarrow s}]$. Since $\rho_l \geq \rho_s$, $F_{k\rightarrow l} = p_{k\rightarrow l}f_{k\rightarrow l}$. On the other hand, for link s, when $p_{k\rightarrow s} \gg p_{k\rightarrow l}$, we approximate $F_{k\rightarrow s}$ by $p_{k\rightarrow s}f_{k\rightarrow s}$, and approximate $F_{k\rightarrow s}$ by $p_{k\rightarrow s}f_{k\rightarrow l}$ when $p_{k\rightarrow s} \ll p_{k\rightarrow l}$.

The link model (and the above choice of flow transfer function) rely on an important assumption, which is that the density and flow along each link are homogeneous. In the presence of traffic signals, particularly in transient regimes, this assumption may break down. For example, if the upstream link is initially at the jamming density ρ_j, then $J_k = 0$ and consequently $F_{k\rightarrow l} = 0$. In reality however, the flow on link l is non-zero if $\rho_l < \rho_j$, and may even be very large if ρ_l is small. The reason is that the flow close to the downstream end of link k can be rather different from the bulk link flow J_k of link k. Nevertheless, as we will see, the link model provides quite a good approximation of stationary behavior for relatively homogeneous links.

2.3 Domain Wall Model

Domain walls are shocks separating two regions of different density. We assume the width of such shocks is small compared to the system size, and so we can consider the position of the domain wall to be localized to the boundary between cells. The motion of such a domain wall $W_{l|r}$, separating states with density and flow (ρ_l, J_l) to its left and (ρ_r, J_r) to its right, is described by a simple biased random walk with hopping rates $R_l = \frac{J_l}{\rho_r - \rho_l}$, and $R_r = \frac{J_r}{\rho_r - \rho_l}$, for moves to the left and right, respectively.

In the disruption and recovery processes for two-dimensional networks, we allow the possibility of multiple domain walls coexisting in the system simul-

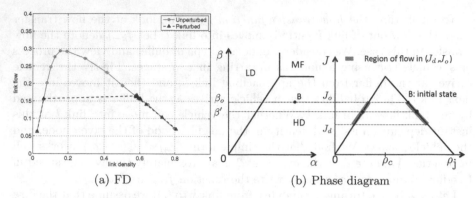

(a) FD   (b) Phase diagram

Fig. 2. (a) Unperturbed and perturbed FD for the link immediately upstream of the defect in the OP network. Simulated data is taken from [17]. (b) Phase diagram and FD for the boundary outlink in the downstream subsystem.

taneously. We assume that the dynamics of each wall is independent of all the other walls, unless two walls choose to move to the same site. In such a case the two walls immediately merge to form a single wall.

3 Simulation

In this section, we begin by recalling the impact of the disruption on the fundamental diagram (FD), and then compare the perturbed stationary state predicted by the link model with the CA simulation results. We then apply the link model as input to the DW model in order to study the transient behavior.

3.1 Stationary State

Fundamental Diagram
It is easy to see that for a one-dimensional system of capacity J_c, as discussed in [17], the introduction of a lane reduction defect reduces the capacity to some value $J_d < J_c$. If the initial flow J_o prior to the imposition of the defect is smaller than J_d, then the defect has no impact on the density or flow of the system. Otherwise, the flow drops to J_d, and the defect induces phase separation. Let ρ_r and $\rho_\neg$ be the unique densities satisfying $J(\rho_r) = J_d = J(\rho_\neg)$ with respect to the unperturbed FD, where $\rho_r < \rho_c < \rho_\neg$, and ρ_c is the critical density at which the unperturbed system obtains maximum flow J_c. In the presence of the defect, the upstream region becomes congested and has density $\rho_\neg$, whereas the downstream region becomes free-flow and has density ρ_r. The resulting perturbed FD has a trapezoidal shape, in contrast to the triangular unperturbed FD.

The above argument is also generally applicable to the defect route in a two-dimensional network. Fig. 2 shows the unperturbed and perturbed FDs for the link immediately upstream of the defect in the network shown in Fig. 1(a). The two-dimensional network is more complicated however since links along the defect routes have different densities at perturbed stationarity, due to the external inflow from and outflow to side streets of the defect route. Such heterogeneity was studied via CA simulation in [17]. In the current article, we use the link model to predict the densities of the links in the defect route.

Density Heterogeneity at Perturbed Stationarity

We first simplify the link model by making two reasonable assumptions. i) The network is homogenous prior to the disruption. I.e., $\rho_l = \rho_k$ for all l, k. ii) Since $p_T \ll 1$, the states of the side streets adjacent to the defect route are not affected by the disruption. Thus, $\rho_s = \rho_o$ and $J_s = J_o$ for all side streets s, where ρ_o and J_o are the initial density and flow.

During the disruption process, the defect partitions the defect route into two subsystems, and also divides the defect link into two parts. Let links $l-1$, l and $l+1$ be consecutive links along the defect route with $l-1$ upstream of l, and l upstream of $l+1$. Following Eq. (1), the dynamics on link l is given by

$$L \frac{d\rho_l}{dt} = F_{s \to l} + F_{l-1 \to l} - F_{l \to l+1} - F_{l \to s}$$

$$= \begin{cases} 2p_T f(J_o, \rho_l) + (1 - 2p_T) f(J_{l-1}, \rho_l) - f(J_l, \rho_{l+1}) & \text{upstream sub-sys;} \\ 2p_T f(J_o, \rho_l) + (1 - 2p_T) f(J_{l-1}, \rho_l) \\ \quad -(1 - 2p_T) f(J_l, \rho_{l+1}) - 2p_T f(J_l, \rho_o) & \text{downstream sub-sys.} \end{cases}$$

Note that we are employing a slight abuse of notation here in writing $F_{s \to l}$ and $F_{l \to s}$, in that s does not refer to a specific link, but any generic side street, all of which we are considering to be identical. We note that, for the upstream subsystem, flow $F_{l \to s}$ was set to $2p_T f_{l \to l+1}$, because $2p_T \ll 1 - 2p_T$ and $\rho_o < \rho_{l+1}$.

For the upstream subsystem, the upstream part of the defect link plays the role of the boundary outlink with a constant density $\rho_\neg$. On the other hand, since the inflow rate is constant, we assume that the boundary inlink has a constant flow J_o [3]. Initially, each link l is in the initial stationary state with $\rho_l(0) = \rho_o$. Were the defect to remain indefinitely, each link would eventually relax to a perturbed stationary state, whose density would in general differ from ρ_o.

For the downstream subsystem, the downstream part of the defect link acts as the boundary inlink with a constant flow $J(\rho_\neg)$. Let ρ_o' be the density satisfying $J(\rho_o') = J_o$ with $\rho_o' \leq \rho_c$. The density of the boundary outlink will be ρ_o'. Unless the network is initially at high density, we have $\rho_o' = \rho_o$. For the network initially at high density, a simple argument explains why $\rho_o' < \rho_c$ at perturbed stationarity. Firstly, we note that the defect link provides a flow of J_d, and the side streets can provide flows not greater than J_o because the majority of their traffic goes to congested links and the turning probability to the defect route is very low. Thus, the perturbed flow of the boundary outlink lies in (J_d, J_o).

---

[3] The upstream subsystem consists of five bulk links. The constant inflow may result in very high density for the boundary inlink, which may cause a significant difference in the bulk flow and the flow at the approaching side of the node. As mentioned in Subsection 2.2, this could reduce the accuracy of the link model. We therefore put the upstream subsystem into a larger system consisting of eight bulk links with the same boundary inlink and outlink settings as described above and took the results for the most downstream five links.

Table 1. Comparison of the link density and flow in the perturbed stationary state between the simulated results $\bar{\rho}_l, \bar{J}_l$ and the analytical solutions ρ_l, J_l produced by the link model for the 8 by 8 network shown in Fig. 1(a)

link	MC($\alpha = 0.6, \beta = 0.9$)		LD($\alpha = 0.25, \beta = 0.9$)		HD($\alpha = 0.6, \beta = 0.3$)	
	$\bar{\rho}_l$	ρ_l	$\bar{\rho}_l$	ρ_l	$\bar{\rho}_l$	ρ_l
1	0.6705 ± 0.0058	0.658	0.6291 ± 0.0069	0.629	0.5970 ± 0.0072	0.604
2	0.6504 ± 0.0046	0.631	0.6191 ± 0.0059	0.614	0.5917 ± 0.0073	0.598
3	0.6271 ± 0.0068	0.625	0.6024 ± 0.0048	0.609	0.5897 ± 0.0067	0.595
4	0.6086 ± 0.0064	0.609	0.5957 ± 0.0050	0.600	0.5738 ± 0.0048	0.591
5	0.5997 ± 0.0036	0.598	0.5824 ± 0.0054	0.593	0.5833 ± 0.0046	0.588
6*	0.3151 ± 0.0015	0.323	0.3170 ± 0.0015	0.323	0.3176 ± 0.0014	0.323
7	0.0703 ± 0.0009	0.069	0.0687 ± 0.0008	0.065	0.0696 ± 0.0010	0.066
link	$\bar{J}_l$	J_l	$\bar{J}_l$	J_l	$\bar{J}_l$	J_l
1	0.1265 ± 0.0031	0.134	0.1443 ± 0.0030	0.146	0.1578 ± 0.0039	0.155
2	0.1318 ± 0.0020	0.145	0.1482 ± 0.0029	0.151	0.1597 ± 0.0037	0.157
3	0.1451 ± 0.0033	0.147	0.1535 ± 0.0029	0.153	0.1591 ± 0.0034	0.158
4	0.1523 ± 0.0026	0.153	0.1558 ± 0.0031	0.156	0.1680 ± 0.0029	0.159
5	0.1587 ± 0.0023	0.157	0.1617 ± 0.0027	0.159	0.1642 ± 0.0023	0.160
6	0.1689 ± 0.0015	0.161	0.1652 ± 0.0018	0.161	0.1653 ± 0.0014	0.161
7	0.1754 ± 0.0021	0.174	0.1726 ± 0.0019	0.167	0.1706 ± 0.0018	0.168

*: Defect link: The defect is placed in the middle of the link. Thus, the upstream and downstream parts of the defect link have densities $\rho_\neg$ and $\rho_\vdash$ respectively, implying its mean density is $(\rho_\vdash + \rho_\neg)/2$.

Secondly, as illustrated in Fig. 2(b), since β_o that produces J_o is greater than the outflow rate β' that produces a flow in (J_d, J_o), the perturbed state of the outlink must be determined by the inflow rate, and, therefore, is in low density. Then the perturbed stationary density for bulk links can be obtained in the same way as we have described for the upstream system.

We simulated the NetNaSch model for the network shown in Fig. 1(a) in three different regimes: maximum current (MC), low density (LD) and high density (HD) with $(\alpha, \beta) = (0.6, 0.9), (0.25, 0.9)$ and $(0.6, 0.3)$ respectively, for all of which $J_o > J_d$. Table 1 compares the simulation results for links in the perturbed stationary state with the results obtained by the link model. The link model is capable of reproducing the density heterogeneity in the upstream (downstream) subsystem of the defect route. The predictions by the link model are in a good agreement with the CA simulation results.

3.2   Transient Regime

Disruption and Recovery Processes
The detailed analysis of the domain wall motion along the defect route during the disruption and recovery processes has been given in [17]. We now briefly describe the processes. During the disruption process, introducing the defect induces a high-density region in the subsystem upstream of the defect. The traffic state of this region is link dependent, and thus we denote it as C_l for link l. It follows that

a domain wall $W_{\mathcal{U}_l|\mathcal{C}_l}$ forms, separating $\mathcal{C}_l$ and the initial density region, $\mathcal{U}_l$, of link l and drifts upstream. Conversely, the defect causes a low-density region $\mathcal{F}_l$ in the downstream subsystem. A domain wall $W_{\mathcal{F}_l|\mathcal{U}_l}$ forms and drifts downstream. The defect route has reached the perturbed stationary state when both of the walls have arrived at the boundaries, where they then remain localized.

During the recovery process, the removal of the defect induces a maximum-flow region $\mathcal{M}_l$, which expands via the motion of two domain walls, $W_{\mathcal{C}_l|\mathcal{M}_l}$ and $W_{\mathcal{M}_l|\mathcal{F}_l}$, which drift upstream and downstream respectively. When $W_{\mathcal{U}_l|\mathcal{C}_l}$ and $W_{\mathcal{C}_l|\mathcal{M}_l}$ ($W_{\mathcal{M}_l|\mathcal{F}_l}$ and $W_{\mathcal{F}_l|\mathcal{U}_l}$) meet, they merge to form $W_{\mathcal{U}_l|\mathcal{M}_l}$ ($W_{\mathcal{M}_l|\mathcal{U}_l}$) provided that $\mathcal{U}_l \neq \mathcal{M}_l$. The defect route returns to the initial stationary state when $W_{\mathcal{U}_l|\mathcal{M}_l}$ and $W_{\mathcal{M}_l|\mathcal{U}_l}$ merge.

The traffic state of $\mathcal{U}_l$ is the unperturbed stationary state of link l, whereas the traffic states of $\mathcal{C}_l$ and $\mathcal{F}_l$ are the perturbed stationary state. By definition, $\rho_{\mathcal{U}_l} = \rho_o$ and $J_{\mathcal{U}_l} = J_o$ for all l. Because the FD is unimodal, as shown in Fig. 2, the maximum flow regime $\mathcal{M}_l$ is the same for all links. The density $\rho_{\mathcal{C}_l}$ and flow $J_{\mathcal{C}_l}$ (or $\rho_{\mathcal{F}_l}$ and $J_{\mathcal{F}_l}$) correspond to the perturbed stationary density ρ_l and flow J_l listed in Table. 1. We note that, for the defect link, the densities of the upstream and downstream parts need to be considered separately.

Comparison of Analytical and Simulation Results

Fig. 3 compares the results derived from the DW model with the numerical results from the simulation of the NetNaSch model in various initial regimes. Figs. 3(a)-(b) show the link observables for links upstream of the defect, when the system was initially at MC. The link-dependent time translation in Figs. 3(a)-(b) is the same as that used in [17]. Figs. 3(c)-(e) show the route-aggregated observables at MC, LD and HD. We observe that the DW results are in a good agreement with the CA simulations. This is not surprising given that the link model has provided a good approximation of the perturbed stationary density and flow for each individual link along the defect route.

4   Discussion

In this paper, we have extended our previous study [17] of the impact of a lane-reduction defect on two-dimensional traffic networks by introducing the link model to predict the perturbed stationary state for each link along the defect route. We compared the link model predictions with the numerical results of CA simulations and found good agreement. We then combined the link model results with the extended DW model to predict the transient behavior of the defect route, due to the imposition and subsequent removal of the defect. Again, the DW predictions and the CA simulations show a good agreement.

The link model presented here should be considered a prototype, and the results presented in this paper are preliminary. The flow transfer function, which is a key component of the link model, assumes a homogeneous density distribution within each link. For realistic traffic signal systems, the density heterogeneity will in general be non-negligible. In addition, how flows from one source (upstream link) into multiple sinks (downstream links) interfere with each other requires

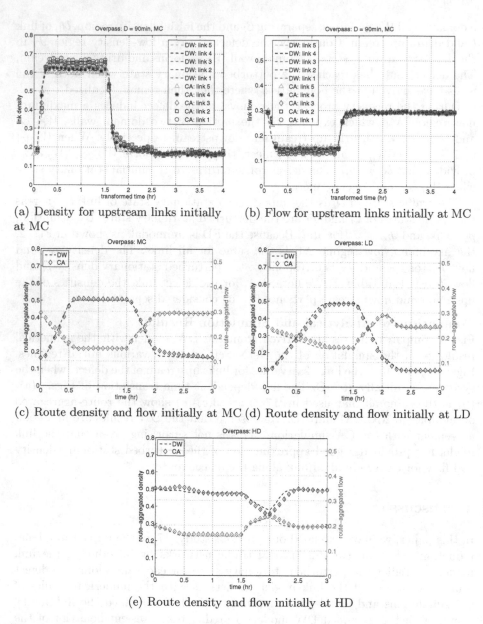

(a) Density for upstream links initially at MC

(b) Flow for upstream links initially at MC

(c) Route density and flow initially at MC (d) Route density and flow initially at LD

(e) Route density and flow initially at HD

Fig. 3. Comparison of density and flow derived from the DW-link model with CA simulations in various initial states. Error bars corresponding to one standard deviation are shown but usually smaller than symbol sizes. Simulation data here is taken from [17]. The DW-link results are similar to those DW-CA results presented in [17] since the link model predictions of the perturbed states for the links along the defect route are in good agreement with the numerical results.

further investigation. It remains a challenge to improve the flow transfer function and the link model in order to provide qualitative and quantitative predictions for networks with realistic signal systems.

References

1. Diedrich, G., Santen, L., Schadschneider, A., Zittartz, J.: Effects of on- and off-ramps in cellular automata models for traffic flow. International Journal of Modern Physics C 11(3), 519–529 (2002)
2. Ebersbach, A., Schneider, J.J.: Two-lane traffic with places of obstruction to traffic. International Journal of Modern Physics C 15, 535–544 (2004)
3. de Gier, J., Garoni, T.M., Rojas, O.: Traffic flow on realistic road networks with adaptive traffic lights. Journal of Statistical Mechanics: Theory and Experiment 2011, P04008 (2011)
4. Hanaura, H., Nagatani, T., Tanaka, K.: Jam formation in traffic flow on a highway with some slowdown sections. Physica A: Statistical Mechanics and its Applications 374, 419–430 (2007)
5. Ishibashi, Y., Fukui, M.: The bottleneck effect on high-speed car traffic. Journal of the Physical Society of Japan 70, 1237–1239 (2001)
6. Janowsky, S.A., Lebowitz, J.L.: Finite-size effects and shock fluctuations in the asymmetric simple-exclusion process. Physical Review A 45, 618–625 (1992)
7. Janowsky, S.A., Lebowitz, J.L.: Exact results for the asymmetric simple exclusion process with a blockage. Journal of Statistical Physics 77, 35–51 (1994)
8. Jia, B., Jiang, R., Wu, Q.S.: The traffic bottleneck effects caused by the lane closing in the cellular automata model. International Journal of Modern Physics C 14, 1295–1303 (2003)
9. Kolomeisky, A.B.: Asymmetric simple exclusion model with local inhomogeneity. Journal of Physics A: Mathematical and General 31, 1153–1164 (1998)
10. Kolomeisky, A.B., Schutz, G.M., Kolomeisky, E.B., Straley, J.P.: Phase diagram of one-dimensional driven lattice gases with open boundaries. Journal of Physics A: Mathematical and General 31, 6911–6919 (1998)
11. Komada, K., Masukura, S., Nagatani, T.: Effect of gravitational force upon traffic flow with gradients. Physica A 388, 2880–2894 (2009)
12. Nagai, R., Hanaura, H., Tanaka, K., Nagatani, T.: Discontinuity at edge of traffic jam induced by slowdown. Physica A: Statistical Mechanics and its Applications 364, 464–472 (2006)
13. Nagel, K., Schreckenberg, M.: A cellular automaton model for freeway traffic. Journal de Physique I 2, 2221–2229 (1992)
14. Santen, L., Appert, C.: The asymmetric exclusion process revisited: Fluctuations and dynamics in the domain wall picture. Journal of Statistical Physics 106, 187–199 (2002)
15. Tanaka, K., Nagai, R., Nagatani, T.: Traffic jam and discontinuity induced by slowdown in two-stage optimal-velocity model. Physica A: Statistical Mechanics and its Applications 370, 756–768 (2006)
16. Zhang, J., Li, X., Wang, R., Sun, X., Cui, X.: Traffic bottleneck characteristics caused by the reduction of lanes in an optimal velocity model. Physica A 391, 2381–2389 (2012)
17. Zhang, L., de Gier, J., Garoni, T.M.: Traffic disruption and recovery in road networks. Physica A: Statistical Mechanics and its Applications 401, 82–102 (2014)

Simulation of Pedestrians Behavior
in a Shopping Mall

Paweł Kłeczek and Jarosław Wąs

AGH University of Science and Technology
al. Mickiewicza 30, 30-059 Kraków, Poland
pkleczek@student.agh.edu.pl, jarek@agh.edu.pl
http://www.agh.edu.pl/en

Abstract. The knowledge of phenomena connected with pedestrian movement and behavior is important in retail and service sectors. Such a belief finds confirmation in numerous researches, which proved true a strong relationship between shops' profitability and the way customers move inside them. The goal of the article is to work out a model of pedestrian behavior in a shopping mall based on a multi-agent approach on the basis of some already-existing successful solutions, namely we combine PED4 and Social Distances algorithms into one simulation framework.

1 Introduction

The significance of the issue of simulating pedestrian movement and behavior in shopping areas was confirmed in numerous projects. One of the best known approaches in this area is a research conducted by Aloys Borges and Harry Timmermans [1]). They proved a strong relationship between shops' profitability and the way customers move inside them. This problem is quite complex and may be considered on different levels of abstraction depending on the purpose of the developed model. Decision-making issue in shopping behaviors was also addressed by Dijkstra, Timmermans and de Vries in [2]. Agent approach to pedestrian modeling was described in [3] and recently in [12], while interactions between agents in high densities was addressed by Bandini, Mondini and Vizzari in [4].

The goal of our project is to work out a model of pedestrian behavior in a shopping mall (based on *Galeria Krakowska* - a shopping arcade in Krakow) and to create a computer simulation. The area of a shopping mall is relatively small thus it is necessary to consider movement of a single pedestrian on microscopic level. To match the scale of the studied phenomenon the model was based on a multi-agent approach and all decisions are taken in different phases: strategic, tactical and operational. Similar approach, however using only tactical and operational approach, has been used by Rauh, Schenk and Schödl in [5].

J. Wąs, G.C. Sirakoulis, and S. Bandini (Eds.): ACRI 2014, LNCS 8751, pp. 650–659, 2014.

2   The Proposed Model of a Shopping Mall

2.1   Agents

Agents are described by parameters affecting their movement in the operational phase such as: maximal number of potential POIs to be used in one simulation cycle, tendency to swap with other agents, current position and orientation etc. Some of these parameters describe agents behavior, rather than their state and their values are initialized using special configuration lists. Those lists contains general characterization of some of client archetypes which may be observed in a mall such as a *adolescent* (a person who tend to move quickly), an *aged person* (who generally prefers a slow walk) and many other groups and subgroups.

2.2   Mall's Topology

The model of a shopping mall consists of maps of both its layout (i.e. the arrangement of obstacles like walls, benches etc. and the arrangement of movement algorithms applied to different regions of a mall, Fig. 1), as well as locations of special areas which, in an active way, influence the pedestrians' behavior (Fig. 2). The latter items are *attractors*, *queues* and *waiting areas*. They help simulate of such behaviors as *grouping* or *queuing* through modifications of the default movement algorithm of the tactical phase.

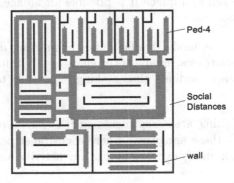

Fig. 1. A sample layout of rooms and combination of different movement algorithms in a hypothetical mall

Although this research is limited to one-storey malls, the presented solution is scalable. Multi-storey building may be treated as a set of independent simulations interconnected only with entrance and exit fields.

Attractors. Attractors are objects or phenomenons which attract clients attention thus causing a *crowding* effect (eg. shop windows, stalls, information desks). They originate a spherical gradient field which influences agents' behavior. Attractors vary in type and different types attract different kind of agents

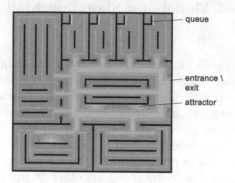

Fig. 2. A sample map of special features in a hypothetical mall

what reflects differences in preferences of customers visiting a mall. To simplify computations the actual superposed value of the attraction is precomputed for every cell.

Queues. Queues model the *strict queuing* effect which may be observed for instance by the counter or on escalators. Such a behavior does not arise from the basic movement model thus needs to be handled explicitly. A queue can be regarded as a stretch of attractors which influence agents so intensively that after stepping on one cell of a queue it is possible for an agent only to move on another cell of a queue.

Passages. Passage areas model traffic routes connecting different parts of a mall, i.e. accesses to staircases, escalators or elevators. Within passages distance preferences of agents are modified thus making it possible to reduce distances between agents.

Waiting Areas. Waiting areas represents such elements of a shopping mall as benches or tables - these are places where a customer perch for a moment. They simply hold back an agent from taking any activity for a certain number of simulation cycles.

3   Pedestrian Movement

In order to organize the structure of the simulation, we have divided agent's decision-making process into three phases: strategic, tactical and operational. Agent's activities regarding decision-making process are presented in Fig. 3 and it is inpired by former works by authors [8,9].

3.1   Strategic Phase

Strategic phase of agent's movement concerns selection of final POI and/or intermediate POI from a set of available POIs. Generally, the aim of the strategic

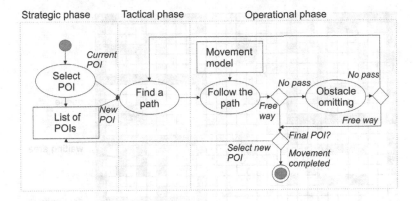

Fig. 3. Activity diagram of movement phases

phase is to reflect the general intentions of every client (represented as an agent) regarding their visit in a shopping mall.

Choice of POIs. Firstly, a number of POIs are picked and sorted so that the total length of a path connecting them is minimized. This approach allows to describe various pedestrian behaviors on a local level.

3.2 Tactical Phase

The purpose of a tactical phase is to determine a path leading from one destination to another. In this phase only the layout of a mall (including a map of special areas) is taken into account, factors like position of other agents (even if they block a corridor) are passed over (Fig. 4).

Routes Finding. In order to determine routes leading to destination points the A* algorithm has been applied. It is a complete algorithm, meaning it always finds an optimal solution. A* makes use of a heuristic which speeds up the process of cost estimation by examining only the most promising path's vertices. Depending on the heuristic used, A* is able to find either optimal or suboptimal paths. As in the real world a pedestrian is seldom able to accurately determine the real "cost" of a path, a complex admissible heuristic has been applied in this model. It results in finding sub-optimal solutions.

Deviation of Paths. The deviation of path takes place during the search for a (sub)optimal path in order to facilitate the happening of certain effects such as attraction. The deviation was achieved by modification of the A* heuristic - every cell on a map of distribution of special areas has two values associated with it: *attraction* and *hold time*.

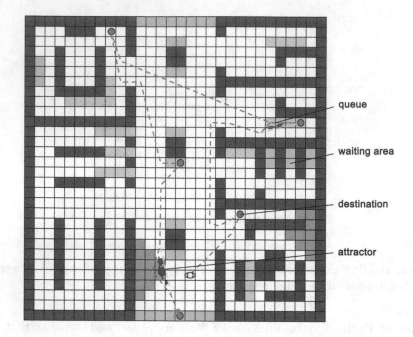

Fig. 4. Scope of application of the strategic and tactical phases

The *attraction* parameter is responsible for attracting agents to certain areas of a mall. A* heuristic multiplies the cost of a path by this value to encourage agents to enter such areas of interest.

Additionally, the heuristic is burdened with weight $\epsilon = 5$ which allows to quickly generate paths of the given cost (i.e. such a cost which does not exceeds ϵ-times the cost of an optimal path).

Intermediate Destinations. The tactical phase ends with choosing a certain (small) number of indirect points which lie on the outlined path - they serve as beacons for an agent to help him find the right way.

3.3 Operational Phase

In the operational phase for each agent a decision about his further movement is taken based on information from his local neighborhood (Fig. 5). In particular various possibilities of collision avoidance (with other agents and obstacles) are considered (to achieve this *Ped-4* and *Social Distances* algorithms are used) and various behaviors are taken into account (such as grouping, flocking and path following).

The operational phase consists of four stages (repeatedly executed):

1. For each agent check if he/she reached the current destination. If so, then assign a next destination or (if it was the final destination and no new destinations is available) enter a "wander about" mode.
2. Agents setup (set variables used by movement algorithms).
3. Compute available movement points (based on both personal conditioning and environmental factors).
4. Perform the movement of agents.

A destination can be reached either by stepping on a destination cell or by stepping on a cell in the neighborhood of the destination cell. In the latter case the likelihood of acknowledging the movement as destination-reaching is inversely proportional to the distance to the actual destination cell.

In the movement stage agents are examined cyclically. In one cycle each agent may take only one action such as *wait* or *move one field forward*. This approach ensures equal opportunities for all agents, i.e. no agent is biased in favor in the process of accessing cells.

3.4   Ped-4

The *Ped-4* algorithm [6], which is an extension of a bi-directional model by Blue and Adler [10], describes well the movement of people in alleys and corridors as it facilitates the formation of pedestrian flows into lanes.

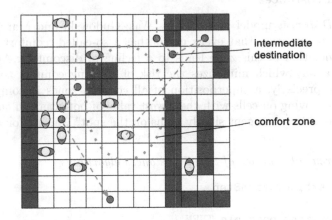

Fig. 5. Scope of application of the operational phase

The *Ped-4* algorithm consists of the following stages:

1. **Adjustment of movement direction** - when the angle between current movement direction and the direction to target exceeds a threshold an agent turns towards the target.

2. **Change of a lane** - numbers of free cells on the currently occupied and adjacent lanes are counted. An agent will occupy this lane which at the moment allows him to cover the maximal distance. The current lane is the preferred one. In case the currently occupied lane is not free (i.e. another agent is approaching from the opposite direction) to avoid a collision an agent tries to "hide" behind another agent which already heads in the same direction but on an adjacent lane.

3. **Step forward** - in case the cell directly in front of an agent (i.e. according to his movement direction) is free he makes an attempt to take it. If not then a swap with the blocking agent is feasible. Such a swap illustrates a situation when pedestrians twist their torsos to squeeze past one another. The *step forward* stage is repeated multiple times until all agents use up their movement points.

Different swap types occur with different likelihood, the preferred order is:

1. between agents on the same lane walking in opposite directions
2. between agents on adjacent lanes walking in opposite directions
3. between agents walking in perpendicular directions

A pedestrian may make a swap only if his swap-counterpart has not moved yet. If a swap of the first type will not take place, the next one from the list is examined (in a crowd people are more willing to squeeze past others).

3.5 Social Distances

The *Social Distances* model proposed by Was, Gudowski and Matuszyk [7] is based on an observation that every person has a so-called "comfort zone" and that every violation of this zone leads to a feeling of discomfort. Agents tend to move in a way which minimizes the risk of entering comfort zones of the others. More precisely, a superposition of all comfort zones is computed and agents prefer moving on cells with the lowest value of potential. In case none of adjacent cells is free an agent simply "runs on the spot" waiting for any cell to vacate.

Forward movement routines of Social Distances algorithms

```
PROCEDURE nextIterationStep
BEGIN
    IF no movement possible THEN
        turn agent;      // it allows to examine new possibilities
                         // in next iteration
    ELSE
        target := determine_cell_with_highest_potential();
        move agent to the target cell;
        reflect the movement direction by adjusting the
            agent's rotation;
END
```

```
FUNCTION determine_cell_with_highest_potential
BEGIN
    available_fields := determine_available_fields()
    FOR each available field DO
        take into account overlapping potential fields of other
            agents and distance to target;

    IF agent is tired THEN
        increase potential of the field which lies closest to
            the target;

    RETURN fields with highest potential and closest to target;
END

FUNCTION determine_available_fields
BEGIN
    agent_cells := cells in von Neumann neighborhood lying in
        the hemisphere determined by agent's orientation;
    target_cells := cells in von Neumann neighborhood lying in
        the hemisphere determined by direction to target;
    RETURN cells which are both in agent_ and target_cells sets;
END
```

The *determine_ available_ fields* function restricts possible movements to either proceeding along the same path or turning towards the destination point.

The potential of a field is computed as a superposition of "comfort zones" of other agents (negative components) and distance of a cell to the destination (positive component). When an agent tries to reach one destination for too long (i.e. the distance covered so far significantly exceeds the minimal distance needed to reach the next destination) it tends to stop paying too much attention to other agents on his path – this effect was modeled by adding an extra positive value of potential to the cell which lies closest to the destination.

4   Simulation and Analysis of Results

In tests a map of the ground floor of "Galeria Krakowska" shopping arcade has been used (Fig. 6). It accurately presents layout of the object (walls).

The path-finding algorithm described in Sec. 3 leads to the choice of realistic destination points (POIs) (Fig. 7).

A "temperature map" proves that as in a real shopping mall agents prefer to move through the center of corridors as long as it is not too crowded. They also tend to form lanes on straight segments and faster agents pass slower ones only if no one is approaching from the opposite direction. Some natural behaviors such as looking at shop windows and path deviation are observed.

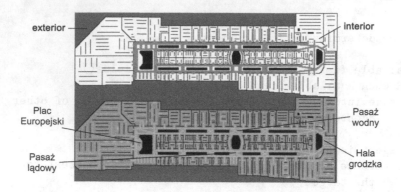

Fig. 6. Maps of the ground floor of *Galeria Krakowska* shopping arcade

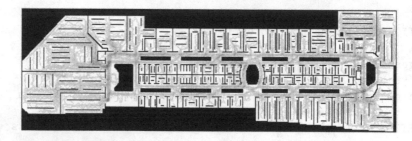

Fig. 7. A realistic routing of agents in a shopping mall

The performance of the presented model may be measured using several metrics. The Ped-4 part can be assessed by calculating the proportion of Ped-4 fields which constitute lanes (according to criteria of crowd's density and occurrence of a dominant movement direction) and the consistency of lanes (i.e. single lanes do not interleave). The Social Distances part can be assessed by calculating the average ratio of distance to target actually covered to the minimal distance to target and by measuring the number of agents "lost" (i.e. those who cannot reach target because they are blocked by the influence of social fields of other agents and thus revisit same fields multiple times).

5 Conclusions

The idea of combining various approaches to the issue of pedestrian dynamics seems quite promising. It contributes to a growth of realism of the simulation by providing a more diverse (thus more accurate) model of pedestrian behavior in different situations.

One model used was a *Ped-4* algorithm worked out by V. Blue and J. Adler which originally was used to describe pedestrian flows in long halls and corridors of Grand Central Station in New York. The second one was *Social Distances* model which takes into account patterns of movement without previously organized space.

In order to illustrate a practical application of this approach, the authors have proposed a model of pedestrian behavior inside a *Galeria Krakowska* shopping arcade. Space in the model is represented as a square, regular lattice of CA. Each pedestrian occupies one cell. Depending on the algorithm used, in one time-step-slice pedestrian can transfer into another cell in Moore or von Neumann neighborhood of radius $r = 1$. Thus, an inhomogeneous an asynchronous cellular automaton is an excellent basis of agent-based system mimicking behavior of pedestrians in a shopping mall.

References

1. Borgers, A., Timmermans, H.J.P.: A Model of Pedestrian Route Choice and Demand for Retail Facilities within Inner-City Shopping Areas. Geographical Analysis (1986)
2. Dijkstra, J., Timmermans, H.J.P., de Vries, B.: Modeling impulse and non-impulse store choice processes in a multi-agent simulation of pedestrian activity in shopping environments. In: Timmermans, H.J.P. (ed.) Pedestrian Behavior Models: Data Collection and Applications, pp. 63–87. Emerald, Bingley (2009)
3. Bandini, S., Manzoni, S., Vizzari, G.: Agent-based Modeling and simulation. In: Meyers, R.A. (ed.) Computational Complexity, pp. 105–117. Springer, New York (2012)
4. Bandini, S., Mondini, M., Vizzari, G.: Modelling negative interactions among pedestrians in high density situations. Transportation Research Part C: Emerging Technologies 40, 251–270 (2014)
5. Rauh, J., Schenk, T., Schödl, D.: The Simulated consumer - an agent-based approach to shopping behaviour (2011)
6. Blue, V., Adler, J.: Modelling Four Directional Pedestrian Movements (2000)
7. Wąs, J., Gudowski, B., Matuszyk, P.: Social Distances Model of Pedestrian Dynamics (2006)
8. Wąs, J., Lubaś, R.: Adapting Social Distances Model for Mass Evacuation Simulation. Journal of Cellular Automata 8(5-6), 395–405 (2013)
9. Wąs, J., Lubaś, R.: Towards realistic and effective Agent-based models of crowd dynamics. Neurocomputing (accepted)
10. Blue, V., Adler, J.: Cellular automata microsimulation for modeling bi-directional pedestrian walkways (2001)
11. Bitgood, S., Dukes, S.: Economy of Movement and Pedestrian Choice Point Behavior in Shopping Malls (2005)
12. Bandini, S., Gorrini, A., Vizzari, G.: Towards an integrated approach to crowd analysis and crowd synthesis: A case study and first results. Pattern Recognition Letters 44, 16–29 (2014)

How Agents Can Form a Specific Pattern

Rolf Hoffmann

Technische Universität Darmstadt,
FB Informatik, FG Rechnerarchitektur,
Hochschulstr. 10, 64289 Darmstadt, Germany
hoffmann@informatik.tu-darmstadt.de

Abstract. A multi-agent system is considered, comprised of a square
2D cell field of cells with uniform agents controlled by finite state machines (FSMs). Each cell contains a particle with one out of four colors,
which can be changed by the agents. Initially the agents and colors are
randomly distributed. The objective is to form a specific target pattern
belonging to a predefined pattern class. The target patterns (path patterns) shall consist of preferably long narrow paths with the same color.
The quality of the path patterns is measured by a degree of order, which
is computed by counting matching 3 x 3 patterns (templates). The used
agents can perform 32 actions, combinations of moving, turning and coloring. They react on the own color, the color in front, and blocking
situations. The agents' behavior is determined by an embedded FSM
with 6 states. For a given 8 x 8 field, near optimal FSMs were evolved by
a genetic procedure separately for $k = 1 .. 48$ agents. The evolved agents
are capable to form path patterns with a high degree of order. Agents,
evolved for a 8 x 8 field, are able to structure a 16 x 16 field successfully,
too. The whole multi-agent system was modeled by cellular automata. In
the implementation of the system, the CA-w model (cellular automata
with write access) was used in order to reduce the implementation effort
and speed up the simulation.

Keywords: Multi-Agent System, Cellular Automata Agents, Pattern
Formation, Evolving and Learning FSM Behavior, CA-w.

1 Introduction

The Agents'Task. Given is a square field of $N = n \times n$ cells with border, and
we assume an even number for n. Each cell, except the border cells, contains
a particle with a certain $color \in \{0, 1, 2, 3\}$. A given number k of agents can
move around in the field and can change the colors at the sites they are situated
on. Initially the colors, the agents, and the agent's directions are randomly distributed. The task is to end up in a global state where a certain *target pattern*
appears, belonging to a predefined pattern class. As an example we defined the
path pattern class which is characterized by preferably long paths of width = 1,
where all the neighboring cells have another color or are border cells. The paths
may have branches and may form loops (as shown in Fig. 5b). The objective is

J. Wąs, G.C. Sirakoulis, and S. Bandini (Eds.): ACRI 2014, LNCS 8751, pp. 660–669, 2014.
© Springer International Publishing Switzerland 2014

to find the behavior of the agents that can solve this task with a certain quality. The capabilities of the agents shall be constrained, e.g. the number of control states, the action set, and the details of the perceived environment.

Motivation. The original idea for this research was to find artificial patterns which are to a certain extend creative and impressive from the artistic point of view. As artistic patterns are difficult to evaluate in a formal way, the more modest objective was to find patterns with a certain interesting or valuable structure. Then experiments were conducted to find certain global patterns, like a black box in the center of the field, or with a global symmetry. It turned out, until now, that it is very difficult to find agents that can comply with such strict global objectives. Then, the objective was even more relaxed, namely to find global patterns that obey to intrinsic local rules (local matching patterns, templates). For this work, the Moore-Neighborhood (3 x 3) was used for the templates, but it could be enlarged in order to form more interesting global patterns. – Benefit of the presented results could also be taken when nano-structures have to be constructed by nano-robots or by beaming focused energy onto certain cells in order to change their physical state [1–3]. Other applications of this research can be imagined when the task is to form biological [14], chemical or computational structures with specific properties.

Why Agents? What is the advantage to solve this task by agents? Generally speaking, agents can behave very flexible, powerful and coordinated because of their intelligence and their specific sensors and actuators. Important properties that can be achieved by agents are

- *Scalability*. The problem can be solved with a variable number of agents, and faster or better with more agents.
- *Tuneability*. Increasing the agent's intelligence, the problem can be solved faster or more effective (better quality of solutions).
- *Versatility*. Similar problems can be solved by the same agents, e.g. by changing the shape or size of the environment.
- *Updating-tolerance*. Usually the time-evoluted global state depends only marginally on the updating-scheme (synchronous, asynchronous).
- *Fault-tolerance*. When obstacles are introduced or not all agents work correctly, the problem can still be solved in a gracefully degraded way.

Because agents are very flexible, they can be employed to design, model, analyze, simulate, and solve problems in the areas of complex systems, real and artificial worlds, games, distributed algorithms and mathematical questions.

Related Work. (i) *FSM controlled agents:* In former investigations we have tried to find the best algorithms for the *Creature's Exploration Problem* [4], in which the agents have the task to visit all empty cells in shortest time, for the *All-to-All Communication Task* [5], in which each agent has to distribute its information to all the others, and for the *Target Searching Task* [7]. The FSMs for these tasks have been evolved using, i.e., genetic algorithms, genetic programming [6], and sophisticated enumeration methods. Other related works are a multi-agent system modeled in CA for image processing [8], and modeling the agent's behavior by an FSM with a restricted number of states [9]. An important pioneering work about FSM controlled agents is [10].

(ii) *Pattern-formation:* Agent-based pattern formations in nature and physics are studied in [15, 16]. A programming language is presented in [17] for pattern-formation of locally-interacting, identically-programmed agents; as example the layout of an CMOS inverter is formed by agents. In [19] a general framework is proposed to discover rules that produce special spatial patterns based on a combination of Machine Learning strategies including Genetic Algorithms and Artificial Neural Networks. In [20] a methodology based on different learning-techniques is introduced that helps the designer to model the behavior of the agents for a multi-agent system.

(iii) *Modeling moving agents/particles:* Here the agents are modeled by classical CA or CA-w as described in Sect. 3. Other modeling concepts related to CA are lattice-gas cellular automata, block substitutions, or partitioned CA as used in [5]. The concept of transactional CA was proposed in [18] to implement agent mobility in CA, and it was shown that scheduling policies and conflict resolution strategies have an impact on the global behavior of the system.

2   Target Patterns and Degree of Order

How can the class of target patterns be characterized? The idea is to use a set of small local matching patterns as building blocks, also called *templates*, that can successfully tile the field (with overlaps). In the color structures arranged by the agents such templates are expected with a high frequency. The 41 templates used here are shown in Fig. 1a. They describe the target *path patterns*. E.g. the *plank* template means that there are 3 consecutive cells of the same color (depicted in black), enclosed by 3 + 3 cells in another color (depicted in grey). The plank can be rotated by 90 degrees, giving the second form of this type. Altogether, under reflection and rotation, there are 41 distinct templates. The templates can be depicted in a condensed form (Fig. 1b), using *don't care* neighbors that can have any color. E.g. the template T4 does not care about the West and East neighbor.

The patterns created by the agents have to be evaluated, how well do they fit into the defined path pattern class. In order to evaluate a given pattern, all templates are applied (tested) on each cell. If a match (hit) is found, a dot is used to mark this cell. Then, all dots are summed up which gives the total number of hits h. This number is also called *degree of order*. The terminal cells of a path will not be taken into account when the path length is computed. Thus a consecutive path of 3 cells has only a length count of 1. The reason is to avoid searching for very short paths of length ≤ 2. The theoretically maximum order is $h_{max} = n \times n - 4$. The relative order is h/h_{max}. The maximum could be reached by nesting squares with different colors into each other. In Fig. 1b there are 6 templates that match, leading to 9 hits.

It can be observed that the testing for templates hits corresponds to the application of an equivalent CA rule. From the formal language point of view, the templates can be seen as the generators of a 2D pattern language.

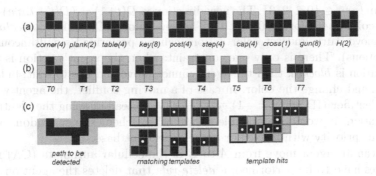

Fig. 1. (a) Templates are small building blocks which are expected to appear in a target pattern. A path cell is colored in black. Grey represents another color. The number of symmetric templates by rotation and reflection is given in the brackets. (b) The same templates, described in condensed form. (c) A path (part of the target pattern) can be tiled (with overlaps) by matching templates. Each matching template produces a hit (dot). All hits are summed up and give the degree of order.

3   Modeling the System by Cellular Automata

Standard in CA is that the cells are uniform, meaning that they are all similar and obey to the same rule. The rule changes the state of each cell by taking into account the own cell's state and the states of its neighbors. Nevertheless the cell's rule has to react on non-uniform situations, e.g. whether there is an agent situated on a cell or not. Therefore the cell's state is modeled as record $(Type, Color, Agent)$ comprising a type tag, where

$Type \in \{Border, Particle, AgentAndParticle\}$, and
$Agent = (Identifier, Direction, ControlState)$.

When designing a system with agents (multi-agent system MAS), then the capabilities of the agents have to be defined before designing or searching for the behavior of the agents to solve a given task. The main capabilities are: The perceivable inputs from the environment, the actions an agent can perform, and the size of its memory (number of possible control states, optionally additional data states). In our system, an agent shall react on the following inputs in a certain combination

- the **own color** C of the cell the agent is situated on
- the **color in front** C_F (in moving/viewing direction)
- a **border** cell in front
- the **blocked** situation/condition, caused either by a border, another agent in front, or when another prior agent can move to the front cell in case of a conflict. The inverse condition is called *free*.

An agent has a moving/viewing $Direction = D \in \{0, 1, 2, 3\} = \{toN, toE, toS, toW\}$. Note that in the used model an agent cannot observe the direction and control state of another agent in the neighborhood. The actions that an agent shall be able to perform are

- **move**: $move \in \{0, 1\} = \{wait, go\}$

- **turn:** $turn \in \{0, 1, 2, 3\}$. The new direction is $D(t+1) = (D(t)+turn) \ mod \ 4$.
- **set color:** $setcolor \in \{0, 1, 2, 3\}$. The new color is $C(t+1) = setcolor$.

The move, turn and set color actions can be performed simultaneously (32 combinations). There is only one constraint: when the agent's action is *go* and the situation is *blocked*, then the agent cannot move and has to wait, but still it can turn and change the color. In case of a moving conflict, the agent with the lowest identifier (ID = 0 .. $k-1$) gets priority. Instead of using the identifier for prioritization, it would be possible to use other schemes, e.g. random priority, or a cyclic priority with a fixed or space dependent base.

How can an agent move from A to B in the cellular automata (CA) model? Two rules have to be performed, a *delete-rule* that deletes the agent on A, and a *copy-rule* that copies the agent to B. In CA both rules have to compute the same blocking condition, this means a redundant computation. In order to avoid this redundancy, a two-phase updating scheme could be used (first compute the moving condition, second use it in cell A and B), or the *cellular automata with write-access model* (CA-w) [11]. When using the CA-w model, the moving condition is computed by cell A, and if it is true, A applies a rule that deletes the agents on A and copies it to B. The simulation program was implemented by the CA-w model, although it is possible to implement the system in standard CA with redundant computation.

The CA-w model was introduced in order to describe moving agents, moving particles or dynamic changing activities. This model allows to write information onto a neighbor. This method has the advantage that a neighbor can directly be activated or deactivated, or data can be sent actively to it by an agent. The CA-w model is a restricted case of the more general, *"Global"* GCA-w model [12, 13]. In GCA-w any cell of the whole array can be modified whereas in the CA-w model only the local neighbors can be. Usually the cells of these models are a composition of (data, pointers). The neighbors are accessed via pointers, that can be changed dynamically like the data by an appropriate rule from generation to generation. Comparing CA and CA-w, a CA equivalent to a CA-w with neighborhood N_1 can be found by extending N_1 to N_2 (N_1 extended by write-distance). For example, an 1D CA-w with neighborhood distance 1 (read and write) is equivalent to a CA with neighborhood distance 2.

The behavior of an agent shall be determined by an embedded finite state control automaton (FSM) (Fig. 2). We also formulate that an agent has/obeys to a certain (control) algorithm. Each CA cell contains an FSM which is active when an agent is situated on it. The FSM contains a *state table* (also called *next state/output table*). Outputs are the actions (move, turn, setcolor) and the next control state. Inputs are the control state and the relevant input situations x. The *input mapping* reduces all possible input combinations of (border, blocked, color, front color) to an index $x \in X = \{0, 1, \ldots, |X| - 1\}$ that is used in combination with the control state to select the actual line of the state table.

The following input mapping is used. If the situation is *free* the index x is the color in front: $x = C_F$. If the situation is *blocked* by a border cell in front, then $x = 4$. If the blocking is caused by another agent in front, or by a prior agent in the case of a conflict, then the own color is directly mapped to the index with an offset $x = C + 5$. It is possible to choose other input mappings, with less or more x values, or other assignments, e.g. in the case of blocking, the direction of the agent could be used $(x = D + 5)$, instead of the own color.

The used updating scheme is *synchronous*; exemplarily simulation experiments showed, that the results with asynchronous updating are quite similar.

4 Evolving the Agent's Behavior by a Genetic Procedure

The goal is to find a general applicable FSM which is optimal for a large set of different initial configurations covering the whole area of applications (different size and shape of the field, different number of agents). As we cannot optimize for a very large set of initial configurations within a limited amount of computation time, we used a fixed field size of 8 x 8 and optimized separately for $k = 1, 2, 4, 8, 16, 32, 48$ agents, and used 100 training fields for each k. This means that we searched for specialists and not for all-rounders.

As the search space for different FSMs (algorithms) is very large, we are not able to check all possible behaviors by enumeration. The number of FSMs which can be coded by a state table is $Z = (|s||y|)^{(|s||x|)}$ where $|s|$ is the number of control states, $|x|$ is the number of different inputs and $|y|$ is the number of different outputs. As the search space increases exponentially, we use a genetic procedure in order to find the best behavior with reasonable computational cost. Even with a genetic approach the number of states, inputs and outputs have to be kept low in order to find a good solution in acceptable time.

A possible solution (genome of one individual in the genetic) corresponds to the contents of the FSM's state table (Fig. 2b). The column index j is defined by a certain combination of (x, s). Each column j defines $(s', y) = (nextstate, setcolor, move, turn)$. The used genetic procedure per iteration is

1. $A' \leftarrow mutate(A)$
2. $(A, B) \leftarrow deleteDuplicates(sort(A, A', B))$
3. $(A, B) \leftarrow exchange(b, A, B)$.

One population of N individuals is stored in two lists (A, B) with $N/2$ individuals each. (Step 1) During each iteration $N/2$ offspring are produced from list A by mutation. (Step 2) The union of the current N individuals and the $N/2$ offspring are sorted according to their fitness, duplicates are deleted and the number of individuals is then reduced to the limit of N in the pool. (Step 3) In order not to get stuck in local minima and to allow a certain diversity in the gene pool, the first b individuals from B are exchanged with the last b individuals from A. We used $N = 20$ and $b = 3$, therefore the individuals 8, 9, 10 are exchanged with the individuals 11, 12, 13, when the individuals are numbered from 1 to N.

An offspring is produced by modifying separately with a certain probability p each $action \in \{nextstate, setcolor, move, turn\}$:

$action \leftarrow (action + 1) \bmod N_{action}$.

We restricted the number of states to $N_{states} = 6$, and used $N_{setcolor} = 4$, $N_{move} = 2$, and $N_{turn} = 4$. We tested different probabilities, and we achieved good results with $p = 35\%$.

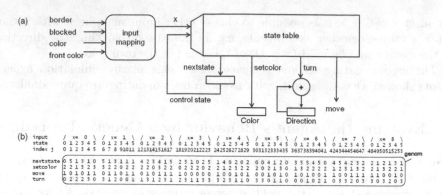

(a)

(b)
```
input      /  x= 0  \  /  x= 1  \  /  x= 2  \  /  x= 3  \  /  x= 4  \  /  x= 5  \  /  x= 6  \  /  x= 7  \  /  x= 8  \
state      0 1 2 3 4 5  0 1 2 3 4 5  0 1 2 3 4 5  0 1 2 3 4 5  0 1 2 3 4 5  0 1 2 3 4 5  0 1 2 3 4 5  0 1 2 3 4 5  0 1 2 3 4 5
index j    0 1 2 3 4 5  6 7 8 91011  121314151617 181920212223 242526272829 303132333435 363738394041 424344454647 484950515253
                                                                                                                          genom
nextstate  0 5 1 3 1 0  5 1 3 1 1 1  4 2 3 4 1 5  2 3 1 0 2 5  1 4 0 2 0 2  0 0 4 1 2 0  3 5 5 4 5 0  4 5 4 2 3 2  2 1 2 1 3 1
setcolor   2 2 1 3 2 3  3 2 2 0 2 2  2 2 0 3 2 2  0 2 2 2 0 2  2 1 2 3 2 2  2 0 2 1 3 0  1 3 2 2 2 2  1 2 3 1 3 2  2 1 3 2 2 1
move       1 0 1 0 1 1  0 1 1 0 1 1  0 1 0 1 1 1  1 0 0 0 0 0  1 0 0 1 0 1  0 0 1 0 1 0  1 0 1 0 0 1  1 0 0 1 1 1  1 1 0 0 1 0
turn       0 2 2 2 3 0  3 1 2 0 0 1  1 3 1 2 3 1  2 3 1 1 3 3  3 2 3 1 1 0  3 3 0 1 1 0  0 0 1 0 2 1  0 3 3 2 0 3  3 0 3 2 0 3
```

Fig. 2. (a) Finite state machine (FSM). The state table defines the next control state, the setting of the color, the agent's new direction, and whether to move or not. (b) Example for a state table. It represents the best found, near optimal TopFSM(16) for a 8 x 8 field with 16 agents.

The fitness of our multi-agent system is defined as the number t of time steps which is necessary to emerge successfully a target pattern with a given degree h_1 of order, averaged over all given randomized initial configurations (color distribution, position and directions of the agents). As the behavior of the whole system depends on the behavior of the agents, we search for the agents' FSM that can solve the problem successfully with a minimum number of steps for a large number of initial configurations. Successfully means that a target pattern with $h \geq h_1$ was found. The fitness function F is evaluated by simulating the agent system with a tentative FSM on a given initial configuration.

$$F(FSM, config) = \begin{cases} TimeSteps & \text{if } successful \text{ within } TimeLimit \\ HighConstant & \text{otherwise} \end{cases} \quad (1)$$

Then the mean fitness $\overline{F}(FSM)$ is computed by averaging over all given initial configurations. The mean fitness $\overline{F}$ is then used to rank and sort the FSMs. The parameters used were $TimeLimit = 5,000$ and $HighConstant = 100,000$. The genetic procedure starts with $N = 20$ random FSMs. Usually there is no FSM in the initial population that is successful. After some generations, some successful FSMs are found. Then, after further generations, FSMs are expected to be evolved that are completely successful on all or most of the given initial configurations. It turned out, that it is very difficult and time consuming to find good solutions. Therefore the genetic procedure was divided into several phases with increasing difficulty. (1) The system with $k = 16$ agents was optimized (1a) on 10 initial configuration (may also be called *field* for short) with an increasing degree of order ($h_1 = 30, 40, 48$), then (1b) on 20 fields with $h_1 = 48$, and then (1c) on 100 fields with $h_1 = 48$. Then (2 .. 7) the other systems with $k = 1, 2, 4, 8, 32, 48$ were optimized in the same way. Note that the highest degree of order is $h_{max} = 60$ for the 8 x 8 field. Thus the aimed relative degree of order was $h_1/h_{max} = 48/60 = 80\%$. Experiments showed that a higher h can be

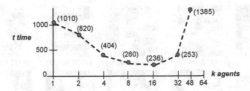

Fig. 3. Time to form the desired patterns with an 80% degree of order by the TopFSMs specifically evolved for $k = 1 .. 48$ agents. Field size is 8 x 8.

reached sometimes, but not always within the limited capabilities of the agents, the system, and the time limit. – 4500 generations (simulations with 10 mutated FSMs on up to 100 fields) were computed for each k. The overall computation time on a processor Intel Xeon QuadCore 2 GHz was around two weeks. The implementation language was Object Pascal under the platform Lazarus.

The Evolved top FSMs. The best found FSM for 16 agents (TopFSM(16)) is shown in Fig. 2b. All found TopFSM(k) for $k = 1, 2, 4, 8, 16, 32, 48$ are able to form a target pattern with an 80% degree of order for all 100 random initial configurations. The time to form the patterns reaches a minimum for 16 agents (Fig. 3), and a maximum for 48 agents. No solution within the constraints was found for 64 agents (fully packed, agents cannot move – only turn). It can be observed that a certain density of the agents (here $25\% = 48/64$) is optimal in order to reach the minimal time. It can be concluded that an agent can work only optimal if it is responsible for a certain "personal" local area (here 4 cells). One explanation could be that an agent uses the colors in its neighborhood in a stigmergic way (like pheromones, indirect communication mainly with itself – self-feedback memory) to be at last successful. If the field is overcrowded or sparsely populated, the performance is lowered. It was also interesting to observe, that the task can even be solved by one agent only. From the cost investment point of view ($cost = time \times agents$), one agent alone is most economical.

Simulations. (Fig. 4) The evolved TopFSM(k) were simulated and visualized. The snapshots show how the path patterns are being built. It can be seen that at the end two colors are dominating (red and yellow). The other two colors rapidly decrease and may disappear at the end. In the optimization procedure and simulation it was not forbidden to reduce the number of colors (to require an almost even color distribution of the 4 colors at the end is a too hard condition as experiments have shown). It can be seen, that the agents prefer to move on a path with the same color. Note that the degree of order was set to $\geq 80\%$. When this limit is surpassed the simulation is successful and terminates.

Versatility Test. (Fig. 5) This test was undertaken in order to prove that agents, which are optimized for special field, can be successful on another given (here larger) field with another number of agents (here larger). The test was really successful and showed that agents (as usually) can cope with different environments. The original field was of size 8 x 8, with 16 agents. The test field was of size 16 x 16, with 64 agents (the same density as in the original field).

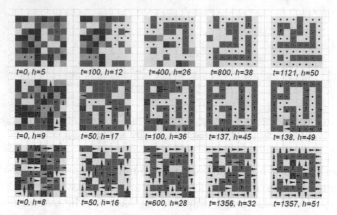

Fig. 4. Snapshots showing how path patterns are formed by k agents; $k = 1$ (top row), 16 (middle row), 48 (bottom row). h = degree of order. Dots represent template hits.

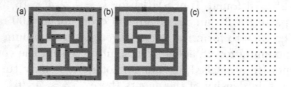

Fig. 5. The TopFSM(16) evolved on a 8 x 8 field can also solve the problem on a 16 x 16 field. (a) Agents and colors, (b) colors only, (c) template hits.

The degree of order was also set to 80%. The mean time to successfully form a path pattern for the larger field was $t_2 = 1259$, averaged over 100 random initial configurations. For comparison, the mean time on the original field was $t_1 = 236$. The ratio of the field areas is 4, and the ratio $t_2/t_1 = 5.33$, which is not extremely more.

5   Conclusion

The objective was to find FSM controlled agents that can form specific path patterns. The class of path patterns was defined by a set of templates, small 3 x 3 local patterns. The number of templates that can be found in a given pattern defines the degree of order. For a 8 x 8 field near optimal FSMs were evolved for a different number of agents. The agents are able to form successfully with an 80% degree of order the aimed path patterns. The task can be solved fastest with 16 agents (density 25%), and around five times slower with one agent only. The FSM(16) evolved for a 8 x 8 field can also handle a 16 x 16 field with the same density of agents. This means that an evolved specialist can also be successful on another field size. The general result is that specific pattern generation by CA agents can be constructed in a methodic way. It would be of interest to enhance and apply this method in order to generate more complex patterns.

References

1. Shi, D., He, P., Lian, J., Chaud, X., et al.: Magnetic alignment of carbon nanofibers in polymer composites and anisotropy of mechanical properties. Journal of Applied Physics 97, 064312 (2005)
2. Itoh, M., Takahira, M., Yatagai, T.: Spatial Arrangement of Small Particles by Imaging Laser Trapping System. Optical Review 5(I), 55–58 (1998)
3. Jiang, Y., Narushima, T., Okamoto, H.: Nonlinear optical effects in trapping nanoparticles with femtosecond pulses. Nature Physics 6, 1005–1009 (2010)
4. Halbach, M., Hoffmann, R., Both, L.: Optimal 6-state algorithms for the behavior of several moving creatures. In: El Yacoubi, S., Chopard, B., Bandini, S. (eds.) ACRI 2006. LNCS, vol. 4173, pp. 571–581. Springer, Heidelberg (2006)
5. Hoffmann, R., Désérable, D.: CA Agents for All-to-All Communication Are Faster in the Triangulate Grid. In: Malyshkin, V. (ed.) PaCT 2013. LNCS, vol. 7979, pp. 316–329. Springer, Heidelberg (2013)
6. Komann, M., Ediger, P., Fey, D., Hoffmann, R.: On the Effectiveness of Evolution Compared to Time-Consuming Full Search of Optimal 6-State Automata. In: Vanneschi, L., Gustafson, S., Moraglio, A., De Falco, I., Ebner, M. (eds.) EuroGP 2009. LNCS, vol. 5481, pp. 280–291. Springer, Heidelberg (2009)
7. Ediger, P., Hoffmann, R.: CA Models for Target Searching Agents. Automata 2009, J. Electronic Notes in Theor. Comp. Science (ENTCS) 252, 41–54 (2009)
8. Komann, M., Mainka, A., Fey, D.: Comparison of evolving uniform, non-uniform cellular automaton, and genetic programming for centroid detection with hardware agents. In: Malyshkin, V. (ed.) PaCT 2007. LNCS, vol. 4671, pp. 432–441. Springer, Heidelberg (2007)
9. Mesot, B., Sanchez, E., Peña, C.-A., Perez-Uribe, A.: SOS++: Finding Smart Behaviors Using Learning and Evolution. In: Artificial Life VIII, pp. 264–273. MIT Press, Cambridge (2002)
10. Blum, M., Sakoda, W.: On the capability of finite automata in 2 and 3 dimensional space. In: 18th IEEE Symp. on Foundations of Computer Science, pp. 147–161 (1977)
11. Hoffmann, R.: Rotor-routing algorithms described by CA-w. Acta Phys. Polonica B Proc. Suppl. 5(1), 53–68 (2012)
12. Hoffmann, R.: The GCA-w massively parallel model. In: Malyshkin, V. (ed.) PaCT 2009. LNCS, vol. 5698, pp. 194–206. Springer, Heidelberg (2009)
13. Hoffmann, R.: GCA-w algorithms for traffic simulation. Acta Phys. Polonica B Proc. Suppl. 4(2), 183–200 (2011)
14. Deutsch, A., Dormann, S.: Cellular Automaton Modeling of Biological Pattern Formation. Birkäuser (2005)
15. Bonabeau, E.: From Classical Models of Morphogenesis to Agent-Based Models of Pattern Formation. Santa Fe Institute Working Paper: 1997-07-063
16. Hamann, H.: Pattern Formation as a Transient Phenomenon in the Nonlinear Dynamics of a Multi-Agent System. In: Proc. of MATHMOD 2009 (2009)
17. Nagpal, R.: Programmable Pattern-Formation and Scale-Independence. MIT Artificial Intelligence Lab (2002)
18. Spicher, A., Fatèz, N., Simonin, O.: From Reactive Multi-Agents Models to Cellular Automata - Illustration on a Diffusion-Limited Aggregation Model. In: ICAART 2009, pp. 422–429 (2009)
19. Bandini, S., Vanneschi, L., Wuensche, A., Shehata, A.B.: A Neuro-Genetic Framework for Pattern Recognition in Complex Systems. Fundam. Inform. 87(2), 207–226 (2008)
20. Junges, R., Klügl, F.: Programming Agent Behavior by Learning in Simulation Models. Applied Artificial Intelligence 26(4), 349–375 (2012)

An Integrated Model for the Simulation
of Pedestrian Crossings

Luca Crociani and Giuseppe Vizzari

CSAI - Complex Systems & Artificial Intelligence Research Center,
University of Milano-Bicocca,
Viale Sarca 336, 20126, Milano, Italy
{name.surname}@disco.unimib.it

Abstract. The present paper represents an approach to the modeling of pedestrians and vehicles interaction in the area of a zebra crossing, either signalised or not, employing two existing models devoted to the simulation of the specific pedestrian and vehicular sub-systems and integrating them in a comprehensive agent *environment*. The latter acts as a bridge allowing mutual perception of the different heterogeneous agents that cooperate to avoid accidents: vehicles give way to perceived pedestrians whenever they can safely brake to let them pass, pedestrians yield whenever they perceive cars that would not be able to stop before the zebra crossing. The paper presents the model and shows results in simple crossing scenarios.

Keywords: Agent-based Simulation, Pedestrian-Vehicle Interactions.

1 Introduction and Related Works

The micro-simulation of cars and vehicular traffic is a consolidated research area that produced results whose level of maturity led to a significant impact both on the activity of traffic engineers and planners, as well as to the creation of successful companies developing commercial simulation systems or providing consultancy on their employment. From pioneering works, such as [1], several successful models for the simulation of different aspects of vehicular traffic have been developed and applied: see, for instance, [2] for a review of different approaches, which include both discrete models (mainly cellular automata), also applied to complicated road sections such as roundabouts [3], and continuous ones, like car-following models [4]. In parallel, models for the micro-simulation of pedestrians have also emerged and affirmed as supports to the design of environments subject to crowding situations. Also in this case, successful researches have produced discrete approaches, like the floor-field Cellular Automata model [5], and continuous ones, like the social force model [6]; like for vehicular traffic, also for pedestrians successful commercial simulation systems can be found in the market.

Whereas separately micro-simulation approaches have produced a significant impact, preceded by a body or relevant research, efforts characterised by an integrated micro-simulation model considering the simultaneous presence of cars

J. Wąs, G.C. Sirakoulis, and S. Bandini (Eds.): ACRI 2014, LNCS 8751, pp. 670–679, 2014.

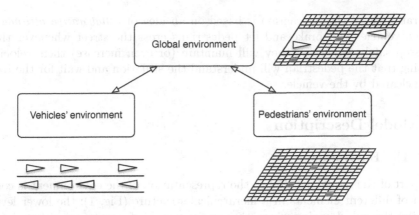

Fig. 1. Structure of the global environment composed of the vehicular and pedestrian sub-environments

(and other vehicular traffic like trucks or buses) and vulnerable road users (in particular pedestrians, but also bicycles) are not as frequent or advanced as isolated vehicular traffic and pedestrian models. Although observation studies of pedestrian and driver behaviour in crossing can be found, both in normal conditions [7] and with respect to the presence of crossing warning systems [8], few attempts towards the modelling of this kind of scenario have been performed. With the notable exception of [9], most efforts in this direction are relatively recent, such as [10], and they just analyse simple scenarios and they are not validated against real data. The most significant and recent work in this direction is represented by [11] which adapt the social force model to this kind of scenario, considering vehicles as generators of a repulsive force for pedestrians; while this work considers real world data, the analysed scenario is characterised by a signalised crosswalk in which only turning cars can actually interact with pedestrians and their behaviour is not thoroughly analysed. Similarly, some of the most relevant commercial products for traffic simulation provide the possibility to perform some kind of integration of simplified pedestrian models inside the overall simulated scenario, but the level of integration of the two represented phenomena is generally sketchy and the possibility to achieve plausible results severely increases the overall effort of the modeller.

The present paper represents an approach to the modeling of pedestrians and vehicles interaction in the area of a zebra crossing, either signalised or not, employing two existing models devoted to the simulation of the specific pedestrian [5] and vehicular [12] sub-systems and integrating them in a comprehensive agent *environment* [13]. We consider vehicles and pedestrians as *agents*, whose behavioural specification is based on the original models plus specific behavioural rules regulating the coordination of their actions based on their mutual perception. This perception is allowed by an integrated representation of the global environment, comprising the road section, represented in the vehicular sub-system, and the sidewalk and zebra crossing, represented in the pedestrian sub-system.

The rationale of the interaction is based on an idea of *collaborative attitude* of agents: vehicles will brake and let pedestrians cross the street whenever they can stop safely, otherwise they will maintain (or even increase) their velocity, trusting that the pedestrian will understand the situation and wait for the road to be cleared by the vehicle.

2   Model Description

2.1   The Environment

The part of the model devoted to the representation of the environment is composed of different elements in a hierarchical structure (Fig. 1): the lower levels describe the sub-domains where the specific types of agents are situated (respectively cars and pedestrians) and their union grants a comprehensive view of the overall situation. This approach is aimed at exploiting the different representations (discrete and bi-dimensional for pedestrians, continuous and mono-dimensional for vehicles) allowing relatively simple behavioural specifications for the respective agents. In this way, therefore, the global environment allows hosting different types of entities, which can act in different portions of the environment with different representations and also different dimensions. Of course, since the two types of entities must interact (i.e. perceive each other in specific situations and modify their actions accordingly) the global environment also acts as a bridge allowing a form of comminication among the sub-domains.

The information for realizing the simulation scenario is introduced by annotating the global environment with *spatial markers*, that are, special portions of space that describe relevant elements for the simulation and in particular: (i) **Start area**, for the introduction of pedestrian agents in the environment, which can be done by a user-defined frequency; (ii) **End area**, representing final targets of pedestrian agents; (iii) **Street**, the portion of the space where the *cars* sub-environments are situated. Each lane of the street will instantiate one sub-environment, since lane changing and perception between cars of different lanes is not considered; (iv) **Obstacle**, to represent eventual obstacles in the sideways; (v) **Crossing area**, the shared space between the different entities; it can be *regulated* by semaphores or not.

Vehicular sub-environment – The vehicular sub-domain $Street = \{q_1, \ldots, q_l\}$ is represented by the set of l continuous mono-dimensional queues, each one representing one single lane of the street. Each queue is modeled by another couple $\langle Dir, V \rangle$, where Dir is the direction of the roadway and V is the set of vehicles. Each car is represented in the environment as $\langle x_i, \nu_i \rangle$, which are the position and velocity of the vehicle i of the simulation.

Pedestrian sub-environment – The pedestrian environment is discrete and represented by a set of grids, with the same size, of square cells of 40 cm side, in order to represent the average space occupation of a person [14]. The main grid describes the structure of environment, having a state function, initially computed with the annotated global environment, which informs pedestrian agents about cells usability at a given step: $state(c) : Cells \rightarrow \{Sidewalk, Str, ZebraCrs,$ $ZebraBrd, Obs, Ped\}$. By means of this function, indeed, pedestrian space is specialized with respect to the relevant elements of this scenario. Street, obstacles and cells already occupied by a pedestrian describe not usable spaces during the simulation. Among the usable space, the zebra crossing is specialized as $ZebraCrs$, the shared portion of the street, and $ZebraBrd$ which describes its two borders. This annotation will be exploited by the interactions mechanism, supporting reciprocal perception of the different entities.

Space annotation allows the definition of virtual grids of the environment as containers of information for agents and their movement, developing the *floor field* approach [5]. This method is based on the generation of a set of superimposed grids (similar to the grid of the environment) starting from the information derived from spatial markers. Floor field values are spread on the grid as a gradient and they are used to support pedestrians in the navigation of the environment, representing their interactions with static object (i.e., destination areas and obstacles) or with other pedestrians. In this model *static floor field* is used, that indicates for every cell the distance S_{ij} from one destination area (i.e. one floor field is computed for each pedestrian destination).

2.2 Vehicular Traffic Model

The behavioral model of cars has been designed on the basis of the work in [12], which is a simplified version of the well-known Gipps car-following model [15]. We chose this continuous abstraction of the traffic dynamics, because it considers aspects like the *limited* acceleration and deceleration capability of a car, leading to a precise definition of a *safe* velocity per car at a given step.

The model is continuous in space and discrete in time, defining the step as the reaction time of the car drivers. It is, therefore, assumed than all the simulated drivers have the same reaction time, fixed to 1 second. The car behavior is based on a small set of formulas which describe the speed of a car n_i at a step $t + 1$ by considering three fundamental factors: (i) its current speed; (ii) the gap g between it and the preceding vehicle n_{i-1}; (iii) the speed of the preceding vehicle n_{i-1}, to calculate the velocity which allows to maintain a safe state (i.e. to not have a collision with n_{i-1} even if it applies the maximum deceleration). The velocity ν of a vehicle at a turn t is defined by the following (*ran* describe a random choice between the two elements): $\nu(t + 1) = ran(\nu_0, \nu_1)$, with $\nu_0 = min(\nu(t) + b, \nu_{max}, \nu_{safe})$, and $\nu_1 = \nu_0 - \epsilon \cdot \{\nu_0 - [\nu(t) - b]\}$.

In particular, ν_0 represents two potential cases: when the vehicle has sufficient headway it can increase the velocity considering its previous value and its maximum acceleration b (that also describes the maximum deceleration) but not beyond the maximum velocity ν_{max}; on the other hand, if the headway is not sufficient for maintaining or increasing the velocity, since a preceding vehicle is getting too close, the maximum safe velocity ν_{safe} must be adopted. ν_{safe} is computed in order to avoid a crash in the following turns even if the preceding vehicle should perform the maximum possible brake until a complete stop. Choosing the minimum value among the three assures that the most appropriate

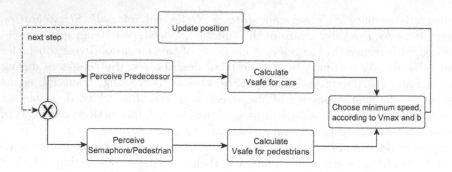

Fig. 2. Vehicles life-cycle updated to consider pedestrian presence

one is selected. ν_1, instead, introduces a sort of small random additional drop on the adopted velocity, being essentially based on ν_0 decreased by a small (potentially zero, but not negative). For sake of space the formula for ν_{safe} is omitted, but the adopted car-following model is more thoroughly described in [12].

Managing Interactions with Pedestrians – While the above mechanism is conceived to manage interactions among vehicles, we have to define how interactions between vehicles and pedestrians are managed. The rationale is to adopt an altruistic attitude, from the car perspective. The function for the calculation of the highest safe speed ν_{safe} can also be used to let vehicles calculate a velocity that will let them avoid accidents with crossing pedestrians, as well as to stop for allowing pedestrians in the crossing nearby to proceed. The extended mechanism is shown in Fig. 2.

The perception capability of car drivers has been extended to let them perceive also the x-coordinate of the closest entity between their position and the end of the crossing zone. The value of ν_{safe}^{ped} is calculated considering the possibly perceived position of pedestrians, and it describes the highest safe speed that car drivers can assume to avoid accidents with pedestrians to let them cross the street. ν_{safe}^{ped} is computed analogously as ν_{safe}, only considering that pedestrian will mostly move along the y axis, not changing its x-coordinate. The choice among the velocity values associated to the different cases will therefore also include a case causing braking due the perception of a pedestrian close to a crossing site the the vehicle can safely let pass.

2.3   Pedestrian Behavior Model

Base-line pedestrian behavior has been modeled by using the floor-field model [5], able to reproduce a wide range of pedestrian dynamics despite its simplicity. The overall agent life-cycle per step is described by the following two-phase procedure: (i) according to its final destination, each agent perceives values S_{ij} of cells of its Moore neighborhood, to understand the direction to take. With the perception phase, values ϵ_{ij} and $\eta_{ij} \in \{0, 1\}$ are also computed, indicating respectively the presence of a not usable cell (in our case a cell c is not usable if $state(c) = Obs$

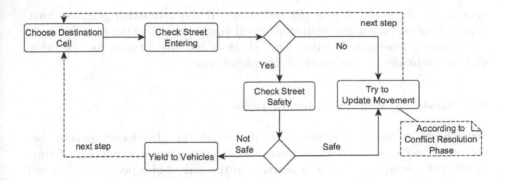

Fig. 3. Pedestrian life-cycle considering interactions with vehicles

or $state(c) =$ Str) and a cell occupied by pedestrians. Using this information, in step (ii), agents calculate the probability to choose each movement according to the function $p_{ij} = N\epsilon_{ij}\exp(\kappa_s S_{ij})(1 - \phi\eta_{ij})$, where N is a normalization factor, κ_s, $\phi \in [0, 1]$ are calibration weights. Note that the second parameter allows the utilization of cells already occupied by pedestrians: this mechanism can be exploited for managing high-density situations, where the arise of consistent jamming can lead to stalemate of simulation. Since pedestrian high-densities are out from the scope of this work, the results shown in Sec. 3 have been achieved with $\phi = 1$. The model uses a *parallel* update strategy, so at each step the agents do not perform directly the movement they chose. Conflicts arisen for the choice of the same cell by more agents are, in fact, managed by the conflict resolution phase, which allows the movement of only one of the agents involved in the conflict, randomly chosen.

Managing Interactions with Vehicles – From the pedestrian point of view, interactions with vehicles are managed with the procedure shown in Fig. 3. The designed behavior is not as collaborative as for vehicles: once the agent has reached the crossing its objective is to cross the street safely, so it has to verify that no cars are present nearby or the present ones are able to stop before the crossing. This form reasoning has been realized by means the following two procedures (l denotes the number of lanes of the street): $checkSE : Cells^2 \to$ {true, false}, $checkSafety : \mathbb{R}^{l+1} \to$ {true, false}.

The meaning of $checkSE$ is to let agents understand that they are entering the crossing, formally explained by the proposition $state(p) ==$ ZebraBrd $\wedge$ $state(d) ==$ ZebraCross where p and d the cells describing position and chosen destination of the agent respectively.

Function $checkSafety$ checks the speed of the closest approaching car to the crossing for each lane. Formally, $checkSafety(Street, p) =$ true iff for all not empty $q = \langle Dir, V \rangle \in Street$:

$$\exists \langle x_i, \nu_i \rangle \in V : \{(x_i < x_p) \wedge (\nexists \langle x_j, \nu_j \rangle \in V : \{x_i < x_j < x_p\}) \wedge (\nu_i > \nu_{safe,i}^{ped})\}$$

where $\nu_{safe,i}^{ped}$ is the highest speed the car i can assume, in order to be able to stop before the position p of the pedestrian. If the pedestrian *perceives* that approaching cars are not able to stop, it will yield to them. In the above formula we assume a left-right direction for each lane, but the formula for the other direction is analogous and omitted for sake of space.

2.4   Modeling Regulated Interactions

Semaphores in the system are managed through the global environment, being essentially objects that can change their state given the passage of time (fixed cycle semaphores) or as a reaction to the arrival of a pedestrian (on call semaphore). In both the above cases, the semaphore is simply perceived by cars as an additional obstacle in the queue whenever the semaphore shows them the red light, causing the triggering of their braking. Similarly, whenever the semaphore shows a red light to pedestrians it is perceived as the presence of a car causing *checkSafety* to be uniformly false, irrespectively of the actual road conditions.

3   Simulation Results

Before evaluating the integrated model we validated the basic pedestrian and vehicular sub-models separately, in a very simple road section comprising a single lane for vehicles and a single zebra crossing not regulated by a semaphore. Although these models are not original but essentially derived from the literature, we needed to be sure that they were properly implemented and employing reasonable values for the different parameters. To this aim, we performed tests with vehicles and no pedestrians and also the other way around, checking the fact that no accidents were generated among cars and also generating fundamental diagrams to estimate the plausibility of the generated results (e.g. drop of the flow with the growth of the density, for both vehicular and pedestrian models, but also maximum vehicular flow in line wit and other qualitative phenomena such as the capability to generate "traffic out of nowhere").

After this first phase we tried to evaluate the capability of the model of generating a drop in the vehicular flow with a growing number of pedestrians trying to cross the road the above described scenario. Pedestrians are created randomly on one of the sidewalks according to a predefined frequency of generation and they try to cross the road according to their behavioural specification described in Sect. 2; similarly also vehicles are initially positioned in the simulated road section (configured as a toroid) to be able to achieve a certain and stable level of vehicular density. By altering the number of cars and the frequency of pedestrian generation, we were able to achieve a fundamental diagram in which both the variation in the vehicular and pedestrian density were considered. The results are shown in Figure 4: each point is associated to one hour of simulated time and we can see that the maximum flow of vehicles drops from about 1700 vehicles per hour per lane to less than half of this value when the frequency of pedestrian

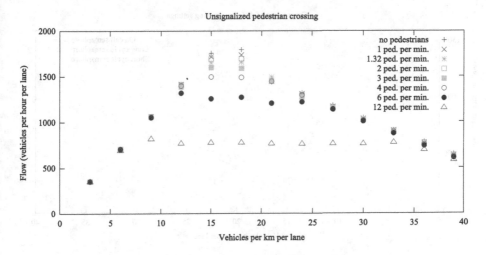

Fig. 4. Fundamental diagram of vehicle flow with different pedestrian crossing frequencies in an unsignalised intersection

generation reaches 12 pedestrians per minute (one approaching the zebra crossing every 5 seconds). Moreover, the critical density decreases with the growth of the frequency of pedestrian arrival.

A second set of experiments was conducted to evaluate the effect of the introduction of a semaphore in the scenario; in particular, we actually tested the introduction of three different types of semaphore: two of them have a fixed cycle, respectively a "long" one (50 seconds of green light for cars, 40 for pedestrians) and a short one (in which both the timings are halved), and the last one is an *on call* semaphore, activated manually by an approaching pedestrian, generating a short green light period for pedestrians (25 seconds) whose end inhibits additional activations for a similar amount of time (30 seconds). We tested the three configurations of the crossing in a similar way as the unsignalised intersection, varying the vehicular traffic conditions, but actually fixing a certain rate of arrival for pedestrians. In particular, we simulated one hour in which the rate of arrival of pedestrians is generally low (about 3 pedestrians per minute) but for a few peak minutes in which the number of pedestrians grows to about 60 pedestrians per minute, a demand whose shape is similar to a gaussian bell. The presence of a semaphore should reduce the impact of pedestrians on the vehicular flow while, at the same time, assuring a safe crossing possibility to the pedestrians.

The results of this experimentation are shown in Figure 5 and they are in line with our expectations: in particular, the fixed cycle semaphores cause a significant reduction of the vehicular flow and, among them, the long cycle configuration assures a slightly higher flow, granting a higher "global welfare" although at the cost of a potentially lower "local wellfare" due to a higher maximum waiting time for both pedestrians and vehicles (although this data is not shown in

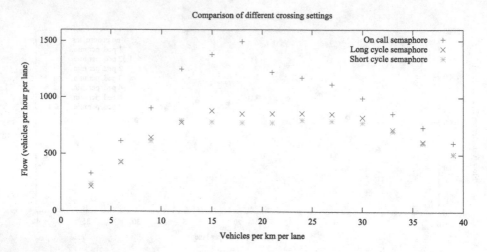

Fig. 5. Fundamental diagram of vehicle flow in different intersection configurations, respectively considering an on call semaphore, a long and short fixed cycle semaphore

the figure). The on call semaphore configuration, with this kind of pedestrian demand, is actually able to grant a vehicular flow only slightly lower than a situation of unsignalised intersection with no pedestrians crossing the street: in fact, when very few pedestrians approach the crossing, the semaphore is rarely red for vehicles. On the other hand, when a large number of pedestrians approach the crossing, the semaphore acts as a sort of dam, accumulating pedestrians that want to cross the street in the green phase for vehicles, which is assured thanks to the 30 seconds inhibition phase following the green phase for pedestrians, arbitrating the access to the shared resource. The on call semaphore configuration, considering this model and therefore a compliant behaviour of the involved stakeholders, seems the one able to assure a reduced impact on the vehicular traffic in case of low pedestrian presence, while at the same time providing a sense of safety to the pedestrians.

4   Conclusions and Future Works

The paper has presented an integrated model for the interaction of pedestrians and vehicles in crossing situations. We employ existing models for the pedestrian and vehicular subsystems, for the management of the ordinary behaviour of the managed entities, extending them for allowing the mutual perception of the relevant entities. The interaction is based on a collaborative attitude, in which cars give way to pedestrians whenever they can actually safely brake to let them pass, and pedestrians yield whenever they perceive that the vehicle would not be able to stop in time. Future works are aimed at a proper validation employing real world data and at the representation and management of more complex situations (e.g. intersections) and behaviours (e.g. possibility of having non-compliant behaviours for both vehicles and pedestrians, car overtaking).

Acknowledgments. The authors would like to thank Massimo Sporchia for his work on the implementation and experimentation of the model.

References

1. Nagel, K., Schreckenberg, M.: A cellular automaton model for freeway traffic. Journal de Physique I 2, 2221–2229 (1992)
2. Nagel, K., Wagner, P., Woesler, R.: Still Flowing: Approaches to Traffic Flow and Traffic Jam Modeling. Operations Research 51, 681–710 (2003)
3. Wang, R., Ruskin, H.J.: Modelling Traffic Flow at Multi-Lane Urban Roundabouts. International Journal of Modern Physics C 17, 693–710 (2006)
4. Kesting, A., Treiber, M., Helbing, D.: General Lane-Changing Model MOBIL for Car-Following Models. Transportation Research Record 1999, 86–94 (2007)
5. Burstedde, C., Klauck, K., Schadschneider, A., Zittartz, J.: Simulation of pedestrian dynamics using a two-dimensional cellular automaton. Physica A 295, 507–525 (2001)
6. Helbing, D., Molnár, P.: Social force model for pedestrian dynamics. Phys. Rev. E 51, 4282–4286 (1995)
7. Hamed, M.M.: Analysis of pedestrians' behavior at pedestrian crossings. Safety Science 38, 63–82 (2001)
8. Hakkert, A., Gitelman, V., Ben-Shabat, E.: An evaluation of crosswalk warning systems: effects on pedestrian and vehicle behaviour. Transportation Research Part F 5, 275–292 (2002)
9. Helbing, D., Jiang, R., Treiber, M.: Analytical investigation of oscillations in intersecting flows of pedestrian and vehicle traffic. Physical Review E 72, 046130 (2005)
10. Godara, A., Lassarre, S., Banos, A.: Simulating Pedestrian-Vehicle Interaction in an Urban Network Using Cellular Automata and Multi-Agent Models. In: Traffic and Granular Flow 2005, pp. 411–418 (2007)
11. Zeng, W., Chen, P., Nakamura, H., Iryo-Asano, M.: Application of social force model to pedestrian behavior analysis at signalized crosswalk. Transportation Research Part C 40, 143–159 (2014)
12. Krauss, S., Wagner, P., Gawron, C.: Metastable states in a microscopic model of traffic flow. Phys. Rev. E 55, 5597–5602 (1997)
13. Weyns, D., Omicini, A., Odell, J.: Environment as a first class abstraction in multiagent systems. Autonomous Agents Multi-Agent Systems 14, 5–30 (2007)
14. Weidmann, U.: Transporttechnik der fussgänger - transporttechnische eigenschaften des fussgängerverkehrs (literaturstudie). Literature Research 90, Institut für Verkehrsplanung, Transporttechnik, Strassen- und Eisenbahnbau IVT an der ETH Zürich (1993)
15. Gipps, P.G.: A behavioural car-following model for computer simulation. Transportation Research Part B: Methodological 15, 105–111 (1981)

Agent-Based Pedestrian Activity Simulation in Shopping Environments Using a Choice Network Approach

Jan Dijkstra and A. Joran Jessurun

Department of the Built Environment, Design Systems,
Eindhoven University of Technology,
P.O. Box 513, 5600MB Eindhoven, The Netherlands
{J.Dijkstra,A.J.Jessurun}@tue.nl

Abstract. Most of current approaches for processing agent-based pedestrian activity simulations propose movement choice networks. Choice mechanisms include where to stop, in what order, and which overall route to take. In our network approach, the movement choice network is approximated using a lattice of irregular cells representing streets and shops. In this approach, cell centroids are considered the nodes of an implicit movement network. A pedestrian agent is located in a node and can move on the implicit movement network to other nodes and is situated randomly in the cell related to that node. In this paper, the focus is on the generation of the movement network and the underlying behavioral rules that conducts the activation of pedestrians on the network representing a shopping environment.

Keywords: Agent-based Simulation, Pedestrian Dynamics, Irregular Network.

1 Introduction

Agent-based modeling is a computational methodology that allows us to create, analyze, and experiment with artificial worlds populated by agents. A specific research area is micro-scale agent-based modeling that can be used for the simulation of pedestrian movement for low and high density scenarios and for the effect of changes in the environment. Such models can also be used for pedestrian dynamics in city centers to show design effects in the shopping environment. In this context Ali and Moulin [1] describe their multi-agent simulation prototype of customers' shopping behavior in a mall. It turns out that a multi-agent model is well suited to simulate pedestrian dynamic destination, where the simulation of movement patterns is embedded in a more comprehensive model of activity travel behavior.

Representation is a main issue in simulating pedestrian dynamics. One can distinguish the representation of the pedestrian environment and the representation of pedestrians. In the domain of a city center, representation of a pedestrian environment includes the geometry of the shopping environment such as shops and streets, the network as a cellular grid, and pedestrian objects. It is assumed that pedestrians perceive their environment and that they are supposed to carry out a set of activities. As a consequence, the activity of pedestrians influences their behavior over the network.

J. Wąs, G.C. Sirakoulis, and S. Bandini (Eds.): ACRI 2014, LNCS 8751, pp. 680–687, 2014.

Although a 3D presentation of pedestrian movement is the ultimate goal, it is nevertheless meaningful to test the underlying principles in an appropriate 2D representation of pedestrians and their environment. Repast Simphony[1] and NetLogo[2] can be used as modeling and simulation toolkit because they provide a suitable simulation framework that supports skeletons of agents and their environment, and their interoperability (e.g. GIS). In our approach, we use Repast as guideline for the theoretical framework of the simulation process. On the other hand, we will use NetLogo for the actual simulation because it easily allows the empirical testing of the principles of the simulation approach.

In this paper, the focus is on the realization of pedestrian movement on a choice network approach. Herein, the network is an irregular lattice of cells and the choice of movement direction is determined by activation of pedestrians' activities. The domain of the agent-based modeling approach is pedestrian behavior in a shopping environment and the choice mechanism that are involved. It shows some similarity with other models that investigate pedestrian movement with fine-scale considerations (e.g. [2]), pedestrians' shop-around behavior (e.g. [3]), or principles of bounded rationality [4]. In tackling the combined MAS-CA approach, the inspiring 'situated cellular agents' approach [5] is worth mentioning. Rooted on basic principles of CA, this approach takes into account the heterogeneity of agents and provides interaction between agents locally and at-a-distance interaction; also the notion of perception and action is included in affective agents [6].

This paper discusses successively the concept of pedestrian agent and its environment, the engineering basis of the simulation process, and the simulation of pedestrian activity and pedestrian movement. A discussion part will conclude this paper.

2   Pedestrian Agent and Environment

Figure 1 shows the initial concept of a pedestrian agent description as a basis for an agent structure that can be applied. By declaring the methods *perceive*, *interpret* and *updEnv* private, the agent has its own control of the methods. The declaration of behavior represents the set of possible attitudes. In this diagram it is not worked out.

The environment consists of streets, a set of shops and pedestrians represented by agents. Streets are presented as an lattice of cells (cellular grid), which is used to simulate agent movement. A pedestrian agent moves with his own behavior and personal characteristics. At each time step, there is an update about pedestrian agents' positions. In fact, each cell in the cellular grid can be considered as an information container object; it contains information about the area size, street or shop characteristics, and agents' positions. We regard a restricted environment E of a pedestrian agent in the cellular grid. The cellular grid provides percepts to the pedestrian agent and the pedestrian agent perform actions in them.

---

[1] http://repast.sourceforge.net/
[2] http://ccl.northwestern.edu/netlogo/

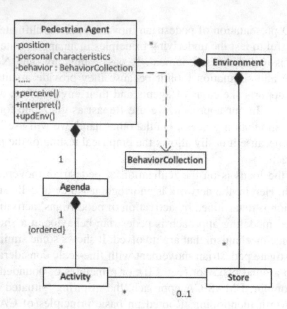

Fig. 1. Pedestrian agent structure

Therefore, we distinguish the functions *perceive* and *interpret*:

Perceive: E → P*

The function *perceive* represents the perception process of the agent. It maps the environment E to a set of percepts. The function *interpret* presents the decision making process of the agent and has a more complex form because an agent has an internal state, which includes the built-in knowledge.

Interpret: P* x I x G → A*

The *interpret* function maps the perception (P) of the environment, the current internal state (I) and the current activity agenda (G) into a list of one or more actions A. the *interpret* function updates the internal state based on its percepts and the activity agenda; select actions (*act*) based on the updated activity agenda and the updated internal state.

UpdStatePandG: P* x I x G → I x G
act: I x G → A*

The function *updEnv* represents the reaction of the environment to the agents' actions.

UpdEnv: E x A* → E

A new state of the environment is realized.

3   Simulation Process

In the previous section discussed the basis of the pedestrian agent structure and associated environment. This section provides some understanding in the engineering basis of the simulation of pedestrian movement. This basis is rooted in agent-based modeling and simulation, which is currently a fundamental tool for predicting the behavior of complex systems. As mentioned in the introduction, we use the principles of Repast Simphony creating the model [7].

The model structure in Repast Simphony is based on *contexts* and *projections*. The core data structure is called a *context* that represents that represents from a modeling perspective an abstract population: the objects in these populations are referred as agents.

The *context* provides the basic infrastructure to define a population and the interactions of that population; it creates an abstract environment in which agents exist at a given point in the simulation. The *context* also holds its own internal state for maintaining the collection of agents. This state can consist of multiple types of data. These provide agents with information about the world in which they interact. In addition, *data fields* can be maintained by the *context*. A *data field* is a n-dimensional field of values with which the agents in a *context* interact. These *data fields* can be directly associated with a physical space. The field is generic, which means each value is derived from a set of coordinates.

Projections take the population as defined in a *context* and impose a new structure on it. This structure defines and imposes relationships on the population by using semantics defined in the *projection*; therefore an agent is population is realized once a *projection* is applied to it. This means that *projections* are added to a *context* to allow agents to interact with each other. Each *context* can have an arbitrary number of *projections* associated with it (1-n relationship); in our case it concerns about two *projections*.

A feature of Repast Simphony is the ability to integrate GIS data directly to the simulation; it provides a set of classes that allow *shapefiles* to displayed. A *shapefile* is a storage format for storing geometric and associated attribute information. For example, *shapefiles* can be provided by Mapinfo and ArcGIS. A GIS contains multiple layers of data; each layer is made up of a number of elements. Each feature in the layer has aspects to it; its geographical coordinates (but it could be also a polygon, a polyline or polypoint) and the data associated with it [8]. GIS store data about layers in database files, with each record in the file referring to a feature in GIS. Actually, integration with GIS means *shapefile* integration while they use the same *shapefile.*. Agents are created using these data, and the simulation process (the *context* creator) provides the population. Agents, can be created, recreated and destroyed at each simulation step. Figure 2 shows A*gent Loop* of the context creator.

The interaction with environment is provided by the *shapefile* containing GIS data and the other one for the generated network from this GIS data. The *context* needs this GIS data for the *data fields* which provides the information from the environment.

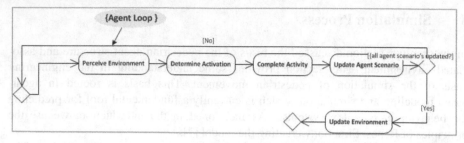

Fig. 2. Activity diagram part of the agent loop of the *context* creator

In our approach, the environment consists of polygons representing the network of shops and streets. In Mapinfo, feature data will be connected to cells of the network and layers will be created. After that, Mapinfo provides the Mapinfo GIS database that can be used in NetLogo for environmental information for pedestrian agents perceiving this environment.

4   Simulation of Pedestrian Activity and Pedestrian Movement

As mentioned in the previous section, the environment consists of polygons representing the network of shops and streets. Polygons are used to indicate borders, functional areas like walkways. Adjacent cells means that connections are possible, for instance pedestrian agents can move from one cell to an adjacent cell. If cells are not strictly adjacent, no movement from each other is possible.

Each cell in the network has a node. Therefore, the network consists of N nodes and L links. A subset of these N nodes are linked to J shops, and a subset E of these N nodes represents the entry/departure points of the simulation system. The link between a street_cell and a shop_cell will be established by the adjacent part of the polygon representing the shop and the street_cell. Actually, pedestrian agents are situated in the cells of the network, namely a street_cell or a shop_cell and bounded to a node on the underlying representation, and pedestrian agents can move on the implicit generated network to other nodes if they are linked together. The network is irregular because a clear border between a shop_cell and adjacent cell is desired.

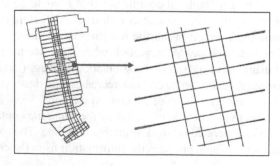

Fig. 3. Main street of the city center (segment) and the zooming in on a part of this segment

The test ground is the inner-city center of Eindhoven. We will perform the simulation on a segment of a section of this city center (Figure 3). Figure 4 shows the nodes in this part of the segment.

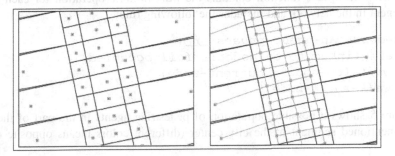

Fig. 4. Layers *Nodes* on (left) - Layer *Nodes* and *Links* on (right)

As mentioned before, we use a network of irregular cells. In research areas like geo-computation, land-use change, and urban planning, one can find extensions on the traditional formalization of CA to include an irregular spatial structure [9] [10][11]. These models are based on uniform CA transition rules.

Tomassini [12] pointed out that standard lattice cellular automata and random Boolean networks can be extended to a wider class of generalized automat networks that can be built on any connected graph. In this approach, there is no uniform transition function; the change is in the local transition function.

We have no uniform lattice of cells and no uniform transition rules; transition rules in the sense that the transition of cell i at time t depends on the state of the neighboring cells. In our approach, a street_cell i in the network is bounded to the stay of a maximum number of pedestrian agents related to node i.

Pedestrian behavior and pedestrian profile characteristics result in pedestrian activity and choice moments. That results in position change from a current position in cell i linked to node i to a next position in cell j linked to node j. Strictly speaking, our approach is not CA-based; nevertheless at each time step there is an update of the network according to 'network rules'.

A pedestrian agent will be introduced in the simulation by setting an entry position, which will be done by Monte Carlo method. Also a pedestrian agent receives a pedestrian profile including pedestrian characteristics, desired speed, activity agenda, etc. At a certain point of time, the network of shop-cells and street-cells is populated with pedestrian agents. At this point of time, all pedestrian agents have their current-node and according cell position. For each pedestrian agent, the to-node will be derived from the execution of pedestrian's activity. The following 'network characteristics' applies:

Let L consists of a lattice of cells representing the network of shop-cells and street-cells, and let $C = \{c_1, c_2,\ldots, c_n\}$ the set of cells of with n = number of cells. Furthermore, let S the set of finite states, whereby $S = S_{k_1}^{m_1} o S_{k_2}^{m_2} o \ldots o S_{k_n}^{m_n}$ with $S_{k_i}^{m_i}$ is the state of cell c_i with k_i pedestrian agents $\wedge$ maximum of m_i pedestrian agents in cell c_i.

A configuration Q_t: $L \rightarrow S$ is a function that associates a network configuration state of the lattice L. The network update function f changes a configuration Q_t into a new configuration Q_{t+1}: $Q_{t+1}(s) = f(\{Q_t(r)|r, s \in S\})$.

The network update function contains the *walk-to-node* operation for each pedestrian agent in the network and includes the following rule:

```
If  pedestrian-agent pauses or
    cell linked to to-node is full occupied
Then wait {to-node = current-node}
Else walk-to to-node
```

Figure 5 shows a possible population of pedestrian agents in the part of the previous mentioned segment of the city center (different colors means opposite direction).

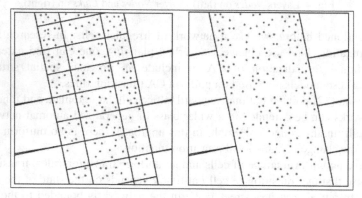

Fig. 5. Layers *Nodes* and *Links* off – Layer *Streets* on (left) and layer *Streets* off (right)

5   Discussion

In this paper, we presented a simulation platform for performing pedestrian movement simulation in a shopping environment. Pedestrian movement depends on pedestrian behavior, which depends of behavioral principles like perception, activation and completing an activity. The outcome of pedestrian activation is pedestrian movement on the network of shops and streets. In our approach, pedestrians are represented by agents and the network of shops and streets are represented by a lattice of irregular cells; each represented by their node. Pedestrian agents move from node to node and are situated into the cells related to those nodes. They are situated randomly in those cells, but if the area is occupied they cannot move to that cell. This reduces the complexity of the simulation by ignoring collisions and with that collision detection. This approach makes the simulation feasible because computer power is less binding.

The next phase is incorporating activity agenda's for pedestrian agents, including planned and unplanned shop stops, and subsequently validate the simulation in a 2D environment.

Future developments should make the pedestrian agent model suitable for a 3D environment with lifelike virtual persons. In that case, the pedestrian agent movement will be realized from cell point to cell point considering collision detection. Finally, this will result in a virtual environment of a real situation, populated with virtual persons and a real person (user) moving amongst these virtual persons. In that case, a user can assess an environment that has high reality content. For city managers or designer, it is possible to gain deeper insight into pedestrian activity behavior in city centers, even for those that do not exist yet.

References

1. Ali, W., Moulin, B.: How Artificial Intelligent Agents Do Shopping in a Virtual Mall: A 'Believable' and 'Usable' Multiagent-Based Simulation of Customers' Shopping Behavior in a Mall. In: Lamontagne, L., Marchand, M. (eds.) Canadian AI 2006. LNCS (LNAI), vol. 4013, pp. 73–85. Springer, Heidelberg (2006)
2. Kitazawa, K., Tanaka, H., Shibasaki, R.: A Study for Sget-based Modeling of Migration Behavior of Shoppers. In: 8th Conference on Computers in Urban Planning & Urban Management Conference, CUPUM 2003, Shendai, Japan (2003)
3. Yoshida, T., Kandea, T.: An Architecture and Development Framework for Pedestrians' Shop-around Behavior Model Inside Commercial District by Using Agent-based Approach. In: 10th Conference on Computers in Urban Planning & Urban Management Conference, CUPUM 2007, Iguassu, Brazil (2007)
4. Zhu, W., Timmermans, H.J.P.: Cut-off Models for the 'go-home' Decision of Pedestrians in Shopping Streets. Environment and Planning B: Planning and Design 35(2), 248–260 (2008)
5. Bandini, S., Federica, M.L., Vizzari, G.: Situated Cellular Agents Approach to Crowd Modeling and Simulation. Cybernetics and Systems 38(7), 729–753 (2007)
6. Bandini, S., Manzoni, S.: Towards Affective Situated Cellular Agents. In: El Yacoubi, S., Chopard, B., Bandini, S. (eds.) ACRI 2006. LNCS, vol. 4173, pp. 686–689. Springer, Heidelberg (2006)
7. Howe, T.R., Collier, N.T., North, M.J., Paker, M.T., Vos, J.R.: Repast for GIS. In: Sallach, D., Macal, C.M., North, M.J. (eds.) Proceedings of the Agent 2006 Conference on Social Agents: Results and Procspects, Chicago, Illinois, pp. 107–116 (2006)
8. Najlis, R., North, M.J.: Repast for GIS. In: Macal, C.M., Sallach, D., North, M.J. (eds.) Proceedings of the Agent 2004 Conference on Social Dynamics: Interaction, Reflexivity and Emergence, Chicago, Illinois, pp. 225–260 (2004)
9. Stevens, D., Dragićević, S.: A GIS-based Irregular Cellular Automata Model of Land-use Change. Environment and Planning B: Planning and Design 34, 708–724 (2007)
10. Stevens, D., Dragićević, S., Rothley, K.: iCity: A GIS-CA Modeling Tool for Urban Planning and Decision Making. Environmental Modelling & Software 22, 761–773 (2007)
11. Pinto, N.N., Sntunes, A.P.: A Cellular Automata Model Based on Irregular Cells: Application to Small Urban Areas. Environment and Planning B: Planning and Design 37, 1095–1114 (2010)
12. Tomassini, M.: Generalized Automata Networks. In: El Yacoubi, S., Chopard, B., Bandini, S. (eds.) ACRI 2006. LNCS, vol. 4173, pp. 14–28. Springer, Heidelberg (2006)

Software Implementation of Population of Cognitive Agents Learning to Cross a Highway

Anna T. Lawniczak[1], Bruno N. Di Stefano[2], and Jason B. Ernst[3]

[1] Department of Mathematics and Statistics, University of Guelph, Guelph, Ontario, Canada
alawnicz@uoguelph.ca
[2] Nuptek Systems Ltd, Toronto, Ontario, Canada
bruno.distefano@nupteksystems.com, b.distefano@ieee.org
[3] School of Computer Science, University of Guelph, Guelph, Ontario, Canada
jernst@uoguelph.ca

Abstract. We describe the model and the software implementation of population of simple cognitive agents, naïve creatures experiencing fear and/or desire while learning to cross a highway. The creatures use an observational learning mechanism for adoption or rejection of a strategy to cross the highway. Presented simulation results are consistent with the fact that crossing a highway becomes more difficult with increase of cars density and it is affected by the creatures' fears and desires. The transfer the knowledge base acquired in one environment to another one combined with creatures ability to change a crossing point improves creatures success of crossing a highway.

Keywords: Agents, Cognitive Agents, Learning, Knowledge Base, Cellular Automata, Nagel-Schreckenberg model.

1 Introduction

In many situations, such as unmanned space exploration, rovers & robots must be autonomous because tele-operation is impractical and unreliable, [1]. To increase reliability it is possible to replace complex robots with swarms of micro-bots, entities with minimal memory size and minimal logical primitives (e.g., conjunction, disjunction, and negation), but still exhibiting some learning & decision ability, that can be modelled with cognitive agents, [2], [3], [4], [5], [6]. We study what is a minimal requirement of micro-bots intelligence. We believe that natural evolution happened because of the actions of entities unable to deal with crisp values & to express or compute complex mathematical formulas. Thus, we experiment with very primitive creatures and we model using *biomimicry*. We are not interested in studying abstract decision mechanisms and coordination in conditions of uncertainty. We use "observational learning", a type of "social learning (*"imitate what works and don't do what doesn't work "*), [5]. We developed a simulator of our model and conducted various experiments to assess the impact of the learning algorithm for the population under investigation, [7]. This paper is about a cognitive agent model of naïve creatures

J. Wąs, G.C. Sirakoulis, and S. Bandini (Eds.): ACRI 2014, LNCS 8751, pp. 688–697, 2014.

learning to cross a highway, their learning algorithm and their virtual environment & is structured as follows. In Section 2 we briefly outline the model and in Section 3 we describe its software implementation. In Section 4 we report selected simulation results. In Section 5 we provide our conclusions and outline future work.

2 The Model

Our model of cognitive agent is described in [8]. We can summarize saying that: (1) the environment is a vehicular traffic highway, either single lane or multi-lane, either unidirectional or bidirectional, without any intersection; (2) the agent is a creature with a strong instinct to survive; (3) all creatures are born on one side of the highway; (4) each creature wants to cross the highway to get to the opposite side of the highway; (5) crossing the highway may or may not be successful; i.e. (5a) if successful, the creature simply crosses the highway and never crosses again; (5b) otherwise the creature is struck by a vehicle and dies; (6) crossing may happen at any point of the highway; (7) creatures see what happened to other creatures who have previously crossed and if under similar conditions the crossing was successful they will cross too, otherwise they will not cross and wait; (8) if a creature cannot cross the highway at its current location, due to unsafe conditions, it may move to a different potential crossing point to cross at, either up stream or down stream traffic.

We assume that the creatures under consideration are not capable of evaluating precisely distance and velocity. In reality most human beings are not capable of evaluating precisely distance and velocity of moving vehicles. The creatures can rank the position of the vehicle with respect to its crossing location according to a discrete number of categories (e.g., {far, mid range, close} or, alternatively, {very far, far, mid range, close, very close}, etc.). The larger the number of categories, the higher is the precision of the estimate, but also the higher the complexity of the "brain" of the creature and, potentially, the higher is the cost of a possible hardware implementation of the creature. A similar thing can be said for the velocity.

Information whether a creature crossed the highway successfully or not is recorded into the knowledge base of all the creatures. The columns of the knowledge base table store information about verbal descriptions of velocity and the rows of the table store information about verbal descriptions of the distance. The knowledge base table is initialized as "*tabula rasa*"; i.e. a "blank slate", represented with "0" at each location in the assumption that all possible (distance, velocity) combinations allow crossing. If a creature successfully crosses the highway the perceived (distance, velocity) score in the knowledge base table is increased by one point. If the creature was killed, it is decreased by one point. When a new creature arrives at the top of the queue, the creature consults the knowledge base table to decide if it is safe or not to cross. The decision is based on the naïve creature with fear and/or desire implemented intelligence/learning algorithm.

We impose a special initial condition for each (distance, velocity) pair to encourage creatures crossing the highway: (1) creatures pay no attention to their knowledge-base table or to their fear and/or desire at the start of the simulation; (2) this lasts until the first successful crossing of a creature, or five consecutive unsuccessful crossing of the creatures, whichever comes first.

After this initialization, each randomly generated creature makes its decision to cross or not to cross the highway for a given (distance, velocity) pair by combining the "*success ratio*" of crossing the highway for this (distance, velocity) pair with the creature's fear and/or desire probabilities, as follows: (1) if a creature has both fear and desire, then it will base its decision on the following formula: "*success ratio + probability of desire – probability of fear*"; (2) if a creature has only fear then it will base its decision on the formula: "*success ratio – probability of fear*"; (3) if a creature has only desire then it will base its decision on the formula: "*success ratio + probability of desire*". If for a creature and a given (distance, velocity) combination the value of the respective formula is: (1) non-negative, then the creature will attempt to cross the highway; (2) less than zero, then the creature will not attempt to cross the highway under this condition and it will wait for a configuration for which the value of the formula is non-negative. For each (distance, velocity) pair at each time step the numerator in the *success ratio* is the number of "*successful crossing*" minus the number of "*unsuccessful crossings*" for this (distance, velocity) pair up to this time; i.e. it is the value from the knowledge base table corresponding to this (distance, velocity) pair at this time. The denominator is the total number of creatures who have crossed successfully the highway regardless of the (distance, velocity) combination up to this time; i.e. it is the number describing the creatures' entire population success up to this time. If for some (distance, velocity) configuration at the start, all creatures are killed then the ratio becomes "-5/0". In this case, we set the *success ratio* to zero.

3   Simulator Software Implementation

The simulator: (1) executes in batch mode; (2) has no graphical user interface; (3) communicates with the outside world by means of text files; (4) is implemented in the C++ programming language; (5) has been designed according to the object-oriented paradigm and implemented in ANSI C++.

Once, the simulator has been compiled for the correct environment, it executes in the same way under UNIX/Linux and under MS Windows by means of: (1) a configuration file to read information about the experiment that is being run; (2) a knowledge base file containing information about knowledge acquired during previous executions; (3) a result file containing information with the results of the execution; (4) a full trace file.

The highway traffic is modeled by means of the Nagel-Schreckenberg model, [9]. For our investigation its implementation requires to modify the Cellular Automata (CA) paradigm and to make the evolution of the CA not only dependent on the state of the neighborhood but also on the current velocity of each vehicle. This implies that each cell is characterized not only by presence or absence of a vehicle but also by a pointer to a data structure containing the current velocity of the vehicle. As customary in discrete traffic modelling, we model each lane of unidirectional traffic of a highway as a large number of adjacent cells, with each cell representing a segment of highway of 7.5 m in length, [9], [10]. At each time step in the simulation, for each lane, a new car may be generated with a probability specified in the configuration file as car creation probability p. If there is already a car in the first cell because it hasn't sped up enough, or traffic is congested, the generated car is added to a queue of cars waiting to enter the highway. The entrance point is always cell zero of each lane. Cars accelerate by one until they reach their maximum speed, which is specified in the configuration file. The creatures are generated similarly to the cars. As cars they also use queues. If a creature at a top of the queue has not yet crossed the highway then the newly created creatures will line up behind it. The creatures are generated randomly (with a creation probability and fear and/or desire probabilities specified in configuration file) at each time step at a crossing point. The motion of the creature is modeled similarly to the motion of the vehicle; i.e. with a CA-like approach.

The simulator is based on 6 classes: Experiment, Simulation, Cell, Car, Creature, and Result.

An instance of class Experiment may generate multiple instances of class Simulation and is a collection of simulations. Each Simulation instance has a highway, which is a vector of lanes, where each lane has a direction (left or right) and is made of cells (objects of class Cell) that have the same direction associated with them. This dictates how the movement of cars within the lane operates. A cell can contain a single car (object of class Car) or a single creature (object of class Creature). If any cell contains both, a car and a creature, at any time, it means a car has hit the creature. If a car passes over a cell that contains a creature, the creature is also considered hit by the car. A simulation is also associated with a vector of results (each being an object of class Result). This vector is also known as the "Knowledge Base". A creature is also associated with an object of class Result. Each lane the creature advances through adds another temporary result to the creature. This is done because the creature may encounter different conditions as it passes across each lane in a multi-lane highway. If the creature makes it across all lanes successfully, all of these crossing conditions will be considered successful in the knowledge base table (i.e., the vector of results). Conversely, if a creature is hit, all of these configurations will be considered unsuccessful.

The number of simulations created, as specified in the configuration file, depends on: (1) the number of repeats of a single simulation configuration; (2) the range of a particular configuration value (e.g., creature creation probability from 0.1 to 1.0); (3) the increment value of a particular configuration value (e.g., creature creation probability increment by 0.1).

Classes Creature, Car, and Simulation use a pseudo-random number generator class, that allows to instantiate as many independent pseudo-random number generators as required without having to keep track of how many have been instantiated.

The class Experiment contains the main function of the software simulator package, the function that is executed automatically at the start of the program. The first thing that the program does is to read the configuration file of the experiment that will be running. The contents of this configuration file include: (1) the maximum number of simulation cycles; (2) the maximum number of creatures to be generated; (3) the maximum number of cars to be generated; (4) the length of the segment of highway under observation expressed as number of cell; (5) the number of lanes of the highway under observation; (6) an integer variable indicating by how many cell, as a range, a creature can move from its original location to look for more favorable crossing conditions; (7) an integer variable by how many cells per time step a creature can move to look for more favorable crossing conditions; (8) a vector of positive integers to quantize and classify the distances; (9) a vector of positive integers to quantize and classify the velocities; (10) a vector of positive integers to store the Boolean flags identifying the direction associated to each cell (i.e., If false, left-to-right. If true right-to-left.); (11) the maximum speed that a car can achieve; (12) a Boolean flag to indicate if the random deceleration has to be applied to the car; (13) an integer identifying the "intelligence" algorithm to be used by the creatures; (14) an integer variable defining how many distinct classes of values are associated to distance and velocity; (15) a Boolean flag to be set if we want to save a knowledge base file at the end of the simulation; (16) a Boolean flag to be set if we want to save a trace file at the end of the simulation; (17) the car creation probability, between 0.0 and 1.0; (18) the creature creation probability, between 0.0 and 1.0; (19) the amount of fear to cross that a creature may feel; i.e. the fear probability between 0.0 and 1.0; (20) the amount of desire to cross that a creature may feel; i.e. the desire probability between 0.0 and 1.0; (21) in the event that a creature at some instance of time does not cross the highway because it is "afraid", then (21a) it waits for more favorable conditions to cross and the newly generated creatures will build up in the queue behind it until it crosses, or (21b) it moves up stream or down stream of the traffic along the highway (to search for a new crossing point to cross from), in each case with probability 1/3, or it stays in its current location with probability 1/3; (22) a vector of positive integers to store the cell numbers at which the creatures may cross (also called "cross points").

After the program reads in the configuration and knowledge base, the main loop executes once for every time step in the simulation. At each time step there are several tasks: (1) generate cars at each lane of the highway using the car creation probability p; (2) generate creatures at each predefined cross point, as specified in the configuration file, using the creature creation probability; (3) update the car speeds. This accelerates the cars according the Nagel-Schreckenberg model; (4) move the creatures from the cross point queues into the highway (if the decision algorithm indicates this should occur); (5) move the cars on the highway including passing other cars and the logic to check if any creature has been hit; (6) advance the current time step.

After the simulation has completed, the results are written to output files using an output function, as defined by class Result.

Class Simulation "contains" all other classes except Experiment (which actually "contains" Simulation). Simulation is associated by a "has a" relationship to classes Car, Cell, Creature, and Results, in all case with a multiplicity "one to many".

The class Simulation is instantiated from within the execution of Experiment using the data read from the configuration file. Experiment passes the following parameters to the constructor: maximum simulation time (expressed as simulation cycles), length of the segment of highway under observation (expressed as number of cells), number of lanes, maximum speed that a car can achieve (expressed as cells per simulation cycle), car creation probability, creature creation probability, a vector containing the coordinates of all cross points specified in the configuration file (expressed as cell numbers), an experiment ID, and the direction of traffic on the road. Class Simulation is also responsible for setting up the output data streams to store the simulation result outputs, the knowledge base output, and the trace file. Class Cell is associated to class Car and class Creature by a "has a" relationship. This means that class Car and class Creature must be explicitly declared inside the header file of class Cell to allow the compilation of class Cell. Class Car is contained inside the class Cell, meaning that class Cell "has a" "Car" (i.e., the cell may contain a car). Similarly, class Simulation "has a" a "Car" (i.e., the simulation may contain one or more cars; i.e. with multiplicity "one to many"). Class Car is explicitly declared inside class Cell.

To allow tracing the route of cars an output data stream is produced and written to a data file. It contains all the relevant information about a particular car, i.e. unique car ID, car creation time, car start time, current time (i.e., the time when the data is sampled and stored), maximum speed associated to the car, exit location if the car leaves the road (i.e., lane number and cell number), and current car position, expressed as lane number and cell number, where current means time when the data is sampled and stored. Time information stored in the output file is expressed in number of simulation cycles.

4 Selected Simulation Results

The selected simulation results show learning performance of a population of naïve creatures using *naïve learning algorithm with fear and/or desire* for various values of fear and desire probabilities p_f and p_d (listed in the first columns of the figures) when the creatures are learning to cross a one lane unidirectional highway under various traffic conditions characterized by car creation probability p and without "erratic drivers". For each experimental set up the experiment was repeated 30 times for different random seed values. The creatures learning performance is measured by: (1) how many creatures crossed the highway; (2) how many creatures were killed during a simulation run; (3) how many creatures arc still queuing at the end of the simulation. We consider only one crossing point at the cell number 45 in the highway at the initialization step.

In the figures we display by dots and whiskers the mean values and one standard deviations of numbers of creatures that: (1) crossed the highway successfully (green colour); (2) were killed while crossing a highway (red colour); (3) are still queuing at the end of the simulation run (blue colour). These mean values and standard deviations are calculated over 30 simulation runs for each car traffic density, measured by the car creation probability, p; i.e., for $p=0.1$, 0.3, 0.5, 0.7, and 0.9, respectively. Additionally, on each figure we show best-fit lines for the mean values of the numbers of successful creatures (green lines), killed creatures (red lines) and queued creatures (blue lines). Figure 1 displays the results when the creatures are not allowed to leave their crossing point at cell 45. Figure 2 displays the results when they are allowed to leave the crossing points (randomly one cell up or down stream of car traffic per time step with maximum displacement of 5 cells in both directions of the initial crossing

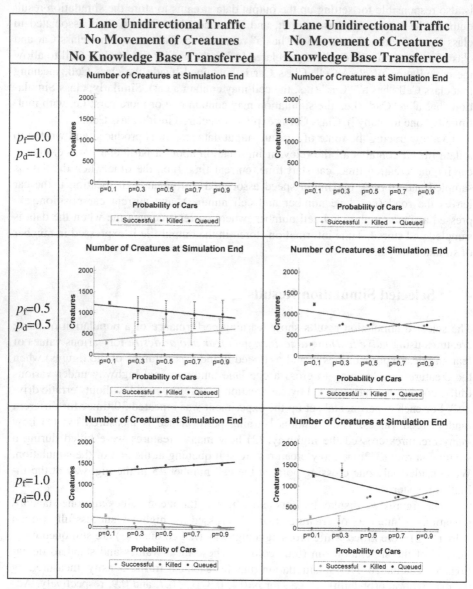

Fig. 1. Plots of best fit lines (solid graphs), means (dots) and one standard deviations (whiskers centered at the dots) of number of creatures, at the crossing point 45 of a one lane unidirectional highway, crossing successfully (green colour), killed (red colour) and queuing (blue colour), respectively, for car creation probability $p = 0.1, 0.3, 0.5, 0.7, 0.9$. The fear and desire probabilities p_f and p_d are listed in the first column. The creatures are not allowed to change the crossing point 45 to another one to cross from. The cars are not allowed to drive "erratically".

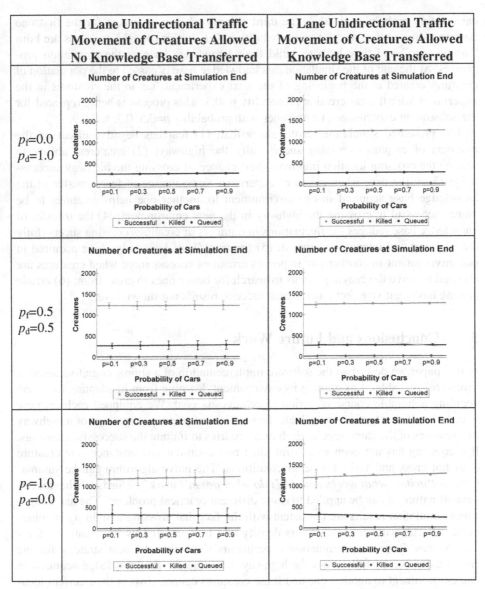

Fig. 2. Plots of best fit lines (solid graphs), means (dots) and one standard deviations (whiskers centered at the dots) of number of creatures, at the crossing point 45 of a one lane unidirectional highway, crossing successfully (green colour), killed (red colour) and queuing (blue colour), respectively, for car creation probability $p = 0.1, 0.3, 0.5, 0.7, 0.9$. The fear and desire probabilities p_f and p_d are listed in the first column. The creatures are allowed to change the crossing point 45 to another one to cross from. The cars are not allowed to drive "erratically".

point at cell 45), if they cannot cross at the current locations, in order to search for a better ones to cross from. In both figures the second column displays the results when the knowledge base is not transferred from one experiment to the next one, indexed by car creation probability p, while the third column when it is, except for the first one corresponding to the car creation probability $p=0.1$. In this case the creatures are born "*tabula rasa*" and they have to build their knowledge base as the simulation progresses. At the end of the simulation this knowledge base is passed to the population of creatures created at the beginning of the next experiment; i.e. to the creatures in the experiment with the car creation probability $p=0.3$. This process is being repeated for the subsequent experiments; i.e. the ones with probability $p=0.5, 0.7$, and 0.9.

The presented simulation results show that: (1) fear has negative effect on the numbers of creatures crossing successfully the highway; (2) creatures' ability to change the crossing location improves their chance of crossing the highway successfully; (3) in the case when creatures experience some degree of fear, transfer of the knowledge base acquired in one environment to another one helps creatures to be more successful in crossing the highway in the new environment; (4) the transfer of knowledge base reduces the fluctuations in numbers of creatures crossing successfully the highway and queuing to cross it; (5) the transfer of knowledge base acquired in one environment to another one improves creatures success more when creatures are allowed to leave the crossing points to search for better ones to cross from; (6) erratic driving has negative effect on creatures success, results not shown here.

5   Conclusions and Future Work

In this paper we described the software implementation of a simple cognitive agent, a "creature", capable of examining its environment, learning from it, adapting to it, and deciding a suitable course of action to achieve its goal. We equipped each creature with a simple mechanism to evaluate the outcome of previous crossings of a highway by creatures of the same specie. Each creature tries to imitate the successful crossings. If a crossing has not been successful, then under similar circumstances the creature does not cross and waits for better conditions. The naïve algorithm can be summarized as "*imitate what works and don't do what doesn't work*". This is a behaviour of general nature. It can be applied to many different practical problems. The naïve algorithm simulation results are consistent with the fact that crossing a highway becomes more difficult with increase of cars density and it is affected by the creatures' fears and desires. Results of simulation experiments show that the best strategy for the creatures to successfully cross the highway is to transfer the knowledge acquired in one environment to another one and if the creatures cannot cross at their current locations is to leave them to search for better ones to cross from. We reported selected simulation results, while more extensive results will their detailed analysis will be reported elsewhere.

Acknowledgments. A.T. L. & B.N. Di S. acknowledge hospitality of The Fields Institute for Research in Mathematical Sciences where part of this research was conducted. A.T. L. acknowledges partial financial support from the NSERC of Canada. B.N. Di S. acknowledges full financial support from Nuptek Systems Ltd., J.E. acknowledges full financial support from a SHARCNET Research Fellowship provided by A.T. L.

References

1. Bajracharya, M., Maimone, M.W., Helmick, D.: Autonomy for mars rovers: Past, present, and future. IEEE Computer 41(12), 44–50 (2008)
2. Ferber, J.: Multi-Agent Systems. An Introduction to Distributed Artificial Intelligence. Addison Wesley, London (1999)
3. Wooldridge, M.: An Introduction to MultiAgent Systems. John Wiley & Sons, Ltd., Chichester (2009)
4. Uhrmacher, A.M., Weyns, D.: Multi-Agent Systems Simulation and Applications. CRC Press, Taylor & Francis Group, Boca Raton, Fl. (2009)
5. Alonso, E., d'Inverno, M., Kudenko, D., Luck, M., Noble, J.: Learning in multi-agent systems. Knowledge Engineering Review 16(3), 277–284 (2001)
6. Lawniczak, A.T., Di Stefano, B.N.: Computational intelligence based architecture for cognitive agents. In: Proc. of ICCS 2010, Amsterdam, Holland, May 31-June 2. Elsevier Procedia Computer Science, vol. 1(1), pp. 2221–2229 (2010)
7. Lawniczak, A.T., Ernst, J.B., Di Stefano, B.N.: Simulated Naïve Creature Crossing a Highway. Procedia Computer Science 18, 2611–2614 (2013)
8. Lawniczak, A.T., Ernst, J.B., Di Stefano, B.N.: Improved Performance of Naïve Creature Learning to Cross a Highway. In: IEEE CCECE 2014, May 4-7, pp. 1269–1274 (2014)
9. Nagel, K., Schreckenberg, M.: A cellular automaton model for freeway traffic. J. Physique I 2, 2221–2229 (1992)
10. Lawniczak, A.T., Di Stefano, B.N.: Digital Laboratory of Agent-Based Highway Traffic Model. Acta Physica Polonica B Proc. Supplement 3(2), 479–493 (2010)

The Effects of Supraregional Innovation and Production Collaboration on Technology Development in a Multiregional World: A Spatial Agent-Based Model Study[*]

Ben Vermeulen and Andreas Pyka

Institute of Innovation Economics, Universitt Hohenheim,
Wollgrasweg 23, 70599 Stuttgart, Germany
{b.vermeulen,a.pyka}@uni-hohenheim.de

Abstract. With globalization, firms acquire locally unavailable inputs from and collaborate in innovation with firms in other regions. We contend that, depending on the collaboration distances feasible and spatial layout of regions, a core-periphery structure of regions emerges, in which core regions produce more advanced and complex products. We develop a spatial agent-based model of (supraregional) firm collaboration in production and innovation to study technological progress. We find that when collaboration is possible over greater distances, agents produce more advanced and more complex products. Moreover, we find that, in general, the core-periphery structure indeed emerges. However, for some layouts, the core-periphery structure vanishes almost immediately, while for others first becomes stronger, peaks and then vanishes with an increase in collaboration distance. Moreover, we find that the properties of the technology structure play a prominent mediating role, e.g. the effect of supraregional collaboration on technological progress may be strong for some and relatively weak for other structures.

Keywords: Spatial agent-based model, cellular world, technology development, innovation collaboration, production network.

1 Introduction

The last couple of decades, production and innovation collaboration became more global. In production, firms look for cheaper labor and locally unavailable inputs, while, in innovation, firms look for technological capabilities and knowledge alien to their region to realize breakthrough innovations [1,2]. Given limitations in the distance over which collaboration in production is economically and innovation is technically feasible, firms in certain regions have an advantage

[*] This work was realized with financial support of the Dutch science foundation NWO, grant 458-03-112, and the DACH research program *Innovation Networks for Regional Development* partly funded by the German science foundation DFG, grant PY 70/8-1, and partly funded by the Austrian science foundation FWF, grant I 886-G11.

J. Wąs, G.C. Sirakoulis, and S. Bandini (Eds.): ACRI 2014, LNCS 8751, pp. 698–707, 2014.
© Springer International Publishing Switzerland 2014

in acquiring inputs and recombining knowledge. Due to this, regional differences may emerge, forming a core-periphery structure, where firms in core regions have more advanced and complex products. However, we contend that also the structure of how technological elements in products and technological knowledge relate to one another determines how (ir)relevant the geographical dimension is in regional development. To realize breakthrough innovations, firms may need 'pipelines' to firms in possibly remote regions to use knowledge which is alien to the region yet technologically related [1,2]. To do justice to the effect of both the technological *and* geographical dimension in networking for production and innovation, we combine elements from models of multiregional development in the cellular automata tradition that take into account the geographical space (cf. [3] and [4]) and neo-Schumpeterian agent-based models of technology development in which agents form networks to combine knowledge or production facilities [5,6]. In this paper, we conduct an agent-based model simulation study on the effects of supraregional collaboration of firms in production and innovation (in conjunction) on the technological progress[1]. While the products that are produced may become more advanced and more complex with an increase in the distance over which collaboration is possible, the extent of this positive effect depends on both the structure of the technology and the spatial layout of regions over the world. To study the effect of the structure of the technology, we extend our novel operational 'artifact-transformation' model[2] of technology development, see [7]. Our model borrows notions on production systems from common operations management: an artifact is manufactured by a network of production units, where each production unit transforms input artifacts (acquired 'upstream') through transformations into output artifacts (delivered 'downstream'). In our model, there are one or more 'firm agents', and each agent has a portfolio of transformations and searches for feasibly producible artifacts by connecting transformations by their input-output artifact specifications. In this work, we assume that there is a 'transformation blueprint', which is a fixed, universal directed graph that defines how advanced transformations depend on more primitive ones. The transformation blueprint and input-output specifications of the transformations specify the technology structure. This technology structure is a mediating experimental variable in our simulation study. We study the effect of the distance over which collaboration is possible in both production and innovation on technological progress for different technological structures.

---

[1] With 'technology', we mean both production capabilities and the products produced with these production capabilities. With 'production', we mean the construction of products out of input products or resources using production capabilities. With 'technology development', we mean the activities in discovering new production options and thus allowing producing more advanced and more complex products. There is technological progress if production options and manufactured products become more advanced and/or more complex. A product is a hierarchical tree of input products, where each input is itself produced by a transformation of lower level inputs or raw resources.

[2] We use the terms 'artifacts' and 'transformations' in the operational model as the operationally defined counterparts of 'products' and 'production capabilities'.

Moreover, we conduct simulations for several stylized 'worlds' of spatial configurations of regions.

In the next section, we provide the in-depth operationalization of the technology development model (and notably the generation of the blueprint and the search heuristics), followed by a section with an operational definition of the spatial agent-based simulation model, then a section with an overview and discussion of simulation results. The last section provides conclusions.

2 Technology Development Model

In this work, technology is developed by economic agents, either in collaboration or alone. An economic agent has a repository of transformations (production capabilities, requiring physical activities, skills, know-how, etc) and produces artifacts (products). An agent searches for 'feasibly producible' artifacts by building trees of input artifacts by connecting transformations on the basis of their input-output artifact specification. As such, there is a direct correspondence of the artifact tree and the tree of transformations.

Apart from artifact search exploiting the existing repositories of transformations, there is also transformation search to expand repositories. Given the cumulative character of technological development [8], we assume that the 'unlocking' of advanced transformations requires the mastering of particular primitive transformations first. For instance, man needs to be able to 'control fire' and 'make container for liquid' before it can unlock a transformation like 'boiling'. We assume that there is a 'transformation blueprint', which is a fixed directed graph of precedence of transformations and equal for all agents. With the discovery of new transformations, new artifacts can be produced, with which yet new transformations become possible, etc. This accumulation effectively bootstraps technological developments.

Operationally, this blueprint of transformations starts from several root transformations (at what we call tier $t = 0$) and extends indefinitely to more advanced transformations. With probability p, a transformation at tier $t-1$ splits into two transformations at tier t, while, with probability $1-p$, a transformation τ at tier $t-1$ is merged with a second transformation τ' at a tier $\leq t-1$ producing one transformation at tier t. We introduce a second parameter q which defines where this second transformation τ' comes from. Let $\Omega(\tau)$ be the set of all transformations that are ancestors of transformation τ. With probability q, the second transformation τ' is uniform randomly drawn from the set $\Omega(\tau)$, which we dub as 'conservative' accumulation. With probability $1 - q$, the second transformation τ' is drawn uniform randomly from all transformations at tiers $\leq t$ minus $\Omega(\tau)$, i.e. all eligible transformations that are not ancestors of τ, which we dub 'progressive' accumulation. Figure 1 contains plots of transformation blueprints for $p = 0, q = 0$, $p = 0, q = 1$ and $p = 1, q = 0$, generated from tier 0 through to tier 6. Note that for $p = 1.0$, there is no merging, so the blueprint does not change with changes in q.

The blueprint only defines how transformations relate to one another, it does not specify which inputs are transformed in which outputs. In this work,

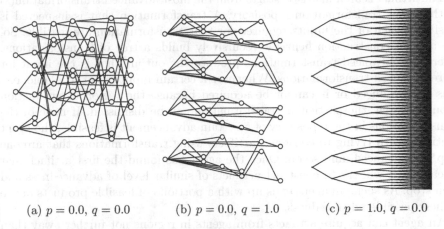

(a) $p = 0.0$, $q = 0.0$ (b) $p = 0.0$, $q = 1.0$ (c) $p = 1.0$, $q = 0.0$

Fig. 1. Transformation blueprints plotted from tier $t = 0$ (left) to tier $t = 6$ (right) for different splitting-merging probabilities p and progressive-conservative merging probabilities q. The fixed, universal blueprint specifies how transformation nodes are connected. Each transformation node specifies which input artifacts are transformed into which output artifact, but this artifact information is not visualized.

transformations at tier $t \in \{0, 1, \ldots\}$ take inputs of advancedness t and produce output of advancedness $t+1$. The descending transformation(s) at tier $t+1$ take uniform randomly drawn inputs of advancedness t and produces a unique output of advancedness $t + 1$, both in case of a split as well as in case of a merger. Although the assumptions for the generation of the transformation blueprint and input-output structure per transformation are generic and nonrestrictive in mapping it to real world technology in general, we are aware that also other assumptions may apply for particular technologies.

3 Spatial Agent-Based Model

In the agent-based simulation model, there are R regions, M raw resources that are (for the moment) ubiquitously available in each region. In the present setup, each region hosts only one firm that is engaged in both production and innovation. Each firm starts with its own unique primitive transformation that processes only a uniform random combination of 2 raw resources. In each period of the simulation, all agents first conduct transformation research and then each agent constructs artifacts. Whenever agents collaborate in innovation, each of them gets the transformations discovered, if any.

3.1 Search Heuristics

Agents have a research partner search heuristic, an artifact construction heuristic and a research heuristic to 'unlock' more advanced transformations (that can subsequently possibly be used to build more advanced artifacts).

The artifact search heuristic starts from the most advanced transformation(s) in the agent transformation repository. A transformation that is inspected is feasible if each of the inputs required for that transformation are feasible. So, the artifact construction heuristic recursively builds a tree of transformations, where less advanced transformations produce the output that is the input for more advanced transformations. Whenever a certain input is not available, e.g. it is not produced or it cannot be acquired because the region of production is out of reach, the particular transformation can be dismissed. If none of the transformations in the repository of a certain advancement is feasible, the agent continues with trying to construct artifacts using transformations that are one step less advanced, and so on. Once the agent has found the first artifact that is feasible, it will try to construct artifacts of similar level of advancedness and then stop. As such, an agent ends up with a portfolio of feasible products of the highest possible advancedness.

An agent can acquire artifacts from agents in regions not further away than m regions away (i.e. at distance m at most). Consequently, an agent can use all the transformations owned by firms in those regions in trying to construct artifacts.

The transformation search heuristic selects 'splitting search' to investigate whether a single transformation splits into two with probability p and 'merging search' to investigate whether two transformations can be combined into a new one with probability $1 - p$. In 'merging search', the investigating agent picks the first transformation (uniform randomly) from its own transformation repository and then with probability q from the transformation repository from a (uniform randomly) selected firm within distance n and with probability $1 - q$ again from its own repository. Whenever an agent conducts splitting search on a transformation that actually also splits in the blueprint, it will discover the two new transformations in the blueprint. Whenever an agent conducts merging search on two transformations that are actually also merged in the blueprint, it will discover that one new transformation. If two agents collaboratively 'unlock' the merged transformation, both agents add the transformation to their repository.

We assume that an agent does not seek to develop futuristic transformations, i.e. transformations that are more advanced than its most advanced artifact, because it will not be of immediate use in developing a new artifact.

Moreover, an agent registers the transformations it has tried to split and has tried to combine. In splitting search, the agent will uniform randomly draw from not yet inspected, "non-futuristics" transformations. If it has tried to split all the non-futuristic transformations in its repository, it will conduct merging research regardless of the merging-splitting probability p. In merging search, the agent will randomly draw two unique, non-futuristic transformations that have not yet been inspected together. They are non-futuristic because we assume that firm agents first concentrate on unlocking transformations that provide the inputs necessary for the most advanced transformations that it already has.

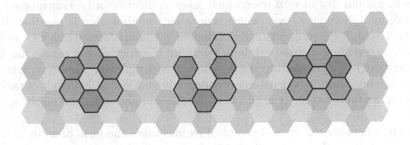

Fig. 2. Examples of the various configurations of cells, notably a circle, a string and a cluster, each consisting of six cells

3.2 Cellular World of Regions

In the simulation model, there is a two-dimensional hexagonal space composed of cells that are either 'sea' or 'land'. In the present setup, each agent is located in a single land cell and can transport artifacts only over land cells and can only collaborate in research to unlock transformations with firms that can be reached over land cells. The land cells can now be spatially configured in different ways, e.g. a string of cells each with only one or two neighbors, a cluster of cells, or a circle of cells each with two neighbors, see Figure 2.

4   Simulation Results

We run the simulation model for four different experimental blueprint settings ($p = 0.2, 0.8$; $q = 0.2, 0.8$), i.e. four extreme scenarios in a contingency table of high-merging-low-splitting ($p = 0.2$) and low-merging-high-splitting ($p = 0.8$) versus high-progressive-low-conservative merging ($q = 0.2$) and low-progressive-high-conservative merging ($q = 0.8$). We study the effect of these differently structured transformation blueprints in several spatial configurations of regions: a circle, a string, and a cluster (see Figure 2). We run 50 cases per scenario and, per region, we compute the average complexity of artifacts produced and determine the complexity in the 95%, 50% (median) and 5%-percentile case. In the present work, the complexity of an artifact is the depth of the artifact tree. An artifact of advancedness $t = 4$ is constructed by using transformation that uses two inputs of advancedness[3] 3, each taking two inputs of advancedness 2, etc, until at the but-one-lowest tier each eight artifacts takes two raw resources. In this case the depth of the tree and thereby the complexity is five.

In general, it is so that there is an increase in the average, minimum and maximum complexity of the artifacts that are produced whenever there is an increase

---

[3] Unlike previous work, in this work, transformations of advancedness t exclusively take inputs of advancedness $t-1$ (so, not lower), such that the complexity is perfectly correlated with the advancedness.

in the maximum distance m over which input artifacts can be transported and the maximum distance n over which innovation collaboration is possible. However, there may be strong regional differences in the artifact complexity and -in particular- revealing a core-periphery structure in which a core region has high complexity, while surrounding regions have low complexity. However, whether such a core-periphery structure emerges depends on the spatial layout of regions. Moreover, we find that also the effects of distances m and n depend on the spatial layout.

Firstly, whenever the spatial layout of regions takes the form of a circle, there may be regional differences in individual cases (e.g. in a particular simulation instance, firms in one region may produce rather complex artifacts while in others firms produce rather primitive artifacts), but over 50 different seeds, there is no structural difference.

Secondly, in a cluster layout, there are regional differences in technological performance (i.e. in advancedness of transformations and complexity of artifacts) discovered, but only for low maximum production collaboration distance $m \leq 1$. As soon as m is higher, the complexity in all regions is about the same. Figure 3 contains a plot of the spatial layout with in each region written the average complexity over 50 runs (and 5% and 95%-percentiles between square brackets) of the most advanced artifact feasible after $T = 600$ periods in each run. In Figure 3a, we see that the core region has relatively high average artifact complexity. For $m = 1$, the central region has access to artifacts (used as inputs) in all regions, but the peripheral regions have access to artifacts provided in only a subset of regions. Whenever the production collaboration distance is $m = 2$, the peripheral regions have now also access to input artifacts in all regions and the average complexity is about the same as that of the core region. The artifacts in the periphery regions become substantially more complex and the core-periphery structure vanishes. This is explained from the fact that whenever firms fail to produce artifacts of a complexity higher than t due to absence of particular inputs, they will focus on innovations in transformations with an advancedness of $t - 1$ and lower, but not higher. So, the rationale behind the effect of m is that by increasing the distance over which inputs can be acquired, artifact complexity goes up in expectation. In fact, this technological progress is amplified as firms subsequently also engage in search for more advanced transformations (in turn providing more advanced artifacts, potentially). In fact, for low $m \leq 1$, the maximum distance n over which firms collaborate in innovation has little effect on the artifact complexity. It is primarily the $q = 0.2$ case in which n does have (a moderate) effect on the artifact complexity, caused by the cross-linking in the transformation blueprint. In Figure 3, we have plotted the cases for, $p = 0.8$ and $q = 0.8$, however, for all four combinations of $p = 0.2, 0.8$ and $q = 0.2, 0.8$, a similar core-periphery structure emerges (although slightly less polarized, particularly for lower p) and similarly vanishes with an increase in m.

Thirdly, there is a particularly strong core-periphery structure in case of a string layout in which four regions have only two neighbors and the two regions on either ends of the string only one neighbor. In line with intuition,

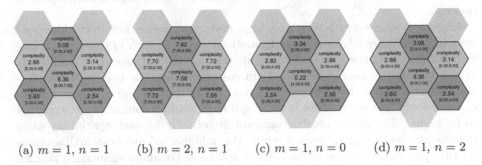

(a) $m = 1, n = 1$ (b) $m = 2, n = 1$ (c) $m = 1, n = 0$ (d) $m = 1, n = 2$

Fig. 3. Average artifact complexity after $T = 600$ periods in a cluster for various maximum production collaboration distances $m = 1, 2$

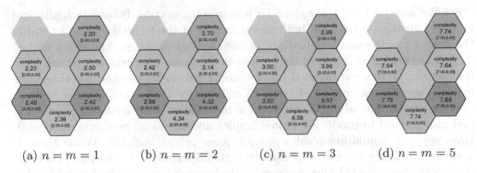

(a) $n = m = 1$ (b) $n = m = 2$ (c) $n = m = 3$ (d) $n = m = 5$

Fig. 4. Average artifact complexity after $T = 600$ periods in a string for various maximum production and innovation collaboration distances $m = n$

the middle two regions have the highest complexity (and hence transformation advancedness) and the two at the ends the lowest, in general. However, this core-periphery emerges not for low, nor for high n, m, but is particularly strong when the distance over which innovation and production collaboration is possible is somewhere in the middle. The discrepancy between the highest and the lowest level of artifact complexity in the various regions follows an inverted-U shape. The reason is because the maximum difference in the number of regions that can be accessed is then highest: when $n, m = 2$ ($n, m = 5$), a firm in the middle region can access four (five) regions excluding its own, while a firms in an end region can access two (five) other regions.

Apart from the spatial layout of regions and distances n, m, also the technological structure defined by p and q affects the emerging levels of artifact complexity in the various regions. Whenever the transformation blueprint is conservative (q is high), recombination of transformations *within* the regions will already unlock more advanced transformations and thereby allow production of relatively complex artifacts. So, whenever q is high, artifact complexity in the region is relatively high and collaboration in innovation across regional boundaries has relatively little impact. Simulation results confirm this for each spatial layout of regions.

Moreover, whenever p is relatively high, many transformations in the blueprint split into two more advanced transformations, whereby each of these two transformations, say at tier t, takes two inputs that are the outputs of two uniformly drawn transformations at tier $t - 1$. In case of a split, one primitive transformation gives rise to two options to create an artifact of higher advancedness. Consequently, whenever there is more splitting, artifact complexity is expected to be higher. Simulation results confirm this robustly for each spatial layout of regions. Access to more potential inputs (i.e. a higher m) increases artifact complexity, particularly when there is more splitting. For more simulation results, the reader is referred to [9].

5 Conclusion

We have showed that the extent to which collaboration boosts technological progress greatly depends on both the structure of the technology (and notably the innate transformation blueprint defined by our model parameters p and q) as well as the spatial layout of the regions in the world (and whether or not these regions can be reached, defined by our model parameters m and n). Whenever firms in a particular region are able to collaborate with firms in other regions, they discover more advanced production technology (transformations) in R&D and also succeed in producing more complex and advanced products (artifacts). However, our simulation results provide more refined insights. While there is a strong tendency for a core-periphery regional structure to emerge, this core-periphery structure vanishes as soon as the geographical scope of collaboration is non-trivial, but for strings, this core-periphery structure first becomes increasingly pronounced, peaks and then levels off with possible collaboration distance. Moreover, we see that this core-periphery effect is stronger whenever production technologies are 'fusions' of primitive production technologies (more merging in the transformation blueprint) and particularly whenever these 'fused' production technologies are technological relatively unrelated (the merging of transformations is progressive). Whenever production technologies primarily extend ideas already enclosed in more primitive related production technologies (the transformation blueprint is conservative, q is high), both products and production technologies can already quickly advance to high levels and we found that collaboration in innovation across regional boundaries has relatively little impact. In real world cases, it is however quite hard to tell ex ante whether a particular technological knowledge base can be progressed by cross-fertilization with other knowledge bases, let alone how much technological developments in specialized regions would benefit from collaboration with firms in other regions. However, we can tell whether old production technologies can be often applied singularly in several new, more advanced production systems (transformations in the blueprint split often, p is high and q has little effect). Note that, in that particular case, innovation and production networks need not extend beyond the regional boundaries to boost production (transformation) and product (artifact) advancedness. Particularly whenever there is a lot of merging of technologically relatively unrelated production systems (p is low and q is low), being able to collaborate in innovation over greater distances has a strong effect on the technological progress in terms of complexity. So, whenever the technological structure has such properties, firms should codify technological knowledge or -alternatively- facilitate R&D representatives to meet each other for face-to-face cross-fertilization of knowledge more frequently.

References

1. Rallet, A., Torre, A.: Is geographical proximity necessary in the innovation networks in the era of global economy? Geo Journal 49(4), 373–380 (1999)
2. Bathelt, H., Malmberg, A., Maskell, P.: Clusters and knowledge: local buzz, global pipelines and the process of knowledge creation. Progress in Human Geography 28(1), 31–56 (2004)
3. White, R., Engelen, G.: Cellular automata as the basis of integrated dynamic regional modelling. Environment and Planning. B 24, 235–246 (1997)
4. Caruso, G., Peeters, D., Cavailhes, J., Rounsevell, M.: Spatial configurations in a periurban city. A cellular automata-based microeconomic model. Regional Science and Urban Economics 37, 542–567 (2007)
5. Gilbert, N., Pyka, A., Ahrweiler, P.: Innovation networks: A simulation approach. Journal of Artificial Societies and Social Simulation 4(3) (2001),
   http://www.soc.surrey.ac.uk/JASSS/4/3/8.html
6. Morone, P., Taylor, R.: Knowledge diffusion and innovation: Modelling complex entrepreneurial behaviours. Edward Elgar Publishing (2010)
7. Vermeulen, B., Pyka, A.: Technological progress and effects of (supra)regional innovation and production collaboration. An agent-based model simulation study. In: Proceedings of IEEE Conference on Computational Intelligence for Financial Engineering & Economics, CIFEr (2014)
8. Basalla, G.: The Evolution of Technology. Cambridge University Press (1988)
9. Vermeulen, B., Pyka, A.: The effects of supraregional innovation and production collaboration on technology development in a multiregional world. A spatial agent-based model study. Forschungszentrum Innovation und Dienstleistung, Discussion Paper (2014)

Author Index